MW00985895

THE
DOCTRINE AND COVENANTS

CONTAINING REVELATIONS

Given to

JOSEPH SMITH, JR., THE PROPHET

With an

INTRODUCTION
and HISTORICAL AND EXEGETICAL NOTES

BY

HYRUM M. SMITH
of the Council of The Twelve Apostles

AND

JANNE M. SJODAHL

Revised Edition

Salt Lake City, Utah

D E S E R E T   B O O K   C O M P A N Y

1978

CONTENTS

PREFACE

While engaged in studying the Standard Works of the Church, I have been deeply impressed with the thought—which I believe to be the fact also—that the Revelations contained in the Doctrine and Covenants are pre-eminently the Scriptures of the Dispensation of the Fulness of Times. Every phrase, sentence, and paragraph is so instructive and enlightening; so pregnant with wisdom and purpose, and throws such a flood of light upon the gospel, as to bear convincing witness of their Divine Source, and proclaim them to be the very Word of God.

Splendid and glorious as are the ancient and meridian Hebrew and Nephite Scriptures, their splendor and glory are infinitely enhanced by the light these modern Scriptures cast upon them. As a group of great lights are more brilliant and beautiful than the light of one of them alone, so the Scriptures of different periods, when brought together, illuminate each, making clearer the meaning of the other. Such has been the effect of joining the "Light of Truth" as contained in the Bible and the Book of Mormon—the "Sticks of Judah and of Ephraim." When the "Light of Truth" in the Revelations in the Doctrine and Covenants is added, the Word of God and the "Way of Life" are revealed in all their power and purity and straightforwardness.

Without the light of these Revelations, many of the truths of the Bible would still be obscure, or seen dimly, "as through a glass darkly"; its prophecies, miracles, and history would be as unintelligible, meaningless, and mythical to the Latter-day Saints as they are to the world. Without it, the Church of Jesus Christ of Latter-day Saints could not have been organized; the Kingdom of God could not have been established in these days. It would have been impossible to designate the offices and officers, and set in order the quorums of the Holy Priesthood, and indicate the proper duties and calling of each. Very little would be known about the gathering of Israel and the building up of Zion in the last days. The appointed times and places, when and where the ancient predictions concerning these matters were to be fulfilled, would be veiled in darkness. Temple building, its object and purpose, and the doctrine of baptisms for the salvation and redemption of the unnumbered dead would be shrouded in impenetrable mystery. The coming of the Son of Man, His Millennial reign on the earth, the resurrection of the dead; eternal judgments, executed in justice and mercy according to the works of men, with everlasting rewards and punishments, would remain "rocks of offense," and discord upon which mankind would continue to split and be rent asunder.

All these principles, and many others pertaining to the gospel of Jesus Christ and the fulness of times, are made as clear as the cloudless noonday in the Revelations given to Joseph the Prophet.

In view of this, and the fact that the Lord has commanded His people to, "Search these commandments, for they are true and faithful, and the prophecies and promises which are in them shall all be fulfilled," it has been felt that the Priesthood, and members of the Church, in all departments, and in every place, should diligently study the Doctrine and Covenants; that they should become more familiar with the Word of the Lord and His great latter-day work; that they should sense more fully that they are living in the "hour of His judgment," the signs of which are terribly apparent, the world over, to all who have eyes to see, and ears to hear, and hearts open to understanding; and that they might realize the eternal importance of setting themselves and their houses in order, and thereby be ready to meet the Lord whose coming is at the very doors.

To this end the historical and explanatory notes relating to the coming forth, context, and import of each of these Revelations have been prepared. They are humbly offered to the Saints, and to all men, in the hope that those who read, may do so with faith and prayerful hearts, and thereby come to a fuller knowledge of the truth, and find added charm and interest in, and increased love for, the Word of the Lord, as well as a higher conception of the inspiration and greatness of Joseph Smith, the Prophet, and a broader understanding of the magnitude of the "marvelous" and "wonderful" work inaugurated by him.

To Elder J. M. Sjodahl, our fellow-laborer and companion in the service, is chief credit due, for his faithful and untiring efforts in searching out the references from the sermons of the Presidents, Apostles, and leading Elders of the Church, as well as from historical and other sources available, and for his other valuable labors in connection with this work.

We pray our heavenly Father, in the name of Jesus Christ, His Son, to bless His word and seal it upon the hearts of His children by the sanctifying power and witness of the Holy Ghost, for to know the Truth and continue in it, is to be made free and have Eternal Life.

HYRUM M. SMITH.

PREFACE

To The Revised Edition Of The

DOCTRINE AND COVENANTS COMMENTARY

While laboring in the European Missions, Elder Hyrum M. Smith, of the Council of the Twelve Apostles, and Elder Janne M. Sjodahl, were impressed very fervently with the desire to prepare a commentary dealing with the revelations given by the Lord to the Prophet Joseph Smith. In their odd moments, when not otherwise engaged, during the years 1913-1916, these brethren carried on a careful research and study and prepared this volume which has met with popular favor.

For a number of years the commentary has been out of circulation, and because of the increasing demand for it, the First Presidency instructed the Publication Committee to take the matter in hand and revise the volume ready for a re-printing. This the committee has done and after many months of labor has fulfilled the assignment given.

Since the time of the first publication many world-wide events of the greatest importance have occurred many of which have a bearing on the fulfillment of the prophecies found in the Doctrine and Covenants; these have been noted. The Doctrine and Covenants is a sacred volume of Scripture, and in the revision and preparation of this book, the members of the committee have felt their weakness in commenting on these sacred commandments and revelations coming from the Lord.

THE PUBLICATION COMMITTEE.

JOSEPH FIELDING SMITH
HAROLD B. LEE
MARION G. ROMNEY

INTRODUCTION

INTRODUCTION

The Latter-day Saints accept four volumes as the standard works of the Church. These are the Bible, the Book of Mormon, the Doctrine and Covenants, and the Pearl of Great Price. By unanimous vote of a General Conference, these four have been declared to be the established rule or test, by which the belief, the teachings, and the conduct of men must be judged. In the words of Isaiah, "To the law and the testimony: if they speak not according to this word, it is because there is no light in them" (Isa. 8:20). This applies with equal force to all these volumes. They are in perfect harmony one with the other, as the four Gospels in the New Testament. The same eternal truths are taught in each volume, and what is the word of God in the Bible, must be the word of God in the Book of Mormon, when found there; or in the Doctrine and Covenants, or in the Pearl of Great Price.

The Doctrine and Covenants occupies a unique and highly important position among this sacred literature.

The Bible is a collection of books—a library—written during a period of many centuries, from Moses, 1500 B. C., to St. John, who, towards the close of the first century of our era, wrote his Gospel, probably the last of the New Testament writings. These books, sixty-six in all, deal with the history of the kingdom of God on earth, chiefly on the eastern hemisphere. They contain a brief record of the origin and development of the Hebrew nation; a biography of our Lord while on earth; the rise and earliest struggles of the Church, together with sacred songs, proverbs, dramatic compositions, and letters. Scattered all through is found a vast amount of predictions relating to the future destiny of the Hebrews, the Church of Christ, and the human race. Among these prophecies are some concerning the coming forth of the Book of Mormon and the Church in our day, preparatory to the establishment of the Millennial reign of our Lord. But by far the largest part of the Bible refers to the past history of the people of God; some of it, to events so remote, and to present-day readers so obscure, as to render the brief references to them unintelligible. There are no first manuscripts of any of the books of the Bible extant. The text has been reconstructed from more or less defective copies found in all parts of the Old World, and this text has been translated to the best ability of uninspired scholars, and therefore, neither the text, nor any translation made, is perfect.

The Book of Mormon is also a collection of books, originally written between the years 600 B. C. and 400 A.D. It deals with the history of the kingdom of God on the western hemisphere. For centuries, inspired men in that part of the world kept historical records, until the leading events of a thousand years were covered. From this voluminous material, Mormon, the historian, prophet, and general, made an abridgment, or synopsis, and added his own inspired book. There is also an ecclesiastical history, by the prophet Nephi, and a brief history of the inhabitants of the "North Country," by Moroni, the son of Mormon, who completed the abridgment of his father, and wrote the last book of the collection. There is, of course, no facsimile of the original text extant. The plates from which the Prophet Joseph made his translation, through the power of God, are now hidden to mortal eye, as are the tables of stone upon which the Decalogue was written. They may be unveiled again, in the due time of the Lord. The Book of Mormon, too, has some remarkable predictions concerning the day in which we live, but the greater part of it relates to the past. Nephi incorporates in his writings portions of the prophecies of Isaiah, and thus the Book of Mormon becomes a witness for the Bible against the onslaughts of a ruthless, negative criticism, just as the Bible is a witness for the Book of Mormon against the infidelity that rejects that volume, notwithstanding the overwhelming evidence on which its claims rest.

The Pearl of Great Price is "a selection from revelations, translations, and narrations of Joseph Smith." It contains some visions of Moses as revealed to the Prophet, a translation of records found in Egypt, some of the writings of Joseph Smith, and the Articles of Faith. The Pearl of Great Price, therefore, also contains much matter which refers to the past. In it we obtain a clearer view of the Creation, the fall, and redemption, and a fuller account of the history of Abraham and the effect of his mission to Egypt. It was necessary that these things should be more clearly revealed in this dispensation. For this is the time when the hearts of the children are to be turned to their fathers, as well as the hearts of the fathers to their children, and this implies that the children should know something about their fathers and ancestors, and their work in the past on which they have built in all ages, and are still building. Through the Book of Abraham, in the Pearl of Great Price, a great deal of light has been shed upon the history of Egypt, to which country European civilization is so highly indebted.

The Doctrine and Covenants is different from these three volumes. It is in every respect a modern book. It contains revelations given during a period extending from 1823 to 1847. It covers the rise and development of the Church, restored in our day. It enables us to follow the tender watchcare of God over the infant Church, during its days of numerical weakness and the incessant assaults of the adversary, in the form of persecution, temptations, and apostasy, and to watch the retreat of the people of God into the wilderness. It contains "doctrines," "covenants," and predictions, all of the utmost importance to every nation and every individual on earth. The writings of Moses and the Prophets concerned, in the first place, the Hebrew nation and its neighbors in an age that is past. The writings of the Apostles were intended, in the first place, for the churches and saints of their age. The Doctrine and Covenants has been given to us for our instruction and salvation. We are interested in it, and should study it diligently and intelligently. Moses directed that the Law, that is, the Book of Moses, be read before all Israel (Deut. 31:11), and that the king should read it every day of his life (Deut. 17:19). In the same spirit Isaiah exhorted the people to search the Book of the Lord (Isa. 34:16), which, probably, contained the prophecies then collected, and Paul instructed the churches concerning the reading of his inspired epistles (Col. 4:16). The same instructions may be applied now to the Doctrine and Covenants.

As the name implies, and as already stated, this volume of

Scripture contains doctrine and covenants. "Doctrine" means "teaching," "instruction." It denotes more especially what is taught as truth, for us to believe, as distinct from precepts, by which rules, to be obeyed, are given. "Doctrine" refers to belief; precept to conduct.

In the Doctrine and Covenants our Lord teaches us what to believe concerning the Godhead, the Church, the Priesthood, the Millennium, the resurrection, the state of man after death in eternal glory, or the opposite, and many other subjects about which it is necessary to have true information.

The word "covenant" is a term by which God indicates the settled arrangement between Him and His people. In the great Council in heaven, before the creation of the earth, the Father covenanted with His Son, when He said, "Thou art my Son: this day have I begotten thee. Ask of me, and I shall give thee the heathen for thine inheritance, and the uttermost parts of the earth for thy possession (Psalm 2:7, 8). It was in pursuance of this decree, that the Son came to redeem the world; wherefore Isaiah (9:6) calls Him "Counsellor," or, as it has been rendered, the "Angel [or Messenger] of the Great Council." This covenant concerning the salvation of the human race, entered into in eternity, was made known to Adam, Noah, Abraham, and others, and, finally, through the Prophet Joseph, to the people of God in our day. It is the "everlasting" covenant, because it is from eternity to eternity. The new and everlasting covenant is the Gospel of Jesus Christ.

In it are revealed the organization of the Church, the authority of the Priesthood, the laws and rules by which, if we obey them, we can obtain citizenship in the kingdom of God, and salvation, both temporal and eternal. The covenant made with Israel has been called the Covenant of Works, and that made with Abraham, the Covenant of Promise. The covenant of the gospel is the covenant of "Truth and Grace." It is the covenant of "Faith," as expressed in obedience to all the laws of God. It is the covenant of a Father with His children, the covenant of adoption and heirship. The nature of this covenant is revealed to us in this precious volume of the word of God. It shows us what obligations we take upon ourselves in baptism, and what blessings we secure; what covenants we renew by partaking of the Sacrament, and what promises accompany that ordinance. In one word, it teaches us how to worship God in Spirit and in truth, and reveals to us the way opened up, back to the presence of God.

Furthermore, the Doctrine and Covenants contains predictions in which every nation in the world is interested. Some of these, as for instance, that of the Civil War in the United States, and the more recent world conflicts of 1914 and 1939, have been fulfilled, and there are others regarding wars and distress among the nations awaiting fulfillment because the peoples of the earth will not repent and receive the Gospel. The predictions concerning the establishment of the kingdom of God, and the events through which this will be accomplished, in large measure await fulfillment. These predictions are a Voice of Warning to the nations. "Hear, O heavens, and give ear, O earth, for the Lord hath spoken."

Each age has had its own questions to discuss. The first age of our era, when the Greek mind was predominant, dealt with the question of the Deity, and, finally, formulated the doctrine of the Trinity, as now known in the so-called orthodox world. To the following age, under Roman influence, fell the task of studying man in his relation to God, and the doctrine of sin and grace, as taught by Augustine and later church fathers. The age of the Reformation took up the question of God's plan of salvation, and formulated the doctrine of justification by faith, as promulgated by Luther and others. But it is evident to all who know the Scriptures, that the world has not been led into the truth on any of these important questions. In the doctrine of the Deity the influence of pagan philosophy is more prominent than that of the Bible. The doctrine of predestination, as traced to Augustine, is, essentially, fatalism, such as was taught by the Stoics. The doctrine of justification by faith has, in some respects, become a cover for spiritual indolence, and even for licentiousness, so thick as to keep the justice of God out of view. It was, therefore, highly necessary that new light should be shed upon these questions, from the only Source of light and truth, through Revelation, and this God has graciously and mercifully done in the Revelations recorded in the volume called Doctrine and Covenants. And He has done more. As each previous age had its problem to solve, so our age also is face to face with questions peculiarly its own. These relate to the Church; its nature, attributes, prerogatives, and organization; and also to man's state after death; the Millennium, resurrection, and judgment. All these questions belong particularly to the time in which we are living, and the Lord has been pleased to give Revelations on all these subjects, for the purpose of keeping His people from falling into the errors of former ages, and that the truth may be preserved unadulterated and pure.

It may be remarked here, that the Book of Doctrine and Covenants resembles the Bible in this respect, that it does not present the truths revealed, in systematic order. It resembles Nature too, God's other great book. The Creator has not given us, in Nature, a systematized, classified exhibition of facts or objects. He has created the objects, but He leaves it to man to study and classify them for himself, for the purpose of learning the laws by which all things are governed, and thus become proficient in astronomy, chemistry, biology, etc. It is the same with the Scriptures. Truths are there revealed; facts are there recorded, in order that the student may be able to form a system of theology, just as the student of Nature is enabled, through study, to construct the various branches of natural science. God intends us to do this. He intends us to study the Scriptures, to memorize them, to classify the doctrines they teach, and to apply the knowledge thus obtained to our daily lives. As the facts of Nature are all related, so the Scripture truths revealed are all related and form a grand whole; but we must discover what the relationship is. "As He [God] wills that men should study His works and discover their wonderful organic relation and harmonious combination, so it is His will that we should study His Word, and learn that, like the stars, its truths are not isolated points, but systems, cycles, epicycles, in unending harmony and grandeur." (Hodge, *Systematic Theology,* Vol. I., p. 3).

Only by such study and application of the Word to our lives will it influence our character and fit us for exaltation hereafter. The mere reading does not avail. The standing before a mirror serves no useful purpose, unless we set ourselves in order, so that we become fit to associate with our fellowmen. It is so with reading the Word of God. If we read so as to govern our lives in accordance with the mind and will of God, our characters will be formed thereby, and we shall be fit to associate with those who are permitted to enter His presence.

The book of Doctrine and Covenants formerly contained a series of seven lectures on Faith, which deal with the existence and attributes of God, and the nature of that principle which we call faith. The lectures were delivered before a theological class of the School of Elders at Kirtland, in 1835, and incorporated in the Doctrine and Covenants, "in consequence of their embracing the important doctrine of salvation" (Preface of the First Edition).*

This sacred volume consists of one hundred and thirty-six sections, and is called "Covenants and Commandments." The first section is "The Lord's Preface" to the volume, given by divine inspiration.

It is instructive to note the dates of the various sections. The introduction was given November 1, 1831, when, at a special conference held at Hiram, Portage Co., Ohio, it was decided to publish the first edition. The other one hundred and thirty-one sections were given as follows:

1	in	the	year	1823.	2	in	the	year	1835.
1	"	"	1828.	3	"	"	1836.
15	"	"	1829.	1	"	"	1837.
19	"	"	1830.	8	"	"	1838.
35	"	"	1831.	3	"	"	1839.
16	"	"	1832.	3	"	"	1841.
13	"	"	1833.	2	"	"	1842.
5	"	"	1834.	4	"	"	1843.

The greatest number of revelations was given, as will be seen from this table, during the years 1829-33, when the Church was

* These Lectures were removed from the Doctrine and Covenants in the edition of 1921, not because they were called in question, for they are excellent lectures of great value on the principle of faith, but because they were not revelations. When they were received and ordered printed in the Doctrine and Covenants it was with the understanding as expressed by Elder John Smith, "that the lectures were judiciously arranged and compiled, and were profitable for doctrine." (D.H.C. 2:244.) The Prophet Joseph Smith revised and prepared these Lectures himself, and they are still "profitable for doctrine."

being formed and strengthened for life's struggle. Then the Saints needed special instructions and special care.

It is also instructive to note the various places in which the Revelations were given. Four came to the Prophet at Manchester, Ontario Co., New York; fifteen at Harmony, Susquehanna Co., Pennsylvania; fourteen at Fayette, Seneca Co., New York; forty-three at Kirtland, Geauga Co., Ohio; one at Thompson, Geauga Co., Ohio; eight in Jackson Co., Missouri; two at McIlwaine's Bend, on the Missouri River; fifteen at Hiram, Portage Co., Ohio; one at Orange, Cuyahoga Co., Ohio; one at Amherst, Lorain Co., Ohio; one at Perrysburgh, New York; one at Fishing River, Missouri; six at Far West, Caldwell Co., Missouri; one near Wight's Ferry, Missouri; three in Liberty Jail, Clay Co., Missouri; seven at Nauvoo, Hancock Co., Illinois; one at Ramus, Illinois; and one at Winter Quarters. There are thirteen sections for which no place is given in the headlines.

The first revelation (Sec. 2) was given to the Prophet in his father's house, through an angel, on the 21st of September, 1823. It relates to the restoration of the Priesthood. Some of the Revelations given at Harmony and Fayette concerned the bringing forth of the Book of Mormon, and the establishment of the Church. A number of glorious Revelations were given at Kirtland, including the Word of Wisdom and Section 88, on the future destiny of man. At Hiram, Portage Co., Ohio, many Revelations were given on the correct interpretation of the Scriptures, including I. Cor. 7:14, and the Revelation by John. There the Prophet Joseph and Sidney Rigdon were favored with the grand vision recorded in Section 76, while they were pondering the meaning of John 5:29. Important Revelations concerning the future of the Church were given at Far West. The Revelation on the eternity of the marriage covenant was first written at Nauvoo. And thus we see a gradual unfoldment of truth, each revelation containing just what the people at each time needed for instruction, encouragement, or correction.

Some of the Revelations, as Sections 2 and 27, were given through heavenly messengers; others, as Sections 76 and 110, through "visions": "The veil was taken from our minds, and the eyes of our understanding were opened" (Sec. 110:1).

Others came through divine inspiration, or quickening of the faculties to keener perception of things spiritual, than enjoyed under ordinary circumstances. By what token the Prophet knew that the Revelations so given were from God, we may judge from what the Lord told Oliver Cowdery concerning translation, "You must study it out in your mind; then you must ask me if it be right, and if it is right, I will cause that your bosom shall burn within you; therefore you shall feel that it is right" (Doc. and Cov. 9:8). When the Spirit of the Lord burns within, there is no mistaking that sacred fire. The Prophet Joseph says that the visions at times rolled like an overflowing surge before his mind (*History of the Church*, Vol. V., p. 339); and that the "still small voice, * * * oftentimes it maketh my bones to quake while it maketh manifest" (Doc. and Cov. 85:6). When God speaks, there is no room for doubt.

Many Revelations were given in the presence of witnesses. Section 29, for instance, contains a Revelation inspired in the presence of six elders. Parley P. Pratt, who was present when the revelation in Section 51 was received, relates how the Prophet caused the Revelations to be committed to writing. He says, "Each sentence was uttered slowly and very distinctly, and with a pause between each, sufficiently long for it to be recorded by an ordinary writer in long hand. This was the manner in which all his written Revelations were dictated and written. There was never any hesitation, reviewing, or reading back, in order to keep the run of the subject; neither did any of these communications undergo revisions, interlinings, or corrections. As he dictated them, so they stood, so far as I have witnessed; and I was present to witness the dictation of several communications of several pages each" (Parley P. Pratt, *Autobiography*, pp. 65-66). This statement Elder Brigham H. Roberts (*History of the Church*, Vol. I., p. 173) supplements by the information that some of the early Revelations published in the *Book of Commandments* in 1833, were revised by the Prophet himself; errors made by scribes and publishers were corrected, and some additional clauses, which also had been given by revelation, were added. The addition of Verses 65 and 67, in Section 20, is an example.

The Prophet Joseph never entertained any doubt concerning the divine inspiration of the Revelations he received for the guidance of the Church. To some of his associates their authority was not always equally clear. Oliver Cowdery, shortly after the establishment of the Church in 1830, informed the Prophet that he had discovered an error in Section 20, Verse 37. He demanded that it be corrected. He had succeeded in influencing the Whitmers in favor of this view, and the Prophet seemed to face a schism which might become fatal to the Church. Had the Prophet Joseph been conscious of a human origin of the work in which he was engaged, wisdom would have suggested that he yield to his co-laborers; but he knew that the Revelations were not his, to change and alter at will. Consequently, he asked Oliver Cowdery by what authority he commanded him "to alter or erase, to add to, or diminish from, a Revelation or commandment from Almighty God" (*History of the Church,* Vol. I., p. 105). Later, Cowdery and the Whitmers freely acknowledged that they had been in error.

Shortly after the Revelation contained in Section 26 had been received, in July, 1830, the Prophet Joseph began to arrange and copy the Revelations so far given, and in this work John Whitmer assisted him. At a special conference held at Hiram, Portage Co., Ohio, November 1st, 1831, it was decided that ten thousand copies should be printed, and that the title should be, *Book of Commandments.* It was also decided to send Oliver Cowdery to Independence, Mo., to supervise the printing there. The manuscript was to be ready for the press by the 15th of November, that year. It was at this time that Section 1 was given (November 1st), and Section 133 (November 3rd). At a conference held at Hiram, on November 12th, 1831, the Saints by vote expressed their appreciation of the Revelations given. Oliver Cowdery and John Whitmer were set apart to publish the book, and the manuscript and the means entrusted to them to carry to Zion were dedicated to the Lord by prayer. At the same time Joseph Smith, Jr., Martin Harris, Oliver Cowdery, John Whitmer, Sidney Rigdon, and William W. Phelps were, by revelation (Doc. and Cov. 70), appointed a committee— "stewards"—to look after the business of the publication and distribution of the book; if they should receive more than needful for their necessities, the surplus was to be consecrated for the benefit of the inhabitants of Zion. On the 26th of April, 1832, a general Council of the Church was held at Independence, Mo., which was in session for several days. On the 1st of May, that year, it was decided that, instead of printing ten thousand copies of the *Book of Commandments,* the first edition should be limited to three thousand copies. William W. Phelps, Oliver Cowdery, and John Whitmer were appointed to "review and prepare such Revelations for the press as shall be deemed proper for publication, and print them as soon as possible, at Independence, Mo., the announcement to be made that they are published by W. W. Phelps and Co." For the Saints believe all that God "does now reveal," as well as all that He "has revealed," and that the publication of Revelations now given through the inspired servants of the Lord is as necessary as the placing of former-day revelations on record.

After the Revelation in Section 1, called "The Lord's Preface," had been received at Hiram, Portage Co., Ohio, on the 1st of November, 1831, a number of the brethren who were present at the conference arose and testified to the truth of the *Book of Commandments.* But notwithstanding this fact, some of the brethren criticised the language in which they were recorded, as imperfect. The Prophet Joseph did not take any notice of these critics; if the Lord should select some other instrument through whom to speak to the Church, it would be agreeable to him. But the Lord had no such purpose. He gave the critics a test, in these words, "Now seek ye out of the Book of Commandments, even the least that is among them, and appoint him that is the most wise among you; or, if there be any among you, that shall make one like unto it, then ye are justified in saying that ye do not know that they are true. But if ye cannot make one like unto it, ye are under condemnation if ye do not bear record that they are true" (Doc. and Cov. 67:6-8). That was the test.

William E. M'Lellin accepted the challenge and did his best to bring forth a literary production that should compare favorably with the Revelations given through the Prophet. He was regarded as a learned man at that time, and when he utterly failed, the testimony of the elders was strengthened, and they renewed their allegiance to the Lord and their loyalty to the Prophet. Accordingly, the following declaration was drawn up:

"The testimony of the witnesses to the book of the Lord's Commandments, which He gave to His Church through Joseph Smith, Jr., who was appointed by the voice of the Church for this purpose; we therefore feel willing to bear testimony to all the world of mankind, to every creature upon the face of all the earth and upon the islands of the sea, that the Lord has borne record to our souls, through the Holy Ghost, shed forth upon us, that these commandments were given by inspiration of God, and are profitable for all men, and are verily true. We give this testimony unto the world, the Lord being our helper; and it is through the grace of God, the Father, and His Son, Jesus Christ, that we are permitted to have this privilege of bearing this testimony unto the world, that the children of men may be profited thereby."

Among the elders present at the special conference by which this question was decided were: Joseph Smith, Jr., Oliver Cowdery, David Whitmer, John Whitmer, Peter Whitmer, Jr., Sidney Rigdon, William E. M'Lellin, Orson Hyde, Luke Johnson, and Lyman E. Johnson (*History of the Church,* Vol. I., p. 226). In July 1833, a mob destroyed the press before the *Book of Commandments* was completed and only a portion of the forms were preserved. For this reason the testimony of these brethren was not published with the small collection of revelations later published as the *Book of Commandments.*

On the 24th of September, 1834, a general assembly of Saints appointed a committee, consisting of Joseph Smith, Oliver Cowdery, and F. G. Williams to collect and arrange the Revelations so far given. This work was completed, and on August 17th, 1835, it was presented to a general assembly at Kirtland, under the name of The Doctrine and Covenants. It was accepted by unanimous vote, as a "law and a rule of faith and practice to the Church," on motion of Oliver Cowdery, on behalf of the committee. Many testimonies were borne to the truth of the Revelations. W. W. Phelps read the written testimony of the Twelve,

which was almost identical with that given previously with refer-
ence to the *Book of Commandments*. The Twelve at that time
were: Thomas B. Marsh, David W. Patten, Brigham Young,
Heber C. Kimball, Orson Hyde, William E. M'Lellin, Parley
P. Pratt, Luke S. Johnson, William Smith, Orson Pratt, John F.
Boynton, and Lyman E. Johnson.

After the labors of the committee had been accepted, W. W.
Phelps read an article on "Marriage," and Oliver Cowdery read
one on "Government and Laws in General."*

On the 5th of May, 1879, Elder Orson Pratt, who was then
on a mission in England, received a letter from President John
Taylor, informing him that the Twelve had decided that he
should obtain electro-plates for a new edition of the Doctrine
and Covenants. He divided the text into verses, and added the
references. He was assisted by Elders John Nicholson, Hugh
Findlay, John Rider, and Moroni Snow.

The Christian world should not consider it strange that the
Lord, our God, again reveals His will to His children. Ancient
prophets, speaking of the last days, declare that the Spirit of
God will be poured out upon all flesh, and the result will be
visions, dreams, and prophecies (Isaiah 44:3; Ezek. 11:19;
36:27; Joel 2:28; Zech. 12:10; Acts 2:16-20). The pouring out
of the Spirit upon all flesh is followed by a general Pentecostal
manisfestation.

Joseph Smith was a great man, raised up for the work he
did. He came at the time when the world was prepared for
it. At no other time previously could the Church have been
established. He came in the country where the foundations could
be laid, because the ground had been prepared by liberal laws
and religious influences. In no other country could the foundations of the Church have been laid at that time. He came through

---

* These articles were prepared by Oliver Cowdery, and both were ordered printed,
in the volume of *The Doctrine and Covenants*. Neither of these articles is a revelation and they were not presented as being such. It should be noted that the Prophet
Joseph Smith was not in attendance at this General Assembly, nor was his second
counselor, Frederick G. Williams. They were in Canada at the time and therefore
had no opportunity to pass upon these articles before the action of the Assembly.
(D.H.C. 2:243, 253.) The article on Government is found as Section 134. That on
Marriage is not included in this volume since the Lord has revealed further light
on this subject.

a lineage selected for his earthly mission, equipped with the very characteristics, gifts, and graces of a messenger from God and a martyr. God formed him for his mission. Therefore, he was great in his day and generation; towering over his fellowmen, and yet full of love towards all, willing to serve on all occasions, though mighty in words and deeds.

The subjoined description of the personality of the Prophet Joseph is by Parley P. Pratt:

"President Joseph Smith was in person tall and well built, strong and active, of a light complexion, light hair, blue eyes, very little beard, and of an expression peculiar to himself, on which the eye naturally rested with interest, and was never weary of beholding. His countenance was ever mild, affable, beaming with intelligence and benevolence; mingled with a look of interest and an unconscious smile, a cheerfulness, and entirely free from all restraint or affectation of gravity; and there was something connected with the serene and penetrating glance of his eye, as if he would penetrate the deepest abyss of the human heart, gaze into eternity, penetrate the heavens, and comprehend all worlds.

"He possessed a noble boldness and independence of character; his manner was easy and familiar; his rebuke terrible as the lion; his benevolence unbounded as the ocean; his intelligence universal, and his language abounding in original eloquence, peculiar to himself—not polished—not studied—not smoothed and softened by education and refined by art; but flowing forth in its own native simplicity, and profusely abounding in variety of subject and manner. He interested and edified, while at the same time, amused and entertained his audience; and none listened to him that were ever weary with his discourse. I have even known him to retain a congregation of willing and anxious listeners for many hours together in the midst of cold or sunshine, rain or wind, while they were laughing at one moment, and weeping the next. Even his most bitter enemies were overcome, generally, if he could once get their ears.

"I have known him, when chained and surrounded with armed murderers and assassins who were heaping upon him every possible insult and abuse, rise up in the majesty of a son of God and rebuke them, in the name of Jesus Christ, till they quailed before him, dropped their weapons, and, on their knees, begged his pardon, and ceased their abuse.

"In short, in him the character of a Daniel and a Cyrus were wonderfully blended. The gifts, wisdom and devotion of a Daniel were united with the boldness, courage, temperance, perseverance and generosity of a Cyrus. And had he been spared a martyr's fate until mature manhood and age he was certainly imbued with powers and ability to have revolutionized the world in many respects, and to have transmitted to posterity a name associated with more brilliant and glorious facts than have yet fallen to the lot of mortal. As it is, his work will live to endless ages, and unnumbered millions yet unborn will mention his name with honor, as a noble instrument in the hands of God, who, during his short and youthful career, laid the foundation of that kingdom spoken of by Daniel, the Prophet, which should break in pieces all other kingdoms and stand forever."

Such was the Prophet through whom God gave to the world the Doctrine and Covenants.

DOCTRINE AND COVENANTS

THE

DOCTRINE AND COVENANTS

SECTION 1.

REVELATION *given through Joseph Smith, the Prophet, during a special conference of Elders of the Church of Jesus Christ of Latter-day Saints, held at Hiram, Ohio, November 1, 1831. Many revelations had been received from the Lord prior to this time; and the compilation of these for publication in book form was one of the principal subjects passed upon at the conference. See History of the Church, vol. 1, page 222. This Section constitutes the Lord's Preface to the doctrines, covenants, and commandments given in this dispensation.——Proclamation of warning and commandment to the Church and to the inhabitants of the earth at large—The authority of the Priesthood in this dispensation attested—Second advent of the Lord Jesus Christ foretold—Authenticity of the Book of Mormon affirmed.*

HEARKEN, O ye people of my church, saith the voice of him who dwells on high, and whose eyes are upon all men; yea, verily I say: Hearken ye people from afar; and ye that are upon the islands of the sea, listen together.

2. For verily the voice of the Lord is unto all men, and there is none to escape; and there is no eye that shall not see, neither ear that shall not hear, neither heart that shall not be penetrated.

3. And the rebellious shall be pierced with much sorrow; for their iniquities shall be spoken upon the housetops, and their secret acts shall be revealed.

4. And the voice of warning shall be unto all people, by the mouths of my disciples, whom I have chosen in these last days.

5. And they shall go forth and none shall stay them, for I the Lord have commanded them.

Covenants and Commandments] "You will find in the book of Doctrine and Covenants that these commandments [Exodus 20] have been renewed unto us. The Lord says in one place, All old covenants have I caused to be done away; and this is a new and everlasting covenant. It is even that which was in the beginning; it is that covenant which was made in the days of Jesus. It is that same covenant which the Almighty revealed to Father Adam in the Garden of Eden; but it has been renewed in these last days, and hence it is a new and everlasting covenant. Those covenants that we have made with God were also made in the beginning of creation. They are now renewed to us; and revelations of this kind are just as binding upon you and me as the words and counsels that come from President Young and others. We are acting in the same capacity that the apostles and prophets of former dispensations have acted, and our word will have the same effect upon this generation that theirs had upon the generations in which they lived. We have the same God to worship; the same Jesus lives to save, and He has spoken and renewed this covenant to us and for us, and to remain with us forever and forever" (Heber C. Kimball, *Journal of Discourses,* Vol. VIII, pp. 330, 331).

The term "covenant" signifies the settled arrangement between God and man, whereby the eternal Father undertakes to save His children. This arrangement is also called His "oath," His "counsel," and His "promise" (Psalm 89:3, 4; Heb. 6:13-20). "Commandments" are the laws, or rules man must obey as a condition of obtaining salvation. Divine covenants are ratified with a sacrifice, to show us in a most impressive manner that the wages of sin is death, and that eternal life can be gained only through atonement. Jesus Christ is both the Sacrifice and the Mediator of the new and everlasting covenant (Heb. 9:16). Some fail to understand how God can enter into a covenant with man, since a "covenant" means mutual obligations and benefits, and in the relations between the Creator and the creature, they say, both the benefits and obligations are all on one side, the side of man; but that is hardly the entire truth. In so far as God, the eternal Father, can be said to yearn for the salvation and exaltation of His children, He is benefited by their keeping the covenant faithfully. Their salvation is His joy, and His Glory, in the same sense that the success of all children is the joy of their loving parents. Our Savior prayed, "Glorify thy Son, that thy Son also may glorify thee" (John 17:1), and that prayer all God's children may properly repeat. The salvation of man adds to the glory of God. "For behold, this is my work and my glory—to bring to pass the immortality and eternal life of man" (Pearl of Great Price, Book of Moses 1:39).

1. In this revelation God addresses the members of the Church, at that time only eighteen months old, and sorely persecuted; and also the inhabitants of the earth generally. There is no doubt, therefore, that the Doctrine and Covenants is a book intended for the instruction of all. This is still more emphasized in verse 2.

3. *The "rebellious"*] This expression refers to every soul who rejects the everlasting Gospel. When the Church of Jesus Christ of Latter-day Saints was established, this position was made clear to all the world. When the light comes, they can no longer hide their errors, their iniquities, their secret acts. The light reveals these things. That is the true cause of the enmity toward the Church. They want the light extinguished. It hurts them.

4-5. But, notwithstanding all enmity, the servants of the Lord are commanded, and authorized, to lift up their Voice of Warning in all the world, and "none shall stay them."

6. Behold, this is mine authority, and the authority of my servants, and my preface unto the book of my commandments, which I have given them to publish unto you, O inhabitants of the earth.

7. Wherefore, fear and tremble, O ye people, for what I the Lord have decreed in them shall be fulfilled.

8. And verily I say unto you, that they who go forth, bearing these tidings unto the inhabitants of the earth, to them is power given to seal both on earth and in heaven, the unbelieving and rebellious;

9. Yea, verily, to seal them up unto the day when the wrath of God shall be poured out upon the wicked without measure—

10. Unto the day when the Lord shall come to recompense unto every man according to his work, and measure to every man according to the measure which he has measured to his fellow man.

6. *This is mine authority*] This section contains the divine authority, and also the authority of God's servants, "whom I have chosen in these last days" (v. 4), to re-establish the Church: that is, the credentials given by our Lord to the Prophet Joseph and his associates in the ministry, and by them transmitted to others, regularly called and ordained, giving them divine authority to preach the gospel and warn the world. It is also God's preface to the Book of Commandments, the title under which the Doctrine and Covenants was first published.

7. God's decrees never fail. Some of those contained in this volume, have been remarkably fulfilled to the letter. All will be fulfilled in the same way.

8-10. The servants of the Lord have been given "power to seal." Ancient seals were used either to stamp the name of the owner, or some other mark of identification, on a document, or other object. Some seals were signet rings, worn on the hand; others were quite large affairs. In Ezek. 9:4-6, the man in linen garment was commanded to place a "mark"—the letter *Tav,* our T—on the foreheads of those who did not partake in the abominations practiced in Jerusalem. As *Tav* is the last letter in the Hebrew alphabet, it might properly be used as an abbreviation of the name of Him who is the First and the Last. In Rev. 7:4-8, an angel has the commission to seal the servants of God in their foreheads, and from Rev. 14:1, it appears that the "mark" used at the time there referred to was the name of God, the Father of our Lord, in full. That sealing, or marking, was done, as the sprinkling of the blood upon the door-posts of the houses on the night of the exodus from Egypt, in order to save those who were so marked, from destruction. The power to seal conferred upon the servants of the Lord in this, the last dispensation, extends to the "unbelieving" and "rebellious." They have power to discern between truth and error, right and wrong, and to declare, authoritatively, that such and such doctrine is true, and the opposite false; that such and such conduct is in accordance with the mind and will of God, and that the contrary conduct is sinful. They have power to put the seal of disapprobation upon the children of men who persist in unbelief and rebellion, and those who are thus "sealed" and remain in that condition, will suffer the wrath of God. This sealing concerns the "unbelievers," those who refuse to accept the gospel message; and the "rebellious," i.e., those who turn against the servants of the Lord, especially those who do so after having enjoyed the privileges and blessings of membership in the Church.

11. Wherefore the voice of the Lord is unto the ends of the earth, that all that will hear may hear:

12. Prepare ye, prepare ye for that which is to come, for the Lord is nigh;

13. And the anger of the Lord is kindled, and his sword is bathed in heaven, and it shall fall upon the inhabitants of the earth.

14. And the arm of the Lord shall be revealed; and the day cometh that they who will not hear the voice of the Lord, neither the voice of his servants, neither give heed to the words of the prophets and apostles, shall be cut off from among the people;

15. For they have strayed from mine ordinances, and have broken mine everlasting covenant;

16. They seek not the Lord to establish his righteousness, but every man walketh in his own way, and after the image of his own God, whose image is in the likeness of the world, and whose substance is that of an idol, which waxeth old and shall perish in Babylon, even Babylon the great, which shall fall.

11-12. The message of the Lord to the inhabitants of the Earth, through His authorized servants, is here stated, "Prepare ye for that which is to come, for *the Lord is nigh.*" Hitherto the adversary has reigned supreme; now the day of the Lord is at hand.

13. *Anger of the Lord*] God is long-suffering, and infinitely patient, but His anger is now kindled, and He has unsheathed His sword. It is "bathed in heaven." This is a very expressive term from Isaiah 34:5, where it is used to signify the pouring out of the indignation of the Lord upon all nations and His fury upon their armies, delivering them to destruction and slaughter. The Lord here tells us that the day predicted by Isaiah, and other prophets, as the day of the Lord, has come, and that it is a day of war and slaughter. For the armaments of nations must be destroyed before the reign of peace can be established.

15-16. The reason why the children of men came to be in such a condition, that nothing but bloodshed could save them, is here given. They have strayed from the ordinances of the Lord: changed them, and added to them, or abolished them. Baptism has been changed to infant sprinkling, and the Lord's supper, to a sacrificial rite. One church has added five sacraments to the two instituted by our Lord; another disregards both baptism and the supper. That is one reason. Furthermore, they have broken the everlasting covenant, by pursuing another plan of salvation than that agreed upon in the Council of heaven before the creation of the world. That plan was founded upon individual freedom and the honor and glory of God. Men have, very largely, adopted the plan of the adversary and established a reign of compulsion for the aggrandizement of man. They have made an "image," a likeness of God, that is but a likeness of the world. A God without body, parts, or passions, is the god of the world, "whose substance is that of an idol"; there is nothing more substantial to that conception of God than there is to the pagan conception, that finds expression in an idol. Speaking of a God without body, parts, or passions, Parley P. Pratt observes: "It is painful to the human mind to be compelled to admit, that such wonderful inconsistencies of language, or ideas, have ever found place in any human creed. Yet, so it is. It is but another way of saying, that there is a God who does not exist, a God who is composed of nonentity, who is the negative of all existence, who occupies no space, who exists in no time, who is composed of no substance, known, or unknown, and who has no powers or properties in common with any thing or being known to exist, or which can possibly be conceived of, as existing either in the heavens or on the earth" (*Key to Theology,* p. 27).

17. Wherefore, I the Lord, knowing the calamity which should come upon the inhabitants of the earth, called upon my servant Joseph Smith, Jun., and spake unto him from heaven, and gave him commandments;

18. And also gave commandments to others, that they should proclaim these things unto the world; and all this that it might be fulfilled, which was written by the prophets—

19. The weak things of the world shall come forth and break down the mighty and strong ones, that man should not counsel his fellow man, neither trust in the arm of flesh—

20. But that every man might speak in the name of God the Lord, even the Savior of the world;

21. That faith also might increase in the earth;

22. That mine everlasting covenant might be established;

23. That the fulness of my gospel might be proclaimed by the weak and the simple unto the ends of the world, and before kings and rulers.

24. Behold, I am God and have spoken it; these commandments are of me, and were given unto my servants in their weakness, after the manner of their language, that they might come to understanding.

25. And inasmuch as they erred it might be made known;

26. And inasmuch as they sought wisdom they might be instructed;

27. And inasmuch as they sinned they might be chastened, that they might repent;

28. And inasmuch as they were humble they might be made strong, and blessed from on high, and receive knowledge from time to time.

29. And after having received the record of the Nephites, yea, even my servant Joseph Smith, Jun., might have power to translate through the mercy of God, by the power of God, the Book of Mormon.

30. And also those to whom these commandments were

given, might have power to lay the foundation of this church, and to bring it forth out of obscurity and out of darkness, the only true and living church upon the face of the whole earth, with which I, the Lord, am well pleased, speaking unto the church collectively and not individually—

31. For I the Lord cannot look upon sin with the least degree of allowance;

32. Nevertheless, he that repents and does the commandments of the Lord shall be forgiven;

33. And he that repents not, from him shall be taken even the light which he has received; for my Spirit shall not always strive with man, saith the Lord of Hosts.

17-19. The Lord knew that calamities would overtake the world, in the form of wars, famine, pestilence, earthquakes, floods, etc., because of the apostate condition of Christendom; for that reason He commissioned Joseph Smith and others to sound a voice of warning and find a place of refuge for those who would accept their message. They were weak in the estimation of the world. So was Paul (I.Cor.2:3).

24. *Weakness*] "When the Lord reveals anything to men, He reveals it in language that accords with their own. If any of you were to converse with an angel, and you used strictly grammatical language, he would do the same. But if you used two negatives in a sentence, the heavenly messenger would use language to correspond with your understanding, and this very objection to the Book of Mormon is an evidence in its favor" (George A. Smith, *Journal of Discourses,* Vol. VII., p. 335).

25-29. But through their testimony faith was to be increased in the earth (v. 21), the everlasting covenant established (v. 22), and the fulness of the gospel proclaimed (v. 23). Errors were to be revealed (v. 25), sins reproved (v. 27), and the humble to be made strong and receive knowledge. It is to be noted that God, who gave the Prophet Joseph power to translate the Book of Mormon, and lay the foundations of the Church, also gave him the Revelations in this volume (v. 24, 30). They are from the same Source, and of equal importance.

30-33. Through his instrumentality the Church was brought forth "out of obscurity." John, the Revelator, saw the Church fleeing into the wilderness (Rev. 12:6), where it was to remain 1260 "days." This period expired in 1830, and then the Church came forth, and was revealed in its pristine glory, power, and purity. The Lord was "well pleased" with the Church, its doctrines, precepts, and organization, and also with the members generally; however, there were some with whom He was not pleased, for He does not condone sin in Church members because of their membership (v. 31), any more than in anybody else. They, too, must repent, if they want forgiveness (v. 32), and if they do not repent, the light will be taken from them. The Spirit will be withdrawn (v. 33).

"The Church should be cleansed from bad men, and the Lord will take His own way to cleanse the Church" (Orson Spencer, *History of the Church,* Vol. VI, p. 273). "Every tree that bringeth not forth good fruit, God Almighty (not Joseph Smith) shall hew it down and cast it into the fire" (Joseph Smith, *Ibid.* p. 274).

34. And again, verily I say unto you, O inhabitants of the earth: I the Lord am willing to make these things known unto all flesh;

35. For I am no respecter of persons, and will that all men shall know that the day speedily cometh; the hour is not yet, but is nigh at hand, when peace shall be taken from the earth, and the devil shall have power over his own dominion.

36. And also the Lord shall have power over his saints, and shall reign in their midst, and shall come down in judgment upon Idumea, or the world.

34-36. The Lord reiterates His warning to all the inhabitants of the earth. The day is coming, when peace shall be taken from the Earth. "The hour is not yet (when this revelation was given,) but it is nigh at hand." The beginning of the fulfillment of this day when peace was taken from the earth appears to be at the commencement of the Civil War. This is implied in the first verse of the revelation on War. Surely it is plain to see after the great conflicts in which the entire world has been involved in war and bloodshed, distress and wickedness, that peace is not found today on the earth. Never before in the history of the world, as far as we have knowledge, has there been the turmoil, contention, strife among nations and unrest and uncertainty that is found today in this troubled world. Wickedness and disregard for every sacred principle predominate in the world in the lives of men. We can say as the Lord said to Noah, "all flesh had corrupted its way upon the earth." All these wars are really a struggle of the adversary of all righteousness against our Lord, for dominion, but the outcome will be that the Lord shall reign and the world be judged.

37. Search these commandments, for they are true and faithful, and the prophecies and promises which are in them shall all be fulfilled.

38. What I the Lord have spoken, I have spoken, and I excuse not myself; and though the heavens and the earth pass away, my word shall not pass away, but shall all be fulfilled,

whether by mine own voice or by the voice of my servants, it is the same.

39. For behold, and lo, the Lord is God, and the Spirit beareth record, and the record is true, and the truth abideth forever and ever. Amen.

37-39. The concluding verses are a commandment to study this book, for it contains the truth. Every word will be fulfilled. Can we receive a testimony of the truth? Yes, for the Spirit beareth record of the truth. And so does history.

GENERAL NOTES

Hiram, Portage Co., Ohio, where this Revelation was given, together with fourteen others, is a small village situated about 30 miles from Kirtland. In 1831, "Father" Johnson, who lived there, invited the Prophet Joseph to come and stay with him, which invitation was accepted. During his residence there, the Prophet was engaged in Bible study and translation, Sidney Rigdon assisting him as scribe. He held several conferences there, and preached on the Sabbath days, and many were baptized. This aroused persecution. It was there, on the 25th of March, 1832, that a mob planned to assassinate him; but this God did not permit them to do. The Prophet and Sidney Rigdon were maltreated during the night by fiends in human form. Sidney Rigdon almost lost his life on this occasion. When the Prophet, in the morning, went to see him, he found his co-laborer delirious. During the mobbing a twin child of John Murdock, which Mrs. Emma Smith had adopted, took a severe cold, that, a few days later, ended fatally. Both of the children were at the time sick with measles. The mob was composed of members of various denominations. It was under such circumstances that some of these glorious Revelations were received. Paul was given a "thorn in the flesh," a "messenger," or angel, "from Satan, to buffet him, lest he should be exalted through the abundance of revelations" (II. Cor. 12: 7), and it may well be that troubles are necessary to keep the servants of the Lord humble when they are highly favored with revelations.

FIRST PERIOD, 1823-1830, SECTIONS 2-37.

SECTION 2.

WORDS SPOKEN BY MORONI, *the Angel, to Joseph Smith the Prophet, while in his father's house at Manchester, New York, on the evening of September 21, 1823. See History of the Church, vol. 1, page 12. Moroni was the last of a long line of historians who had made the record that is now before the world as the Book of Mormon. Compare Malachi 4:5, 6. See also Sections 27:9 and 110:13-16.*

BEHOLD, I will reveal unto you the Priesthood, by the hand of Elijah the prophet, before the coming of the great and dreadful day of the Lord.

2. And he shall plant in the hearts of the children the promises made to the fathers, and the hearts of the children shall turn to their fathers.

3. If it were not so, the whole earth would be utterly wasted at his coming.

This Revelation is part of the message which Moroni delivered to the Prophet on the 21st day of September, 1823. In the evening of that day, after he had retired, Joseph engaged in prayer, asking for forgiveness for his past sins and imperfections, and for some manifestation of divine favor. While he thus prayed, the room gradually became light until it was lighter than at noon, and in the light appeared a personage, standing by the bedside. His robe was exceedingly white and his person glorious beyond description. At first the youthful Prophet was afraid, but presently all fear left him. The heavenly visitor called him by name and introduced himself as a messenger sent from the presence of God, whose name was Moroni. He then delivered his message. God had a work for him (Joseph) to do. If he would do it, he should be spoken of among all nations "for good and evil." The nature of the work was then explained. An ancient record had been deposited in a certain place, containing an account of the former inhabitants of the American continents, including the fulness of the gospel as it was preached to them. These records were to be recovered and translated.

Continuing his revelations, Moroni quoted passages from the book of Malachi, the last of the Old Testament prophets; for the work about to begin was but the fulfilment of ancient prophecies. "The revelation of God," as students of theology know, "is always continuous. Each fresh step is developed out of, and is in harmony with, those which went before."

Among the paragraphs quoted by Moroni was this: "For behold, the day cometh that shall burn as an oven, and all the proud, yea, and all that do wickedly shall burn as stubble; for they that come shall burn them, saith the Lord of hosts, that it shall leave them neither root nor branch" (Mal. 4:1). Then he quoted the 5th and 6th verses of the same chapter, as found in this Section. He quoted other passages of the scriptures, with explanations, and gave certain instructions regarding the records referred to, and then he withdrew, but appeared again and again the same night.

1. *The great and dreadful day of the Lord*] This "day" of judgment is to follow the coming of Elijah and the turning of the hearts of the children to their fathers and the hearts of the fathers to the children. It is necessary that the keys of this sealing power held by Elijah be restored that there might come to pass the sealing of parents to each other and children to their parents, of the righteous who are living, and in behalf of the dead who would have received the fulness of the Gospel had the privilege come to them. (D.H.C. Vol. 2:180). This will be a dreadful day to all the rebellious who have refused to receive these sealing ordinances by which families become united for time and all eternity.

Moroni informed the Prophet that great judgments were about to come upon the earth, in the form of famine, sword and pestilence, in the present generation, but not until the Priesthood had been revealed, and the sealing power by the hand of Elijah was restored so that husbands and wives could be sealed to each other and children sealed to their parents. That which makes the day to come so great and terrible, is not confined to the distress of peoples and nations, because of famine and war, but more particularly will it be great and dreadful to all of those who find themselves outside of the great family of our Father in heaven because they have not obtained these everlasting sealing ordinances, so essential to the exaltation.

"That great prophet, apostle, and martyr, Joseph Smith, was the Elias, the Restorer, the presiding messenger, holding the keys of the *Dispensation of the fulness of times;* yes, that extraordinary man * * * was the chosen vessel * * * to be a messenger in the spirit and power of Elijah, to prepare the way of the Lord! For, behold, he will suddenly come to his temple" (*Key to Theology*, p. 79).

Joseph Smith, after receiving the keys of restoration from John the Baptist, Peter, James and John, Elias, Moses and Elijah, and all other prophets who held keys of dispensations, also became a restorer, an Elias called to prepare the way before the coming of the Lord. In this point Elder Parley P. Pratt has said:

"The United States of America was the favored nation raised up, with institutions adapted to the protection and free-development of the necessary truths, and their practical results. And that great Prophet, and Martyr, Joseph Smith, was the Elias, the Restorer, the presiding Messenger, holding the keys of the *'Dispensation of the Fulness of Times.'*" "Yes, that extraordinary man, * * * was the chosen vessel honored of God, and ordained by angels, to ordain other Apostles and Elders, to restore the Church and Kingdom of God, the gifts of the Holy Spirit, and to be a messenger in the spirit and power of Elijah, to prepare the way of the Lord! For behold, he will suddenly come to his temple!"

The prophecy of Malachi has a double fulfillment. It was fulfilled in the coming of John, wherein he declared: "Behold, I will send my messenger, and he shall prepare the way before me: and the Lord, whom ye seek, shall suddenly come to his temple, even the messenger of the covenant, whom ye delight in: behold, he shall come, saith the Lord of hosts." The prevailing opinion is that this passage has reference to John, and that too, with reference to his first coming to prepare the way for the ministry of Jesus Christ. A careful reading, however, will reveal that this coming of the messenger to prepare the way was to have its fulfillment in the last days, not the days of our Lord's ministry. It is very apparent that in the former day the offering of Judah and Jerusalem was not pleasant, nor did the sons of Levi in that day offer an offering that was pleasant, but all of this to the contrary. The Lord did not at that time come as a swift messenger against the sorcerers, and against the adulterers, etc. But when he comes again all of this will be fulfilled. Joseph Smith was called to be an Elias in this dispensation to prepare the way before him.

In the Old Testament the name of the great prophet to whom Malachi refers is *Elijah*. This is the Hebrew form of the word. In the New Testament the Greek form, *Elias,* is used. Both mean the same and refer to the same person, and the same office. In later writings the two forms of the names occur indiscriminately. But we know from the Doctrine and Covenants (Sec. 110) that there are two personages, and two offices, one called Elias, and the other Elijah. No further information is given concerning the life, or history, of Elias, but he appeared in the Kirtland temple to Joseph and Oliver Cowdery and "committed the dispensation of the gospel of Abraham, saying, that in us and our seed, all generations after us should be blessed" (Doc. and Cov. 110:12). The Prophet Joseph draws a sharp distinction between the spirit and office of the two, and retains for the one the Old Testament form of the name, and for the other the New. He says:—

"I saw an angel, and he laid his hands upon my head, and ordained me to a priest after the order of Aaron * * * But I was informed that this office did not extend to the laying on of hands for the giving of the Holy Ghost * * * but that my ordination was a preparatory work, or a going before, which was the spirit of Elias."

*   *   *

"The spirit of Elias is to prepare the way for a greater revelation of God, which is the Priesthood of Elias, or the Priesthood that Aaron was ordained into. And when God sends a man into the world to prepare for a greater work, holding the keys of the power of Elias, it was called the doctrine of Elias, even from the early ages of the world."

*   *   *

"The spirit, power, and calling of Elijah is, that ye have power to hold the key of the revelation, ordinances, oracles, powers, and en- dowments of the fulness of the Melchizedek Priesthood and of the kingdom of God on the earth; and to receive, obtain, and perform all the ordinances belonging to the kingdom of God, even unto the turning of the hearts of the fathers unto the children, and the hearts of the children unto their fathers, even those who are in heaven" (*History of the Church,* Vol. VI, pp. 250-1).

It has already been stated that "the day of the Lord" is a day of judgment upon nations. In the prophecies of Zephaniah (1:14-18) that day is described as a day of battle and assault upon "fenced cities," and also a day of "trouble and distress," "wasteness and desolation," "dark- ness and gloominess," and "trumpet and alarm." It is the *dies irae* of the poet—the day of wrath.

"The day of the Lord is the day of His self-revelation to judge evil and bring His work of redemption among men to completion. On the one side His revelation of Himself fills men with terror and anguish; on the other side it is the cause of universal gladness, for the oppressions under which the world groaned come to an end and the reign of God begins: 'The Lord is king; let the earth rejoice; let the multitude of isles be glad * * * for he cometh to rule the earth; he shall rule the earth with righteousness, and the people with equity' (Psalms 97:1; 98-9). * * * The judgment of the day of the Lord is a judgment on the known world, on Israel and the historical nations lying within its horizon, and the nation that executes the judgment is some fierce and wild people emerg- ing from the dark places of the earth lying beyond the confines of the known world" (*Cambridge Bible,* Notes under Zephaniah, pp. 117-8).

Note, that Elijah, according to the Scriptures, was to restore the Priesthood before the coming of that day.

1. *Priesthood*] This is authority to act in the name of our Lord.

"What is this power that is conferred upon us in the holy Priesthood? What particular power do you give when you send a man to some other land to transact business in your name? You give him a power of attorney, authorizing him to transact in your name the business that you wish to be performed; and in that letter of appointment would be conveyed all your power, your authority, and ability to transact that business, even as effectually as if you yourself were present to perform it with your own hand" (Orson Hyde, *Journal of Discourses,* Vol. VIII., p. 20).

"It is in the order of heavenly things that God should always send a new dispensation into the world when men have apostatized from the truth and lost the Priesthood; but when men come out and build upon other men's foundations, they do it on their own responsibility, without authority from God" (Joseph Smith, *History of the Church,* Vol. VI., p. 474).

2. *And he shall plant,* etc.] The mission of the Prophet Elijah is here stated. It is to restore the keys that will bring to pass the promise made by Malachi, to plant in the hearts of the children the promises made to the fathers etc. The fathers are our ancestors for whom the work of salvation could not be done while they were living. *This includes all from the beginning down to and including this dispensation who were denied the knowledge of the Gospel and the privilege of the ordinances thereof.* The children are those who are living since the restoration of the keys of salvation and exaltation who now have the privilege of working in behalf of their dead, performing the ordinances vicariously and preparing the way that these ordinances may be accomplished for the dead.

If it were not so, the whole earth would be utterly wasted at his coming.] This implies that if the keys of the sealing power were not restored so that the families might be sealed and thus their unity made eternally sure, the entire work of the Lord would fail and be utterly wasted at the coming of the Lord. The crowning blessing in the kingdom of God is the preservation of the family, and this earth is to be the eternal abode of the righteous.

SECTION 3.

REVELATION *given to Joseph Smith the Prophet, at Harmony, Pennsylvania, July, 1828, relating to the loss of certain manuscripts of the first part of the Book of Mormon, which Joseph had reluctantly allowed to pass from his custody to that of Martin Harris, who had served for a brief period as scribe in the translation of the Book of Mormon. This revelation was given through the Urim and Thummim. See History of the Church, vol. 1, p. 21. Compare Section 10.*

THE works, and the designs, and the purposes of God cannot be frustrated, neither can they come to naught.

2. For God doth not walk in crooked paths, neither doth he turn to the right hand nor to the left, neither doth he vary from that which he hath said, therefore his paths are straight, and his course is one eternal round.

3. Remember, remember that it is not the work of God that is frustrated, but the work of men;

4. For although a man may have many revelations, and have power to do many mighty works, yet if he boasts in his own strength, and sets at naught the counsels of God, and follows after the dictates of his own will and carnal desires, he must fall and incur the vengeance of a just God upon him.

The Prophet Joseph had found, in Martin Harris, a valuable friend, whose friendship, however, was not altogether free from danger. Harris was a prosperous farmer. He gave freely of his means to help the Prophet in his poverty. He took a facsimile of some of the characters engraved on the Book of Mormon plates to scientists in New York, Professor Charles Anthon and Dr. Samuel L. Mitchell, and returned satisfied in his own mind, from the interviews, that the writings were genuine. He went to the Prophet's temporary home in Harmony, Pennsylvania, and acted as a scribe for him, manifesting great interest in the work. But, when he had written 116 pages, he began to importune the Prophet for permission to carry the manuscript home and show it to his friends. He urged the Prophet to inquire of the Lord, through Urim and Thummim. The Prophet, yielding to the pertinacity of his friend, laid the matter before the Lord. The answer received was in the negative. But Martin Harris would not take "No" for an answer. In all probability he was anxious to convince his friends of the truth of the cause in which he had become interested, and, no doubt, he hoped to be able to do so by submitting the manuscript for their inspection. At all events, he prevailed upon the Prophet to ask the Lord again. The reply was another refusal. But Martin Harris still persisted. Finally, the Lord permitted him to take the manuscript and show it to his wife, his father, mother, and brother, and to his wife's sister, but to nobody else. To this he agreed. But alas! he did not keep the agreement, and the precious writings were lost and never recovered. For a short time the Urim and Thummim was taken from the Prophet. When he again was entrusted with the guardianship of this sacred instrument, he went before the Lord, in humility, and received this Revelation.

1. *Cannot be frustrated*] The disappearance of the manuscript was a great loss, but the Lord here takes occasion to assert that His plans and purposes can never be frustrated, or brought to naught, by anything man can do. His government is supreme; His providence is over all. Nor can He be turned out of the established course, or be made to vary from His word. It is the privilege of God's children to pray, but, if, like Martin Harris, they ask God to break His word, prayer is not acceptable.

3. *The work of men*] This is often frustrated; the work of God, never. Even when to our view God's plans appear to be upset, His eternal purposes are being worked out.

This suggests a word or two about the providence of God. He preserves and governs all His creatures, and directs their actions, so that the ultimate results will serve the ends He has in view. The universe and all that it contains is sustained by His power; it would go back into chaos, if He should withdraw that power. He overrules the affairs of nations. "He changeth the times and the seasons; he removeth kings and setteth up kings" (Daniel 2:21). In the same way He governs individuals. There is an old adage which says, "Man proposes, but God disposes." The Lord turns the acts of men and nations to his purposes although they may design to overthrow His work and establish their own. While it may appear, at times, that the work of the Lord is defeated, it is only for a short period of time. "The Lord killeth and maketh alive; he bringeth down to the grave and bringeth up. The Lord maketh poor and maketh rich, he bringeth low and lifteth up" (I. Sam. 2:6, 7). He is the Lord, the absolute Ruler, (Isaiah 45:5), but He governs without interfering with the free agency of man. He overrules all for good. Notwithstanding the wicked conduct of men, thirst for plunder, war, and bloodshed, the world has been so shaped and formed that the gospel can be preached in it and the Church send out its light from the mountain tops. The very persecution of the Saints in the early days, resulted in the firmer establishment of the Church, and its triumphant rise and advance. Thus God governs supreme, and this glorious doctrine, the consolation of His people in all ages, is here re-affirmed. It may be contrary to the teachings of philosophers of worldly schools, but it is the gospel, and, therefore, the truth.

4. *A man may have many revelations,* etc.] Man may fall, notwithstanding revelations and spiritual gifts, but God's work will go on just the same. This is amply illustrated in the history of the Church. Some of the most gifted and most trusted men fell by the wayside, because they were proud, set aside God's counsel, and followed their own will and carnal desires, but their fall did not impede the progress of the Church.

5. Behold, you have been entrusted with these things, but

how strict were your commandments; and remember also the promises which were made to you, if you did not transgress them.

6. And behold, how oft you have transgressed the commandments and the laws of God, and have gone on in the persuasions of men.

7. For, behold, you should not have feared man more than God. Although men set at naught the counsels of God, and despise his words—

8. Yet you should have been faithful; and he would have extended his arm and supported you against all the fiery darts of the adversary; and he would have been with you in every time of trouble.

5. *These things*] The manuscript which Martin Harris carried away.

How strict were your commandments] The angel Moroni had instructed the Prophet not to show the Book of Mormon plates to anyone, except those to whom he should be commanded to exhibit them; if he did, he would be destroyed. That equally strict instructions had been given regarding the translated copy is probable. The angel met Joseph on at least four different occasions after the visit in 1823. On each of these, minute instructions were imparted regarding the publication of the Book of Mormon.

6. *Transgressed*] Joseph transgressed by listening to the continued pleadings of his friend. It should be realized that Joseph Smith at this time was but a youth with confidence in the promise of his friends. His faith in God was absolutely firm, but he lacked experience in trusting his untried friend in his constant pleadings. He learned his lesson. From this time on he made no other such mistake. A great man does not repeat his mistakes. Joseph was a great man and he profited by his experiences.

9. Behold, thou art Joseph, and thou wast chosen to do the work of the Lord, but because of transgression, if thou art not aware thou wilt fall.

10. But remember, God is merciful; therefore, repent of that which thou hast done which is contrary to the commandment which I gave you, and thou art still chosen, and art again called to the work;

11. Except thou do this, thou shalt be delivered up and become as other men, and have no more gift.

9. *Thou wast chosen*] The Prophet Joseph was chosen to do the work of the Lord. So was Isaiah (Isa. 49:5); Jeremiah (Jer. 1:5); Paul (Acts 9:15), and many others. But although God had selected him to be His instrument, unless he kept the commandments and instructions imparted to him, he would fall and lose his gift. God does not pre-ordain man's fate, except conditionally. If He has decreed that men shall live by food, He has also made it necessary to prepare and to eat the food in order to enjoy the gift and blessings of life. That is the condition. He chose Israel to be His people, but only on the condition that they would keep His commandments. When they rejected Him, He rejected them. There is no other predestination.

12. And when thou deliveredst up that which God had given thee sight and power to translate, thou deliveredst up that which was sacred into the hands of a wicked man,

13. Who has set at naught the counsels of God, and has broken the most sacred promises which were made before God, and has depended upon his own judgment, and boasted in his own wisdom.

14. And this is the reason that thou hast lost thy privileges for a season—

15. For thou hast suffered the counsel of thy director to be trampled upon from the beginning.

12. *A wicked man*] Martin Harris was "wicked" in persisting to ask for what God at first refused to grant. He was "wicked" in not keeping the sacred pledge to guard the manuscript. But otherwise he was not a wicked man, as that term is generally understood. A father will sometimes call his boy "wicked," meaning disobedient for the time being.

15. *Thy director*] The Urim and Thummim. There is difference of opinion among Bible students concerning the use of this sacred instrument; but it is generally admitted that through it the divine will on important questions was ascertained in some manner not described. In the original Hebrew text of I. Sam. 14:41, presupposed by the translators of the *Septuagint,* we read, "And Saul said, O Jehovah, the God of Israel, why hast thou not answered thy servant this day? If the iniquity be in me, or in Jonathan my son, *give Urim;* and if it be in thy people Israel, *give Thummim.*" "(The Hebrew words rendered * * * Give a perfect (lot) are a mutilated fragment of the longer text preserved in the *Septuagint* * * *). The priest who cast the lots on this occasion was evidently Ahijah" (*Cambridge Bible,* Notes under Exodus, p. 314). This shows that the people of God anciently enquired of the Lord through Urim and Thummim. When, however, the Spirit of prophecy was poured out in great abundance, the sacred instrument was not necessarily needed.

After the organization of the Church the Prophet Joseph could ascertain the mind and will of the Lord without any outward aid. The office of the Spirit is to lead into all truth.

16. Nevertheless, my work shall go forth, for inasmuch as the knowledge of a Savior has come unto the world, through the testimony of the Jews, even so shall the knowledge of a Savior come unto my people—

17. And to the Nephites, and the Jacobites, and the Josephites, and the Zoramites, through the testimony of their fathers—

18. And this testimony shall come to the knowledge of the Lamanites, and the Lemuelites, and the Ishmaelites, who dwindled in unbelief because of the iniquity of their fathers, whom the Lord has suffered to destroy their brethren the Nephites, because of their iniquities and their abominations.

19. And for this very purpose are these plates preserved, which contain these records—that the promises of the Lord might be fulfilled, which he made to his people;

20. And that the Lamanites might come to the knowledge of their fathers, and that they might know the promises of the Lord, and that they may believe the gospel and rely upon the merits of Jesus Christ, and be glorified through faith in his name, and that through their repentance they might be saved. Amen.

16. *My work shall go forth*] The Book of Mormon. The time had come for the publication of that Book, and, therefore, it "shall go forth."

My people] God's scattered children who were to be gathered from all the nations of the earth.

17. *Nephites*] At the beginning of our era, one section of America was divided into two great divisions, one being the *Land of Nephi,* and the other, *Zarahemla.* The Nephites generally occupied Zarahemla. A desert separated the two countries.

Jacobites] One of the tribes of the Nephites, the descendants of Jacob, the son of Lehi.

Josephites] Another tribe of the Nephites, the descendants of Joseph, a son of Lehi.

Zoramites] A family of the Nephites, the descendants of Zoram, the servant of Laban.

Lamanites] These were the descendants of Laman, the eldest son of Lehi. They separated themselves from their brethren, the Nephites, waged war upon them, and, finally, destroyed them.

Lemuelites] The descendants of Lemuel. They formed a tribe of the Lamanites.

Ishmaelites] Descendants of that Ishmael who, with his family, accompanied Lehi on the journey to the American Continents.

In course of time, all these mixed, so that the names became a religious rather than a racial distinction:

"Now the people which were not Lamanites, were Nephites; nevertheless, they were called Nephites, Jacobites, Josephites, Zoramites, Lamanites, Lemuelites, and Ishmaelites (Book of Mormon, Jacob 1:13).

19. *For this very purpose*] The Book of Mormon plates were preserved and translated in order that all these should be brought to a knowledge of the Savior. It may be concluded, then, that among the American Indians and the Polynesians who are mostly the descendants of the Lamanites, is also a sprinkling of the descendants of the Nephites who may have escaped the general destruction.

SECTION 4.

REVELATION *given through Joseph Smith the Prophet, to his father, Joseph Smith, Sen., at Harmony, Pennsylvania, February, 1829.——Qualifications for the labors of the ministry are set forth.*

NOW behold, a marvelous work is about to come forth among the children of men.

2. Therefore, O ye that embark in the service of God, see that ye serve him with all your heart, might, mind and strength, that ye may stand blameless before God at the last day.

3. Therefore, if ye have desires to serve God ye are called to the work;

4. For behold the field is white already to harvest; and lo, he that thrusteth in his sickle with his might, the same layeth up in store that he perisheth not, but bringeth salvation to his soul;

5. And faith, hope, charity and love, with an eye single to the glory of God, qualify him for the work.

6. Remember faith, virtue, knowledge, temperance, patience, brotherly kindness, godliness, charity, humility, diligence.

7. Ask, and ye shall receive; knock, and it shall be opened unto you. Amen.

Joseph Smith, Sr., the father of the Prophet, was among the first to accept the calling of his remarkable son as from God. When, after repeated visits of the angel Moroni, during the night of September 21st, 1823, and the following forenoon, Joseph was physically exhausted and sorely in need of a friend and confidant, he unburdened his soul, by a full statement of what had transpired, to his father. Joseph Smith, Sr., this God's nobleman, did not scoff; he was not even impatient. He listened reverently to the wonderful story told by his boy, and then, his mind enlightened by a flash of intelligence from the divine Spirit of truth, he declared that the message was from God, and counseled Joseph to do as the angel had commanded him.

Now Joseph Smith, Sr., came to Harmony, Pa., where his son, Joseph, had taken refuge on account of persecution by the mob in the State of New York. He came, undoubtedly, to learn more of the work, to the divinity of which he had already borne testimony. Then the Prophet received this Revelation for his beloved father.

Joseph Smith, Sr., was baptized on the day the Church was organized. Later, he was ordained a Patriarch, and a President of the High Priesthood, in which offices he was singularly blessed.

The following is part of a patriarchal blessing which he pronounced upon his son Hyrum, in Kirtland, on December 18, 1833. It shows a high degree of spirituality, as well as clear thought and easy command of language.

"I now ask my heavenly Father in the name of Jesus Christ, to bless thee with the same blessing with which Jacob blessed his son Joseph, for thou art his true descendant, and thy posterity shall be numbered with the house of Ephraim, and with them thou shalt stand up to crown the tribes of Israel, when they come shouting to Zion. * * * The Lord will multiply His choice blessings upon thee and thy seed after thee, and thou with them shalt have an inheritance in Zion, and they shall possess it from generation to generation, and thy name shall never be blotted out from among the just, for the righteous shall rise up, and also thy children after thee, and say thy memory is just, that thou wert a just man and perfect in thy day."

In this Revelation God (1) declares that a "marvelous work" was about to come forth; (2) exhorts His servants to be sincere; and (3) indicates some of the qualities necessary for success in His service.

1. *Marvelous work*] The Book of Mormon is a marvelous work, no matter from what angle it is viewed. It was marvelous because it was brought to light by immortal hands. It was marvelous that a young man, with only a limited school education, and poor as far as this world's riches go, should be called upon to translate and publish it. It is marvelous in the story it tells, the teachings it gives and the prophecies it contains. It is marvelous in the effects it has produced. It has encountered the most bitter opposition. Is it because it is a fable? No, there are many works of fiction, ranging all the way from Aesop's

far-famed *Fables,* or the *Arabian Nights,* down to Cervantes' *Don Quixote,* Rider Haggard's *He,* or Muenchausen's absurdities; but none of them has aroused a storm, except the Book of Mormon. That sacred volume is not fable. Owing to its influence, thousands upon thousands of God's children have been saved from spiritual and temporal poverty, degradation, and sin, and lifted up to the highest level. The prediction of Isaiah has been fulfilled literally, "The deaf shall hear the words of the book, and the eyes of the blind shall see out of obscurity and out of darkness. The meek also shall increase their joy in the Lord, and the poor among men shall rejoice in the Holy One in Israel" (Isaiah 29: 18, 19). However, the marvelous work is not confined to the coming forth of the Book of Mormon, but has reference to all that pertains to the restoration in the Dispensation of the Fulness of Times.

2. *Serve him,* etc. Because the Lord was about to begin a marvelous work among the children of men. He needed servants who were willing to give themselves entirely to that work—"heart, might, mind, and strength"; that is affections, will-power, reasoning faculty, and physical strength, all must be dedicated to the service of the Lord in this latter-day work.

3. *A desire* to serve God is an indication that the Spirit of the Lord is calling one to do that work; but the desire is not the same as an ordination, by which authority to perform it is conferred.

4. *Behold the field*] The field was ripe for harvest at the time the Lord established the Church. The world had been prepared during many centuries, by religious movements. To thrust in the sickle and reap is to lay up a store for the future. Sowing and reaping follow each other. The early period of the Church was a time of reaping. Later, missionary labor became more like gleaning, and then sowing.

5-7. There are certain things the servants of the Lord must have, as their equipment, if they desire success. They must have faith, hope, charity, love, and an eye single to the glory of God; further, virtue, knowledge, temperance, patience, brotherly kindness, godliness, humility, and diligence. "Faith" and "charity" are enumerated twice in this list of a missionary's equipment, for he needs these in abundance. And then he must be prayerful; "Ask and ye shall receive, knock and it shall be opened unto you."

5. *Faith*] Not only the fundamental principle of trust, but that more complete realization of God's presence that enables one to "remove mountains."

Hope] That which makes one a true optimist. "Tribulation worketh patience; and patience, experience; and experience, hope; and hope maketh not ashamed" (Rom. 5:3-5).

Charity] "The pure love of Christ" (Moroni 7:47).

Love]. Love "suffereth long and is kind; it boasts not, and does not behave itself unseemly," for it is always considerate; "it seeketh not its own, is not easily provoked, thinketh no evil. It beareth all things, believeth all things, hopeth all things.

Where love of God and fellow men is, there are also the other qualities necessary to successful missionary labor.

GENERAL NOTES

Joseph was instructed by the angel to impart to his father that which he had learned of the purposes of God. "He obeyed at once, and standing there in the harvest field, related to his father all that had passed. The inspiration of heaven rested upon the elder Joseph as he heard the lad's words; and when the account was finished, he said, 'My son, these things are of God; take heed that you proceed in all holiness to do His will' " (George Q. Cannon, *Life of Joseph Smith*, p. 15).

SECTION 5.

REVELATION *given through Joseph Smith the Prophet, at Harmony, Pennsylvania, March, 1829.——Three witnesses to the Book of Mormon are promised, of whom Martin Harris is to be one if he shall prove himself worthy—Baptism is foreshadowed, but as no one had at this time been ordained to administer the ordinance, patient waiting is enjoined—Note that ordination followed, a few weeks later; see Section 13.*

BEHOLD, I say unto you, that as my servant Martin Harris has desired a witness at my hand, that you, my servant Joseph Smith, Jun., have got the plates of which you have testified and borne record that you have received of me;

Martin Harris had already received a remarkable proof of the truth of the claims made by the Prophet Joseph regarding the Book of Mormon, when he carried a facsimile of the engravings to New York scientists. Professor Anthon had told him, as he himself states, that the "hieroglyphics were true characters." He had also, through the Prophet received revelations (Sec. 3:12). But he was not yet satisfied. He seems to have asked for further evidence that the Prophet Joseph actually had the plates from which the lost manuscript had been translated. To some, faith in God is as natural as it is for little children to trust their parents; others seem to be struggling with doubts continually. This Revelation was given in answer to the desire of Martin Harris for further evidence. In it the Lord declares (1) that the plates were hidden from public view for a wise purpose, which would be made known at some future time; (2) that the testimony of the three witnesses would be added to the Prophet's testimony; (3) that condemnation would be the consequence of rejection of this testimony; and (4) that it was necessary to keep the commandments of the Lord and to be humble, in order to receive and retain a testimony of the truth.

2. And now, behold, this shall you say unto him—he who spake unto you, said unto you: I, the Lord, am God, and have given these things unto you, my servant, Joseph Smith, Jun., and have commanded you that you should stand as a witness of these things;

3. And I have caused you that you should enter into a covenant with me, that you should not show them except to those persons to whom I commanded you; and you have no power over them except I grant it unto you.

4. And you have a gift to translate the plates; and this is the first gift that I bestowed upon you; and I have commanded that you should pretend to no other gift until my purpose is fulfilled in this; for I will grant unto you no other gift until it is finished.

5. Verily, I say unto you, that woe shall come unto the inhabitants of the earth if they will not hearken unto my words;

6. For hereafter you shall be ordained and go forth and deliver my words unto the children of men.

7. Behold, if they will not believe my words, they would not believe you, my servant Joseph, if it were possible that you should show them all these things which I have committed unto you.

8. Oh, this unbelieving and stiffnecked generation—mine anger is kindled against them.

9. Behold, verily I say unto you, I have reserved those things which I have entrusted unto you, my servant Joseph, for a wise purpose in me, and it shall be made known unto future generations;

10. But this generation shall have my word through you;

2. *Behold, this shall you say*] God's answer to Martin Harris contains a doctrine, the importance of which has been made clear in later years, viz., that there is on Earth only one main channel at a time, through

which divine revelations flow. "I have," the Lord says, "given these things unto *you*, my servant, Joseph Smith" (v. 2).

3. *I have caused you*] The responsibility was laid upon him, and he did not have discretionary power as to whom he should take into his confidence.

4. *And you have a gift*] The gift of translating had been bestowed upon the Prophet Joseph, and that was the only special gift he had received so far. And it would be withdrawn if not used in accordance with the instructions imparted. It was a loan, as are all God's other gifts.

5-10. But if the prophet would use it and be faithful, he should receive other gifts, and "this generation shall have my word through you."

11. And in addition to your testimony, the testimony of three of my servants, whom I shall call and ordain, unto whom I will show these things, and they shall go forth with my words that are given through you.

12. Yea, they shall know of a surety that these things are true, for from heaven will I declare it unto them.

13. I will give them power that they may behold and view these things as they are;

14. And to none else will I grant this power, to receive this same testimony among this generation, in this the beginning of the rising up and the coming forth of my church out of the wilderness—clear as the moon, and fair as the sun, and terrible as an army with banners.

11-14. *Three of my servants*] Here is a gracious promise. The Lord would call and ordain three witnesses to the Book of Mormon, and thus the responsibility would be divided and unbelief be without excuse.

*Clear as the moon * * * banners*] This is a quotation from the Song of Songs (6:4, 10), where Shulamite is said to be fair as the moon, clear as the sun, and terrible as an army with banners"; that is, indescribably beautiful, but at the same time inaccessible to flatterers, unconquerable, as an army under banners. Here and elsewhere in the Doctrine and Covenants (105:31; 109:73) this expression is applied to the Church. When the Prophet was revising by inspiration the books of the Bible the Lord revealed to him that the Song of Solomon is not an inspired book, therefore the Prophet did not include it in his revision. This beautiful expression, it is reasonable to suppose, is not original with this uninspired book and, we may well suppose, was a current expression in ancient times. The fact remains no matter what view we take of it that an expression of this kind full of beauty and poetry could be found even in an uninspired book. Even should this be the case it is no reason why the Lord could not use it in a revelation given to the Church in our own day.

15. And the testimony of three witnesses will I send forth of my word.

16. And behold, whosoever believeth on my words, them will I visit with the manifestation of my Spirit; and they shall be born of me, even of water and of the Spirit—

17. And you must wait yet a little while, for ye are not yet ordained—

18. And their testimony shall also go forth unto the condemnation of this generation if they harden their hearts against them;

19. For a desolating scourge shall go forth among the inhabitants of the earth, and shall continue to be poured out from time to time, if they repent not, until the earth is empty, and the inhabitants thereof are consumed away and utterly destroyed by the brightness of my coming.

20. Behold, I tell you these things, even as I also told the people of the destruction of Jerusalem; and my word shall be verified at this time as it hath hitherto been verified.

19. *A desolating scourge*] The consequence of the rejection of the testimony of the Prophet and the three witnesses would be "a desolating scourge," in the form of pestilence, floods, earthquakes, wars, etc., until the final destruction by the coming of Christ.

Brightness of my coming]. This expression is used by Paul (II. Thess. 2:8), and means literally "the presence," or "arrival" of Christ. It denotes the advent of our Lord in glory, when He will come to judge the nations and establish His kingdom.

20. *Behold, I tell you these things*] Careful observers noted during the years following the establishment of the Church many of the calamities predicted, and they have multiplied in our own day. But men are slow to comprehend the signs of the times, even when they are predicted. "When spots (signs) appear in the sun * * * a natural cause is assigned. When all nature is illumed by the commotion of the starry heavens, as was the case in 1833, it is nothing but meteors. When the howling tempest and furious tornadoes come, rolling the sea (waves) beyond its bounds, desolating cities, sweeping off its thousands, * * * the wind has blown a little harder than usual. When the bellowing earthquakes rend the earth * * * the naturalist is again set to work to

prove that God has no hand in it" (*Times and Seasons,* Vol. II., p. 352).
The same is true of other signs.

21. And now I command you, my servant Joseph, to repent
and walk more uprightly before me, and to yield to the persuasions of men no more;

22. And that you be firm in keeping the commandments
wherewith I have commanded you; and if you do this, behold
I grant unto you eternal life, even if you should be slain.

21. *Walk more uprightly*] The Prophet's mistake was that he listened to the persuasive efforts of his friends and yielded to them, even
when they, as Martin Harris, unwisely asked for privileges which the
Lord had decided to withhold. Hence the admonition that follows.

22. *Be firm in keeping the commandments*] The Prophet learned this
important lesson gradually.

Slain] An indication, at this early day, that the Prophet would die,
a martyr.

23. And now, again, I speak unto you, my servant Joseph,
concerning the man that desires the witness—

24. Behold, I say unto him, he exalts himself and does not
humble himself sufficiently before me; but if he will bow down
before me, and humble himself in mighty prayer and faith, in
the sincerity of his heart, then will I grant unto him a view of
the things which he desires to see.

25. And then he shall say unto the people of this generation:
Behold, I have seen the things which the Lord hath shown unto
Joseph Smith, Jun., and I know of a surety that they are true,
for I have seen them, for they have been shown unto me by the
power of God and not of man.

26. And I the Lord command him, my servant Martin
Harris, that he shall say no more unto them concerning these
things, except he shall say: I have seen them, and they have been
shown unto me by the power of God; and these are the words
which he shall say.

27. But if he deny this he will break the covenant which he
has before covenanted with me, and behold, he is condemned.

28. And now, except he humble himself and acknowledge
unto me the things that he has done which are wrong, and
covenant with me that he will keep my commandments, and

exercise faith in me, behold, I say unto him, he shall have no such views, for I will grant unto him no views of the things of which I have spoken.

24. *If he bow down before me * * * to see*] Here is a promise, in answer to prayer, that if Martin Harris would be humble, he should be permitted to see the Book of Mormon plates himself.

25. *Then he shall say,* etc.] After having been granted such a privilege, it would be his duty to testify thereof to the world. If he should refuse, he would be condemned.

29. And if this be the case, I command you, my servant Joseph, that you shall say unto him, that he shall do no more, nor trouble me any more concerning this matter.

30. And if this be the case, behold, I say unto thee Joseph, when thou hast translated a few more pages thou shalt stop for a season, even until I command thee again; then thou mayest translate again.

31. And except thou do this, behold, thou shalt have no more gift, and I will take away the things which I have entrusted with thee.

29. *That he shall do no more*] The Lord placed before Martin Harris the conditions on which he could obtain a view of the plates. He was to be humble and willing to bear his testimony to the world. He was at liberty to accept, or reject, these conditions, for God does not deprive man of his free agency. If he refused to comply with the requirements, he was to be told not to "trouble" the Lord any more.

30. *Stop for a season*] The Lord directed the Prophet to discontinue the work of translation for the time being. He was about to raise up another friend to him, who would take the place of Martin Harris as an assistant and scribe.

31. *Except thou do this*] Unless the Prophet followed the instructions here given, the plates and the sacred instrument would be taken from him.

This is a remarkable Revelation. It furnishes an irrefutable proof that the Prophet Joseph actually had the plates. He promised that Martin Harris, on certain conditions, which he could easily comply with, should obtain a view of them. Such a promise, if the records had not been in existence, would have been impossible to redeem. It would have been mere buffoonery. The fraud would have been detected at once. The promise was repeated a few months later (Sec. 17) to two more witnesses. Joseph had the plates and the Urim and Thummim, and this Revelation proves the truth of that assertion.

32. And now, because I foresee the lying in wait to destroy thee, yea, I foresee that if my servant Martin Harris humbleth not himself and receive a witness from my hand, that he will fall into transgression;

33. And there are many that lie in wait to destroy thee from off the face of the earth; and for this cause, that thy days may be prolonged, I have given unto thee these commandments.

34. Yea, for this cause I have said: Stop, and stand still until I command thee, and I will provide means whereby thou mayest accomplish the thing which I have commanded thee.

35. And if thou art faithful in keeping my commandments, thou shalt be lifted up at the last day. Amen.

32-35. Here the warning is repeated and a promise added. Unless Martin Harris would humble himself, he would fall into transgression. There is strength in humility; weakness in pride. Unless Joseph followed the directions regarding postponement of his work of translation, he would be destroyed. That is the warning. If he would keep the commandments given, he would be "lifted up" at the last day. That is the promise.

Lifted up] This term in the New Testament sometimes refers to the Crucifixion. Christ was "lifted up" on the Cross. Here it means to be exalted and receive honor and glory.

GENERAL NOTES

"We never inquire at the hand of God for special revelation only in case of there being no previous revelation to suit the case; and that in a council of High Priests."

*   *   *

"It is a great thing to inquire at the hands of God, or to come into His presence; and we feel fearful to approach Him on subjects that are of little or no consequence, * * * especially about things the knowledge of which men ought to obtain in all sincerity, before God, for themselves" (Joseph Smith, *History of the Church*, Vol. I., p. 339).

SECTION 6.

REVELATION *given to Joseph Smith the Prophet, and Oliver Cowdery, at Harmony, Pennsylvania, April, 1829. Oliver Cowdery began his labors as scribe, in the translation of the Book of Mormon, April 7, 1829. He had already received a divine manifestation attesting the truth of Joseph's testimony respecting the plates on which was engraved the Book of Mormon record. Joseph inquired of the Lord through the Urim and Thummim and received this response. See History of the Church, vol. 1, pp. 32-35.—Oliver's willingness to serve is commended; and both to him and to Joseph blessings of great import are promised.*

A GREAT and marvelous work is about to come forth unto the children of men.

2. Behold, I am God; give heed unto my word, which is quick and powerful, sharper than a two-edged sword, to the dividing asunder of both joints and marrow; therefore give heed unto my words.

3. Behold, the field is white already to harvest; therefore whoso desireth to reap, let him thrust in his sickle with his might, and reap while the day lasts, that he may treasure up for his soul everlasting salvation in the kingdom of God.

4. Yea, whosoever will thrust in his sickle and reap, the same is called of God.

5. Therefore, if you will ask of me you shall receive; if you will knock it shall be opened unto you.

On the 5th of April, 1829, Oliver Cowdery came to Harmony, Pa. He had been teaching school in the neighborhood of Manchester, N. Y., and for some time boarded in the home of the Smith family. While there he had heard the wonderful story of the Book of Mormon, and he was impressed to go to Harmony and visit the Prophet, to see for himself and learn more about the Book. Oliver Cowdery was an intimate friend of the Whitmers, and on his way to Harmony he called at their house, and at that time he promised David Whitmer, who also heard many conflicting rumors about the finding of the plates, to inform him of the result of his investigation. The first converts to "Mormonism" did not accept it without prayerful investigation. Oliver Cowdery, after his arrival in Harmony, soon became convinced that Joseph was called of God, and wrote to that effect to David Whitmer. The Lord now prompted His servant, Joseph, to resume the work of translation which had been interrupted by the vacillation of Martin Harris. Oliver Cowdery acted as amanuensis. According to his own statement at Council Bluffs on October 21st, 1848, Oliver Cowdery wrote the entire Book (save a few pages) as the words fell from the lips of the Prophet, "as he translated it by the gift and power of God, by the means of the

Urim and Thummim, or, as it is called by that Book, 'holy interpreters.' "
So that the testimony of Oliver Cowdery was as firm in 1848, two years
before his death, as it was in 1829, when he first accepted the gospel,
although he had been outside the Church for eleven years. When Joseph
and Oliver had been engaged on the Book of Mormon a few days, this
Revelation was received.

1. *Great and marvelous work*] To the father of the Prophet the Lord
declared (Sec. 4) that a "marvelous" work was about to come forth.
But it would also be a "great" work. This has proved true. The Church
stands in the world today, "a great and marvelous work" and a
testimony to the fact that he who uttered this prophecy in 1829, before
the Church was organized, was a true prophet.

About the time the Church of Jesus Christ was founded in the United
States, Mr. Edward Irving, a gifted minister in London, constructed his
church. He, too, appointed apostles, prophets, evangelists, "angels" or
bishops, elders, and deacons. He, too, claimed that the spiritual gifts
had been restored. He, too, preached the second coming of our Lord.
The Irvingites gained adherents in Great Britain, the United States, and
the European continent, and there was every prospect that they would
bring forth a great and marvelous work. But where is that church
today? Irving called it the *Catholic Apostolic Church.* Even the name is
unknown to most Christians, while that of the Church of Jesus Christ
of Latter-day Saints and, to a still greater extent, that of the Prophet
Joseph, have become famous throughout the world. Mr. Irving was a
clergyman, learned, eloquent and earnest. Joseph Smith was an unlettered, unknown youth, but his work stood the test, because it was
God's work. It has become great, indeed.

2. *Give heed unto my word*] The Word of God is "quick"; it is
"living," and not dead. It is "powerful"; it is a force, like compressed
steam, or electricity. As a sharp, two-edged sword it pierces and cuts,
and penetrates to the inmost parts of man, being a "discerner of the
thoughts and intents of the heart" (Heb. 4:12. Compare Isa. 49:2; Eph.
6:17; Rev. 2:16; 19:15). But the power of the Word of God does not
consist in oratory, nor in philosophy, but in the "demonstration of the
Spirit" (I. Cor. 2:4). Some modern preaching is accompanied by no
greater "demonstration of the Spirit" than would attend the reading
of one of Cicero's essays. The Word of God is different.

3. *Behold the field is white*] See Section 4:4.

4. *Whosoever will thrust in his sickle*] See Section 4:4.

5. *If you will ask of me, etc.*] Compare Matt. 7:7; Doc. and Cov.
5:24, 41:2; 52:15; 103:36. God hears the prayers of His children and
answers them.

"And now, my beloved brethren, I perceive that ye ponder still
in your hearts; and it grieveth me that I must speak concerning this

thing. For if ye would hearken unto the Spirit which teacheth a man to pray ye would know that ye must pray; for the evil spirit teacheth not a man to pray, but teacheth him that he must not pray. But behold, I say unto you that ye must pray always, and not faint; that ye must not perform anything unto the Lord save in the first place ye shall pray unto the Father in the name of Christ, that he will consecrate thy performance unto thee, that thy performance may be for the welfare of thy soul." (2 Nephi 32: 8-9.)

6. Now, as you have asked, behold, I say unto you, keep my commandments, and seek to bring forth and establish the cause of Zion;

7. Seek not for riches but for wisdom, and behold, the mysteries of God shall be unfolded unto you, and then shall you be made rich. Behold, he that hath eternal life is rich.

8. Verily, verily, I say unto you, even as you desire of me so it shall be unto you; and if you desire, you shall be the means of doing much good in this generation.

7. *Seek not for riches*] Solomon sought for wisdom and received both wisdom and riches. The promise here given is that the "mysteries" of the kingdom shall be unfolded to him who seeks for wisdom. He who spends his time and exerts his energy in the pursuit of wealth only, will never know the mysteries of the kingdom of God. Materialism and spiritual interests cannot unite. A materialistic age does not comprehend the gospel of Christ.

9. Say nothing but repentance unto this generation; keep my commandments, and assist to bring forth my work, according to my commandments, and you shall be blessed.

10. Behold thou hast a gift, and blessed art thou because of thy gift. Remember it is sacred and cometh from above—

11. And if thou wilt inquire, thou shalt know mysteries which are great and marvelous; therefore thou shalt exercise thy gift, that thou mayest find out mysteries, that thou mayest bring many to the knowledge of the truth, yea, convince them of the error of their ways.

12. Make not thy gift known unto any save it be those who are of thy faith. Trifle not with sacred things.

13. If thou wilt do good, yea, and hold out faithful to the end, thou shalt be saved in the kingdom of God, which is the

greatest of all the gifts of God; for there is no gift greater than the gift of salvation.

9. *Repentance*] That is the message of the gospel to this generation. Repentance is a complete change of mind, which brings about an equally complete change of practice as far as wrong-doing is concerned. He who truly repents is sorry because of his sins, and ceases sinning. If he has wronged anyone, he rights the wrong done, as far as lies in his power to do so. He confesses his sins to God and to those whom he may have injured, and makes whatever restitution he can. That is true repentance.

Keep my commandments] He who cries repentance must himself keep the commandments, in order to enjoy the blessings of that labor.

10. *Behold thou hast a gift*] Oliver Cowdery's gift was the spirit of revelation (Section 8:3, 4), by which he could obtain knowledge of things divine. He also had the gift of Aaron. Aaron was the spokesman of Moses, and Oliver Cowdery became the first spokesman of the Prophet, or of the Church, when, on the 30th of April, 1830, he preached the first public discourse in this dispensation.

12. *Make not thy gift known*] The gifts of the Spirit are not for public display.

13. *Salvation*] Salvation is the greatest gift; it includes all other gifts. All other gifts are subservient to it. Salvation means deliverance from outward dangers, victory over enemies, remission of sins through acceptance of Christ and obedience to His laws, and eternal exaltation. (Compare Exodus 14:13; I. Sam. 14:45; Luke 1:77; 19:9.) "Wherefore let him that thinketh he standeth take heed lest he fall." (1 Cor. 10:12.)

"Salvation is for man to be saved from all his enemies: for, until a man can triumph over death, he is not saved. A knowledge of the Priesthood [and obedience] alone will do this" (Joseph Smith, *History of the Church*, Vol. V., p. 403).

14. Verily, verily, I say unto thee, blessed art thou for what thou hast done; for thou hast inquired of me, and behold, as often as thou hast inquired thou hast received instruction of my Spirit. If it had not been so, thou wouldst not have come to the place where thou art at this time.

15. Behold, thou knowest that thou hast inquired of me and I did enlighten thy mind; and now I tell thee these things that thou mayest know that thou hast been enlightened by the Spirit of truth;

16. Yea, I tell thee, that thou mayest know that there is

none else save God that knowest thy thoughts and the intents of thy heart.

17. I tell thee these things as a witness unto thee—that the words or the work which thou hast been writing are true.

14-17. *Verily, verily, I say unto thee, * * * True*] Nathanael believed that Jesus was the Messiah, when He told him that He had seen him under the fig tree. (John 1:48-50.) Oliver Cowdery had a similar experience. Before he came to Harmony, Pa., to see the Prophet, he had prayed earnestly to the Lord, in the seclusion of his own room, for light, and the Lord had manifested Himself to him by filling his heart with that peace which passeth understanding. No other human being knew of this. And yet, in this Revelation the Lord reminded him of that prayer and the answer. This was a testimony to Oliver Cowdery, similar to that which Nathanael received.

18. Therefore be diligent; stand by my servant Joseph, faithfully, in whatsoever difficult circumstances he may be for the word's sake.

19. Admonish him in his faults, and also receive admonition of him. Be patient; be sober; be temperate; have patience, faith, hope and charity.

20. Behold, thou art Oliver, and I have spoken unto thee because of thy desires; therefore treasure up these words in thy heart. Be faithful and diligent in keeping the commandments of God, and I will encircle thee in the arms of my love.

21. Behold, I am Jesus Christ, the Son of God. I am the same that came unto mine own, and mine own received me not. I am the light which shineth in darkness, and the darkness comprehendeth it not.

18. *For the word's sake*] For the sake of the Book of Mormon.

19. *Admonish him,* etc.] This is an important principle.
"When any of you receive a rebuke, or a correction, acknowledge it at once, and say to the one who administers it, 'Thank you, brother; God bless you! And may the Almighty give me power to do right' " (Heber C. Kimball, *Journal of Discourses,* Vol. IX., p. 41).

21. *Behold, I am Jesus Christ*] Jesus Christ, our Lord, is the source of these Revelations. He is the WORD, as well as the Redeemer of the world. He is the Light which shineth in darkness; not which *shone* formerly, but which *now* shineth. The Darkness is that condition of the world, which is unaffected by the light of divine revelation, because

of the ignorance, superstition, and enmity of men. In that condition the world does not comprehend the light of revelation. That kind of darkness remains apart, unyielding, unpenetrated, now as in the day when John wrote his Gospel (John 1:5).

22. Verily, verily, I say unto you, if you desire a further witness, cast your mind upon the night that you cried unto me in your heart, that you might know concerning the truth of these things.

23. Did I not speak peace to your mind concerning the matter? What greater witness can you have than from God?

24. And now, behold, you have received a witness; for if I have told you things which no man knoweth have you not received a witness?

22. *A further witness*] The Lord again reminds Oliver Cowdery of the night of prayer, and the testimony he received in answer to his supplications. There is no surer testimony than that of the Spirit of God in the heart.

25. And, behold, I grant unto you a gift, if you desire of me, to translate, even as my servant Joseph.

26. Verily, verily, I say unto you, that there are records which contain much of my gospel, which have been kept back because of the wickedness of the people;

27. And now I command you, that if you have good desires —a desire to lay up treasures for yourself in heaven—then shall you assist in bringing to light, with your gift, those parts of my scriptures which have been hidden because of iniquity.

25. *To translate even as my servant Joseph*] This is a divine promise to Oliver Cowdery. A great many records have been kept since the beginning of history, which are now hidden. God was willing to make the contents of some of them known to the world through Oliver Cowdery. To man those records are lost, but to God, they are only "hidden", and He can bring their contents to light. This promise would, undoubtedly, have been fulfilled, if Oliver Cowdery had remained faithful.

28. And now, behold, I give unto you, and also unto my servant Joseph, the keys of this gift, which shall bring to light this ministry; and in the mouth of two or three witnesses shall every word be established.

28. *Unto you, and also unto my servant Joseph*] Both were endowed with the power and gift of translation. There is no monopoly in the kingdom of God.

29. Verily, verily, I say unto you, if they reject my words, and this part of my gospel and ministry, blessed are ye, for they can do no more unto you than unto me.

30. And even if they do unto you even as they have done unto me, blessed are ye, for you shall dwell with me in glory.

31. But if they reject not my words, which shall be established by the testimony which shall be given, blessed are they, and then shall ye have joy in the fruit of your labors.

29-31. Faithful missionaries are blessed whether the world receives, or rejects, their testimony. There is great happiness in the performance of duty.

32. Verily, verily, I say unto you, as I said unto my disciples, where two or three are gathered together in my name, as touching one thing, behold, there will I be in the midst of them— even so am I in the midst of you.

33. Fear not to do good, my sons, for whatsoever ye sow, that shall ye also reap; therefore, if ye sow good ye shall also reap good for your reward.

34. Therefore, fear not, little flock; do good; let earth and hell combine against you, for if ye are built upon my rock, they cannot prevail.

35. Behold, I do not condemn you; go your ways and sin no more; perform with soberness the work which I have commanded you.

36. Look unto me in every thought; doubt not, fear not.

37. Behold the wounds which pierced my side, and also the prints of the nails in my hands and feet; be faithful, keep my commandments, and ye shall inherit the kingdom of heaven. Amen.

32-36. Instructions and encouragement in every line.

35. *The work which I have commanded you*] The translation of the Book of Mormon.

37. *Behold the wounds, etc.*] Contemplate the sacrifice of the Savior and His atonement, and receive from Him the power necessary to remain

faithful, to keep the commandments, and to gain an inheritance in the kingdom of heaven. Jesus was "the first begotten of the Father, full of grace and truth; and suffered His body to be broken and His blood to be spilled, doing 'not His own will, but the will of Him that sent Him,' not to accomplish His own purpose particularly, but the purpose of Him that sent Him" (John Taylor, *Journal of Discourses*, Vol. X., p. 115).

SECTION 7.

REVELATION *given to Joseph Smith the Prophet, and Oliver Cowdery, at Harmony, Pennsylvania, April, 1829, when they inquired through the Urim and Thummim as to whether John, the beloved disciple, tarried in the flesh or had died. The revelation is the translated version of the record made on parchment by John and hidden up by himself. See History of the Church, vol. 1, pp. 35, 36.*

AND the Lord said unto me: John, my beloved, what desirest thou? For if you shall ask what you will, it shall be granted unto you.

2. And I said unto him: Lord, give unto me power over death, that I may live and bring souls unto thee.

3. And the Lord said unto me: Verily, verily, I say unto thee, because thou desirest this thou shalt tarry until I come in my glory, and shalt prophesy before nations, kindreds, tongues and people.

4. And for this cause the Lord said unto Peter: If I will that he tarry till I come, what is that to thee? For he desired of me that he might bring souls unto me, but thou desiredst that thou mightest speedily come unto me in my kingdom.

5. I say unto thee, Peter, this was a good desire; but my beloved has desired that he might do more, or a greater work yet among men than what he has before done.

6. Yea, he has undertaken a greater work; therefore I will make him as flaming fire and a ministering angel; he shall minister for those who shall be heirs of salvation who dwell on the earth.

7. And I will make thee to minister for him and for thy

brother James; and unto you three I will give this power and the keys of this ministry until I come.

8. Verily I say unto you, ye shall both have according to your desires, for ye both joy in that which ye have desired.

In the Gospel account as given by John (21:21-23.) he modestly refers to the question by Peter concerning John and the Savior's answer in the following words:

"Peter seeing him (John) saith to Jesus, Lord, and what shall this man do?

"Jesus saith unto him, If I will that he tarry till I come, what is that to thee? Follow thou me.

"Then went this saying abroad among the brethren, that that disciple should not die: yet Jesus said not unto him, He shall not die; but, If I will that he tarry till I come, what is that to thee?"

We learn from this that there was a general understanding among the apostles that John should not die until the second coming of our Lord. This revelation confirms that view.

The prophet Joseph Smith and Oliver Cowdery, one day, discussed this passage of the Scriptures, and expressed different views on the meaning of it. In order to come to unity of faith on that question, the Prophet inquired of the Lord and received this Revelation.

The question might be asked, whether the Prophet had actually seen the parchment written and hidden by John, or a copy of it; if so, where and when did he obtain it, and what became of it?

The history of the Prophet does not furnish information on these subjects. But it is not necessary to suppose that the Prophet had St. John's parchment, or a copy of it, before him, when he received this Revelation. It was the contents of the document that were revealed. It was just as easy for the Spirit of the Lord to communicate the contents of that record to the Prophet, without the actual presence of it, as it would have been to enable him to understand the language in which John wrote it, whether Greek or Aramæan, which languages neither Joseph nor Oliver could have read, except by special divine interposition, even if they had had the manuscript before them. The miracle would have been practically the same.

Our Lord saw, from the mountain top, "all the kingdoms of the world in a moment of time" (Luke 4:5). They were, of course, not actually present on the mountain. He saw them in a vision. The Prophet Joseph heard the words which were spoken to Moses on a high mountain; that is to say, those words were repeated to him by revelation (Pearl of Great Price, Book of Moses 1:1-42). He was given, by revelation, part of the contents of the Book of Enoch (Doc. and Cov. 107:57). President Brigham Young saw the Salt Lake Temple, in a vision, one day in July, 1847, over five years before the ground whereupon it stands was broken for the foundation, on the 14th of February, 1853. He relates:

"I scarcely ever say much about revelations, or visions, but suffice it to say, five years ago last July I was here, and saw in the spirit the Temple, not ten feet from where we have laid the chief corner stone. I have not inquired what kind of a Temple we should build. Why? Because it was represented before me. I have never looked upon that ground but the vision of it was there" (From an address by Brigham Young, April 6th, 1853. *Journal of Discourses,* Vol. I., p. 133).

There is, therefore, no difficulty in accepting the proposition that God could make the contents of John's parchment known to His Servants, whether the document was accessible to them or not. That John committed our Lord's last promise to him and Peter to writing is probable. It must have made a deep and lasting impression on him. That the incident is recorded in the Gospel in an abbreviated form, is certain.

3. *Until I come in my glory*] This expression is almost identical with that used by our Lord on another occasion, when He said. "For the Son of man shall come in the glory of his Father * * * Verily I say unto you, There be some standing here, which shall not taste death, till they see the Son of man coming in his kingdom" (Matt. 16:28; Mark 9:1; Luke 9:27). Peter suffered martyrdom probably in the year 64 or 65 A.D., at least five years before the fall of Jerusalem. James the Less, also called the Just, was martyred in the year 62 A.D., and James, the brother of John, in the year 42. Many of the other Apostles were slain.

John had "power over death." Tradition says that on one occasion he came unharmed from a cauldron of boiling oil; and that on another occasion he was a captive among a band of robbers, whose chieftain became converted through his preaching.

He "prophesied before nations, kindred, tongues and people" through the Book of Revelation, in which the history of the world, as committed to the records of heaven before the foundations of the world were laid, is outlined. He prophesied more particularly about the general apostasy (Rev. 9:20, 21; 13:1-18); and the restoration of the Gospel (10:1-11; 14: 1-13).

6. *A ministering angel*] John received the promise that he would be a "ministering angel" for the benefit of the heirs of salvation on earth. The bishops of the seven Asiatic churches are addressed as *angels,* and the inference is that it was a common title at that time of all bishops, in Europe and Africa, as well as Asia. The word *angel* means *messenger.* It is almost synonymous with the word *apostle,* which also means *messenger.*

The following is suggestive:

"Men are made a little lower than the angels for the suffering of death, but when men are clothed with the holy Priesthood and sent forth to minister the word of life, the comparison between them and the angels is somewhat different. And of his angels he saith, Who maketh his angels spirits, and his ministers a flame of fire." While in the act of ministering the gospel, the servants of God may be considered angels. * * * The servants of God are angels in one sense, sent forth to gather the house of Israel from the four corners of the earth; and the Elders of this Church in their labors have fulfilled, partly, the sayings of the Savior, when they have found two working in the field, one has received the gospel and been gathered, and the other left; two lying in a bed, the one has been taken and the other left" (Heber C. Kimball, *Journal of Discourses,* Vol. X, p. 103. Compare Doc. and Cov. 129:1).

Peter, James, and John hold the "power and keys" of the ministry. John wrote his Gospel about the year 97 A.D.—almost at the end of the first century of our era. After that he passes out of view, as far as history knows, until he, in company with Peter and James, appears on the banks of the Susquehanna River and confers the Melchizedek Priesthood upon Joseph Smith and Oliver Cowdery, not many days after the 15th of May, 1829.

John was the last surviving member of the first Apostles chosen of the Lamb, and, as the last tone of the bell always sounds longer than the preceding ones, so the sweet influence of his sacred compositions— the Gospel and the Epistles—seem to have been more lasting and to have had a deeper effect upon the religious thought and life of men, than that of any other writer, inspired, or profane. The very name of John has become more popular than any other name, except those of the Deity, judging from the almost innumerable forms in which it occurs throughout the Christian world.

For an account of the three Nephites who obtained the promise that they should not "taste of death," see III. Nephi 28:1-33.

SECTION 8.

REVELATION *given through Joseph Smith the Prophet, to Oliver Cowdery, at Harmony, Pennsylvania, April, 1829. In the course of the translation of the Book of Mormon, Oliver, who continued to serve as scribe, writing at the prophet's dictation, desired to be endowed with the gift of translation—The Lord responded to his supplication by granting this revelation.—— The spirit of revelation is defined, and the gift of Aaron specified.*

OLIVER Cowdery, verily, verily, I say unto you, that assuredly as the Lord liveth, who is your God and your Redeemer, even so surely shall you receive a knowledge of whatsoever things you shall ask in faith, with an honest heart, believing that you shall receive a knowledge concerning the engravings of old records, which are ancient, which contain those parts of my scripture of which has been spoken by the manifestation of my Spirit.

2. Yea, behold, I will tell you in your mind and in your heart, by the Holy Ghost, which shall come upon you and which shall dwell in your heart.

Church historians briefly state that Oliver Cowdery, while acting as secretary to the Prophet, became anxious to have the gift to translate bestowed upon him, and that this Revelation, and the following, were received, for his benefit, on that subject.

1. *Knowledge concerning the engravings*] This is another promise to Oliver Cowdery, that he should receive a knowledge concerning the characters on the plates, if he would pray for it in faith. The same promise was given to him in a previous Revelation (6:25-27). The truth of the record had been made manifest to him by the Spirit.

2. *I will tell you in your mind*] The same Spirit would make known to him the meaning of the strange writing.

3. Now, behold, this is the spirit of revelation; behold, this is the spirit by which Moses brought the children of Israel through the Red Sea on dry ground.

4. Therefore this is thy gift; apply unto it, and blessed art thou, for it shall deliver you out of the hands of your enemies, when, if it were not so, they would slay you and bring your soul to destruction.

5. Oh, remember these words, and keep my commandments. Remember, this is your gift.

3. *The Spirit of revelation*] The Holy Ghost is the Spirit of revelation. It is the Spirit by whose directions Moses led the children of Israel safely through their perilous journey.

4. *This is thy gift*] It was Oliver Cowdery's special gift to understand the "still, small voice" of the Spirit, and if he would follow it, he would be delivered from the hand of the enemy.

6. Now this is not all thy gift; for you have another gift, which is the gift of Aaron; behold, it has told you many things;

7. Behold, there is no other power, save the power of God, that can cause this gift of Aaron to be with you.

8. Therefore, doubt not, for it is the gift of God; and you

shall hold it in your hands, and do marvelous works; and no power shall be able to take it away out of your hands, for it is the work of God.

6. *The gift of Aaron*] Oliver Cowdery also had the "gift of Aaron." Aaron was the elder brother of Moses. Being prompted by the Spirit of the Lord, he met his younger brother in the wilderness and accompanied him to Egypt. He introduced him to the children of Israel in the land of Goshen. He was his spokesman before Pharaoh, and he assisted him in opening up the dispensation which Moses was commissioned to proclaim (Exodus 4:27-31). This was the gift of Aaron. In some respects Oliver Cowdery was the Aaron of the new and last dispensation.

8. *It is the gift of God*] The gift to translate is not the only gift God bestows. Other gifts are also from Him. Compare I. Corinthians 12:4-11; Moroni 10:8-17; Doc. and Cov. 46:11-26).

9. And, therefore, whatsoever you shall ask me to tell you by that means, that will I grant unto you, and you shall have knowledge concerning it.

10. Remember that without faith you can do nothing; therefore ask in faith. Trifle not with these things; do not ask for that which you ought not.

11. Ask that you may know the mysteries of God, and that you may translate and receive knowledge from all those ancient records which have been hid up, that are sacred; and according to your faith shall it be done unto you.

12. Behold, it is I that have spoken it; and I am the same that spake unto you from the beginning. Amen.

10. *Without faith you can do nothing*] The power of faith is wonderful. Speaking of faithful Elders, President John Taylor says that, "If they possess the principle of intelligence, there will be a power and an influence manifested in and accompanying all their words." He mentions the name of one Brother Attwood, who first heard the gospel preached in a tongue foreign to him, and which he did not understand. Nevertheless, he felt the power of the testimony, and an influence that accorded with his own feelings and spirit (*Journal of Discourses,* Vol. X., p. 37). A somewhat similar experience is related of Elders Franklin D. Richards and Karl G. Maeser, two men eminently prominent in the history of the Church. When they first met, they conversed, one speaking English and the other German, and although neither understood the language of the other, except imperfectly, both were in such accord with each other that Elder Maeser grasped the instructions Elder Richards

imparted to him, and he rejoiced greatly, as one truth after another was unfolded to him in this manner. "Without faith you can do nothing," but by faith frail man may draw, as it were, on the unlimited resources and power of the Almighty.

SECTION 9.

REVELATION *given through Joseph Smith the Prophet, to Oliver Cowdery, at Harmony, Pennsylvania, April, 1829. Oliver is admonished to patience, and is urged to be content to write, for the time being, at the dictation of the translator, rather than to attempt to translate.——It is not sufficient for one merely to ask for a divine gift, without prayerful thought and study— Oliver loses such small measure of the gift of translation as he had temporarily possessed.*

BEHOLD, I say unto you, my son, that because you did not translate according to that which you desired of me, and did commence again to write for my servant, Joseph Smith, Jun., even so I would that ye should continue until you have finished this record, which I have entrusted unto him.

2. And then, behold, other records have I, that I will give unto you power that you may assist to translate.

3. Be patient, my son, for it is wisdom in me, and it is not expedient that you should translate at this present time.

4. Behold, the work which you are called to do is to write for my servant Joseph.

5. And, behold, it is because that you did not continue as you commenced, when you began to translate, that I have taken away this privilege from you.

6. Do not murmur, my son, for it is wisdom in me that I have dealt with you after this manner.

It seems that Oliver Cowdery, although he had been promised the gift to translate, neglected to seek diligently to obtain it, or that he neglected to cultivate it. For this he was gently rebuked. He did, however, continue to write, as the Prophet dictated. For this he was commended.

2. *Other records*] Other Nephite records. Oliver Cowdery, if he had remained faithful, would have had the privilege of assisting in their

translation. He, however, was outside the Church, because of transgression, for eleven years, and although he was again received in full fellowship, some of the blessings he had lost could not be recovered.

3. *My son*] In this revelation our Lord calls Oliver, "my son." He speaks for the Father, and represents the Father, and is, therefore, in that sense both the Father and the Son. "Because he dwelleth in flesh he shall be called the Son of God, and having subjected the flesh to the will of the Father, being the Father and the Son" (Mosiah 15:2).

7. Behold, you have not understood; you have supposed that I would give it unto you, when you took no thought save it was to ask me.

8. But, behold, I say unto you, that you must study it out in your mind; then you must ask me if it be right, and if it is right I will cause that your bosom shall burn within you; therefore, you shall feel that it is right.

9. But if it be not right you shall have no such feelings, but you shall have a stupor of thought that shall cause you to forget the thing which is wrong; therefore, you cannot write that which is sacred save it be given you from me.

10. Now, if you had known this you could have translated; nevertheless, it is not expedient that you should translate now.

11. Behold, it was expedient when you commenced; but you feared, and the time is past, and it is not expedient now;

12. For, do you not behold that I have given unto my servant Joseph sufficient strength, whereby it is made up? And neither of you have I condemned.

13. Do this thing which I have commanded you, and you shall prosper. Be faithful, and yield to no temptation.

14. Stand fast in the work wherewith I have called you, and a hair of your head shall not be lost, and you shall be lifted up at the last day. Amen.

7. *You have not understood*] Oliver Cowdery, as many others, seems to have been of the opinion that revelation ought to come through some indefinable, mystic process, without the exertion of the human faculties. Our Lord corrects this erroneous view.

8. *You must study it out in your own mind*] After study and prayer the Lord will make it manifest whether the result obtained is right or wrong; if right, He will cause the spirit within to "burn"; if wrong, there will be no such manifestation.

12. *I have given to my servant Joseph sufficient strength*] Oliver
Cowdery needed to be reminded of this; for he was inclined, at least
later, to regard himself as indispensable to the Church. President Brigham
Young says:

"I have seen men who belonged to this kingdom, and who really
thought that if they were not associated with it, it could not progress.
One man especially, whom I now think of, was peculiarly gifted in self-
reliance and general ability. He said as much to the Prophet Joseph,
a number of times; as much as to say that if he left this kingdom, it
could not progress any further. I speak of Oliver Cowdery. He forsook
it, and it still rolled on and still triumphed over every opposing foe,
and bore off safely all those who clung to it" (*Journal of Discourses,* Vol.
XI., p. 252).

God does not need any one in particular. We need Him. Oliver
Cowdery seems to have lacked humility until, after his experience outside the Church, he returned to the fold. Then he was humble. To the
special High Council that heard his case, in November, 1848, he said:
"I am not a member of the Church, but I wish to become a member of
it. I wish to come in at the door. I know the door. I have not come here
to seek precedence. I come humbly and throw myself upon the decisions
of this body, knowing as I do, that its decisions are right and should be
obeyed" (Andrew Jenson, *Historical Record,* p. 201).

GENERAL NOTES

"Other records" are referred to in the 2nd paragraph of this Section.
On that subject President Brigham Young makes the following statement:

"When Joseph got the plates, the angel instructed him to carry them
back to the hill Cumorah, which he did. Oliver says that when Joseph
and Oliver went there, the hill opened, and they walked into a cave, in
which there was a large and spacious room. He says he did not think, at
the time, whether they had the light of the sun, or artificial light; but it
was just as light as day. They laid the plates on a table; it was a large
table that stood in the room. Under this table there was a pile of plates
as much as two feet high, and there were altogether in this room more
plates than, probably, many wagon loads; they were piled up in the
corners and along the walls. The first time they went there, the sword
of Laban hung upon the wall; but when they went again, it had been
taken down and laid upon the table across the gold plates; it was unsheathed, and on it were written these words, 'This sword will never be
sheathed again until the kingdoms of this world become the kingdom
of our God and His Christ.' I take the liberty of referring to those
things so that they will not be forgotten and lost. Carlos Smith was a
young man of as much veracity as any young man we had, and he was
a witness to these things. Samuel Smith saw some things, and Hyrum
saw a good many things, but Joseph was the leader.

"Now, you may think I am unwise in publicly telling these things, thinking, perhaps, I should preserve them in my own breast; but such is not in my mind. I would like the people called Latter-day Saints to understand some little things with regard to the workings and dealings of the Lord with His people here upon the earth. I could relate to you a great many more, all of which are familiar to many of our brethren and sisters" (*Journal of Discourses*, Vol. XIX., p. 38).

SECTION 10.

REVELATION *given to Joseph Smith the Prophet, at Harmony, Pennsylvania, in the summer of 1828.——Herein the Lord informs Joseph of alterations made by wicked men in the 116 manuscript pages of the Book of Mormon, which had been lost from the possession of Martin Harris, to whom the sheets had been temporarily entrusted. Compare Section 3. See History of the Church, vol. 1, pp. 21, 23. The evil design was to await the expected re-translation of the matter covered by the stolen pages, and then to discredit the translator by showing the discrepancies created by the alterations. That this wicked purpose had been conceived by the evil one, and was known to the Lord even while Mormon, the ancient Nephite historian, was making his abridgment of the accumulated plates is shown in the Book of Mormon. See The Words of Mormon 3-7.*

NOW, behold, I say unto you, that because you delivered up those writings which you had power given unto you to translate by the means of the Urim and Thummim, into the hands of a wicked man, you have lost them.

2. And you also lost your gift at the same time, and your mind became darkened.

3. Nevertheless, it is now restored unto you again; therefore see that you are faithful and continue on unto the finishing of the remainder of the work of translation as you have begun.

4. Do not run faster or labor more than you have strength and means provided to enable you to translate; but be diligent unto the end.

5. Pray always, that you may come off conqueror; yea, that

you may conquer Satan, and that you may escape the hands of the servants of Satan that do uphold his work.

This Revelation should be read in connection with Sec. 3.

As soon as the 116 pages of manuscript had been lost through the carelessness of Martin Harris, the Urim and Thummim was taken from the Prophet. The sacred instrument was restored after a short time, and the Revelation in Section 3, especially rebuking Martin Harris, was received. Then both the plates and the Urim and Thummim were removed for a few days. It was necessary that the young Prophet should learn the lesson that he was entirely dependent on the Lord. When they were restored, he received the Revelation in Section 10, containing instructions to himself with regard to the lost portion of the manuscript (See *History of the Church*, Vol. I., p. 23, Footnote.).

The Prophet was sorely punished for his continuous importuning of the Lord, which was an important lesson which he never forgot. The Lord has given us instruction not to be overly insistent in having some of our prayers answered. He has said:

"Whatsoever ye ask the Father in my name it shall be given unto you, that is expedient for you;

"And if ye ask anything that is not expedient for you, it shall turn unto your condemnation." (Doc. and Cov. 88:64-65.)

1. *Because you delivered up those writings*] The Prophet Joseph did not deliver the manuscript to Martin Harris, except upon persistent requests and after divine permission had been obtained, although reluctantly; but it was, none the less, displeasing to God. Our heavenly Father sometimes grants the unwise requests of His children, in order that they may learn, through their experience, that they are dependent on Him for guidance in all things. Israel demanded a king and God consented; but He did not approve of the change in the form of the government of His people. Baalam obtained permission to go to Balak, but the angel of the Lord, nevertheless, met the false prophet in the road and opposed him. Joseph should have refused to listen to Martin Harris.

A wicked man] Martin Harris is again referred to as a "wicked man." This is explained in the 6th and 7th verses, where the Lord says, "Even the man in whom you have trusted, has sought to destroy you. And for this cause I said that he is a wicked man." Martin Harris on the suggestion of wicked men, had adopted a course, which, but for divine interposition, would have led the Prophet to destruction. He associated with wicked men, probably without perceiving what the consequences might be.

The experience with the lost folios taught all concerned the necessity of keeping constant watch over the precious manuscript. And so, when the translation was completed Oliver Cowdery, complying with a command of God (See *History of the Prophet Joseph* by Mother Smith, p.

142), made a transcript of the entire volume for the printer. This copy was delivered at the printing office, a few folios at a time, and as soon as they were printed, they were taken care of by the Prophet. There were, therefore, two written copies of the Book of Mormon, and any alteration in the printed text would have been detected at once.

The first written copy was, in the year 1841, placed in a stone box in the southwest corner of the Nauvoo House, by the Prophet Joseph. Part of it was destroyed by dampness. What remained was eventually obtained and taken care of by President Joseph F. Smith. The copy used by the printer fell into the hands of David Whitmer, who kept it as a most sacred relic. But, notwithstanding all precautions, an effort was made, while the book was being printed, to foist a spurious version of it upon the world. Many attempts by wicked men were undertaken to get possession of the plates of the Book of Mormon and to destroy the translated work, but they all failed. The Prophet learned that the greatest vigilance had to be used for the preservation of the sacred record and the translation he had made.

Urim and Thummim] See notes on Sections 3:15; 17:1.

2. *You also lost your gift*] The gift of translating by inspiration. "Your mind became darkened"—a natural consequence of disobedience and the withdrawal of the Spirit.

3. *It is now restored*] "The Lord is merciful and gracious, slow to anger, and plenteous in mercy. He will not always chide: neither will He keep His anger for ever" (Psalm 103:8, 9).

5. *Pray always*] The Prophet is constantly admonished to pray. This is one evidence, among many, that he was a man of God. A pretender would not have been admonished to pray, but to repent. Hypocrites do not pray, though they may say long prayers. One who prays earnestly will not be led astray: nor will he lead others into error, as long as he communes with God and follows the guidance of the Holy Spirit.

6 Behold, they have sought to destroy you; yea, even the man in whom you have trusted has sought to destroy you.

7. And for this cause I said that he is a wicked man, for he has sought to take away the things wherewith you have been entrusted; and he has also sought to destroy your gift.

8. And because you have delivered the writings into his hands, behold, wicked men have taken them from you.

9. Therefore, you have delivered them up, yea, that which was sacred, unto wickedness.

10. And, behold, Satan hath put it into their hearts to alter the words which you have caused to be written, or which you have translated, which have gone out of your hands.

11. And behold, I say unto you, that because they have altered the words, they read contrary from that which you translated and caused to be written;

12. And, on this wise, the devil has sought to lay a cunning plan, that he may destroy this work;

13. For he hath put into their hearts to do this, that by lying they may say they have caught you in the words which you have pretended to translate.

10. *Satan has put it into their hearts*] The plot was executed by wicked men, through the aid of Martin Harris, but the great enemy of God and man was the instigator of it. It was his plan.

The word "satan" means "adversary." It is the same as "devil," which is generally rendered "accuser." Satan is also known as the "Evil One," "Angel of the Bottomless Pit," the "Prince of this World," the "Prince of the Power of the Air," the "God of this World," "Apollyon," "Abaddon," "Belial," "Beelzebub," etc. Originally he belonged to the heavenly hosts and was a chief among them. He was known as *Lucifer,* which means "light-bearer"; also as the "Son of the Morning," or "Morning Star."

Lucifer was from "the beginning." In the great Council in heaven he proposed to redeem mankind by compulsion, if God would give him His honor. That proposition was rejected by the Council, and another, made by the Beloved Son, was adopted. Satan, instead of yielding to the majority, in accordance with the rule of the kingdom of heaven, rebelled and, at the head of other rebellious spirits, endeavored to carry out his plan, in opposition to that which had been accepted. Then he was "cast down" and became Satan (Pearl of Great Price, Book of Moses, 4:1-4).

"When the devil and his host were sent from heaven because of disobedience, they came to this world. And wherever the children of men are, there also those evil spirits exist to tempt the children of men to do evil, and everything that leads to destruction and misery, and woe originates from that source, but everything that leads to exaltation, virtue, holiness, goodness, glory, immortality, and eternal life is from the hand of God. The Lord is the strongest power, and He will prevail at last" (Wilford Woodruff, *Journal of Discourses,* Vol. XI., p. 66).

14. Verily, I say unto you, that I will not suffer that Satan shall accomplish his evil design in this thing.

15. For behold, he has put it into their hearts to get thee to tempt the Lord thy God, in asking to translate it over again.

16. And then, behold, they say and think in their hearts— We will see if God has given him power to translate; if so, he will also give him power again;

17. And if God giveth him power again, or if he translates again, or, in other words, if he bringeth forth the same words, behold, we have the same with us, and we have altered them;

18. Therefore they will not agree, and we will say that he has lied in his words, and that he has no gift, and that he has no power;

19. Therefore we will destroy him, and also the work; and we will do this that we may not be ashamed in the end, and that we may get glory of the world.

20. Verily, verily, I say unto you, that Satan has great hold upon their hearts; he stirreth them up to iniquity against that which is good;

21. And their hearts are corrupt, and full of wickedness and abominations; and they love darkness rather than light, because their deeds are evil; therefore they will not ask of me.

22. Satan stirreth them up, that he may lead their souls to destruction.

23. And thus he has laid a cunning plan, thinking to destroy the work of God; but I will require this at their hands, and it shall turn to their shame and condemnation in the day of judgment.

24. Yea, he stirreth up their hearts to anger against this work.

25. Yea, he saith unto them: Deceive and lie in wait to catch, that ye may destroy; behold, this is no harm. And thus he flattereth them, and telleth them that it is no sin to lie that they may catch a man in a lie, that they may destroy him.

26. And thus he flattereth them, and leadeth them along until he draggeth their souls down to hell; and thus he causeth them to catch themselves in their own snare.

27. And thus he goeth up and down, to and fro in the earth, seeking to destroy the souls of men.

14. *Satan shall not accomplish his evil design*] The plan was very cunning. If the Prophet attempted another translation, his enemies would "prove" that he was merely a pretender, by giving publicity to the stolen manuscript, changed to suit their purposes.

25. *Deceive and lie in wait*] Satan had told these "wicked men" that it is no sin to lie, if by lying an enemy can be caught and destroyed.

This doctrine is here stamped as "Satanic."

27. *Seeking to destroy*] It is one of the doctrines by which he is seeking to destroy the souls of men.

28. Verily, verily, I say unto you, wo be unto him that lieth to deceive because he supposeth that another lieth to deceive, for such are not exempt from the justice of God.

29. Now, behold, they have altered these words, because Satan saith unto them: He hath deceived you—and thus he flattereth them away to do iniquity, to get thee to tempt the Lord thy God.

28. *Wo be unto him that lieth to deceive*] Lying is always a sin, even when it is done in the interest of moral reform, and those who use falsehood as their weapon, be it of offense or defense, are under this condemnation.

29. *To get thee to tempt the Lord thy God*] To pray for a translation of 116 written pages, word for word the same as the missing portion, would be "tempting" the Lord. It would be asking for a miracle as great as that by which Satan suggested that our Lord prove his Divine commission, which suggestion Christ declined by quoting Deut. 6:16, "Thou shalt not tempt the Lord thy God" (Matt. 4:5-7). If we expect God to perform miracles in our behalf, when we bring trouble upon ourselves by disobedience, we "tempt" God.

30. Behold, I say unto you, that you shall not translate again those words which have gone forth out of your hands;

31. For, behold, they shall not accomplish their evil designs in lying against those words. For, behold, if you should bring forth the same words they will say that you have lied and that you have pretended to translate, but that you have contradicted yourself.

32. And, behold, they will publish this, and Satan will harden the hearts of the people to stir them up to anger against you, that they will not believe my words.

33. Thus Satan thinketh to overpower your testimony in this generation, that the work may not come forth in this generation.

34. But behold, here is wisdom, and because I show unto you wisdom, and give you commandments concerning these things, what you shall do, show it not unto the world until you have accomplished the work of translation.

35. Marvel not that I said unto you: Here is wisdom, show it not unto the world—for I said, show it not unto the world, that you may be preserved.

36. Behold, I do not say that you shall not show it unto the righteous;

37. But as you cannot always judge the righteous, or as you cannot always tell the wicked from the righteous, therefore I say unto you, hold your peace until I shall see fit to make all things known unto the world concerning the matter.

30. *You shall not translate again*] The Prophet is now directed not to translate the lost portion a second time.

34. *Here is wisdom*] The Lord had a better course for him to follow. But this course he should keep to himself for the present. (v. 37).

38. And now, verily I say unto you, that an account of those things that you have written, which have gone out of your hands, is engraven upon the plates of Nephi;

39. Yea, and you remember it was said in those writings that a more particular account was given of these things upon the plates of Nephi.

40. And now, because the account which is engraven upon the plates of Nephi is more particular concerning the things which, in my wisdom, I would bring to the knowledge of the people in this account—

41. Therefore, you shall translate the engravings which are on the plates of Nephi, down even till you come to the reign of king Benjamin, or until you come to that which you have translated, which you have retained;

42. And behold, you shall publish it as the record of Nephi; and thus I will confound those who have altered my words.

38. *An account of these things that you have written*] Nephi made two records. In one he preserved an account of his father Lehi's life and genealogy, and the history of his people. This history was continued for many generations, by historians, such as Mosiah, Alma, Helaman, etc. The Prophet Mormon made an abridgment from this vast amount of historical material. The Prophet Joseph translated this abridgment, and it was the first part of that translation which was lost.

But Nephi also made another record. In this he preserved an account of events connected with the departure of his father from Jerusalem.

and their landing in America. This history was continued for 400 years, down to the reign of King Benjamin. It was chiefly an ecclesiastical history.

The Prophet Mormon found these "smaller plates" of Nephi and attached them to his own abridgment of the "larger plates." And thus there was a double line of history of the Nephites for 400 years. The Prophet Mormon says he added the smaller plates to his abridgment "for a wise purpose" (Mormon 1: 7), "for thus it whispereth me, according to the working of the Spirit of the Lord which is in me," and Nephi says he made those smaller plates in obedience to a commandment of God, given for some reason unknown to him (I, Nephi 9: 5).

41-2. *Therefore you shall translate * * * my words*] The Prophet Joseph was directed not to translate the lost portion of the manuscript a second time, but to substitute for it the account of the smaller plates of Nephi.

43. I will not suffer that they shall destroy my work; yea, I will show unto them that my wisdom is greater than the cunning of the devil.

44. Behold, they have only got a part, or an abridgment of the account of Nephi.

45. Behold, there are many things engraven upon the plates of Nephi which do throw greater views upon my gospel; therefore, it is wisdom in me that you should translate this first part of the engravings of Nephi; and send forth in this work.

46. And, behold, all the remainder of this work does contain all those parts of my gospel which my holy prophets, yea, and also my disciples, desired in their prayers should come forth unto this people.

47. And I said unto them, that it should be granted unto them according to their faith in their prayers;

45. *There are many things, etc.*] As is always the case, the plans of the Evil One turn out contrary to his evil intentions. The loss of the one hundred and sixteen pages of manuscript proved a gain. For, "There are many things engraven on the Plates of Nephi which do throw greater views upon my gospel."

The Prophet Joseph, from the very beginning of his prophetic calling, learned the truth so well expressed in Luther's great battle-hymn:

> "Our old, malignant foe,
> Fain would us overthrow,
> With cunning and great might."

But he also learned that:

> "Our God, He is a mighty tower,
> A bulwark that availeth;
> A present help in danger's hour,
> When trouble us assaileth."

48. Yea, and his was their faith—that my gospel, which I gave unto them that they might preach in their days, might come unto their brethren the Lamanites, and also all that had become Lamanites because of their dissensions.

49. Now, this is not all—their faith in their prayers was that this gospel should be made known also, if it were possible that other nations should possess this land;

50. And thus they did leave a blessing upon this land in their prayers, that whosoever should believe in this gospel in this land might have eternal life;

51. Yea, that it might be free unto all of whatsoever nation, kindred, tongue, or people they may be.

48-50. *This was their faith * * * eternal life*] Why did the last prophets of the Nephites abridge the records of their forefathers and carefully deposit their literary work in the ground? The answer to these questions is found here. They hoped and prayed that the gospel that was preached among the ancient inhabitants of the American Continents might, by that means, reach the descendants of the Lamanites and those associated with them (Section 3:18), and also to other nations that might come to the Western World.

52. And now, behold, according to their faith in their prayers will I bring this part of my gospel to the knowledge of my people. Behold, I do not bring it to destroy that which they have received, but to build it up.

53. And for this cause have I said: If this generation harden not their hearts, I will establish my church among them.

54. Now I do not say this to destroy my church, but I say this to build up my church;

55. Therefore, whosoever belongeth to my church need not fear, for such shall inherit the kingdom of heaven.

56. But it is they who do not fear me, neither keep my commandments but build up churches unto themselves to get gain, yea, and all those that do wickedly and build up the kingdom

of the devil—yea, verily, verily, I say unto you, that it is they that I will disturb, and cause to tremble and shake to the center.

52. *According to their faith in their prayers*] God always hears the prayers of faith, and now He raised up the Prophet Joseph to publish the ancient records, and thus the faith manifested in the prayers of those who preserved those records, was proved not to have been in vain.

Not to destroy that which they have received] The Book of Mormon does not take the place of the Bible; it confirms that sacred record, at a time when so-called Higher Critics are doing all in their power to destroy the belief in the divine authority of the Scriptures. It is a "New Witness" for the authenticity of the Bible. It claims no other position in sacred literature. It is the "Stick of Ephraim" joined to the "Stick of Judah," according to the word of the Lord (Ezekiel 37:15-19).

54. *Not to destroy * * * to build up my church*] When the Lord undertook to establish again His Church among the children of men, He did not intend to set aside any truth they had discovered, or in which they believed. "Mormonism" embraces all truth, no matter where found. It is a fact that the Latter-day Saints, as the late Bishop F. S. Spalding (Episcopalian), of Salt Lake City, expressed it, believed all the truth that other Christians believe, and then something more. "Mormonism" is constructive, not destructive. It recognizes truth everywhere, and it builds on such truth. Truth is its building material.

The cosmopolitan character of the Church of Jesus Christ of Latter-day Saints has often been noted. Here is a striking illustration. On the 1st of June, 1834, services were held in Zion's Camp, near Jacksonville. Many strangers attended. Heber C. Kimball, in his Journal, says that some of these were very much interested, but they could not make out what church the speakers represented. They said they thought that Joseph Young was a Methodist, Brigham Young a Close Communion Baptist, Orson Hyde a Campbellite, Lyman E. Johnson a Presbyterian, and Orson Pratt a "Restorationer" (*Times and Seasons*, Vol. VI., p. 773).

55. *Kingdom of heaven*] The Kingdom of Heaven is the Church. Sometimes the "Kingdom of Heaven" means the entire domain in which the government of God has been established—the kingdom in which God is acknowledged to be the Supreme Ruler. This kingdom is, and has always been, in "heaven." It is on Earth in the Church and will be extended over the whole Earth during the Millennium, and during its glorified state. But in this passage the Church especially seems to be meant. The Prophet Joseph uses the term in that sense, when he says. "The Kingdom of heaven is like unto a mustard seed. Behold, then, is not this the Kingdom of heaven that is raising its head in the last days in the majesty of its God, even the Church of the Latter-day Saints?" (*History of the Church*, Vol. II, p. 268).

56. *They who do not fear me*] Those who are rebellious and go on

building up churches for temporal profit have every reason to fear. For when the Church is established, their condemnation will follow, unless they repent.

Kingdom of the devil] There is also a "kingdom of the devil," and those who are engaged in building up this kingdom, have cause to fear the triumph of the Church.

57. Behold, I am Jesus Christ, the Son of God. I came unto mine own, and mine own received me not.

58. I am the light which shineth in darkness, and the darkness comprehendeth it not.

59. I am he who said—Other sheep have I which are not of this fold—unto my disciples, and many there were that understood me not.

60. And I will show unto this people that I had other sheep, and that they were a branch of the house of Jacob.

61. And I will bring to light their marvelous works, which they did in my name;

62. Yea, and I will also bring to light my gospel which was ministered unto them, and, behold, they shall not deny that which you have received, but they shall build it up, and shall bring to light the true points of my doctrine, yea, and the only doctrine which is in me.

63. And this I do that I may establish my gospel, that there may not be so much contention; yea, Satan doth stir up the hearts of the people to contention concerning the points of my doctrine; and in these things they do err, for they do wrest the scriptures and do not understand them.

64. Therefore, I will unfold unto them this great mystery.

65. For, behold, I will gather them as a hen gathereth her chickens under her wings, if they will not harden their hearts.

66. Yea, if they will come, they may, and partake of the waters of life freely.

57. *Behold, I am Jesus Christ*] It is our Lord and Savior who gives these Revelations—He who came to His own and was not received (John 1:11); He who is the Light which the darkness does not comprehend (John 1:5), He who said that He had other sheep, besides the Jews, and that, as a shepherd, He would bring also them to the fold (John 10:16).

59. *Other sheep*] On the American continents (III. Nephi 15:17-24).

60. *I will show unto this people*] the present inhabitants of America. God was about to show them, in the Book of Mormon, the history of these "other sheep"—their marvelous works in the past, and the principles they were taught. And this would be done, in order that contention might cease among Christians, and unity be established. Christians today realize the need of union of Christian effort. But how can they obtain it? The Gospel has been restored to make unity possible.

67. Behold, this is my doctrine—whosoever repenteth and cometh unto me, the same is my church.

68. Whosoever declareth more or less than this, the same is not of me, but is against me; therefore he is not of my church.

69. And now, behold, whosoever is of my church, and endureth of my church to the end, him will I establish upon my rock, and the gates of hell shall not prevail against them.

70. And now, remember the words of him who is the life and light of the world, your Redeemer, your Lord and your God. Amen.

67. *This is my doctrine,* etc.] The doctrine of the Lord is that, "Whosoever repenteth and cometh unto me, the same is [of] my church." To repent is to turn from evil; to "come to Christ" is to believe on Him and obey His commandments. Our Lord does not acknowledge repentance, no matter how crushing the sorrow may be, unless the repentant sinner proves his sincerity by coming to Him for pardon and regeneration.

Is [of] *my Church*] "Of" should be inserted, as in the 68th and 69th paragraphs.

69. *Gates of hell*] This, in the New Testament (Matt. 16:18), means the power of the unseen world, *Hades* or *Sheol,* and especially the power of death. The faithful members of the Church will not be overcome by the destructive forces, but triumph over them and live for ever.

SECTION 11.

REVELATION *given through Joseph Smith the Prophet, to his brother, Hyrum Smith, at Harmony, Pennsylvania, May, 1829. This revelation was received through the Urim and Thummim in answer to Joseph's supplication and inquiry.——The coming forth of a great and marvelous work proclaimed—Hyrum restrained from preaching for the time being, he not being yet*

baptized and ordained—He is assured of the gift of God await-
ing his preparation to receive—The organization of the Church
foreshadowed—Hyrum admonished to learn the word of God
before attempting to proclaim it—Warned against denying the
spirit of revelation and prophecy.

A GREAT and marvelous work is about to come forth among
the children of men.

2. Behold, I am God; give heed to my word, which is quick
and powerful, sharper than a two-edged sword, to the dividing
asunder of both joints and marrow; therefore give heed unto
my word.

3. Behold, the field is white already to harvest; therefore,
whoso desireth to reap let him thrust in his sickle with his
might, and reap while the day lasts, that he may treasure up
for his soul everlasting salvation in the kingdom of God.

4. Yea, whosoever will thrust in his sickle and reap, the
same is called of God.

5. Therefore, if you will ask of me you shall receive; if you
will knock it shall be opened unto you.

6. Now, as you have asked, behold, I say unto you, keep
my commandments, and seek to bring forth and establish the
cause of Zion.

7. Seek not for riches but for wisdom; and, behold, the mysteries of God shall be unfolded unto you, and then shall you
be made rich. Behold, he that hath eternal life is rich.

8. Verily, verily, I say unto you, even as you desire of me
so it shall be done unto you; and, if you desire, you shall be
the means of doing much good in this generation.

9. Say nothing but repentance unto this generation. Keep
my commandments, and assist to bring forth my work, according to my commandments, and you shall be blessed.

Hyrum Smith, who was born on the 9th day of February, 1800, was
the second son of Joseph Smith, Sr., and his wife, Lucy, and the oldest
of the children living at this time. He was a Presbyterian, but when he
heard of the finding of the Book of Mormon plates and learned that
his brother, Joseph, was translating them, he went to Harmony, Pa.,
where the young Prophet lived temporarily, to investigate the matter.
At his earnest request, Joseph prayed for a Revelation for him and

received the one contained in this Section. Hyrum became convinced of the truth, and was baptized in June, 1829. Shortly afterwards he became one of the Eight Witnesses to the Book of Mormon.

Between Joseph and Hyrum there was a sacred bond of genuine friendship, unselfish and tender; a friendship of that pure quality of which there are but few instances on record. We may recall the beautiful story of David and Jonathan, or, that of Damon and Pythias; the friendship between Joseph and Hyrum was all that those names stand for, and, in addition, the sympathy engendered by natural affection, and made sacred by a common interest in the salvation of their fellow men. Hyrum watched tenderly over Joseph. He was a peacemaker. He was faithful to death, and shared the martyr wreath with his illustrious, younger brother.

The following sentiment was expressed by the Prophet Joseph on the 11th of August, 1842:

"Brother Hyrum, what a faithful heart you have got! Oh, may the Eternal Jehovah crown eternal blessings upon your head, as a reward for the care you have had for my soul! O how many are the sorrows we have shared together; and again we find ourselves shackled with the unrelenting hand of oppression. Hyrum, thy name shall be written in the *Book of the Law of the Lord*,* for those who come after thee to look upon, that they may pattern after thy works" (*History of the Church,* Vol. V., pp. 107-8).

That the Lord was well pleased with this faithful witness, is clear from the following, "Verily I say unto you, blessed is my servant Hyrum Smith, for I, the Lord, love him because of the integrity of his heart, and because he loveth that which is right before me, saith the Lord" (Doc. and Cov. 124:15). Like Abraham, Hyrum Smith was a Patriarch, and as such he was a great man; but he was greater still as "the friend of God."

The Revelation in this Section was given to him in order that he might know the truth.

1-9. These verses are identical with Section 6:1-9. There are some remarkable repetitions in the Bible, too. See, for instance, Isaiah 2:2-4 and Micah 5:1-3.

10. Behold, thou hast a gift, or thou shalt have a gift if thou wilt desire of me in faith, with an honest heart, believing in the power of Jesus Christ, or in my power which speaketh unto thee;

11. For, behold, it is I that speak; behold, I am the light

---

* The Prophet kept a record which he called "The Book of the Law of the Lord," in which he recorded in love and gratitude the names of those who had proved themselves loyal to him and the Church. It also contained some important revelations.

which shineth in darkness, and by my power I give these
words unto thee.

12. And now, verily, verily, I say unto thee, put your trust
in that Spirit which leadeth to do good—yea, to do justly, to walk
humbly, to judge righteously; and this is my Spirit.

13. Verily, verily, I say unto you, I will impart unto you
of my Spirit, which shall enlighten your mind, which shall fill
your soul with joy;

14. And then shall ye know, or by this shall you know, all
things whatsoever you desire of me, which are pertaining unto
things of righteousness, in faith believing in me that you shall
receive.

10. *Thou hast a gift*] Hyrum Smith was a very gifted man, but his
special gift, as indicated in these paragraphs, was the possession, in an
abundant measure, of the Spirit of Christ Jesus (v. 12). That is the
Spirit "which leadeth to do good: yea, to do justly, to walk humbly, to
judge righteously." Justice, humility, and righteousness, and, it may be
added, a merciful disposition, were exemplified in the life of Hyrum
Smith, because he had the Spirit of Christ and was guided by it.

13. *Enlighten your mind*] Orson Pratt remarks:
"The Apostles heard, during three years and a half, many sermons [by
our Lord], and a vast amount of conversation and private teaching. The
office of the Spirit of Truth was to bring to their remembrance the things
that Jesus had formerly taught them. So it is the office of the same
Spirit in these days to bring to our remembrance the words of the ancient Prophets and Apostles, and the words of Jesus, inasmuch as we
have faith and confidence in God" (*Journal of Discourses*, Vol. VI., p.
349).

15. Behold, I command you that you need not suppose that
you are called to preach until you are called.

16. Wait a little longer, until you shall have my word, my
rock, my church, and my gospel, that you may know of a
surety my doctrine.

17. And then, behold, according to your desires, yea, even
according to your faith shall it be done unto you.

18. Keep my commandments; hold your peace; appeal unto
my Spirit;

19. Yea, cleave unto me with all your heart, that you may
assist in bringing to light those things of which has been spoken

—yea, the translation of my work; be patient until you shall accomplish it.

20. Behold, this is your work, to keep my commandments, yea, with all your might, mind and strength.

21. Seek not to declare my word, but first seek to obtain my word, and then shall your tongue be loosed; then, if you desire, you shall have my Spirit and my word, yea, the power of God unto the convincing of men.

22. But now hold your peace; study my word which hath gone forth among the children of men, and also study my word which shall come forth among the children of men, or that which is now translating, yea, until you have obtained all which I shall grant unto the children of men in this generation, and then shall all things be added thereto.

15. *Called to preach*] Hyrum Smith had a desire to engage in public speaking, as a minister. It was, therefore, necessary to correct certain prevalent errors concerning preaching, for the benefit of the little circle of friends who, under divine guidance, now were laying the foundations of the Church. One of these errors was the assumption that a minister can prove that he has divine authority, by quoting the commission of our Lord to His first Apostles. The Lord therefore instructs His servant not to suppose that he is sent to preach until he is actually called, as were the Twelve. On the other hand, one who is so called must not refuse to obey (v. 25). This was illustrated in the case of Leman Copley, who was tried before the High Council in Kirtland, in 1833, for having neglected to go on a mission, when called (*Journal of Discourses,* Vol. XI., p. 8). D.H.C. 1:354.

16. *Wait a little longer*] The instructions here given are applicable to all who desire to engage in the ministry. They must have the word of God; they must have revelation; they must belong to the Church; they must be instructed in the gospel and know that it is true. These are necessary qualifications of a minister. See also Sec. 4:5-7.

My rock] My revelation.

"Jesus says, 'Upon this rock I will build my Church, and the gates of hell shall not prevail against it.' What rock? Revelation" (Joseph Smith, *Hist. of Church,* Vol. V., p. 258).

18-22. Further instructions are given here. "Keep my commandments." Assist in the bringing forth of the Book of Mormon (v. 19). "First seek to obtain my Word" (v. 21). This involves prayerful study. The command is repeated (v. 22), "Study my word which hath gone forth" (the Bible), "and also study my word which shall come forth" (the Book of Mormon). The Lord does not employ ignorant preachers.

"It is impossible for a man to be saved in ignorance" (Doc. and Cov. 131:6). Much less can one be a savior in ignorance.

23. Behold thou art Hyrum, my son; seek the kingdom of God, and all things shall be added according to that which is just.

24. Build upon my rock, which is my gospel;

25. Deny not the spirit of revelation, nor the spirit of prophecy, for wo unto him that denieth these things;

26. Therefore, treasure up in your heart until the time which is in my wisdom that you shall go forth.

27. Behold, I speak unto all who have good desires, and have thrust in their sickle to reap.

28. Behold, I am Jesus Christ, the Son of God. I am the life and the light of the world.

29. I am the same who came unto mine own and mine own received me not;

30. But verily, verily, I say unto you, that as many as receive me, to them will I give power to become the sons of God, even to them that believe on my name. Amen.

23. *Thou art Hyrum*] The word *hyrum,* or *hiram,* is supposed to mean "noble"; "thou art noble." The founders of the Church were noblemen in God's Kingdom.

24. *Build upon my rock*] My revelation (v. 16). It is also "my gospel." The "rock" is not Peter but the revealed truth that Jesus is the Christ, the Son of the living God. That is the "rock," the gospel, upon which Christ builds His Church by continuously revealed truth in regard to both doctrine and organization.

25. *Deny not the Spirit of revelation*] The Spirit of Revelation operates in different ways: sometimes by means of vision, as in the case of the writing on the wall of the palace of Belshazzar; sometimes by the hearing of voices; frequently, seeing and hearing are combined, as in the case of the vision of the Prophet Joseph of the Father and the Son, and the wonderful manifestations in the Kirtland Temple (Doc. and Cov. 110). The giving of the Law on Mount Sinai and the testimony concerning the Book of Mormon given to the Three Witnesses were such manifestations. Israel saw the clouds indicating the presence of Jehovah, and heard His voice in rolling thunders. The Three Witnesses heard and saw the angel of the Lord. There could be no deception. The revelation was as real as that which Saul had on the road to Damascus. Sometimes Revelations are given in dreams. A notable instance is a dream

in which the Prophet Joseph saw certain false friends appear to him as snakes, while others were surrounded by wild beasts and appealed to him for help, after they had thrown him into a pit, bound hand and foot. Generally revelations come by the voice of the Spirit within. Most of the Revelations in the Doctrine and Covenants were received by this means. But no matter *how* the Spirit speaks, its voice must be heeded. One of the great sins of the Christian world today is that it denies the Spirit of revelation.

Nor the Spirit of prophecy] The Spirit of revelation is the Spirit of prophecy; it reveals things past, present, and future. To deny this Spirit is one form of atheism.

30. *But verily, * * * my name*] This is quoted from John 1:12. It means that all who accept Jesus Christ as their Savior receive of Him the right to possess all the privileges of God's children, whether they be Gentiles or Jews. Those who believe *on* His name receive that right. To believe on His name is to accept Him as being all that the name stands for. "Jesus" means "savior," "Christ" means "the anointed one," the incarnate Son of God, and to believe on His name is to be His follower.

GENERAL NOTES

Hyrum Smith was one of the Eight Witnesses to the Book of Mormon. He suffered a great deal of persecution because of his testimony. In December, 1839, he wrote a letter to the scattered Saints, in which he told them of the sufferings he had endured in the State of Missouri, and reaffirmed his testimony. He said, in part:

"I had been abused and thrust into a dungeon, and confined for months on account of my faith and the testimony of Jesus Christ. However, I thank God that I felt a determination to die, rather than deny the things which my eyes had seen, which my hands had handled, and which I had borne testimony to, wherever my lot had been cast; and I can assure my beloved brethren that I was enabled to bear as strong a testimony, when nothing but death presented itself, as ever I did in my life" (*Times and Seasons*, Vol. I., p. 23).

SECTION 12.

REVELATION *given through Joseph Smith the Prophet, to Joseph Knight, Sen., at Harmony, Pennsylvania, May, 1829. Joseph Knight believed the declarations of Joseph Smith, concerning his possession of the Book of Mormon plates, and the work of translation then in progress, and had given material assistance to the translator and his scribe. See History of the*

Church, vol. 1, p. 47.——Great and marvelous character of the Lord's work—Personal participation in the bringing forth and establishment of the cause of Zion open to all who have earnest desires and who possess the requisite qualifications.

A GREAT and marvelous work is about to come forth among the children of men.

2. Behold, I am God; give heed to my word, which is quick and powerful, sharper than a two-edged sword, to the dividing asunder of both joints and marrow; therefore, give heed unto my word.

3. Behold, the field is white already to harvest; therefore, whoso desireth to reap let him thrust in his sickle with his might, and reap while the day lasts, that he may treasure up for his soul everlasting salvation in the kingdom of God.

4. Yea, whosoever will thrust in his sickle and reap, the same is called of God.

5. Therefore, if you will ask of me you shall receive: if you will knock it shall be opened unto you.

6. Now, as you have asked, behold, I say unto you, keep my commandments, and seek to bring forth and establish the cause of Zion.

Joseph Knight, Sr., of Colesville, N. Y., having heard of the work in which the Prophet Joseph was engaged, was prompted to go to Harmony, Pa., with a load of provisions, to enable the Prophet and his associates to continue the translation. He brought supplies several times, a distance of thirty miles. The Lord thus taught His young servants to trust in Him. He gave them their first lesson in laboring without "purse and scrip." Knight was a Universalist, but he was liberal, hospitable, and kind, and was of great assistance in laying the foundations of the Church. During his visit with the Prophet in May, 1829, this Revelation was received.

1-6. See notes on Sec. 6:1-6. The first six verses are identical with the first part of Section Eleven, which contains a Revelation to Hyrum Smith; also with the first part of the Revelation to Oliver Cowdery, Sec. 6. There are elementary truths which the Spirit of God deemed it necessary to impress upon the minds of all who had a desire to engage in the ministry: (1) The work about to come forth was "great and marvelous," even the marvelous work predicted by Isaiah (29:14); (2) He who gave these Revelations, Jesus Christ, is God, and His word must be obeyed; (3) the field was ripe, ready for the harvest; the time had come; (4) only those who were willing to work would be called; (5) by prayer great things would be accomplished; and, finally, it would be necessary, for success, to keep the commandments of God.

7. Behold, I speak unto you, and also to all those who have desires to bring forth and establish this work;

8. And no one can assist in this work except he shall be humble and full of love, having faith, hope, and charity, being temperate in all things, whatsoever shall be entrusted to his care.

9. Behold, I am the light and the life of the world, that speak these words, therefore give heed with your might, and then you are called. Amen.

8. *No one can assist in this work, except,* etc.] Joseph Knight had shown a generous willingness to sacrifice both his means and his time, and his assistance was gratefully accepted. But he needed instruction. The Lord, therefore, told him that those who would assist in the furtherance of His work must be humble, full of love, faith, hope, and charity, and be temperate in all things—in eating and drinking, and all the enjoyments of life. All temporal blessings are to be enjoyed in moderation, for indulgence may become a hindrance to effectual work in the service of God.

Humble] Humility is a Christian virtue. Heathen philosophers—Aristotle, for instance—regarded meekness as a defect, and not a virtue. The world generally holds that view. Humility is submission to the will of God. Christ was "meek and lowly," and He is the pattern. Humility is the opposite of self-assertion and pride.

9. *I am the light and the life of the world*] It is our Lord who is speaking. He calls Himself the Light and the Life of the World, adopting the terms which the Apostle John loved so well (John 1:4, 9; 3:19; 6:35; 12:35; 14:6). The Savior frequently quotes in these Revelations; or, rather, expressions familiar to the readers of John's writing meet us here again and again. John had a prominent part in the ushering in of this dispensation. On the Isle of Patmos he saw the coming, in our day, of the "mighty angel" with the "little book open," and it was said to him, "Thou must prophesy again before many peoples, and nations, and tongues, and kings" (Rev. 10:11). In fulfilment of this prediction, he and two fellow Apostles conferred the Melchizedek Priesthood upon Joseph Smith and Oliver Cowdery. No wonder if the spirit of the teachings of these Apostles, and especially that of John, the last of the first Twelve, should be discernible in these Revelations.

SECTION 13.

ORDINATION *of Joseph Smith and Oliver Cowdery to the Aaronic Priesthood, at Harmony, Pennsylvania, May 15, 1829, under the hands of an Angel, who announced himself as John, the same that is called John the Baptist in the New Testament. The angelic visitant averred that he was acting under the direction of Peter, James, and John, the ancient Apostles, who held the keys of the higher Priesthood, which was called the Priesthood of Melchizedek. The promise was given to Joseph and Oliver that in due time the Priesthood of Melchizedek would be conferred upon them. See History of the Church, vol. 1, p. 39. Compare Section 27:7, 8, 12.*

UPON you my fellow servants, in the name of Messiah I confer the Priesthood of Aaron, which holds the keys of the ministering of angels, and of the gospel of repentance, and of baptism by immersion for the remission of sins; and this shall never be taken again from the earth, until the sons of Levi do offer again an offering unto the Lord in righteousness.

The Section contains the words which John the Baptist spoke when he conferred upon Joseph Smith and Oliver Cowdery the keys of the Aaronic Priesthood. John held these keys in the dispensation of the Meridian of Time, and because of this authority he was sent in the dispensation of the Fulness of Times to confer these keys in the day of restoration of all things. This Priesthood we are informed holds the keys of the preparatory Gospel, which is the Gospel of faith, repentance and the remission of sins by baptism by immersion, but does not hold the authority of laying on of hands for the gift of the Holy Ghost, they were informed by John that he was acting under the direction of Peter, James and John, who held the keys of the Priesthood of Melchizedek, and that this Priesthood would in due time be conferred upon them, and Joseph Smith should be called the first Elder of the Church and Oliver Cowdery the second. This Priesthood held the keys of the higher ordinances, including the laying on of hands for the gift of the Holy Ghost. (D.H.C. 1:39-40.)

This promise was fulfilled shortly afterwards, when Peter, James, and John appeared in the wilderness between Harmony, Pa., and Colesville, N. Y., on the banks of the Susquehanna River, declaring that they held the keys of the Kingdom and of the Dispensation of the Fulness of Times (Doc. and Cov. 128-20), and ordaining and confirming the Prophet and Oliver to "be apostles and especial witnesses of my name"

(Doc. and Cov. 27:12). *When* this ordination took place is not known, but Elder B. H. Roberts, *Hist. of the Church*, Vol. I., pp. 40, 41) fixes the date, from the historical material available, at some day between the 15th of May and the latter part of June, 1829.

The Priesthood of Aaron] There are two Priesthoods, the Melchizedek and the Aaronic, but "the Melchizedek Priesthood comprehends the Aaronic, or Levitical, "Priesthood" (Joseph Smith). Moses held the Melchizedek Priesthood, "and sought diligently to sanctify his people * * * but they hardened their hearts * * * therefore, he took Moses out of their midst, and the holy Priesthood also; and the lesser Priesthood continued" (Doc. and Cov. 84:23-27). This Lesser, or Aaronic Priesthood holds the Keys; that is, it has and confers authority to receive the ministration of angels, to preach the gospel of repentance, to baptize for the remission of sins, and to administer "the law of carnal commandments." Those who held this Priesthood in the Old Dispensation, attended to the Tabernacle and the Temple service, including the sacrifices; they took care of everything belonging to the Sanctuary. The duties of that Priesthood are of a similar nature now.

The Priests of the Aaronic Priesthood in the Mosaic Dispensation kept the fire upon the altar burning continually (Lev. 1:13). They dressed the burnt offerings (II. Chron. 29:34) and killed the pascal lamb (Ezra 6:20); they received the blood of the sacrifices in basins (Ex. 24:6) and sprinkled it round the altar; they disposed of the meat offerings, as prescribed by law, and of other offerings; they performed the ceremonies of purification (Lev. 12:6, 7) and judged cases of leprosy, etc.

The presiding officer was called the High Priest. His duties were to offer a meat offering every morning and evening, to officiate on the Day of Atonement, to arrange the shew-bread every Sabbath, to adjudicate legal differences, and to ascertain the mind and will of the Lord. Under his direction the Priests took the Tabernacle to pieces, when the people were to move forward, and reconstructed it, when they camped. He also appointed the Levites to their various duties and blessed the people (Num. 6:23-27).

The garments worn by the Priests consisted of linen drawers (Ex. 28:42) and a coat of fine linen, or cotton (Ex. 39:27), which, according to Josephus, reached to the feet, sat close to the body, had sleeves, and was girded to the chest by a girdle: it had an aperture for the head, and was tied with strings.

The dress of the High Priest was similar, but, in addition, he wore a robe, an ephod, a breastplate in which he carried the Urim and Thummim, and a mitre (Ex. 28:4; 29:9). There is difference of opinion as to whether the ephod was a waistcoat or an apron.* The Urim and Thummim was carried in a pocket, called the "breastplate," either above or

---

* Facsimile No. 3 in the Book of Abraham throws some light on the vestments of the bearers of the Priesthood in ancient times. Abraham is there depicted with a mitre, or crown, on his head, emblematic of the grand Presidency in heaven, or the Melchizedek Priesthood. Shulem wears an apron, and this may be emblematic of the Lesser Priesthood.

upon the ephod. This pocket was about nine inches square, and was adorned with twelve precious stones, on each of which was engraved the name of one of the twelve tribes of Israel.

Speaking of the Aaronic Priesthood, the Prophet says:

"The offering of sacrifice has ever been connected with and forms a part of, the duties of the Priesthood. It began with the Priesthood, and will be continued until after the coming of Christ, from generation to generation. We frequently have mention made of the offering of sacrifice by the servants of the Most High in ancient days, prior to the Law of Moses; which ordinances will be continued when the Priesthood is restored with all its authority, power, and blessings" (*History of the Church*, Vol. IV., p. 207).

Until the sons of Levi do offer again, etc.] This does not mean that the Aaronic Priesthood will be taken from Earth when the sons of Levi are re-instated in their calling, but that, as a result of the restoration of that Priesthood, the sons of Levi would again offer sacrifices, as of yore. Oliver Cowdery, in an article in the *Times and Seasons,* reproduced in the Pearl of Great Price, quotes John the Baptist thus:

"Upon you my fellow servants, in the name of Messiah, I confer the Priesthood and this authority, which shall remain upon Earth, that the sons of Levi may yet offer an offering unto the Lord in righteousness," giving the true sense of the words of John in this Revelation.

SECTION 14.

REVELATION *given through Joseph Smith the Prophet, to David Whitmer, at Fayette, New York, June, 1829. The Whitmer family had become greatly interested in the translating of the Book of Mormon. Joseph changed his residence to the Whitmer home, where he dwelt until the work of translation was carried to completion and the copyright on the forthcoming book secured. Each of the three sons, having received a testimony as to the genuineness of the work, became deeply concerned over the matter of his individual duty; and the Prophet inquired of the Lord respecting the matter. This revelation and the two next following (Sections 15 and 16) were given in answer, through the Urim and Thummim. See History of the Church, vol. 1, p. 48. David Whitmer later became one of the Three Witnesses to the Book of Mormon.——Conditions of attaining eternal life specified—The Lord's purpose of bringing the fulness of his Gospel from the Gentiles to the house of*

Israel—David Whitmer informed of his call to assist in the latter-day work—His reward, conditioned by his faithfulness, is promised.

A GREAT and marvelous work is about to come forth unto the children of men.

2. Behold, I am God; give heed to my word, which is quick and powerful, sharper than a two-edged sword, to the dividing asunder of both joints and marrow; therefore give heed unto my word.

3. Behold, the field is white already to harvest; therefore, whoso desireth to reap let him thrust in his sickle with his might, and reap while the day lasts, that he may treasure up for his soul everlasting salvation in the kingdom of God.

4. Yea, whosoever will thrust in his sickle and reap, the same is called of God.

5. Therefore, if you will ask of me you shall receive; if you will knock it shall be opened unto you.

David Whitmer was the son of a prosperous farmer, Peter Whitmer, living in the western part of the state of New York. On a business trip to Palmyra he became acquainted with Oliver Cowdery and heard the story of the finding of the Book of Mormon plates by Joseph Smith. It was the subject of common conversation in the community. This was in the year 1828. David, who had been brought up a strict Presbyterian, at first paid little attention to the rumor. Cowdery said there must be some foundation for it, and that he intended to make an investigation. David returned home. Some months after this visit to Palmyra, Cowdery visited the Whitmers. He was then on his way to Harmony, Pa., to see the Prophet Joseph. David Whitmer asked him to let him know the results of his investigation. Some time later he received a letter from Cowdery, in which that latter stated that he was convinced that Joseph the Prophet, had the plates, as claimed. Several letters passed between them, and finally David Whitmer went to Harmony with a conveyance and brought Joseph Smith, his wife, and Oliver Cowdery to his home, where they were hospitably received. The very next day after the arrival, the work on the Book of Mormon was resumed and continued for a month, from June the 1st to July the 1st, 1829. David Whitmer states that the translation was done in the presence of all of his father's family, Mrs. Smith, Oliver Cowdery, and Martin Harris, through the aid of the Urim and Thummim (*Millennial Star,* Vol. XLIII., p. 421). While this work was being done in the Whitmer home, David, John, and Peter Whitmer were anxious to know the will of God concerning them, and the Revelations contained in Sections 14, 15 and 16 were received.

1-5. These verses are identical with the first five verses of Sec. 6.

6. Seek to bring forth and establish my Zion. Keep my commandments in all things.

7. And, if you keep my commandments and endure to the end you shall have eternal life, which gift is the greatest of all the gifts of God.

8. And it shall come to pass, that if you shall ask the Father in my name, in faith believing, you shall receive the Holy Ghost, which giveth utterance, that you may stand as a witness of the things of which you shall both hear and see, and also that you may declare repentance unto this generation.

9. Behold, I am Jesus Christ, the Son of the living God, who created the heavens and the earth, a light which cannot be hid in darkness;

10. Wherefore, I must bring forth the fulness of my gospel from the Gentiles unto the house of Israel.

11. And behold, thou art David, and thou art called to assist; which thing if ye do, and are faithful, ye shall be blessed both spiritually and temporally, and great shall be your reward. Amen.

6. *Keep my commandments*] David Whitmer is told to seek to bring forth Zion and to do whatever God should command him.

7. *Endure to the end*] The promise is that, if he would do so and remain faithful to the end, he should receive eternal life. The Spirit of Prophecy indicated, even before David Whitmer joined the Church, the danger of not enduring to the end.

David Whitmer was baptized during the month of June 1829, and was privileged to become one of the Three Witnesses to the Book of Mormon. He was one of the original six members of the Church. He shared in the trials of the Saints, was appointed president of the High Council in Clay County, July 3, 1834, and took a leading part in the Church in Missouri. When the saints settled in Far West, he was sustained as their president there. But, notwithstanding all this, he was excommunicated on April 13th, 1838. Had he given heed to this Revelation, he might have remained faithful to the end. He did not return to the Church, but he remained faithful to the testimony to the Book of Mormon until the day of his death.

9. *Behold, I am Jesus Christ*] Our Lord here presents Himself as the Son of God "who created heaven and earth"; God who reveals Himself in the history of the creation, in whose image man was created—

not the God of erring theology. He was instructed to pray to a living God, all-powerful and good.

10. *I must bring forth,* etc.] Our Lord says He "must bring forth the fulness of His gospel to the house of Israel. That was the work which began with the publication of the Book of Mormon. It "must" be done. Jesus, our Savior, had undertaken to complete the plan of salvation; He was under obligation to His heavenly Father to do so.

11. *Thou art David*] David Whitmer was called to assist, and given the promise that, if he would do so, he would be blessed both temporally and spiritually.

GENERAL NOTES

Some imagine that the first associates of the Prophet were dupes, who took his words at par without evidence. This is far from true. They believed because the evidence was overwhelming. This is clear from the history of Samuel Smith, Hyrum Smith, Martin Harris, Oliver Cowdery, and David Whitmer. The latter relates the following:

"Soon after this [the arrival of a letter from Oliver Cowdery] Joseph sent for me to come to Harmony to get him and Oliver, to bring them to my father's house. I did not know what to do. I was pressed with my work. I had some twenty acres to plow, so I concluded I would finish plowing and then go. I got up one morning to go to work as usual, and on going to the field, found between 5 and 7 acres of my ground had been plowed during the night. I do not know who did it, but it was done just as I would have done it myself, and the plow was left standing in the furrow."

This incident was related to Orson Pratt and Joseph F. Smith by David Whitmer, on the 7th of September, 1878, forty years after he had left the Church. It was to him a miraculous evidence, the force of which he never denied.

SECTION 15.

REVELATION *given through Joseph Smith the Prophet, to John Whitmer, at Fayette, New York, June, 1829. See heading to Section 14. John Whitmer later became one of the Eight Witnesses to the Book of Mormon.———The message is intimately and impressively personal, in that the Lord tells of what was known only to John Whitmer and himself—The recipient blessed for his worthy desire—The thing of greatest worth to him.*

HEARKEN, my servant John, and listen to the words of Jesus Christ, your Lord and your Redeemer.

2. For behold, I speak unto you with sharpness and with power, for mine arm is over all the earth.

3. And I will tell you that which no man knoweth save me and thee alone—

4. For many times you have desired of me to know that which would be of the most worth unto you.

5. Behold, blessed are you for this thing, and for speaking my words which I have given you according to my commandments.

6. And now, behold, I say unto you, that the thing which will be of the most worth unto you will be to declare repentance unto this people, that you may bring souls unto me, that you may rest with them in the kingdom of my Father. Amen.

John Whitmer, the third son of Peter Whitmer, Sr., was baptized by Oliver Cowdery shortly after the arrival of the Prophet at the Whitmer home. He assisted Joseph as secretary; accompanied him to Colesville, where a Branch was organized; was Church historian; went with Oliver Cowdery to Jackson County, in 1831, to direct the publication of the *Book of Commandments,* and he was one of the Eight Witnesses to the Book of Mormon. But he did not remain faithful. He was excommunicated by the High Council at Far West, 1838, the charge being that he, together with David Whitmer and W. W. Phelps, had failed to account properly for $2,000 of the funds of the Church. He did not return to the Church, but he always maintained that his testimony concerning the Book of Mormon was true.

2. *With sharpness*] The word of the Lord is like a "two-edged sword." See note on Section 6:2.

My arm] God's power, which is over all the Earth; wherefore the gospel is to be made known everywhere, for the salvation of the children of men. See Isa. 53:1; John 12:38.

3-5. The Lord made Himself known to John Whitmer, as He had done to Oliver Cowdery (Doc. and Cov. 6:15), and to Nathanael (John 1:48).

6. *Declare repentance*] To engage in the ministry is to labor in a calling which is worth more than any other. This great truth John Whitmer eventually forgot.

GENERAL NOTES

During the persecution in Missouri, Elders Heber C. Kimball and Theodore Turley came to Far West, to render any assistance they could. On the 5th of April, 1839, fifty men swore that they would neither eat nor drink until they had killed the Prophet. At the same time eight men presented a paper to Elder Turley, containing a Revelation predicting that the Apostles would take leave of the Saints on the Temple ground at Far West, on the 26th of April, 1839 (Doc. and Cov. 118:5). This, they said, could not be done; if any of the Twelve should attempt it, they would be killed; here, then, they said, was a false prophecy. Turley replied, "In the name of God, that Revelation will be fulfilled." Then he turned to John Whitmer and observed, "There are many things published that they say are true, and again turn around and say they are false." "Do you hint at me?" Whitmer asked. Turley said, "If the cap fits, you may wear it; all I know is that you have published to the world that an angel did present those plates to Joseph Smith." Then John Whitmer, in that company, made this statement, "I now say, I handled those plates; there were fine engravings on both sides, I handled them; they were shown to me by supernatural power." (*Historical Record,* p. 458).

SECTION 16.

REVELATION *given through Joseph Smith the Prophet, to Peter Whitmer, Jun., at Fayette, New York, June, 1829. See heading to Section 14. Peter Whitmer, Jun., later became one of the Eight Witnesses to the Book of Mormon.*

HEARKEN, my servant Peter, and listen to the words of Jesus Christ, your Lord and your Redeemer.

2. For behold, I speak unto you with sharpness and with power, for mine arm is over all the earth.

3. And I will tell you that which no man knoweth save me and thee alone—

4. For many times you have desired of me to know that which would be of the most worth unto you.

5. Behold, blessed are you for this thing, and for speaking my words which I have given unto you according to my commandments.

6. And now, behold, I say unto you, that the thing which will be of the most worth unto you will be to declare repentance unto this people, that you may bring souls unto me, that you may rest with them in the kingdom of my Father. Amen.

Peter Whitmer, Jr., was the fifth son of Peter Whitmer. He was baptized in the month of June, 1829, and in September, 1830, he was called to the ministry. The following month he was sent to accompany Elders Parley P. Pratt, Oliver Cowdery, and Ziba Peterson on a mission to the Lamanites (Doc. and Cov. 32). Peter Whitmer took an active part with the Saints in Jackson County and Clay County. He died on a farm about two miles from Liberty, Clay County, Sept. 22nd, 1836. He was one of the Eight Witnesses to the Book of Mormon, and one of the original six founders of the Church, and he remained faithful to the last. This Revelation is identical with Section 15.

SECTION 17.

REVELATION *given through Joseph Smith the Prophet, to Oliver Cowdery, David Whitmer and Martin Harris, at Fayette, New York, June, 1829, prior to their viewing the engraved plates that contained the Book of Mormon record. Joseph and his scribe, Oliver Cowdery, had learned from the translation of certain passages on the Book of Mormon plates that three special witnesses would be designated. See Ether 5:2-4; also 2 Nephi 11:3, and 27:12. Oliver Cowdery, David Whitmer and Martin Harris were moved upon by an inspired desire to be the three special witnesses. The Prophet inquired of the Lord, and this revelation was given in answer, through the Urim and Thummim. See History of the Church, vol. 1, p. 52.——The three conditionally promised that they shall be permitted to view not only the plates but also other sacred relics of Book of Mormon record—Only by faith like unto that of the prophets of old can they be thus privileged—They to testify of what they shall see—Joseph Smith's solemn avowals to be supported— The Lord declares that as he lives the translation is true.*

BEHOLD, I say unto you, that you must rely upon my word, which if you do with full purpose of heart, you shall have a view of the plates, and also of the breastplate, the sword of

Laban, the Urim and Thummim, which were given to the brother of Jared upon the mount, when he talked with the Lord face to face, and the miraculous directors which were given to Lehi while in the wilderness, on the borders of the Red Sea.

Some time during the month of March, 1829, when Martin Harris expressed a desire to receive a divine confirmation of the testimony of the Prophet Joseph that he actually had the plates, the Lord promised His servant that three men should be called and ordained to become witnesses to the world (Sec. 5:11-15), after they had seen the plates and heard the heavenly voice declare the truth to them. As the translation of the Book of Mormon proceeded, they learned from the book itself (II. Nephi 11:3; Ether 5:2-4) that there were to be three witnesses to the Book, and then Oliver Cowdery, David Whitmer, and Martin Harris desired the Prophet to ask the Lord that they might be chosen. In answer to the Prophet's prayer this Revelation was received.

1. *You must rely upon my word*] Only by faith could they obtain the privilege they desired. Faith is the force by which everything in the Kingdom of God takes place. By faith Abel offered unto God a more acceptable sacrifice than Cain; by faith Enoch was translated; by faith Noah was warned of the flood; by faith Abraham received Isaac back from the dead, figuratively speaking (Heb. 11), and by faith the Three Witnesses saw the Book of Mormon plates.

The plates] The records were engraved on plates which had the appearance of gold. Each plate was nearly seven by eight inches in width and length, being not quite as thick as common tin. They had engravings on both sides and were bound together in a volume as the leaves of a book, and fastened at one edge with three rings running through the whole. The volume was about six inches in thickness, and part of it was sealed (Andrew Jenson, *Historical Record*, p. 363).

Urim and Thummim] See notes on Sec. 3:15; also Mosiah 8:13-19; 28:13-20; Ether 4:5. The place where God resides is a Urim and Thummim, and this Earth is to become one, in its sanctified state (Doc. and Cov. 130:8, 9). John describes the earth, in its sanctified state, as a "sea of glass." (Rev. 4:6; 15:2. D. & C. 130:7.)

Given to the brother of Jared] The instrument which Joseph had was that which was given to the brother of Jared (Ether 3:23), and deposited with the Jaredite Record, also known as the Book of Ether. It was entrusted to the care of Alma, the son of Alma, and finally hidden in the hill Cumorah. What became of the sacred instrument which the High Priest of Israel had is not known. From Ezra 2:63, and Nehemiah 7:65, it appears that it had been lost, but that its restoration was looked for. The meaning of the two words *Urim and Thummim* has been given as "lights" and "perfections"; or "manifestation" and "truth." Judges in Egypt presiding at trials, wore, suspended from their necks, an image of the Goddess of Truth, a custom in all probability handed down to them from the time of the Patriarchs, if these, as the High Priest of Israel, wore the Urim and Thummim when they entered the presence of God.

The breast plate] See notes, Section 13.

The sword of Laban] "The hilt thereof was of pure gold, and the workmanship exceeding fine, and * * * the blade * * * of the most precious steel" (I. Nephi 4:9). This sword played an important part in the history of the Nephites. It was wielded with great strength by Nephi and by King Benjamin, but steel cannot save a people from destruction. The Nephites fell, and the sword was buried with their records.

Miraculous directors] When the time had come for Lehi to leave the Valley of Lemuel, the voice of the Lord came to him during the night, commanding him to begin the perilous journey across the desert. It was no easy undertaking. Who was to act as guide? Undoubtedly, Lehi spent the night in prayer, asking for light and guidance. Early in the morning he stood in the tent door, anxiously surveying the surroundings, and then he beheld on the ground a brass ball. On examining this, he found that it had two spindles, one of which pointed the way (I. Nephi 16:10). When Lehi perceived the wonderful qualities of this instrument, he exclaimed, in ecstasy, *Liahona!* and that became its name (Alma 37:38). Liahona is a Hebrew word with, possibly, a Nephite termination, added later. *L* means "to"; *Jah* is an abbreviated form of the sacred name, "Jehovah," and *on* means "light." The meaning, then, is, "To Jehovah is light"; that is, "God has light; light comes from God," for He had answered his prayers for light and guidance. Similarly, Hagar, after having seen the Angel of the Lord, said, *Beer-lahai-roi;* that is, "The well of the Living One who seeth me" (Gen. 16:13).

The Prophet Joseph renders the word, "compass," as the nearest modern equivalent to it, just as one might properly apply the modern term "dreadnought" to an ancient viking ship; but it was not a compass, for it pointed out only the way the travelers were to follow, and it worked according to their faith; it was not dependent on the magnetic pole.

2. And it is by your faith that you shall obtain a view of them, even by that faith which was had by the prophets of old.

2. *Faith*] If we would know what faith is, and what it can accomplish, we must study the lives of the Prophets of God.

"Thus grave the lesson on thy soul—
  Faith, hope, and love—and thou shalt find
Strength when life's surges rudest roll,
  Light when thou else wert blind."—Schiller.

3. And after that you have obtained faith, and have seen

them with your eyes, you shall testify of them, by the power of God;

4. And this you shall do that my servant Joseph Smith, Jun., may not be destroyed, that I may bring about my righteous purposes unto the children of men in this work.

5. And ye shall testify that you have seen them, even as my servant Joseph Smith, Jun., has seen them; for it is by my power that he has seen them, and it is because he had faith.

6. And he has translated the book, even that part which I have commanded him, and as your Lord and God liveth it is true.

7. Wherefore, you have received the same power, and the same faith, and the same gift like unto him;

8. And if you do these last commandments of mine, which I have given you, the gates of hell shall not prevail against you; for my grace is sufficient for you, and you shall be lifted up at the last day.

9. And I, Jesus Christ, your Lord and your God, have spoken it unto you, that I might bring about my righteous purposes unto the children of men. Amen.

3. *You shall testify*] Favors impose duties. When the witnesses obtained a view of the plates, it became their duty to testify of that which they had seen and heard.

6. *It is true*] The Spirit here testifies to the truth of the Book of Mormon. May we not, in view of this solemn affirmation, "As your Lord and God liveth," inscribe, on the fly leaf of that volume, something like this:

> "Within this awful volume lies
> The mystery of mysteries.
> Happiest he of human race
> To whom our God has given grace
> To read, to fear, to hope, to pray,
> To lift the latch, and force the way;
> And better had he ne'er been born
> Who reads to doubt, or reads to scorn."

These lines were written by Sir Walter Scott and copied by Lord Byron in his Bible. Are they not appropriate on the title page of that companion volume to the Bible, of which the Three Witnesses testify?

GENERAL NOTES

One day a short time after this Revelation had been received, and after the customary morning devotions, the Prophet Joseph said to

Martin Harris, "You must humble yourself before your God this day, that you may obtain a forgiveness of your sins. If you do, it is the will of God that you should look upon the plates in company with Oliver Cowdery and David Whitmer" (*History of the Prophet Joseph,* by Mother Smith).

A place had been selected, not very far from Whitmer's house, and the Prophet and his three friends went there. They all prayed in rotation, but at first there was no answer. Then Martin Harris withdrew. They prayed again, and now, as they poured out their souls in fervent petitions, there was a light around them, and an angel appeared who held in his hands the plates and turned them over, one by one. To Whitmer the angel said, "David, blessed is the Lord, and he that keeps His commandments." And then a voice came from above, "These plates have been revealed by the power of God, and they have been translated by the power of God. The translation of them which you have seen is correct, and I command you to bear record of what you now see and hear."

Joseph now went to look for Martin Harris and found him engaged in prayer. He joined him, and presently Martin Harris cried out, full of joy, " 'Tis enough; mine eyes have beheld," and jumping up, he shouted, "Hosanna." He had seen the same vision and heard the same voice.

It was between 3 and 4 p.m. when the men returned home. Mrs. Whitmer, Mr. Joseph Smith, Sr., and Mrs. Lucy Smith were sitting in the bedroom at the time. Joseph went straight to his mother and exclaimed, "Father, mother, you do not know how happy I am; the Lord has now caused the plates to be shown to three more besides myself. They have seen an angel, who has testified to them, and they will have to bear witness to the truth of what I have said, for now they know for themselves that I do not go about to deceive people, and I feel as if I were relieved of a burden which was almost too heavy for me to bear, and it rejoices my soul that I am not any longer to be entirely alone in the world."

Elder Edward Stephenson declares:

"I have often heard him [Oliver Cowdery] bear a faithful testimony to the restoration of the gospel by the visitation of an angel, in whose presence he stood in company with the Prophet Joseph Smith, and David Whitmer" (*Millennial Star,* Vol. XLVIII., p. 420).

David Whitmer, on the 7th of September, 1878, in a conversation with Elders Orson Pratt and Joseph F. Smith, said, in part:

"Joseph, Oliver, and myself were together when I saw them [the plates]. We not only saw the plates of the Book of Mormon, but also the brass plates, the plates of the Book of Ether * * * and many other plates * * * there appeared, as it were, a table with many records, or plates, upon it, besides the plates of the Book of Mormon, also the sword of Laban, the directors [i.e., the ball which Lehi had], and the interpreters. I saw them just as plainly as I see this bed (striking the bed beside him with his hand), and I heard the voice of the Lord, as distinctly as I ever heard anything in my life, declaring that the records of the plates of the Book of Mormon were translated by the gift and power of God" (Andrew Jenson, *Historical Record*, p. 208).

Martin Harris, while estranged from the Church, was on one occasion asked whether he actually believed that he had seen an angel. He replied:

"Gentlemen, what I have said is true, from the fact that my belief is swallowed up in knowledge; for I want to say to you that, as the Lord lives, I do know that I stood with the Prophet Joseph Smith in the presence of the angel, and it was in the brightness of day" (*Historical Record*, p. 217).

SECTION 18.

REVELATION *to Joseph Smith the Prophet, Oliver Cowdery and David Whitmer, given at Fayette, New York, June, 1829: Making known the calling of Twelve Apostles in these last days; and also containing instructions relative to building up the Church of Christ according to the fulness of the Gospel. When the Aaronic Priesthood was conferred, the bestowal of the Melchizedek Priesthood was promised. See heading to Section 13. In response to fervent supplication for greater knowledge on the matter the Lord gave this revelation. See History of the Church, vol. 1, pp. 60-64.——Diligence enjoined—Oliver Cowdery and David Whitmer called with the calling of Paul the Apostle of old—The value of souls emphasized—The great joy attending conversion of souls to the Gospel of Christ—The calling of twelve to assist in the ministry foreshadowed—The Twelve, here called disciples but later named Apostles, to be chosen from among those who desire to take upon them the name of Christ with full purpose of heart—Oliver Cowdery and David Whitmer commissioned to search out the Twelve.*

NOW, behold, because of the thing which you, my servant Oliver Cowdery, have desired to know of me, I give unto you these words:

2. Behold, I have manifested unto you, by my Spirit in many

instances, that the things which you have written are true; where-fore you know that they are true.

3. And if you know that they are true, behold, I give unto you a commandment, that you rely upon the things which are written;

4. For in them are all things written concerning the founda-tion of my church, my gospel, and my rock.

5. Wherefore, if you shall build up my church, upon the foundation of my gospel and my rock, the gates of hell shall not prevail against you.

After the glorious manifestations referred to in Section 17, Joseph and Oliver became anxious to receive the holy Melchizedek Priesthood, promised by John the Baptist when he conferred upon them the Aaronic Priesthood (Sec. 13), and they, together with David Whitmer, made this the subject of earnest prayer. One day, while thus engaged in a secluded chamber in Whitmer's house, the word of the Lord came to them, commanding Joseph and Oliver to ordain each other Elders, and then ordain others to the same office, as the Spirit should direct. But this ordination was not to take place until the Church should be organ-ized and the members have an opportunity of sanctioning it by their vote, for Common Consent is one of the fundamental principles in the government of the Kingdom of God (Section 26:2; 28:13). When the time for the ordination came, they were further instructed to partake of the Sacrament and afterwards to ordain each other and those selected by the voice of the Spirit, and, finally, confer the gift of the Holy Ghost by the laying on of hands upon those who had been baptized. All this was done on the 6th day of April, 1830, the day on which the Church was organized. Shortly after having received these instructions, Joseph Smith, Oliver Cowdery, and David Whitmer were given this Revelation concern-ing the calling of the Twelve Apostles and the building up of the Church.

1. *The thing which you have desired to know*] Oliver Cowdery de-sired special instructions concerning the building up of the Church. In the following paragraphs (vv. 2-4) the answer to his prayers on this subject is given. It was, in substance: You have received a testimony that the Book of Mormon is true; rely on that truth. In that Volume all things are written concerning the foundation of the Church. No further Revelations, covering the same ground, were needed. Where the written Word is sufficient, no special Revelation may be expected.

5. *Gates of hell*] See Notes, Section 10:69.

The Spirit manifested to Oliver Cowdery that the Book of Mormon was true.

"I say to all, both Saint and sinner, that there is not an individual who has heard the sound of the gospel of salvation, the report of this work of the last days, of the coming forth of the Book of Mormon, and of the mission of Joseph Smith, but the Spirit of the Lord in a greater or less degree accompanied the report with power, and with a testimony of its truth, no matter as to the character of the individual, nor yet whether he embraces or rejects the truth" (Brigham Young, *Journal of Discourses,* Vol. I., p. 88).

6. Behold, the world is ripening in iniquity; and it must needs be that the children of men are stirred up unto repentance, both the Gentiles and also the house of Israel.

7. Wherefore, as thou hast been baptized by the hands of my servant Joseph Smith, Jun., according to that which I have commanded him, he hath fulfilled the thing which I commanded him.

8. And now, marvel not that I have called him unto mine own purpose, which purpose is known in me; wherefore, if he shall be diligent in keeping my commandments he shall be blessed unto eternal life; and his name is Joseph.

6. *Ripening in iniquity*] As fruit, when ripe, falls, so the world, when ripened in iniquity, is destroyed. The Lord, therefore, commanded His servants to preach repentance, to avert destruction. The most conspicuous sin of the world in this age, as when Paul wrote his letter to the Romans (Rom. 1:26), is unchastity. Consequently, the voice of the Church has been raised against that sin with more emphasis than against any other evil.

8. *Marvel not*] Oliver Cowdery may have thought it strange that Joseph should have been called to do the work in which he was engaged, wherefore the Lord says, "Marvel not." God knew why He had called him. There were sufficient reasons, even if they were not apparent to man.

His name is Joseph] Attention is called to the name, because the Scriptures predict the coming of a great deliverer in the latter days, so named. Nephi says that Joseph, the Patriarch, predicted the coming forth of the House of Israel on the American continents, of a "righteous branch" and a Seer, whose name, he said, "shall be called after me" (Joseph), and after the name of his father (II. Nephi 3:1-15). In Isaiah, too, there is an apocalyptic reference to the name, Joseph, in connection with the establishment of the Kingdom of God. That Prophet (Chapter 3) describes the judgment on his people and dissolution of the social order, as a consequence of greed, selfishness, and indulgence in luxury by the "upper classes." Then he predicts (Chapter 4) the restoration, when "the Branch of the Lord"—"the righteous Branch, of II. Nephi—shall be "beautiful and glorious." At the beginning of this time of restoration, Isaiah says, something unusual is to occur. "Seven women shall take hold of one man," and ask him for the privilege of bearing his name, "to take away our reproach." This, we say, may well be considered as an allusion to the name and mission of the Prophet Joseph; for *Joseph* is said to mean, "God hath taken away my reproach" (Gen. 30:23).

9. And now, Oliver Cowdery, I speak unto you, and also unto David Whitmer, by the way of commandment; for, behold, I command all men everywhere to repent, and I speak unto you, even as unto Paul mine apostle, for you are called even with that same calling with which he was called.

10. Remember the worth of souls is great in the sight of God;

11. For, behold, the Lord your Redeemer suffered death in the flesh; wherefore he suffered the pain of all men, that all men might repent and come unto him.

12. And he hath risen again from the dead, that he might bring all men unto him, on conditions of repentance.

13. And how great is his joy in the soul that repenteth!

14. Wherefore, you are called to cry repentance unto this people.

15. And if it so be that you should labor all your days in crying repentance unto this people, and bring, save it be one soul unto me, how great shall be your joy with him in the kingdom of my Father!

16. And now, if your joy will be great with one soul that you have brought unto me into the kingdom of my Father, how great will be your joy if you should bring many souls unto me!

17. Behold, you have my gospel before you, and my rock, and my salvation.

18. Ask the Father in my name, in faith believing that you shall receive, and you shall have the Holy Ghost, which manifesteth all things which are expedient unto the children of men.

19. And if you have not faith, hope, and charity, you can do nothing.

20. Contend against no church, save it be the church of the devil.

21. Take upon you the name of Christ, and speak the truth in soberness.

22. And as many as repent and are baptized in my name,

which is Jesus Christ, and endure to the end, the same shall be saved.

23. Behold, Jesus Christ is the name which is given of the Father, and there is none other name given whereby man can be saved;

24. Wherefore, all men must take upon them the name which is given of the Father, for in that name shall they be called at the last day;

25. Wherefore, if they know not the name by which they are called, they cannot have place in the kingdom of my Father.

9-25. These verses contain special instructions to Oliver Cowdery and David Whitmer concerning the building up of the Church. They were called with the same calling as Paul (v. 9). They were to remember that souls are so precious in the sight of God that our Redeemer suffered death in order to make it possible for all men to repent and come to Him; and not only did He die, but He rose, victorious over death, in order that He might bring *all men* unto Him, on condition of repentance (vv. 10-12). They were to remember that even if they should labor a life-time and bring only one soul to Christ, their joy would be great, and that they would have correspondingly greater joy, if they should win many souls (vv. 13-16). They had His gospel; if they would pray, they would also receive the Holy Ghost, and thus be fully equipped for the ministry, for the Holy Spirit manifests all things to the children of men; yet, unless they also had faith, hope, and charity, they could do nothing (vv. 17-19). But charity is the pure love of Christ, and it endureth forever; and whoso is found possessed of it at the last day, it shall be well with him. (Moroni 7:47.)

"And now abideth faith, hope and charity, these three; but the greatest of these is charity" (I. Cor. 13:13).

"Faith receives the promises of God as true. * * * Hope, as an anchor of the soul, keeps it steadfast amid all the storms and temptations of life; but the exercise of faith and hope is limited to the present imperfect state. The one shall be exchanged for sight, and the other shall be swallowed up in fruition. Love is superior to both, as the end is greater than the means; as that which is unchangeable is superior to that which is transitory" (Lothian).

"Faith and hope are our own: love is diffused among others" (Calvin).

20. *Contend against no church*] It is the calling of a minister of the Lord to preach the gospel and not to engage in endless and unprofitable controversies (II. Tim. 2:15, 16). Contention is of the Devil (III. Nephi 11:29).

Church of the devil] The Devil has his church, his kingdom. "I beheld this great and abominable church; and I saw the devil, that he was the foundation of it" (I. Nephi 13:6). "There are two churches only; the one is the church of the Lamb of God, and the other is the church of the devil" (I. Nephi 14:10). The church of the adversary may be known by its fundamental principle of government. In the beginning he declared himself in favor of salvation by compulsion, and although he was cast out of heaven for refusing to submit to the divine Council, he has continued his agitation for that plan among the children of men ever since. His church consists of those who adopt his plan and seek to destroy the free agency of man by brute force. In the Church of the Lamb of God the "law of liberty," which is the law of "common consent," prevails. The church of the adversary may also be known by contention and strife, by false doctrines, and by all manner of iniquity. A minister of the Lord makes war upon the domain of the adversary by the sword of the Spirit; not by persecution.

21. *Take upon you the name of Christ*] To take upon one's self the name of Christ, is to acknowledge Him as the Master. Slaves, in olden times, sometimes had the name of their master on their foreheads.

Christ revealed Himself in the Old Testament as "I am,"—Hebrew, *'Ehyeh 'asher 'Ehyeh* (Ex. 3:14), which implies that, while He *is,* or exists, and is therefore different from all non-existing deities of merely human imagination, He is not an abstract existence without form or substance, but He is a real Being, manifesting Himself in history ever anew; He is always with His people, active for their welfare.

In the New Testament He has revealed Himself as Jesus, the Savior, and Christ, the Anointed One (see v. 22). "Thou shalt call His name JESUS: for he shall save his people from their sins" (Matt. 1:21). To take upon oneself His name is, therefore, more than to become a disciple; it is to engage in His service for the salvation of men. JESUS CHRIST is the name given of the Father, and there is no other through which man can be saved. It is the name in which men shall be called at the last day—the day of judgment (Mosiah 5:9)—and those who know not the Name can have no place in the Kingdom of God (vv. 23-25).

The modern tendency to insert the definite article and read, "Jesus, the Christ" is not consistent with this revelation.

26. And now, behold, there are others who are called to declare my gospel, both unto Gentile and unto Jew;

27. Yea, even twelve; and the Twelve shall be my disciples, and they shall take upon them my name; and the Twelve are they who shall desire to take upon them my name with full purpose of heart.

28. And if they desire to take upon them my name with full purpose of heart, they are called to go into all the world to preach my gospel unto every creature.

29. And they are they who are ordained of me to baptize in my name, according to that which is written;

30. And you have that which is written before you; wherefore, you must perform it according to the words which are written.

26-29. The Lord, in these paragraphs, makes known His purpose to select, as of old, Twelve Apostles, to proclaim His gospel, both unto Gentile and Jew. These must "take upon them" the name of the Lord and be prepared to go to all parts of the world and preach to every creature. No man on Earth can sink so low that he is not entitled, through the mercy of God, to hear the gospel, for every human being is one of God's "creatures." The Twelve would also be authorized to baptize in the name of Jesus; i.e., in His stead, as His representatives, but the ordinance must be performed in accordance with the written word.

Some hold that the office and calling of the Twelve ended with the death of the Apostles first ordained by our Lord. Theologians tell us that, "The office of the Apostles as described in the New Testament, was, from its nature, incapable of being transmitted, and has not in fact been perpetuated." They say that, "There is no command given in the New Testament to keep up the succession of Apostles," and when it is pointed out that Matthias was selected to fill the vacancy caused by the apostasy of Judas, and that Paul was called to the Apostleship by our Lord Himself, while Barnabas, Silas, Timothy, Titus, and Apollos may, for all we know, have been members of the Apostles' Council, it is argued, in reply, that there is no record of the appointment of any of these to the Apostleship, except Matthias. The fact remains, however, that God gave to the Church both Apostles, Prophets, Evangelists, Pastors, and Teachers, for the perfecting of the Saints, the work of the ministry, and the edifying of the body of Christ, and that they were to continue, till we all come in the unity of the faith (Eph. 4:11-13). Apostles, according to the New Testament, are just as much needed as Pastors, Evangelists, and Teachers.

The calling of the Twelve neither began nor ended with the organization of which Peter, James, and John were prominent members. A Council of Twelve was appointed by Moses, in obedience to a divine command, shortly after the Exodus (Numb. 1:1-16). This Council consisted of one representative of each tribe of Israel, and they had, to a very large extent, the responsibility of leadership among the people. They are called "Princes* of Israel," and when the Tabernacle was dedicated, they brought the offerings of the people before the Lord (Numb. 7:1-83; Joshua 3:12; 4:2-9).

There was then a permanent Council of Twelve in ancient Israel, al-

---

* "Prince," from PRINCEPS, one who takes the first place, a leader.

though the Melchizedek Priesthood had been taken away. Our Lord appointed a Council of Twelve, to whom He committed the affairs of the Church on earth during His absence. He selected a Council of Twelve among the ancient people of the American continents (III. Nephi 12:1; 19:4), and He has again, in our day, appointed Twelve to be His special servants.

The duty of the Twelve is to carry the message of Christ to the world. They are His messengers. They have power over unclean spirits and diseases. They have the "keys of the kingdom of God"; that is, authority to act in the name of Christ. They are witnesses. They must know for themselves that their message is true, for they cannot testify to what they know only by hearsay.

31. And now I speak unto you, the Twelve—Behold, my grace is sufficient for you; you must walk uprightly before me and sin not.

32. And, behold, you are they who are ordained of me to ordain priests and teachers; to declare my gospel, according to the power of the Holy Ghost which is in you, and according to the callings and gifts of God unto men;

33. And I, Jesus Christ, your Lord and your God, have spoken it.

34. These words are not of men nor of man, but of me; wherefore, you shall testify they are of me and not of man;

25. For it is my voice which speaketh them unto you; for they are given by my Spirit unto you, and by my power you can read them one to another; and save it were by my power you could not have them;

36. Wherefore, you can testify that you have heard my voice, and know my words.

31-36. These are special instructions to the Twelve that were to be called in this dispensation. They must walk uprightly and sin not; they must have integrity. They were to ordain Priests and Teachers, to preach by the power of the Holy Ghost, and to testify of the Lord that they have heard His voice and know His words.

31. *Sin not*] No man is perfect, but one who strives earnestly to conquer weaknesses and grow unto perfection does not "sin." That is to say, he is not a "sinner." A sinner is one who indulges in sin habitually because he takes pleasure in it.

36. *Testify*] "All these, your brethren, who are called to the Apostleship, and to minister in the midst of the house of Israel, are endowed,

or ought to be endowed richly, with the spirit of their calling. For instance, these twelve disciples of Christ are supposed to be eye and ear witnesses of the divine mission of Jesus Christ. It is not permissible for them to simply say, I believe; I have accepted it, just because I believe it. Read the Revelation. The Lord informs us that they must *know,* they must get the knowledge for themselves, it must be with them as if they had seen with their eyes and heard with their ears, and they know the truth. That is their mission, to testify of Jesus Christ and Him crucified, and risen from the dead and clothed now with almighty power at the right hand of God, the Savior of the world. That is their mission, and their duty; and that is the doctrine and the truth; that is their duty to preach to the world, and see that it is preached to the world. Where they cannot go themselves, they are to have help of others called to their assistance—the Seventies first, also the Elders and the High Priests. Those who hold the Melchizedek Priesthood, not otherwise appointed, are under their direction to preach the gospel to the world and to declare the truth—that Jesus is the Christ, and that Joseph is a Prophet of God and was authorized and qualified to lay the foundation of the Kingdom of God (President Joseph F. Smith, *Millennial Star,* Vol. LXXVII., p. 336).

37. And now, behold, I give unto you, Oliver Cowdery, and also unto David Whitmer, that you shall search out the Twelve, who shall have the desires of which I have spoken;

38. And by their desires and their works you shall know them.

39. And when you have found them you shall show these things unto them.

40. And you shall fall down and worship the Father in my name.

41. And you must preach unto the world, saying: You must repent and be baptized, in the name of Jesus Christ;

42. For all men must repent and be baptized, and not only men, but women, and children who have arrived at the years of accountability.

37. *Search out the Twelve*] Oliver Cowdery and David Whitmer are here commissioned to select the Twelve.

38. *Their desires and their works*] They were to be guided in their choice by the desires of those that might be considered, and by what these had already accomplished.

This divine command was complied with on the 14th of February, 1835, at a special meeting held in Kirtland, when the Three Witnesses selected twelve men to form the first Council of Apostles.

43. And now, after that you have received this, you must keep my commandments in all things;

44. And by your hands I will work a marvelous work among the children of men, unto the convincing of many of their sins, that they may come unto repentance, and that they may come unto the kingdom of my Father.

45. Wherefore, the blessings which I give unto you are above all things.

46. And after that you have received this, if you keep not my commandments you cannot be saved in the kingdom of my Father.

47. Behold, I, Jesus Christ, your Lord and your God, and your Redeemer, by the power of my Spirit have spoken it. Amen.

43-46. Those who are favored with divine instructions must follow them; if they do not, they cannot be saved in the Kingdom of God.

SECTION 19.

A COMMANDMENT OF GOD, *and not of man, revealed through Joseph Smith the Prophet, to Martin Harris, at Manchester, New York, March, 1830, by him who is Eternal.——Christ affirms his omnipotence—Declares that punishment and suffering are inevitable consequences of unrepented sins—Explains the signification of endless torment and eternal damnation—Reaffirms the actuality of his own suffering in the flesh—Emphasizes the necessity of prayer—Gives specific commandment to Martin Harris.*

I AM Alpha and Omega, Christ the Lord; yea, even I am he, the beginning and the end, the Redeemer of the world.

This Revelation is the first received in the year 1830, the year of the organization of the Church. In it our Lord (1) gives His names and character (v. 1); (2) reveals Himself as ruler of the world (2-3); (3) explains the nature of endless punishment (4-12); (4) commands Martin Harris (a) to repent (13-20), (b) to preach repentance (21-24), (c) to refrain from sin (25), (d) to give liberally for the purpose of enabling Joseph to print the Book of Mormon (26, 27), (e) to pray and to preach (28-31). Then the Lord warns Martin Harris that this would be the last word to him regarding the publication of the Book of Mormon (32) and tells him that he would be miserable, if he failed to obey, but happy, if he complied (33-38). The closing verses (39-41) contain searching questions.

1. NAMES AND CHARACTERS OF OUR LORD.

Our Lord begins this Revelation by introducing Himself under five different names, each indicating His nature or work:

Alpha and Omega] The first and the last letter of the Greek alphabet, used as symbols of the beginning and the ending. Christ is so called, because He is the Author and the Preserver of all things (Heb. 1:2, 10).

Christ the Lord] "Christ" means "anointed." Prophets, Priests, and Kings were anointed, and our Lord unites all these offices in Him. He is the anointed Lord. The Greek word Christ is the same as the Hebrew Messiah (Mashiac), the title used in John 1:41, and 4:25.

I am He] This is equivalent to Jehovah (See notes on Sec. 18:21).

The Beginning and the End] He was in the beginning and will remain throughout all eternities. He is endless (v. 4).

The Redeemer of the World] Christ is our Redeemer. He delivers those who turn to Him from the bondage of sin and guilt. He has "bought" us (I. Cor. 6:20; 7:23; II. Pet. 2:1). And the world will in due time be delivered from the power of Satan, from sin and all its consequences, such as war, poverty, ignorance, sickness, and even death.

What a glorious constellation of divine names meets our wondering eyes in this Revelation, indicating that the Son of Righteousness is again about to rise effulgent on the world, through the establishment of the Church!

2. I, having accomplished and finished the will of him whose I am, even the Father, concerning me—having done this that I might subdue all things unto myself—

3. Retaining all power, even to the destroying of Satan and his works at the end of the world, and the last great day of judgment, which I shall pass upon the inhabitants thereof, judging every man according to his works and the deeds which he hath done.

2. CHRIST THE RULER OF THE WORLD.

2. Our Lord, by His life and death, complied with the will of the Father and accomplished that for which He was sent to the Earth, and was faithful in all things.

3. He has all power, even over Satan and his works, and through this power the influence of the adversary will be destroyed, when judgment shall be passed upon the inhabitants of the Earth, at the "end of the world." Our Lord has *all* power. The kingdom is His. "And when I

say 'Kingdom' of God, I mean what I say. Christ is the King—not man. No man is king of the Kingdom of God; God is the King of it, and we acknowledge Him, and Him only, as Sovereign of His Kingdom" (President Joseph F. Smith).

It is only a little while before the empires symbolized by beasts shall give way to the Kingdom of Immanuel. Then the pollutions of paganism and the sufferings due to error will be no more. Then the name of the Redeemer will be everywhere adored. Truth, freedom, love shall spread their mantle over every nation, and man will be permitted to fulfil his destiny unhampered by sin and suffering.

End of the World] This expression does not mean, as sometimes supposed, the destruction of the Earth, but the termination of a dispensation by some act of final judgment upon the inhabitants of the Earth. The flood was the "end" of the antediluvian world. The destruction of Jerusalem by Titus was the end of "the world" to which the first Christians were looking forward. The next "end of the world" will be the overthrow of the kingdoms of the world and the establishment of the Millennium.

"The end of the world is the destruction of the wicked; the harvest and the end of the world have an allusion directly to the human family in the last days, instead of the Earth, as many have imagined" (Joseph Smith, *History of the Church,* Vol. II., p. 271).

Judging every man] Every man shall be judged according to his works, but it will make a difference whether we stand before God as children in the presence of a father, as hired servants expecting wages, as criminals before a judge, or as enemies before the conqueror. The Lord tells us (Doc. and Cov. Sec. 76:111) that those who shall inherit telestial glory "shall be judged according to their works" and "receive according to their works." He also declares (John 5:24) that "He that heareth my word and believeth him that sent me, hath eternal life, and cometh *not into judgment,* but hath passed out of death into life (Revised Version). The believer does not come to judgment as a hired servant, nor as a criminal, or an enemy.

4. And surely every man must repent or suffer, for I, God, am endless.

5. Wherefore, I revoke not the judgments which I shall pass, but woes shall go forth, weeping, wailing and gnashing of teeth. yea, to those who are found on my left hand.

6. Nevertheless, it is not written that there shall be no end to this torment, but it is written *endless torment.*

7. Again, it is written *eternal damnation;* wherefore it is more express than other scriptures, that it might work upon the hearts of the children of men, altogether for my name's glory.

8. Wherefore, I will explain unto you this mystery, for it is meet unto you to know even as mine apostles.

9. I speak unto you that are chosen in this thing, even as one, that you may enter into my rest.

10. For, behold, the mystery of godliness, how great is it! For, behold, I am endless, and the punishment which is given from my hand is endless punishment, for Endless is my name. Wherefore—

11. Eternal punishment is God's punishment.

12. Endless punishment is God's punishment.

3. Endless Punishment.

4-12. This is an explanation of the doctrine of eternal damnation. Why, it may be asked, was an exposition of this doctrine necessary at this time, even before the organization of the Church? Because it is necessary that God's children have a correct understanding of His character and power, lest they should be influenced by a fear of Satan instead of by love of God. The story is told of Luther that, when examining a candidate for the pulpit to ascertain his qualifications as a minister, he asked him first of all, "What do you know about the Devil?" That may sound absurd; but one who has false notions about the adversary is not likely to conquer him. Satan is a mighty potentate, but he is not as strong as some imagine. At the time this Revelation was given, preachers used to declare that unless sinners repented and believed, they would be cast into a lake of burning brimstone and there be tormented in all eternity. Then they tried to explain the duration of eternity. "I have heard men," says George A. Smith, "spend hours in endeavoring to explain how long this hell would last. It was frequently illustrated in this manner, 'Suppose a bird could carry a drop of water from this planet to another, and be gone a year on the journey, and continue this until every drop of water on the earth was carried away, and then should take a particle of sand and go to another planet and be gone a thousand years, and carry one particle of sand at a time until every particle of matter of which this globe is composed was carried away; then, this eternal punishment would have just commenced" (*Journal of Discourses,* Vol. XII., p. 333). How is it possible to believe in God, if He is powerless against such a condition, or to love Him, if He suffers the Devil to revenge himself upon His erring children? This Revelation sheds a flood of truth upon the future condition of sinners.

4. *God is endless*] He is the Eternal One.

5. *I revoke not the judgments*] His judgments are irrevocable. From them there is no appeal. They are final. In that sense they are everlasting.

6-12. *Endless torment*] "Endless torment," "eternal damnation" are expressions which denote the punishment inflicted by the Endless One, the Eternal One. "Eternal punishment" is contrasted with such punishment as man can inflict on man in time here on earth.

13. Wherefore, I command you to repent, and keep the commandments which you have received by the hand of my servant Joseph Smith, Jun., in my name;

14. And it is by my almighty power that you have received them;

15. Therefore I command you to repent—repent, lest I smite you by the rod of my mouth, and by my wrath, and by my anger, and your sufferings be sore—how sore you know not, how exquisite you know not, yea, how hard to bear you know not.

16. For behold, I, God, have suffered these things for all, that they might not suffer if they would repent;

17. But if they would not repent they must suffer even as I;

18. Which suffering caused myself, even God, the greatest of all, to tremble because of pain, and to bleed at every pore, and to suffer both body and spirit—and would that I might not drink the bitter cup, and shrink—

19. Nevertheless, glory be to the Father, and I partook and finished my preparations unto the children of men.

20. Wherefore, I command you again to repent, lest I humble you with my almighty power; and that you confess your sins, lest you suffer these punishments of which I have spoken, of which in the smallest, yea, even in the least degree you have tasted at the time I withdrew my Spirit.

21. And I command you that you preach naught but repentance, and show not these things unto the world until it is wisdom in me.

22. For, they cannot bear meat now, but milk they must receive; wherefore, they must not know these things, lest they perish.

23. Learn of me, and listen to my words; walk in the meekness of my Spirit, and you shall have peace in me.

24. I am Jesus Christ: I came by the will of the Father, and I do his will.

25. And again, I command thee that thou shalt not covet thy neighbor's wife; nor seek thy neighbor's life.

26. And again, I command thee that thou shalt not covet thine own property, but impart it freely to the printing of the Book of Mormon, which contains the truth and the word of God—

27. Which is my word to the Gentile, that soon it may go to the Jew, of whom the Lamanites are a remnant, that they may believe the gospel, and look not for a Messiah to come who has already come.

28. And again, I command thee that thou shalt pray vocally as well as in thy heart; yea, before the world as well as in secret, in public as well as in private.

29. And thou shalt declare glad tidings, yea, publish it upon the mountains, and upon every high place, and among every people that thou shalt be permitted to see.

30. And thou shalt do it with all humility, trusting in me, reviling not against revilers.

31. And of tenets thou shalt not talk, but thou shalt declare repentance and faith on the Savior, and remission of sins by baptism, and by fire, yea, even the Holy Ghost.

32. Behold, this is a great and the last commandment which I shall give unto you concerning this matter; for this shall suffice for thy daily walk, even unto the end of thy life.

33. And misery thou shalt receive if thou wilt slight these counsels, yea, even the destruction of thyself and property.

34. Impart a portion of thy property, yea, even part of thy lands, and all save the support of thy family.

35. Pay the debt thou hast contracted with the printer. Release thyself from bondage.

36. Leave thy house and home, except when thou shalt desire to see thy family;

37. And speak freely to all; yea, preach, exhort, declare the truth, even with a loud voice, with a sound of rejoicing, crying—Hosanna, hosanna, blessed be the name of the Lord God!

38. Pray always, and I will pour out my Spirit upon you, and great shall be your blessing—yea, even more than if you

should obtain treasures of earth and corruptibleness to the extent
thereof.

4. INSTRUCTIONS TO MARTIN HARRIS.

13-38. These verses contain special instructions to Martin Harris.
Notwithstanding the many manifestations he had received concerning
the Book of Mormon, he was still tormented with doubts, to such an
extent that it became sinful. Skepticism has its legitimate use, in so far
as it prompts one to investigate, but to doubt in the face of overwhelming evidence is perversity.

13. *Repent*] In his case skepticism was a sin.

15. *The rod of my mouth*] Unless he repented, the Lord would smite
him with the rod of His mouth, an expression equivalent to "the spirit
of his mouth" (II. Thess. 2:8), and "the sword of my mouth" (Rev.
2:16). He would be in the same category as the followers of the antichrist and the apostates from the church at Pergamos.

21. *Nought but repentance*] He was also instructed not to preach
anything but repentance. He, evidently, was anxious to tell about the
Revelations, which the world could not understand.

26. *Thine own property*] Martin Harris is here told that he must
not covet "his own" property any more than his neighbor's wife, or his
life. This may be strange, but in the language of President Joseph F.
Smith, "We are here on His [Christ's] Earth, we breathe His air, we
behold His sunlight. We eat His food, we wear His clothing." Our "own"
property belongs to Him.

28. *Pray*] Without prayer life is not a success. Prayer is just as
necessary as work. Working without prayer is a form of atheism which
takes no cognizance of God.
"Those who go farthest on in the school of prayer and learn most
of its hidden secrets often develop a sort of prescience which comes
nearest to the prophetic spirit, the Holy Spirit showing them 'things
to come.' They seem, like Savonarola, to know something of the
purpose of God, to anticipate His plans, and to forecast the history of
their own times. The great supplicators have been also the great seers"
(Arthur T. Pierson).

31. *Tenets*] Martin Harris was also commanded to preach but not
"tenets"; not dogmas, or opinions, but the gospel message.

32. *This is the great and the last commandment*] The Spirit of the
Lord does not always strive with man. Sometimes He withdraws, if man
does not obey.

35. *Pay the debt * * * printer*] An agreement had been made with
Mr. Egberth Grandon, of Palmyra, for the printing of 5,000 copies of

the Book of Mormon, for $3,000, and it was necessary that this obliga-
tion should be met promptly.

39. Behold, canst thou read this without rejoicing and lifting up thy heart for gladness?
40. Or canst thou run about longer as a blind guide?
41. Or canst thou be humble and meek, and conduct thyself
wisely before me? Yea, come unto me thy Savior. Amen.

39-41. The closing verses contain questions which must have revealed
Martin Harris' thoughts to him in their true light.

GENERAL NOTE

Martin Harris was a prosperous farmer and had means enough for
the furtherance of the great latter-day work, but when he became dis-
associated from the Church, he did not continue to prosper. In 1870, at
the age of 87 years,* the Spirit prompted him to go to Utah. Elder
Edward Stevenson, consequently, raised the money necessary among
the Saints in Utah, and some of the Saints at Des Moines, Iowa, gave
him a new suit of clothes. But Martin Harris, in his days of poverty,
was never troubled with doubts. While prosperous, he frequently merited
chastisement. He died in full fellowship with the Church, a faithful
witness to the last.

SECTION 20.

REVELATION *on Church Organization and Government, given
through Joseph Smith the Prophet, April, 1830. Preceding his
record of this revelation the Prophet wrote: We obtained of
him [Jesus Christ] the following, by the spirit of prophecy and
revelation; which not only gave us much information, but also
pointed out to us the precise day upon which, according to his
will and commandment, we should proceed to organize his
Church once more here upon the earth.——The Lord again
attests the genuineness of the Book of Mormon—He gives commandment respecting baptism—Defines the functions of the
several offices in the Priesthood—Specifies the duties of members—Prescribes the mode of baptism, and of administering*

* He was born May 18th, 1783.

the sacrament of bread and wine—Directs the keeping of records of Church membership.

THE rise of the Church of Christ in these last days, being one thousand eight hundred and thirty years since the coming of our Lord and Savior Jesus Christ in the flesh, it being regularly organized and established agreeable to the laws of our country, by the will and commandments of God, in the fourth month, and on the sixth day of the month which is called April—

2. Which commandments were given to Joseph Smith, Jun., who was called of God, and ordained an apostle of Jesus Christ, to be the first elder of this church;

3. And to Oliver Cowdery, who was also called of God, an apostle of Jesus Christ, to be the second elder of this church, and ordained under his hand;

4. And this according to the grace of our Lord and Savior Jesus Christ, to whom be all glory, both now and forever. Amen.

The time was now drawing near for the organization of the Church, and the Spirit of Revelation indicated the date for that event. This Revelation (1) states that the Church should "rise" out of obscurity and darkness, (Sec. 1:30); in the year 1830 (1-4); (2) gives a brief review of events preceding the organization (5-12); (3) presents the solemn testimony of the two Elders (13-16); (4) sets forth some of the truths established by the Book of Mormon (17-28; and 29-36); (5) imparts instructions regarding (a) baptism (37); (b) duties of officers (38-67); (c) duties of members (68-71); (d) the manner of the administration of the Sacraments (72-79); (e) transgressors (80), and (f) conferences and records (81-84).

1. THE RISE OF THE CHURCH.

1. The Church was organized on the 6th of April, 1830. This date was chosen in accordance with a divine command. In all probability the 6th of April is the anniversary of the birthday of our Lord. There is no authentic record of the date of the birth of Christ, but scholars (Griswell, among others) consider it probable that He was born on the tenth day of the Jewish month of Nisan, which in the year of the Nativity has been calculated to correspond to Saturday, April the 5th. But as He was born at night, and Saturday expired at sunset, the date would be more precisely, April the 6th, and that would be the beginning of Sunday, "our Lord's day." On this supposition the date was most appropriate.

Agreeable to the laws] The Church was organized under the laws

of the State of New York, which required that a society should have no
fewer than six members, to be recognized under the law. It was organized in accordance with a divine command, for God requires His children to conform to all just laws. From the first the Church was taught
loyalty.

Joseph and Oliver had, by this time, conferred upon them the
Melchizedek Priesthood. They had authority to organize the Church,
receive commandments, and take charge of the affairs of the Kingdom
of God, according to the grace of our Lord the Savior.

5. After it was truly manifested unto this first elder that he
had received a remission of his sins, he was entangled again in
the vanities of the world;

6. But after repenting, and humbling himself sincerely,
through faith, God ministered unto him by an holy angel, whose
countenance was as lightning, and whose garments were pure
and white above all other whiteness;

7. And gave unto him commandments which inspired him;

8. And gave him power from on high, by the means which
were before prepared, to translate the Book of Mormon;

9. Which contains a record of a fallen people, and the fulness
of the gospel of Jesus Christ to the Gentiles and to the Jews
also;

10. Which was given by inspiration, and is confirmed to
others by the ministering of angels, and is declared unto the
world by them—

11. Proving to the world that the holy scriptures are true,
and that God does inspire men and call them to his holy work
in this age and generation, as well as in generations of old;

12. Thereby showing that he is the same God yesterday,
today, and forever. Amen.

5-12. A brief review of events preceding the establishment of the
Church.

2. EVENTS PRECEDING.

5. *Remission of his sins*] Joseph had received a marvelous manifestation of divine favor, in the answer given to his first prayer, but afterwards he was "entangled again in the vanities of the world." In his autobiography the Prophet ascribes this, in part, to the unkind treatment accorded him by the religious people. He was young and inexperienced;
they ostracized and slandered him, and, consequently, he "was left to
all kinds of temptations." And this is placed on record for our instruc-

tion. Christians cannot be too careful in their conduct among their fellow men. It is a mark of integrity and veracity that this weakness of youth is made as prominent in the record as are the divine manifestations. In the sacred Scriptures the failings of Moses, or the difficulties between Paul and Peter, are recorded as well as their good qualities and victories over sin. A mere human history would conceal such imperfections, as far as possible. God places them on record for the instruction of others.

6. *God ministered unto him*] When he repented and sought God in prayer the angel Moroni was sent to him. This was another marvelous manifestation that his repentance had been accepted and his sins forgiven.

8. *The means which were before prepared*] The Urim and Thummim.

9. *Fulness of the gospel*] The Book of Mormon contains the "fulness of the gospel of Jesus Christ to Gentiles and Jews." The word "fulness" means "abundance," "completeness." In the epistles of Paul (Eph. 1:23; Col. 1:19) it means, as Lightfoot has shown, the completed condition, as when a rent is mended. Gnostics taught that between the Infinite and finite man there was a chasm which none could cross except over a bridge of divine "emanations," or æons. These were their *pleroma,* or "fulness." Paul teaches us that Christ is the bridge, the fulness, between God and man. He is the Intermediary. In Him the cleft is mended, the ideal realized. In the same meaning of the word, the Book of Mormon contains the "fulness" of the gospel. It is the bridge between the Church of former ages and ours.

11. *Proving to the world*] The Book of Mormon proves the divine inspiration of such prophecies as Isaiah 29:1-14; Ezekiel 37:15-28; Revelation 9:18-21; 10:1-11; 14:6, and many others. It is, particularly, a witness for the Isaianic authorship of the latter part of the book of Isaiah, which some scholars have questioned.

12. *He is the same*] It proves that God is the same today as He was yesterday, that Christ is the same, and that His Priesthood is unchangeable. Comp. Heb. 13:8; 7:24. The unchangeableness of Christ and His Priesthood proves that the gospel is also the same as it has been. We must not follow "diverse and strange doctrines."

13. Therefore, having so great witnesses, by them shall the world be judged, even as many as shall hereafter come to a knowledge of this work.

14. And those who receive it in faith, and work righteousness, shall receive a crown of eternal life;

15. But those who harden their hearts in unbelief, and reject it, it shall turn to their own condemnation—

16. For the Lord God has spoken it; and we, the elders of the church, have heard and bear witness to the words of the glorious Majesty on high, to whom be glory forever and ever. Amen.

3. TESTIMONY OF THE ELDERS.

13-16. In the Book of Mormon the reader will find the solemn testimony of Three Witnesses, and also of Eight, to the authenticity of that Volume. Here is added the solemn testimony of the Prophet Joseph and Oliver Cowdery.

13. *So great witnesses*] The Bible and the Book of Mormon (v. 11). The world shall be judged by them. Those who receive the testimony in faith, will be crowned with eternal life; those who reject it, will be condemned.

16. *The elders of the Church*] Joseph and Oliver. They were the first and second Elders, respectively, and they testify that they heard the words of the glorious Majesty on high. Here again it is the unchangeableness of God that is kept in view (see also Psalm 145:12, 13). God's Kingdom is everlasting, the same in all ages; hence His Majesty is glorious. It is everlasting.

17. By these things we know that there is a God in heaven, who is infinite and eternal, from everlasting to everlasting the same unchangeable God, the framer of heaven and earth, and all things which are in them;

18. And that he created man, male and female, after his own image and in his own likeness, created he them;

19. And gave unto them commandments that they should love and serve him, the only living and true God, and that he should be the only being whom they should worship.

20. But by the transgression of these holy laws man became sensual and devilish, and became fallen man.

21. Wherefore, the Almighty God gave his Only Begotten Son, as it is written in those scriptures which have been given of him.

22. He suffered temptations but gave no heed unto them.

23. He was crucified, died, and rose again the third day;

24. And ascended into heaven, to sit down on the right hand of the Father, to reign with almighty power according to the will of the Father;

25. That as many as would believe and be baptized in his holy name, and endure in faith to the end, should be saved—

26. Not only those who believed after he came in the meridian of time, in the flesh, but all those from the beginning, even as many as were before he came, who believed in the words of the holy prophets, who spake as they were inspired by the gift of the Holy Ghost, who truly testified of him in all things, should have eternal life,

27. As well as those who should come after, who should believe in the gifts and callings of God by the Holy Ghost, which beareth record of the Father and of the Son;

28. Which Father, Son, and Holy Ghost are one God, infinite and eternal, without end. Amen.

4. BOOK OF MORMON TRUTHS.

17-28. These are some of the important truths set forth in the Book of Mormon.

17. *By these things*] By the Book of Mormon and the heavenly voice attesting its truth, as well as by the Bible.

We know] Not "we believe," but we *know* that God exists; that He is infinite and eternal; unchangeable; the Creator of the heavens and the Earth and all things that are in them. The world is not the work of chance; nor is it self-existent; it is "created." The elements have been organized by an Infinite Intelligence. This the Saints *know*.

We know that God created man, male and female, after His own "image" in His own "likeness." Our first parents were in the image of God, in the same sense that Seth was in the image of Adam (Gen. 5:1-3). " 'Image' suggests reproduction in form and substance, physical or spiritual; 'likeness' gives the idea of resemblance and outward similarity" (The *Cambridge Bible,* Genesis, p. 20).* Woman, as well as man, was made after the image, in the likeness, of God.

We know that man fell (v. 19), and that God gave His Son, to atone for the sin of Adam and to open the way for all to life eternal, through faith and obedience. The disobedience of Adam brought upon him and his descendants, death—physical, moral, and legal. The atonement of Christ restored all that was lost through Adam. By justification men are freed from the legal condemnation; by sanctification their moral status is restored; and by glorification physical death, the last enemy, will be overcome.

"Is justice dishonored? No, it is satisfied, the debt is paid. Is righteous-

---

* The commentator quoted thinks it improbable, however, that the word "likeness" is used in Genesis to indicate an outward resemblance, though that is the idea it conveys. Is it improbable that it means what it says?

ness departed from? No, this is a righteous act. All requirements are met. Is judgment violated? No, its demands are fulfilled. Is mercy triumphant? No, she simply claims her own. Justice, judgment, mercy, and truth, all harmonize as the attributes of Deity" (John Taylor, *Mediation and Atonement*, p. 171).

"A divine debt has been contracted by the children, and the Father demands recompense. He says to His children on this Earth, who are in sin and transgression, It is impossible for you to pay this debt; I have prepared a Sacrifice; I will send my Only Begotten Son to pay this debt. Was it necessary, then, that Jesus should die? Do we understand why He should sacrifice His life? The idea that the Son of God, who never committed sin, should sacrifice His life, is unquestionably pre-posterous to the minds of many in the Christian world. But the fact exists that the Father * * * provided this Sacrifice and sent His Son to die for us; and it is also a great fact that the Son came to do the will of the Father, and that He has paid the debt, in fulfilment of the Scripture which says, 'He was the Lamb slain from the foundation of the world. Is it so on any other earth? * * * (Brigham Young, *Jour. of Dis.,* Vol. XIV., p. 71; comp. Doc. and Cov. 88:51-61).

28. *Father, Son, and Holy Ghost are one God*] They are one in essence, in purpose, in spirit, in attributes, in power, and glory, but they are, nevertheless, *three* personages.

"The Scriptural facts are, (a) the Father says I; the Son says I; the Spirit says I. (b) The Father says Thou to the Son, and the Son says Thou to the Father; and in like manner the Father and the Son use the pronouns He and Him in reference to the Spirit. (c) The Father loves the Son; the Son loves the Father; the Spirit testifies of the Son. The Father, Son, and Spirit are severally subject and object. They act and are acted upon, or are the objects of action * * * The Son is of the Father, and the Spirit is of the Father and the Son. The Father sends the Son, and the Father and the Son send the Spirit. The Father operates through the Son, and the Father and Son operate through the Spirit" (Charles Hodge, D.D., *Systematic Theology,* Vol. 1., pp. 444-5).

This is a correct statement of the leading Scripture facts relating to the distinct personalities of the Father, Son, and Holy Ghost, although the author of it holds the orthodox, not Scriptural, view that the three Persons are one Being.

29. And we know that all men must repent and believe on the name of Jesus Christ, and worship the Father in his name, and endure in faith on his name to the end, or they cannot be saved in the kingdom of God.

30. And we know that justification through the grace of our Lord and Savior Jesus Christ is just and true;

31. And we know also, that sanctification through the grace of our Lord and Savior Jesus Christ is just and true, to all those who love and serve God with all their mights, minds, and strength.

32. But there is a possibility that many may fall from grace and depart from the living God;

33. Therefore let the church take heed and pray always, lest they fall into temptation;

34. Yea, and even let those who are sanctified take heed also.

35. And we know that these things are true and according to the revelations of John, neither adding to, nor diminishing from the prophecy of his book, the holy scriptures, or the revelations of God which shall come hereafter by the gift and power of the Holy Ghost, the voice of God, or the ministering of angels.

36. And the Lord God has spoken it; and honor, power and glory be rendered to his holy name, both now and ever. Amen.

29-36. In these verses the subject is still further pursued and truths set forth in the Book of Mormon are enumerated.

29. We know that all men must repent (II. Nephi 2:21); believe (Hel. 14:29); and endure to the end (II. Nephi 31:15).

30. We know that justification through Christ is just and true (II. Nephi 2:5; Rom. 5:1). Justification is a judicial act, whereby God declares that the sinner who repents and by faith accepts the sacrifice of the Lamb of God, and who is baptized according to the Word of God, is acquitted and received into His Kingdom.

31. Sanctification is the work of the Holy Spirit by which he who is justified is enabled to keep the Commandments of God and grow in holiness (Helaman, 3:35).

32. We know that man, even after he has been justified and sanctified, may fall in sin. Therefore, the Saints must always watch and pray (v. 34).

How do we know that these things are true? Because the Lord God has spoken them (v. 36). Not always with a voice audible to the ear, but through the Spirit.

"The spirit of revelation is not so mysterious and incomprehensible as many imagine it to be. Men have imagined that it is something they cannot understand, and that men in possession of it must differ very remarkably from those who are destitute of it. But the Lord in His dealings with the children of men never produced monstrosities. His servants were not so remarkable in appearance as to strike everybody who saw them with surprise. * * * It is a glorious privilege we possess, of living so before the Lord our God, that we can have the testimony constantly within us, that we are operating and laboring in conformity with the requirements of Heaven" (George Q. Cannon, *Journal of Discourses,* Vol. XII, p. 42).

37. *And again, by way of commandment to the church concerning the manner of baptism*—All those who humble themselves before God, and desire to be baptized, and come forth with broken hearts and contrite spirits, and witness before the church that they have truly repented of all their sins, and are willing to take upon them the name of Jesus Christ, having a determination to serve him to the end, and truly manifest by their works that they have received of the Spirit of Christ unto the remission of their sins, shall be received by baptism into his church.

5. INSTRUCTIONS.

There are three requirements of an applicant for baptism: (1) He must be humble, so that he asks for it as a favor. He who comes with broken heart and contrite spirit is in the proper frame of mind for that ordinance; (2) He must show before the Church that he is repentant and willing to take upon him the name of Jesus Christ (Sec. 18:21). This confession is made before the Church when it is made in the presence of an Elder, or Elders, representing the Church; (3) he must manifest by his works that he has received the Spirit. An infant cannot comply with these conditions.

38. *The duty of the elders, priests, teachers, deacons, and members of the church of Christ*—An apostle is an elder, and it is his calling to baptize;

39. And to ordain other elders, priests, teachers, and deacons;

40. And to administer bread and wine—the emblems of the flesh and blood of Christ—

41. And to confirm those who are baptized into the church, by the laying on of hands for the baptism of fire and the Holy Ghost, according to the scriptures;

42. And to teach, expound, exhort, baptize, and watch over the church;

43. And to confirm the church by the laying on of the hands, and the giving of the Holy Ghost;

44. And to take the lead of all meetings.

45. The elders are to conduct the meetings as they are led by the Holy Ghost, according to the commandments and revelations of God.

46. The priest's duty is to preach, teach, expound, exhort, and baptize, and administer the sacrament,

47. And visit the house of each member, and exhort them to pray vocally and in secret and attend to all family duties.

48. And he may also ordain other priests, teachers, and deacons.

49. And he is to take the lead of meetings when there is no elder present;

50. But when there is an elder present, he is only to preach, teach, expound, exhort, and baptize,

51. And visit the house of each member, exhorting them to pray vocally and in secret and attend to all family duties.

52. In all these duties the priest is to assist the elder if occasion requires.

53. The teacher's duty is to watch over the church always, and be with and strengthen them;

54. And see that there is no iniquity in the church, neither hardness with each other, neither lying, backbiting, nor evil speaking;

55. And see that the church meet together often, and also see that all the members do their duty.

56. And he is to take the lead of meetings in the absence of the elder or priest—

57. And is to be assisted always, in all his duties in the church, by the deacons, if occasion requires.

58. But neither teachers nor deacons have authority to baptize, administer the sacrament, or lay on hands;

59. They are, however, to warn, expound, exhort, and teach, and invite all to come unto Christ.

60. Every elder, priest, teacher, or deacon is to be ordained according to the gifts and callings of God unto him; and he is to be ordained by the power of the Holy Ghost, which is in the one who ordains him.

61. The several elders composing this church of Christ are

to meet in conference once in three months, or from time to time as said conferences shall direct or appoint;

62. And said conferences are to do whatever church business is necessary to be done at the time.

63. The elders are to receive their licenses from other elders, by vote of the church to which they belong, or from the conferences.

64. Each priest, teacher, or deacon, who is ordained by a priest, may take a certificate from him at the time, which certificate, when presented to an elder, shall entitle him to a license, which shall authorize him to perform the duties of his calling, or he may receive it from a conference.

65. No person is to be ordained to any office in this church, where there is a regularly organized branch of the same, without the vote of that church;

66. But the presiding elders, traveling bishops, high councilors, high priests, and elders, may have the privilege of ordaining, where there is no branch of the church that a vote may be called.

67. Every president of the high priesthood (or presiding elder), bishop, high councilor, and high priest, is to be ordained by the direction of a high council or general conference.

38. *An Apostle is an Elder*] Peter calls himself an Elder (I. Pet. 5:1). So does John (II. John 1; III, John 1).

39-44. An Apostle's duties are enumerated here.
"The Twelve are not subject to any other than the First Presidency" (Joseph Smith, *Hist. of Church,* Vol. II., p. 374).

45. *The Elders*] It is the duty of the Elders in the Church to conduct the meetings of worship, when called upon to do so. There were Elders among the Hebrews as far back as their history takes us. When Jacob was buried, the Elders in Egypt accompanied the remains (Gen. 50:7). They were the representatives of the people. When Moses came to the Children of Israel with the message of deliverance, he called together the Elders and gave the people the word of the Lord through them (Ex. 3:16). The Seventy were chosen from the Elders (Numb. 11:24), and so were, undoubtedly, the "rulers of thousands, rulers of hundreds, rulers of fifties, and rulers of tens" (Ex. 18:25), who were judges and held a position similar to that of Bishops of Wards in the Church; and also the Twelve Princes (Numb. 1:4). When Israel settled in Canaan, there were Elders in every city (Deut. 19:12; 21:3, 19: Ezra 10:14). In the

New Testament, Elder is a title comprising, as in the Church today, all who hold the Melchizedek Priesthood (I. Tim. 5:17). Apostles, as we have seen (v. 38), are Elders, as are also Bishops (Tit. 1:5-7).

"A person who is ordained to the office of an Elder in this Kingdom has the same Priesthood that the High Priests, that the Twelve Apostles, that the Seventies, and that the First Presidency hold: but all are not called to be one of the Twelve Apostles, nor are all called to be one of the First Presidency, nor to be one of the First Presidents of all the Seventies, nor to be one of the Presidents of a Quorum of Seventy, nor to preside over the High Priests' Quorum; but every man in his order."* (Brigham Young, *Journal of Discourses,* Vol. IX., p. 89).

46-52. The duties of a Priest are here enumerated. His office is the most advanced in the Aaronic Priesthood. In the Mosaic dispensation the Priests were ordained to instruct and pray for the people, and to offer sacrifices for them. In the Church the Priest's duty is to preach, exhort, baptize, administer the Sacrament, visit Church members, pray for them, and watch over them.

"From a retrospect of the requirements of the servants of God to preach the gospel, we find few qualified even to be Priests, and if a Priest understands his duty, his calling, and ministers and preaches by the Holy Ghost, his enjoyment is as great as if he were one of the Presidency, and his services are necessary in the body, as are also those of Teachers and Deacons" (Joseph Smith, *History of the Church,* Vol. 11., p. 478).

53-56. The duties of Teachers. The Teacher also holds the Aaronic Priesthood. His duty is to watch over the Church, and to warn the members against all kinds of evil.

57-59. The duty of Deacons is to assist the Teachers. A Deacon holds the power and authority first bestowed in the Aaronic Priesthood. One who performs those duties well, thereby qualifies himself for the more advanced positions.

"It was customary in Paul's days to ordain mature men to the office of Deacons, because the conditions of the Saints were such that only elderly people could be used to advantage. The Church was new, and adults were converted; perhaps only few, if any, were born and educated in the Church. But even in our day * * * There are many men holding the office of Deacon, and many men who hold the higher Priesthood who act in the office of Deacon. It is true the Priesthood is conferred on boys of twelve and thirteen who are found faithful and worthy. But that is no sign that such action is not acceptable to God. * * * The appointment of boys to the Deaconship is done under the direction of the constituted authority of the Lord, though the exact date of its beginning is perhaps not on record" (*Improvement Era,* Vol. XVIII., p. 452).

---

* That is, an office in the Priesthood.

60. Ordination to these callings is to be according to the guidance of the Holy Spirit; in the Church there must be no office-seeking, no rivalry, no nepotism.

61-62. Conferences are appointed by God. They are part of the divinely-instituted organization of the Church. A memorable conference of the New Testament church was that held in Jerusalem (Acts 15), when the Apostles, Elders, and brethren decided not to require that Gentile converts should be circumcised and obliged to keep the Mosaic law as a condition of membership in the Church. The first Conference of the Church of Jesus Christ of Latter-day Saints was held June 9th, 1830. On that occasion the Spirit came upon those assembled with such power that some prophesied, and others saw the heavens opened. Newel Knight beheld our Lord seated on the right hand of God, and the future of the Church was unfolded to him (*History of Church*, Vol. 1, p. 85).

65-67. These verses were added some time after those preceding them. The organization of the Church was not completed at one time. Revelations were given gradually, as the Church required them.

The Lord teaches us in these paragraphs that no person can assume authority or take honor unto himself. All things are done by common consent and every man appointed, or ordained, to office must receive his calling by proper authority. Any other course would lead to confusion and disintegration of the Church. President Joseph F. Smith has said:

"The house of God is a house of order, and not a house of confusion"; and it could not be thus, if there were not those who had authority to preside, to direct, to counsel, to lead in the affairs of the Church. No house would be a house of order if it were not properly organized, as the Church of Jesus Christ of Latter-day Saints is organized. Take away the organization of the Church and its power would cease. Every part of its organization is necessary and essential to its perfect existence. Disregard, ignore, or omit any part, and you start imperfection in the Church; and if we should continue in that way we would find ourselves like those of old, being led by error, superstition, ignorance, and by the cunning and craftiness of men." (*Gospel Doctrine*, p. 185.)

"The duties and powers of a Bishop cease the moment he steps over the Aaronic Priesthood, which is to officiate in temporal things; when he passes this, he immediately begins to officiate by the authority and power of the Melchizedek Priesthood, though he may not know it. * * * It is chiefly because of the ignorance of the people that we often concentrate in one man these offices and callings, but when the people are sufficiently informed, and have advanced further in the knowledge of the truth, it will not be so, but every Branch will have its full quota of officers—a Patriarch, President, Bishop, High Council, and all officers that are necessary for the work of the ministry" (Brigham Young, *Journal of Discourses,* Vol. X., p. 96).

68. *The duty of the members after they are received by baptism.*—The elders or priests are to have a sufficient time to expound all things concerning the church of Christ to their understanding, previous to their partaking of the sacrament and being confirmed by the laying on of the hands of the elders, so that all things may be done in order.

69. And the members shall manifest before the church, and also before the elders, by a godly walk and conversation, that they are worthy of it, that there may be works and faith agreeable to the holy scriptures—walking in holiness before the Lord.

70. Every member of the church of Christ having children is to bring them unto the elders before the church, who are to lay their hands upon them in the name of Jesus Christ, and bless them in his name.

71. No one can be received into the church of Christ unless he has arrived unto the years of accountability before God, and is capable of repentance.

68-71. By baptism we enter into a solemn covenant with God. We must, therefore, learn to know our duties as baptized members of the Church. Church members, above all others, should, in the language of the Prophet Joseph, "be kindly affectionate, one towards another; that the fathers should be kind to their children, husbands to their wives, masters to their slaves, or servants, children obedient to their parents, wives to their husbands, and slaves or servants to their masters" (*History of the Church,* Vol. II., p. 263).

72. Baptism is to be administered in the following manner unto all those who repent—

73. The person who is called of God and has authority from Jesus Christ to baptize, shall go down into the water with the person who has presented himself or herself for baptism, and shall say, calling him or her by name: Having been commissioned of Jesus Christ, I baptize you in the name of the Father, and of the Son, and of the Holy Ghost. Amen.

74. Then shall he immerse him or her in the water, and come forth again out of the water.

74. *Then shall he immerse*] Immersion is the only *mode* of baptism. No other mode is *baptism.*

75. It is expedient that the church meet together often to partake of bread and wine in the remembrance of the Lord Jesus;

76. And the elder or priest shall administer it; and after this manner shall he administer it—he shall kneel with the church and call upon the Father in solemn prayer, saying:

77. O God, the Eternal Father, we ask thee in the name of thy Son, Jesus Christ, to bless and sanctify this bread to the souls of all those who partake of it, that they may eat in remembrance of the body of thy Son, and witness unto thee, O God, the Eternal Father, that they are willing to take upon them the name of thy Son, and always remember him and keep his commandments which he has given them; that they may always have his Spirit to be with them. Amen.

78. The manner of administering the wine—he shall take the cup also, and say:

79. O God, the Eternal Father, we ask thee in the name of thy Son, Jesus Christ, to bless and sanctify this wine to the souls of all those who drink of it, that they may do it in remembrance of the blood of thy Son, which was shed for them; that they may witness unto thee, O God, the Eternal Father, that they do always remember him, that they may have his Spirit to be with them. Amen.

75. *Meet together often*] Church members should meet for public worship and to partake of the Sacrament often; not occasionally. See also Sections 59:9, 10.

Bread and wine] These are the Emblems. Bread is the proper emblem of the spiritual food we receive in the Sacrament. "Wine" is here used as a synonym for the *Cup,* the term found in Matt. 26:27; Mark 14:23; Luke 22:20; 1. Cor. 11:25. (Sec. 27:2). The essential part of the Sacrament is that those who partake of it receive broken bread and drink of the cup, in remembrance of the broken body and spilt blood of the Redeemer, for the broken bread and the cup are the emblems; both must be blessed, and both must be received by the communicants.

"When we partake of the bread, let us pray the Father that strength may be given to our bodies that they may not wither, but be strengthened to reach a good old age; when we partake of the wine, or water, which is emblematic of His blood, let us ask the Father that our blood may never be spilt, unless it is necessary for the advancement of His Kingdom and the glory of God" (Heber C. Kimball, *Journal of Discourses,* Vol. X., p. 102).

80. Any member of the church of Christ transgressing, or being overtaken in a fault, shall be dealt with as the scriptures direct.

80. How to deal with offenders is briefly stated here. Compare Section 42:74-93. The Church does not inflict temporal punishments. But it does not shield law-breakers from the arm of the law.

81. It shall be the duty of the several churches, composing the church of Christ, to send one or more of their teachers to attend the several conferences held by the elders of the church,

82. With a list of the names of the several members uniting themselves with the church since the last conference; or send by the hand of some priest; so that a regular list of all the names of the whole church may be kept in a book by one of the elders, whomsoever the other elders shall appoint from time to time;

83. And also, if any have been expelled from the church, so that their names may be blotted out of the general church record of names.

84. All members removing from the church where they reside, if going to a church where they are not known, may take a letter certifying that they are regular members and in good standing, which certificate may be signed by any elder or priest if the member receiving the letter is personally acquainted with the elder or priest, or it may be signed by the teachers or deacons of the church.

81-84. It is the duty of the "several churches," i.e., the several Stakes, Wards, or Branches, composing the Church to send representatives to the conferences, with complete records of the membership. Comp. Sec. 21:1; 47:3; 128:4-6.

GENERAL NOTES

The Church was organized on the 6th of April, 1830, in the home of Peter Whitmer, Sr., at Fayette, N. Y. After prayer the Prophet asked those present if they were willing to accept him and Oliver Cowdery as teachers and to organize the Church. The vote was affirmative and unanimous. Then the Prophet ordained Oliver Cowdery an Elder, where-upon Oliver ordained him to the same office. They had received the Melchizedek Priesthood under the hands of Peter, James and John, out of which all the offices in the Church come. On this day of the organi-zation, they complied with the instruction given them by John the Baptist, and ordained each other to the office of Elder by and with the consent of their brethren. After the ordination, they partook of the Sacrament, and then they confirmed all the members present. The Spirit of the Lord fell upon the little group of Saints. Some prophesied; all were filled with joy. The six original members of the Church were, Joseph Smith, Jr., Hyrum Smith, Samuel H. Smith, Oliver Cowdery, Peter Whitmer, Jr., and David Whitmer, and thus, as Elder Orson F. Whitney says, "arose, as a system, what the world terms Mormonism, universally regarded as the most remarkable religious movement of modern times; detested and denounced throughout Christendom as a dangerous and soul-destroying imposture, but revered and defended by its disciples as the wonderful work of the Almighty, the veritable 'marvelous work and wonder' foretold by Isaiah and other ancient seers."

A widely-prevalent conception of the Church of Christ is that it is invisible, because consisting of true believers only, who, it is argued, are found in all churches, often hidden among those who have the form but not the substance, and who, therefore, are known to our Lord and not to man. St. Augustine speaks of the "Twofold body" of Christ,— the true and the commingled, or the true and feigned body. This invisible church is also called the "mystical body" of Christ. "Whatsoever we read in Scripture," says Hooker, "concerning endless love and saving mercy which God sheweth to His church, the only proper subject thereof is this Church." But does not this view stamp the churches that are visible organizations as "feigned," excluding them from the influence of that saving mercy which is reserved for the so-called mystical body only?

President Brigham Young says: "When this Kingdom is organized in any age, the spirit of it dwells in the hearts of the faithful, while its visible department exists among the people, with laws, ordinances, helps, governments, officers, administrators, and every other appendage neces-sary for its complete operation to the attainment of the end in view" (*Journal of Discourses,* Vol. X., p. 18).

The Church is said to be the "body" of Christ (Eph. 1:23). As a "body" it may have its limitations, and even failings, for the human element in it has not reached perfection; but as long as it has the Holy Priesthood and is true to Him, keeping His commandments, observing His ordinances, and promulgating His gospel, it is His "body," the object of His love. He is the "head," although He is on the other side of the veil; for He rules and guides its affairs, and is as really present in the Church, as if He were among us in the flesh. The Tabernacle in the wilderness had two compartments, separated by a veil,—the Holy and the Most Holy. The Presence of God rested on the Mercy Seat in the Most Holy place, but from there it was manifested throughout the entire camp, and all Israel was guided by it. The Church, too, has two grand divisions, one on this side of the veil, and one on the other side. Christ is now, in a special sense, with the Church on the other side, but His presence here is none the less real, for there is only a veil between this side and the other.

The Hebrews, anciently, had their Assembly, which was a representative and ruling body. This institution survived in the ruling body of the Synagogue, which was called the "Church" (Matt. 18:17). The Greek republics also had their representative assemblies, known as "churches" (ecclesiæ). They were visible bodies, and so is the Church of Christ. It is an assembly as tangible as any Congress or Parliament.

On "The Origin of Man" (v. 18) see an article in the *Improvement Era,* Vol. XIII., p. 75-81.

Salvation comes through the power of God; yet, only those who "endure to the end" will be saved (v. 25), and, generally speaking, those who feel too sure of their salvation are farthest from it. Soren Kjerkegaard has expressed this thought in the following quaint paradox: "If you fear, then fear not; but if you do not fear, then fear."

SECTION 21.

REVELATION *given to Joseph Smith the Prophet, at Fayette, New York, April 6, 1830. This revelation was given at the organization of the Church of Jesus Christ of Latter-day Saints, on the date named, in the home of Peter Whitmer, Sen. Six men, who had previously been baptized, participated. By unanimous vote these expressed their desire and determination to organize, according to the commandment of God; see Section 20. They also voted to accept and sustain Joseph Smith, Jun., and Oliver Cowdery as the presiding officers of the Church. With the laying on of hands, Joseph then ordained Oliver an Elder of the Church of Jesus Christ of Latter-day Saints; and Oliver similarly ordained Joseph. After administration of the sacrament, Joseph and Oliver laid hands upon the participants individually, for the bestowal of the Holy Ghost, and for the confirmation of each as a member of the Church. See History of the Church, vol. 1, p. 75.——Church records—The Lord manifests acceptance of the Church, and recognition of the presiding officers.*

BEHOLD, there shall be a record kept among you; and in it thou shalt be called a seer, a translator, a prophet, an apostle of Jesus Christ, an elder of the church through the will of God the Father, and the grace of your Lord, Jesus Christ,

2. Being inspired of the Holy Ghost to lay the foundation thereof, and to build it up unto the most holy faith.

3. Which church was organized and established in the year of your Lord eighteen hundred and thirty, in the fourth month, and on the sixth day of the month which is called April.

This Revelation was given while the meeting called for the organization of the Church was still in session. The Prophet Joseph received several Revelations in the presence of his brethren. A Revelation concerning the Apostleship, for instance, came while Brigham Young and Joseph Young were at his home. Brigham Young relates:

"After we returned from Missouri, my father, Joseph Young, and myself had been singing after preaching in a meeting; and when the meeting was dismissed, Brother Joseph Smith said, 'come, go down to my house with me.' We went, and sang to him a long time, and talked with him. He then opened the subject of the Twelve and Seventies for the first time I ever thought of it. He said, 'Brethren, I am going to call out Twelve Apostles. I think we will get together by and by and select Twelve Apostles, and a Quorum of Seventy from those who have been up to Zion, out of the camp boys.' * * * He had a Revelation when we were singing to him. Those who were acquainted with him knew when the Spirit of Revelation was upon him, for his countenance wore an expression peculiar to himself while under that influence. He preached by the Spirit of Revelation, and taught in Council by it, and those who were acquainted with him could discover it at once, for at such times there was a peculiar clearness and transparency in his face" (*Journal of Discourses,* Vol. IX., p. 89).

1-3. The Spirit here directs the Saints to keep an historical record, and defines the duties and responsibilities of the Prophet. The titles enumerated are not those of honor and emoluments but of duty, each indicating some line of service.

1. *Seer*] A Seer has the divine gift of "seeing," or having visions. Moses, Samuel, Isaiah, Ezekiel, and many others were seers, so called because they were privileged to have a nearer view of the divine glory and power than other mortals have. Joseph Smith also was a seer. (See Mosiah 8:13).

Translator] A translator renders the spoken, or written, word into another language. Here it means one who does so by the gift of divine inspiration.

Prophet] A prophet is one who speaks for another. Aaron was the prophet of Moses (Ex. 7:1), when, as his brother's spokesman, he appeared before Pharaoh. Paul (Titus 1:12) quotes Epimenides, a Cretan poet, as a prophet. A Prophet of God is one who speaks for the Almighty, by divine authority. He does not always foretell future events. Sometimes he reveals the past; sometimes he speaks of the present, and sometimes he predicts things to come. Some of the Old Testament Prophets were eminent statesmen, historians, and privy councilors of kings; others occupied less prominent positions, but all were the divinely inspired instructors of the people, whose special function it was to maintain the worship of Jehovah against adverse influences.

Originally the Hebrews called the Prophets, Seers (I. Sam. 9:9), and that designation is used by Lehi, when he blesses his sons and quotes to them the prophecies of his ancestor, Joseph (II. Nephi 3:5-22). Is this not a proof of the antiquity and authenticity of the prophecies quoted by Lehi?

Apostle] An Apostle is a messenger and special witness of Jesus Christ; one who has a divine message to all men.

Elder] Holding the Melchizedek Priesthood (Sec. 20:45).

Through the will of God] Joseph Smith was called, as was Paul, through the divine will, not human agency (Rom. 1:1).

3. See Section 20:1.

4. Wherefore, meaning the church, thou shalt give heed unto all his words and commandments which he shall give unto you as he receiveth them, walking in all holiness before me;

5. For his word ye shall receive, as if from mine own mouth, in all patience and faith.

6. For by doing these things the gates of hell shall not prevail against you; yea, and the Lord God will disperse the powers of darkness from before you, and cause the heavens to shake for your good, and his name's glory.

4-6. It is the duty of the Church to obey God's commandments through the Prophet, because victory over the adversary can be obtained only by obedience. But God does not demand blind obedience. He gives reason for submission.

7. For thus saith the Lord God: Him have I inspired to move the cause of Zion in mighty power for good, and his diligence I know, and his prayers I have heard.

8. Yea, his weeping for Zion I have seen, and I will cause that he shall mourn for her no longer; for his days of rejoicing are come unto the remission of his sins, and the manifestations of my blessings upon his works.

9. For, behold, I will bless all those who labor in my vineyard with a mighty blessing, and they shall believe on his words, which are given him through me by the Comforter, which manifesteth that Jesus was crucified by sinful men for the sins of the world, yea, for the remission of sins unto the contrite heart.

7-9. The Lord inspired Joseph to take up the cause of desolate Zion, as He inspired Moses to champion the cause of enslaved Israel. He wept when he contemplated the fallen condition of Christendom, as Jeremiah wept on the ruins of Jerusalem. God saw his tears; every tear was a prayer.

9. *I will bless all those who labor*] Labor in the Lord's vineyard is never in vain. The laborers always receive a blessing. One reward promised is increased faith in the atonement of our Savior, who was crucified for the sins of the world. This great, central truth of the gospel is made manifest by the Comforter—the Spirit of Revelation.

10. Wherefore it behooveth me that he should be ordained by you, Oliver Cowdery mine apostle;

11. This being an ordinance unto you, that you are an elder under his hand, he being the first unto you, that you might be an elder unto this church of Christ, bearing my name—

12. And the first preacher of this church unto the church, and before the world, yea, before the Gentiles; yea, and thus saith the Lord God, lo, lo! to the Jews also. Amen.

10-12. Because of his high and holy calling, Joseph was ordained by Oliver Cowdery, on behalf of the Church.

10. *It behoveth me*] It is necessary. The word "behoveth" is used in the sense in which it occurs in Luke 24:46. Was not his ordination by Peter, James, and John all sufficient? It was, as far as the Lord required. But in the Kingdom of God common consent is the law. It was, therefore, the privilege of the Church to signify its willingness to accept the divine appointment, or reject it. The Church accepted it, and the ordination by Oliver Cowdery, in behalf of the Church, was the final act of acceptance.

12. *The first preacher*] Oliver Cowdery was to be the first to proclaim the gospel in this dispensation. He delivered the first public discourse on

the 11th of April, 1830, in the home of Peter Whitmer, Sr., at Fayette. On that day, six new members were added to the Church. Among these were Christian, Annie, Jacob, and Elizabeth Whitmer. Peter Whitmer, Sr., Mary and Elizabeth Ann Whitmer, and some others were baptized on the 18th of the same month.

Oliver Cowdery was called to go on a mission to the Lamanites. He was accompanied by Parley P. Pratt, Peter Whitmer, Jr., and Ziba Peterson. On this mission he first preached to an Indian nation near Buffalo. Later, he and Parley P. Pratt labored among the Delaware Indians. And thus he became the first preacher to the Gentiles, and also to the "Jews," as the Revelation says; for the founders of the Church sometimes referred to the Lamanites as "Jews." Compare Section 57:4.

SECTION 22.

REVELATION *given through Joseph Smith the Prophet, to The Church of Jesus Christ of Latter-day Saints, which was established in these last days, in the year of our Lord one thousand eight hundred and thirty. Given at Manchester, New York, April, 1830, in consequence of some who had previously been baptized desiring to unite with the Church without re-baptism.——The indispensability of baptism in the way prescribed and through the authority given by the Lord is set forth.*

BEHOLD, I say unto you that all old covenants have I caused to be done away in this thing; and this is a new and an everlasting covenant, even that which was from the beginning.

2. Wherefore, although a man should be baptized an hundred times it availeth him nothing, for you cannot enter in at the strait gate by the law of Moses, neither by your dead works.

3. For it is because of your dead works that I have caused this last covenant and this church to be built up unto me, even as in days of old.

4. Wherefore, enter ye in at the gate, as I have commanded, and seek not to counsel your God. Amen.

The question having arisen whether baptism, performed by a Baptist minister, or any other who practices immersion, might be accepted as valid, this Revelation, answering that question in the negative, was

received. Romanists hold that, in the case of an emergency, anybody
—man or woman, Jew, pagan, or atheist, may administer baptism, and
that it is valid, provided the administrator really intended to baptize. In
an emergency authority is not needed. The Protestant view is that it is
not proper for a layman to preach or to administer the Sacraments in
a "settled state of the church," without having been ordained, but that
neither the preaching nor the administration of the Sacraments is thereby
rendered invalid. In this Revelation we are taught that divine authority
is as essential as the correct mode of administration.

4. *Enter ye at the gate*] Baptism is the "gate" to the Church.

SECTION 23.

REVELATION *given through Joseph Smith the Prophet, at
Manchester, New York, April, 1830, to Oliver Cowdery, Hyrum
Smith, Samuel H. Smith, Joseph Smith, Sen., and Joseph Knight,
Sen. As the result of earnest desire on the part of the five per-
sons named, the Prophet inquired of the Lord, and received this
revelation in response.*

BEHOLD, I speak unto you, Oliver, a few words. Behold, thou
art blessed, and art under no condemnation. But beware of pride,
lest thou shouldst enter into temptation.

2. Make known thy calling unto the church, and also before
the world, and thy heart shall be opened to preach the truth
from henceforth and forever. Amen.

The brethren here mentioned being anxious to learn the mind and
the will of the Lord concerning them, this Revelation was given. It is
perfectly clear that these intimate friends and close associates of the
Prophet, were fully convinced that God spoke through him. If not, they
would not have asked him to inquire of the Lord for them.

1. *Thou are blessed*] Oliver Cowdery was highly favored by the Lord.
He was one of the first six members of the Church. He was an Elder
and an Apostle.* He was the first messenger to the world from the
Church. He took a leading part in the affairs of the Church. On the 18th
of December, 1833, when the printing press was dedicated at Kirtland,
the Prophet Joseph recorded the following: "Blessed of the Lord is

---

* However, he was not at any time a member of the Council of the Twelve.
The term "apostle," as applied to him, signified that he was a special witness of
the Savior and of the origin of the Book of Mormon.

Brother Oliver; nevertheless, there are two evils in him that he must needs forsake, or he cannot altogether forsake [escape?] the buffetings of the adversary. If he forsake these evils, he shall be forgiven, and shall be made like unto the bow which the Lord hath set in the heavens; he shall be a sign and an ensign unto the nations" (*Historical Record*, p. 199). What these two evils were the Prophet does not place on record. However, on the 11th of April, 1838, charges were preferred against him which show that *pride* and covetousness were the sins that beset him. He did not heed this Revelation warning him of pride, and the consequence was that he lost his membership in the Church. Later in life he became humble and returned to the Church. To the High Council that considered his application for reinstatement, he said, "Brethren, for a number of years I have been separated from you. I now desire to come back. I wish to come humbly and to be one in your midst. I seek no station, I only wish to be identified with you." He was re-baptized (*Historical Record*, p. 201).

3. Behold, I speak unto you, Hyrum, a few words; for thou also art under no condemnation, and thy heart is opened, and thy tongue loosed; and thy calling is to exhortation, and to strengthen the church continually. Wherefore thy duty is unto the church forever, and this because of thy family. Amen.

3. *Thy duty is unto the Church for ever*] Hyrum Smith, the beloved brother of Joseph, successfully proclaimed the gospel, after his tongue had been loosened. On November 7th, 1837, he was appointed a counselor to the Prophet instead of Fred. G. Williams, who was rejected by the Conference at Far West. On January 19th, 1841, he was appointed Patriarch to the Church, for which office he had been blessed by his father, it being his by birthright. He was continually strengthening the Church. See also notes, Sec. 11.

"There is another thing of great significance in this brief blessing to Hyrum Smith (Sec. 23:3) which is: 'Wherefore thy duty is unto the church forever, and this because of thy family. Amen.' It is doubtful if the Prophet Joseph fully understood the meaning of this expression when this revelation was given. In later years it was made clear. Evidently it has reference to the office of Patriarch and in this office, it was his duty and that of his family forever.'" ("Church History and Modern Revelation," series 1, p. 113.)

4. Behold, I speak a few words unto you, Samuel; for thou also art under no condemnation, and thy calling is to exhortation, and to strengthen the church; and thou art not as yet called to preach before the world. Amen.

4. Samuel H. Smith, the fourth son of Joseph Smith, Sen., was born

on the 13th of March, 1808, and was baptized on the 15th of May, 1829, the same day as Joseph and Oliver were baptized. He was one of the first six members of the Church, and one of the Eight Witnesses. On the 13th of June, 1830, he was sent on a mission with some copies of the Book of Mormon. Tracting was uphill work, then as now. Samuel was turned away from most of the houses he approached. At an inn the landlord abused him, as soon as he stated what the Book of Mormon contained, calling him a liar and ordering him out of the house. Sick at heart, he left the place and washed his feet in a brook as a testimony against that man; then he laid his weary head to rest under an apple tree. He learned, a few days later, that the inn-keeper had died of smallpox.

Samuel H. Smith had some wonderful experiences. After the engagement with a mob, known as the Crooked River battle, he went to Illinois, in company with about twenty others, through a wild part of the country. They were pursued by fifty well-armed men, who had orders to bring them back, dead or alive. Soon only four miles of prairie lay between them and their pursuers. Then a snowstorm came, with such a fury that they were completely hidden from the enemy, and escaped. Later on, their provisions gave out, and they subsisted on lynne buds and slippery elm bark. One evening the company appointed Samuel H. Smith their president, and prayed to the Lord for a revelation. That night the Spirit of the Lord came upon him, and he said: "Thus saith the Lord; my servant Joseph is not injured, nor any of his brethren that are with him; but they will all be delivered out of the hands of their enemies; your families are all well, but anxious about you. Let your hearts be comforted, for I, the Lord, will provide food for you on the morrow." This Revelation proved true in every detail. The next day they came upon an Indian camp, where they received a supply of good bread (*Historical Record*, p. 618). On his deathbed Joseph Smith, Sr., gave his son Samuel this blessing:

"Samuel, you have been a faithful and obedient son. By your faithfulness you have brought many into the Church. The Lord has seen your diligence, and you are blessed, in that He has never chastised you, but has called you home to rest; and there is a crown laid up for you, which shall grow brighter and brighter unto the perfect day."

Samuel H. Smith died July 30th, 1844, shortly after his two brothers, Joseph and Hyrum, had passed beyond the veil, martyrs for the cause of truth and liberty.

5. Behold, I speak a few words unto you, Joseph; for thou also art under no condemnation, and thy calling also is to exhortation, and to strengthen the church; and this is thy duty from henceforth and forever. Amen.

Joseph Smith, Sr., the father of the Prophet, was born July 12th, 1771.

He was the first to receive the testimony of his illustrious son, after the Angel had visited the Prophet on the 22nd of September, 1823, and he was baptized the 6th of April, 1830. On December 18th, 1833, he was ordained a Patriarch, an office that was to continue from father to son. (See Section 107:40; 124:91). He died September 14th, 1840.

The Revelations to Joseph Smith, Sr., and Hyrum Smith contain an identical prediction to the effect that it was their calling to strengthen the Church *forever*. This could not refer to their personal ministry on Earth, but it has been fulfilled in the ministry of their descendants, and will, no doubt, come true, as the Revelations say, "forever."

6. Behold, I manifest unto you, Joseph Knight, by these words, that you must take up your cross, in the which you must pray vocally before the world as well as in secret, and in your family, and among your friends, and in all places.

7. And, behold, it is your duty to unite with the true church, and give your language to exhortation continually, that you may receive the reward of the laborer. Amen.

Joseph Knight, Sr., was of great assistance to the Prophet during the early days of persecution. In this Revelation he is enjoined to pray vocally, before the world, and not only in secret; to join the Church, and to labor in the vineyard. He obeyed, and was baptized in June, 1830. See also Sec. 12.

SECTION 24.

REVELATION *given to Joseph Smith the Prophet and Oliver Cowdery, at Harmony, Pennsylvania, July, 1830. Though less than four months had elapsed since the Church was organized, persecution had become intense, and the leaders had to seek safety in partial seclusion. See History of the Church, vol. 1, p. 101.——The Lord combines encouragement with reproof— Gives individual commandments to Joseph and Oliver, respectively.*

BEHOLD, thou wast called and chosen to write the Book of Mormon, and to my ministry; and I have lifted thee up out of thine afflictions, and have counseled thee, that thou hast been delivered from all thine enemies, and thou hast been delivered from the powers of Satan and from darkness!

2. Nevertheless, thou art not excusable in thy transgressions; nevertheless, go thy way and sin no more.

3. Magnify thine office; and after thou hast sowed thy fields and secured them, go speedily unto the church which is in Colesville, Fayette, and Manchester, and they shall support thee; and I will bless them both spiritually and temporally;

4. But if they receive thee not, I will send upon them a cursing instead of a blessing.

As the Church membership increased, the adversary marshalled his forces, and the fires of persecution were kindled. At Colesville, where many were anxious to join the Church, a mob tried to prevent this by tearing up a dam which had been built over a stream, to get a convenient place for baptism. The dam was rebuilt and the ordinance performed. The mob then surrounded the house of Joseph Knight, where the Prophet bravely confronted them. At the house of Newel Knight, Joseph was arrested on the charge of "setting the country in an uproar" by preaching the Book of Mormon. The purpose, it has been supposed, was to waylay the Prophet on his way to court, but this plan was not carried out. Witnesses had been summoned, who were expected to testify that the Prophet had received property from them, by fraud, but they testified to the contrary, and he was acquitted. Again he was arrested. The officer treated him very harshly, and the rabble rejoiced. But again he was acquitted. This infuriated the mob, and the bitterness increased, as they realized that their attempts at persecution by the aid of the courts were futile. *See History of the Church,* Vol. 1., pp. 86, 90.

It was shortly after this trying time that the Prophet received the Revelation called "Visions of Moses" (Pearl of Great Price, p. 1), and Sections 24, 25, and 26, Doc. and Cov.

1. *Called and chosen*] The Prophet Joseph was "called and chosen" to give to the world the Book of Mormon and to engage in the ministry. God called him, through the Angel, and when he manifested his willingness to obey the call, he was chosen for the work. The call preceded the election. "Many are called, but few are chosen" (Matt. 22:14). "When I called, ye did not answer" (Isa. 65:12). The call always precedes the election: "Give diligence to make your calling and election sure" (II. Peter 1:10). He who is called, is sure of his election, if he obeys the call.

I have lifted thee up] God had rescued the Prophet from the persecutors, as He had delivered him from the power of the adversary when he first sought God in prayer.

2. *Sin no more*] The Prophet Joseph did not claim to be perfect; nor would the Lord have permitted him to indulge in Pharisaic self-admiration, even if he had been so inclined, for He reminded him of his failing

and his need of repentance, when necessary, to keep him humble. The Prophet had not fallen into transgression, but in one highly favored by the Lord, a word, an act, which would hardly be noticed in another, may be a "sin."

3-4. The Saints in Colesville, Fayette, and Manchester are here told to contribute to the support of the Prophet; not to pay him a salary, but to supply his wants. The law of tithing had not yet been given to the Church.

5. And thou shalt continue in calling upon God in my name, and writing the things which shall be given thee by the Comforter, and expounding all scriptures unto the church.

6. And it shall be given thee in the very moment what thou shalt speak and write, and they shall hear it, or I will send unto them a cursing instead of a blessing.

7. For thou shalt devote all thy service in Zion; and in this thou shalt have strength.

8. Be patient in afflictions, for thou shalt have many; but endure them, for, lo, I am with thee, even unto the end of thy days.

9. And in temporal labors thou shalt not have strength, for this is not thy calling. Attend to thy calling and thou shalt have wherewith to magnify thine office, and to expound all scriptures, and continue in laying on of the hands and confirming the churches.

5-9. The Prophet Joseph's gifts were of a spiritual, not financial nature, but the Lord promised him that, if he would magnify his calling, he would always have what he needed. Financial ability is also a gift that can be used for the glory of God, but the Prophet was not a financier. He did not live for the accumulation of wealth. The Kingdom of God was his first and chief concern. It has been stated that the sum total of his worldly possessions, probably, never at any time exceeded two or three thousands dollars, though he always contributed liberally towards all public, worthy objects. At his death the administrator could allow the widow only $124 a year from the estate (Tullidge, *Life of Joseph The Prophet,* p. 744).

10. And thy brother Oliver shall continue in bearing my name before the world, and also to the church. And he shall not suppose that he can say enough in my cause; and lo, I am with him to the end.

11. In me he shall have glory, and not of himself, whether in weakness or in strength, whether in bonds or free;

12. And at all times, and in all places, he shall open his mouth and declare my gospel as with the voice of a trump, both day and night. And I will give unto him strength such as is not known among men.

10-12. One evidence of the divine origin of the Church is found in the fact that each member was given the work for which he was best equipped. Oliver Cowdery was instructed to continue preaching the gospel, his special gift being eloquence, as is apparent from his graphic description of the ordination to the Priesthood, Pearl of Great Price, pp. 98-99.

13. Require not miracles, except I shall command you, except casting out devils, healing the sick, and against poisonous serpents, and against deadly poisons;

14. And these things ye shall not do, except it be required of you by them who desire it, that the scriptures might be fulfilled; for ye shall do according to that which is written.

13-14. Miracles are not to be asked for as evidences of the truth of the gospel; the Spirit will testify of the truth of it. And yet, when required by those who humbly desire a blessing, to cast out demons, to heal the sick, or to counteract the effects of poison, a servant of the Lord must not refuse to administer. The Scriptures must be fulfilled.

14. *Do accordingly to that which is written*] The written word, properly interpreted, is the pattern.

15. And in whatsoever place ye shall enter, and they receive you not in my name, ye shall leave a cursing instead of a blessing, by casting off the dust of your feet against them as a testimony, and cleansing your feet by the wayside.

16. And it shall come to pass, that whosoever shall lay their hands upon you by violence, ye shall command to be smitten in my name: and, behold, I will smite them according to your words, in mine own due time.

17. And whosoever shall go to law with thee shall be cursed by the law.

18. And thou shalt take no purse nor scrip, neither staves, neither two coats, for the church shall give unto thee in the very hour what thou needest for food and for raiment, and for shoes and for money and for scrip.

19. For thou art called to prune my vineyard with a mighty pruning, yea, even for the last time. Yea, and also all those whom thou hast ordained, and they shall do even according to this pattern. Amen.

15-19. These verses contain instructions to missionaries.

15. *A cursing instead of a blessing*] The entrance of an Elder into a home with the gospel message will be either a blessing or the opposite, just as the mild spring rain and genial sunshine bring luxuriant verdure to the living plants, but dissolution to the stubble that is dead.

Casting off the dust] Our Lord instructed His Disciples to shake the dust off their feet, when departing from a house where they had not been received (Matt. 10: 14). Paul did so when leaving Antioch, in Pisidia (Acts 13:51). Those who rejected the gospel message were to be considered as pagans, with whom Jews held no social intercourse. Even the dust of their dwellings and their cities, was to be treated as defilement, necessitating a cleansing. But this is not an act to be performed on slight provocation. A disciple of the Lord must learn of Him patience and long-suffering.

16. The Lord endowed His servants with power and authority, but these must be used for the salvation of souls.

17. *Cursed by the law*] Oliver Cowdery needed this warning. One of the charges brought against him in 1838 was that he had turned from his calling to the practice of law, "for filthy lucre," and that he had been urging vexatious lawsuits. He needed to be reminded that those who would persecute others by law would be "cursed by the law."

Lawsuits are to be avoided, if possible.

"Does the Lord love your conduct when you drag each other before the ungodly? When you run after difficulties, contentions, broils, and strife? Do you think He has fellowship with your conduct in such things? No, you do not. Do you suppose that Jesus Christ has? No. Do you believe that angels and good men can fellowship your conduct? You do not?" (Brigham Young, *Jour. of Dis.*, Vol. III., p. 239).

Brigham Young adds that there is not a righteous person who has difficulties that cannot be settled by arbitrators.

18. *No purse nor scrip*] To go without "purse and scrip" is, in modern language, to travel without money and trunk. "Scrip" is a "satchel," a "knapsack." When our Lord sent His Apostles on their first missionary journey, He charged them not to take with them money or money belts; nor "scrip," such as David carried when he went to meet Goliath; nor a change of clothes. Simplicity was to be one of their characteristics. Socrates, long before this time, wore only one coat, or tunic, went without sandals, and subsisted on the bare necessaries of life. Epicurus taught, "To whom a little is not enough, nothing is enough,"

and it was said of him, "This fellow is bringing in a new philosophy; he preaches hunger, and disciples follow him." Our Lord, too, taught the philosophy of the simple life. He taught His followers to rely on God for all their needs. The same lesson is taught in this Revelation. Brigham Young says:

"For me to travel and preach without purse and scrip was never hard; I never saw the day, I never was in the place, nor went into a house when I was alone, or when I would take the lead and do the talking, but what I could get all I wanted. * * * I could make the acquaintance of the family, and sit and sing to them and chat with them, and they would be friendly" (*Jour. of Dis.,* Vol. IV., p. 34).

Revelations and miracles do not keep men from falling.

"I recollect, in the upper room of the Temple in Kirtland, Ohio, when we were assembled there, a very noted man, Sylvester Smith, bore testimony of what he had seen of the Prophet of God, of angels, etc. He said '* * * I have spoken by what you call the Holy Ghost; the eyes of my understanding have been touched, and I have seen convoy after convoy of angels; I have laid hands on the lame, and they have leaped like a hart; I have spoken with tongues and had the interpretation thereof; but, let me tell you, everything I have seen, and everything you have seen, is the height of idiotism.' This was Sylvester Smith, after he had apostatized" (Jedediah M. Grant, *Jour. of Dis.,* Vol. VI., p. 254).

SECTION 25.

REVELATION *given through Joseph Smith the Prophet, at Harmony, Pennsylvania, July 1830.——The word of the Lord directed to Emma Smith, the Prophet's wife—Her duties defined, and glorious possibilities of achievement set forth—The Lord's admonitions are applied to all.*

HEARKEN unto the voice of the Lord your God, while I speak unto you, Emma Smith, my daughter; for verily I say unto you, all those who receive my gospel are sons and daughters in my kingdom.

Emma Smith, the wife of the Prophet, was not always free from doubts regarding the wonderful story of the coming forth of the Book of Mormon. From the fourth verse it is evident that she had murmured because she had not been privileged to see the plates. As the wife of the Prophet she seemed to feel that she was entitled to be admitted into the secret councils of her husband and his brethren.

1. *Sons and daughters in my kingdom*] All Men and Women are the offspring of God (Acts 17:28-29) and they will become sons and daughters of God through obedience to all ordinances and covenants of the Gospel. (Rom. 8:14-17. D. & C. 76:53-58.)

2. A revelation I give unto you concerning my will; and if thou art faithful and walk in the paths of virtue before me, I will preserve thy life, and thou shalt receive an inheritance in Zion.

2. *An inheritance in Zion*] Emma was highly favored, but she could not obtain an inheritance in Zion on any other condition than faithful observance of the laws of God and "walking in the paths of virtue." These paths are often narrow and steep, and "walking"—slowly and warily—is the only mode of progress possible.

3. Behold, thy sins are forgiven thee, and thou art an elect lady, whom I have called.

3. *An elect lady*] The Prophet Joseph, when organizing the Relief Society, at Nauvoo, March 17th, 1842, explained that an "elect lady" is one who is elected to do a certain work in the Church, and that this Revelation was fulfilled when Emma was elected president of that organization. Her calling was, therefore, one of the greatest importance. Not only did she become the head of a benevolent society, but a pioneer in the great work of the emancipation of women—a movement which has grown like an avalanche. The women generally do not yet realize how much they owe to the organization of which Emma Smith was the first president—the first "elect lady."

4. Murmur not because of the things which thou hast not seen, for they are withheld from thee and from the world, which is wisdom in me in a time to come.

4. *Murmur not*] Emma had no just reason for dissatisfaction, although she had not seen the Book of Mormon plates; they had been hidden for a wise purpose which would be revealed in due time.

5. And the office of thy calling shall be a comfort unto thy servant, Joseph Smith, Jun., thy husband, in his afflictions, with consoling words, in the spirit of meekness.

6. And thou shalt go with him at the time of his going, and be unto him for a scribe, while there is no one to be a scribe for him, that I may send my servant, Oliver Cowdery, withersoever I will.

7. And thou shalt be ordained under his hand to expound scriptures, and to exhort the church, according as it shall be given thee by my Spirit.

8. For he shall lay his hands upon thee, and thou shalt receive the Holy Ghost, and thy time shall be given to writing, and to learning much.

9. And thou needest not fear, for thy husband shall support thee in the church; for unto them is his calling, that all things might be revealed unto them, whatsoever I will, according to their faith.

10. And verily I say unto thee that thou shalt lay aside the things of this world, and seek for the things of a better.

11. And it shall be given thee, also, to make a selection of sacred hymns, as it shall be given thee, which is pleasing unto me, to be had in my church.

12. For my soul delighteth in the song of the heart; yea, the song of the righteous is a prayer unto me, and it shall be answered with a blessing upon their heads.

5-12. Some of the duties of Emma Smith are here enumerated. And, first of all, she was to be a comfort to her husband. Her public duties were to come next.

5. *A comfort to my servant*] This comes first, A woman's first and highest calling is to be the guiding spirit of the home, under her husband, who is the head of the household. The home is a divine institution. The Church depends on it. If the home is not a sanctuary where God is present, the church will be cold and cheerless. But the home depends, largely, on the wife and mother. Therefore, her first duty is to the home. Emma was also privileged to act as scribe, or amanuensis, to Joseph for a brief period.

7. *Expound Scriptures and exhort*] This Revelation was given at a time when women were not admitted to the higher institutes of learning, much less to the pulpits as exhorters. Emma was set apart to this calling. She was also called to compile a hymn book for the use of the Church (v. 11).

12. *The song of the heart*] God delights in the song of the heart; not in the mere sounds of the lips. Singing from the heart is worship; wherefore Paul says, "I will sing with the spirit, and I will sing with the understanding also" (I. Cor. 14:15). In such singing God takes delight. No music is as sweet as religious compositions; none is so majestic, so inspiring. Martial music stirs up the animal in man. So-

called "ragtime" breeds frivolity, and appeals to the vulgar. Set to sacred text, it may produce a sensation of distressing incongruity. "Jazz" is an abomination, an evidence of recrudescence of savagery.

13. Wherefore, lift up thy heart and rejoice, and cleave unto the covenants which thou hast made.

14. Continue in the spirit of meekness, and beware of pride. Let thy soul delight in thy husband, and the glory which shall come upon him.

15. Keep my commandments continually, and a crown of righteousness thou shalt receive. And except thou do this, where I am you cannot come.

16. And verily, verily, I say unto you, that this is my voice unto all. Amen.

13-16. These exhortations are not given to Emma Smith only. "This is my voice to all."

General Notes

Emma Smith did not accompany the Saints in their exodus from Nauvoo. At that time, the Nauvoo House, which the Saints, obeying a divine command (Doc. and Cov. 124:22-24, 60-64), had begun to build, became her property, the Prophet Joseph having been a large stock holder. She also retained some other property, including the "old homestead" and a small farm. The Nauvoo House subsequently passed into the hands of her second husband, Mr. Bidamon, who was not a member of the Church. He put part of the building under roof and fitted it up for a hotel.

In the year 1860 Elder Joseph F. Smith visited Nauvoo. He relates:

"In the large dining room, which I had last entered in my childhood to witness the slain bodies of the two martyrs, some sixteen years before, we found Aunt Emma sitting, tailor like, on the large side-table. I knew her instantly. She was sewing. Frederick remarked. 'Mother, do you know these young men?' She instantly raised her eyes, lifted her glasses on to her forehead, and, looking at me, said 'Why, as I live, it is Joseph! Why, Joseph, I would have known you in—; you look so much like your father.' These were her exact words. They fell with bewildering surprise upon my ears, and I shall never forget them" (*Hist. Rec.* p. 190).

SECTION 26.

REVELATION *given to Joseph Smith the Prophet, Oliver Cowdery, and John Whitmer, at Harmony, Pennsylvania, July, 1830.* ——*Instructions as to immediate duty*—*Reaffirmation of the principle of common consent in Church affairs.*

BEHOLD, I say unto you that you shall let your time be devoted to the studying of the scriptures, and to preaching, and to confirming the church at Colesville, and to performing your labors on the land, such as is required, until after you shall go to the west to hold the next conference; and then it shall be made known what you shall do.

2. And all things shall be done by common consent in the church, by much prayer and faith, for all things you shall receive by faith. Amen.

1. *Go to the west*] Refers to the second conference of the Church, at Fayette, Sept. 26th, 1830 (*History of the Church,* Vol. 1., p. 110).

2. *Common consent*] There are two forms of government. The *one-man* form does not recognize the right of the governed to a voice in the government. This is called autocracy, and is frequently referred to as "paternalism." Government by the "people" means the rule of the majority, no matter by what means or methods that majority has been obtained. This is democracy. All human forms of government belong to one of these; they are either autocracies or democracies, or modifications of them. Both have merits, and also defects. In autocracies there is a tendency to disregard individual rights for the benefit of the few; in democracies the danger is that the worst element may obtain preponderance, because citizens of that class will employ means to gain their ends, which citizens with a hig moral standard would never adopt. Democracies with party rule sometimes are exposed to all the evils of mob rule.

In the Church of Christ where the government is that of the Kingdom of Heaven, neither autocracy nor democracy obtains, but government by *Common Consent.* That is to say, the initiative in all that pertains to the government of the Church rests with the Head of the Church, even our Lord Jesus Christ, and He exercises this sovereign function through his authorized servants, upon whom He has bestowed the Holy Priesthood: but it is the privilege of the people to accept, or reject, His laws and ordinances, for God has given every individual free agency. Obedience must be voluntary. The government of the Church has been called a *Theo-democracy*. It is the form of government that will be general during the Millennium.

GENERAL NOTES

The Prophet Joseph was a loyal patriot. He firmly held that the United States Constitution was an inspired document, but he never was an enthusiastic party politician. On January 23rd, 1843, he wrote to a newspaper editor:

"I have of late had repeated solicitations to have something to do in relation to the political farce about dividing the County; but as my feelings revolt at the idea of having anything to do with politics, I have declined, in every instance, having anything to do on the subject. I think it would be well for politicians to regulate their own affairs. I wish to be let alone, that I may attend strictly to the spiritual welfare of the Church" (*History of the Church*, Vol. V., p. 259).

On Dec. 20th, 1841, he wrote to the *Times and Seasons:*

"In the next canvass, we shall be influenced by no party consideration, and no Carthagenian coalescence or collusion with our people will be suffered to affect, or operate against General Bennett, or any other of our tried friends, already semi-officially in the field; so the partisans in this country, who expect to divide the friends of humanity and equal rights will find themselves mistaken—we care not a fig for Whig or Democrat; they are both alike to us, but we shall go for our friends, our tried friends, and the cause or human liberty, which is the cause of God" (*History of the Church,* Vol. IV., p. 480).

Prayer and faith. These are the two mighty forces in the government of the Church.

> "Boast not your lightning wires to bear the news,
> Such tardy means the Saint would never choose;
> Too slow your fluid, and too short the wires
> For heavenly converse, such as love inspires.
> If man would fain commune with worlds above,
> Angels transport the news on wings of love."

—Parley P. Pratt.

The government of the Kingdom of God embodies the best features of human governments, and avoid the defects. In that Kingdom the inspired representatives of the Lord teach the people correct principles; that ends their responsibility in the matter. Every individual must then accept, for himself, the responsibility for the course he pursues, be it one of obedience or disobedience. Even the Decalogue was submitted to the people under the law of Common Consent (Ex. 19:1-8). President Brigham Young says:

"Who called Joseph Smith to be a Prophet? Did the people or God? God, and not the people, called him. Had the people gathered together and appointed one of their number to be a prophet, he would have been accountable to the people; but inasmuch as he was called by God, and not the people, he is accountable to God only and the angel who committed the gospel to him, and not to any man on Earth. The Twelve are accountable to the Prophet, and not to the Church, for the course they pursue" (*History of the Church,* Vol. V., p. 521).

This is in accord with the doctrine of Common Consent. The Prophet is responsible to God, and the Twelve are accountable to the Prophet for the manner in which they perform the duties of their offices, but as members or officers of the Church, they are also subject to the laws and rules of the Church, as much so as any member or officer. Compare Doctrine and Covenants, Sec. 107:81-84.

SECTION 27.

REVELATION *given to Joseph Smith the Prophet, at Harmony, Pennsylvania, August, 1830. In preparation for a religious service at which the sacrament of bread and wine was to be administered, Joseph set out to procure wine for the occasion. He was met by a heavenly messenger, and received this revelation, the first four paragraphs of which were written at the time, and the remainder in the September following. Water is commonly used instead of wine in the sacramental services of the Church.——Warning against the use of wine of unassured purity in the sacrament—Many ancient prophets named, with whom, as with the latter-day prophets, the Lord promises to partake at a time yet to come—The prior ordination of Joseph Smith, Jun., and Oliver Cowdery to the Apostleship avowed—Encouraging admonition given.*

LISTEN to the voice of Jesus Christ, your Lord, your God, and your Redeemer, whose word is quick and powerful.

2. For, behold, I say unto you, that it mattereth not what ye shall eat or what ye shall drink when ye partake of the sacrament, if it so be that ye do it with an eye single to my glory—remembering unto the Father my body which was laid down for you, and my blood which was shed for the remission of your sins.

3. Wherefore, a commandment I give unto you, that you shall not purchase wine neither strong drink of your enemies;

4. Wherefore, you shall partake of none except it is made new among you; yea, in this my Father's kingdom which shall be built up on the earth.

About this time Newel Knight and his wife, of Colesville, N. Y., paid the Prophet a visit at Harmony, Pa. They had been baptized, but were not confirmed. This was also the case with Emma Smith. It was therefore decided to hold a Sacrament meeting and to confirm them. Joseph went to obtain some wine, but a heavenly messenger met him and communicated to him the truths contained in this Section. In consequence of this they celebrated the sacrament with "wine" which they themselves prepared and which undoubtedly was non-alcoholic.

1-4. The important truth is here made known that it is not necessary to use wine as an emblem of the atoning blood of the Redeemer, and that, when it is to be used, it should not be purchased of enemies. This was a necessary Revelation, for the time would come when the Saints would be commanded to abstain from intoxicants at all times.

2. *It matters not what ye shall eat, or what ye shall drink*] Hitherto the Church had used bread and wine as the sacred emblems (See Sec. 20:79). Wine was also one of the two Sacramental emblems of the ancient Church in Book-of-Mormon lands (Moroni 5:1, 2). The New Testament churches used wine diluted with water. In our day the Lord has commanded the use of pure water instead of adulterated wine, and this is by no means contrary to the Scriptures. In their accounts of the institution of the Sacrament, Matthew, Mark, Luke, and Paul—the latter having received his information of the Lord Himself (I. Cor. 11:23) make it clear that it is the eating of the broken bread and the partaking of the common *Cup*—the contents are not once mentioned—that constitute the essential elements of the Sacrament. Compare I. Cor. 11:26.

*Remembering * * * my body * * * and my blood*] The purpose of the Sacrament is to commemorate His death, and to partake, by faith, in the blessings of the New and Everlasting Covenant, ratified by the shedding of His blood. It is not a sacrifice, but it is a representation of the sacrifice on Calvary. By partaking of the consecrated emblems, we testify that we accept the sacrifice and are willing to keep the commandments of our Savior.

4. *Except it is made new*] The Lord, in His infinite wisdom, directed the Saints not to buy wine or any other strong drink, of enemies, and, consequently, not to use wine in the Sacrament, unless they themselves had made it; and then it should be "new wine." Dr. F. W. Farrar says that "new wine" (Luke 5:37) means unfermented wine, or "must"—a beverage which can be kept for years and which improves with age; it is "a rich and refreshing, but non-intoxicating beverage."

In this my Father's kingdom] When the kingdom of God is fully established on Earth, our Lord will associate with His people here, in person. The promise was given to His Apostles, that they should "eat and drink at my table in my kingdom" (Luke 22:29, 30).

5. Behold, this is wisdom in me; wherefore, marvel not, for the hour cometh that I will drink of the fruit of the vine with you on the earth, and with Moroni, whom I have sent unto you to reveal the Book of Mormon, containing the fulness of my everlasting gospel, to whom I have committed the keys of the record of the stick of Ephraim;

6. And also with Elias, to whom I have committed the keys of bringing to pass the restoration of all things spoken by the mouth of all the holy prophets since the world began, concerning the last days;

7. And also John the son of Zacharias, which Zacharias he (Elias) visited and gave promise that he should have a son, and his name should be John, and he should be filled with the spirit of Elias;

8. Which John I have sent unto you, my servants, Joseph Smith, Jun., and Oliver Cowdery, to ordain you unto the first priesthood which you have received, that you might be called and ordained even as Aaron;

9. And also Elijah, unto whom I have committed the keys of the power of turning the hearts of the fathers to the children, and the hearts of the children to the fathers, that the whole earth may not be smitten with a curse;

10. And also with Joseph and Jacob, and Isaac, and Abraham, your fathers, by whom the promises remain;

11. And also with Michael, or Adam, the father of all, the prince of all, the ancient of days;

12. And also with Peter, and James, and John, whom I have sent unto you, by whom I have ordained you and confirmed you to be apostles, and especial witnesses of my name, and bear the keys of your ministry and of the same things which I revealed unto them;

13. Unto whom I have committed the keys of my kingdom, and a dispensation of the gospel for the last times; and for the fulness of times, in the which I will gather together in one all things, both which are in heaven, and which are on earth;

14. And also with all those whom my Father hath given me out of the world.

5-14. To most Christians, the statement that our Lord, in His glorified state, can partake of earthly food, is incomprehensible. Hence the admonition, "Marvel not!" though He speaks about eating on Earth with His people. After His resurrection He ate with His disciples. The Tree of Life will bear fruit on the glorified Earth. Do not marvel at these things; rather believe. What a glorious company! *Moroni* will be there; and *Elias;* and *John;* the Baptist; and *Elijah;* and *Joseph, Jacob, Isaac,* and *Abraham;* and also *Adam,* who is Michael, the *Ancient of Days;* and *Peter, James,* and *John,* and finally, "all those whom my Father hath given me out of the world." (See Sec. 27)

Michael (v. 11) means, "Who is as God?" a name properly given to Adam, who was created in the image of God. In Daniel (10:13-21; 12:1) we learn that Michael is "one of the chief princes," and that he has special charge of Israel. Jude refers to his controversy with Satan regarding the body of Moses, and in Rev. 12:7-9 he and his angels are represented as warring with Satan and his angels.

13. *Dispensation * * * for the last times.*] Paul writing to the Ephesian Saints declared "That in the dispensation of the fulness of times he (Christ) might gather together in one all things in Christ, both which are in heaven, and which are on earth; even in him." (Eph. 1:10.) According to Peter the Father spoke by the mouths of all the holy prophets since the world began, of the day when there should come the restitution of all things since the world began. (Acts 3:21.) This restoration was to be in the Dispensation of the Fulness of Times.

"By a dispensation, in connection with the work of God, we mean 'the opening of the heavens to men, the bestowing of the Holy Priesthood with all its powers upon them, and the organization and building up of the Church of Christ upon the earth, for the salvation of all who will obey the gospel.' (Jaques Catechism p. 77.) By the dispensation of the Fulness of Times we mean the last dispensation, the one in which all things, in Christ, whether in heaven or in earth, shall be gathered together in one; a dispensation which will include all other dispensations—one which will encompass all truth. As the rivers of the earth all eventually find their way to the ocean and empty into it, so all former dispensations will run into, and become part of, the Dispensation of the Fulness of Times, in which the work of God, in respect to the salvation of man and the redemption of the earth, will be consummated." (B. H. Roberts, *Outlines of Ecclesiastical History,* P. 303.)

14. *Whom my Father hath given me*] Christ has redeemed His flock with the ransom paid by Himself, and yet He regards it as a gift of the Father. John 6:37 is a parallel passage, "All that the Father giveth me shall come to me."

15. Wherefore, lift up your hearts and rejoice, and gird up your loins, and take upon you my whole armor, that ye may be able to withstand the evil day, having done all, that ye may be able to stand.

16. Stand, therefore, having your loins girt about with truth, having on the breastplate of righteousness, and your feet shod with the preparation of the gospel of peace, which I have sent mine angels to commit unto you;

17. Taking the shield of faith wherewith ye shall be able to quench all the fiery darts of the wicked;

18. And take the helmet of salvation, and the sword of my Spirit, which I will pour out upon you, and my word which I reveal unto you, and be agreed as touching all things whatsoever ye ask of me, and be faithful until I come, and ye shall be caught up, that where I am ye shall be also. Amen.

15-18. Those who have come to Christ are His in a special sense, and yet, unless they overcome all evil influences and gain the victory in life's struggle, they will not come where He is. In order to gain the victory, we must take up the "whole armor of God." Compare Ephesians 6:13-18.

15. *Rejoice*] The servants of God are full of joy, though they are arming themselves for a struggle against powers, principalities, "rulers of the darkness of this world," and "spiritual wickedness in high places." They go to the front voluntarily, rejoicing, and not as unwilling conscripts.

Gird up your loins] The girdle kept together the soldier's uniform and lent firmness to his manly frame. Be firm!

Ye may be able to stand] The meaning is, having girded up your loins and taken upon you my whole armor, you may be able to hold the ground on the day of battle and be ready to meet the next assault. The followers of Christ must hold the positions in which He has placed them.

16. *Truth*] That is the girdle; truth in the abstract, sincerity, integrity, the very opposite of hypocrisy. He who embraces the gospel is strong only when he is sincere.

Breastplate] This is for the protection of the heart. In this connection "heart" means the source of human understanding, courage, grief, affection, etc. This must be well protected against evil influences.

Righteousness] This is the breastplate. Righteousness means such conduct as will stand the scrutiny of a just and competent judge; and also the legal status of one who has been acquitted of an accusation. One who has received such approval of God is righteous, and that righteousness is his breastplate. God must be the judge; not man. He is "the Lord our Righteousness." It is His judgment that must be opposed to the attacks of the accuser. It is the armor of God we must rely on, not one of our own make.

Preparation of the gospel of peace] "Preparation" is the word used in Eph. 6:15, where it means "equipment." He who desires victory in this conflict, must have the entire equipment of the gospel. This includes the holy Priesthood, the ordinances of the Church, continuous revelation, and all other divinely-appointed means of salvation.

The gospel is the "gospel of peace." "How beautiful upon the mountains are the feet of him that bringeth good tidings, that publisheth peace" (Isa. 52:7). Where the gospel principles prevail, there can be no war, except for self-defence, and in the Book of Mormon we read of a people that, under the influence of the Spirit of God, refused to take up arms even in self-defense (Alma 24:17-24). The gospel enjoins upon the Church to "lift up an ensign of peace * * * to all people" (Doc. and Cov. 105:38), and to make a proclamation for peace "unto the ends of the earth." The Prophet Joseph was a true messenger of peace. His sentiments on bloodshed may be gathered from the following incident. When Zion's Camp was traveling from Kirtland, the brethren one day came to a thick wood of recent growth. The Prophet felt very much depressed. He said that a great deal of blood had been shed in that place, and added these memorable words: "Whenever a man of God is in a place where many have been killed, he will feel lonesome and unpleasant, and his spirits will sink" (*History of the Church*, Vol. II., p. 66).

17. *Shield of faith*] Faith in God is a protecting shield, for the same reason that a child's implicit trust in its parents is to it a safeguard, when manifested in obedience (Psalm 25:15; Moroni 10:23).

Quench all the fiery darts] Burning arrows were used in warfare anciently. It was necessary to extinguish these "fiery darts," and the shield was useful for this purpose.

18. *Helmet of salvation*] Salvation is deliverance from sin and guilt and all other enemies, through the gospel.

The sword of my spirit] This is the word of God (Heb. 4:12; Doc. and Cov. 6:2). In this conflict the defenders must be well versed in the Scriptures, and be in touch with the Spirit of Revelation, in order to expound the truth.

Finally, they must pray, and be faithful "until I come."

GENERAL NOTES

There have been serious controversies concerning the emblems of the Sacrament. Unleavened bread was used by our Lord, and the Latin church maintains that no other kind should be permitted, while the

Greek church condemns the use of unleavened bread as a remnant of Judaism. The Lutherans have adopted the Latin view, while the Reformed church regards the quality of the bread as unimportant. The Reformed views agree with this Revelation.

There has also been contention concerning the contents of the Cup. In the early churches the wine was mixed with water, as was the custom of the Jews, for their wine, as an ancient writer, quoted by Lightfoot, says, "was very strong, and not fit to drinking, unless water was mixed with it." In most churches the wine used for the Sacrament is diluted with water, and at one time clergymen were instructed to mix the wine with "a little pure and clean water." In the early centuries of our era some converts demanded that water be used instead of wine. From one of their leaders, Tatian, they are called *Tatiani*. They are also known as *Hydroparastatæ*, or *Aquarii*. They were centuries ahead of their time and therefore condemned as heretics.

Michael is Adam. This we know from revelation. Very few names of angels are on record. Among the later Jews, according to Edersheim, Michael, Gabriel, Uriel, and Raphael were the names known. In the Apocryphal book of Tobit (12:15) and also in Rev. 8:2, seven angels are referred to, but no names given. In the so-called Book of Enoch (8:1-17, translation by John Baty) seven names occur, Uriel, Raphael, Raguel, Michael, Sarakiel, Gabriel, and Phanuel. How the names not found in the Scriptures were obtained is not known. The Prophet Joseph tells us that Gabriel is Noah, and that "he stands next in authority to Adam in the Priesthood" (B. H. Roberts, *Doctrine of the Deity*, p. 244). In the Doctrine and Covenants, Raphael is mentioned, but without further identification. From modern Revelations we know that Moroni, John the Baptist, James, Peter, and John are angels, and that "there are no angels who minister to this Earth but those who belong, or have belonged, to it" (Doc. and Cov. 130:5).

SECTION 28.

REVELATION *given through Joseph Smith the Prophet, to Oliver Cowdery, at Fayette, New York, September, 1830. Hiram Page, a member of the Church, had a certain stone, and professed to be receiving revelations by its aid concerning the upbuilding of Zion and the order of the Church. Several members had been deceived by these claims, and even Oliver Cowdery was wrongly influenced thereby. Just prior to an appointed conference, the Prophet inquired earnestly of the Lord concerning the matter and this revelation followed. See History of the Church, vol. 1, p. 109.——Joseph's position of presidency defined—Oliver warned against undue assumption—Oliver's mission to the Lamanites stated—He to labor with Hiram Page, whom Satan had deceived—Hiram Page not appointed by the Lord nor accepted by the people as a revelator to the Church.*

BEHOLD, I say unto thee, Oliver, that it shall be given unto thee that thou shalt be heard by the church in all things whatsoever thou shalt teach them by the Comforter, concerning the revelations and commandments which I have given.

2. But, behold, verily, verily, I say unto thee, no one shall be appointed to receive commandments and revelations in this church excepting my servant Joseph Smith, Jun., for he receiveth them even as Moses.

3. And thou shalt be obedient unto the things which I shall give unto him, even as Aaron, to declare faithfully the commandments and the revelations, with power and authority unto the church.

4. And if thou art led at any time by the Comforter to speak or teach, or at all times by the way of commandment unto the church, thou mayest do it.

5. But thou shalt not write by way of commandment, but by wisdom;

6. And thou shalt not command him who is at thy head, and at the head of the church;

7. For I have given him the keys of the mysteries, and the revelations which are sealed, until I shall appoint them another in his stead.

The spirit of persecution being rampant in the City of Harmony, Pa., the Prophet Joseph moved to Fayette, N. Y., to Mr. Whitmer's house. On arriving there, he learned that Hiram Page had obtained a stone by means of which, as he thought, he received revelations concerning the upbuilding of Zion and the government of the Church, and that Oliver Cowdery, the Whitmers, and others were inclined to accept those revelations as the word of God. The Prophet felt concerned about the matter, for he perceived the cunning of the adversary. In answer to his earnest prayers, the Lord gave this Revelation, addressed especially to Oliver Cowdery, in which He (1) reveals fully the great principle that divine revelations come only through the regular channels; (2) appoints Oliver Cowdery a missionary to the Lamanites; (3) instructs him to obey counsel, and (4) to set Hiram Page right before leaving on his mission; and (5) assures him of divine guidance while in the service of the master.

1. *Thou shalt be heard by the church*] Oliver Cowdery was one of the six original members of the Church and a special witness to the divinity of the work. He held the Melchizedek Priesthood, and had every claim to a hearing by the Church, but only as he, in his utterances, was guided by the Spirit. His calling was to teach the truths already revealed.

2. *No one shall be appointed to receive commandments * * * excepting my servant Joseph*] When the Lord had a new commandment to give, or a new revelation to make, He would do so through him who had been appointed for that purpose (Comp. Sec. 5:2). God always honors and sustains His servants in their various positions, as He did when He directed Cornelius to send for Peter, to whom the preaching of the gospel had been entrusted (Acts 10:32).

Thou shalt be obedient] To the voice of God. When the bugle sounds, those concerned govern themselves accordingly because a higher will than that of the bugler is heard in the call.

Oliver Cowdery might speak and teach, and even command, as long as he confined himself to the Revelations God had given, (v. 3); he might write as a wise counselor (v. 5) but, not as having authority, and he could not issue commands to the Prophet whom God had placed at the head of the Church, under His Son, our Redeemer (v. 6). It is the gift of the Prophet to declare mysteries and truths not known (v. 7).

Mysteries] A mystery is a truth that cannot be known except through divine revelation—a sacred secret. In the days of Paul the important truth that Gentiles were to be admitted to the Kingdom of God without observing the Law of Moses was a "mystery" (Eph. 1:9-11; Col. 1:25-27). In our day such great truths as those pertaining to the restoration of the Priesthood, the work for the dead, and the re-establishment of the Church are "mysteries," because they could not have been discovered except by revelation.

It should be noted that when God revealed a truth to anyone, through the Prophet Joseph, President Brigham Young, or any of their successors, that truth was just as true, and just as binding, as if Peter, James, John, Gabriel, or Michael had been sent with the message. He who does not believe the word of God through a mortal messenger, would not believe one from the other side of mortality (Luke 16:31).

8. And now, behold, I say unto you that you shall go unto the Lamanites and preach my gospel unto them; and inasmuch as they receive thy teachings thou shalt cause my church to be established among them; and thou shalt have revelations, but write them not by way of commandment.

9. And now, behold, I say unto you that it is not revealed, and no man knoweth where the city Zion shall be built, but it shall be given hereafter. Behold, I say unto you that it shall be on the borders by the Lamanites.

8. *You shall go unto the Lamanites*] Oliver Cowdery was the first one called to go on a mission among the American Indians. This mission had a two-fold purpose: One was to establish the Church among the Lamanites; another, to call the attention of the Saints to the place where the New Jerusalem, the City of Zion, should be built.

9. *No man knoweth where the city shall be built*] It is not improbable that some of the pseudo-revelations of Hiram Page related to this very subject. The Saints were full of enthusiasm, looking for the immediate fulfilment of the prophecies. The Lord now made it known that the locality of that holy city had not yet been revealed, but that it might be looked for "on the borders by the Lamanites." Further revelation on this subject would come later (Sec. 57:2, 3).

10. Thou shalt not leave this place until after the conference; and my servant Joseph shall be appointed to preside over the conference by the voice of it, and what he saith to thee thou shalt tell.

11. And again, thou shalt take thy brother, Hiram Page, between him and thee alone, and tell him that those things which he hath written from that stone are not of me, and that Satan deceiveth him;

12. For, behold, these things have not been appointed unto him, neither shall anything be appointed unto any of this church contrary to the church covenants.

13. For all things must be done in order, and by common consent in the church, by the prayer of faith.

14. And thou shalt assist to settle all these things, according to the covenants of the church, before thou shalt take thy journey among the Lamanites.

10. *Conference*] The second Conference of the Church which convened September 26th, 1830 (Sec. 26:1).

11. *Thou shalt take thy brother, Hiram Page, etc.*] The Lord, having revealed the error of Hiram Page in the matter of the "seer-stone," directed Oliver Cowdery to labor with him and show him, in all kindness, that he was being deceived by the Evil one.

13. *Common consent*] See Section 26:2.

14. *Settle all these things*] Oliver Cowdery could not go on his important mission to the Lamanites, until he had settled this difficulty. When the Church is weakened by schisms, missionary efforts cannot have the same success as when unity and harmony prevail. The strength of an army in the field depends largely on the conditions at the bases of supply. It is so with the missionary forces of the Church.

15. And it shall be given thee from the time thou shalt go, until the time thou shalt return, what thou shalt do.

16. And thou must open thy mouth at all times, declaring my gospel with the sound of rejoicing. Amen.

15. When a missionary goes out into the world, in obedience to a divine call, being in full fellowship with the Church, and leaving no unsettled incidents behind, he may rely on the Lord for protection and guidance.

16. *Rejoicing*] The gospel should be preached with joy, and not as a message of sorrow and gloom. The labors of a missionary should not be a hard but a pleasant duty.

GENERAL NOTES

The case of Hiram Page was submitted to the Conference and settled in accordance with this Revelation.

In Acts (chap. 15) we have a remarkable record of a difficulty in the early church, which also was settled in a general conference. Some of the brethren taught, in opposition to Paul and Barnabas, that Gentile converts were under the necessity of being circumcised before joining the Church. The question was laid before a conference at Jerusalem, and, after some discussion, Peter moved that it be the sense of the Conference (if a modern expression be permitted) that both Jews and Gentiles are saved "by the grace of Christ"; that is, by the gospel. James seconded this motion and added the suggestion that the decision of the Conference be embodied in a letter to the Gentile churches. This was adopted, but the schism had threatened the Church for years.

The question of the proper channels of revelation was fully settled in the Conference at Fayette, September 26th, 1830.

Hiram Page was born in the year 1800, and, when a young man, traveled considerably as a physician. He joined the Church on the 11th of April, 1830, and became one of the Eight Witnesses to the Book of Mormon. In due time he removed to Independence, Mo., and later became one of the pioneers of the City of Far West. In 1838, however, he drifted away from the Church. He never rescinded his testimony. He died on the 12th of August, 1852.

The doctrine revealed in this Revelation (1-7) was well known to the former-day Saints. In the Patriarchal dispensation no one could take the place of the Patriarch. In the Mosaic dispensation no one could take the position of Moses (See, for instance, Numb., chap. 16). Aaron was the spokesman; Moses was to him "instead of God" (Ex. 4:14-16).

The Lamanite mission was a very important movement of the young but vigorous Church. Oliver Cowdery was the first-appointed member of the party. Peter Whitmer, Jr., was added by Revelation (Sec. 30); and then Parley P. Pratt and Ziba Peterson (Sec. 32). Soon after the Conference the little party set out on the perilous journey of about 1,500 miles. They started on foot, trusting in the Lord to open the way. Near Buffalo they visited the Catteraugus Indians and left the Book of Mormon with them. Then they proceeded to Kirtland, Ohio. Here they visited Sidney Rigdon, then a popular Campbellite minister. He and some of his friends joined the Church. Night and day, for some time, the missionaries were teaching the people in Kirtland and vicinity. After having ordained Rigdon, Isaac Morley, John Murdock, Lyman Wight and others, to the ministry, the missionaries left for the West. Near Sandusky they visited the Wyandot tribe and preached the gospel. In Cincinnati and St. Louis they met with very little success. At the latter place their progress was impeded by heavy snowstorms. With the opening of the New Year, 1831, they continued their journey, traveling on foot 300 miles over prairies, without shelter and fire, living on frozen corn, bread and raw pork. At length they reached Independence, Mo., on the extreme western frontier of the State. They had traveled four months and suffered untold hardships; they had preached to two Indian nations and to thousands of white people, and organized several strong branches of the Church.

After having rested a little at Independence, three of the brethren crossed the frontier and visited the Shawnee Indians. Then they went among the Delawares. These manifested a great deal of interest in the Book of Mormon. Therefore the jealousy of ministers was aroused and these prevailed upon the Indian agents to expel the missionaries from the Indian country. They, accordingly, returned to Jackson county, where they labored for some time with encouraging success.

SECTION 29.

REVELATION *given through Joseph Smith the Prophet, in the presence of six Elders, at Fayette, New York, September, 1830. This revelation was given some days prior to the conference beginning September 26, 1830.——The gathering of the elect specified—The imminence of the Lord's advent affirmed— Calamities incident to the sinful state of the world—The Millennium and scenes of judgment to follow—Distinction between the spiritual and temporal creations—Purpose of the mortal probation—The agency of man—The assured redemption of children who die in infancy.*

LISTEN to the voice of Jesus Christ, your Redeemer, the Great I Am, whose arm of mercy hath atoned for your sins;

2. Who will gather his people even as a hen gathereth her chickens under her wings, even as many as will hearken to my voice and humble themselves before me, and call upon me in mighty prayer.

3. Behold, verily, verily, I say unto you, that at this time your sins are forgiven you, therefore ye receive these things; but remember to sin no more, lest perils shall come upon you.

4. Verily, I say unto you that ye are chosen out of the world to declare my gospel with the sound of rejoicing, as with the voice of a trump.

5. Lift up your hearts and be glad, for I am in your midst, and am your advocate with the Father; and it is his good will to give you the kingdom.

6. And, as it is written—Whatsoever ye shall ask in faith, being united in prayer according to my command, ye shall receive.

7. And ye are called to bring to pass the gathering of mine elect; for mine elect hear my voice and harden not their hearts;

8. Wherefore the decree hath gone forth from the Father that they shall be gathered in unto one place upon the face of this land, to prepare their hearts and be prepared in all things against the day when tribulation and desolation are sent forth upon the wicked.

The Saints at Fayette were looking forward with anticipation to the conference that was to be held on the 26th of September, 1830. The first conference had been the occasion of a Pentecostal outpouring of the Holy Spirit, and there was every reason to believe that the second would be a similar spiritual feast. Some time before the September Conference this Revelation was given in the presence of six Elders. In it the Lord (1) reveals the doctrine of gathering (1-8); (2) makes the important announcement that the second Advent and the Millennium are near (9-11); (3) makes known the position of the first Apostles in the coming of the Kingdom (12); (4) speaks of the first resurrection (13), (5) and the signs preceding the Advent (14-21); and (6) of events after the

Millennium and the general resurrection (22-29); (7) reveals important truths regarding the creation (30-35), the fall (36-45), and the innocence of little children (46-50).

1. *I Am*] The same as JEHOVAH. Jesus Christ is Jehovah.

Arm of mercy] This is an unusual expression, but it occurs in the Book of Mormon (Jacob 6:5, III. Nephi 9:14), where it refers to Christ's gracious offer of salvation. It is the equivalent to His love, which prompted Him to make the atonement for the sins of the world. In Isa. 51:5, the Lord declares that His "arms" shall judge the people. That is, He shall exert His mighty power in judgment; in this Revelation He promises to exert that power in mercy. He is as "mighty to save" as to judge.

2. *Who will gather His people*] Our Lord, immediately before the end of His earthly mission, exclaimed, "O Jerusalem, Jerusalem, * * * how often would I have gathered thy children together * * * and ye would not" (Matt. 23:37). By gathering they might have been saved from the destruction that awaited the City. But they would not, and so, "Behold, your house is left unto you desolate." The dispensation that followed was not a gathering dispensation, but rather a scattering. Our dispensation is one of gathering.

8. *The decree hath gone forth*] In the councils of heaven it had been decreed that the Saints should gather to one place on the American continent, in order to be prepared against the last great tribulations of the world.

Gathered in unto one place] Jackson County, Mo., is the central gathering place of the Saints. On this subject the Prophet Joseph, in a letter to the Elders of the Church, dated September 1st, 1835, and published in the *Messenger and Advocate,* said, in part:—

"I received, by a heavenly vision, a commandment in June following [1831], to take my journey to the Western boundaries of the State of Missouri, and there designate the very spot which was to be the central place for the commencement of the gathering together of those who embrace the fulness of the everlasting gospel. Accordingly I undertook the journey, with certain ones of my brethren, and, after a long and tedious journey, suffering many privations and hardships, arrived in Jackson County, Mo., and after viewing the country, seeking diligently at the hand of God, He manifested Himself unto us, and designated unto me and others, the very spot upon which He designed to commence the work of the gathering, and the upbuilding of an Holy City: which should be called Zion—Zion, because it is a place of righteousness, and all who build thereon are to worship the true and living God, and all believe in one doctrine, even the doctrine of our Lord and Savior, Jesus Christ" (*History of the Church,* Vol. II, p. 254).

The Saints were scattered, and established themselves in the Rocky Mountains, according to the prophetic word (Sec. 35:24; 49:25), but

"Zion" was not "moved out of her place," and the Saints will return and build it up. "Will our mission end here [in Utah]? Is the State of Utah the proper monument of the 'Mormon' people? No. * * * The monument to 'Mormonism' will stand in Jackson County, Mo. There the great City will be built: There Zion will arise and shine, 'the joy of the whole Earth,' and there the Lord will come to His temple in His own time, when His people shall have made the required preparation" (Orson F. Whitney, in an address, Salt Lake City, April 9, 1916).

9. For the hour is nigh and the day soon at hand when the earth is ripe; and all the proud and they that do wickedly shall be as stubble; and I will burn them up, saith the Lord of Hosts, that wickedness shall not be upon the earth;

10. For the hour is nigh, and that which was spoken by mine apostles must be fulfilled; for as they spoke so shall it come to pass;

11. For I will reveal myself from heaven with power and great glory, with all the hosts thereof, and dwell in righteousness with men on earth a thousand years, and the wicked shall not stand.

9. *The hour is nigh*] The hour of judgment. The world was ripe; the harvest was about to begin; the wheat would be gathered in and the stubble burned. The warning is repeated (v. 10) because of its great importance.

That which was spoken] By Paul, John the Revelator, and other prophets, concerning the coming of the Lord and the judgments of the latter days; all was about to be fulfilled. The great and terrible "day of the Lord" was nigh, when this Revelation was given. We have seen the dawn of it in blood.

11. *I will reveal myself*] Before this stormy "day" is ended, the Lord will reveal himself in power and glory.

A thousand years] The Millennium will then begin. Our Lord will dwell with men on Earth for a thousand years, as He blessed His disciples with His visible presence after His resurrection, for forty days. His Kingdom is then on Earth.

"It may be asked what I mean by the Kingdom of God. The Church of Jesus Christ has been established now for many years, and the Kingdom of God has got to be established, even that Kingdom which will circumscribe all the kingdoms of this world. It will yet give laws to every nation that exists upon the Earth. This is the kingdom that Daniel, the Prophet, saw should be set up in the last days. * * * If the Latter-day Saints think, when the Kingdom of God is established on the Earth, that all the inhabitants of the Earth will join the Church called Latter-day Saints, they are egregiously mistaken. I presume there will be as many sects and parties then as now. Still, when the Kingdom of God triumphs, every knee shall bow and every tongue confess that Jesus is the Christ, to the glory of the Father. Even the Jews will do it then: but will the Jews and Gentiles be obliged to belong to the Church of Jesus Christ of Latter-day Saints? No, not by any means. Jesus said to His disciples, 'In my Father's house are many mansions; were it not so I would have told you; I go to prepare a place for you, that where I am, there ye may be also.' There are mansions in sufficient numbers to suit the different classes of mankind, and a variety will always exist to all eternity, requiring a classification and an arrangement into societies and communities in the many mansions which are in the Lord's house, and this will be so for ever and ever" (Brigham Young, *Journal of Discourses,* Vol. XI., p. 275).

It should be noted, however, that the preaching of the Gospel will continue during the millennium with greater power than ever before. Satan will be bound so that he will have no power to tempt any man, (Doc. and Cov. 101:28) and men will be more susceptible to the teachings of the elders of the Church who go forth to instruct them, until practically all have been brought into the Church. The Lord revealed to Isaiah that in that day the Lord in righteousness "shall judge the poor, and reprove with equity for the meek of the earth: and he shall smite the earth with the rod of his mouth, and with the breath of his lips shall he slay the wicked. And righteousness shall be the girdle of his loins, and faithfulness the girdle of his reins. The wolf also shall dwell with the lamb, and the leopard shall lie down with the kid; and the calf and the young lion and the fatling together; and a little child shall lead them. * * * They shall not hurt nor destroy in all my holy mountain: for the earth shall be full of the knowledge of the Lord, as the waters cover the sea." (Isa. 11:4-9.) If righteousness is to cover the earth as the waters cover the sea, there cannot be many wicked men left. "There shall be no more thence an infant of days, nor an old man that hath not filled his days; for the child shall die an hundred years old; but the sinner being an hundred years old shall be accursed." (Isa. 65:20.)

"Christ and the resurrected Saints will reign over the earth during the thousand years. They will not probably dwell upon the earth, but will visit it when they please, or when it is necessary to govern it. There will be wicked men on the earth during the thousand years. The heathen nations who will not come up to worship will be visited with the judgments of God, and must eventually be destroyed from the earth. (D.H.C. 5:212. Teachings 268-269.)

"The Prophet's statement that there will be wicked men on the earth during the Millennium has caused considerable confusion in the minds of many who have read in the Scriptures in many places that when Christ comes the earth shall be cleansed from its wickedness, and that the wicked shall not stand, but shall be consumed. See Doc. and Cov. 5:18-19, 29:8-10, 101:23-25. Isa. 24:1-3. Malachi 4:1. The evil-minded inhabitants, those 'who love and make a lie' and are guilty of all manner of corruption, will be consumed and pass away when Christ comes. In using the term 'wicked men' in this instruction at the home of Judge Adams, the Prophet did so in the same sense in which the Lord uses it in the eighty-fourth section of the *Doctrine and Covenants* 49-53. The Lord in this scripture speaks of those who have not received the Gospel as being under the bondage of sin, and hence 'wicked.' However, many of these people are honorable, clean living men, but they have not embraced the Gospel. The inhabitants of the terrestrial order will remain on the earth during the Millennium and this class is without the Gospel ordinances. See Doc. and Cov. 76:73-76." (Footnote, *Teachings of the Prophet Joseph Smith,* pp. 268-269.)

It should be noted that our Lord does not state any time for the beginning of the thousand years. The famous Adventist, William Miller, in the year 1831, committed the error of predicting that the Millennium would be established in 1843. The Prophet Joseph took the charitable view that Miller was misled through certain errors in the Bible translations extant (*History of the Church,* Vol. V., p. 272), and emphasized the fact that certain signs, such as the darkening of the sun and the turning of the moon into blood, must precede the coming of Christ. The Lord has given His people certain signs by which those who watch and pray may know that the time is near; but He has not told them the time or the season.

12. And again, verily, verily, I say unto you, and it hath gone forth in a firm decree, by the will of the Father, that mine apostles, the Twelve which were with me in my ministry at Jerusalem, shall stand at my right hand at the day of my coming in a pillar of fire, being clothed with robes of righteousness, with crowns upon their heads, in glory even as I am, to judge the whole house of Israel, even as many as have loved me and kept my commandments, and none else.

A firm decree] Our Lord prepared a special reward for His first Apostles. He promised them, while yet with them in the flesh, that, seated on thrones of glory, they should judge the twelve tribes of Israel. Here we are informed that the promise had been ratified by the Father, and that a firm decree had been issued, making that fact known. When our Lord comes to judgment, His Apostles will take the places promised to them, arrayed in the robes of their office.

13. For a trump shall sound both long and loud, even as upon Mount Sinai, and all the earth shall quake, and they shall

come forth—yea, even the dead which died in me, to receive a crown of righteousness, and to be clothed upon, even as I am, to be with me, that we may be one.

They shall come forth] Not the Twelve alone, but all "the dead which died in me." All will receive crowns and robes. The victor at the Olympian games won, perhaps, a crown of olive branches, and he who was triumphant at the Pythian contests rejoiced in a laurel wreath; but those who conquer in life's conflicts, will wear a crown of righteousness. Their very righteousness in this life will be their glory hereafter.

A trump shall sound] The resurrection will be accompanied by divine manifestations similar to those that accompanied the giving of the Law on Sinai. The dead will hear and answer the summons. "If the spirit honors the body and the body honors the spirit while they are here united, the particles of matter that compose the mortal tabernacle will be resurrected and brought forth to immortality and eternal life: but it cannot be brought forth and made immortal, except it undergoes a change, by which it is prepared to dwell in the presence of God."

14. But, behold, I say unto you that before this great day shall come the sun shall be darkened, and the moon shall be turned into blood, and the stars shall fall from heaven, and there shall be greater signs in heaven above and in the earth beneath;

15. And there shall be weeping and wailing among the hosts of men;

16. And there shall be a great hailstorm sent forth to destroy the crops of the earth.

17. And it shall come to pass, because of the wickedness of the world, that I will take vengeance upon the wicked, for they will not repent; for the cup of mine indignation is full; for behold, my blood shall not cleanse them if they hear me not.

18. Wherefore, I the Lord God will send forth flies upon the face of the earth, which shall take hold of the inhabitants thereof, and shall eat their flesh, and shall cause maggots to come in upon them;

19. And their tongues shall be stayed that they shall not utter against me; and their flesh shall fall from off their bones, and their eyes from their sockets;

20. And it shall come to pass that the beasts of the forest and the fowls of the air shall devour them up.

21. And the great and abominable church, which is the whore of all the earth, shall be cast down by devouring fire, according as it is spoken by the mouth of Ezekiel the prophet, who spoke of these things, which have not come to pass but surely must, as I live, for abominations shall not reign.

14-21. In these paragraphs some of the signs that are to precede and indicate the coming of the Lord to judge the world are given. (1) There shall be unusual manifestations among the heavenly luminaries; (2) men shall weep and wail; (3) crops shall be destroyed, causing shortages of food; (4) "flies" shall cause painful and nauseating diseases; (5) beasts shall multiply and destroy many; and (6) the "great and abominable church" shall be cast down. Such are "the signs of the times" which the people of God must be looking for. And they do not belong to a distant future only.

14. *The sun shall be darkened.*] The prediction by the prophets and confirmed by our Lord, that shortly preceding his second coming the sun shall be darkened and the moon appear like a ball of blood, will be a literal appearance of these heavenly bodies, and not a figure of speech. After speaking of the calamities, wars and bloodshed which shall come to plague the nations just preceding his coming, the Savior said:

"Immediately after the tribulation of those days shall the sun be darkened, and the moon shall not give her light, and the stars shall fall from heaven, and the powers of the heavens shall be shaken. And then shall appear the sign of the Son of man in heaven: and then shall all the tribes of the earth mourn, and they shall see the Son of man coming in the clouds of heaven with power and great glory." (Matt. 24:29-30.) Joel also speaks of this great day: "And I will shew wonders in the heavens and in the earth, blood, and fire, and pillars of smoke. The sun shall be turned into darkness, and the moon into blood, before the great and terrible day of the Lord come." (Joel 2:30-31.) On this same theme the Prophet Joseph Smith has said: "Men profess to prophesy. I will prophesy that the signs of the coming of the Son of Man are already commenced. One pestilence will desolate after another. We shall soon have war and bloodshed. The moon will be turned into blood. I testify of these things, and that the coming of the Son of Man is nigh, even at our doors. If our souls and our bodies are not looking forth for the coming of the Son of Man; and after we are dead, if we are not looking forth, we shall be among those who are calling for the rocks to fall upon them." (*Teachings,* p. 160.) "There will be wars and rumors of wars, signs in the heavens above and on the earth beneath, the sun turned into darkness and the moon to blood, earthquakes in divers places, the seas heaving beyond their bounds: then will appear one grand sign of the Son of Man in heaven.

But what will the world do? They will say it is a planet, a comet, etc. But the Son of Man will come as the sign of the coming of the Son of Man, which will be as the light of the morning cometh out of the east." (*Teachings,* p. 286-7.)

15. *Weeping and wailing*] The wicked pay little heed to the many warnings of the impending judgment which await them, and they put off the dreadful day in their thoughtless indulgence in sin. When destruction overtakes them then they weep and wail as did the Nephites of old. "O that we had repented before this great and terrible day, and then would our brethren have been spared, and they would not have been burned * * * O that we had repented before this great and terrible day, and had not killed and stoned the prophets, and cast them out." (3 Nephi 8:24-25.) Wo shall it be in that great day when the sun shall be darkened, the moon turned to blood and calamity overtakes the world.

16. *A great hailstorm*] In this great day of judgment, there shall come a great hailstorm to destroy the crops. When men turn from God he is under no obligation to protect them and they bring punishments upon themselves, floods, winds, hailstorms, fire and plagues. All of these would be turned away if men would keep the commandments of the Lord, this is his promise.

17. *My blood shall not cleanse them*] This indicates that, at the time of the end, the children of men would appeal to the atonement of Christ in vain. Perhaps there never was a time when professed Christians rested in greater security than they do today, hoping that the blood of the Lamb will be their shield. Here is a warning that His atoning blood does not cleanse them, unless they are willing to obey Him. Destruction will go forth, for the day of vengeance has come.

18. *Flies*] This prediction of the plague of flies is also spoken of by Zechariah:

"And this shall be the plague wherewith the Lord will smite all the people that have fought against Jerusalem; Their flesh shall consume away while they stand upon their feet, and their eyes shall consume away in their holes, and their tongues shall consume away in their mouth." (Zech. 14:12.) There is no promise that this great plague of hail, destruction and disease shall be confined to any one section of the earth. It is a calamity which will come upon the wicked because they will not repent. We may well believe that in addition to the plague of flies there shall be included in this prediction the plague of microbes, or bacilli, new to the scientific world and with which they will not be able to cope, much of which will be the result of impure lives.

19. Some kind of loathsome disease is here described, the symptoms of which resemble somewhat those of leprosy (*Elephantiasis Groecorum, or Lepra Arabum*), which some doctors consider to be one form of an unmentionable disease.

20. *Beasts * * * shall devour them*] When a country is devastated by war, wild beasts multiply in it, and men, weakened by disease, cannot successfully combat them.

The great and abominable church] This is the great church spoken of by Nephi (1 Nephi 13:5-9; 26-28, and also by John in Revelation 17.) The Lord declares that this abominable church shall be cast down when Christ comes, when all things corrupt shall be consumed. Compare also Revelation 18.)

22. And again, verily, verily, I say unto you that when the thousand years are ended, and men again begin to deny their God, then will I spare the earth but for a little season;

23. And the end shall come, and the heaven and the earth shall be consumed and pass away, and there shall be a new heaven and a new earth.

24. For all old things shall pass away, and all things shall become new, even the heaven and the earth, and all the fulness thereof, both men and beasts, the fowls of the air, and the fishes of the sea;

25. And not one hair, neither mote, shall be lost, for it is the workmanship of mine hand.

26. But, behold, verily I say unto you, before the earth shall pass away, Michael, mine arch-angel, shall sound his trump, and then shall all the dead awake, for their graves shall be opened, and they shall come forth—yea, even all.

27. And the righteous shall be gathered on my right hand unto eternal life; and the wicked on my left hand will I be ashamed to own before the Father;

28. Wherefore I will say unto them—Depart from me, ye cursed, into everlasting fire, prepared for the devil and his angels.

29. And now, behold, I say unto you, never at any time have I declared from mine own mouth that they should return, for where I am they cannot come, for they have no power.

22-29. Here a view is presented of the condition of the world after the Millennium. (1) Men shall again deny God (v. 22); (2) for a "little season" the Earth will be spared, but the end is inevitable (vv. 23-25); (3) before the end, Michael will summon the dead; all shall rise—the righteous to eternal life, and the wicked to eternal fire (vv. 26-29; Rev. 20:7-15).

22. *Again begin to deny their God*] During the thousand years Satan will be bound so that he cannot tempt any man. During this time temples will be erected in all parts of the land and the work of salvation for the dead will be continued until it is accomplished and the Lord will reveal all things pertaining to his kingdom. The Lord and other resurrected beings will visit the earth from time to time and give instruction to those still in mortality so that eventually the knowledge of the Lord will cover the earth as the waters do the sea. (Isa. 11:9; Heb. 2:14.) After the Millennium Satan will be loosed and will go forth again to receive the nations, and then will come the great conflict with Gog and Magog. (Rev. 20:8.)

23. *Earth shall be consumed*] Not only the kingdoms of the Earth and human authority, as in former catastrophes, but Earth itself shall pass through fire and be "born again," and become a habitation fit for celestial beings. In its new state it will be a Urim and Thummim (Sec. 130:9), like the place where God dwells.

24. *Old things shall pass and all things become new*] After the thousand years are ended and the "little season" when Satan shall gather his forces and come to the final judgment, all things mortal shall come to an end and pass away; then shall come the restoration in the resurrection of all creatures "both men and beasts, the fowls of the air, and the fishes of the sea; and not one hair, neither mote, shall be lost, for it is the workmanship of mine hand," the Lord declares. The Lord created nothing that is not to be eternal. Paul wrote: "Because the creature itself also shall be delivered from the bondage of corruption into the glorious liberty of the children of God. For we know that the whole creation groaneth and travaileth in pain together until now." (Rom. 8:21-22.) "I know that, whatsoever God doeth, it shall be for ever: nothing can be put to it, nor anything taken from it; and God doeth it, that men should fear before him." (Eccl. 3:14.) When the celestialized heaven and earth shall come, then will all creatures be free from mortal bondage and be permitted to partake of the blessings of immortality in the "glorious liberty" granted to all our Father's creations.

25. *Workmanship*] Everything created is God's handiwork and will be taken care of. Paul (Eph. 2:10, and Rom. 1:20) speaks of everything created as His "workmanship," or "making." The word he uses is one from which our word "poem" is derived, as if he would say that the works of creation are God's poetic compositions—His poems.

*Michael * * * shall sound his trump*] The world generally represents Gabriel as sounding the trump that summons the dead. Here we learn that it is Michael. How appropriate that the Ancestor of the race should perform this function! That the father should call his children in the morning of the resurrection day!

27-29. The language here employed is like that found in Matt. 25:31-46, where the Lord speaks of judgment upon nations. There has been a separation of nations, so that while some have the blessings of light, others are groping in darkness. Finally, there will be a similar separation of individuals.

28. *Depart from me, ye cursed*] This is the final fate of the sons of perdition (See 76:32-39). It should be noted that in Matthew those on the right side are "blessed of my Father," while those of the left side are "cursed." This curse they bring upon themselves by their disobedience, and not because it pleases the Creator to see them punished. "For behold, justice exerciseth all his demands, and also mercy claimeth all which is her own; and thus, none but the truly penitent are saved. What, do ye suppose that mercy can rob justice? I say unto you, nay; not one whit. If so, God would cease to be God." (Alma 42:24-25.)

29. Those whose fate is the everlasting fire are finally lost. There is no "return" for them. The details of their sufferings are not revealed (See Sec. 76:45, 46); only that they will not return (See Rev. 20:7-10).
Power] The power of the Spirit of God. The Spirit has left them. There remains only torment.

30. But remember that all my judgments are not given unto men; and as the words have gone forth out of my mouth even so shall they be fulfilled, that the first shall be last, and that the last shall be first in all things whatsoever I have created by the word of my power, which is the power of my Spirit.

31. For by the power of my Spirit created I them; yea, all things both spiritual and temporal—

32. First spiritual, secondly temporal, which is the beginning of my work; and again, first temporal, and secondly spiritual, which is the last of my work—

33. Speaking unto you that you may naturally understand; but unto myself my works have no end, neither beginning; but it is given unto you that ye may understand, because ye have asked it of me and are agreed.

34. Wherefore, verily I say unto you that all things unto me are spiritual, and not at any time have I given unto you a law which was temporal; neither any man, nor the children of men; neither Adam, your father, whom I created.

35. Behold, I gave unto him that he should be an agent unto himself; and I gave unto him commandment, but no temporal commandment gave I unto him, for my commandments are spiritual; they are not natural nor temporal, neither carnal nor sensual.

30. *All my judgments are not given unto men*] Our Lord has not revealed all the rewards in store for the righteous. There will be an infinite variety in the conditions of the blessed. Nor has He revealed the final fate of the wicked. But one truth is clearly revealed:—"The first shall be the last, and the last the first."

31. All things, both temporal and spiritual, are created. There is a pre-existence.

32. The first creation was spiritual, the second temporal. The temporal will again become spiritual, and the first will become the last, as the last is the first, or, in other words, the spiritual existence is both first and last.

33. However, the expression "first" and "last" are only employed for the sake of human understanding. From the divine point of view there is neither beginning nor end. God's works are as eternal as He is. This is beyond human understanding, except in so far as the poetic imagination offers an explanation:

> "Nature is but a name for an effect
> Whose cause is God. He feeds the secret fire
> By which the mighty process is maintained.
> [All things] are under one. One Spirit, His
> Who wore the platted thorns with bleeding brows,
> Rules Universal nature."—Cowper.

And are agreed] Note that this Revelation was given in answer to united prayer by the Elders in the house of the Prophet.

34-35. *Not at any time * * * law which was temporal*] Man makes a distinction between temporal and spiritual laws, and some are very much concerned about keeping the two separate. To the Lord everything is both spiritual and temporal, and the laws He gives are consequently spiritual, because they concern spiritual beings. When He commanded Adam to eat bread in the sweat of his brow, or Moses to strike the rock that the people might drink, or the Prophet Joseph to erect the Nauvoo House, or the Saints in Utah to build fences and roads, such laws were for their spiritual welfare, as well as physical. To obey such laws, when given, is a spiritual duty. One who performs his daily labor "as to the Lord, and not to men" (Eph. 6:7) derives spiritual benefit from whatever his duties are.

> "A servant with this clause
> Makes drudgery divine;
> Who sweeps a room as for thy laws
> Makes that and th' action fine."—Herbert.

36. And it came to pass that Adam, being tempted of the devil—for, behold, the devil was before Adam, for he rebelled against me, saying, Give me thine honor, which is my power; and also a third part of the hosts of heaven turned he away from me because of their agency;

37. And they were thrust down, and thus came the devil and his angels;

38. And, behold, there is a place prepared for them from the beginning, which place is hell.

39. And it must needs be that the devil should tempt the children of men, or they could not be agents unto themselves; for if they never should have bitter they could not know the sweet—

40. Wherefore, it came to pass that the devil tempted Adam, and he partook of the forbidden fruit and transgressed the commandment, wherein he became subject to the will of the devil, because he yielded unto temptation.

41. Wherefore, I, the Lord God, caused that he should be cast out from the Garden of Eden, from my presence, because of his transgression, wherein he became spiritually dead, which is the first death, even that same death which is the last death, which is spiritual, which shall be pronounced upon the wicked when I shall say: Depart, ye cursed.

42. But, behold, I say unto you that I, the Lord God, gave unto Adam and unto his seed, that they should not die as to the temporal death, until I, the Lord God, should send forth angels to declare unto them repentance and redemption, through faith on the name of mine Only Begotten Son.

43. And thus did I, the Lord God, appoint unto man the days of his probation—that by his natural death he might be raised in immortality unto eternal life, even as many as would believe;

44. And they that believe not unto eternal damnation; for they cannot be redeemed from their spiritual fall, because they repent not;

45. For they love darkness rather than light, and their deeds are evil, and they receive their wages of whom they list to obey.

36-45. In these paragraphs the Lord reveals some important truths relating to the fall of man. (1) Adam was tempted (v. 36). (2) The devil was the tempter (vv. 36-40). (3) Adam fell and was expelled from the Garden of Eden (v. 41). (4) The penalty was death (vv. 41-42). (5) Through death man goes to eternal life (v. 43); or to damnation (vv. 44, 45).

36. *Adam being tempted*] Our first ancestor was actually tempted. This was possible, because he was endowed with free agency. There can be no free agency where there is no possibility to choose between right and wrong. If only one course of action is open to us, we are not free agents. Freedom presupposes a law which can be broken as well as kept. Hence, God gave the law concerning the fruit of the trees in the garden. Adam was tempted, but, as Paul informs us, "he was not deceived" (1. Tim. 2:14), as was Eve. He partook of the forbidden fruit in order not to be separated from his wife, fully understanding the consequences. "Adam fell that man might be" (II. Nephi. 2:25).

The devil] The adversary of God and His Son, Jesus Christ, and the tempter and accuser of man. He is called the "angel of the bottomless pit," the "messenger" or representative, of the "abysm," (Rev. 9:11), as our Lord is the Messenger of the Great Council, or Counselor, (Is. 9:6; Sec. 10:10). The word "devil," from "diabolus," means "calumniator," "accuser," and calumny is his principal weapon of warfare. No wonder if the children of this world, whose "god" he is, employ that weapon against the Saints of the Most High!

37. *They were thrust down*] See Sec. 10:10. This has reference to the rebellion in heaven. See P. of G. P., Moses 4:3-4. Revelation 12:4.

38. *Hell*] This is the place prepared for the devil and his angels, his adherents, from the beginning; that is, from the moment they were thrust out of heaven.

After our Savior has finished his work and has gained the victory over death, (1. Cor. 15:24-26.) then the devil and his angels will go to their own place which the Lord has prepared for them, sometimes spoken of as "outer darkness," and "the bottomless pit."

39. The origin of evil is not a mystery, if we understand that there cannot be free agents without temptation and a possibility of falling.

43. *He might be raised in immortality*] Adam transgressed and was cast out of the Garden of Eden. He was spiritually dead, because banished from the presence of God. He was subject to physical death, and we may say he was legally dead, as one under death sentence. But by the gospel which was preached to him, he came to understand that he would be raised to immortality even through the process of death.

"And in that day Adam blessed God and was filled, and began to prophesy concerning all the families of the Earth, saying, Blessed be the name of God, for because of my transgression my eyes are opened, and in this life I shall have joy, and again in the flesh I shall see God. And Eve, his wife, heard all these things and was glad, saying, Were it not for our transgression we never should have had seed, and never should have known good and evil, and the joy of our redemption, and the eternal life which God giveth unto all" (Pearl of Great Price, Book of Moses 5:10-11).

44. *Eternal damnation*] Eternal damnation is the punishment meted out to all those who die in their sins. "And in fine, wo unto all those who die in their sins; for they shall return to God, and behold his face, and remain in their sins. (II. Nephi 9:38.) "God had decreed that all who will not obey His voice shall not escape the damnation of hell. What is the damnation of hell? To go with that society who have not obeyed His commands." (*Teachings,* p. 198.) Damnation is to be stopped, or barred from partaking of blessings, because of disobedience that could be partaken of through obedience to the laws of God. The word "damnation" means, in the New Testament, "judgment."

46. But behold, I say unto you, that little children are redeemed from the foundation of the world through mine Only Begotten;

47. Wherefore, they cannot sin, for power is not given unto Satan to tempt little children, until they begin to become accountable before me;

48. For it is given unto them even as I will, according to mine own pleasure, that great things may be required at the hand of their fathers.

49. And, again, I say unto you, that whoso having knowledge, have I not commanded to repent?

50. And he that hath no understanding, it remaineth in me to do according as it is written. And now I declare no more unto you at this time. Amen.

46-50. The status of little children is a subject closely connected with that of the fall. The Lord here declares that the children are redeemed through Jesus Christ; that they cannot sin; and that they cannot be tempted.

GENERAL NOTES

"With regard to the future state of those who die in infancy I do not feel authorized to say much. There has been a great deal of theory, and many views have been expressed on this subject, but there are many things connected with it which the Lord has probably never revealed to any of the prophets or patriarchs who ever appeared on Earth * * * It is sufficient for me to know that our children are saved, and that, if we ourselves keep the faith and do our duty before the Lord.

if we keep the celestial law, we shall be preserved by that law, and our children will be given unto us there, as they have been given here in this world of sorrow, affliction, pain and distress" (Wilford Woodruff, *Journal of Discourses*, Vol. XVIII, p. 32).

That our Lord will reign upon this Earth, and that the Saints will reign with Him for a thousand years, is clearly revealed. This truth was generally accepted among the Christians till the fourth century. From that time till the Reformation, the general opinion was against a literal Millennium. At the time of the Reformation, the so-called *Anabaptists* declared their belief in it, and that was enough to damn the doctrine in the eyes of their bigoted opponents. In England it was condemned as "Jewish dotage." Later, Rome declared against a literal Millennium, while Protestants took the opposite view. Some who believe in a Millennium hold that Christianity will be gradually diffused until the entire race is Christianized, and that will be the Millennium. This is an error. The world will be redeemed through the mighty arm of Jehovah; through judgments and tribulation. The general conversion will take place during the Millennium.

Zion means the pure in heart, as well as a place of gathering, and it is to be noted that no place can be Zion, unless it is inhabited by those who are pure in heart. Jackson County, Mo., is to be the central place of Zion, and there the New Jerusalem will be built, and this will be just as soon as the Lord has a people prepared to make a Zion and a New Jerusalem there. "When the Lord shall build up Zion, he shall appear in his glory" (Psalm 102:16).

Some have asserted that the story of the fall is but a myth, or an allegory, but it is given in the Scriptures as part of the history of the human family, and must be either accepted as such, or rejected as fiction. The fall was as necessary for the development of the race as was the creation. The story of the first fall is, moreover, the story of every sin, Temptation begins with doubt as to the truth of the prohibition. "Has God said * * * ?" It is continued by a contemplation of the pleasure that may be derived from doing that which has been prohibited. It ends with a sense of shame and degradation and dread of the presence of God. Such is the beginning and development of every transgression.

There are many theories of the origin of sin. The Scriptures tell us that our first parents fell, and that sin thereby was introduced into the world. That there is sin in the world, cannot be denied. What is sin, then, and how did it happen to come among men? Where did it come from? Such are the questions asked by philosophy and theology alike. Some assume the existence of two eternal principles—one good and one evil, and they say that sin comes from the latter. Gnostics and Manichæans regarded matter as evil and sin as a result of the contact of the spirit with matter. Others have held that sin is merely an absence of good, a negation, a limitation. God, they say, is the one good Being, all others being inferior to Him in attributes, and, therefore, sinful.

"Evil is what is finite," says Baur. "If other beings than God are to exist, there must be in them, so far as they are not infinite as God is, for that very reason, a minimum of evil." Leibnitz holds that sin is due to the imperfection of all that is created. No created being can be perfect. His knowledge is limited and so is his power, and sin comes because of this necessary limitation. "Evil is hidden under good as under a mask." Another theory derives sin from selfishness, but fails to account for the origin of selfishness, which itself is sinful. Another theory holds that sin is necessary, since all men must be developed by antagonism, and a moral world without sin would be as a stagnant pool. Professor Muller characterized this theory as an approach to "pansatanism."

How different from all these speculations is the revealed truth! Man has free agency. This presupposes a law and freedom to obey or disobey. The law was given, and man, tempted by the fallen angel, disobeyed. Through Christ Jesus his redemption was accomplished, by which he regained infinitely more than he lost, and thus the fall, as someone has said, became a "fall upwards." Sin, in its outward manifestations, is the breaking of the law.

SECTION 30.

REVELATION *given through Joseph Smith the Prophet, to David Whitmer, Peter Whitmer, Jun., and John Whitmer, at Fayette, New York, September, 1830, following the three days' conference at Fayette, but before the Elders of the Church had separated. See History of the Church, vol. 1, p. 115.——Individual instruction is given, and the fact of Oliver Cowdery's mission to the Lamanites is reiterated.*

BEHOLD, I say unto you, David, that you have feared man and have not relied on me for strength as you ought.

2. But your mind has been on the things of the earth more than on the things of me, your Maker, and the ministry whereunto you have been called; and you have not given heed unto my Spirit, and to those who were set over you, but have been persuaded by those whom I have not commanded.

3. Wherefore, you are left to inquire for yourself at my hand, and ponder upon the things which you have received.

4. And your home shall be at your father's house, until I give unto you further commandments. And you shall attend to

the ministry in the church, and before the world, and in the regions round about. Amen.

There is some discrepancy in the records regarding the date of the second Conference of the Church, but Elder B. H. Roberts, in *History of the Church,* Vol. I., p. 110, gives sufficient reasons for accepting the 26th of September, 1830, rather than the first of that month, as the correct date. When this Conference convened, the question of the seer-stone of Hiram Page was discussed. The error was thoroughly exposed and acknowledged (Sec. 28:11), and harmony and unity were fully restored. The Saints partook of the Sacrament, and the Spirit of the Lord was poured out upon them in abundant measure. While the conference was still in session this Revelation and the following were received.

This Revelation contains three sections; one is addressed to David Whitmer, one to Peter Whitmer, Jr., and one to John Whitmer.

1-4. David Whitmer is mildly rebuked for listening to Hiram Page, and perhaps for using his influence over other members of the family in favor of the supposed seer-stone. He was told that he had feared man, and set his mind on earthly things, instead of taking care of the ministry and listening to the Spirit and the inspired Prophet, with the result that he had been left to inquire for himself; the Prophet could not inquire for him. He was also commanded to remain at home, until further instruction should be given, and confine his labors, for the time being, to the Church and the world in the neighborhood. Deviation from the narrow path always brings with it some consequences which remain after the sin has been pardoned. See also notes, Sec. 14.

5. Behold, I say unto you, Peter, that you shall take your journey with your brother Oliver; for the time has come that it is expedient in me that you shall open your mouth to declare my gospel; therefore, fear not, but give heed unto the words and advice of your brother, which he shall give you.

6. And be you afflicted in all his afflictions, ever lifting up your heart unto me in prayer and faith, for his and your deliverance; for I have given unto him power to build up my church among the Lamanites;

7. And none have I appointed to be his counselor over him in the church, concerning church matters, except it is his brother, Joseph Smith, Jun.

8. Wherefore, give heed unto these things and be diligent in keeping my commandments, and you shall be blessed unto eternal life. Amen.

5-8. **Peter Whitmer is not rebuked.** He, in all probability, was inno-cent in the matter of the seer-stone. He was called to go with Oliver Cowdery on the long and perilous mission to the Lamanites (Sec. 28:8), and he was admonished to give heed to him, follow his advice, share with him the trials and sufferings before him, and always pray and exercise faith. If he would do these things and keep God's command-ments, he would have eternal life. Missionary labor is complete only when the missionary is willing to follow counsel and keep the com-mandments of God. See notes, Sec. 16.

9. Behold, I say unto you, my servant John, that thou shalt commence from this time forth to proclaim my gospel, as with the voice of a trump.

10. And your labor shall be at your brother Philip Bur-roughs', and in that region round about, yea, wherever you can be heard, until I command you to go from hence.

11. And your whole labor shall be in Zion, with all your soul, from henceforth; yea, you shall ever open your mouth in my cause, not fearing what man can do, for I am with you. Amen.

9-11. **John Whitmer** is called at this time to labor especially among the Saints. He was very active in the Church as an aid to the Prophet. He assisted in the compilation of the Revelations, and accompanied Oliver Cowdery to Jackson County to superintend the printing of them. He was one of the seven High Priests appointed to preside in the Church in Jackson County. He was Church historian and editor of important Church publications. But he did not remain faithful. See notes Sec. 15.

SECTION 31.

REVELATION *given through Joseph Smith the Prophet, to Thomas B. Marsh, September, 1830. Thomas B. Marsh had been baptized earlier in the month, and had already been or-dained an Elder in the Church when this revelation was given.* ———*Commended for obedience and faithfulness—Assured as to the welfare of his family—Appointed to preach and administer—Promised the guidance of the Comforter in his ministry.*

THOMAS, my son, blessed are you because of your faith in my work.

2. Behold, you have had many afflictions because of your

family; nevertheless, I will bless you and your family, yea, your little ones; and the day cometh that they will believe and know the truth and be one with you in my church.

3. Lift up your heart and rejoice, for the hour of your mission is come; and your tongue shall be loosed, and you shall declare glad tidings of great joy unto this generation.

4. You shall declare the things which have been revealed to my servant, Joseph Smith, Jun. You shall begin to preach from this time forth, yea, to reap in the field which is white already to be burned.

5. Therefore, thrust in your sickle with all your soul, and your sins are forgiven you, and you shall be laden with sheaves upon your back, for the laborer is worthy of his hire. Wherefore, your family shall live.

6. Behold, verily I say unto you, go from them only for a little time, and declare my word, and I will prepare a place for them.

7. Yea, I will open the hearts of the people, and they will receive you. And I will establish a church by your hand;

8. And you shall strengthen them and prepare them against the time when they shall be gathered.

This Revelation was also received while the second Conference of the Church was in session. It was given for the benefit of Thomas B. Marsh especially.

Thomas B. Marsh was born at Acton, Mass., Nov. 1st, 1799. He came on a visit to Palmyra at the time when the Book of Mormon was being printed, and Martin Harris gave him a sheet containing the first sixteen pages of that book. He read these pages and showed them to his wife, and both received a testimony that the book was of God. When he learned that the Church had been organized, he moved to Palmyra and was baptized by David Whitmer. This was in the month of September, 1830, shortly before this Revelation was received. After a career of varied experiences, Marsh moved to Kirtland, where he was called to the Apostleship. In July and August, 1837, he accompanied the Prophet Joseph and Sidney Rigdon on a mission to Canada, and the following year he and David W. Patten were appointed presidents of the Church in Missouri, until the arrival of the Prophet. In August, 1838, a year of apostasy, he became disaffected and turned traitor to his brethren. He made an affidavit to the effect that the "Mormons" had a company called "Danites," organized for the purpose of murdering "enemies"—a statement he certainly knew to be false. After that he became a vagabond, without resting-place, without peace, for many years.

In 1857, he came to Salt Lake City, and asked forgiveness and reinstatement in the Church. President Young introduced him to the audience in the Bowery, on the 6th of September. He told the congregation that he had suffered greatly during his absence from the Church, but that he acknowledged the hand of the Lord in the chastisement he had received. He made the following significant remark concerning the beginning of his apostasy:

"I became jealous of the Prophet, and then I saw double and overlooked everything that was right, and spent all my time in looking for the evil. * * * I saw a beam in Brother Joseph's eye, but it was nothing but a mote, and my own eye was filled with the beam. * * * I talked with Brother Brigham and Brother Heber, and I wanted them to be mad like myself; and I saw they were not mad, and I got madder still because they were not. Brother Brigham, with a cautious look, said, 'are you the leader of the Church, Brother Thomas?' I answered, 'No!' 'Well then,' said he, 'Why do you not let that alone?' Well, this was about the amount of my hypocrisy. I meddled with that which was not my business" (*Journal of Discourses,* Vol. V., p. 207).

At the conclusion of his address he was by unanimous vote received into full fellowship as a member of the Church.

1. *Blessed are you because of your faith*] Thomas B. Marsh had embraced the gospel on the testimony of the Spirit concerning sixteen pages of the Book of Mormon, and he moved to Palmyra in order to join the Church. This was faith. Many "inquirers" cannot be moved, though they have an entire library from which to draw information. God commends him for his faith.

2. *You have had many afflictions*] The trials he had passed through, because of the unbelief of his relatives, were not unknown to his heavenly Father. "My Father knows!" This assurance was accompanied by the promise, "I bless you and your family." God blesses the families of his faithful servants. That is part of their reward. Children often owe their success in life to the faith of their parents. Israel was blessed because of the faith of Abraham, their ancestor.

3. *Your tongue shall be loosed*] As long as Thomas B. Marsh was faithful he was an eloquent speaker. At the time of the troubles in Clay County, Mo., he was elected a member of a committee to lay the grievances of the Saints before the authorities of the State. On that occasion he spoke so impressively that General Atchison, who was present, shed tears, and the meeting passed resolutions to assist the Saints in finding a new location.

4. *The things which have been revealed*] Marsh was here given his commission to preach the gospel as revealed through the Prophet.

Even as an Apostle of our Lord, he had no other commission. As long as he was faithful to this charge, he was singularly blessed, but when, through envy and pride, he turned away from the leadership of the Prophet, he fell.

7. *Establish a church by your hand*] Thomas B. Marsh was very active as a missionary, but whatever success he had was the work of God. No missionary has any reason to be proud, for he is but an instrument—a brush in the hand of an artist, a tool in the hand of an architect. Still, the divine Master-builder acknowledges the services of those through whose instrumentality His work is done.

8. *Strengthen them * * * they shall be gathered*] The principle of gathering had just been revealed (Sec. 29:2-8). Marsh was to be one of the servants of the Almighty whose duty it would be to strengthen and prepare the people for gathering. It takes both strength of character and preparation to gather to Zion, and this will be still more the case, when the City of Zion is to be built up, and the laws of God must be observed. Marsh, in the autumn of 1832, led a company of Saints to Jackson Co., Mo.

9. Be patient in afflictions, revile not against those that revile. Govern your house in meekness, and be steadfast.

10. Behold, I say unto you that you shall be a physician unto the church, but not unto the world, for they will not receive you.

11. Go your way whithersoever I will, and it shall be given you by the Comforter what you shall do and whither you shall go.

12. Pray always, lest you enter into temptation and lose your reward.

13. Be faithful unto the end, and lo, I am with you. These words are not of man nor of men, but of me, even Jesus Christ, your Redeemer, by the will of the Father. Amen.

9-13. The Lord here imparts special instructions for the guidance of His servant. Among these are:—Be patient in afflictions; revile not against those that revile; govern your house and be steadfast; pray always, lest you enter into temptation and lose your reward; and be faithful unto the end.

The Lord knew the dangers threatening Thomas B. Marsh and warned him of them.

General Notes

Thomas B. Marsh was commanded to govern his house in meekness, and to be steadfast. In this he utterly failed. And for that reason he apostatized and became active in drawing the mob against the Saints in Missouri, in persecution. George A. Smith, in an address delivered in Salt Lake City, April 6th, 1856, tells the story. When the Saints were living in Far West, the wife of Marsh and Sister Harris agreed to exchange milk, in order to enable each of them to make a larger cheese than they could do separately. Each was to take to the other the "strippings" as well as the rest of the milk. Mrs. Harris performed her part of the agreement, but Mrs. Marsh kept a pint of "strippings" from each cow. When this became known the matter was brought before the Teachers, and these decided against Mrs. Marsh. An appeal was taken to the Bishop. He sustained the Teachers. If Marsh had obeyed the Revelation and governed his house in humility and with steadfastness, he would have righted the wrong done, but, instead of doing so, he appealed to the High Council. Marsh, who at the time was President of the Twelve, possibly thought that the Council would favor him, but that body confirmed the Bishop's decision. He was not yet satisfied, but appealed to the First Presidency, and Joseph, the Prophet, and his two Counsellors consented to review the case. They approved the finding of the High Council. Was Marsh satisfied then? No. With the persistency of Lucifer himself, he declared that he would uphold the character of his wife, "even if he had to go to hell for it." Elder George A. Smith observes:

"The then President of the Twelve Apostles, the man who should have been the first to do justice and cause reparation to be made for wrong, committed by any member of his family, took that position, and what next? He went before a magistrate and swore that the 'Mormons' were hostile to the State of Missouri. That affidavit brought from the government of Missouri an exterminating order, which drove some 15,000 Saints from their homes and habitations, and some thousands perished through suffering the exposure consequent on this state of affairs" (*Journal of Discourses*, Vol. III., p. 284).

Marsh appears before us in the early history of the Church as a man of great faith. This attribute again became prominent, when, after many years of apostasy and suffering, he wended his way to Utah to confess his sins and ask for pardon. With all his efforts he could raise only five dollars and ten cents, and with this sum he started on his way from Harrison Co., Mo., to Salt Lake City. He looked at this money and said, "Lord, if you will help me, I will go." He says, "Before I got out of the State, the Lord had changed my fortune, and I had $65.05. I then concluded within myself that the Lord was with me."

At the time Marsh was reinstated as a member of the Church, President Brigham Young referred to the fact that Marsh said he was an old man. President Young said,

"Brother Thomas considers himself very aged and infirm, and you can see that he is, brethren and sisters! What is the cause of it? He left the gospel of salvation. What do you think is the difference between his age and mine? One year and seven months to a day; and he is one year, seven months, and fourteen days older than Brother Heber C. Kimball. 'Mormonism' keeps men and women young and handsome; and where they are full of the Spirit of God, there are none of them but will have a glow upon their countenances; and that is what makes you and me young; for the Spirit of God is with us, and within us" (*Journal of Discourses,* Vol. V., p. 210).

SECTION 32.

REVELATION *given through Joseph Smith the Prophet, to Parley P. Pratt and Ziba Peterson, October, 1830. Great interest and yearning desires were felt by the Elders respecting the Lamanites, of whose predicted blessings the Church had learned from the Book of Mormon. In consequence, supplication was made that the Lord would indicate his will as to whether Elders should be sent at that time to the Indian tribes in the West. The revelation followed. See History of the Church, vol. 1, p. 118.— The missionaries admonished to confine themselves to the expounding of the written word, as they shall be given understanding thereof.*

AND now concerning my servant Parley P. Pratt, behold, I say unto him that as I live I will that he shall declare my gospel and learn of me, and be meek and lowly of heart.

2. And that which I have appointed unto him is that he shall go with my servants, Oliver Cowdery and Peter Whitmer, Jun., into the wilderness among the Lamanites.

3. And Ziba Peterson also shall go with them; and I myself will go with them and be in their midst; and I am their advocate with the Father, and nothing shall prevail against them.

4. And they shall give heed to that which is written, and pretend to no other revelation; and they shall pray always that I may unfold the same to their understanding.

5. And they shall give heed unto these words and trifle not, and I will bless them. Amen.

Oliver Cowdery and Peter Whitmer had been called to go on a mission to the Lamanites (Sec. 28:8; 30:5). There was great interest among the Saints in this mission, for it was hoped that the time had come for the redemption of the scattered Remnant, according to the promises in the Book of Mormon (I Nephi 15:13-18, and many other places). The Prophet laid the matter before the Lord in prayer and received this Revelation, in which Parley P. Pratt and Ziba Peterson were called to join Oliver Cowdery and Peter Whitmer, Jr., on that important mission.

Parley P. Pratt was born on the 12th of April, 1807, in Burlington, N. Y., a descendant of a venerable Pilgrim family that came with the Rev. Thomas Hooker and settled at Hartford, Conn., 1636. In September, 1830, he started on a journey east from his home in Ohio and, in the providence of God, obtained a copy of the Book of Mormon. He believed and hastened to Palmyra to investigate. At Manchester he met Hyrum Smith, who related to him the wonderful story of the coming forth of that Book. In company with Hyrum Smith he went to Fayette, where he was baptized by Oliver Cowdery, in September, 1830. He now continued his journey eastward. His brother, Orson Pratt, heard the gospel and was baptized by him. Then he went back to Fayette, attended the Conference and received his call to go on a mission. Parley P. Pratt, previous to joining the Church, had identified himself with the Campbellite movement. After several successful missionary journeys, he was called to the Apostleship, in February, 1835, and in 1840 he accompanied Brigham Young and others to England, where he commenced the publication of the *Millennial Star*, at Manchester. In 1846 he again performed a mission to Great Britain, having left his family at Council Bluffs upon the broad prairie, without adequate shelter. The following year he came to Salt Lake Valley. In the year 1857, on the 13th of May, his earthly life of usefulness and self-sacrifice was ended. His *Voice of Warning* and *Key to Theology* are known wherever there are Latter-day Saints.

Of Ziba Peterson less is known. He* was baptized on the 18th of April, 1830, together with Peter Whitmer, Sen., Mary Whitmer, William Jolly, and Elizabeth Ann Whitmer, Oliver Cowdery officiating. He went on a mission to the Lamanites, but, unfortunately, afterwards, he proved himself unworthy of being entrusted with further responsibilities, and the Lord commanded that that which had been bestowed upon him be taken away (Sec. 58:60). He had committed sins in secret, and refused to confess them.

---

* In the Church History there appears among the names of those baptized on that date that of Richard B. Peterson. In the "Historical Record" the name is Richard Z. Peterson. In the Revelations we have Ziba Peterson.

1. *Be meek and lowly*] Parley P. Pratt, just before joining the Church, had decided to become a Campbellite preacher, and needed this admonition. The great majority of preachers are too proud to receive instruction from the servants of the Lord. Their attitude towards the gospel is one of assumed hauteur. Christ was "meek and lowly in heart" (Matt. 11:29), and His disciples must learn of Him.

3. *I am their advocate*] A most delicate warning to Ziba Peterson especially, to beware of sin. For this expression is found in a passage of the New Testament which reads, "My little children, these things write I unto you, that ye sin not. And if any man sin, we have an advocate with the Father, Jesus Christ, the righteous (I. John 2:1). The very mention of the word "advocate" should have called to his mind the preceding warning, "Sin not." It should also have reminded him that, if he should be overcome and fall, it would not be necessary to remain in sin, for we have an Advocate with the Father. An "advocate" is one who acts as the spokesman, or intercessor, for another, Christ intercedes for the repentant sinner. The Spirit also "maketh intercession" for us (Rom. 8:26). Against these divine Advocates "nothing shall prevail."

4. *Give heed to that which is written*] This is another admonition not to go beyond the written word or pretend to receive or accept false revelation.

GENERAL NOTES

Concerning the mission to the Lamanites, Oliver Cowdery wrote from Kaw Township, Mo., May 7th, 1831:—

"Brother Ziba Peterson and myself went into the county east, which is Lafayette, about forty miles; and in the name of Jesus, we called on the people to repent, many of whom are, I believe, earnestly searching for truth, and if sincerely, I pray they may find that precious treasure, for it seems to be wholly fallen in the streets; and equity cannot enter. The letter we received from you, informed us that the opposition was great against you. Now, our beloved brethren, we verily believe that we also can rejoice that we are counted worthy to suffer shame for His name; for almost the whole country, consisting of Universalists, Atheists, Deists, Presbyterians, Methodists, Baptists, and other professed Christians, priests and people, with all the devils from the eternal pit, are united and foaming out their shame [against us]. God forbid that I should bring a railing accusation against them, for vengeance belongeth to Him who is able to repay" (*History of the Church*, Vol. I., p. 182).

Parley P. Pratt was admonished to be meek and lowly of heart. In the year 1837, there were "jarrings and discord" in the Church at Kirtland, and he was overcome with that spirit. He even tried to turn John Taylor from the Prophet by pointing out to him what he regarded as Joseph's error. Elder Taylor rebuked him as a brother, and Parley P.

Pratt went to the Prophet in tears and confessed his sin, whereupon the Prophet frankly forgave him, prayed with him, and blessed him. This was meekness. It was also manliness. Only a really strong character can possess true humility.

SECTION 33.

REVELATION *given through Joseph Smith the Prophet, to Ezra Thayre and Northrop Sweet, at Fayette, New York, October, 1830. In recording this revelation the Prophet avers that the Lord is ever ready to instruct such as diligently seek in faith. ——The corrupted state of the world declared—Call for laborers in the ministry—Bringing forth of the Church from the wilderness and its establishment by the Lord—Commission of the Elders to proclaim repentance and baptism—Imminence of the Lord's coming.*

BEHOLD, I say unto you, my servants Ezra and Northrop, open ye your ears and hearken to the voice of the Lord your God, whose word is quick and powerful, sharper than a two-edged sword, to the dividing asunder of the joints and marrow, soul and spirit; and is a discerner of the thoughts and intents of the heart.

2. For verily, verily, I say unto you that ye are called to lift up your voices as with the sound of a trump, to declare my gospel unto a crooked and perverse generation.

3. For behold, the field is white already to harvest; and it is the eleventh hour, and the last time that I shall call laborers into my vineyard.

4. And my vineyard has become corrupted every whit; and there is none which doeth good save it be a few; and they err in many instances because of priestcrafts, all having corrupt minds.

5. And verily, verily, I say unto you, that this church have I established and called forth out of the wilderness.

6. And even so will I gather mine elect from the four quarters of the earth, even as many as will believe in me, and hearken unto my voice.

7. Yea, verily, verily, I say unto you, that the field is white already to harvest; wherefore, thrust in your sickles, and reap with all your might, mind, and strength.

8. Open your mouths and they shall be filled, and you shall become even as Nephi of old, who journeyed from Jerusalem in the wilderness.

9. Yea, open your mouths and spare not, and you shall be laden with sheaves upon your backs, for lo, I am with you.

In this Revelation the Lord calls Ezra Thayre and Northrop Sweet to missionary labors. It contains (1) a description of the condition in which the world is, and urges them to go to work (2-9); (2) states what they should preach (10-12); (3) gives special instructions relating to the ministry (13-18).

1. *Open ye your ears and hearken*] Only he whose ears are open to hear the voice of God and who is willing to obey, is qualified to be a messenger of the Almighty. God's ambassadors must be in touch with Him and know His will at all times.

Quick and powerful] See Sec. 6:2.

Soul and spirit] The union of the spirit and the body is the soul (Sec. 88:15), and, if that definition is the only one, the expression is somewhat difficult to analyze. But "soul" also means "life," and this seems to be the meaning here.

2. *Perverse generation*] Our Lord employed this expression, when He came down from the Mountain of Transfiguration and saw how weak in faith were His disciples, how great power the demons had over a human being, and how senseless were the disputations of the scribes and Pharisees in view of the actual condition of the people.

3. *It is the eleventh hour*] This expression is from Matt. 20:6. Our Lord had taught the Twelve that it was almost impossible for a rich man to enter the Kingdom of Heaven. Then the disciples said, in substance, "We, at any rate, left all and followed Thee; what shall our reward be?" Christ's answer was the parable of the Laborers in the Vineyard, in which He taught them that all His servants should have a great reward, but that those who are called last will receive just as much as the first. The time in which we live is the eleventh hour, and those who obey the call now will receive just as much as the laborers of former dispensations. The reward which God gives is not on the same basis as that which obtains in the world of industry among men. It is, after all, a gift. "The *wages* of sin is death; but the *gift* of God is eternal life through Jesus Christ our Lord" (Rom. 6:23). "The wage at best is a free gift; for on the basis of strict accounting who of us is not in debt to God?" (Dr. James E. Talmage, *Jesus the Christ*, p. 482).

4. *Corrupted every whit*] "Whit" means a very small part of a thing, a particle, and when the Lord says that His vineyard has become corrupted, "every whit," He teaches us that the corruption is total: that there is not a spot in all the world that has not been affected by the apostasy from His sovereignty. Hence the urgent necessity of faithful laborers at this, the eleventh and last hour.

Many object to the teachings of the gospel on the subject of the deviation from the original pattern. They take exception to the picture of total corruption presented but this only confirms the truth of the gospel. We have in holy writ successive portraits of human nature taken at various times. One was taken before the deluge: "All flesh had corrupted his way upon the earth" (Gen. 6:12). Another is presented by Eliphaz, in Job: "Man, which drinketh iniquity like water" (Job 15:16). David viewed the conditions in this light: "The Lord looked down from heaven upon the children of men, to see if there were any that did understand, and seek God. They are all gone aside; they are all together become filthy; there is none that doeth good, no, not one" (Psalm 14:2, 3). Paul, in his day, repeats this and draws a terrible picture of man outside the influence of the gospel (Rom. 3:10-18). "There is," he says, "no fear of God before their eyes." The picture presented in the Revelations given in our day has the same features. "They [the sects] were all wrong." "My vineyard has been corrupted, every whit." Let the reader compare these statements with those quoted from the Bible, and he will feel convinced that they originated in the same source—the Foundation of truth. The purpose of God in presenting these pictures is to call men to repentance. Even those who are doing good, according to the best of their understanding, err in many respects because of "priestcraft."

6. *Mine elect*] The "elect" are those who "will believe in me, and hearken unto my voice." The Lord regards the "will," the "desire" of man. Many are prevented from believing and obeying the gospel, by ignorance or prejudices. But they are honest, even in their mistakes and errors. Such will eventually be brought to a knowledge of the truth. All who will believe and obey are the "elect.'

7. *The field is white already to harvest*] When our Lord uttered these memorable words to His first disciples (John 4:35), He was sitting at the famous well, near Sychar (the modern Nablus). He had had a "gospel conversation" with a Samaritan woman, and she had gone into the City and told the people of that wonderful conversation. The people were hastening to the well. It was at this moment that our Lord noticed the Samaritans coming over the fields, and called the attention of the disciples to the approaching multitude: "Lift up your eyes and look on the fields; for they are white already to harvest." Christ saw in the flocking of these Samaritans to him the beginning of an abundant harvest of souls. So there was, in the first conversions, in our dispensation, an

assurance of an abundant harvest. There was no reason to hesitate to go to work.

8. *As Nephi of old*] This is a promise that if they would "open their mouths," that is, consecrate their gift of speech to the service of the Lord, He would accept them and make them as Nephi of old, who was a leader of men, because of his faith and obedience. The promise is repeated in verse 9.

10. Yea, open your mouths and they shall be filled, saying: Repent, repent, and prepare ye the way of the Lord, and make his paths straight; for the kingdom of heaven is at hand;

11. Yea, repent and be baptized, every one of you, for a remission of your sins; yea, be baptized even by water, and then cometh the baptism of fire and of the Holy Ghost.

12. Behold, verily, verily, I say unto you, this is my gospel; and remember that they shall have faith in me or they can in nowise be saved;

10-12. The servants of the Lord are here instructed what to preach to the world. This is their message:

10. (1) *Repent*] This is the *alpha and omega* of their mission (see Sec. 3:20; 6:9; 11:9; 15:6, etc.).

(2) *Prepare the way of the Lord*] Eastern potentates, when traveling from one part of the kingdom to another, would proclaim their coming and order their subjects to prepare the way for them, by building roads where there were none, if necessary; by leveling hills and filling up depressions, and straightening out the winding paths. Semiramis is said to have had roads constructed especially for her journeys. In modern times the Turkish government built a good road from Jaffa to Jerusalem, when the German Emperor signified his intention of visiting the Holy City. To prepare the way of the Lord and make His paths straight is to acknowledge His sovereignty and to make all necessary preparations for His reception. He will not come to reign until all necessary preparations for his coming have been made. "Hear this, O Earth! The Lord will not come to reign over the righteous, in this world, in 1843 [as was expected by Miller] nor until everything for the Bridegroom is ready" (Joseph Smith, *History of the Church,* Vol. V., p. 291).

11. (4) *Be baptized*] Baptism for the remission of sins is a necessary part of the preparation.

(5) Baptism "of fire and the Holy Ghost" is equally necessary. Baptism in water and in that fire which is "holy spirit" is but one baptism. Any ceremony which does not embrace both is empty and void.

12. (6) *They shall have faith in me*] Faith is also necessary, for without faith there is no salvation. "Faith comes by hearing the word of God, through the testimony of the servants of God" (Joseph Smith, *History of the Church,* Vol. III., p. 379).

These six subjects embrace the entire gospel. Repentance, acceptance of Christ as the Sovereign whose coming is near, baptism in water, reception of the Holy Ghost, and faith form the complete and perfect basis of true religion.

13. And upon this rock I will build my church; yea, upon this rock ye are built, and if ye continue, the gates of hell shall not prevail against you.

14. And ye shall remember the church articles and covenants to keep them.

15. And whoso having faith you shall confirm in my church, by the laying on of the hands, and I will bestow the gift of the Holy Ghost upon them.

16. And the Book of Mormon and the holy scriptures are given of me for your instruction; and the power of my Spirit quickeneth all things.

17. Wherefore, be faithful, praying always, having your lamps trimmed and burning, and oil with you, that you may be ready at the coming of the Bridegroom—

18. For behold, verily, verily, I say unto you, that I come quickly. Even so. Amen.

Upon this rock] The Lord reveals in this verse that it was not on Peter, but upon the rock of revelation that he built His church. President George A. Smith, counselor to President Brigham Young, in a discourse delivered June 24, 1855, said:

" * * * But, says the Savior, 'Whom do you say that I am?' Why, says Peter: 'Thou art the Christ the Son of the living God.' The Savior replied, 'Blessed art thou, Simon Barjona, for flesh and blood hath not revealed this unto thee, but my Father who is in heaven; I say unto thee thou art Peter, and upon this rock will I build my Church, and the gates of hell shall not prevail against it.'

"This argument would be introduced by those who believe that Christ built His church upon St. Peter, and you then come to read the passage, and what do you learn by it? You simply learn that Peter had made the discovery, by revelation, that Jesus was the Son of the living God, and that upon the rock (revelation) He (Christ) would build His church, and upon nothing else, and that the gates of hell should not prevail against it." (George A. Smith, Tabernacle, June 24, 1855.)

Gates of hell] See Sec. 10:69.

The special instructions here given to Ezra Thayre and Northrop Sweet are of general application. Remember the Church articles and covenants to keep them (14); confirm those who have faith (15); seek knowledge by studying the Book of Mormon and the Bible (16); be faithful, prayerful, prepared to meet the Savior (17).

18. The Revelation ends with the same assurance that our Lord gave to John on Patmos, "I come quickly."

At that time He came in judgment upon an apostate church in the form of invasions from Asia, by which the candlesticks were removed and the world was plunged in darkness. Again the Lord's voice is heard, "I come quickly." This time He is coming to sit in judgment upon the nations and lay the foundations for His Millennial reign.

Northrop Sweet, it seems, notwithstanding this Revelation, very soon joined Wycom Clark and four other individuals and formed what they called "The Pure Church of Christ." Their organization did not live long.

SECTION 34.

REVELATION *given through Joseph Smith the Prophet, to Orson Pratt, at Fayette, New York, November 4, 1830. The recipient was nineteen years old at the time. He had been converted and baptized when he first heard the preaching of the restored Gospel by his brother, Parley P. Pratt, six weeks before. See History of the Church, vol. 1, p. 127.——Commended for obedience—Commanded to preach and to prophesy as the Holy Ghost shall give utterance—Certainty of the Lord's advent.*

MY son Orson, hearken and hear and behold what I, the Lord God, shall say unto you, even Jesus Christ your Redeemer;

2. The light and the life of the world, a light which shineth in darkness and the darkness comprehendeth it not;

3. Who so loved the world that he gave his own life, that as many as would believe might become the sons of God. Wherefore you are my son;

4. And blessed are you because you have believed;

5. And more blessed are you because you are called of me to preach my gospel—

6. To lift up your voice as with the sound of a trump, both

long and loud, and cry repentance unto a crooked and perverse generation, preparing the way of the Lord for his second coming.

7. For behold, verily, verily, I say unto you, the time is soon at hand that I shall come in a cloud with power and great glory.

8. And it shall be a great day at the time of my coming, for all nations shall tremble.

About this time Orson Pratt came to Fayette. He was then only 19 years of age, having been born on the 19th of September, 1811. His brother Parley had told him of the Book of Mormon and he had accepted the message and been baptized, on the 19th of September, 1830, his birthday. Orson was a studious boy, but, like Abraham Lincoln, he was under the necessity of relying mainly upon his own resources. He paid special attention to mathematics, grammar, geography, surveying, etc. In later years he delved into the mysteries of astronomy, theology, and languages, and became one of the most profound thinkers and logical speakers and writers of the early days of the Church.

As stated, Orson Pratt had just become a member of the Church, and he now came to Fayette to inquire of the Lord, through the Prophet, about the will of the Lord concerning him. This Revelation was then received, in which (1) he was called to preach the gospel (1-8); (2) was given some signs by which to know that the coming of the Lord was near (9); and (3) was assured of divine assistance, on condition of faithfulness.

1-3. The Lord first introduces Himself as Jesus Christ, the Redeemer, the Light and the Life of the world; the Light which shineth in darkness, though the darkness does not comprehend it; and He who so loved the world that He gave His own life. These are reasons why we should hearken to Him, when He speaks. See also Sec. 6:21; 11:30.

1. *Redeemer*] Christ is our Redeemer. Redemption means deliverance by means of ransom. There is a deliverance from *guilt* (Eph. 1:7; Col. 1:14); from the power and dominance of *sin,* through the sanctifying influence of the Holy Spirit (I. Peter 1:18); and from *death* through the resurrection (Rom. 8:23). There is, finally, a deliverance from all evil (Eph. 1:14; 4:30; I. Cor. 1:30; Titus 2:14). All this is the work of Christ, through obedience to the gospel.

4-5. *Blessed are you*] Doubly blessed is he who accepts the Redeemer, through faith, and who is called to proclaim Him to the world. Living faith must precede the call to the ministry. God does not call unbelievers to preach the gospel. Blessed is he who believes and is called to preach. The reverse of this is, Wo to him who preaches without being authorized to do so.

"The ordinances of the gospel, being of divine origin, require divine authority in their administration. * * * No company, firm, society, court, or government would acknowledge or become responsible for the acts of any but its duly appointed and properly accredited agents. Why, then, should the great King endorse the doings of men who take upon themselves duties not required of them, or bestow, through their unauthorized performance, blessings that only belong to the administrations of His chosen ambassadors?" (Charles W. Penrose).

The following trenchant comments on Heb. 5:4, dealing with authority, are recommended to the thoughtful and intelligent reader:

"We have here the second qualification for Priesthood. A man's own caprice must not be the bishop which ordains him. He must be conscious of a divine call. Great stress is laid on this point in Scripture (Ex. 28:1). 'Any stranger that cometh nigh'—i.e., that intruded unbidden into the Priesthood—was to be put to death (Num. 3:10). The fate of Korah and his company (Num. 16:40), and of Uzziah, king though he was (II. Chron. 26:18-21), served as a terrible warning, and it was recorded as a special aggravation of Jeroboam's impiety that 'he made priests of the lowest of the people, which were not of the sons of Levi' (I. Kings 12:31). In one of the Jewish Midrashim, Moses says to Korah, 'If Aaron, my brother, had *taken upon himself* the priesthood, ye would be excusable for murmuring against him; but God gave it to him'" (Dean Farrar, Hebrews, Cambridge Bible, p. 97).

"Whenever men can find out the will of God and find an administrator legally authorized from God, there is the kingdom of God; but where these are not, the kingdom of God is not. All the ordinances, systems, and administrations on the Earth are of no use to the children of men, unless they are ordained and authorized of God; for nothing will save a man but a legal administrator; for none others will be acknowledged either by God or angels" (Joseph Smith, *History of the Church*, Vol. V., p. 259).

6. *Both long and loud*] Orson Pratt's mission was not to be obscure or of short duration. He was to be heard throughout the world, as the silver trumpets of the sons of Aaron were heard throughout the camp of Israel (Num. 10:2), and his ministry was to be "long." This was literally fulfilled. Orson Pratt was ordained an Elder on Dec. 1st, 1830, not quite three months after his baptism, and went immediately on a mission to Colesville. From that day until his death, Oct. 3rd, 1881, in Salt Lake City, his life was that of a missionary. From April 26th, 1835, he was a member of the Council of Twelve, holding that exalted position for 46 years—longer than any of the other Apostles appointed in 1835. And during this ministry he became generally known as the champion of the Church. This prediction, therefore, came true to the letter.

Preparing the way of the Lord for His coming] This was Orson Pratt's mission. In his sermons and writings, the dominant note is always the coming of the Lord. "Divine Authority," "Kingdom of God," "Authenticity of the Book of Mormon," "New Jerusalem," "The First

Principles of the Gospel"—such are the themes to which he recurs again and again in writing and speech, as a bee to a beautiful field of flowers, returning each time with sweet honey.

8. *My coming*] The day of the Lord is a day in which the nations shall "tremble." The explanation of their fear is found in the next paragraph, which gives some of the signs that, to the watcher, indicate the coming of the day of the Lord.

9. But before that great day shall come, the sun shall be darkened, and the moon be turned into blood; and the stars shall refuse their shining, and some shall fall, and great destructions await the wicked.

The sun shall be darkened, etc.] See Sec. 29:14. When thrones begin to fall and the kingdoms are torn to pieces, the coming of the Lord is near.

10. Wherefore, lift up your voice and spare not, for the Lord God hath spoken; therefore prophesy, and it shall be given by the power of the Holy Ghost.

11. And if you are faithful, behold, I am with you until I come—

12. And verily, verily, I say unto you, I come quickly. I am your Lord and your Redeemer. Even so. Amen.

10. *Wherefore lift up your voice*] Because the day of the Lord is near, preach, and "spare not;" that is, do not be "sparing," or niggard, in preaching the gospel. Preach it in season, out of season (II. Tim. 4:2).

Prophesy] To prophesy is to speak in the name of the Lord, whether the message relates to the future, the present, or the past. It is the testimony of Jesus that is the spirit of prophecy (Rev. 19:10). He who has that testimony is a prophet, and a "fellow servant" of the messengers, or angels, who come from the presence of God.

11. *If you are faithful*] Orson Pratt was faithful. In the obituary the Editor of the *Deseret News* said:

"Orson Pratt was a true Apostle of the Lord. Full of integrity, firm as a rock to his convictions, true to his brethren and his God, earnest and zealous in defense and the proclamation of the truth, ever ready to bear testimony to the Latter-day work, he had a mind stored with Scripture, ancient and modern, was an eloquent speaker, a powerful minister, a logical and convincing writer, an honest man and a great soul who reached out after eternal things, grasped them with the gift of inspiration, and brought them down to the level and comprehension of the common mind. Thousands have been brought into the Church through his preaching in many lands, thousands more by his writings. He set but little store on the wealth of this world, but he has laid up treasures in heaven which will make him eternally rich."

12. *I come quickly*]. See Sec. 33:18.

GENERAL NOTES

One truly amusing incident in the remarkable career of Orson Pratt may be recalled, viz., his debate with Dr. J. P. Newman. There has always been an impression in the world that the "Mormons" are ignorant. Dr. Newman thought so, too, and decided to display his learning in their midst. He came from Washington to Salt Lake City for the express purpose of engaging in a public debate with President Brigham Young, and he fairly seemed to gloat over the prospect of overwhelming him in an argument. Newman was the chaplain of the United States Senate. Brigham Young accepted the challenge and selected Orson Pratt to represent him. The Tabernacle was filled during three sessions, on the 12th, 13th, and 14th of August, 1870. Dr. Newman in his first address, fairly bristled with Greek, probably in order to impress the audience. In his second address he resorted to Hebrew, confident that he would have the field all to himself. To his astonishment Orson Pratt followed him, went into the argument and tore Dr. Newman's Hebrew and exegesis all to pieces. The learned gentleman from Washington had made himself ridiculous. He did not know that Orson Pratt had studied Hebrew in the school of the Elders at Kirtland under a competent instructor.

SECTION 35.

REVELATION *given to Joseph Smith the Prophet, and Sidney Rigdon, December, 1830. As a preface to his record of this revelation the Prophet wrote: In December Sidney Rigdon came to inquire of the Lord, and with him came Edward Partridge; the latter was a pattern of piety, and one of the Lord's great men. See History of the Church, vol. 1, p. 128.——How men may become sons of God—Sidney is promised that through him the Holy Ghost shall be given, as by the Apostles of old—Directed to assist the Prophet Joseph, and assured of the eventual redemption of Israel.*

LISTEN to the voice of the Lord your God, even Alpha and Omega, the beginning and the end, whose course is one eternal round, the same today as yesterday, and forever.

2. I am Jesus Christ, the Son of God, who was crucified for the sins of the world, even as many as will believe on my name, that they may become the sons of God, even one in me as I am one in the Father, as the Father is one in me, that we may be one.

Sidney Rigdon, who became noted in Church history, was born in Saint Claire, Pa., Feb. 19th, 1793. At the age of 25 years he joined a Baptist church. In 1819 he obtained a license as a minister, and a couple of years later he received a call to take charge of a church at Pittsburg, Pa. While engaged in this ministry, he became convinced that some of the doctrines of the Baptists were not Scriptural, and he resigned his position and joined his brother-in-law in the tanning business. At this time he became acquainted with Alexander Campbell, the reputed founder of the church known as "Disciples," or "Campbellites," and with one Mr. Walter Scott, and these three started that religious movement. Rigdon left Pittsburg and went to Bainbridge, and later to Mentor, preaching faith, repentance, baptism by immersion for the remission of sins, and righteous conduct. He had many adherents.

In the fall of 1830, Parley P. Pratt, Ziba Peterson, Oliver Cowdery, and Peter Whitmer, Jr., who were on their mission to the Lamanites, called at the house of Sidney Rigdon, and Parley P. Pratt, who knew him, presented him a copy of the Book of Mormon and related its story. He believed and was baptized, as were many members of his church in that vicinity. Sidney Rigdon and Edward Partridge shortly afterwards went to Fayette for the purpose of visiting the Prophet and learning something about the will of God concerning them.

Sidney Rigdon accompanied the Prophet to Ohio, visited Missouri, suffered persecution at Hiram, Ohio, received wonderful manifestations in Kirtland, labored as counselor in the First Presidency, visited Canada and the Eastern States, shared prison at Liberty with the Prophet, went to Washington on behalf of the persecuted Saints, and assisted in building up the Church. Unfortunately, he did not endure to the end. When the crucial trial came, he proved himself untrue and sought to lead the Saints astray. After the death of the Prophet he aspired to the leadership of the Church and refused to submit to the decision of the Apostles, which had been sustained by the people, and because he continued his agitation he was excommunicated by the High Council in Nauvoo, Sept. 8th, 1844. He died outside the Church on the 14th of July, 1876.

In this Revelation to Sidney Rigdon the Lord (1) introduces Himself, as He had done in the Revelation to Orson Pratt, and others (1, 2); then (2) He explains the difference between the ministry in which Rigdon had been engaged and that to which he would be called now (3-6); the Lord, next (3), sets before him what the true gospel is and the fruits of it (7-19); then follows (4) the divine appointment of Sidney Rigdon to his place in the Church (20-23). The Revelation closes (5) with promises to Sidney Rigdon and the Saints generally (24-27).

1. *Listen to the voice of the Lord your God*] Who is He that commands attention in these Revelations? The Lord your God, even He who spoke to John on Patmos, in the marvelous revelations recorded in the Apocalypse; whose course is "one eternal round," unchangeable as the courses of the worlds in their orbits.

2. *I am Jesus Christ*] Jesus is both the Son of God and God (v. 1). This is the doctrine of Paul, who calls Him, "Our great God and Savior, Jesus Christ" (Titus 2:13, Revised Version). It is the doctrine of the Book of Mormon: "Because he dwelleth in the flesh, he shall be called the Son of God: and having subjected the flesh to the will of the Father, being the Father and the Son; the Father because he was conceived by the power of God; and the Son, because of the flesh; thus becoming the Father and Son; and they are one God, yea, the very eternal Father of heaven and earth" (Mosiah 15:2-4). Jesus, being the Son of God, partakes of the nature of God.

*Crucified for the sins of the world, * * * name*] For whom did Christ die? is a much-discussed question. Some hold, with Augustine, that God elected a certain number of the human race, and that our Lord died for them only. Opponents of this doctrine maintain that He, through His death, made it possible for all to gain salvation. In this Revelation we learn that Christ was crucified for the sins of the whole world, but that only those who believe on His name become the "sons of God."

Sin is a matter which concerns the individual. We are taught in the Second Article of Faith that men will be punished for their own sins and not for Adam's transgression. It would be contrary to the law of justice to punish all of Adam's posterity for his sin, although this doctrine has prevailed in the world in the midst of its spiritual darkness. While it is true, that we all partake of the mortal death because of the fall, this death is not a sin and from it we are redeemed by our Savior Jesus Christ.

"For as death hath passed upon all men, to fulfill the merciful plan of the great Creator, there must needs be a power of resurrection, and the resurrection must needs come unto man by reason of the fall; and the fall came by reason of transgression; and because man became fallen they were cut off from the presence of the Lord.

"Wherefore, it must needs be an infinite atonement—save it should be an infinite atonement this corruption could not put on incorruption. Wherefore, the first judgment which came upon man must needs have remained to an endless duration. And if so, this flesh must have laid down to rot and to crumble to its mother earth, to rise no more. * * *

"O how great the goodness of our God, who prepareth a way for our escape from the grasp of this awful monster; yea, that monster, death and hell, which I call the death of the body, and also the death of the spirit.

"And because of the way of deliverance of our God, the Holy One of

Israel, this death, of which I have spoken, which is the temporal, shall deliver up its dead; which death is the grave." (2 Nephi 9:6-11.)

One in me] The oneness of the Saints of God with their Redeemer is the same as that of the Son with the Father. Concerning this divine unity John Taylor writes:

" 'His name shall be called Immanuel,' which being interpreted is, 'God with us.' Hence He is not only called the Son of God, the First Begotten of the Father, the Well Beloved, the Head, Ruler, and Dictator of all things, Jehovah, the I Am, the Alpha and Omega, but He is also called the very Eternal Father. Does not this mean that in Him were the attributes and power of the very Eternal Father?" (*Mediation and Atonement,* p. 138).

3. Behold, verily, verily, I say unto my servant Sidney, I have looked upon thee and thy works. I have heard thy prayers, and prepared thee for a greater work.

4. Thou art blessed, for thou shalt do great things. Behold thou wast sent forth, even as John, to prepare the way before me, and before Elijah which should come, and thou knewest it not.

5. Thou didst baptize by water unto repentance, but they received not the Holy Ghost;

6. But now I give unto thee a commandment, that thou shalt baptize by water, and they shall receive the Holy Ghost by the laying on of the hands, even as the apostles of old.

3-6. Here the Lord gives Sidney Rigdon to understand that his efforts as a minister, previous to his acceptance of the gospel, had not been in vain. The eye of the Lord had been upon him, and his prayers had been heard; wherefore now he was prepared to do greater work. The Church of Jesus Christ is infinitely greater than any mere human organization. Sidney Rigdon had been sent forth, as this Revelation states, even as John the Baptist, to prepare the way before the Lord. There have been many forerunners of the great Latter-day work. The reformers who broke the chains of tyranny; Columbus, who discovered a new world where the oppressed of all nations might find a refuge; the Pilgrim Fathers, who laid the solid foundations of a great, free nation; the authors of the Constitution that guaranteed the freedom the Fathers had come to the New World to enjoy; and, finally, the heroes who fought and died for the right of man—all were forerunners of the Church and Kingdom of our Lord.

Sidney Rigdon had been baptized in water unto repentance; he was now to baptize and to impart the Holy Ghost by the laying on of hands

(v. 5). The "Holy Ghost" in this paragraph is the same as the "Holy Spirit."

"The terms are frequently used synonymously. We often say the Spirit of God when we mean the Holy Ghost; we likewise say the Holy Ghost when we mean the Spirit of God. The Holy Ghost is a personage in the Godhead, and is not that which lighteth every man that comes into the world" (President Joseph F. Smith).

7. And it shall come to pass that there shall be a great work in the land, even among the Gentiles, for their folly and their abominations shall be made manifest in the eyes of all people.

8. For I am God, and mine arm is not shortened; and I will show miracles, signs, and wonders, unto all those who believe on my name.

9. And whoso shall ask it in my name in faith, they shall cast out devils; they shall heal the sick; they shall cause the blind to receive their sight, and the deaf to hear, and the dumb to speak, and the lame to walk.

10. And the time speedily cometh that great things are to be shown forth unto the children of men;

11. But without faith shall not anything be shown forth except desolations upon Babylon, the same which has made all nations drink of the wine of the wrath of her fornication.

12. And there are none that doeth good except those who are ready to receive the fulness of my gospel, which I have sent forth unto this generation.

13. Wherefore, I call upon the weak things of the world, those who are unlearned and despised, to thrash the nations by the power of my Spirit;

14. And their arm shall be my arm, and I will be their shield and their buckler; and I will gird up their loins, and they shall fight manfully for me; and their enemies shall be under their feet; and I will let fall the sword in their behalf, and by the fire of mine indignation will I preserve them.

15. And the poor and the meek shall have the gospel preached unto them, and they shall be looking forth for the time of my coming, for it is nigh at hand—

16. And they shall learn the parable of the fig-tree, for even now already summer is nigh.

17. And I have sent forth the fulness of my gospel by the hand of my servant Joseph; and in weakness have I blessed him;

18. And I have given unto him the keys of the mystery of those things which have been sealed, even things which were from the foundation of the world, and the things which shall come from this time until the time of my coming, if he abide in me, and if not, another will I plant in his stead.

19. Wherefore, watch over him that his faith fail not, and it shall be given by the Comforter, the Holy Ghost, that knoweth all things.

7-19. Here we learn what the gospel is and what some of its fruits are.

7. *There shall be a great work in the land*] God, from the very beginning, declared that the work to which He had selected the Prophet Joseph would be "great." This truth is already realized. But it is, as yet, only in its beginning. It will, ultimately, fill the world, as the stone in the dream of Nebuchadnezzar.

Among the Gentiles] "Gentiles" means "nations," as distinct from the Jews. It is the *goyim* of the Hebrews—a term applied to all outside the Mosaic faith. In the Church literature "Gentile" is not a term of disrespect, but merely one of convenience. It is not used frequently in our day.

*Their folly * * * manifest*] See Section 84:117.

8. *I will show miracles*] The preaching of the gospel was accompanied by miraculous manifestations. In the New Testament there are four words denoting such manifestations. In Mark 5:30 there is a word meaning "power" (*dynamis*), which has also been translated "virtue." It is the same as "miracles" in this paragraph. Another word is *semeia*, rendered "signs," and another, *terata*, translated "wonders." Miracles, or "powers," are "mighty works," such as God alone can do. When they are viewed as proofs of the divine authority of those through whom they are performed, they are called "signs." When regarded as miraculous manifestations, they are said to be "wonders." John frequently calls miracles the "works" (*erga*) of God (John 6:28), for miracles are but ordinary works to Him.

Unto all those who believe] Miracles are not given as a foundation for faith, but to confirm the faith that has been built already upon the Word of God. The promise is given that those who, in faith, ask for the gift of miracles shall cast out devils and heal the sick, but without faith no other miraculous manifestation shall be given than the desolation of Babylon. That, according to God's unchangeable decree, will come to pass, whether anybody believes it, or not.

9. *Cast out devils*] "Devils" here means demons, or evil spirits in the service of the Devil, the fallen angel. The Jews, anciently, believed that physical and mental derangements, such as insanity, melancholia, etc., were due to the possession of the afflicted individual, by evil spirits. In Luke 8:31 demons are said to supplicate our Lord not to command them to "go out into the deep"—the *tehom,* or abyss, of Gen. 1:2; the "bottomless pit" of Rev. 9:1—the cold, empty space, without a resting-place. They preferred an abode in the material creation, no matter where; even the body of an unclean animal was acceptable.

11. *Babylon*] "Babylon" is the name the Prophets give to the capital of the domain of antichrist, because ancient Babylon represented the power under which the Hebrews suffered oppression for many years.

"The preaching of the everlasting gospel shakes the foundations of antichrist in the world. * * * The greatness of the papal Babylon will not prevent her fall, but will make it more dreadful and remarkable" (Henry and Scott, Rev. 14:8).

13. *Called upon the weak*] See I. Cor. 1:26-31. In the Kingdom of God the humble triumph over the haughty, the weak over the strong; kings kneel at the cross. Humility, weakness, ignominy are not in themselves a power unto salvation, but God uses as His instruments only those who, because they are weak and humble realize their need of His aid, put their trust in Him alone.

Thresh the nations] This expression is found in Habakkuk 3:12. Threshing, in olden times, was done by treading out the grain on a threshing-floor. The going forth of the messengers of the gospel among the nations is like trampling the wheat sheaves on the hard floor. The valuable kernels are carefully gathered up; the straw is left.

14. This paragraph contains a gracious promise of divine protection. Even the sword will fall, if necessary, in behalf of the servants of the Lord.

16. *The parable of the fig tree*] "Behold the fig tree and all trees; when they now shoot forth, ye see and know of your own selves that summer now is nigh at hand" (Luke 21:29-30).

"This sign of events near at hand was equally applicable to the premonitory conditions which were to herald the fall of Jerusalem and the termination of the Jewish autonomy, and to the developments by which the Lord's second advent shall be immediately preceded" (Dr. James E. Talmage, *Jesus the Christ,* p. 574).

18. In the dispensation of the Fulness of Times all things, both in Heaven and which are on earth, are to be revealed. This restoration was to continue until all things were consummated pertaining to the rounding out of the destiny of this earth preparatory for its sanctification. All of the keys of the dispensations past were to be conferred upon

the Prophet Joseph Smith, and by these keys he would receive knowledge of things which had been sealed and by decree before the foundation of the earth, were to be made known in this the dispensation of the Fulness of Times. Not only did this refer to the restoration of knowledge in ancient records, but also in the things kept from the world pertaining to the salvation and exaltation of all those who were just and true. Among these mysteries which had been sealed were the sealing powers in relation to the salvation of both the living and the dead as performed in the Temples of the Lord. (Doc. and Cov. 124:41.)

19. *Watch over him*] The Prophet Joseph, notwithstanding his extraordinary gifts, needed the tender watchcare of his brethren, against the wiles of the adversary.

20. And a commandment I give unto thee—that thou shalt write for him; and the scriptures shall be given, even as they are in mine own bosom, to the salvation of mine own elect;

21. For they will hear my voice, and shall see me, and shall not be asleep, and shall abide the day of my coming; for they shall be purified, even as I am pure.

22. And now I say unto you, tarry with him, and he shall journey with you; forsake him not, and surely these things shall be fulfilled.

23. And inasmuch as ye do not write, behold, it shall be given unto him to prophesy; and thou shalt preach my gospel and call on the holy prophets to prove his words, as they shall be given him.

24. Keep all the commandments and covenants by which ye are bound; and I will cause the heavens to shake for your good, and Satan shall tremble and Zion shall rejoice upon the hills and flourish;

25. And Israel shall be saved in mine own due time; and by the keys which I have given shall they be led, and no more be confounded at all.

26. Lift up your hearts and be glad, your redemption draweth nigh.

27. Fear not, little flock, the kingdom is yours until I come. Behold, I come quickly. Even so. Amen.

20-23. Here the Lord assigns Sidney Rigdon his special duty in the Church. He was to be the secretary of the prophet. Through the faithful co-operation of the two, by the inspiration of the Spirit, the Scriptures would be given to the world, for the salvation of the elect. He was to stay with the Prophet (v. 22) and accompany him on his travels. When they were not engaged in writing, the Prophet was to "Prophesy;" that is, to preach the gospel, and Rigdon was to prove from the Scriptures that the doctrines preached were true (v. 23). This was Sidney Rigdon's appointment. The Lord well knew that Rigdon, left to himself, would encounter insurmountable difficulties, but that by the side of the Prophet he would be a great help.

24. *Keep all the commandments and covenants*] On this condition the promises with which the Revelation closes were given.

GENERAL NOTES

Sidney Rigdon, it has been said, was the real inspirer, if not author, of the Book of Mormon. The story is that a mentally feeble clergyman, named Spaulding, wrote a book which he called the *Manuscript Found,* and which was left with a printer in Pittsburgh, Mr. Patterson, who did not print it because he failed in business. Then, it is alleged, it fell into the hands of Sidney Rigdon, and he induced the Prophet to publish it as the Book of Mormon. This untrue and highly improbable tale was, undoubtedly, invented by Doctor P. Hurlburt,* a worthless character, who had been cut off from the Church for transgression, and who had vowed vengeance. Sidney Rigdon, however, maintained to the last that he had never seen or heard of the Book of Mormon until a copy of it was presented to him by Parley P. Pratt. And this is the truth. John W. Rigdon, his son, in the fall of 1865, put the question to his father, who replied:

"My son, I can swear before high heaven that what I have told you of the origin of the book is true. Your mother and sister, Mrs. Athalia Robinson, were present when that book was handed to me in Mentor, Ohio, and all I ever knew about the origin of the book was what Parley P. Pratt, Oliver Cowdery, Joseph Smith, and the Witnesses who claimed they saw the plates, told me; and in all my intimacy with Joseph Smith he never told me but the one story, and that was that he found it engraved upon gold plates in a hill near Palmyra, N. Y., and that an angel had appeared to him and directed him where to find it; and I have never, to you or anyone else, told but the one story, and that I now repeat to you."

The Prophet could not have assured Rigdon that he had taken the plates from the hill Cumorah, if Rigdon had been, as alleged, the originator of the scheme.

John W. Rigdon also gives another bit of information which may be

* "This said 'Doctor,' wrote Rigdon, in 1839, to the Boston Journal, was never a physician . . . He was the seventh son, and his parents called him 'Doctor'; it was his name, and not the title of his profession" (*Hist. of the Church,* Vol. I., p. 355).

referred to here. It has been claimed that the Prophet Joseph set his son Joseph apart to be his successor, when "young Joseph" one day visited his father in Liberty jail. Asked about this, Sidney Rigdon replied that no such act was performed while he was imprisoned there with the Prophet. He was absolutely certain of this.

The power to cast out devils was necessary for the progress of the Church. There were many odd manifestations in Kirtland when the Prophet first came there. There was a society with communistic ideas of property, and they had a negro, known as Black Pete, for "revelator." Sometimes these folks would be put through the most wonderful distortions, and these were to them an evidence that they had the Holy Spirit. One of the early converts in Kirtland was Ezra Booth, a Methodist minister. He was present in a log schoolhouse, in June, 1831, when the Prophet, under the influence of the power of God, set apart some of the Elders to the High Priesthood. The evil spirit came over Ezra Booth, and he was, as George A. Smith expressed it, "bound" and his countenance was distorted. The Prophet rebuked the evil spirit and commanded it to depart. Booth was relieved.

From paragraph 24 of this Section it appears that the Spirit of Prophecy, at this early date of the existence of the Church, directed the attention of God's people to the fact that Zion, His Church, would flourish in "the hills," meaning, as we now know from Church history, the Rocky Mountains. And this was at a time when the Rocky Mountain region was almost unknown to the people in the Eastern States. Later the prophecies on this subject became clearer, and the Prophet, before his death, was fully aware that the Saints would go to the Rocky Mountains and there become a mighty people. Brigham Young tells us:

"Remarks have been made as to our staying here in the Rockies. I will tell you how long we shall stay here. If we live our religion, we shall stay here in these mountains for ever and for ever, worlds without end, and a portion of the Priesthood will go and redeem and build up the Center* Stake of Zion * * * In the days of Joseph we have sat many hours at a time conversing about this very country. Joseph has often said, 'If I were only in the Rocky Mountains with a hundred faithful men, I would then be happy, and ask no odds of mobocrats'" (*Jour. of Dis.*, Vol. XI., p. 16).

---

* It has become customary to speak of the "Center Stake of Zion." It might, therefore, be well to remember that no Stake was ever organized in Jackson County. Following the figure given by Isaiah Ch. 33:20 and 54:2 we cannot speak of a "center stake of Zion." The term "Stake of Zion" was first used in a revelation given in November, 1831. (Sec. 68.) It is a comparison to the stakes which bind a tent. Isaiah says: "Look upon Zion, the city of our solemnities; thine eyes shall see Jerusalem a quiet habitation, a tabernacle that shall not be taken down; not one of the stakes thereof shall ever be removed, neither shall any of the cords thereof be broken." Again, "Enlarge the place of thy tent and let them stretch forth the curtains of thine habitations: spare not, lengthen thy cords, and strengthen thy stakes." Zion is the tent, and how can the tent be a stake?

SECTION 36.

REVELATION *given through Joseph Smith the Prophet, to Edward Partridge, December, 1830. See heading to Section 35. ——The recipient instructed to preach—Every man may be commissioned in the ministry if he will comply with the Lord's requirements.*

THUS saith the Lord God, the Mighty One of Israel: Behold, I say unto you, my servant Edward, that you are blessed, and your sins are forgiven you, and you are called to preach my gospel as with the voice of a trump;

2. And I will lay my hand upon you by the hand of my servant Sidney Rigdon, and you shall receive my Spirit, the Holy Ghost, even the Comforter, which shall teach you the peaceable things of the kingdom;

3. And you shall declare it with a loud voice, saying: Hosanna, blessed be the name of the most high God.

4. And now this calling and commandment give I unto you concerning all men—

5. That as many as shall come before my servants Sidney Rigdon and Joseph Smith, Jun., embracing this calling and commandment, shall be ordained and sent forth to preach the everlasting gospel among the nations—

6. Crying repentance, saying: Save yourselves from this untoward generation, and come forth out of the fire, hating even the garments spotted with the flesh.

7. And this commandment shall be given unto the elders of my church, that every man which will embrace it with singleness of heart may be ordained and sent forth, even as I have spoken.

8. I am Jesus Christ, the Son of God; wherefore, gird up your loins and I will suddenly come to my temple. Even so. Amen.

Edward Partridge was born at Pittsfield, Mass., the 27th of August, 1793. His ancestors came from Scotland. At the age of twenty he became impressed with the doctrine of "universal restoration," and in 1828 he joined the so-called Campbellites. At the time he lived at Painsville, Ohio. When Oliver Cowdery and companions came to Ohio, on their mission to the Lamanites, he obtained a copy of the Book of Mormon and began to investigate. In 1830 he accompanied Sidney Rigdon to Fayette, and on the 11th of December, that year, he was baptized by the Prophet Joseph. Edward Partridge had a prominent part in the development of the Church. He was called to the Bishopric February 4th, 1831 (Sec. 41:9), and on that occasion the Lord declared that he was pure before Him, "like unto Nathanael of old." As the Bishop, it became his duty to divide unto the Saints their inheritances in Zion, and to make preparations for the settlement of the Saints who were journeying to Zion from Ohio. He suffered persecution on sundry occasions. One day in July, 1833, a mob at Independence violently seized him and one Charles Allen, and dragged them to the public square. Here they were offered the alternatives of renouncing the Book of Mormon or going into exile. As American citizens they refused to comply with this un-American demand, but Bishop Partridge said he was willing to suffer for the Master. His voice was drowned in the tumult that followed. Some of the mob cried, "Call upon your God to deliver you!" Others cursed. Finally, the two brethren were stripped and maltreated by the persecutors, but they suffered in silence and with dignity, as true martyrs. Edward Partridge died in Nauvoo, May 27th, 1840, the same year in which Joseph Smith, Sr., and some other faithful Saints departed, in consequence of the effects of the persecutions in Missouri.

1. *The Mighty One of Israel*] In this Revelation our Lord announces Himself as "the Mighty One of Israel." This name also occurs in Isaiah (1:24; 30:29). It means JEHOVAH, the Lord of Hosts, who led His people out of Egypt, with a strong arm. While the "mighty one" of Assyria was a winged bull, and while earthly kingdoms adopt images of eagles, lions, etc., as emblems of strength, the "Mighty One" of the Kingdom of God is JEHOVAH.

As with the voice of a trump] Edward Partridge was called to preach the gospel; not timidly, but boldly; not as a whisper, but as a trumpet blast. In the wilderness, Israel was warned by means of trumpets to advance, or to halt. They were called to their assemblies, or to the defense of the camp, by the same means. The trumpet announced the new moons, the festivals, the years of jubilee. The preaching of the gospel should be to us even more than the fanfares of trumpets were to Israel, anciently.

2. *I will lay my hand upon you by * * * Rigdon*] Edward Partridge was called to the ministry by revelation, but it was, nevertheless, necessary that he should receive the spirit of his calling by the laying on of hands, and the Lord assured him that He would perform that ordinance by the hands of Sidney Rigdon. God regards the administrations of His authorized servants as though they were performed by Himself.

The peaceable things of the kingdom] The things that bring peace to men. They are of God. Those that engender strife and contention are not from Him.

Hosanna, blessed be the name of the most High God] A thought suggested here is this, that, as the disciples of our Lord and the multitude accompanied Him into Jerusalem, before His death, with songs of joy, and caused commotion among the entire populace, so His heralds at this time should fill the whole world with the proclamation of His advent. *Hosanna means*, "Save, I beseech you!" Here it is a prayer for the salvation of the world. Preaching, without praying, is in vain.

5. *Shall be ordained and sent forth*] Not only those who were called specially to the ministry, but all who held the Priesthood, were to be ordained and sent forth.

6. *Garments spotted with the flesh*] This expression is also found in Jude 23. The garment, a tunic worn next to the body, was thought of as polluted by indulgence in carnal sins, or defiled by the stains of diseases caused by transgression. The Elders of the Church were to cry repentance as the only means of salvation from the burning fires of the lusts of the flesh.

8. *To my temple*] This is the first intimation in these Revelations that temples were to be built in this dispensation. The Revelations were given, as was the translation of the Book of Mormon, "line upon line," although the entire plan was present before God from the beginning.

GENERAL NOTES

The imposition of hands for the reception of the Holy Ghost is an ordinance that was clearly understood in the primitive church. In Acts (8:5-17) we read that Philip preached in Samaria, and that many believed and were baptized. Philip was one of seven appointed to take charge of the temporal affairs of the church in Jerusalem (Acts 6:1-6). When compelled to leave the city, because of persecution, he went to Samaria, but, although he had been preaching the gospel to the Samaritans, he did not impart the gift of the Holy Ghost. In all probability he did not hold the Melchizedek Priesthood at that time. But when the brethren in Jerusalem heard that Samaritans had received the gospel, they sent Peter and John to them, and these Apostles confirmed those who had been baptized, and they received the Holy Ghost.

In this Revelation the Lord places the possession of the Holy Spirit first among the qualifications necessary for the ministry. On this subject Brigham Young well says:

"The idea generally prevails in Christian countries, that it requires men to be qualified, and learned, and eloquent, to stand before the people and act as religious teachers. I will give you the reason why this is so. When a false theory has to be maintained, it requires to be set forth with much care; it requires study, and learning, and cunning sophistry to guild over a falsehood and give it the semblance of truth, and make it plausible and congenial to the feelings of the people; but the most simple and unlearned person can tell the truth. A child can tell the truth. * * * Education is a good thing, and blessed is the man who has it, and can use it for the dissemination of the gospel without being puffed up with pride. But God hath chosen the foolish things of the world to confound the wise; and God hath chosen the weak things of the world to confound the things which are mighty * * * that no flesh should glory in His presence" (*Journal of Discourses,* Vol. XI., p. 214).

SECTION 37.

REVELATION *given to Joseph Smith the Prophet, and Sidney Rigdon, December, 1830. Herein is given the first command-ment respecting gathering in this dispensation.——The future migration of the Church westward—Duties of the Elders in strengthening the Church.*

BEHOLD, I say unto you that it is not expedient in me that ye should translate any more until ye shall go to the Ohio, and this because of the enemy and for your sakes.

2. And again, I say unto you that ye shall not go until ye have preached my gospel in those parts, and have strengthened up the church whithersoever it is found, and more especially in Colesville; for, behold, they pray unto me in much faith.

3. And again, a commandment I give unto the church, that it is expedient in me that they should assemble together at the Ohio, against the time that my servant Oliver Cowdery shall return unto them.

4. Behold, here is wisdom, and let every man choose for himself until I come. Even so. Amen.

Before the close of this year, the first of the existence of the Church, the Prophet Joseph commenced preparing a new English version of the Bible. It is referred to as an inspired "translation," although that term, in its generally accepted meaning of rendition of the spoken, or written, word from one language into another, hardly gives a cor-rect idea of the character of that work. But if by "translate" we mean, to render sentences which are obscure and difficult to understand, into language more easy of comprehension, and free from ambiguity and contradiction, then the attempted revision is a translation. For that is what the Prophet aimed at, by the guidance of the Holy Spirit. Sidney Rigdon aided him as secretary. On the 2nd of February, 1833, the

New Testament was completed, and on the 2nd of July, the same year, the Old Testament, was completed, as far as the Prophet was directed to revise these records up to that time. This work of revision was never completed fully, and the Prophet intended to take up this work in Nauvoo, but persecution and difficulties prevented him from finishing this work.

Regarding the publication of this work, the Prophet, in a letter to W. W. Phelps, dated June 25th, 1833, wrote: "In regard to the printing of the New Translation: It cannot be done until we can attend to it ourselves, and this we will do, as soon as the Lord permits" (*History of the Church,* Vol. I., p. 365). From this it is clear that the publication of this version is not authorized. "It cannot be done *until we can attend to it ourselves.*"

The prophet expected some indication from the Lord that the time for publication had come. But, during the later years of his life, events crowded upon him so fast that it became a physical impossibility for him to give his personal attention to everything that seemed to be necessary. The publication of the New Translation would, no doubt, have involved a final revision by himself; that no one else could do; and he did not do it; the Lord did not command him to put the finishing touch to the work, and, therefore, it remained in manuscript, unpublished.

But we must not suppose that the patient labor spent on the study of the Old and New Testament was lost. It was while Joseph Smith and Sidney Rigdon were engaged in this work that they received the wonderful Revelation on the resurrection, recorded in Section 76; also the Key to John's Revelation, recorded in Section 77. It was during the same time that the Prophet received the Revelation explaining I. Cor. 7:14. There can be no doubt that the close study of the Scriptures, such as that in which the Prophet engaged during these years particularly—for he was always a Bible student—was one of the means by which the Holy Spirit revealed to him the grand and glorious truths concerning the salvation of the children of men, before he sealed his testimony with his blood.

1. *It is not expedient in me*] Not advisable. The Lord watched over the Prophet, and the Prophet was guided by Him in his labors. At this time God directed His servant to discontinue his work on the Bible translation for the time being, because of the enemy.

Until ye shall go to the Ohio] The Ohio valley. The work was resumed at Hiram, Portage Co., Ohio, during the forepart of October, 1831.

2. *Strengthened the Church*] Joseph and Sidney were to go to Ohio, but not hurriedly; they were to set the Church in order first; and especially the branch in Colesville; for, "behold, they pray unto me in much faith." The prayer of faith is the secret of the strength of the Church. There is no progress without prayer.

3. *Assemble together at the Ohio*] This is the first revelation direct-

ing the Saints to gather at a central place. The doctrine of gathering was taught before (Sects. 10:65; 29:8); here a gathering-place is designated. When Oliver Cowdery returned from his mission to the Lamanites, the Saints were to meet him.

GENERAL NOTES

This is the last of the nineteen revelations given in the year 1830.

During the year 1829, the Prophet was engaged in translating and preparing the Book of Mormon for publication, and answering questions concerning the finding of the plates, the report having gone abroad and caused many inquirers to come to the Prophet to ascertain the truth for themselves, or to engage in controversy with him. During this year the foundations of the Church were laid by the Almighty Himself. Not only did He reveal the existence of the plates, and endow the Prophet with the gift of reading the contents, but He also made it possible for him to publish the sacred record, an achievement that would have been as much beyond the reach of the unlettered young man, without financial resources, as would the translation have been without the inspiration of the Holy Spirit. It was entirely the work of God. Martin Harris, notwithstanding his naturally suspicious disposition and vacillating character, came to the aid of the Prophet. Oliver Cowdery arrived just when his services were needed. The Whitmers opened their home when there were no other visible resources. Joseph Knight was on hand when provisions and the protecting hand of a friend were needed. And thus the Lord took care of the work and of his Prophet during the first development of the Church. It was just as much of a miracle as the maintenance of the Prophet Elijah by ravens at the brook Cherith, or in the house of the widow of Zarephath (I. Kings 17:1-16). During this year, also, the manifestations solemnly attested by the Witnesses were given.

During the year 1830, the Book of Mormon was published; a Revelation on Church government was given (Sec. 20); the Church was organized (Sec. 21); the duties of the Prophet Joseph, Oliver Cowdery, Hyrum Smith, Samuel Smith, and Emma Smith were defined by divine Revelation, as were those of Thomas B. Marsh (Sec. 31), the Pratts (Sec. 32 and 34), Sidney Rigdon (Sec. 35) and Edward Partridge (Sec. 36). The Revelation to Emma Smith (Sec. 25) calling her to great prominence in the Church is particularly noteworthy, because it was given years before the women in the English speaking world had ever thought of an organized effort for "woman's rights." That Revelation is the very beginning of the emancipation movement in the world. During this year were also revealed the important doctrine of Common Consent, which is one of the cornerstones in the government of the Kingdom of God (Sec. 26); the propriety of using water instead of wine in the Sacrament (Sec. 27), which may be regarded as the beginning of the great Prohibition movement in the Christian world; and the doctrine of the gathering (Sec. 29). The first mission to the Lamanites was undertaken, and the first gathering-place of the Saints indicated (Sec. 37).

If we consider only the work accomplished during this one year; or study, in their practical bearing upon human affairs, the wonderful truths revealed, we are overwhelmed with the vastness of the vistas opened up before us. It is like trying to penetrate the infinite depths of space, where the handiworks of God bear witness of His majesty, wisdom, power, and love, and where each glistening spark of light, on close examination, turns out to be a world.

SECTION 38.

REVELATION *given through Joseph Smith the Prophet, at Fayette, New York, January 2, 1831, at a conference of the Church.——Jesus Christ proclaims himself as the Creator—Doom of the wicked depicted—Goodly inheritance promised to the righteous—Definite promise of endowment with power from on high—The riches of eternity extolled—Diligent service required of every member of the Church.*

THUS saith the Lord your God, even Jesus Christ, the Great I AM, Alpha and Omega, the beginning and the end, the same which looketh upon the wide expanse of eternity, and all the seraphic hosts of heaven, before the world was made;

2. The same which knoweth all things, for all things are present before mine eyes;

3. I am the same which spake, and the world was made, and all things came by me.

4. I am the same which have taken the Zion of Enoch into mine own bosom; and verily, I say, even as many as have believed in my name, for I am Christ, and in mine own name, by the virtue of the blood which I have spilt, have I pleaded before the Father for them.

5. But behold, the residue of the wicked have I kept in chains of darkness until the judgment of the great day, which shall come at the end of the earth;

6. And even so will I cause the wicked to be kept, that will not hear my voice but harden their hearts, and wo, wo, wo, is their doom.

On January 2nd, 1831, the third general Conference of the Church was held at Fayette, at the house of Peter Whitmer, Sr. On this occasion the Revelation in this Section was received.

In this Revelation our Lord (1) presents Himself to the Church under several names, expressing so many different attributes (1-6); then (2) He promises to appear, visibly, to the Saints (7-12), and (3) warns them of certain dangers that threaten them (13-14); then (4) He makes a covenant with them regarding the land of gathering (15-22), and (5) exhorts them to be united (23-27); and finally (6), He charges them to gather out "from the wicked," in order to escape the coming judgments (28-42).

1-6. In these paragraphs our Lord reveals Himself to the Church under these names: Lord and God, Jesus Christ, I Am, Alpha and Omega, the Beginning and the End. See Section 35:1. He further describes Himself as pre-existent, all-knowing, the Creator of the world, and the Savior of His people. Well may we exclaim, in the language of the Hebrew poet, "O God, who is like unto thee!" (Psalm 71:19).

1. *Wide expanse of eternity*] A somewhat difficult expression; but the language of the Doctrine and Covenants is flavored with Biblical terms, which is but natural, since the Spirit of Revelation chose as an instrument through whom to make these communications, one whose literary achievements were derived, chiefly, from that volume. In the language of the Old Testament (Hebrew) an idea for which we use an adjective, is often expressed by a noun. The "wide expanse of eternity" would, if a Hebraism, mean, "the wide, eternal expanse," or "boundless space," which is different from the expanse (*raquia*) of Genesis 1:6-8, that appeared on the second day of the creation. The grand truth conveyed here is, that our Lord existed before the world was made, and that, with some object in view, He surveyed space and all it contained.

Seraphic hosts of heaven] In a vision of the Prophet Isaiah (6:2-3) seraphim are standing *over** the throne of God, in the attitude of service. They are the attendants of Jehovah, reflecting His glory and majesty, and, in His presence, they sing in chorus, "Holy, holy, holy is the Lord of Hosts: The whole Earth is full of His glory." Our Lord looked upon these hosts. They were standing before Him, awaiting His commands, even before the Earth had been created.

2. *Knoweth all Things*] Our Eternal Father is all-knowing. It has been taught erroneously by some that God cannot know all things; that he is like a chemist in a laboratory searching for and constantly discovering hidden truth which was unknown to Him and that even the mind of God is limited and He cannot survey the universe and take cognizance of the innumerable changes occurring every moment. These

---

* "Above" is not a good translation.

critics declare that if He knows all things he must cease to progress for there is no place to go further if He is on the pinnacle of knowledge, etc., but to retrogress and that "eternal progress" means that he is still learning. There could not be a greater fallacy than this. If he is still laboring as a scientist experimenting and seeking hidden truth, then there must be some power greater than He is. He teaches us that "He knoweth all things, and there is not anything save He knows it." (II Nephi 9:20.) which truth is confirmed by our Lord's words in the first paragraph of this revelation. "And He comprehendeth all things, and all things are before him, and all things are round about him; and he is above all things, and in all things, and is through all things; and all things are by Him, and of Him, even God, forever and ever." * * * . . . he hath given a law unto all things, by which they move in their times and their seasons." (Doc. and Cov. 88:41-42.) The Lord has said, "There is no end to my works, neither to my words. For behold, this is my work and my glory—to bring to pass the immortality and eternal life of man." (Moses 1:38-39.) He is continually progressing in his works, expanding his dominions, creating worlds to be peopled by His children, and thus he is progressing, but in knowledge, wisdom, love, justice and other like virtues, He dwells in perfection.

3. *All things came by me*] Our Lord is the Creator.
"This creative and administrative work of Christ the Word in the natural order of things is always emphasized in the writings of the Apostles when they touch on the doctrine of His person * * * With ourselves this idea has retired very much in the background * * * How much more hearty would be the sympathy of theologians with the revelations of science and the developments of history, if they habitually connected them with operations of the same divine Word who is the center of all their religious aspirations" (Lightfoot, *Colossians*).

4. *Zion of Enoch*] This city called "Zion" because its inhabitants were all righteous and "pure in heart" (Doc. and Cov. 97:21.) will return when the Millennial reign is come. (Pearl of Great Price, Book of Moses 7:63.)
Enoch, the seventh from Adam (Jude 14) built a city called Zion, after the people of God, so named by the Lord, because they were united, righteous, and prosperous. This city of Enoch flourished for three hundred and sixty-five years and then the Lord, by some process not known to us, took it with all its inhabitants, "to His bosom," thus saving them from destruction in the flood that was to come. "And from thence went forth the saying, Zion is fled" (Pearl of Great Price, Book of Moses 7:18, 19, 68, 69). The building up of another Zion in the latter days was predicted by the prophets of old. David, for instance, says, "When the Lord shall build up Zion, he shall appear in his glory" (Psalm 102:16). That the people of God in the latter days should be found in a mountain region, was also foretold. "O Zion, that bringest

good tidings, get thee up into a high mountain" (Isaiah 40:9, see also Ezekiel 40:2, etc.)

Christ, by virtue of His atonement, is the Savior of those who believe. A repentant sinner needs someone to plead for him. Our Lord does that. In the presence of the Father He represents His people, and as a beloved Son in whom the Father is well pleased—He having kept the everlasting covenant and fulfilled its conditions—He is in a position to be the Author of their salvation. His atonement is the foundation for salvation. By faith, active in repentance and obedience, the inestimable gift is received.

5-7. The wicked, the disobedient, must plead their own cause. They are kept in "chains of darkness"—in a condition in which the light of revelation does not set them free from ignorance and prejudices, and in that condition they will be overtaken by the day of judgment.

7. But behold, verily, verily, I say unto you that mine eyes are upon you. I am in your midst and ye cannot see me;

8. But the day soon cometh that ye shall see me, and know that I am; for the veil of darkness shall soon be rent, and he that is not purified shall not abide the day.

9. Wherefore, gird up your loins and be prepared. Behold, the kingdom is yours, and the enemy shall not overcome.

10. Verily I say unto you, ye are clean, but not all; and there is none else with whom I am well pleased;

11. For all flesh is corrupted before me; and the powers of darkness prevail upon the earth, among the children of men, in the presence of all the hosts of heaven—

12. Which causeth silence to reign, and all eternity is pained, and the angels are waiting the great command to reap down the earth, to gather the tares that they may be burned; and, behold, the enemy is combined.

7-12. Another promise that the Lord will soon appear.

7. *I am in your midst*] The Lord had already come to His people, but they had not seen Him; or, if they had seen Him, had not known Him. President Brigham Young helps us to understand this mystery, when he says, "The Lord Jesus Christ might come among us and we would not know Him: and if He were to come in our midst and speak unto us today, we might suppose Him to be one of the returned missionaries" (*Jour. of Dis.*, Vol. XI., p. 41.) When our Lord had ascended to glory, two heavenly messengers—"men" Luke calls them—appeared to the disciples and said to them, "This same Jesus, which is taken up from you into heaven, shall so come in like manner as ye

have seen him go into heaven" (Acts 1:11). We generally think that when the Lord comes, He will be accompanied by His Saints, and the lightnings will be flashing, the thunders rolling, mountains falling, trumpets sounding, waves roaring, and the terror-stricken mortals crying out to mountains and to rocks, "fall on us, and hide us from the face of him that sitteth on the throne, and from the wrath of the Lamb" (Rev. 6:16); but we should not, while contemplating this grand Scriptural picture of the Advent, forget the promise that our Lord would return as He ascended from the Mount before He should come in majesty and glory. He came in like manner as He ascended when He first appeared to the Prophet Joseph, and He has remained with the Church ever since, though invisible except on a few occasions, as, for instance, at the time of the manifestations in the Kirtland Temple. As far as the world was concerned, our Lord did come without warning, "as a thief in the night."

8. *The day soon cometh that ye shall see me*] The day is near, when the veil between this world and the next will be removed. The Tabernacle in the wilderness and the Temple in Jerusalem were divided into two compartments, separated from each other by a heavy veil, or curtain. In the inner room the presence of Jehovah was manifested on the Ark of Covenant, between the Cherubim. God dwelt in the midst of Israel, though not seen by the people. There was a veil between Him and them. In our dispensation the Lord is also present in the Church, in more than a figurative sense, though we do not see Him with our natural eyes. He is hidden by the veil that limits the range of vision of our spirits. But this veil will be rent. The Lord will come forth and all shall see Him but those who have not been purified by the sanctifying influence of the Holy Spirit will not be able to abide His appearing. They will flee, but find no place of refuge.

9. *Gird up your loins*] In Biblical language, to "gird up the loins" is to prepare for a journey, or for work. The Hebrews wore girdles when traveling, and when at work. On such occasions they girt their clothes about them to ensure free movement of the limbs. The servants of the Lord must be prepared to do His work, and to go when He calls.

10-11. Here the Lord draws a distinction between His people and the world. "Ye are clean * * * the powers of darkness prevail upon the earth." Witness the ignorance, superstition, the poverty, the sickness, sin, and wickedness existing among the children of men!

12. *The angels are waiting*] The destroying angels, at the time when this Revelation was given, were ready, only waiting for the divine command to pour out their vials on Earth—to gather the tares for the fire.

The revelations that are in the Bible, the predictions of the Patriarchs and Prophets who saw by vision and revelation the last dispensation and fulness of times plainly tell us what is to come to pass. The 49th chapter of Isaiah is having its fulfillment I have often said in my teachings, if the world want to know what is coming to pass, let them read the revelations of St. John. Read of the Judgments of God that are going to overtake the world in the last dispensation. Read the papers and see what is taking place in our own nation and in the nations of the earth, and what does it all mean? It means the commencement of the fulfillment of what the Prophets of God have predicted. In the Doctrine and Covenants there are many revelations given through the mouth of the Prophet of God; these revelations will all have their fulfilment, as the Lord lives, and no power can hinder it. In one of the revelations the Lord told Joseph Smith:

"Behold, Verily I say unto you, the angels are crying unto the Lord day and night, who are ready and waiting to be sent forth to reap down the fields:

"But the Lord saith unto them, Pluck not up the tares while the blade is yet tender (for verily your faith is weak), lest you destroy the wheat also.

"Therefore let the wheat and the tares grow together until the harvest is fully ripe, then ye shall first gather out the wheat from among the tares, and after the gathering of the wheat, behold and Lo! the tares are bound in bundles, and the field remaineth to be burned."

I want to bear testimony to this congregation, and to the heavens and the earth, that the day is come when those angels are privileged to go forth and commence their work. They are laboring in the United States of America; they are laboring among the nations of the earth; and they will continue. We need not marvel or wonder at anything that is transpiring in the earth. The world do not comprehend the revelations of God. They did not in the days of the Jews; yet all that the Prophets had spoken concerning them came to pass. So in our day these things will come to pass. I heard the Prophet Joseph bear his testimony to these events that would transpire in the earth. * * * We cannot draw a veil over the events that await this generation. No man that is inspired by the Spirit and power of God can close his ears, his eyes or his lips to these things. (Mil. Star, 58:738-9.)

13. And now I show unto you a mystery, a thing which is had in secret chambers, to bring to pass even your destruction in process of time, and ye knew it not;

14. But now I tell it unto you, and ye are blessed, not because of your iniquity, neither your hearts of unbelief; for verily some of you are guilty before me, but I will be merciful unto your weakness.

13-14. In these paragraphs the Lord utters a warning to the Church.

13. *I show unto you a mystery*] "Mystery" here means a "profound secret and refers to the last sentence in the previous verse, "Behold the enemy is combined." In the "secret chambers the enemy of the Church plotted her destruction. They meant to keep it secret. The Lord revealed it. No information is at hand as to what secret society this refers to.

14. It was necessary to put away iniquity and unbelief in order to be able to stand against the adversary.

Merciful unto your weakness] The Lord does not "look upon sin with the least degree of allowance," and yet He is as merciful as He is Holy and just, and it is not *weakness* in His children, but wilful *rebellion,* that calls down His wrath upon them.

> "Like as a father pitieth his children.
> So the Lord pitieth them that fear Him.
> For He knoweth our frame;
> He remembereth that we are dust."
>
> Psalm 103:13, 14.

15. Therefore, be ye strong from henceforth; fear not, for the kingdom is yours.

16. And for your salvation I give unto you a commandment, for I have heard your prayers, and the poor have complained before me, and the rich have I made, and all flesh is mine, and I am no respecter of persons.

17. And I have made the earth rich, and behold it is my footstool, wherefore, again I will stand upon it.

18. And I hold forth and deign to give unto you greater riches, even a land of promise, a land flowing with milk and honey, upon which there shall be no curse when the Lord cometh;

19. And I will give it unto you for the land of your inheritance, if you seek it with all your hearts.

20. And this shall be my covenant with you, ye shall have it for the land of your inheritance, and for the inheritance of your children forever, while the earth shall stand, and ye shall possess it again in eternity, no more to pass away.

21. But, verily I say unto you that in time ye shall have no king nor ruler, for I will be your king and watch over you.

22. Wherefore, hear my voice and follow me, and you shall be a free people, and ye shall have no laws but my laws when I come, for I am your lawgiver, and what can stay my hand?

15-22. In the last Revelation given in the year 1830 (Sec. 37), the Saints were commanded to gather in Ohio. In this Revelation our Lord explains that the command was given for their salvation, and He establishes the *Covenant of Gathering* (v. 20).

16. *For your salvation*] Why were the Saints instructed to gather? One reason is stated in the twelfth verse. The enemies were combining against them, and gathering would be a means of escape from their plots. Another reason is given in this paragraph, as follows:

The poor have complained] In the world there is an artificial and mischievous distinction between rich and poor. The Lord was mindful of His destitute children, as well as those who were wealthy, and He commanded His people to gather in a place where that class distinction could be wiped away.

18. *Great riches*] God's design was to give to His gathered people great riches, even a land of promise, "upon which there shall be no curse [of destitution] when the Lord cometh."

19. The Lord promises to give His Saints such a land, if they will seek it with all their hearts. It cannot be obtained except through diligent, God-directed effort.

20. *This shall be my Covenant with you*] A covenant is an agreement between two parties—in this instance, between our Lord and His Saints. The Lord promises to give to the Saints a land of inheritance, just as He formerly gave Canaan to Israel,—a land which they shall possess, while the Earth stands, and then in a glorified state after the transformation of the globe and the general resurrection.

21. The Saints, in accepting this promise, agree to yield allegiance to Him as the Supreme King and Ruler.

22. And to hearken to Him and follow Him. On this condition they would be a free people, and their laws would be His laws, He being the Law-giver.

The gathering-place of the Saints, then, was designed to be a place of temporal as well as eternal salvation; a place from which every "curse" shall be removed; a place in which our Lord shall be the Supreme Ruler, and the laws be His laws.

"We have to learn that, in the first place, the Lord sent His servants forth to preach the principles of the gospel, to impress upon the inhabitants of the Earth the necessity of believing in Jesus Christ as the Savior of the world, repenting of their sins, and being baptized for the remission of them, and receive the Holy Ghost by the laying on of hands, and it was hoped and expected that when the Holy Ghost descended upon men and women they would be filled with the spirit of obedience, and that their understandings would be so awakened that they would begin to comprehend the object God had in view in restoring the everlasting gospel to the Earth. It has had that effect, but it has been slowly manifested; it has dawned upon us ray by ray, gradually opening our minds to the comprehension of the great work the Lord has established on the earth; and today, after years of experience, the Church of Christ has barely commenced to comprehend the great work God had in view in establishing His kingdom on the Earth. But we are learning it now more rapidly than we have in past years" (George Q. Cannon, *Jour. of Dis.*, Vol. XI., pp. 32-3).

23. But, verily, I say unto you, teach one another according to the office wherewith I have appointed you;

24. And let every man esteem his brother as himself, and practise virtue and holiness before me.

25. And again I say unto you, let every man esteem his brother as himself.

26. For what man among you having twelve sons, and is no respecter of them, and they serve him obediently, and he saith unto the one: Be thou clothed in robes and sit thou here; and to the other: Be thou clothed in rags and sit thou there—and looketh upon his sons and saith I am just?

27. Behold, this I have given unto you as a parable, and it is even as I am. I say unto you, be one; and if ye are not one ye are not mine.

23-27. In the previous paragraphs our Lord has stated the conditions on which He would make a covenant with the Saints. He adds an admonition to unity: "If you are not one, ye are not mine."

23. *Teach one another*] One of the means by which unity is preserved among the Saints is teaching. Everyone appointed to an office in the Church must magnify that office, and every member must sustain him in it. That brings unity.

24. *Let every man esteem his brother as himself*] This is made possible in the kingdom of God, because there the standard of superiority is different from that which governs in the world. It is, in fact, inverted: "He that is greatest among you shall be your servant" (Matt. 23:11). There is no exalted position in the kingdom of God but that of service. "I," saith the Lord, "am among you as he that serveth" (Luke 22:27). In this kingdom, therefore, there can be no competition for "first" places; no envy, no agitation for offices. And it is, consequently, not impossible for every man to "esteem his brother as himself."

25. This injunction is repeated, because of its importance.

26-27. *I have given unto you a parable*] The illustration in the previous paragraph shows the effects of class distinction among men. What would happen in a family where some children should be clothed in rags and made to suffer want, while others live sumptuously every day? There would be discontent, revolt, perhaps crime. The results are no less serious in society where unjust lines are drawn between classes. God does not make such lines. In the Church they must be obliterated, as they were in Enoch's Zion. "And the Lord called His people Zion, because they were of one heart and one mind, and dwelt in righteousness; and there was no poor among them" (Book of Moses 7:18). See also IV. Nephi 1:1-3. In these two verses, together with verses 24 and 25, the Lord sets forth the principle that the members of his Church are to look after the temporal needs of worthy poor Church members. This is the basic principle underlying the United Order and the Church Welfare Plan.

28. And again, I say unto you that the enemy in the secret chambers seeketh your lives.

Again the warning is repeated: "The enemy in the secret chambers seeketh your lives."

"It has ever been the desire of the wicked to destroy the people of God. They have never slackened their efforts, nor failed to use all the means in their power, nor hesitated to resort to the most cruel, foul, and fiendish acts to accomplish their nefarious purpose * * * What a host of apostasies there have been since the organization of the Church! There have been Rigdonites, Strangites, Benemites, Wightites, Gladdenites, Cutlerites, Morrisites, * * * but what does the world care about these? Nothing. Why? Because they have forfeited the Priesthood, they have not the power, nor the principles of salvation except in part; they have deserted the cause, have struck hands alike with the infidel and the bigot, and formed an alliance with the maligners and persecutors of the saints, and therefore they are harmless in the eyes of the world" (Joseph F. Smith, *Journal of Discourses,* Vol. XIX., pp. 24-5).

29. Ye hear of wars in far countries, and you say that there will soon be great wars in far countries, but ye know not the hearts of men in your own land.

30. I tell you these things because of your prayers; wherefore, treasure up wisdom in your bosoms, lest the wickedness of men reveal these things unto you by their wickedness, in a manner which shall speak in your ears with a voice louder than that which shall shake the earth; but if ye are prepared ye shall not fear.

31. And that ye might escape the power of the enemy, and

be gathered unto me a righteous people, without spot and blameless—

32. Wherefore, for this cause I gave unto you the commandment that ye should go to the Ohio; and there I will give unto you my law; and there you shall be endowed with power from on high;

33. And from thence, whosoever I will shall go forth among all nations, and it shall be told them what they shall do; for I have a great work laid up in store, for Israel shall be saved, and I will lead them whithersoever I will, and no power shall stay my hand.

34. And now, I give unto the church in these parts a commandment, that certain men among them shall be appointed, and they shall be appointed by the voice of the church;

35. And they shall look to the poor and the needy, and administer to their relief that they shall not suffer; and send them forth to the place which I have commanded them;

36. And this shall be their work, to govern the affairs of the property of this church.

37. And they that have farms that cannot be sold, let them be left or rented as seemeth them good.

38. See that all things are preserved; and when men are endowed with power from on high and sent forth, all these things shall be gathered unto the bosom of the church.

39. And if ye seek the riches which it is the will of the Father to give unto you, ye shall be the richest of all people, for ye shall have the riches of eternity; and it must needs be that the riches of the earth are mine to give; but beware of pride, lest ye become as the Nephites of old.

40. And again, I say unto you, I give unto you a commandment, that every man, both elder, priest, teacher, and also member, go to with his might, with the labor of his hands, to prepare and accomplish the things which I have commanded.

41. And let your preaching be the warning voice, every man to his neighbor, in mildness and in meekness.

42. And go ye out from among the wicked. Save yourselves. Be ye clean that bear the vessels of the Lord. Even so. Amen.

29. *Wars in far countries*] Only a few months previous to the date of this Revelation (July 27th, 1830), France was shaken by a revolution which forced Charles X to abdicate and flee from the country. The disturbances in France were felt in Belgium, and on the 25th of August the performance of a revolutionary opera at Brussels was the signal for an insurrection that spread from town to town throughout the Southern Netherlands. In the autumn of 1830 an outbreak occurred in Poland, which required the concentration of all the military forces of the Czar to quell it. It was about this time that the Brazilians compelled their Emperor, Dom Pedro, to resign.

There will soon be great wars] The Belgian revolution threatened to involve all Europe in war, because it broke up a kingdom established by a general treaty.

Ye know not the hearts of men in your own land] In the United States the opinion prevailed that internal troubles, such as those from which France, Belgium, Poland, and some other countries suffered, could not arise in the great Republic. The people generally did not know what was in the hearts of men, but the Lord knew, and He gave, in this paragraph, the first intimation that there would be civil war in the United States.

30. *Treasure up wisdom*] Our Lord gave this indirect, but none the less clear, prophecy concerning the Civil War in the United States, and then admonished the Saints to be wise. If they were wise, they would prepare themselves by gathering to one place. As a matter of fact the Saints did, in due time, go to the valleys of the Rocky Mountains, and in those impregnable "chambers" they were effectively secluded "for a little moment, until the indignation be overpast" (Isa. 26:20).

32. *To the Ohio*] The Ohio valley was the first gathering place. The Saints were promised a Pentecostal outpouring of power. There they received some of the grandest manifestations and most glorious Revelations ever vouchsafed to man in mortality (Secs. 101 and 110, for instance).

35. *Look to the poor and needy*] Our Lord had said, in this Revelation, that there should be no "curse" of destitution in the land of gathering (vv. 16-18). He now commands the Saints to select men to look after the worthy poor and help them to gather. The worthy poor are precious in His sight. Lazarus may be a fit companion for Abraham.

39. *Ye shall be the richest of all people*] By the possession of eternal riches; and also the wealth of the Earth. Our Lord does not object to his people's being rich. It all depends on *how* they *obtain* wealth, and how they *use* it. Wealth obtained by dishonesty and oppression is a curse. Wealth used for selfish purposes is a snare. Money received of the Lord, through His blessings, and used for the furtherance of His kingdom is a means of eternal exaltation.

40. *The things which I have commanded*] The gathering. Everyone, Elder, Priest, Teacher, is commanded to labor diligently to make the gathering possible. There is no "hierarchy" in the Church.

42. The last exhortation in this Revelation on gathering, "Go ye out from the wicked! Save yourselves! Be clean!"

GENERAL NOTES

Concerning the subject of gathering, the Prophet Joseph says:

"All that the prophets have written, from the days of righteous Abel, down to the last man that has left any testimony on record for our consideration, in speaking of the salvation of Israel in the last days, goes directly to show that it consists in the work of gathering" (*History of the Church*, Vol. II., p. 260; see Deut. 30:1-4; Rev. 21:3; III. Nephi 20:22; Ether 13:1-12).

It is evident, from this Revelation, that the Lord, from the beginning, intended to teach the members of the Church the principle of the United Order or consecration.

To acknowledge the Lord as the Supreme Ruler is not to be disloyal to any earthly government, but for any government to fail to acknowledge the Supreme Ruler, is an act of disloyalty to the Supreme Ruler.

SECTION 39.

REVELATION *given through Joseph Smith the Prophet, to James Covill, at Fayette, New York, January 5, 1831. James Covill covenanted that he would obey any command that the Lord would give to him through Joseph the Prophet. See History of the Church, vol. 1, p. 143.——The Lord Jesus Christ specifies the conditions under which men may become his sons —James Covill promised blessing beyond all he had ever known conditioned on his obedience to the Lord's commandments.*

HEARKEN and listen to the voice of him who is from all eternity, the Great I AM, even Jesus Christ—

2. The light and the life of the world; a light which shineth in darkness and the darkness comprehendeth it not;

3. The same which came in the meridian of time unto mine own, and mine own received me not;

4. But to as many as received me, gave I power to become

my sons; and even so will I give unto as many as will receive me, power to become my sons.

5. And verily, verily, I say unto you, he that receiveth my gospel receiveth me; and he that receiveth not my gospel receiveth not me.

Shortly after the conference, a gentleman, James Covill, who had been a Baptist minister for forty years, came to the Prophet at Fayette, and expressed a desire to yield obedience to any commandment God should be pleased to give him, through His servant. This Revelation came in answer to prayer on that subject. In it our Lord (1) introduces Himself as on former occasions (1-5); then (2) He makes known what the true gospel is (6); and (3) He tells James Covill what is required of him, and promises him great blessings if he will yield obedience (7-21).

1-5. The names under which our Lord here reveals Himself are all significant. See Secs. 29:1, 33; 6:21.

1. *From all eternity to all eternity*] The Eternal One. Moses uses the same expression, when he says:

> "Before the mountains were brought forth,
> Or ever thou hadst formed the Earth and the world,
> Even from everlasting to everlasting, thou art God."
>
> —Psalm 90:2.

The word "eternity" in the Scriptures does not mean "never-ending duration." It means a "period," an "age." In Matt. 13:39, the word is translated "world," although a literal rendering would be, "The harvest is the completion of this age." But when the Lord says He is "From all eternity to all eternity," He states, as clearly as can be done in human language, that He exists in all ages: past, present, and future. He is everlasting.

6. And this is my gospel—repentance and baptism by water, and then cometh the baptism of fire and the Holy Ghost, even the Comforter, which showeth all things, and teacheth the peaceable things of the kingdom.

This is my gospel] Mr. Covill was a Baptist. The Baptists are a rather venerable sect, in point of age. In the early days of ecclesiastical history there were many who protested against the changing of the ordinances, and the worldliness of the church. In Africa the Donatists refused to accept as valid the ordinances performed by the dominant church. In England Britons refused to "perform the office of baptizing according to the custom of the holy Roman church" (The Venerable Bede, in the year 731). Later, Waldenses, Albigenses, Petrobrusians, and others contended for baptism for believers. The Anabaptists at the time of the Reformation were the descendants of sects which had taught baptism by immersion. In Holland they were called Mennonites, after Menno Simonis; in England, Baptists. They believe in baptism by immersion after a confession of belief in our Lord and repentance of past sins. To them baptism is but an outward sign of inward grace, not essential to salvation but necessary to those who will "fulfil all righteousness." The Lord now states to Mr. Covill what *His* gospel is. It is repentance, and baptism in water and the Holy Ghost, and obedience to the teachings of the Comforter regarding "the peaceable things of the kingdom" (See Sec. 36:2).

7. And now, behold, I say unto you, my servant James, I have looked upon thy works and I know thee.

8. And verily I say unto thee, thine heart is now right before me at this time; and, behold, I have bestowed great blessings upon thy head;

9. Nevertheless, thou hast seen great sorrow, for thou hast rejected me many times because of pride and the cares of the world.

10. But, behold, the days of thy deliverance are come, if thou wilt hearken to my voice, which saith unto thee: Arise and be baptized, and wash away your sins, calling on my name, and you shall receive my Spirit, and a blessing so great as you never have known.

11. And if thou do this, I have prepared thee for a greater work. Thou shalt preach the fulness of my gospel, which I have sent forth in these last days, the covenant which I have sent forth to recover my people, which are of the house of Israel.

12. And it shall come to pass that power shall rest upon thee; thou shalt have great faith, and I will be with thee and go before thy face.

13. Thou art called to labor in my vineyard, and to build up my church, and to bring forth Zion, that it may rejoice upon the hills and flourish.

14. Behold, verily, verily, I say unto thee, thou art not called to go into the eastern countries, but thou art called to go to the Ohio.

15. And inasmuch as my people shall assemble themselves at the Ohio, I have kept in store a blessing such as is not known

among the children of men, and it shall be poured forth upon their heads. And from thence men shall go forth into all nations.

16. Behold, verily, verily, I say unto you, that the people in Ohio call upon me in much faith, thinking I will stay my hand in judgment upon the nations, but I cannot deny my word.

17. Wherefore lay to with your might and call faithful laborers into my vineyard, that it may be pruned for the last time.

18. And inasmuch as they do repent and receive the fulness of my gospel, and become sanctified, I will stay mine hand in judgment.

19. Wherefore, go forth, crying with a loud voice, saying: The kingdom of heaven is at hand; crying: Hosanna! blessed be the name of the Most High God.

20. Go forth baptizing with water, preparing the way before my face for the time of my coming;

21. For the time is at hand; the day or the hour no man knoweth; but it surely shall come.

22. And he that receiveth these things receiveth me; and they shall be gathered unto me in time and in eternity.

23. And again, it shall come to pass that on as many as ye shall baptize with water, ye shall lay your hands, and they shall receive the gift of the Holy Ghost, and shall be looking forth for the signs of my coming, and shall know me.

24. Behold, I come quickly. Even so. Amen.

7-24. In these paragraphs our Lord is pleased to give special instructions to James Covill and to offer him special blessings.

7. *I have looked upon thy works*] The Lord recognizes the honest efforts of all His children.

10. *The days of thy deliverance have come*] James Covill had experienced sorrow and tribulation, because pride and worldly cares had caused him to neglect his duty to God. But the Lord now offered him another opportunity of deliverance. "Arise and be baptized, and wash away your sins." That is the way to salvation which God has appointed.

11. *If you do this,* etc.] His baptism would be the preparation for a much greater work than he had done as a Baptist minister. As an Elder in the Church he would be authorized to preach the gospel in its fulness and to assist in the work of gathering Israel.

12. *Thou shalt have great faith*] The Lord would give him the "moving power" necessary for the work, if he were willing to obey the call

13. *Upon the hills*] See Sec. 35:24.

16. *People in Ohio*] There were at this time in Kirtland, Ohio, some who had been baptized but not fully instructed. Some of these had a strange spirit, and many, it appears, were praying that the judgments decreed upon the nations would not be executed. These prayers the Lord could not grant, unless the sinners repented and received the gospel (v. 18). Hence the necessity of "crying with a loud voice," proclaiming the coming of the Lord.

SECTION 40.

REVELATION *given to Joseph Smith the Prophet and Sidney Rigdon, at Fayette, New York, January, 1831. Preceding the record of this revelation, the Prophet wrote: As James Covill rejected the word of the Lord, and returned to his former principles and people, the Lord gave unto me and Sidney Rigdon the following revelation:*

BEHOLD, verily I say unto you, that the heart of my servant James Covill was right before me, for he covenanted with me that he would obey my word.

2. And he received the word with gladness, but straightway Satan tempted him; and the fear of persecution and the cares of the world caused him to reject the word.

3. Wherefore he broke my covenant, and it remaineth with me to do with him as seemeth me good. Amen.

One would naturally suppose that one who had made a covenant with the Lord to obey Him, and received such instructions and promises as those contained in Section 39, would have endeavored to keep faith with God; but James Covill, fearing persecution, fell a victim to the temptations of the adversary. He lost a great opportunity.

2. *Satan tempted him*] Note that fear of persecution and of inability to obtain the necessaries of life if we serve the Lord, is a temptation that must be overcome by faith. God is able to stay the hand of the persecutor, and to bestow upon His children temporal, as well as eternal salvation. If we love God, we have no fear for the future. "There is no fear in love; but perfect love casteth out fear" (I. John 4:18).

GENERAL NOTES

Baptism is an ordinance instituted for the benefit of God's children. The Prophet Joseph tells us that when he and Oliver Cowdery were baptized, the Holy Ghost fell upon them, and they prophesied. And, further,

"Our minds being now enlightened, we began to have the Scriptures laid open to our understandings, and the true meaning and intention of their more mysterious passages revealed unto us in a manner which we never could attain to previously, nor ever before had thought of" (*History of the Church,* Vol. I., p. 43).

SECTION 41.

REVELATION *given through Joseph Smith the Prophet, to the Church, at Kirtland, Ohio, February 4, 1831. The Kirtland branch of the Church at this time was rapidly increasing in numbers, and the Saints generally were striving to live according to the commandments of the Lord; but, the Prophet states, some strange notions and false spirits had crept in among them. See History of the Church, vol. 1, p. 146.——Commandment regarding the observance of the law of the Lord—Promise of greater knowledge as to the government of the Church—Edward Partridge named as the first Bishop unto the Church.*

HEARKEN and hear, O ye my people, saith the Lord and your God, ye whom I delight to bless with the greatest of all blessings, ye that hear me; and ye that hear me not will I curse, that have professed my name, with the heaviest of cursings.

2. Hearken, O ye elders of my church whom I have called, behold I give unto you a commandment, that ye shall assemble yourselves together to agree upon my word;

3. And by the prayer of your faith ye shall receive my law, that ye may know how to govern my church and have all things right before me.

4. And I will be your ruler when I come; and behold, I come quickly, and ye shall see that my law is kept.

5. He that receiveth my law and doeth it, the same is my disciple; and he that saith he receiveth it and doeth it not, the same is not my disciple, and shall be cast out from among you;

6. For it is not meet that the things which belong to the children of the kingdom should be given to them that are not worthy, or to dogs, or the pearls to be cast before swine.

In the latter part of January, 1831, the Prophet Joseph, accompanied by his wife, Sidney Rigdon, and Edward Partridge, started for Kirtland, Ohio, in compliance with the Revelation, (Sec. 37). They had a journey of about 200 miles before them. The following graphic account of their arrival at their destination is from the *Contributor,* Vol. VI., p. 125:

"About the first of February, 1831, a sleigh containing four persons drove through the streets of Kirtland and drew up at the door of Gilbert and Whitney's mercantile establishment * * * One of the men, a young and stalwart personage, alighted, and, springing up the steps, walked into the store and to where the junior partner was standing.

" 'Newel K. Whitney! Thou art the man!' he exclaimed, extending his hand cordially, as if to an old and familiar acquaintance.

" 'You have the advantage of me,' replied the one addressed, as he mechanically took the proffered hand—a half-amused, half-mystified look overspreading his countenance—'I could not call you by name, as you have me.'

" 'I am Joseph, the Prophet,' said the stranger. 'You have prayed me here; now what do you want of me?'

"Mr. Whitney astonished, but no less delighted, as soon as his surprise would permit, conducted the party * * * across the street to his house on the corner, and introduced them to his wife. She shared fully his surprise and ecstasy."

There were about a hundred members in the Kirtland Branch of the Church, at this time.

In order to understand this Revelation, it may be well to recall the conditions that existed. There was, for instance, a society, sometimes called the Morley Family, because located on the farm of Isaac Morley. They had been baptized, but knew very little about the gospel. "Black Pete," a negro, was their "revelator." They claimed to see angels and to receive letters from heaven. There was one Wycom Clark, who claimed to be a revelator, and he organized "The Pure Church." The Prophet says, "the Branch of the Church in this part of the Lord's vineyard * * * were striving to do the will of God, so far as they knew it, though some strange notions and false spirits had crept in among them. With a little caution and some wisdom, I soon assisted the brethren and sisters to overcome them." (*History of the Church,* Vol. I., p. 146.)

In this Revelation, the first given in Kirtland, our Lord (1) commands obedience to His law (1-6); and (2) indicates His will concerning the Prophet and his two companions (7-12).

2. *Assemble * * * to agree upon my word*] Our Lord required of the Saints in Kirtland that they should obey *His* word; not the word of anyone that claimed to be a revelator. He required the Elders to assemble for the purpose of agreeing upon His word. The wisdom of this is apparent. Impostors succeed best when they can address each in-

dividual separately. When a number of persons meet, all desirous of knowing the truth, and praying for truth, the adversary has little chance of deceiving them.

3. *By the prayer of your faith ye shall receive my law*] This is an important principle in the kingdom of God. Christ is the Lawgiver. But He does not force His law upon anybody. He gives it in answer to prayer.

4. *I will be your Ruler*] Christ will be the Supreme Ruler, when he comes. It is, therefore, necessary that his people should have some of His laws, and learn to obey before He comes, otherwise He would have no people, no kingdom, to come to.

6. *It is not meet,* etc.] Our Lord does not give His laws to those who refuse to receive them. They belong only to the "children of the kingdom."

7. And again, it is meet that my servant Joseph Smith, Jun., should have a house built, in which to live and translate.

8. And again, it is meet that my servant Sidney Rigdon should live as seemeth him good, inasmuch as he keepeth my commandments.

9. And again, I have called my servant Edward Partridge; and I give a commandment, that he should be appointed by the voice of the church, and ordained a bishop unto the church, to leave his merchandise and to spend all his time in the labors of the church;

10. To see to all things as it shall be appointed unto him in my laws in the day that I shall give them.

11. And this because his heart is pure before me, for he is like unto Nathanael of old, in whom there is no guile.

12. These words are given unto you, and they are pure before me; wherefore, beware how you hold them, for they are to be answered upon your souls in the day of judgment. Even so. Amen.

7. Our Lord is the Lawgiver. He had appointed the Prophet Joseph His mouthpiece. His people could do no less, to show their appreciation of the blessings they had received, and would receive, than to provide the servants of the Lord a humble dwelling place. Even that would, finally, be their own gain, for "Inasmuch as ye have done it unto the least of these my brethren, ye have done it unto me" (Matt. 24:40).

8. *As seemeth him good*] This applies to Sidney Rigdon. The Saints were instructed to provide him with whatever accommodation he should

need. As one who keeps the commandments of God, he would not ask for a palatial residence, or a luxurious office.

9-11. Edward Partridge (see Sec. 36) is here called to the office of Bishop, and as such to spend all his time laboring for the Church, in accordance with the law of God, "because his heart is pure before me." In the kingdom of God it takes men with pure hearts to manage the temporal, as well as the spiritual affairs.

GENERAL NOTES

The laws defining the duties of the Bishopric were not yet fully revealed, but in a general way it was understood that the gathering of the Saints was commanded for their temporary salvation, and that the office was instituted with this end in view. The Revelation concerning gathering (Sec. 38) also contained more than an intimation of the United Order (vv. 24-27). Orson F. Whitney well remarks:

"An order of unity and equality, a system of consecration and stewardships, the abolition of fraud and monopoly in all their phases, a sinking of individual into and for the purpose of the common good, the sacrifice of self at the shrine of principle—of pure religion, whose incense—call it charity, philanthropy, or what we will, is the pure love of God and humanity. It was to the establishment of such an order,—one object of which, in the arcana of the faith, was to pave the way for the Zion of Enoch, which the Saints believe will yet descend to Earth, the planet whence it was taken,—that Joseph Smith, as early as February, 1831, more than fifty years before Edward Bellamy and his ingenious book 'Looking Backward' were heard of, directed his thoughts and labors. A movement to that end was the organization of the Bishopric, representing the temporal wing of the Mormon Church government. The Apostleship, which pertains to the Priesthood of Melchizedek, through possessing general powers, has a special calling to minister in spiritual things; while the Bishopric, which is the presidency of the Priesthood of Aaron, administers, under the direction of the higher authority, in things temporal" (*History of Utah,* Vol. I., p. 85). See also Secs. 42:30-32; 51:3-6 and 13-17.

The controversy over the meaning of "Bishop" has never been settled satisfactorily in the world. The New Testament has no office into which the Bishops of the various churches fit, and therefore they are at a loss to explain their duties. They notice that the Bishops in the Bible are sometimes called Elders and sometimes Bishops, and they are confused because they cannot understand how a Bishop can be an Elder. In Eph. 4:11, the Bishops are "Pastors," or Shepherds, and are placed next to the teachers. This is another puzzle. The fact is, that the Apostles appointed some to superintend the spiritual, and others to have charge of the temporal wants of the churches. The latter were called "Bishops," which means "overseers." To the Latter-day Saints, the controversy, in the light of modern revelation, is meaningless.

SECTION 42.

REVELATION *given through Joseph Smith the Prophet, at Kirtland, Ohio, February 9, 1831, in the presence of twelve Elders, and in fulfilment of the Lord's promise previously made; see Section 38:32. The Prophet specifies this revelation as embracing the law of the Church.——Elders commanded to go forth two by two westward, preaching and baptizing, according to the Bible and the Book of Mormon, and according to the latter-day revelations already given and to be given—Several commandments comprised in the decalog reiterated—Church members who commit crimes to be handed over to the law of the land—Members required to impart of their substance for the needs of the poor and the building up of the Church—Site of the New Jerusalem to be revealed later—Pride of heart and costly apparel forbidden—The idler denounced—Administration to the afflicted by the laying on of hands of the Elders— Comforting assurance concerning those who die in the Lord— Sexual sin proclaimed against—The fundamental principles of Church discipline.*

HEARKEN, O ye elders of my church, who have assembled yourselves together in my name, even Jesus Christ the Son of the living God, the Savior of the world; inasmuch as ye believe on my name and keep my commandments.

2. Again I say unto you, hearken and hear and obey the law which I shall give unto you.

3. For verily I say, as ye have assembled yourselves together according to the commandment wherewith I commanded you, and are agreed as touching this one thing, and have asked the Father in my name, even so ye shall receive.

In the Revelation given at Fayette, January 2nd, 1831, our Lord promised the Saints that He would give to them His law, if they would gather in Ohio (Sec. 38:32). On the 4th of February following, He added that they should receive the Law in answer to prayer. On the 9th of February these promises were fulfilled in this Revelation, which was given in the presence of twelve Elders and which is called the Law (v. 2). It is the Law of the Gospel. It may conveniently be studied under the following divisions: (1) Introduction (1-3); (2) the law of propaganda (4-10); (3) the law of ordination (11-17); (4) the law of moral conduct (18-29); (5) the law of charity (30-34); (6) the law of consecration (35-36); (7) the law of discipline (37-39); (8) the law of sundry duties (40-69); (9) the law of remuneration for services (70-73); (10) the law concerning new members (74-77); and (11) the law concerning transgressors (78-93).

1-3. This is the introduction to the Law. "Hearken, O ye Elders of my Church." They had gathered to hear the word of God; they had prayed for it; now their duty was to obey.

4. Behold, verily I say unto you, I give unto you this first commandment, that ye shall go forth in my name, every one of you, excepting my servants Joseph Smith, Jun., and Sidney Rigdon.

5. And I give unto them a commandment that they shall go forth for a little season, and it shall be given by the power of the Spirit when they shall return.

6. And ye shall go forth in the power of my Spirit, preaching my gospel, two by two, in my name, lifting up your voices as with the sound of a trump, declaring my word like unto angels of God.

7. And ye shall go forth baptizing with water, saying: Repent ye, repent ye, for the kingdom of heaven is at hand.

8. And from this place ye shall go forth into the regions westward; and inasmuch as ye shall find them that will receive you ye shall build up my church in every region—

9. Until the time shall come when it shall be revealed unto you from on high, when the city of the New Jerusalem shall be prepared, that ye may be gathered in one, that ye may be my people and I will be your God.

10. And again, I say unto you, that my servant Edward Partridge shall stand in the office whereunto I have appointed him. And it shall come to pass, that if he transgress another shall be appointed in his stead. Even so. Amen.

4-10. This is the law concerning the preaching of the gospel. It was given for the instruction of the Elders present when the Revelation came, but the principles it embodies are of general interest and application.

4. *Ye shall go forth in my name*] Those who go out to preach the gospel must go in the name of Jesus Christ; that is, on his behalf, in his stead. They are His ambassadors.

6. *In the power of my Spirit*] They must have the Spirit of God. That is the first requisite.

*Lifting up your voices as * * * a trump*] They must make themselves heard, in order that the world may have no excuse.

*Repent ye * * * the kingdom of heaven is at hand*] This is the gospel message. A true messenger of the Lord may be put to this test. He preaches repentance and proclaims the coming of the kingdom of heaven. He knows something about this kingdom. A pretender may preach philosophical or ethical discourses. He may read essays on civic or political problems, but he does not deliver *the* all-important message of the gospel.

9. *Until the time * * * of the New Jerusalem*] When Oliver Cowdery was called to go on a mission to the Lamanites, our Lord told him that "the City" would be built on the western border of the Country (Sec. 28:9). The Saints, therefore, knew that they were to build the New Jerusalem, but the place had not yet been revealed. In the meantime, the Elders were to build up "my Church in every region," until the time for the preparation of the City should come. The author of the 102nd Psalm had this City of Zion in view, when he said, "The people which shall be created shall praise the Lord. For he hath looked down from the heights of his sanctuary * * * to hear the groaning of the prisoner; to loose those that are appointed to death; to declare the name of the Lord in Zion, and his praise in Jerusalem (Ps. 102:18-21). This Zion is a *place* where those who have been "loosed" from death shall declare the name of the Lord. And it is necessary for the Lord to reveal where it shall be located and when it shall be built.

10. *Edward Partridge shall stand in office*] He, too, shall go on a mission (v. 4), but retain his office (Sec. 41:9).

*If he transgresses * * * another shall be appointed*] The office was to be permanent. Note the almost identical expression regarding a successor to the Prophet Joseph (Sec. 35:18). The law of succession is the same.

11. Again, I say unto you, that it shall not be given to any one to go forth to preach my gospel, or to build up my church, except he be ordained by some one who has authority, and it is known to the church that he has authority and has been regularly ordained by the heads of the church.

12. And again, the elders, priests and teachers of this church shall teach the principles of my gospel, which are in the Bible

and the Book of Mormon, in the which is the fulness of the gospel.

13. And they shall observe the covenants and church articles to do them, and these shall be their teachings, as they shall be directed by the Spirit.

14. And the Spirit shall be given unto you by the prayer of faith; and if ye receive not the Spirit ye shall not teach.

15. And all this ye shall observe to do as I have commanded concerning your teaching, until the fulness of my scriptures is given.

16. And as ye shall lift up your voices by the Comforter, ye shall speak and prophesy as seemeth me good;

17. For, behold, the Comforter knoweth all things, and beareth record of the Father and of the Son.

11-17. The law of ordination is here stated: No one shall go forth to preach the gospel except he be ordained by one who has authority, and who is known to hold such authority. Those who are so ordained must teach the principles of the gospel as contained in the Bible, the Book of Mormon, and the Covenants and Church Articles, and to do so as they shall be directed by the Holy Spirit.

11. *Ordained*] In the early days of the Church the term "Ordain" was used quite generally in the dictionary interpretation, "to appoint or establish," to set apart. This term was used in relation to the setting apart of sisters in the Relief Society. As time advanced, the term "ordain" came to mean in the Church the conferring of office in the order of the Priesthood, such as Elder, Seventy, High Priest, and in the case of those called to officiate in some office by virtue of their Priesthood, the expression "set apart" has become universal. We set apart a Bishop, after he has been ordained, a President of a Stake who has previously been ordained to the office of High Priest.

In the Bible and the Book of Mormon] The ministers of the Church are instructed to teach the principles of the Gospel as contained in these two volumes. This does not mean, necessarily, that they should always select a text from these books to preach from; but they should study these volumes, and know them, and teach what they contain. The Doctrine and Covenants was not published at this time.

15. *Fulness of my Scripture*] Refers especially to the new English version of the Bible which the Prophet and Sidney Rigdon were preparing vv. 56-58. At the October conference, 1880, the Doctrine and Covenants and the Pearl of Great Price were accepted as standard works of the Church, in addition to the Bible and the Book of Mormon (*Millennial Star,* Vol. XLII., p. 274).

18. And now, behold, I speak unto the church. Thou shalt not kill; and he that kills shall not have forgiveness in this world, nor in the world to come.

19. And again, I say, thou shalt not kill; but he that killeth shall die.

20. Thou shalt not steal; and he that stealeth and will not repent shall be cast out.

21. Thou shalt not lie; he that lieth and will not repent shall be cast out.

22. Thou shalt love thy wife with all thy heart, and shalt cleave unto her and none else.

23. And he that looketh upon a woman to lust after her shall deny the faith, and shall not have the Spirit; and if he repents not he shall be cast out.

24. Thou shalt not commit adultery; and he that committeth adultery, and repenteth not, shall be cast out.

25. But he that has committed adultery and repents with all his heart, and forsaketh it, and doeth it no more, thou shalt forgive;

26. But if he doeth it again, he shall not be forgiven, but shall be cast out.

27. Thou shalt not speak evil of thy neighbor, nor do him any harm.

28. Thou knowest my laws concerning these things are given in my scriptures; he that sinneth and repenteth not shall be cast out.

29. If thou lovest me thou shalt serve me and keep all my commandments.

18-29. This is the law of moral conduct, given especially to the Church, as the Decalogue was given to ancient Israel.

There are different kinds of divine laws. Some are binding for no other reason, as far as known to man, than the explicit command of God. They are called *positive* laws.

The commandment to Adam to offer sacrifices belongs to this class, for Adam knew of no reason for doing it, "save the Lord commanded me" (Pearl of Great Price, Book of Moses 5:6). Some are binding because of peculiar conditions or relations that may exist, and cease to be binding with the end of those conditions. New conditions require new laws, Israel in a settled condition in Canaan needed many rules and regulations which would have been inapplicable to their national life while in the wilderness. Laws regarding property, marriage, etc., belong to this class. Some laws are binding because they are founded on the nature and attributes of God. If God is love, it is our duty to love Him and teach others. If He is just, merciful, pure, it is our duty to conform our lives to the divine standards of justice, mercy, and holiness. And from this springs another class of laws which are founded on the permanent relations of men in their present state of existence. They are called the *moral* laws to distinguish them from *statutes,* which are founded on temporary relations of man to man. Statutes may vary from time to time and in different countries. Moral laws are permanent.

President J. Reuben Clark in the Improvement Era for November 1933:

"An illustration of how a regulation may be abrogated because not applicable to changed conditions, may be added. We take it from the law of health of ancient Israel. For evidently the Lord's law is as already indicated, that his people must be healthy and clean.

"To Moses was given a dietary and sanitary code that was to govern Israel. It was a code founded on scientific principles. It was the most complete not only of its own time, but of the millenniums that followed. It would be difficult for any student to escape the conclusion that the Mosaic dietary and sanitary code was dictated from a full knowledge of biological laws as well as a complete knowledge of human physiology and of advanced medical and scientific principles. One of the prohibitions of that code ran against the use by the Israelites of sea foods 'that have not fins and scales.'

"Today we eat many wholesome sea foods that do not meet this ancient requirement. Again it must be said that it is not for me to attempt to suggest the reasons why the Lord gave this great law, nor the reasons why he made this and other dietary distinctions. But looking at the matter from the point of view of human knowledge, one reason why the Lord forbade such things to ancient Israel might have been the extreme perishability of certain sea foods which would not be found either in the Wilderness or in Palestine, sea foods which rapidly decay, and which, in decaying, generate poisons, destructive of health and, indeed, of life itself. Ancient Israel had no such rapid transportation as would enable the delivery of such food materials while they were still fresh, and no refrigerating processes by which they might preserve such sea food materials pending the time they were to be eaten. Under such conditions, even a wise human lawgiver would today enact such a law as was given to ancient Israel, and for the reasons I have suggested. But however that may be, the Lord made to Israel an absolute prohibition against the eating of certain of such foods.

"But in our time, with our rapid transportation, our efficient refrigeration, such sea foods may be properly preserved and, so preserved, seem as wholesome as other sea foods that have fins and scales; the Lord has not forbidden these foods to us and we eat them.

"Thus the law that God's people must be clean and healthy has not changed, but the rule prescribed to secure obedience to the law has changed with the change in the manner of living."

18. *Thou shalt not kill*] This, as our Lord explains it (Matt. 5:22), stamps anger "without a cause," or malice in all its manifestations, as a crime. There is a difference between the anger that is but malice or thirst for revenge, and the emotion that is felt in the presence of injustice and wrong. It is malice that is forbidden. To take the life of a fellow-being in order to gratify malice is the highest crime one human being can commit against another. The Prophet Joseph recognized this when he said, "A murderer, for instance, one that sheds innocent blood, cannot have forgiveness." This commandment prohibits dueling, because dueling is but manslaughter, actual or potential. It prohibits suicide, which is self-murder. It condemns unjustifiable wars, which are but wholesale murders. There have been wars which are justifiable from the standpoint of one side of the contesting parties, but when the nations have courts of arbitration there will be no justification for any war, any more than there is for murder. The moral law must be applied to nations as well as individuals. "He that killeth shall die" (v. 19).

Statement of the First Presidency delivered at the General Conference on April 6, 1942:

"When therefore a constitutional law, obedience to those principles (meaning the principles laid down in the scriptures which have been previously cited) calls the manhood of the Church into the armed service of any country to which they owe allegiance, their high civic duty requires that they meet that call. If hearkening to that call and obeying those in command over them, they shall take the lives of those who fight against them, that will not make of them murderers nor subject them to the penalty that God has described for those who kill, beyond the principle to be mentioned shortly, for it would be a cruel God that would punish his children as moral sinners for acts done by them as the innocent instrumentalities of a sovereign whom he had told them to obey and whose will they were powerless to resist."

20. *Thou shalt not steal*] This commandment forbids all violations of the rights of property. But it also forbids those who have property and the power and influence that go with it, to use these in such a way as to prevent others from acquiring a just proportion of the resources of nature, or the accumulated wealth of mankind. Monopolies may be just as condemnable as anarchist plots. Dishonesty in the payment of wages, in weights and measures, in quality of commodities for which payment is exacted—all is stealing.

The gospel has been given to save the world from sin against this commandment, as well as from all other sins. "He that stealeth and will not repent, shall be cast out of the Church."

21. *Thou shalt not lie*] This commandment forbids the violation of all obligations of truth. It should be noted that lying is a crime, not merely a fault, or a weakness. To bear false witness against a neighbor is an aggravated form of offense against this law, but to lie about him, or her, in private circles is very little better than testifying falsely in court. Falsehoods have been divided into pernicious, benevolent, and jocose. The first includes all that are instigated by an evil motive and are designed to promote an evil end. The second are so-called "white lies," and the third are mirth-promoting and supposed to be harmless, because there is no pretence that they are true. To these should be added another class, the falsehoods of innocence. A man may be deceived and honestly believe that he is telling the truth, when, in fact, he is but repeating a falsehood. There are in the world both theologians and philosophers to whom this applies. It has been claimed, in support of the doctrine of infallibility, that a man may be a liar as a man and yet trustworthy as an official. It might just as well be alleged that an individual may be intoxicated as a man, and, at the same time, sober, as a clergyman. Lying and hypocrisy, in its various forms, are crimes, and "He that lieth and will not repent, shall be cast out" of the Church.

22-26. In these paragraphs our Lord forbids impurity in behavior, words, and thought. Compare Matthew 5:28. There is, perhaps, no sin which has caused more sorrow, more ruined homes, more sickness, more bloodshed, than the one here prohibited. None has caused more falling away from the Church. George A. Smith observes:

"I have been conversant with early elders, and I am satisfied that a large number of them fell from their positions in the Kingdom of God because they yielded to the spirit of adultery; this was the cause of their destruction. There was an Elder named John Smith, who lived in Indiana, who was quite popular in that part of the country as a preacher. He apostatized but did not know it. In talking about his faith and how firm he was, he said, 'I have proved the Revelation given to Joseph Smith untrue, which says that if a man shall commit adultery he shall lose the Spirit of God and deny the faith. I have proved that not to be true.' He was so blind that he could not see through the darkness that the spirit of adultery had placed upon his head the great apostasy which seemed to shake the Church, and tried men's souls" (*Journal of Discourses,* Vol. XI. p. 10).

Marriage is ordained of God and a commandment to his children as well as it was to Adam. Being ordained of God, marriage should be performed in accordance with His laws and that would be for time and all eternity in the Temple of the Lord. It was never intended that marriage should end at the death of the covenanting parties. Our Lord declared that when a man and a woman are married according to divine law, they twain become one flesh; therefore they are *no more* twain, but one "flesh." His laws are eternal, not temporary laws. Marriage in the world for time only are based on a misconception of the word of the Lord to the Sadducees who did not believe in the resurrection.

Celibacy virtually denies the sacred character of the marriage relation. It is contrary to the Word of God. Men and women should be taught to marry young and to keep themselves pure. If they have a correct understanding of their mission on earth, their duties and privileges as husbands and wives, fathers and mothers, they will no more be guilty of violating the laws of chastity, than of treating with disrespect anything that is sacred—the emblems of the Sacrament, for instance, or the revelations of the Lord.

27. "Thou shalt not speak evil of thy neighbor nor do him any harm." Lying is condemned and the liar who will not repent is not to remain in the Church; neither shall backbiting, evil speaking, nor bearing false witness, be tolerated by the Lord, and those who indulge in these evil habits will receive their reward in punishment. It is better never to speak in derision or ridicule of anyone or even to expose their follies or circulate their sins, than to do so to their harm. Speaking evil of one is classed as a sin against the law of the Gospel. It may be necessary when on the witness stand, or before an ecclesiastical court, to testify of one's sins, but to do so promiscuously is a sin. Even when called upon to testify, the testimony should be given in the spirit of brotherly kindness, not in the spirit of vindictiveness or gloating over the predicament of a fellow being where punishment awaits him. Speaking words that may prove harmful to another is a crime. Such words constitute the "idle words" condemned by our Savior, for which there will come a day of judgment. (Matt. 12:35-36.) "The lip of truth shall be established for ever: but a lying tongue is but for a moment." (Prov. 12:19.) A very common way in which this law is broken is by attacking in caricatures intended to convey some falsehood about individuals.

29. *If thou lovest me*] The Lord expects His children to keep His laws because they love Him. Love of God gives "boldness in the day of judgment" (I. John 4:17).

30. And behold, thou wilt remember the poor, and consecrate of thy properties for their support that which thou hast to impart unto them, with a covenant and a deed which cannot be broken.

31. And inasmuch as ye impart of your substance unto the poor, ye will do it unto me; and they shall be laid before the bishop of my church and his counselors, two of the elders, or

high priests,* such as he shall appoint or has appointed and set apart for that purpose.

32. And it shall come to pass, that after they are laid before the bishop of my church, and after that he has received these testimonies concerning the consecration of the properties of my church, that they cannot be taken from the church, agreeable to my commandments, every man shall be made accountable unto me, a steward over his own property, or that which he has received by consecration, as much as is sufficient for himself and family.

33. And again, if there shall be properties in the hands of the church, or any individuals of it, more than is necessary for their support after this first consecration, which is a residue to be consecrated unto the bishop, it shall be kept to administer to those who have not, from time to time, that every man who has need may be amply supplied and receive according to his wants.

34. Therefore, the residue shall be kept in my storehouse, to administer to the poor and the needy, as shall be appointed by the high council of the church,* and the bishop and his council;

30-34. The true law of charity is stated here. These paragraphs should be read in connection with the preceding one, "If thou lovest me * * * behold, thou wilt remember the poor." Christ's poor should be remembered for His sake.

30. *Consecrate of thy properties*] The ultimate aim our Lord had in view was the abolition of poverty among His children, but in the meantime it was a duty of the Church members to consecrate some of their property for the support of the poor and needy. Property so consecrated was turned over to the Presiding Bishop and his counselors (v. 31) by legal instruments ("testimonies," v. 32) so that the title to it would be good.

32. *Steward over his own property*] A man might turn his property over to the Bishop, but then he should receive back enough for the support of himself and family, and use it as the Lord's steward.

33. Any surplus should be kept for the poor and needy.

35. And for the purpose of purchasing lands for the public benefit of the church, and building houses of worship, and building up of the New Jerusalem which is hereafter to be revealed—

° The words, "or High Priests," were added by the Prophet some years after; and also the words, "High Council," in the 34th verse.

36. That my covenant people may be gathered in one in that day when I shall come to my temple. And this I do for the salvation of my people.

35-36. The law of charity is, in the kingdom of God, connected with the law of consecration, for the building up of the New Jerusalem, the gathering of Israel, and the coming of the Lord.

A word may be said here of the religio-social system by which the temporal salvation of the world is to be accomplished. According to the Revelations on the subject, each individual is to deed to the Bishop, his, or her, property, *in toto*. It would then belong to the Bishop. After all property has been thus "consecrated," all members are equal in ownership. Then the Bishop deeds back to each individual a portion of the common property. A man would probably receive back the same farm, or the same factory, that he owned before. Whatever he needs for himself and family is his, and the surplus goes back into the common treasury (See Whitney's *History of Utah,* Vol. I., p. 84). These are the main outlines of the "United Order," or "Order of Enoch." In all probability further revelations as to details are needed, before the Order can be established on a practical basis.

"Those who are inspired by the Holy Spirit to comprehend the dealings of God with His people, both ancient and modern, may be able to look forward to the future and behold a prosperous and happy people that should be one in temporal things, and rich in the enjoyment of heavenly things, and among whom there will be no poor or rich, having all things common, so far as property is concerned, when no one will say, "this is mine, and I have a right to do just as I please with it" (Erastus Snow, *Jour. of Dis.,* Vol. XIX., p. 179).

36. *For the salvation of my people*] The prevalent idea seems to be that "salvation" means happiness hereafter. Salvation should begin here, and one of the evils from which the gospel will save men, is poverty and destitution.

37. And it shall come to pass, that he that sinneth and repenteth not shall be cast out of the church, and shall not receive again that which he has consecrated unto the poor and the needy of my church, or in other words, unto me—

38. For inasmuch as ye do it unto the least of these, ye do it unto me.

39. For it shall come to pass, that which I spake by the mouths of my prophets shall be fulfilled; for I will consecrate of the riches of those who embrace my gospel among the Gentiles unto the poor of my people who are of the house of Israel

37-39. The law concerning transgressors is that unrepentant offenders, when cast out of the Church, lose their standing in the Order also. This is necessary; for a community of this kind must be founded on morality. It is just, too. For those who consecrate their property to the Lord's service must do it with the understanding that they cannot demand the return of it whenever they experience a change of mind (See Sec. 85:11).

40. And again, thou shalt not be proud in thy heart; let all thy garments be plain, and their beauty the beauty of the work of thine own hands;

41. And let all things be done in cleanliness before me.

42. Thou shalt not be idle; for he that is idle shall not eat the bread nor wear the garments of the laborer.

43. And whosoever among you are sick, and have not faith to be healed, but believe, shall be nourished with all tenderness, with herbs and mild food, and that not by the hand of an enemy.

44. And the elders of the church, two or more, shall be called, and shall pray for and lay their hands upon them in my name; and if they die they shall die unto me, and if they live they shall live unto me.

45. Thou shalt live together in love, insomuch that thou shalt weep for the loss of them that die, and more especially for those that have not hope of a glorious resurrection.

46. And it shall come to pass that those that die in me shall not taste of death, for it shall be sweet unto them;

47. And they that die not in me, wo unto them, for their death is bitter.

48. And again, it shall come to pass that he that hath faith in me to be healed, and is not appointed unto death, shall be healed.

49. He who hath faith to see shall see.

50. He who hath faith to hear shall hear.

51. The lame who hath faith to leap shall leap.

52. And they who have not faith to do these things, but believe in me, have power to become my sons; and inasmuch as they break not my laws thou shalt bear their infirmities.

53. Thou shalt stand in the place of thy stewardship.

54. Thou shalt not take thy brother's garment; thou shalt pay for that which thou shalt receive of thy brother.

55. And if thou obtainest more than that which would be for thy support, thou shalt give it into my storehouse, that all things may be done according to that which I have said.

56. Thou shalt ask, and my scriptures shall be given as I have appointed, and they shall be preserved in safety;

57. And it is expedient that thou shouldst hold thy peace concerning them, and not teach them until ye have received them in full.

58. And I give unto you a commandment that then ye shall teach them unto all men; for they shall be taught unto all nations, kindreds, tongues and people.

59. Thou shalt take the things which thou hast received, which have been given unto thee in my scriptures for a law, to be my law to govern my church;

60. And he that doeth according to these things shall be saved, and he that doeth them not shall be damned if he so continue.

61. If thou shalt ask, thou shalt receive revelation upon revelation, knowledge upon knowledge, that thou mayest know the mysteries and peaceable things—that which bringeth joy, that which bringeth life eternal.

62. Thou shalt ask, and it shall be revealed unto you in mine own due time where the New Jerusalem shall be built.

63. And behold, it shall come to pass that my servants shall be sent forth to the east and to the west, to the north and to the south.

64. And even now, let him that goeth to the east teach them that shall be converted to flee to the west, and this in consequence of that which is coming on the earth, and of secret combinations.

65. Behold, thou shalt observe all these things, and great shall be thy reward; for unto you it is given to know the mysteries of the kingdom, but unto the world it is not given to know them.

66. Ye shall observe the laws which ye have received and be faithful.

67. And ye shall hereafter receive church covenants, such

as shall be sufficient to establish you, both here and in the New Jerusalem.

68. Therefore, he that lacketh wisdom, let him ask of me, and I will give him liberally and upbraid him not.

69. Lift up your hearts and rejoice, for unto you the kingdom, or in other words, the keys of the church have been given. Even so. Amen.

49-69. Various duties of the Latter-day Saints are set forth in these paragraphs. All are important.

40. *Thou shalt not be proud in thy heart*]

> "These six things doth the Lord hate:
> Yea, seven are an abomination unto him:
> A proud look, a lying tongue,
> And hands that shed innocent blood,
> A heart that deviseth wicked imaginations,
> Feet that be swift in running to mischief,
> A false witness that speaketh lies,
> And he that soweth discord among brethren."
> —(Prov. 6:16-19).

The opposite of pride is humility, and this beautiful virtue manifests itself by deference to others. "All of you be subject one to another, and be clothed with humility; for God resisteth the proud" (I. Pet. 5:5).

Let thy garments be plain] There is in every age a tendency to exaggerate personal adornment. Paul (I. Tim. 2:9) takes note of the "broided hair," gold, pearls, and costly array of his day. Peter (I. Pet. 3:3) warns against making the womanly adornment consist of "plating the hair," wearing of gold, or "putting on of apparel." The women of Greece and Rome, at that time, braided their hair and intertwined in it chains of gold and strings of pearls, while they imported cloth for their gowns, or garments, from factories known for the fineness and costliness of their fabrics. The Christians were not to adorn themselves with such things, but with the virtues that make up a beautiful character. Our Lord gives the same law in this dispensation.

41. *Let all things be done in cleanliness*] This is, after all, the chief adornment. He who keeps himself clean in body, in habits, in clothes, in habitations, is well adorned, even if his garments are patched and threadbare.

42. *Thou shalt not be idle*] If all are workers, there will be ample time for amusement and improvement for all.

"The non-producer must live on the products of those who labor. There is no other way. If we all labor a few hours a day, we could then spend the remainder of our time in rest and the improvement of our minds. This would give an opportunity to the children to be educated in the learning of the day, and to possess all the wisdom of man" (Brigham Young, *Jour. of Dis.*, Vol. XIX., p. 47).

43-44. The Latter-day Saints believe in the healing virtue of the prayer of faith, but they do not proscribe the use of "herbs and mild food," nor the aid of a physician. In the month of November, 1842, Brigham Young was seriously ill. In his diary the Prophet Joseph notes that, "He was suddenly and severely attacked by disease, with strong symptoms of apoplexy," and then he adds, "We immediately administered to him by laying on of hands and prayer, accompanied with the use of herbs" (*History of the Church*, Vol. V., p. 126).

Under date of December 26th, 1842, the Prophet writes:

"General Law gave me in custody of Doctor Richards, with whom I visited Sister Morey, who was severely afflicted. We prescribed *Lobelia* for her, among other things, which is excellent in its place" (*ibid.*, p. 209).

If they die] All who have any experience in the Church know of instances of miraculous healing, but there is no promise that all afflicted persons for whom the Elders pray shall recover. But the promise to the Church members is that, if they die, "they shall die unto me."

45. *Thou shalt weep for the loss of them*] It is natural to feel sorrow when death parts us from our loved ones.

"Parting, at best, is underlaid with tears and pain."

46. *Not taste death*] But we must not mourn as those who are "without hope" of a reunion. To those who die in the Lord death is not bitter. To them it does not taste like death. It is sweet.

> "Passing out of the shadow
> Into eternal day
> Why do we call it dying,
> This sweet passing away?"

"That which we call death is merely the slumber and rest of this mortal clay, and that only for a little season, while the spirit, the life, has gone to enjoy again the presence and society of those whence it came, and to whom it is joy again to return. And this will be the condition of the righteous until the morning of the resurrection, when the spirit will have power to call forth the lifeless frame to be united again, and they both become a living soul, an immortal being, filled with the light and power of God * * * What reason have we to mourn? None, except that we are deprived for a few days of the society of one whom we love" (Joseph F. Smith, *Jour. of Dis.*, Vol. XIX., p. 263).

48-52. *Appointed to death*] Sometimes God intervenes even when the decree of death has gone forth, as in the case of King Hezekiah (II. Kings 20:1-7); but the rule is that he whose time for departure has come must follow the beck and call of the silent messenger. It is best so. But he who "is not appointed to death" shall be healed, in accordance with his faith. And those who have not faith to be healed may yet have faith in the Lord to become His children. It is a peculiar fact that it is easier to believe that the Lord is willing to give us celestial glory, than it is to feel absolutely certain that He will give us what we need in life. Many believe that He can give them back their body, in resurrection, but deny His power to heal them this side of the grave.

A most remarkable manifestation of the healing power of God was given in the early days of Nauvoo. Many of the Saints, driven from Missouri and weakened by the exposures, were taken sick, in the moist, malarial air of the new settlements. On the 22nd of July, 1839, the Prophet arose from a bed of sickness and went forth in the power of God to administer to the sick. Heber C. Kimball describes what followed thus:

"He commenced with the sick in his own house, then visited those who were camping in tents in his own dooryard, commanding the sick in the name of the Lord Jesus Christ to arise from their beds and be whole, when they were healed according to his words. He then went from house to house, and from tent to tent, upon the bank of the river, healing the sick by the power of Israel's God as he went among them. He did not miss a single house, wagon, or tent, and continued this work up to the 'the upper stone house,' where he crossed the river in a boat, accompanied by Parley P. Pratt, Orson Pratt, John E. Page, John Taylor, and myself, and landed at Montrose. He then walked into the cabin of Brother Brigham Young, who was lying very sick, and commanded him in the name of the Lord Jesus Christ to arise and be made whole. He arose, healed of his sickness, and thus accompanied Joseph and his brethren of the Twelve, and went into the house of Elijah Fordham, who was insensible, and considered by his family and friends to be in the hands of death. Joseph stepped to his bedside, looked him in the eye for a minute without speaking, then took him by the hand and commanded him in the name of Jesus Christ to arise from his bed and walk. Brother Fordham immediately leaped out of his bed, threw off all his poultices and bandages, dressed himself, called for a bowl of bread and milk, which he ate, and followed us into the street. We then went into the house of Joseph B. Noble, who was also very sick, and he was healed in the same manner" (Orson F. Whitney, *Life of Heber C. Kimball,* p. 273-4).

On this occasion, the Prophet, being importuned to come and administer to the twin children of a stranger, handed his handkerchief to Elder Wilford Woodruff and asked him to go with the stranger, and wipe the faces of the little sufferers with it. Elder Woodruff did so, and they recovered.

53. *Thou*] Refers to all the Saints, as in paragraphs 42 and 45.

54. *Thou shalt not take thy brother's garment*] Business must be coupled with humane considerations. Do not exact the "pound of flesh."

Thou shalt pay] Avoid debt. On this point modern legislators might study the Mosaic legislation with profit.

56. *My Scriptures shall be given*] The new English version (v. 15).

57. *Until ye have received them in full*] Note the injunction against teaching the new version as long as it was incomplete.

59-60. *The things which thou has received*] Refers to the Revelations given. They are the law by which the Church shall be governed. According to that law men will be saved or condemned.

61-64. Here is a promise that, in answer to prayer, the Saints shall receive revelations and knowledge. The Spirit of Revelation is with the Saints whose hearts are opened to let the light in. The promise embraces especially a Revelation concerning the location of the New Jerusalem.

68-69. In view of such promises it is the duty of the Saints to pray for wisdom and to rejoice before the Lord.

70. The priests and teachers shall have their stewardships, even as the members.

71. And the elders or high priests* who are appointed to assist the bishop as counselors in all things, are to have their families supported out of the property which is consecrated to the bishop, for the good of the poor, and for other purposes, as before mentioned;

72. Or they are to receive a just remuneration for all their services, either a stewardship or otherwise, as may be thought best or decided by the counselors and bishop.

73. And the bishop, also, shall receive his support, or a just remuneration for all his services in the church.

70-73. The law of remuneration is that those who administer in spiritual affairs must have their stewardships and labor for their living, "even as the members." This is wisdom. For in that position they are absolutely independent and can preach the truth without fear. Those who administer in temporal affairs and give their entire time to public business are to have a just remuneration. If they were to earn a living for themselves, they could not give all their time and energy to the community.

74.† Behold, verily I say unto you, that whatever persons among you, having put away their companions for the cause of fornication, or in other words, if they shall testify before you

* The words, "or High Priests," were added by the Prophet some years after.—Orson Pratt.

† Verses 74-93 were given some days after the first 73 verses.

in all lowliness of heart that this is the case, ye shall not cast them out from among you;

75. But if ye shall find that any persons have left their companions for the sake of adultery, and they themselves are the offenders, and their companions are living, they shall be cast out from among you.

76. And again, I say unto you, that ye shall be watchful and careful, with all inquiry, that ye receive none such among you if they are married;

77. And if they are not married, they shall repent of all their sins or ye shall not receive them.

78. And again, every person who belongeth to this church of Christ, shall observe to keep all the commandments and covenants of the church.

79. And it shall come to pass, that if any persons among you shall kill they shall be delivered up and dealt with according to the laws of the land; for remember that he hath no forgiveness; and it shall be proved according to the laws of the land.

80. And if any man or woman shall commit adultery, he or she shall be tried before two elders of the church, or more, and every word shall be established against him or her by two witnesses of the church, and not of the enemy; but if there are more than two witnesses it is better.

81. But he or she shall be condemned by the mouth of two witnesses; and the elders shall lay the case before the church, and the church shall lift up their hands against him or her, that they may be dealt with according to the law of God.

82. And if it can be, it is necessary that the bishop be present also.

83. And thus ye shall do in all cases which shall come before you.

84. And if a man or woman shall rob, he or she shall be delivered up unto the law of the land.

85. And if he or she shall steal, he or she shall be delivered up unto the law of the land.

86. And if he or she shall lie, he or she shall be delivered up unto the law of the land.

87.   And if he or she do any manner of iniquity, he or she shall be delivered up unto the law, even that of God.

88.   And if thy brother or sister offend thee, thou shalt take him or her between him or her and thee alone; and if he or she confess thou shalt be reconciled.

89.   And if he or she confess not thou shalt deliver him or her up unto the church, not to the members, but to the elders. And it shall be done in a meeting, and that not before the world.

90.   And if thy brother or sister offend many, he or she shall be chastened before many.

91.   And if any one offend openly, he or she shall be rebuked openly, that he or she may be ashamed. And if he or she confess not, he or she shall be delivered up unto the law of God.

92.   If any shall offend in secret, he or she shall be rebuked in secret, that he or she may have opportunity to confess in secret to him or her whom he or she has offended, and to God, that the church may not speak reproachfully of him or her.

93.   And thus shall ye conduct in all things.

74-93.   This is the law concerning transgressors.

74.   *Fornication*]   This term is sometimes used for all kinds of sexual sins (See I. Cor. 7:2; Matt. 5:32; I. Cor. 5:1), and also, figuratively, for idolatry (II. Chron. 21:11). But generally it stands for the sin of impurity when committed between unmarried persons. At the time when St. Paul wrote his Epistles, the pagans generally were guilty of this sin to such an extent that many actually believed that the body was made for licentiousness. The Apostles contradict this false view. He says (I. Cor. 6:13), "The body is not for fornication, but for the Lord." The Lord, he argues, will raise it up, if we keep it for Him, but by joining a harlot we become one with her and have no further claim on Christ. Nevertheless, according to this Revelation, if one has fallen into this sin and confesses it in humility, he is not to be cast out of the Church.

75.   *Adultery*]   A case of adultery is different. That sin is one of impurity where one or both offenders are married. Anciently this wickedness was punished by death so the Lord commanded. (Lev. 20:10.) "Sexual union is lawful in wedlock, and if participated in with right intent is honorable and sanctifying. But without the bonds of marriage, sexual indulgence is a debasing sin, abominable in the sight of Deity." (President Joseph F. Smith—*Gospel Doctrine*, pp. 386-7.)

"We accept without reservation or qualification the affirmation of Deity, through an ancient Nephite prophet: "For I the Lord God, delight in the chastity of women. And whoredoms are an abomination before me; thus saith the Lord of Hosts (Jacob 2:28.) * * * We hold that sexual sin is second only to the shedding of innocent blood in the category of personal crimes; and that the adulterer shall have no part in the exaltation of the blessed." (President Joseph F. Smith, *Gospel Doctrine*, p. 388).

76. *Be watchful and careful*] Watch, so that offenders of this class be not accepted as members, "if they are married;" that is, if the party sinned against still has a claim upon him or her.

79. *If any * * * shall kill*] A murderer has no forgiveness. He must be delivered up to the law of the land. It is the business of the regularly-constituted authorities to decide whether the killing is murder or manslaughter.

80-83. An adulterer, or adulteress, who is a Church member, is to be tried before a Church court and dealt with according to the Law of God (v. 75-77).

Others to be given up to the law of the land are, robbers (v. 84), thieves (v. 85), liars (v. 86). Those guilty of any other kind of iniquity are to be delivered up unto the Law of God (v. 87).

Note the perfect equality in responsibility of the sexes, in the Law of God. "If he or she" is guilty, the consequences are the same. There is no sex in crime. Equal "rights," to use a familiar expression, presuppose equality in responsibility.

88-92. This is the rule of procedure in case a brother or sister offend thee. The offender is to be labored with and brought to confess, and then there is to be forgiveness and reconciliation. The confession is to be as public as the offense and no more.

It may be remarked here that the Romanists have a sacrament which they call *Penance,* by means of which they deal with transgressors in their church. It is, they hold, a divine institution by which sins committed after baptism are remitted. It consists of contrition, confession, and satisfaction, on the part of the sinner, and absolution, on the part of the clergyman. By contrition is meant sorrow, or remorse. Confession is confiding whatever is done, to the priest. It must be "auricular" and include all "mortal sins," because "a sin not confessed is not forgiven." Confession, however, does not, in the Roman view, entitle the offender to obtain remission of temporal punishments or torture in purgatory, but if he makes "satisfaction" as directed by the priest, and the priest grants him "absolution," he escapes eternal death. Hence, a thief and a murderer may have to suffer here and in purgatory, though he may receive eternal bliss through penance. It is very instructive to compare this view with the law concerning transgression and transgressors, as enunciated in this Revelation.

In the special Bishops' meeting held at the April Conference, on the evening of April 5, 1946, President Clark said this:

"There is in the Church, as Bishop Richards said, the power to remit sins, but I do not believe that it resides in the bishops. That is a power that must be exercised under the proper authority of the priesthood and by those who hold the keys that pertain to that function. Rue back every sinner, forgive them personally, the Lord has said that. Do all you can, but short of that formal remission the matter then rests between the transgressor and the Lord who is merciful, who knows all the circumstances, who has no disposition but to aid his children, give them comfort, build them up, and help them, but the Lord has said, 'I can not look upon sin with the least degree of allowance,' so we leave it with him and our prayers go with the prayers of the transgressor that God will forgive him, but the path of the sinner was never smooth and I believe it never will be. We must pay the penalty, but God's mercy tempers his justice. His love is boundless, his desire to save us is infinite and he will be good to us. All of us have done something that would have been better left undone; all of us need the mercy of God and His love, and we should look at all others as our brothers and sisters, knowing that we with them have something for which to be forgiven, but we must remember that we must pay whatever the price may be that the Lord exacts."

GENERAL NOTES

This Revelation is called the Law of Christ (v. 2). In the Scriptures the Law of God is always a manifestation of His will. In nature the laws of nature are His laws. God's will determines the moral standards. It is the rule of conduct. It is necessary that God should give laws to His children. There is in every man a disposition to lord it over others. Everyone, as soon as he has formed an opinion on a subject, is inclined to force it upon others, just as Lucifer proposed to do with regard to the plan of salvation. But when God manifests *His* will, all men and women are brought to a level of equality, without which there can be no true liberty. Hence, under the divine law liberty is possible, since all are under equal obligation to obey, and have an equal chance of obtaining the reward of obedience.

The ministers of the Church are instructed to teach the principles of the gospel, as found in the Scriptures, "as they shall be directed by the Spirit" (12-14). Studying the Scriptures without the guidance of the Spirit does not reveal their true meaning to us. But if we have the Spirit, we shall not fall into error, even if we are not great Bible scholars. As an illustration of this truth we may quote George Q. Cannon:

"I remember hearing related Brother Parley P. Pratt's first interview with the Saints at Fayette, Seneca County, where the Church was organized * * * On that occasion he was called upon to speak; the Prophet Joseph was not present at the time. He brought forth from the prophecies of Isaiah, Jeremiah, Ezekiel, and other prophets, abundant proofs concerning the work which the Lord had established through His servant Joseph. A great many of the Latter-day Saints were surprised that there were so many evidences existing in the Bible concerning this work. The Church had then been organized some five months, but the members had never heard from any of the Elders these proofs and evidences which existed in the Bible. And, if I remember correctly, he told me that Oliver Cowdery and the Prophet Joseph himself were surprised at the great amount of evidence there was in the Bible concerning these things. The Prophet Joseph was inspired of God to teach the doctrines of life and salvation, and he did so without reference to what the ancient prophets had said. I have heard President Young make the same remarks" (*Jour. of Dis.,* Vol. XIX., p. 105).

The penalty for murder, adultery in certain cases, and a number of other crimes was, under the Mosaic law, death. The object of the severity was to keep Israel pure. Criminal tendencies were extinguished by the enforcement of a rigorous law, the possibility of transmitting them to the next generation, by inheritance, being done away with. It should be remembered, if the Mosaic law is thought too severe, considering the infinite mercy of God, that Israel had a judiciary, a Priesthood, with access to the presence of Jehovah, who was the Supreme Judge and whose mind and will could be ascertained by means of urim and thummim. There was no danger of a wrong verdict, as long as the judges were in communication with God.

SECTION 43.

REVELATION *given through Joseph Smith the Prophet, at Kirtland, Ohio, in February, 1831. At this time some members of the Church were disturbed by people making false claims as revelators. See History of the Church, vol. 1, p. 154.——— First part of the revelation addressed to the Elders of the Church—Revelations to the Church given only through the one appointed to receive such—Elders warned against spurious claims and false teachings of others—Elders sent forth to teach according to the spirit of revelation and not to be taught in the precepts of men—Assurances of the Lord's future advent— Calamities to precede his coming—Latter part of the revelation addressed to the nations of the earth—Warning, proclamation, and commandment.*

O HEARKEN, ye elders of my church, and give ear to the words which I shall speak unto you.

2. For behold, verily, verily, I say unto you, that ye have received a commandment for a law unto my church, through him whom I have appointed unto you to receive commandments and revelations from my hand.

3. And this ye shall know assuredly—that there is none other appointed unto you to receive commandments and revelations until he be taken, if he abide in me.

4. But verily, verily, I say unto you, that none else shall be appointed unto this gift except it be through him; for if it be taken from him he shall not have power except to appoint another in his stead.

5. And this shall be a law unto you, that ye receive not the teachings of any that shall come before you as revelations or commandments;

6. And this I give unto you that you may not be deceived, that you may know they are not of me.

7. For verily I say unto you, that he that is ordained of me shall come in at the gate and be ordained as I have told you before, to teach those revelations which you have received and shall receive through him whom I have appointed.

A short time after the Revelation in Section 42 was given, a woman named Hubble came to the Prophet Joseph and made the claim that she had received divine revelations. She was one claimant of many, at this time. Elder George A. Smith relates that, "There was a prevalent spirit all through the early history of this Church, which prompted the Elders to suppose that they knew more than the Prophet. Elders would tell you that the Prophet was going wrong" (*Jour. of Dis.,* Vol. XI., p. 7.) On one occasion Sidney Rigdon began a sermon by saying that the Church and Kingdom had been rent from them and given to another people. Joseph was absent, and when he came home, he found Rigdon acting very strangely. There was a man named Hawley who said the Lord had commanded him to go to Kirtland and tell the Prophet that he had lost his office, because he had caused John Noah, a pretended prophet, to be cut off from the Church. Many were bewildered by the different voices and consequent confusion. It was therefore necessary to ask the Lord for light and guidance with regard to this matter, and this Revelation came in answer to prayer.

In this important communication to the Church our Lord (1) gives the law concerning the leadership of the Church and the succession (1-7); (2) states the duties of the officers and members with regard to (a) public assemblies (8-10); (b) the divinely-appointed leader (11-14);

(c) the world (15-16) (d) in view of the advent of the Lord (17-28); and (3) gives a promise of the coming of the Millennium (29-35).

1-7. In these paragraphs the Lord declares that there is only *one* appointed at a time to receive divine Revelations and commandments for the Church. This law was more than adumbrated in a Revelation addressed to Oliver Cowdery in September, 1830 (Sec. 28:2-7); and again in a Revelation to Joseph Smith and Sidney Rigdon, in December, the same year (Sec. 35:18). Here it is again stated.

2. *A Commandment for a law*] Refers to Sec. 42. This Law of the Church was received through the Prophet Joseph; not through any of his associates; much less through any of the numerous pretenders that appeared in Kirtland at this time. This ought to have been sufficient evidence to the Saints that God had chosen Joseph as the Prophet through whom He would speak to the Church.

3. *There is none other appointed*] The Lord has declared that his house is a house of order and therefore only the President of the Church is appointed to receive revelation for the Church. There was some difficulty in the early years of the Church because men assumed the privilege of receiving revelation for the Church. This led to confusion and some were deceived. It was due to this condition that the Lord decreed that only Joseph Smith was authorized to receive revelation for the Church, and this was to be the law to the Church.

4. *Except through him*] If Joseph should prove not faithful, the gift would be taken from him, and in that case he would have "no power, except to appoint another in his stead."

"It was necessary at that time that some provision be made for the perpetuity of the Priesthood with its keys and powers, and especially the prophetic office, in case that Joseph Smith should not prove faithful to the great trust in the days of his preparation and qualification, and before he became thoroughly seasoned and fitted for this important calling. In such an emergency the power of necessity must have been conferred by Joseph Smith on his successor, for he held the keys; therefore the Lord declared that in case of the Prophet's transgression, or removal, he would still retain the power in that case to ordain his successor, and to confer upon such successor, whom the Lord was to choose, the keys and authority that had been conferred upon him" (Joseph Fielding Smith, Origin of the *'Reorganized'* Church, p. 39).

Except to appoint another in his stead] This clause, at first sight, may appear difficult to understand. If the Prophet should be removed through apostasy, for instance, would he, in his fallen condition, be willing, or have authority, to ordain a successor? Would he not, more probably, make an effort to retain the position for himself? Would Sidney Rigdon, when he aspired to the Presidency, have appointed somebody else, even at the request of the Church? On the other hand, if the Prophet should be removed by death, how could he "appoint another in his stead?" But whatever difficulty the passage may present, has been removed by God, when He inspired His servant to appoint a Council of Twelve Apostles and to confer upon this body all the keys, power, and authority which he held himself. Thus provision was made for a successor appointed and ordained, as the Revelation says he should be, through, or by, the Prophet, before his removal, fully equipped to step into the vacant place.

Note that this arrangement is the same as that which our Savior made when He was here in the flesh. He told the Twelve that it was the Father's good pleasure to give *them* the kingdom (Luke 12:32). Shortly before His death He said to the Twelve, "I appoint unto you a kingdom, as my Father hath appointed unto me" (Luke 22:29); and again, in His prayer, after the last passover, He said, "As thou hast sent me into the world, even so have I also sent them into the world" (John 17-18). He committed the Kingdom with its duties and responsibilities to their care. They were to administer it after His departure. Even so, in our day, He has provided that the leadership of the affairs of the Kingdom should devolve on the Twelve, in the case of the removal, by one cause or another, of the Prophet; see Secs. 90:4; 107:24 and 112:30-32.

President Anthon H. Lund, commenting on John 21:15-17, observes:

"The word which is here [v. 16] translated "feed" is different in the Greek text from the word so translated above. The word first used is *boske,* which is translated, "graze," "feed," "nourish." The word used in the second place is *poimaine,* which has been translated "feed," but which has a much broader meaning. My lexicon gives the following translation of *poimaine,* "to herd"; "to be a shepherd"; "to rule"; "to take care of"; "to tend." Peter was, therefore, called to be the shepherd, the caretaker, the ruler of the Church. * * * I consider that the charge which Jesus gave to Peter and the Apostles was that they should direct and take charge of His church here upon the Earth. Following the history of the Apostles, as it is given [in the Acts], we find that when any dissensions arose in the Church, men were sent to Peter and James and John at Jerusalem, to learn from them what was the Word of God on those matters, and the decision of the Apostles was the end of the controversy. There we have the precedent given us, that when the President of the Church was taken away, the Apostles took the place. Jesus presided over the Church while He lived in the flesh upon the Earth; He continued to preside over the Church through His Spirit, and revealed His Word to his servants, but His earthly representatives were the Apostles, and they took charge of the Church. So when the Prophet Joseph was martyred, the responsibility rested where he had placed it. There was no talk of heredity; there was nothing said about his relatives taking charge; but there was the Quorum of the Apostles, and upon them rested the responsibility of carrying on the work, and they did so, they continued the work that Joseph had commenced so well" (From a Conference Address given at Salt Lake City and quoted by the *Liahona*).

5. *This shall be a law*] It *must* be observed. It is not merely a rule that *may* or may not be observed.

7. *At the gate*] No one can enter the Church except through the gate —baptism. Nor can anyone enter the office held by the Prophet except through ordination.

8. And now, behold, I give unto you a commandment, that when ye are assembled together ye shall instruct and edify each other, that ye may know how to act and direct my church, how to act upon the points of my law and commandments, which I have given.

9. And thus ye shall become instructed in the law of my church, and be sanctified by that which ye have received, and ye shall bind yourselves to act in all holiness before me—

10. That inasmuch as ye do this, glory shall be added to the kingdom which ye have received. Inasmuch as ye do it not, it shall be taken, even that which ye have received.

8-10. It is the duty of the Saints, when they assemble, to instruct each other in the Laws and Commandments already given, in order that all may be instructed, and edified, and sanctified by that which has been received; not to endeavor to bring forth new Revelations.

8. *Instruct * * * each other*] The Law is for instruction. It is significant that the Lord here uses the very word which the Hebrews gave to the Law. They called it *Torah* (Instructions); "an instructor of the foolish, a teacher of babes" (Rom. 2:20).

9. *Be sanctified*] This means to be made clean and pure and fit for the service of the Lord, as, for instance, Ex. 19:10, "Go unto the people, and sanctify them today and tomorrow, and let them wash their clothes, and be ready against the third day," viz., to receive the Law. By obedience to the Law of Christ the Saints are sanctified.

11. Purge ye out the iniquity which is among you; sanctify yourselves before me;

12. And if ye desire the glories of the kingdom, appoint ye my servant Joseph Smith, Jun., and uphold him before me by the prayer of faith.

13. And again, I say unto you, that if ye desire the mysteries of the kingdom, provide for him food and raiment and whatsoever thing he needeth to accomplish the work wherewith I have commanded him;

14.   And if ye do it not he shall remain unto them that have received him, that I may reserve unto myself a pure people before me.

11-14. It is the duty of the Saints to sustain the Prophet God appoints, by prayer and by their works. There is an illustration of the latter in the history of the Prophet. When he, owing to the persecution in Missouri, was reduced to poverty, the Twelve addressed an appeal to the branches of the Church at Lima, Ramus, Augusta, and other places, and immediately the Saints sent him several wagon loads of grain and other provisions. Paul was in the same way relieved by the generosity of the Saints in Philippi (Phil. 4:16). It is not an idle ceremony to sustain the authorities at the general conferences. It means that we are willing to aid them by all honorable means at our disposal.

15.   Again I say, hearken ye elders of my church, whom I have appointed: Ye are not sent forth to be taught, but to teach the children of men the things which I have put into your hands by the power of my Spirit;

16.   And ye are to be taught from on high. Sanctify yourselves and ye shall be endowed with power, that ye may give even as I have spoken.

15-16. The duty of the Elders who are sent forth into the world is to teach the children of men that which the Lord has revealed; they are to be taught from on High. Elders sometimes come before audiences and confess that they have nothing to say; they are not prepared; or, that they never did give much time to study, or to meetings, etc. It is all wrong. If they are appointed to go forth into the world, they are ambassadors of the Lord, with a special message to the world, and they must deliver it by the power of the Holy Spirit. Before God they may be humble and confess their ignorance and weakness; but before the world they must magnify their office and calling.

17.   Hearken ye, for, behold, the great day of the Lord is nigh at hand.

18.   For the day cometh that the Lord shall utter his voice out of heaven; the heavens shall shake and the earth shall tremble, and the trump of God shall sound both long and loud, and shall say to the sleeping nations: Ye saints arise and live; ye sinners stay and sleep until I shall call again.

19.   Wherefore gird up your loins lest ye be found among the wicked.

20.   Lift up your voices and spare not. Call upon the nations

to repent, both old and young, both bond and free, saying: Prepare yourselves for the great day of the Lord;

21. For if I, who am a man, do lift up my voice and call upon you to repent, and ye hate me, what will ye say when the day cometh when the thunders shall utter their voices from the ends of the earth, speaking to the ears of all that live, saying—Repent, and prepare for the great day of the Lord?

22. Yea, and again, when the lightnings shall streak forth from the east unto the west, and shall utter forth their voices unto all that live, and make the ears of all tingle that hear, saying these words—Repent ye, for the great day of the Lord is come?

23. And again, the Lord shall utter his voice out of heaven, saying: Hearken, O ye nations of the earth, and hear the words of that God who made you.

24. O, ye nations of the earth, how often would I have gathered you together as a hen gathereth her chickens under her wings, but ye would not!

25. How oft have I called upon you by the mouth of my servants, and by the ministering of angels, and by mine own voice, and by the voice of thunderings, and by the voice of lightnings, and by the voice of tempests, and by the voice of earthquakes, and great hailstorms, and by the voice of famines and pestilences of every kind, and by the great sound of a trump, and by the voice of judgment, and by the voice of mercy all the day long, and by the voice of glory and honor and the riches of eternal life, and would have saved you with an everlasting salvation, but ye would not!

26. Behold, the day has come, when the cup of the wrath of mine indignation is full.

27. Behold, verily I say unto you, that these are the words of the Lord your God.

28. Wherefore, labor ye, labor ye in my vineyard for the last time—for the last time call upon the inhabitants of the earth.

17-28. There are certain duties the Saints must perform in view of the coming of the day of the Lord. Among these are the following:— They must separate themselves from the wicked (v. 19); they must call upon the nations to repent (v. 20); they must take up the labor in the vineyard for the last time (v. 28).

17. *The great day of the Lord is nigh at hand*] This is the message that the Prophet Joseph brought to the earth. At a general Conference in Nauvoo, April 6th, 1843, he said, "There are those of the rising generation who shall not taste death till Christ comes." At the same time he was well aware that the coming of the Lord in the clouds was not to be expected immediately. Our Savior had told him, in answer to prayer, that, "If thou livest until thou art eighty-five years old, thou shalt see the face of the Son of Man" (Sec. 130:15); but he was left in doubt as to whether this meant that Christ would come in power and glory at the end of the year 1890, or whether he (the Prophet) at that time, should be admitted to His presence. The Prophet says, "I took the liberty to conclude that if I did live till that time, He would make his appearance" (*Hist. of the Church,* Vol. V., p. 336). This conclusion does not appear improbable. The work the Lord did accomplish through the Prophet Joseph in a few years, from 1830 to 1844, was certainly wonderful. What would it have been in 60 years! At the same time, the Prophet knew that many great events were to precede the Millennium. At the Conference referred to, he said: .

"Judah must return, Jerusalem must be rebuilt, and the temple, and water come out from under the temple, and the waters of the Dead Sea be healed. It will take some time to rebuild the walls of the City and the temple, etc., and all this must be done before the Son of Man will make His appearance. There will be wars and rumors of wars, signs in the heavens above and on the earth beneath, the sun turned into darkness and the moon to blood, earthquakes in divers places, the seas heaving beyond their bounds; then will appear one grand sign of the Son of Man in heaven. But what will the world do? They will say it is a planet, a comet, etc. But the Son of Man will come as the sign of the coming of the Son of Man, which will be as the light of the morning cometh out of the east" (*Hist. of the Church,* Vol. V., p. 337).

18. *The heavens shall shake*] See Sec. 21:6.

19. *Gird up your loins*] Take up your journey and depart from the wicked.

21. *When the Thunders shall utter their voices*] This is to be taken literally. It is predicted that calamity and destruction await the inhabitants of the earth if they continue to reject the Gospel and fill the cup of their iniquity. This punishment will come when "the wrath of God shall be poured out upon the wicked without measure." (Doc. and Cov. 1:9.) It will come after the elders of Israel have declared their message to all the world. Then will come the testimony of wrath and indignation; the testimony of earthquakes, the voice of thunders and lightnings and tempests and the waves heaving themselves beyond their bounds. (Doc. and Cov. 88:88-91.) "Do you think there is calamity abroad now among the people? Not much. All we have yet heard and all we have experienced is scarcely a preface to the sermon that is going to be preached.

When the testimony of the Elders ceases to be given, and the Lord says to them, 'Come home; I will now preach my own sermons to the nations of the earth,' all you now know can scarcely be called a preface to the sermon that will be preached with fire and sword, tempests, earthquakes, hail, rain, thunders and lightnings, and fearful destruction. * * * The sea will heave itself beyond its bounds, engulfing mighty cities. Famine will spread over the nations, and nation will rise against nation, kingdom against kingdom, and states against states, in our own country and in foreign lands; and they will destroy each other, caring not for the blood and lives of their neighbors, of their families, or for their own lives. They will be like the Jaredites who preceded the Nephites upon this continent, and will destroy each other to the last man, through the anger that the Devil will place in their hearts because they have rejected the words of life and are given over to Satan to do whatsoever he listeth to do with them."—(President Brigham Young, July 15, 1860.)

22. *Lightnings*] In this great day of tribulation the thunders of heaven and the lightning streaking from the East to the West, will be more terrible than man has witnessed before. This is to be taken literally as an event to come when the cup of iniquity is full.

23. *Again, the Lord shall utter His voice*] If we understand this prophecy correctly, it means that after the warning voices of the thunders and lightnings and world wars, God will again speak to the children of men. In other words, the gospel sound will be heard. The Lord will explain to men, through His servants, why the calamities have come, viz., to cause men to repent and be saved (v. 24-27).

29. For in mine own due time will I come upon the earth in judgment, and my people shall be redeemed and shall reign with me on earth.

30. For the great Millennium, of which I have spoken by the mouth of my servants, shall come.

31. For Satan shall be bound, and when he is loosed again he shall only reign for a little season, and then cometh the end of the earth.

32. And he that liveth in righteousness shall be changed in the twinkling of an eye, and the earth shall pass away so as by fire.

33. And the wicked shall go away into unquenchable fire, and their end no man knoweth on earth, nor ever shall know, until they come before me in judgment.

34. Hearken ye to these words. Behold, I am Jesus Christ, the Savior of the world. Treasure these things up in your hearts, and let the solemnities of eternity rest upon your minds.

35. Be sober. Keep all my commandments. Even so. Amen.

29-35. The Lord, in this Revelation, as in others, has placed before the world a picture of distress on Earth, as a consequence of divine wrath. He ends by a promise that after the day of judgment upon the nations, His people will be redeemed, and the Millennial reign established on Earth. In the revelations of God to man the final view is always one of redemption, glory, and alleluias. It is not Paradise Lost, but Paradise Regained, that is the purpose of the message of God to man.

31. *Satan shall be bound*] Persecution shall cease; liberty shall prevail; peace shall be permanent and universal. Satan's reign is characterized by religious persecution, political oppression, and strife everywhere. After the Millennium he will again be in evidence for "a little season," and then comes the end.

32. *He that liveth in righteousness shall be changed*] During the Millennium the Saints will be changed (I. Thess. 4:16, 17). Again, at the time of the end of the Earth, after the Millennium, those who are faithful will be changed "in the twinkling of an eye."

The Earth shall pass away] Parley P. Pratt observes:

"Righteousness will abide upon its face, during a thousand years, and the Savior will bless it with His personal presence, after which the end soon comes, and the earth itself will die, and its elements be dissolved through the agency of fire. This death, or dissolution of the Earth, is a penalty of the original sin. Infants and righteous men die, not as a penalty of their own sins, but because Adam sinned; so the Earth dies, or undergoes a similar change, not because of the transgression of the children of Adam, but because of the original transgression. But all mankind are made alive from the first death through the resurrection, so the Earth will again be renewed, its elements will again be collected, they will be recombined and reorganized, as when it first issued from the womb of chaos" (*Jour. of Dis.,* Vol. I., p. 331).

SECTION 44.

REVELATION *given to Joseph Smith the Prophet and Sidney Rigdon, at Kirtland, Ohio, in the latter part of February, 1831. In compliance with the requirements herein set forth the Church appointed a conference to be held early in the month of June following.——The Elders to assemble to receive further instruction—To organize according to the laws of the land, thus strengthening themselves against the machinations of their opponents.*

BEHOLD, thus saith the Lord unto you my servants, it is expedient in me that the elders of my church should be called together, from the east and from the west, and from the north and from the south, by letter or some other way.

In the latter part of February, 1831, the Lord directed that the missionaries who had gone to the various parts of the Country be summoned to Kirtland to meet in a general Conference. Three Conferences had been held before, viz., one on June 9th, 1830; one on September 26th, the same year, and one on January 2nd, 1831. These were all held at Fayette, N. Y. The Conference referred to in this Revelation convened at Kirtland, June 3rd, 1831. It was the Fourth General Conference of the Church, and the first gathering of its kind in Kirtland.

2. And it shall come to pass, that inasmuch as they are faithful, and exercise faith in me, I will pour out my Spirit upon them in the day that they assemble themselves together.

3. And it shall come to pass that they shall go forth into the regions round about, and preach repentance unto the people.

4. And many shall be converted, insomuch that ye shall obtain power to organize yourselves according to the laws of man;

5. That your enemies may not have power over you; that you may be preserved in all things; that you may be enabled to keep my laws; that every bond may be broken wherewith the enemy seeketh to destroy my people.

6. Behold, I say unto you, that ye must visit the poor and the needy and administer to their relief, that they may be kept until all things may be done according to my law which ye have received. Amen.

2. *I will pour out my Spirit*] A promise that was fulfilled during the Conference.

3-5. One of the purposes of the Conference was to call Elders and send them forth to do missionary work in the neighborhood of Kirtland, in order that the Church might become so strong, numerically, as to be able to claim the protection of the law (v. 4). Then the enemies would have no power, that is, legal power, to destroy the work (v. 5).

6. *My law*] Refers to the law given for the temporal salvation of the Saints. See Sec. 40:30-36.

GENERAL NOTES

"The grand principle upon which the Gospel of life and salvation is founded and on which Zion is to be built, is brotherly love and good will to man. This was the theme of the angels of God in announcing the birth of the Savior. Hitherto, under the old systems, it has been, 'Every man for himself' * * * but the principle which the Lord proposes is that we should square our lives by a higher and holier one, namely, 'Everyone for the whole, and God for us all'" (Erastus Snow, *Jour. of Dis.,* Vol. XVII., p. 75).

The Conference which convened in accordance with this Revelation was attended by about two thousand souls. And the Church was only fourteen months old! On that occasion the Saints again had wonderful manifestations of the divine power, and "the man of sin," the Prophet tells us, was also revealed. Several Elders were ordained High Priests—the first ordination to that position in the Melchizedek Priesthood in this dispensation. "The Spirit of the Lord," the record says, "fell upon Joseph in an unusual manner, and he prophesied that John the Revelator was then among the Ten Tribes of Israel that had been led away by Shalmaneser, king of Assyria, to prepare them for their return from their long dispersion, to again possess the land of their fathers." Lyman Wight, who was among those ordained High Priests, prophesied concerning the coming of Christ, and said that some of his brethren would suffer martyrdom. "He saw the heavens opened and the Son of Man sitting on the right hand of the Father. He said that God would do a work in these last days that tongue cannot express and the mind is not capable to conceive. The glory of the Lord shone around" (*History of the Church,* Vol. I., p. 176).

SECTION 45.

REVELATION *given through Joseph Smith the Prophet, to the Church, at Kirtland, Ohio, March 7, 1831. Prefacing his record of this revelation, the Prophet states that at this age of the Church many false reports and foolish stories were published and circulated, to prevent people from investigating the work or embracing the faith. See History of the Church, vol. 1, p. 158.——Jesus Christ the advocate for His people with the Father—Blessed state of Enoch and his people—Prediction made to the disciples in former days cited—Times of the Gentiles signalized by the light of the Gospel—In the same genera-*

*tion the times of the Gentiles to be fulfilled—A desolating
sickness named among the many tribulations preceding the
coming of the Lord in judgment—Significance of the parable of
the fig-trees and that of the ten virgins—Gathering of the people
from the eastern lands into the western countries—Promise of
the establishment of the New Jerusalem—Eventual triumph of
Zion.*

HEARKEN, O ye people of my church, to whom the kingdom
has been given; hearken ye and give ear to him who laid the
foundation of the earth, who made the heavens and all the
hosts thereof, and by whom all things were made which live,
and move, and have a being.

2. And again I say, hearken unto my voice, lest death shall
overtake you; in an hour when ye think not the summer shall
be past, and the harvest ended, and your souls not saved.

3. Listen to him who is the advocate with the Father, who
is pleading your cause before him—

4. Saying: Father, behold the sufferings and death of him
who did no sin, in whom thou wast well pleased; behold the
blood of thy Son which was shed, the blood of him whom thou
gavest that thyself might be glorified;

5. Wherefore, Father, spare these my brethren that believe
on my name, that they may come unto me and have everlasting
life.

6. Hearken, O ye people of my church, and ye elders listen
together, and hear my voice while it is called today, and harden
not your hearts;

7. For verily I say unto you that I am Alpha and Omega,
the beginning and the end, the light and the life of the world—
a light that shineth in darkness and the darkness comprehendeth
it not.

8. I came unto mine own, and mine own received me not;
but unto as many as received me gave I power to do many
miracles, and to become the sons of God; and even unto them
that believed on my name gave I power to obtain eternal life.

9. And even so I have sent mine everlasting covenant into
the world, to be a light to the world, and to be a standard for

my people, and for the Gentiles to seek to it, and to be a messenger before my face to prepare the way before me.

10. Wherefore, come ye unto it, and with him that cometh I will reason as with men in days of old, and I will show unto you my strong reasoning.

11. Wherefore, hearken ye together and let me show unto you even my wisdom—the wisdom of him whom ye say is the God of Enoch, and his brethren,

12. Who were separated from the earth, and were received unto myself—a city reserved until a day of righteousness shall come—a day which was sought for by all holy men, and they found it not because of wickedness and abominations;

13. And confessed they were strangers and pilgrims on the earth;

14. But obtained a promise that they should find it and see it in their flesh.

It is noted in the *History of the Church* that in the early spring of 1831, numerous false reports and foolish stories were circulated about the Saints in Kirtland, who were tried sorely on account of the enmity aroused against them by such means, for persecution is never pleasant to a refined, sensitive human being. But while the adversary was raging against them, our Lord inspired this Revelation, which may be divided into three parts:—(1) God's appeal to His people for obedience (1-15); (2) a revelation concerning the day of redemption (16-59); and (3) instructions regarding the new English Bible translation, the gathering of the Saints, and the building of the New Jerusalem (60-75).

In these paragraphs our Savior appeals to the members of the Church for obedience to His word. Many reasons are given why we should render implicit obedience.

1. *Kingdom has been given*] That is one reason. Our Lord *has* committed His Kingdom to the Saints. That is a settled arrangement, an accomplished fact. In vain do the "heathen rage" and the mighty ones take counsel together against the Lord, saying, "Let us break the bands asunder." For "He that sitteth in heaven shall laugh: the Lord shall have them in derision. Then shall he speak unto them in his wrath * * * 'Yet have I set my king upon my holy hill of Zion'" (Psalm 2:1-6). The adversaries of God are too late in their plans. The Kingdom belongs to the Son of God, and He has already given it to His Saints (Dan. 7, 22). That is one reason why we should obey Him.

Laid the foundation of the earth] That is another reason. In obeying Jesus Christ, we obey the Creator of the heavens and all the hosts thereof—all the worlds in our big universe—as well as the Earth and all it contains. There is no mightier ruler, no greater potentate, to whom we can yield obedience. And not only is he powerful but he is also wise and good, as is clearly seen in all that he has called into existence. He is, therefore, both able and willing to reward those who obey Him.

2. *Lest death shall overtake you*] That is another important reason why we should obey our Lord. Death is certain. Life at best is short and uncertain.

> "The days of our years—therein are threescore and ten,
> And if we be of much strength, fourscore years:
> And their pride is but travail and misery.
> For it is swiftly past, and we have taken flight."
> —Psalms 90:10; translation by Dr. Kirkpatrick, Cambridge Bible.

If life is so uncertain, we are wise, if by obedience we prepare for the hereafter.

3. *Him who is the advocate with the Father*] That is another reason for obedience. Christ, our Lord, is our legal representative at the eternal bar of justice. He pleads our cause. But a client must follow the counsel of his advocate, or lose his case.

4-5. *Behold the sufferings and death * * * spare these my brethren*] This is the plea of the Son. In the Mosaic dispensation the priest presented before God a sacrifice slain in behalf of the Israelites. That was a type of Christ's sacrifice, who presents Himself as the Lamb of God, slain for us, and intercedes in our behalf, on the condition that we are willing to obey Him and leave our cause in His hands. There is but one Mediator between God and man, and that is our blessed Savior. His redeemed and sanctified brethren may pray for one another, but they cannot enter behind the veil in behalf of others, or even in behalf of themselves. Our justification, our salvation, is due only to the mediation of Christ.

That thyself might be glorified] Christ died, that His Father might be glorified, and the salvation of His children is His glory.

6. *Hearken * * * while it is called today*] Every day; obedience to His voice is necessary every day. It is necessary that His Spirit should be with us in our homes, in our offices, in our workshops, in our fields and on our farms, as well as in church or school.

Harden not your hearts] Like Pharaoh, who refused to obey, notwithstanding the signs and wonders performed in his presence.

7-10. Here is another reason for yielding obedience. The Lord has again established the Everlasting Covenant in the world, as a preparation for His advent. Once before He came to His own, but was rejected. The Jews were "His own" then. They did not, as a nation, receive Him, but to those who did receive Him He gave power to work miracles, to become the sons of God and obtain eternal life. Let it not be said a second time, that Christ has come to "His own," even to His Church in this dispensation, but "His own" refused to hearken to Him.

It may be noted that the language here used is that of John (1:10-12). The meaning there, more fully explained, is that Christ came to His own *inheritance,* His own vineyard, the Holy Land (*ta idia*), but His own people (*hoi idioi*) did not receive Him. The Lord was about to come again in our dispensation to His own inheritance, the New Jerusalem in the land of Zion; let His people, the members of the Church, receive Him.

11-14. In these paragraphs another reason for obedience is stated. If the people would listen to Him, He would once more manifest the wisdom which was shown in the establishment of the City of Enoch, the inhabitants of which were taken from the earth and preserved from destruction by the flood. This is a divine promise that the conditions which prevailed in the City of Enoch will again be established, when God's people will obey Him.

"There was a remarkable work performed then [in the days of Enoch], according to the revelations which have been given to us, which will be more fully developed when the Lord shall see fit to reveal other things associated therewith. But we learn that there was a Church organized about as ours may be; we learn that they went forth and preached the gospel; we learn that they were gathered together to a place called Zion; we learn that the people of Zion were under the guidance, direction, and teaching of the Almighty; in order that they might be prepared for another Zion in the grand drama associated with the dealings of God and His purposes pertaining to the earth and the heavens * * * Enoch preached the gospel to the people, and so did hundreds of Elders, as they are doing today; and they gathered the people together and build up a Zion to the Lord, and when Enoch was not, but was caught up, Enoch's city was not, but was caught up, and there were certain things associated therewith that are very peculiar. And what came next? Why, the destruction of the world. It was overflowed, we read, by the flood" (John Taylor, *Jour. of Dis.,* Vol. XXVI., p. 34).

12. *Until a day of righteousness shall come*] The ultimate aim of our Lord in proclaiming the gospel is to bring about the day of righteousness on Earth—the day when all God's children shall be one great and happy family. How far off that day seems to be! Brigham Young on one occasion said:

"The Lord revealed to Joseph, that the people would gather out from Babylon, and establish the Kingdom of God upon the principles of heaven. They went up to Jackson Co., Mo., with this in their faith, and with the express understanding that when they got there, everything was to be laid at the feet of the Bishop * * * who was to distribute it among the people, according to the Revelation given for that purpose, for their benefit. But they could not bear this; consequently, they were driven from Jackson County, and finally they were driven from the State. This was in the fall of 1838 * * * While we were in Winter Quarters, the Lord gave to me a Revelation just as much as He ever gave one to anybody. He opened my mind, and showed me the organization of the Kingdom of God in family capacity. I talked it to my brethren; I would throw out a few words here, and a few words there, to my first counselor, to my second counselor, and the Twelve Apostles, but with the exception of one or two of the Twelve, it would not touch a man. They believed it would come. O yes, but it would be by and by" (*Jour. of Dis.*, Vol. XVIII., pp. 242, 244).

13. *Strangers and pilgrims*] Holy men of old were looking for Zion and hoping for the dawn of the day of that universal brotherhood, but in vain; they found it not; only wickedness and abominations. They looked for liberty, and found oppression; for brotherly love, and found selfishness; for happiness in righteousness, and found misery. The government of heaven was not on Earth, and, consequently, they felt that they were only "strangers," and "pilgrims" on Earth, "declaring plainly that they seek a country," (Heb. 11:14)—a land in which the Lord is the Ruler, and in which they would not be "strangers" or aliens. Abraham was a stranger in Palestine, though the land was his by promise. The saints are strangers in the world, until the reign of their Lord and Redeemer is established, though the promise is that they shall inherit the Earth.

14. *See it in their flesh*] When the Millennial reign comes, the holy men of old shall see it in their "flesh," for they will be resurrected and take their place among the Saints.

15. Wherefore, hearken and I will reason with you, and I will speak unto you and prophesy, as unto men in days of old.

15. *Hearken*] In the preceding verses, our Lord appealed to His people for obedience, on many grounds: He is their Creator (v. 1); life is short and uncertain (v. 2); He is their legal representative (v. 3); He will again come to His own inheritance, and if His people will receive Him, by obeying Him (vv. 6-14), He will establish Zion as the center of a great Brotherhood of Man. In this verse our Lord again exhorts His people to hearken to Him, while He unfolds to them the Revelation which He gave to the Twelve on the Mount of Olives, concerning His coming and the signs preceding His day of judgment.

16. And I will show it plainly as I showed it unto my disciples as I stood before them in the flesh, and spake unto them, saying: As ye have asked of me concerning the signs of my

coming, in the day when I shall come in my glory in the clouds of heaven, to fulfil the promises that I have made unto your fathers,

17. For as ye have looked upon the long absence of your spirits from your bodies to be a bondage, I will show unto you how the day of redemption shall come, and also the restoration of the scattered Israel.

18. And now ye behold this temple which is in Jerusalem, which ye call the house of God, and your enemies say that this house shall never fall.

19. But, verily I say unto you, that desolation shall come upon this generation as a thief in the night, and this people shall be destroyed and scattered among all nations.

20. And this temple which ye now see shall be thrown down that there shall not be left one stone upon another.

21. And it shall come to pass, that this generation of Jews shall not pass away until every desolation which I have told you concerning them shall come to pass.

22. Ye say that ye know that the end of the world cometh; ye say also that ye know that the heavens and the earth shall pass away;

23. And in this ye say truly, for so it is; but these things which I have told you shall not pass away until all shall be fulfilled.

24. And this I have told you concerning Jerusalem; and when that day shall come, shall a remnant be scattered among all nations;

25. But they shall be gathered again; but they shall remain until the times of the Gentiles be fulfilled.

26. And in that day shall be heard of wars and rumors of wars, and the whole earth shall be in commotion, and men's hearts shall fail them, and they shall say that Christ delayeth his coming until the end of the earth.

27. And the love of men shall wax cold, and iniquity shall abound.

28. And when the times of the Gentiles is come in, a light shall break forth among them that sit in darkness, and it shall be the fulness of my gospel;

29. But they receive it not; for they perceive not the light, and they turn their hearts from me because of the precepts of men.

30. And in that generation shall the times of the Gentiles be fulfilled.

31. And there shall be men standing in that generation, that shall not pass until they shall see an overflowing scourge; for a desolating sickness shall cover the land.

32. But my disciples shall stand in holy places, and shall not be moved; but among the wicked, men shall lift up their voices and curse God and die.

33. And there shall be earthquakes also in divers places, and many desolations; yet men will harden their hearts against me, and they will take up the sword, one against another, and they will kill one another.

34. And now, when I the Lord had spoken these words unto my disciples, they were troubled.

35. And I said unto them: Be not troubled, for, when all these things shall come to pass, ye may know that the promises which have been made unto you shall be fulfilled.

36. And when the light shall begin to break forth, it shall be with them like unto a parable which I will show you—

37. Ye look and behold the fig-trees, and ye see them with your eyes, and ye say when they begin to shoot forth, and their leaves are yet tender, that summer is now nigh at hand;

38. Even so it shall be in that day when they shall see all these things, then shall they know that the hour is nigh.

39. And it shall come to pass that he that feareth me shall be looking forth for the great day of the Lord to come, even for the signs of the coming of the Son of Man.

40. And they shall see signs and wonders, for they shall be shown forth in the heavens above, and in the earth beneath.

41. And they shall behold blood, and fire, and vapors of smoke.

42. And before the day of the Lord shall come, the sun shall be darkened, and the moon be turned into blood, and the stars fall from heaven.

43. And the remnant shall be gathered unto this place;

44. And then they shall look for me, and, behold, I will come; and they shall see me in the clouds of heaven, clothed with power and great glory; with all the holy angels; and he that watches not for me shall be cut off.

45. But before the arm of the Lord shall fall, an angel shall sound his trump, and the saints that have slept shall come forth to meet me in the cloud.

46. Wherefore, if ye have slept in peace blessed are you; for as you now behold me and know that I am, even so shall ye come unto me and your souls shall live, and your redemption shall be perfected; and the saints shall come forth from the four quarters of the earth.

47. Then shall the arm of the Lord fall upon the nations.

48. And then shall the Lord set his foot upon this mount, and it shall cleave in twain, and the earth shall tremble, and reel to and fro, and the heavens also shall shake.

49. And the Lord shall utter his voice, and all the ends of the earth shall hear it; and the nations of the earth shall mourn, and they that have laughed shall see their folly.

50. And calamity shall cover the mocker, and the scorner shall be consumed; and they that have watched for iniquity shall be hewn down and cast into the fire.

51. And then shall the Jews look upon me and say: What are these wounds in thine hands and in thy feet?

52. Then shall they know that I am the Lord; for I will say unto them: These wounds are the wounds with which I was wounded in the house of my friends. I am he who was lifted up. I am Jesus that was crucified. I am the Son of God.

53. And then shall they weep because of their iniquities; then shall they lament because they persecuted their king.

54. And then shall the heathen nations be redeemed, and they that knew no law shall have part in the first resurrection; and it shall be tolerable for them.

55. And Satan shall be bound, that he shall have no place in the hearts of the children of men.

56. And at that day, when I shall come in my glory, shall the parable be fulfilled which I spake concerning the ten virgins.

57. For they that are wise and have received the truth, and

have taken the Holy Spirit for their guide, and have not been deceived—verily I say unto you, they shall not be hewn down and cast into the fire, but shall abide the day.

58. And the earth shall be given unto them for an inheritance; and they shall multiply and wax strong, and their children shall grow up without sin unto salvation.

59. For the Lord shall be in their midst, and his glory shall be upon them, and he will be their king and their lawgiver.

16-59. In these paragraphs our Lord repeats to the Prophet Joseph the substance of His address to the Twelve on the Mount of Olives, on His coming and the end of the world, as recorded in Matt. 24:1-35. Many details are added, which throw a wonderful light upon that exceedingly important portion of the Word of God.

16. *Ye have asked concerning the signs of my coming*] (Matt. 24:3). Our Lord has just delivered His denunciatory address to the Jews (Matt. 23), by which He broke irrevocably His connection with the Jewish hierarchy and announced the coming judgment: "Your house is left unto you desolate." Your temple is doomed to destruction, and your city to ruin. The address must have made an impression like a deep wound upon His disciples who believed their Master's words. With sad hearts and heavy steps the little group left the temple ground, crossed the Brook of Kidron and ascended the slope of the Mount of Olives. Having arrived at their usual resting place, where the wonderful temple building and the City could be seen as a beautiful panorama illuminated by the fire of the setting sun, the disciples seized the opportunity of asking the Master for definite information concerning the time when the awful catastrophe He had predicted should take place, and what would be the signs by which they might know that the end was drawing near.

17. *A bondage*] One reason for their anxiety to know the signs is here stated. The separation of the spirits from the bodies is, even to those who are Christ's own, a "bondage," which is ended only by a glorious resurrection, and they were interested in knowing by what signs they might recognize that their day of redemption was drawing near, when spirit and body should be united. The departed saints are, we may be sure, looking for the signs of the coming of the Lord, with an intense interest as the saints still in mortality. Jesus graciously showed them "how the day of redemption shall come, and also the restoration of scattered Israel." The two events are inseparably connected.

18. *Ye behold this temple*] It was a magnificent structure. It was built on Mount Moriah, on the ground purchased by David from Araunah, the Jebusite. The first temple on that site was erected by Solomon and dedicated in the year B. C. 1004. It was destroyed by the

Chaldeans, B. C. 588. Zerubbabel erected the second temple on the same site. It was much inferior in splendor. It did not contain the ark. The *Shekinah,* or presence of the Lord, had departed. The sacred fire, and the urim and thummim had been lost. Antiochus Epiphanes profaned it, B. C. 163, and Judas Maccabeus purified it three years later. This temple was used for five centuries, and Herod the Great undertook to repair and reconstruct it, a few years before the birth of our Savior. He employed thousands of laborers, who worked for nine years on it, and no expense was spared to make it a beautiful building. Long after Herod's death the work of enlargement and ornamentation was continued, so that, at the time our Lord spoke of it (John 2:20), it had been forty-six years in building. And, strange to say, the destruction began by riots among the temple workingmen, themselves. For, when they were discharged and could procure no suitable employment, they caused the tumults and seditions which ended in the overthrow of the Jewish state and ruin of both the city and the sacred edifice.

In the construction of this sanctuary many stones of prodigious size had been used. Josephus says some were 45 cubits long, 5 high, and 6 broad—something like 78x8x10 feet. How improbable it must have appeared that the time could ever come when one stone should not be left upon another (v. 20)! Yet, in the year 70 A. D., in the same month and on the same day that witnessed the destruction of the temple of Solomon, this temple was demolished. Roman soldiers, it is said, ploughed the ground on which it had stood.

19. *Destroyed and scattered*] Desolation came, as our Savior said would be the case, as a "thief," unexpected, not looked for. In the year 66 A. D., Cestus Gallus marched into Judea and threatened Jerusalem. He might have taken the City, but he retreated and met with defeat near Beth-Horon. The Christians in the City, remembering the words of our Lord, fled to the little city of Pella, but the Jews were fired, by their temporary success, to renewed resistance. Vespasian was then sent from Rome to crush the rebellion. He took some of the strongholds of the Country and approached Jerusalem. Internal strife prevailed there, and such horrors were perpetrated that Vespasian decided to give his army a rest, while the Jews destroyed each other. Vespasian was elevated to the throne, and his son, Titus, was left to continue the conquest. The siege began in the year 70 A. D. Soon famine prevailed. Citizens who ventured outside the walls to search for roots to eat, if seized, were crucified by the Roman soldiers. Sometimes hundreds in that awful position could be seen from the walls. A trench was dug around the City, in order to make its isolation complete. Prisoners of war were cut open, while alive, to enable soldiers to search their bodies for gold which they might have swallowed. Six hundred thousand persons died within the walls, and the dead bodies, too numerous to be buried, were left in the houses. The Zealots, a fanatical sect whose members maintained that God would save them at the last moment, went about

murdering and urging the people to resistance. Even Titus was sick at heart at the daily horrors he witnessed or heard of. At length the temple became a fort. Titus attacked it as such. A Roman soldier, contrary to order, set fire to it. After a while the scene was one of carnage and plunder. Six thousand Jews perished in the flames. In this awful war more than a million and a half of the Jews perished, and many were sold into slavery, and thus "scattered among all nations."

21. *This generation of Jews*] Our Lord told the Twelve that the generation of Jews then living should not pass away until the desolation predicted should come. The prophesy was delivered 37 years before its fulfilment.

22. *Ye say ye know,* etc.] Our Lord reminded His Disciples of the fact that they knew that the "end of the world" was drawing near; also that the heavens and the Earth would pass away. They knew that these were two distinct and separate events, the end of the "world" being at the time of Christ's coming, and the passing away of the heavens and the Earth being the purification of this Earth by fire.

23. *Ye say truly*] This, He adds, is true, but the heavens and the earth shall not pass away, until every prophecy has been fulfilled. Some believe that the Earth may pass away any day; for instance, by collision with some dead world drifting about in space, as a derelict on the ocean; or by a volcanic outburst, an earthquake, or an internal explosion. But this is an error. The end will not come until every word God has spoken concerning it, is fulfilled.

24. *This I have told you concerning Jerusalem*] This revelation beginning with the 16th verse is an explanation of the instruction given by the Lord to His Apostles on the Mount of Olives when they made inquiry of him about his second coming and the end of the world. Up to this 24th verse he had been speaking of the destruction of Jerusalem, and now he is about to launch forth on the events which should follow that dire calamity which was to come upon that city and the Jews. The siege of Jerusalem by the Romans was one of the most dreadful events in the history of the world.

25. *Thy shall be gathered again*] But the dispersion was not to be the last episode of Jewish history. The scattered shall be gathered, but not until "the times of the Gentiles be fulfilled."

"The times of the Gentiles" is their opportunity to hear and embrace the gospel (Rom. 11:25).

"Jesus came to the lost sheep of the house of Israel, but they rejected him, and the Apostles were moved upon to say, 'Lo, we turn to the Gentiles;' and they did so, the Jews having proved themselves unworthy of eternal life, 'and the kingdom of God shall be taken from you,' says the Savior, and given to a nation bringing forth the fruits thereof. The

Gentiles, to whom the gospel was to be given, received it, and the gifts and graces of the Church, which were before enjoyed by Israel were now manifested among the Gentiles. But behold, they corrupted themselves, after having received the kingdom" (Orson Pratt, *Jour. of Dis.,* Vol. XVIII., p. 225).

26. *In that day shall be heard of wars,* etc.] Note that this is given as one of the signs that the "times of the Gentiles" are about to be fulfilled. There shall be heard of wars, and rumors of wars, and the whole Earth shall be in commotion, and so dreadful shall be the experiences of men, that their hearts shall fail them. It would not be surprising if this were meant for literal "heart failure," as well as for "fear." The time of the end is too strenuous for many human beings.

Christ delayeth His coming] Another sign of the end of the times of the Gentiles is this, that men shall teach that Christ will not come until the end of the Earth. That is, even now, a very orthodox doctrine. In fact, the common doctrine of the world is that Christ will not come. until a majority of the race is converted, the Jews gathered and antichrist conquered, and then, it is taught, come the judgment and the destruction of the Earth. It is one of the signs of the end, that men shall teach that there will be no Millennium, no personal reign of Christ on Earth.

27. *The love of men shall wax cold*] This is another sign of the end of the times of the Gentiles. The expression is the same as that found in Matt. 24:12, where we read (translated literally), "And because lawlessness has abounded, the love of the many [this indicates more than a few] shall wax cold." "Love" here means Christian unity, harmony. Where in the Christian world does that love, that oneness, prevail? There is an abundance of co-operation based on self-interest, or family connections: but where is there genuine Christian love, true, unselfish, constant? Its absence in the majority of men is one of the signs of the end. Paul experienced the coldness here referred to when, at his first trial in Rome, "no man stood" with him (II. Tim. 4:16). The Latter-day Saints, in their days of trials, always have been attacked for believing in being united in the bonds of brotherly love. And yet, unity is the main characteristic of the Church of Christ.

28. *A light shall break forth*] This is another sign by which the end of the times of the Gentiles may be known. This light is the "fulness of the gospel," as revealed through the Prophet Joseph. It came at the time of the end.

30. *In that generation*] That is, in the generation during the existence of which the fulness of the gospel should shine forth as a light in the darkness, the end of the times of the Gentiles would come.

31. *An overflowing scourge*] But in that generation there are some who shall not pass away, until they see an "overflowing scourge," in the

form of desolating sickness, covering the land. All the medical skill of the world cannot overcome the epidemics God sends.

32. *Holy places*] During these calamities God's people will be gathered in the "holy places" in the mountains, selected for their safety, and in other places purified and cleansed, and they shall not be moved from their settlements and homes, as they were from Missouri and Illinois.

33. *Earthquakes and desolations*] This is another sign of the end. Men will harden their hearts against God and take up the sword one against another, "and they will kill one another"—a terrible arraignment of militarism. Our Lord says those who "take up the sword one against another" are those who, like Pharaoh, harden their hearts against God, defying Him, notwithstanding wars, earthquakes, and other signs of the end. Is this not the strongest possible condemnation of the international policy that trusts to armies and navies, instead of courts of arbitration, for the adjustment of international difficulties?

34-38. The disciples were troubled when they heard our Lord speaking about wars and earthquakes, and the hardening of the hearts of men against God, but He told them that these things were indications of the coming of the Son of God, just as the budding of the trees is an indication of the approach of summer. A wise statesman, when observing a state of decay of morals, prevalence of sordid selfishness in business and politics, widening of the gulf between classes, and love of ease and luxury, knows, by those signs, that the end of such a condition cannot be delayed long. For similar reasons the people of God know, from the signs enumerated by our Lord, that the end of a dispensation is approaching. Deviation from the teachings of the servants of God in any dispensation brings war and bloodshed among men. Revolt from the Priesthood of the Son of God means increased power of the adversary, and he will exert that power not only by seducing mortals to sin, but by causing sickness, and destruction by the forces of nature, to the extent that this is possible for him to do, and, undoubtedly, as "the prince of the power of the air," and "the spirit that now worketh in the children of disobedience" (Eph. 2:2), his power to inflict injury is considerable, wherever the protecting hand of God is wholly, or partly, withdrawn, because of disobedience and sin. Hence, the unrestrained activity of the adversary in any dispensation is a sign that it is nearing the end. And when, towards the end, the gospel light "begins to break forth," then, "summer is nigh at hand." The change from one dispensation to another, radical though it be, is as gradual as the change from one season to another.

39-44. In the preceding paragraphs our Lord gave His disciples a number of signs by which they might know that the times of the Gentiles were about to be completed. Here He enumerates the signs immediately preceding "the day of the Lord."

39. *Looking forth for the great day*] Those who fear the Lord will be looking for His day and the signs of His coming. That is, toward the end there will be a notable revival of the belief in the Scriptural doctrine of the second advent of our Redeemer and His Millennial reign. This is one of the signs. The world in general will deny the doctrine, but those who fear the Lord will believe it and be eagerly looking for the signs of the advent.

40. *They shall see signs and wonders*] This is another sign that the end is approaching. Compare Sec. 88:88-91.

41. *Blood, fire, and vapors of smoke*] Evidently referring to the destructive agencies of modern warfare and their death-dealing effects —"blood." This is another sign. There have been wars before (v. 26), but the armed conflicts immediately preceding the coming of our Savior in glory will be more destructive than any previous wars.

42. *The sun shall be darkened,* etc.] This is another great sign. See Section 29:14.

43. *The remnant shall be gathered*] This has reference to the return of the Jews to Jerusalem. This is another important sign of the coming of our Lord. In the day in which we live the children of God have been taught to gather at the various places appointed by revelation, in order to assist in the building up of the Kingdom of God preparatory to the second advent. The spirit of gathering accompanies the acceptance of the gospel. Those who receive the glad message generally have a desire to go where the people of God dwell, without being instructed to do so by any man. Saints flock together as naturally as each individual creature of God's creation is attracted to its own genus or species.

44. *Then shall they look for me*] When they are gathered. The very purpose of the gathering is that there may be a people prepared for the coming of the Lord.

"When He comes again He comes to take vengeance and to bring deliverance unto His Saints; 'for the day of vengeance,' it is said, 'is in my heart and the year of my redeemed is come.' It behooves us to be made well aware of which class we belong to" (Orson Hyde, *Jour. of Dis.,* Vol. X., p. 116).

45-59. Having indicated the signs of the end, our Lord now proceeds to enumerate some of the events that will occur at his coming.

45. *The Saints * * * shall come forth*] First, the departed Saints will be resurrected and "meet the Savior in the cloud."

46. The Saints everywhere will be quickened "in the twinkling of an eye" and join the resurrected Saints and ascend with them.

47-50. Then the judgment upon the nations shall be held. Our Lord will descend with His Saints. He will again stand upon "this mountain," the Mount of Olives. There will be an earthquake; the Mount will be cleft, and the whole "earth" shall hear it. The Lord will speak, as from Mount Sinai, and the nations of the Earth will hear it and mourn for their folly.

51-53. The Jews, gathered to Palestine, will accept the crucified Nazarene as their deliverer and King.

54. *Heathen Nations*] "The heathen nations who have not known God shall have their part in the first resurrection. The extent of their blessing, or degree of salvation is not stated, but the Lord says it will be "tolerable" for them. Tolerable, according to the dictionary means "passably good; commonplace." The Lord being just to all men, we may be assured that he will give to them in justice and according to divine law.

55. *At that time "Satan shall be bound"* (Section 43:31).

56-59. The Parable of the Ten Virgins will be seen to be true when the Lord comes. For even among those who have gone out to meet the Bridegroom, some will be foolish, not being fully prepared for His coming (Matt. 25:1-13). The wise virgins are described in this Section, v. 57.

58-59. *The earth shall be given to them*] The faithful members of the Church, compared to the five wise virgins, who have kept the faith, are not to be hewn and cast into the fire when the Lord comes, but shall abide the day. In that day the earth will be cleansed from its wickedness, and the "greatness of the kingdom under the whole heaven, shall be given to the people of the saints," (Daniel 7:27) and the earth shall be given unto them for an inheritance. During this thousand years "they shall multiply and wax strong, and their children shall grow up without sin unto salvation." They will have the advantage of having the Lord in their midst and the Saints who have received the resurrection shall be their instructors.

59. For the Lord will be in their midst and He will be their King and Lawgiver.

Some of the grandest chapters in human history are here outlined in prophecy. Our Lord and Savior will return and establish His reign upon this Earth during a thousand years, preliminary to His celestial reign, which shall last forever.

"By and by, when all things are prepared—when the Jews have received their scourging, and Jesus has descended upon the Mount of Olives, the Ten Tribes will leave Zion, and will go to Palestine, to inherit the land that was given to their ancient fathers, and it will be divided among the descendants of Abraham, Isaac, and Jacob by the inspiration of the Holy Ghost. They will go there to dwell in peace in their own land from that time, until the Earth shall pass away. But Zion, after their departure. will still remain upon the Western hemisphere, and she will be crowned with glory as well as old Jerusalem, and, as the Psalmist David says, she will become the joy of the whole Earth * * * Zion will be caught up when Jesus comes, to meet Him. Jesus will descend not only upon the Mount of Olives, but He will descend and stand upon Mount Zion. But before He stands upon it, it will be caught up to meet Him in the air. Will the buildings of Zion be caught up? Yes. And its land? Yes. And Jesus will stand upon Mount Zion according to the prediction of John the Revelator, and He will reign over His people during a thousand years; and His associates will be the resurrected righteous of all former dispensations" (Orson Pratt, *Jour. of Dis.*, Vol. XVIII., p. 66).

60.   And now, behold, I say unto you, it shall not be given unto you to know any further concerning this chapter, until the New Testament be translated, and in it all these things shall be made known;

61.   Wherefore I give unto you that ye may now translate it, that ye may be prepared for the things to come.

62.   For verily I say unto you, that great things await you;

60-62.   In December, 1830, the Prophet Joseph and Sidney Rigdon were instructed not to continue the translation of the Bible until their arrival in Ohio (Sec. 37:1); now they were living in that State and were given permission to resume the work. They were to make themselves familiar with the Scriptures, in order to "be prepared for the things to come."

63.   Ye hear of wars in foreign lands; but, behold, I say unto you, they are nigh, even at your doors, and not many years hence ye shall hear of wars in your own lands.

63.   *In your own lands*] See Sec. 38:29. The Spirit of Revelation again, through the Prophet Joseph, predicts the American Civil War. And these prophecies were uttered at a time when, humanly speaking, a war between the Northern and Southern States was highly improbable. The first indication of serious trouble came when South Carolina declared that the tariff laws enacted by Congress were not binding within her territory, and fixed February 1st, 1833, as the date of abrogation. But this dispute was settled by an agreement which gave the State an opportunity to retire from its defiant position without humiliation. See Sec. 87.

64.   Wherefore I, the Lord, have said, gather ye out from the eastern lands, assemble ye yourselves together ye elders of my church; go ye forth into the western countries, call upon the

inhabitants to repent, and inasmuch as they do repent, build up churches unto me.

65. And with one heart and with one mind, gather up your riches that ye may purchase an inheritance which shall hereafter be appointed unto you.

66. And it shall be called the New Jerusalem, a land of peace, a city of refuge, a place of safety for the saints of the Most High God;

67. And the glory of the Lord shall be there, and the terror of the Lord also shall be there, insomuch that the wicked will not come unto it, and it shall be called Zion.

64. *Gather ye*] The Prophet Joseph says:
"Pestilence, hail, famine, and earthquake will sweep the wicked of this generation, from off the face of the land, to open and prepare the way for the lost tribes of Israel from the north country. The people of the Lord, those who have complied with the requirements of the new covenant, have already commenced gathering together to Zion * * * Repent ye, repent ye, and embrace the everlasting covenant, and flee to Zion, before the overflowing scourge overtake you, for there are those now living upon the Earth whose eyes shall not be closed in death until they see all these things, which I have spoken, fulfilled" (*History of the Church,* Vol. I., p. 315).

67. *The terror of the Lord*] The glory of the Lord shall fill the New Jerusalem, when it is built; but the terror of the Lord shall also be there, so that it will be no place for the wicked. The Laws of God will be enforced.

68. And it shall come to pass among the wicked, that every man that will not take his sword against his neighbor must needs flee unto Zion for safety.

69. And there shall be gathered unto it out of every nation under heaven; and it shall be the only people that shall not be at war one with another.

70. And it shall be said among the wicked: Let us not go up to battle against Zion, for the inhabitants of Zion are terrible; wherefore we cannot stand.

71. And it shall come to pass that the righteous shall be gathered out from among all nations, and shall come to Zion, singing with songs of everlasting joy.

68. *Must needs flee to Zion for safety*] The Lord abhorring war and

bloodshed, commanded His people to gather and build up Zion, in order to have peace, when all the world is at war. "It shall be called the New Jerusalem, a land of peace" (v. 66).

71. *The righteous shall be gathered*]
"Why does the Lord gather them out? As the Prophet Isaiah has said in another place, He gathers them out to the mountains, and they say one to another, 'Come, let us go up to the mountain of the Lord and to the house of the God of Jacob.' What for? 'That he may teach us his ways, and that we may walk in his paths.' It seems, then, that the Lord will have one people somewhere on the face of the Earth, up in the mountainous region, who are going to teach the nations His ways, and how to walk in His paths" (Orson Pratt, *Jour. of Dis.,* Vol. XVIII., p. 46).

72. And now I say unto you, keep these things from going abroad unto the world until it is expedient in me, that ye may accomplish this work in the eyes of the people, and in the eyes of your enemies, that they may not know your works until ye have accomplished the thing which I have commanded you;

73. That when they shall know it, that they may consider these things.

74. For when the Lord shall appear he shall be terrible unto them, that fear may seize upon them, and they shall stand afar off and tremble.

75. And all nations shall be afraid because of the terror of the Lord, and the power of his might. Even so. Amen.

GENERAL NOTES

Our Lord, in this Revelation calls upon His people to obey Him. Is this not a hard requirement? Not if we love Him. "Love is the fulfilment of the law" (Rom. 13:10). Obedience prompted by love is the greatest happiness a man can enjoy, and that is the only kind of obedience God values: not the obedience of a servant, but that of a loving child.

The word "generation" (v. 30) is generally used to denote the race of men existing at the same time. In that sense it has been suggested that the duration of a generation would be about a hundred years. But it also means a "race," a "family," or a "nation."

The expression "signs in the heavens," such as the darkening of sun and moon, and the falling of stars, when used metaphorically, means the overthrow of kingdoms and the fall of potentates. But the last days will also be marked by strange phenomena in the sky. The Prophet

Joseph notes in his diary for March 10, 1843, that he and others, about 7 p.m., saw a stream of light in the southwest quarter of the sky, which had the shape of a sword, with the hilt downward, the blade raised, and he took this as a sign that there would be a sanguinary war before long (*Hist. of the Church,* Vol. V., p. 301). This stream of light appeared for several evenings and formed itself into a large ring round the moon, two balls immediately appearing in the ring opposite each other. On the 21st of the same month the pilot and officers of the steamer *William Penn,* on the Ohio river, observed a great light in the sky, in the form of a serpent. It changed form and became letters, and observers thought it spelt G, O, D, thus blazing forth a warning in the sky to turn from the serpent and to God (*Ibid.* p. 309).

Heber C. Kimball relates the following:

"I had retired to bed, [Sep. 22nd, 1827], when John P. Greene, who was living within a hundred steps of my house, came and woke me up, calling upon me to come out and behold the scenery in the heavens. * * * We looked to the eastern horizon, and beheld a white smoke arise towards the heavens; as it ascended it formed itself into a belt, and made a noise like the sound of a mighty wind, and continued southwest, forming a regular bow dipping in the western horizon. * * * In this bow an army moved, commencing from the east and marching to the west. * * * They moved in platoons, and walked so close that the rear ranks trod in the steps of their file leaders, until the whole bow was literally crowded with soldiers. We could distinctly see the muskets, bayonets, and knapsacks of the men, who wore caps and feathers like those used by the American soldiers. When the front rank reached the western horizon a battle ensued. * * * This scene was gazed upon for hours, until it began to disappear. After I became acquainted with Mormonism, I learned that this took place the same evening Joseph Smith received the records of the Book of Mormon from the angel Moroni" (Whitney's *Life of Heber C. Kimball,* pp. 3-31).

Wars are calamities. The New Jerusalem will be a "land of peace." War was the last recourse of Lucifer, after he had been defeated in the Council. Peace is the rule in the Kingdom of God, for our Lord is the Prince of Peace, but His gospel of peace and good will came into a world where strife prevailed, and there has been a struggle between pacifism, so-called, and militarism ever since. Many of the first Christians refused to serve in the Roman legions, but after the great apostasy militarism obtained control of the church. But there have always been a few peacemakers in the world. Erasmus, the great New Testament student, was of the opinion that the settlement of disputes between nations by war was contrary to the teachings of Christ. Grotius, the first great constructive pacifist, suggested a world court of arbitration. Emanuel Kant, the great philosopher, in his tract, *Eternal Peace,* insisted that courts must supplant war, federations of nations drive away selfish individualism, treaties take the place of guns, and democracy render oppressive dynasties obsolete. Henry IV, of France, dreamed of a League of Nations on a plan similar to that so forcibly advocated by President Wilson, of the United States. The Revelations of our Lord to the Prophet Joseph make it clear that peace will finally be established on the Earth permanently, and that implements of war will be turned into agricultural tools.

SECTION 46.

REVELATION *given through Joseph Smith the Prophet, to the Church, at Kirtland, Ohio, March 8, 1831. A custom of admitting to the sacrament meetings and other assemblies of the Church only members and earnest investigators had become somewhat general. See History of the Church, vol. 1, p. 163.——— Meetings of the Church to be conducted as the Holy Spirit shall guide—Neither members nor earnest seekers after the truth to be excluded from sacramental services—Many of the gifts of the Holy Spirit enumerated—Power of discernment promised so that manifestations not inspired by the Spirit of God may be recognized.*

HEARKEN, O ye people of my church; for verily I say unto you that these things were spoken unto you for your profit and learning.

2. But notwithstanding those things which are written, it always has been given to the elders of my church from the beginning, and ever shall be, to conduct all meetings as they are directed and guided by the Holy Spirit.

3. Nevertheless ye are commanded never to cast any one out from your public meetings, which are held before the world.

4. Ye are also commanded not to cast any one who belongeth to the church out of your sacrament meetings; nevertheless, if any have trespassed, let him not partake until he makes reconciliation.

5. And again I say unto you, ye shall not cast any out of your sacrament meetings who are earnestly seeking the kingdom —I speak this concerning those who are not of the church.

6. And again I say unto you, concerning your confirmation meetings, that if there be any that are not of the church, that

are earnestly seeking after the kingdom, ye shall not cast them out.

7. But ye are commanded in all things to ask of God, who giveth liberally; and that which the Spirit testifies unto you even so I would that ye should do in all holiness of heart, walking uprightly before me, considering the end of your salvation, doing all things with prayer and thanksgiving, that ye may not be seduced by evil spirits, or doctrines of devils, or the commandments of men; for some are of men, and others of devils.

This Revelation was received the day after that recorded in the preceding Section. Elder B. H. Roberts (*Hist. of the Church,* Vol. I., p. 163) quotes John Whitmer to the effect that some of the Saints used to exclude unbelievers from their meetings, although this is forbidden in the Book of Mormon (III. Nephi 18:22, 23). The Lord, therefore, at this time (1) gave instructions regarding the meetings of the Saints (1-7); (2) explained why spiritual gifts are given (8-9); and (3) enumerated those gifts (10-33).

1. CONCERNING MEETINGS.

3. *Ye are commanded*] From the preceding verses it is learned that the meetings of the Saints are conducted as the Elders "are directed by the Holy Spirit." The selection of hymns, the prayers, the choice of speakers, all must be according as the Spirit shall prompt. There must be no set, stereotyped forms limiting and hindering the free operation of the Spirit of God. Those who preside, those who speak, pray, sing, and those who listen must all be under the sacred Influence. In this verse a commandment is added that none is to be refused admittance to the public meetings of the Saints. All must be given a chance to hear the Gospel.

4-5. *Sacrament meetings*] The Sacrament meetings are also to be open to all; but Church members who have trespassed must make reconciliation before partaking of the sacred emblems.

Trespasses are, chiefly, sins against our fellowmen. The Law of God is so broad, the occasions to sin so numerous, that we should always be on our guard, and we should search ourselves each time we come to partake of the Sacrament, and make sure that we are not unworthy guests. During the Mosaic Covenant atonement was made specially for trespasses "in the holy things of the Lord" (Lev. 5:15, 16), by which God was defrauded in the payment of tithes and offerings. This should be a lesson to the people of God in all ages. It is inconsistent to come to the Lord's table and not be honest in tithes and offerings.

7. *Ask of God*] This is a commandment to pray always and to walk

uprightly before God, to escape being seduced, or led astray, by false doctrines.

Note that some false doctrines come from men, while others are originated by the devil. The former may depend on human imperfection of preception or deductions. We do not always understand the Word of God correctly, and we are apt to draw hasty conclusions, and if we teach these for doctrine, we err. The latter are inspired by the adversary to deceive man.

8.   Wherefore, beware lest ye are deceived; and that ye may not be deceived seek ye earnestly the best gifts, always remembering for what they are given;

9.   For verily I say unto you, they are given for the benefit of those who love me and keep all my commandments, and him that seeketh so to do; that all may be benefited that seek or that ask of me, that ask and not for a sign that they may consume it upon their lusts.

2. WHY SPIRITUAL GIFTS ARE GIVEN.

8-9.   There are many gifts of the Spirit. There is the "fruit of the Spirit," which all Saints enjoy, such as "love, joy, peace, longsuffering, gentleness, goodness, faith, meekness, temperance" (Gal. 5:22, 23). But there are also special gifts (Paul calls them *Charismata*, I. Cor. 7:7) vouchsafed by God to the Saints, for the benefit of those who love Him.

They are given in answer to prayer, but there is one kind of prayer that God does not grant—prayer for gifts to gratify carnal desires.

10.   And again, verily I say unto you, I would that ye should always remember, and always retain in your minds what those gifts are, that are given unto the church.

11.   For all have not every gift given unto them; for there are many gifts, and to every man is given a gift by the Spirit of God.

12.   To some is given one, and to some is given another, that all may be profited thereby.

13.   To some it is given by the Holy Ghost to know that Jesus Christ is the Son of God, and that he was crucified for the sins of the world.

14.   To others it is given to believe on their words, that they also might have eternal life if they continue faithful.

15.   And again, to some it is given by the Holy Ghost to know the differences of administration, as it will be pleasing unto the

same Lord, according as the Lord will, suiting his mercies according to the conditions of the children of men.

16. And again, it is given by the Holy Ghost to some to know the diversities of operations, whether they be of God, that the manifestations of the Spirit may be given to every man to profit withal.

17. And again, verily I say unto you, to some is given, by the Spirit of God, the word of wisdom.

18. To another is given the word of knowledge, that all may be taught to be wise and to have knowledge.

19. And again, to some it is given to have faith to be heaied;

20. And to others it is given to have faith to heal.

21. And again, to some is given the working of miracles;

22. And to others it is given to prophesy;

23. And to others the discerning of spirits.

24. And again, it is given to some to speak with tongues;

25. And to another is given the interpretation of tongues.

26. And all these gifts come from God, for the benefit of the children of God.

27. And unto the bishop of the church, and unto such as God shall appoint and ordain to watch over the church and to be elders unto the church, are to have it given unto them to discern all those gifts lest there shall be any among you professing and yet be not of God.

28. And it shall come to pass that he that asketh in Spirit shall receive in Spirit;

29. That unto some it may be given to have all those gifts, that there may be a head, in order that every member may be profited thereby.

30. He that asketh in the Spirit asketh, according to the will of God; wherefore it is done even as he asketh.

31. And again, I say unto you, all things must be done in the name of Christ, whatsoever you do in the Spirit;

32. And ye must give thanks unto God in the Spirit for whatsoever blessing ye are blessed with.

33. And ye must practise virtue and holiness before me continually. Even so. Amen.

3. WHAT ARE THE SPIRITUAL GIFTS?

10-33. The main spiritual gifts are enumerated in these paragraphs. They are, (1) knowledge; (2) faith; (3) administration; (4) recognition of the operations of the Spirit; (5) wisdom; (6) gift to instruct; (7) faith to be healed; (8) faith to heal; (9) power to work other miracles; (10) gift to prophesy; (11) gift to discern spirits; (12) gift of tongues; (13) gift of interpretation; (14) gift to discern all these gifts.

13. *To know that Jesus is Christ*] This knowledge is placed first among the special gifts, because it is obtained only by revelation. To *believe* that Jesus of Nazareth was the Anointed One, the Messiah, and that He was crucified for the sins of the world, is not to *know* it. Knowledge is a special gift.

14. *To believe on their words*] That faith which enables us to realize divine things and obtain life eternal is another special gift. But it is one which God is willing to bestow upon His children.

15. *To know the difference of administration*] This is another special gift. The term, as used by Paul (I. Cor. 12:5) means the different divisions or courses of the priests and Levites engaged in the temple service, and in this Revelation it may refer to the different duties and responsibilities of the Priesthood in its two divisions, the Melchizedek and Aaronic. To know this is a gift of the Spirit.

16. *The diversities of operations*] This refers to various spiritual influences at work, for instance such as are manifested in Spiritism, anarchism, and the numerous other "isms." To know whether an influence with a professedly moral, or reformatory, aim is from the Holy Spirit, or from another source, is a special gift.

17. *The word of wisdom*] This means a discourse or a testimony characterized by and productive of wisdom. Wisdom, according to Philo, was the highest of the divine attributes, and human wisdom is a reflection of the divine.

18. *The word of knowledge*] Refers to the gift to instruct others. There is a difference between wisdom, knowledge, and ability to instruct. According to Coleridge, "common sense in an uncommon degree" is what men call *wisdom*. It is almost a direct operation of intuition. *Knowledge* is a carefully-stored-up supply of facts, generally slowly acquired. The *ability* to *instruct* is the gift to impart of this supply to others. Each is a gift of God.

19. *Faith to be healed*] This is a gift of the Spirit, and it should be earnestly sought for, because our Lord is willing both to forgive sins, if we repent of them, and to heal *all diseases* (Psalm 103:3), as long as the appointment to death has not been made.

20. *Faith to heal*] This also is a gift.

21. *Working of miracles*] A special divine power is needed for the working of miracles. The Prophet Joseph had this power in a very high degree. It was one of the evidences that he had the authority of the holy Priesthood. One of the numerous miracles God performed through him was the healing of one Mrs. Johnson, who, in company with others, visited his home in Kirtland, 1831. She had, for some time, been afflicted with a lame arm. She could not raise it to her head. The conversation turned on supernatural power, and someone in the company asked if there was anybody on Earth that could heal Mrs. Johnson for instance. The Prophet arose, walked over to Mrs. Johnson, took her by the hand and said, "Woman, in the name of the Lord Jesus Christ, I command thee to be whole," whereupon he left the room. Mrs. Johnson at once lifted up her arm, and the next day was able to do her washing (*History of the Church,* Vol. I., p. 215).

22. *To prophesy*] That is, to speak in the name of the Lord, whether of things present, past, or future. This is a special gift. The Prophet Joseph had it in the highest degree. Heber C. Kimball also had the gift highly developed. At times he could see into the future as if it were an open book. During the time of famine in Salt Lake valley in 1847, when many subsisted on roots and hides of animals, and knew not where to obtain bread or clothing necessary, owing to the devastation by crickets, President Kimball declared in a public meeting that, within a short time, "state goods" would be sold in the streets of Salt Lake City cheaper than in New York, and that the people should be abundantly supplied with food and clothing. Many who heard him refused to believe. He himself said he was afraid he had missed it. But the prophecy came true. Very soon the California gold-hunters came through the Valley. Salt Lake City became their resting-place, and they were glad to exchange their goods for whatever they could get. Many of them threw goods away, or sold them for a song, in order to lighten their wagons and be able to make better progress (Whitney's *Life of Heber C. Kimball,* p. 401-2).

23. *Discerning of spirits*] What this means may be illustrated by relating a remarkable experience which the Prophet records. On the 9th of November, 1835, a man came to his home and introduced himself as a Jewish minister whose name was Joshua. The Prophet entertained him hospitably, as he always did both strangers and friends who visited him. One day Mr. Joshua said that he was a lineal descendant of Matthias, and a re-incarnation of this Apostle. The Prophet writes:

"I told him that his doctrine was of the Devil, that he was in reality in possession of a wicked and depraved spirit, although he professed to be the spirit of truth itself. He said also that he possessed the Spirit of Christ. He tarried until Wednesday, 11th, when, after breakfast, I told him that my God told me that his god was the Devil, and I could not keep him any longer" (*Hist. of the Church,* Vol. II., p. 307).

Thus the Prophet Joseph had the gift to discern spirits.

"We may look for angels and receive their ministration, but we are to try the spirits and prove them, for it is often the case that men make a mistake in regard to these things. God had so ordained that, when he has communicated, no vision is to be taken but what you see by the seeing of the eye, or what you hear by the hearing of the ear. When you see a vision, pray for the interpretation. If you get not this, shut it up" (Joseph Smith, *Jour. of Dis.,* Vol. VI., p. 240).

24. *To speak with tongues*] The Prophet Joseph says:
"Be not so curious about tongues; do not speak in tongues except there be an interpreter present; the ultimate design of tongues is to speak to foreigners, and if persons are very anxious to display their intelligence, let them speak to such in their own tongues. The gifts of God are all useful in their places, but when they are applied to that which God does not intend, they prove an injury, a snare, and a curse instead of a blessing" (*Hist. of the Church,* Vol. V., p. 31).

25. *Interpretation of tongues*] This is another of the special gifts. "If therefore the whole Church be come together in one place, and all speak with tongues, and there come in those that are unlearned, or unbelievers, will they not say that ye are mad?" (I. Cor. 14:23).

"However well calculated the gift of tongues might be to arrest and compel attention when used properly, it is clear, says the Apostle, that its introduction at the public assemblies of the Church was not a proper use of it, unless (v. 27) it were restricted in its use by wise rulers. If not so restricted, so far from its being a sign to unbelievers, it would give them, as well as the great body of Christian laity, occasion of complaint, and even ridicule" (*Cambridge Bible,* I. Cor., p. 136).

27. *To discern all those gifts*] That is the great gift which the Bishops and others whom God appoints to watch over the Church must seek to obtain, lest hypocrites should go undetected.

29. Some may have all these gifts.

30. *Asketh in the Spirit*] He who prays "in the Spirit—that is, as the Spirit dictates—receives an answer, for the Spirit of God prompts him to ask in accordance with the will of God.

31. *In the name of Christ*] A prayer dictated by the Spirit is always offered in the name of Him who is the Mediator between God and man.

32. *Must give thanks*] Thanksgiving for the blessings received, always accompanies acceptable prayers. God's children are constantly enjoying many blessings for which they are grateful, and it is pleasing to God when they praise Him for His goodness in bestowing them.

33. *Virtue and holiness*] God's children must practice these, if they

desire to possess the spiritual gifts and receive a favorable answer to their prayers.

GENERAL NOTES

Our Lord, in His own life, has given His followers an example to imitate. He began His public career by baptism and prayer (Luke 3:21), and a forty days' fast. After a day of strenuous work, He prayed in order to find rest (Luke 5:16). He prayed at the beginning of the day in order to have strength for the work before Him (Mark 1:35). He prayed when He was about to take any decisive step in His ministry. Before He selected the Twelve, He continued a whole night in prayer, in order to have the wisdom necessary for that important duty (Luke 6:12). He prayed in order to have power over evil spirits (Mark 9:29). He prayed to have strength to bear up in the supreme hour of trial, as in Gethsemane, and, finally, in the hour of death, on the cross. He taught His disciples to pray always, "and not to faint" (Luke 18:1). A Christian life without prayer would not be real, active life. It might be unconscious existence, as if in a swoon, and end in spiritual death.

The Prophet Joseph knew the power of prayer. It was while praying *that he received the glorious* vision of the Father and the Son. The Church was founded and built up and every stone cemented to the rest of the structure, with prayer. Every new Revelation given, every new vision, came in answer to prayer. Many remarkable instances of prayer are recorded in the biography of the Prophet. On the 11th of January, 1834, he and some of his co-laborers united in prayer, asking the Lord that their lives might be spared and that angels would be given charge concerning them and their families, that they might prevail over their enemies, and especially one who had threatened to take the life of the Prophet; that the Lord would provide the Presiding Bishop at Kirtland with means to discharge every obligation; that he would protect the printing press, and that He would deliver Zion and gather His scattered people; and "finally, that God, in the name of Jesus, would gather His elect speedily, and unveil His face that His Saints might behold His glory, and dwell with Him" (*Hist. of the Church*, Vol. II., pp. 2, 3). He prayed to the Lord "that three thousand subscribers would be added to the [*Evening and Morning Star*] in the time of three years" (*Ibid.* p. 24). He prayed for "strength and wisdom and understanding to lead the people of the Lord, and to gather and establish the Saints upon the land of their inheritances, and organize them according to the will of heaven, that they may be no more cast down for ever" (*Ibid.* p. 51). He prayed when in trials and difficulties, privately and publicly, every day of his life, and his last word in mortality was a prayer committing himself into the hands of his Father in heaven—"O Lord, my God!"

There can be no spiritual progress, no growth of the Church, no victory over evil, without prayer. If faithful work is the steam that keeps the engines in motion, prayer is the sacred fire without which there is no steam.

"A praying heart is the one thing that the devil cannot easily counterfeit. It is easy enough to imitate praying lips, so that hypocrites and Pharisees feign devoutness. But only God can open in the heart's depths those springs of supplication that often find no channel in language, but flow out in groanings which cannot be uttered" (ARTHUR PIERSON).

SECTION 47.

REVELATION *given through Joseph Smith the Prophet, in Kirtland, Ohio, March 8, 1831. Prior to this time Oliver Cowdery had acted as Church historian and recorder. John Whitmer had not sought an appointment as historian, but, being desired to serve in this capacity had said that he would obey the will of the Lord in the matter. See History of the Church, vol. 1, p. 166.——John Whitmer designated as the keeper of the history of the Church.*

BEHOLD, it is expedient in me that my servant John should write and keep a regular history, and assist you, my servant Joseph, in transcribing all things which shall be given you, until he is called to further duties.

2. Again, verily I say unto you that he can also lift up his voice in meetings, whenever it shall be expedient.

3. And again, I say unto you that it shall be appointed unto him to keep the church record and history continually; for Oliver Cowdery I have appointed to another office.

4. Wherefore, it shall be given him, inasmuch as he is faithful, by the Comforter, to write these things. Even so. Amen.

1. *My servant John*] For biographical notes see Sec. 15.

GENERAL NOTES

Previous to this time Oliver Cowdery had been the historian and recorder of the Church. When the suggestion was made that John Whitmer be appointed to do this important work, he expressed the wish that the Lord would make His will manifest through the Prophet Joseph. Then this revelation was received.

John Whitmer was now appointed custodian of the records of the Church. When he was excommunicated, March 10, 1838, at Far West, he refused to deliver up the documents in his possession, and at his death they were taken charge of by his nephew, John C. Whitmer, of Richmond, Mo.

The position of the Church Historian is one of great importance. One of the epoch-making events in the history of the world took place when the Church was organized. But without a specially-appointed recorder, that event would have passed almost unnoticed, or it would have been described from the viewpoint of enemies. The development of the Church would have had no proper place in the annals of man but for a truthful historian, well acquainted with and instructed in that part of human history. The Prophet began his history on May 2nd, 1831, "to disabuse the public mind, and put all inquirers after the truth into possession of the facts, as they have transpired, in relation to both myself and the Church, so far as I have such facts in my possession" (*History of the Church*, Vol. I., p. 1), and that is the great reason for the existence of the office of the Historian of the Church.

SECTION 48.

REVELATION *given through Joseph Smith the Prophet, at Kirtland, Ohio, March, 1831. Joseph had inquired of the Lord as to the mode of procedure in procuring lands for the settlement of the Saints, this being an important matter in view of the migration of members of the Church from New York State, in obedience to the Lord's command that they should assemble in Ohio.——The people already established in Ohio to share their holdings with new arrivals—Lands to be purchased as required—The people to follow the counsel of their presiding officers in the matter.*

IT is necessary that ye should remain for the present time in your places of abode, as it shall be suitable to your circumstances.

2. And inasmuch as ye have lands, ye shall impart to the eastern brethren;

3. And inasmuch as ye have not lands, let them buy for the present time in those regions round about, as seemeth them good, for it must needs be necessary that they have places to live for the present time.

4. It must needs be necessary that ye save all the money that ye can, and that ye obtain all that ye can in righteousness, that in time ye may be enabled to purchase land for an inheritance, even the city.

5. The place is not yet to be revealed; but after your brethren come from the east there are to be certain men appointed, and to them it shall be given to know the place, or to them it shall be revealed.

6. And they shall be appointed to purchase the lands, and to make a commencement to lay the foundation of the city; and then shall ye begin to be gathered with your families, every man according to his family, according to his circumstances, and as is appointed to him by the presidency and the bishop of the church, according to the laws and commandments which ye have received, and which ye shall hereafter receive. Even so. Amen.

1-6. In former Revelations (Secs. 37:3; 38:32; 39:15) our Lord had commanded the Saints in the East to gather in Ohio, where they would be "endowed with power from on high." The spirit of gathering was poured out upon them, and in the spring of 1831, shortly after the arrival of the Prophet Joseph in Kirtland, many Saints began the westward move from the State of New York. The Saints in Kirtland then began to make inquiries as to how the newcomers could obtain land to settle upon, and where they should make a permanent location. This Revelation was given in answer to their inquiries.

1. *Remain for the present*] The Saints in Ohio should not yet move westward. The place of the gathering and of the city had not yet been revealed, but would be, after the arrival of the Saints from the East (v. 5).

2. *Impart to the eastern brethren*] They should divide their land with the brethren from the East, and if there was not enough land for all, those who could not buy of the Saints, should buy wherever there was an opportunity (v. 3). They were also instructed to earn all they could, and save the money, so that they would be in a position to buy land for an inheritance wherever God indicated that the City should be built.

6. *Then shall ye begin to gather*] Then the time would come for the great gathering of the Saints to the place of the City of Zion.

GENERAL NOTES

This is a dispensation of gathering. "Gather my Saints together unto me: those that have made covenant with me by sacrifice" (Psalm 50:5).

And not only does the spirit of gathering rest upon the Saints. The nations of the world have also become partakers of the same spirit. Zionism among the Jews, pan-Hellenism among the Greeks, pan-Slavism, etc. are illustrations of the operation of the Holy Spirit among the children of men toward the unification of all into a great brotherhood. And it is all due to the establishment of the Church in this age of the world.

See General Notes, p. 269.

SECTION 49.

REVELATION *given through Joseph Smith the Prophet, to Sidney Rigdon, Parley P. Pratt and Leman Copley, at Kirtland, Ohio, March, 1831. See History of the Church, vol. 1, p. 167. Leman Copley had embraced the Gospel, but still held to some of the teachings of the Shakers, or Shaking Quakers, of whom he had formerly been one. Many of these people were honest-hearted, and the Lord directed his servants to labor amongst them.——Exact time of the Lord's advent not to be revealed prior to the great event—Sanctity of marriage as a law of God unto man—Complete abstinence from meat not required—Development of Lamanites and establishment of Zion to precede the coming of the great day of the Lord.*

HEARKEN unto my word, my servants Sidney, and Parley, and Leman; for behold, verily I say unto you, that I give unto you a commandment that you shall go and preach my gospel which ye have received, even as ye have received it, unto the Shakers.

2. Behold, I say unto you, that they desire to know the truth in part, but not all, for they are not right before me and must needs repent.

3. Wherefore, I send you, my servants Sidney and Parley, to preach the gospel unto them.

4. And my servant Leman shall be ordained unto this work, that he may reason with them, not according to that which he has received of them, but according to that which shall be taught him by you my servants; and by so doing I will bless him, otherwise he shall not prosper.

In this Revelation the Lord appoints a special mission to a sect generally known as *Shakers* or *Shaking Quakers*.

The Elders who were set apart for that mission, shortly afterwards visited one of their settlements near Cleveland, Ohio, but were not received. The Lord (1) names the Elders selected for the mission (1-4); (2) in a brief synopsis of the gospel indicates the nature of their message (5-14); (3) points out some of the errors of the sect (15-23); (4) gives a prophecy concerning the future of Zion (24-25); and (5) gives His servants certain promises (26-28).

1. THE ELDERS SELECTED FOR THE MISSION.

1. *Sidney*] See biographical notes, Sec. 32.

Leman] Leman Copley had been a Shaker. When he embraced the gospel he was anxious to impart the truth to his former associates. He was, therefore, by revelation, chosen to accompany Sidney Rigdon and Parley P. Pratt on a mission to them.

Shakers] The Shakers call themselves, *The United Society of Believers in Christ's Second Appearing*. In 1747, James Wardley and wife, English Quakers, united with some French members of that church and protested against all existing churches. Ten years later, Ann Lee joined this society and testified especially against what she called "the lust of generation." She became the "spiritual mother" of the Society. About the year 1772 Mother Ann had a "revelation," directing her to repair to America. Many of her friends emigrated with her, and they left Liverpool and landed in New York in the year 1774. In 1776 they moved first to Albany, and then to Watervliet. This was the origin of the sect.

They believed that "the true Christian church is a congregation of souls baptized with the degree of the Christ spirit which harvests them *from the generative plane,* and from the selfish, sinful elements of the world; consecrates their lives to God; absolves them from the bondage of sin and the power of sinful temptations, and opens their souls to receive continuous revelations of light, truth, love, mercy, charity, and forgiveness of penitents, combined with impartiality and merciful judgment from heaven's eternal fountain" (*What the World Believes,* edited by George J. Hagar).

The Society is now defunct.

5. Thus saith the Lord; for I am God, and have sent mine Only Begotten Son into the world for the redemption of the world, and have decreed that he that receiveth him shall be saved, and he that receiveth him not shall be damned—

6. And they have done unto the Son of Man even as they listed; and he has taken his power on the right hand of his glory, and now reigneth in the heavens, and will reign till he descends

on the earth to put all enemies under his feet, which time is nigh at hand—

7. I, the Lord God, have spoken it; but the hour and the day no man knoweth, neither the angels in heaven, nor shall they know until he comes.

8. Wherefore, I will that all men shall repent, for all are under sin, except those which I have reserved unto myself, holy men that ye know not of.

9. Wherefore I say unto you that I have sent unto you mine everlasting covenant, even that which was from the beginning.

10. And that which I have promised I have so fulfilled, and the nations of the earth shall bow to it; and, if not of themselves, they shall come down, for that which is now exalted of itself shall be laid low of power.

11. Wherefore, I give unto you a commandment that ye go among this people, and say unto them, like unto mine apostle of old, whose name was Peter:

12. Believe on the name of the Lord Jesus, who was on the earth, and is to come, the beginning and the end;

13. Repent and be baptized in the name of Jesus Christ, according to the holy commandment, for the remission of sins;

14. And whoso doeth this shall receive the gift of the Holy Ghost, by the laying on of the hands of the elders of the church.

2. The Gospel Message to the Shakers.

5-14. The gospel message to the Shakers is the same as that to all the children of men.

5. *Thus saith the Lord*] These Revelations contain the Word of the Lord, not of man.

Have sent mine Only Begotten] Jesus Christ is the "Only Begotten" of the Father, in the flesh. He is the Firstborn in the spirit. He is the only Savior of man. Without Him there is no salvation in this life; nor hereafter.

6. *Now reigneth in the heavens*] Our Lord was given *all power* in heaven and on earth. He reigns supreme in heaven; on this Earth His supremacy has not yet been fully recognized, but it will be: for *all* enemies will be put under His feet, and the will of God will be done as it is done in heaven.

8. *I will that all men shall repent*] There can be no entrance into the kingdom of God when it is celestialized, except through perfect faith

and repentance. "And no unclean thing can enter into his kingdom; therefore nothing entereth into his rest save it be those who have washed their garments in my blood, because of their faith, and the repentance of all their sins, and their faithfulness unto the end." (3 Nephi 27:19.) The Lord here speaks of holy men whom he has reserved to himself, "that ye know not of." These holy men without sin, unknown to the Prophet Joseph Smith and the elders of the Church, must have been the translated prophets reserved by the Lord to remain on the earth until his second coming, for all other men, not in the church, were still under the bondage of sin having not been baptized.

12. *Believe on the name of the Lord Jesus*] This is the first principle of the gospel. It is a commandment of God. We can and must obey it.

13. *Repent and be baptized*] These are the second and third principles of the gospel. Man's unbelief is the ground on which he stands condemned before God, who commands men everywhere to believe, repent, and be baptized. If, through unbelief, we fail to obey, we are condemned. The Shakers did not believe in baptism in water; nor in the Sacrament. On these ordinances of the Church they held views similar to those of the Quakers.

Since God commands all His children to believe, the question may be asked, "Can man regulate his belief?" "Is not belief the necessary consequence of the peculiar mental make-up of each individual?" The gospel does not give us an affirmative answer to these questions. It commands us to accept the truth, taking our ability to do so for granted. By attending to evidence and contemplating the truth, we become convinced, and faith is produced. Man is so constituted that he cannot fail to believe the truth, when he perceives it. Nobody can doubt that two and two make four, if he understands the proposition, or that the whole is equal to its parts.

"Faith and affection are both influenced, not by analyzing them or by violently attempting to strengthen and to purify them, but by examining truth and holding communion with the objects that deserve and claim our love" (Joseph Angus, M.A., D.D.).

15. And again, verily I say unto you, that whoso forbiddeth to marry is not ordained of God, for marriage is ordained of God unto man.

16. Wherefore, it is lawful that he should have one wife, and they twain shall be one flesh, and all this that the earth might answer the end of its creation;

17. And that it might be filled with the measure of man, according to his creation before the world was made.

18. And whoso forbiddeth to abstain from meats, that man should not eat the same, is not ordained of God;

19. For, behold, the beasts of the field and the fowls of the air, and that which cometh of the earth, is ordained for the use of man for food and for raiment, and that he might have in abundance.

20. But it is not given that one man should possess that which is above another, wherefore the world lieth in sin.

21. And wo be unto man that sheddeth blood or that wasteth flesh and hath no need.

22. And again, verily I say unto you, that the Son of Man cometh not in the form of a woman, neither of a man traveling on the earth.

23. Wherefore, be not deceived, but continue in steadfastness, looking forth for the heavens to be shaken, and the earth to tremble and to reel to and fro as a drunken man, and for the valleys to be exalted, and for the mountains to be made low, and for the rough places to become smooth—and all this when the angel shall sound his trumpet.

3. SOME ERRORS CORRECTED.

15. *Marriage is ordained of God*] The Shakers taught that only a "virgin life" was consistent with "purity of mind and body." The gospel teaches that marriage is a divine institution. The Shakers taught that a desire for offspring is the "root of human depravity." The gospel teaches that it is lawful for men and women to marry, and that under no other condition can the Earth "answer the measure of its creation."

"The doctrine which degrades marriage by making it a less holy state, has its foundation in Manicheism or Gnosticism. It assumes that evil is essentially connected with matter; that sin has its seat and source in the body; that holiness is attainable only through asceticism and 'neglecting of the body;' that because the *vita angelica* [the angelic life] is a higher form of life* than that of men here on Earth, therefore marriage is a degradation. The doctrine * * * is thoroughly antichristian. It rests on principles derived from the philosophy of the heathen. It presupposes that God is not the author of matter; and that He did not make man pure, when He invested him with a body" (Charles Hodge, D. D., *Systematic Theology,* Vol. III., p. 369).

18. *Whoso forbiddeth to abstain from meats * * * is not ordained*

---

*This is itself a misunderstanding of the Scriptures. "In the celestial glory there are three heavens or degrees; and in order to obtain the highest, a man must enter into this order of the Priesthood, and if he does not, he cannot obtain it. He may enter into the other, but that is the end of his kingdom; he cannot have an increase" (Joseph Smith, Hist. of the Church, Vol. V., p. 392. See Sec. 131:1-4).

of God] A purely vegetarian diet cannot be urged on religious grounds.

Forbiddeth] "Forbiddeth" here stands for "biddeth" or commandeth. The context is perfectly clear.

"And again, verily I say unto you, all wholesome herbs God hath ordained for the constitution, nature, and use of man. Every herb in the season thereof, and every fruit in the season thereof. All these to be used with prudence and thanksgiving. Yea, flesh of the beasts and fowls of the air, I the Lord have ordained for the use of man with thanksgiving. Nevertheless, they should be used sparingly; and it is pleasing unto me, that they should not be used only in times of winter, or of cold, or famine. All grain is ordained for the use of man, and of beasts, to be the staff of life, not only for man, but for the beasts of the field, and the fowls of heaven, and all the wild animals that run or creep on the earth; and these hath God made for the use of man only in times of famine, and excess of hunger" (Hyrum Smith, *Times and Seasons,* Vol. III., p. 799).

But although God has ordained animals for the use of man, He has not sanctioned the order of things under which some have an abundance of food and clothing, while others are destitute; for that very reason "the world lieth in sin" (v. 20). Nor must man waste animal life. To kill, when not necessary, is a sin akin to murder. "A righteous man regardeth the life of his beast" (Prov. 12:10). Man has been entrusted with sovereignty over the animal kingdom (Gen. 1:21), that he may learn to govern, as God rules, by the power of love and justice, and become fit for his eternal destiny as a ruler of worlds. A tyrant who has learned nothing but selfishness and cruelty can hope for no position of trust hereafter in the kingdom of the Father.

22. *Not in the form of a woman*] The Shakers taught that "in this Christ-order there is neither male nor female, in the fleshly generative sense." This originated the notion that our Savior might come as a woman just as well as a man. The idea that the Son of God, our elder Brother, is without sex, is contrary to the Word of God.

Neither of a man traveling] When He comes, He will appear in the Temples erected to receive Him, and not as a homeless wanderer.

23. *The heavens to be shaken, and the earth to tremble*] This is the manner in which His presence will be manifest. The term "Quakers"—applied to the so-called Shakers, as well as to the mother society—was given to followers of George Fox, it is said, by a magistrate whom he had bidden to "tremble at the word of God." When Christ appears, both the heavens and the earth will shake and tremble.

24. But before the great day of the Lord shall come, Jacob shall flourish in the wilderness, and the Lamanites shall blossom as the rose.

25. Zion shall flourish upon the hills and rejoice upon the

mountains, and shall be assembled together unto the place which I have appointed.

4. REGARDING THE FUTURE OF ZION.

24-25. The Shakers established their communities in the Eastern States. In 1886 they had no fewer than seventeen settlements scattered principally over the States of New York, Massachusetts, New Hampshire, Maine, and Connecticut. The Spirit of Prophecy, therefore, revealed to the Saints that the gathering place He had chosen was in the Western mountains, in what was then known as the great American Desert, not in the East. This is the second intimation (see also Sec. 35:24) that the Saints would find a gathering-place in the Rocky Mountains, a region almost unknown in 1831, when this remarkable prophecy was given.

There are two distinct predictions in these paragraphs. One says that "Jacob shall flourish in the wilderness, and the Lamanites shall blossom as the rose," before the great day of the Lord shall come; the second tells us that "Zion shall flourish upon the hills and rejoice upon the mountains.' The first of these predictions refers to the Indians; the second, to the Latter-day Saints. Have they been fulfilled?

The American Indians are, indeed, flourishing today. On Government reservations they enjoy a measure of prosperity beyond the dreams of their fathers. In Indian Territory they have attained a high degree of both civilization and prosperity. Indians now occupy Government offices and seats in legislative assemblies, in schools and pulpits, and in every walk of life. They are flourishing. This is all the more remarkable because at one time the general belief was that they were a vanishing race. When the United States became an independent nation, the number of Indians in North America was estimated at three millions, and in the year 1876 at only one million three hundred thousand. In 1907 the decrease had been checked, and an increase to one million four hundred and seventy-four thousand was reported. Only a prophet inspired by God could have foreseen such a decided turn in the tide of Indian affairs.

The Latter-day Saints, it is hardly necessary to say, by their location in the Rocky Mountains and their prosperity, are an irrefutable proof of the truth of the second part of this prophecy.

26. Behold, I say unto you, go forth as I have commanded you; repent of all your sins; ask and ye shall receive; knock and it shall be opened unto you.

27. Behold, I will go before you and be your rearward; and I will be in your midst, and you shall not be confounded.

28. Behold, I am Jesus Christ, and I come quickly. Even so. Amen.

5. PROMISES TO THE MISSIONARIES.

26-28. If the missionaries would repent of their sins, pray, and labor diligently ("knock"), the Lord would be with them, and they should not be "confounded."

27. *Confounded*] This word means "baffled," "confuted," "disappointed." The mission to the Shakers may have appeared to be a failure. But was it without effect? It is certain that there are now no prominent Shaker communities. They have vanished from public view. If they rejected the message God sent to them, they certainly have not prospered. A few years ago their principal community was dissolved, their experiment having proved a failure.

GENERAL NOTES

A wedding at Kirtland is noted in the *History of the Church,* Vol. II., p. 320. The Prophet Joseph writes under date of November 24, 1835: "I had an invitation to attend a wedding at Brother Hyrum Smith's in the evening; also to solemnize the matrimonial ceremony between Newel Knight and Lydia Goldthwaite. My wife accompanied me. On our arrival a considerable company had collected. The bridegroom and bride came in, and took their seats, which gave me to understand that they were ready. After prayers, I requested them to rise and join hands. I then remarked that marriage was an institution of heaven, instituted in the Garden of Eden; that it was necessary it should be solemnized by the authority of the everlasting Priesthood. The ceremony was original with me, and in substance as follows—you covenant to be each other's companions through life, and discharge the duties of husband and wife in every respect; to which they assented. I then pronounced them husband and wife in the name of God, and also pronounced upon them the blessings that the Lord conferred upon Adam and Eve in the Garden of Eden, that is, to multiply and replenish the Earth, with the addition of long life and prosperity."

John Whitmer, in his *History,* says "The above-named brethren [v. 1] went and proclaimed [the gospel] according to the Revelation given them, but the Shakers hearkened not to their words and received not the gospel at that time; for they are bound in tradition and priestcraft; and thus they are led away with foolish and vain imaginations" (*Hist. of the Church,* Vol. IV., p. 169).

SECTION 50.

REVELATION *given through Joseph Smith the Prophet, at Kirtland, Ohio, May, 1831. The Prophet states that some of the Elders present did not understand the manifestations of different spirits abroad in the earth, and that this revelation was given in response to his special inquiry on the matter. So-called spiritual phenomena were not uncommon among the members, some of whom claimed to be receiving visions and revelations. See History of the Church, vol. 1, p. 170.——False spirits deceiving the world—Means by which they may be detected—Between their manifestations and those of the Spirit of the Lord there is difference as between light and darkness—Special service required of certain Elders—Greater knowledge promised as the people shall grow in grace and truth—The Lord is the Good Shepherd and the Stone of Israel.*

HEARKEN, O ye elders of my church, and give ear to the voice of the living God; and attend to the words of wisdom which shall be given unto you, according as ye have asked and are agreed as touching the church, and the spirits which have gone abroad in the earth.

2. Behold, verily I say unto you, that there are many spirits which are false spirits, which have gone forth in the earth, deceiving the world.

3. And also Satan hath sought to deceive you, that he might overthrow you.

4. Behold, I, the Lord, have looked upon you, and have seen abominations in the church that profess my name.

5. But blessed are they who are faithful and endure, whether in life or in death, for they shall inherit eternal life.

6. But wo unto them that are deceivers and hypocrites, for, thus saith the Lord, I will bring them to judgment.

7. Behold, verily I say unto you, there are hypocrites among you, who have deceived some, which has given the adversary power; but behold such shall be reclaimed;

8. But the hypocrites shall be detected and shall be cut off, either in life or in death, even as I will; and wo unto them who are cut off from my church, for the same are overcome of the world.

9. Wherefore, let every man beware lest he do that which is not in truth and righteousness before me.

Parley P. Pratt, in his *Autobiography,* says that, as he went forth among the different branches of the Church, he saw some very strange spiritual operations. Some persons would seem to swoon away and make unseemly gestures, and be drawn and disfigured in their countenances. Others would fall into ecstacies and be drawn into contortions, cramps, fits, etc. Others claimed to have visions and revelations. All these things had developed since Elder Pratt left for his mission to the Lamanites and before the arrival of the Prophet Joseph in Kirtland. On account of these strange phenomena, Parley P. Pratt, John Murdock, and several other Elders asked the Prophet to inquire of the Lord concerning these manifestations. They all united in prayer in the translating room of the Prophet, and this Revelation was received after the prayer. In it the Lord (1) warns them against false spirits, deception, and hypocrisy (1-9); (2) gives instructions on how to discern between false and true spirits (10-36); (3) gives personal directions to some of the Elders and encouragement to all (37-46).

1. WARNING AGAINST FALSE SPIRITS.

1. *Words of Wisdom*] That is the name given to this Revelation concerning "the Church and the spirits which have gone abroad in the Earth." Section 89 is also called "A Word of Wisdom."

2. *False Spirits*] Elder George A. Smith says:
"There was a prevalent spirit all through the early history of the Church, which prompted the Elders to suppose that they knew more than the Prophet. Elders would tell you that the Prophet was going wrong. Men who thought they knew all about this work, some of them thirty or forty years before the Lord revealed it, tried to 'steady the ark.' The Church was constantly afflicted with such a class of men" (*Jour. of Discourses*. Vol. XI., p. 7).

4. *Abominations in the church*] Elder George A. Smith refers to a "church" formed by apostates, in which the president accused the bishop of impure conduct, and the bishop retaliated by charging his accuser with stealing. Their "church" lasted only a few months. There were abominations in it.

6-8. The Lord, in these paragraphs denounces deceivers. It is possible to save "sinners," when they repent, but a hypocrite cannot repent, until he becomes honest before God and men. The Prophet Joseph was not a deceiver.

10. And now come, saith the Lord, by the Spirit, unto the elders of his church, and let us reason together, that ye may understand;

11. Let us reason even as a man reasoneth one with another face to face.

12. Now, when a man reasoneth he is understood of man,

because he reasoneth as a man; even so will I, the Lord, reason with you that you may understand.

13. Wherefore, I the Lord ask you this question—unto what were ye ordained?

14. To preach my gospel by the Spirit, even the Comforter which was sent forth to teach the truth.

15. And then received ye spirits which ye could not understand, and received them to be of God; and in this are ye justified?

16. Behold ye shall answer this question yourselves; nevertheless, I will be merciful unto you; he that is weak among you hereafter shall be made strong.

17. Verily I say unto you, he that is ordained of me and sent forth to preach the word of truth by the Comforter, in the Spirit of truth, doth he preach it by the Spirit of truth or some other way?

18. And if it be by some other way it is not of God.

19. And again, he that receiveth the word of truth, doth he receive it by the Spirit of truth or some other way?

20. If it be some other way it is not of God.

21. Therefore, why is it that ye cannot understand and know, that he that receiveth the word by the Spirit of truth receiveth it as it is preached by the Spirit of truth?

22. Wherefore, he that preacheth and he that receiveth, understand one another, and both are edified and rejoice together.

23. And that which doth not edify is not of God, and is darkness.

24. That which is of God is light; and he that receiveth light, and continueth in God, receiveth more light; and that light groweth brighter and brighter until the perfect day.

25. And again, verily I say unto you, and I say it that you may know the truth, that you may chase darkness from among you;

26. He that is ordained of God and sent forth, the same is appointed to be the greatest, notwithstanding he is the least and the servant of all.

27. Wherefore, he is possessor of all things; for all things

are subject unto him, both in heaven and on the earth, the life and the light, the Spirit and the power, sent forth by the will of the Father through Jesus Christ, his Son.

28.   But no man is possessor of all things except he be purified and cleansed from all sin.

29.   And if ye are purified and cleansed from all sin, ye shall ask whatsoever you will in the name of Jesus and it shall be done.

30.   But know this, it shall be given you what you shall ask; and as ye are appointed to the head, the spirits shall be subject unto you.

31.   Wherefore, it shall come to pass, that if you behold a spirit manifested that you cannot understand, and you receive not that spirit, ye shall ask of the Father in the name of Jesus; and if he give not unto you that spirit, then you may know that it is not of God.

32.   And it shall be given unto you, power over that spirit; and you shall proclaim against that spirit with a loud voice that it is not of God—

33.   Not with railing accusation, that ye be not overcome, neither with boasting nor rejoicing, lest you be seized therewith.

34.   He that receiveth of God, let him account it of God; and let him rejoice that he is accounted of God worthy to receive.

35.   And by giving heed and doing these things which ye have received, and which ye shall hereafter receive—and the kingdom is given you of the Father, and power to overcome all things which are not ordained of him—

36.   And behold, verily I say unto you, blessed are you who are now hearing these words of mine from the mouth of my servant, for your sins are forgiven you.

2. How to Discern Between False and True Spirits.

14.   *Preach my gospel by the Spirit*] The Elders of the Church are ordained to preach as directed by the Spirit (Sec. 42:13, 14). They have no other authority.

19-20.   *The word of truth*] That which comes from the Spirit of God is the word of truth, and it comes through the channels He has appointed. This is *one* sure sign of a true doctrine or any divine manifestation.

Both are edified] Another sign of truth is this, that both he who speaks it and those who hear it, who have the Spirit of God, are edified thereby. "That which doth not edify is not of God" (v. 23).

24. *Receiveth more light*] Another characteristic of truth is that it opens the way for revelation of more truth. The light of truth grows ever brighter, while falsehood envelops the mind in a veil of darkness, ever increasing in density.

31. *A spirit * * * that you cannot understand*] He who is ordained of God, and is purified from sin (v. 29), has recourse to prayer when he beholds manifestations which he cannot understand. He is prompted to ask God for light, in the name of Jesus, and if he does not, under the influence of prayer, receive the same spirit, then he knows that it is not of God, and that he may rebuke it, though not with "railing accusation." Evil spirits must be fought in humility, lest, through pride, they gain power over those who rebuke them (v. 33). Elder George A. Smith explains that these paragraphs refer particularly to Hiram Page. See Sec. 28:11.

36. *Your sins are forgiven you*] The Elders to whom this Revelation was given were "blessed" because the Kingdom had been given to them by the Father, and they had power, by the Spirit, to overcome all things, but the greatest blessing of all was that their sins were forgiven.

37. Let my servant Joseph Wakefield, in whom I am well pleased, and my servant Parley P. Pratt go forth among the churches and strengthen them by the word of exhortation;

38. And also my servant John Corrill, or as many of my servants as are ordained unto this office, and let them labor in the vineyard; and let no man hinder them doing that which I have appointed unto them—

39. Wherefore, in this thing my servant Edward Partridge is not justified; nevertheless let him repent and he shall be forgiven.

40. Behold, ye are little children and ye cannot bear all things now; ye must grow in grace and in the knowledge of the truth.

41. Fear not, little children, for you are mine, and I have overcome the world, and you are of them that my Father hath given me;

42. And none of them that my Father hath given me shall be lost.

43. And the Father and I are one. I am in the Father and the

Father in me; and inasmuch as ye have received me, ye are in me and I in you.

44. Wherefore, I am in your midst, and I am the good shepherd, and the stone of Israel. He that buildeth upon this rock shall never fall.

45. And the day cometh that you shall hear my voice and see me, and know that I am.

46. Watch, therefore, that ye may be ready. Even so. Amen.

3. Personal and General Instructions.

37. Joseph Wakefield and Parley P. Pratt are here instructed to labor among the Branches of the Church. Elder George A. Smith, relating his early experiences, says:

"During the fall of 1830, a gentleman who lived in our neighborhood went to western New York and saw the Prophet, got baptized and ordained an Elder; and that was Elder Solomon Humphrey [See Sec. 52: 35]. Very few knew the old gentleman: he died in Missouri in 1835. He was a very faithful man. Previous to joining the Church he was a Baptist exhorter. He came back to our place of residence in company with a man named Wakefield, * * * They came and preached and baptized for the remission of sins" (*Jour. of Dis.,* Vol. V., p. 104).

Elder George A. Smith was baptized by Joseph Wakefield, September 10, 1832.

38. John Corrill was also appointed to labor in the Church. He took a prominent part in the affairs of the Church for some time. In 1832 he baptized Emily Dow Partridge, a daughter of Edward Partridge, at Independence, Jackson Co., Mo. About that time he was one of seven High Priests appointed to preside over the Saints of Zion. The others were, Oliver Cowdery, W. W. Phelps, John Whitmer, Sidney Gilbert, Edward Partridge, and Isaac Morley. In 1837 he was made keeper of the Lord's storehouse, by the same Conference that sustained David Whitmer as president of the Church in Missouri, and John Whitmer and W. W. Phelps as his counselors. But notwithstanding the trust placed in him, when the fires of persecution raged with terrifying fury, he faltered, and signified his intention of publishing a booklet called, *Mormonism Fairly Delineated,* the appearance of which the mob looked forward to with hopeful anticipation (*Historical Record,* p. 458). At a special conference at Quincy, Ill., March 17, 1839, he was excommunicated for acting against the interests of the Saints. Among others who were similarly dealt with at that time were Geo. M. Hinckle, Sampson Avard, W. W. Phelps, Frederick G. Williams, and Thomas B. Marsh—all of whom were, at one time, prominent in the Church.

39. Edward Partridge is admonished to repent of some errors of

judgment, or mistake, by which those appointed to labor in the Branches were hindered from doing so (v. 38).

40. *Ye are little children*] Of such is the kingdom of heaven. When a man or woman becomes as a little child, humble, willing to learn, obedient, he, or she, is fit for citizenship in that Kingdom.

42. *None of them * * * shall be lost*] Not that the sheep cannot go astray, but the vigilance of the Shepherd is such that no wolf can slay them, as long as they remain with the flock.

45-46. The revelation closes with an assurance that the "day cometh that you shall hear my voice, and see me, and know that I am." Watch, therefore, and be ready.

General Notes

Since our Lord says, "None of them that my Father hath given me shall be lost," the question might be asked, "Was not John Corrill, who in all probability was present when this Revelation was given 'lost,' although the Lord said, You are of them that my Father hath given me?" It might seem like entering the field of fruitless speculation to consider that question. But it must be remembered that there are two entirely different classes of apostates. One class consists of members too weak to resist temptations and persecutions, wherefore they fall by the wayside, when the storms sweep over them. The other class deliberately join the forces of the adversary and make war upon Christ and His followers, because they love sin and hate righteousness. Who shall say that those who have fallen because of weakness will not ultimately be reclaimed by our Savior and given some degree of glory, although they may have lost their grandest opportunity? Who can say that they are "lost," in the same sense as the enemies who die in hatred? John Corrill at one time offered, with others, to give himself to the mob as ransom for the Church, but the mob refused the sacrifice. It was when the persecution raged at its worst in Missouri that he fell.

SECTION 51.

REVELATION *given through Joseph Smith the Prophet, at Thompson, Ohio, May, 1831. At this time the Saints migrating from the State of New York began to arrive in Ohio; and it became necessary to make definite arrangements for their settlement. As this undertaking belonged particularly to the bishop's office, Bishop Edward Partridge sought instruction on the matter; and the Prophet inquired of the Lord. See History of the*

Church, vol. 1, p. 173.——Provision made for the allotment of property to the immigrant members—Care and proper use of moneys and other possessions—Gathering place in Ohio consecrated to the Church for a little season only.

HEARKEN unto me, saith the Lord your God, and I will speak unto my servant Edward Partridge, and give unto him directions; for it must needs be that he receive directions how to organize this people.

2. For it must needs be that they be organized according to my laws; if otherwise, they will be cut off.

3. Wherefore, let my servant Edward Partridge, and those whom he has chosen, in whom I am well pleased, appoint unto this people their portions, every man equal according to his family, according to his circumstances and his wants and needs.

Shortly after the Revelation recorded in Section 50 had been received, the Saints from Colesville, N. Y., began to arrive in Ohio. They had been directed to gather in that locality (Sec. 37:3) and they had been promised that there they would receive The Law (Sec. 38:32). The Saints in Ohio had been instructed to divide their land with their Eastern brethren (Sec. 48:2), and it was the duty of Edward Partridge, who had been appointed Bishop (Sec. 36) to take care of the newcomers, as far as possible. Under the circumstances, Bishop Partridge asked for divine guidance. The Prophet inquired of the Lord for him, and received this answer to his prayers.

In this Revelation our Lord gives instructions concerning the temporal organizations of His people. We learn from it that it was the special duty of the Bishopric to have charge of the temporal affairs of the Church, under the direction of the Prophet. The temporal organization (1) must be effected in accordance with the Law of God (1-3); (2) it must include (a) the just and equitable treatment of transgressors (4-6); (b) the appointment of an agent for the community (7-9); (c) just and equitable dealing with other churches (10-12); (d) the establishment of a storehouse and a provision for adequate compensation for services rendered (13-15); (3) the location of the Colesville Saints in Ohio was only temporary (16-17); but (4) their organization was, nevertheless, to be a pattern for the future (13-19); (5) Christ's promise to His people (20).

1. TEMPORAL ORGANIZATION.

1. *Need*] Read, "needs," as in verse 2, and elsewhere. The word is originally a genitive form and means, "of need," "of necessity," but it is used as an adverb for "necessarily."

2. *According to my laws*] Even the temporary organization of the people of God must be effected in accordance with the laws of God. All things are spiritual to God (Sec. 29:34, 35). All things should be spiritual to man.

Cut off] Unless the organization is in accordance with divine laws, it will not be permanent. There have been many attempts in the world to create a Utopia on the basis of the consolidation of interests. Their failure is due chiefly to the fact that God has not been consulted in their organization. An individualistic society is not much of a success without God; and a communistic society without Him is impossible. God warned His people at the outset of the consequences of attempting an organization, such as contemplated in the Revelations, except in accordance with His law; they will be "cut off" as the dry branches of a tree, that have become useless.

3. *Equal according to their * * * needs*] The Lord here instructs Bishop Partridge and the two counselors, whom he had chosen, to locate the Colesville Saints at Thompson, a place not far from Kirtland, and to see that each man received a portion of property equal to his needs. Equality in a community organized according to the laws of God does not mean a division of property in equal shares, but in shares equal to the needs of each family or person. One who has a large family needs a larger portion than he who has but few to take care of. One who has a large business to manage needs more capital than one who works for wages. But there is perfect equality when each has what he needs and no more, and that is the ideal state of society, under the law of God.

4. And let my servant Edward Partridge, when he shall appoint a man his portion, give unto him a writing that shall secure unto him his portion, that he shall hold it, even this right and this inheritance in the church, until he transgresses and is not accounted worthy by the voice of the church, according to the laws and covenants of the church, to belong to the church.

5. And if he shall transgress and is not accounted worthy to belong to the church, he shall not have power to claim that portion which he has consecrated unto the bishop for the poor and needy of my church; therefore, he shall not retain the gift, but shall only have claim on that portion that is deeded unto him.

6. And thus all things shall be made sure, according to the laws of the land.

2. Equitable Treatment of Transgressors.

4. *Give unto him a writing*] In the community there would always be some who would wish to draw out and, perhaps, embarrass the rest by lawsuits, or otherwise. In order to prevent such designs, just and equitable provisions were to be made and secured by legal agreements. The plan was that everybody should transfer his property to the Bishop. Then the Bishop should deed back whatever each one needed. This was his stewardship. The surplus was to be retained by the Bishop for the benefit of those who, through sickness or age, were unable to contribute their share to the common fund of labor. If anyone transgressed and was counted unworthy of membership in the Church, he also lost his standing in the society, but in that case he was to retain the property deeded to him, but have no claim on the portion set apart for the maintenance of the poor and needy.

7. And let that which belongs to this people be appointed unto this people.

8. And the money which is left unto this people—let there be an agent appointed unto this people, to take the money to provide food and raiment, according to the wants of this people.

9. And let every man deal honestly, and be alike among this people, and receive alike, that ye may be one, even as I have commanded you.

3. The Agent and His Duties.

7. *That which belongs to this people*] The stewardship of each individual was to be secured to him by a legal deed; in the same way, the common property was to be secured to the people.

8. *Let there be an agent appointed*] The community was to be represented by an Agent, whose special duty it would be to handle the money required for food and clothing by the people. There is great wisdom manifested in the distribution of responsibilities. The Bishopric would receive the property, distribute it in "stewardships," and receive the earnings of each stewardship; the Agent would see to it that property was not unduly accumulated, but that the needs of all were supplied.

9. *Be alike*] By this means it would be possible to preserve equality and unity, as God has commanded (See Sec. 49:20). The plan was admirable in every respect. Under it, every member would have been absolutely independent. All would have had the benefit of whatever inventive genius, productive power, or business ability, existed in the community. Not only would poverty have been abolished, but all would have been wealthy, by having a share in the common resources. Honesty, however, would have been absolutely necessary. There can be no success, in a communistic society, unless the members are first made honest, through the gospel. It is a notable fact that when nations, now-a-days, because of war or other calamities, are in danger of a shortage of food, for instance, a wise government immediately takes possession of all the supplies on hand and forces the people, to that extent, into a united order, with distributing agents. Individualism is then abandoned as inadequate. But if this arrangement is superior in times of scarcity, why would it not be equally superior in times of abundance? In 1857 Heber C. Kimball told the saints in Salt Lake City:

"In the house of Israel there is now clothing enough to last us ten years and make us comfortable, if it could be put into the storehouse of God and properly distributed, to clothe men, and their wives, and children, who may be worthy and needy. That is the Apostle's doctrine, you know" (*Jour. of Dis.,* Vol. V., p. 33).

How many years' supply would there be in Israel now, if all necessaries of life were stored and distributed according to this plan?

10. And let that which belongeth to this people not be taken and given unto that of another church.

11. Wherefore, if another church would receive money of this church, let them pay unto this church again according as they shall agree;

12. And this shall be done through the bishop or the agent, which shall be appointed by the voice of the church.

4. EACH COMMUNITY INDEPENDENT.

10. *That which belongeth to this people, * * * church*] The word "church" in this paragraph stands for "Branch," as in Sec. 20:81; 45:64, and elsewhere. The meaning conveyed is that the property owned by the Colesville Branch could not be claimed by any other Branch.

11. *If another church would receive money*] In their business transactions with each other the Branches of the Church were to follow the business rules that honorable men observe as individuals.

12. *The bishop or the agent*] Business representatives of the community.

13. And again, let the bishop appoint a storehouse unto this church; and let all things both in money and in meat, which are more than is needful for the wants of this people, be kept in the hands of the bishop.

14. And let him also reserve unto himself for his own wants, and for the wants of his family, as he shall be employed in doing this business.

15.   And thus I grant unto this people a privilege of organizing themselves according to my laws.

5. The Storehouse and Compensation.

13.   *Appoint a storehouse*] A general storehouse would be needed, in which to care properly for such products of the community, as grain, vegetables, meat, raw materials of every kind, manufactured articles, works of art, etc., as well as money.

14.   *Let him also reserve unto himself for his own wants*] The bishop was given the custody of the storehouse with the privilege of reserving unto himself the substance needed for the wants of his family while he was employed in the business of the Church.

15.   *Grant unto this people a privilege*] The law of the United Order was given to the Colesville Branch as a boon, *a privilege*. God, who knew the weakness of His people, did not, at this time, give it with the force of a peremptory command. But some day the Saints will be required to observe this law, for Zion cannot be redeemed without it.

16.   And I consecrate unto them this land for a little season, until I, the Lord, shall provide for them otherwise, and command them to go hence;

17.   And the hour and the day is not given unto them, wherefore let them act upon this land as for years, and this shall turn unto them for their good.

6. A Temporary Location.

16.   *For a little season*] The location of the Saints at Thompson was only temporary. Those who came there did not generally accept the order revealed to them (Sec. 56:6), wherefore the humble and contrite among them were given permission to go to Missouri (Sec. 56:7).

17.   *Let them act * * * as for years*] They were, however, to perform their temporal duties, as if they were to remain at Thompson for years. That is always a good rule, "Whatsoever thy hand findeth to do, do it with thy might" (Ecclesiastes 9:10).

18.   Behold, this shall be an example unto my servant Edward Partridge, in other places, in all churches.

19.   And whoso is found a faithful, a just, and a wise steward shall enter into the joy of his Lord, and shall inherit eternal life.

7. The Colesville Organization A Pattern.

18.   *This shall be an example*] The instructions to the Colesville Saints

regarding their temporal affairs were to be a pattern to other Branches of the Church.

Churches] See verse 10.

19. *Whoso is found faithful * * * eternal life*] The Lord promises those who are faithful, just, and wise as His "stewards" over the temporal things entrusted to their care an entrance into the "joy of his Lord" and eternal life. We are apt to regard a blissful hereafter as a reward for the faithful performance of such duties as attending meetings, praying, engaging in devotional studies, giving alms, etc., and all such manifestations of a new life are as natural to those who are born again of the water and the Spirit, as are breathing, eating, etc. to man's physical existence. But we must not forget that to take care of whatever material and temporal gifts we may have is just as much the duty of a Latter-day Saint, as to attend meetings and to pray. All our talents should be used for the furtherance of the Kingdom of Christ. There is no such real distinction between things temporal and eternal as men frequently draw. The fact is that we are now in eternity, as much as we ever will be, and we are surrounded everywhere by things of eternal portent.

20. Verily, I say unto you, I am Jesus Christ, who cometh quickly, in an hour you think not. Even so. Amen.

8. CHRIST'S PROMISE.

20. *Who cometh quickly*] The Lord again promises His people that He will come quickly. This fact He impresses upon our minds again and again. May we realize it.

"Even so, come, Lord Jesus" (Rev. 22:20).

GENERAL NOTES.

There have been some successful attempts to practice unity in temporal affairs. Enoch preached the gospel in his day, and those who believed were gathered and lived in a United Order. "They were of one heart and one mind, and dwelt in righteousness; and there was no poor among them" (Pearl of Great Price, Book of Moses, 7:18). Their city existed for 365 years, and then the Lord took Enoch and his Zion up to Him, before the flood came. They were translated or changed in a moment, as the Saints of the latter days will be at His coming.

In the year 36 A. D. a great many Nephites and Lamanites were converted and united in a society in which all property was held common. "Therefore they were not rich and poor, bond and free, but they were all made free, and partakers of the heavenly gift" (IV. Nephi v. 3). This blessed condition lasted more than 150 years [George Reynolds, *Story of the Book of Mormon*, p. 484], when they began to be lifted up in pride and to wear costly clothes and ornaments. "And from that time forth they did have their goods and their substance no more common among them" (IV. Nephi v. 25). Pride was the death of brotherhood.

The first converts in Jerusalem, who embraced the gospel at the time of Pentecost, sold their "possessions and goods" and distributed to all according to the needs of each. It may be supposed that they retained their homes, as provided by the Mosaic law, and also other things necessary for their own maintenance, and that they sold the rest for the benefit of the needy Saints, at the same time extending their hospitality to all (Acts 2:45). That which was intended for distribution was laid at the feet of the Apostles. They were the representatives of the Lord, and the money was, therefore, in fact, given to Him. Not one of them said that his possessions were his, but everyone considered himself as the Lord's steward. The consecration of their property was entirely voluntary, as is clear from the story of Ananias (Acts 5:4). In all ages, when the Spirit of God has been poured out upon the people in an abundant measure, they have proved their love of God by an unselfish love of their fellowmen, God's children.

SECTION 52.

REVELATION *given through Joseph Smith the Prophet, to the Elders of the Church, at Kirtland, Ohio, June 7, 1831. A conference had been held at Kirtland, beginning on the 3rd, and closing on the 6th. At this conference the first distinctive ordinations to the office of High Priest were made; and certain manifestations of false and deceiving spirits were discerned and rebuked. See History of the Church, vol. 1, p. 175.——Missouri designated as the place for the next succeeding conference— Elders named with their respective appointments to travel two by two, preaching and baptizing.*

BEHOLD, thus saith the Lord unto the elders whom he hath called and chosen in these last days, by the voice of his Spirit—

2. Saying: I, the Lord, will make known unto you what I will that ye shall do from this time until the next conference, which shall be held in Missouri, upon the land which I will consecrate unto my people, which are a remnant of Jacob, and those who are heirs according to the covenant.

On June 3, 1831, the elders who had been laboring in the country, in different parts, met in Kirtland, to attend the Fourth General Conference of the Church, which convened by a Revelation (Sec. 44).

Though the Church was only fourteen months old at this time, there were about two thousand attendants at the Conference. Among the elders present was Parley P. Pratt, who had returned from his mission to the Lamanites (See Sec. 32:2), to report his labors, while Oliver Cowdery, Ziba Peterson, and Peter Whitmer, Jr., his fellow-laborers in that Mission, remained in Missouri.

The Conference convened, probably on the third day of June, and lasted for three days. As had been promised in a Revelation (Sec. 44), the Spirit of the Lord was manifested in mighty power. The special office of High Priest was bestowed upon several Elders, this being done for the first time in the Church. The power of the adversary was also manifested. Two brethren, Harvey Whitlock and John Murdock, were "bound," so that they could not speak, and others were similarly affected, but the Prophet rebuked the adversary in the name of Jesus Christ, and the evil spirit departed. Lyman Wight, after having been ordained a High Priest, prophesied of the coming of the Lord and testified that he saw the heavens opened and the Son of Man sitting at the right hand of the Father (*Hist. of the Church,* Vol. I., pp. 175-6).

The next day after the Conference this Revelation was received, in which the Lord (1) appoints another Conference, to be held in some place in Missouri (1-2); (2) instructs Joseph Smith and Sidney Rigdon to go to Missouri (3-6); (3) calls Lyman Wight, John Corrill, John Murdock, and Hyrum Smith to take a journey to Missouri (7-13); (4) gives to the Elders instructions enabling them to discern between false and true spirits (14-21); (5) calls a number of Elders to go on a mission to Missouri (22-34); (6) calls two Elders to go east (35-36); (7) gives miscellaneous instructions (37-42); and (8) closes with a great promise (43-44).

1. NEXT CONFERENCE.

2. *Next Conference*] The next General Conference was to be held in Missouri, upon ground that would be consecrated for the people of God, both Lamanites and Gentiles (See Sec. 49:24, 25). The time was drawing near for the promised Revelation of the place where the City of Zion, the New Jerusalem, should be built (See Sec. 42:62).

3. Wherefore, verily I say unto you, let my servants Joseph Smith, Jun., and Sidney Rigdon take their journey as soon as preparations can be made to leave their homes, and journey to the land of Missouri.

4. And inasmuch as they are faithful unto me, it shall be made known unto them what they shall do;

5. And it shall also, inasmuch as they are faithful, be made known unto them the land of your inheritance.

6. And inasmuch as they are not faithful, they shall be cut off, even as I will, as seemeth me good.

2. JOSEPH SMITH AND SIDNEY RIGDON TO GO TO MISSOURI.

3. *As soon as preparations can be made*] A journey of a thousand miles, from Kirtland to Independence, during those early days was quite an undertaking.

4-5. But if they would be faithful in the performance of that duty, the Lord would reveal to them what to do, from time to time, and also make known to them the location of the land of their inheritance.

6. *Inasmuch as they are not faithful, they shall be cut off*] In the service of God everything depends on faith and faithfulness. Strong faith enables us to remain faithful under all circumstances.

7. And again, verily I say unto you, let my servant Lyman Wight and my servant John Corrill take their journey speedily;

8. And also my servant John Murdock, and my servant Hyrum Smith, take their journey unto the same place by the way of Detroit.

9. And let them journey from thence preaching the word by the way, saying none other things than that which the prophets and apostles have written, and that which is taught them by the Comforter through the prayer of faith.

10. Let them go two by two, and thus let them preach by the way in every congregation, baptizing by water, and the laying on of the hands by the water's side.

11. For thus saith the Lord, I will cut my work short in righteousness, for the days come that I will send forth judgment unto victory.

12. And let my servant Lyman Wight beware, for Satan desireth to sift him as chaff.

13. And behold, he that is faithful shall be made ruler over many things.

3. APPOINTMENT FOR THE MISSION TO MISSOURI.

9. *Saying none other thing,* etc.] The Elders mentioned (vv. 7 and 8) were to depart speedily and preach along the route, from the things that were written and which were taught them by the Holy Spirit, through the prayer of faith.

12. *Let my servant Lyman Wight beware*] He had been ordained a High Priest at the Conference and had received a vision. He was a most zealous and successful missionary. He was fearless as a lion in the defense of the Saints, and he was a terror to the enemy. At the April Conference, 1841, he was appointed an Apostle. But, notwithstanding all, there was a flaw in his character which the Lord saw, and of which He warned him in this Revelation. In April, 1844, he was tried before the High Council at Far West for teaching false doctrine. He acknowledged his fault then and was forgiven. But, after the martyrdom of the Prophet, he declared that he would not turn his hand over to be one of the Twelve, and when the Saints went to the Rocky Mountains, as the Prophet Joseph had predicted they would do, he and George Miller led a small company to Texas. Wight died in that State, March 31, 1858. The Lord told him to "beware," but the warning was forgotten in the hour of greatest danger.

14. And again, I will give unto you a pattern in all things, that ye may not be deceived; for Satan is abroad in the land, and he goeth forth deceiving the nations—

15. Wherefore he that prayeth, whose spirit is contrite, the same is accepted of me if he obey mine ordinances.

16. He that speaketh, whose spirit is contrite, whose language is meek and edifieth, the same is of God if he obey mine ordinances.

17. And again, he that trembleth under my power shall be made strong, and shall bring forth fruits of praise and wisdom, according to the revelations and truths which I have given you.

18. And again, he that is overcome and bringeth not forth fruits, even according to this pattern, is not of me.

19. Wherefore, by this pattern ye shall know the spirits in all cases under the whole heavens.

20. And the days have come; according to men's faith it shall be done unto them.

21. Behold, this commandment is given unto all the elders whom I have chosen.

4. How to Discern Between False and True Spirits.

15. *He that prayeth*] Prayer offered by one whose spirit is contrite; one who is humble enough to obey God's ordinances, is accepted of God. "Contrite" means "humble." "The sacrifices of God are a broken spirit: a broken and a contrite heart, O God, thou wilt not despise" (Psalm 51:17); a broken spirit and a contrite heart are those in which the

obstinacy of pride has been replaced by the humility of repentance, frequently brought about by sorrow and affliction.

16. *He that speaketh*] The hearers may know whether a speaker is from God, by the humility of the spirit and the effect of the words. Are they edifying? If not, they are not from God. Does the speaker obey God's ordinances? If not, he is not of God.

Ordinances] Abraham is said to have kept the commandments and ordinances of God (Gen. 26:5, LXX. version). The same is said of Jehoshaphat (II. Chron. 17:4). In Hebrews 9:1, "ordinances" means the requirements of the ceremonial law, as distinct from "Commandments," which refers to moral precepts. The ordinances of the gospel are, more especially, baptism, the laying on of hands for the reception of the Holy Spirit, the sacrament, and the rules and regulations of the Church given by divine inspiration. He who is sent of God obeys God's ordinances, as well as His commandments. Comp. Sec. 53:3, 6.

17. *He that trembleth*] This is another indication of the presence of the Lord, with which the Elders of Israel are familiar; for they almost invariably have that experience when they stand before a congregation to address it. The promise is that he who feels his weakness under the power of God shall be made strong and be able to feed those who hear him, with "fruits of praise and wisdom."

"Often, when I stand up here, I have the feelings of a person that is unable to convey his ideas, because I have not the advantages of language. However, I do not very frequently complain of that, but I rise to do the best I can and to give the people the best I have for them at the time" (Brigham Young, *Jour. of Dis.,* Vol. V., p. 97).

18. *He that is overcome * * * is not of me*] There were some in these early days who were not fully converted, and their spirits not being contrite they failed in their ministry, and did not follow the pattern of prayer, humility and faith. Such was the case with James Covill. See Sections 39, 40.

22.   And again, verily I say unto you, let my servant Thomas B. Marsh and my servant Ezra Thayre take their journey also, preaching the word by the way unto this same land.

23.   And again, let my servant Isaac Morley and my servant Ezra Booth take their journey, also preaching the word by the way unto this same land.

24.   And again, let my servants Edward Partridge and Martin Harris take their journey with my servants Sidney Rigdon and Joseph Smith, Jun.

25.   Let my servants David Whitmer and Harvey Whitlock

also take their journey, and preach by the way unto this same land.

26. And let my servants Parley P. Pratt and Orson Pratt take their journey, and preach by the way, even unto this same land.

27. And let my servants Solomon Hancock and Simeon Carter also take their journey unto this same land, and preach by the way.

28. Let my servants Edson Fuller and Jacob Scott also take their journey.

29. Let my servants Levi W. Hancock and Zebedee Coltrin also take their journey.

30. Let my servants Reynolds Cahoon and Samuel H. Smith also take their journey.

31. Let my servants Wheeler Baldwin and William Carter also take their journey.

32. And let my servants Newell Knight and Selah J. Griffin both be ordained, and also take their journey.

33. Yea, verily I say, let all these take their journey unto one place, in their several courses, and one man shall not build upon another's foundation, neither journey in another's track.

34. He that is faithful, the same shall be kept and blessed with much fruit.

5. FURTHER APPOINTMENTS FOR MISSOURI.

22. *Thomas B. Marsh*] Sec. 31:1.

Ezra Thayre] Secs. 33:1; 56:5; 75:31. Ezra Thayre was a member of Zion's camp, and was, later, with others who were selected to form the First Quorum of Seventy, ordained February 28th, 1835.

23. *Isaac Morley*] Among the prominent men who in the early days of the Church joined its ranks at Kirtland, was Isaac Morley. Previous to that time, he was one of the leaders of a society that practiced communistic principles and was sometimes called the "Morley Family," because a number were living on his farm. He was ordained to the ministry at the same time as Sidney Rigdon, Lyman Wight, and Edward Partridge, by the brethren who passed through Kirtland on their Indian mission, and the newly baptized Saints in Kirtland and vicinity were left to their care. He passed through the many storms that swept over the Church and cast his lot with the Saints in Utah.

Ezra Booth] Ezra Booth was a Methodist minister. He was brought into the Church through a miracle, having witnessed the healing of the wife of Father Johnson, through the instrumentality of the Prophet

Joseph (p. 275). He began to preach immediately, but soon apostatized. In his darkened condition he wrote a series of letters that were published in the Ohio *Star,* though they were full of falsehoods, and Elder George A. Smith says that "his apostasy culminated in collecting a mob who tarred and feathered Joseph Smith, and inflicted upon his family the loss of one of its members at Hiram, Portage Co., Ohio" (*Jour. of Dis.,* Vol. XI., p. 5. See also Doctrine and Covenants, Sec. 64:15).

24. *Edward Partridge*] Sec. 36.
Martin Harris] Sec. 3. These two were called to join Joseph Smith and Sidney Rigdon (v. 3).

25. *David Whitmer*] Sec. 14.

26. *Parley P. Pratt*] Sec. 32.
Orson Pratt] Sec. 34.

27. *Solomon Hancock*] He was among a party of fifteen brethren who were called to go from Clay County to Kirtland, on June 23, 1834, to receive their endowments, because "they had proved themselves faithful and true during the late persecutions." A month afterwards he was appointed a member of the High Council in Clay County.
Simeon Carter] The same note may refer to him. Parley P. Pratt, while on his mission to the Lamanites, stayed at the house of Simeon Carter, fifty miles west of Kirtland. They were in the act of reading the Book of Mormon, when an officer entered and arrested Elder Pratt. The book was left in the house. Pratt managed to escape, and Carter read the Book of Mormon with great interest. He was baptized and ordained an Elder, and soon organized a Branch of sixty members.

29. *Levi Hancock*] He was one of the First Council of Seventies, organized in Kirtland, in 1835.
Zebedee Coltrin] He was another member of the Council.

30. *Reynolds Cahoon and Samuel Smith*] While on this journey, they preached the gospel to William E. McLellin, and so much impressed was he, that he wound up his business and followed them to Jackson County. In 1838 Cahoon was appointed first counselor to John Smith, who was made president of a Stake of Zion organized at Adam-ondi-Ahman. Lyman Wight was the second counselor. The following year, these three presided over the Saints in Iowa. In 1848, when President Brigham Young led a company of 1,229 souls across the plains to the Mountain valleys, Isaac Morley was appointed president, with Reynolds Cahoon and William W. Major as counselors.
Samuel Smith] See note, Sec. 23.

31. *William Carter*] One of the Utah Pioneers who put the first ploughs into the ground and planted the first potatoes in Salt Lake Valley. George W. Brown and Shadrach Roundy were the others (Whitney's *History of Utah,* Vol. I., p. 331).

32. *Newel Knight*] A son of Joseph Knight, of Colesville, N. Y. He attended the meetings of the Saints at Colesville and became interested in the gospel. The Prophet tried to prevail upon him to pray in public, but being timid, he refused, and the result was that an evil spirit seized him and distorted his face, twisted his limbs, and tossed him about fearfully. The afflicted youth earnestly besought the Prophet to cast out the evil spirit. Joseph did so in the name of the Lord. Newel Knight then came under the influence of the Holy Spirit, and visions of eternity were open to his view.

The Knight family were Universalists, and this miracle, the first performed in the Church, must have made a deep impression upon them. Newel Knight says that under the influence of the Spirit of God he was lifted up bodily from the floor, so that his head pressed against the ceiling.

Newel Knight was the leader of the Saints of the Colesville Branch in their migration from Ohio to Missouri (See Sec. 54:2).

Selah J. Griffin] He was, later, instructed to accompany Thomas B. Marsh (Sec. 56:5).

35. And again, I say unto you, let my servants Joseph Wakefield and Solomon Humphrey take their journey into the eastern lands;

36. Let them labor with their families, declaring none other things than the prophets and apostles, that which they have seen and heard and most assuredly believe, that the prophecies may be fulfilled.

6. Two Elders to go East.

35. *Joseph Wakefield and Solomon Humphrey*] See notes, Sec. 50:37. These two Elders were to go East and labor with their families.

37. In consequence of transgression, let that which was bestowed upon Heman Basset be taken from him, and placed upon the head of Simonds Ryder.

38. And again, verily I say unto you, let Jared Carter be ordained a priest, and also George James be ordained a priest.

39. Let the residue of the elders watch over the churches, and declare the word in the regions round about them; and let them labor with their own hands that there be no idolatry nor wickedness practised.

40. And remember in all things the poor and the needy, the sick and the afflicted, for he that doeth not these things, the same is not my disciple.

41. And again, let my servants Joseph Smith, Jun., and Sidney Rigdon and Edward Partridge take with them a recommend from the church. And let there be one obtained for my servant Oliver Cowdery also.

42. And thus, even as I have said, if ye are faithful ye shall assemble yourselves together to rejoice upon the land of Missouri, which is the land of your inheritance, which is now the land of your enemies.

7. MISCELLANEOUS INSTRUCTIONS.

37. *Simonds Rider*] Shortly after this, Rider joined Ezra Booth and the Johnson boys in inflicting the outrage upon the Prophet Joseph and Sidney Rigdon, at Hiram, on the 25th of March, 1832 (Andrew Jenson, *Hist Rec.*, p. 112).

39. *Labor with their own hands*] It is an excellent rule in the Kingdom of God that those who labor in the ministry be independent. For the word of God does not always suit those who are rebuked by it, and if these hold the purse-strings, they are liable to draw them tight and strangle truth. Paul, in his farewell address to the Elders at Ephesus (Acts 20:34, 35), charged them to follow his example in this respect. "Ye yourselves know," he said, "that these hands have ministered unto my necessities, and to them that were with me." I have shown you, he added, that as I have labored to support the weak, so ye ought to labor, and to "remember the words of the Lord Jesus, how He said, It is more blessed to give than to receive." Paul was a tent-maker, and it has been suggested that he and Philemon were partners in that business (See Philemon 17). It is not displeasing to God if the Saints share temporal blessings with those who minister to them in spiritual things, as long as it is voluntary and an expression of gratitude and love, but to preach for hire is, according to the gospel, to encourage "idolatry" and "wickedness."

40. *Remember * * * the afflicted*] This is mandatory upon the Elders as well as the members of the Church.

41. *Let my servants * * * take with them a recommend*] Joseph Smith, Sidney Rigdon, Edward Partridge, and Oliver Cowdery were appointed by Revelation, but they were also to have some proof that they were sustained by the Church. Some preach, and claim that God has authorized them to do so, because they have a desire to be preachers. The desire, they say, is from God. But even if this were true, they would not be fully qualified until the Church had sustained them, for the law of God is that of "common consent," and He honors His own law

42. *Land of your inheritance*] Missouri is again so designated (See also v. 2).

43. But, behold, I, the Lord, will hasten the city in its time, and will crown the faithful with joy and with rejoicing.

44. Behold, I am Jesus Christ, the Son of God, and I will lift them up at the last day. Even so. Amen.

8. CHRIST'S PROMISE.

43. *Will hasten the city*] The Lord assured the Elders about to depart for Missouri, that He would hasten the time for the building of the New Jerusalem, and crown the faithful with joy. He is ready; whenever His people are ready, they may look for the redemption of Zion.

44. See Sec. 5:35.

GENERAL NOTES

Lyman Wight was a peculiar character. At times his faith seemed strong enough to move mountains. After the Saints were driven out of Jackson County, into Clay County, volunteers were called for to go to Kirtland to report the situation to the Prophet. Several Elders excused themselves. Lyman Wight volunteered. Asked what the circumstances were in which his family would be placed, he told the Bishop that his wife had been placed by the side of a log in the woods, for shelter, and that she had a child three days old. They had provisions for three days. Under such circumstances he went on a mission to Kirtland, in company with Parley P. Pratt.

On one occasion he was offered any office in the State he would name, if he would swear to a testimony against Joseph Smith. If you do not do it, the tempter added, you will be shot tomorrow at 8 o'clock. Wight replied, "General, you are entirely mistaken in your man, both in regard to myself and Joseph Smith. Joseph Smith is not an enemy to mankind; he is not your enemy, and is as good a friend as you have got. Had it not been for him, you would have been in hell long ago, for I should have sent you there, and no other man than Joseph Smith could have prevented me, and you may thank him for your life. And now, if you will give me the boys I brought from Diahman yesterday, I will whip your whole army." General Wilson said, "Wight, you are a strange man; but if you will not accept my proposal, you will be shot tomorrow morning at eight." Wight only made the characteristic reply that has become famous. "Shoot and be damned."

SECTION 53.

REVELATION *given through Joseph Smith the Prophet, to Algernon Sidney Gilbert, at Kirtland, Ohio, June, 1831. The Prophet had inquired of the Lord as to Gilbert's work and appointment in the Church.——Gilbert to be ordained an Elder —Also to be an agent unto the Church as the Bishop shall appoint.*

BEHOLD, I say unto you, my servant Sidney Gilbert, that I have heard your prayers; and you have called upon me that it should be made known unto you, of the Lord your God, concerning your calling and election in the church, which I, the Lord, have raised up in these last days.

2. Behold, I, the Lord, who was crucified for the sins of the world, give unto you a commandment that you shall forsake the world.

3. Take upon you mine ordination, even that of an elder, to preach faith and repentance and remission of sins, according to my word, and the reception of the Holy Spirit by the laying on of hands;

4. And also to be an agent unto this church in the place which shall be appointed by the bishop, according to commandments which shall be given hereafter.

5. And again, verily I say unto you, you shall take your journey with my servants Joseph Smith, Jun., and Sidney Rigdon.

6. Behold, these are the first ordinances which you shall receive; and the residue shall be made known in a time to come, according to your labor in my vineyard.

7. And again, I would that ye should learn that he only is saved who endureth unto the end. Even so. Amen.

Elder B. H. Roberts, in a footnote on Page 118, Vol. II., *Hist. of the Church,* makes the remark that the Lord has had few more devoted servants in this dispensation than Algernon Sidney Gilbert. Where he was born is not known, but his father's family resided in Connecticut. For some years he was a successful merchant in Painesville, Ohio, and there the gospel found him in 1830. In the persecution that came upon the Saints in Jackson County he sacrificed all his goods. He was one of the six who offered their lives for their friends. He was a man of great practical sense, as is evidenced by the correspondence he and others engaged in with Governor Dunklin, on behalf of the brethren, but, nevertheless, he shrank from speaking publicly, and it appears that, when called to go on a mission to preach the gospel, he said he would rather die. Not long afterwards he was attacked by cholera, and the disease proved fatal.

Shortly after the Revelation in Section 52 was received, Gilbert requested the Prophet to inquire of the Lord for him. The Prophet Joseph did so, and this communication was given, in which the Lord called him to forsake the world and give his services to the Church, as an Elder and an agent (Business representative).

1. *I have heard your prayers*] This is a gracious assurance. Sidney Gilbert had asked his heavenly Father to make known to him his calling and election in the Church; the prayer had been heard and granted.

3. *Take upon you mine ordination*] (See Sec. 52:15). The verse is an appeal from Him who was crucified for the sins of the world to His servant, to take up the calling as a preacher of the first principles of the gospel.

4. *And also to be an agent*] Sidney Gilbert was an able business man. The crucified Redeemer asks him to give his business talents to the Church. The Lord was about to gather His Saints in a new locality, even in Missouri, and they needed men like Sidney Gilbert to transact business for them. Business talents, when consecrated to the service of mankind, are just as good and necessary as so-called spiritual gifts. It is only when they are used to serve the purposes of selfishness and greed that they become a snare and a curse. In the service of the Lord they are a blessing. As an agent he could help in building up the Church.

5. *You shall take your journey*] He was next directed to join the Prophet Joseph Smith and Sidney Rigdon in their journey to Missouri (See Sec. 52:3).

6. *These are the first ordinances*] Others would be given in the future, as required by the labor in the vineyard.

7. *That endureth unto the end*] No one else is saved. "If you all live your religion and are faithful to the end of your days, that proves that you were chosen as were Jesus and John, who were prophesied of many hundred years before they came, as were many others. Mary, the mother of Jesus, was raised up to bear the Savior. Elizabeth was ordained and set apart to come along near the meridian of time, and we were ordained to come along near the end of time" (Heber C. Kimball, *Jour. of Dis.*, Vol. V., p. 34).

SECTION 54.

REVELATION *given through Joseph Smith the Prophet, to Newel Knight, at Kirtland, Ohio, June, 1831. Members of the Church in the branch at Thompson, Ohio, were divided on certain questions of Church administration, and selfishness was manifest amongst them. Newel Knight and other Elders had come to the Prophet asking how to proceed. See History of the Church, vol. 1, p. 180.——Some who had entered the Church had broken their covenants—Newel Knight to journey to Missouri.*

BEHOLD, thus saith the Lord, even Alpha and Omega, the beginning and the end, even he who was crucified for the sins of the world—

2. Behold, verily, verily, I say unto you, my servant Newel Knight, you shall stand fast in the office whereunto I have appointed you.

3. And if your brethren desire to escape their enemies, let them repent of all their sins, and become truly humble before me and contrite.

4. And as the covenant which they made unto me has been broken, even so it has become void and of none effect.

5. And wo to him by whom this offense cometh, for it had been better for him that he had been drowned in the depth of the sea.

6. But blessed are they who have kept the covenant and observed the commandment, for they shall obtain mercy.

Bishop Partridge had been instructed to organize the Colesville Saints who were located at Thompson, near Kirtland, according to the laws of the United Order (Sec. 51), but all of them did not keep the covenants they had entered into, and the result was confusion. In their troubles, the Saints sent Newel Knight to Kirtland to receive counsel of the Prophet Joseph. In this Revelation, which was received in answer to prayer, the Lord (1) releases the Saints at Thompson from the obligation of the vows that had been broken and were, therefore, void, and pronounces wo upon him through whom the offense had come (1-6); (2) commands all to repent and to flee to Missouri (7-10).

1. THE COVENANTS BROKEN.

1. *Thus saith the Lord*] Our Lord addressed Newel Knight, and the Colesville Saints through him, as their Lord, their Master. He reminds them of their allegiance to Him. He also speaks to them as the Existing One, the Beginning and the End, and the Redeemer of the world (See Sec. 19:1; 35:1). When our Lord, in the Book of Revelation (5:9, 10), undertakes to execute the decrees of the Father, He does so by virtue of His sacrifice of Himself, for, as a Lamb slain, He is the center of adoration; and the "new song" of the Saints, "Thou art worthy to take the book and to open the seals thereof: for thou wast slain, and hast redeemed us to God by thy blood," fills the heavens and the Earth with sweet harmony. God rules the world through the Redeemer of it—through the One who gave His own life for it; not through a conqueror who came to destroy the life of others.

2. *Stand fast in the office*] Newel Knight was to carry out the mission to which he had been called (Sec. 52:32), notwithstanding what had happened at Thompson. That was his office.

3. *Let them repent*] The Colesville Saints at Thompson were in jeopardy because of the enemies of the Kingdom of God; if they wanted to escape, they must repent and become contrite. Most of the evils that befall us are due to disobedience. Repentance is the true remedy.

4. *Covenant * * * has been broken*] "It is difficult, says Elder B. H. Roberts (*Hist. of the Church,* Vol. I., p. 180), "to determine with exactness in what the transgressions of the Saints at Thompson consisted; but it is evident that selfishness and rebellion were at the bottom of their troubles, and that Leman Copley and Ezra Thayre were immediately concerned in it."

The Colesville Saints had been given permission to form a United Order, and some of the Saints at Thompson, Copley and Thayre among others, had agreed to enter the Order with them. Copley had land which he offered to place at the disposal of the brethren. A contract was drawn up and work begun, but Copley, it seems, broke the agreement. That Ezra Thayre was guilty of some such offense appears from Section 56:8.

5. *Wo to him by whom this offense cometh*] As the world is constituted, offenses will come. Some individuals will always place stumbling-blocks in the paths of their brethren. But wo to him who does it! The fate of one lying at the bottom of the sea with a millstone around his neck is, as our Savior declares, better than that of those who cause offenses among the people of God (Luke 17:2).

6. *Blessed are they who kept the covenant*] "They shall obtain mercy," but in the meantime they suffered through the conduct of the covenant-

breakers. However, they were assured of divine comfort. There is a difference between the sufferings of those who are innocent of wrong-doing and those of wrong-doers, who must feel the tortures of an accusing conscience, in addition to the evil consequences of transgression.

7. Wherefore, go to now and flee the land, lest your enemies come upon you; and take your journey, and appoint whom you will to be your leader, and to pay moneys for you.

8. And thus you shall take your journey into the regions westward, unto the land of Missouri, unto the borders of the Lamanites.

9. And after you have done journeying, behold, I say unto you, seek ye a living like unto men, until I prepare a place for you.

10. And again, be patient in tribulation until I come; and, behold, I come quickly, and my reward is with me, and they who have sought me early shall find rest to their souls. Even so. Amen.

2. FLEE TO MISSOURI.

7-8. The Colesville Saints are here directed to leave Ohio and continue their journey westward, to Missouri.

9-10. In Missouri they were to make a living, as other men, until a place should be prepared for them. The Lord again promises that He will come quickly. If they were patient in tribulations, they would be rewarded at His coming. The Lord knew that the saints who went to Missouri, in search of the promised land, would meet tribulations; hence the promise of reward for patience. Saints bound for Zion should always remember the truth expressed in Eliza R. Snow's beautiful hymn,

"Think not, when you gather to Zion,
    Your troubles and trials are through;
That nothing but comfort and pleasure
    Are waiting in Zion for you:
No, no; 'tis designed as a furnace,
    All substance, all textures to try,
To burn all the 'wood, hay, and stubble,'
    The gold from the dross purify."

SECTION 55.

REVELATION *given through Joseph Smith the Prophet, to William W. Phelps, at Kirtland, Ohio, June, 1831. William W. Phelps and his family had just arrived at Kirtland; and the Prophet sought of the Lord information concerning him.——— William W. Phelps designated as one called and chosen— Directed to be baptized and confirmed—Ordination as an Elder to follow—Appointed to assist Oliver Cowdery in literary work for the Church.*

BEHOLD, thus saith the Lord unto you, my servant William, yea, even the Lord of the whole earth, thou art called and chosen; and after thou hast been baptized by water, which if you do with an eye single to my glory, you shall have a remission of your sins and a reception of the Holy Spirit by the laying on of hands;

2. And then thou shalt be ordained by the hand of my servant Joseph Smith, Jun., to be an elder unto this church, to preach repentance and remission of sins by way of baptism in the name of Jesus Christ, the Son of the living God.

3. And on whomsoever you shall lay your hands, if they are contrite before me, you shall have power to give the Holy Spirit.

About the middle of June, 1831, William W. Phelps with his family, arrived in Kirtland. He was born at Hanover, Morris County, N. J., February 17th, 1792. In the State of New York he had edited a newspaper and taken an active part in politics. In Missouri, whither he went in company with the Prophet Joseph, he founded *The Evening and Morning Star,* a monthly magazine devoted to the interests of the Church, and published by the Church. Its first number appeared at Independence, June, 1832. The printing office was destroyed by a mob in July, 1833, but in the following December another printing office was established at Kirtland, and the publication of the *Star* was resumed there. Phelps, in 1837, was appointed to act, with David and John Whitmer, as a President of the Church in Zion. In 1848 he came to Utah, where he attained some prominence. He assisted in the drafting of the Constitution of Deseret, and became preceptor in the University. He died in Salt Lake City, March 7th, 1872, eighty years of age. Many inspiring hymns, popular among the Latter-day Saints, were composed by him.

As stated, he came to Kirtland to learn the will of God concerning him, whereupon he received this Revelation, through the Prophet. The Lord (1) calls him to the ministry (1-3); and (2) gives him the special mission of assisting Oliver Cowdery in educational work in Zion (4-6).

1. CALLED TO THE MINISTRY.

1. *Thus saith the Lord*] Our Lord addresses William W. Phelps in the character of "the Lord of the whole earth." This Earth belongs to Jesus Christ. As the Lord of the Earth, "He shall choose our inheritance for us, the excellency of Jacob whom he loved" (Ps. 47:4). In these Revelations the Saints, when about to leave for a far-away land, were reminded that the sovereignty of every country was vested in Him who commanded them to go.

Thou art called and chosen] W. W. Phelps had been both called and chosen, but it was also his duty to be baptized in water and receive the Holy Spirit by the laying on of hands. There is no other entrance to the Kingdom of God.

One who wants to hold an office in a kingdom must take upon himself certain obligations as a citizen. He must be naturalized, if his citizenship is not one of birthright. He must enter into certain covenants as to loyalty, morality, etc. The rule is the same in the Kingdom of Heaven. We enter it through baptism and the laying on of hands, taking upon us the obligations of citizens in that Kingdom, and receiving the Holy Spirit which permeates it. Then we are qualified for appointment for such offices as the King may call us to take charge of.

The instruction of our Savior to His first disciples regarding baptism was, "Teach all nations, baptizing them;" that is, "Make disciples everywhere, in all nations, by baptizing them in the name of the Father, and of the Son, and of the Holy Ghost; and by instructing them to observe all things whatsoever I have commanded you" (Matt. 28:19, 20, paraphrased). He has given the same instruction to His people in our day.

If baptism is performed and accepted with an eye single to the glory of God, remission of sins is granted. But that is the condition. Baptism for selfish purposes has no such promise. It is but an empty ceremony. Christ undertook to carry out the plan of redemption for the glory of God. If we are His disciples, we follow Him for the glory of God.

Laying on of hands] This ordinance is as necessary as baptism. By it the Lord gives us of His Spirit, through His authorized servants. Paul longed to see the Saints in Rome, "that I may impart unto you some Spiritual gift, to the end that ye may be established (Rom. 1:11); for, although they had been baptized, they had not yet been *established* under the hands of an Apostle of our Lord. John says, "Hereby know we that we dwell in him, and he in us, because he hath given us of his Spirit" (I. John 4:13).

2. *Thou shalt be ordained*] Having received citizenship in the Kingdom of God, Phelps was qualified for ordination to the Priesthood. Our Lord promised him that he would be ordained an Elder under the

hands of the Prophet, and thus receive authority to preach and administer the ordinances of the gospel.

3. *Power to give the Holy Spirit*] He would also have power, as well as authority, to give to others the gift of the Holy Spirit, by the laying on of hands. This is a decisive refutation of the theory that the power to impart the Holy Spirit was confined to the Twelve and ceased with their departure. This view is contrary to history, as well as to the Scriptures, for Justin Martyr, Tertullian, and Cyprian, all testify that the supernatural gifts existed in the Church of Christ long after the time of the first Apostles.

4. And again, you shall be ordained to assist my servant Oliver Cowdery to do the work of printing, and of selecting and writing books for schools in this church, that little children also may receive instruction before me as is pleasing unto me.

5. And again, verily I say unto you, for this cause you shall take your journey with my servants Joseph Smith, Jun., and Sidney Rigdon, that you may be planted in the land of your inheritance to do this work.

6. And again, let my servant Joseph Coe also take his journey with them. The residue shall be made known hereafter, even as I will. Amen.

2. SPECIAL CALLING OF WILLIAM W. PHELPS.

4. *Ordained to * * * the work of printing*] William W. Phelps was familiar with the printing and publishing business, and his talent would be used for the furtherance of the Kingdom of God.

Books for schools] It would be his calling to assist Oliver Cowdery in selecting and writing books suitable for the children, so that these might receive proper instruction.

"The Latter-day Saints have always been far in advance of the majority of their neighbors in regard to education of their children. Even in the earliest days they had schools that made real men and women; not schools that produced weaklings and sycophants. The old schools made for character and real worth; they took the raw material, and moulded it into beings of personality and culture" (Levi Edgar Young).

5. Phelps is called to accompany the Prophet Joseph and Sidney Rigdon to Missouri "for the cause."

6. *Joseph Coe*] He was also called to accompany the Prophet to Missouri, and became prominent in the Church. He was appointed a member of the first High Council at Kirtland, organized February 17th, 1834 (Sec. 102:3). He was one of eight men present when the Temple site, west of Independence, was dedicated, August 3rd, 1831. Unfortu-

nately for himself, he did not remain in the Church. In the year 1837 he cast his lot with John F. Boynton, Luke S. Johnson, Warren Parrish, and others who had been disfellowshiped, and together they set up a church of their own, which they called the "Church of Christ." They alleged that Joseph Smith was a "fallen prophet," teaching false doctrines. For some time these dissenters took a leading part in the persecution of the Saints at Kirtland, but their efforts to build up a church came to naught. They were swept away, as chaff before the wind (Psalm 1:4).

SECTION 56.

REVELATION *given through Joseph Smith the Prophet, at Kirtland, Ohio, June, 1831. Elder Ezra Thayre, who had been appointed to travel in the ministry with Elder Thomas B. Marsh, was unable to start on his mission when the latter was ready, and the Lord answered the Prophet's inquiry on the matter by giving this revelation.——The Lord may and does revoke as well as command—Ezra Thayre rebuked for pride and selfishness—Selah J. Griffin appointed in his place to travel with Thomas B. Marsh—Offenders reproved, both rich and poor —Necessity of repentance as expressed by the broken heart and contrite spirit.*

HEARKEN, O ye people who profess my name, saith the Lord your God; for behold, mine anger is kindled against the rebellious, and they shall know mine arm and mine indignation, in the day of visitation and of wrath upon the nations.

2. And he that will not take up his cross and follow me, and keep my commandments, the same shall not be saved.

3. Behold, I, the Lord, command; and he that will not obey shall be cut off in mine own due time, after I have commanded and the commandment is broken.

One more Revelation was given before the Prophet Joseph and companions started upon the epoch-making journey to the western part of Missouri. It was given at the solicitation of Thomas B. Marsh. In this Revelation the Lord (1) declares His anger against the rebellious (1-3); (2) sets forth His freedom of action (4-7); (3) calls Ezra Thayre to repentance (8-11); (4) assures the Prophet that He will provide (12-13); (5) calls the Saints to repentance (14-17); and (6) promises blessings to the pure in heart (18-20).

1. GOD'S ANGER AGAINST THE REBELLIOUS.

1. *Mine anger is kindled*] The Lord has, on several occasions declared His anger against the rebellious (Comp. 1:13; 5:8; 19:5, and many other passages). Those who believe in a God without passions must deny that He can feel anger, and love too, for that matter, but the Word of God is clear on this point. Sin and wickedness kindle the anger of the Lord, when persisted in. But the great difference between the divine passion and that of man is this, that in God's anger there is no element of malice. It is the "wrath of the Lamb" (Rev. 6:16).

In the day of visitation] The rebellious will come under the wrath of God, when it is poured out upon the nations.

2. *He that will not follow me * * * not be saved*] The commandments of God are all given for our salvation; if we do not keep them, we are lost. When a ship is sinking, the orders of the captain must be obeyed implicitly. Disobedience by the crew might mean the loss of ship and all. Noah could not have been saved except by building the Ark. "According to all that God commanded him, so did he" (Gen. 6:22). That was his salvation. It is so now. The salvation of the world is possible only by obedience to the commandments of God.

3. *Shall be cut off*] All who are disobedient will be "cut off" in the due time of the Lord, when a divine commandment has been given and broken, without true repentance following. God does not condemn man for trespassing in ignorance, but for wilful sin against the light offered, as Paul declared at Athens, "The times of ignorance God winked at [overlooked], but now commandeth all men everywhere to repent" (Acts 17:30).

4. Wherefore I, the Lord, command and revoke, as it seemeth me good; and all this to be answered upon the heads of the rebellious, saith the Lord.

5. Wherefore, I revoke the commandment which was given unto my servants Thomas B. Marsh and Ezra Thayre, and give a new commandment unto my servant Thomas, that he shall take up his journey speedily to the land of Missouri, and my servant Selah J. Griffin shall also go with him.

6. For behold, I revoke the commandment which was given unto my servants Selah J. Griffin and Newel Knight, in consequence of the stiffneckedness of my people which are in Thompson, and their rebellions.

7. Wherefore, let my servant Newel Knight remain with them; and as many as will go may go, that are contrite before me, and be led by him to the land which I have appointed.

2. FREE AGENCY.

4. *I, the Lord, command and revoke*] The laws of God are immutable. He is the Father of lights, "with whom is no variableness, neither shadow of turning" (James 1:17). "Hath he said, and shall he not do it? Or hath he spoken, and shall he not make it good" (Num. 23:19)? "The Counsel of the Lord standeth for ever; the thoughts of his heart to all generations" (Psalm 33:11). He is the same yesterday, today, and for ever.

Some take this to mean that the plans of God are never changed, never modified. Here we learn that He commands and revokes, as seemeth Him good; that is, not capriciously, but for good and sufficient reasons. God is a *free agent*. We must not suppose that His immutability deprives Him of free agency. And because He is a free agent, He can command and revoke at will. But those who make it necessary for God, because of rebellion, to revoke laws given for the benefit of His children, will be held responsible.

5. *Commandment* * * * *unto my servants Thomas B. Marsh and Ezra Thayre*] See Sec. 52:22. This was now revoked, because of the rebellion of the latter (Sec. 54:4), and Marsh was instructed to take Selah J. Griffin for companion on his journey.

6. The commandment given to Selah J. Griffin and Newel Knight (See Sec. 52:32) was revoked, because of the "stiffneckedness" of some of the Saints at Thompson.

7. *Let my servant Newel Knight remain with them*] Instead of proceeding to Missouri immediately, Knight was to remain with the Saints at Thompson long enough to organize a company which he should lead to the Promised Land. He performed this duty well, for about a week after the arrival of the Prophet Joseph in Independence, a company of Colesville Saints, who had lived at Thompson temporarily, arrived and settled in Kaw Township, not far from the site of Kansas City.

8. And again, verily I say unto you, that my servant Ezra Thayre must repent of his pride, and of his selfishness, and obey the former commandment which I have given him concerning the place upon which he lives.

9. And if he will do this, as there shall be no divisions made upon the land, he shall be appointed still to go to the land of Missouri;

10. Otherwise he shall receive the money which he has paid, and shall leave the place, and shall be cut off out of my church, saith the Lord God of hosts;

11. And though the heaven and the earth pass away, these words shall not pass away, but shall be fulfilled.

3. EZRA THAYRE CALLED TO REPENTANCE.

8. *Must repent*] Ezra Thayre, undoubtedly, was, to some extent, responsible for the failure of the Colesville Saints to organize themselves under the law of consecration, but the Lord did not cast him off without giving him another chance. If he would obey the Lord with regard to the land on which he lived, he would still have a chance of going to Missouri (v. 9).

9. *There shall be no divisions made upon the land*] This phrase, says B. H. Roberts, "undoubtedly has reference to the land upon which Ezra Thayre was living at Thompson, and which he had covenanted, under some arrangement for compensation, to grant to the Church, and which contract he attempted, at least, to repudiate" (*Hist. of the Church,* Vol. I., p. 188).

10. *Otherwise he shall receive the money which he has paid*] He would not lose money by persisting in rebellion, but he would lose the companionship of the brethren, as Lot lost the companionship of Abraham, when he went to dwell in Sodom. He must have repented, for in 1834 he held the position of High Priest. He was also a member of Zion's Camp, an organization formed for the purpose of assisting the Saints who had been driven out of Jackson County, Mo. He was one of the first who were stricken with cholera on the 21st of June, 1834, before the organization was disbanded.

12. And if my servant Joseph Smith, Jun., must needs pay the money, behold, I, the Lord, will pay it unto him again in the land of Missouri, that those of whom he shall receive may be rewarded again according to that which they do;

13. For according to that which they do they shall receive, even in lands for their inheritance.

4. GOD WILL PROVIDE.

12. *If my servant Joseph Smith, Jr. must needs pay*] If the money to be returned to Ezra Thayre (v. 10) was to be furnished by the Prophet Joseph Smith, the Lord would refund it to him in Missouri. The meaning seems to be that anybody who would, by contributions, enable the Prophet to discharge whatever financial obligations remained as a result of the annulling of the agreements with the Colesville Saints, would be rewarded by receiving land in Missouri, according to the contributions made.

13. "For, according to that which they do, they shall receive."

14. Behold, thus saith the Lord unto my people—you have many things to do and to repent of; for behold, your sins have come up unto me, and are not pardoned, because you seek to counsel in your own ways.

15. And your hearts are not satisfied. And ye obey not the truth, but have pleasure in unrighteousness.

16. Wo unto you rich men, that will not give your substance to the poor, for your riches will canker your souls; and this shall be your lamentation in the day of visitation, and of judgment, and of indignation: The harvest is past, the summer is ended, and my soul is not saved!

17. Wo unto you poor men, whose hearts are not broken, whose spirits are not contrite, and whose bellies are not satisfied, and whose hands are not stayed from laying hold upon other men's goods, whose eyes are full of greediness, and who will not labor with your own hands!

5. The Saints Called to Repentance.

14. *Many things to do and to repent of*] "To do and to repent" are inseparably connected. Repentance is primarily a change of mind (*metanoya*), but it is a change of mind that produces a change from wrong conduct. For instance, "A certain man had two sons; and he came to the first and said, Son, go work today in my vineyard. He answered and said, I will not; but afterwards repented and went" (Matt. 21:28, 29). That was genuine repentance. The word in Romans 11:29 (*metameleia*), translated "repentance," means "regret," or a "change of plan," without implying a change of mind.

True repentance is both a change of mind and of conduct.

Repentance is not accomplished once for all. It is a spiritual experience that is completed only when this Earthly existence is ended. For, no matter how far advanced we may be, there is always something to better, something to improve, and the first step to improvement is repentance. The Saints always "have many things to do and to repent of," until they reach the stage of perfection. Our Lord, who told Peter, the Apostle, that he had yet to be converted (Luke 22:32), also taught the Colesville Saints that they, though members of the Church, had many things to repent of.

Your sins have come up unto me] This refers to the sin of not organizing under the law of consecration. Those who were responsible for the failure to do so had not been pardoned, because they preferred their own counsel to that of God.

15. *Truth * * * unrighteousness*] The law of consecration represents

truth. They refused to obey it. The order adopted by the world is more adapted to the practice of unrighteousness. That they delighted in.

16. *Wo unto you rich men*] In this and the following verse the Lord indicates the main reasons why the United Order cannot be practiced on Earth at present. The rich are not willing to serve the poor with their substance. They love mammon, not their fellowmen.

17. *Wo unto you poor men*] But not only the rich are to blame. The poor are also responsible, for many of them are not humble, nor honest. Many of them are dishonest; many are as greedy as any miser, and many are lazy, or given to violence on the slightest provocation. A United Order cannot be built up of mammon-slaves and belly-worshipers, be they rich or poor. Both classes must repent, and enter upon a new life before the highest ideal of a human society can be realized. Compare James 5:1-9. St. James tells the rich, to whom he wrote, that they had been so foolish as to heap up for themselves a treasure in "the last days." They were living in the last days of the Mosaic dispensation when that was written, and in the chaos attendant upon the cataclysm in which the old dispensation expired, the treasures heaped up were of but little use to the possessors. Wealthy Jews, when Jerusalem fell, were first marked out for torture and plunder. Again, the world is passing through the last days of a dispensation. When the vials of wrath are poured out, gold will bring but small comfort.

18. But blessed are the poor who are pure in heart, whose hearts are broken, and whose spirits are contrite, for they shall see the kingdom of God coming in power and great glory unto their deliverance; for the fatness of the earth shall be theirs.

19. For behold, the Lord shall come, and his recompense shall be with him, and he shall reward every man, and the poor shall rejoice;

20. And their generations shall inherit the earth from generation to generation, forever and ever. And now I make an end of speaking unto you. Even so. Amen.

6. A BLESSING PRONOUNCED.

18. *Blessed are the poor who are pure in heart*] It is the state of the heart, not outward circumstances, that makes us "blessed" or happy. "Pure in heart" means pure in affections, unselfish in one's love of fellowmen. Purity of doctrine is not sufficient; nor the most faithful observance of ceremonies. It is the "pure in heart" that shall see God (Matt. 5:8). They are happy because they can see Him in the wonderful works of His hands; in the events of history; in their own experiences, and in their fellowmen; and they will, finally, be admitted to His

presence; not because they are *poor* but *pure*. To be poor, says Sœren Kjærkegaard, is not to be a Christian, but it is a good introduction to it.

*The fatness of the Earth * * * theirs*] The Earth in its celestial state will be theirs.

20. *And their generations * * * for ever*] Their descendants. For they shall increase in all eternity.

GENERAL NOTES

The following reference to Thomas B. Marsh made by John Taylor in a sermon in Salt Lake City, 1857, may be quoted here:

"You that do not know him, have heard of Thomas B. Marsh, who was formerly the president of the Twelve Apostles, but who apostatized some years ago in Missouri. He is on his way here, a poor, decrepit, broken-down, old man. He has had a paralytic stroke—one of his arms hangs down * * * In meeting with some of the apostates, he said to them, 'you do not know what you are about; if you want to see the fruits of apostasy, look on me' " (*Jour. of Dis.,* Vol. V., p. 115).

The Prophet was now ready to go on the journey to Missouri, as the Lord had commanded (Sec. 52:3). On the 19th of June, 1831, he left Kirtland, in company with Sidney Rigdon, Martin Harris, Edward Partridge, William W. Phelps, Joseph Coe, and Sidney Gilbert and wife. They went by wagon, canal boats, and stages to Cincinnati. In this city they took a steamer to Louisville, Ky. Here they were detained three days waiting for a steamer to St. Louis. The Prophet, Martin Harris, William W. Phelps, Edward Partridge, and Joseph Coe proceeded on foot from St. Louis to Independence, and arrived there about the middle of July. The rest of the company came a few days later, having traveled by water. The Prophet notes that an evil spirit was manifested towards them at many places, on account of their belief in the Book of Mormon, but God was with them.

In Independence they met Oliver Cowdery, Peter Whitmer, Jr., and Ziba Peterson, who had been on a mission to the Lamanites, and also Frederick G. Williams. It was a glorious meeting. It was a notable fulfilment of a prediction given in December, 1830 (Sec. 37:3). And now the Prophet of God, surrounded by a few friends, was standing on the western border of civilization, looking westward into an unknown expanse and veiled future. "How natural it was," he writes, "to observe the degradation, leanness of intellect, perversity and jealousy of a people that were nearly a century behind the time, and to feel for those who roamed about without the benefit of civilization, refinement, or religion; yea, and exclaim in the language of the prophets, 'When will the wilderness blossom as the rose?' When will Zion be built up in her glory, and where will thy temple stand, unto which all nations shall come in the last day?"

SECTION 57.

REVELATION *given through Joseph Smith the Prophet, in Zion, Jackson County, Missouri, July, 1831. In compliance with the Lord's command, the Elders had journeyed from Kirtland to Missouri with many varied experiences and some opposition. In contemplating the degraded state of the Lamanites and the lack of civilization, refinement and religion among the people generally, the Prophet exclaimed in yearning prayer: When will the wilderness blossom as the rose? When will Zion be built up in her glory, and where will thy Temple stand, unto which all nations shall come in the last days? See History of the Church, vol. 1, p. 189.——The land appointed and consecrated—The land of promise—The place for the city of Zion—The center place specified—The Saints directed to purchase land—Commanded to make preparation for others who are to come.*

HEARKEN, O ye elders of my church, saith the Lord your God, who have assembled yourselves together, according to my commandments, in this land, which is the land of Missouri, which is the land which I have appointed and consecrated for the gathering of the saints.

2. Wherefore, this is the land of promise, and the place for the city of Zion.

3. And thus saith the Lord your God, if you will receive wisdom here is wisdom. Behold, the place which is now called Independence is the center place; and a spot for the temple is lying westward, upon a lot which is not far from the court-house.

In the Book of Mormon the Saints were told (Ether 13:1-12), that the new Jerusalem and Holy Sanctuary of the Lord should be located in America (Comp. III. Nephi 20:22; 21:23), and they were anxious to know *where* the site for the City was. In September, 1830, the Lord gave them to understand that the City should be erected "on the borders by the Lamanites" (Sec. 28:9). In February, 1831, they were promised that a Revelation should be given on that subject, if they would pray for it (Sec. 42:62). On the 7th of March, the same year, they were given to understand that the gathering from the eastern States and the sending out of Elders on the mission to the West were preparatory steps to the establishment of that City, wherefore the Saints should gather up their riches and purchase an inheritance in the place to be indicated, which should be a place of refuge for the Saints of the most High God (Sec. 45:64-66). The time had now come for the fulfilment of the promise referred to (Sec. 42:62), and this Revelation was received. In it the Lord (1) designates the location of the City and the Temple site (1-3); (2) instructs the Saints how to locate (4-5); (3) gives special directions concerning the first settlement (6-15); and (4) closes with a promise (16).

1. Zion and the Temple.

1. *The land of Missouri*] That is the land which, in the providence of God, has been appointed and consecrated for the gathering of the Saints.

2. *The land of promise*] To the Latter-day Saints Missouri is the land of promise. There the City of Zion will be established. There the City of Enoch, coming down from heaven, will meet the City of the Saints, and the two will be united and known as the New Jerusalem.

3. *The center place*] Independence is designated as the center place, and the Temple site is pointed out on "a lot not far from the court house." Zion, it may be added, has not been removed, though her children have been scattered (Secs. 90:37; 101:17).

On the 2nd of August, 1831, the Prophet assisted the Colesville Saints, who had just arrived from Thompson, O., to lay the first log for a house, as a foundation of Zion in Kaw Township, twelve miles southwest of Independence. The log was carried by twelve men, each representing one of the twelve tribes of Israel, and the land was dedicated by Sidney Rigdon for the gathering of the Saints. On the 3rd day of August the Temple site was dedicated. This sacred act of the holy Priesthood is as binding today as it was then.

Brigham Young, before the Saints were driven out of the State of Missouri, was shown in a vision that they were scattered in all directions, but that they eventually returned to Jackson county, from the west. He says, "When this people return to the Center* Stake of Zion, they will go from the west" (*Jour. of Dis.*, Vol. XI., p. 17).

4. Wherefore, it is wisdom that the land should be purchased by the saints, and also every tract lying westward, even unto the line running directly between Jew and Gentile;

5. And also every tract bordering by the prairies, inasmuch as my disciples are enabled to buy lands. Behold, this is wisdom, that they may obtain it for an everlasting inheritance.

2. How to Obtain Land.

4. *Should be purchased*] The Saints were to be strictly honest in all

* See page 189, footnote.

their dealings with their fellowmen. Jackson County at this time was sparsely settled. There was a great deal of unoccupied land, and this could be secured at the price of $1.25 an acre.

5. *An everlasting inheritance*] The land so purchased would be a permanent possession.

6. And let my servant Sidney Gilbert stand in the office to which I have appointed him, to receive moneys, to be an agent unto the church, to buy land in all the regions round about, inasmuch as can be done in righteousness, and as wisdom shall direct.

7. And let my servant Edward Partridge stand in the office to which I have appointed him, and divide unto the saints their inheritance, even as I have commanded; and also those whom he has appointed to assist him.

8. And again, verily I say unto you, let my servant Sidney Gilbert plant himself in this place, and establish a store, that he may sell goods without fraud, that he may obtain money to buy lands for the good of the saints, and that he may obtain whatsoever things the disciples may need to plant them in their inheritance.

9. And also let my servant Sidney Gilbert obtain a license—behold here is wisdom, and whoso readeth let him understand—that he may send goods also unto the people, even by whom he will as clerks employed in his service;

10. And thus provide for my saints, that my gospel may be preached unto those who sit in darkness and in the region and shadow of death.

11. And again, verily I say unto you, let my servant William W. Phelps be planted in this place, and be established as a printer unto the church.

12. And lo, if the world receive his writings—behold here is wisdom—let him obtain whatsoever he can in righteousness, for the good of the saints.

13. And let my servant Oliver Cowdery assist him, even as I have commanded, in whatsoever place I shall appoint unto him, to copy, and to correct, and select, that all things may be right before me, as it shall be proved by the Spirit through him.

330 DOCTRINE AND COVENANTS [SEC. 57.

14. And thus let those of whom I have spoken be planted in the land of Zion, as speedily as can be, with their families, to do those things even as I have spoken.

15. And now concerning the gathering—Let the bishop and the agent make preparations for those families which have been commanded to come to this land, as soon as possible, and plant them in their inheritance.

3. INSTRUCTIONS REGARDING SETTLEMENT.

6. *Sidney Gilbert * * * to be an agent*] He had been appointed to that position (Sec. 53:4). He was to buy land in righteousness and wisdom.

7. *Edward Partridge * * * to divide the Saints their inheritance*] That was his calling (Sec. 41:9; 42:10).

8. *That he may sell goods without fraud*] Sidney Gilbert was instructed to establish a store, sell goods without fraud, and use the profits for the good of the Saints.

" 'Sell goods without fraud.' That is a point I wish our merchants to look at; if that does not hit them squarely in the face, I am mistaken" (Brigham Young, *Jour. of Dis.,* Vol. XI., p. 326).

Sidney Gilbert's store was not a money-making scheme for him. His business was to be conducted as for the Lord. The profit was to be used for the building up of Zion.

9-10. For that reason his traveling agents were also to labor with the end in view of enabling the Saints to preach the gospel.

11. *William W. Phelps * * * a printer unto the Church*] That was his calling (Sec. 55:4).

12. *Let him obtain * * * for the good of the saints*] He, too, was to labor for the Saints. The Lord recognizes the importance of the printed word, and enlists the press in His service, for the building up of Zion.

13. *Let * * * Oliver Cowdery assist him*] In Sec. 55:4, Phelps is appointed to assist Cowdery; here Cowdery is mentioned as the assistant. There is no discrepancy in this. It only shows that God intended them to assist each other as fellow-laborers in the same service.

15. *Concerning the gathering*] The Bishop and the agent are here instructed to make preparations for the reception of the Colesville Saints who, in obedience to the divine command (Sec. 54:7, 8), were on the road to Zion.

16. And unto the residue of both elders and members further directions shall be given hereafter. Even so. Amen.

4. A DIVINE PROMISE.

16. The Lord, in closing this Revelation, promises to give further instructions, as needed. God gives Revelations only when they are needed. Says President Brigham Young:

"I am thankful that I do not hear, of late, since the Spirit has been generally diffused among the people, 'O Lord, give Revelations to Brother Brigham.' I wish to fulfil what we have received before I ask for more. I said to Brother Joseph, the spring before he was killed, 'You are laying out work for twenty years.' He replied, 'You have as yet scarcely begun to work; but I will set you enough to last you during your lives, for I am going to rest" (*Journal of Discourses,* Vol. V., p. 331).

GENERAL NOTES

The city of Independence is situated in one of the most attractive and healthful parts of Missouri, 338 feet above the level of the Missouri River, and 1,075 feet above sea level. It is an old town. It was laid out in 1827, but in 1831 it was only a village. It is now a suburb of Kansas City.

As soon as this Revelation had been received, Edward Partridge and the other brethren, appointed to "plant" themselves in Zion, began the work of building. During the first winter the settlers put up with many inconveniences. In some log cabins, without windows and with the frozen ground for floor, several families were living together. They had very little to eat, but they were united, and their hearts were filled with brotherly love and a fervent desire to build up Zion. As a consequence, their meetings were times of refreshing, and in their family devotions they were blessed with the presence of the Holy Spirit. And as soon as the Saints in Ohio and elsewhere learned that the site of the City of Zion had been made known, the spirit of gathering was poured out upon them, and many sent money to Sidney Gilbert, the agent, and instructed him to secure land for them. So rapidly did they gather, that in 1832 there were 830 souls in the new settlements, and a certain degree of prosperity had begun to attend their efforts.

Very soon the spirit of the world entered the Church in Zion. Seven High Priests, Oliver Cowdery, William W. Phelps, John Whitmer, Sidney Gilbert, Edward Partridge, Isaac Morley, and John Corrill, had been appointed to preside over the Saints in Missouri, but many of those who came, refused to acknowledge their authority. Others did not obey the Law of Consecration. Jealousies, covetousness, light-mindedness were followed by neglect to keep the commandments of God, and His wrath was kindled against Zion. A word of warning seemed to have the desired effect, for a general assembly was called and the Saints promised repentance. However, the Spirit of Revelation indicated that they must pass through tribulation, before they could receive the blessings in Zion.

This remarkable prediction was fulfilled, for they were driven out of Missouri, and the persecution extended into Illinois, until the Church had no resting-place within the confines of the United States, but was compelled to go to the Mountains, as foretold by the Prophet.

In 1845, Brigham Young and associates addressed letters to all the Governors of the States and Territories in the Union, except Missouri and Illinois, for obvious reasons, asking them for an asylum, within their borders, for the Saints. Everyone of them, with the single exception of the Governor of Arkansas (See Whitney's *Hist. of Utah,* Vol. I., p. 243), either refused to comply with the request or neglected to reply. Three members of Congress advised the Saints to leave the Country. They took this advice and went to Utah, which then was part of Mexico. The Lord led His people to the Valleys of the Mountains. He will also lead them back to the Land of Promise; not all of them; but such as are prepared to live in accordance with His laws and commandments.

"Will the time ever come that we can commence and organize this people as a family? It will. Do we know that? Yes; what was lacking in these revelations from Joseph to enable us to do so was revealed to me" (Brigham Young, *Jour. of Dis.,* Vol. XI., p. 326).

"Several very important facts are here presented for the consideration of God's people. In the first place, they are reminded of the great object for which this latter-day work was instituted, namely, the building up of Zion, preparatory to the glorious coming of the Lord. Prior to that expulsion, the place for the City, New Jerusalem, unto which a people will gather, to make the preparation that is absolutely essential before the Lord will come—the very place for the City had been designated, and from this Revelation we learn why those who had been sent to Jackson County to build up Zion were not permitted to accomplish the work at that time. Inferentially—nay, directly, we are told what kind of people will be permitted to do that work, namely, 'the pure in heart,' for that is the meaning of Zion, according to the word of the Lord. A prophecy is contained in this Revelation (Sec. 10:18): "The colony driven from that land in 1833, or their descendants, joined with Zion's other children, or a people gathered out from among them, a pure-hearted people, are eventually to return and build up the waste places of Zion. In the meantime other places, likewise appointed of God, are to be inhabited by the Latter-day Saints" (Orson F. Whitney, Address delivered in Salt Lake City, April 9, 1916).

SECTION 58.

REVELATION *given through Joseph Smith the Prophet, in Zion, Jackson County, Missouri, August 1, 1831. On the first Sabbath after the arrival of the Prophet and party in Jackson*

County, Missouri, a religious service was held and two members were received by baptism. During that week, members of the Colesville branch and others arrived. See History of the Church, vol. 1, p. 190. Many were eager to learn the will of the Lord concerning them in the new place of gathering.——Great things to follow, with glory, after much tribulation—Certain duties of the Bishopric—The Bishop is warned—People instructed to observe the laws of the land, and to regard the commandments given through revelation as the laws of the Church—Servants not to be compelled in all things but to be diligent and active—Lands to be purchased in Independence—Some of the people to stay, others to travel in the ministry—Assignment of duty to individual Elders—Those returning to the East to bear record of what they have seen and know concerning the land of Zion—Gathering of the Saints not to be conducted in haste.

HEARKEN, O ye elders of my church, and give ear to my word, and learn of me what I will concerning you, and also concerning this land unto which I have sent you.

The Colesville Branch had just arrived; also Sidney Rigdon, Sidney Gilbert and wife, and Elders Isaac Morley and Ezra Booth. This Revelation concerning the Elders of the Church and the land of Zion was then received. In it the Lord (1) promises glory to the faithful, and warns the Elders of tribulation (2-5); (2) sets forth the reasons why they had been commanded to go to Missouri (6-14); (3) warns Edward Partridge (15-33); (4 gives further directions concerning the land and its settlement (34-65).

2. For verily I say unto you, blessed is he that keepeth my commandments, whether in life or in death; and he that is faithful in tribulation, the reward of the same is greater in the kingdom of heaven.

3. Ye cannot behold with your natural eyes, for the present time, the design of your God concerning those things which shall come hereafter, and the glory which shall follow after much tribulation.

4. For after much tribulation come the blessings. Wherefore the day cometh that ye shall be crowned with much glory; the hour is not yet, but is nigh at hand.

5. Remember this, which I tell you before, that you may lay it to heart, and receive that which is to follow.

1. GLORY PROMISED AFTER TRIBULATION.

In these paragraphs the Lord warns the Elders and Saints against expecting a life of ease, free from trials, in Zion. They were to receive blessings, but not until they had endured tribulation. They were to be crowned with glory, but only after severe trials. They did not comprehend this, and needed the warning given in this Revelation. Many of them had gone west to escape persecution, as did the Pilgrim Fathers in their day. Were they to encounter new outbursts of violence in their God-given home? We know now how the tribulation came, but when the prediction was first given, it must have been to most of the Saints almost a riddle.

2. *Blessed is he that keepeth my commandments*] Tribulations were to come, but those who were faithful and kept the commandments of God were "blessed" or happy, in life or death.

Note that one of the first predictions regarding Zion made it known to the Saints that they would meet tribulation there; and yet they gathered; so strong was their faith.

3. *Ye cannot behold * * * the design of your God*] The Saints could not, at that time, comprehend that they were facing a most serious problem, involving the very existence of the Church. They were in a new, sparsely-settled country. Usually settlers are welcome in such places. They lived under a flag that waves as an emblem of liberty over a Republic proclaimed to be a place of refuge for the oppressed of all the world. Whence could any serious trial come? God knew; and also that glory would follow.

4. *After much tribulation * * * blessings*] When the Saints were driven from Missouri, and then from Illinois, some of their enemies thought the end of the Church had come. But less than twenty years after the exodus, the Saints were prospering in their new home in the mountain valleys. Says Elder George A. Smith, in a sermon delivered at Salt Lake City, in 1865:

"Notwithstanding the many drawbacks and difficulties encountered, in the shape of drouth, crickets, grasshoppers, and the cold, sterile climate, the Spirit of the Lord was hovering over the great basin. * * * I never was at the crossing of the Sevier River in summer for seven years after our settlement in Iron County had been established, without experiencing frost; and now the Sevier Valley produces luxuriant fields of grain and vegetables in the season thereof * * * To have told the mountaineers ten years ago that grain could be raised in the upper valleys of the Weber, where they encountered heavy frosts every month in summer, would have incurred their ridicule; but the genial influence of the Spirit of the Almighty has softened the rigor of the climate, and the flourishing counties of Morgan and Summit are the result. I suppose that Provo Valley, this season, with all its losses, will raise not less than thirty thousand bushels of grain and vegetables. * * * Go to Pottawatomie, Iowa; Nauvoo, Ill.; or Kirtland, Ohio, and ask for apples and peaches, and you will find them few and far between. In February, 1857, I visited my former field of labor in Western Virginia, and inquired of an old friend for fruit; his reply was, 'My peach trees are all killed, and I have not been able to raise any peaches for six years * * * ' It is so wherever the Saints have lived and been driven away—their glory has departed to return no more, until the land is dedicated and consecrated to God and occupied by the Saints" (*Journal of Discourses,* Vol. XI., pp. 177-8).

Blessings came to the Saints after the tribulation. They will yet be crowned with glory in Zion.

The hour is not yet, but is nigh at hand] It must be much nearer now than when this inspired line was first penned.

5. *Remember this*] The Lord desires His people to remember the prophecies given, in order that, when they see them fulfilled, they may have faith to obey His word.

6. Behold, verily I say unto you, for this cause I have sent you—that you might be obedient, and that your hearts might be prepared to bear testimony of the things which are to come;

7. And also that you might be honored in laying the foundation, and in bearing record of the land upon which the Zion of God shall stand;

8. And also that a feast of fat things might be prepared for the poor; yea, a feast of fat things, of wine on the lees well refined, that the earth may know that the mouths of the prophets shall not fail;

9. Yea, a supper of the house of the Lord, well prepared, unto which all nations shall be invited.

10. First, the rich and the learned, the wise and the noble;

11. And after that cometh the day of my power; then shall the poor, the lame, and the blind, and the deaf, come in unto the marriage of the Lamb, and partake of the supper of the Lord, prepared for the great day to come.

12. Behold, I, the Lord, have spoken it.

13. And that the testimony might go forth from Zion, yea, from the mouth of the city of the heritage of God—

14. Yea, for this cause I have sent you hither, and have selected my servant Edward Partridge, and have appointed unto him his mission in this land.

2. REASONS WHY THE SAINTS AND ELDERS WERE IN ZION.

The Lord here gives six reasons for calling the Elders and Saints to go to the land of Zion.

6. *That you may be obedient*] This is the first reason. Obedience is absolutely necessary for the furtherance of the Kingdom of God. There must be *one* directing will. This is necessary in earthly concerns—a factory, a ship, a railroad system. It is equally necessary in the kingdom of God. His will must be supreme there.

To render obedience to lawful authority, is not humiliating or degrading. Even the Son learned obedience (Heb. 5:8), before He became the Author of eternal salvation. Disobedience, or rebellion, is as bad as idolatry (I. Sam. 15:23). The Lord does not stand personally in the midst of His people to direct their affairs but He speaks to them through His inspired servants. When we obey their counsel, we obey God. Those who refuse to obey them, would refuse to obey the Lord, even if He spoke to them Himself, in person.

That your hearts might be prepared to bear testimony] This is another reason. There were truths which the Lord would reveal only in Zion. Those who were there could testify of those truths, as witnesses. They could bear witness of that which they had heard.

7. *Laying the foundation*] This is the third reason. It was to be their privilege to lay the foundation. They might have expected to be given the honor of building the City and constructing the Temple, but the promise was that they would lay the foundation. This they did; they dedicated the land and the Temple site, and, we may say, prepared, to some extent, the people from whom the builders will come, for their future great mission.

Bearing record of the land] This is the fourth reason. They were to testify, not only of what they had heard but of what they had seen themselves, of the land.

8. *That a feast * * * for the poor*] This is the fifth reason. One great purpose of God in establishing Zion is to save the world, through its laws and institutions, from the curse of poverty and destitution. The object is to give to the world an entirely new social order, to establish a community in which even the poor would share the "fat things" with "the rich and the learned, the wise and the noble" (v. 10). Zion is to be a place for the "supper of the house of the Lord"—a banquet hall —"unto which all nations shall be invited." There "the marriage feast of the Lamb" will be held when the time has come for God Omnipotent to reign upon this Earth (Rev. 19:7-9). It is the New Jerusalem, con-

sisting of the City of Zion and the "Jerusalem which is above," that is, "the Bride of the Lamb" (Rev. 21:2; Gal. 4:26; Eph. 5:27). The two will be united when our Savior comes in His glory. "Blessed are they who are called unto the marriage supper of the Lamb." Yea, blessed are they who will be called to become citizens in the City of Zion.

11. *After that cometh the day of my power*] Zion will be built. The Temple will be reared. Enoch's Zion, the "Jerusalem which is above," will meet the Saints who have part in the first resurrection, and those who will be changed in the twinkling of an eye, and they will all be united. Then will come the day of God's power. The poor and the lame, the blind and the deaf will all be invited to partake of the blessings of the Millennium. The Earth will not be freed from all defects at once. The work of redemption will be gradual.

13. *That the testimony might go forth from Zion*] That is the sixth reason. The law must go forth from Zion, as the light from a lighthouse.

15. But if he repent not of his sins, which are unbelief and blindness of heart, let him take heed lest he fall.

16. Behold his mission is given unto him, and it shall not be given again.

17. And whoso standeth in this mission is appointed to be a judge in Israel, like as it was in ancient days, to divide the lands of the heritage of God unto his children;

18. And to judge his people by the testimony of the just, and by the assistance of his counselors, according to the laws of the kingdom which are given by the prophets of God.

19. For verily I say unto you, my law shall be kept on this land.

20. Let no man think he is ruler; but let God rule him that judgeth, according to the counsel of his own will, or, in other words, him that counseleth or sitteth upon the judgment seat.

21. Let no man break the laws of the land, for he that keepeth the laws of God hath no need to break the laws of the land.

22. Wherefore, be subject to the powers that be, until he reigns whose right it is to reign, and subdues all enemies under his feet.

23. Behold, the laws which ye have received from my hand are the laws of the church, and in this light ye shall hold them forth. Behold, here is wisdom.

24. And now, as I spake concerning my servant Edward Partridge, this land is the land of his residence, and those whom he has appointed for his counselors; and also the land of the residence of him whom I have appointed to keep my storehouse;

25. Wherefore, let them bring their families to this land, as they shall counsel between themselves and me.

26. For behold, it is not meet that I should command in all things; for he that is compelled in all things, the same is a slothful and not a wise servant; wherefore he receiveth no reward.

27. Verily I say, men should be anxiously engaged in a good cause, and do many things of their own free will, and bring to pass much righteousness;

28. For the power is in them, wherein they are agents unto themselves. And inasmuch as men do good they shall in nowise lose their reward.

29. But he that doeth not anything until he is commanded, and receiveth a commandment with doubtful heart, and keepeth it with slothfulness, the same is damned.

30. Who am I that made man, saith the Lord, that will hold him guiltless that obeys not my commandments?

31. Who am I, saith the Lord, that have promised and have not fulfilled?

32. I command and men obey not; I revoke and they receive not the blessing.

33. Then they say in their hearts: This is not the work of the Lord, for his promises are not fulfilled. But wo unto such, for their reward lurketh beneath, and not from above.

3. INSTRUCTIONS TO EDWARD PARTRIDGE.

15. *If he repent not*] The Lord requires His servant to repent of his sins, and he is told what they are, namely, "unbelief and blindness of heart." "Blindness of heart" means affections not guided by the light of the Spirit. Those who place their affection upon wrong objects, such as belong to the world, in preference to those that pertain to the Kingdom of God, are blind at heart, no matter how clear the physical or mental vision may be. He that loveth his own kindred more than the Lord, is blind at heart, for he is not worthy of the Lord, and, consequently, not of His household (Matt. 10:37).

"Unbelief," in this case means "weak faith" (as in Mark 9:24), and it was, perhaps, the cause of the blindness of heart.

Unbelief and blindness are sins. They must be repented of. Some teach that we are not responsible for our beliefs. This is not the Lord's view. If we are weak in faith and blind in affections, we need to go to this Great Physician, who can heal us, and if we neglect to do this, we are guilty.

17. *Judge in Israel*] The calling of Edward Partridge was that of a judge among the Saints. As such he was to divide the land among them. The Patriarchs during their dispensation divided the land by divine revelation (Comp. Acts. 17:26) among the nations. The judges in Israel performed the same office for the Twelve Tribes. Partridge and his successors were to distribute God's inheritance among the Saints in the same way.

18. *To judge his people*] And also to arbitrate among the people and adjust differences in accordance with the testimony of the just and the demands of the laws of God. The Saints should not have lawsuits. Arbitration is a better way.

"There is not a righteous person in this community, who will have difficulties that cannot be settled by arbitrators, the Bishop's court, or the High Council * * * far better and more satisfactorily than to contend with each other in law courts, which directly tends to destroy the best interests of the community, and to lead scores of men away from their duties, as good and industrious citizens" (Brigham Young, *Jour. of Dis.,* Vol. III., p. 238).

19. *My law shall be kept*] Section 42.

20. *Let no man think he is ruler*] In the Kingdom of God, Jesus Christ is the Ruler. Judges and counselors are but His servants. There is no "hierarchy" in the Church.

21. *Let no man break the laws of the land*] Refers to the Constitution and all laws that are Constitutional.

22. *Be subject to the powers that be*] The Latter-day Saints do not aspire to political supremacy. They are looking forward to the time when He, "whose right it is to reign," even the Lord Jesus Christ, will rule the Earth.

Civil authority is of divine origin. It may be more or less adapted to the needs of man; more or less just and benevolent, but, even at its worst, it is better than anarchy. Revolutionary movements that aim at the abolition of government itself are contrary to the law of God; those which are aimed at the correction of abuses are not wrong. Despotism is not supported by Divine law, but it must be abolished through the influence of the gospel. Christ will subdue all enemies; tyranny is one of them.

23. *The laws of the Church*] These do not conflict with any Constitutional laws of the land; nor do they supersede them. The Latter-day Saints who keep the laws of the Church are, for that reason, the most loyal citizens, or subjects, of the respective countries in which their lot has been cast.

24-29. Having imparted these instructions, the Lord commanded Edward Partridge, his counselors, and Sidney Gilbert to bring their families to Missouri and to settle there. They were to apply themselves with all diligence to their respective callings and not wait for a Revelation concerning every duty. They were to act as intelligent beings on their own initiative. All those engaged in the Lord's service are expected to act as intelligent, free agents, and not to move as a watch, which depends on somebody to wind it up.

33. *Say in their hearts * * * not fulfilled*] The Saints sometimes fail to do their duty and to keep the commandments of God. But they expect Him to make good to them the promises He has given to the faithful. If He does not, they complain. They neglect their prayers; they absent themselves from their meetings; they break the Word of Wisdom; they withhold their tithing; but when sickness comes and falls like a dark, terrifying shadow across their path, they expect immediate Divine interference in their behalf, through the administration of the Elders. If their expectations are not realized, they say, in a rebellious spirit, "His promises are not fulfilled." The reply of the Lord to that is, "Their reward lurketh beneath." They must look "beneath" for their reward; they have no claim on heaven.

34. And now I give unto you further directions concerning this land.

35. It is wisdom in me that my servant Martin Harris should be an example unto the church, in laying his moneys before the bishop of the church.

36. And also, this is a law unto every man that cometh unto this land to receive an inheritance; and he shall do with his moneys according as the law directs.

37. And it is wisdom also that there should be lands purchased in Independence, for the place of the storehouse, and also for the house of the printing.

38. And other directions concerning my servant Martin Harris shall be given him of the Spirit, that he may receive his inheritance as seemeth him good;

39. And let him repent of his sins, for he seeketh the praise of the world.

40. And also let my servant William W. Phelps stand in the office to which I have appointed him, and receive his inheritance in the land;

41. And also he hath need to repent, for I, the Lord, am not well pleased with him, for he seeketh to excel, and he is not sufficiently meek before me.

42. Behold, he who has repented of his sins, the same is forgiven, and I, the Lord, remember them no more.

43. By this ye may know if a man repenteth of his sins—behold, he will confess them and forsake them.

44. And now, verily, I say concerning the residue of the elders of my church, the time has not yet come, for many years, for them to receive their inheritance in this land, except they desire it through the prayer of faith, only as it shall be appointed unto them of the Lord.

45. For, behold, they shall push the people together from the ends of the earth.

46. Wherefore, assemble yourselves together; and they who are not appointed to stay in this land, let them preach the gospel in the regions round about; and after that let them return to their homes.

47. Let them preach by the way, and bear testimony of the truth in all places, and call upon the rich, the high and the low, and the poor to repent.

48. And let them build up churches, inasmuch as the inhabitants of the earth will repent.

49. And let there be an agent appointed by the voice of the church, unto the church in Ohio, to receive moneys to purchase lands in Zion.

50. And I give unto my servant Sidney Rigdon a commandment, that he shall write a description of the land of Zion, and a statement of the will of God, as it shall be made known by the Spirit unto him;

51. And an epistle and subscription, to be presented unto all the churches to obtain moneys, to be put into the hands of the bishop, of himself or the agent, as seemeth him good or as he shall direct, to purchase lands for an inheritance for the children of God.

52. For, behold, verily I say unto you, the Lord willeth that the disciples and the children of men should open their hearts, even to purchase this whole region of country, as soon as time will permit.

53. Behold, here is wisdom. Let them do this lest they receive none inheritance, save it be by the shedding of blood.

54. And again, inasmuch as there is land obtained, let there be workmen sent forth of all kinds unto this land, to labor for the saints of God.

55. Let all these things be done in order; and let the privileges of the lands be made known from time to time, by the bishop or the agent of the church.

56. And let the work of the gathering be not in haste, nor by flight; but let it be done as it shall be counseled by the elders of the church at the conferences, according to the knowledge which they receive from time to time.

57. And let my servant Sidney Rigdon consecrate and dedicate this land, and the spot for the temple, unto the Lord.

58. And let a conference meeting be called; and after that let my servants Sidney Rigdon and Joseph Smith, Jun., return, and also Oliver Cowdery with them, to accomplish the residue of the work which I have appointed unto them in their own land, and the residue as shall be ruled by the conferences.

59. And let no man return from this land except he bear record by the way, of that which he knows and most assuredly believes.

60. Let that which has been bestowed upon Ziba Peterson be taken from him; and let him stand as a member in the church, and labor with his own hands, with the brethren, until he is sufficiently chastened for all his sins; for he confesseth them not, and he thinketh to hide them.

61. Let the residue of the elders of this church, who are coming to this land, some of whom are exceedingly blessed even above measure, also hold a conference upon this land.

62. And let my servant Edward Partridge direct the conference which shall be held by them.

63. And let them also return, preaching the gospel by the way, bearing record of the things which are revealed unto them.

64. For, verily, the sound must go forth from this place into all the world, and unto the uttermost parts of the earth—the gospel must be preached unto every creature, with signs following them that believe.

65. And behold the Son of Man cometh. Amen.

4. FURTHER DIRECTIONS CONCERNING ZION.

35. *Martin Harris * * * an example*] Martin Harris was called to be the first to obey the Law of Consecration in the Land of Zion.

36. *A law unto every man*] But all were under equal obligation to obey that law. For, "Zion cannot be built up unless it is by the principles of the law of the celestial kingdom" (Sec. 105:5). In the celestial kingdom the children of God are united. They are all one family.

During the Patriarchal Dispensation, the family government, which was patterned after the government in the celestial kingdom, obtained. In our dispensation, which is the Dispensation of the Fulness of Times, that form of government must be restored, in order that the Saints may learn something of celestial government, by their experience here.

39. *Let him repent*] Martin Harris was also admonished to repent of his sins—those that were caused by his desire to obtain "the praise of the world." Men would probably not regard such a desire as sinful; they might call it a "weakness," or a "failing"; or it might even be considered laudable "ambition." God classes it as *sin*.

40. *William W. Phelps stands in the office, etc.*] This refers to the important office of publisher. Phelps was to hold that office and to receive an inheritance in the land.

41. *Also he hath need to repent*] He lacked humility and was anxious to "excel," that is to say, to be in public view as the foremost among his associates. That disposition is born of selfishness and pride, and, unless it is overcome, it will disqualify one for the celestial kingdom. To excel and to be unconscious of it is the disposition of a humble disciple of Christ. Comp. Luke 17:10.

These revelations are remarkable because in them men are told of their sins and admonished to repent. This is one mark of their divine origin. If the Prophet Joseph had been an impostor, it would have been immaterial to him whether his associates were humble or proud; whether they were looking for the approbation of the world, or not. He would not have rebuked them, as he did, at the risk of losing their support. He could not have admonished them to repent, for they would have known his true character. But he was no impostor. He told his friends the truth, and they knew that the Spirit of God spoke through him. This is a proof of his divine calling, for it is one of the functions of a Prophet of God to show His people their sins. Micah 3:8.

42. *He who has repented * * * forgiven*] Repentance brings forgiveness, and when God forgives sins, He remembers them no more. See Isaiah 43:25; 44:22; Ezekiel 33:16; I. Peter 2:24.

43. *Confess them and forsake them*] These are marks of genuine repentance. A repentant sinner confesses his sins unto God, and to those against whom he has sinned. He makes restitution, as far as possible, for whatever wrong he may have done toward his fellow-men; and he forsakes the sins he confesses.

44. *The residue of the elders*] The Elders not specially mentioned in this Revelation were instructed not to hasten to establish themselves in Zion. "The time has not yet come," and would not come, they were told, "for many years" for them to receive their inheritances, except as the Lord should appoint unto them, in answer to their prayers. This is an important principle of gathering. Many have gathered with the people of God and become disappointed. They did not wait to go till the Lord opened up the way for them in answer to their prayers of faith, but they went very much for the same reasons as emigrants go to any other part of the world, and with no nobler motives. This is not in accordance with the spirit of the gospel. Possibly the Saints in those early days were too much in a hurry to build up Zion.

45. *Push the people together*] The calling of the rest of the Elders was to gather the honest in heart in all parts of the Earth, and to begin by preaching the gospel in the vicinity of Independence (v. 46) and on the way back to their homes (v. 47-48). The faithful performance of this mission was one mode of building up Zion.

49. *An agent * * * by the voice of the church*] The Saints in Ohio were to have an agent to render those who desired to go to Zion the necessary assistance, and he was to be appointed "by the voice of the Church." In the Kingdom of God the people must share the responsibilities of their servants. God has given the Church a voice in the government, and corresponding responsibility.

50. *Sidney Rigdon*] His special calling at the time was to write a description of the land and a statement of the will of God concerning it, as it would be made known to him by the Spirit.

51. *Epistle and Subscription*] The description was to be accompanied by a circular letter, with subscription lists, soliciting funds, of Church members, to enable the Bishop, or the agent, to purchase land for the Saints.

54. *Let there be workmen sent forth*] The land purchased was not to be left unimproved. Labor was to be expended upon it. God never promises His children an existence in idleness. Even the Garden of Eden was a place in which to work, for man was placed there by the Creator "to dress it and to keep it" (Gen. 2:15). The land of Zion, too, was to be build up by labor. Labor is just as important as capital, and God recognizes its worth, whether man does or not. Labor should be sanctified to the service of man.

55. *Let the Privileges of the lands be made known*] One of the duties of the Bishop, or the agent, was to issue reports from time to time concerning the progress of the work.

56. *Gathering be not in haste*] This is another warning against gathering without deliberate consideration of the duties and responsibilities connected with the settlement in Zion. If the Saints need wisdom and wise counsel at any time, it is when they are moved upon by the spirit of gathering.

57. It was also the duty of Sidney Rigdon to consecrate and dedicate the land and the Temple lot unto the Lord.

The land was dedicated the day after that on which this Revelation was received. Sidney Rigdon asked the Saints present:

"Do you receive this land for the land of your inheritance with thankful hearts, from the Lord?"

Answer from all:—"We do."

"Do you pledge yourselves to keep the law of God in this land, which you never have kept in your own lands?"

"We do."

"Do you pledge yourselves to see that others of your brethren who shall come hither do keep the laws of God?"

"We do."

After prayer Elder Rigdon said, "I now pronounce this land consecrated and dedicated unto the Lord for a possession and inheritance for the Saints, and for all the faithful servants of the Lord to the remotest ages of time. In the name of Jesus Christ, having authority from Him. Amen." (*Hist. of the Church,* Vol. I., p. 196).

The Temple lot was dedicated on August 3rd. Joseph Smith the Prophet, Edward Partridge, William W. Phelps, Oliver Cowdery, Martin Harris, and Joseph Coe were present. "The scene," says the Prophet, "was solemn and impressive."

58. *Let a conference meeting be called*] This Conference was held on August 3rd, at the house of Joshua Lewis, in Kaw Township. The Colesville Saints who lived there, about sixty in all, attended. This was the Fifth Conference of the Church, and the first in the Land of Zion.

On the 9th of August, the Prophet and ten Elders left Independence and began the return journey to Kirtland, where they arrived on the 27th of the same month.

64. *The sound must go forth from this place into all the world*] The gospel sound. Zion is to be the light-house from which the rays of truth will radiate in all directions.

"The Lord will have a place whence His Word will go forth, in these last days, in purity; for if Zion will not purify herself, so as to be approved in all things, in His sight, He will seek another people, for His work will go on until Israel is gathered, and they who will not hear his voice, must expect to feel his wrath" (Joseph Smith, *Hist. of the Church*, Vol. I., p. 316).

GENERAL NOTES

The Church will proclaim the Gospel during the Millennium with greater power and with more success than before the advent of our Lord.

The Temple lot, as owned at present by the Church of Christ, commonly called "Hedrickites."* comprises the summit of a hill and consists of about three acres. In 1827 one Jones H. Flournoy owned the quarter section of which it is a part. In 1831 the Saints purchased the land, either the entire section or a portion of it, and subsequently 63 acres and 43 square rods were deeded to Edward Partridge for $130. In 1848 the land became the property of one James Pool, having been sold to him by the heirs of Partridge. Pool sold it to one Maxwell for $1,315. "Maxwell's heirs" divided the land into building-lots and disposed of them to different parties. The Hedrickite brethren, in 1867, secured the three acres they now hold, at a cost of about $1,500. They built a meeting-house of lumber upon the lot. Some years ago, the so-called Reorganized church sought to obtain possession of the part held by the so-called Hedrickites, by means of a law suit, on the ground that their church was, as they alleged, the legal successor of the Church founded through the instrumentality of the Prophet Joseph. The courts took a different view, and the Hedrickite brethren remained in possession.

Concerning the first Elders of the Church mentioned in this Revelation and others, Brigham Young on one occasion said:

"I am a witness * * * that the persons whose names are mentioned, and many others of the first Elders of the Church, were looked upon almost as angels. They were looked upon by the young members as being so filled with the Spirit of God, that we were hardly worthy to converse with them. You hear the names of Bishop Partridge, of Brother W. W. Phelps, who is now sitting on this stand†; of Parley P. Pratt, of David Whitmer, of Oliver Cowdery, and the names of many others of the first Elders who had been up to Zion, and I declare to you the brethren in other parts of the land, those who had not seen the persons named, felt that, should they come into their presence, they would have to pull off their shoes, as the ground would be so holy upon which they trod" (*Jour. of Dis.*, Vol. III., p. 335).

---

* So called after Mr. Granville Hedrick, who became one of the leaders of some apostate Saints in Woodford County, Ill., several years after the martyrdom at Carthage and the exodus of the Church. About the year 1867 he and others moved to Independence, Mo., where he presided, until his death, over the group that originated in Woodford County.

† The discourse was delivered in the Bowery, Salt Lake City, June 15, 1856.

The word "damned," which occurs in this Revelation (v. 29), and elsewhere, means to be deprived of the highest glory. It does not mean "lost." Says Brigham Young:

"To be damned is to be banished from, or be deprived of living in, the presence of the Father and the Son. Who will live with Him? * * * Those who live as Father Abraham did and improve upon every means of grace, and upon every privilege given to them of the Lord. What is going to become of the others? Brother Joseph F. Smith told us the truth this morning. None will become angels to the devil except those who have sinned against the Holy Ghost" (*Jour. of Dis.*, Vol. XI., p. 271).

From the same discourse the following is quoted:

"It was said to Joseph Smith, the Prophet, 'According to your faith and the teachings of your Elders, nobody will be saved but you Mormons; now, Mr. Smith, will all be damned but the Mormons?' Joseph Smith replied, 'Yes, and many of them [the "Mormons"] unless they repent and do better.' "

SECTION 59.

REVELATION *given through Joseph Smith the Prophet, in Zion, Jackson County, Missouri, August 7, 1831. Preceding his record of this revelation, the Prophet writes descriptively of the land of Zion wherein the people were then assembled. See History of the Church, vol. 1, p. 196. The land was conse- crated, as the Lord had directed, and the site for the future Temple was dedicated. The Lord makes these commandments especially applicable to the Saints in Zion.——The people com- mended for their obedience in gathering to Jackson County— Certain of the commandments given in the decalog reiterated— Sanctity of the Sabbath emphasized—Not confessing the hand of God in all things a grievous offense.*

BEHOLD, blessed, saith the Lord, are they who have come up unto this land with an eye single to my glory, according to my commandments.

2. For those that live shall inherit the earth, and those that die shall rest from all their labors, and their works shall follow them; and they shall receive a crown in the mansions of my Father, which I have prepared for them.

3. Yea, blessed are they whose feet stand upon the land of Zion, who have obeyed my gospel; for they shall receive for their reward the good things of the earth, and it shall bring forth in its strength.

4. And they shall also be crowned with blessings from above, yea, and with commandments not a few, and with revelations in their time—they that are faithful and diligent before me.

The Fifth Conference of the Church was held August 4th, 1831 (Sec. 58:58), and on the 7th, the Prophet attended the funeral of Sister Polly Knight, wife of Joseph Knight, Sr. Her health had been failing for some time, and she was very ill during the journey from Kirtland to Independence, but she had a strong desire to see the Land of Zion. She lived to have that wish gratified, and then she slept in peace. She was the first of the Saints to pass away in that country. This Revelation was received on the day of the funeral. In it the Lord (1) assures the Saints in Zion that they are blessed, whether they live or die (1-4); (2) reiterates the great commandments (5-6); (3) shows how love of God is manifested (7-14); (4) promises blessings to the obedient (15-21); and (5) gives further promises (22-24).

1. THE INHABITANTS OF ZION BLESSED.

1. *Blessed * * * they who have come up unto this land*] "Blessed" means "happy." The inhabitants of Zion are happy; but there is a condition: If they have come "with an eye single to my glory, according to my commandments." Those who go there to get wealth and honor have something else in view than the glory of God, and they have no promise of happiness.

2. *They that live * * * the earth*] They that live in Zion, and keep the commandments of God, shall receive their inheritances. This earth is the Lord's, and He will share it with them.

*They that die * * * rest*] They that die shall rest from their labors. Death to them is but a sweet repose, a rest from toil, a refreshing sleep, from which they shall awake in the morning of the resurrection.

Their works shall follow them] We are not to suppose that those who die in Zion before the coming of the Lord lose the reward of witnessing that great event and partaking in its glory. For both they and their good works have as real an existence after death as before. They are resting from their labor, but what good they have accomplished, remains. The architect may rest, but his house stands there, a monument to his genius and diligence.

This is a notable passage. In Rev. 14 we read about the restoration of the gospel in our day, through the instrumentality of an angel flying in mid-heaven, proclaiming the advent of our Lord. The contents of the message are indicated as follows: First, worship God as He is revealed in the story of the Creation; not the God of man-made creeds; second, fallen is Babylon; and, third, doomed to drink of the wrath of God are all who worship the "beast" and his "image." These are characteristics of the everlasting gospel, as regards the living. There is another, which more especially pertains to the dead; for the gospel embraces both living and dead. It is this, "Blessed are the dead which die in the Lord from henceforth" (Rev. 14:13). From henceforth, that is to say, from now onward, since the gospel has been restored, the state between death and resurrection is no longer conceived of as a gloomy existence, torture in hell, or purgatory, unconsciousness, or annihilation, but as a conscious, active existence under the influence of the mercy of the eternal Father. John, in the Revelation, saw this feature of the Gospel of Jesus Christ, as restored to the Earth in our day, and here is a clear indication of the doctrine of the blessedness of the dead as seen by him, by which we may identify the gospel preached by the Prophet Joseph with that proclaimed by the angel in Rev. 14. Later, the glorious truth of vicarious work for the dead, which is here indicated, was more fully revealed.

3. *Blessed * * * upon the land of Zion*] Happy are they who are in Zion, "who have obeyed my gospel." This includes the Word of Wisdom, the Law of Consecration, and all other laws and ordinances of the gospel.

*They shall receive * * * good things of the earth*] God blesses the soil and the labor expended upon it, for the good of His children who keep His commandments.

4. *Blessings from above*] The heavenly influence that will enhance the enjoyment of the good things of the Earth.

And with commandments] Those who love God, love His commandments, as blessings bestowed upon them. Love prompts them to render obedience.

5. Wherefore, I give unto them a commandment, saying thus: Thou shalt love the Lord thy God with all thy heart, with all thy might, mind, and strength; and in the name of Jesus Christ thou shalt serve him.

6. Thou shalt love thy neighbor as thyself. Thou shalt not steal; neither commit adultery, nor kill, nor do anything like unto it.

2. THE TWO GREAT COMMANDMENTS.

5-6. Our Lord has declared that these are the greatest commandments in the Law, because upon them "hang" all the Law and the Prophets. The Word of God presupposes and depends on love of God and fellowmen. If there is no such love, laws and instructions are of but little avail.

Heart, might, mind, and strength] "Heart" stands for "emotions," "sentiment." "Might" here stands for "soul," the term used in Matthew 22:37, and means the spiritual faculties. "Mind" refers to the intellect, and "strength" to the physical attributes. This commandment enjoins on us to love our heavenly Father so that our entire beings—our emotions, our spiritual faculties, our mental and physical activities are all devoted to Him and His service.

In Deuteronomy 6:5, the great commandment reads "Heart," "soul," and "mind"; Matthew has, "Heart," "soul," and "mind,"; Mark has, "Heart," "soul," "mind"; and Luke, "Heart," "soul," "strength," and "mind." In the Doctrine and Covenants the text differs somewhat from all. When the Spirit of the Lord speaks through a human instrument, He acts independently, even when proclaiming truths formerly revealed. Strictly speaking, the Holy Spirit does not quote the Scriptures, but gives Scripture.

Love thy neighbor as thyself] This law is eternal. It was given to Israel (Lev. 19:18): "Thou shalt not avenge, nor bear grudge against the children of thy people, but thou shalt love thy neighbor as thyself." Is it impossible to do this? God does not give a command that cannot be obeyed.

7. Thou shalt thank the Lord thy God in all things.

8. Thou shalt offer a sacrifice unto the Lord thy God in righteousness, even that of a broken heart and a contrite spirit.

9. And that thou mayest more fully keep thyself unspotted from the world, thou shalt go to the house of prayer and offer up thy sacraments upon my holy day;

10. For verily this is a day appointed unto you to rest from your labors, and to pay thy devotions unto the Most High;

11. Nevertheless thy vows shall be offered up in righteousness on all days and at all times;

12. But remember that on this, the Lord's day, thou shalt offer thine oblations and thy sacraments unto the Most High, confessing thy sins unto thy brethren, and before the Lord.

13. And on this day thou shalt do none other thing, only let thy food be prepared with singleness of heart that thy fasting may be perfect, or, in other words, that thy joy may be full.

14. Verily, this is fasting and prayer, or in other words, rejoicing and prayer.

3. How Love of God is Manifested.

7. *Thank the Lord*] Gratitude is a natural manifestation of love. We are commanded to thank God "in all things;" in adversity as well

as prosperity; in sorrow as well as joy; in death as well as life. If we love God, we shall never pray for benefits without thanking Him for blessings already bestowed.

8. *Offer a sacrifice*] Sacrifice is a natural manifestation of love. But the sacrifice God delights in is a "broken heart and a contrite spirit" (See Sec. 52:15). God dwells in "the high and holy place"—at an infinite distance from human greatness and pride, but also with him that is of a "contrite and humble spirit." Humility is the beginning of exaltation.

9. *My holy day*] The day of the Lord. God has given His children the Law of the Sabbath, in order that they may manifest their love for Him by observing that day.

On the Sabbath, the Saints should be in the house of prayer and offer up their "sacraments"; that is, present their devotions before the Lord, in the form of songs of praise, prayer and thanksgiving, testimonies, partaking of the Sacrament, and contemplation of the Word of God. All this is meant by the word "sacrament," which, in its widest range, stands for any sacred rite or ceremony whereby we affirm our allegiance to our divine Lord.

10. *A day * * * to rest from your labors*] Man needs a day of rest every week, in addition to his rest at night.

"Instead of suffering our labors to occupy the Sabbath—instead of planning our business to infringe upon the first day of the week, we should do as little as possible; if it is necessary to cook food, do so; but even if that could be dispensed with, it would be better. * * * Under the new covenant, we should remember to preserve holy one day in the week as a day of rest—as a memorial of the rest of the Lord and the rest of the Saints; also for our temporal advantage, for it is instituted for the express purpose of benefiting man" (Brigham Young, *Jour. of Dis.*, Vol. VI., p. 277).

11. *All days and at all times*]
"We do not believe in worshiping God, or being religious on the Sabbath day only; but we believe it is as necessary to be religious on Monday, Tuesday and every day of the week, as it is on the Sabbath day; we believe that it is as necessary to do unto our neighbors as we would they should do unto us, during the week as it is on the Sabbath. In short, we believe it is necessary to live our religion every day in the week, every hour in the day, and every moment. Believing and acting thus, we become strengthened in our faith, the Spirit of God increases within us, we advance in knowledge, and we are better able to defend the cause we are engaged in" (Joseph F. Smith, *Jour. of Dis.*, Vol. XII., p. 329).

12. *On this the Lord's day * * * thine oblations*] Nevertheless, on the Lord's day, the Saints will devote themselves especially to the service of the Lord in spiritual things, so-called.

Oblations] In the Mosaic dispensation, an oblation, or offering, was anything presented to God to atone for sins, to merit favors, or to express gratitude for favors received. The firstlings of the flock, first fruits, tithes, incense, the shewbread, all these were oblations or offerings; some prescribed by law, some entirely voluntary. In the New and Everlasting Covenant the Lord graciously accepts tithes and offerings, donations and gifts; and the Lord's day is a very proper day upon which to remember such oblations, as well as to confess sins, publicly among the brethren, if necessary; privately before the Lord, which is always necessary.

13. *Do none other thing*] Upon the Sabbath, even the food should be prepared "with singleness of heart"; that is to say, in simplicity. Our hearts, our desires, on that day should not be elaborate feasts, whereby some are prevented from having a Sabbath. A simple meal should suffice. To that extent every Sabbath should be a fast day, one bringing perfect joy.

Our Lord, on one occasion, entered the house of Martha and Mary. Martha was cumbered about much serving, desirous of giving the Master many courses, and all in grand style. Mary was anxious to listen to the Master. To Martha's rebuke of her younger sister, our Lord gently replied, "But one thing is needful." This might well be always remembered on our Lord's day.

14. *Fasting and prayer*] To keep the Sabbath in this manner is fasting and prayer; or, in other words, rejoicing and prayer.

Fasting should be rejoicing.

Fasting, as an expression of sorrow, is natural, for in deep affliction man does not crave nourishment to the same extent as under normal conditions. In the Law of Moses one annual fast day was provided— the day of atonement (Lev. 23:27-29). But on solemn occasions other fast days were observed. Joshua and the leading Elders of Israel were prostate before the Ark one entire day after the defeat in the battle of Ai (Jos. 7:6). David fasted when his child was sick (II. Sam. 12:16). Moses fasted forty days on Mount Horeb. Elijah fasted a similar period, as did our Lord before entering upon His ministry. The children of God, in all ages, have found comfort and strength in fasting and prayer. In answer to prayer with fasting, extending over a period of two days and nights, Alma was healed (Mosiah 27:22, 23). Alma fasted and prayed many days, in order to receive a testimony of the truth (Alma 5:46). There are many instances of fasting recorded in the Book of Mormon. Paul reminded the Saints that he and his companions had proved themselves to be ministers of God in "fastings" as well as in all other circumstances (II. Cor. 6:5). Our Lord warns His disciples not to fast as hypocrites who look sad and distort their countenances, in order to be seen by men, but to appear as if going to a social function, in order that God, "who seeth in secret" may reward them openly

(Matt. 6:16-18). This is in harmony with what God revealed through Joseph the Prophet, that fasting should be rejoicing. It is also in harmony with the view taken by Isaiah (58:3-8). The Latter-day Saints have a Fast Sunday every month, on which they bear testimony to the goodness of the Lord to them, and remember the poor by donations. If they understand the gospel, they will make every Sunday a fast-Sunday, by abstaining from work, partaking of simple food, and devoting the day to spiritual matters.

15. And inasmuch as ye do these things with thanksgiving, with cheerful hearts and countenances, not with much laughter, for this is sin, but with a glad heart and a cheerful countenance—

16. Verily I say, that inasmuch as ye do this, the fulness of the earth is yours, the beasts of the field and the fowls of the air, and that which climbeth upon the trees and walketh upon the earth;

17. Yea, and the herb, and the good things which come of the earth, whether for food or for raiment, or for houses, or for barns, or for orchards, or for gardens, or for vineyards;

18. Yea, all things which come of the earth, in the season thereof, are made for the benefit and the use of man, both to please the eye and to gladden the heart;

19. Yea, for food and for raiment, for taste and for smell, to strengthen the body and to enliven the soul.

20. And it pleaseth God that he hath given all these things unto man; for unto this end were they made to be used, with judgment, not to excess, neither by extortion.

21. And in nothing doth man offend God, or against none is his wrath kindled, save those who confess not his hand in all things, and obey not his commandments.

4. BLESSINGS OF OBEDIENCE.

15-21. In these paragraphs the Lord promises the Saints certain blessings on certain conditions. If we shall keep His law concerning the Sabbath, with thanksgiving and cheerful hearts and countenances, though not with much laughter, He will bless us with the fulness of the Earth.

15. *Not with much laughter*] Much laughter is often an indication of levity, of frivolity, and is, therefore, sinful.

"Never give way to vain laughter. I have seldom laughed aloud for twenty or thirty years without regretting it, and I always blush for those who laugh aloud without meaning. I am often full of joy and gladness, and were I to give way to the promptings of my nature at such times, it would lead to unreasonable levity, which would be a source of mortification and sorrow to me * * * I am satisfied that those persons who stamp, clap hands, whistle, and make other noisy and boisterous demonstrations in the theatres, so untimed and uncalled for, have but little sense, and know not the difference between a happy smile of satisfaction to cheer the countenance of a friend, and a contemptuous sneer that brings the curses of man upon man" (Brigham Young, *Jour. of Dis.*, Vol. IX., p. 290).

16. *The fulness of the Earth*] This blessing includes all that is good to eat and suitable for raiment—every necessity of life, and even luxuries—things to "please the eye and gladden the heart" (v. 18).

19. *To strengthen the body*] This is another blessing. The body is benefited by the observance of the Sabbath.

"We should observe the Sabbath as a day of rest, and if we do it faithfully, we shall live longer; for my impression is, saying nothing about the commandment of the Lord, that nature requires one-seventh of our time for rest, and that when a man has worked fifty-two Sundays in a year, he is at least fifty-two days older than he needs to be, and has not done as much work during the year, as if he had worked only six days and had rested the seventh. * * * The evidence is plain on the face of the Book of Mormon, that when men commence to live in accordance with the laws of the gospel, as the people of Nephi did for about two hundred years after the Savior visited the land Bountiful, they shall be stronger and live longer. Amos, the son of Nephi, kept the records on the plates of Nephi eighty-eight years, and his son Amos kept them one hundred and eleven years (See IV Nephi vv. 20, 21). Previous to this period the Book of Mormon shows that the Nephites were a short-lived race. The observance of the Sabbath, as well as the observance of every other commandment of God, has a tendency to prolong human life" (George A. Smith, *Jour. of Dis.*, Vol. XII., p. 197).

20. *Neither by extortion*] "Extortion" is the act of taking something by violence, by threats, by overcharge, etc., unlawfully. It is lawful to procure, by honest labor, the means whereby the good things of the Earth may be obtained, but it is not lawful to wrest anything from another by methods contrary to this great law: "Thou shalt love thy neighbor as thyself."

22. Behold, this is according to the law and the prophets; wherefore, trouble me no more concerning this matter.

23. But learn that he who doeth the works of righteousness shall receive his reward, even peace in this world, and eternal life in the world to come.

24. I, the Lord, have spoken it, and the Spirit beareth record. Amen.

5. FURTHER PROMISES.

23. *He who doeth the works of righteousness * * * reward*] Here the promises are further emphasized and summed up. Doing the works of righteousness brings peace in this world, and eternal life hereafter. This is a truth which the Saints should "learn." They can learn it only by experience in doing what is right.

GENERAL NOTES

This Revelation is especially intended to instruct the Saints concerning the observance of the Sabbath.

The Lord has always given prominence to the law pertaining to the weekly rest. It is one of the first on record in the Bible. God had no sooner completed the creation than he "blessed the seventh day, and sanctified it; because that in it he had rested from all his work which God created and made" (Gen. 2:3). That the seventh day thus was separated from other days, by God Himself, accounts for the fact that the division of time into weeks has been almost universal. Noah certainly counted days by sevens (Gen. 8:10, 12). So did Laban (Gen. 29:27, 28). Israel observed the Sabbath before the Law was given on Sinai (Ex. 16:23), but when the Decalogue was promulgated, the Sabbath law was incorporated in it among the commandments dealing with man's duty to God. The prophets of Israel pronounce blessings upon those who keep the Sabbath (Is. 56:2). They tell us that when the people polluted the Sabbath the fury of the Lord was poured out upon them (Ez. 20:13), but that Israel restored will again "hallow my Sabbaths" (Ez. 44:24). That the Sabbath was observed by the first Christian churches, with the sanction of the Apostles, is beyond doubt. Jesus proclaimed Himself "Lord also of the Sabbath" (Luke 6:5) and His followers honored Him by observing *His* day, in the spirit of Christ, who taught, contrary to the traditions of the Pharisees, that "the Sabbath was made for man, and not man for the Sabbath" (Mark 2:27). The Saints at Troas assembled to break bread on the Lord's day (Acts 20:7). Paul counseled the Galatian and Corinthian Saints to make their donations on that day, as part of their worship (I. Cor. 16:2). John observed the Lord's day, even in his exile (Rev. 1:10). In the Book of Mormon we read that the people of Nephi kept the Sabbath (Jarom v. 5), and that Alma commanded his people to keep the Sabbath day holy (Mosiah 18:23).

From this Revelation (Sec. 59) we learn that the Sabbath law was among the first that were given in the Land of Zion, after the place for the City had been located and the Temple site designated. And again, when the Pioneers had entered Salt Lake Valley, President Young advised them, and all who should come after them, to observe the Sabbath.

"He told the brethren," says Apostle Woodruff, "that they must not work on Sunday; that they would lose five times as much as they would gain by it. None were to hunt or fish on that day, and there should not any man dwell among us who would not observe these rules" (Whitney's *History of Utah,* Vol. I., p. 133).

It is certain that a community which ignores the Sabbath and the services of the Lord's house will become pagan and sink to a low level of morality. It is not true that man can worship alone, and any day, with as much benefit as he can derive from worshiping in the assemblies of his brethren on the day appointed by the Lord. The "Reign of Terror" stands on the pages of history as an illustration of human government without a Sabbath.

The question may now be asked, "Is the observance of Sunday as the Sabbath acceptable to God?" There is a great deal of confusion in the world on that subject.

Christian observers of Saturday as the Sabbath tell us that some pope is responsible for the change from the seventh to the first day of the week, and almost in the same breath they declare that Constantine the Great is the author of it. Roman Catholics, of course, accept, for the head of their church, the responsibility, but the change was made long before there was an ecclesiastical "head" in Rome. There is no uncertainty in the minds of the Latter-day Saints on the question. This Revelation recognizes Sunday, the Lord's day, as the Sabbath in this dispensation.

It might, further, be observed that the Sabbath law does not, primarily, set apart either Saturday or Sunday as the Sabbath, but A SEVENTH PART OF THE WEEK. "Six days shalt thou labor, but the seventh is the Sabbath of the Lord thy God." It is immaterial where you begin counting, as long as the rule of working six days and resting on the seventh is observed. The rule is the same as that which governs tithe-paying. One dollar out of ten belongs to the Lord. Which one? Any of them. Which day of the seven belongs to the Lord? Any of them, but as the Sabbath is for the entire community, *one* day must be agreed upon for the good of all.

Which day of the week was observed before the exodus of Israel from Egypt, is not known, but, whichever it was, at the time of the exodus some change must have occurred, for a new reckoning began with that event (Ex. 12:2). The month of the exodus became the first month of the Jewish ecclesiastical year and the Sabbaths were, accordingly, rearranged. The beginning of the year was counted from the new moon of the passover, which festival was celebrated between and including the 14th and 21st of the month. The 10th, 14th, and 16th were work days, and could never be Sabbaths (See. Ex. 12:3, 5, 6, 24). From the fact that the Hebrew festivals seem to have been observed on fixed dates, as our Christmas, and were not movable holidays, like Easter, it has been thought that the weekly Sabbaths also were celebrated on fixed dates. If that is correct, the Hebrew Sabbath must have fallen on every day in the week in rotation, as does our New Year's day.

Aside from this argument, it would be impossible to observe as Sabbath any one and the same day all over the Earth, simultaneously. What would be the beginning of the Seventh-day Sabbath—Friday evening at sundown—at a given point in Asia Minor, would be Friday noon in Greenland, Friday morning in Alaska, midnight between Thursday and Friday in Australia, and Thursday evening at a given longitude east of the point of beginning. So, while the Sabbath day cannot be observed all over the Earth on the same day, a seventh part of the week can be dedicated to the service of the Lord everywhere.

Before the Mosaic dispensation, the Sabbath was observed in memory of the creation; Israel celebrated it in memory of the exodus, and the followers of our Savior hold the day sacred to the memory of His Resurrection.

When President Brigham Young said that Sabbath-breakers were not to live among the Saints, he enunciated a true and important principle. The Saints were entitled to rest on that day, but unless all were agreed that needless work should be discontinued for that purpose, there would be but little rest for anybody.

The Sabbath is necessary for the maintenance of free institutions and morality. No one living in a Christian community has the right to undermine these, by his conduct, no matter what his personal views may be.

SECTION 60.

REVELATION *given through Joseph Smith the Prophet, in Jackson County, Missouri, August 8, 1831. The occasion was that of the Elders who had been appointed to return to the East desiring to know how they should proceed, and by what route and manner they should travel.——Reproof for those who neglect to use their talents and who fail to testify of the knowledge they have received—Specific instructions as to the return of Elders to Ohio—Others, yet to arrive in Zion, are to return, proclaiming the word of God.*

BEHOLD, thus saith the Lord unto the elders of his church, who are to return speedily to the land from whence they came: Behold, it pleaseth me, that you have come up hither;

2. But with some I am not well pleased, for they will not open their mouths, but they hide the talent which I have given

unto them, because of the fear of man. Wo unto such, for mine anger is kindled against them.

3. And it shall come to pass, if they are not more faithful unto me, it shall be taken away, even that which they have.

4. For I, the Lord, rule in the heavens above, and among the armies of the earth; and in the day when I shall make up my jewels, all men shall know what it is that bespeaketh the power of God.

Some of the Elders who had come to Independence, but were not to remain, were anxious to learn the will of the Lord concerning them, especially with regard to their return journey. In reply to their prayers this Revelation was given, in which the Lord (1) warns them against yielding to fear of man (1-4); (2) gives instructions regarding the journey (5-9); (3) regarding expenses (10-11); (4) regarding other elders who intended to come to Zion (12-16); and (5) promises further revelations (17).

1. The Fear of Man Displeasing to God.

1. *It pleaseth me*] The Lord was pleased with the Elders who had come to Independence, and He graciously expressed His approbation. Our Father is generous in praise and slow to rebuke. This time He had occasion to voice His displeasure, but He prefaced it by a gracious word of commendation.

2. *Not well pleased*] Some of the Elders, notwithstanding the manifestations they had had of the power and goodness of God, did not speak of these things to their fellowmen, because of their fear of man. This was highly displeasing to the Lord. We should learn from this, that, if we have a testimony of the truth, it is our duty to give that testimony to others, without fear.

3. *It shall be taken away*] Those who neglect to testify of the truth revealed to them, will surely lose the testimony they have.

4. *When I shall make up my jewels*] This is an expression found in Malachi 3:17, where "jewels" refers to the people of God, and where the meaning seems to be that when God segregates His people from the world, His power, as that of a monarch wearing a crown of jewels, will be made manifest to all men. But the testimony concerning the truth must be given to the world before the coming of that day, in order that, when it comes, its portent may be known to all.

5. But, verily, I will speak unto you concerning your journey unto the land from whence you came. Let there be a craft made, or bought, as seemeth you good, it mattereth not unto me, and

take your journey speedily for the place which is called St. Louis.

6. And from thence let my servants, Sidney Rigdon, Joseph Smith, Jun., and Oliver Cowdery, take their journey for Cincinnati;

7. And in this place let them lift up their voice and declare my word with loud voices, without wrath or doubting, lifting up holy hands upon them. For I am able to make you holy, and your sins are forgiven you.

8. And let the residue take their journey from St. Louis, two by two, and preach the word, not in haste, among the congregations of the wicked, until they return to the churches from whence they came.

9. And all this for the good of the churches; for this intent have I sent them.

2. INSTRUCTIONS REGARDING THE JOURNEY.

5-9. These paragraphs contain detailed directions for the return journey to Kirtland, Ohio. The Elders are instructed to preach the gospel by the way, and especially in the City of Cincinnati. Oliver Cowdery and companions, when on their mission to the Lamanites, preached the gospel in that city without a great deal of success, but they were not to pass by the place on that account.

10. And let my servant Edward Partridge impart of the money which I have given him, a portion unto mine elders who are commanded to return;

11. And he that is able, let him return it by the way of the agent; and he that is not, of him it is not required.

3. REGARDING EXPENSES.

10-11. The expenses of the journey might be borne by the common funds, but those who were able to refund the money, were expected to do so.

12. And now I speak of the residue who are to come unto this land.

13. Behold, they have been sent to preach my gospel among the congregations of the wicked; wherefore, I give unto them a commandment, thus: Thou shalt not idle away thy time, neither shalt thou bury thy talent that it may not be known.

14. And after thou hast come up unto the land of Zion, and

hast proclaimed my word, thou shalt speedily return, proclaiming my word among the congregations of the wicked, not in haste, neither in wrath nor with strife.

15. And shake off the dust of thy feet against those who receive thee not, not in their presence, lest thou provoke them, but in secret; and wash thy feet, as a testimony against them in the day of judgment.

16. Behold, this is sufficient for you, and the will of him who hath sent you.

4. REGARDING OTHER ELDERS.

12-16. Other elders were to be appointed to go on a mission to Jackson County. They were to preach the gospel to the world diligently, and not idle their time away (v. 13); and when they had reached their destination, they were to return and continue preaching, without being in a hurry and without stirring up strife (v. 14).

15. *Shake off the dust of thy feet*] Our Lord instructed His first Apostles to shake the dust off their feet, when they departed from a house or a city in which their message had been rejected. Paul and Barnabas did so, when they were forced to leave Antioch in Pisidia (Acts 13:50-1). Paul, at Corinth, when the Jews opposed him and blasphemed, shook his raiment and said, "Your blood be upon your own heads; I am clean" (Acts 18:6). The significance of this solemn act is made clear in Nehemiah 5:13. This prophet, after having taken a promise of the priests, shook his lap and said, "God shake out every man from his house, and from his labor, that performeth not this promise, even thus be he shaken out and empty." To shake the dust of the feet signified the same thing. The Elders of the Church were to perform this act in secret, as a testimony against scoffers and persecutors on the day of judgment, and only when prompted by the Spirit, lest they should make a serious mistake.

17. And by the mouth of my servant Joseph Smith, Jun., it shall be made known concerning Sidney Rigdon and Oliver Cowdery. The residue hereafter. Even so. Amen.

17. Further Revelations are promised, when needed.

SECTION 61.

REVELATION *given through Joseph Smith the Prophet, on the bank of the Missouri river, McIlwaine's Bend, August 12, 1831.*

The Prophet and ten Elders had traveled down the river in canoes. On the first day of the journey many dangers were experienced. Elder William W. Phelps, in daylight vision, saw the destroyer riding in power upon the face of the waters. See History of the Church, vol. 1, p. 203.——Elders not to travel swiftly upon the river, thus losing opportunity to preach—Elders had been permitted to come thus far by boat that they might bear record of the power of the destroyer over the waters— Those who come later to Zion to be warned thereof—Attention of the First Presidency needed in the organized branches— Special labor of declaring the Gospel to non-members left to the Elders thereto appointed.

BEHOLD, and hearken unto the voice of him who has all power, who is from everlasting to everlasting, even Alpha and Omega, the beginning and the end.

On the 8th of August, 1831, the Lord in a Revelation (Sec. 60) directed the Prophet Joseph and his companions to return to Kirtland by way of St. Louis. The following day the Prophet, in company with ten Elders, left Independence in canoes and proceeded down the river. The journey was uneventful, until the third day, when the dangers of river-navigation became manifest. The travelers had landed at McIlwair's, or McIlwaine's, Bend, where they encamped on the bank of the river. While here William W. Phelps had a vision in which he saw "the destroyer" riding upon the face of the waters. Some of the Elders heard a noise, though they did not see anything.

The "destroyer" seen by William W. Phelps in a vision, was, in all probability, the Evil One himself, "the prince of the power of the air"(Eph. 2:2).

The brethren retired that evening, we may feel sure, with peculiar feelings. Their gratitude for the escape from the dangers of the river must have been mixed with misgivings and anxiety for the Saints who were preparing for emigration to the promised land. In the morning they received this Revelation, in which God (1) released them from the obligation of traveling on the river (2-3); (2) declared His decree of destruction on the waters (4-6); (3) urged Sidney Gilbert and William W. Phelps to hasten on their journey (7-12); (4) gave a remarkable revelation concerning the waters (13-22); (5) issued special instructions to Joseph Smith, Oliver Cowdery, and Sidney Rigdon (23); (6) and the Saints (24-29); (7) gave directions concerning the preaching of the gospel (30-32); and (8) the journey of other Elders (33-35); and (9) closed with general instructions and promises (36-39).

2. Behold, verily thus saith the Lord unto you, O ye elders of my church, who are assembled upon this spot, whose sins are now forgiven you, for I, the Lord, forgive sins, and am merciful unto those who confess their sins with humble hearts;

3. But verily I say unto you, that it is not needful for this whole company of mine elders to be moving swiftly upon the waters, whilst the inhabitants on either side are perishing in unbelief.

1. RELEASED FROM THE RIVER.

2. *Whose sins are now forgiven you*] It appears from this that some of the Elders, in their conduct, had displeased the Lord (See verse 20). Possibly, they had refused to go any farther on the river, although their instruction was to go as far as St. Louis. Possibly, as soon as they encountered a little danger, they were seized with fear and insisted upon landing. But the vision of the destroyer seems to have had the effect of making them humble; they had sought the Lord and obtained forgiveness.

3. *Not needful * * * to be moving swiftly*] The Lord released them from the obligation to travel by the more speedy river route, and permitted them to travel more slowly and preach the gospel as they went along.

4. Nevertheless, I suffered it that ye might bear record; behold, there are many dangers upon the waters, and more especially hereafter;

5. For I, the Lord, have decreed in mine anger many destructions upon the waters; yea, and especially upon these waters.

6. Nevertheless, all flesh is in mine hand, and he that is faithful among you shall not perish by the waters.

2. DESTRUCTION OF THE WATERS.

4. *I suffered it * * * record*] God commanded the Elders to travel on the river, in order that they might benefit others by bearing record of their experience.

5. *Decreed * * * destruction*] Destruction had been decreed upon these rivers, and the Saints were to be warned.

Destructive tornadoes have visited the depression through which the Missouri and Mississippi rivers flow, many times. On May 7th, 1840, the city of Natchez was laid in ruins. The people were at dinner when, suddenly, the place was enveloped in darkness, the rain descended in torrents, and the strongest buildings shook as if tossed by an earthquake. Hundreds of lives were lost (*Times and Seasons*, Vol. I., pp. 104-5). During the year 1843, it was estimated that for a number of weeks the loss of steamboats averaged one a day.

6. *He that is faithful * * * not perish*] This promise has been fulfilled. Even unbelievers have had a sense of security in the company of the Saints.

7. Wherefore, it is expedient that my servant Sidney Gilbert and my servant William W. Phelps be in haste upon their errand and mission.

8. Nevertheless, I would not suffer that ye should part until you were chastened for all your sins, that you might be one, that you might not perish in wickedness;

9. But now, verily I say, it behooveth me that ye should part. Wherefore let my servants Sidney Gilbert and William W. Phelps take their former company, and let them take their journey in haste that they may fill their mission, and through faith they shall overcome;

10. And inasmuch as they are faithful they shall be preserved, and I, the Lord, will be with them.

11. And let the residue take that which is needful for clothing.

12. Let my servant Sidney Gilbert take that which is not needful with him, as you shall agree.

3. SIDNEY GILBERT AND W. W. PHELPS.

7. *Be in haste*] Sidney Gilbert had been selected to be the head of a merchant establishment in Zion, and William W. Phelps to establish a publishing house there (Sec. 57:9). They were now returning to their homes, in order to make the necessary arrangements to engage in their respective callings, and they were to make haste.

These two were directed to continue their journey on the river (vv. 9-12). The little company was, consequently, divided. They met at St. Louis, but from there they again took separate routes to Kirtland.

13. And now, behold, for your good I gave unto you a commandment concerning these things; and I, the Lord, will reason with you as with men in days of old.

14. Behold, I, the Lord, in the beginning blessed the waters;

but in the last days, by the mouth of my servant John, I cursed the waters.

15. Wherefore, the days will come that no flesh shall be safe upon the waters.

16. And it shall be said in days to come that none is able to go up to the land of Zion upon the waters, but he that is upright in heart.

17. And, as I, the Lord, in the beginning cursed the land, even so in the last days have I blessed it, in its time, for the use of my saints, that they may partake the fatness thereof.

18. And now I give unto you a commandment that what I say unto one I say unto all, that you shall forewarn your brethren concerning these waters, that they come not in journeying upon them, lest their faith fail and they are caught in snares;

19. I, the Lord, have decreed, and the destroyer rideth upon the face thereof, and I revoke not the decree.

20. I, the Lord, was angry with you yesterday, but today mine anger is turned away.

21. Wherefore, let those concerning whom I have spoken, that should take their journey in haste—again I say unto you, let them take their journey in haste.

22. And it mattereth not unto me, after a little, if it so be that they fill their mission, whether they go by water or by land; let this be as it is made known unto them according to their judgments hereafter.

4. REVELATION CONCERNING THE WATERS.

14. *Behold I, the Lord, in the beginning blessed the waters*]
In the beginning the Spirit of God "moved upon the face of the waters," and life and order came forth from chaos.

> "Darkness profound
> Covered the abyss; but on the watery calm
> His* brooding wings the Spirit of God outspread,
> And vital virtue infused, and vital warmth,
> Throughout the fluid mass."—Milton, *Paradise Lost.*

*In the last days * * * I cursed the waters*] "By the mouth of my servant John." In the Revelation by John, sixteenth chapter, we read

---

* Milton uses the masculine pronoun, but the Hebrew noun (Ruach) is feminine, as is the participle of the verb, "moved upon" (Merakephet). The simile is that of a mother-bird bringing an egg to life by tender care.

that seven angels poured out vials of wrath on the Earth. The third of these was poured out upon the rivers and fountains of waters, "and they became blood" (Rev. 16:4). That this refers to convulsions in nature and sanguinary conflicts, by which persecutors and enemies of the Church will be visited before the coming of the Lord in His glory, is the opinion of most commentators.

15. *No flesh * * * safe upon the waters*] This is a prophecy re-ferring to ocean as well as river traffic. Enoch prophesied concerning the latter days, as follows:

"But before that day he saw great tribulations among the wicked; and he also saw the sea, that it was troubled, and men's hearts failing them, looking forth with fear for the judgments of Almighty God, which should come upon the wicked" (Pearl of Great Price, Book of Moses 7:66).

Many have seen in the world war that broke out in 1914 a remarkable fulfilment of these predictions concerning troubles upon the waters. The extent of the losses of ships and lives is hardly realized. On the 21st of March, 1916, it was reported from Washington that more than 2,000 merchant vessels had been sunk by U-boats and mines. Submarine warfare is something new. It dates no farther back than 1885. Through the ingenuity of militarism the waters have been "cursed" by torpedoes and mines. The latter is a diabolical memento of the Russo-Japanese war, mines being for the first time extensively used at Port Arthur. The conflict in 1914, defies description for its horrors both on land and on the waters, but its successor, the con-flict of 1939, far outstripped the first in the horrors of destruction both on land and on the sea.

16. *None is able to go up to the land of Zion * * * heart*] Note that only those who are upright in heart have promise of protection while traveling among the dangers of the sea, to Zion.

17. *In the beginning cursed the land*] "Cursed is the ground for thy sake," God said to Adam (Gen. 3:17). Man was to overcome the adverse forces of nature by laborious toil, and then receive for reward only a small part of the wealth hidden in the bosom of Mother Earth.

In the last days have I blessed it, in its time, for the use of my saints] While it is true that the Lord pours out his blessings upon the unjust as well as the just, "for he maketh his sun to rise on the evil and on the good, and sendeth rain on the just and on the unjust" (Matt. 5:45), yet he has in store for his Saints great blessings upon the land *in its time*. He has promised to give to them the fulness of the earth, and all he has asked is that we keep his commandments. "Yea, blessed are they whose feet stand upon the land of Zion, who have obeyed my gospel; for they shall receive for their reward the good things of the earth, and it shall bring forth in its strength" (Doc. and Cov. 59:3). Compare the blessings to Israel, Deut. 28.

23. And now, concerning my servants, Sidney Rigdon, Joseph Smith, Jun., and Oliver Cowdery, let them come not again upon the waters, save it be upon the canal, while journeying unto their homes; or in other words they shall not come upon the waters to journey, save upon the canal.

5. SIDNEY RIGDON, JOSEPH SMITH, AND OLIVER COWDERY.

23. *The canal*] There were several canals. Some took the travelers around the rapids in the large rivers; others connected navigable rivers. The instruction not to journey on the river did not include such artificial waterways.

24. Behold, I, the Lord, have appointed a way for the journeying of my saints; and behold, this is the way—that after they leave the canal they shall journey by land, inasmuch as they are commanded to journey and go up unto the land of Zion;

25. And they shall do like unto the children of Israel, pitching their tents by the way.

26. And, behold, this commandment you shall give unto all your brethren.

27. Nevertheless, unto whom is given power to command the waters, unto him it is given by the Spirit to know all his ways;

28. Wherefore, let him do as the Spirit of the living God commandeth him, whether upon the land or upon the waters, as it remaineth with me to do hereafter.

29. And unto you is given the course for the saints, or the way for the saints of the camp of the Lord, to journey.

6. INSTRUCTIONS FOR IMMIGRATING SAINTS.

24. *They shall journey by land*] God can protect His people on the water as well as on land, but He does save them miraculously from the dangers they can avoid by using common precautions.

The Mississippi river is navigable a distance of 2,500 miles. As late as 1866 there were seventy-one steamers plying on the part of the river that flows through the State of Missouri alone. Twenty years later this number had dwindled to ten, three of which were tow boats. It is very remarkable that the Prophet, as far back as 1831, was led to anticipate the cessation of passenger traffic on this mighty water-way, by establishing a land route for the Saints.

25. *Pitching their tents by the way*] By traveling on land and camping together at night, the Saints had the advantage of common devotional exercises every day.

29. *The course for the Saints*] It was one of the duties of the Prophet Joseph to map out the course which the Lord's camp should follow on its way to the promised land. The Saints were to be led by the Spirit of revelation.

30. And again, verily I say unto you, my servants, Sidney Rigdon, Joseph Smith, Jun., and Oliver Cowdery, shall not open their mouths in the congregations of the wicked until they arrive at Cincinnati;

31. And in that place they shall lift up their voices unto God against that people, yea, unto him whose anger is kindled against their wickedness, a people who are well-nigh ripened for destruction.

32. And from thence let them journey for the congregations of their brethren, for their labors even now are wanted more abundantly among them than among the congregations of the wicked.

7. Instructions Concerning Preaching the Gospel.

30. Sidney Rigdon, Joseph Smith, and Oliver Cowdery were not to bear their testimony, until they came to Cincinnati, Ohio. The people of that city had been warned, but they were to be called to repentance again.

33. And now, concerning the residue, let them journey and declare the word among the congregations of the wicked, inasmuch as it is given;

34. And inasmuch as they do this they shall rid their garments, and they shall be spotless before me.

35. And let them journey together, or two by two, as seemeth them good, only let my servant Reynolds Cahoon, and my servant Samuel H. Smith, with whom I am well pleased, be not separated until they return to their homes, and this for a wise purpose in me.

8. Concerning Other Elders.

33. *Declare the word * * * as it is given*] There were eleven Elders in the company. Special instructions had been given to Joseph Smith, Oliver Cowdery, Sidney Gilbert, William W. Phelps, and Sidney Rigdon. The other six were to travel, either all together or two and two, and preach the gospel.

34. *Rid their garments*] See Sec. 60:15.

35. *Two by two*] Our Lord sent His disciples out in pairs. It is not good for men to be alone; nor to travel alone. In congenial companionship there is spiritual strength. It is, moreover, desirable that baptisms and other ordinances be performed in the presence of witnesses. For these reasons the Lord sends His messengers forth in pairs or companies. Reynolds Cahoon and Samuel H. Smith, however, were to travel together (Compare Section 52:30). Elders traveling two by two became a protection to each other against false accusers.

Reynolds Cahoon held many important positions in the Church. In 1833 he was associated with Hyrum Smith and Jared Carter in a committee appointed to raise money for a house of the Lord in Kirtland, in which to accommodate the Elders who might come there to receive instructions before engaging in missionary work. In 1839 he was appointed second counselor to John Smith, who, at that time, presided over the Saints in Iowa. In 1840 he was a member of a committee appointed to superintend the building of the Nauvoo Temple.

Samuel H. Smith] See Sec. 23:4.

36. And now, verily I say unto you, and what I say unto one I say unto all, be of good cheer, little children; for I am in your midst, and I have not forsaken you;

37. And inasmuch as you have humbled yourselves before me, the blessings of the kingdom are yours.

38. Gird up your loins and be watchful and be sober, looking forth for the coming of the Son of Man, for he cometh in an hour you think not.

39. Pray always that you enter not into temptation, that you may abide the day of his coming, whether in life or in death. Even so. Amen.

9. GENERAL INSTRUCTIONS AND PROMISES.

36. *I am in your midst*] The Lord was with the Saints in their journeys, their struggles, their triumphs, or short-comings, as really as He was with the children of Israel in the wilderness. There is no other ground on which to account for the marvelous progress of the Church in the face of the enmity of man.

37. *The blessings of the kingdom are yours*] The blessings and privileges of citizenship in the kingdom of Heaven.

GENERAL NOTES

The prophecy in this Section furnishes a good illustration of *double application* of the prophetic word. There are many such "double" prophecies in the Scriptures. To that class belong the promises to

Abraham (Gen. 15), the predictions of Jacob concerning Judah and the sons of Joseph (Gen. 49); of Balaam (Numb. 24:17); of Nathan (II Sam. 7:12-17); our Lord's prediction concerning the destruction of Jerusalem, and prophecies concerning the restoration of Israel. In this Section the Elders are shown the destroyer making the great rivers of North America unsafe for navigation, and at the same time the vision is opened up and they are made aware of the general application of the "curse" in the latter days.

God's educational methods are wonderful. He commanded the Elders to go by the river to St. Louis. They complied with this command until, on the third day of their voyage, they met with an experience which caused them to land. The destroyer then appeared, and that vision was followed by the Revelation concerning destruction upon the waters. And thus the lesson was impressed on their minds.

Our Lord says He has blessed the land for the use of the Saints. These paragraphs from a sermon by Elder George A. Smith are to the point:

"We came to this land [Utah] because it was so desert, desolate and God-forsaken that no mortal upon Earth ever would covet it; but, as Colonel Fremont reported, that at the mouth of the Bear River, in the early part of August, his thermometer stood at 29 degrees Fahrenheit, three degrees below the freezing-point, which would kill grain, fruit, or vegetables, our enemies said, 'You Mormons may go there and welcome,' chuckling to each other over what seemed to them our annihilation. * * * The newspapers recorded the joy, and gratification felt at the utter end of 'Mormonism.' * * * Notwithstanding, however, the many drawbacks and difficulties encountered in the shape of drought, crickets, grasshoppers, and the cold, sterile climate, the Spirit of the Lord was hovering over the Great Basin * * * and the climate became genial and soft" (*Jour. of Dis.*, Vol. XI., p. 177).

SECTION 62.

REVELATION *given through Joseph Smith the Prophet, on the bank of the Missouri River, August 13, 1831. On this day the Prophet and his Counselors met several Elders who were on their way to the land of Zion, and after joyful salutations, received this revelation to the encouragement of all.——Labors of faithful Elders commended—Those on their way to Zion told of their prospective return in continuation of their ministry.*

BEHOLD, and hearken, O ye elders of my church, saith the Lord your God, even Jesus Christ, your advocate, who knoweth the weakness of man and how to succor them who are tempted.

2. And verily mine eyes are upon those who have not as yet gone up unto the land of Zion; wherefore your mission is not yet full.

3. Nevertheless, ye are blessed, for the testimony which ye have borne is recorded in heaven for the angels to look upon; and they rejoice over you, and your sins are forgiven you.

4. And now continue your journey. Assemble yourselves upon the land of Zion; and hold a meeting and rejoice together, and offer a sacrament unto the Most High.

5. And then you may return to bear record, yea, even altogether, or two by two, as seemeth you good, it mattereth not unto me; only be faithful, and declare glad tidings unto the inhabitants of the earth, or among the congregations of the wicked.

6. Behold, I, the Lord, have brought you together that the promise might be fulfilled, that the faithful among you should be preserved and rejoice together in the land of Missouri. I, the Lord, promise the faithful and cannot lie.

7. I, the Lord, am willing, if any among you desire to ride upon horses, or upon mules, or in chariots, he shall receive this blessing, if he receive it from the hand of the Lord, with a thankful heart in all things.

8. These things remain with you to do according to judgment and the directions of the Spirit.

9. Behold, the kingdom is yours. And behold, and lo, I am with the faithful always. Even so. Amen.

On the 13th of August, the day after the Revelation regarding the curse upon the waters had been given, the Prophet met a company of Elders from Kirtland, presumably some of those called on the 7th of June to go to Missouri on a mission (See Sec. 52). There was great rejoicing when the two companies met.

Our Lord, on one occasion, gave an interview to some Greeks who had come to Jerusalem to worship. He saw in the presence of those strangers an assurance of the coming of the day when He shall be glorified and, being lifted up, draw all men unto Him (John 12:20-32). In the same way, we may be assured, the Prophet Joseph, on this occasion, looked far into the future, when from every land and every direction, multitudes, and not only a few Elders, would go up to redeem Zion, with songs of everlasting joy. On this inspiring occasion the Revelation in this Section was received.

1. *Succor them who are tempted*] Our Lord addresses the Elders as their advocate (comp. Sec. 29:5), who knoweth the weakness of man, and how to succor those who are tempted. He suffered temptation. Not only did He pass through two great crises—one at the beginning of His ministry, in the desert, and one at its close, in Gethsemane—but His entire life on Earth was a trial, such as no other human being can comprehend. Can we imagine a man with an unstained character, pure, refined, unselfish, and beautiful in soul, compelled to live, for some time, in association with fellow-beings the very opposite of all this—morally crippled and deformed, full of bigotry, hatred, selfishness? If so, we can vaguely understand some of the sufferings of our Lord while on this Earth. But, thank God! because of the temptations He endured, He can sympathize with His brethren and plead their cause. Someone has well said, "By His *passion,* He acquired *compassion.*"

2. *Your mission is not yet full*] As long as there were those who would go to Zion, through the missionary labors of the Elders, their mission was not completed.

3. *Testimony * * * recorded in heaven*] The Elders are blessed, for the testimony they had borne had been recorded in heaven for the angels to look upon. St. Peter uses a similar expression (I. Peter 1:12). He teaches us that prophets have diligently searched to find out the time indicated by the Spirit of Christ, when it testified of His sufferings and the glory that should follow. "These things, he says, "angels desire to look into." In this Revelation we are told that angels are scrutinizing the records kept of the testimonies of the Elders, and that they rejoice over the witnesses. It appears from this that the ministry on earth has its effects beyond the veil as well as on this side. An Elder who bears his faithful testimony to the truth does not know how far-reaching the result may be, though his visible audience may consist of but few.

4. *Offer a sacrament*] Comp. Sec. 59:9, 12.

6. *That the promise might be fulfilled*] Comp. Sec. 28:9; 42:9, 35, 62, 67; 45:64-71).

9. *Behold, the kingdom is yours*] The Kingdom of Heaven, the center of which here on Earth is, or will be, the land of promise toward which the Elders addressed were traveling. Great faith may have been required to see in the sparsely settled region of Western Missouri a portion of the Kingdom of God; but does not the entire Earth belong to our Lord, as His Kingdom, whether men acknowledge that fact or not?

General Notes

Orson Pratt, on the 14th of July, 1849, closed a treatise on *The Kingdom of God* with this prophetic utterance:

"Awake, for troublous times are at hand! Nations shall no longer sit at ease! The troubled elements shall foment and rage, and dash with tremendous fury. A voice is heard unto the ends of the Earth. A sound of terror and dismay! A sound of nations rushing to battle: fierce and dreadful is the contest; mighty kingdoms and empires melt away. The destroyer has gone forth, the pestilence that walketh in darkness. The plagues of the last days are at hand, and who shall escape? None but the righteous; none but the upright in heart; none but the children of the Kingdom. They shall be gathered out from among the nations; they shall stand in holy places and not be moved. But among the wicked, men shall lift up their voices and curse God because of His sore judgments, and die. And there shall be a voice of mourning and lamentation unto the ends of the Earth; for the cup of the indignation of the Almighty shall be poured out without mixture of mercy, because they would not receive His messengers, but hardened their hearts against the warning proclamation; against the gospel of the Kingdom, and against the great, preparatory work for the universal reign of the King of kings and Lord of lords."

It is difficult to decide which is the more striking feature of this prophecy: The resemblance of the language to that of the ancient prophets, or the literal fulfilment that is now, since 1914, a matter of history.

SECTION 63.

REVELATION *given through Joseph Smith the Prophet, at Kirtland, Ohio, August, 1831. Prefacing his record of this revelation the Prophet wrote: In these infant days of the Church, there was a great anxiety to obtain the word of the Lord upon every subject that in any way concerned our salvation; and as the land of Zion was now the most important temporal object in view, I inquired of the Lord for further information upon the gathering of the Saints, and the purchase of the land, and other matters. See History of the Church, vol. 1, p. 207.——Solemn warning to the wicked—Divine manifestations, and signs wrought by evil powers—Sin of adultery especially condemned—Saints commanded to gather to Zion as they are able, but not with undue haste lest confusion result—Lands to be secured by purchase and not by seizure—Blessed are they who die in the Lord—Condition of those who shall die during the Millennium—Sidney Rigdon rebuked for pride—Those who use the name of the Lord without authority declared to be under condemnation.*

HEARKEN, O ye people, and open your hearts and give ear from afar; and listen, you that call yourselves the people of the Lord, and hear the word of the Lord and his will concerning you.

2. Yea, verily, I say, hear the word of him whose anger is kindled against the wicked and rebellious;

3. Who willeth to take even them whom he will take, and preserveth in life them whom he will preserve;

4. Who buildeth up at his own will and pleasure; and destroyeth when he pleases, and is able to cast the soul down to hell.

5. Behold, I, the Lord, utter my voice, and it shall be obeyed.

The Prophet Joseph and his companions arrived in Kirtland on August 27th, 1831, having traveled by stage from St. Louis. The building up of Zion and the gathering of the Saints were now the most important objects in view. Wherefore the Prophet humbly asked the Lord for further information on those subjects. Then he received this Revelation, in which the Lord (1) calls for the attention of the Saints to His Word (1-5); (2) warns the wicked (6-21); (3) commands the Saints to gather (22-31); (4) gives an important reason for gathering (32-37), and (5) some special directions (38-47); (6) promises blessings (48-54); (7) warns Sidney Rigdon (55-56); (8) directs that ministers be ordained (57-58); and (9) closes with warnings and a promise (59-66).

1. GOD DEMANDS THE ATTENTION OF HIS PEOPLE.

Our heavenly Father is the sovereign Ruler of the worlds, and when He speaks, He is entitled to our undivided attention and implicit obedience.

1. *Hearken * * * open your hearts * * * give ear * * * listen*] Note that God expects His people to exert themselves to learn His will and do it. He does not reveal His will to us without an earnest effort on our part to learn it. To "hearken" is to hear, as a judge hears a case on which he must give a decision. To "open" one's "heart" is to listen to the Word of God with love and affection, and with an eager desire to understand it and to do the will of God. To "give ear" is to devote the sense of hearing to the search for truth, and to "listen" is to give attention, lest any word escape.

2. *Anger is kindled against the wicked*] It is necessary to hear and obey, lest we be found among those against whom His anger is kindled. God is love, but He is also a "consuming fire" (Heb. 12:29), in the presence of rebellion and apostasy. The same sun that gives life to the humblest living plant parches the grass that is dead.

3. *Who willeth to take * * * preserve*] It is necessary to hear and

obey, because God is the Lord over life and death. He takes life and preserves life at will.

4. *Who buildeth up * * * and destroyeth*] There are always sufficient reasons for the decrees of God. He is not governed by caprice; nor by selfishness, but by love; yet He is supreme and from His decrees there is no appeal. As Paul expresses it, "Nay but, O man, who art thou that replieth against God? Shall the thing formed say to him that formed it, why hast thou made me thus? Hath not the potter power over the clay, of the same lump to make one vessel unto honor, and another unto dishonor" (Rom. 9:20, 21)? This is perhaps one of the things in the writings of Paul to which Peter refers as "hard to be understood" (II. Pet. 3:16), but Heber C. Kimball's comment in his famous sermon on the Clay and the Potter removes every difficulty from it. He says:

"The potter tried to bring a lump of clay into subjection, and he worked and tugged at it, but the clay was rebellious and would not submit to the will of the potter, and marred in his hands. Then of course he had to cut it from the wheel and throw it into the mill to be ground over in order that it might become passive; after which he takes it again and makes of it a vessel unto honor, out of the same lump that was dishonored * * * Ten thousand millions of men may go to hell, because they dishonor themselves and will not be subject, and after that they will be taken and made vessels unto honor, if they will become obedient" (Whitney's *Life of Heber C. Kimball,* pp. 475-6).

5. *My voice * * * shall be obeyed*] God has decreed that His voice must finally be obeyed, and this will be brought about without interference with the free agency of man. Disobedience is useless. It does not nullify God's plans. By it we only bring sufferings upon ourselves.

6. Wherefore, verily I say, let the wicked take heed, and let the rebellious fear and tremble; and let the unbelieving hold their lips, for the day of wrath shall come upon them as a whirlwind, and all flesh shall know that I am God.

7. And he that seeketh signs shall see signs, but not unto salvation.

8. Verily, I say unto you, there are those among you who seek signs, and there have been such even from the beginning;

9. But, behold, faith cometh not by signs, but signs follow those that believe.

10. Yea, signs come by faith, not by the will of men, nor as they please, but by the will of God.

11. Yea, signs come by faith, unto mighty works, for without faith no man pleaseth God; and with whom God is angry he is

not well pleased; wherefore, unto such he showeth no signs, only in wrath unto their condemnation.

12. Wherefore, I, the Lord, am not pleased with those among you who have sought after signs and wonders for faith, and not for the good of men unto my glory.

13. Nevertheless, I give commandments, and many have turned away from my commandments and have not kept them.

14. There were among you adulterers and adulteresses; some of whom have turned away from you, and others remain with you that hereafter shall be revealed.

15. Let such beware and repent speedily, lest judgment shall come upon them as a snare, and their folly shall be made manifest, and their works shall follow them in the eyes of the people.

16. And verily I say unto you, as I have said before, he that looketh on a woman to lust after her, or if any shall commit adultery in their hearts, they shall not have the Spirit, but shall deny the faith and shall fear.

17. Wherefore, I, the Lord, have said that the fearful, and the unbelieving, and all liars, and whosoever loveth and maketh a lie, and the whoremonger, and the sorcerer, shall have their part in that lake which burneth with fire and brimstone, which is the second death.

18. Verily I say, that they shall not have part in the first resurrection.

19. And now behold, I, the Lord, say unto you that ye are not justified, because these things are among you.

20. Nevertheless, he that endureth in faith and doeth my will, the same shall overcome, and shall receive an inheritance upon the earth when the day of transfiguration shall come;

21. When the earth shall be transfigured, even according to the pattern which was shown unto mine apostles upon the mount; of which account the fulness ye have not yet received.

2. THE WICKED WARNED.

6-21. In these paragraphs the Lord warns the wicked, especially apostates and unbelievers, but also those who only profess to be Church members, of the day of wrath, and reminds them of the reward they will lose, when the Earth shall be transfigured.

6. *Let the unbelieving hold their lips*] It is a general characteristic of unbelievers that they want to argue with others and tear up the foundations of the faith of others. Unbelief loves a discussion for the sake of the controversy itself, not as a means of the discovery of truth. The Lord warns quarrelsome unbelievers of the coming of His day, when the truth will be manifest.

He that seeketh signs] Some unbelievers are asking for signs. They are here promised signs, but not unto salvation. The Prophet Joseph relates an incident which may be of interest in this connection. He was holding a meeting in Philadelphia on one occasion, when a man asked for a sign. The Prophet writes:

"After the sermon he again asked for a sign. I told the congregation the man was an adulterer; that a wicked and adulterous generation seeketh after signs; and that the Lord had said to me in a Revelation, that any man who wanted a sign was an adulterous person. 'It is true,' cried one, * * * and the man afterwards confessed" (*Hist. of the Church,* Vol. V., p. 268).

9. *Faith cometh not by signs*] Ezra Booth (Comp. Sec. 52:23) is an illustration of this truth. Those who swear allegiance to Christ only for the sake of the loaves and fishes, are not true to Him (John 6:15, 26).

Signs follow faith] Mark 16:17. Hundreds of miracles have been performed in this dispensation, through the power of God. Signs and miraculous manifestations prove the genuineness of man's faith; they do not produce it. The speed of the vessel proves the good quality of her engines and the skill of the designer and builders; it does not produce these qualities or that skill.

12. *Am not pleased,* etc.] Signs and wonders are intended for the good of man and the glory of God. When our Lord healed the sick and raised the dead, He had these objects in view.

13. *Many have turned away*] They were looking for signs, but disregarded the commandments of God.

14. *There were among you,* etc.] The Lord here lays bare some of the sores of the Church at Kirtland, with a view to their healing. There were transgressors among them. Some of these had left the Church. Others were still claiming membership, but they were sinning in secret.

15. *Folly shall be made manifest*] The Lord here declares their secret sins, their "folly," would be made known. Sin is folly. It is folly to expect pleasure from secret sins, and it is still greater folly to suppose that sins can remain hidden.

16. *He that looketh on a woman*] With a view to possessing her unlawfully. In the world, only the act is, as a rule, regarded as sin. Our Lord teaches us that transgression begins in the thoughts and

desires of the heart, and that the outcome of cherishing such things is apostasy. The Spirit leaves the impure heart; then the door is open for doubt, denial, and fear.

17. *The fearful and the unbelieving * * * lake of fire*] Compare Rev. 19:20; 20:10, 14; 21:8. It is, perhaps, idle to speculate on the nature of this "lake of fire." It is the final destination of the "beast," the "false prophet," the devil, the grave (*hades*), and death, as well as of the "fearful," the unbelieving and the "abominable," and murderers, whore-mongers, sorcerers, idolaters, liars, and all who love and make a lie.

The second death] The death of the body is not the end of the exist-ence of the individual that passes through that experience. There is a life hereafter, and there is a death more terrible than the first. There is a death by which the sinner is separated from God forever.

18. *The first resurrection*] Compare Rev. 20:4-6. After the over-throw of the antichrist, the departed Saints will, in a resurrected state, join the translated Saints, and together they will meet the Savior. That is called the first resurrection.

On the 30th of December, 1842, the Prophet Joseph, in a conversation with Judge Adams, Springfield, said:

"Christ and the resurrected Saints will reign over the Earth during the thousand years. They will not, probably, dwell upon the Earth, but will visit it when they please, or when it is necessary to govern it. There will be wicked men on the Earth during the thousand years. The heathen nations who will not come up to worship will be visited with the judgments of God, and must eventually be destroyed from the Earth" (*Hist. of the Church*, Vol. V., p. 212).

20. *An inheritance upon the earth*] Those who endure in faith and do the will of the Lord have the promise of an inheritance on Earth after its "transfiguration." The earth is to pass through fire and become "sanctified and immortal"; it will be made like unto crystal, and be a urim and thummim, "whereby all things pertaining to an inferior king-dom * * * will be manifest to those who dwell on it." (Sec. 130:9.) The Scriptures teach us that there will be a restitution of all things (Matt. 17:11; Acts 3:21); a "regeneration" (Matt. 19:28), which begins with the Millennium and will be completed when the Earth is re-born and sanctified, fit for an abode of celestial bodies. Then those who are faith-ful will have an inheritance on the glorified Earth. "Blessed are the meek; for they shall inherit the Earth" (Matt. 5:5).

22. And now, verily I say unto you, that as I said that I would make known my will unto you, behold I will make it known unto you, not by the way of commandment, for there are many who observe not to keep my commandments.

23. But unto him that keepeth my commandments I will give

the mysteries of my kingdom, and the same shall be in him a well of living water, springing up unto everlasting life.

24. And now, behold, this is the will of the Lord your God concerning his saints, that they should assemble themselves together unto the land of Zion, not in haste, lest there be confusion, which bringeth pestilence.

25. Behold, the land of Zion—I, the Lord, hold it in mine own hands;

26. Nevertheless, I, the Lord, render unto Cæsar the things which are Cæsar's.

27. Wherefore, I the Lord will that you should purchase the lands, that you may have advantage of the world, that you may have claim on the world, that they may not be stirred up unto anger.

28. For Satan putteth it into their hearts to anger against you, and to the shedding of blood.

29. Wherefore, the land of Zion shall not be obtained but by purchase or by blood, otherwise there is none inheritance for you.

30. And if by purchase, behold you are blessed;

31. And if by blood, as you are forbidden to shed blood, lo, your enemies are upon you, and ye shall be scourged from city to city, and from synagogue to synagogue, and but few shall stand to receive an inheritance.

3. THE SAINTS COMMANDED TO GATHER.

22. *My will unto you*] The Lord gave the Saints at this time the Law of Gathering more as counsel than as commandment, because "there are many who observe not to keep my commandments." The Word of Wisdom was at first given in a similar manner (Sec. 89:1, 2). God is mindful of the weakness of His Saints. "He knoweth our *frame; he* remembereth that we are dust" (Psalm 103:14). He would not give a commandment which He knew would be broken by many of those who were dear to Him. But, when He says, this is my will concerning you, that should be a commandment to all who revere and love Him.

23. *I will give the mysteries*] Knowledge of the things pertaining to the Kingdom of God is given only to those who are obedient. If we accept the first principles, we shall receive further light. If we obey the laws given, others will be revealed.

"It was the design of the councils of heaven before the world was, that the principles and laws of the Priesthood should be predicated upon the gathering of the people in every age of the world. Jesus did everything to gather the people, and they would not be gathered" (Joseph Smith, *History of the Church*, Vol. V., p. 423).

"Why gather the people together in this place (Jackson County, Mo.)? For the same purpose that Jesus wanted to gather the Jews—to receive the ordinances, the blessings, and glories that God has in store for His Saints" (*Ib.,* p. 427).

24-31. In these paragraphs special instructions concerning gathering are given. It was not to be undertaken in haste, but after due preparation, "lest there should be confusion, which bringeth pestilence" (v. 24). If they went on the long journey without the necessary preparations, proper food and suitable clothing, the consequence would be sickness. This was the experience of some American military training camps during the war with Spain, in 1898. Here a truth is revealed, in 1831, of which the world, half a century later, had but little knowledge.

The land of gathering belonged to the Lord (v. 25), but the Saints, mindful of the injunction of Christ, to "render unto Cæsar the things which are Cæsar's," were to purchase their inheritance (v. 27). A contrary course would lead to bloodshed (v. 28). But that would mean that the Saints would be slaughtered, for they were forbidden to shed blood (v. 31). They would be "scourged from city to city, and from synagogue to synagogue."

The Latter-day Saints are forbidden to make war in order to secure a gathering-place, and especially such a sacred place as that in which the greatest of all God's temples is to be located. They are not forbidden to defend their lives, their homes, their loved ones, their liberty and country, against murderers and thieves, but they are forbidden to be the aggressors.

32. I, the Lord, am angry with the wicked; I am holding my Spirit from the inhabitants of the earth.

33. I have sworn in my wrath, and decreed wars upon the face of the earth, and the wicked shall slay the wicked, and fear shall come upon every man;

34. And the saints also shall hardly escape; nevertheless, I, the Lord, am with them, and will come down in heaven from the presence of my Father and consume the wicked with unquenchable fire.

35. And behold, this is not yet, but by and by.

36. Wherefore, seeing that I, the Lord, have decreed all these things upon the face of the earth, I will that my saints should be assembled upon the land of Zion;

37. And that every man should take righteousness in his hands and faithfulness upon his loins, and lift a warning voice unto the inhabitants of the earth; and declare both by word and by flight that desolation shall come upon the wicked.

4. REASONS FOR GATHERING.

32-37. In these paragraphs our Lord states one of the most solemn reasons for the gathering of His Saints—a reason which concerns the entire world. He is angry with the wicked (v. 32), and He has decreed wars upon Earth; "the wicked shall slay the wicked" (v. 33). In order that the Saints might escape this general slaughter, they were commanded to gather upon the land of Zion (v. 36). Our Savior, when He had predicted the destruction of Jerusalem, directed His people to "flee into the mountains"; that is, to gather in the mountain region, when they should see the desolating armies surround the City and the Roman Eagles planted upon the battlements. In the same way, in this dispensation, He provided a place of gathering, in order that the Saints might not perish in the general destruction. There are other important reasons for gathering.

"The multitude we see assembled here today are here, because the Kingdom of God is to be built up; for if the Kingdom of God is to be built up, there must be people to constitute it" (Amasa M. Lyman, *Jour. of Dis.,* Vol. X., p. 84).

But our Father in heaven desired, by the law of gathering, to save his people from the doom of the wicked.

32. *I am holding my Spirit from * * * the earth*] This is the most serious calamity that can befall men. "Take away this Spirit," says Orson Pratt, "and you would immediately see some things going up and others down; some moving horizontally; one portion of the Earth would divide from the other; one part would be flying here, and another there" (*Jour. of Dis.,* Vol. IV., p. 340). But for this Spirit, in whom "We live, and move, and have our being" (Acts 17:28), the universe would again resolve itself into a formless, chaotic mass. When that Spirit was partly withdrawn in the days of Noah, the immense masses of water confined below in "the fountains of the great deep" broke their fetters and overflowed the Earth, while, at the same time, the vapors in the atmosphere condensed and fell down in torrents as if "windows of heaven" had been opened (Gen. 7:11), and the result was the destruction of every living creature, except those in the ark. Similarly, in this dispensation, the partial withdrawal of that Spirit will have the effect of upsetting human society and causing a deluge of blood.

34. *The Saints also shall hardly escape*] Because of their neglect to gather and to build up Zion. The world will be a different place to live in when the glory of God fills the Temple in the New Jerusalem.

On January 4th, 1833, the Prophet wrote to a New York paper:

"I declare unto you the warning which the Lord has commanded me to declare unto this generation * * * 'Fear God and give glory to Him, for the hour of His judgment is come.' Repent ye, repent ye, and embrace the everlasting covenant, and flee to Zion, before the overflowing scourge overtake you, for there are those now living upon the Earth whose eyes shall not be closed in death until they see all these things which I have spoken, fulfilled" (*Hist. of the Church,* Vol. I., p. 315).

37. *Righteousness in his hands and faithfulness upon his loins*] The Israelites, when fleeing from Egypt, ate the paschal lamb, their loins girdled and their staffs in hand (Ex. 12:11). The Saints, in their exodus, should also be prepared, but righteousness must be their "staff," and faithfulness their "girdle." No one should go to Zion unless so equipped.

38. Wherefore, let my disciples in Kirtland arrange their temporal concerns, who dwell upon this farm.

39. Let my servant Titus Billings, who has the care thereof, dispose of the land, that he may be prepared in the coming spring to take his journey up unto the land of Zion, with those that dwell upon the face thereof, excepting those whom I shall reserve unto myself, that shall not go until I shall command them.

40. And let all the moneys which can be spared, it mattereth not unto me whether it be little or much, be sent up unto the land of Zion, unto them whom I have appointed to receive.

41. Behold, I, the Lord, will give unto my servant Joseph Smith, Jun., power that he shall be enabled to discern by the Spirit those who shall go up unto the land of Zion, and those of my disciples who shall tarry.

42. Let my servant Newel K. Whitney retain his store, or in other words, the store, yet for a little season.

43. Nevertheless, let him impart all the money which he can impart, to be sent up unto the land of Zion.

44. Behold, these things are in his own hands, let him do according to wisdom.

45. Verily I say, let him be ordained as an agent unto the disciples that shall tarry, and let him be ordained unto this power;

46. And now speedily visit the churches, expounding these

things unto them, with my servant Oliver Cowdery. Behold, this is my will, obtaining moneys even as I have directed.

47. He that is faithful and endureth shall overcome the world.

5. Special Instructions.

38-47. The Lord, through His Prophet, instructs the Saints in Kirtland to settle their affairs, (v. 38), dispose of their land, and go to the Land of Zion in the spring (v. 39); and to send funds to the agent in Zion (v. 40); He promises to give to the Prophet power to discern, by the spirit of God, who should go (v. 41); He directs that Newel K. Whitney be appointed an agent for those who were to remain (vv. 42-45); and that he and Oliver Cowdery visit the Branches and collect funds for the building up of Zion (v. 46).

38. *Upon this farm*] Refers, probably, to the Morley farm. See p. 307. Isaac Morley accompanied the Colesville Saints to Jackson County and arrived there in the latter part of June, 1831.

Titus Billings] In the month of April, 1832, he led a company of Saints from Kirtland to Jackson County. He is said to have been the second person baptized in Kirtland, having joined the Church in Kirtland in November, 1830. In 1837, at Far West, he was appointed second counselor to Bishop Partridge, Isaac Morley being the first counselor, and in 1849 he became a member of the Salt Lake Stake High Council.

40. *Whom I have appointed to receive*] Edward Partridge and Sidney Gilbert. See Section 57:6-9.

48. He that sendeth up treasures unto the land of Zion shall receive an inheritance in this world, and his works shall follow him, and also a reward in the world to come.

49. Yea, and blessed are the dead that die in the Lord, from henceforth, when the Lord shall come, and old things pass away, and all things become new, they shall rise from the dead and shall not die after, and shall receive an inheritance before the Lord, in the holy city.

50. And he that liveth when the Lord shall come, and hath kept the faith, blessed is he; nevertheless, it is appointed to him to die at the age of man.

51. Wherefore, children shall grow up until they become old; old men shall die; but they shall not sleep in the dust, but they shall be changed in the twinkling of an eye.

52. Wherefore, for this cause preached the apostles unto the world the resurrection of the dead.

53. These things are the things that ye must look for; and, speaking after the manner of the Lord, they are now nigh at hand, and in a time to come, even in the day of the coming of the Son of Man.

54. And until that hour there will be foolish virgins among the wise; and at that hour cometh an entire separation of the righteous and the wicked; and in that day will I send mine angels to pluck out the wicked and cast them into unquenchable fire.

6. BLESSINGS PROMISED.

48. *He that sendeth up treasures,* etc.] It is a peculiar fact that, in the service of the Lord, the more we spend the more we have. It is like distributing five loaves and two fishes among five thousand and then gathering up twelve basketfuls of food yet left.

49. *Shall receive an inheritance*] This is a remarkable promise. Even those who pass away, if they died in the Lord, will obtain an inheritance in the holy city.

50. *He that liveth * * * blessed is he*] He, too, must die, but he will not sleep in the dust but be changed in the twinkling of an eye. Comp I. Thess. 4:13-18.

> "Heaven's broad day hath o'er me broken
> Far above Earth's span of sky!
> Am I dead? Nay, by this token,
> Know that I have ceased to die."

53. *They are nigh at hand*] As God counts time, the events spoken of in this Revelation, including the first resurrection and the change of the living from mortality to immortality, were near at hand.

54. *Foolish among the wise*] Until the Lord comes, there will always be two classes among the people of God: some will be wise and keep His commandments; others will be foolish and neglect their duties.

"Tradition has taught us that the great purpose of religion is to prepare people to die; that when they have passed through a change of heart and become converted, they are ready for glory at any moment, and to dwell with the Father and the Son in the heavens to all eternity. This is a mistake; for they have to improve, become substantially changed from bad to good, from sin to holiness, here or somewhere else, before they are prepared for the society they anticipate enjoying" (Brigham Young, *Jour. of Dis.,* Vol. X., p. 172).

Foolish virgins are those who suppose that they need less preparation for their attendance at the Court on High than they would need if they were to attend the court function of an earthly monarch.

55. And now behold, verily I say unto you, I, the Lord, am

not pleased with my servant Sidney Rigdon; he exalted himself in his heart, and received not counsel, but grieved the Spirit;

56. Wherefore his writing is not acceptable unto the Lord, and he shall make another; and if the Lord receive it not, behold he standeth no longer in the office to which I have appointed him.

7. SIDNEY RIGDON WARNED.

55-6. Sidney Rigdon had been instructed, by revelation (Sec. 58:50), to write a description of the Land of Zion. His first effort was not acceptable to God. The reason for his failure is stated. He was too proud to receive counsel. He was, however, given another chance, and his second effort proved a success and was accepted.

57. And again, verily I say unto you, those who desire in their hearts, in meekness, to warn sinners to repentance, let them be ordained unto this power.

58. For this is a day of warning, and not a day of many words. For I, the Lord, am not to be mocked in the last days.

8. MINISTERS MUST BE ORDAINED.

57. *Let them be ordained*] See Section 5:6. A desire to preach is not sufficient; ordination is necessary.

58. *Am not to be mocked*] To speak in the name of the Lord without authorization is to "mock" Him. That word denotes not merely an attempt to deceive, but deception accompanied by a gesture of contempt. Those guilty of that terrible sin will be overtaken by disaster, as surely as reaping follows sowing. "Be not deceived; God is not mocked; for whatsoever a man soweth, that shall he also reap" (Gal. 6:7).

59. Behold, I am from above, and my power lieth beneath. I am over all, and in all, and through all, and search all things, and the day cometh that all things shall be subject unto me.

60. Behold, I am Alpha and Omega, even Jesus Christ.

61. Wherefore, let all men beware how they take my name in their lips—

62. For behold, verily I say, that many there be who are under this condemnation, who use the name of the Lord, and use it in vain, having not authority.

63. Wherefore, let the church repent of their sins, and I, the Lord, will own them; otherwise they shall be cut off.

64. Remember that that which cometh from above is sacred, and must be spoken with care, and by constraint of the Spirit; and in this there is no condemnation, and ye receive the Spirit through prayer; wherefore, without this there remaineth condemnation.

65. Let my servants, Joseph Smith, Jun., and Sidney Rigdon, seek them a home, as they are taught through prayer by the Spirit.

66. These things remain to overcome through patience, that such may receive a more exceeding and eternal weight of glory, otherwise, a greater condemnation. Amen.

9. WARNINGS AND PROMISES.

59-66. Our Lord again addresses the Saints in His divine character of Alpha and Omega, and His name and title, Jesus [the] Christ, the Anointed One (v. 60). He warns them not to take His name in vain (vv. 61, 62), and calls upon them to repent of their sins (v. 63); counsels the Prophet Joseph and Sidney Rigdon regarding their temporal affairs (v. 65), and closes this important Revelation with the promise that those who overcome, through patience, shall receive eternal glory (v. 66).

61. *Beware how they take my name in their lips*] "Thou shalt not take the name of the Lord thy God in vain; for the Lord will not hold him guiltless that taketh His name in vain." This means, in the first place, thou shalt not swear falsely. To utter the sacred name in such swearing, is to call upon the Lord to affirm a falsehood. That is blasphemy. It means, in the second place, Thou shalt not use His name irreverently on any occasion whatever; nor refer to Him carelessly, or unnecessarily, for any purpose. Men and women are wont to use the sacred name merely as an interjection, expressing astonishment, or fear, or temper, or merriment. It is all wrong, and the Saints are warned against it.

In the common formulas, such as "adieu!" "good-bye" etc., few recognize the divine name, although the meaning is, "to God!" and, "God be with ye!" If the expressions are used reverently, there can be no objection, but in many cases they are spoken without any meaning and might as well be omitted. (Comp. Doc. and Cov. 112:24-26; 121:18-22; 136:21.)

The prohibition means, in the third place, Thou shalt not pretend to speak in the name of the Lord, or as His representative, when He has not sent thee (v. 62). That is an offense as serious as false swearing. It was the sin of Korah, Dathan, and Abiram (Numbers 16:31-33).

GENERAL NOTES

Before leaving this Section, we may recall the important fact that the gathering of the Saints is for a purpose entirely different from that which emigrants to a foreign country usually have in view. If they have the spirit of the gospel, their gathering will be for the purpose of building up the Kingdom of God and, as far as depends on them, hasten on the day when the Millennial reign shall begin. Consequently, they will go to Zion duly prepared. They will repent of their weaknesses and imperfections; they will go according to counsel (v. 41), and they will realize that to gather to Zion is a religious undertaking similar to that of joining the Church.

"The City of Zion, in beauty and magnificence, will outstrip anything that is now known upon the Earth. The curse will be taken from the Earth, and sin and corruption will be swept from its face" (Brigham Young, *Jour. of Dis.,* Vol. X., p. 172).

The doctrine of the sovereignty of God, as stated in the first five verses of this Section, is in perfect accord with all that God has revealed in the Scriptures on this subject. In the Revelations of St. John, the Elders, representing the Church, declare, "Thou art worthy, O Lord, to receive glory, and honor, and power: for thou hast created all things, and for thy pleasure they are and were created" (Rev. 4:11). The Lord Himself declares, "As truly as I live, all the Earth shall be filled with the glory of the Lord" (Num. 14:21). Again, "For mine own sake, even for mine own sake, will I do it; for how should my name be polluted? And I will not give my glory unto another" (Is. 48:11). God's sovereignty is absolute, but the exaltation and happiness of His creation and of His children are His glory. His absolutism is that of a loving Father who knows of no greater happiness than the promotion of the welfare of his family.

How sovereignty in God can be exercised upon free agents, may be difficult to explain, but we know that yielding obedience voluntarily does not take away our free agency. Sometimes we know beforehand how we are going to act in a certain case; it is determined; and yet we are conscious of being free agents. There is, therefore no inconsistency in the doctrine of God's sovereignty and man's freedom.

In this Revelation and others, especially those relating to Temple work, the Latter-day Saints are committed to the cause of peace. "You are forbidden to shed blood" for the building up of Zion (v. 31); and this Revelation was given at a time when that cause was but little known. Since then the peace propaganda has taken more or less definite shape, and peace friends are confidently looking forward to the birth of a League of Nations for the maintenance of peace in a United Nations league; but there will be no peace again among the nations of the earth, until the Prince of Peace comes to cleanse the earth and establish His righteousness. (Doc. and Cov. 97:23.)

The peace propaganda is not a movement of modern origin. See pp. 269-70. In our own day such men as Victor Hugo, Cobden, William Ladd, and many of the foremost statesmen now living, have lifted their voices for universal peace. Among the greatest peace advocates of modern times we must place the Prophet Joseph, who, by proclaiming the gospel of peace, prepared the field, as far as his influence went, for the precious seed which philosophers and statesmen before him had sown in soil but imperfectly prepared.

The Church of Jesus Christ of Latter-day Saints takes the stand held by our Lord and His first followers on the question of peace and war. He enunciated the principle of the Fatherhood of God and the brotherhood of man. This doctrine He proclaimed in a world where militarism held sway. It made many converts, for even at that time men were weary of bloodshed and sick of brutality. Many of the Christians preferred death as martyrs to that of murderers in the Roman legions. But militarism obtained control of the early church, and it has dominated it ever since. That was one result of the general apostasy from our Lord Jesus Christ and the placing of usurpers on His throne in the church.

What the first followers of Christ thought of militarism may be gathered from the early ecclesiastical writers.

Justin Martyr, who died about 165 A. D., proclaims, "that the prophecy is fulfilled we have good reason to believe, for we [Christians], who in the past killed one another, do not fight our enemies."

Irenaeus, about 140-202 A. D., boasts that "The Christians have changed their swords and their lances into instruments of peace, and they know not how to fight."

Clement of Alexandria (second century) writes: "The followers of Christ use none of the implements of war."

Tertullian (150-230 A. D.) asks, "How shall a Christian go to war, how shall he carry arms in a time of peace, when the Lord has forbidden the sword to us?"

Origen (185-230 A. D.) says: "For no longer do we take arms against any race, or learn to wage war, inasmuch as we have been made sons of peace through Jesus."

Cyprian (200-257 A. D.) says: "Christians do not in turn assail their assailants, since it is not lawful for the innocent even to kill the guilty; but they readily deliver up their lives and blood."

Athanasius (296-373 A. D.) says that when people "hear the teaching of Christ, straightway, instead of fighting, they turn to husbandry, and instead of arming their hands with weapons they raise them in prayer."

Augustine (354-430 A. D.) holds that "defensive wars are the only just and lawful ones; it is in these alone that the soldier may be allowed to kill, when he cannot otherwise protect his city and his brethren."

To these testimonies of early church fathers, that of the scholarly

Erasmus may be added. He declares: "If there is in the affairs of mortal men any one thing which is proper to explode, and incumbent upon every man by every lawful means to avoid, to deprecate, to oppose, that one thing is doubtless war" (From an article in the *Christian Work*).

The gospel of Jesus Christ, as proclaimed by the Prophet Joseph, is, on this question, as on others affecting the welfare of the human race, in full accord with the best thought of all ages.

SECTION 64.

REVELATION *given through Joseph Smith the Prophet, to the Elders of the Church, at Kirtland, Ohio, September 11, 1831. A company of brethren who had been commanded to journey to Zion were busily engaged in making preparations to leave in October.——The Lord's rebuke to sinners—Forgiveness for the repentant sinner whose sin is not unto death—Forgive one another, and all men—Instruction to individuals—The intervening time, until the coming of the Son of Man, called today—This is a time of sacrifice and for the tithing of the people—The Saints warned against debt—Liars, hypocrites, and those who falsely pretend to be Apostles and Prophets to be exposed.*

BEHOLD, thus saith the Lord your God unto you, O ye elders of my church, hearken ye and hear, and receive my will concerning you.

2. For verily I say unto you, I will that ye should overcome the world; wherefore I will have compassion upon you.

The Prophet Joseph during the first part of September, 1831, made preparations for removing to Hiram, about 30 miles from Kirtland. This place was the home of Father Johnson, who invited the Prophet to come and stay with him while he was engaged upon the revision of the Bible. Joseph accepted the invitation gladly,* and moved there on the 12th of September. The day before, the Revelation contained in this Section was given, in which the Lord (1) rebukes some of the leading men in the Church (3-17); (2) gives special direction concerning Zion

---

* The Prophet Joseph frequently found himself in circumstances similar to those of our Lord, who did not have "where to lay his head" (Matt. 8:20). At a conference held at Orange, Oct. 25th, 1831, he said he had nothing to consecrate to the Lord, of the things of the Earth; yet he felt to consecrate himself and family (Hist. of the Church, Vol. I., p. 220).

(18-25); (3) warns against contracting debts with enemies (26-33); and (4) gives further instructions and promises (34-43).

2. *Overcome the world*] This is another expressive Johannean term, of which there are many in this inspired volume. John, in his First Epistle, says: "Whatever is born of God overcometh the world, (5:4); and, "who is he that overcometh the world, but he that believeth that Jesus is the Son of God" (v. 5)? What he wants to say is that as long as we follow our desires to conform to the habits and customs of the world, the commandments of God are hard; but when we overcome that desire and do not conform to the spirit of the world, then His commandments are not difficult, and, if we really believe that Jesus is the Son of God, we shall not take any notice of the world, which is in rebellion against Him. In this Revelation the Lord, making use of an expression by the disciple whom He loved, tells the Elders of the Church that they should not conform to the world in their worship, in their life, in their amusements. Some had failed in this respect.

3. There are those among you who have sinned; but verily I say, for this once, for mine own glory, and for the salvation of souls, I have forgiven you your sins.

4. I will be merciful unto you, for I have given unto you the kingdom.

5. And the keys of the mysteries of the kingdom shall not be taken from my servant Joseph Smith, Jun., through the means I have appointed, while he liveth, inasmuch as he obeyeth mine ordinances.

6. There are those who have sought occasion against him without cause;

7. Nevertheless, he has sinned; but verily I say unto you, I, the Lord, forgive sins unto those who confess their sins before me and ask forgiveness, who have not sinned unto death.

8. My disciples, in days of old, sought occasion against one another and forgave not one another in their hearts; and for this evil they were afflicted and sorely chastened.

9. Wherefore, I say unto you, that ye ought to forgive one another; for he that forgiveth not his brother his trespasses standeth condemned before the Lord; for there remaineth in him the greater sin.

10. I, the Lord, will forgive whom I will forgive, but of you it is required to forgive all men.

11. And ye ought to say in your hearts—let God judge between me and thee, and reward thee according to thy deeds.

12. And him that repenteth not of his sins, and confesseth them not, ye shall bring before the church, and do with him as the scripture saith unto you, either by commandment or by revelation.

13. And this ye shall do that God may be glorified—not because ye forgive not, having not compassion, but that ye may be justified in the eyes of the law, that ye may not offend him who is your lawgiver—

14. Verily I say, for this cause ye shall do these things.

15. Behold, I, the Lord, was angry with him who was my servant Ezra Booth, and also my servant Isaac Morley, for they kept not the law, neither the commandment;

16. They sought evil in their hearts, and I, the Lord, withheld my Spirit. They condemned for evil that thing in which there was no evil; nevertheless I have forgiven my servant Isaac Morley.

17. And also my servant Edward Partridge, behold, he hath sinned, and Satan seeketh to destroy his soul; but when these things are made known unto them, and they repent of the evil, they shall be forgiven.

1. Leading Men Rebuked.

3. *There are those * * * who have sinned*] It was about this time that Ezra Booth, Jacob Scott, Simons Rider, Eli Johnson, and others apostatized, "The spirit of apostasy," says George A. Smith (*Jour. of Dis.,* Vol. XI., p. 4), "was little known, but when these men apostatized, they became more violent, more cruel, and manifested a greater spirit of persecution than any other of our enemies." Ezra Booth became particularly bitter. His apostasy culminated in the gathering of the mob that tried to assassinate the Prophet Joseph and Sidney Rigdon at Hiram.

I have forgiven you] There were others, besides those whose sins have led them into apostasy, who had fallen into error, but the Lord had forgiven them, for His own glory and the salvation of souls. "The Lord is merciful and gracious, slow to anger, and plenteous in mercy" (Psalm 103:8).

5. The *keys * * * shall not be taken from my servant Joseph*] The *keys;* that is, the authority, shall not depart from him, as the glory of God from the temple in Jerusalem, while he lives, if he complies with what God ordains.

6. *There are those who have sought occasion against him*] One man named Hawley came from the State of New York and declared that God had rejected the Prophet because he had suffered John Noah, a false prophet, to be cut off from the Church, and also because women in the Church were permitted to wear caps. Some of the Saints listened to him, and it became necessary to call a Bishop's Council to investigate the charges. Oliver Cowdery and others searched the Bible for passages permitting or forbidding women to wear caps and veils, and the outcome of the trial was that the man was expelled for having a false spirit. To quote:

"There was a prevalent spirit all through the early history of the Church, which prompted [some of] the Elders to suppose that they knew more than the Prophet. Elders would tell you that the Prophet was going wrong. Men who thought they knew all about this work, some of them thirty or forty years before the Lord revealed it, tried to 'steady the ark.' The Church was constantly afflicted with such a class of men" (George A. Smith, *Jour. of Dis.*, Vol. XI., p. 7).

7. *Nevertheless he has sinned*] Men assailed the Prophet without cause, calling that which God has not condemned, sin, while that which God censured but pardoned, when confessed repentantly, they did not even see. The Prophet was not sinless, but he was a good man. Brigham Young observes:

"If ever Joseph got wrong, it was before the public, in the face and eyes of the people; but he never did a wrong in private that I knew of. In his private instructions to the Saints, the angel Gabriel could not have given better * * * and my firm conviction is, that Joseph Smith was as good a man as any Prophet or Apostle that ever lived upon this Earth, the Savior excepted" (*Jour. of Dis.*, Vol. X., p. 364).

8-11. Here the Lord teaches the Saints that it is their duty to forgive one another (v. 9), for he who does not forgive his brother "stands condemned before the Lord" and is the greater sinner of the two. They are also taught to forgive "all men," and leave it with the Lord, whether He will forgive or not (v. 10).

"Forgive as we forgive," that is the prayer of the followers of Christ, and our Savior comments as follows:

"For if we forgive men their trespasses your Heavenly Father will forgive you; but if we forgive not men their trespasses, neither will your Father forgive your trespasses." Read also His denunciation of those who treat their brethren with taunts and sneers and contempt (Matt. 5:22). Some people who call themselves Christians are bitter and arrogant. The religion of Christ is humanity and love.

One of the worst traits of human nature is that exhibited by the debtor who said to his fellow-servant, "Pay me what thou owest." But we are all apt to feel that way. We flame into anger at the smallest provocation. We brood over injuries and magnify them. We often hear the coarse threat, "I'll get even."

"When thou sayest 'I will not forgive,' and standest before God with thy precious *pater noster,* and mumblest with thy mouth 'Forgive us our debts, as we forgive our debtors,' what is it but saying: 'I do not forgive him, so do not Thou, God, forgive me' "—Luther.

12. *He that repenteth not * * * bring him before the Church*] Not out of vindictiveness, but for the glory of God (v. 13), and that of the Church may be blameless.

15. *Ezra Booth * * * Isaac Morley*] Note the difference. Booth, the Lord says, *was* my servant. Morley is still recognized as such. Both had failed to keep the Law. Both had condemned as evil that which was not evil. Both had lost the spirit (v. 16). But Ezra Booth persisted in evil-doing, while Isaac Morley repented and was forgiven.

17. *Edward Partridge*] He, too, had sinned; perhaps by listening to the traducers of the Prophet; but he repented and was forgiven.

18. And now, verily I say that it is expedient in me that my servant Sidney Gilbert, after a few weeks, shall return upon his business, and to his agency in the land of Zion;

19. And that which he hath seen and heard may be made known unto my disciples, that they perish not. And for this cause have I spoken these things.

20. And again, I say unto you, that my servant Isaac Morley may not be tempted above that which he is able to bear, and counsel wrongfully to your hurt, I gave commandment that his farm should be sold.

21. I will not that my servant Frederick G. Williams should sell his farm, for I, the Lord, will to retain a strong hold in the land of Kirtland, for the space of five years, in the which I will not overthrow the wicked, that thereby I may save some.

22. And after that day, I, the Lord, will not hold any guilty that shall go with an open heart up to the land of Zion; for I, the Lord, require the hearts of the children of men.

23. Behold, now it is called today until the coming of the Son of Man, and verily it is a day of sacrifice, and a day for the tithing of my people; for he that is tithed shall not be burned at his coming.

24. For after today cometh the burning—this is speaking after the manner of the Lord—for verily I say, tomorrow all the

proud and they that do wickedly shall be as stubble; and I will burn them up, for I am the Lord of Hosts; and I will not spare any that remain in Babylon.

25. Wherefore, if ye believe me, ye will labor while it is called today.

2. SPECIAL DIRECTIONS CONCERNING ZION.

18-19. *Sidney Gilbert*] He is directed to return to Zion, to his business and agency. The Saints there needed his experience and knowledge, "that they perish not." To settle and to build up a new country is an ardent task, full of trials and perils. In a letter dated Kirtland, April 21, 1833, the Prophet Joseph, referring to Brother Gilbert, wrote:

"We are well aware of the great care upon his mind, in consequence of much business, but he must put his trust in God, and he may rest assured that he has our prayers day and night, that he may have strength to overcome every difficulty. We have learned of the Lord that it is his duty to assist all the poor brethren that are pure in heart, and that he has done wrong in withholding credit from them, as they must have assistance; and the Lord established him in Zion for that express purpose" (*History of the Church,* Vol. I., p. 341).

20. *Isaac Morley*] His farm had been sold, and the Lord here explains the reason. As the owner of the farm, Morley was not a safe counselor. When he had been released from the responsibilities of the ownership of the land, his talents could be fully utilized, and in Zion he was first called to be one of the counselors to Bishop Partridge, and then to be the second Bishop in Zion. Later he was one of seven presidents appointed to preside over the Church in Zion.

21. *Frederick G. Williams*] He was directed to retain his farm, for the time being, for this reason, "I, the Lord, will to retain a strong hold in the land of Kirtland, for the space of five years." George A. Smith comments as follows:

"The word of the Lord given in September, 1831 * * * to make Kirtland a strong hold for the space of five years, gave rise to a new development in the feelings and sentiments of the Saints. The Prophet said, purchase land in the vicinity of Kirtland; men were induced to buy farms, and to go to work and build houses, to quarry rock, and haul them on the ground, to build a Temple" (*Journal of Discourses,* Vol. XI., p. 9).

But for this Revelation, the Kirtland Temple might not have been built, and the glorious manifestations in that sacred structure would not have been received.

23. *Now it is called to-day*] "To-day" is the time before the coming of the Lord. The expression is found in Psalm 95:7, and Heb. 3:13. The Psalm referred to was sung at the dedication of the second temple, and it means, *now,* that we had this manifestation of the goodness of God, "harden not your heart." The introduction of this phrase here is a prophetic allusion to the building of the Kirtland Temple and the manifestations there to be given, if the Saints would not harden their hearts.

A day of sacrifice and a day for the tithing] "Sacrifice" and "tithing" seem to be used as synonymous terms here, for the law of tithing had not yet been introduced. The law of consecration was still in force. The law of tithing was first given as the standing law of the Church on the 8th of July, 1838, at Far West.

"This event signalized the discontinuance of the United Order, which had practically been dissolved some time before * * * The law of tithing * * * bears about the same relation to the order of Enoch as the Mosaic law to the gospel of Christ" (Whitney's *Hist. of Utah,* Vol. I., p. 141).

The mention of tithing here is prophetic, indicating a restoration of that lesser law, instead of the greater.

Shall not be burned] The importance of the law of tithing is here shown. In the day of the Lord the proud and the evil-doers will be destroyed, as completely as straw in a furnace (Mal. 4:1, 2). Those who obey this law will not be counted as "straw" on that day (v. 24).

26. And it is not meet that my servants, Newel K. Whitney and Sidney Gilbert, should sell their store and their possessions here; for this is not wisdom until the residue of the church, which remaineth in this place, shall go up unto the land of Zion.

27. Behold, it is said in my laws, or forbidden, to get in debt to thine enemies;

28. But behold, it is not said at any time that the Lord should not take when he please, and pay as seemeth him good.

29. Wherefore, as ye are agents, ye are on the Lord's errand; and whatever ye do according to the will of the Lord is the Lord's business.

30. And he hath set you to provide for his saints in these last days, that they may obtain an inheritance in the land of Zion.

31. And behold, I, the Lord, declare unto you, and my words are sure and shall not fail, that they shall obtain it.

32. But all things must come to pass in their time.

33. Wherefore, be not weary in well-doing, for ye are laying the foundation of a great work. And out of small things proceedeth that which is great.

3. Regarding Debt To Enemies.

26-33. In these paragraphs Newel K. Whitney and Sidney Gilbert are warned against contracting debt with enemies. The Lord reminds them that He can take from His inexhaustible storehouse whenever He pleases, and pay the debt contracted on His behalf (v. 28). He acknowledges Whitney and Gilbert as His agents (v. 29), to conduct His business (v. 30), as long as they were acting in accordance with His instructions. But it was not His will that His people should be in debt to enemies, and they were not authorized to conduct His business on principles involving such obligations. Nor was it necessary to do so, for what God has said will surely come to pass (v. 32); wherefore they were not to be discouraged, but lay the foundations of Zion and always remember that "out of small things proceedeth that which is great" (v. 33).

34. Behold, the Lord requireth the heart and a willing mind; and the willing and obedient shall eat the good of the land of Zion in these last days.

35. And the rebellious shall be cut off out of the land of Zion, and shall be sent away, and shall not inherit the land.

36. For, verily I say that the rebellious are not of the blood of Ephraim, wherefore they shall be plucked out.

37. Behold, I, the Lord, have made my church in these last days like unto a judge sitting on a hill, or in a high place, to judge the nations.

38. For it shall come to pass that the inhabitants of Zion shall judge all things pertaining to Zion.

39. And liars and hypocrites shall be proved by them, and they who are not apostles and prophets shall be known.

40. And even the bishop, who is a judge, and his counselors, if they are not faithful in their stewardships shall be condemned, and others shall be planted in their stead.

41. For, behold, I say unto you that Zion shall flourish, and the glory of the Lord shall be upon her;

42. And she shall be an ensign unto the people, and there shall come unto her out of every nation under heaven.

43. And the day shall come when the nations of the earth shall tremble because of her, and shall fear because of her terrible ones. The Lord hath spoken it. Amen.

4. GENERAL INSTRUCTIONS.

35. *The rebellious shall be cut off*] Those who rebelled against the laws of God, including the law of consecration, were not worthy of an inheritance in Zion. The spirit of rebellion must not exist in the Church. Those afflicted with it are to be cut off.

37-42. This is a sifting dispensation. Zion must be purged and cleansed. Then she will be in a position to take her part in international affairs—to "judge the nations" (v. 37). She will also judge the affairs pertaining to Zion, and prove, that is to say, expose, liars and hypocrites and those who falsely claim to be apostles and prophets (vv. 38, 39). And the day will come when the nations—those who reject our Lord —shall fear because of Zion and her "terrible ones" (v. 43).

"Would to God that all the people were prophets! Why? Then they would all have the light of truth in them, and the knowledge of truth that would save them. If this was the case, what would be among the results? Sinners in Zion would be afraid, and fearfulness would surprise the hypocrite. Why? Because they would feel uneasy, for this simple reason: They would know that they were not honest, and they would be afraid lest they should be overtaken in their guilt" (*Jour. of Dis.*, Vol. V., p. 37).

SECTION 65.

REVELATION *given through Joseph Smith the Prophet, at Hiram, Ohio, October, 1831. The Prophet designates this revelation as a prayer.——Commitment of the keys of the kingdom of God unto man—The kingdom of God and the kingdom of Heaven named separately—Supplication that the kingdom of God, already on earth, may go forth that the kingdom of Heaven may come.*

HEARKEN, and lo, a voice as of one sent down from on high, who is mighty and powerful, whose going forth is unto the ends of the earth, yea, whose voice is unto men—Prepare ye the way of the Lord, make his paths straight.

2. The keys of the kingdom of God are committed unto man on the earth, and from thence shall the gospel roll forth unto the ends of the earth, as the stone which is cut out of the mountain without hands shall roll forth, until it has filled the whole earth.

3. Yea, a voice crying—Prepare ye the way of the Lord, prepare ye the supper of the Lamb, make ready for the Bridegroom.

4. Pray unto the Lord, call upon his holy name, make known his wonderful works among the people.

5. Call upon the Lord, that his kingdom may go forth upon the earth, that the inhabitants thereof may receive it, and be prepared for the days to come, in the which the Son of Man shall come down in heaven, clothed in the brightness of his glory, to meet the kingdom of God which is set up on the earth.

6. Wherefore, may the kingdom of God go forth, that the kingdom of heaven may come, that thou, O God, mayest be glorified in heaven so on earth, that thine enemies may be subdued; for thine is the honor, power and glory, forever and ever. Amen.

The prophet Joseph was now living at Hiram, about thirty miles south-east of Kirtland. He had gone there, on invitation of Father Johnson, in order to devote himself to his work on the Bible revision. From Sept. 12, 1831, until the first of October, he did little more than prepare to re-commence the translation of the Bible" *Hist. of the Church,* Vol. I., p. 215). What the preparations consisted in is not stated, but this Revelation, which is an inspired prayer, indicates that an important part of such preparation was communion with God in prayer.

At Hiram, several important conferences were held. There thirteen Revelations were received, including the memorable vision recorded in Section 76. There a mob, excited by the agitation of Ezra Booth, who had denied the faith and become an enemy, tried to take the life of the Prophet and Sidney Rigdon. No doubt, this Revelation came to strengthen them for the work and experiences before them. By prayer we obtain the faith which is the grasp of our immortal spirit upon the realities and verities of an unseen world. By prayer we receive strength to "walk with God" in obedience and defy the wind and waves of human opposition.

1. *Hearken, and lo, a voice as from one on high*] The prophet Joseph, in his retreat at Father Johnson's, like John on Patmos, heard a voice, and naturally turned to see where it came from (Comp. Rev. 1:10-12). This is implied in "hearken," and "lo." The voice which John heard sounded like a trumpet. That which Joseph heard was "as from one on high," a messenger from heaven. It was "mighty and powerful," like thunder, rolling forth "unto the ends of the earth." And this Revelation contains the message.

*Prepare ye the way * * * make his paths straight*] The message begins with this proclamation, quoted from Isaiah 40:3 and Malachi 3:1. The coming of the Lord is near at hand. Prayer should be preceded by a preparation for His reception. The paths must be made straight and level.

This imagery is Oriental. An Eastern ruler, anciently, when about to visit the provinces, sent a messenger to proclaim his coming and to instruct the people to be prepared to receive him. Among the preparations was road-building. Crooked paths along which he would travel were to be made straight, and uneven roads to be leveled out. Loyal subjects would comply with the instructions, and if they had favors to ask, they could present their petitions with confidence, because of their loyalty. The application is obvious. Our Lord has sent His messengers to proclaim His coming and to instruct His people to be prepared to receive Him. When we comply with His commandments and prepare for His advent, our prayers are acceptable to Him.

2. *The keys to the kingdom of God*] "Keys" signifies authority to administer the ordinances, teach the doctrines, and take part in the government of the Church. Compare Matt. 16:19. The "key" is a symbol of authority (Is. 22:22). See *Gospel Doctrine*, p. 169, edition of 1928.

From thence] From the Church, and more especially from Zion.

As the stone which is cut out of the mountains] The gospel of Jesus Christ is destined to fill the Earth, as the stone in Nebuchadnezzar's dream (Dan. 2:35). The Church will fill the Earth before the end of the Millennium, but the principles of the Gospel will roll forth, as that stone, and prevail from one end of the Earth to another. Even now, many of the truths revealed through the Prophet Joseph are being preached from pulpits in which to name him with reverence would be deemed sacrilege.

3. *Yea, a voice crying*] The Prophet seems to pause here for a moment in contemplation, until the voice resumes, "*Prepare ye the way of the Lord.*" He comes as a bridegroom. "Prepare ye the supper of the Lamb." His coming must be a festivity, a banquet.

4. *Pray unto the Lord*] While waiting for Him, pray to Him; call upon His holy name; make known His wonderful work among the people. Prayer and preaching must go together. A sermon without prayer may be a perfect specimen of homiletic effort; it may be a marvelous piece of rhetoric; it may be a correct ethical discourse, or an admirable philosophical essay; it may be amusing, entertaining, and instructive; and yet, without the power that comes from prayer, it will be barren of spiritual results.

5. *That His kingdom may go forth*] This should be the subject of our prayers. "Thy kingdom come!"

6. *That thou, O God, mayest be glorified*] This is the end and aim of the establishment of His kingdom on Earth. In the salvation of man, God is glorified.

GENERAL NOTES

Luther was at Wartburg, hidden by friends, when he began his Bible translation. The Prophet Joseph wrote a large part of his Bible revision among friends at Hiram.

Our Savior taught His disciples the prayer that has become known in every land and clime. "Our Father, who art in heaven." The central thought in this sublime address to God is, "Thy kingdom come." He closed His last celebration of the passover, with an equally sublime prayer, in which the same thought predominated (John 17). Again, in this Revelation on prayer, which the Prophet seems to have heard, the prayer is that the Kingdom of God may come.

In this Revelation the two expressions, the kingdom of God, and the kingdom of heaven, occur. The Prophet Joseph tells us that the kingdom of heaven is the Church. "The kingdom of heaven," he says, "is like unto a mustard seed. Behold, then, is not this the kingdom of heaven that is raising its head in the last days in the majesty of its God, even the Church of Latter-day Saints?" (*Hist. of the Church*, Vol. II., p. 268.) He also states that, "Where there is a prophet, a priest, or a righteous man unto whom God gives His oracles, there is the kingdom of God" (*Ibid.*, Vol. V., p. 268). The Church, then, is also the Kingdom of God. The two terms seem to be used as synonyms, but there may be this distinction between them, if a distinction it be, that the domain of God on the other side of the veil is referred to in a particular sense as the Kingdom of Heaven, while that on this side is the Church or Kingdom of God. The two constitute the Kingdom of God. One is God's Kingdom in heaven; the other is His Kingdom on Earth.

The interesting question whether all men on Earth during the Millennium will belong to the Church, is answered by Brigham Young, in the paragraph quoted on pages 147-8.

SECTION 66.

REVELATION *given through Joseph Smith the Prophet, to William E. M'Lellin, at Orange, Ohio, October 25, 1831. This was the first day of an important conference. See History of the Church, vol. 1, p. 219.——The recipient commended for his repentance and reformation—Warning against personal weaknesses and liability to specific temptation—Great achievements in righteousness, with consequent blessings, predicted on condition of devotion to the work of the ministry.*

BEHOLD, thus saith the Lord unto my servant William E. M'Lellin—Blessed are you, inasmuch as you have turned away from your iniquities, and have received my truths, saith the Lord your Redeemer, the Savior of the world, even of as many as believe on my name.

2. Verily I say unto you, blessed are you for receiving mine everlasting covenant, even the fulness of my gospel, sent forth unto the children of men, that they might have life and be made partakers of the glories which are to be revealed in the last days, as it was written by the prophets and apostles in days of old.

3. Verily I say unto you, my servant William, that you are clean, but not all; repent, therefore, of those things which are not pleasing in my sight, saith the Lord, for the Lord will show them unto you.

A conference was held at Orange, Ohio, on the 25th of October, 1931. There were present, twelve High Priests, seventeen Elders, four Priests, three Teachers, four Deacons, and a large congregation. The subject of consecration of property was considered, and many of those present expressed a willingness to give all they had for the furtherance of the cause of God. The divine presence was felt in these conferences, and where God is, parsimony is stifled. Among those present was William E. McLellin. He desired to know the will of the Lord concerning him, and, in answer to prayer, the Prophet received this Revelation, in which the Lord (1) commends him for having embraced the gospel and urges him to further repentance (1-3); (2) calls him to the ministry (4-11) and gives him a promise (12-13).

1. COMMENDATION AND ADMONITION

1. *Blessed are you*] "Blessed" means "happy." It is the same expression as that used by our Lord in the Sermon on the Mount. McLellin was happy because he had turned away from his iniquities and received the gospel.

3. *You are clean, but not all*] The Lord knew McLellin. He could see what no human eye could perceive. And when the Prophet uttered this sentence, sharp as a two-edged sword, McLellin knew, no doubt, by the testimony of his own conscience, that it was true. The word of revelation was to him a mirror in which he saw himself reflected.

4. And now, verily, I, the Lord, will show unto you what I will concerning you, or what is my will concerning you.

5. Behold, verily I say unto you, that it is my will that you should proclaim my gospel from land to land, and from city to city, yea, in those regions round about where it has not been proclaimed.

6. Tarry not many days in this place; go not up unto the land of Zion as yet; but inasmuch as you can send, send; otherwise, think not of thy property.

7. Go unto the eastern lands, bear testimony in every place, unto every people and in their synagogues, reasoning with the people.

8. Let my servant Samuel H. Smith go with you, and forsake him not, and give him thine instructions; and he that is faithful shall be made strong in every place; and I, the Lord, will go with you.

9. Lay your hands upon the sick, and they shall recover. Return not till I, the Lord, shall send you. Be patient in affliction. Ask, and ye shall receive; knock, and it shall be opened unto you.

10. Seek not to be cumbered. Forsake all unrighteousness. Commit not adultery—a temptation with which thou hast been troubled.

11. Keep these sayings, for they are true and faithful; and thou shalt magnify thine office, and push many people to Zion with songs of everlasting joy upon their heads.

2. A CALL TO THE MINISTRY.

4-11. In these paragraphs the Lord calls McLellin to the Ministry. The call includes (1) that he should send whatever money he could spare to Zion, but not to go there as yet (v. 6); (2) that he should take Samuel Smith for a companion on his mission (v. 8); (3) that he should lay his hands on the sick and heal them (v. 9); (4) that he should forsake all unrighteousness (v. 10); (5) and that he should be faithful and magnify his office (v. 11).

12. Continue in these things even unto the end, and you shall have a crown of eternal life at the right hand of my Father, who is full of grace and truth.

13. Verily, thus saith the Lord your God, your Redeemer, even Jesus Christ. Amen.

3. A PROMISE AND THE CONDITION.

12. *A crown of eternal life*] That is the promise. A crown is a costly ornament. Many crowns are worth a fortune each. But they are not merely ornaments; they are the symbols of power and excellency. Eternal life, considered as a crown, is a beautiful life, the life of a king.

Continue in these things even unto the end] Such is the condition. It is he who is faithful unto death that will have a crown of life (Rev. 2:10).

GENERAL NOTES

William E. McLellin was born in the State of Tennessee. He was about a year younger than the Prophet. Having heard Samuel H. Smith and Reynolds Cahoon preach the gospel, in the early summer of 1831, when they were on their way from Kirtland to Independence, he accompanied these two Elders, and was baptized and ordained an Elder by them. Shortly afterwards he returned to Kirtland and met the Prophet Joseph at a conference held at Orange. Later he became prominent in the Church. He was at one time a member of the first Council of Apostles. However, unfortunately for him, he did not heed the warning given in this Revelation. He fell, and on May 11th, 1838, he was severed from the Church, at Far West.

Healing the sick was part of the commission of McLellin. It was one of his special gifts. In January, 1836, important meetings were held at Kirtland and holy ordinances administered. On one of these occasions the Prophet had remarkable visions. He saw the Apostles standing in a circle, their clothes tattered and their feet swollen, and Jesus standing in their midst. He saw McLellin standing upon a hill and surrounded by a multitude, and a lame man standing before him, who was healed through the power of God. He saw Brigham Young in a strange land, in a desert place, upon a rock in the midst of about a dozen men of color, who appeared hostile, but the angel of God stood above him, though he did not see him. Finally, the Prophet saw the Twelve in the celestial kingdom of God (*Hist. of the Church*, Vol. II., p. 381).

There are two kinds of healing. One is mental; the other we may call spiritual. Mental healing is as old as the race. It is done through "suggestion," or even "auto-suggestion." The spirit within is an intelligent being and is greatly helped, in its efforts to repair tissue or withstand the attacks of adverse agencies, by the suggestion of others who have great will-power; or even by auto-suggestion. The disciples of the Pharisees cast out demons by that power, and many modern "healers" operate under the law of suggestion. This is mental healing. Spiritual healing is by the Spirit of God, through the Priesthood. It is healing effected by the

Holy Spirit imparting the strength necessary to overcome the causes of diseases, and it often operates instantaneously. Its power is circumscribed, for all men must die; but those who live so that they are receptive to the healing influences of the Holy Spirit should live to a ripe age, and then fall "asleep" in sweet slumber, conscious of the beginning of a new life in the morning of the resurrection. Spiritual healing is divine healing. It is part of the gospel. Mental healing is human. It is good in its place, but it is not part of the gospel any more than common therapeutics, or surgery.

SECTION 67.

REVELATION *given through Joseph Smith the Prophet, at Hiram, Ohio, November, 1831. The occasion was that of a special conference, and the publication of the revelations already received from the Lord through Joseph Smith the Prophet was considered and acted upon. See heading to Section 1. Many of the brethren bore solemn testimony that the revelations then compiled for publication are verily true as was witnessed unto them by the Holy Ghost shed forth upon them. The Prophet records that after the revelation known as Section 1 had been received, some conversation was had concerning revelations and language. The present revelation followed.——The Lord affirms the truth of the commandments—Secret ambitions of some there present to express themselves in language superior to that of the revelations exposed—The Lord's challenge to even the wisest to imitate the least of the revelations.*

BEHOLD and hearken, O ye elders of my church, who have assembled yourselves together, whose prayers I have heard, and whose hearts I know, and whose desires have come up before me.

2. Behold and lo, mine eyes are upon you, and the heavens and the earth are in mine hands, and the riches of eternity are mine to give.

A special conference was held at Hiram, Ohio, on the first day of November, 1831. Oliver Cowdery and John Whitmer were making preparations for the journey to Independence, where the Revelations received up to this time were to be published, and the brethren devoted a great deal of time to the consideration of this important undertaking. The conference authorized the printing of ten thousand copies under the title of the *Book of Commandments.* The Revelation contained in Section 1, and known as *The Lord's Preface* to the Book of Commandments (Sec. 1:6) was also received on this occasion. The Prophet asked what testimony those present were willing to bear to the Commandments. Several declared that they were willing to testify that they were of the Lord. On the second day of the Conference, Oliver Cowdery read *The Lord's Preface,* and then the brethren arose, and each in turn testified to the truth of all of the Revelations received (*Hist. of the Church,* Vol. I., p. 222).

However, there was not perfect harmony among the brethren. A few criticized the language found in some of the Revelations. They forgot that the spirit of God uses as they are, the instruments through which He communicates with man, just as an author, when writing, makes use of whatever pen, paper, and ink he may be able to obtain. They forgot that God calls to the prophetic office men as He finds them, be it behind the plough, among the sheep, in the royal courts, or the study of the scholar.

Some of the brethren did not fully realize that divine inspiration is independent of university education, and they were wavering in their faith. The Lord, therefore, gave this Revelation in which He (1) assured them of His presence (1-2); (2) gave the reasons why blessings are withheld (3); (3) offered them a test of the divine origin the Revelations received (4-9); and (4) closed with promises and admonitions (10-14).

1. An Assurance of the Divine Presence.

1. *Behold, and hearken*] Our Lord assured the Elders assembled at this important Conference that He had heard their prayers; that He knew their hearts, and that His eyes were upon them (v. 2). He was in their midst and demanded their attention: "Behold and hearken!" Attention to the Word of God is of the utmost importance. There can be no faith without it. Without intelligent attention we find no charm in the singing of birds, no delight in the exquisite form and sweet fragrance of flowers, no inspiration in the grandeur of nature, and no appreciation of the gifts God bestows upon us and, consequently, no faith on, no love of, the Giver. God demands our attention, as a father or a teacher demands the attention of the children. Why should mortals pay attention to His Word? Because He has "the riches of eternity" to *give,* not to sell.

3. Ye endeavored to believe that ye should receive the blessing which was offered unto you; but behold, verily I say unto you there were fears in your hearts, and verily this is the reason that ye did not receive.

2. WHY BLESSINGS ARE WITHHELD.

3. *There were fears in your hearts*] The assembled Elders, or some of them, failed to receive a blessing which they had expected. What that blessing was is not stated. It might have been a special manifestation concerning the *Book of Commandments* (v. 4); or, some miraculous manifestation after the laying on of hands by the Prophet (v. 14). But whatever it was, some had failed to receive what they expected, and the reason is here stated: they lacked faith, and were consequently, dominated by fear.

4. And now I, the Lord, give unto you a testimony of the truth of these commandments which are lying before you.

5. Your eyes have been upon my servant Joseph Smith, Jun., and his language you have known, and his imperfections you have known; and you have sought in your hearts knowledge that you might express beyond his language; this you also know.

6. Now, seek ye out of the Book of Commandments, even the least that is among them, and appoint him that is the most wise among you;

7. Or, if there be any among you that shall make one like unto it, then ye are justified in saying that ye do not know that they are true;

8. But if ye cannot make one like unto it, ye are under condemnation if ye do not bear record that they are true.

9. For ye know that there is no unrighteousness in them, and that which is righteous cometh down from above, from the Father of lights.

3. A TEST OF DIVINE INSPIRATION.

4. *A testimony of the truth*] To those who have failed to receive the manifestation expected (v. 3) and, therefore, were tempted to doubt, the Lord offered the test stated in vv. 5-8.

5-8. The *Book of Commandments* was before the Conference, in manuscript. Any Church member might examine it and select the Revelation which might be considered the least (v. 6). Then the wisest among them might be appointed to compose one like it; if he succeeded, the Saints would be justified in concluding that the book was of no higher than human origin (v. 7); if he failed, they would be under obligation to accept it as divinely inspired, and to bear testimony to the truth of it (v. 8).

9. *No unrighteousness in them*] This is an additional test. None of the Revelations contains anything that has a tendency to produce unrighteousness, or to condone it. On the contrary, by obedience to them righteousness is promoted among the children of men. As Truth, by the appearance of the Book of Mormon, sprang out of the Earth, so Righteousness, in these Revelations, looked down from heaven (Psalm 85:11); for "that which is righteous cometh down from above" (v. 9).

Wm. E. McLellin accepted the offer and, in a spirit of presumption, undertook to imitate the Revelations of the Lord. His effort to produce a Revelation was witnessed with great interest by the Elders, and when they became aware of his complete failure, all doubt concerning the Revelations of God vanished, and they signified their willingness to testify of their truth. Accordingly, a document containing their testimony was drawn up and given to the world (*Hist. of the Church*, Vol. I., p. 226; see also the Introduction to this Volume, pp. 15-17).

10. And again, verily I say unto you that it is your privilege, and a promise I give unto you that have been ordained unto this ministry, that inasmuch as you strip yourselves from jealousies and fears, and humble yourselves before me, for ye are not sufficiently humble, the veil shall be rent and you shall see me and know that I am—not with the carnal neither natural mind, but with the spiritual.

11. For no man has seen God at any time in the flesh, except quickened by the Spirit of God.

12. Neither can any natural man abide the presence of God, neither after the carnal mind.

13. Ye are not able to abide the presence of God now, neither the ministering of angels; wherefore, continue in patience until ye are perfected.

14. Let not your minds turn back; and when ye are worthy, in mine own due time, ye shall see and know that which was conferred upon you by the hands of my servant Joseph Smith, Jun. Amen.

4. DIVINE PROMISES AND ADMONITIONS.

10. *You shall see me and know that I AM*] This is a promise which no man could have given with the hope of fulfilling it. But it was fulfilled. On the evening of the first day of the dedication of the Kirtland Temple, there was a gathering of Elders, numbering over four hundred, and many of them testified that they had visions. They heard a sound of a mighty wind. "Almost every man in the house," one report says, "arose, and

hundreds of them were speaking in tongues, prophesying and declaring visions, almost with one voice" (*Jour. of Dis.*, Vol. XI., p. 10). Frederick G. Williams testified that he saw the Savior on that occasion.

Not with the carnal mind, etc.] Visions of our Lord are not perceived with the outward eye, or reflected in the natural mind, but with the spiritual eye. There is a spirit within, whose range of vision is limited by the capacity of physical organs, so that it can neither see nor hear that which lies beyond the boundaries of what we call "matter," but when the veil is lifted, the spirit can perceive the spiritual world.

12-13. But such a temporary removal of the veil is only partial. Natural man cannot see God, or abide in His presence, nor in the presence of angels, unless he be "quickened" by the Spirit of God. Comp. Dan. 10:7-10; 1. Cor. 13:12; Rev. 1:17.

GENERAL NOTES

Miraculous manifestations do not keep men from falling away. Referring to some of the Elders who had seen great visions, Elder George A. Smith asks:

"Where are those men? A number of men who manifested the greatest gifts, and had the greatest manifestations have fallen out by the wayside. You look around you, and they are not here. Many who received the knowledge of the things of God by the power of His Spirit, and sought not after signs and wonders, and when the Spirit rested upon them, it seemed to produce no visible demonstration—you look around among the Saints in the Valleys of the Mountains, and you find they are here with us, bearing on high the standard of Zion, or have descended into honorable graves" (*Jour. of Dis.*, Vol. XI., p. 10).

According to the order of the kingdom of God, there is only one man appointed at any one time to receive revelations for the Church. McLellin, had he been faithful and humble, might have received revelations for himself, though not for the Church. On this subject Heber C. Kimball observes:

"Oliver Cowdery received revelations and wrote them; so did David Whitmer, and so did Thomas B. Marsh. About the time he was preparing to leave this Church, he received a Revelation in the printing office. He retired to himself, and prayed, and was humble, and God gave him a Revelation, and he wrote it. There were from three to five pages of it; and, when it came out, he read it to Brother Brigham and me. In it God told him what to do, and that was to sustain Brother Joseph and to believe that what Brother Joseph had said was true" (*Jour. of Dis.*, Vol. V., p. 28).

SECTION 68.

REVELATION *given through Joseph Smith the Prophet, at Hiram, Ohio, November, 1831, concerning Orson Hyde, Luke S. Johnson, Lyman E. Johnson, and William E. M'Lellin. This was given in response to supplication that the mind of the Lord be made known concerning the Elders named.——Utterances of men ordained to the Holy Priesthood when they speak as moved upon by the Holy Ghost designated as Scripture—Ordination of additional Bishops foreshadowed—Right of literal descendants of Aaron—High Priests may be ordained Bishops—Duties of parents respecting their children, particularly as to the teaching of the principles of the Gospel—Observance of the Sabbath as a holy day—Idleness and greed for worldly things condemned.*

MY servant, Orson Hyde, was called by his ordination to proclaim the everlasting gospel, by the Spirit of the living God, from people to people, and from land to land, in the congregations of the wicked, in their synagogues, reasoning with and expounding all scriptures unto them.

2. And, behold, and lo, this is an ensample unto all those who were ordained unto this priesthood, whose mission is appointed unto them to go forth—

3. And this is the ensample unto them, that they shall speak as they are moved upon by the Holy Ghost.

4. And whatsoever they shall speak when moved upon by the Holy Ghost shall be scripture, shall be the will of the Lord, shall be the mind of the Lord, shall be the word of the Lord, shall be the voice of the Lord, and the power of God unto salvation.

5. Behold, this is the promise of the Lord unto you, O ye my servants.

5. Wherefore, be of good cheer, and do not fear, for I the Lord am with you, and will stand by you; and ye shall bear record of me, even Jesus Christ, that I am the Son of the living God, that I was, that I am, and that I am to come.

7. This is the word of the Lord unto you, my servant Orson

Hyde, and also unto my servant Luke Johnson, and unto my servant Lyman Johnson, and unto my servant William E. M'Lellin, and unto all the faithful elders of my church—

8. Go ye into all the world, preach the gospel to every creature, acting in the authority which I have given you, baptizing in the name of the Father, and of the Son, and of the Holy Ghost.

9. And he that believeth and is baptized shall be saved, and he that believeth not shall be damned.

10. And he that believeth shall be blest with signs following, even as it is written.

11. And unto you it shall be given to know the signs of the times, and the signs of the coming of the Son of Man;

12. And of as many as the Father shall bear record, to you shall be given power to seal them up unto eternal life. Amen.

Elders Orson Hyde, Luke S. Johnson, Lyman E. Johnson, and William E. M'Lellin being anxious to learn the will of God concerning them, the Prophet inquired and received this Revelation. It is divided into two main parts. The first (1-12) contains directions to the Elders mentioned and to all who are called to the ministry. The second (13-35) contains (a) instructions on the Bishopric (13-24); (b) on the duty of parents toward their children (25-28); (c) on the Sabbath (29-30) and (d) rebuke and commandments (31-35).

1. DIRECTIONS CONCERNING THE MINISTRY.

1. *Orson Hyde*] He was born January 8th, 1805, at Oxford, Conn. At the age of fourteen he came to Ohio, and was, a few years later, engaged as clerk in the store of Gilbert and Whitney. In 1827 he joined the Methodists. Then he accepted the Campbellite creed. When Oliver Cowdery and his companions, on their mission to the Lamanites, came to Kirtland with the gospel message, he embraced it, was baptized, and, shortly afterwards, was ordained a High Priest. In company with Hyrum Smith he performed a mission among the Campbellites and organized several branches.

The prophecy in this verse was literally fulfilled. Orson Hyde proclaimed the gospel "from people to people, from land to land." In 1832, he and Samuel H. Smith traveled in the States of New York, Massachusetts, Maine, and Rhode Island—two thousand miles—on foot. In 1835 he was ordained an Apostle, and in 1837 he went on a mission to England. In 1840 he was sent on a mission to Jerusalem. He crossed the Ocean, traveled through England and Germany, visited Constantinople, Cairo, and Alexandria, and, finally, reached the Holy City. On October 24th, 1841, he went up on the Mount of Olives and offered a prayer, dedicating Palestine for the gathering of the Jews.

3. *They shall speak as they are moved upon*] The ministers of the gospel of Jesus Christ must be "in tune with" the Holy Spirit. They may gather information from all pure sources, but they must rely on the Spirit of God to bring forth, from that which has been stored up, the instructions needed on each particular occasion.

4. *Shall be Scripture*] Whatever is thus spoken, or written, by the inspiration of the Holy Spirit is authoritative.

6. *Ye shall bear record of me*] This is the very essence of the message of the Elders of the Church. They are sent into the world, to testify of the Lord Jesus Christ, not to speak of themselves. Their mission is to tell the world that He is the Son of God; to bear witness of His work in the past, as the One to whom God, our Father, entrusted the plan of Salvation; of His present work in carrying out that plan; and of His future exaltation and glory, when He comes into His kingdom. This embraces the entire message of the Elders.

7-12. This section contains the commission to all Elders in the ministry. It is their duty to go to every part of the world (v. 8) and preach the gospel to every "creature"; i.e., to every human being. No one stands so low down in the scale of civilization, or is so degraded, that he is not one of God's creatures. The gospel message is for him, or her. Those who believe and repent are to be baptized, and signs will follow faith. Comp. Mark 16:15-18.

Two special promises are given to the faithful Elders; one is this that they shall know the "signs of the coming of the Son of Man" (v. 11). To many, wars, pestilence, famine, and commotion among the nations are but ordinary events of history, but to the Saints they are "signs" indicating the advent of our Savior. They read these signs, as the navigator reads the indications of the sky or the meaning of the lights that pass his view at night. Another promise is this that they shall have authority to "seal up to eternal life" as many as the Father shall indicate to them (v. 12).

Luke Johnson] He was born November 3rd, 1807, and was baptized May 10th, 1831, by the Prophet Joseph. On February 14th, 1835, he was ordained an Apostle. He was one of the prominent men who fell away in 1838, but he repented and was re-instated in the Church in 1846. In 1847 he came to Salt Lake Valley. In 1858 he was appointed Bishop of St. John's Ward, Tooele County. He died in Salt Lake City, at the home of Orson Hyde, December 9th, 1861.

Lyman Johnson] He was a brother of Luke Johnson. He was born October 24th, 1811, and baptized in February, 1834, by Sidney Rigdon. He performed successful missions, went with Zion's Camp to Missouri, and was ordained an Apostle, February 14th, 1835. He, too, was disfellowshiped in 1838, but remained friendly to his former associates in the Church. He lost his life by drowning, in the Mississippi River, December 20th, 1856.

Luke S. and Lyman E. Johnson were sons of John Johnson, at whose home in Hiram the Prophet found the welcome hospitality that enabled him to attend to his study of the Bible and to other important work for the Church.

M'Lellin] See Sec. 66. M'Lellin, unlike the Johnson brothers, became a bitter enemy of the Prophet Joseph and the Church, when he fell by the wayside. In 1838 he confessed before a Bishop's court at Far West that he had ceased praying and keeping the commandments of the Lord, but, when he was disfellowshiped, he, nevertheless, tried to establish a church of his own. Failing in this, he took an active part in the persecution by which the Saints were driven from Missouri (*Hist. Record,* p. 38).

13. And now, concerning the items in addition to the covenants and commandments, they are these—

14. There remain hereafter, in the due time of the Lord, other bishops to be set apart unto the church, to minister even according to the first;

15. Wherefore they shall be high priests who are worthy, and they shall be appointed by the First Presidency of the Melchizedek Priesthood, except they be literal descendants of Aaron.

16. And if they be literal descendants of Aaron they have a legal right to the bishopric, if they are the firstborn among the sons of Aaron;

17. For the firstborn holds the right of the presidency over this priesthood, and the keys or authority of the same.

18. No man has a legal right to this office, to hold the keys of this priesthood, except he be a literal descendant and the firstborn of Aaron.

19. But, as a high priest of the Melchizedek Priesthood has authority to officiate in all the lesser offices he may officiate in the office of bishop when no literal descendant of Aaron can be found, provided he is called and set apart and ordained unto this power, under the hands of the First Presidency of the Melchizedek Priesthood.

20. And a literal descendant of Aaron, also, must be designated by this Presidency, and found worthy, and anointed, and ordained under the hands of this Presidency, otherwise they are not legally authorized to officiate in their priesthood.

21. But, by virtue of the decree concerning their right of the priesthood descending from father to son, they may claim their anointing if at any time they can prove their lineage, or do ascertain it by revelation from the Lord under the hands of the above named Presidency.

22. And again, no bishop or high priest who shall be set apart for this ministry shall be tried or condemned for any crime, save it be before the First Presidency of the church;

23. And inasmuch as he is found guilty before this Presidency, by testimony that cannot be impeached, he shall be condemned;

24. And if he repent he shall be forgiven, according to the covenants and commandments of the church.

25. And again, inasmuch as parents have children in Zion, or in any of her stakes which are organized, that teach them not to understand the doctrine of repentance, faith in Christ the Son of the living God, and of baptism and the gift of the Holy Ghost by the laying on of the hands, when eight years old, the sin be upon the heads of the parents.

26. For this shall be a law unto the inhabitants of Zion, or in any of her stakes which are organized.

27. And their children shall be baptized for the remission of their sins when eight years old, and receive the laying on of the hands.

28. And they shall also teach their children to pray, and to walk uprightly before the Lord.

29. And the inhabitants of Zion shall also observe the Sabbath day to keep it holy.

30. And the inhabitants of Zion also shall remember their labors, inasmuch as they are appointed to labor, in all faithfulness; for the idler shall be had in remembrance before the Lord.

31. Now, I, the Lord, am not well pleased with the inhabitants of Zion, for there are idlers among them; and their children are also growing up in wickedness; they also seek not earnestly the riches of eternity, but their eyes are full of greediness.

32. These things ought not to be, and must be done away

from among them; wherefore, let my servant Oliver Cowdery carry these sayings unto the land of Zion.

33. And a commandment I give unto them—that he that observeth not his prayers before the Lord in the season thereof, let him be had in remembrance before the judge of my people.

34. These sayings are true and faithful; wherefore, transgress them not, neither take therefrom.

35. Behold, I am Alpha and Omega, and I come quickly. Amen.

2. INSTRUCTIONS ON VARIOUS TOPICS.

(a) On the Bishopric.

13-24. In these paragraphs the Lord gives instructions regarding the appointment of Bishops. Edward Partridge was the first Bishop appointed (Sec. 41:9). Other Bishops were to be called in due time (v. 14). It was, therefore, necessary to have instructions concerning their appointment. Isaac Morley and John Corrill, who had been Bishop Partridge's counselors, were selected as second and third Bishops respectively. Morley was to select Christian Whitmer and Newel Knight for his counselors; and Corrill, Daniel Stanton and Hezekiah Peck (*Hist. of the Church*, Vol. I., p. 363).

Bishops must be High Priests, and they must be *worthy;* they must be appointed by the First Presidency of the Melchizedek Priesthood, unless they are literal descendants of Aaron (v. 15); in which case, if they are firstborn, they have a right to the Bishopric, as heirs; but even a lineal descendant of Aaron must be designated, found worthy, anointed, and ordained by the First Presidency (v. 20); any High Priest of the Melchizedek Priesthood may officiate in the Bishopric, if he is called, ordained, and set apart by the First Presidency.

The Bishop, with his counselors, is the head of the *Ward,* under the direction of the President of the *Stake,* of which the Ward is an ecclesiastical division. He presides over the Aaronic Priesthood.

"You may see him in charge of the Sunday Sacrament meetings, the fast meetings, and the Priesthood meetings. He is to be seen at the Quorum meetings, at the Sabbath school, and at the Young People's Mutual Improvement meetings—and at all times observing what is going on, and often giving instruction and counsel. His official duties require him to visit the homes of the members, administering comfort and blessing to the sick and needy, and encouragement to all; besides this, he mingles freely with the people in a social way. On account of this constant paternal watch-care over all, he is affectionately styled 'the father of the Ward.'" Joseph B. Keeler, *First Steps in Church Government,* p. 13).

One of the prerogatives of the office of the *Presiding Bishop* is, that the incumbent can be tried only before the First Presidency of the Church (vv. 22-4).

(b) On the Duty of Parents Toward Children.

25-8. Many people in the world consider that they have done their full duty to their children, when they have given them shelter, food, clothing, and education, and accumulated property for them to inherit. But Latter-day Saints have a still more important duty, as parents. They must teach their children, when they are eight years old, the doctrines of the gospel—faith, repentance, baptism, and the gift of the Holy Ghost (v. 25). It is not enough to send them to Primaries, Sunday-schools, and day-schools. The parents themselves have a personal duty to perform as teachers of their children. They must see to it that the little ones are baptized at the age of eight years (v. 27), and that they are taught to pray and walk uprightly before the Lord (v. 28). If parents will do this, they will be blessed. God says of Abraham, that "he shall surely become a great and mighty nation * * * for I know him, that he will command his children and his household after him, and they shall keep the way of the Lord, to do justice and judgment" (Gen. 18:17-19). God could make Abraham the head of a numerous posterity, because of his faithfulness in teaching his children to keep the commandments.

"Now, my brethren and sisters, will you try to take care of your children, and look after them on the Sabbath day, see where they are, bring them to meeting and teach them something they do not know? I recollect, when on my mission in England, I visited a number of my relatives there. They were what we might call sectarian; they did not believe the true gospel * * * but when the Sabbath day came, their children were called in, and if they did not go to meeting, they were taught to take a book and read, and the parents sat down and taught them and they read by turns and explained passages of Scripture and history, and they talked to and instructed one another, and thus they spent the day, and when evening came the children had learned something, their minds were improved, and they were better than when the day began" (Joseph F. Smith, *Jour. of Dis.,* Vol. XIV., p. 286).

(c) On the Sabbath.

29-30. See Sec. 59:9, 12. The inhabitants of Zion are commanded to observe the Sabbath; but also to work on other days. They were members of one family, and if one of them shirked his duties, the others would be imposed upon to that extent. Idlers were to be "had in remembrance before the Lord"; their case was to be handled in the Church courts. "Joseph Smith never tolerated in the least indolence, idleness, slothfulness, drunkenness, or anything of the kind wherein exists sin" (Brigham Young, *Jour. of Dis.,* Vol. X., p. 364)

(d) *Rebuke and Commandments.*

31-5. The Lord found idlers in Zion; also children growing up in wickedness, and Church members who thought more of money than of the riches of eternity (v. 31). These things He condemned (v. 32). He also found those who did not pray regularly; they were to be dealt with by the Church (v. 33).

GENERAL NOTES

Speaking of the authority of Bishops, President Brigham Young says:
"Now and then one believes that he has a right, when ordained a Bishop, to officiate and preside over every temporal and spiritual interest in his district, by virtue of the Bishopric; he believes that he ought to go into a Seventies' Council in his Ward and preside because he is a Bishop; and under this impression he dictates, guides, and directs all things in his district; he baptizes, confirms, and administers the Sacrament as a Bishop, performing, under this impression, every spiritual and temporal duty. * * * The duties and powers of a Bishop cease the very moment he steps over the Aaronic Priesthood, which is to officiate in temporal things; when he passes this, he immediately begins to officiate by the authority and power of the Melchizedek Priesthood, though he may not know it" (*Jour. of Dis.,* Vol. X., p. 96).

From the Sixth Chapter of Acts we may gather what the duties of a Bishop in the Church are. There we read that, when the disciples multiplied, a complaint was made that the widows of men of Grecian descent were discriminated against in the daily distribution of supplies. The Twelve, therefore, suggested that seven men be appointed to attend to this business, since it was not meet that they themselves, should leave the Word of God and serve at the tables, where the contributions were placed. Accordingly, seven men were chosen and ordained to have charge of the temporal affairs of the Church. Bible commentators generally refer to these seven men as "Deacons," but without sufficient grounds. They were, rather, Bishops (*Episcopoi*). Stephen, the powerful preacher and first martyr of the Church, was one of them. Philip, also a mighty witness for the Lord and a successful missionary, was another.

In this Revelation important instructions are given to parents concerning their children. Children are a precious gift of God, and should be taken care of as such. And yet, in the world there are those who advocate —perhaps for so-called eugenic reasons—the limitation of child-birth, while others are guilty of practices that should be classed as infanticide. The Latter-day Saints have been taught that "some of the most noble spirits are waiting with the Father to this day, to come forth through the right channel and the right kind of men and women," and that "there are thousands, and millions, of spirits waiting to obtain bodies upon this Earth" (Heber C. Kimball, *Jour. of Dis.,* Vol. V., p. 92). The Latter-day Saints know, therefore, that it depends largely upon parents whether the spirits to whom they give bodies of their own flesh and blood will be able to profit to the fullest extent by their experience on Earth. To the immortal spirits waiting for an opportunity to pass through mortality, a body bred on the principles that obtain in the production of race horses, or meat for the table, is of infinitely less importance than a tabernacle morally pure, in which the Spirit of God can dwell.

On the subject of the rearing of children, President Brigham Young on one occasion made these pertinent remarks:

"Kind words and loving actions towards children, will subdue their uneducated natures a great deal better than the rod, or, in other words, than physical punishment, although it is written that 'The rod and reproof give wisdom, but a child left to himself bringeth his mother to shame'; and, 'He that spareth the rod hateth his son, but he that loveth him chastens him betimes.' These quotations refer to wise and prudent corrections. Children who have lived in the sunbeams of parental kindness and affection, when made aware of a parent's displeasure, and receiving kind reproof from parental lips, are more thoroughly chastened than by any physical punishment that could be applied to their persons. * * * When children are reared under the rod * * * it not infrequently occurs, that they become so stupefied and lost to every hightoned feeling and sentiment that though you bray them in a mortar among wheat, with a pestle, yet will not their foolishness depart from them" (*Jour. of Dis.,* Vol. X., p. 360-1).

SECTION 69.

REVELATION *given through Joseph Smith the Prophet, at Hiram, Ohio, November, 1831. The compilation of revelations intended for early publication had been passed upon at the special conference of November 1st. On the 3rd the revelation herein appearing as Section 133 was added to the Doctrine and Covenants, and called the Appendix. By action of the conference, Oliver Cowdery was appointed to carry the manuscript of the compiled revelations and commandments to Independence, Missouri, for printing. He was also to take with him moneys that had been contributed for the building up of the Church in Missouri. The course of travel would lead him through a sparsely settled country to the frontier. A traveling companion was desirable. See History of the Church, vol. 1, p. 234.——John Whitmer to accompany Oliver Cowdery, for the latter's safety and sake—John Whitmer to continue his duties as historian and recorder—Reports and accounts from the traveling Elders to be forwarded to the land of Zion, of which Independence, Missouri, was the center place.*

HEARKEN unto me, saith the Lord your God, for my servant Oliver Cowdery's sake. It is not wisdom in me that he should be entrusted with the commandments and the moneys which he shall carry unto the land of Zion, except one go with him who will be true and faithful.

2. Wherefore, I, the Lord, will that my servant, John Whitmer, should go with my servant Oliver Cowdery;

3. And also that he shall continue in writing and making a history of all the important things which he shall observe and know concerning my church;

4. And also that he receive counsel and assistance from my servant Oliver Cowdery and others.

5. And also, my servants who are abroad in the earth should send forth the accounts of their stewardships to the land of Zion;

6. For the land of Zion shall be a seat and a place to receive and do all these things.

7. Nevertheless, let my servant John Whitmer travel many times from place to place, and from church to church, that he may the more easily obtain knowledge—

8. Preaching and expounding, writing, copying, selecting, and obtaining all things which shall be for the good of the church, and for the rising generations that shall grow up on the land of Zion, to possess it from generation to generation, forever and ever. Amen.

At the Conference held at Hiram, November 1st and 2nd, 1831, it had been decided that Oliver Cowdery should take the *Commandments and Revelations, in manuscript,* to Independence, Mo., and publish them there; also that the Prophet should dedicate the work to God. After the dedicatory prayer, he received this Revelation, in which he was instructed to send John Whitmer with Oliver Cowdery, and charge him (Whitmer) to continue his labors as Church Historian.

1. *It is not wisdom * * * except one go with him*] Notwithstanding the fact that Oliver Cowdery finally yielded to the temptation to greed,

leaving his high and holy calling for that of law-practice, there is no reason to believe that the Prophet at this time had any reason not to trust him with the funds necessary for the publication of the Revelations. But, as Elder B. H. Roberts points out (*Hist. of the Church,* Vol. I., p. 234), the journey from Kirtland to Independence, through a sparsely settled frontier country, was full of dangers for a lonely traveler carrying money or valuables; for that reason the Lord instructed the Prophet to send John Whitmer with him.

3. *Continue * * * making a history*] John Whitmer was to continue his labor as historian. The historical records of the Church are exceedingly valuable documents, and, as years go by, they increase in historical value to the entire world. In the Records of the Church Historians will always be found reliable sources of information concerning the Church. Other historians either ignore the Church or write about it from a prejudiced, or even hostile, point of view. But for the conscientious labor of the Church Historians, there would be no Church history; only tradition and myth.

SECTION 70.

REVELATION *given through Joseph Smith the Prophet, at Kirtland, Ohio, November, 1831. The documentary history written by the Prophet states that four special conferences were held from the 1st to the 12th of November, inclusive. In the last of these assemblies the great importance of the Book of Commandments, later called the Doctrine and Covenants, was considered; and the Prophet refers to it as being the foundation of the Church in these last days, and a benefit to the world, showing that the keys of the mysteries of the kingdom of our Savior are again entrusted to man. See History of the Church, vol. 1, p. 235.——Management of printing and distributing the books entrusted to the Prophet and the other Elders named—Any surplus means accruing from the undertaking to be consecrated for the benefit of the Church—Provision to be made for the temporal support of the ministry—The diligent laborer worthy of his hire, whether appointed to temporal or spiritual duties.*

BEHOLD, and hearken, O ye inhabitants of Zion, and all ye people of my church who are afar off, and hear the word of the Lord which I give unto my servant Joseph Smith, Jun., and also unto my servant Martin Harris, and also unto my servant

Oliver Cowdery, and also unto my servant John Whitmer, and also unto my servant Sidney Rigdon, and also unto my servant William W. Phelps, by the way of commandment unto them.

2. For I give unto them a commandment; wherefore hearken and hear, for thus saith the Lord unto them—

3. I, the Lord, have appointed them, and ordained them to be stewards over the revelations and commandments which I have given unto them, and which I shall hereafter give unto them;

4. And an account of this stewardship will I require of them in the day of judgment.

5. Wherefore, I have appointed unto them, and this is their business in the church of God, to manage them and the concerns thereof, yea, the benefits thereof.

This Revelation also contains instructions concerning the publication of the book of *Commandments and Revelations*. At the Conference held at Hiram, November 12th, 1831, the Saints, by vote, expressed their appreciation of that work, whereupon the Prophet suggested that Oliver Cowdery and John Whitmer, who were about to leave for Independence with the priceless manuscript (Sec. 69:1, 2), be dedicated to the Lord by prayer. He also suggested that the Church grant Sidney Rigdon, Oliver Cowdery, Martin Harris, and himself some compensation for their labors in the Church. "I feel," said he, "that it will be according to the mind of the Spirit, for by IT these things were put into my heart which I know to be the Spirit of Truth." The Conference decided that the Prophet should dedicate the manuscript and the two Elders who had charge of it; also that Joseph Smith, Oliver Cowdery, John Whitmer, and Sidney Rigdon be appointed a committee to manage the publication in accordance with the laws of the Church and the commandments of God; and, further, that the families of Joseph Smith, Hyrum Smith, Peter Whitmer, Christian Whitmer, Jacob Whitmer, Hiram Page, and David Whitmer, who had administered to their wants, and also Samuei H. Smith, Peter Whitmer, Jr., William Smith, and Don Carlos Smith, for labor performed, be remembered to the Bishop in Zion as worthy of inheritances there. See *Hist. of the Church,* Vol. I., pp. 235-6.

It was about this time that the Revelation in the present Section was received, in which our Lord (1) appoints a committee to manage the business connected with the printing of the *Commandments and Revelations* (1-5); (2) instructs this committee concerning the disposition of the proceeds (6-14); and (3) assures them of His favor (15-18).

1. STEWARDS APPOINTED.

1-5. To the committee appointed by the Conference the Lord adds the names of Martin Harris and W. W. Phelps (v. 1). It was an important

position, for the Lord would ask them for an account of their stewardship in the day of judgment.

6. Wherefore, a commandment I give unto them, that they
shall not give these things unto the church, neither unto the
world;

7. Nevertheless, inasmuch as they receive more than is needful for their necessities and their wants, it shall be given into my
storehouse;

8. And the benefits shall be consecrated unto the inhabitants
of Zion, and unto their generations, inasmuch as they become
heirs according to the laws of the kingdom.

9. Behold, this is what the Lord requires of every man in
his stewardship, even as I, the Lord, have appointed or shall
hereafter appoint unto any man.

10. And behold, none are exempt from this law who belong
to the church of the living God;

11. Yea, neither the bishop, neither the agent who keepeth
the Lord's storehouse, neither he who is appointed in a stewardship over temporal things.

12. He who is appointed to administer spiritual things, the
same is worthy of his hire, even as those who are appointed to
a stewardship to administer in temporal things;

13. Yea, even more abundantly, which abundance is multiplied unto them through the manifestations of the Spirit.

14. Nevertheless, in your temporal things you shall be equal,
and this not grudgingly, otherwise the abundance of the manifestations of the Spirit shall be withheld.

2. CONCERNING THE PROCEEDS.

6-14. As to the "benefits," these were not to be given to the Church
entirely, nor to the world (v. 6), but if more were realized than the
Elders in charge needed, the surplus was to be turned over to the Lord's
storehouse (v. 7), and thus become a perpetual benefit to the inhabitants
of Zion (v. 8). The business part was, in other words, to be conducted
in accordance with the Law of God relating to the United Order. According to that Law, all share alike; one who administers in spiritual
things is "worthy of his hire" (v. 12) equal with one who manages some
business, though the world generally rates business ability higher than
spiritual excellence. "In your temporal things you shall be equal" (v. 14).
That is the law of the Kingdom of God.

15. Now, this commandment I give unto my servants for their benefit while they remain, for a manifestation of my blessings upon their heads, and for a reward of their diligence and for their security;

16. For food and for raiment; for an inheritance; for houses and for lands, in whatsoever circumstances I, the Lord, shall place them, and whithersoever I, the Lord, shall send them.

17. For they have been faithful over many things, and have done well inasmuch as they have not sinned.

18. Behold, I, the Lord, am merciful and will bless them, and they shall enter into the joy of these things. Even so. Amen.

3. An Assurance of Divine Favor.

15-18. In these paragraphs the Lord says that this commandment (concerning the stewardship of the Elders named in verse 1) was given as a manifestation, or token, of God's willingness to bless them with temporal blessings, as well as spiritual (v. 16). To those who receive temporal blessings from the Lord, and acknowledge His hand in everything, there is joy in the possession of those things; for the Earth, and the fulness thereof, are the Lord's, the same as the heavens and their fulness. Those who can enjoy heaven can enjoy the Earth, also.

SECTION 71.

REVELATION *given to Joseph Smith the Prophet and Sidney Rigdon, at Hiram, Ohio, December 1, 1831. The Prophet had resumed the translation of the Scriptures with Sidney Rigdon as his scribe; and the two so labored until this revelation was received.——Circumstances of the times required that the two devote themselves to travel and preaching for a season—To meet the opponents of the Church, both in public and in private— To bear testimony of the commandments that have been received and in preparation for others yet to come.*

BEHOLD, thus saith the Lord unto you my servants Joseph Smith, Jun., and Sidney Rigdon, that the time has verily come that it is necessary and expedient in me that you should open your mouths in proclaiming my gospel, the things of the kingdom, expounding the mysteries thereof out of the scriptures, according to that portion of Spirit and power which shall be given unto you, even as I will.

2. Verily I say unto you, proclaim unto the world in the regions round about, and in the church also, for the space of a season, even until it shall be made known unto you.

3. Verily this is a mission for a season, which I give unto you.

4. Wherefore, labor ye in my vineyard. Call upon the inhabitants of the earth, and bear record, and prepare the way for the commandments and revelations which are to come.

5. Now, behold this is wisdom; whoso readeth, let him understand and receive also;

6. For unto him that receiveth it shall be given more abundantly, even power.

7. Wherefore, confound your enemies; call upon them to meet you both in public and in private; and inasmuch as ye are faithful their shame shall be made manifest.

8. Wherefore, let them bring forth their strong reasons against the Lord.

9. Verily, thus saith the Lord unto you—there is no weapon that is formed against you shall prosper;

10. And if any man lift his voice against you he shall be confounded in mine own due time.

11. Wherefore, keep my commandments; they are true and faithful. Even so. Amen.

Oliver Cowdery and John Whitmer left, at the appointed time, for Independence, and the Prophet resumed his work on the Bible revision, with Sidney Rigdon as secretary. On December 1st, however, this Revelation was received, in which they were instructed to discontinue, for the time being, their Bible studies, and to take up missionary work in the neighborhood of Kirtland, and elsewhere. This was necessary because of the enmity that had been aroused, and the ignorance concerning the Church, that prevailed among the people generally.

1. *Expounding the mysteries*] The Prophet, by this time, had learned many great and glorious truths, partly by the direct Revelations he had received, and partly by close study of the Scriptures. To the world, many of these truths were "mysteries." The time had come to reveal them, and when they were revealed, or unveiled, they would be mysteries no longer. When the gospel of Christ was first preached by Peter, Paul, and the

other Apostles of their day, the doctrine of the Incarnation was a mystery (I. Cor. 2:7; I. Tim. 3:16); the doctrine of the resurrection (I. Cor. 15:51), and the gathering of the Gentiles into the Church (Col. 1:26, 27) were mysteries. In our dispensation, the doctrines of the gathering and of the building of temples and the City of Zion are as great mysteries, until they are explained by the Holy Spirit of Promise. The Prophet Joseph and Sidney Rigdon were now to go forth and proclaim these and other truths to the Church and the world, for a season (vv. 2, 3).

4. *Prepare the way*] One object was to prepare the public for the appearance of the book of *Commandments and Revelations,* which was about to be published. The world generally supposed that the volume containing divine Revelations had been closed, and that no further revelations would be given. This error they were to correct as a preparation for the acceptance of the new volume.

7. *Confound your enemies*] Another object was to meet and refute slanderers. "Call upon them to meet you both in public and in private." "Let them bring forth their strong reasons *against the Lord*" (v. 8). Attacks upon the servants of the Lord are really directed against *Him.*

Ezra Booth had just published a series of anti-"Mormon" letters, in an Ohio paper. These letters, the Prophet says, "by their coloring, falsity, and vain calculations to overthrow the work of the Lord, exposed his weakness, wickedness, and folly, and left him a monument of his own shame for the world to wonder at." It was to meet the situation that had been created by this hostile agitation, that Joseph and Sidney were called to take this mission. Sometimes it is wise to ignore the attacks of the wicked; at other times it is necessary to meet them, fearlessly and with ability.

GENERAL NOTES

Referring to this mission, the Prophet Joseph says:

"From this time [December 4th, 1831] until the 8th or 10th of January, 1832, myself and Elder Rigdon continued to preach in Shalersville, Ravenna, and other places, setting forth the truth, vindicating the cause of our Redeemer: showing that the day of vengeance was coming upon this generation like a thief in the night; that prejudice, blindness and darkness filled the minds of many, and caused them to persecute the true Church, and reject the true light; by which means we did much towards allaying the excited feelings which were growing out of the scandalous letters then being published in the *Ohio Star,* at Ravenna, by the before mentioned Ezra Booth" (*Hist. of the Church,* Vol. I., p. 241).

One reason why the Church is hated is that it is practical. It makes men and women *practice* what they profess to believe. The world is fond of something pretty, something poetical, in religion. It delights in eloquent, glowing descriptions of the land "over there," which no living mortal has seen in the flesh; it likes to hear about crowns, harps, white robes, and angels' wings; it enjoys elegies of dead heroes, and, to a moderate extent, mild suggestions concerning social reforms, which nobody needs to take offense at. But the Church is not such a nerve-soothing, caressing religion. It is a message from Almighty God to a world steeped in idolatry and sin; it comes like the rolling thunders of Sinai, or the prophecies of Elijah to Ahab and Jezebel, and it makes Carmel ring with the frantic cries of the prophets of Baal. It does something. It takes the poor out of the clutches of oppression and makes them free and independent. It interferes with the profits of those who live on human weakness and shame. It opens a new era in which there will be no room for the government of Satan. No wonder it is hated! Christ, too, was hated because He did something. He might have denounced with impunity the Pharisees as hypocrites and whited sepulchers, but when He interfered with the money-bags on the temple ground, He was crucified. It was always thus.

SECTION 72.

REVELATION *given through Joseph Smith the Prophet, at Kirtland, Ohio, December 4, 1831. Several Elders and members had assembled to learn their duty and to be further edified in the teachings of the Church. See History of the Church, vol. 1, p. 239.——The need of another Bishop being appointed, he to attend to the affairs pertaining to the Bishopric in the eastern branches—His records to be delivered to the Bishop in Zion— Newel K. Whitney named as the second Bishop to be ordained in the Church—Duties of the Bishop enlarged upon—Certificates of membership provided for.*

HEARKEN, and listen to the voice of the Lord, O ye who have assembled yourselves together, who are the high priests of my church, to whom the kingdom and power have been given.

2. For verily thus saith the Lord, it is expedient in me for a bishop to be appointed unto you, or of you, unto the church in this part of the Lord's vineyard.

3. And verily in this thing ye have done wisely, for it is required of the Lord, at the hand of every steward, to render an account of his stewardship, both in time and in eternity.

4. For he who is faithful and wise in time is accounted worthy to inherit the mansions prepared for him of my Father.

5. Verily I say unto you, the elders of the church in this part of my vineyard shall render an account of their stewardship unto the bishop, who shall be appointed of me in this part of my vineyard.

6. These things shall be had on record, to be handed over unto the bishop in Zion.

7. And the duty of the bishop shall be made known by the commandments which have been given, and the voice of the conference.

8. And now, verily I say unto you, my servant Newel K. Whitney is the man who shall be appointed and ordained unto this power. This is the will of the Lord your God, your Redeemer. Even so. Amen.

Having received the call to perform special missionary labors (Sec. 71), the Prophet and Sidney Rigdon went to Kirtland, September 3rd, 1831. The following day a number of Elders met with them, and after they had been conversing on their temporal and spiritual welfare, the Prophet received this Revelation, in which the Lord (1) designates Newel K. Whitney to be Bishop in Kirtland (1-8); (2) enumerates his duties (9-23); and (3) adds instructions regarding the credentials of Saints going to Zion (24-6).

1. A BISHOP FOR KIRTLAND.

1. *High Priests of my Church*] At the Conference in Kirtland, June 1st, 1831, a number of Elders were ordained High Priests. "A High Priest," the Prophet Joseph explains, "is a member of the same Melchizedek Priesthood with the Presidency, but not of the same power and authority in the Church" (*Hist. of the Church,* Vol. II., p. 447).

3. *In this thing ye have done wisely*] Those assembled had, it seems, agreed upon the appointment of a Bishop in Kirtland, and the Lord commended them for this, adding that every steward must render an account of his stewardship "both in time and eternity."

4. *He who is faithful and wise in time * * * to inherit the mansions prepared*] Brigham Young says:

"We are trying to teach this people to use their brains, that they may obtain knowledge and wisdom to sustain themselves and to dictate for others; that they may be worthy to be made Priests and Kings to God, which they never can be unless they learn, here or somewhere else, to govern, manage, legislate, and sustain themselves, their families, and friends, even to the making of nations, and nation after nation. If they cannot attain to this they will have to be servants somewhere" (*Jour. of Dis.*, Vol. XI., p. 328).

8. *Newel K. Whitney*] See Secs. 63:42; 64:26. He is the first Bishop appointed specially for Kirtland. The organization of the Church was a gradual unfoldment, as the needs of the people required.

9. The word of the Lord, in addition to the law which has been given, making known the duty of the bishop who has been ordained unto the church in this part of the vineyard, which is verily this—

10. To keep the Lord's storehouse; to receive the funds of the church in this part of the vineyard;

11. To take an account of the elders as before has been commanded; and to administer to their wants, who shall pay for that which they receive, inasmuch as they have wherewith to pay;

12. That this also may be consecrated to the good of the church, to the poor and needy.

13. And he who hath not wherewith to pay, an account shall be taken and handed over to the bishop of Zion, who shall pay the debt out of that which the Lord shall put into his hands.

14. And the labors of the faithful who labor in spiritual things, in administering the gospel and the things of the kingdom unto the church, and unto the world, shall answer the debt unto the bishop in Zion;

15. Thus it cometh out of the church, for according to the law every man that cometh up to Zion must lay all things before the bishop in Zion.

16. And now, verily I say unto you, that as every elder in this part of the vineyard must give an account of his stewardship unto the bishop in this part of the vineyard—

17. A certificate from the judge or bishop in this part of the vineyard, unto the bishop in Zion, rendereth every man acceptable, and answereth all things, for an inheritance, and to be received as a wise steward and as a faithful laborer;

18. Otherwise he shall not be accepted of the bishop of Zion.

19. And now, verily I say unto you, let every elder who shall

give an account unto the bishop of the church in this part of the vineyard be recommended by the church or churches, in which he labors, that he may render himself and his accounts approved in all things.

20. And again, let my servants who are appointed as stewards over the literary concerns of my church have claim for assistance upon the bishop or bishops in all things—

21. That the revelations may be published, and go forth unto the ends of the earth; that they also may obtain funds which shall benefit the church in all things;

22. That they also may render themselves approved in all things, and be accounted as wise stewards.

23. And now, behold, this shall be an ensample for all the extensive branches of my church, in whatsoever land they shall be established. And now I make an end of my sayings. Amen.

2. DUTIES OF THE BISHOP IN KIRTLAND.

The duties of the Bishop in Kirtland are here enumerated. They are, (a) to keep the Lord's storehouse and receive the funds of the Church in that part of the vineyard (v. 10); that is, to look after the needy and preside over the temporal affairs of the Church; (b) to keep an account of property consecrated for public use, as commanded (Sec. 42:31-2), and administer to the need of the Elders (v. 11), whether these were able to pay for the services rendered, or not (vv. 12-13); the Lord here makes it clear that faithful service in administering in spiritual things is also a contribution to the general funds (vv. 14-15). (c) The Bishop is, further, under obligation to furnish every Elder entitled to it, a certificate, by which the Bishop in Zion may know that the bearer has the right to receive an inheritance (vv. 16-18); he is (d) to receive an account of the labors of every Elder, in order that these might be properly recommended to the Branches they might visit (v. 19); (e) he was, finally, to aid, financially, the "stewards" appointed to look after the literary interests of the Church (Sec. 72:20). "This," we read, "shall be an ensample"—a pattern, or model for imitation—for all Branches of the Church (v. 23). All were to have Bishops with similar duties to perform.

24. A few words in addition to the laws of the kingdom, respecting the members of the church—they that are appointed by the Holy Spirit to go up unto Zion, and they who are privileged to go up unto Zion—

25. Let them carry up unto the bishop a certificate from three elders of the church, or a certificate from the bishop;

26. Otherwise he who shall go up unto the land of Zion shall not be accounted as a wise steward. This is also an ensample. Amen.

3. CONCERNING CREDENTIALS.

24-6. Members of the Church going to Zion were to carry a Bishop's certificate, or recommend, to show their standing in the Church. "Otherwise he * * * shall not be accounted as a wise steward" (v. 26). Wisdom was required in those who went to Zion. They would show their wisdom in the management of their temporal affairs.

Brigham Young is a striking illustration of wise management. In September, 1833, he came to Kirtland, absolutely destitute, a widower with two children to take care of. He had borrowed a pair of shoes and some other articles of clothing, and he had spent every dollar he had on missionary labors. Of the thirty or forty Elders who came to Kirtland that fall, he was the only one who remained there during the winter. The others went wherever they could obtain higher wages than in Kirtland. He went to work for Brother William F. Cahoon, one of the trustees of the Temple. As for wages, Brother Cahoon divided what little he had with Brigham Young. But, when the work was done, the balance due was paid, and it was subsequently found that none of those who had left Kirtland for higher wages had been able to save as much as he had. He stayed in Kirtland till the year 1837, and then he practically abandoned property valued at $5,000. In Nauvoo he also left some houses, and came to Utah without a farthing, except a span of horses, a carriage and harness, all of which had been given him in payment for a house in Nauvoo. See *Journal of Discourses,* Vol. XI., pp. 295-6. Brigham Young was a wise steward, because he always placed the interests of the Kingdom of God first.

GENERAL NOTES

This is the last of thirty-seven Revelations given during the year 1831, the second of the existence of the Church. The development was marvelous. During this year the Prophet moved to Kirtland, and this city was shortly afterwards designated as a gathering place of the Saints. The important office of the Bishopric was instituted (Secs. 41 and 72); the Revelation on Church government was given (Sec. 42); a Church Historian was appointed (47:4), and missionaries were sent to Missouri (Sec. 52). Rules were given for the United Order (Sec. 51), and High Priests were ordained; the Prophet made a trip to Missouri, and shortly afterwards a Revelation was received designating Independence, Jackson County, in that State, as the center of the Land of Zion (Sec. 57); the foundations of Zion were then laid, and the Temple ground dedicated, and at the same time it was predicted that the "blessings" would come after "much tribulation"; that is, that the Saints would pass through many trials before Zion would be redeemed. The vision of the Destroyer on the waters was received on the return journey to Kirtland (Sec. 61); a press was bought for the printing of a Church paper at Independence, *The Evening and Morning Star,* and arrangements were made for the publication of the Book of *Commandments and Revelations* at the same place.

There is a wonderful feature connected with these Revelations—their *Unity.* Although neither the Prophet Joseph nor his associates had any pre-arranged plan regarding the work in which they were engaged, yet every Revelation fits into its place perfectly, as does each separate stone which the skilful architect lays in the walls of his magnificent cathedral, and as we follow the development from Section to Section, we perceive that there is a plan so grand, so beautiful, and so well adapted to human needs, as to leave no room for doubt concerning its divine origin. Each Revelation, considered by itself, though full of beauty, may be but a stone detached from the building to which it belongs, but seen as a part of the entire structure, it speaks with convincing eloquence of the wisdom, power, and love of the Divine Builder of the Church, our Lord Jesus Christ.

THIRD PERIOD. 1832. Sections 73-88.

SECTION 73.

REVELATION *given to Joseph Smith the Prophet, and Sidney Rigdon, at Hiram, Ohio, January 10, 1832. Since the early part of the preceding December, Joseph and Sidney had been engaged in preaching, and by these means much was accomplished in allaying the excited feelings that had been aroused through the publication of scandalous communications to the press. See History of the Church, vol. 1, p. 241.——Elders instructed to continue their preaching and exhortation—Joseph Smith and Sidney Rigdon to resume the work of translation.*

FOR verily, thus saith the Lord, it is expedient in me that they should continue preaching the gospel, and in exhortation to the churches in the regions round about, until conference;

2. And then, behold, it shall be made known unto them, by the voice of the conference, their several missions.

3. Now, verily I say unto you my servants, Joseph Smith, Jun., and Sidney Rigdon, saith the Lord, it is expedient to translate again;

4. And, inasmuch as it is practicable, to preach in the regions round about until conference; and after that it is expedient to continue the work of translation until it be finished.

5. And let this be a pattern unto the elders until further knowledge, even as it is written.

6. Now I give no more unto you at this time. Gird up your loins and be sober. Even so. Amen.

A Conference had been appointed to be held at Amherst, Ohio, January 25th, 1832. The Elders (for their names see Sec. 75) while waiting for Conference time, were anxious to know the will of the Lord, whereupon the Prophet received this Revelation, in which He (1) directs the Elders to preach the gospel to the world and exhort the churches, until Conference (vv. 1-2); (2) instructs the Prophet Joseph and Sidney Rigdon to resume the Bible revision and to preach whenever convenient, until Conference time (vv. 3-4).

6. *Gird up your loins*] Be ready for a journey, or for work in the Lord's service, always. "Gird up the loins of your minds" (I. Peter 1:13). That is, let your minds be prepared for the work in which you are engaged; let it be free from the cares, lusts, and aspirations that make you less proficient in the Master's service.

Be sober] "Sober" means "not excited by intoxicants," but it also means "cool," "deliberate," "serious," and "subdued in demeanor." A minister of the gospel should be "sober" in every sense of the word.

SECTION 74.

BY REVELATION *to Joseph Smith the Prophet, this explanation of the First Epistle of Paul to the Corinthians, chapter 7, verse 14, was given, at Hiram, Ohio, January, 1832.*

FOR the unbelieving husband is sanctified by the wife, and the unbelieving wife is sanctified by the husband; else were your children unclean, but now are they holy.

2. Now, in the days of the apostles the law of circumcision was had among all the Jews who believed not the gospel of Jesus Christ.

3. And it came to pass that there arose a great contention among the people concerning the law of circumcision, for the unbelieving husband was desirous that his children should be circumcised and become subject to the law of Moses, which law was fulfilled.

4. And it came to pass that the children, being brought up in subjection to the law of Moses, gave heed to the traditions of their fathers and believed not the gospel of Christ, wherein they became unholy.

5. Wherefore, for this cause the apostle wrote unto the church, giving unto them a commandment, not of the Lord,

but of himself, that a believer should not be united to an unbeliever; except the law of Moses should be done away among them,

6. That their children might remain without circumcision; and that the tradition might be done away, which saith that little children are unholy; for it was had among the Jews;

7. But little children are holy, being sanctified through the atonement of Jesus Christ; and this is what the scriptures mean.

Complying with the instructions in the previous Section, the Prophet Joseph resumed his Bible studies, whereupon he received this Revelation. The central thought expressed here is found in the first and last verses, and may be stated thus: Little children, sanctified through the atonement of Jesus Christ, are holy.

Two conclusions follow from this proposition. The first, fully set forth in this Revelation, is, that little children do not need circumcision to become sanctified, as taught by the adherents of the Mosaic faith. The second is equally important, that is, little children are holy being sanctified through the atonement of Jesus Christ.

In the Corinthian Church, some evidently held that when the husband, or wife, had been converted, he, or she, ought to abandon the unconverted partner as unclean and contaminating. Not at all! St. Paul says, in substance, that the conversion of one of the partners has brought a sanctifying influence into the family. As Meyer puts it, "The non-believing partner in a marriage * * * becomes partaker—as if by sacred contagion—of the higher, divinely consecrated character of his consort." "Else," the Apostle argues, "were your children unclean." If the wife—this is the argument—must abandon a husband because he is not a Church member, she would also be obliged to abandon her children. But this is not required.

The consecration of the believing parent includes the children. They are sanctified through the atonement of our Lord. They need no ordinance, until they arrive at the age of accountability, when they should be baptized, after proper instruction. Christians were forbidden to marry outside the Church (II. Cor. 6:14), but marriages contracted before conversion were not to be broken up, if the unconverted partner desired to continue the marriage relation.

2. *Among all the Jews*] Corinth was a Grecian city, the most considerable in the country of the Hellenes at the time Paul visited the place, but there were also many Jews, living there in exile, in consequence of a decree issued by Emperor Claudius (Acts 18:2), expelling the Hebrews from Rome. Some of them had joined the Church. This accounts for a controversy, in a Greek city, concerning a Mosaic rite (v. 3).

SECTION 75.

REVELATION *given through Joseph Smith the Prophet, at Amherst, Ohio, January 25, 1832. The occasion was that of a conference before appointed. Certain Elders, who had encountered difficulty in bringing men to an understanding of their message, desired to learn more in detail as to their immediate duties. This revelation followed. See History of the Church, vol. 1, p. 242.——Instructions for individual guidance of Elders who are to travel two by two—Necessity of constant prayer and unwavering faith—Directions for the care and support of the families of absent Elders.*

VERILY, verily, I say unto you, I who speak even by the voice of my Spirit, even Alpha and Omega, your Lord and your God—

2. Hearken, O ye who have given your names to go forth to proclaim my gospel, and to prune my vineyard.

The date of the Amherst Conference* had now arrived. The Elders who had been promised instructions, by revelation, concerning their duties as missionaries, were present, and eager for the word of the Lord through His inspired servant. In answer to prayer this Revelation was received, in which the Lord (1) demands the attention of his servants (1-2); (2) calls them to go on missions (3-5); (3) selects especially (a) M'Lellin and Luke Johnson (6-12); (b Orson Hyde and Samuel H. Smith (13); (c) Lyman Johnson and Orson Pratt (14); (d) Asa Dodds and Calves Wilson (15-16); and (e) Major N. Ashly and Burr Riggs (17); (4) gives general instructions (a) to the Elders (18-22), and (b) to the Church members (23-9); and (5) calls a number of missionaries (30-6).

1. THE LORD DEMANDS ATTENTION.

2. *Hearken*] When the Elders of the Church can say, in all sincerity, with Samuel of old, "Speak; for thy servant heareth" (I. Sam. 3:10), then the Lord can use them in the ministry.

3. Behold, I say unto you that it is my will that you should go forth and not tarry, neither be idle but labor with your might—

---

* At this Conference the Prophet Joseph was ordained as President of the High Priesthood.

4. Lifting up your voices as with the sound of a trump, proclaiming the truth according to the revelations and commandments which I have given you.

5. And thus, if ye are faithful ye shall be laden with many sheaves, and crowned with honor, and glory, and immortality, and eternal life.

2. CALLS THE ELDERS FOR THE MINISTRY.

3. *Labor with your might*] Our Lord is the great "householder" (Matt. 20:1). He has work that must be done, and He calls His laborers to do it; He needs their services, but they need the wages which He pays. He expects them to labor faithfully. There must be no idlers in His service.

4. *Lifting up your voices as with the sound of a trump*] A trumpet is heard far and wide. The year of jubilee was announced in ancient Israel, from hill top to hill top, by blasts of trumpets. That is the way to proclaim the gospel. The sound of harps and lutes, caressing like the soft, warm breath of love, can not be compared to the vigor and earnestness with which the truth must be *proclaimed*.

5. *If faithful * * * laden with many sheaves*] Elders who go out to preach the gospel sometimes return and report that they know not whether they have been the means of converting anybody or not. But if they have been faithful, the harvest is sure. The seed they have sown may sprout and come to maturity years after they have been released. At all events, faithful Elders have the promise that they will be crowned with "honor, and glory, and immortality, and eternal life."

6. Therefore, verily I say unto my servant William E. M'Lellin, I revoke the commission which I gave unto him to go unto the eastern countries;

7. And I give unto him a new commission and a new commandment, in the which I, the Lord, chasten him for the murmurings of his heart;

8. And he sinned; nevertheless, I forgive him and say unto him again, Go ye into the south countries.

9. And let my servant Luke Johnson go with him, and proclaim the things which I have commanded them—

10. Calling on the name of the Lord for the Comforter, which shall teach them all things that are expedient for them—

11. Praying always that they faint not; and inasmuch as they do this, I will be with them even unto the end.

12. Behold, this is the will of the Lord your God concerning you. Even so. Amen.

(a) *M'Lellin and Luke Johnson.*

6. *William E. M'Lellin*] See Sec. 66:1; 68:7.

7. *New commission*] M'Lellin had, it seems, been called to go to the Eastern States, but had neglected to obey the call. The Lord, in this Revelation, rebuked him for the "murmurings of his heart," but gave him another chance.

8. *Into the south countries*] The Southern States.

9. *Luke Johnson*] See Sec. 68:7.

10. *Calling * * * for the Comforter*] They were commanded (v. 4) to preach the truth "according to the revelations and commandments" given. They were to keep strictly to the revealed word, but even this they could not do without the aid of the Comforter, the Holy Spirit of God. Studying alone does not qualify an Elder for preaching the truth. It is the Spirit that qualifies.

11. *Praying always*] Some Elders put all their faith in preaching. The Latter-day Saints generally will endorse the following, though uttered by one not a member of the Church:

"What is preaching without praying! Sermons are but pulpit performances, learned essays, rhetorical orations, popular lectures, or it may be political harangues, until God gives, in answer to earnest prayer, the preparation of the heart, and the answer of the tongue. It is only he who prays that can truly preach. Many a sermon that has shown no intellectual genius and has violated all homiletic rules and standards has had dynamic spiritual force. Somehow it has moved men, melted them, moulded them. The man whose lips are touched by God's living coal from off the altar may even stammer, but his hearers soon find out that he is on fire with one consuming passion to save souls" (Arthur T. Pierson, *The Fundamentals,* Vol. IX., p. 67).

Even unto the end] The end of their mission. The Lord will be with His servants, as long as they are laboring faithfully in their calling.

13. And again, verily thus saith the Lord, let my servant Orson Hyde and my servant Samuel H. Smith take their journey into the eastern countries, and proclaim the things which I have commanded them; and inasmuch as they are faithful, lo, I will be with them even unto the end.

(b) *Orson Hyde and Samuel H. Smith.*

13. *Orson Hyde.* See Sec. 68:1, 7. *Samuel H. Smith.* See Sec. 23:4. Orson Hyde and Samuel H. Smith, during this mission to the Eastern

States, traveled on foot two thousand miles, through the States of New York, Massachusetts, Maine, and Rhode Island.

14. And again, verily I say unto my servant Lyman Johnson, and unto my servant Orson Pratt, they shall also take their journey into the eastern countries; and behold, and lo, I am with them also, even unto the end.

(c) Lyman Johnson and Orson Pratt.

14. Lyman Johnson. See Sec. 68:7. Orson Pratt. See Sec. 34:1. Orson Pratt left for this mission February 2nd, 1832. He traveled through the States of Ohio, Pennsylvania, New Jersey, New York, Vermont, New Hampshire, and Connecticut, returning home in the fall of the same year. Lyman E. Johnson undoubtedly accompanied him on this journey of four thousand miles, during which one hundred and four persons were baptized and several branches organized.

15. And again, I say unto my servant Asa Dodds, and unto my servant Calves Wilson, that they also shall take their journey unto the western countries, and proclaim my gospel, even as I have commanded them.

16. And he who is faithful shall overcome all things, and shall be lifted up at the last day.

(d) Asa Dodds and Calves Wilson.

15-16. In the Doctrine and Covenants, as in the New Testament and the other inspired writings, there are names of whose bearers nothing more is placed on record. There are several such names in Rom. 16, and there are some in this Revelation. Asa Dodds and Calves Wilson are among them. They were assigned to a mission in the Western States, and were promised victory and exaltation as a reward of faithfulness. Note that the Lord rewards faithfulness, whether the visible success is great, or not.

17. And again, I say unto my servant Major N. Ashley, and my servant Burr Riggs, let them take their journey also into the south country.

(e) Major N. Ashley and Burr Riggs.

17. Burr Riggs] The name appears in the minutes of the proceedings of the High Council at Kirtland, February 13th, 1833, on which occasion he was charged with neglect of duty, and especially with failure to magnify his calling as a High Priest. He admitted the charge and expressed a desire to repent, but this he evidently failed to do, for he was

severed from the Church on the 26th of the same month. In all probability, his neglect of duty began by failure to perform the mission to which he was called, or by neglecting his duties as a missionary. Faithful missionaries are generally faithful members of the Priesthood and of the Church.

18. Yea, let all those take their journey, as I have commanded them, going from house to house, and from village to village, and from city to city.

19. And in whatsoever house ye enter, and they receive you, leave your blessing upon that house.

20. And in whatsoever house ye enter, and they receive you not, ye shall depart speedily from that house, and shake off the dust of your feet as a testimony against them.

21. And you shall be filled with joy and gladness; and know this, that in the day of judgment you shall be judges of that house, and condemn them;

22. And it shall be more tolerable for the heathen in the day of judgment, than for that house; therefore, gird up your loins and be faithful, and ye shall overcome all things, and be lifted up at the last day. Even so. Amen.

3. General Instructions to the Elders.

18. *From house to house*] Their mission was to warn all men. They were not to go over the field hurriedly.

19. *Leave your blessing*] Wherever they were received, they were to bring true and lasting happiness with them.

20. *Shake off the dust of your feet*] "As a testimony." See Section 60:15.

21. *You shall be judges of that house*] The Father "hath committed all judgment unto the Son" (John 5:22). And He will judge in accordance with the testimony of His servants. In the world, the Elders are not considered of great importance, at present, but when the Judge of all the Earth is seated on His throne, they also will occupy thrones and assist in the final adjustment of all things. Matt. 19:28.

23. And again, thus saith the Lord unto you, O ye elders of my church, who have given your names that you might know his will concerning you—

24. Behold, I say unto you, that it is the duty of the church to assist in supporting the families of those, and also to support

the families of those who are called and must needs be sent unto the world to proclaim the gospel unto the world.

25. Wherefore, I, the Lord, give unto you this commandment, that ye obtain places for your families, inasmuch as your brethren are willing to open their hearts.

26. And let all such as can obtain places for their families, and support of the church for them, not fail to go into the world, whether to the east or to the west, or to the north, or to the south.

27. Let them ask and they shall receive, knock and it shall be opened unto them, and be made known from on high, even by the Comforter, whither they shall go.

28. And again, verily I say unto you, that every man who is obliged to provide for his own family, let him provide, and he shall in nowise lose his crown; and let him labor in the church.

29. Let every man be diligent in all things. And the idler shall not have place in the church, except he repent and mend his ways.

4. INSTRUCTIONS TO CHURCH MEMBERS.

23-9. In these paragraphs the Lord provides that the families of the missionaries be looked after by the Church members (v. 24); the Elders, before leaving, were to obtain places for those dependent on them, "inasmuch as your brethren are willing to open their hearts" (v. 25). Those who were able to obtain places and support for their families during their absence, were to perform, without fail, the missions to which they had been called (v. 26). To those who were under the necessity of providing for their families, themselves, the Lord says, "Let him provide, and he shall in no wise lose his crown" (v. 28).

30. Wherefore, let my servant Simeon Carter and my servant Emer Harris be united in the ministry;

31. And also my servant Ezra Thayre and my servant Thomas B. Marsh;

32. Also my servant Hyrum Smith and my servant Reynolds Cahoon;

33. And also my servant Daniel Stanton and my servant Seymour Brunson;

34. And also my servant Sylvester Smith and my servant Gideon Carter;

35. And also my servant Ruggles Eames and my servant Stephen Bt rnett;

36. And also my servant Micah B. Welton and also my servant Eden Smith. Even so. Amen.

5. MISSIONARIES CALLED.

30. *Simeon Carter*] See Section 52:27.

Emer Harris] A brother of Martin Harris. Simeon Carter and Emer Harris, at the Conference at Orange, Oct. 25th, 1831, were appointed members of a committee charged with the duty of instructing the Saints on how to conduct their meetings. David Whitmer and Reynolds Cahoon, appointed by the Conference at Hiram, Oct. 11th, 1831, were members of the same committee, as were also Orson Hyde and Hyrum Smith.

31. *Ezra Thayre*] Sec. 33:1; *Thomas B. Marsh*, Sec. 31:1.

32. *Hyrum Smith*] Secs. 11; 23:3; *Reynolds Cahoon;* see Sec. 52:30.

33. *Daniel Stanton*] When a Stake of Zion was organized at Adam-ondi-Ahman, he was made a member of the High Council, June 28th, 1838.

Seymour Brunson] Andrew Jenson, *Historical Record,* notes that he was "a lieutenant-colonel in the Nauvoo Legion, and a prominent Elder in the Church; died in Nauvoo, August 10th, 1840, aged 40 years, 10 months, and 23 days." He solemnized the marriage of Louisa Maria Tanner to Amasa M. Lyman, in Kirtland, 1835 (*Hist. Rec.,* p. 125). In 1838 he preferred the charges against Oliver Cowdery on which this prominent witness to the great Latter-day work was tried by the High Council at Far West. He was also a member of the first High Council organized at Commerce in 1839.

34. *Sylvester Smith*] He occupied several prominent positions in the Church. In 1834 the first High Council of the Church was organized at Kirtland, and he was chosen a member. In 1835, when the First Council of Seventies was organized, he was made one of the Presidents. Having been ordained a High Priest, previously, he was advised to join the High Priest Quorum, and his place was filled by the appointment of John Gaylord as one of seven Presidents of Seventies. Other Presidents of Seventies, who had been ordained High Priests previously, were also released, and the vacancies were filled by Seventies. Sylvester Smith was a member of Zion's Camp, but it appears that his heart was not right at that time, for on one occasion he was in open rebellion and was severely rebuked. On the 28th of August, 1834, he appeared before the High Council in Kirtland to answer to a charge of violation of the laws of the Church, and more especially for having circulated false rumors about the conduct of the Prophet during the journey of Zion's Camp. The Council found that the charge had been proved, and ordered him

to sign an acknowledgment of his error. He did so, though not in a spirit of humility. Later, however, he sent a communication to the *Messenger and Advocate* in which he vindicated the Prophet completely and humbly confessed his own fault (*Hist. of the Church*, Vol. II., p. 160).

Gideon Carter] He was killed in an encounter with a mob near Far West, in what is known as "the Crooked River Battle," Oct. 24th, 1838. At that time word had reached Far West that one Samuel Bogart, with a band of seventy-five marauders, was committing depredations. Judge Elias Higbee then ordered the military authorities to disperse the mob, and Captain David W. Patten and others volunteered for that expedition. With a company of about seventy-five men, Patten met the marauders at a point near Crooked River, and routed them completely. But in the melee David W. Patten, Gideon Carter, and Patrick O'Bannion were mortally wounded. Carter was left on the ground dead, but his body was afterwards recovered and buried.

35-6. Stephen Burnett and Eden Smith were appointed, a month later, to go on a mission. See Section 80.

General Notes

Referring to the subject of the servants of the Lord being judges, at the end of this dispensation, Parley P. Pratt says:

"He [Joseph Smith] will continue holding those keys through all eternity, and will stand—yes, again in the flesh upon this Earth, as the head of the Latter-day Saints, under Jesus Christ, and under Peter, James and John. He will hold the keys to judge the generation to whom he was sent, and will judge my brethren that preside over me; and will judge me, together with the Apostles ordained by the word of the Lord through him and under his administration. When this is done, those Apostles will judge this generation and the Latter-day Saints; and they will judge them with that judgment which Jesus Christ will give unto them; and they will have the same spirit and the same mind as Jesus Christ, and their judgment will be His judgment, for they will be one * * * Brother Brigham, who now presides over us, will hold the keys under Brother Joseph; and he and his brethren, who hold the keys with him, or under his direction, will judge the people; for they will hold those keys to all eternity, worlds without end. By those keys they will have to judge this generation; and Peter, James, and John will hold the keys to preside over, and judge, and direct Brother Joseph to all eternity; and Jesus Christ will hold the keys over them and over us, under His Father, to whom be all the glory" (*Jour. of Dis.*, Vol. V., p. 196).

"With regard to preaching, let a man present himself before the Saints, or go into the world before the nobles and great men of the earth, and let him stand up, full of the Holy Ghost, full of the power of God, and though he may use words and sentences in an awkward style, he will convince and convict more of the truth, than can the most polished orator destitute of the Holy Ghost" (Brigham Young, *Jour. of Dis.*, Vol. IV., p. 21).

Speaking of the financial support of missionaries of the Church, Brigham Young, on one occasion said:

"I came into this Church in the spring of 1832. Previous to my being baptized, I took a mission to Canada at my own expense; and from the time that I was baptized until the day of our sorrow and affliction, at the martyrdom of Joseph and Hyrum, no summer passed over my head but what I was traveling and preaching, and the only thing I ever received from the Church, during over twelve years, that I now recollect, was in 1842, when Brother Joseph sent me the half of a small pig that the brethren had brought to him * * * and that fall Brother Heber C. Kimball * * * was credited $2 in the Church books for one day's services, by Brother Willard Richards, who was then keeping these books. Brother Heber said, 'Blot it out, for I do not want it.' * * * I have traveled and preached, and, at the same time, sustained my family by my labor and economy" (*Ibid.*, p. 34).

Brigham Young states that it was never hard for him to travel without purse and scrip. As an illustration, he relates his experience in England in 1839. He and his companions had left home, sick and without money. Some time after their arrival in Preston, they decided to begin the publication of a magazine, under the name of *The Millennial Star,* with Parley P. Pratt as editor. The *Star* was printed and paid for with borrowed money. Three thousand hymn-books, five thousand Books of Mormon, and thousands of tracts were also printed. Brigham Young remained in England a few days over a year. During that time he paid out $380, expenses incurred by the establishment of the Church in London, in addition to the means expended for printing. When he left, he had paid the debt. He had books, for the mission, to the value of $2,500, and money to pay for the passage home. "And that," he says, "though I had not a sixpence when we first landed in Preston, and I do not know that one of the Twelve had" (*Ibid.*, p. 36).

SECTION 76.

A VISION, *given to Joseph Smith the Prophet, and Sidney Rigdon, at Hiram, Ohio, February 16, 1832. Prefacing his record of this vision the Prophet wrote: "From sundry revelations which had been received, it was apparent that many important points touching the salvation of man had been taken from the Bible, or lost before it was compiled. It appeared self-*

evident from what truths were left, that if God rewarded every one according to the deeds done in the body, the term Heaven, as intended for the Saints' eternal home, must include more kingdoms than one." While he and Sidney Rigdon were engaged in studious and doubtless prayerful consideration of this matter, the glorious vision here recorded was given them. See History of the Church, vol. 1, p. 245.——Revelation of truth, wisdom, and even mysteries promised unto those who are worthy—The eventual resurrection of both just and unjust—The two Elders bear solemn personal testimony that Jesus Christ lives—The expulsion of Lucifer, and his evil activities as Satan on the earth —Awful fate of those who become sons of perdition—Distinctive glories of the celestial, the terrestrial, and the telestial states— Qualifications of souls that shall be assigned to each—Glorious consummation of the Savior's work.

HEAR, O ye heavens, and give ear, O earth, and rejoice ye inhabitants thereof, for the Lord is God, and beside him there is no Savior.

2. Great is his wisdom, marvelous are his ways, and the extent of his doings none can find out.

3. His purposes fail not, neither are there any who can stay his hand.

4. From eternity to eternity he is the same, and his years never fail.

5. For thus saith the Lord—I, the Lord, am merciful and gracious unto those who fear me, and delight to honor those who serve me in righteousness and in truth unto the end.

6. Great shall be their reward and eternal shall be their glory.

7. And to them will I reveal all mysteries, yea, all the hidden mysteries of my kingdom from days of old, and for ages to come, will I make known unto them the good pleasure of my will concerning all things pertaining to my kingdom.

8. Yea, even the wonders of eternity shall they know, and things to come will I show them, even the things of many generations.

9. And their wisdom shall be great, and their understanding reach to heaven; and before them the wisdom of the wise shall

perish, and the understanding of the prudent shall come to naught.

10. For by my Spirit will I enlighten them, and by my power will I make known unto them the secrets of my will—yea, even those things which eye has not seen, nor ear heard, nor yet entered into the heart of man.

This is one of the grandest and, in some respects, most remarkable visions ever vouchsafed to man in mortality. Human language can but imperfectly portray the glory in the midst of which the various scenes, as a panorama, passed before the minds of the enraptured Prophets of God, quickened by the divine Spirit. "The glory of the Lord shone round about," as on the Mount of Transfiguration. They saw and conversed with the Redeemer of the world, and were given to understand the very mysteries of eternities.

The Prophet Joseph says of this Revelation:

"Every law, every commandment, every promise, every truth, and every point touching the destiny of man, from Genesis to Revelation, where the purity of the Scriptures remains unsullied by the folly of men, goes to show the perfection of the theory, and witnesses the fact that that document is a transcript from the records of the eternal world. The sublimity of the ideas; the purity of the language; the scope for action; the continued duration for completion, in order that the heirs of salvation may confess the Lord and bow the knee; the rewards for faithfulness, and the punishments of sins, are so much beyond the narrowmindedness of men, that every honest man is constrained to exclaim, 'It came from God' " (*Hist. of the Church,* Vol. I., p. 252).

Charles W. Penrose, in a sermon delivered in Salt Lake City, March 4th, 1883, expressed the appreciation of the Church for this Revelation, in the following words:

"There is nothing in the book called the Bible that can compare with it. It is full of light; it is full of truth; it is full of glory; it is full of beauty. It portrays the future of all the inhabitants of the earth, dividing them into three grand classes or divisions—celestial, terrestrial, and telestial, or as compared to the glory of the sun, the glory of the moon, and the glory of the stars. It shows who will be redeemed, and what redemption they will enjoy; and describes the position the inhabitants of the earth will occupy when they enter into the future state" (*Jour. of Dis.,* Vol. XXIV., p. 92).

This Revelation was received shortly after the return of the Prophet to Hiram, from the Amherst Conference, where he had been ordained President of the High Priesthood. It contains, (1) an introduction (1-10); (2) a statement of the circumstances under which it was given (11-19); (3) a vision of the glory of the Son (20-4); (4) a vision of the fall of Satan (25-9); (5) a vision of the sufferings of the lost (30-49); (6) a vision of those who will come forth in the resurrection of the just (50-70); (7) a vision of the terrestrial world (71-80); (8) a vision of the telestial glory (81-8); (9) a comparison between the three glories (89-112); and (10) the conclusion (113-19).

1. THE INTRODUCTION.

1. *Hear, O ye heavens, and give ear, O earth*] Here is a Revelation intended for those in heaven as well as on Earth. Spirits beyond the veil must receive their information through the prophets of the Lord. They are as anxious to learn what God reveals to man as we are. (Comp. Dan. 8:13; I. Pet. 1:12).

The Lord is God] There is an all-sufficient reason why all should listen to this Revelation. It is the Lord that speaks; it is Jehovah, and He is God. "Know that Jehovah is God; He it is that made us, and we are His; His people and the sheep of His pasture" (Ps. 100:3). He made Israel of old to be a people for Himself (Deut. 32:6, 15). He gathered, and is still gathering, His Saints, and He owns them as *His* people. He is God. He is also the Redeemer, and besides Him there is no Savior.

Savior] Deliverer. The expression is used by Isaiah (43:3, 11) where the Lord promises the redemption of Israel; "I gave Egypt for thy ransom, Ethiopia, and Seba for thee." In the same way He is the Savior, the Redeemer, of His latter-day Zion. There is none besides Him. He will surely "ransom" His inheritance in due time.

The world has almost forgotten that Jehovah, our Lord and Savior, Jesus Christ, is God. When they think of God, they endeavor to perceive either an imperceptible Being without body and without direct influence on the events of history; or a Thor hurling his flashing, murderous hammer in every direction; or an angry judge opening dungeons and ordering tortures, for His own glory. It is high time the world should hear again that Christ is God, and learn to worship Him who is revealed in Christ Jesus. The only true idea we have of God is the one we can obtain by seeing Him as revealed in His Son. Hence this important Revelation to which the attention of all the world is directed. The Lord Jesus Christ, is God.

2. *Great is his wisdom*] In Him "are hid all the treasures of wisdom and knowledge" (Col. 2:3). He is "the wisdom of God" (I. Cor. 1:24). World-wisdom, or philosophy, such as that in which the Greek masters of St. Paul's day gloried, was "foolishness" in the sight of God. The gospel, in which Jesus Christ is the central figure, is God's wisdom, though men deem it foolish.

Marvelous are his ways] See Isaiah 29:14, where the Prophet predicts the destruction of the wisdom of the wise men, and the concealment of their understanding, and gives the assurance that the Lord will "do a marvelous work" among the people. This was literally fulfilled when the Prophet Joseph was called to lay the foundations of the Church in this dispensation. Again and again the Lord declared, through the Prophet, "Now behold, a marvelous work is about to come forth" (Doctrine and Covenants, Secs. 4:1; 11:1; 18:44). This work far surpassed all human conceptions and calculations.

3. *His purposes fail not*] *We* can do very little; *God* can do whatever He wills. "Ah Lord God! behold, thou hast made the heaven and the earth by thy great power and stretched-out arm; and there is nothing too hard for thee" (Jer. 32:17). He is omnipotent; not in the sense that He calls forth something out of nothing, or that He deprives any of His children of their free agency, but in the sense that He has unlimited resources at His supreme command, and innumerable means whereby to accomplish His purposes.

4. *From eternity to eternity he is the same*] He is immutable, because His wisdom is infinite. His plans and purposes are perfect in conception. "The counsel of the Lord standeth for ever; the thoughts of his heart to all generations" (Psalm 33:11). Truth is immutable. It can never change. What is true today has always been true, and will always remain true. The gospel continues the same from eternity, because it is truth.

His years never fail] Never come to an end. There will never be a last year of His existence.

5. *Merciful and gracious*] Mercy is kindness exercised toward those who are unfortunate and miserable. Grace is love, or benevolence, extended toward those who have not earned it. In both are included pity, forbearance, gentleness, and compassion. In the proper government of the family the justice of the parent is always tempered with mercy. In the same way, God, in His dealings with His children, is both merciful and gracious. "Like as a father pitieth his children, so the Lord pitieth them that fear Him" (Psalm 103:13). He saves His repentant children. "That in the ages to come he might show the exceeding riches of his grace in his kindness toward us, through Christ Jesus (Ephesians 2:7).

In the Gospels, several occasions are noted on which our Savior manifested His compassion. When He saw the scattered, fainting multitude, without shepherd to take care of them, He was "moved with compassion" (Matt. 9:36; 14:14). He was full of compassion when He met lepers (Mark 1:41), blind (Matt. 20:34); mourners (Luke 7:13), and when He contemplated the fate of Jerusalem in the hands of blind leaders, in rebellion against God (Luke 19:41).

Honor those who serve me] As He is merciful and gracious to those who *fear* Him, so He takes delight in honoring those who *serve* Him in righteousness and in truth to the end. Note the difference between these two classes—those that fear Him, and those that serve Him.

7. *Will I reveal all mysteries*] See Sec. 28:7. One of the rewards promised to God's faithful servants is revelations of the mysteries of the kingdom of God. The Lord will teach them all that pertains

to that kingdom, in order that they may be qualified as citizens, and take part in His government. He will teach them to be efficient legislators, executives, judges, diplomats, etc., in the kingdom.

8. *The wonders of eternity*] The history of the past and events yet to come are included in this curriculum. Through the Spirit of God His faithful servants will have the past, present, and future opened to their view.

10. *By my Spirit will I enlighten them*] If we have the Spirit of God, we are, to that extent, part of the Deity, and partake of the knowledge and wisdom which God has, "For the Spirit searcheth all things, yea, the deep things of God" (I. Cor. 2:10). Through the Spirit the knowledge of God is communicated to man as readily as a Marconigram is sent from one place to another. Knowledge thus communicated from God to man, we call revelation.

11. We, Joseph Smith, Jun., and Sidney Rigdon, being in the Spirit on the sixteenth day of February, in the year of our Lord one thousand eight hundred and thirty-two—

12. By the power of the Spirit our eyes were opened and our understandings were enlightened, so as to see and understand the things of God—

13. Even those things which were from the beginning before the world was, which were ordained of the Father, through his Only Begotten Son, who was in the bosom of the Father, even from the beginning;

14. Of whom we bear record; and the record which we bear is the fulness of the gospel of Jesus Christ, who is the Son, whom we saw and with whom we conversed in the heavenly vision.

15. For while we were doing the work of translation, which the Lord had appointed unto us, we came to the twenty-ninth verse of the fifth chapter of John, which was given unto us as follows:

16. Speaking of the resurrection of the dead, concerning those who shall hear the voice of the Son of Man, and shall come forth—

17. They who have done good in the resurrection of the just, and they who have done evil in the resurrection of the unjust—

18. Now this caused us to marvel, for it was given unto us of the Spirit.

19. And while we meditated upon these things, the Lord touched the eyes of our understandings and they were opened, and the glory of the Lord shone round about.

2. CIRCUMSTANCES UNDER WHICH THIS VISION WAS RECEIVED.

11-19. Upon the return of the Prophet Joseph and Sidney Rigdon from the Amherst Conference, the work on the Bible revision was resumed. While studying the Scriptures, they were led to reflect on the great truth that in the hereafter, God will reward all men according to the deeds done in the body, and the conclusion seemed inevitable that "heaven" must include more than one glory. When, in the Bible reading, they came to John 5:29, "And shall come forth; they that have done good, unto the resurrection of life; and they that have done evil, unto the resurrection of damnation," the whole subject was opened up before their minds in visions, and they were commanded to write them as they saw them in the spirit.

11. *Being in the Spirit*] Joseph Smith and Sidney Rigdon were in a state of spiritual rapture, as John on Patmos (Rev. 1:10); or Ezekiel (3:12); or Paul (II. Cor. 12:2-4). The veil was lifted from their mortal senses, and they could see and hear things spiritually, with their spiritual senses.

14. *Of whom we bear record*] They saw and conversed with Jesus Christ, in a heavenly vision, and testify to that fact, and that testimony is the fulness of the gospel.

17. *Resurrection of the just * * * unjust*] The rendition differs somewhat from that in the English Authorized Version, but not in meaning.

19. *The Lord touched the eyes of our understandings*] When the Lord opens the eyes of men, the glory of the Lord can be seen.

20. And we beheld the glory of the Son, on the right hand of the Father, and received of his fulness;

21. And saw the holy angels, and them who are sanctified before his throne, worshiping God, and the Lamb, who worship him forever and ever.

22. And now, after the many testimonies which have been given of him, this is the testimony, last of all, which we give of him: That he lives!

23. For we saw him, even on the right hand of God; and we heard the voice bearing record that he is the Only Begotten of the Father—

24. That by him, and through him, and of him, the worlds are and were created, and the inhabitants thereof are begotten sons and daughters unto God.

3. VISION OF THE GLORY OF THE SON.

20-24. The first vision given was one of the glory of the Son on the right hand of the Father. They saw holy angels and those "who are sanctified" before His throne, worshiping God and the Lamb. They also heard a voice testifying that the Son is the Only begotten of the Father and the Creator.

20. *His fulness*] In Christ dwelt the totality of the divine powers and attributes (Col. 1:19), and through His human body they were made manifest to man (Col. 2:9), and especially to the Church, which is His "fulness" (Eph. 1:23). To receive of His fulness is to receive of that divine Spirit which fills Him and makes us one with those who belong to Him—His Church.

21. *They who are sanctified*] See Section 88:2.

22. *The testimony last of all*] Our Lord was seen, after His resurrection, by Peter and the Twelve; by more than five hundred brethren at once; by Stephen, the martyr; by Saul, afterwards called Paul; by John on Patmos; by Joseph Smith alone in the initial vision of this dispensation, and by Joseph Smith and Sidney Rigdon in the vision placed on record in this Section. This is the last testimony to the fact that He lives, a resurrected and glorified Being; not the *final* testimony, but the last up to the time of this vision.

23. *The only begotten of the Father*] "God the Eternal Father, whom we designate by the exalted name-title Elohim, is the literal Parent of our Lord and Savior Jesus Christ, and of the spirits of the human race * * * Jesus Christ is the Son of Elohim, both as spiritual and bodily offspring; that is to say, Elohim is literally the Father of the spirit of Jesus Christ, and also of the body in which Jesus Christ performed His mission in the flesh, and which body died on the cross, and was afterwards taken up by the process of resurrection, and is now the immortalized tabernacle of the eternal spirit of our Lord and Savior."

*   *   *   *

"There is no impropriety, therefore, in speaking of Jesus Christ as the Elder Brother of the rest of human kind. That He is by spiritual birth Brother to the rest of us, is indicated in Hebrews: 'Wherefore in all things it behoved him to be made like unto his brethren, that he might be a merciful and faithful High Priest in things pertaining to God, to make reconciliation for the sins of the people' (Heb. 2:17). Let it not be forgotten, however, that He is essentially greater than any and all others, by reason (1) of His seniority as the oldest and firstborn;

(2) of His unique status in the flesh as the offspring of a mortal mother and of an immortal, or resurrected and glorified Father; (3) of His selection and foreordination as the one and only Redeemer and Savior of the race; and (4) of His transcendent sinlessness" (*The Father and the Son,* a Doctrinal Exposition by the First Presidency and the Twelve, *Millennial Star,* Vol. LXXVIII., pp. 482, 500).

24. *The worlds * * * created*] It has been usual to refer to the Father of our Lord as the Creator, and this is true in the sense that He is the originator of the plan. But the worlds were created through the Son. He was the great Architect, the Executive of the Great Council in heaven, through whom the plan of creation was made a reality, as well as the plan of redemption (Comp. Heb. 1:2).

Note that the worlds were "created," which means, "formed," "organized." They were not "made" out of "nothing," or *ex nihilo,* as the learned express that impossible proposition. Nor are they without beginning, in their present form. The world, as we know it, has a beginning; it will have an end. Matter itself has neither beginning nor end, as far as mortals can know.

John, the beloved, in his visions on Patmos, saw the Lord in the midst of the seven candlesticks, or the seven principal churches in Asia Minor, among which the Apostle had been laboring for some years. He describes His appearance (Rev. 1:13-16). John had known the Master intimately in the flesh, but in His glory He inspired even John with terror (v. 17). In this vision of Joseph and Sidney, the element of terror was absent. The Lord had opened their eyes and quickened them beforehand, so that they could gaze on His glory though its radiance surpassed that of the sun.

25. And this we saw also, and bear record, that an angel of God who was in authority in the presence of God, who rebelled against the Only Begotten Son whom the Father loved and who was in the bosom of the Father, was thrust down from the presence of God and the Son,

26. And was called Perdition, for the heavens wept over him —he was Lucifer, a son of the morning.

27. And we beheld, and lo, he is fallen! is fallen, even a son of the morning!

28. And while we were yet in the Spirit, the Lord commanded us that we should write the vision; for we beheld Satan, that old serpent, even the devil, who rebelled against God, and sought to take the kingdom of our God and his Christ—

29. Wherefore, he maketh war with the saints of God, and encompasseth them round about.

4. Vision of the Fall of Lucifer.

25-9. The curtain here falls on the glorious scene in which the throne of God and His Son form the radiant center, and another picture is rolled up before the view of the awe-stricken spectators. They see Lucifer rebelling against the Son (v. 25), and thrust down from the divine presence; they see the heavens weeping over him, as he goes to perdition, a fallen being; they see him continuing in rebellion and making war upon the Saints, for the purpose of taking away the kingdom from the Son of God.

25. *Angel of God * * * rebelled*] In the Pearl of Great Price, Book of Moses, 4:1-4, and Book of Abraham, 3:27, 28, we read the particulars of this rebellion. There was a great Council in heaven deliberating concerning the redemption of man. And God said, "Whom shall I send?" We may infer from Scripture passages that there were many mighty angels in that assembly. Lucifer was one of them. He was one of the chief princes. He rose and spoke, "Behold, here am I; send me. I will be thy son, and I will redeem mankind, that one soul shall not be lost, and surely I will do it; wherefore give me thine honor."

God's well-beloved Son was also there and He said, "Here am I, send me." But He added, "Father, thy will be done, and the glory be thine forever."

Lucifer proposed to destroy the free agency of man and save every soul by *compulsion*. The Son of God proposed salvation by free choice on the part of man.

Christ's proposition was accepted; wherefore Lucifer decided to carry out his plan without the consent of the heavenly Council, and to subject the human race to his will. He began his agitation for followers among the spirits, and such was his eloquence and influence that he turned away one-third part of the hosts of heaven from the Son of God (Sec. 29:36, 37). He and his followers were cast out. But they have never ceased to oppose the Son of God. They have never ceased to endeavor to establish their kingdom among the children of men, and their efforts are visible in false doctrines, corrupt morals, strife and contention, persecution, and abortive efforts to combat sin by legislation instead of by the influence of the gospel.

Lucifer] The name means "Light-bearer" and indicates the exalted position of him who was so called, for a "light-bearer" is a sun in the firmament. But when he was cast out, he was called *Perdition*.

29. *Maketh war with the Saints*] As the opponent of the Son of God, he makes war on the Saints of God. He has always acted on the false supposition that by imprisoning, burning and otherwise torturing, and murdering the Saints, they would deny Christ, and others would be deterred from joining His people. He is still acting on the same principle, for although prisons are not generally opened to the Saints, yet false-

hoods of the blackest dye are told about them in pulpit and press, publicly and privately, until ignorant men and women shun them as they would lepers, while they are coddling to their bosoms the emissaries of the devil who lead them to destruction. The fallen angel still hopes, we may presume, to obtain a large enough following among the children of men to form a strong kingdom of his own.

30. And we saw a vision of the sufferings of those with whom he made war and overcame, for thus came the voice of the Lord unto us:

31. Thus saith the Lord concerning all those who know my power, and have been made partakers thereof, and suffered themselves through the power of the devil to be overcome, and to deny the truth and defy my power—

32. They are they who are the sons of perdition, of whom I say that it had been better for them never to have been born;

33. For they are vessels of wrath, doomed to suffer the wrath of God, with the devil and his angels in eternity;

34. Concerning whom I have said there is no forgiveness in this world nor in the world to come—

35. Having denied the Holy Spirit after having received it, and having denied the Only Begotten Son of the Father, having crucified him unto themselves and put him to an open shame.

36. These are they who shall go away into the lake of fire and brimstone, with the devil and his angels—

37. And the only ones on whom the second death shall have any power;

38. Yea, verily, the only ones who shall not be redeemed in the due time of the Lord, after the sufferings of his wrath.

39. For all the rest shall be brought forth by the resurrection of the dead, through the triumph and the glory of the Lamb, who was slain, who was in the bosom of the Father before the worlds were made.

40. And this is the gospel, the glad tidings, which the voice out of the heavens bore record unto us—

41. That he came into the world, even Jesus, to be crucified for the world, and to bear the sins of the world, and to sanctify the world, and to cleanse it from all unrighteousness;

42. That through him all might be saved whom the Father had put into his power and made by him;

43. Who glorifies the Father, and saves all the works of his hands, except those sons of perdition who deny the Son after the Father has revealed him.

44. Wherefore, he saves all except them—they shall go away into everlasting punishment, which is endless punishment, which is eternal punishment, to reign with the devil and his angels in eternity, where their worm dieth not, and the fire is not quenched, which is their torment—

45. And the end thereof, neither the place thereof, nor their torment, no man knows;

46. Neither was it revealed, neither is, neither will be revealed unto man, except to them who are made partakers thereof;

47. Nevertheless, I, the Lord, show it by vision unto many, but straightway shut it up again;

48. Wherefore, the end, the width, the height, the depth, and the misery thereof, they understand not, neither any man except those who are ordained unto this condemnation.

49. And we heard the voice, saying: Write the vision, for lo, this is the end of the vision of the sufferings of the ungodly.

5. A VISION OF THE SUFFERING OF THE LOST.

Again the scene changes. The shadows deepen as the picture of mystery and despair comes into view for a brief moment and then fades away. Some of the children of men will finally be lost, through the influence of the adversary, and this vision is concerning them.

Two questions are involved in the subject of this vision: (a) Who are the lost? (b) What is their fate? To these important questions this Revelation gives the answer.

30. *Made war and overcame*] Lucifer, cast out of heaven as a rebel, makes war upon the people of God and becomes the master of some of them. These, if they remain in that servitude, are, finally, lost. Some further details follow:

31. *Know my power*] Those who are finally lost are such as have had actual knowledge of the power of God; they have been made partakers thereof; they have not only heard of it or seen its manifestations in others, but they have received it themselves. Paul (Heb. 6:4) uses the expression, "enlightened," which is equivalent to "baptized," and is so understood by early Christian authors, because Christian baptism is followed by the reception of the Holy Ghost, who gives light and leads into all truth. He adds, "and have tasted the heavenly gift and were made partakers of the Holy Ghost." In other words, they have been

regenerated by the gospel and received the blessings bestowed through the ordinances thereof; and then they have "suffered themselves to be overcome." They have *denied* the truth and have *defied* the power of God. They have become rebels, like Lucifer. Their status is that of apostasy. The 35th verse should be read here. They have denied the Holy Spirit, after having received it; they have denied the Only Begotten Son, and by that denial, crucified Him, as it were. They have been the servants of Christ but are now enlisted in the service of Lucifer, as were those who crucified the Lord; they belong to the same class.

"The 'sons of perdition' are those who have received the gospel, those to whom the Father has revealed the Son; those who know something concerning the plan of salvation; those who have had keys placed in their hands by which they could unlock the mysteries of eternity; those who received power sufficient to overcome all things, and who, instead of using it for their own salvation, and in the interest of the salvation of others, prostituted that power and turned away from that which they knew to be true, denying the Son of God and putting Him to open shame. All such live in the spirit of error, and they love it and roll it under their tongue as a sweet morsel; they are governed by Satan; becoming servants to him whom they list to obey, they become the sons of perdition, doomed to suffer the wrath of God reserved for the Devil and his angels," Charles W. Penrose, *Journal of Discourses,* Vol. XXIV., p. 93).

It follows from what has been revealed concerning the sons of Perdition, that they are but a small portion of the human race. Formerly, the gloomy view was widely held that the greater number by far of human beings were doomed to eternal hell-fire. A theologian of the old school said that souls were daily falling into the sulphury lake, as numerous as snowflakes during a winter storm. But this is all wrong. John the Revelator represents the redeemed as "a great multitude which no man could number" (Rev. 7:9). The lost are nowhere so represented. Our Lord will finally triumph over the adversary, even in regard to the number of His followers. Glory to Him for evermore!

36-49. The fate, or the final destiny, of the sons of Perdition, is set forth in these paragraphs, as far as God has deemed it wise to give any revelation upon that subject.

36. *Lake of fire and brimstone*] In all probability this expression has reference to *Gehenna,* the place outside Jerusalem where all kinds of garbage was consumed by fire, and where, consequently, the flames were never quenched. The bodies of criminals were cremated there. "Hell fire," in the New Testament, means the "burning Gehenna" (Matt. 5:22). "Damnation of hell" (Matt. 23:33) means the judgment of "Gehenna." The "gates of hell" (Matt. 16:18) does not refer to Gehenna but to Hades, and means the evil forces of the unseen world. It should be noted that, although "the lake of fire" may be a figurative expression, deriving its meaning from a place in which, not living transgressors but

their lifeless bodies were consumed, this does not lessen the awfulness of the fate awaiting the lost. Let those who have no reverence for the exalted Majesty of God, and no regard for His infinite mercy extended to them in the message of the gospel, take warning by the solemn truth placed before them in this metaphor, depicting the final consequences of rebellion under the leadership of Lucifer (Jacob 3:11; see also page 377).

37. *Second death*] The end of the lost is also called the "second death." The first is spiritual death. When Adam was expelled from the Garden of Eden, "he became spiritually dead, which was the first death." But spiritual death is also the last, "which shall be pronounced upon the wicked, when I shall say, Depart, ye cursed" (Sec. 29:41).

38. *The only ones who shall not be redeemed*] All but sons of perdition will be redeemed from Satan's power and will find some place outside of his domain. The inhabitants of this earth will be assigned to the telestial, the terrestrial or the celestial kingdom according to the law which they have kept while in mortality. Redemption does not mean exaltation, but to be released from Satan's chains. These sons of perdition have willed to go with the prince of darkness. They have reached a stage where they cannot repent, for repentance is a gift of God, and they have placed themselves beyond its influence and power.

39-43. These paragraphs point to the fact that all but sons of perdition will be redeemed and obtain some place in one of the three kingdoms. See verses 111-112. Alma states that sons of perdition, while not redeemed because they partake of the second death cannot die again:

"Then I say unto you, they shall be as though there had been no redemption made; for they cannot be redeemed (i.e. from Satan's power) according to God's justice; and they cannot die, seeing there is no more corruption. (Alma 12:17-18.)

44. *Everlasting punishment*] The subject of the fate of the lost is resumed here (See Sec. 19:4-12).

To reign with the devil] This is a peculiar, but a highly significant expression. The Lord is the sovereign ruler. He reigns. Sin is said to reign, when men submit to its behests. Grace is also said to reign (Rom. 5:21). The Saints will reign with Christ. But here the sons of Perdition are said to "reign" with the Devil and his angels in eternity, in the place where the worm dieth not and the fire is not quenched. The conflict between Lucifer and the Son has been, from the beginning, for sovereignty. Men have ranged themselves on one side or the other. The Saints are, and will be, citizens and officials in the Kingdom of God and there they will "reign," as citizens in a free country. The sons of Perdition are, and will remain, citizens and officials in the kingdom of Lucifer. But that kingdom will, finally, be confined to *Gehenna*. There they will *"reign,"* under such laws and rules as obtain in the kingdom of the Devil, and of which we have had numerous illustrations in human history, during the dark ages of ignorance, superstition, tyranny, and iniquity. Think of a place where the evil passions of human beings and evil spirits rage, unrestrained by the influence of the gospel! Such is the kingdom of the Devil, where the sons of Perdition will reign.

Which is their torment] Not literal fire! The necessity of living in a place where the Devil is the supreme ruler and applies the law of compulsion to minutest details of existence, and where, consequently, hatred consumes every heart, is torment enough.

45. *The end thereof*] Is there an end? If so, it is not known to man. Neither is the place known. But there is a place. The kingdom of the lost is not only a condition, a state. It is a real place. Nor can any man fathom the intensity of the misery of the lost. (I. Ne. 15:34, 35.)

46. *Neither was it revealed *.* * * unto man*] These things have not been revealed.

47. *I, the Lord, show it by vision*] Many have had a vision of the final destiny of the lost, but the Lord closes the view immediately, and no man can form any conception of it.

48. *Except them who are ordained unto this condemnation*] Not foreordained, in the sense of pre-elected by God, to condemnation. God has ordained that rebellion against Him shall result, if persisted in to the end, in misery, but He has not foreordained anyone to that fate. A legislature may ordain that thieves must be imprisoned and murderers killed, but that does not mean that it has foreordained any individual, or any number of individuals, to do that which ends in imprisonment, or death. The sons of Perdition pursue their course according to their own choice, and not as victims of inexorable destiny.

50. And again we bear record—for we saw and heard, and this is the testimony of the gospel of Christ concerning them who shall come forth in the resurrection of the just—

51. They are they who received the testimony of Jesus, and believed on his name and were baptized after the manner of his burial, being buried in the water in his name, and this according to the commandment which he has given—

52. That by keeping the commandments they might be washed and cleansed from all their sins, and receive the Holy Spirit by the laying on of the hands of him who is ordained and sealed unto this power;

53. And who overcome by faith, and are sealed by the Holy Spirit of promise, which the Father sheds forth upon all those who are just and true.

54. They are they who are the church of the Firstborn.

55. They are they into whose hands the Father has given all things—

56. They are they who are priests and kings, who have received of his fulness, and of his glory;

57. And are priests of the Most High, after the order of Melchizedek, which was after the order of Enoch, which was after the order of the Only Begotten Son.

58. Wherefore, as it is written, they are gods, even the sons of God—

59. Wherefore, all things are theirs, whether life or death, or things present, or things to come; all are theirs and they are Christ's, and Christ is God's.

60. And they shall overcome all things.

61. Wherefore, let no man glory in man, but rather let him glory in God, who shall subdue all enemies under his feet.

62. These shall dwell in the presence of God and his Christ forever and ever.

63. These are they whom he shall bring with him, when he shall come in the clouds of heaven to reign on the earth over his people.

64. These are they who shall have part in the first resurrection.

65. These are they who shall come forth in the resurrection of the just.

66. These are they who are come unto Mount Zion, and unto the city of the living God, the heavenly place, the holiest of all.

67. These are they who have come to an innumerable company of angels, to the general assembly and church of Enoch, and of the Firstborn.

68. These are they whose names are written in heaven, where God and Christ are the judge of all.

69. These are they who are just men made perfect through Jesus the mediator of the new covenant, who wrought out this perfect atonement through the shedding of his own blood.

70. These are they whose bodies are celestial, whose glory is that of the sun, even the glory of God, the highest of all,

whose glory the sun of the firmament is written of as being typical.

6. Vision of the Resurrection of the Just.

50-70. From a sense of dark despair, the vision again changes, this time to one of effulgent glory, as those who come forth in the resurrection of the just pass before view.

Two questions are here answered: (a) Who are those resurrected beings? (b) What will be their final glory?

(a) Who are They?

51. *Received the testimony*] Those who come forth in the resurrection of the just are they who accepted the gospel of Jesus Christ and were baptized, as He commanded.

52. *Washed and cleansed from all their sins*] That is the effect of baptism when performed in accordance with the divine command, by one having authority from God. Baptism, notwithstanding exegetical sophistries, is "the washing of regeneration" (Titus 3:5), and the members of the Church are sanctified by it (Eph. 5:26). It is the door to the kingdom of God.

Receive the Holy Spirit] They have not only been baptized in water, but have received the Holy Spirit by the laying on of hands. They are "born" of water and the Spirit; not of water alone; nor of Spirit alone; neither alone would be a complete baptism.

53. *Who overcome by faith*] They have not only been cleansed from sin and have received the Holy Spirit, but they have, by faith, endured all trials, and been "sealed" by the Holy Spirit of Promise. This sealing refers to the gifts of the Holy Spirit, by which that Spirit attests the reality of the conversion and claims the convert.

54. *Church of the firstborn*] They are members of the Church of the Firstborn, even Jesus Christ.

55. *Into whose hands the Father has given all things*] "All things are yours; whether Paul, or Apollos, or Cephas, or the world, or life, or death, or things present, or things to come; all are yours" (I. Cor. 3:21, 22).

56. *Priests and Kings*] They hold these exalted offices, by promise now, but they will assume the full duties of them on coming forth in the first resurrection.

57. *After the order of Melchizedek*] They hold the holy Melchizedek Priesthood.

58. *They are gods, even the sons of God*] Because of their Priesthood, their office, their possession of all things, they are gods, even the sons of God. Comp. Sec. 132:20.

Some take exception to the glorious doctrine here taught, that those who are called forth in the first resurrection are destined to become gods. There is no valid reason for objection. The expression "gods" is applied to men, in the Bible as well as here. The Lord said to Moses, "I have made thee a God to Pharaoh" (Ex. 7:1). The Psalmist declares that "God standeth in the congregation of the mighty; he judgeth among the gods" (82:1). And again, "I have said, Ye are gods; and all of you are the children of the Most High (Ps. 82:6). Here the judges in Israel are called gods, and they are rebuked for dishonoring their exalted position by judging unjustly. Our Lord was accused of blasphemy because He claimed Godhood. His answer was an appeal to this Psalm (John 10:34). The judges of old, He said, were called gods and sons of the Most High, by virtue of their calling; was it, then, blasphemy for Him to call Himself the "Son of God?" The doctrine, therefore, is perfectly Scriptural, and is denied only by those who, like the opponents of our Lord, do not know the Scriptures. Says Brigham Young:

"Jesus is the elder Brother, and all the brethren shall come in for a share with Him; for an equal share according to their works and calling, and they shall be crowned with Him. Do you read of any such thing as the Savior praying that the Saints may be one with Him, as He and the Father are one? The Bible is full of such doctrine, and there is no harm in it, as long as it agrees with the New Testament * * * The Lord created you and me for the purpose of becoming gods * * * How many will become thus privileged? Those who honor the Father and the Son; those who receive the Holy Ghost, and magnify their calling; and are found pure and holy; they shall be crowned in the presence of the Father and the Son" (*Jour. of Dis.,* Vol. III., p. 93).

"The Scriptures are a mixture of very strange doctrines to the Christian world, who are blindly led by the blind. I will refer to another Scripture. 'Now,' says God, when He visited Moses in the bush * * * 'Thou shalt be a god unto the children of Israel.' God said, 'Thou shalt be a god unto Aaron, and he shall be thy spokesman.' I believe those gods that God reveals as gods to be sons of God, who exalt themselves to be gods even from before the foundation of the world, and are the only gods I have reverence for (Joseph Smith, *Hist. of the Church,* Vol. VI., p. 478).

"Gods have an ascendancy over the angels, who are ministering servants. In the resurrection, some are raised to be angels; others are raised to become gods" (Joseph Smith, *Hist. of the Church,* Vol. V., p. 426).

(b) What is their final glory?

62. *Dwell in the presence of God and his Christ*] This is the sum total of glory and honor and exaltation. They shall have access to the presence of the Father and the Son. A citizen in a kingdom can have no greater honor than to be a welcome visitor in the palaces of the king. This is the privilege of those who come forth in the resurrection of the just.

63. *Whom he shall bring with him*] Christ will bring them with Him when He comes to take possession of the Kingdom on this Earth.

64. *The first resurrection*] For they will be resurrected at His coming, and together with the living Saints, who will be changed in a moment, they will meet Him "in the air," and return with Him (Compare I. Thes. 4:15-17; Jude 14, 15).

65. *Resurrection of the just*] This is also called the first resurrection, but the truth is here taught that only those who are *just* will have part in it. To be *just* is to be upright and sincere in one's actions and dealings with others. It is to be like Christ, who suffered, the just for the unjust (I. Pet. 3:18). To be just is also to be justified. That is to say, one who is just is, by God Himself, declared to be as he ought to be. Such are they who have part in the first resurrection.

66. *Who have come unto Mount Zion*] They have accepted the gospel and cast their lot with the people of God in Mount Zion and the New Jerusalem, "the heavenly place, the holiest of all."

67. *To an innumerable company of angels,* etc.] In mortality they cast their lot with the Saints of God. As resurrected beings they gather with angels, with the Saints of Enoch's Zion, and with those of the Church of the Firstborn, even Jesus Christ, our Lord.

68. *Whose names are written in heaven*] There is a special record which is called the "Book of God," or the "Book of Life," which contains the names of those who shall rise from the dead in the first resurrection. Moses, on one occasion, asked the Lord to forgive; "and if not," he said, "blot me, I pray thee, out of the book which thou hast written." The Lord's reply was, "Whosoever hath sinned against me, him will I blot out of my book" (Ex. 32:32-3). The disciples of our Lord, after their first missionary journey, returned to their Master full of enthusiasm, and reported that even demons were subject to them in His name. Jesus replied, "Notwithstanding in this rejoice not * * * but rather rejoice, because your names are written in heaven" (Luke 10:20). In the Revelation by John it is stated that all who dwell on Earth, "whose names are not written in the Book of Life of the Lamb" shall worship the "beast" with seven heads and ten horns (Rev. 13:8). Here is one mark by which it may be known in this life, whether our names are "written in heaven." There are two classes of children of men. One consists of the followers of the Lamb; the other, of the followers of the beast. For there are only two churches (I. Nephi 14:10-17). The names of the members of one are recorded in the Book of God; those of the other are not found there.

Where God and Christ are judge of all] That insures absolute justice and perfection in the Record. No name will be entered by mistake; none will be left out by mistake. No one worthy of a place in the Book will be forgotten; no unworthy name will be inscribed. Both the Father and the Son are interested in the Record. Infinite justice and infinite mercy stand guardians over its pages.

69. *Just men made perfect*] Those who have part in the first resurrection are made perfect. They have passed from their first existence to one in mortality, and from mortality to immortality again, with celestialized tabernacles. They are now made perfect. And this life in perfection they owe to the atonement of Jesus, the Mediator (Comp. Rom. 2:7; I. Tim. 6:16).

70. *Bodies are celestial*] Their resurrected bodies are "celestial." Their glory is that of God, "the highest of all," typified by the sun.

On January 21st, 1836, while the Prophet Joseph and his associates were attending to holy ordinances in Kirtland, the heavens were opened to their vision. The Prophet says he beheld the Celestial Kingdom of God and the glory thereof. He saw the gate through which the heirs of that Kingdom will enter, and it appeared to him like circling flames of fire; also the radiant throne of God, whereon were seated the Father and the Son. He saw streets which seemed to be paved with gold. He saw also Adam, Abraham, his own father and mother, and his brother Alvin, who departed this life in 1824, and he marveled. Then the voice of the Lord came to him:

"All who have died without a knowledge of this gospel, who would have received it if they had been permitted to tarry shall be heirs of the Celestial Kingdom of God; also all that shall die henceforth without a knowledge of it, who would have received it with all their hearts, shall be heirs of that Kingdom, for I, the Lord, will judge all men according to their works, according to the desire of their hearts."

The Prophet, further, beheld that all children who die before they arrive at the years of accountability, are saved in the celestial kingdom of heaven (*Hist. of the Church,* Vol. II., p. 380-1).

In an address at Nauvoo, May 12th, 1844, the Prophet said, in part:

"All men who are immortal dwell in everlasting burnings.

"In order for you to receive your children to yourselves you must have a promise—some ordinance, some blessing, in order to ascend above principalities, or else it may be an angel. They must rise just as they died; we can there hail our lovely infants with the same glory— the same loveliness in the celestial glory, where they all enjoy alike. They differ in stature, in size; the same glorious spirit gives them the likeness of glory and bloom; the old man with his silvery hairs will glory in bloom and beauty. No man can describe it to you—no man can write it" (*Ibid.,* Vol. VI., p. 366).

71. And again, we saw the terrestrial world, and behold and lo, these are they who are of the terrestrial, whose glory differs from that of the church of the Firstborn who have received the fulness of the Father, even as that of the moon differs from the sun in the firmament.

72. Behold, these are they who died without law;

73. And also they who are the spirits of men kept in prison, whom the Son visited, and preached the gospel unto them, that they might be judged according to men in the flesh;

74. Who received not the testimony of Jesus in the flesh, but afterwards received it.

75. These are they who are honorable men of the earth, who were blinded by the craftiness of men.

76. These are they who receive of his glory, but not of his fulness.

77. These are they who receive of the presence of the Son, but not of the fulness of the Father.

78. Wherefore, they are bodies terrestrial, and not bodies celestial, and differ in glory as the moon differs from the sun.

79. These are they who are not valiant in the testimony of Jesus; wherefore, they obtain not the crown over the kingdom of our God.

80. And now this is the end of the vision which we saw of the terrestrial, that the Lord commanded us to write while we were yet in the Spirit.

7. VISION OF THE TERRESTRIAL WORLD.

71-80. Another grand scene is now presented. The seers have been given a view of the celestial world and have learned that those who have accepted the gospel in this world, and remained faithful, and all who have lived before the restoration of the gospel and would have accepted it, had they heard it; also those who live now in ignorance of the gospel and who would gladly believe, if they had an opportunity of hearing it; and, finally, all infants who die before the age of accountability, will have an inheritance in the celestial kingdom. But what about those who have heard the gospel and rejected it, and yet have remained morally upright men and women? What about those who have passed away, and those who live, in ignorance of the truth, and who would not have accepted it here, even if they had heard it? These questions are answered in this vision. There is a terrestrial, as well as a celestial world. There is the glory of the moon, as well as of the sun, and they will be partakers of this lesser glory.

71. *Terrestrial world*] This glory differs from that inherited by the members of the Church of the Firstborn; and yet it is, undoubtedly, all that those who inherit it can endure.

73. *Spirits of men kept in prison*] This has reference not only to those who rejected the teachings of Noah and others before the flood,

but also all who in like manner refused to receive the message of salvation when living from the beginning to the time of Christ. In the spirit world they accepted the "testimony of Jesus," and repented of their sin of rejection. This class is composed of those who were clean in their lives, "honorable men who were blinded by the craftiness of men." Because they rejected the message when living on the earth but afterwards received it they are awarded with a place in the terrestrial kingdom. The same reward will be given to honorable men since the restoration of the Gospel, who refused to receive it, as well as to those who lived before the crucifixion of our Savior.

76-78. *Receive of his glory* * * * *They are bodies terrestrial*] Because they were honorable men, free from lying, adultery and kindred sins, they will receive of the Savior's glory. In other words they will be entitled to visits from the Son, but not from the Father. They do not "obtain the crown over the kingdom of our God."

79. *They who are not valiant in the testimony of Jesus*] This is another class which will be composed of those assigned to the terrestrial kingdom. These are members of the Church who have had the gift of the Holy Ghost, many of whom have filled missions and in other ways have been active in the Church, but they have not endured in faithfulness, or have not been valiant to the end. This class could not be composed of those who had never been in the Church, for no one outside of the Church could be valiant in the testimony of Jesus, for they have not had the gift of the Holy Ghost. (See John 14:17 and I. Cor. 12:3.)

"Are we all magnifying our calling? No; we are not! We have indeed a sort of skeleton fixed up; but I think sometimes it needs flesh on the bones and the breath of life, the Spirit of the Living God breathed into it. We need to realize the position we occupy and the duties devolving upon us. We see this in almost everything around us associated with the Church and kingdom of God. While many men are diligent and their whole hearts are engaged in the work of God, there are a great many astride of the fence * * * And yet they are High Priests, and Seventies and Elders. What will be the condition of such? We are told that 'Many will say to me in that day, Lord, Lord, have we not prophesied in Thy name and in Thy name have cast out devils, and in Thy name done many wonderful works?' Yet to all such he will say; 'Depart from me, ye that work iniquity.' You say that means the outsiders? No, it does not. Do they do many wonderful works in the name of Jesus? No; if they do anything, it is done in the name of themselves or of the devil. Sometimes they will do things in the name of God; but it is simply an act of blasphemy. This means you, Latter-day Saints, who heal the sick, cast out devils and do many wonderful things in the name of Jesus. And yet how many we see among this people of this class, that become careless, and treat lightly the ordinances of God's house and the Priesthood of the Son of God; yet they think they are going by and by, to slide into the kingdom of God; but I tell you unless they are righteous and keep their covenants they will never go there. Hear it, ye Latter-day Saints! Hear it, ye Seventies and ye High Priests! Whatsoever a man soweth that shall he reap. * * * You have the Priesthood, and if you do not magnify that Priesthood, God will require it at your hands. He expects us all to be alive and energetic, honoring our callings, our Priesthood and our God; for he expects it of all of us. Now hear it, for as sure as God lives it will be so. * * * If you aim at a celestial glory you must have a celestial spirit and be governed by it. You must be honest, virtuous and benevolent; you must be men full of the Holy Ghost, magnifying your Priesthood, if you would obtain an entrance into the kingdom of God."—President John Taylor, Salt Lake Stake Conference, January 6, 1879.

80. *Write while * * * yet in the spirit*] The Lord commanded the seers to write this and the previous vision, while they were yet "in the spirit;" that is, while the vision of their spirits was yet unobstructed by their outward senses. This proves that, although they were in a condition of ecstasy, they had full control of all their faculties. They were not in a trance, which is described as a condition in which voluntary movement is suspended and all evidence of mental activity removed. They were, still less, in an epileptic condition. They had full control of all their faculties, and deception was impossible, for both heard the same words and saw the same vision, and the record was made while the impression was still deep on their minds. The reality of these visions is, therefore, fully attested.

Speaking of the departed ones, President Brigham Young (*Jour. of Dis.,* Vol. III., p. 95) makes the statement that the spirits of the righteous and those of the ungodly, all go to "prison" after death. If the word "prison" is used as a synonym for *hades,* the statement is perfectly correct, for *hades* is understood to be the domain of all the dead. But the righteous and the unrighteous are, of course, not in the same locality in that domain. President Young also explains that the wicked, after death, are unhappy, while the righteous dead have passed beyond the reach of the adversary and are resting in peace until the morning of the resurrection, and this makes it clear that he did not mean to say that all the departed spirits are in the same place or the same condition.

The prison into which the antediluvians who perished in the flood were cast is the same place where the spirits of men all through the ages have gone. The Lord said to Enoch: "But behold, these which thine eyes are upon shall perish in the floods; and behold, I will shut them up; a prison have I prepared for them. And That which I have chosen hath plead before my face, wherefore, he suffereth for their sins; inasmuch as they will repent in the day that my Chosen shall return unto me, and until that day they shall be in torment."—(Moses 7:38-39.) Alma tells us that the righteous are received in a state of happiness, which is called paradise, a state of rest, but those who have done evil are "cast out into outer darkness" where they are in a state of "awful, fearful looking for the fiery indignation of the wrath of God upon them."— (Alma 40:12-14.)

"If we accept the record of St. Peter's speeches in the Acts as a true record, and compare the assured clearness and freedom of his teaching there with his imperfect insight into the character of our Lord's work during the whole period of His ministry prior to the resurrection, we can scarcely fail to see in the interpretation of His words, 'Thou shalt not leave my soul in hell,' the first fruits of the method of prophetic interpretation which he had learned from our Lord Himself when He expounded to His disciples the things that were written concerning Himself in the Law, and the Prophets, and the Psalms (Luke 24:44)" (*Cambridge Bible,* Note on I. Peter 3:19).

St. Peter, then, had heard from Christ Himself of His descent into hades, the visit to the "prison," and the preaching of the gospel there.

81. And again, we saw the glory of the telestial, which glory is that of the lesser, even as the glory of the stars differs from that of the glory of the moon in the firmament.

82. These are they who received not the gospel of Christ, neither the testimony of Jesus.

83. These are they who deny not the Holy Spirit.

84. These are they who are thrust down to hell.

85. These are they who shall not be redeemed from the devil until the last resurrection, until the Lord, even Christ the Lamb, shall have finished his work.

86. These are they who receive not of his fulness in the eternal world, but of the Holy Spirit through the ministration of the terrestrial;

87. And the terrestrial through the ministration of the celestial.

88. And also the telestial receive it of the administering of angels who are appointed to minister for them, or who are appointed to be ministering spirits for them; for they shall be heirs of salvation.

8. VISION OF TELESTIAL GLORY.

81-88. Again there is a change of scene. A lesser glory than the terrestrial passes before the view of the seers. When the gospel had been preached on both sides of the veil, and those who have accepted it are gathered into celestial, or terrestrial, spheres, there still remains a large class, consisting of those who have not received the gospel, and yet not committed the unpardonable sin of denying the Holy Spirit.

What will be their fate? And who are they? For them there is the telestial glory.

82. *Received not the gospel*] They did not receive the gospel here; nor the testimony of Jesus on the other side of the veil.

83. *Deny not the Holy Spirit*] But they had not denied the Holy Spirit, because they had never known His power, or tasted of the heavenly gift; they had never been "enlightened" by baptism in water and spirit.

84. *Thrust down to hell*] Those who partake of the telestial kingdom are the unclean inhabitants of the earth; those who have defiled themselves with immoral practices, the liars, sorcerers, thieves, blasphemers, and all who have loved wickedness. Because of their evil practices they bring down upon themselves the wrath of God. These are turned over to Satan and become subject to his rule and suffer his buffetings until the day of the earth, or their redemption which is the resurrection which will not come until the end of the earth, or the "fulness of times," or when our Savior has finished his work; then they shall be brought forth after they have paid the "uttermost farthing," and have learned by the things they have suffered that "crime does not pay."

85. *The last resurrection*] This will take place after the Millennial reign of our Lord. Then they will be "redeemed," that is, ressurrected: for, "the resurrection of the dead is the redemption of the soul" (Sec. 88:16).

86. *Receive not of his fulness*] As those of the terrestrial kingdom do not receive a fulness of the glory of the Father, so these do not receive a fulness of the glory of either the Father or the Son. They will, however, receive of the Holy Spirit. The celestials are admitted to the presence of the Father and the Son; the terrestrials, only to the presence of the Son; and the telestials, only to the presence of the Holy Spirit, and that divine presence will be manifested only through the ministry of terrestrial beings, and through angels appointed to minister in the telestial world (v. 88).

87. *The terrestrial through the * * * celestial*] The meaning seems to be that whatever glory is given to those of the terrestrial world comes from God, through the celestial world, and it reaches the telestial world from the terrestrial. It is all one kingdom under one supreme Ruler, but the conditions of those who inhabit it are as different as here indicated.

88. *Shall be heirs of salvation*] Those of telestial glory are also heirs of salvation, but their glory is that of the stars, contrasted with that of the moon and sun.

Can anybody who has been thrust down to hell] be an "heir of salvation?" Yes. (v. 88.) Hell must deliver up its dead (Rev. 20:13) and they are to be judged according to their works. The Lord calls this a kingdom of glory, and therefore it is a kingdom of salvation as they are freed from the devil and his angels in the final resurrection. Salvation is condition of degree. The inhabitants of this kingdom do not get what is called an exaltation, for this blessing is reversed for those who become heirs of the celestial kingdom. Those who enter the telestial kingdom are judged at death and thrust down to hell. They receive their final judgment at the last day.

"How much does it take to prepare a man or woman, or any other being, to become angels to the devil, to suffer with him to all eternity? Just as much as it does to prepare a man to go into the celestial kingdom, into the presence of the Father and the Son, and to be made an heir to His kingdom and all his glory, and be crowned with crowns of glory, immortality, and eternal lives" (Brigham Young, *Jour. of Dis.,* Vol. III., p. 93).

89. And thus we saw, in the heavenly vision, the glory of the telestial, which surpasses all understanding;

90. And no man knows it except him to whom God has revealed it.

91. And thus we saw the glory of the terrestrial which excels in all things the glory of the telestial, even in glory, and in power, and in might, and in dominion.

92. And thus we saw the glory of the celestial, which excels in all things—where God, even the Father, reigns upon his throne forever and ever;

93. Before whose throne all things bow in humble reverence, and give him glory forever and ever.

94. They who dwell in his presence are the church of the Firstborn; and they see as they are seen, and know as they are known, having received of his fulness and of his grace;

95. And he makes them equal in power, and in might, and in dominion.

96. And the glory of the celestial is one, even as the glory of the sun is one.

97. And the glory of the terrestrial is one, even as the glory of the moon is one.

98. And the glory of the telestial is one, even as the glory of the stars is one; for as one star differs from another star in glory, even so differs one from another in glory in the telestial world;

99. For these are they who are of Paul, and of Apollos, and of Cephas.

100. These are they who say they are some of one and some of another—some of Christ and some of John, and some of Moses, and some of Elias, and some of Esaias, and some of Isaiah, and some of Enoch;

101. But received not the gospel, neither the testimony of Jesus, neither the prophets, neither the everlasting covenant.

102. Last of all, these all are they who will not be gathered with the saints, to be caught up unto the church of the First-born, and received into the cloud.

103. These are they who are liars, and sorcerers, and adulterers, and whoremongers, and whosoever loves and makes a lie.

104. These are they who suffer the wrath of God on earth.

105. These are they who suffer the vengeance of eternal fire.

106. These are they who are cast down to hell and suffer the wrath of Almighty God, until the fulness of times, when Christ shall have subdued all enemies under his feet, and shall have perfected his work;

107. When he shall deliver up the kingdom, and present it unto the Father, spotless, saying: I have overcome and have trodden the wine-press alone, even the wine-press of the fierceness of the wrath of Almighty God.

108. Then shall he be crowned with the crown of his glory, to sit on the throne of his power to reign forever and ever.

109. But behold, and lo, we saw the glory and the inhabitants of the telestial world, that they were as innumerable as the stars in the firmament of heaven, or as the sand upon the seashore;

110. And heard the voice of the Lord saying: These all shall bow the knee, and every tongue shall confess to him who sits upon the throne forever and ever;

111. For they shall be judged according to their works, and every man shall receive according to his own works, his own dominion, in the mansions which are prepared;

112. And they shall be servants of the Most High; but where God and Christ dwell they cannot come, worlds without end.

9. THE THREE GLORIES FURTHER EXPLAINED.

89. *The telestial*] Even the telestial glory "surpasses understanding." It cannot be conceived of by human mind, except as revealed (v. 90). We receive impressions through our senses. We analyze these impressions, classify them, and form deductions from them, and thus we obtain some knowledge of things both seen and unseen; but we cannot gain any knowledge of the glories beyond any such process. It must be revealed. Revelation is also a source of knowledge, and ignorant indeed is he who rejects it.

91. *The terrestrial*] Note that the glory of the terrestrial world exceeds that of the telestial "in all things."

In glory] This means in power, knowledge, privilege and dominion, the celestial exceeds the other kingdoms in that its inhabitants have obtained the fulness and have become the sons of God. The terrestrial, while limited, has greater privileges and knowledge than the telestial.

In power] In the world beyond, as here, there are "powers that be," officials who hold authority delegated to them by the Lord. In the terrestrial world such divine authority exceeds by far that held in the telestial sphere.

In might, and in dominion] The remark just made applies also to these. "Might" refers to the ability to do, or perform whatever must be done; "dominion" refers to the extent of the field of action. The terrestrials have more intelligence, more authority, more strength, and a larger expanse in which to operate, than the telestials.

Paul also speaks of "thrones, or dominions, or principalities, or powers" (Col. 1:16); and of "principality, and power, and might, and dominion," (Eph. 1:21) alluding to different degrees of authority in the government of the world beyond. They were created, or appointed by our Lord, and when He was resurrected He was placed "far above" all these various authorities, namely upon the right hand of the Supreme Throne, as co-regent with the Father (Eph. 1:20-1).

92. *The celestial*] This glory excels in all things. It is the glory in which the eternal Father dwells and reigns; the glory that surrounds His throne.

93. *In humble reverence*] These all bow in humility and give glory (praise for ever and ever). Isaiah (6:3) heard the song that is sung there: "Holy, holy, holy, is the Lord God of hosts: the whole earth is full of his glory;" for the glory of God is manifest in all His creation.

95. *Equal in power, and in might, and in dominion*] Those who dwell in the presence of God are faithful members of the Church of the Firstborn. They are equal. In the celestial world all the ransomed are equal in authority, in strength, in opportunities, and in possessions. Is it any wonder, then, that our Lord instituted the United Order, with equality, in the Church, as a school in which to obtain some understanding of, and training for, a place in celestial glory? Can anyone, after a life of selfishness, fill a position in a kingdom where all are equal?

96-8. This is a repetition of the wonderful truth that one glory differs from another in degree, and another important truth is added, that in the telestial glory there are many degrees, just as there are many gradations of brilliancy among the stars.

99-112. These paragraphs contain additional information concerning the inhabitants of the telestial sphere. Among them are those who have followed religious leaders and formed churches and sects, but who have refused to accept the gospel here, or the testimony of Jesus beyond the veil; they have refused to enter into the everlasting covenant and to gather with the Saints (vv. 99-102).

Among them are also "liars, and sorcerers, and adulterers, and whoremongers, and whosoever loves and makes a lie" (v. 103). In the Revelation by John this class is said to be excluded from the celestial city (Rev. 22:15). The reader of this portion of the Revelation by John might ask, Why are they not in the bottomless pit with the sons of Perdition? The answer is found in this Section of the Doctrine and Covenants: Because they had not committed the unpardonable sin. Having suffered all the consequences of their transgressions and paid the "uttermost farthing," they have been released. They have suffered "the wrath of God on the earth" (v. 104), for even here the way of the transgressor is hard. "They have suffered the vengeance of eternal fire," and through these sufferings they have learned submission to the will of God (v. 110), and they can, therefore, enjoy telestial happiness (v. 105), through the redemption of Jesus Christ (vv. 106-8). Their redemption is the completion of Christ's work as a Savior.

109. *Innumerable as the stars*] Note the great number of telestials. The celestials must also be numerous, since departed infants belong to that class. The telestials are innumerable.

111. *Judged according to their works*] There are, as has been stated, various degrees of glory in the telestial sphere, and each individual will, in the judgment, receive that "dominion" in the "mansions" of God for which he has, by his works, proved himself fit.

112. *They shall be servants of the Most High*] That is also an honorable position, indeed, but it is different to being "kings and priests." "Where God and Christ dwell, they cannot come, worlds without end."

113. This is the end of the vision which we saw, which we were commanded to write while we were yet in the Spirit.

114. But great and marvelous are the works of the Lord, and the mysteries of his kingdom which he showed unto us, which surpass all understanding in glory, and in might, and in dominion;

115. Which he commanded us we should not write while we were yet in the Spirit, and are not lawful for man to utter;

116. Neither is man capable to make them known, for they are only to be seen and understood by the power of the Holy Spirit, which God bestows on those who love him, and purify themselves before him;

117. To whom he grants this privilege of seeing and knowing for themselves;

118. That through the power and manisfestation of the Spirit, while in the flesh, they may be able to bear his presence in the world of glory.

119. And to God and the Lamb be glory, and honor, and dominion forever and ever. Amen.

10. Conclusion.

113-19. The vision here recorded is one of the most remarkable that any mortal ever had. The record, however, contains but a part of that which passed before the view of the favored seers.

General Notes

In one portion of this Revelation the eternal misery of a certain class of apostates is graphically set forth. But if such opponents of the Kingdom of God would tell the truth about themselves, they would reveal the fact that their sufferings have already commenced. Lyman E. Johnson, the first to be called to the Apostleship when the first Council of Twelve was organized,* left the Church, but he never had a really happy day after that. According to President Brigham Young he, on one occasion, said, at a meeting of the Council:

"Brethren,—I will call you brethren—I will tell you the truth. If I could believe Mormonism—it is no matter whether it is true or not—but If I could believe Mormonism as I did when I traveled with you and preached, if I possessed the world I would give it. I would give anything. I would suffer my right hand to be cut off, if I could believe it again. Then I was full of joy and gladness. My dreams were pleasant. When I awoke in the morning, my spirit was cheerful. I was happy by day and by night, full of peace and joy and thanksgiving. But now it is darkness, pain, sorrow, misery in the extreme. I have never since seen a happy moment" (*Jour. of Dis.,* Vol. XIX., p. 41).

All men will be judged "according to their works," but all will not be judged in the same way, or at the same time, "He that heareth my word, and believeth on him that sent me, hath everlasting life, and shall

---

* Brigham Young was the second, and Heber C. Kimball the third.

not come into condemnation" (John 5:24). "Condemnation" here means "judgment."* They shall not come into "judgment." There is a difference between the status of a son, or daughter, appearing before a father, and a stranger standing as a transgressor before a judge. "If we become the sons of God, we shall be joint heirs with Jesus Christ to all the inheritances that the Father hath prepared for the faithful."

Some people deny the existence of the Devil and evil spirits. Heber C. Kimball relates:

"When I was in England, Brother George D. Watt was the first man baptized * * * The night previous * * * I had a vision * * * I saw legions of wicked spirits that night, as plain as I now see you, and they came as near to me as you now are, and company after company of them rushed towards me; and Brother Hyde and Brother Richards also saw them. It was near the break of day, and I looked upon them, as I now look upon you" (*Jour. of Dis.,* Vol. III., p. 229).

Brigham Young: "When Lucifer, the Son of the Morning, was cast out * * * he came here, and one-third part of the spirits in heaven came with him. Do you suppose that one-third part of all the beings that existed in eternity came with him? No, but one-third part of the spirits that were begotten and organized and brought forth to become tenants of fleshly bodies to dwell upon this Earth; they forsook Jesus Christ, the rightful heir, and joined with Lucifer, the Son of the Morning, and came to this Earth; they got here first. As soon as Mother Eve made her appearance in the Garden of Eden, the Devil was on hand" (*Ibid.,* p. 368-9).

"The Lamanites, or Indians, are just as much the children of our Father and God as we are. So also are the Africans. But *we* are also the children of adoption through obedience to the gospel of His Son. Why are so many of the inhabitants of the Earth cursed with a skin of blackness? It comes in consequence of their fathers rejecting the power of the Holy Priesthood, and the law of God. They will go down to death. And when all the rest of the children have received their blessings in the Holy Priesthood, then that curse will be removed from the seed of Cain, and they will then come up and possess the Priesthood, and receive all the blessings which we now are entitled to" (Brigham Young, *Jour. of Dis.,* Vol. XI., p. 272).

SECTION 77.

REVELATION *given to Joseph Smith the Prophet, at Hiram, Ohio, March, 1832.——An explanation of part of the Revelation of John.*

---

* The word in the original is KRISIS.

Q. WHAT is the sea of glass spoken of by John, 4th chapter, and 6th verse of the Revelation?

A. It is the earth, in its sanctified, immortal, and eternal state.

1. *Sea of glass*] St. John, in this chapter of the Revelation, is taken up to heaven, where thrones were placed. There was the central Throne, and seated upon it One "who was to look like a jasper and a sardine stone." There were twenty-four thrones occupied by Elders in white raiment. There were seven lamps burning symbolizing the "seven spirits of God," and there was a "sea of glass like unto crystal." In the Temple of Solomon there was an immense basin called "a molten sea" (I. Kings 7:23). In the Temple in heaven, of which the temples on Earth are feeble representations, there is a *glassy* sea, calm, transparent, and solid, and here we are informed that this "sea" is "the Earth in its sanctified, immortal, and eternal state." The "sea" connected with the temples of God is a baptismal font. It represents the Earth. All who desire access to the Church of Jesus Christ must come through the baptismal font, and be buried with Christ.

"This Earth will become a celestial body—be like a sea of glass, or like a Urim and Thummim; and when you wish to know anything, you can look in this Earth and see all the eternities of God. We shall make our homes here, and go on our missions as we do now" (Brigham Young, *Jour. of Dis.,* Vol. VIII., p. 200). See also Sec. 130:9.

2. Q. What are we to understand by the four beasts, spoken of in the same verse?

A. They are figurative expressions, used by the Revelator, John, in describing heaven, the paradise of God, the happiness of man, and of beasts, and of creeping things, and of the fowls of the air; that which is spiritual being in the likeness of that which is temporal; and that which is temporal in the likeness of that which is spiritual; the spirit of man in the likeness of his person, as also the spirit of the beast, and every other creature which God has created.

2. *Four beasts*] The Revelator saw "four beasts," or rather "four living creatures," "in the midst of the throne, and round about it." They were, possibly, supporting it, as the Cherubim in Ez. 1:4-22. Here we have an explanation of these living creatures. They represent the happiness enjoyed in that part of heaven which is called the Paradise of God, by men, by the larger animals, and by creeping things and fowls of the air. For the things on Earth are but a counterpart of things in heaven.

3. Q. Are the four beasts limited to individual beasts, or do they represent classes or orders?

A. They are limited to four individual beasts, which were shown to John, to represent the glory of the classes of beings in their destined order or sphere of creation, in the enjoyment of their eternal felicity.

3. *Individual beasts*] In the vision, John saw four individual living creatures, but each represented a class having attained glory and happiness.

4. Q. What are we to understand by the eyes and wings, which the beasts had?

A. Their eyes are a representation of light and knowledge, that is, they are full of knowledge; and their wings are a representation of power, to move, to act, etc.

4. *Eyes and wings*] These living creatures are different to any seen by former prophets. One is like a lion; another like a calf; another has a face resembling that of a man, and another looks like a flying eagle. Each of them has six wings, and they have eyes "round about and within" (Rev. 4:8).

It is needless to say that many opinions have been expressed concerning these creatures. One very ancient idea is that they represent the four gospels, Mark being the lion, Matthew the man, Luke the ox, and John the eagle. Others see in them a representation of all created beings, and others hold that the lion represents Christ's royalty; the calf His sacrifice; the man His humanity, and the eagle His union with the Father. The explanation in the text is natural, easy of comprehension, and full of meaning.

5. Q. What are we to understand by the four and twenty elders, spoken of by John?

A. We are to understand that these elders whom John saw, were elders who had been faithful in the work of the ministry and were dead; who belonged to the seven churches, and were then in the paradise of God.

5. *Four and twenty elders*] It is most generally supposed that these Elders were the twelve sons of Jacob, as heads of the ancient Israel, and the first twelve Apostles, as heads of the Church, but that is an arbitrary interpretation. Is it probable that John would see himself seated on one of those thrones? The explanation in the text is correct.

6. Q. What are we to understand by the book which John saw, which was sealed on the back with seven seals?

A. We are to understand that it contains the revealed will, mysteries, and works of God; the hidden things of his economy concerning this earth during the seven thousand years of its continuance, or its temporal existence.

6. *The book * * * sealed*] The book which is sealed contains the history of the seven thousand years of the temporal existence of the earth.

"By the seven thousand years of temporal existence is meant the time of the earth's duration from the fall of Adam to the end of time, which will come after the Millennium and 'a little season' which will follow. The earth and all on it were in a spiritual condition before the fall, for mortality had not come bringing temporal conditions. We are now living in the second period of the earth's history, which is referred to as being a telestial condition. In other words, a condition where wickedness and all the vicissitudes of mortality endure. It is the earth and its inhabitants in the fallen state which Adam brought through his transgression. This condition will continue until Christ comes." (*Ch. History and Modern Revelation,* p. 64, second series.)

7. Q. What are we to understand by the seven seals with which it was sealed?

A. We are to understand that the first seal contains the things of the first thousand years, and the second also of the second thousand years, and so on until the seventh:

7. *The seven seals*] The number seven denotes completeness. The plans of God are hidden completely, until they are revealed by Himself. So these seven seals signify the seven thousand years of temporal existence.

Some ancient books consisted of parchment rolled round a piece of wood. This book contained seven skins, rolled upon one another. When the first seal was broken, the first skin was unrolled, and was found to contain a hieroglyphic painting, as described in ch. 6:2-12. Each skin contained some drawing. Ancient books of the East were often beautifully illustrated in this manner.

8. Q. What are we to understand by the four angels, spoken of in the 7th chapter and 1st verse of Revelation?

A. We are to understand that they are four angels sent forth from God, to whom is given power over the four parts of the earth, to save life and to destroy; these are they who have the everlasting gospel to commit to every nation, kindred, tongue, and people; having power to shut up the heavens, to seal up unto life, or to cast down to the regions of darkness.

8. *Four angels*] Four messengers from God with extraordinary powers over life and death, and having a commission to preach the everlasting gospel in all the world.

9. Q. What are we to understand by the angel ascending from the east, Revelation 7th chapter and 2nd verse?

A. We are to understand that the angel ascending from the east is he to whom is given the seal of the living God over the twelve tribes of Israel; wherefore, he crieth unto the four angels having the everlasting gospel, saying: Hurt not the earth, neither the sea, nor the trees, till we have sealed the servants of our God in their foreheads. And, if you will receive it, this is Elias which was to come to gather together the tribes of Israel and restore all things.

9. *Angel ascending from the east*] John stands before the Temple in heaven, looking down upon the Earth, and the then known world is spread out before him as a map. On this map he sees four angels stationed, one at each corner, holding back the winds of destruction. Then another angel ascends from the East high enough to be seen or heard by the four. He had the seal of God, and he cried, "Hurt not the Earth, neither the sea, nor the trees, till we have sealed the servants of our God in their foreheads." This angel is Elias, who has the commission to gather Israel and restore all things (Comp. Secs. 27:6; 76:100).

10. Q. What time are the things spoken of in this chapter to be accomplished?

A. They are to be accomplished in the sixth thousand years, or the opening of the sixth seal.

10. *What time?*] The things spoken of in this chapter (Rev. 7) belong to the sixth seal, or sixth millennium (See v. 7).

11. Q. What are we to understand by sealing the one hundred and forty-four thousand, out of all the tribes of Israel—twelve thousand out of every tribe?

A. We are to understand that those who are sealed are high priests, ordained unto the holy order of God, to administer the everlasting gospel; for they are they who are ordained out of every nation, kindred, tongue, and people, by the angels to whom is given power over the nations of the earth, to bring as many as will come to the church of the Firstborn.

11. *Out of all the tribes of Israel*] One hundred and forty-four thousand were sealed, 12,000 of each tribe. Opinions are divided as to whether this refers to Israel, literally, or to believers generally. The explanation in the text favors the latter opinion. In the enumeration of the Twelve Tribes in the Revelation, there are some peculiarities. Judah is named first and Reuben second. The name of Ephraim is omitted, while that of Manasseh is retained. Joseph's name is inserted. Dan's is left out. There is a tradition to the effect that this name was omitted, because antichrist was to come from the tribe of Dan. That is only surmise, but the very irregularity of the enumeration may indicate that it is not Israel, as constituted anciently, that is had in view here.

12. Q. What are we to understand by the sounding of the trumpets, mentioned in the 8th chapter of Revelation?

A. We are to understand that as God made the world in six days, and on the seventh day he finished his work, and sanctified it, and also formed man out of the dust of the earth, even so, in the beginning of the seventh thousand years will the Lord God sanctify the earth, and complete the salvation of man, and judge all things, and shall redeem all things, except that which he hath not put into his power, when he shall have sealed all things, unto the end of all things; and the sounding of the trumpets of the seven angels are the preparing and finishing of his work, in the beginning of the seventh thousand years—the preparing of the way before the time of his coming.

12. *The sounding of trumpets*] This forms the contents of the seventh seal of the book, which is the completion of man's salvation in the seventh millennium.

13. Q. When are the things to be accomplished, which are written in the 9th chapter of Revelation?

A. They are to be accomplished after the opening of the seventh seal, before the coming of Christ.

13. *The ninth chapter of Revelations*] The events placed before us in this chapter are to be accomplished just before the coming of Christ. The fifth and sixth trumpets take us to the very last days.

14. Q. What are we to understand by the little book which was eaten by John, as mentioned in the 10th chapter of Revelation?

A. We are to understand that it was a mission, and an ordinance, for him to gather the tribes of Israel; behold, this is Elias, who, as it is written, must come and restore all things.

14. *The little book*] In the previous chapter, John saw destruction overwhelming that part of the world in which the first Christian churches had been planted. He saw that idolatry, violence, and impurity prevailed there, where the gospel of peace, love, and holiness had been preached by himself and other inspired men. When he beheld the extent of the apostasy, the question, naturally, arose in his mind, Is this, then, the end of the Church of Christ? Is it destined to perish in error and iniquity, as the antediluvians perished in the flood? That question is answered in the vision recorded in the tenth chapter. In this vision John sees another mighty angel, or messenger, coming from heaven. This angel had a "little book" open, and he cried out his message with a loud voice, declaring solemnly that there would be "time no longer," —no more delay—but that when the seventh angel begins to sound, the mystery of God—God's plan of salvation—will be completed. This is a vision of the restoration of the Church through the instrumentality of the Prophet Joseph, who came as a messenger from God and declared that the Church was to be restored, preparatory to the second coming of Christ. The coming forth of the "little book" was the beginning of a new prophetic era, for John was told (Rev. 10:11): "Thou must prophesy again before many peoples, and nations, and tongues, and kings." The establishment of the Church in our day is foretold in this chapter of the Revelation as clearly as the birth of Christ is predicted in Isaiah 9:6, 7.

15. Q. What is to be understood by the two witnesses, in the eleventh chapter of Revelation?

A. They are two prophets that are to be raised up to the Jewish nation in the last days, at the time of the restoration. and to prophesy to the Jews after they are gathered and have built the city of Jerusalem in the land of their fathers.

15. *Two witnesses*] One tradition is that the two witnesses will be Enoch and Elijah. Some suggest Moses and Elijah. But it is useless to speculate any further than the Revelation warrants. Two witnesses will be raised up in the last days, and when their testimony is finished, some terrible calamity will strike the Earth, whereupon men will turn to God and give glory to Him (Rev. 11:13).

GENERAL NOTES

In the opening words of the Revelation John says, "Blessed is he that readeth, and they that hear the words of this prophecy, and keep

478   DOCTRINE AND COVENANTS   [SEC. 77.

those things which are written therein" (1:3), but, notwithstanding
this promise, the book is commonly left unread. The prophetic part of
it is mostly regarded as an unsolvable riddle. And to those who read it,
a multitude of opinions concerning the meaning of the visions described
present themselves, until Apocalyptic exegesis appears to be a Babylonian babble.

The reason for this confusion is that the modern interpreters have
lost the key to the book. The Revelation of John can never be understood by anyone who supposes that the Church of Christ has remained
in uninterrupted activity and development from its first organization
till the present time. That book was written to show that the Church
would conquer paganism, but that it would itself be driven into exile
and remain in absolute obscurity for 1260 "days"—prophetic years of
354 days each—and that then it would again be established by messengers from heaven, preparatory to the second advent and the Millennium. If this purpose of the book is kept in view, it becomes intelligible.
It is then also seen why he who reads it and they who hear are blessed;
they have in this sublime record the "more sure word of prophecy,"
shining as a light in a dark place, indicating the entrance to the true
Church of latter days. In the 10th chapter they see the coming of the
mighty angel with the "Little book" open, and hear his message to the
world. In the 14th chapter again, they view the angel with the everlasting
gospel, flying in midheaven, and delivering his divine message.

The Book of Revelation is one of the grandest books in sacred
literature, and the Lord clearly designs that the Saints should become
familiar with it. Else, why this Revelation in the Doctrine and Covenants?

But this Revelation is not a complete interpretation of the book. It
is a *key*. A key is a very small part of the house. It unlocks the door
through which an entrance may be gained, but after the key has been
turned, the searcher for treasure must find it for himself. It is like
entering a museum in which the students must find out for themselves
what they desire to know. The sources of information are there.

The Lord has, in this Section, given His people a key to the book.
He explains the "sea of glass," the "four living creatures," the "four
and twenty Elders," the "book," the "seals," the "four angels," and the
fifth angel with the "seal" of God; the "sealing," the "sounding of
trumpets," the "locusts," the "four angels" from Euphrates, an "angel
with the little book," and the "two witnesses." From the key thus given,
from the Old Testament prophecies, and from history, ecclesiastical and
political, it should be possible to interpret the rest. As Champollion, by
the key furnished in the brief test on the Rosetta stone, was able to
open the secrets of Egyptian hieroglyphics, so the Bible student should
be able to read the Apocalypse with a better understanding of it, by the
aid of this key.

SECTION 78.

REVELATION *given through Joseph Smith the Prophet, at Hiram, Ohio, March, 1832. The Order given of the Lord to Enoch* [*Joseph Smith, Jun.*] *for the purpose of establishing the poor. In the documentary history of the Church, vol. 1, p. 255, appears this note: It was not always desirable that the individuals whom the Lord addressed in revelations should at the time be known by the world, and hence in this and in some subsequent revelations the brethren were addressed by other than their own names. The temporary necessity having passed for keeping the names of the individuals addressed unknown, their real names were subsequently given in brackets.——A fuller organization of the people for the regulation of their temporal affairs necessary—Spirit of equality among the Saints inculcated—Additional revelation from time to time to be given—Membership in the Church of the Firstborn defined.*

THE Lord spake unto Enoch [Joseph Smith, Jun.], saying: Hearken unto me, saith the Lord your God, who are ordained unto the high priesthood of my church, who have assembled yourselves together;

2. And listen to the counsel of him who has ordained you from on high, who shall speak in your ears the words of wisdom, that salvation may be unto you in that thing which you have presented before me, saith the Lord God.

3. For verily I say unto you, the time has come, and is now at hand; and behold, and lo, it must needs be that there be an organization of my people, in regulating and establishing the affairs of the storehouse for the poor of my people, both in this place and in the land of Zion—

4. Or in other words, the city of Enoch [Joseph], for a permanent and everlasting establishment and order unto my church, to advance the cause, which ye have espoused, to the salvation of man, and to the glory of your Father, who is in heaven;

5. That you may be equal in the bonds of heavenly things, yea, and earthly things also, for the obtaining of heavenly things.

6. For if ye are not equal in earthly things ye cannot be equal in obtaining heavenly things;

7. For if you will that I give unto you a place in the celestial world, you must prepare yourselves by doing the things which I have commanded you and required of you.

During the month of March, 1832, the Prophet Joseph was engaged on the Bible revision. He continued to reside at the house of Father Johnson, at Hiram. This is one of the four Revelations received during that month. It is addressed to the High Priesthood of the Church. In it, the Lord taught His people (1) that equality was necessary (1-7); and (2) that the Saints in Zion needed counsel (8-10); (3) gave them a commandment to organize themselves (11-16); and (4) promised certain blessings (17-22).

1. EQUALITY NECESSARY.

1. *Enoch*] For some reason it was at first not deemed advisable to publish the names of those addressed in this Revelation, wherefore fictitious names were used. Subsequently, when the reason for concealing the identity of the brethren referred to no longer existed, their real names were added in parentheses. This applies also to some Revelations given later. Enoch, in the opinion of some, means "Experienced."

2. *That which you have presented before me*] We can judge only from the Revelation itself what this refers to. It appears that some members of the High Priesthood had asked for a Revelation regarding the United Order, the fundamental principles of which had been revealed February 9th, 1831 (Sec. 42:30-36).

3. *The time has come*] The answer was that the time for more complete organization had come.

6. *Equal in earthly things*] The principle is here taught that the Latter-day Saints must be equal in things pertaining to this Earth. In celestial glory there is perfect equality (Sec. 76:95). But if they have not practiced equality here, they are not prepared to live under that law there.

7. *You must prepare yourselves*] This important truth is further stated in this verse. Let not the rich man, who has only crumbs for Lazarus, think that he is fit for celestial glory!

8. And now, verily thus saith the Lord, it is expedient that all things be done unto my glory, by you who are joined together in this order;

9. Or, in other words, let my servant Ahashdah [Newel K. Whitney] and my servant Gazelam, or Enoch, [Joseph Smith,

Jun.] and my servant Pelagoram [Sidney Rigdon], sit in council with the saints which are in Zion;

10. Otherwise Satan seeketh to turn their hearts away from the truth, that they become blinded and understand not the things which are prepared for them.

2. COUNSEL NEEDED.

8. *Unto my glory*] Efforts had been made by social reformers to establish communism in various forms, but the United Order, revealed to the Prophet Joseph, was different to all previous efforts, in this respect that, while its results would be the social and economic elevation of man, its sole object was the honor and glory of God. There can be no successful United Order until the selfishness of man is swallowed up by his desire to glorify his Father in heaven.

9. *Let my servant * * * sit in council with the saints which are in Zion*] The Saints in Zion needed the counsel of the servants of the Lord at this time. Shortly after this Revelation had been received, the Prophet went to Missouri on his second visit to the land of Zion.

11. Wherefore, a commandment I give unto you, to prepare and organize yourselves by a bond or everlasting covenant that cannot be broken.

12. And he who breaketh it shall lose his office and standing in the church, and shall be delivered over to the buffetings of Satan until the day of redemption.

13. Behold, this is the preparation wherewith I prepare you, and the foundation, and the ensample which I give unto you, whereby you may accomplish the commandments which are given you;

14. That through my providence, notwithstanding the tribulation which shall descend upon you, that the church may stand independent above all other creatures beneath the celestial world;

15. That you may come up unto the crown prepared for you, and be made rulers over many kingdoms, saith the Lord God, the Holy One of Zion, who hath established the foundations of Adam-ondi-Ahman;

16. Who hath appointed Michael your prince, and established his feet, and set him upon high, and given unto him the keys of salvation under the counsel and direction of the Holy One, who is without beginning of days or end of life.

3. A COMMANDMENT TO ORGANIZE.

11. *A bond or everlasting covenant*] The legal instrument—bond or everlasting covenant—whereby property was conveyed to the Bishop, as trustee-in-trust of the Church, stated that the donor, having become a member of the Church of Christ, of his own free will and accord granted and gave the property described to——, "for the purpose of purchasing land in Jackson County, Missouri, and building up the New Jerusalem, even Zion, and for relieving the wants of the poor and needy." The Bishop bound himself to use the property for the purposes mentioned "to the satisfaction of the said Church."

In the legal document securing to the donor his stewardship, the Bishop leased to him the property described to be used "as to him shall seem meet and proper." The donor agreed to pay the taxes and to turn over to the Bishop all the accumulations over and above what he needed for the support of himself and family. The Bishop bound himself to support the donor out of the Church funds, in case of sickness and inability to work, while he was a Church member (Whitney's *History of Utah,* Vol. I., p. 90-1).

12. *He who breaketh it,* etc.] The penalty for breaking this covenant was the loss of office and Church membership.

14. *That the Church may stand independent*] The purpose of revealing the celestial order of society was to enable the Church to pass through all trials safely. God knew that persecutions and sufferings would come. He also knew that obedience to the law revealed would make the Church independent of enemies.

Above all other creatures beneath the celestial world] The term "creatures" is used here in its widest meaning, to signify all that is created, and refers especially to the various organizations in the world, whether ecclesiastical, political, financial, or industrial.

15. *Rulers over many kingdoms*] Another purpose is stated in this verse: "That you may come up unto the crown prepared for you and be made rulers over many kingdoms." The crown is prepared, but it also takes preparation to wear it; that is to say, to exercise the power and authority symbolized by that emblem. The self-abnegation, the unselfish devotion to duty, the all-comprising, brotherly love necessary in the United Order, are excellent qualities with which to enter upon celestial existence. No one can rule a kingdom, or many kingdoms, under the great King of Kings, without having acquired those qualities in His service somewhere.

Adam-ondi-Ahman] Rendered, by Orson Pratt, "the Valley of God." He says:

"Adam-ondi-Ahman, the Valley of God, where Adam dwelt, was located about fifty miles north of Jackson County, in the State of Missouri. The Lord has revealed to us that Adam dwelt there toward the latter period of his probation. Whether he had lived in that region of country from the earliest period of his existence on the Earth, we know not. He might have lived thousands of miles distant, in his early days" (*Jour. of Dis.,* Vol. XVI., p. 48). Comp. Sec. 116.

The place was settled by Lyman Wight in 1836 or 37. In the spring of 1838 the Prophet Joseph, Sidney Rigdon, and George W. Robinson went up to Wight's Ferry for the purpose of selecting a city plat. They did so at a place which was called Spring Hill, but which the Prophet named Adam-ondi-Ahman, as instructed by the Lord, "because," said He, "it is the place where Adam should come to visit his people, or the Ancient of Days shall sit, as spoken of by Daniel the Prophet." Settlers flocked rapidly to the place, and that summer about 200 houses had been built, while many families lived in their wagons. On the 28th of June, 1838, a Stake was organized, with John Smith as president and Reynolds Cahoon and Lyman Wight as counselors. The influx of Church members and the rapid growth of the new settlement excited the animosity of the neighbors. When an armed mob threatened Far West, Lyman Wight, with 120 mounted men went from Adam-ondi-Ahman to assist the Saints at Far West, and in their absence a mob despoiled their homes and destroyed the prosperous settlement. The site of the city is now in a pasture, and nothing remains but broken rock and brick to mark the spots where there once were homes and business houses.

16. *Michael your prince*] Michael is Adam (See Sec. 107:53-57). He holds the keys of salvation, under the counsel and direction of Him who is without beginning of days, or end of life.

17. Verily, verily, I say unto you, ye are little children, and ye have not as yet understood how great blessings the Father hath in his own hands and prepared for you;

18. And ye cannot bear all things now; nevertheless, be of good cheer, for I will lead you along. The kingdom is yours and the blessings thereof are yours, and the riches of eternity are yours.

19. And he who receiveth all things with thankfulness shall be made glorious; and the things of this earth shall be added unto him, even an hundred fold, yea, more.

20. Wherefore, do the things which I have commanded you, saith your Redeemer, even the Son Ahman, who prepareth all things before he taketh you;

21. For ye are the church of the Firstborn, and he will take you up in a cloud, and appoint every man his portion.

22. And he that is a faithful and wise steward shall inherit all things. Amen.

4. BLESSINGS PROMISED.

17. *Little children*] Not only children, but little children. Our Lord uses this expression when addressing the Twelve on the occasion of the institution of the Sacrament (John 13:33), and it is a favorite expression in the Epistles of John (I. John 2:1, 12, 28; 3:7, 18; 4:4; 5:21). It is a term of endearment. It means that the Church of Christ is, or will be when perfected, a family, a brotherhood, such as contemplated in the United Order. It also means that man, notwithstanding he may have been favored with Revelations and been given the holy Priesthood, is but uninformed and weak. "Ye have not as yet understood how great blessings the Father has * * * prepared for you; and ye cannot bear all things now" (v. 18).

19. *The things of this earth shall be added*] The Lord promises His "little children" the blessings of His kingdom and the riches of eternity, but also the things of this Earth, on the condition that they will do "the things which I have commanded you," as stated in verse 20. This promise has been gloriously fulfilled in the case of the faithful Latter-day Saints; for each time they have been driven from their possessions, for the testimony of Jesus, they have found a better location and become more prosperous. Those who were despoiled of humble cottage homes, nearly always found themselves in possession of mansions afterwards. Deserts became gardens.

20. *Ahman*] This word in the pure language, Orson Pratt says, signifies God. The word is possibly akin to "Amen." In Isaiah (65:16) the Almighty is called "God of Amen," but the translators have made it, "God of truth." In Rev. 3:14, our Lord calls Himself by that name: "These things saith the *Amen,* the faithful and true witness." There is also the word *Amon,* the name which Egyptians gave a Deity, in whose honor the magnificent temple at Karnak was reared. Amon, the "Unrevealed" corresponds to the Greek *Zeus.*

22. *A faithful and wise steward*] The members of the United Order were to be "stewards" over the property entrusted to their care. Those who were faithful and wise were here promised that they should inherit "all things." With God's promise as security, there is no risk.

SECTION 79.

REVELATION *given through Joseph Smith the Prophet, at Hiram, Ohio, March, 1832.——Jared Carter directed to go again into the eastern country—Conditional promise of great reward.*

VERILY I say unto you, that it is my will that my servant Jared Carter should go again into the eastern countries, from place to place, and from city to city, in the power of the ordination wherewith he has been ordained, proclaiming glad tidings of great joy, even the everlasting gospel.

2. And I will send upon him the Comforter, which shall teach him the truth and the way whither he shall go;

3. And inasmuch as he is faithful, I will crown him again with sheaves.

4. Wherefore, let your heart be glad, my servant Jared Carter, and fear not, saith your Lord, even Jesus Christ. Amen.

1-4. In this Revelation, Jared Carter, who had been ordained a Priest, according to a divine command given June 7th, 1831 (Sec. 52:38), is called to perform a mission to the Eastern States (v. 1). He is given the promise that the Comforter would guide him where to go, as well as teach him the truth (v. 2); and that he would be "crowned with sheaves" (v. 3).

The early missionaries of the Church followed the promptings of the Spirit very closely. That was one reason for their success. Wilford Woodruff's experience in the British mission in 1840 is a wonderful illustration of this truth. On his arrival in Preston, he was sent to the Staffordshire potteries, where he labored with success, until Spring prompted him to go south. He did so. At Worcester he heard of the United Brethren, who had separated themselves from the Wesleyan Methodists. He began to labor among them, and after eight months, 1,800 persons had been baptized, including all the United Brethren but one.

SECTION 80.

REVELATION *given through Joseph Smith the Prophet, at Hiram, Ohio, March, 1832.——Commandment concerning ministerial labors to Stephen Burnett and Eden Smith.*

VERILY, thus saith the Lord unto you my servant Stephen Burnett: Go ye, go ye into the world and preach the gospel to every creature that cometh under the sound of your voice.

2. And inasmuch as you desire a companion, I will give unto you my servant Eden Smith.

3. Wherefore, go ye and preach my gospel, whether to the

north or to the south, to the east or to the west, it mattereth not, for ye cannot go amiss.

4. Therefore, declare the things which ye have heard, and verily believe, and know to be true.

5. Behold, this is the will of him who hath called you, your Redeemer, even Jesus Christ. Amen.

1-5. In this Revelation Stephen Burnett is called to go out into the world to preach the gospel, and Eden Smith was designated as his companion (See Sec. 75:35). It was optional with them whether they would go north, south, east, or west. But their commission was to "declare the things which ye have heard and verily believe, and *know* to be true." Missionaries are *witnesses*. They must testify to what they *know*.

SECTION 81.

REVELATION *given through Joseph Smith the Prophet, at Hiram, Ohio, March, 1832.——Frederick G. Williams called to be a High Priest and a Counselor in the First Presidency of the Church.*

VERILY, verily, I say unto you my servant Frederick G. Williams: Listen to the voice of him who speaketh, to the word of the Lord your God, and hearken to the calling wherewith you are called, even to be a high priest in my church, and a counselor unto my servant Joseph Smith, Jun.;

2. Unto whom I have given the keys of the kingdom, which belong always unto the Presidency of the High Priesthood:

3. Therefore, verily I acknowledge him and will bless him and also thee, inasmuch as thou art faithful in counsel, in the office which I have appointed unto you, in prayer always, vocally and in thy heart, in public and in private, also in thy ministry in proclaiming the gospel in the land of the living, and among thy brethren.

4. And in doing these things thou wilt do the greatest good unto thy fellow beings, and wilt promote the glory of him who is your Lord.

5. Wherefore, be faithful; stand in the office which I have

appointed unto you; succor the weak, lift up the hands which hang down, and strengthen the feeble knees.

6. And if thou art faithful unto the end thou shalt have a crown of immortality, and eternal life in the mansions which I have prepared in the house of my Father.

7. Behold, and lo, these are the words of Alpha and Omega, even Jesus Christ. Amen.

1-7. Frederick G. Williams was not ordained a counselor in the First Presidency until March 18th, 1833. A Revelation was given on March 8th, that year, on that subject (See Sec. 90:6). This Revelation seems to have been given to prepare him for the important calling that awaited him. The Lord told him that the keys of the kingdom had been given to Joseph. Rebellion against the Prophet would, therefore, be disloyalty to Him who gave Joseph the keys. He promised Williams blessings, if he would be faithful. His duties were, to "succor the weak, lift up the hands which hang down, and strengthen the feeble knees." The office of the First Presidency, as here outlined, is one of salvation under the great Captain of Salvation. Of Him, too, it was said, "A bruised reed shall He not break, and smoking flax shall he not quench, till he send forth judgment unto victory" (Matt. 12:20). To Frederick G. Williams our Lord says, "If thou art faithful unto the end, thou shalt have a crown of immortality." See also Sec. 64:21.

GENERAL NOTES

Attention may be called, at this time, to the fact that on the 25th of March, 1832, the Prophet Joseph and Sidney Rigdon were violently assaulted by a mob consisting of apostates and individuals whose passions had been excited by false and libelous newspaper articles written by Ezra Booth. But there is no Revelation occasioned by that event. There is no denunciation of the brutes who thirsted for the blood of the servants of God. In the Revelation given immediately after that event, the Lord says, "Leave judgment alone with me, for it is mine, and I will repay" (See 82:23). Never was the Spirit of Christ manifested to a greater degree. The mobbing took place on a Saturday night, and the Prophet and his friends spent many hours attending to his injuries, but the next morning, he preached the gospel as usual, and among the audience were some of the mobbers, including Simonds Ryder.

Some people apostatize for very trivial reasons. Simonds Ryder furnishes an illustration of this. He received a letter at one time, in which the Prophet Joseph and Sidney Rigdon informed him that it was the will of the Lord that he should preach the gospel. In this letter, as in the Revelation (Sec. 52:37), his surname was spelled with an "i" instead of "y," and that was his pretext for apostatizing (*Hist. of the Church*, Vol. I., p. 261).

Many of the individuals who took part in this murderous assault came to a tragic end. One had an attack of a spinal affection; another died of cholera, and another ended his days in the penitentiary, convicted of some grave crime. (*Millennial Star,* Vol. XXVI., pp. 834-5).

SECTION 82.

REVELATION *given to Joseph Smith the Prophet, in Jackson County, Missouri, April 26, 1832, showing the order given to Enoch, and the Church in his day. The occasion was a general council of the Church, at which Joseph Smith the Prophet was sustained as the President of the High Priesthood, to which office he had previously been ordained at a conference of High Priests, Elders and members, at Amherst, Ohio, January 25, 1832. See History of the Church, vol. 1, p. 267. For explanation of unusual names see heading to Section 78.——The Lord reproves for sin and commends for repentance—Those who seek the mind of the Lord and then fail to abide by it are transgressors—The Lord is bound when his commandments are complied with—The Saints commanded to enter into covenant in the administration of their stewardships—Selfishness to be curbed and every man to seek the interest of his neighbor.*

VERILY, verily, I say unto you, my servants, that inasmuch as you have forgiven one another your trespasses, even so I, the Lord, forgive you.

2. Nevertheless, there are those among you who have sinned exceedingly; yea, even all of you have sinned; but verily I say unto you, beware from henceforth, and refrain from sin, lest sore judgments fall upon your heads.

3. For of him unto whom much is given much is required; and he who sins against the greater light shall receive the greater condemnation.

In the Revelation recorded in Section 78, our Savior commanded His servants of the High Priesthood to effect an organization for the temporal benefit of the people, and directed the Prophet Joseph, Newel K. Whitney, and Sidney Rigdon to go from Hiram, Ohio, to Missouri, and "sit in council with the Saints which are in Zion," on that matter. The Prophet commenced the journey on April 1st, 1832, accompanied by Newel K. Whitney, Peter Whitmer, and Jesse Gause, and they were joined by

Sidney Rigdon at Warren, the same day. The excitement of the mob in Kirtland, owing to the falsehoods circulated by apostates, was so intense that the Prophet and his companions avoided passing through the city. Some of the mobbers followed them all the way to Cleveland, but the protecting hand of the Lord was over His servants. The captain who took them to Louisville protected them in his boat, and gave them their meals, free of charge. They arrived at Independence, Missouri, on the 24th of April, and were greeted with joy by the Saints.

On the 26th a general council of the Church was called. The Prophet was acknowledged as the President of the High Priesthood, to which exalted position he had been ordained at the Conference at Amherst, Ohio, Jan. 25th, 1832. Bishop Partridge gave him the right hand of fellowship in behalf of the Church.

On this occasion a misunderstanding between Sidney Rigdon and Edward Partridge was cleared up, and unity and peace prevailed. The Lord then gave this Revelation, in which He (1) warns the Saints against sinning, lest judgments fall upon them (1-3); (2) sets forth the necessity of obeying the laws revealed (4-7); (3) gives them a commandment concerning the Order of Enoch (8-19); and (4) closes with admonitions and promises (20-24).

1. WARNING AGAINST SIN.

1. *My servants*] Refers to Sidney Rigdon and Edward Partridge. Even those who stand highest among the Church leaders have their human weaknesses. Paul may have to rebuke Peter (Gal. 2:11-13). But when they forgive each other, God forgives them. "It is a true sentiment that great men may err; a higher finish with such is, that their greatness is enhanced by acknowledging their errors" (Orson Spencer).

2. *All of you have sinned*] Sidney Rigdon and Edward Partridge were not the only ones who had erred; all had sinned, some exceedingly. The Revelation does not give the particulars. But Church historians note that although the settlements in Zion increased rapidly, and were exceedingly prosperous, many of the Saints failed to obey the counsel of the authorities. Some refused to submit to the law of consecration, preferring to obtain property for themselves, and jealousy, covetousness, and general neglect of duty. Some of the High Priests and Elders ignored the seven Presidents appointed to have charge of the Branches in Zion, viz., Oliver Cowdery, W. W. Phelps, John Whitmer, Sidney Gilbert, Edward Partridge, Isaac Morley, and John Corrill, and took the leadership into their own hands. Hence the warning, "Refrain from sin, lest sore judgments fall upon you."

4. Ye call upon my name for revelations, and I give them unto you; and inasmuch as ye keep not my sayings, which I give unto you, ye become transgressors; and justice and judgment are the penalty which is affixed unto my law.

5. Therefore, what I say unto one I say unto all: Watch, for the adversary spreadeth his dominions, and darkness reigneth;

6. And the anger of God kindleth against the inhabitants of the earth; and none doeth good, for all have gone out of the way.

7. And now, verily I say unto you, I, the Lord, will not lay any sin to your charge; go your ways and sin no more; but unto that soul who sinneth shall the former sins return, saith the Lord your God.

2. NECESSITY OF OBEDIENCE.

4-7. The Saints in Zion prayed for, and received, Revelations. But if they did not keep the laws received, they became transgressors and incurred the penalties affixed to the law. The adversary holds sway in the world, and Zion is surrounded by darkness; the Saints must, therefore, be on their watch continually; for if they permit the darkness to come in, the anger of God will come with it.

5. *Darkness reigneth*] "Darkness" here, as in John 1:5, means the condition of the world outside divine revelation. It refers to both spiritual and moral error. Revelation from God gives light, but when divine revelation is rejected, the adversary spreads his dominion among the children of men.

7. *Unto the soul who sinneth shall the former sins return*] Note this exceedingly grave truth. Ezekiel preached the same doctrine, "But when the righteous turneth away from his righteousness, and committeth iniquity, and doeth according to all the abominations that the wicked man doeth, shall he live? All his righteousness that he hath done shall not be mentioned" (Ez. 18:24). God forgives the repentant sinner so completely that "his transgressions shall not be mentioned unto him"; on the other hand, the righteous, who turns away from righteousness, cannot hope that his former life will save him. The principle works both ways, and is, therefore, eminently just.

8. And again, I say unto you, I give unto you a new commandment, that you may understand my will concerning you;

9. Or, in other words, I give unto you directions how you may act before me, that it may turn to you for your salvation.

10. I, the Lord, am bound when ye do what I say; but when ye do not what I say, ye have no promise.

11. Therefore, verily I say unto you, that it is expedient for my servants Alam and Ahashdah [Newel K. Whitney], Mahalaleel and Pelagoram [Sidney Rigdon], and my servant Gazelam

[Joseph Smith], and Horah and Olihah [Oliver Cowdery], and Shalemanasseh and Mahemson [Martin Harris], to be bound together by a bond and covenant that cannot be broken by transgression, except judgment shall immediately follow, in your several stewardships—

12. To manage the affairs of the poor, and all things pertaining to the bishopric both in the land of Zion and in the land of Shinehah [Kirtland];

13. For I have consecrated the land of Shinehah [Kirtland] in mine own due time for the benefit of the saints of the Most High, and for a stake to Zion.

14. For Zion must increase in beauty, and in holiness; her borders must be enlarged; her stakes must be strengthened; yea, verily I say unto you, Zion must arise and put on her beautiful garments.

15. Therefore, I give unto you this commandment, that ye bind yourselves by this covenant, and it shall be done according to the laws of the Lord.

16. Behold, here is wisdom also in me for your good.

17. And you are to be equal, or in other words, you are to have equal claims on the properties, for the benefit of managing the concerns of your stewardships, every man according to his wants and his needs, inasmuch as his wants are just—

18. And all this for the benefit of the church of the living God, that every man may improve upon his talent, that every man may gain other talents, yea, even an hundred fold, to be cast into the Lord's storehouse, to become the common property of the whole church—

19. Every man seeking the interest of his neighbor, and doing all things with an eye single to the glory of God.

3. Concerning the Order of Enoch.

8-19. The Saints had prayed for new revelations (v. 4); the Lord, at this time, gave them directions regarding the management of the temporal affairs of the Church, for the benefit of the poor, both in Missouri and in Kirtland (v. 12). The brethren mentioned in verse 11 were to form a corporation under the law of consecration and stewardship (v. 15). Each of them was to have an equal claim on the common property, for the management of the particular work over which he had been made a steward (v. 17), for the benefit of the Church (v. 18); and each one was to promote the interests of his neighbor, and in all things have "an eye single to the glory of God" (v. 19).

8. *A New commandment*] In the year 1831 the Lord revealed certain laws by which the Saints would have been made one in temporal, as well as spiritual affairs. But they did not comply with that celestial law. Then the Lord decided to give them a new, less exacting law. This has been called the Order of Enoch, or the law of Enoch.

"The law of Enoch is so named in the book of Doctrine and Covenants, but, in other words, it is the law given by Joseph Smith, Jr. The word 'Enoch' did not exist in the original copy; neither did some other names. The names that were incorporated when it was printed, did not exist there, when the manuscript revelations were given, for I saw them myself. Some of them I copied. And when the Lord was about to have the Book of Covenants given to the world, it was thought wisdom, in consequence of the persecutions of our enemies in Kirtland and some of the regions around, that some of the names should be changed, and Joseph was called *Baurak Ale,* which was a Hebrew word meaning, 'God bless you.' He was also called *Gazelam,* being a person to whom the Lord had given the Urim and Thummim. He was also called *Enoch.* Sidney Rigdon was called *Baneemy* and the Revelation where it read so many *dollars* into the treasury was changed to *talents.* And the name of the City of New York was changed to *Cainhannoch.* Therefore, when I speak of the Order of Enoch, I do not mean the Order of ancient Enoch; I mean the Order that was given to Joseph Smith in 1832-3-4, which is a law inferior to the celestial law, because the celestial law required the consecration of all that a man had. The law of Enoch only required a part. The law of consecration in full required that all the people should consecrate everything that they had; and none were exempt. The law of Enoch called upon certain men only to consecrate" (Orson Pratt, *Jour. of Dis.,* Vol. XVI., p. 156).

11. In this paragraph the Lord selects nine of His servants to form an association under the Order of Enoch. Five are identified in parentheses.

"Now, did the people keep this second law, inferior to the first? The Lord picked out some of the best men in the Church, and tried them, if they would keep it. 'Now I will,' says He, 'try the best men I have in the Church, not with the celestial law, but they shall consecrate in part, and have a common stock property among them.' And in order to stir them up in diligence, He fixed certain penalties to this law, such as, 'he shall be delivered up to the buffetings of Satan'; 'sins that have been remitted shall return to him and be answered upon his head.' How did they get along then? The Lord tells us that the covenant had been broken. And consequently it remained with Him to do with them as seemed to Him good. Many have apostatized since that day. Sidney Rigdon for one, Oliver for another, and John Johnson for another. Why have they apostatized? They did not comply with the covenant that they made in regard to the law given to Joseph Smith, that was afterwards called the Law of Enoch" (Orson Pratt, *Ibid.*).

17. *You are to be equal*] Equality does not mean an equal division of property. It means a division by which each has what he needs.

"Does every man receive an exact equality? No. Why not? Because some men have more ability for managing a stewardship than other men. Some men, perhaps all their lifetime, have been accustomed to carrying on great establishments and know how to conduct great establishments. Is it to be supposed that such a man would be limited to the same amount of stewardship as the man who has fifty acres of land? It may require twenty, or a hundred times the amount of stewardship to be placed in the hands of such a man, than what is required of other stewards who manage farming only. Does not that make them unequal? No. They are all stewards. The property belongs to the Lord" (Orson Pratt, *Ibid.*, p. 154).

20. This order I have appointed to be an everlasting order unto you, and unto your successors, inasmuch as you sin not.

21. And the soul that sins against this covenant, and hardeneth his heart against it, shall be dealt with according to the laws of my church, and shall be delivered over to the buffetings of Satan until the day of redemption.

22. And now, verily I say unto you, and this is wisdom, make unto yourselves friends with the mammon of unrighteousness, and they will not destroy you.

23. Leave judgment alone with me, for it is mine and I will repay. Peace be with you; my blessings continue with you.

24. For even yet the kingdom is yours, and shall be forever, if you fall not from your steadfastness. Even so. Amen.

20. *An everlasting covenant*] The Order here referred to would have been permanent, if the Saints had lived up to it, and it would have made them capable of practicing the higher, or celestial, Order. But it was not accepted and practiced with an eye single to the glory of God. In 1839, the Prophet Joseph wrote to the Saints:

"We would suggest to the brethren, that there be no organization of large bodies upon common stock principles, until the Lord shall signify it in a proper manner, as it opens such a field for the avaricious, the indolent, and the corrupt-hearted, to prey upon the virtuous, the industrious, and the honest. We have reason to believe that many things were introduced among the Saints, before God had signified the time, and notwithstanding the principles and the plans may have been good, yet aspiring men, who had the form of Godliness, but not the substance, by their aspiring notions brought trouble both upon themselves and the

Saints at large. However, the time is coming, when God will signify many things which are expected, for the well-being of the Saints" (*Millennial Star,* Vol. V., p. 71).

This letter was written in Liberty Jail. It was signed by Joseph Smith, Jr., Hyrum Smith, Lyman Wight, Caleb Baldwin, and Alexander McRay, and parts of it are embodied in the Revelations contained in Sections 121 and 123.

23. *I will repay*] In the history of persecution and mobbings of the Church, there are many instances of retributive justice, illustrating this truth, although the Saints themselves did not lift a hand against their persecutors. George A. Smith tells an anecdote, which may be retold here. One Samuel C. Owen, with eleven men, was engaged in raising the mob in Jackson county, in 1834. They had made speeches and worked up an excitement. In the evening, he, James Campbell, and others, commenced to cross the Missouri river on their way home again. The boat sprung a leak, and Owen said to the company on the ferry, "We must strip to the bone, or we shall all perish." Campbell replied that he would rather be "damned." He was drowned. Owen, stripped of clothing, floated down the river with the current and, finally, landed on the Jackson side. In this condition he made his way back to the settlements against which he had tried to raise a mob (*Jour. of Dis.,* Vol. II., p. 24).

SECTION 83.

REVELATION *given through Joseph Smith the Prophet, at Independence, Missouri, April 30, 1832. This revelation was received as the Prophet sat in council with his brethren.——— Claims of women and children for support upon their husbands and fathers—Claims of widows and orphans upon the Church.*

VERILY, thus saith the Lord, in addition to the laws of the church concerning women and children, those who belong to the church, who have lost their husbands or fathers:

2. Women have claim on their husbands for their maintenance, until their husbands are taken; and if they are not found transgressors they shall have fellowship in the church.

3. And if they are not faithful they shall not have fellowship in the church; yet they may remain upon their inheritances according to the laws of the land.

4. All children have claim upon their parents for their maintenance until they are of age.

5. And after that, they have claim upon the church, or in

other words upon the Lord's storehouse, if their parents have not wherewith to give them inheritances.

6. And the storehouse shall be kept by the consecrations of the church; and widows and orphans shall be provided for, as also the poor. Amen.

1-6. After the council meeting on the 26th of April, 1832, the Prophet visited the Saints of the Colesville Branch, situated in Kaw township, and other Saints, and transacted a great deal of business necessitated by the fact that the Church members were settling among bitter opponents. "It was my endeavor," he says, "to so organize the Church, that the brethren might eventually be independent of every incumbrance beneath the celestial kingdom, by bonds and covenants of mutual friendship and mutual love" (*Hist. of the Church*, Vol. I., p. 269). On the 30th, the council meeting was resumed. It is probable that the question came up, "What, under the law of Enoch, would be the status of women and children, whose natural protectors were dead?" In answer to some such inquiry, the Revelation in this Section was received. Widows, if faithful, have fellowship in the Church, and, therefore, a claim on the Church; if not in the Church, they were, nevertheless, to remain on their inheritances, according to the law (1-3). Children have a claim upon the Church, if the parents are unable to provide for them (4-6).

The rule laid down in the New Testament, for the support of widows, is found in I. Tim. 5:8-11. There Paul teaches that it is the duty of the husband to provide for "his own," and not leave the family destitute at his death, and that he who neglects this, is "worse than an unbeliever," having fallen below the normal standard recognized even among the pagans. But when it was necessary to support the widows from public funds, none under sixty years should be enrolled as a widow; and they were to have a good reputation as mothers, neighbors, and church members.

5. *They have a claim upon the church*] The children. This is a wise provision. If the Church undertakes to care for orphans and poor children in the spirit of the gospel, they will be saved from the curse of child-labor in factories; and also from the curse of that idleness which is the mother of crime. They will be given necessary education and training to become good and useful citizens.

SECTION 84.

REVELATION *given through Joseph Smith the Prophet, at Kirtland, Ohio, September 22 and 23, 1832. During the month of September, Elders had begun to return from their missions*

in the eastern States, and to make reports of their labors. It was while they were together in this season of joy that the following communication was received. The Prophet designates it a Revelation on Priesthood. See History of the Church, vol. 1, p. 286.
———A Temple to be built in the land of Zion during this generation—The line of the Holy Priesthood from Moses back to Adam—Relation between the Holy Priesthood and the Lesser Priesthood—Bearers of these two Priesthoods called the sons of Moses and of Aaron respectively—Blessings and privileges of those who attain to these Priesthoods—The bondage of sin—The new and everlasting covenant—Gifts of the spirit specified—The Lord calls his servants, friends—Missionary service imperative—Plagues impending because of wickedness.

A REVELATION of Jesus Christ unto his servant Joseph Smith, Jun., and six elders, as they united their hearts and lifted their voices on high.

2. Yea, the word of the Lord concerning his church, established in the last days for the restoration of his people, as he has spoken by the mouth of his prophets, and for the gathering of his saints to stand upon Mount Zion, which shall be the city of New Jerusalem.

During the month of September, 1832, the Elders who had been doing missionary work in the Eastern States began to return to Kirtland, where the Prophet now resided, and on the 22nd and 23rd of the month, this Revelation was received, in the presence of six Elders. It is called, "A Revelation of Jesus Christ unto His Servant Joseph Smith, Jr.," and, "The Word of the Lord concerning His Church." (vv. 1-2.) It contains (1) a promise regarding the place and the time of the building of the New Jerusalem and the Temple (3-5); (2) A Revelation on the Temple service, including the Priesthood (6-34); (3) a Revelation on the importance of the Priesthood (35-59); (4) a commission to preach the gospel (60-102); and (5) special directions (103-120).

3. Which city shall be built, beginning at the temple lot, which is appointed by the finger of the Lord, in the western boundaries of the State of Missouri, and dedicated by the hand of Joseph Smith, Jun., and others with whom the Lord was well pleased.

4. Verily this is the word of the Lord, that the city New

Jerusalem shall be built by the gathering of the saints, beginning at this place, even the place of the temple, which temple shall be reared in this generation.

5. For verily this generation shall not all pass away until an house shall be built unto the Lord, and a cloud shall rest upon it, which cloud shall be even the glory of the Lord, which shall fill the house.

1. THE NEW JERUSALEM AND THE TEMPLE.

3-5. In these paragraphs the Lord promises that the New Jerusalem will be built on the spot dedicated for that purpose. No matter what trials and difficulties the Saints might have to pass through, the place had been selected, and the Lord would keep His word (v. 3-4).

3. *The temple lot*] Dedicated August 3rd, 1831. (Comp. Sec. 57:3.)

4. *Beginning at this place*] The New Jerusalem would be built by the gathering of the Saints, and the beginning was to be made at the Temple lot.

5. *This generation shall not all pass away*, etc.] "This statement has been a stumbling block to some and there have been various interpretations of the meaning of a generation. It is held by some that a generation is one hundred years; by others that it is one hundred and twenty-years; by others that a generation as expressed in this and other scriptures has reference to a period of time which is indefinite. The Savior said: "An evil and adulterous generation seeketh after a sign." This did not have reference to a period of years, but to a period of wickedness. A generation may mean the time of the present dispensation. Moreover, the statement is qualified in this revelation in the above quotation." (Church History and Modern Revelation, p. 102, second series.)

This is quite generally understood to be the meaning of this prophecy; but it is quite possible that a complete explanation of it cannot be obtained until it is fulfilled. That is the case with many divine predictions. When they are fulfilled they are clear.

A cloud shall rest upon it] The Lord manifested Himself in ancient Israel in a cloud, shaped as a pillar, which became luminous at night. It guided the people on the journey to Canaan. It stood at the entrance to the Sanctuary, and in it God spoke to Moses. It rested on the Sanctuary and filled it, when that sacred tent was set up. It was the visible sign of God's guiding and protecting care over His people. This glory of the Lord is known as the *Shekinah*. When the first temple was dedicated, it filled the house (II. Chron. 7:1-3), and the people bowed down and worshiped. The Shekinah departed when the Temple was profaned (Ez. 10:19; 11:22), but Ezekiel, in his vision of the Temple in the latter days, saw the glory of the Lord returning (Ez. 43:2-3). The presence of the Lord will be manifested in this Temple of the Latter-day Zion.

2. The Temple Service.

6. And the sons of Moses,

This is the beginning of a sentence which is continued in paragraph 31. All that intervenes is parenthetic, containing a statement regarding the lineage through which the Priesthood came to Moses and Aaron, and how it was restored in our day.

A History of the Priesthood.

according to the Holy Priesthood which he received under the hand of his father-in-law, Jethro;

7. And Jethro received it under the hand of Caleb;

8. And Caleb received it under the hand of Elihu;

9. And Elihu under the hand of Jeremy;

10. And Jeremy under the hand of Gad;

11. And Gad under the hand of Esaias;

12. And Esaias received it under the hand of God.

13. Esaias also lived in the days of Abraham, and was blessed of him—

14. Which Abraham received the priesthood from Melchizedek, who received it through the lineage of his fathers, even till Noah;

15. And from Noah till Enoch, through the lineage of their fathers;

16. And from Enoch to Abel, who was slain by the conspiracy of his brother, who received the priesthood by the commandments of God, by the hand of his father Adam, who was the first man—

17. Which priesthood continueth in the church of God in all generations, and is without beginning of days or end of years.

18. And the Lord confirmed a priesthood also upon Aaron and his seed, throughout all their generations, which priesthood also continueth and abideth forever with the priesthood which is after the holiest order of God.

19. And this greater priesthood administereth the gospel and holdeth the key of the mysteries of the kingdom, even the key of the knowledge of God.

20. Therefore, in the ordinances thereof, the power of godliness is manifest.

21. And without the ordinances thereof, and the authority of the priesthood, the power of godliness is not manifest unto men in the flesh;

22. For without this no man can see the face of God, even the Father, and live.

23. Now this Moses plainly taught to the children of Israel in the wilderness, and sought diligently to sanctify his people that they might behold the face of God;

24. But they hardened their hearts and could not endure his presence; therefore, the Lord in his wrath, for his anger was kindled against them, swore that they should not enter into his rest while in the wilderness, which rest is the fulness of his glory.

25. Therefore, he took Moses out of their midst, and the Holy Priesthood also;

26. And the lesser priesthood continued, which priesthood holdeth the key of the ministering of angels and the preparatory gospel;

27. Which gospel is the gospel of repentance and of baptism, and the remission of sins, and the law of carnal commandments, which the Lord in his wrath caused to continue with the house of Aaron among the children of Israel until John, whom God raised up, being filled with the Holy Ghost from his mother's womb.

28. For he was baptized while he was in his childhood, and was ordained by the angel of God at the time he was eight days old unto this power, to overthrow the kingdom of the Jews, and to make straight the way of the Lord before the face of his people, to prepare them for the coming of the Lord, in whose hand is given all power.

29. And again, the offices of elder and bishop are necessary appendages belonging unto the high priesthood.

30. And again, the offices of teacher and deacon are necessary appendages belonging to the lesser priesthood, which priesthood was confirmed upon Aaron and his sons.

6-16. *The Holy Priesthood which he received*] These verses give us by revelation a clear order of descent of the Priesthood from Adam to Moses, and in the following paragraphs (17-18) we are informed that the

"Priesthood continueth in the Church of God in all generations, without beginning of days or end of years." Among the scholars who are uninspired, there is doubt as to who Jethro was. In Exodus 3:1, he is called the father-in-law of Moses, but these scholars say the name may mean any male relative by marriage. In Exodus 2:18, Reuel, or Raguel, appears as the name of the father-in-law of Moses. Then it is maintained that the transaction related of Jethro in Exodus 18:12-27, is told of Hobab in Numbers 10:29. These may have been names given to Jethro by different scribes, or in different countries. We know, however, by the information given in this revelation that Jethro was the father-in-law of Moses and that Moses received the Priesthood from him. This has been a mystery to some, who have thought that only the children of Israel were blessed with the authority of Priesthood. We know that the Midianites were descendants of Abraham who had sons by his wife Keturah, they were named, Zimran, Jokshan, Medan and Midian, Ishbak and Shuah. Evidently among the "gifts" which Abraham gave his other sons was the authority of the Priesthood. We know that the "Midianites" held it. We read that Balak of Moab, sent for Balaam, of the "elders of Midian," to come and curse Israel. The story which follows strongly implies that Balaam was a prophet, and the Lord commanded him what he should say. (Num. 22-24.)

14. *Abraham * * * Noah*] From the flood to the birth of Abraham there was a period of 352 years. But Noah lived 350 years after the flood, and when he died, Nahor, Abraham's brother, was 58 years old. Of Melchizedek's lineage nothing is known, but it is easily understood, by the chronological data available, that the Priesthood could have come from Noah to Abraham through Melchizedek.

16. *Adam who was the first man*] In these days, when the Lord has sent into the world "strong delusion, that they should believe a lie: that they all might be damned who believe not the truth, but had pleasure in unrighteousness," (II. Thess. 2:11-12) it has become popular among the wise in the world, to declare that Adam was not the first man, and that he did not transgress and bring death into the world. In this scripture the Lord definitely declares that Adam was the first man, and in other scriptures this is definitely affirmed, for instance in the Pearl of Great Price, (3:7) we read: "And I the Lord God, formed man from the dust of the ground, and breathed into his nostrils the breath of life; and man became a living soul, the first flesh upon the earth, the first man also; nevertheless, all things were before created; but spiritually were they created and made according to my word."

"Adam, our great progenitor, the first man, was, like Christ, a pre-existent spirit, and like Christ he took upon him an appropriate body, the body of a man, a 'living soul,' The doctrine of the pre-existence—revealed so plainly, particularly in latter days—pours a wonderful flood of light upon the otherwise mysterious problem of man's origin. It shows that man, as a spirit, was begotten and born of heavenly parents, and reared to maturity in the eternal mansions of the Father prior to coming upon the earth, in a temporal body to undergo experience in mortality. It teaches that all men existed in the spirit before any man existed in the flesh, and that all who have inhabited the earth since Adam have taken bodies and become souls in like manner.

"It is held by some that Adam was not the first man upon this earth, and that the original human was a development from lower orders of the animal creation. These, however, are the theories of men. The word of the Lord declares that Adam was 'the first man of all men,' (Moses 1:34) and we are therefore in duty bound to regard him as the primal parent of our race.

> "Joseph F. Smith,
> "John R. Winder,
> "Anthon H. Lund.

"First Presidency of the Church of Jesus Christ of Latter-day Saints" (Era. 13:75-81).

The genealogy of the Savior given in the Inspired Version, states this "And of Enos, and of Seth, and of Adam, who was formed of God, and the first man upon the earth" (Luke 3:45).

17. *Without beginning * * * or end*]

"The Priesthood was first given to Adam; he obtained the First Presidency, and held the keys of it from generation to generation. He obtained it in the creation, before the world was formed, as [related] in Genesis 1:26-28. He had dominion given him over every living creature. He is Michael, the archangel, spoken of in the Scriptures. Then to Noah who is Gabriel; he stands next in authority to Adam in the Priesthood; he was called of God to this office, and was the father of all living in his day, and to him was given the dominion. These men held keys first on Earth, and then in heaven. The Priesthood is an everlasting principle, and existed with God from eternity, and will to eternity, without beginning of days or end of years. The keys have to be brought from heaven whenever the gospel is sent. When they are revealed from heaven, it is by Adam's authority" (Joseph Smith, *Hist. of the Church,* Vol. III., p. 385).

18. *Also upon Aaron and his seed*]

"There are two Priesthoods spoken of in the Scriptures, viz., the Melchizedek and the Aaronic, or Levitical. Although there are two Priesthoods, yet the Melchizedek Priesthood comprehends the Aaronic, or Levitical Priesthood, and is the grand head, and holds the highest authority which pertains to the Priesthood, and the keys of the kingdom of God in all ages of the world to the latest posterity in the Earth, and is the channel through which all knowledge, doctrine, the plan of salvation, and every important matter is revealed from heaven" (Joseph Smith, *Hist. of the Church,* Vol. IV., p. 207).

Speaking of the importance of the Aaronic Priesthood, the Prophet says:

"From a retrospect of the requirements of the servants of God to preach the gospel, we find few qualified even to be Priests, and if a Priest understands his duty, his calling, and ministry, and preaches by the Holy Ghost, his enjoyment is as great as if he were one of the presidency; and his services are necessary in the body, as are also those of Teachers and Deacons. Therefore, in viewing the Church as a whole, we may strictly denominate it one Priesthood" (Joseph Smith, *Ibid.*, Vol. II., p. 778).

Abideth forever] The Aaronic Priesthood is never to be abolished. It remains forever with the Melchizedek Priesthood.

19-22. The mission and authority of the greater Priesthood are here set forth. It administers in the gospel, and reveals the "mysteries of the kingdom"—even the knowledge concerning God, without which there would be no eternal life (v. 19). It administers the ordinances of the gospel, in which the power of godliness is manifest (v. 20); and it holds the authority which enables man to see God, even the Father, and live (v. 22). To quote again from the *History of the Church*:

"President Joseph Smith, Jun., addressed the assembly and said, the Melchizedek High Priesthood was no other than the Priesthood of the Son of God; that there are certain ordinances which belong to the Priesthood, from which flow certain results; and the Presidents or Presidency are over the Church; and revelations of the mind and will of God to the Church, are to come through the Presidency. This is the order of heaven, and the power and privilege of the Priesthood. It is also the privilege of any officer in the Church to obtain revelations, so far as relates to his particular calling and duty in the Church. All are bound by the principles of virtue and happiness, but one great privilege of the Priesthood is to obtain revelations of the mind and will of God. It is also the privilege of the Melchizedek Priesthood, to reprove, rebuke, and admonish, as well as to receive revelation" (Vol. II., p. 477).

23. *This Moses plainly taught to the children of Israel*] The Lord also gave to Israel in the wilderness a book of "Doctrine and Covenants" (Ex. 24:7, 8) which is found in Exodus 20:22 to 23:33. This was accepted by the people, by common consent, and the acceptance was solemnly ratified by sacrifice. In the 19th chapter of Exodus we read that God promised His people that if they would keep the covenant, He would make them "a peculiar treasure"; that is, His own special and private possession, "and ye shall be unto me a kingdom of priests and a holy nation." This is what Moses tried to teach the people. He tried to sanctify them through the Priesthood. See also I. Pet. 2:9. The Saints of God are there referred to as a "holy Priesthood."

24-25. But Israel did not keep the covenant, and the result was that Moses was taken from them, and with him the greater Priesthood (v. 25).

26. *The lesser Priesthood continued*] It was, as Paul calls the Law

(Gal. 3:24), "our schoolmaster to bring us to Christ." It was confined to one tribe, that of Levi, and the presidency was vested in one family, that of Aaron. Hence its name, the Aaronic, or Levitic Priesthood.

"The Children of Israel were not capable of living up to all the requirements of the Higher or Holy Priesthood and the law of the Gospel, so the Lord, through Moses, gave them a new law and order of the Holy Priesthood, and another set of officers to administer to the people under the new conditions. How long did the Israelites sojourn in Egypt? * * * .

"This new authority, or new Priesthood, or rather this new adaptation of and order of the old Priesthood, is called the 'Lesser Priesthood.' It is an appendage of the Higher Priesthood, because it belongs to or grows out of it." (Joseph B. Keeler, *"The Lesser Priesthood,"* p. 8.) The Lord had promised to Israel that if the people would obey His voice he would make of them a royal Priesthood, and He would give them the fulness of the Priesthood and the Gospel, but they hardened their hearts against him. Through Moses he said: "Now, therefore, if ye will obey my voice indeed, and keep my covenant, then ye shall be a peculiar treasure unto me above all people: for all the earth is mine. And ye shall be unto me a kingdom of Priests (i.e. of the Melchizedek order), and an holy nation. These are the words which thou shalt speak unto the children of Israel." (Ex. 19:5-6.) "But they hardened their hearts and could not endure His presence, therefore, the Lord in his wrath, for his anger was kindled against them, swore that they should not enter into his rest while in the wilderness, which rest is the fulness of his glory." (V. 24.) This Aaronic Priesthood was to remain with them until the coming of Christ in his ministry.

27. The mission of the Aaronic Priesthood is here stated. It holds the key to the gospel of repentance, baptism, the remission of sins, and the Law of Carnal Commandments—the Law which was in force until John the Baptist.

28. *For he was baptized,* etc.] John was filled with the Holy Ghost, before he was born, when Mary visited Elizabeth (Luke 1:41). When he was eight days old, he was ordained by the Angel of God "to overthrow the kingdom of the Jews," and to make "straight the way of the Lord"; to prepare His people for His coming. John, then, had the authority to close the Mosaic dispensation, after a last call to the people for repentance. He exercised that authority, and the result was the overthrow of the Jewish polity, the destruction of Jerusalem, and the dispersion of the people.

The angel who conferred upon John the power of the Priesthood and the authority to overthrow the kingdom of the Jews, we do not know; but he was one commissioned with all the authority and power to confer these keys, and his name matters not. From this revelation we learn that it was deemed expedient that John should be so blessed at the time he was named, when only eight days old. When he reached the age appointed, he was also baptized and prepared for his ministry when the full time had come.

29-30. The offices of Elder and Bishop are appendages belonging to the High Priesthood, and again, the offices of Teacher and Deacon are here mentioned as appendages to the lesser Priesthood.

While it is here stated that these offices are "necessary appendages" to the Priesthood, this does not signify, as some have supposed, that the other offices in the Priesthoods are not appendages. All the offices grow out of, and are appendages to the Priesthood as well as those mentioned here. (Doc. and Cov. 107:5.)

31. Therefore, as I said concerning the sons of Moses—for the sons of Moses and also the sons of Aaron shall offer an acceptable offering and sacrifice in the house of the Lord, which house shall be built unto the Lord in this generation, upon the consecrated spot as I have appointed—

32. And the sons of Moses and of Aaron shall be filled with the glory of the Lord, upon Mount Zion in the Lord's house, whose sons are ye; and also many whom I have called and sent forth to build up my church.

33. For whoso is faithful unto the obtaining these two priesthoods of which I have spoken, and the magnifying of their calling, are sanctified by the Spirit unto the renewing of their bodies.

34. They become the sons of Moses and of Aaron and the seed of Abraham, and the church and kingdom, and the elect of God.

31-4. The subject introduced by the first words of the 6th paragraph is resumed here. The house of the Lord is to be reared in Zion before "this generation" has passed away, and the sons of Moses and the sons of Aaron shall officiate therein (v. 31), and be filled with the glory of the Lord. However, "sons of Moses," and "sons of Aaron" do not refer to their literal descendants only, for all who are faithful and obtain these Priesthoods, and magnify their calling, are sanctified by the Spirit and become the "sons" of Moses and of Aaron, and the seed of Abraham, as well as the Church and Kingdom, and the elect of God (v. 34). Paul expresses this thought as follows, "Know ye therefore that they which are of faith, the same are the children of Abraham" (Gal. 3:7).

31. *Offering sacrifice*]

"It is generally supposed that sacrifice was entirely done away with, when the great Sacrifice was offered up, and that there will be no necessity for the ordinance of sacrifice in the future; but those who assert this are certainly not acquainted with the duties, privileges, and authority of the Priesthood, or with the Prophets. The offering of sacrifice has ever been connected with, and forms a part of the duties of the Priesthood. It began with the Priesthood and will be continued until after the coming of Christ, from generation to generation" (Joseph Smith, *History of the Church,* Vol. IV., p. 207).

35. And also all they who receive this priesthood receive me, saith the Lord;

36. For he that receiveth my servants receiveth me;

37. And he that receiveth me receiveth my Father;

38. And he that receiveth my Father receiveth my Father's kingdom; therefore all that my Father hath shall be given unto him.

39. And this is according to the oath and covenant which belongeth to the priesthood.

40. Therefore, all those who receive the priesthood, receive this oath and covenant of my Father, which he cannot break, neither can it be moved.

41. But whoso breaketh this covenant after he hath received it, and altogether turneth therefrom, shall not have forgiveness of sins in this world nor in the world to come.

42. And wo unto all those who come not unto this priesthood which ye have received, which I now confirm upon you who are present this day, by mine own voice out of the heavens; and even I have given the heavenly hosts and mine angels charge concerning you.

43. And I now give unto you a commandment to beware concerning yourselves, to give diligent heed to the words of eternal life.

44. For you shall live by every word that proceedeth forth from the mouth of God.

45. For the word of the Lord is truth, and whatsoever is truth is light, and whatsoever is light is Spirit, even the Spirit of Jesus Christ.

46. And the Spirit giveth light to every man that cometh into the world; and the Spirit enlighteneth every man through the world, that hearkeneth to the voice of the Spirit.

47. And every one that hearkeneth to the voice of the Spirit cometh unto God, even the Father.

48. And the Father teacheth him of the covenant which he has renewed and confirmed upon you, which is confirmed upon you for your sakes, and not for your sakes only, but for the sake of the whole world.

49. And the whole world lieth in sin, and groaneth under darkness and under the bondage of sin.

50. And by this you may know they are under the bondage of sin, because they come not unto me.

51. For whoso cometh not unto me is under the bondage of sin.

52. And whoso receiveth not my voice is not acquainted with my voice, and is not of me.

53. And by this you may know the righteous from the wicked, and that the whole world groaneth under sin and darkness even now.

54. And your minds in times past have been darkened because of unbelief, and because you have treated lightly the things you have received—

55. Which vanity and unbelief have brought the whole church under condemnation.

56. And this condemnation resteth upon the children of Zion, even all.

57. And they shall remain under this condemnation until they repent and remember the new covenant, even the Book of Mormon and the former commandments which I have given them, not only to say, but to do according to that which I have written—

58. That they may bring forth fruit meet for their Father's kingdom; otherwise there remaineth a scourge and judgment to be poured out upon the children of Zion.

59. For shall the children of the kingdom pollute my holy land? Verily, I say unto you, Nay.

3. IMPORTANCE OF THE PRIESTHOOD.

35-42. Here the importance of the holy Priesthood is shown. Those who receive the Priesthood in sincerity, thereby prove that they receive the servants of the Lord, as His servants; for they would not accept their administration, if they did not regard them as His representatives; and when they so receive them, they receive the Savior, whose ambassadors

His servants are, and when they receive Him, they receive the Father, who sent Him, and His Father's kingdom. He who receives an ambassador, receives the king, the government, and the entire kingdom which that official represents. What mortal can fully realize the importance of receiving the holy Priesthood, or the consequences of breaking the covenants belonging to the Priesthood, which includes, on the part of man, obedience to the laws of God and loyalty to His cause.

39. *Oath and covenant*] These two terms stand for the arrangement between God and man regarding the plan of salvation. The covenant is, in the Scriptures, sometimes called God's "counsel," and sometimes His "oath," and His "promise" (Comp. Ps. 89:3, 4, 105:8, 11; Heb. 6:13-20; Luke 1:68-75; Gal. 3:15-18). All these terms mean His "covenant."

Here in these verses (33-41) we learn that the Lord has promised to all those who are faithful, and who magnify their calling, that they shall be in fellowship with both the Father and the Son, and if they continue faithful, they shall eventually inherit "all that my Father hath." This means that they shall become the sons of God, joint heirs with Jesus Christ, and as expressed in Section 76:55-60, they shall receive the fulness of His glory. When the Lord offers the fulness of His glory on conditions of faithfulness, he attaches a penalty for the breaking of such a glorious and far-reaching covenant. Therefore he has decreed that all those who trample this covenant (which every person receiving the Melchizedek Priesthood receives) under his feet, "and altogether turneth therefrom, shall not have forgiveness of sins in this world nor in the world to come." This means that all who treat this covenant of the Priesthood with contempt shall never have the privilege of exercising it in the world to come. Therefore they will be barred from celestial exaltation.

The Prophet has written:

The Melchizedek Priesthood holds the right from the eternal God, and not by descent from father and mother; and that priesthood is as eternal as God Himself, having neither beginning of days nor end of life.

The 2nd Priesthood is Patriarchal authority. Go to and finish the temple, and God will fill in with power, and you will then receive more knowledge concerning this priesthood.

The 3rd is what is called the Levitical Priesthood, consisting of priests to administer in outward ordinance, made without an oath; but the Priesthood of Melchizedek is by an oath and covenant.

(Aug. 27, 1843.) D.H.C. 5:554-556.

42. *I have given * * * charge concerning you*] Note that the Lord, in conferring the Priesthood upon the Elders present when this Revelation was given, assured them that angels had been appointed to guard them. The first Christians believed in guardian angels. Luke says the angel of the Lord on one occasion opened the prison doors by night and liberated the Apostles (Acts 5:19); and on another occasion Peter was set free by an angel, and when he appeared among the Saints at

the house of Mary, the mother of Mark, they at first said, "It is his angel" (Acts 12:15). Paul asks, "Are they not all ministering spirits sent forth to minister for them who shall be heirs of salvation? (Heb. 1:14. Comp. Ps. 91:11, 12; Matt. 4:6, 7). How important, then, that those who bear the Holy Priesthood should live so, that they are fit companions for angels!

The following anecdote, which was told by David Whitmer to Elders Orson Pratt and Joseph F. Smith in 1878, may be retold here:

"When I was returning to Fayette, with Joseph and Oliver, all of us riding in the wagon, Oliver and I on an old fashioned wooden spring-seat, and Joseph behind us—when traveling along in a clear, open space, a very pleasant, nice-looking old man suddenly appeared by the side of the wagon and saluted us with, "Good morning, it is very warm," at the same time wiping his face or forehead with his hand. We returned the salutation, and, by a sign from Joseph, I invited him to ride, if he was going our way. But he said very pleasantly, 'No, I am going to Cumorah.' This name was something new to me. I did not know what Cumorah meant. We all gazed at him and at each other, and as I looked around inquiringly at Joseph, the old man instantly disappeared, so that I did not see him again." Whitmer described his appearance and added, "It was the messenger who had the plates [of the Book of Mormon], who had taken them from Joseph just prior to our starting for Harmony" (Andrew Jenson, *Historical Record*, p. 209).

43-53. Our Lord teaches the important truth that His Spirit, or Spirit of Jesus Christ, gives light to every man who comes into the world and hearkens to its voice (v. 46), and that those who hearken to that voice come to God; that is, they receive the gospel (v. 47), and God will teach them of the covenant which He has renewed; that is to say, God, through His Spirit, will bear witness to the truth of the gospel (v. 48). However, the world is in darkness and under the bondage of sin, and the proof of that is, that men refuse to come to God by accepting the gospel (v. 51). By this the righteous may be known from the wicked (v. 53).

46. *The Spirit giveth light to every man that cometh into the world*] On this subject Brigham Young says:

"I do not believe for one moment that there has been a man or woman upon the face of the Earth, from the days of Adam, to this day, who has not been enlightened, instructed, and taught by the revelations of Jesus Christ. 'What! the ignorant heathen? Yes, every human being who has possessed a sound mind. I am far from believing that the children of men have been deprived of the privilege of receiving the Spirit of the Lord to teach them right from wrong.

" 'Do you suppose the Hindoos have the light of the Spirit of Christ?' I know they have; and so have the Hottentots, and so has every nation and kingdom on the face of the Earth, even though some of them may be cannibals, indulging in a practice most repugnant to our refined feel-

ings of any we know of among any people * * * But when the light
of the knowledge of God comes to a man and he rejects it, that is his
condemnation. When I have told all I have been authorized to declare
to him in the name of the Lord, if he does not have visions of eternity,
it is all nonsense to him. To know the truth of my testimony he must
have the visions and revelations of God for himself. And when he gets
them, and turns aside, becoming a traitor to the cause of righteousness,
the wrath of God will beat upon him, and the vengeance of the Almighty
will be heavy upon him" (*Jour. of Dis.*, Vol. II., pp. 139, 140).

"We often say the Spirit of God when we mean the Holy Ghost; we,
likewise, say the Holy Ghost when we mean the Spirit of God. The
Holy Ghost is a personage in the Godhead, and is not that which
lighteth every man that comes into the world. It is the Spirit of God
which proceeds through Christ to the world, that enlightens every man
that comes into the world, and that strives with the children of men,
and will continue to strive with them, until it brings them to a knowledge
of truth and the possession of the greater light and testimony of the
Holy Ghost" (Joseph F. Smith, *Gospel Doctrine,* page 82 (1st edition),
page 67 (later edition). (Compare John 1:4-9).

"For behold, the Spirit of Christ is given to every man, that he may
know good from evil; wherefore I show unto you the way to judge;
for everything which inviteth to do good, and to persuade to believe in
Christ, is sent forth by the power and gift of Christ; wherefore ye may
know with a perfect knowledge it is of God." (Moroni 7:16).

54-59. The Lord, having told His servants that the world is in darkness, turns to them, and reproves them, because they had been in the
dark, as a consequence of having treated the things received, lightly,
thereby causing the whole Church to be brought under condemnation
(v. 55). And this condition, they were told, would remain until the
Saints had repented. Nothing but sincere repentance can turn away
the wrath of God (v. 57).

54. *The things you have received*] Referring to the Book of Mormon
(v. 57) and the Revelations given to the Church.

55. The effect of "vanity and unbelief" upon the Saints was terrible.
The example was contagious; the disease spread and general condemnation ensued. The Elders ought to be the lights in the darkness. If they
become darkened, too, through treating the Revelations lightly, the
darkness will become impenetrable.

56. *Condemnation resteth upon * * * even all*] God warned the
Elders and the children of Zion of the condition existing, in order that
they might repent and, by repentance, avert the disaster that befell them
later.

58. *A scourge and a judgment*] Referring to the expulsion from Missouri and, probably, the plague by which many of the Saints were
stricken.

59. *Shall the children of the kingdom pollute my holy land?*] The children of the world have not the same responsibility as the Saints. If these pollute the holy land, their sin is greater than the same sin committed by the children of the world.

60. Verily, verily, I say unto you who now hear my words, which are my voice, blessed are ye inasmuch as you receive these things;

61. For I will forgive you of your sins with this commandment—that you remain steadfast in your minds in solemnity and the spirit of prayer, in bearing testimony to all the world of those things which are communicated unto you.

62. Therefore, go ye into all the world; and unto whatsoever place ye cannot go ye shall send, that the testimony may go from you into all the world unto every creature.

63. And as I said unto mine apostles, even so I say unto you, for you are mine apostles, even God's high priests; ye are they whom my Father hath given me; ye are my friends;

64. Therefore, as I said unto mine apostles I say unto you again, that every soul who believeth on your words, and is baptized by water for the remission of sins, shall receive the Holy Ghost.

65. And these signs shall follow them that believe—

66. In my name they shall do many wonderful works;

67. In my name they shall cast out devils;

68. In my name they shall heal the sick;

69. In my name they shall open the eyes of the blind, and unstop the ears of the deaf;

70. And the tongue of the dumb shall speak;

71. And if any man shall administer poison unto them it shall not hurt them;

72. And the poison of a serpent shall not have power to harm them.

73. But a commandment I give unto them, that they shall not boast themselves of these things, neither speak them before the world; for these things are given unto you for your profit and for salvation.

74. Verily, verily, I say unto you, they who believe not on your words, and are not baptized in water in my name, for the

remission of their sins, that they may receive the Holy Ghost, shall be damned, and shall not come into my Father's kingdom where my Father and I am.

75. And this revelation unto you, and commandment, is in force from this very hour upon all the world, and the gospel is unto all who have not received it.

76. But, verily I say unto all those to whom the kingdom has been given—from you it must be preached unto them, that they shall repent of their former evil works; for they are to be upbraided for their evil hearts of unbelief, and your brethren in Zion for their rebellion against you at the time I sent you.

77. And again I say unto you, my friends, for from henceforth I shall call you friends, it is expedient that I give unto you this commandment, that ye become even as my friends in days when I was with them, traveling to preach the gospel in my power;

78. For I suffered them not to have purse or scrip, neither two coats.

79. Behold, I send you out to prove the world, and the laborer is worthy of his hire.

80. And any man that shall go and preach this gospel of the kingdom, and fail not to continue faithful in all things, shall not be weary in mind, neither darkened, neither in body, limb, nor joint; and a hair of his head shall not fall to the ground unnoticed. And they shall not go hungry, neither athirst.

81. Therefore, take ye no thought for the morrow, for what ye shall eat, or what ye shall drink, or wherewithal ye shall be clothed.

82. For, consider the lilies of the field, how they grow, they toil not, neither do they spin; and the kingdoms of the world, in all their glory, are not arrayed like one of these.

83. For your Father, who is in heaven, knoweth that you have need of all these things.

84. Therefore, let the morrow take thought for the things of itself.

85. Neither take ye thought beforehand what ye shall say; but treasure up in your minds continually the words of life, and

it shall be given you in the very hour that portion that shall be meted unto every man.

86.   Therefore, let no man among you, for this commandment is unto all the faithful who are called of God in the church unto the ministry, from this hour take purse or scrip, that goeth forth to proclaim this gospel of the kingdom.

87.   Behold, I send you out to reprove the world of all their unrighteous deeds, and to teach them of a judgment which is to come.

88.   And whoso receiveth you, there I will be also, for I will go before your face. I will be on your right hand and on your left, and my Spirit shall be in your hearts, and mine angels round about you, to bear you up.

89.   Whoso receiveth you receiveth me; and the same will feed you, and clothe you, and give you money.

90.   And he who feeds you, or clothes you, or gives you money, shall in nowise lose his reward.

91.   And he that doeth not these things is not my disciple; by this you may know my disciples.

92.   He that receiveth you not, go away from him alone by yourselves, and cleanse your feet even with water, pure water, whether in heat or in cold, and bear testimony of it unto your Father which is in heaven, and return not again unto that man.

93.   And in whatsoever village or city ye enter, do likewise.

94.   Nevertheless, search diligently and spare not; and wo unto that house, or that village or city that rejecteth you, or your words, or your testimony concerning me.

95.   Wo, I say again, unto that house, or that village or city that rejecteth you, or your words, or your testimony of me;

96.   For I, the Almighty, have laid my hands upon the nations, to scourge them for their wickedness.

97.   And plagues shall go forth, and they shall not be taken from the earth until I have completed my work, which shall be cut short in righteousness—

98.   Until all shall know me, who remain, even from the least unto the greatest, and shall be filled with the knowledge of the Lord, and shall see eye to eye, and shall lift up their voice, and with the voice together sing this new song, saying:

99.   The Lord hath brought again Zion;
The Lord hath redeemed his people, Israel,
According to the election of grace,
Which was brought to pass by the faith
And covenant of their fathers.

100.   The Lord hath redeemed his people;
And Satan is bound and time is no longer.
The Lord hath gathered all things in one.
The Lord hath brought down Zion from above.
The Lord hath brought up Zion from beneath.

101.   The earth hath travailed and brought forth her strength;
And truth is established in her bowels;
And the heavens have smiled upon her;
And she is clothed with the glory of her God;
For he stands in the midst of his people.

102.   Glory, and honor, and power, and might,
Be ascribed to our God; for he is full of mercy,
Justice, grace and truth, and peace,
Forever and ever, Amen.

4. A Commission to Preach the Gospel.

(a) *Where to Preach.*

60-2. *All the world*] The commission of the servants of God is valid
in all the world (62). They are not confined to a parish, or a city, nor
even to a continent. Their field is the world. This Globe must be reclaimed for our Lord Jesus Christ.

(b) *Effects of the Preaching.*

63-73. Several effects of the proclamation of the gospel are noted
here. Those who believe and are baptized in water for the remission
of sins, shall receive the Holy Ghost (v. 64). Signs shall follow also those
who believe (v. 65). A "sign" is a miraculous manifestation *designed*
to confirm a message for which the claim is made that it is from God.

66. *Wonderful works*] The same as miracles.* Some of the signs and
wonders that may be looked for as a result of faith are enumerated.

67. *They shall cast out devils*] The case of Newel Knight whom the
Prophet rescued from the power of an evil spirit, is known as the first
miracle performed after the organization of the Church (*Hist. of the
Church,* Vol. I., pp. 82-3). The opening of the British Mission was at-

---

* The word "miracle" is derived from *Mirari,* "to wonder" and means that which
excites wonder.

tended by combats with evil spirits. On July 30th, 1837, at daybreak, Elder Isaac Russell, one of the first British missionaries, called Elder Heber C. Kimball out of bed and implored him to deliver him from the evil spirits that were tormenting him to such a degree that he felt that he must succumb. Elder Heber C. Kimball arose immediately, and so did Orson Hyde, who was sleeping in the same bed. Both laid hands on him and prayed and rebuked the evil spirits. Heber C. Kimball relates:

"While thus engaged, I was struck with great force by some invisible power, and fell senseless to the floor. The first thing I recollected was being supported by Elders Hyde and Richards, who were praying for me * * * Elders Hyde and Richards then assisted me to get on the bed * * * when a vision was opened to our minds, and we could distinctly see the evil spirits, who foamed and gnashed their teeth at us. We gazed upon them about an hour and a half (by Willard's watch). We were not looking towards the window, but towards the wall. Space appeared before us, and we saw the devils coming in legions, with their leaders, who came within a few feet of us. They came towards us like armies rushing to battle. They appeared to be men of full stature, possessing every form and feature of men in the flesh who are angry and desperate; and I shall never forget the vindictive malignity depicted on their countenances as they looked me in the eye * * * We distinctly heard those spirits talk and express their wrath and hellish designs against us. However, the Lord delivered us from them, and blessed us exceedingly that day" (See also p. 471).

Elder Orson Hyde, in a letter addressed to Heber C. Kimball several years later, says in part:

"After you were overcome by them and fallen, their awful rush upon me with knives, threats, imprecations, and hellish grins, amply convinced me that they were no friends of mine. When you were apparently senseless and lifeless on the floor and upon the bed * * * I stood between you and the devils and fought them and contended with them face to face, until they began to diminish in number and to retreat from the room" (Whitney's *Life of Heber C. Kimball,* pp. 144-5).

68. *In my name they shall heal the sick*] In the ministry of our Lord, the healing of the sick formed an important part. He must have restored thousands of sufferers to health, for it is said, again and again, that they brought their sick to Him and that He healed them all. He made no marked distinction between the health of the soul and that of the body. He recognized the unmistakable connection between physical health and spiritual life. He gave to His disciples the gift of healing, and these conferred it upon others, so that hundreds, perhaps thousands, were so endowed. And now, in this dispensation, the same great gift is promised to those that believe. The Latter-day Saints enjoy this gift. Among them, the healing of the sick by divine power is a well-known fact. Elder George Q. Cannon appeals to the presence in the Church of this

gift, and others, as an evidence of the divine mission of the Prophet Joseph. He says:

"In all the churches of which we have any knowledge, there has yet to be heard the promise made by one of its ministers to the humble believer who submits to its ordinances, that he shall receive the Holy Ghost as they did in ancient days, with its accompanying gifts and blessings and powers. Joseph Smith made this promise. The world has the opportunity of testing it. If people did not receive the Holy Ghost, then he was an impostor. If they did receive it, then his ministry was sealed by the power of God, and it was indisputable" (*Jour. of Dis.,* Vol. XXIV., p. 136).

71. *Poison * * * not hurt them*] The Prophet Joseph relates the following, which may serve as an illustration:

"While at this place [Greenville, Indiana, where he stayed with Newel K. Whitney during May, 1832, the latter suffering from a fractured leg] I frequently walked out in the woods, where I saw several fresh graves; and one day, when I rose from the dinner table, I walked directly to the door and commenced vomiting most profusely. I raised large quantities of blood and poisonous matter, and so great were the muscular contortions of my system, that my jaw, in a few moments, was dislocated. This I succeeded in replacing with my own hands, and made my way to Brother Whitney (who was on the bed), as speedily as possible; he laid his hands on me and administered to me in the name of the Lord, and I was healed in an instant * * * Thanks be to my heavenly Father for his interference in my behalf at this critical moment, in the name of Jesus Christ. Amen" (*Hist. of the Church,* Vol. I., p. 271).

72. *The poison of a serpent shall not have power to harm them*] Paul, on one occasion, shook a venomous snake from his hand, and was not injured by it (Acts 28:3-6). No less remarkable is an incident from the famous march of Zion's Camp. The members of that organization often encountered reptiles on the prairie. One day Solomon Humphrey laid himself down for a little rest, being weary. When he awoke, he saw a rattlesnake coiled up not more than a few inches from his head. Some proposed to kill it, but Brother Humphrey said, "Let it alone; we have had a good nap together." It was on this occasion that the Prophet Joseph instructed the brethren not to kill serpents, or any other animals, unless absolutely necessary. "Men," said he, "must first become harmless themselves, before they can expect the brute creation to be so" (Andrew Jenson, *Hist. Rec.,* p. 835).

A. Clarke observes that there is no record or tradition indicating that any of the Apostles of our Lord ever suffered death by poison, while Mohammed came to his end by that means, as did, it may be added, Socrates. The promise of immunity from poison is, therefore, very remarkable.

73. *They shall not boast themselves of these things*] The spiritual

gifts are not to be exhibited in public, as sparkling rings and necklaces are worn for personal adornment; they are given for the edification and nourishment of the Church.

It has been asserted that miracles are impossible, because they are contrary to the laws of nature, and that the supernatural element in the history of religion is, in our enlightened age, the main difficulty in the way of its acceptance. It is assumed that the so-called laws of nature are immutable, and that nothing can take place that appears to be contrary to such laws. To this objection the answer is, that we do not know *all* the laws of nature. We can, therefore, not maintain that the miracles performed by the servants of the Lord are not in perfect accord with some law of which we are ignorant. All we can say is that they do not belong to any of the classes of ordinary events with which men are familiar. But that is far from saying that they are impossible. As a matter of fact, violations of the best established laws of nature appear to be occurring constantly. We raise a weight from the ground. That seems to be contrary to the law of gravitation. Our bodies, for years, resist decay because of the action of the life-force within. That seems to be contrary to chemical laws governing matter. One force counteracts another; and besides, God's universe is not exclusively controlled by physical forces. Superior to these, directing and controlling them, is the divine will. As a captain, with a word of command, turns his immense ship in whatever direction he chooses, and controls his engines and everything, so God directs and controls His universe and all that pertains thereto, not contrary to, but in conformity with, laws and forces known to Him, even though unknown to us.

(c) *Effects on those who Reject the Gospel.*

74-6. Spiritual gifts were to follow acceptance of the message of the Gospel. Here we are told that those who do not believe and, therefore, are not baptized, shall be damned.

74. *Shall not come into my Father's kingdom*] This is an explanation of the meaning in which the word "damned" is used in these Revelations. "My Father's kingdom, where my Father and I am" means celestial glory.

75. *And this Revelation * * * is in force from this very hour upon all the world*] How necessary, then, that the world should be made acquainted with the truths it contains!

76. *They are to be upbraided*] The children of the world. The word "upbraid" seems to be used here in the same sense as "reprove" in John 16:8. There it means "convict." It is the office of the Holy Spirit to convict the world of sin, of righteousness, and of judgment, in order to bring men and women to repentance. If those who are sent to the world with the gospel message are filled with the Holy Spirit, the result will be the conviction of sinners, and conviction will be followed by

either condemnation or salvation—salvation, if the gospel is accepted; condemnation, if it is rejected.

Your brethren in Zion for their rebellion] It is evident from the history of the Church that not all the brethren in Zion were actuated by that spirit of brotherly love, unselfishness, and willingness to follow counsel, which should predominate in such a place. At the general Council of the Church held on the 26th of April, 1832, "all the differences [were] settled and the hearts of all were united together in love," but the perfect condition had not yet come. Therefore, they, as well as the children of the world, were to be upbraided.

In obedience to this commandment a conference of twelve High Priests, held at Kirtland, January 14th, 1833, appointed Orson Hyde and Hyrum Smith to address a letter "to the Bishop, his Council, and the inhabitants of Zion," and warn them, on behalf of the Conference, of the consequences of rebellion. The letter was written, and received the endorsement of the brethren.

In this epistle it was pointed out that the children of Zion were under condemnation, until they repented and remembered the new covenant and the commandments of God; and a scourge and a judgment would be poured out upon them, if they did not repent (*Hist. of the Church,* Vol. I., pp. 317-21). The letter was not without effect, for the Saints of Zion began to humble themselves, and the Lord took notice of the change of heart (Sec. 90:34).

(d) *Equipment of a Herald of the Gospel.*

77-86. When a young man of the world decides to devote his life to ministerial, or missionary, work in the interest of one of the popular churches, he generally enters some college, or university, in order to get a special education for such a position. That is part of his equipment. Having obtained the necessary instruction in the art of preparing sermons, he seeks an opportunity to come in contact with the members of the board of some missionary society with ample means, or the trustees of some church, in order that he may secure a salary, and, if everything is agreeable, he obligates himself to preach certain doctrines at so much a year. The salary is an essential part of the equipment. All arrangements being made, the missionary starts for his field with so many trunks and boxes that he needs several beasts of burden to carry them, unless he can load them on a railroad car.

The Lord did not want His servants to travel in this manner. They were commanded to go without both purse and scrip, which means without salary and baggage (v. 78). They were not even to take two coats with them. If they were faithful, the Lord would provide for them, so that they would not grow weary, nor go hungry or thirsty (v. 80). As missionaries, they were not to take any thought "for tomorrow" concerning what to eat and drink, etc. (v. 81). Neither were they to take any thought beforehand as to what to say. If they would but treasure up in their minds continually the words of life, they would, on each occasion, be given what to say (v. 85). The command is repeated, "Let no man among you. * * * from this hour take purse or scrip, that goeth forth to proclaim the gospel of the kingdom" (v. 86). An ideal, different from that of the world!

Young missionaries are apt to make the mistake of supposing that the main strength of a sermon can be drawn from books, and they read good authors and repeat their arguments and illustrations faithfully, and then they wonder why their efforts fall flat. The substance of a discourse should be drawn from experience, rather than from the printed page. Good books are helpful, but that which we bring forth from our own experience is that which is of the greatest value to those who hear us. A man who prays can speak of prayer, because he knows something about communion with God, by his experience. One who keeps the Word of Wisdom, or obeys the Law of Tithing, can speak on these principles with authority. Only those who live pure lives can speak convincingly of the happiness virtue gives. This rule obtains in everything. One who desires to teach his neighbor agriculture, must, himself, have practical knowledge of the subject. A pilot must have personal knowledge of the course over which he undertakes to steer the ship. The soldier who has been at the front, can speak to some purpose about the trials and hardships of life in the trenches. No study of books can take the place of personal experience.

86. *Scrip*] See Section 24:18.

(e) *What to Preach.*

87. *Reprove the world*] "Reprove," as stated (v. 76) is to "convict." God's messengers, as it were, are lawyers before the bar of God. It is their duty to "convict" the world of sin, and to warn all men of the "judgment which is to come." They are not sent out to entertain the world with philosophical lectures, or ethical discourses, or flowery oratory, or amusing anecdotes. Their one duty is to secure conviction and, if possible, repentance and salvation. The sermon of Peter on the day of Pentecost is an illustration of a "convicting" discourse, for many of those who heard it "were pricked in their heart, and said unto Peter and to the rest of the apostles, men and brethren, what shall we do?" (Acts 2:37). The message delivered had had the intended effect. The preaching of Jonah in Nineveh is another illustration.

Judgment which is to come] The servants of the Lord must know, through the spirit of prophecy and the prophetic word of God, something of the judgments that are to pass over the Earth, and the fate that necessarily will befall unrepentant sinners, and it is their duty to tell the world of these things. The Prophet Joseph and his associates warned the people everywhere of judgments in the form of wars, pestilence, famine, etc. (Sec. 1:17-18), unless, for some special reason, they were commanded to "talk not of judgment" (Sec. 105:24). The law of God regarding this subject is: "When I say unto the wicked, Thou shalt surely die; and thou givest him not warning, nor speakest to warn the wicked from his wicked way, to save his life; the same wicked man shall die in his iniquity; but his blood will I require at thine hand. Yet, if thou warn the wicked, and he turn not from his wickedness, nor from his wicked way, he shall die in his iniquity; but thou hast delivered thy soul" (Ezekiel 3:18, 19).

(f) *God's Messengers Well Protected.*

88-94. In these paragraphs the Lord promises His servants that He will be their companion; that His Spirit will be in their hearts; and His angels round about them (v. 88). What a glorious promise!

89. *Whoso receiveth you receiveth me*] Those who receive the servants of the Lord as teachers and guests, receive the Lord, whose embassadors and representatives they are, and their reward is sure (v. 90). They will receive such reward as the Lord's messengers have (See Matt. 10:40-42), and our Lord Himself will reward them hereafter. (See v. 36.)

91. *By this you may know my disciples*] Hospitality toward the messengers of the Lord is a true mark of discipleship. Genuine faith is always active in good works.

92. *Cleanse your feet*] See Sec. 60:15.

(g) *Coming Judgments.*

95-7. Our Lord, in loving kindness, warns all men against rejecting His messengers and their testimony, as He warned the cities in which His mighty works were performed during His earthly ministry. Though He was meek and lowly, and though His boundless love impelled Him to sacrifice Himself on the cross, yet He pronounced a woe upon Chorazin and Bethsaida and warned Capernaum that it would be brought down from its exalted position and fall lower than the cities in which His mighty works had not been done (Matt. 11:20-24).

97. *Plagues shall go forth*] The Prophet Joseph noted (in May, 1833), that the signs of the times continued to attract the attention of the world. The cholera was then raging in Cuba and Portugal. Influenza carried off many victims in Russia.

Shall not be taken from the earth] It is a fact that, although medical science has performed wonders, by way of stamping out some diseases and mitigating the horrors of others, yet plagues are more common than ever and defy all attempts at staying their onward course. Witness the reports of tuberculosis congresses, or statistics on the growth of cancer. This is only to be expected; for the Lord declared that plagues would continue until His work is completed.

*My work * * * cut short*] Several circumstances helped to shorten the duration of the siege of Jerusalem by Titus, as promised by the Lord (Matt. 24:22). The supply of provisions was cut off; important fortifications were abandoned, and internal dissension prevented the defenders from utilizing their resources to the best advantage. Similarly, during the time of trouble that is to precede the Millennium, circumstances will occur to shorten that period for the sake of the elect. The time of trouble will not be prolonged beyond the time necessary for the redemption of the human race from the power of evil, through repentance.

When the Lord cuts short his work in righteousness it has a far more significant meaning than bringing his purposes to pass by calamity and punishment. He will cut short the time of preaching the gospel, and "will hasten my (his) work in its time." (Sec. 88:73.) We can see how this will be accomplished. The missionaries who are sent forth are not going forth in sufficient numbers to contact all the peoples of the earth, but the Lord will use other agencies in order to get his message before the people—the press, radio, television, and other wonderful ways to get the message before the world where the elders will not be able to go. All of this will help to hasten His work to its end.

(h) Coming Glory.

98-102. The prophetic word does not leave us in contemplation of the gloomy view of wrath and judgment. It bids us look beyond and see the glories of the Millennial reign of the Redeemer, when all shall know the Lord, and see eye to eye (v. 98) and sing the new song of the redeemed (v. 99-102).

98. *All shall know me*] See Jer. 31:33-34.
And shall see eye to eye] When our Lord comes to His Zion, the New Jerusalem, He shall be seen in person, as clearly as when two men look each other in the face.
This new song] In the Revelations contained in the Doctrine and Covenants, reference is frequently made to the songs of Zion. See Secs. 25:12; 45:71; 66:11; 101:18; 133:33. The Saints are to come to Zion with songs of everlasting joy, and when the Lord comes to His people in the New Jerusalem, they will sing the new song. The Latter-day Saints are famous for their love of singing and music. There is, perhaps, no other community on Earth of an equal size, in which the divine art has as many, as ardent devotees.

99. *Lord hath brought again Zion*] The City of Zion has again been established on Earth, and God has gathered His Israel.

100. *Brought down Zion from above*] Enoch's Zion, which "God received up into His bosom (Book of Moses 7:69).
Brought up Zion from beneath] The City of the Saints; for the former-day Zion and the latter-day Zion shall meet (Book of Moses 7:21, 60-67).

103. And again, verily, verily, I say unto you, it is expedient

that every man who goes forth to proclaim mine everlasting gospel, that inasmuch as they have families, and receive money by gift, that they should send it unto them or make use of it for their benefit, as the Lord shall direct them, for thus it seemeth me good.

104. And let all those who have not families, who receive money, send it up unto the bishop in Zion, or unto the bishop in Ohio, that it may be consecrated for the bringing forth of the revelations and the printing thereof, and for establishing Zion.

105. And if any man shall give unto any of you a coat, or a suit, take the old and cast it unto the poor, and go on your way rejoicing.

5. SPECIAL DIRECTIONS.

(a) Concerning the Offerings of Friends.

103-105. Missionaries with families were to send the money which friends might put into their hands, to their families (v. 103); those without home-ties were to remit such gifts to the Bishop in Zion, or in Ohio, to be used for the propagation of the gospel (v. 104). Clothes given should be accepted, and the old pieces of clothing given to the poor (v. 105). The missionary should not attempt to accumulate means, while preaching the gospel. He should not refuse gifts offered in a spirit of kindness and love, but he should use them wisely and for the blessing of others. He should not pile them up for his own benefit. And thus the temptation to a miserly, sordid course was removed from their path, if they would obey this divine counsel. They would never have any use for purse, nor scrip.

106. And if any man among you be strong in the Spirit, let him take with him him that is weak, that he may be edified in all meekness, that he may become strong also.

107. Therefore, take with you those who are ordained unto the lesser priesthood, and send them before you to make appointments, and to prepare the way, and to fill appointments that you yourselves are not able to fill.

108. Behold, this is the way that mine apostles, in ancient days, built up my church unto me.

109. Therefore, let every man stand in his own office, and labor in his own calling; and let not the head say unto the feet it hath no need of the feet; for without the feet how shall the body be able to stand?

110. Also the body hath need of every member, that all may be edified together, that the system may be kept perfect.

111. And behold, the high priests should travel, and also the elders, and also the lesser priests; but the deacons and teachers should be appointed to watch over the church, to be standing ministers unto the church.

(b) *Concerning the Weak.*

106-11. The rule in the kingdom of God is that the strong shall take care of the weak. In the world the rule is to leave the weak behind to perish. The expressions "strong" and "weak" are evidently adapted from Rom. 15:1, where they mean "able" and "unable" respectively. The idea is, further, that those who are able should bear, or carry, the infirmities of those that are not so able. But to carry a burden involves not only strength but also patience and perseverance to the higher Priesthood, because of their age and experience (v. 106). In compliance with this rule those who were ordained should take with them those holding the lesser Priesthood and give them every opportunity to learn and to develop (v. 107). This follows from the fact that all are members of the same body, each having need of all the others (109, 110). All may travel except Teachers and Deacons (v. 111).

108. *This is the way that mine * * * apostles built up my church*] See, for instance II. Tim. 4:9-13. Our Lord, too, employed His disciples in the ministry (Luke 10:1).

109. *Let not the head say unto the feet*] The unity and equality of the Saints are not those of anarchy, but those obtaining under the most perfect system of organization and coordination conceivable—that of the human body. In the body each member has its own function to perform. God did not intend that the foot should see, or hear, but walk. Nor did He design the eye to see for itself alone, but for the benefit of the entire body; or the ear to hear for its own service, but for all. In the body each organ performs its own function for the preservation and building up of the whole organization. When we fully understand this great truth, we shall realize that it does not matter whether we are doing the work of the head or the foot, as long as we are faithful. Well says Chrysostom, "Is the head crowned? All the man is glorified. Do the lips speak? The eyes also laugh and rejoice."

112. And the bishop, Newel K. Whitney, also should travel round about and among all the churches, searching after the poor to administer to their wants by humbling the rich and the proud.

113. He should also employ an agent to take charge and to do his secular business as he shall direct.

(c) *Concerning the Poor.*

112-13. Newel K. Whitney had been appointed Bishop at Kirtland (See Sec. 72:2, 8). One of his duties was to travel among the churches and look after the poor.

112. *By humbling the rich and the proud*] The gospel message would make the rich humble enough to place sufficient means in the hands of the Bishop to enable him to administer to the wants of the poor. No true Latter-day Saint can hoard his means and neglect the poor. The words of our Lord, "Ye have the poor always with you," are frequently repeated as an excuse for the condition of destitution in which even the Christian world has left so great a portion of God's children. But He does not say, "The poor ye *must* always have with you." Poverty is one of the problems which the gospel undertakes to solve, and if anyone is of the opinion that the gospel is not applicable to our temporal conditions, he may as well contend that the gospel is not a power of God to salvation from sin; for if it saves from sin, it saves from the consequences of sin, among which are poverty and destitution, sickness, and death.

114. Nevertheless, let the bishop go unto the city of New York, also to the city of Albany, and also to the city of Boston, and warn the people of those cities with the sound of the gospel, with a loud voice, of the desolation and utter abolishment which await them if they do reject these things.

115. For if they do reject these things the hour of their judgment is nigh, and their house shall be left unto them desolate.

116. Let him trust in me and he shall not be confounded; and a hair of his head shall not fall to the ground unnoticed.

(d) *Concerning Those who Reject the Gospel.*

114-16. Bishop Newel K. Whitney was given a special mission to go to the cities mentioned (v. 114) and warn the inhabitants that the hour of judgment was near at hand, if they should reject the gospel message (v. 115). The promise was added that he should go and return in safety, if he would trust in the Lord (v. 116).

Shortly after this Revelation was given, the Prophet Joseph, accompanied by Bishop Whitney, took a hurried journey to Albany, New York, and Boston. In the *Millennial Star,* Vol. X., p. 286, there is an extract from an article from the *Albany Express,* in which a conflagration is described, by which buildings and property to the value of $2,000,000 was destroyed at Albany. Several lives were lost and many business men were utterly ruined.

Ancient prophets and the Lord Himself by prophetic vision have seen the great calamities and destructions which await great cities, countries in these last days because they will not repent and forsake their iniquities. Isaiah (Ch. 24) speaks of the time when "the land shall be utterly emptied, and utterly spoiled," and a "curse devoureth the earth," and there shall be few men left.

117. And verily I say unto you, the rest of my servants, go ye forth as your circumstances shall permit, in your several callings, unto the great and notable cities and villages, reproving the world in righteousness of all their unrighteous and ungodly deeds, setting forth clearly and understandingly the desolation of abomination in the last days.

118. For, with you saith the Lord Almighty, I will rend their kingdoms; I will not only shake the earth, but the starry heavens shall tremble.

119. For I, the Lord, have put forth my hand to exert the powers of heaven; ye cannot see it now, yet a little while and ye shall see it, and know that I am, and that I will come and reign with my people.

120. I am Alpha and Omega, the beginning and the end. Amen.

(e) Concerning the End.

117-20. The servants of the Lord are called upon to warn the world and to set forth, clearly and understandingly, the "desolation of abomination" in the last days. This expression is found in Daniel (11:31), where it refers to the pollution of the Temple and the destruction of Jerusalem by the Romans. Compare Matthew 24:15. In this Revelation it has a similar meaning, referring, however, to different agents of destruction. The "abomination of desolation" is "the abomination that maketh desolate." It is, in other words, sin and transgression, and especially the profanation of sacred things, for in the wake of sin follows destruction, sooner or later. When the Roman standards were planted on the battlements of the sacred precincts, desolation was near, but those pagan insignia were but symbolical of the apostasy that had taken place, which was *the* abomination which caused desolation.

118. *With you * * * I will rend their kingdoms*] This indicates the nature of the desolation spoken of. Kingdoms are to be rent, and that through the influence of the gospel which the servants of the Lord are proclaiming. They are very humble and unobtrusive, but as missionaries of the gospel, they are they who—in the language of Bishop Ryle—"Shake the universe." Yes, "These are they who change the

fortunes of kingdoms by their prayers; these are they who are the active workers for spreading the knowledge of pure religion and undefiled; these are the life-blood of a country, the shield, the defense, the stay, and the support of any nation to which they belong."*

119. This Revelation, as many others, closes with the promise that the Lord will come and reign on Earth. The message of the second advent extends through the Doctrine and Covenants, from the beginning to the end.

General Notes

As an illustration of the power of God made manifest in our dispensation, this incident, published in a Welsh paper, *The Merlin,* may be retold:

"During the night of Friday week (September 22nd, 1848), between the hours of eleven and twelve, a very extraordinary occurrence took place in Newport. A young man named Reuben Brinkworth was, in 1840, at Bermuda, on board the *Terror,* * * * when, in the midst of thunder and lightning, he was suddenly deprived of both hearing and speech; and in this deplorable condition returned to Stroud in England, of which place he was a native. He has since been residing with Mr. Naish, basket maker, Market Street, Newport, who, with several other persons, is attached to the community of the people known as 'Mormons.' Persons of this denomination have been able to communicate their doctrines to Brinkworth, by means of writing, signs, and the finger alphabet. * * * On Friday night week, the young man was suddenly seized with a kind of fit, in which he continued some time; and on his recovery he was called upon by signs to believe in the Savior, that the healing power of God might be exercised in his behalf. He was, moreover, earnestly entreated to be baptized; but this was very strongly opposed by a person in the room. The deaf and dumb man, however, signified his acquiescence. He was taken to the canal and baptized in the name of our Savior; and immediately on coming up out of the water, he cried out, 'Thank the Lord, I can speak and hear again, as well as any of you' " (*Millennial Star,* Vol. X., p. 349).

If only a small part of all the miraculous manifestations of the power of God witnessed by Latter-day Saints, were recorded, they would fill volumes. But the Saints do not boast of miracles. They do not expect the Lord to interpose miraculously in their behalf at all times. Brigham Young says on this subject:

"If we are sick, and ask the Lord to heal us, and to do all for us that is necessary to be done, according to my understanding of the gospel of salvation, I might as well ask the Lord to cause my wheat

---

° Bishop Ryle is speaking of the members of what has been called "the invisible church," but what he says is more applicable to the true members of the visible Church of Christ, and His ambassadors.

and corn to grow, without my plowing the ground and casting in the seed. It appears consistent to me to apply every remedy that comes within the range of my knowledge, and to ask my Father in heaven, in the name of Jesus Christ, to sanctify that application to the healing of my body" (*Jour. of Dis.,* Vol. IV., p. 24).

Some would have us believe that miracles of healing are no longer necessary. But the fact is that such miracles are inseparably connected with the gospel. He who forgives sins, also heals "all thy diseases" (Psalm 103:3). When the healing power of God is separated from the gospel, it is no longer the gospel our Lord committed to His disciples to preach to all the world.

There is, however, such a thing as "lying wonders." There are signs and wonders that owe their origin to evil spirits and that are designed to promote error instead of truth. Only through the Spirit of the Lord can we discern, between the true and the false.

The Elders are charged with the duty of warning the world of judgments. But not unless directed to do so by the Holy Spirit. In the *Evening and Morning Star,* published in July, 1932, we read:

"You are to walk in the valley of humility, and pray for the salvation of all; yea, you are to pray for your enemies and warn in compassion without threatening the wicked with judgments which are to be poured out upon the world hereafter. You have no right to take the judgments which fell upon the ungodly before the flood, and pour them upon the head of this generation; you have no authority to use the judgments which God sent upon Pharaoh in Egypt, to terrify the inhabitants of America, neither have you any direction by commandment, to collect the calamities of six thousand years and paint them upon the curtain of these last days to scare mankind to repentance; no, you are to preach the gospel, which is the power of God unto salvation, even glad tidings of great joy unto all people" (*Hist. of the Church,* Vol, I., p. 280).

SECTION 85.

REVELATION *given through Joseph Smith the Prophet, at Kirtland, Ohio, November 27, 1832, concerning the Saints in Zion, Missouri. See History of the Church, vol. 1, p. 298.——— Inheritances in Zion to be received through consecration—Provision made for the assignment of inheritances among the Saints.*

IT is the duty of the Lord's clerk, whom he has appointed, to keep a history, and a general church record of all things that transpire in Zion, and of all those who consecrate properties, and receive inheritances legally from the bishop;

2. And also their manner of life, their faith, and works; and also of the apostates who apostatize after receiving their inheritances.

3. It is contrary to the will and commandment of God that those who receive not their inheritance by consecration, agreeable to his law, which he has given, that he may tithe his people, to prepare them against the day of vengeance and burning, should have their names enrolled with the people of God.

4. Neither is their genealogy to be kept, or to be had where it may be found on any of the records or history of the church.

5. Their names shall not be found, neither the names of the fathers, nor the names of the children written in the book of the law of God, saith the Lord of Hosts.

About this time the Prophet Joseph received letters from the brethren in Missouri concerning the conditions there. In his reply, he says he fancies to himself that William W. Phelps was saying or thinking something like this:

"My God, great and mighty art thou; therefore show unto Thy servant what shall become of all those who are essaying to come up into Zion, in order to keep the commandments of God, and yet receive not their inheritance by consecrations, by order or deed from the Bishop, the man that God has appointed in a legal way, agreeably to the law given to organize and regulate the Church, and all the affairs of the same."

The Prophet then goes on to dictate the instructions contained in this Section.

A GENERAL CHURCH RECORD.

1-5. It is the duty of the Lord's clerk to keep a History and a general Church Record, containing the particulars mentioned in these paragraphs. But those who receive not their inheritance by consecration shall not have their names enrolled in that Record.

3. *That he may tithe his people*] The law of tithing had not yet been introduced. The Order of Enoch was still in force. See also Sec. 64:23. But the law of tithing was known.

6. Yea, thus saith the still small voice, which whispereth through and pierceth all things, and often times it maketh my bones to quake while it maketh manifest, saying:

7. And it shall come to pass that I, the Lord God, will send one mighty and strong, holding the scepter of power in his hand, clothed with light for a covering, whose mouth shall utter words.

eternal words; while his bowels shall be a fountain of truth, to set in order the house of God, and to arrange by lot the inheritances of the saints whose names are found, and the names of their fathers, and of their children, enrolled in the book of the law of God;

8. While that man, who was called of God and appointed, that putteth forth his hand to steady the ark of God, shall fall by the shaft of death, like as a tree that is smitten by the vivid shaft of lightning.

9. And all they who are not found written in the book of remembrance shall find none inheritance in that day, but they shall be cut asunder, and their portion shall be appointed them among unbelievers, where are wailing and gnashing of teeth.

10. These things I say not of myself; therefore, as the Lord speaketh, he will also fulfil.

11. And they who are of the High Priesthood, whose names are not found written in the book of the law, or that are found to have apostatized, or to have been cut off from the church, as well as the lesser priesthood, or the members, in that day shall not find an inheritance among the saints of the Most High;

12. Therefore, it shall be done unto them as unto the children of the priest, as will be found recorded in the second chapter and sixty-first and second verses of Ezra.

ONE MIGHTY AND STRONG.

7-12. It was necessary that the Church Record should be kept correctly, for "it shall come to pass that I, the Lord God, will send one mighty and strong * * * to set in order the house of God, and to arrange by lot the inheritances of the saints, whose names are found * * * enrolled" in that Record—"the book of the law of God" (v. 7), or, "book of remembrance" (v. 9).

Who is this Mighty and Strong?

In an article over the signatures of Joseph F. Smith, John R. Winder, and Anthon H. Lund, First Presidency, published in the *Deseret News,* November 13, 1905, that question is comprehensively and clearly discussed. After having quoted in full the letter of the Prophet Joseph to William W. Phelps, the authors of the article say:

"It is to be observed first of all that the subject of this whole letter, as also the part of it subsequently accepted as a revelation, relates to the affairs of the Church in Missouri, the gathering of the Saints to that land, and obtaining their inheritances under the law of consecration and stewardship; and the Prophet deals especially with the matter of what is to become of those who fail to receive their inheritances by order or deed from the Bishop."

It is then pointed out that Edward Partridge, the Bishop of the Church, was the one "called and appointed to divide by lot unto the Saints their inheritances." But was Edward Partridge the one who, in 1832, was "putting forth his hand to steady the ark," and was threatened with falling "by the shaft of death like as a tree that is smitten by the vivid shaft of lightning"? In the article quoted, this question is answered in the affirmative. It is shown that Edward Partridge, though a worthy man, one whom God loved, at times arrayed himself in opposition to the Prophet, so strenuously that Ezra Booth made their differences an excuse for his apostasy. On the 26th of April, 1832, Partridge gave the Prophet the right hand of fellowship, and it was supposed that all differences were settled, but afterwards he brought them up again. Edward Partridge was, when this Revelation was written, neglecting his own duty and putting "forth his hand to steady the ark"; hence the warning. Partridge repented, in part at least, but in March, 1833, the Lord again took occasion to say that He was "not well pleased with him" and others. In the midst of the troubles and persecution of Missouri, Partridge acted a most noble and self-sacrificing part, offering himself as one of five willing to suffer and be put to death by the mob, if by so doing they could secure freedom for the rest of the Saints. He bore persecution with meekness and dignity, and the Lord, in November, 1835, said He was well pleased with him. But that he was the man threatened with sudden and untimely death "there can be no question."

But let us quote again:

"Now as to the 'one mighty and strong' who shall be sent of God, to 'set in order the house of God, and to arrange by lot the inheritances of the Saints'; who is he? What position will he hold in the Church? In what manner will he come to his calling? We draw attention first of all to the fact that this whole letter to William W. Phelps, as well as the part afterwards accepted as the word of the Lord, related to the affairs of the Church in Zion, Independence, Jackson County, Missouri: and inasmuch as through his repentance and sacrifices and suffering, Bishop Edward Partridge undoubtedly obtained a mitigation of the threatened judgment against him of falling 'by the shaft of death, like as a tree that is smitten by the vivid shaft of lightning,' so the occasion for sending another to fill his station—'one mighty and strong to set in order the house of God, and to arrange by lot the inheritance of the Saints'—may also be considered as having passed away and the whole incident of the prophecy closed."

*   *   *   *

"If, however, there are those who will still insist that the prophecy concerning the coming of 'one mighty and strong' is still to be regarded as relating to the future, let the Latter-day Saints know that he will be a future Bishop of the Church who will be with the Saints in Zion, Jackson County, Missouri, when the Lord shall establish them in that land; and he will also be blessed with the spirit and power of his calling, that he will be able to set in order the house of God, pertaining to the department of the work under his jurisdiction; and in righteousness and justice he will 'arrange by lot the inheritances of the Saints.' He will hold the same high and exalted station that Edward Partridge held."

SECTION 86.

REVELATION *given through Joseph Smith the Prophet, at Kirtland, Ohio, December 6, 1832.——Exposition of the Lord's parable concerning the wheat and the tares—Its application to the latter days.*

VERILY, thus saith the Lord unto you my servants, concerning the parable of the wheat and of the tares:

2. Behold, verily I say, the field was the world, and the apostles were the sowers of the seed;

3. And after they have fallen asleep the great persecutor of the church, the apostate, the whore, even Babylon, that maketh all nations to drink of her cup, in whose hearts the enemy, even Satan, sitteth to reign—behold he soweth the tares; wherefore, the tares choke the wheat and drive the church into the wilderness.

4. But behold, in the last days, even now while the Lord is beginning to bring forth the word, and the blade is springing up and is yet tender—

5. Behold, verily I say unto you, the angels are crying unto the Lord day and night, who are ready and waiting to be sent forth to reap down the fields;

6. But the Lord saith unto them, pluck not up the tares while the blade is yet tender (for verily your faith is weak), lest you destroy the wheat also.

7. Therefore, let the wheat and the tares grow together until the harvest is fully ripe; then ye shall first gather out the wheat from among the tares, and after the gathering of the wheat, behold and lo, the tares are bound in bundles, and the field remaineth to be burned.

8. Therefore, thus saith the Lord unto you, with whom the priesthood hath continued through the lineage of your fathers—

9. For ye are lawful heirs, according to the flesh, and have been hid from the world with Christ in God—

10. Therefore your life and the priesthood have remained, and must needs remain through you and your lineage until the restoration of all things spoken by the mouths of all the holy prophets since the world began.

11. Therefore, blessed are ye if ye continue in my goodness, a light unto the Gentiles, and through this priesthood, a savior unto my people Israel. The Lord hath said it. Amen.

The Wheat and the Tares.

1-11. "So important is the lesson embodied in this parable, and so assured is the literal fulfilment of its contained predictions, that the Lord has given a further explication through revelation in the current dispensation, a period in which the application is direct and immediate" (Dr. James E. Talmage, *Jesus the Christ,* p. 288).

2. *The apostles were the sowers*] Our Lord (Matt. 13:37) explains that *the* Sower is the Son of Man. After His mission on Earth, He does the sowing through His Apostles.

3. *Behold he soweth the tares*] Satan. "The enemy is the devil" (Matt. 13:39). As the work of sowing good seed is done by Christ through His Apostles, so the work of sowing tares is done by the adversary through the agency of the leaders of an apostate, persecuting church. A persecuting church, be it remembered, is always a false church. Persecution is from the evil one. For, as has been well said by a student of history, "While it is true that victims of persecution have *sometimes* been wrong, it is equally true that the persecutors have *always* been wrong."

6. *Pluck not up the tares*] In this parable the good seed is the "children of the kingdom," and the tares are "the children of the wicked one" (Matt. 13:38). In the world, which is the field, the two classes grow together, and while the blade is yet tender, even the angels may not readily distinguish between them.

7. *Until the harvest is fully ripe*] That is the time of separation. That is the time of gathering of the wheat, before the tares are destroyed by fire.

10. *Until the restoration of all things*] The gathering dispensation has been ushered in with the restoration of the Priesthood and the organization of the Church.

"The angels are the reapers and still, angels, you say, are coming to Earth no more. This won't do, for the reapers are the angels * * * in another place it is said, 'And he shall send his angels with a great sound of a trumpet, and they shall gather together his elect from four winds, from one end of heaven to the other.' And yet the present Christian world would say that angels have no more to do; of course, then they do not look for anything of this kind; their faith does not embrace the sayings of the Savior and His Apostles, touching the winding-up scene: and without faith it is impossible to please God; consequently, they cannot share in the blessings of the gathering dispensation of the last days; their unbelief excludes them" (Orson Hyde, *Jour. of Dis.,* Vol. II., p. 64-5).

SECTION 87.

REVELATION AND PROPHECY ON WAR, *given through Joseph Smith the Prophet, December 25, 1832.——Wars predicted— Division between the Northern States and the Southern States —Great calamities in manifestation of the chastening hand of God.*

VERILY, thus saith the Lord concerning the wars that will shortly come to pass, beginning at the rebellion of South Carolina, which will eventually terminate in the death and misery of many souls;

2.   And the time will come that war will be poured out upon all nations, beginning at this place.

3.   For behold, the Southern States shall be divided against the Northern States, and the Southern States will call on other nations, even the nation of Great Britain, as it is called, and they shall also call upon other nations, in order to defend themselves against other nations; and then war shall be poured out upon all nations.

4.   And it shall come to pass, after many days, slaves shall rise up against their masters, who shall be marshaled and disciplined for war.

5.   And it shall come to pass also that the remnants who are left of the land will marshal themselves, and shall become ex-

ceedingly angry, and shall vex the Gentiles with a sore vexation.

6. And thus, with the sword and by bloodshed the inhabitants of the earth shall mourn; and with famine, and plague, and earthquake, and the thunder of heaven, and the fierce and vivid lightning also, shall the inhabitants of the earth be made to feel the wrath, and indignation, and chastening hand of an Almighty God, until the consumption decreed hath made a full end of all nations;

7. That the cry of the saints, and of the blood of the saints, shall cease to come up into the ears of the Lord of Sabaoth, from the earth, to be avenged of their enemies.

8. Wherefore, stand ye in holy places, and be not moved, until the day of the Lord come; for behold, it cometh quickly, saith the Lord. Amen.

This remarkable Revelation was given through the Prophet Joseph on Christmas day, 1832.

At that time there was considerable commotion in the United States. The tariff question was one of great issue. The State of New York, before its acceptance of the Federal Constitution, surrounded itself with protective tariffs, and this policy was gradually approved by other Northern States. The Southern States, on the other hand, regarded free trade as best serving their interests, as their products were limited to a few articles of raw material, which they exported, while they imported practically all the manufactured commodities they needed. In 1824, Congress enacted a protective-tariff bill. A few years later, a stricter measure was adopted against Great Britain, in retaliation for efforts to exclude American trade from the British West Indies. This met with vigorous opposition in the South, especially in South Carolina. In this State, in 1832, a convention of the citizens declared that the tariff acts of 1828 and 1832 were not binding within their territory, and fixed February 1st, 1833, as the date after which they would be considered abrogated, unless Congress should, before then, remove the difficulty. Many Northerners were in favor of carrying the laws of the Union into effect by means of arms, at that time, and a bill empowering the President to use force was introduced in Congress. It was during this political agitation that the Prophet Joseph made the condition of his Country the subject of prayer and received this Revelation (See Sec. 130:12, 13).

While all of these differences existing between the North and the South had a tendency to drive the people apart, yet it was the question of slavery, and the contention over the expansion of new territory and the creation of new states and whether or not slavery should be permitted in such new territory, that became the crux which brought upon the people the great Civil War. The historian, John Fisk wrote:

"The story of the disputes over slavery, which led to the Civil War, is inseparably connected with the story of the westward expansion of the United States." (*History of the United States for Schools,* p. 349.)

"The longer the dispute about slavery in the new territory went on, the hotter it grew. Three methods of settlement were proposed. The extreme Southern men said, Every citizen of the United States has the right to go to any part of the country he pleases, and take his property—including his negroes—with him. Give us, said they, that right, and we ask no more. But the advocates of the 'Wilmot Proviso' and other Free-Soil men answered, we will have no more slave states. All territory shall be free. Finally, a third class said: Congress has no right to meddle in this matter, one way or the other. The people of the territories are the sovereigns; let them decide for themselves between freedom and slavery." (D. H. Montgomery, *Leading Facts of American History,* p. 273.)

In this revelation on war, the Lord reveals to the Prophet:

(1) That the agitation will lead to war;

(2) That South Carolina will take the initiative;

(3) That the war will bring death and misery to many souls;

(4) That the rebellion in South Carolina is only the beginning;

(5) That there will be a division between Southern and Northern States;

(6) That the South will appeal to Great Britain and other nations for aid;

(7) That finally nations shall rise against nations, until war is poured out upon all.

Have all these predictions been fulfilled?

(1.) All the world now knows that the agitation in the United States in the first part of the last century resulted in a long, devastating war. But at the time this prophecy was given, American statesmen and the American people generally firmly believed that the problem could be solved by constitutional means. In fact, a settlement was agreed on, the basis of which was a law providing for a gradual, moderate reduction of the tariff. This law enabled South Carolina to withdraw her Nullification Ordinance, while the necessity for the Force Bill was removed. Thus it was hoped that the crisis was passed. The Lord, however, declared, through His Prophet, that war would come. No statesmanship could avert the calamity.

(2.) South Carolina took the initiative. From a mere human point of view this appeared improbable. The probability was that the Northern States, conscious of their numerical and financial strength, would throw down the gauntlet. A bill was before Congress authorizing President Andrew Jackson to use force in defense of the Union. But, notwithstanding this, the North did not begin the war. South Carolina took the first step, by recalling her representatives in the United States Senate, November 10, 1860. This was followed by an ordinance of secession, passed by the State Legislature on the 17th of November, the same year. And on the 12th of April, 1861, the first shot of the war was fired by General Beauregard against Fort Sumpter, and thus the conflict was begun by South Carolina, as foretold by the Prophet, and not by any of the Northern States.

(3.) It was a war that brought death and misery to many souls. The entire loss on both sides, including deaths from diseases and wounds, is estimated at a million men,—an enormous total at that time. The sufferings of prisoners in forts where food was scarce and sanitary arrangements imperfect, and in hospitals where there were but few facilities for the proper treatment of wounds, were beyond anything that can be imagined.

"To the terrible loss of life and property let there be added the consideration of the suffering of the wounded and the sick who languished in loathsome prisons; the sorrow of widows and orphans who looked in vain for the return of husbands and fathers who marched in the fulness of manly strength to the war; the anguish of parents, whose dim eyes looked in vain for sons thrown into unknown graves; and the gentler yet equally tender sorrow of sisters who in the fierce war lost the companion of their childhood. Let all this, I say, be taken into account, and the fact that Joseph Smith was a Prophet of the living God will be found written in characters of blood to this generation, and witnessed by the heartache and tears of millions" (B. H. Roberts, *A New Witness for God*, p. 330).

(4-5.) The Southern and Northern States were divided against each other. No State escaped. All became involved, as stated in the prophecy. This no mere human wisdom could have foreseen. But the Spirit of prophecy knew. South Carolina led the way in December, 1860. Would any other States follow the lead? Let history answer. Mississippi, Florida, Alabama, Georgia, and Louisiana seceded during the month of January, 1861; Texas in February; Virginia in April; Arkansas, and North Carolina in May; and Tennessee in June, 1861, and thus the prophecy concerning the division between the South and the North was fulfilled.

(6.) Did the South appeal to Great Britain and other nations for aid? Historians tell us that in May, 1861, the Southern States sent commissioners abroad to seek recognition for the Confederacy. Mr. William L. Yancy, of Alabama, was sent to England; Mr. P. A. Rost, of Louisiana, to France; and Mr. A. Dudley Mann, of Virginia, to Holland and Belgium. In October, the same year, James M. Mason and John Slidell were appointed ambassadors to England and France, respectively, to induce those countries to aid the Southern cause. That their mission failed was due to the firm stand taken by the workingmen of the United Kingdom, who regarded the cause of the North as a righteous cause, even though they suffered greatly through the Northern blockade of Southern ports, especially on account of the "cotton famine" resulting therefrom.

(7.) Thus far, the prophecy deals with the American Civil War. Then it takes a wider scope and predicts a general world war, something like the prediction of our Lord concerning the destruction of Jerusalem, which connects His second coming with that local catastrophe. The Prophet declares (v. 2) that "the days will come that war will be poured out upon all nations," and that the fire kindled in South Carolina was but the beginning of a general conflagration. Great Britain and other nations will, he further says, "call upon other nations" for "aid against other nations"; and thus war shall be poured out upon all nations. We have lived to see this prediction literally fulfilled. We have lived to see war poured out upon every continent and every ocean. And it is a great question whether this war will not be followed by a race war, still more destructive.

The American Civil War was only the beginning of a series of conflicts, each leading up to the world-war of 1914. This is all the more remarkable, because since the middle of the 19th century, the peace movement in the world assumed so definite proportions as to warrant the hope that there would be no war in the 20th century. Peace friends were hopeful that the institution of the *Hague Tribunal* (July 27th, 1899), would mark the end of warfare between civilized nations, but the Prophecy on war has to be fulfilled. The Civil War was, in fact, the beginning of war which was eventually to engulf all nations. There are some critics of this revelation who, shortly after the Civil War, declared that any one could have made the prediction that the Southern States would rise against the Northern States, and that others had declared that such a conflict was inevitable. The fact remains, however, granting this contention, there was no one wise enough to predict that out of and following this conflict, nations would make alliances for their protection and in spite of these alliances eventually war would sweep the nations of the earth. One eminent educator, Dr. David Starr Jordan, in the Salt Lake Tabernacle, and at other times declared as late as 1914:

"What shall we say of the great war of Europe, ever threatening, ever impending and which never comes. We shall say that it will never come. Humanly speaking, it is impossible, not in the physical sense, of course, for with weak, restless and godless men nothing evil is impossible. It may be, of course, that some half-crazed Arch-Duke, or some harassed minister of state shall half knowing, give the signal for Europe's conflagration. * * *

"The bankers will not find the money for such a fight, the industries of Europe will not and statesmen cannot. No matter whatever the bluster of apparent provocation, it comes to the same thing at the end. There will be no general war until the master directs the fighters to fight. The masters have much to gain, but vastly more to lose and their signal will not be given." (Quoted from remarks by Elder Charles H. Hart, Conference pamphlet, Oct. 6, 1914.)

Yet, within a few weeks following this repeated prediction as given in the Salt Lake Tabernacle, the whole world was thrown into turmoil and bloodshed in the struggle of 1914-1918. Then again, with more terrible loss of life and property the world was plunged into the second conflict of 1939-1945. Some sneering critic may arise and say, that this prophecy was not fulfilled, for there were some countries which were not engaged in this deadly conflict; but what is war? Does it not partake of many things besides the carrying of arms and open battle? None can deny that every nation on the earth suffered from the effect and ravages of this stupendous struggle. Truly the effects of war reach every quarter of the earth. Nor is this the end. The clouds are now gathering in preparation for another conflict even more terrible and destructive of life and property. League of Nations, or United Nations delegates, cannot stop it, because people will not repent and they have rejected the Gospel. Peace has been taken from the earth (Doc. and Cov. 1) and it will not return until the Lord shall come to establish it. (Doc. and Cov. 97:23.)

The Prophet also indicates (Sec. 130:12, 13) that the slave question might be the outstanding issue in the conflict between the North and South. There were two points on which the two groups of States disagreed. The North wanted protection for manufacturing interests against foreign competition; the South demanded free trade. The South profited by the products of slave labor; the North determined to abolish slavery. The assertion of the rights of the States to secede was prompted by these two issues, but the slave question, which at first was of subordinate importance, soon took the chief place in public view, as the Prophet predicted.

In all these important particulars the prophecy has been fulfilled. There are other parts which yet remain unfulfilled, but they, too, will come to pass, in time. "Slaves are to rise up against their masters" (v. 4), and the "Remnant" is to "vex the Gentiles with a sore vexation" (v. 5). There will, finally, be "famine, and plague, and earthquakes, and the thunder of heaven, and the fierce and vivid lightning also," and thus the inhabitants of the Earth will feel the wrath of God (v. 6).

6. *And thus war * * * nations*] Elder B. H. Roberts gives the following information:

"It reads in the current print of Doctrine and Covenants, 'and "thus" war shall be poured out upon all nations.' But, revising the *History of the Church* some years ago, we found that in the manuscript it read, 'then'; this is, when Great Britain shall call upon other nations to defend herself against other nations, 'then war shall be poured out upon all nations'" (Report of Eighty-seventh Semi-annual Conference, p. 141).

*Thunder * * *]* Not only by sword and cannon were the inhabitants of the earth to be called upon to mourn because of their iniquity, but even the elements were to become angry, and by famine, plague, and the vivid lightnings and thunder, earthquakes and other disturbances, the inhabitants of the earth are to feel the wrath, and indignation, and chastening hand of the Almighty. We have discovered in another revelation (Sec. 43) that the thunders shall utter their voices from the ends of the earth in a manner never witnessed before. This will come after the testimonies of the elders of Israel have been declared.

*Until * * * hath made a full end of all nations*] How long is the time of trouble to last? This is the answer to that question. All the kingdoms of the world will become the kingdom of the Son of God.

7. *The cry of the Saints * * * shall cease to come up*] This is an intimation that these wars will come after many of these holding the Priesthood and the saints have suffered martyrdom and the Church has been denied redress for its wrongs, at the bars of early justice. The Lord promised the saints that He would fight their battles (Sec. 98:37) and the cry of the Saints, and the blood of the martyrs, should cease to plead before His face. (Com. Rev. 6:10.) The Saints do not thirst for revenge, for this belongs to the Lord; but there is a divine law of retribution, or recompense, and peace and justice cannot be perfect until every wrong is righted.

8. *Until the day of the Lord come*] Until that day of war and calamities, here predicted, come. For that is part of the great events of the day of the Lord.

General Notes

We have seen that this prophecy has been literally fulfilled. Was it not written after the Civil War? Orson Pratt tells us:

"When I was a boy, I traveled extensively in the United States and the Canadas, preaching this restored gospel. I had a manuscript copy of this Revelation, which I carried in my pocket, and I was in the habit of reading it to the people among whom I traveled and preached" (*Jour. of Dis.,* Vol. XVIII., p. 224).

Orson Pratt was born in 1811, and was, therefore, only 21 years of age when this Revelation was first given.

President George Q. Cannon says:

"I recollect very well that in the fall of 1860, while going to England, we were invited at Omaha to preach the gospel to the people of that City. A good many of the leading citizens procured the court house for us, and Brother Pratt preached. By request, I read the Revelation given through Joseph Smith, on the 25th of December, 1832, respecting the secession of the Southern States. It created a great sensation, the election of Abraham Lincoln having just been consummated, and it being well known that there was a great deal of feeling in the South in relation to it. A great many persons came forward and examined the book from which the Revelation was read to see the date, to satisfy themselves that it was not a thing of recent manufacture. The Revelation was in the Pearl of Great Price which was published in 1851."

A copy of the edition of 1851 is still preserved in the *Millennial Star* library, Liverpool. It was published by Franklin D. Richards and has a preface by him, dated the 11th of July, that year. That was ten years before the war broke out.

There is no doubt that the prophecy was given in 1832 and circulated in manuscript form; nor that it was read publicly and privately as soon as it was given. There is no doubt that it was committed to the "immortal custody of the press" in 1851.

Christ teaches that the meek shall inherit the Earth, not the warriors. History teaches the same truth.

SECTION 88.

REVELATION *given through Joseph Smith the Prophet, at Kirtland, Ohio, December 27, 1832. Designated by the Prophet, the Olive Leaf. See History of the Church, vol. 1, p. 302.——— Ministrations of the Comforter—The light of truth is the light of Christ—The spirit and the body constitute the soul—Parable of the man sending his servants into the field and visiting them in turn—Search for the truth through study and prayer enjoined— Testimony of the Elders to be followed by that of calamity— Scenes incident to the Lord's coming—The angels sounding their trumpets in turn as appointed—Duties of the Presidency of the School of the Prophets—The ordinance of washing of feet.*

VERILY, thus saith the Lord unto you who have assembled yourselves together to receive his will concerning you:

2. Behold, this is pleasing unto your Lord, and the angels rejoice over you; the alms of your prayers have come up into the ears of the Lord of Sabaoth, and are recorded in the book of the names of the sanctified, even them of the celestial world.

This Revelation is known as *The Olive Leaf.* The Prophet Joseph, in a letter to Elder Wm. W. Phelps, dated Kirtland, January 14th, 1833, referred to it under that name. "I send you," he wrote, "the 'Olive Leaf' which we have plucked from the tree of Paradise, the Lord's message of peace to us." At that time some of the Saints in Zion did not strictly obey the commandments of the Lord, and their feelings towards the

Prophet Joseph were not those of perfect harmony. But the Prophet had only one desire, that the Saints in Zion and in Kirtland would merit the approbation of God. In this spirit he sent a copy of this Revelation to Elder Phelps, who was the editor of the *Evening and Morning Star,* and accompanied it by a letter in which the Saints were admonished to repent. He wrote: "For if Zion will not purify herself, so as to be approved in all things, in His sight, He will seek another people; for His work will go on until Israel is gathered, and they who will not hear His voice, must expect to feel His wrath." A copy of the Revelation was sent to Zion, by the Prophet, as a message of peace, as "oil upon troubled waters"; hence, it was called the "Olive Leaf."

In this Revelation our Lord (1) expresses His gracious approval of the assembly that had convened for the purpose of learning the will of God concerning the Saints (1, 2); (2) promises them another Comforter (3, 4); (3) explains the nature of celestial glory (5-13) and (4) the resurrection (14-24); (5) promises the redemption of the Earth (25-35); (6) reveals the great truth that there are many kingdoms in space, each governed by law (36-62); (7) explains acceptable prayer (63-5) and (8) how to obtain spiritual light (66-9); (9) gives instructions regarding preparations for missionary labor (70-85); (10) sets forth the doctrine of the last days and the Millennium (86-116); and (11) gives special instructions (117-26) and (12) commandments concerning the School of the Prophets (127-41).

1. GOD PLEASED WITH THE ASSEMBLY.

1-2. Evidently, some of the Elders had come together for the purpose of learning something regarding the will of God concerning them. The Revelation on war had just been received, and it must have made a deep impression upon them. They desired further instructions as to their duties in view of the critical times that had been predicted. This was pleasing to God. The angels, too, rejoiced (v. 2).

2. *The alms of your prayers*] An unusual expression, but it conveys the idea that their prayers for a Revelation had been offered up freely, and that God would reward them, as He rewards alms-giving.

Lord of Sabaoth] "Sabaoth" is a Hebrew word meaning "hosts." It sometimes refers to the armies of Israel and other nations; sometimes to the priests officiating in the Sanctuary; sometimes to the people of God generally, and sometimes to the stars and planets in the sky. "Lord of Hosts" is equivalent to the "all-sovereign," or "omnipotent" Lord. When we pray, we should remember that He, to whom we speak, has all power in heaven and on Earth—the Lord of Hosts. The Lord has given His interpretation to this word to be: "The Creator of the first day, the beginning and the end."

Recorded in the book] The prayers were placed on record in the book in which the names of the Sanctified are enrolled.

3. Wherefore, I now send upon you another Comforter, even upon you my friends, that it may abide in your hearts, even the Holy Spirit of promise; which other Comforter is the same that I promised unto my disciples, as is recorded in the testimony of John.

4. This Comforter is the promise which I give unto you of eternal life, even the glory of the celestial kingdom;

2. ANOTHER COMFORTER PROMISED.

3-4. *Another Comforter*] This is the Holy Spirit, who gives to the Saints the assurance of eternal life. See also John 14:16.

5. Which glory is that of the church of the Firstborn, even of God, the holiest of all, through Jesus Christ his Son—

6. He that ascended up on high, as also he descended below all things, in that he comprehended all things, that he might be in all and through all things, the light of truth;

7. Which truth shineth. This is the light of Christ. As also he is in the sun, and the light of the sun, and the power thereof by which it was made.

8. As also he is in the moon, and is the light of the moon, and the power thereof by which it was made;

9. As also the light of the stars, and the power thereof by which they were made;

10. And the earth also, and the power thereof, even the earth upon which you stand.

11. And the light which shineth, which giveth you light, is through him who enlighteneth your eyes, which is the same light that quickeneth your understandings;

12. Which light proceedeth forth from the presence of God to fill the immensity of space—

13. The light which is in all things, which giveth life to all things, which is the law by which all things are governed, even the power of God who sitteth upon his throne, who is in the bosom of eternity, who is in the midst of all things.

3. CELESTIAL GLORY.

5-13. In the world the opinion prevails that celestial glory is of a different *nature* from anything known on Earth. As the poet expresses it:

"We know not, O we know not,
      What joys await us there;
   What radiance of glory,
      What bliss beyond compare."

Paul also says, "Eye hath not seen, nor ear heard, neither have entered into the heart of man, the things which God hath prepared for them that love Him (I. Cor. 2:9). And that is literally true as to the *details* of eternal life in celestial glory. But in this Revelation it is made known to us that celestial glory is not of a different *nature* from that in which God manifests Himself to us on this Earth, in the gospel, in nature, or in the gift of the Holy Spirit. In other words, celestial glory is the glory of truth and love—the glory of the Church of the Firstborn (v. 5); it is the glory of wisdom and power, as manifested in the sun, the moon, the stars, and the Earth (vv. 7-10); it is the glory of intelligence and life, as manifested in the gift of the Holy Spirit (vv. 11-13).

The meaning seems to be this: Our Lord lived with the Father in celestial glory; consequently, the Church is founded upon, and developed by, celestial truth. For the same reason, the universe was framed in accordance with a celestial pattern; the glory and intelligence of the Creator are manifested everywhere. And for the same reason, the gifts of the Holy Spirit—the gift of wisdom, of faith, of knowledge, of healing, of prophecy—are of the same kind, in a small degree, as those powers possessed by our heavenly Father in the celestial realms, in infinite perfection. The change from mortality to immortality is, therefore, not to be compared to taking a fish out of water, or a bird out of the air into the ether of space. It is a change from imperfection to perfection; it is a birth to a life of which the existence on Earth is the beginning.

14. Now, verily I say unto you, that through the redemption which is made for you is brought to pass the resurrection from the dead.

15. And the spirit and the body are the soul of man.

16. And the resurrection from the dead is the redemption of the soul.

17. And the redemption of the soul is through him that quickeneth all things, in whose bosom it is decreed that the poor and the meek of the earth shall inherit it.

18. Therefore, it must needs be sanctified from all unrighteousness, that it may be prepared for the celestial glory;

19. For after it hath filled the measure of its creation, it shall be crowned with glory, even with the presence of God the Father;

20. That bodies who are of the celestial kingdom may possess

it forever and ever; for, for this intent was it made and created, and for this intent are they sanctified.

21. And they who are not sanctified through the law which I have given unto you, even the law of Christ, must inherit another kingdom, even that of a terrestrial kingdom, or that of a telestial kingdom.

22. For he who is not able to abide the law of a celestial kingdom cannot abide a celestial glory.

23. And he who cannot abide the law of a terrestrial kingdom cannot abide a terrestrial glory.

24. And he who cannot abide the law of a telestial kingdom cannot abide a telestial glory; therefore he is not meet for a kingdom of glory. Therefore he must abide a kingdom which is not a kingdom of glory.

4. THE RESURRECTION.

14-24. The entrance to celestial glory is through death and resurrection (v. 14). And the Earth itself must pass through the same process, in order to become the dwelling-place of celestial beings (vv. 18-20). Each one can receive only the glory for which obedience to law has prepared him. Those who have been able to obey celestial law are prepared for celestial glory; This is equally true of those who have obeyed inferior laws (vv. 21-4).

16. *Resurrection * * * redemption of the soul*] The body and spirit united are the soul. Death separates the spirit from the body, whereupon the latter is dissolved into its elementary parts. By the resurrection the spirit and body are again united, and by that union, the soul is redeemed. Says the Prophet Joseph:

"The spirits in the eternal world are like the spirits in this world. When those have come into this world and received tabernacles, then died and again have risen and received glorified bodies, they will have an ascendancy over the spirits who have received no bodies, or kept not their first estate, like the devil" (*Hist. of the Church*, Vol. V., p. 403).

18. *It must needs be sanctified*] The Earth. The opinion that this globe is to be annihilated finds no support in the Word of God. Here, the important truth is revealed that our globe will be sanctified from all unrighteousness, and prepared for celestial glory, so that it will be fit for the presence of God, the Father. It will die (v. 26), but it will be quickened again. It will not remain a dead planet, whirling about aimlessly in space; nor will it be distributed in the form of cosmic dust, throughout the universe. It will be glorified, by celestial glory, and become an abode for resurrected beings (v. 20).

25. And again, verily I say unto you, the earth abideth the law of a celestial kingdom, for it filleth the measure of its creation, and transgresseth not the law—

26. Wherefore, it shall be sanctified; yea, notwithstanding it shall die, it shall be quickened again, and shall abide the power by which it is quickened, and the righteous shall inherit it.

27. For notwithstanding they die, they also shall rise again, a spiritual body.

28. They who are of a celestial spirit shall receive the same body which was a natural body; even ye shall receive your bodies, and your glory shall be that glory by which your bodies are quickened.

29. Ye who are quickened by a portion of the celestial glory shall then receive of the same, even a fulness.

30. And they who are quickened by a portion of the terrestrial glory shall then receive of the same, even a fulness.

31. And also they who are quickened by a portion of the telestial glory shall then receive of the same, even a fulness.

32. And they who remain shall also be quickened; nevertheless, they shall return again to their own place, to enjoy that which they are willing to receive, because they were not willing to enjoy that which they might have received.

33. For what doth it profit a man if a gift is bestowed upon him, and he receive not the gift? Behold, he rejoices not in that which is given unto him, neither rejoices in him who is the giver of the gift.

34. And again, verily I say unto you, that which is governed by law is also preserved by law and perfected and sanctified by the same.

35. That which breaketh a law, and abideth not by law, but seeketh to become a law unto itself, and willeth to abide in sin, and altogether abideth in sin, cannot be sanctified by law, neither by mercy, justice, nor judgment. Therefore, they must remain filthy still.

5. THE REDEMPTION OF THE EARTH.

25-35. The subject of the redemption of the Earth is resumed here. We know from the Bible that "the heavens and the earth, which are now, are reserved unto fire" (II. Pet. 3:7. See also Dan. 7:9, 10, and II. Thess.

1:8). We know also that there are combustible elements in abundance and heat enough to consume many worlds like ours, whenever the torch is applied. Here we are told, that the Earth will abide "the power by which it is quickened"; it will abide the fire and come out of the flames, quickened and purified, like gold out of the refiner's fire, or a beautiful vessel of potter's clay out of the fiery furnace (v. 26). In this sanctified state it will be the residence of celestial beings, resurrected and inhabiting "the same" bodies that they had here, quickened by celestial glory (v. 28). For each individual will receive the glory by which he is quickened (vv. 29-31).

25. *The earth abideth the law of a celestial kingdom*] It fills the measure of its creation, and the inference is that whatever, or whoever is true to the purpose of its, or his, or her existence lives in accordance with celestial law. To do that for which we are not created; to use our bodies or any of its organs, or faculties, for purposes for which they were not created is to break that law.

27. *A spiritual body*] The righteous will rise with the same body that was a natural body, but it will be cleansed and purified.

"So far as we are concerned, we were taken from the earth, and we may expect to return to it again; and that portion of me which is pure, after the dross of this mortality is separated from it, I expect will be Brother Heber. It is that which will be resurrected; but all that is not pure will remain; that is, it will not go back into my body again; and if there are ten parts out of the hundred which are dross and corruption they will remain in the earth; I do not expect to take that up again, but I expect to take up the purified element that will endure for ever; still the dross is beneficial in its place" (Heber C. Kimball, *Jour. of Dis.,* Vol. III., p. 107).

32. *And they who remain shall also be quickened*] A superficial reading of Sec. 76: 38-9 might give the impression that the sons of perdition are not to be resurrected, but here it is expressly stated that they, too, will be quickened, and then return to "their own place." They were not willing to receive a degree of glory, by keeping the law pertaining to either of the glories; wherefore they were to remain under the dominion of him whom they had chosen to serve. On this subject we can quote Elder Charles W. Penrose:

"There is one class which will be different from all the rest. They shall be brought forth, the Lord says, but they will go back into their own place. They would not receive that which they might have had; they would not obey that which they might have obeyed. They received the light and the truth and then would not use it in the way that God had appointed. They would not go on unto perfection by keeping every word that proceeded from the mouth of God, but prostituted the power God had given them to rise to the highest heights, but sunk down to the lowest depths; denying the truth revealed to them; shedding innocent blood;

consenting to the death of Christ; thus sinning against the Holy Ghost and becoming so corrupt and abominable that they cannot be redeemed. But they shall be brought forth from the grave and become subject to the devil and his angels in eternity. What is their end we do not know; nobody knows, the Lord says. Some people are inquiring about the end of those sons of perdition. The Lord says no man knows it, that the end thereof and the height and extent and the depth thereof no man knoweth, and if the Lord does reveal it to some, He shuts up the vision. What, then, is the 'second death'? Why, the Lord tells us what that is, in His Revelation in the twenty-ninth section of the Doctrine and Covenants. It is eternal banishment from His presence. He is the source of light and truth and power and glory and happiness and joy and dominion and increase forever, of which they will all be deprived. Being shut right out from the light, these shall go away into outer darkness, where no ray of light comes, spiritual or physical—no ray of light from sun or moon or twinkling star or even a comet, to be in outer darkness; and no wonder there is 'weeping and wailing and gnashing of teeth,' to use the Scripture expression" (Address at Salt Lake City, October 4th, 1914).

34. *That which is governed by law is also preserved by law*] Every law God has given us is of such a nature that, by keeping it, we are preserved, perfected and sanctified. If we keep the Word of Wisdom, our bodies will be kept pure. If we observe the law of tithing, we shall learn to be unselfish and honest. If we pray, we shall hold communion with the Holy Spirit. If we try to do our duty in everything, we shall come, day by day, nearer to perfection.

On the other hand, those who refuse to be governed by law and are a law unto themselves cannot be sanctified. They are outside the pale of mercy and justice and judgment, as well as law, and must remain "filthy still!" (v. 35). It is only when we try to obey God's laws that we have claim upon His mercy. Justice will take into account, in the judgment, every honest effort to do the will of God.

36. All kingdoms have a law given;

37. And there are many kingdoms; for there is no space in the which there is no kingdom; and there is no kingdom in which there is no space, either a greater or a lesser kingdom.

38. And unto every kingdom is given a law; and unto every law there are certain bounds also and conditions.

39. All beings who abide not in those conditions are not justified.

40. For intelligence cleaveth unto intelligence; wisdom receiveth wisdom; truth embraceth truth; virtue loveth virtue; light cleaveth unto light; mercy hath compassion on mercy and claim-

eth her own; justice continueth its course and claimeth its own; judgment goeth before the face of him who sitteth upon the throne and governeth and executeth all things.

41. He comprehendeth all things, and all things are before him, and all things are round about him; and he is above all things, and in all things, and is through all things, and is round about all things; and all things are by him, and of him, even God, forever and ever.

42. And again, verily I say unto you, he hath given a law unto all things, by which they move in their times and their seasons;

43. And their courses are fixed, even the courses of the heavens and the earth, which comprehend the earth and all the planets.

44. And they give light to each other in their times and in their seasons, in their minutes, in their hours, in their days, in their weeks, in their months, in their years—all these are one year with God, but not with man.

45. The earth rolls upon her wings, and the sun giveth his light by day, and the moon giveth her light by night, and the stars also give their light, as they roll upon their wings in their glory, in the midst of the power of God.

46. Unto what shall I liken these kingdoms, that ye may understand?

47. Behold, all these are kingdoms, and any man who hath seen any or the least of these hath seen God moving in his majesty and power.

48. I say unto you, he hath seen him; nevertheless, he who came unto his own was not comprehended.

49. The light shineth in darkness, and the darkness comprehendeth it not; nevertheless, the day shall come when you shall comprehend even God, being quickened in him and by him.

50. Then shall ye know that ye have seen me, that I am, and that I am the true light that is in you, and that you are in me; otherwise ye could not abound.

51. Behold, I will liken these kingdoms unto a man having a field, and he sent forth his servants into the field to dig in the field.

52. And he said unto the first: Go ye and labor in the field, and in the first hour I will come unto you, and ye shall behold the joy of my countenance.

53. And he said unto the second: Go ye also into the field, and in the second hour I will visit you with the joy of my countenance.

54. And also unto the third, saying: I will visit you;

55. And unto the fourth, and so on unto the twelfth.

56. And the lord of the field went unto the first in the first hour, and tarried with him all that hour, and he was made glad with the light of the countenance of his lord.

57. And then he withdrew from the first that he might visit the second also, and the third, and the fourth, and so on unto the twelfth.

58. And thus they all received the light of the countenance of their lord, every man in his hour, and in his time, and in his season—

59. Beginning at the first, and so on unto the last, and from the last unto the first, and from the first unto the last;

60. Every man in his own order, until his hour was finished, even according as his lord had commanded him, that his lord might be glorified in him, and he in his lord, that they all might be glorified.

61. Therefore, unto this parable I will liken all these kingdoms, and the inhabitants thereof—every kingdom in its hour, and in its time, and in its season, even according to the decree which God hath made.

62. And again, verily I say unto you, my friends, I leave these sayings with you to ponder in your hearts, with this commandment which I give unto you, that ye shall call upon me while I am near—

6. Many Kingdoms, Each Governed by Law.

36-62. We are told here that every part of space is occupied by some "kingdom"; that each kingdom is governed by law, and that the laws are adapted to the conditions that prevail. Some laws are universal. Such is the law of gravitation, for instance; or the great fundamental moral law, "Thou shalt love the Lord thy God with all thy heart, and with all thy soul, and with all thy strength, and with all thy mind; and thy neighbor as thyself." Other laws are limited; they vary as the conditions vary. By kingdoms we understand the planets and orbs that circle in space. God is capable of governing them all, because He "comprehendeth all things, and all things are before Him" (v. 41). God visits all these kingdoms in due time.

37. *Space*] The following data from an article which appeared in the *Literary Digest* may assist us in forming an idea of the immensity of space, with its innumerable kingdoms:

"The sun is making as wild an excursion into the spatial wilderness as the most lunatic comet could contrive. Wilder, indeed; for the comet sooner or later returns, whereas there is no evidence that the sun, with his attendant spheres, is moving otherwise than in the straightest of straight lines. In *Popular Astronomy* (Northfield, Minn.), Professor John Candee Dean tells us some of the things that are known about this solar motion. First suspected by the great astronomer Herschel, it was demonstrated seventy years ago by the Russian Struve, that this movement carries the sun and its system through space with inconceivable velocity in the direction of the constellation Hercules. Later, Mudler, of Dorpat, announced that the sun was moving around a central orb, in a period of 18,000,000 years, but modern astronomers find no evidence that the sun is deviating from a straight line.

" 'It has been found that the sun is moving toward its apex with a velocity of about twelve miles a second. To realize what this means, consider that the muzzle velocity of a shot from a large modern cannon is only 1,500 feet per second, while the sun moves with a speed of 63,000 feet per second, or forty two times as fast. If a cannon-shot could be projected with the velocity of the sun, its energy and penetrating power would be increased 1,700 times, and if a shot could be made that would withstand the enormous pressure and heat generated, it would penetrate 1,500 feet of solid steel. * * * The star called 61 Cygni, in the constellation of the Swan, is the nearest star visible in our latitude. While the sun moves nearly 400,000,000 miles in a year, it would take 100,000 years for it to move over a space equal to the distance that separates us from the nearest star. In the sun's flight toward its apex, it will take over 500,000 years for it to pass the star Vega, but since Vega has a slow motion at right angles to the sun's motion, it follows that the sun will never pass very near that star.

" 'While the sun moves at a uniform rate, and probably in a straight line, the earth, owing to its motion around the sun, describes a huge spiral in space.'

"A remarkable interesting phenomenon of two great drifts of stars, moving in opposite directions, has recently been discovered. About 10,000 stars were dealt with in this investigation. The fast-moving drift is flowing away from the constellation of the Serpent Bearer. The slow-moving drift is flowing from the constellation of the Lynx. The two streams of stars appear to be nearly equally divided, and are completely intermingled with each other.

"The phenomenon is explained on the theory that two great universes have been drawn together, probably by mutual attraction, and are now passing through each other."

Astronomers have since discovered that our sun with all its attendant planets is not traveling in a straight line, but is traveling in its orbit, as are all the stars of our universe around some common center of gravity. So great is this orbit that it will take the sun several billions of years to make one revolution. All of which is in perfect harmony with the revelation of the Lord to Abraham by Urim and Thummim.

Verily, here are many "kingdoms" in space, and they all are governed by law.

41. *He comprehendeth all things,* etc.] He, who "sitteth upon the throne." He not only comprehends all things, but all things are *before* and *round about* Him: He is *above* all things, and *in* all things, and *through* all things, and *round about* all things, and all things are by Him and of Him, even God, for ever and ever. This is one of the most illuminating passages on the divine Omnipresence ever penned. See also Psalm 139:7-13; I. Kings 8:27; Acts 17:28, and Brigham Young, *Jour. of Dis.,* Vol. I., p. 93.

42. *He hath given a law unto all things*] The Saints in Zion needed to be reminded of this truth; they needed to understand that moral laws are as immutable as those by which the courses of the Earth, the planets, and the stars, are governed.

47. *Hath seen God moving in his majesty and power*] To see these majestic orbs, or any of them, and contemplate their motions is to see the power and majesty of God. They are the "garment," the "vesture" of the Almighty (Psalm 102:26); the royal robe and crown by which His majesty is visible to mortal man.

51-61. The Spirit of the Lord prompts the Prophet to compare these orbs to a field into which the Owner sends laborers, whom he visits in rotation. The question is sometimes discussed, whether any other globes than the Earth are inhabited. Prominent astronomers have claimed that they have actually seen irrigation canals on Mars, while others have refused to accept their statements as based on facts. Philosophers, too, have ranged themselves on opposite sides of that question. Some have surmised that many other worlds are inhabited; others, among whom can be mentioned the late Mr. Alfred Russell Wallace, have maintained that only on Earth are the conditions favorable to higher forms of life. This Revelation decides that question. God has sent laborers to each of His worlds, and He visits them, one after another. Parley P. Pratt says:

"I might enlarge the subject by connecting the family of Adam with other branches of Christ's kingdom, and of the celestial family in other planets and worlds, many of which are older and much larger than our

Earth, but peopled by branches of the celestial family, who are of the same kindred and race that we are; viz., the sons and daughters of God. I might also tell you of the continued exertions of creative power by which millions of new worlds will yet be formed and peopled by King Adam and his descendants, in the name and by the authority of Jesus Christ" (From *The Prophet,* quoted in the *Millennial Star,* Vol. V., p. 191.)

62. *Call upon me while I am near*] There are too many who call upon the Lord only in their expediency when they, in desperation need His help. To these he may not be near, but may be slow to hearken to their pleadings. (Doc. and Cov. 101:7-8.) "The Lord is nigh unto all them that call upon him, to all that call upon him in truth. He will fulfill the desire of them that fear him: he also will hear their cry, and will save them." (Ps. 145: 18-19.)

Prayer is the most wonderful institution in the kingdom of God, and none was more familiar with it than the Prophet Joseph. But there are many who have no higher conception of it than to regard it as only a means whereby to obtain gifts from God, most often of a material character. Is the gift bestowed? Then the prayer is answered. Is it withheld? Then God did not hear. "Such theory," as one has said, "is obviously too simple and superficial to be true. Prayer is more subtle than this doctrine implies. It may be described as the soul speaking to God and hearing God speak to it. It is, therefore, the deepest and the most wonderful act of which a man is capable, for in it the whole universe is, as it were, concentrated."

63. Draw near unto me and I will draw near unto you; seek me diligently and ye shall find me; ask, and ye shall receive; knock, and it shall be opened unto you.

64. Whatsoever ye ask the Father in my name it shall be given unto you, that is expedient for you;

65. And if ye ask anything that is not expedient for you, it shall turn unto your condemnation.

7. Acceptable Prayer.

63-5. "Whatsoever ye ask the Father in my name." That is the prayer that is acceptable to God. To pray in the name of the Lord is to ask as one belonging to Him—one accepted by Him. It is to pray according to the dictation of His Spirit. Such prayers God will hear and grant, if "expedient for you." There is quite a difference between the mechanical petition of a street beggar and the request of one who is a friend of the son in the house. The latter is treated as the son. What is good for him he will receive. Bishop Hall well says:

"What God requires and looks at, is neither the arithmetic of our prayers—how many they are; not the rhetoric of our prayers—how eloquent they be; nor the geometry of our prayers—how long they be; nor the music of our prayers—how sweet our voice may be; nor the logic, nor the method, nor even the orthodoxy of our prayers."

God looks to our welfare, even when He does not give us that for which we ask. If we were to pray for, and receive what is not good for us, it would be for our condemnation.

66. Behold, that which you hear is as the voice of one crying in the wilderness—in the wilderness, because you cannot see him—my voice, because my voice is Spirit; my Spirit is truth; truth abideth and hath no end; and if it be in you it shall abound.

67. And if your eye be single to my glory, your whole bodies shall be filled with light, and there shall be no darkness in you; and that body which is filled with light comprehendeth all things.

68. Therefore, sanctify yourselves that your minds become single to God, and the days will come that you shall see him; for he will unveil his face unto you, and it shall be in his own time, and in his own way, and according to his own will.

69. Remember the great and last promise which I have made unto you; cast away your idle thoughts and your excess of laughter far from you.

8. How to Obtain Light.

66-9. The Saints need wisdom and understanding. They need that light that comes from God. They need the Holy Spirit. How can they obtain the divine light? The answer to that question is given in these paragraphs: "If your eye be single to my glory." That is the condition. If we look to the glory of God alone, and not to our own honor and advantage; if we are saved from selfishness, which is the underlying motive of all sin, we shall be filled with divine light. The cause of darkness in the world and of error among the people of God is to be found in the fact that love of self, desire for honor, for wealth, ease, or pleasure, shut the light of heaven out of the soul.

68. *Sanctify yourselves*] The meaning of "sanctification" is explained in the words that follow, "That your minds become single to God." Our Lord had regard only to the glory of the Father, when He undertook the salvation of man. To follow in His footsteps and to be able to say at all times, truthfully, "Thine be the honor," is to be sanctified; that is to be a Saint.

69. *Excess of laughter*] Note that the Lord condemns excess of laughter, which includes boisterous conduct in general. See also Section 59:15.

70. Tarry ye, tarry ye in this place, and call a solemn assembly, even of those who are the first laborers in this last kingdom.

71. And let those whom they have warned in their traveling call on the Lord, and ponder the warning in their hearts which they have received, for a little season.

72. Behold, and lo, I will take care of your flocks, and will raise up elders and send unto them.

73. Behold, I will hasten my work in its time.

74. And I give unto you, who are the first laborers in this last kingdom, a commandment that you assemble yourselves together, and organize yourselves, and prepare yourselves, and sanctify yourselves; yea, purify your hearts, and cleanse your hands and your feet before me, that I may make you clean;

75. That I may testify unto your Father, and your God, and my God, that you are clean from the blood of this wicked generation; that I may fulfill this promise, this great and last promise, which I have made unto you, when I will.

76. Also, I give unto you a commandment that ye shall continue in prayer and fasting from this time forth.

77. And I give unto you a commandment that you shall teach one another the doctrine of the kingdom.

78. Teach ye diligently and my grace shall attend you, that you may be instructed more perfectly in theory, in principle, in doctrine, in the law of the gospel, in all things that pertain unto the kingdom of God, that are expedient for you to understand;

79. Of things both in heaven and in the earth, and under the earth; things which have been, things which are, things which must shortly come to pass; things which are at home, things which are abroad; the wars and the perplexities of the nations, and the judgments which are on the land; and a knowledge also of countries and of kingdoms—

80. That ye may be prepared in all things when I shall send you again to magnify the calling whereunto I have called you, and the mission with which I have commissioned you.

81. Behold, I sent you out to testify and warn the people, and it becometh every man who hath been warned to warn his neighbor.

82. Therefore, they are left without excuse, and their sins are upon their own heads.

83. He that seeketh me early shall find me, and shall not be forsaken.

84. Therefore, tarry ye, and labor diligently, that you may be perfected in your ministry to go forth among the Gentiles for the last time, as many as the mouth of the Lord shall name, to bind up the law and seal up the testimony, and to prepare the saints for the hour of judgment which is to come;

85. That their souls may escape the wrath of God, the desolation of abomination which awaits the wicked, both in this world and in the world to come. Verily, I say unto you, let those who are not the first elders continue in the vineyard until the mouth of the Lord shall call them, for their time is not yet come; their garments are not clean from the blood of this generation.

9. Preparation for Missionary Work.

70-85. Our Lord in this Section, teaches His servants how to prepare themselves for their high and holy calling. They were to be His witnesses (v. 81), and they were commissioned to warn the world to escape the wrath of God (v. 85). Some preparation was needed to do that acceptably; what kind of preparation for the ministry does God require? The answer to this question is twofold: First, call a solemn assembly and purify yourselves from the sins of the world, in order that you may be clean (v. 75); fast and pray (v. 76). Secondly, form a school and teach each other all useful knowledge (vv. 77-9). This is the preparation the Lord requires.

70. *The first laborers*] These included Joseph and Hyrum Smith, Oliver Cowdery, the Whitmers, Samuel Smith, Orson Hyde, the Pratts, Sidney Rigdon, the Johnsons, and many others, mentioned in the Revelations (See Sec. 75). They were to meet in solemn assembly in Kirtland. They now had some experience in proclaiming the gospel, but they needed further preparation for their calling.

74. *Sanctify yourselves*] This was the *first* essential in their preparation for the ministry. A college or university education could be dispensed with, but not sanctification. One who accepts the call to the ministry in the Church of Christ must first be saved from all selfishness, so that he desires only the glory of God (vv. 67 and 68). He must be pure and clean, and be able to bear that testimony before God, the eternal Father.

76. *Prayer and fasting*] These are indispensable in the preparation for the ministry. Our Lord teaches us that there are evil spirits that

cannot be overcome except by those whose spiritual life and faith are made strong by self-denial and communion with God. It is, therefore, of the utmost importance that the servants of the Lord should fast and pray. Through the fasting and prayer of the servants of the Lord, the mouth of Alma was opened, and his limbs strengthened (Mos. 27:22-3). Through fasting and prayer the Nephites "did wax stronger and stronger in their humility, and firmer and firmer in the faith of Christ" (Hel. 3:35).

Fasting has in all ages been an outward sign of sorrow and mourning. When the heart is full of grief, the body does not crave for food as usual. When calamities sweep over a country, or when sinners are awakened to a realization of their condition abstinence from all pleasures, including those of the table, is natural to all who take things seriously. The Elders, however, are not required to fast as a sign of mourning alone, but as one of rejoicing. This is just as natural. For when the heart is filled with joy, the craving for food is forgotten for long periods, as they know who have attended meetings, lasting for many hours, where the Holy Spirit has been poured out upon the assembly. Our Lord warns His people against making a display of their fasting: "When thou fastest, anoint thine head, and wash thy face" (Matt. 6:16-18).

77. *Teach one another*] In this paragraph, and those following, the Lord instructs His servants to apply themselves to the study of various branches of science, and first of all to theology—"the doctrine of the kingdom." They were to study diligently and be instructed "in theory, in principle, in doctrine, in the law of the gospel, in all things that pertain unto the kingdom of God" (v. 78). That comprises the entire range of theology—Exegetical, Historical, Systematic, and Pastoral.

Systematic theology may be divided into (1) *Theology* proper, which includes all that has been revealed concerning the being and attributes of the Godhead, and the relation of God to the world, in the creation and in providence. (2) *Anthropology,* which includes the origin and nature of man; the fall, and the effects of the fall upon the human race. (3) *Soteriology,* which includes the plan of salvation, the work of the Redeemer, and the application of His work for the regeneration, justification, and sanctification of man, (4) *Eschatology,* which includes the doctrines concerning the last things; the state of the human spirit between death and resurrection, the Millennium, the judgment, heaven and hell. (5) *Ecclesiology,* which includes the doctrine, regarding the Church; its organization and attributes, and the Priesthood.

Theology is the most important of all sciences. "There are," says President Brigham Young, "a great many branches of education. Some go to college to learn languages, some to study law, some to study physics, and some to study astronomy and various other branches of science. We want every branch of science taught in this place that is taught in the world. But our favorite study is that branch which particularly belongs to the Elders of Israel, namely, theology. Every Elder should become a profound theologian—should understand this branch better than all the world" (*Jour. of Dis.,* Vol. VI., p. 317).

But theology is not the only subject the Elders should be interested in. They should study:

79. Things both in heaven] Astronomy.

And in the earth] Everything pertaining to the cultivation of the soil.

And under the earth] Mineralogy, geology, etc.

Things which have been] History, in all its branches.

Things which are] Current events.

Things which must shortly come to pass] Prophecies.

*Things which are at home * * * abroad*] Domestic and foreign policies.

*Wars * * * perplexities * * * judgments*] The "signs of the times," by which the observer may know that "the day of the Lord" is at hand.

*A knowledge of countries * * * kingdoms*] Physical and political geography, languages, etc.

These studies, the Lord considers necessary, "That ye may be prepared in all things when I shall send you again to magnify the calling whereunto I have called you (v. 80). God does not require all His servants to become doctors, or professors, or even profound students of these subjects, but He expects them to know enough of these things to be able to magnify their calling as His ambassadors to the world. The Latterday Saints have, as George A. Smith remarks (*Jour. of Dis.,* Vol. VI., p. 84), "been constantly and continually, upon new ground"; they have had to shift for themselves, and it is only because the Elders have tried to live up to this Revelation that they have been able to find a home in a desert and make a Paradise in waste places. It is by the light of this Revelation that the Saints have been able to reach a place in the world of politics, arts, and sciences, second to none. We may say that in the school organized according to this Revelation, the seeds of the future greatness of the Church were sown.

84. Prepare the Saints for the hour of judgment] The following remarks by the Prophet Joseph to the Twelve, in 1835, may be quoted here:

"When you are endowed and prepared to preach the gospel to all nations, kindred, and tongues, in your own languages, you must faithfully warn all, and bind up the testimony, and seal up the law, and the destroying angel will follow close at your heels, and exercise his tremendous mission upon the children of disobedience; and destroy the workers of iniquity, while the Saints will be gathered out from among them, and stand in holy places ready to meet the Bridegroom when He comes" (*Hist. of the Church,* Vol. II., p. 309).

86. Abide ye in the liberty wherewith ye are made free;

entangle not yourselves in sin, but let your hands be clean, until the Lord comes.

87. For not many days hence and the earth shall tremble and reel to and fro as a drunken man; and the sun shall hide his face, and shall refuse to give light; and the moon shall be bathed in blood; and the stars shall become exceedingly angry, and shall cast themselves down as a fig that falleth from off a fig-tree.

88. And after your testimony cometh wrath and indignation upon the people.

89. For after your testimony cometh the testimony of earthquakes, that shall cause groanings in the midst of her, and men shall fall upon the ground and shall not be able to stand.

90. And also cometh the testimony of the voice of thunderings, and the voice of lightnings, and the voice of tempests, and the voice of the waves of the sea heaving themselves beyond their bounds.

91. And all things shall be in commotion; and surely, men's hearts shall fail them; for fear shall come upon all people.

10. EVENTS OF THE LAST DAYS.

86-116. The Revelation, having set forth the necessity of proper preparation for the ministry, lifts a portion of the curtain that veils the future and permits God's servants to view the events that signalize the end of the present dispensation and the establishing of the new, known as the Millennium.

(a) *All things in Commotion.*

85. *Abide ye in the liberty * * * free*] The servants of the Lord must be free. The shackles of ignorance, superstition, and error must be struck from their hands and feet, before they can become the saviors of others; they must be free from the slavery of sin, before they are in a position to open the door of freedom to others. The gospel of Christ is the "perfect Law of Liberty" (James 1:25). It is the truth, and truth makes men free (John 8:32). Anyone who lives a false life; who depends on false pretensions for his position among men, is a slave to falsehood; truth alone can set him free. And when he has been set free, he must abide in liberty. And this is necessary, for the time is coming when all earthly things will be in commotion, and those who do not stand on the rock of truth will fall.

"Robert Speer says that all mankind falls into three classes—the slaves who do the will of another; the knaves who do only their own will; and the freemen who do the will of God. Singularly enough those who do only their own will and defy all law and order seem to think that they are the only free men. President Jordan, of Leland Stanford university, once said that so far as he could see, the life which declared itself free to live laxly, or to live with a low standard was in the most degraded sort of bondage which he could imagine" (Quoted by the Rev. Stephen Paulson in an essay on "The Lord's Prayer").

87. *The earth shall tremble and reel to and fro * * * sun shall hide his face * * * moon shall be bathed in blood * * * stars shall become angry*] All this will take place "not many days hence"—from the date of this Revelation. The expressions quoted may be taken literally, and strange phenomena in the heavens above and on earth below may be looked for, warning the children of men of the approach of the end; but the complete fulfilment will come in the overthrow of governments and kingdoms, through revolutions and wars. See Is. 13:10-14; Ez. 32:1-9.

91. *All things shall be in commotion*] All that men have built up without the guidance of the Spirit of God, whether they be religious, political, or moral structures, will reel to and fro, as storm-tossed ships or buildings affected by seismic disturbances.

92. And angels shall fly through the midst of heaven, crying with a loud voice, sounding the trump of God, saying: Prepare ye, prepare ye, O inhabitants of the earth; for the judgment of our God is come. Behold, and lo, the Bridegroom cometh; go ye out to meet him.

93. And immediately there shall appear a great sign in heaven, and all people shall see it together.

94. And another angel shall sound his trump, saying: That great church, the mother of abominations, that made all nations drink of the wine of the wrath of her fornication, that persecuteth the saints of God, that shed their blood—she who sitteth upon many waters, and upon the islands of the sea—behold, she is the tares of the earth; she is bound in bundles; her hands are made strong, no man can loose them; therefore, she is ready to be burned. And he shall sound his trump both long and loud, and all nations shall hear it.

95. And there shall be silence in heaven for the space of half an hour; and immediately after shall the curtain of heaven be unfolded, as a scroll is unfolded after it is rolled up, and the face of the Lord shall be unveiled;

96. And the saints that are upon the earth, who are alive,

shall be quickened and be caught up to meet him.

97. And they who have slept in their graves shall come forth, for their graves shall be opened; and they also shall be caught up to meet him in the midst of the pillar of heaven—

98. They are Christ's, the first fruits, they who shall descend with him first, and they who are on the earth and in their graves, who are first caught up to meet him; and all this by the voice of the sounding of the trump of the angel of God.

99. And after this another angel shall sound, which is the second trump; and then cometh the redemption of those who are Christ's at his coming; who have received their part in that prison which is prepared for them, that they might receive the gospel, and be judged according to men in the flesh.

100. And again, another trump shall sound, which is the third trump; and then come the spirits of men who are to be judged, and are found under condemnation;

101. And these are the rest of the dead; and they live not again until the thousand years are ended, neither again, until the end of the earth.

102. And another trump shall sound, which is the fourth trump, saying: There are found among those who are to remain until that great and last day, even the end, who shall remain filthy still.

103. And another trump shall sound, which is the fifth trump, which is the fifth angel who committeth the everlasting gospel—flying through the midst of heaven, unto all nations; kindreds, tongues, and people;

104. And this shall be the sound of his trump, saying to all people, both in heaven and in earth, and that are under the earth —for every ear shall hear it, and every knee shall bow, and every tongue shall confess, while they hear the sound of the trump, saying: Fear God, and give glory to him who sitteth upon the throne, forever and ever; for the hour of his judgment is come.

105. And again, another angel shall sound his trump, which is the sixth angel, saying: She is fallen who made all nations drink of the wine of the wrath of her fornication; she is fallen, is fallen!

106. And again, another angel shall sound his trump, which is the seventh angel, saying: It is finished; it is finished! The Lamb of God hath overcome and trodden the wine-press alone, even the wine-press of the fierceness of the wrath of Almighty God.

107. And then shall the angels be crowned with the glory of his might, and the saints shall be filled with his glory, and receive their inheritance and be made equal with him.

(b) *Angels Executing the Decrees of God.*

92. *Angels shall fly through the midst of heaven*] These angels are mighty men of God, messengers of the Almighty, who shall call upon the inhabitants of the Earth to prepare themselves for the coming of the Bridegroom. Moroni was such an angel (Rev. 14:6).

93. *A great sign in heaven*] Immediately after the testimony of these messengers a great sign will appear in heaven, which, like the sun, will be seen all round the world. Our Lord calls it the "Sign of the Son of Man" (Matt. 24:30). What this sign is has not been revealed, but there will be no uncertainty about it, when it appears. In 1843 one Mr. Redding, of Ogle county, Ill., claimed to have seen the sign. The Prophet Joseph then wrote to the *Times and Seasons*:

"Notwithstanding Mr. Redding may have seen a wonderful appearance in the clouds one morning about sunrise (which is not very uncommon in the winter season), he has not seen the sign of the Son of Man, as foretold by Jesus; neither has any man, nor will any man, until after the sun shall have been darkened and the moon bathed in blood; for the Lord hath not shown me any such sign; and as the Prophet saith, so it must be—'Surely the Lord God will do nothing, but he revealeth his secret unto his servants the prophets" (Amos 3:7). Therefore, hear this, O Earth! The Lord will not come to reign over the righteous, in this world, in 1843, nor until everything for the Bridegroom is ready" (*Hist. of the Church,* Vol. V., p. 291).

It may be gathered from this that when the sign appears, God will make its meaning known to the Prophet, Seer and Revelator who at that time may be at the head of the Church, and through him to His people and the world in general.

94-8. *Another angel shall sound his trump*] Here begins a series of world events, each signalized by the sounding of a trump by an angel— a divine messenger. There is some analogy between this vision and that recorded in Revelation 8:7—9:21, although they do not appear to cover the same events.

When the first angel sounds his trump, the doom upon the apostate church is pronounced. "She is ready to be burned." Then there is silence in heaven for half an hour. The heavenly hosts are waiting, awestruck, for the execution of this judgment.

"Whether the half hour here spoken of is according to our reckoning —thirty minutes, or whether it be according to the reckoning of the Lord, we do not know * * * During the period of silence all things are perfectly still; no angels flying during that half hour; no trumpets sounding; no noise in the heaven above; but immediately after this great silence the curtain of heaven shall be unfolded as a scroll is unfolded * * * The face of the Lord will be unveiled, and those who are alive will be quickened, and they will be caught up; and the Saints who are in their graves will come forth and be caught up, together with those who are quickened, and they will be taken into the heavens into the midst of those celestial beings who will make their appearance at that time. These are the ones who are the first fruits at the time of His coming" (Orson Pratt, *Jour. of Dis.,* Vol. XVI., p. 328).

99. *Another angel shall sound*] When the second angel sounds his trump, the time has come for the redemption of the spirits who have accepted Christ in the spirit world up to the time of His second coming. They will be resurrected then, and enter terrestrial glory (See Sec. 76:73).

100. *Another trump shall sound*] When the third angel sounds his trump, those who are worthy of telestial glory will be judged and receive the reward for which they have prepared themselves by their works in the flesh (See Sec. 76:111).

101. *Until the thousand years are ended*] Considerable time will elapse between the sounding of these trumps.

102. *Another trump shall sound*] When the fourth angel sounds his trump, those who remain shall come forth and be returned to their place (See. v. 32; also Sec. 76:44-48).

103-4. When the fifth angel sounds his trump, those who are in heaven as well as on Earth will be summoned to fall down and worship, and give glory to God, who reigns supreme for ever and ever, because the hour of His judgment has come. This call will come to every soul both in heaven and on earth, the spirits of the wicked as well as the spirits of the righteous, even sons of perdition will not be exempt.

105. *Another angel shall sound his trump*] When the sixth angel sounds his trump the judgment on the apostate church will be carried out. "She is fallen! Is fallen!" This angel seems to be the same as that in Rev. 14:8; at least, their messages are identical.

106-7. *Another angel shall sound his trump*] When the seventh angel sounds his trump, the triumphant cry will ascend to heaven and reverberate through the universe, "It is finished!" The plan of redemption as proposed by the Wonderful Counselor in the Council of Heaven, has been carried out in its every detail. "The Lamb of God hath overcome."

Then shall the angels be crowned with glory, and the Saints shall receive their celestial inheritance "and be made equal with Him." The seventh angel is Michael, our glorious ancestor (See v. 112).

108. And then shall the first angel again sound his trump in the ears of all living, and reveal the secret acts of men, and the mighty works of God in the first thousand years.

109. And then shall the second angel sound his trump, and reveal the secret acts of men, and the thoughts and intents of their hearts, and the mighty works of God in the second thousand years—

110. And so on, until the seventh angel shall sound his trump; and he shall stand forth upon the land and upon the sea, and swear in the name of him who sitteth upon the throne, that there shall be time no longer; and Satan shall be bound, that old serpent, who is called the devil, and shall not be loosed for the space of a thousand years.

(c) *God's Plans Made Known.*

108-10. "By and by the whole seven will have sounded, and then they commence to sound a second time. According to the Revelation from which I have read, the second sounding of the trumpets is not to produce destruction among the nations, but the sound of the first one will reveal the secret acts of God, His purposes and doings on the Earth during the first thousand years; the sounding of the second will reveal the doings and purposes of the great Jehovah during the second thousand years, and so on, until the seventh shall sound the second time, and pronounce the work of God finished, so far as the great preparation needful for His second coming is concerned.

Notice now, that it is the first sounding of the first of these seven, when the first resurrection takes place; and all these great works are to be performed on the Earth, and years elapse before Jesus descends with all His Saints; that is, if we understand these things correctly, by what little is revealed upon the subject" (Orson Pratt, *Jour. of Dis.*, Vol. XVI, p. 329).

The seventh angel, our Father Adam, is represented as standing upon "the land and the sea," and solemnly affirming that "there shall be time no longer." A similar expression is applied to the angel with the "little book" in his hand, in Rev. 10:2. The Revelation of John closely follows Daniel, and the prophecies in the Doctrine and Covenants as closely follow John.

111. And then he shall be loosed for a little season, that he may gather together his armies.

112. And Michael, the seventh angel, even the archangel, shall gather together his armies, even the hosts of heaven.

113. And the devil shall gather together his armies; even the hosts of hell, and shall come up to battle against Michael and his armies.

114. And then cometh the battle of the great God; and the devil and his armies shall be cast away into their own place, that they shall not have power over the saints any more at all.

115. For Michael shall fight their battles, and shall overcome him who seeketh the throne of him who sitteth upon the throne, even the Lamb.

116. This is the glory of God, and the sanctified; and they shall not any more see death.

(d) *The Last Battle.*

111. During the Millennium, Satan had been bound, so that he could not lead the children of men astray.

"When the period called the Millennium has passed away, Satan will again be loosed. Now the query arises, Will Satan have power to deceive those who have lived on the Earth and have fallen asleep for a moment, and have received their immortal bodies? No, he will not. When they have passed through their probation, and have received their immortal bodies, Satan will have no power over them. Thus generation after generation will pass away, during the Millennium, but by and by, at the end of that period, unnumbered millions of the posterity of those who lived during the Millennium will be scattered in the four quarters of the Earth, and Satan will be loosed, and will go forth and tempt them, and overcome some of them, so that they will rebel against God; not rebel in ignorance or dwindle in unbelief, as the Lamanites did; but they will sin wilfully against the law of heaven, and so great will the power of Satan be over them, that he will gather them together against the Saints and against the beloved City, and fire will come down out of heaven and consume them" (Orson Pratt, *Jour. of Dis.,* Vol. XVI., p. 322).

This is the last battle between the forces of good and evil, on this Earth, and it will end with the complete overthrow of the adversary.

117. Therefore, verily I say unto you, my friends, call your solemn assembly, as I have commanded you.

118. And as all have not faith, seek ye diligently and teach one another words of wisdom; yea, seek ye out of the best books words of wisdom; seek learning, even by study and also by faith.

119. Organize yourselves; prepare every needful thing; and establish a house, even a house of prayer, a house of fasting, a

house of faith, a house of learning, a house of glory, a house of order, a house of God;

120. That your incomings may be in the name of the Lord; that your outgoing may be in the name of the Lord; that all your salutations may be in the name of the Lord, with uplifted hands unto the Most High.

121. Therefore, cease from all your light speeches, from all laughter, from all your lustful desires, from all your pride and light-mindedness, and from all your wicked doings.

122. Appoint among yourselves a teacher, and let not all be spokesmen at once; but let one speak at a time and let all listen unto his sayings, that when all have spoken that all may be edified of all, and that every man may have an equal privilege.

123. See that ye love one another; cease to be covetous; learn to impart one to another as the gospel requires.

124. Cease to be idle; cease to be unclean; cease to find fault one with another; cease to sleep longer than is needful; retire to thy bed early, that ye may not be weary; arise early, that your bodies and your minds may be invigorated.

125. And above all things, clothe yourselves with the bond of charity, as with a mantle, which is the bond of perfectness and peace.

126. Pray always, that ye may not faint, until I come. Behold, and lo, I will come quickly, and receive you unto myself. Amen.

11. SPECIAL INSTRUCTIONS.

117-126. In this previous section (vv. 86-116) the Lord gave His servants some instruction concerning the future. This was necessary as part of their schooling as His ministers. In these paragraphs He gives them further instructions on a variety of subjects. All are important. They should be studied one by one.

118. *Seek ye out of the best books words of wisdom*] On this subject Orson Pratt says:

"Who does not know that fifteen minutes' study would acquaint persons with discovered and recorded laws which would otherwise take a series of years to become acquainted with? By reasoning and trying to generalize our ideas, we may gain much useful information, but shall we therefore consider books of no use? Is there no wisdom in availing ourselves of the labors of those who have developed truths? It is still knowledge, notwithstanding it has been discovered by others. Truth is truth, and take it wherever you may find it, or from whatever source it comes; it was truth from all eternity, and it will be truth to all eternity. There is a great fund of useful information laid down in books" (*Jour. of Dis.,* Vol. III., p. 294).

119. *Organize yourselves*] This verse contains a commandment to the Elders to establish a school, which would be, at the same time a house of God and a house of learning. The trouble with many schools and institutes of learning is that God has no place in them.

121. *Cease from* * * * *light speeches* * * * *laughter* * * * *lustful desires* * * * *pride and light-mindedness,* * * * *and wicked doings*] These things are but too common among students, of both sexes. They should be banished from this school.

123. *Cease to be covetous*] The Elders must learn, as part of the curriculum, to love one another and to impart of their substance to one another. That is an acquisition, very useful in the missionary field.

124. *Retire to bed early*] All the instructions in this paragraph are notable. They might be included in the Word of Wisdom. Idleness is condemned: Cleanliness is inculcated. Fault-finding is classed as wrong. And this rule is laid down, "Cease to sleep longer than is needful"; retire early; arise early; "that your bodies and your minds may be invigorated." This splendid rule is too often violated. Electric lights and late theaters have transformed night into day and deprived the people of some of their natural sleep, and at the same time of a portion of their physical and mental vigor.

125-6. Note the closing injunctions, Clothe yourselves with charity "as with a mantle;" not as a scanty piece of clothing, but as a generous covering; for charity is "the bond of perfectness and peace." Charity— which means brotherly affection—makes for perfection and *peace*. *Pray always.* Prayer is necessary, if we shall remain faithful till the coming of the Lord.

127. And again, the order of the house prepared for the presidency of the school of the prophets, established for their instruction in all things that are expedient for them, even for all the officers of the church, or in other words, those who are called to the ministry in the church, beginning at the high priests, even down to the deacons—

128. And this shall be the order of the house of the presidency of the school: He that is appointed to be president, or teacher, shall be found standing in his place, in the house which shall be prepared for him.

129. Therefore, he shall be first in the house of God, in a place that the congregation in the house may hear his words carefully and distinctly, not with loud speech.

130. And when he cometh into the house of God, for he should be first in the house—behold, this is beautiful, that he may be an example—

131. Let him offer himself in prayer upon his knees before God, in token or remembrance of the everlasting covenant.

132. And when any shall come in after him, let the teacher arise, and, with uplifted hands to heaven, yea, even directly, salute his brother or brethren with these words:

133. Art thou a brother or brethren? I salute you in the name of the Lord Jesus Christ, in token or remembrance of the everlasting covenant, in which covenant I receive you to fellowship, in a determination that is fixed, immovable, and unchangeable, to be your friend and brother through the grace of God in the bonds of love, to walk in all the commandments of God blameless, in thanksgiving, forever and ever. Amen.

134. And he that is found unworthy of this salutation shall not have place among you; for ye shall not suffer that mine house shall be polluted by him.

135. And he that cometh in and is faithful before me, and is a brother, or if they be brethren, they shall salute the president or teacher with uplifted hands to heaven, with this same prayer and covenant, or by saying Amen, in token of the same.

136. Behold, verily, I say unto you, this is an ensample unto you for a salutation to one another in the house of God, in the school of the prophets.

137. And ye are called to do this by prayer and thanksgiving, as the Spirit shall give utterance in all your doings in the house of the Lord, in the school of the prophets, that it may become a sanctuary, a tabernacle of the Holy Spirit to your edification.

138. And ye shall not receive any among you into this school save he is clean from the blood of this generation;

139. And he shall be received by the ordinance of the washing of feet, for unto this end was the ordinance of the washing of feet instituted.

140. And again, the ordinance of washing feet is to be administered by the president, or presiding elder of the church.

141. It is to be commenced with prayer; and after partaking of bread and wine, he is to gird himself according to the pattern

given in the thirteenth chapter of John's testimony concerning me. Amen.

12. RULES FOR THE SCHOOL OF THE PROPHETS.

127-41. In this section, rules are given for the conduct of the School of the Prophets. This school was to be established for the benefit of all who were called to the ministry in the Church (v. 127). Note the order and etiquette to be observed in everything pertaining to the school. It was to be a house of God and to be respected as such.

GENERAL NOTES

The School of the Prophets was organized, according to the instructions in this Revelation, during the month of February, 1833, and was continued throughout the winter. At this time the Elders and the Saints had many manifestations of the presence of the Spirit of the Lord. The Prophet spoke to a Conference, held in January, that year, in a foreign tongue, and others followed. Says Brigham Young:

"The members of that school were but few at first, and the Prophet commenced to teach them in doctrine to prepare them to go out into the world to preach the gospel unto all people, and gather the select from the four quarters of the Earth, as the prophets anciently have spoken. While this instruction prepared the Elders to administer in word and doctrine, it did not supply the teachings necessary to govern their private, or temporal, lives; it did not say whether they should be merchants, farmers, mechanics, or money-changers. The Prophet began to instruct them how to live, that they might be better prepared to perform the great work they were called to accomplish."

A School of the Prophets was also established in Zion. The Lord approved of this institution, although contention had arisen in it (See Sec. 95:10; 97:3), which called forth severe rebuke. A School of Elders—an extension of the School of the Prophets—was held in the early days of Utah, with President Brigham Young at its head. This was, practically, a theological department of the University of Utah, while that seat of learning was in its infancy.

Some of the leading events in the history of the Church during this year, 1832, may be referred to here.

Early in January, the Prophet Joseph and Sidney Rigdon took a missionary journey to Shalersville, Ravenna, and other places, warning the inhabitants of the wrath to come, and preaching the gospel to them. Through the falsehoods published by apostates, there was great excitement among the people, and a storm of persecution threatened to burst over the Saints. The Prophet and his companion met with some success in allaying the prejudices, but the fire was again fanned into flames by the apostates, and on the 25th of March the two servants of the Lord were seized by a mob at Hiram and barely escaped with their lives. No enemies are so bitter as apostates. None are so unscrupulous, or so dead to the demands of honor and truth.

On the 25th of January, the Seventh General Conference of the Church was held at Amherst, O., on which occasion many Elders were called to go on a mission to various parts of the country (Sec. 75), and as a result of their labors, many Branches of the Church were established in the United States and Canada.

On the 2nd of April, the Prophet, as instructed by a Revelation (Sec. 78:9), left Hiram in order to pay a second visit to the Saints in Missouri. Some difficulties between leading brethren, particularly Edward Partridge and Sidney Rigdon, were settled at a general council of the Church, held at Independence, April 26th. At a meeting on May 1st, it was decided to print 3,000 copies of the *Book of Commandments;* also that other revelations should be prepared for the press, as they might be given from time to time. It was, further, decided that Wm. W. Phelps should publish the hymns selected by Emma Smith for the use of the Saints. Arrangements were also made for the establishment of stores in Missouri and Ohio.

In the month of June, the first number of the *Evening and Morning Star,* published by Wm. W. Phelps & Co., appeared at Independence. This was the first paper published in the interest of the Church.

Some of the most important Revelations were received during this year. Among these were Sec. 76, that grand Vision which shines as a star of the first magnitude among all the Revelations vouchsafed by God to man; Sec. 77, which is a Key to the Revelation by John, with which Bible students should become familiar; Sec. 82, showing the Order of Enoch; Sec. 87, the Prophecy on War, and Sec. 88, the "Olive Leaf."

During this year hundreds of farms were bought in Jackson County, and the Saints gathered there. But they did not keep the laws of God faithfully, notwithstanding the promise given (Sec. 84) that the City of the New Jerusalem should be built in Jackson County "in this generation," provided, of course, that the Saints would be faithful and united.

During the month of November, this year, Brigham Young and Heber C. Kimball came to Kirtland, where they met the Prophet Joseph for the first time. God was already preparing for the future guidance and preservation of the Church, by associating these highly gifted young men with the Prophet, and giving them an opportunity to learn his views, understand his aspirations and become imbued with his spirit. God foresaw that the Church would, before many years, need men schooled in the same school as the Prophet, to take his place and the place of his devoted brother. These were the men. Brigham Young stands forth with prominence on the pages of Church history. But it is difficult to mention his name without remembering that of Heber C. Kimball, too. Brigham and Heber were as inseparable as Joseph and Hyrum.

FOURTH PERIOD, 1833. Sections 89-101.

SECTION 89.

REVELATION *given through Joseph Smith the Prophet, at Kirtland, Ohio, February 27, 1833, known as the Word of Wisdom.*———*Abstinence from wine, strong drink, tobacco and hot drinks enjoined—Moderation in the eating of meat—Wholesome foods—Promises to those who live according to these precepts.*

A WORD of Wisdom, for the benefit of the council of high priests, assembled in Kirtland, and the church, and also the saints in Zion—

2. To be sent greeting; not by commandment or constraint, but by revelation and the word of wisdom, showing forth the order and will of God in the temporal salvation of all saints in the last days—

3. Given for a principle with promise, adapted to the capacity of the weak and the weakest of all saints, who are or can be called saints.

4. Behold, verily, thus saith the Lord unto you: In consequence of evils and designs which do and will exist in the hearts of conspiring men in the last days, I have warned you, and forewarn you, by giving unto you this word of wisdom by revelation—

5. That inasmuch as any man drinketh wine or strong drink among you, behold it is not good, neither meet in the sight of your Father, only in assembling yourselves together to offer up your sacraments before him.

6. And, behold, this should be wine, yea, pure wine of the grape of the vine, of your own make.

7. And, again, strong drinks are not for the belly, but for the washing of your bodies.

8. And again, tobacco is not for the body, neither for the belly, and is not good for man, but is an herb for bruises and all sick cattle, to be used with judgment and skill.

9. And again, hot drinks are not for the body or belly.

10. And again, verily I say unto you, all wholesome herbs God hath ordained for the constitution, nature, and use of man—

11. Every herb in the season thereof, and every fruit in the season thereof; all these to be used with prudence and thanksgiving.

12. Yea, flesh also of beasts and of the fowls of the air, I, the Lord, have ordained for the use of man with thanksgiving; nevertheless they are to be used sparingly;

13. And it is pleasing unto me that they should not be used, only in times of winter, or of cold, or famine.

14. All grain is ordained for the use of man and of beasts, to be the staff of life, not only for man but for the beasts of the field, and the fowls of heaven, and all wild animals that run or creep on the earth;

15. And these hath God made for the use of man only in times of famine and excess of hunger.

16. All grain is good for the food of man; as also the fruit of the vine; that which yieldeth fruit, whether in the ground or above the ground—

17. Nevertheless, wheat for man, and corn for the ox, and oats for the horse, and rye for the fowls and for swine, and for all beasts of the field, and barley for all useful animals, and for mild drinks, as also other grain.

18. And all saints who remember to keep and do these sayings, walking in obedience to the commandments, shall receive health in their navel and marrow to their bones;

19. And shall find wisdom and great treasures of knowledge, even hidden treasures;

20. And shall run and not be weary, and shall walk and not faint.

21. And I, the Lord, give unto them a promise, that the

destroying angel shall pass by them, as the children of Israel, and not slay them. Amen.

There is, possibly, no Revelation in this volume that has been more frequently commented upon by the Elders in their discourses, or more fully explained. There certainly is none that has received stronger confirmation by scientists. It is a Revelation that deals mainly with the proper mode of living, and the rules given, far in advance of anything suggested by scientists, have been amply sanctioned by undisputed authority on hygienic laws, as soon as these have become known through research. Here, the Prophet deals with a subject that belongs properly to the domain of science, and scientists, therefore, without intention on their part, become witnesses to the fact that Joseph Smith spoke by divine inspiration, when they confirm the truths set forth.

It is the first Revelation given after the organization of the School of the Prophets. The Elders who were instructed in that school, as a preparation for the ministry, were to be clean. Brigham Young relates the circumstances that occasioned this Revelation. The first school was held in a small room situated over the Prophet Joseph's kitchen, in a house which belonged to Bishop Whitney. The brethren came to that little room, from near and far, to receive instructions. As was customary at that time, some of them smoked and used tobacco in other forms. Often, when the Prophet entered the room, he would find himself in a cloud of tobacco smoke, and the floor was soiled. The Prophet earnestly sought the Lord for guidance in this difficulty, and received this Revelation.

1. *Word of Wisdom*] It is expressly stated that it is given "not by commandment or constraint," but as a Word of Wisdom—a word dictated by wisdom. It is a commandment that may be compared to that issued by the General Council at Jerusalem to the Gentiles, concerning the abstinence from meats offered to idols, from blood, from things strangled, and from fornication, of which the Apostles wrote, "From which if ye keep yourselves, ye shall do well" (Acts 15:29).

"If we would observe this law or commandment of the Lord—first given not as a commandment nor by constraint but afterwards declared by the mouthpiece of the Lord to be in force as a commandment thereafter to the Latter-day Saints—if, I say, the people would observe the principles of the revelation, there could not exist * * * that most obnoxious institution known as a saloon." (Pres. Joseph F. Smith, Oct. 4, 1908.)

"I said to the Saints at our last annual Conference, The Spirit whispers to me to call upon the Latter-day Saints to observe the Word of Wisdom, to let tea, coffee, and tobacco alone, and to abstain from drinking spirituous drinks" (Brigham Young, *Jour. of Dis.,* Vol. 12, p. 118).

"In the name of the Lord Jesus Christ, command the Elders of Israel * * * to cease drinking strong drink from this time henceforth." (Brigham Young, *Jour. of Dis.*, Vol. 7, p. 337.)

2. *Temporal salvation*] That is what the Word of Wisdom is for. Temporal salvation is so closely interwoven with spiritual redemption that the two cannot be separated. On this subject we may quote Brigham Young:

"In all ages of the world that we have any knowledge of, when there was a people on the Earth whom God acknowledged as His people, He has invariably dictated them in spiritual, as in temporal things. This question was agitated year after year in the days of Joseph. The first two Bishops in the Church—Edward Partridge was the first; I was well acquainted with him; and Newel K. Whitney was the second—questioned the propriety of Joseph having anything to do with temporal things. Joseph would argue the case with them a little, and tell them how things were, and bring up Scripture to show them that it could not be otherwise—that it was impossible for the Lord to dictate people, unless He dictated them in temporal affairs * * * There were William E. McLellin, John F. Boynton, and Lyman Johnson, who belonged to the Twelve; Frederick G. Williams, second counselor to Joseph, and two-thirds of the High Council, all talking about this, and I went into the Temple and just challenged them to show wherein the Lord ever conferred upon any man in the world the power to dictate in spiritual affairs, that he did not in temporal affairs. They could not do it" (*Jour. of Dis.*, Vol. XVIII., p. 243).

5. *Wine or strong drink*] It is not only drunkenness that is prohibited here, but the indulgence in wine or strong drink, no matter how moderately, on all occasions, public or private, except in the Sacrament. This is absolute Prohibition.

6. *Pure wine*] The use of "pure wine" in the Sacrament is permitted. But what is "pure wine" if not the pure juice of the grape, before it has been adulterated by the process of fermentation? No fewer than thirteen Hebrew and Greek terms are rendered in our Bible by the word "wine." There is the pure grape juice, and a kind of grape syrup, the thickness of which made it necessary to mingle water with it previously to drinking (Prov. 9:2, 5). There was a wine made strong and inebriating by the addition of drugs, such as myrrh, mandragora, and opiates (Prov. 23:30; Isa. 5:22). Of the pure wine which was diluted with water, or milk, Wisdom invites her friends to drink freely (Prov. 9:2, 5). There was also "wine on the lees," which is supposed to have been "preserves" or "jellies" (Isa. 25:6). The "pure wine" is not an intoxicating, but a harmless liquid.

7. *Strong drinks are not for the belly*]

"The Lord has told us that 'strong drinks are not good.' Who is it that will say they are, when the Lord says they are not? To the man who says, 'I know that it did me good, for I was fatigued, and feeble, on a certain occasion, and it revived me, and I was invigorated, and that is sufficient proof for me,' I reply, It may be for you, but it would not be for a wise man, for every spirit of this kind will only produce a greater languor when its effects cease to operate upon the human body. But you know that you are benefited. Yes, so does the man who has mortgaged his property, know that he is relieved from his present embarrassments; but his temporary relief only binds the cords of bondage more severely around him. The Lord has not ordained strong drinks for the belly, 'but for the washing of your bodies' " (Hyrum Smith, *Times and Seasons*, Vol. III., p. 799).

8. *Tobacco is not for the body*] Tobacco contains several poisonous alkaloids, the principal one of which is nicotine. There is only one other poison—strychnine—more deadly. A tenth of a grain will, it has been asserted, kill a dog. The evil effects of tobacco on the human frame are summarized in *The Temperance Catechism of the Four-fold Pledge* (Article Tobacco) as follows:

"On the blood, making it poor and thin. On the stomach, weakening the power of digestion, causing loss of appetite, and giving rise to sickness. On the heart, causing weakness and irregular action. On the organs of sense—on the eye by causing confusion and even loss of sight; on the ear, by causing whistling or ringing sounds, and making people unable to hear distinctly. On the brain, by first stimulating and then depressing its action. On the nerves, lessening their power and sensitiveness. On the inside of the mouth, causing enlargement of the tonsils (smoker's throat), redness, dryness, and sometimes peeling, with unnatural firmness, shrinking, or sponginess of the gums; and, worst of all, cancer of the lips, tongue, etc. On the lungs, when they are in an irritable state, by keeping up the irritation and increasing the cough."

It is, as the Revelation says, not for the body.

9. *Hot drinks are not for the body*] "Hot drinks" means tea and coffee, as those two beverages were the only ones in common use among the members of the Church, and drunk at a high temperature, at the time when the Revelation was given. The reason why those beverages were condemned was because they contained a habit-forming drug, rather than because of the temperature at which they were swallowed; although liquids taken into the stomach at too high a temperature, frequently and in large quantities, would be hurtful. But the chief objection to tea and coffee is the drug they contain. It follows logically that any other beverage which contains a hurtful drug or element, is open to the same objection, regardless of the temperature at which it is taken.

" 'Hot drinks are not for the body, or belly.' There are many who wonder what this can mean; whether it refers to tea or coffee, or not. I say it does refer to tea and coffee. Why is it that we are so dull and languid? It is because we break the Word of Wisdom. Disease preys upon our system, our understandings are darkened, and we do not comprehend the things of God. The devil takes advantage of us, and we fall into temptation. Not only are they injurious in their tendency, and baneful in their effects, but importation of foreign products might be the means of thousands of people being poisoned at a future time, through the advantage that an enemy might take of us, if we made use of these things that are thus spoken of as being evil; and be it remembered, that this instruction is given in consequence of evils that do exist in the hearts of conspiring men'" (Hyrum Smith, *Times and Seasons*, Vol. III., p. 799).

10-13. Wholesome herbs and fruit are good for man; also meat.

"Nevertheless, they [the meats] should be used sparingly; and it is pleasing unto me, that they should not be used only in times of winter, or of cold, or famine. * * * And why to be used in time of famine? Because all domesticated animals would naturally die, and might as well be made use of by man as not" (Hyrum Smith, *Ibid.*).

14-17. Grain, fruit, and edible roots are here said to be ordained for the use of man. Undoubtedly man was first taught by God Himself to select and cultivate plants for food. And this was done so far back that there is no record of the first experiments. Tubalcain is mentioned in Genesis (4:22) as a fine worker in metals; Jabal was a cattle king, Jubal a musician, and Lamech somewhat of a poet.

18-21. In these paragraphs, the Lord offers rewards for the faithful observance of the precepts contained in this Revelation. They should be studied closely. Health, wisdom, knowledge, strength, are the rewards promised.

"Let these things be adhered to; let the Saints be wise; let us lay aside our folly and abide by the commandments of God; so shall we be blessed of the great Jehovah in time and in eternity. We shall be healthy, strong, and vigorous; we shall be enabled to resist disease; and wisdom will crown our councils, and our bodies shall become strong and powerful, our progeny will be mighty, and will rise up and call us blessed; the daughters will be beautiful, and the sons the joy of the whole earth; we shall prepare the purposes of Jehovah, for the kingdom of God, for the appearance of Jesus in His glory; out of Zion the perfection of beauty. God will shine, Zion will be exalted, and become the praise of the whole earth." (From the *Times and Seasons*, Vol. III., p. 799.)

GENERAL NOTES

An American physician, Dr. Richard Hoyner, has published a book on *The Art to Grow Old and Keep Young*. From a masterly literary notice in a Stockholm paper, written by Dr. Henrick Berg, it appears that Dr. Hoyner is of the opinion that men and women might reach the age of from 125 to 175 years, if they would live in accordance with the laws of nature. How can they attain that ripe age? The author, first of all, calls attention to the influence of the mind upon the functions of the body. These are normal only when the soul is filled with faith, hope, and charity. Then he takes up the question of diet. Simplicity and temperance are the foundations of his system. He recommends bran and tells how to make bread and pancakes of that part of the grain. He condemns the use of intoxicants, coffee, tea, tobacco, and even chocolate. To tobacco he ascribes many cases of heart failure and anæmia. And, finally, he recommends exercise at regular hours. Here we have a scientific endorsement of the Word of Wisdom.

"Man requires food to build up his body. He requires food that is adapted to the development of bone, muscle, and sinew; but this is not all; he requires food that is suitable to feed his brain and to supply the waste sustained in consequence of the use of his mental faculties. There is a necessity, therefore, to take these things into consideration. My opinion is that it will be most difficult for fathers of families to induce their wives and children to refrain from the use of tea and coffee, if they do not supply their tables with other articles in their place, and unless food, suitable to the requirements of the human system, is provided, our wives and children will be exposed to constant temptation to transgress the counsels that are given in regard to our diet" (George Q. Cannon, *Jour. of Dis.*, Vol. XII., p. 222).

"If you observe faithfully the Word of Wisdom, you will have your dollar, your five dollars, your hundred dollars, yea, you will have your hundreds of dollars to spend for that which will be useful and profitable to you" (Brigham Young, *Jour. of Dis.*, Vol. XII., p. 118).

SECTION 90.

REVELATION *to Joseph Smith the Prophet, given at Kirtland, Ohio, March 8, 1833. Position of Joseph as President of the Church reaffirmed.——Accountability of those who receive the oracles of God—The Gospel to be preached throughout the world—Worthy servants commended and offenders reproved.*

THUS saith the Lord, verily, verily I say unto you my son, thy sins are forgiven thee, according to thy petition, for thy prayers and the prayers of thy brethren have come up into my ears.

2.   Therefore, thou art blessed from henceforth, that bear the keys of the kingdom given unto you; which kingdom is coming forth for the last time.

3.   Verily, I say unto you, the keys of this Kingdom shall never be taken from you, while thou art in the world, neither in the world to come;

4. Nevertheless, through you shall the oracles be given to another; yea, even unto the church.

5. And all they who receive the oracles of God, let them beware how they hold them, lest they are accounted as a light thing, and are brought under condemnation thereby; and stumble and fall, when the storms descend, and the winds blow, and the rains descend, and beat upon their house.

In the Revelation given on the 27th of December, 1832, the Lord instructed His servants that no one was to be received in the School of the Prophets, that was not "clean from the blood of this generation," and that members should be received by the ordinance of washing of feet, which was instituted as a testimony that the recipient was clean in this respect (See Sec. 88:138-9). On January 23rd, when the Elders were assembled in Conference, the Prophet performed that ordinance, and pronounced them "clean from the blood of this generation." He warned them not to sin wilfully after they were thus cleansed, lest they should be given over to the buffetings of Satan. The meeting closed with the administration of the Sacrament. The Elders were now prepared for the ministry.

This Revelation concerning the keys of the kingdom may be considered as a continuation of the glorious manifestations of the beginning of the year. In it the Lord (1) constitutes the Prophet Joseph a guardian of the keys of the kingdom for ever (1-5); (2) defines the position of Sidney Rigdon and Fred G. Williams (6-11); (3) explains the duties of the Prophet and his counselors (12-18); (4) gives instructions on various subjects (19-33); and (5) warns Zion (34-37).

1. The Prophet a Keeper of the Keys for Ever.

1-5. The central thought in these paragraphs is this that the Prophet Joseph would hold the keys of the kingdom for ever, and that, through him, others might also be appointed to receive revelations.

1. *Thy sins are forgiven*] After the great manifestations of the divine Presence during the January Conference, and the sacred ordinance of the washing of feet, the assurance here quoted, and which occurs in v. 6, again, might seem superfluous. For the Prophet had pronounced his brethren "clean" of the blood of this generation, and without question, his status was the same as theirs. But this is a divine recognition of the ordinance they had performed. The power of the Priesthood is such that the acts performed under it are recognized by our Lord Himself and his assurance is His ratification of the ordinance observed according to His word.

Neither the Prophet Joseph, nor his brethren, had any great transgressions, as measured by worldly standards, on their consciences, but no mortal is entirely free from sin. The fact is that, the nearer a man draws to the presence of God, the more keenly he feels his imperfections and shortcomings, and the more natural it is to exclaim with Peter, "Depart from me; for I am a sinful man, O Lord!" (Luke 5:8). It is not surprising, therefore, to learn that the Prophet and his brethren, coming, as it were, from the very presence of the Lord, engaged in prayers for the forgiveness of their sins and received the assurance quoted.

If our minds are open to see and understand things spiritual, we realize that we sin frequently. God has given us beautiful bodies, formed in His own likeness, each part adapted to its own purpose. He has also given us rules for the proper care of this wonderful machinery; how do we follow these rules? How do we honor His laws relating to the preservation of health and the propagation of the race? And how do we keep the great law of God with regard to loving Him more than anything else, and our neighbor as ourselves? We owe even enemies a debt of love; how do we pay it? Truly, there is none without sin, and the assurance, "Thy sins are forgiven thee," is, therefore, sweet to every child of the Eternal Father.

3. *The keys of this kingdom*] The Prophet Joseph, on May 15th, 1829, received the Aaronic Priesthood, under the hands of John the Baptist, and was baptized by Oliver Cowdery, who also had been ordained to that Priesthood. A short time later, he received the Melchizedek Priesthood under the hands of Peter, James, and John. These sealed upon him every power and all the authority belonging to the Apostleship, qualifying him to act as the messenger and representative of our Lord in all that pertains to His Church on Earth. This is meant by "the keys of this kingdom." "Keys" stands for "authority." And this authority would never be taken away from the Prophet. He holds it still.

4. *Oracles of God*] The word in the singular is used to indicate the place where God reveals Himself, as, for instance, the Mercy Seat in the temple (Ex. 25:18, 20; I. Kings 6:5, 16). In the plural it means the Revelations given by God (Rom. 3:2; I. Pet. 4:11).

Be given to another, yea, even unto the Church] In a revelation given in February 1831, the Lord declared that Joseph Smith was the only one appointed to receive revelation and commandments for the Church "until he be taken, if he abide in me," but should the Prophet fail this gift would be taken from him and given to another. (Doc. & Cov. 43:3-4.) Now in March 1833, after the Prophet had been tried and proved, the Lord said that the keys, through which direction, commandment and revelation come, "shall never be taken from you, while thou art in the world, neither in the world to come." Yet when the Prophet should be taken the "oracles" would be given to another, "even to the Church." Therefore after the martyrdom the keys remained and were in possession of the Church and exercised through the presiding council, which at that time was the council of the Twelve Apostles, and in the Church the oracles are found and will continue unto the end of time.

5. *Let them beware*] The oracles of God are not to be treated lightly. His gifts are not to be the object of contention. No campaign for their possession must ever disgrace the Church. Let those who receive them hold them in all humility, as a sacred trust and serve the people of God, as His stewards.

6. And again, verily I say unto thy brethren, Sidney Rigdon and Frederick G. Williams, their sins are forgiven them also, and they are accounted as equal with thee in holding the keys of this last kingdom;

7. As also through your administration the keys of the school of the prophets, which I have commanded to be organized;

8. That thereby they may be perfected in their ministry for the salvation of Zion, and of the nations of Israel, and of the Gentiles, as many as will believe;

9. That through your administration they may receive the word, and through their administration the word may go forth unto the ends of the earth, unto the Gentiles first, and then, behold, and lo, they shall turn unto the Jews.

10. And then cometh the day when the arm of the Lord shall be revealed in power in convincing the nations, the heathen nations, the house of Joseph, of the gospel of their salvation.

11. For it shall come to pass in that day, that every man shall hear the fulness of the gospel in his own tongue, and in his own language, through those who are ordained unto this power, by the administration of the Comforter, shed forth upon them for the revelation of Jesus Christ.

2. SIDNEY RIGDON AND FREDERICK G. WILLIAMS.

6. *Equal with thee*] Ten days after this Revelation had been received, Sidney Rigdon and Frederick G. Williams were ordained counselors to the Prophet Joseph. On that date, March 18th, 1833, the First Presidency of the Church of Jesus Christ of Latter-day Saints was first organized. The occasion was memorable. The High Priests had been organized in the room used by the School of the Prophets, and there was joy among the Saints. The Prophet writes:

"Elder Rigdon expressed a desire that himself and Frederick G. Williams should be ordained to the office to which they had been called, viz., those of Presidents of the High Priesthood, and to be equal in hold-ing the keys of the Kingdom with Brother Joseph Smith, Jun., accord-ing to the Revelation given on the 8th of March, 1833. Accordingly, I laid my hands on Brothers Sidney and Frederick, and ordained them to take part with me in holding the keys of this last kingdom, and to assist in the Presidency of the High Priesthood, as my counselors; after which I exhorted the brethren to faithfulness and diligence in keeping the commandments of God" (*Hist. of the Church*, Vol. I., p. 334).

7. *The keys of the School of the Prophets*] It would not be easy to overestimate the importance attached to this institution. That Sidney Rigdon and Frederick G. Williams should be appointed, together with Joseph Smith, to hold the keys both of the Church and of the School, is significant.

8. *That thereby they may be perfected in their ministry*] That was the object God had in view in bestowing upon His servants this authority. Their mission was to bring the message of salvation to Zion; that is, to the Saints in Jackson County: to the nations of Israel; that is, the nations in which the blood of Israel had been diffused: and to the Gentiles; that is, to those who were not of the seed of Abraham.

9. *That through your administration * * * unto the Jews*] The meaning seems to be this: Through your administration—the administration of the First Presidency—the word of salvation will go to the ends of the Earth, and when Israel has received the message, it will go, first to the Gentiles and then to the Jews.

10. *The arm of the Lord shall be revealed*] Then the power of God will be manifest among all the nations of the Earth. The slums will be cleansed, and children will no longer be brought up naked and hungry, and exposed to temptations and crimes. Mammon-worship will give way to the brotherhood of man. The Sermon on the Mount will be the standard of conduct. Then the prayer for the extinction of tyranny in individuals and multitudes, for the prevalence of righteousness and truth; for the banishment of hypocrisy and fraud, and for the purification of palace and hovel will have received its answer in the establishment of the kingdom of our Lord.

11. *In his own language*] The gospel will be preached in every language under the sun, and the glory of the King will be sung in every tongue. Even during the Millennium there will be a diversity of languages, although, in all probability, one language will be studied as an international language, and by that means intercourse between all nations will be simplified.

12. And now, verily I say unto you, I give unto you a commandment that you continue in the ministry and presidency.

13. And when you have finished the translation of the prophets, you shall from thenceforth preside over the affairs of the church and the school;

14. And from time to time, as shall be manifested by the Comforter, receive revelations to unfold the mysteries of the kingdom;

15. And set in order the churches, and study and learn, and become acquainted with all good books, and with languages, tongues, and people.

16. And this shall be your business and mission in all your lives, to preside in council, and set in order all the affairs of this church and kingdom.

17. Be not ashamed, neither confounded; but be admonished in all your high-mindedness and pride, for it bringeth a snare upon your souls.

18. Set in order your houses; keep slothfulness and uncleanness afar from you.

3. THE DUTIES OF THE PROPHET.

12-18. Some of the duties of the Prophet Joseph are defined in these paragraphs. Although his two Counselors were accounted equal with him, he was to continue in the ministry and Presidency (v. 12) of the Church and the School (v. 13). He was to receive Revelations concerning the mysteries of the kingdom (v. 14); set the Churches, or Branches, in order, and study (v. 15). In these duties the Counselors were to assist him.

13. *The translation of the Prophets*] The Prophet completed the revision of the New Testament on the 2nd of Feb., 1833, and sealed it up, "no more to be opened till it arrived in Zion," where the work was to be printed. When he had finished the Prophets, that is, the last part of the Old Testament, he was to devote his time to the duties of the Presidency.

The Church and the School] This is the second time in this Revelation that the two are mentioned together.

15. *All good books*] The emphasis should be placed on *good*. Bad books—and most books are either bad or useless—should be shunned as a thing contaminated. On that subject, President Brigham Young says:

"If I had charge of such a society as this to which I refer, I would not allow novel-reading; yet it is in my house, in the houses of my Counselors, in the houses of these Apostles, these Seventies and High Priests, in the houses of the High Council in this City, and in other cities, and in the houses of the Bishops, and we permit it; yet it is ten thousand times worse than it is for men* to come here to teach our children the A B C's, good morals, and how to behave themselves—ten

---

* Referring to unprincipled men, or men without moral standards.

thousand times worse! You let your children read novels until they run away, until they get so that they do not care; they are reckless, and their mothers are reckless, and some of their fathers are reckless, and if you do not break their backs and tie them up, they will go to hell. That is rough, is it not? Well, it is a comparison. You have got to check them some way or other, or they will go to destruction. They are perfectly crazy * * * I would not like to get into a society where there were no trials; but I would like to see a society organized to show the Latter-day Saints how to build up the kingdom of God" (*Jour. of Dis.,* Vol. XV., p. 224).

17. *High-mindedness and pride*] God warns His servants against these sins. Man is prone to the proud of talents, of family connections, of education, of social position, of wealth. Nothing is more detrimental to spiritual development and usefulness. "In the last days perilous times shall come. For men shall be lovers of their own selves, covetous, boasters, proud, blasphemers," etc. (II. Tim. 3:1-2). Here, pride has its proper place among such sins as covetousness, boasting, and blasphemy. There is where it belongs.

18. *Set in order your houses*] The commandment in this verse is very important. "Cleanliness is next to godliness." The Holy Spirit is no companion to slothfulness and uncleanness.

19. Now, verily I say unto you, let there be a place provided, as soon as it is possible, for the family of thy counselor and scribe, even Frederick G. Williams.

20. And let mine aged servant, Joseph Smith, Sen., continue with his family upon the place where he now lives; and let it not be sold until the mouth of the Lord shall name.

21. And let my counselor, even Sidney Rigdon, remain where he now resides until the mouth of the Lord shall name.

22. And let the bishop search diligently to obtain an agent, and let him be a man who has got riches in store—a man of God, and of strong faith—

23. That thereby he may be enabled to discharge every debt; that the storehouse of the Lord may not be brought into disrepute before the eyes of the people.

24. Search diligently, pray always, and be believing, and all things shall work together for your good, if ye walk uprightly and remember the covenant wherewith ye have covenanted one with another.

25. Let your families be small, especially mine aged servant

Joseph Smith's, Sen., as pertaining to those who do not belong to your families;

26. That those things that are provided for you, to bring to pass my work, be not taken from you and given to those that are not worthy—

27. And thereby you be hindered in accomplishing those things which I have commanded you.

28. And again, verily I say unto you, it is my will that my handmaid Vienna Jaques should receive money to bear her expenses, and go up unto the land of Zion;

29. And the residue of the money may be consecrated unto me, and she be rewarded in mine own due time.

30. Verily I say unto you, that it is meet in mine eyes that she should go up unto the land of Zion, and receive an inheritance from the hand of the bishop;

31. That she may settle down in peace inasmuch as she is faithful, and not be idle in her days from thenceforth.

32. And behold, verily I say unto you, that ye shall write this commandment, and say unto your brethren in Zion, in love greeting, that I have called you also to preside over Zion in mine own due time.

33. Therefore, let them cease wearying me concerning this matter.

4. Instructions on Miscellaneous Subjects.

19-33. In this section the Lord gives instruction on many subjects, most of them of a temporal character. The Saints were to provide a place of residence for Frederick G. Williams (v. 19). Sidney Rigdon was to remain where he resided, as was the Prophet's father (vv. 20-1). Bishop Whitney was to find a brother who could act as his agent (vv. 22-3. See also Sects. 51:8, 58:49; 84:113). They were to keep down the expense of their households (vv. 25-7); Vienna Jaques was to go to Zion (28-31); and they were to advise the Saints in Zion that the jurisdiction of the First Presidency extended over Jackson County and the West as well as over Kirtland and the East (v. 32). Thus the First Presidency was to be a means of preservation of the unity of the Church.

The primitive church, after the departure of the Apostles, disintegrated and was divided into many groups, each with a head of its own, and, finally, the great division into the Roman and Greek churches occurred, the bishop of Rome and the patriarch of Constantinople, each claiming supreme authority. The Church of Jesus Christ of Latter-day Saints might have been cleft in the same way, into a Western and an Eastern division, with several smaller groups between, but for the Revelation instituting the First Presidency, which is both the symbol of the unity of the Church and the connecting link by which this unity is effected.

Some of the commandments in this Section relate to temporal affairs. Does God care for such matters? Does He notice where His children live, and how? He certainly does, for the Master taught His disciples to make daily bread, as well as the advent of His kingdom, the subject of prayer. God regards the bodily needs of His children. He does not want them to live the unnatural life of hermits and ascetics. He not only teaches us to pray for bread, but guides us through revelation in our wise and honest efforts to obtain it.

34. Behold, I say unto you that your brethren in Zion begin to repent, and the angels rejoice over them.

35. Nevertheless, I am not well pleased with many things; and I am not well pleased with my servant William E. M'Lellin, neither with my servant Sidney Gilbert; and the bishop also, and others have many things to repent of.

36. But verily I say unto you, that I, the Lord, will contend with Zion, and plead with her strong ones, and chasten her until she overcomes and is clean before me.

37. For she shall not be removed out of her place. I, the Lord, have spoken it. Amen.

5. Zion Warned.

34-7. The Revelation closes with a warning and a promise regarding Zion. All the brethren in Zion were not keeping the commandments of God faithfully. Some of them were jealous of the position and influence of the Prophet Joseph, and denied his authority to direct the temporal affairs of the Church. Among them were the men mentioned in Verse 35. In a letter written on behalf of the Church, by Orson Hyde and Hyrum Smith, Jan. 14th, 1833, and addressed to the Bishopric and Saints in Zion, it is pointed out that Sidney Gilbert, in a communication received from him, used "low, dark, and blind insinuations," which were not received "as from the fountain of light." In the same letter Wm. W. Phelps is kindly rebuked for a "lightness of spirit that ill becomes a man placed in the important and responsible station that he is placed in." Furthermore, the Saints in Zion failed to keep the laws of God concerning consecration. Hence the warning: The Lord would contend with Zion, plead with her strong ones, and chasten her "until she overcomes and is clean before me." That is the warning. The promise is: "She shall not be removed out of her place."

34. *Begin to repent*] The letters of warning sent to Zion had the effect of awakening some of the Saints to repentance. In a letter dated, Kirtland, April 21, 1833, the Prophet wrote to the brethren in Zion: "With joy we received your general epistle, written the 26th of February, which contained the confession of our brethren concerned, all of which was to our entire satisfaction." With regard to Sidney Gilbert he observes: "The letter written the 24th of February was not written in that contrition of heart in which it should have been, for it appears to have been written too much in a spirit of justification; but the letter to Brother Whitney of the 20th of March, was written to our entire satisfaction" (*Hist. of the Church*, Vol. I., p. 340-1). "Your brethren in Zion begin to repent," and even this small beginning gave the angels joy.

GENERAL NOTES

"The Lord saw that we were so covetous and filled with the selfish principle instilled into our minds by our forefathers, that we could not give heed to the law which He gave concerning the consecrations that were to be made in Jackson County, Mo., and He determined in His own mind that that should not be a land of Zion unto the present generation of people, take them as a people; and He made this decree, after giving them Revelation upon Revelation, warning them by the mouth of His servant Joseph, who went in person and warned them, and sent up his Revelations a thousand miles from Kirtland and warned them. After they had been sufficiently warned, for some two years and upwards, after the commencement of their settlement of Jackson County, Mo., the Lord fulfilled that which He had spoken concerning them—that they should be driven out of the land of Zion. This was literally fulfilled" (Orson Pratt, *Jour. of Dis.*, Vol. XV., p. 358).

But Zion has not been removed out of her place.

"We shall in due time walk forth into Jackson County and build up the waste places of Zion. We shall erect in that county a beautiful city after the order and pattern that the Lord shall reveal, part of which has already been revealed. God intends to have a city built up that will never be destroyed nor overcome, but that will exist, while eternity shall endure." (*Ibid.*, p. 365).

SECTION 91.

REVELATION *given through Joseph Smith the Prophet, at Kirtland, Ohio, March 9, 1833. The Prophet was at this time engaged in the study of the ancient writings regarded by some as Scripture and known distinctively as the Apocrypha.——— These writings not to be accepted as Scripture—Enlightenment of the Spirit requisite to discernment of the truth contained in these books.*

VERILY, thus saith the Lord unto you concerning the Apocrypha—There are many things contained therein that are true, and it is mostly translated correctly;

2. There are many things contained therein that are not true, which are interpolations by the hands of men.

3. Verily, I say unto you, that it is not needful that the Apocrypha should be translated.

4. Therefore, whoso readeth it, let him understand, for the Spirit manifesteth truth;

5. And whoso is enlightened by the Spirit shall obtain benefit therefrom;

6. And whoso receiveth not by the Spirit, cannot be benefited. Therefore it is not needful that it should be translated. Amen.

When the Prophet, in the course of his Bible revision, came to the writings known as the *Apocrypha,* the question arose as to whether they were to be incorporated in his work. To decide that question, this Revelation was given.

The word "Apocrypha" means "Hidden," and it is applied to certain ancient writings which some regard as part of the Bible, while others consider them as without divine authority. Some of these books illustrate the progress of knowledge among the Jews, their religious character, and their government during the time between the Prophet Malachi and John the Baptist. In some of them, we see the fulfilment of prophecy, and in most of them there are found exalted sentiments and principles. I. and II. *Esdras, Tobit, Judith, Esther, Susanna,* and *The Idol Bel and the Dragon* are regarded as of least value. The first book of the *Maccabees,* gives the history of the deliverance of the Jews through that noble family. The second illustrates the belief of the Jews in a future life. The *Wisdom of Solomon* is an attempt to imitate the style of that illustrious king. *Ecclesiasticus* shows how the Jews expounded the Law.

The Church of Rome, by the Council of Trent, A. D. 1546, declared that the Apocrypha were authentic, although Augustine, in the 5th century, had said, "This reverence have I learnt to give to those books of Scripture only which are called canonical. Others I so read that I think not anything to be true because they so thought it, but because they were able to persuade me either by those canonical authors, or by some probable reason, that it did not swerve from truth."

"As he tells us in *Grace Abounding,* there was a time when John

Bunyan was, in his spiritual strivings, driven to his wit's end and quite giving up the ghost of all hopes of attaining life. Then it was that a sentence fell with weight upon his spirit, 'Look at the generations of old, and see; did ever any trust in God and were confounded?' So fresh and upholding was the saying; it seemed to Bunyan as if it talked with him; but on going to his Bible to find the exact setting, the inspiring words refused to disclose themselves. 'Thus I continued above a year, and could not find the place; but at last, casting my eye upon the Apocryphal books, I found it in Ecclesiasticus, 'Look at the generations of old and see, did ever any trust in the Lord and was confounded; or did any abide in his fear and was forsaken; or whom did he ever despise that called upon him?' This, at first, did somewhat daunt me; but because by this time I had got more experience of the love and kindness of God, it troubled me the less, especially when I considered though it was not in those texts that we call holy and canonical; yet, for as much as this sentence was the sum and substance of many of the promises, it was my duty to take the comfort of it; and I bless God for that word, for it was of good to me: that word doth still ofttimes shine before my face' " (From a Review of Dr. Osterley's *Apocrypha,* in the *Christian Work*).

SECTION 92.

REVELATION *given to Enoch [Joseph Smith the Prophet], at Kirtland, Ohio, March 15, 1833. For explanation of unusual names see heading to Section 78.——Commandment regarding admission to the United Order.*

VERILY, thus saith the Lord, I give unto the united order, organized agreeable to the commandment previously given, a revelation and commandment concerning my servant Shederlaomach [Frederick G. Williams], that ye shall receive him into the order. What I say unto one I say unto all.

2. And again, I say unto you my servant Shederlaomach [Frederick G. Williams], you shall be a lively member in this order; and inasmuch as you are faithful in keeping all former commandments you shall be blessed forever. Amen.

In the Revelation given on April 26th, 1832 (sec. 82), the Lord instructed the Prophet Joseph, Oliver Cowdery, Martin Harris, Sidney Rigdon, Newel K. Whitney, and a few others (v. 11) to unite their temporal interests under the rule of the Order of Enoch. In this Revelation the brethren in that organization are commanded to receive, as a member, Frederick G. Williams, whom the Lord had declared to be the equal of Joseph Smith and Sidney Rigdon in holding the keys of the kingdom (Sec. 90:6). Williams was admonished to be faithful and given the promise that, if he would keep the commandments of God, he would be blessed for ever.

2. *A lively member*] An *active* member. The translators of King James' Version of the Bible used the word "lively" in that sense. See Psalm 38:19; I. Peter 2:5.

Former commandments] See Sec. 64:21; 81:1-7. God demands obedience, but He never imposes upon His servants a burden they cannot bear. To those who are willing to obey, He makes the yoke easy and the burden light.

SECTION 93.

REVELATION *given through Joseph Smith the Prophet, at Kirtland, Ohio, May 6, 1833.——The Lord defines the relation between himself and the Father—The record of John, the Apostle and Revelator—Jesus Christ the Firstborn—Man was in the beginning with God—The elements are eternal—The glory of God is intelligence—Man innocent in the beginning— Erring ones, even though in high authority in the Church, reproved.*

VERILY, thus saith the Lord: It shall come to pass that every soul who forsaketh his sins and cometh unto me, and calleth on my name, and obeyeth my voice, and keepeth my commandments, shall see my face and know that I am;

2. And that I am the true light that lighteth every man that cometh into the world;

3. And that I am in the Father, and the Father in me, and the Father and I are one—

4. The Father because he gave me of his fulness, and the Son because I was in the world and made flesh my tabernacle, and dwelt among the sons of men.

On the 4th of May, 1833, a meeting of High Priests was held at Kirtland, for the purpose of considering ways and means for the building of a house in which to accommodate the School of the Prophets (Sec. 90:6-9). Hyrum Smith, Jared Carter, and Reynolds Cahoon were appointed a committee to obtain subscriptions for that purpose. The

Saints were few and far from wealthy, and an undertaking of that kind must have seemed stupendous to them, but the leaders of the Church were men of God, and their faith was of the practical kind, by which mountains are removed. When this important step had been taken, two instructive Revelations were given on the same date.

In this Section our Lord (1) assures the Saints that obedience is the road to glory (1-4); (2) refers to John's testimony of Him (5-18); (3) instructs them concerning true worship (19-20); (4) teaches pre-existence (21-29); (5) the eternity of truth (30-32) and (6) of the elements (33-37); (7) gives admonitions concerning children (38-50); and (8) closes with special instructions (51-53).

1. To Glory through Obedience.

1-4. The building committee mentioned above had a great work before them, for the success of which they were dependent on the willingness of the Saints to make liberal sacrifices of a temporal character. An appeal was about to be made to their faith and generosity, and the Lord gave them the assurance, as a father his children, that, if they were obedient, they would have the privilege of seeing His face (v. 1), and of receiving knowledge for themselves concerning His divine nature (2-4).

1. *Shall see my face*] While the Lord made the promise that those who are faithful and true to every covenant may receive the presence of the "second Comforter," while still in mortal life, yet this passage implies that those who call on Him and obey His voice and keep His commandments, shall eventually see Him when their reward for their faithfulness shall come, and they shall dwell in His presence.

"On the first day of the dedication, President Frederick G. Williams, one of the counselors of the Prophet, and who occupied the upper pulpit, bore testimony that the Savior, dressed in His vesture without seam, came into the stand and accepted of the dedication of the house; that he saw Him, and he gave a description of His clothing and all things pertaining to it" (George A. Smith, *Jour. of Dis.*, Vol. XI., p. 10).

But the promise is of a general character, as that in I. John 3:2, "Beloved, now are we the sons of God, and it doth not yet appear what we shall be; but we know that when He shall appear, we shall be like him; for we shall see Him as he is." The conditions under which we can obtain a fulfilment of this promise are stated thus: "Every soul who forsaketh his sins and cometh unto me, and calleth on my name, and obeyeth my voice, and keepeth my commandments." Repentance, acceptance of Christ as the Master, prayer, obedience— these are the conditions; this is the road to the glorious presence of the Son of God.

That I am] This is the first great truth God will reveal to those who are obedient to Him—that Jesus Christ is *"I am,"* that is to say, Jehovah.

2. *The true light*] See Sec. 6:21. This is another great truth that can be known only through obedience. Christ is the real, genuine light

that illuminates everyone born into this world. Whatever intelligence man possesses emanates from the Divine Source.

3. *The Father and I are one*] This is another truth we must learn by obedience. Our Lord says He is in the Father, and the Father is in Him. They are absolutely identical in character, aims, sentiment, habits, nature, and essence, although they are two distinct persons. We say that a father lives in his son, if the latter walks in the ways of his parent and resembles him in all essentials. That is how the Father is in the Son, and the Son in the Father. Our Lord explains this in the following.

4. *The Father * * * the Son*] He is the Father, "because he gave me of his fulness; the Son, because I was in the world * * * and dwelt among the sons of men." Compare Mos. 15:2-4; Ether 3:14.

Jesus Christ is the "Father," as the Creator and rightful owner of the heavens and the Earth. He was the Executive of the Father in that work, and stood in His stead. He is the Father of those who are born again through acceptance or His gospel (Doc. and Cov. 34:1-3). He is the Father because a Father's authority is vested in Him. He is the second Adam (I. Cor. 15:45), the head of the human race.

"Jesus Christ is not the Father of the spirits who have taken or yet shall take bodies upon this earth, for He is one of them. He is The Son, as they are sons or daughters of Elohim. So far as the stages of eternal progression and attainment have been made known through divine revelation, we are to understand that only resurrected and glorified beings can become parents of spirit offspring. Only such exalted souls have reached maturity in the appointed course of eternal life; and the spirits born to them in the eternal worlds will pass in due sequence through the several stages or estates by which the glorified parents have attained exaltation (From an article by the First Presidency and the Council of the Twelve Apostles of the Church of Jesus Christ of Latter-day Saints, *Improvement Era*, August, 1916). See also a discourse by President Joseph F. Smith quoted in *Mormon Doctrine of Deity*, pp. 289-94.

5. I was in the world and received of my Father, and the works of him were plainly manifest.

6. And John saw and bore record of the fulness of my glory, and the fulness of John's record is hereafter to be revealed.

7. And he bore record, saying: I saw his glory, that he was in the beginning, before the world was;

8. Therefore, in the beginning the Word was, for he was the Word, even the messenger of salvation—

9. The light and the Redeemer of the world; the Spirit of truth, who came into the world, because the world was made by him, and in him was the life of men and the light of men.

10. The worlds were made by him; men were made by him; all things were made by him, and through him, and of him.

11. And I, John, bear record that I beheld his glory, as the glory of the Only Begotten of the Father, full of grace and truth, even the Spirit of truth, which came and dwelt in the flesh, and dwelt among us.

12. And I, John, saw that he received not of the fulness at the first, but received grace for grace;

13. And he received not of the fulness at first, but continued from grace to grace, until he received a fulness;

14. And thus he was called the Son of God, because he received not of the fulness at the first.

15. And I, John, bear record, and lo, the heavens were opened, and the Holy Ghost descended upon him in the form of a dove, and sat upon him, and there came a voice out of heaven saying: This is my beloved Son.

16. And I, John, bear record that he received a fulness of the glory of the Father;

17. And he received all power, both in heaven and on earth, and the glory of the Father was with him, for he dwelt in him.

18. And it shall come to pass, that if you are faithful you shall receive the fulness of the record of John.

2. THE TESTIMONY OF JOHN.

5. *I was in the world*] Our Lord was a sojourner in this world, when He dwelt here in a tabernacle of flesh. He, the Holy One, left a home of bliss and glory and came to this world of sin and sorrow, in order to save that which was lost.

Received of my Father] While in the world, our Lord was dependent on His Father for wisdom and strength to do the work that was before Him.

*The work of Him * * * manifest*] The works our Lord did were, therefore, the works of the Father. And they were plainly manifest as God's works (John 3:2).

6. *John saw and bore record*] John, the beloved disciple, recorded what had been revealed to him concerning the Savior, but the record as given in the Gospel, is not complete (See John 21:25). Some time it will be made known in greater detail.

7. *He was in the beginning*] "The beginning" can hardly refer to any other moment of time than that with which the story of the creation

in Genesis opens. At that moment our Lord "was." He existed then, and was, therefore, before the world.

8. *He was the word*] John calls Him the *Logos,* which has been translated "the Word," for want of a more intelligible term. Townsend quotes authority for the statement that, in the ancient Jewish writings, *Logos* referred to the Creator, and that the Targums, in many instances, render the sacred name Jehovah by *Logos.* Philo, a contemporary of our Savior, is said to apply the term in that sense.

The messenger of salvation] Isaiah calls Jesus Christ the "Wonderful Counselor"* (Isa. 9:6). He was a Wonderful Counselor when, in the grand council in heaven, He proposed to save man without depriving him of his free agency, and to give the honor and glory to God (Pearl of Great Price, Book of Moses 4:1, 2). But he was not only a Wonderful Counselor; He was also the Messenger of the great council—the "messenger of salvation" to the world (See Introduction p. XIV; p. 450.)

9. *The light*] He was *the* light; the one true light, the Source of both life and intelligence.

Redeemer of the world] Sometimes a "redeemer" is merely a deliverer from peril; but our Lord, as the Redeemer, delivers us by means of the sacrifice of Himself, which act is sometimes called the payment of a ransom. It is thought of as a deliverance of slaves from bondage by the purchase of their liberty.

The Spirit of Truth] He was full of grace and truth (John 1:14), and He was, and is, *the* truth (14:6), being in the form of God, and His representative. He is the truth, and must, therefore, be worshiped in truth, and not in hypocrisy, or falsehood.

The life of Men] The Scriptures trace human life to our Lord as its source; not lower animals. Adam was the son of God (Luke 3:38).

10. *By him, and through him, and of him*] Christ was the actual Maker of the worlds, as an architect is the actual maker of the houses he builds. They were made *by* Him. But they were also made *through* Him; for He was as stated before, the Executive of the Father in the work of creation. They were also made *of* Him; for He is the very source of the light and life that permeate creation.

11. *I, John, bear record*] John saw His glory, and could testify to it.

12. *Not of the fulness at first*] Our Lord, in His mortal tabernacle, did not from the first possess the fulness of glory which He received at the end of His mission on Earth. He increased in grace, as well as in wisdom, stature, and favor with God and man (Luke 2:52).

Grace for grace] This expression is, in Verse 13, correctly rendered "from grace to grace," for the meaning is that, in His life, one grace was bestowed upon Him after another, until His measure was full.

---

* The comma which appears in the English version between these two words should be eliminated.

14. *Thus he was called the Son of God*] See notes, v. 4.

15. *In the form of a dove*] When our Lord had been baptized, the Holy Ghost descended upon Him "like a dove" (John 1:32); or, "in bodily shape, like a dove" (Luke 3:22). The Prophet Joseph explains that the meaning of this expression is that the Holy Ghost descended "in the *sign* of the dove." That is, the descending dove was to John the Baptist the sign of the descent of the Holy Ghost, and a witness that He, upon whom it rested, was the promised Messiah. It was the sign God had given him (John 1:33). Says the Prophet:

"The sign of the dove was instituted before the creation of the world, a witness for the Holy Ghost, and the devil can not come in the sign of a dove. The Holy Ghost is a personage, and is in the form of a personage. It does not confine itself to the *form* of a dove, but in *sign* of the dove. The Holy Ghost cannot be transformed into a dove; but the sign of a dove was given to John to signify the truth of the deed, as the dove is an emblem, or token, of truth and innocence" (*Hist. of the Church,* Vol. V., p. 261).

17. *He received all power*] After He had finished His work on the Earth (Matt. 28:18).

18. See v. 6.

19. I give unto you these sayings that you may understand and know how to worship, and know what you worship, that you may come unto the Father in my name, and in due time receive of his fulness.

20. For if you keep my commandments you shall receive of his fulness, and be glorified in me as I am in the Father; therefore, I say unto you, you shall receive grace for grace.

3. TRUE WORSHIP.

19. *That ye may * * * know how to worship*] The testimony of John concerning our Lord, His divinity and human nature, and His relationship to the Father and the Spirit are here given, in order that the Elders and Saints may know "how to worship," and "what to worship." God wants intelligent worshipers, not devotees who repeat formulated prayers without knowing their meaning.

20. *If you keep my commandments*] That is intelligent worship. It is the highest kind of devotion, and it is the means by which man will receive of the glory of God, "grace for grace."

21. And now, verily I say unto you, I was in the beginning with the Father, and am the Firstborn;

22. And all those who are begotten through me are partakers of the glory of the same, and are the church of the Firstborn.

4. PRE-EXISTENCE.

(a) *Of Christ.*

21. *The firstborn*] "Among the spirit-children of Elohim the firstborn was and is Jehovah or Jesus Christ, to whom all others are juniors. Following are affirmative scriptures bearing upon this great truth. Paul, writing to the Colossians, says of Jesus Christ: 'Who is the image of the invisible God, the firstborn of every creature: For by him were all things created, that are in heaven, and that are in earth, visible and invisible, whether they be thrones or dominions, or principalities, or powers; all things were created by and for him: And he is before all things, and by him all things consist. And he is the head of the body, the church: who is the beginning, the firstborn from the dead; that in all things he might have the pre-eminence. For it pleated the Father that in him should all fulness dwell' (Col. 1:15-19). From this scripture we learn that Jesus Christ was 'the firstborn of every creature,' and it is evident that the seniority here expressed must be with respect to antemortal existence, for Christ was not the senior of all mortals in the flesh" (From a doctrine exposition on *The Father and the Son,* by the First Presidency and the Council of the Twelve Apostles of the Church of Jesus Christ of Latter-day Saints, Salt Lake City, June 30th, 1916).

23. Ye were also in the beginning with the Father; that which is Spirit, even the Spirit of truth;

24. And truth is knowledge of things as they are, and as they were, and as they are to come;

25. And whatsoever is more or less than this is the spirit of that wicked one who was a liar from the beginning.

26. The Spirit of truth is of God. I am the Spirit of truth, and John bore record of me, saying: He received a fulness of truth, yea, even of all truth;

27. And no man receiveth a fulness unless he keepeth his commandments.

28. He that keepeth his commandments receiveth truth and light, until he is glorified in truth and knoweth all things.

29. Man was also in the beginning with God. Intelligence, or the light of truth, was not created or made, neither indeed can be.

(b) *Of Man.*

23-9. In this section the pre-existence of man is clearly taught. Man was in the beginning "with the Father," as was the Son.

There are three theories concerning the origin of the spirit of man, viz., Creation, Traduction, and Pre-existence. The Creation-theory holds that each spirit is created by God, and not generated or derived from the parents. It is the commonly accepted theory. The Traduction-theory is that the spirits are derived from the parents, as truly as are the bodies. The theory of Pre-existence holds that the spirits of men had a separate, conscious, and personal existence before this world was created. Origen held this view but he distorted it by explaining that the spirits sinned in a previous state and were, therefore, doomed to pass through a state of mortality in tabernacles of flesh. The Revelations given in this dispensation tell us of our pre-existence, and of our entrance into this world as a reward for faithfulness in a former state; not as a punishment.

"The spirit of man is not a created being; it existed from eternity, and will exist to eternity. Anything created cannot be eternal: earth, water, etc., had their existence in an elementary state from eternity. Our Savior speaks of children and says, 'Their angels always stand before my Father.' The Father called all spirits before Him at the creation of man, and organized them. He (Adam) is the head, and was told to multiply. The keys were first given to him, and by him to others. He will have to give an account of his stewardship, and they to him" (Joseph Smith, *Jour. of Dis.,* Vol. VI., p. 238).

24. *Truth is knowledge,* etc.] To the important question, "What is truth?" no better answer was ever offered. To be in possession of truth is to know things as they are, as they were, and as they are to come.

26. *The Spirit of truth is of God*] The Spirit of truth could eminate from no other source but from God. Here the Savior declares that He is the Spirit of Truth, and unto John it was revealed that the Son received a fulness of truth, "yea even of all truth." By keeping the commandments the promise is made that man may also receive truth and light, until he is glorified in truth and like the Lord, eventually may know all things. This fulness will never be received by any except those who keep the full law and are obedient to all covenants and commandments. The fulness of truth cannot come to the inhabitants of the terrestrial or the telestial world.

28. *He that keepeth His commandments*] This is the essential condition, without which we cannot receive truth in its fulness. No amount of study can take the place of obedience.

30. All truth is independent in that sphere in which God has placed it, to act for itself, as all intelligence also; otherwise there is no existence.

31. Behold, here is the agency of man, and here is the condemnation of man; because that which was from the beginning is plainly manifest unto them, and they receive not the light.

32. And every man whose spirit receiveth not the light is under condemnation.

5. Truth Eternal.

30-2. The doctrine here taught that truth and intelligence have independent spheres in which to act for themselves, seems to have been before Plato, who taught that ideas are eternal in the divine mind, and that they are living entities, the only true realities, of which material forms are mere shadows.

30. *Otherwise there is no existence*] If the divine ideas are not realities, there is no existence. In other words, if there is no pre-existence, there is not a present existence, and none hereafter.

31. *Behold, here is the agency of man*] Man brings his free agency and responsibility with him from a pre-existent state. There he had the light, "because that which was from the beginning [that is, truth] is plainly manifest unto them" because of the light they had in a previous existence.

32. *Every man whose spirit receiveth not the light is under condemnation*] Why? Because the spirit has had light before it came here, and ought to recognize and love it here, as soon as the years of accountability are reached.

33. For man is spirit. The elements are eternal, and spirit and element, inseparably connected, receive a fulness of joy;

34. And when separated, man cannot receive a fulness of joy.

35. The elements are the tabernacle of God; yea, man is the tabernacle of God, even temples; and whatsoever temple is defiled, God shall destroy that temple.

36. The glory of God is intelligence, or, in other words, light and truth.

37. Light and truth forsake that evil one.

6. Elements Eternal.

33-7. The subject is continued and the additional truth is added, that the elements, too, are eternal. Matter, in its elementary forms, is eternal, and it is only when spirit and matter are inseparably united that there can be perfect happiness.

It is a remarkable fact that the philosophies of the ancient world, notwithstanding the gigantic intellects that originated them, led to materialism, pantheism, fatalism, atheism, and pride, while the philosophy of this wonderful volume, the Doctrine and Covenants, leads men to trust in God, as in the Maker of the worlds and the Father of the spirits. Whence the wisdom possessed by Joseph Smith, which neither ancient nor modern philosophers have found?

33. *Man is spirit*] And God is spirit (John 4:24). "For both he that sanctifieth and they who are sanctified are all of one: for which cause he is not ashamed to call them brethren" (Heb. 2:11).

35. *The elements are the tabernacle of God*] God dwells in the material universe, through His Spirit which pervades everything; not in the pantheistic sense of indwelling, which denies any distinction between matter and mind, body and spirit, God and the world, and affirms, to all intents and purposes, that the universe is God, and God the universe; but in the sense in which we say that God dwelt in the Tabernacle in the wilderness. He dwells in the material world as a king in his palace.

Man is the tabernacle of God] Speaking to members of the Church in Corinth, Paul said: "Know ye not that ye are the temple of God, and that the Spirit of God dwelleth in you? If any man defile the temple of God, him shall God destroy; for the temple of God is holy, which temple ye are." (I. Cor. 3:16-17.) Evidently this verse has reference to those who have become members of the Church with the gift of the Holy Ghost. It is a serious thing to receive the gift of the Holy Ghost, and then defile the body, and those who do so shall be destroyed. Destruction here spoken of does not mean that the individual will be annihilated and cease to exist. Destruction means that the individual shall be banished from the presence of God which is destruction. The body cannot be destroyed permanently because through the atonement of Jesus Christ every spirit and body shall receive the resurrection that they can die no more.

38.   Every spirit of man was innocent in the beginning; and God having redeemed man from the fall, men became again, in their infant state, innocent before God.

39.   And that wicked one cometh and taketh away light and truth, through disobedience, from the children of men, and because of the tradition of their fathers.

40.   But I have commanded you to bring up your children in light and truth.

7. Concerning Children.

(a)   *Children are Innocent but need Instruction.*

38-40.   The orthodox view of the status of children is that they are totally depraved, from the first moment of their existence; that they are contaminated by sin, and that, if they die before they are baptized, they go to destruction as the property of the prince of the lower regions. As soon as a child is capable of moral action, they say, it gives evidence of perverted moral character, in manifestations of anger, malice, selfishness, envy, pride, etc. In short, they are born in sin and begin life as sinners.

Against this gloomy conception of the status of an infant, this Revelation sets forth that the spirit of man comes into the world innocent, redeemed from the fall through the atonement of the Savior. True, there are certain consequences of the fall which remain, and will remain, until Paradise is restored to its first glory, but the infant comes into the world as innocent and pure as our first parents came. As soon, however, as the child begins to awaken to consciousness of its own existence and the existence of the world, the adversary endeavors to take away light and truth from it, by planting within it the spirit of *disobedience.* That is how sin comes into the life of every human being, as, at first, in the Garden of Eden. Parents should, therefore, take up the combat with the adversary from the first, for the mastery of the child, by bringing it up in "light and truth."

"I would now say to parents that their own salvation, as well as that of their children, depends to a certain extent on the bringing up of their children, and educating them in the truth, that their traditions and early impressions may be correct.

"My heart is often pained when I enter a house of the Saints, and find the walls ornamented, and the tables, shelves, and book-cases still groaning as it were with the weight of sectarian paintings, books, and trash. Brethren, I would either sell them at auction to those who wish to purchase, or else I would heap them up and have one good fire; and then I would be to some expense to furnish my family with useful works, such as maps, charts, works of science, and, above all, a good supply of religious information from the true source" (Parley P. Pratt in *the Prophet,* quoted in the *Millennial Star,* Vol. V., pp. 192-3).

41. But verily I say unto you, my servant Frederick G. Williams, you have continued under this condemnation;

42. You have not taught your children light and truth, according to the commandments; and that wicked one hath power as yet, over you, and this is the cause of your affliction.

43. And now a commandment I give unto you—if you will be delivered you shall set in order your own house, for there are many things that are not right in your house.

44. Verily, I say unto my servant Sidney Rigdon, that in some things he hath not kept the commandments concerning his children; therefore, first set in order thy house.

45. Verily, I say unto my servant Joseph Smith, Jun., or in other words, I will call you friends, for you are my friends, and ye shall have an inheritance with me—

46. I called you servants for the world's sake, and ye are their servants for my sake—

47. And now, verily I say unto Joseph Smith, Jun.—You have not kept the commandments, and must needs stand rebuked before the Lord;

48. Your family must needs repent and forsake some things, and give more earnest heed unto your sayings, or be removed out of their place.

49. What I say unto one I say unto all; pray always lest that wicked one have power in you, and remove you out of your place.

50. My servant Newel K. Whitney also, a bishop of my church, hath need to be chastened, and set in order his family, and see that they are more diligent and concerned at home, and pray always, or they shall be removed out of their place.

(b) *Neglect of Children.*

41-50. How general the neglect of the children is among the Latter-day Saints may be inferred from these paragraphs, in which the Lord severely rebukes Frederick G. Williams (vv. 41-3), Sidney Rigdon (v. 44), Joseph Smith (vv. 45-9), and Newel K. Whitney (v. 50), for delinquency in this respect. The Prophet Joseph and Bishop Whitney were plainly told that their families would be removed out of their place. Both held positions of immense importance in the Church, but unless the children proved themselves worthy, these could not expect to obtain similar positions.

51. Now, I say unto you, my friends, let my servant Sidney Rigdon go on his journey, and make haste, and also proclaim the acceptable year of the Lord, and the gospel of salvation, as I shall give him utterance; and by your prayer of faith with one consent I will uphold him.

52. And let my servants Joseph Smith, Jun., and Frederick G. Williams make haste also, and it shall be given them even according to the prayer of faith; and inasmuch as you keep my sayings you shall not be confounded in this world, nor in the world to come.

53. And, verily I say unto you, that it is my will that you should hasten to translate my scriptures, and to obtain a knowledge of history, and of countries, and of kingdoms, of laws of God and man, and all this for the salvation of Zion. Amen.

8. SPECIAL INSTRUCTIONS.

51-3. Sidney Rigdon, the Prophet Joseph, and Frederick G. Williams are here instructed to go on missions, and the Prophet is, further, directed to finish his work on the Bible, and then take up the study of history, geography, politics, and law. Compare Section 88:79.

GENERAL NOTES

The study of history is very important to the Latter-day Saints, for it teaches lessons that should be imprinted on the minds of every one who belongs to a free and sovereign people. It teaches us, for instance, that men, who, like some of the Roman consuls, acquire positions by means of military power, are likely to be stricken down any moment. It teaches us that the Constitution of the United States only provides for the enlargement of the freedom enjoyed under the British Government. Of equal importance is the study of politics and law, for the Saints must be familiar with those subjects, as rulers with Christ in His kingdom.

"When the Prophet proceeded with the deliverance of his message to the world, he * * * proceeded to proclaim him [man] to be a son of God, not only through some means of adoption, but by the very nature of him. He proclaimed him to be an eternal intelligence as to his spirit, and that after the experience of the resurrection from the dead, he would be an immortal personage, a prince of heaven, an heir to all that God possesses, and a joint heir with Jesus Christ, capable of infinite progress and amazing possibilities" (B. H. Roberts, *Improvement Era*, Vol. XIII., p. 434).

SECTION 94.

REVELATION *given through Joseph Smith the Prophet, at Kirtland, Ohio, May 6, 1833.*———*Directions regarding the erection of a house for the work of the Presidency—A printing house to be built—Assignments of certain inheritances.*

AND again, verily I say unto you, my friends, a commandment I give unto you, that ye shall commence a work of laying out and preparing a beginning and foundation of the city of the stake of Zion, here in the land of Kirtland, beginning at my house.

2. And behold, it must be done according to the pattern which I have given unto you.

3. And let the first lot on the south be consecrated unto me

for the building of a house for the presidency, for the work of the presidency, in obtaining revelations; and for the work of the ministry of the presidency, in all things pertaining to the church and kingdom.

4. Verily I say unto you, that it shall be built fifty-five by sixty-five feet in the width thereof and in the length thereof, in the inner court.

5. And there shall be a lower court and a higher court, according to the pattern which shall be given unto you hereafter.

6. And it shall be dedicated unto the Lord from the foundation thereof, according to the order of the priesthood, according to the pattern which shall be given unto you hereafter.

7. And it shall be wholly dedicated unto the Lord for the work of the presidency.

8. And ye shall not suffer any unclean thing to come in unto it; and my glory shall be there, and my presence shall be there.

9. But if there shall come into it any unclean thing, my glory shall not be there; and my presence shall not come into it.

1-9. At a conference held March 23rd, 1833, a committee was appointed to purchase land in Kirtland, upon which to build up a Stake of Zion. Several large farms were bought, and among these was the French farm, so called after its owner. This had an excellent stone quarry and good material for brick-making. A city plant was surveyed, and the Saints gathered from surrounding States, until the Church in Kirtland numbered about 1,500 souls. The Lord, in this Revelation, instructed them to build the city of Kirtland Stake, beginning at His house. He also gave instructions for the consecration of a lot upon which to build a House of the Lord for the ministry of the First Presidency, "in all things pertaining to the church and kingdom." Further particulars about this house are given.

10. And again, verily I say unto you, the second lot on the south shall be dedicated unto me for the building of a house unto me, for the work of the printing of the translation of my scriptures, and all things whatsoever I shall command you.

11. And it shall be fifty-five by sixty-five feet in the width thereof and the length thereof, in the inner court; and there shall be a lower and a higher court.

12. And this house shall be wholly dedicated unto the Lord from the foundation thereof, for the work of the printing, in all

things whatsoever I shall command you, to be holy, undefiled, according to the pattern in all things as it shall be given unto you.

10-12. Another lot was to be dedicated for the building of a house in which to attend to the literary interests of the Church.

13. And on the third lot shall my servant Hyrum Smith receive his inheritance.

14. And on the first and second lots on the north shall my servants Reynolds Cahoon and Jared Carter receive their inheritances—

15. That they may do the work which I have appointed unto them, to be a committee to build mine houses, according to the commandment, which I, the Lord God, have given unto you.

16. These two houses are not to be built until I give unto you a commandment concerning them.

17. And now I give unto you no more at this time. Amen.

13-17. Hyrum Smith, Jared Carter, and Reynolds Cahoon had been appointed a committee to obtain subscriptions for the building of the houses of the Lord. They were to be provided with suitable residences near the Temple lot, but their houses were not to be built until the Lord should give further instructions (v. 16).

SECTION 95.

REVELATION *given through Joseph Smith the Prophet, at Kirtland, Ohio, June 1, 1833.——The people are chastened for their neglect in failing to build the house according to prior command—They are yet promised power to build it if they will abide by the Lord's commandments—Provision to be made for the School of the Apostles.*

VERILY, thus saith the Lord unto you whom I love, and whom I love I also chasten that their sins may be forgiven, for with the chastisement I prepare a way for their deliverance in all things out of temptation, and I have loved you—

2. Wherefore, ye must needs be chastened and stand rebuked before my face;

3. For ye have sinned against me a very grievous sin, in that ye have not considered the great commandment in all things, that I have given unto you concerning the building of mine house;

4. For the preparation wherewith I design to prepare mine apostles to prune my vineyard for the last time, that I may bring to pass my strange act, that I may pour out my Spirit upon all flesh—

5. But behold, verily I say unto you, that there are many who have been ordained among you, whom I have called but few of them are chosen.

6. They who are not chosen have sinned a very grievous sin, in that they are walking in darkness at noon-day.

7. And for this cause I gave unto you a commandment that you should call your solemn assembly, that your fastings and your mourning might come up into the ears of the Lord of Sabaoth, which is by interpretation, the creator of the first day, the beginning and the end.

8. Yea, verily I say unto you, I gave unto you a commandment that you should build a house, in the which house I design to endow those whom I have chosen with power from on high;

9. For this is the promise of the Father unto you; therefore I command you to tarry, even as mine apostles at Jerusalem.

10. Nevertheless, my servants sinned a very grievous sin; and contentions arose in the school of the prophets; which was very grievous unto me, saith your Lord; therefore I sent them forth to be chastened.

11. Verily I say unto you, it is my will that you should build a house. If you keep my commandments you shall have power to build it.

12. If you keep not my commandments, the love of the Father shall not continue with you, therefore you shall walk in darkness.

1-12. In a Revelation dated December 27th, 1832, the Lord instructed the assembled Elders to effect an organization and prepare every thing needful for the building of a house of God (Sec. 88:119-20). The Saints were few, and most of them were poor, and the preparations did not proceed satisfactorily. Hence they are severely rebuked, in this Revelation, for tardiness. Even poverty is no excuse for neglecting to obey a divine command, for when God directs His people to do something, He opens the way for them and provides the means, if He finds that they are willing to do what He requires.

On the 1st of June, 1833, Hyrum Smith, Reynolds Cahoon, and Jared Carter, the building committee (Sec. 94:14, 15), issued a circular to the Saints in which they urged them to exert themselves" to bring about the fulfilment of the command of the Lord concerning the establishing, or preparing of a house, wherein the Elders who have been commanded of the Lord so to do, may gather themselves together, and prepare all things, and call a solemn assembly, and treasure up words of wisdom, that they may go forth to the Gentiles for the last time" (*Hist. of the Church,* Vol. 1., p. 349). This, then, was the object for which this Temple was to be built.

Great interest in this undertaking was now aroused among the Saints, and this Revelation was received, in which the Lord (1) reproves His people for their neglect to begin building the temple (1-12); (2) commands them again to go to work (13-17).

1. TARDINESS REPROVED.

1-12. The Lord characterizes the failure of the Saints to begin work on the Temple without delay, as a "grievous sin." The command was given in December. Six months had passed, and no preparations had as yet been made. They had, so far, failed to do what they ought to have done.

4. *My strange act*] The purpose of the Lord was to prepare His Apostles (that is to say, His messengers) for the labor in the vineyard, for the last time, and bring to pass His "strange act" and pour out His Spirit on all flesh.

The expression quoted is from the Prophet Isaiah (28:21), where it refers to the fact that God would fight against His own people, because of their apostate condition. "Shall I not, as I have done to Samaria and her idols, so do to Jerusalem and her idols (Is. 10:11)? That was, in the estimation of the Jews, who did not realize their apostate condition, "strange." But in this dispensation our Lord was to perform an equally strange act, in revealing His marvelous plan of salvation and making war upon an apostate church which is boasting of its intimate relations with Deity. He was now waiting for the Saints to build that house, in which His messengers were to be prepared for that strange war and endowed with power from on High (v. 8). No wonder that He rebuked them for their tardiness!

10. *Contentions * * * in the school of the prophets*] This was another grievous sin. The Elders who attended this school had had marvelous manifestations of the presence of the Lord. At first they were united and willing to learn, but, gradually, contentions arose. No wonder they

were slow in keeping the command of God! Where contentions prevail, there can be no united effort in any direction.

13. Now here is wisdom, and the mind of the Lord—let the house be built, not after the manner of the world, for I give not unto you that ye shall live after the manner of the world;

14. Therefore, let it be built after the manner which I shall show unto three of you, whom ye shall appoint and ordain unto this power.

15. And the size thereof shall be fifty and five feet in width, and let it be sixty-five feet in length, in the inner court thereof.

16. And let the lower part of the inner court be dedicated unto me for your sacrament offering, and for your preaching, and your fasting, and your praying, and the offering up of your most holy desires unto me, saith your Lord.

17. And let the higher part of the inner court be dedicated unto me for the school of mine apostles, saith Son Ahman; or, in other words, Alphus; or, in other words, Omegus; even Jesus Christ your Lord. Amen.

2. GOD'S COMMAND TO BUILD REPEATED.

13-17. The plan of the Temple was to be revealed (v. 14), and the dimensions are stated 55 by 65 feet, inside measurement. There were to be two stories, or "courts"; the lower for Sacrament meetings, preachings, fasting, and praying, and the upper one for the school of the Apostles (v. 17).

15. *The size thereof shall be fifty and five feet in width, and * * * sixty-five feet in length*] The Tabernacle in the Wilderness was 45 feet in length and 15 feet in width and height. The Temple of Solomon was 90 feet by 30, and 45 feet high (*Cambridge Bible for Schools and Colleges,* I. Kings 6). The temple of Ezekiel's vision appears to have been 150 by 75 feet, outside measurement, while the inside measurement of the holiest place was 30 feet by 30, and that of the Holy, 60 feet by 30, supposing that the cubit of Ezekiel was the same as that of Solomon, and assuming it to be 18 inches.

17. *Son Ahman*] See Sec. 78:20.

*Alphus * * * Omegus*] The same as *Alpha* and *Omega* in Rev. 1:8 and 22:13; the first and the last letters of the Greek alphabet, meaning, "the first and the last." Our Savior is so called, to denote that He is the beginning and the ending: the author, preserver, and upholder of all things, and His glory the end of them. "Thou art worthy, O Lord, to receive glory and honor and power, for thou hast created all things, and for thy pleasure they are and were created" (Rev. 4:11).

GENERAL NOTES

On the 3rd of June, 1833, at a conference of High Priests, assembled in the Translating Room, the dimensions of the Temple were discussed. That was an important question to a community with very limited financial resources. The Prophet, however, had a Revelation on that point, and that was sufficient for the brethren. It was to be fifty-five by sixty-five feet. It should not be built smaller. By the same Conference, the Prophet Joseph, Sidney Rigdon, and Frederick G. Williams were authorized to obtain the first drawings for the building (*Hist. of the Church*, Vol. I., p. 352).

SECTION 96.

REVELATION *given to Enoch [Joseph Smith the Prophet], showing the order of the City or Stake of Zion, Shinehah [Kirtland], at Kirtland, Ohio, June 4, 1833. Given as an ensample to the Saints in Kirtland. For explanation of unusual names see heading to Section 78. The occasion was a conference of High Priests; and the chief subject of consideration was that of certain lands possessed by the Church.——The Kirtland Stake of Zion to be made strong—Admission to the United Order.*

BEHOLD, I say unto you, here is wisdom, whereby ye may know how to act concerning this matter, for it is expedient in me that this stake that I have set for that strength of Zion should be made strong.

2. Therefore, let my servant Ahashdah [Newel K. Whitney] take charge of the place which is named among you, upon which I design to build mine holy house.

3. And again, let it be divided into lots, according to wisdom, for the benefit of those who seek inheritances, as it shall be determined in council among you.

4. Therefore, take heed that ye see to this matter, and that portion that is necessary to benefit mine order, for the purpose of bringing forth my word to the children of men.

5. For behold, verily I say unto you, this is the most expedient in me, that my word should go forth unto the children of men, for the purpose of subduing the hearts of the children of men for your good. Even so. Amen.

On the 4th of June, 1833, the High Priests met in Conference, in the Translating Room, to consider what disposition to make of the French farm, which, together with other real estate, had been bought for the Church. The Conference was not able to agree on a manager, but all were willing to submit the question to the Lord, in prayer. In answer to their petitions, they received this Revelation, in which the Lord directed them (1) to give Bishop Newel K. Whitney charge of the farm (1-5); and (2) to accept John Johnson as a member of the United Order (6-9).

1. BISHOP WHITNEY IN CHARGE.

2. *Ahashdah*] See Sec. 82:11.

Take charge] It was eminently proper to give the Bishop charge of this matter, for it is the special calling of a Bishop to manage the temporal affairs of the kingdom of God. When, in the Church in Jerusalem, the impartiality of the distribution of the funds of the Saints was questioned, the Apostles moved that seven men be appointed to take charge (Acts 6:3). This was done. These seven men were Bishops, in the true meaning of that word—"overseer,"* not Deacons, as generally supposed.

4. *Mine order*] The United Order.

For the purpose of bringing forth my word] That was the purpose of the United Order, and of every institution of the Church. Everything else is, to the Church, of secondary importance. The Church itself exists only for the glory of God and the salvation of the children of men.

6. And again, verily I say unto you, it is wisdom and expedient in me, that my servant Zombre [John Johnson] whose offering I have accepted, and whose prayers I have heard, unto whom I give a promise of eternal life inasmuch as he keepeth my commandments from henceforth—

7. For he is a descendant of Seth [Joseph] and a partaker of the blessings of the promise made unto his fathers—

8. Verily I say unto you, it is expedient in me that he should become a member of the order, that he may assist in bringing forth my word unto the children of men.

9. Therefore ye shall ordain him unto this blessing, and he shall seek diligently to take away incumbrances that are upon the house named among you, that he may dwell therein. Even so. Amen.

---

* Bishop is from the Greek Episcopos, which means "overseer," "superintendent," "inspector."

2. John Johnson Admitted to the Order.

6-9. The Lord instructs the brethren to receive John Johnson as a member of the United Order, as He had instructed them to receive Frederick G. Williams (Sec. 92:1), and others (Sec. 82:11). His special duty would be to find means whereby to lift the indebtedness on a certain property, perhaps the French farm (v. 1).

General Notes

John Johnson was one of the highly favored men in the early days of this dispensation, who did not remain faithful to the end, though at one time he was valiant in the cause.

He had seen his wife miraculously healed by the Prophet Joseph. He opened his home at Hiram to Joseph and his family, while the Prophet was engaged in his great Biblical work. He defended Joseph against a murderous mob, risking his own life. In fact, his collar bone was broken, in the conflict, but he was instantly healed under the hands of David Whitmer. He became a member of the first High Council, and he saw two of his sons, Luke S. and Lyman E., rise to the exalted position of members of the Council of the Twelve Apostles. And yet, when the spirit of apostasy possessed so many Church members in Kirtland, in 1837 and 1838, he, as well as his sons, were affected by it. He died in Kirtland, July 30th, 1843, at the age of 64 years.

SECTION 97.

Revelation *given through Joseph Smith the Prophet at Kirtland, Ohio, August 2, 1833. Ten days before this time the corner stones of the Lord's House in Kirtland were laid, after the order of the Holy Priesthood. See History of the Church, vol. 1, p. 400. This revelation deals particularly with the affairs of the Saints in Zion, Jackson County, Missouri.——Many of the labors of the Saints in Zion are commended—Commendation of the school in Zion—The Lord's will that a house should be built unto him in the land of Zion—Great blessings promised to Zion if her people shall obey this commandment—Zion defined as the pure in heart—Zion to escape the indignation of the Lord if the people are faithful, otherwise many calamities to fall upon them.*

VERILY I say unto you my friends, I speak unto you with my voice, even the voice of my Spirit, that I may show unto you my will concerning your brethren in the land of Zion, many of whom are truly humble and are seeking diligently to learn wisdom and to find truth.

2. Verily, verily I say unto you, blessed are such, for they shall obtain; for I, the Lord, show mercy unto all the meek, and upon all whomsoever I will, that I may be justified when I shall bring them unto judgment.

A brief statement of the condition of the Church at this time may be of some help to the younger students of these Revelations.

In Kirtland, the work on the Temple had commenced. On the 5th of June, 1833, George A. Smith hauled the first load of stone for that sacred building, and Hyrum Smith and Reynolds Cahoon began digging the trench for the walls, which they, later, finished. On the 6th it was decided, by a conference of High Priests, that the Building Committee should obtain stone, brick, lumber, etc., and begin building immediately. On the 23rd of July, the cornerstones were laid. The work was now being prosecuted with vigor, until the building was completed. It was dedicated on March 27th, 1836.

On the 25th of June, 1833, the First Presidency sent letters of instruction to William W. Phelps, Edward Partridge, and the brethren in Zion, and enclosed plans for the future city of Zion and its temples. The first city plat was to be one mile square, divided into blocks containing ten acres each, except the middle range of blocks, which were to contain fifteen acres each. All the blocks, except those containing schools and public buildings, were to be divided into half-acre lots, four by twenty rods each. The dwelling-houses were to stand twenty-four feet from the street. The plat would accommodate from eighteen to twenty thousand inhabitants, and they would need twenty-five buildings for schools and public worship. These buildings would be temples, and none would be less than eighty-seven feet by sixty-one. There were to be no barns or stables in the city, but these were to be situated on lands laid off for that purpose, on the north and south sides of the settlement. The farms would be situated east and west of the city, but the tiller of the soil, as well as the mechanic, merchant, and others, would live in the city. "When this square is thus laid off and supplied, lay off another in the same way," the Prophet wrote, "and so fill up the world in these last days" (*Documentary History,* Vol. 1:357).

What an admirable view of the future cities of the world! For this plan will certainly be adopted when civilization shall have advanced far enough to appreciate it. In such a city the farmer will enjoy every advantage of city life; and yet there will be no slums, and none of the disadvantages of the large cities, in which corrupt politicians, criminals, and dishonest business methods flourish.

Kirtland was growing, notwithstanding the opposition stirred up by apostates. Sidney Rigdon wrote, July 2nd:—"Doors are opening continually for proclaiming the gospel. The spirit of bitterness among the people is fast subsiding, and a spirit of inquiry is taking its place."

The Saints in Missouri, on the 6th of April, 1833, celebrated the third anniversary of the organization of the Church, by a conference at the Ferry, on Big Blue River, a stream a few miles west of Independence. At this time the gospel had been preached in nearly all the States of the Union, and many flourishing branches had been organized. The Saints were contemplating the future of Zion with joy.

In the month of July, however, a mob in Jackson County, led by a Rev. Pixley, began to move against the Saints. This clergyman had published false stories about them, in order to create a hostile sentiment. He carried from house to house a tract, entitled, "Beware of False Prophets," calculated to excite violence against the Church. This was followed by the publication of a manifesto calling for a mass meeting at Independence on the 20th of July, 1833, in which to decide on a course to pursue against the Saints. That the *politicians* of Jackson County eagerly embraced the opportunity of utilizing the adverse sentiment created by religious bigots, is evident from the signatures affixed to the manifesto. The most prominent names are those of political office-holders, such as jailers, justices of the peace, judges, a postmaster, a constable, a colonel, a judge of the court, an Indian agent, and others. In this manifesto the Saints were falsely accused of having invited negroes and mulattoes to become "Mormons" and settle in Missouri; also to have declared that they would, sooner or later, "have possession of our lands for an inheritance." The first of these charges was without any foundation whatever; the second, seemingly, had a foundation of truth, but it was only half a truth and therefore served the same purpose as a falsehood. The Saints had been promised land in Missouri for an inheritance, but only by *purchase;* nobody was to be injured.

On the 20th of July, the mass meeting convened. Inflamed by falsehood strewn broadcast by religious fanatics and political office-seekers, the meeting demanded the discontinuance of the printing office, the closing of the store, and the cessation of all mechanical labor. When the brethren refused to comply with this law-defying dictum, the mob broke down the printing establishment, seized Edward Partridge and Charles Allen, daubed them with tar from head to foot and covered them with feathers, on the public square. Others were frightened from their homes by threats and yells. On the 23rd, the very same day on which the corner stones of the Kirtland Temple were laid, the brethren in Missouri, in order to prevent bloodshed, signed an agreement with the mob leaders to leave the country before the 1st of April, 1834. The brethren immediately sent Oliver Cowdery to Kirtland to report to the First Presidency. He arrived there early in September, 1833.

The Revelation in Sec. 97 was received before the arrival in Kirtland of Oliver Cowdery, and, consequently, before the Prophet knew any particulars of the storm of persecution that raged in the land of Zion.

The Lord (1) states the subject of his Revelation (1-2); (2) expresses his approval of the School of the Prophets in Zion, and of Parley P. Pratt, its superintendent (3-9); (3) instructs the Prophet that a Temple must be built in Zion (10-17); (4) promises that Zion shall prosper, if the Saints there will obey His commandments (18-21); (5) threatens the wicked with vengeance (22-24); while (6) Zion shall escape, if the Saints observe to do according to the Word of God (25-28).

1. THE SUBJECT OF THE REVELATION.

1-2. The Lord, as has been noted, showed to the Prophet Joseph His will concerning the Saints in Zion, before he had received word of the rising of the mob and the agreement the Saints had signed, to leave Jackson County, but when Oliver Cowdery arrived, the Saints in Kirtland were not taken by surprise entirely, their minds having been prepared, by revelation, for the sad tidings of which he was the bearer. Many of the Saints, the Prophet was told (v. 1), were truly humble and willing to learn, and they would find mercy; others were not humble, and they would be brought into judgment (v. 2).

3. Behold, I say unto you, concerning the school in Zion, I, the Lord, am well pleased that there should be a school in Zion, and also with my servant Parley P. Pratt, for he abideth in me.

4. And inasmuch as he continueth to abide in me he shall continue to preside over the school in the land of Zion until I shall give unto him other commandments.

5. And I will bless him with a multiplicity of blessings, in expounding all scriptures and mysteries to the edification of the school, and of the church in Zion.

6. And to the residue of the school, I, the Lord, am willing to show mercy; nevertheless, there are those that must needs be chastened, and their works shall be made known.

7. The ax is laid at the root of the trees; and every tree that bringeth not forth good fruit shall be hewn down and cast into the fire. I, the Lord, have spoken it.

8. Verily I say unto you, all among them who know their hearts are honest, and are broken, and their spirits contrite, and are willing to observe their covenants by sacrifice—yea, every sacrifice which I, the Lord, shall command—they are accepted of me.

9. For I, the Lord, will cause them to bring forth as a very fruitful tree which is planted in a goodly land, by a pure stream, that yieldeth much precious fruit.

2. The School in Zion Approved.

3-9. That the Lord begins His Revelation concerning the Saints in Zion with a word of commendation of the school and its superintendent, Parley P. Pratt, is not accidental. The school was a very important institution of the Church. Parley P. Pratt had given his services to the school under very trying circumstances. The students met in the open air, and he walked six miles, sometimes barefoot, in order to attend. God accepted and acknowledged his labor and sacrifices, in this manner.

5. *A multitude of blessings*] The Lord promises His servant many blessings as a reward for his faithfulness.

6. *The residue of the school*] There were about sixty scholars, and they spent a great part of the time in prayer, prophesying, and the exercise of spiritual gifts.

7. *The axe is laid at the root of the trees*] The "dead trees" were to be cut down. The axe of persecution had already been laid to the root.

10. Verily I say unto you, that it is my will that a house should be built unto me in the land of Zion, like unto the pattern which I have given you.

11. Yea, let it be built speedily, by the tithing of my people.

12. Behold, this is the tithing and the sacrifice which I, the Lord, require at their hands, that there may be a house built unto me for the salvation of Zion—

13. For a place of thanksgiving for all saints, and for a place of instruction for all those who are called to the work of the ministry in all their several callings and offices;

14. That they may be perfected in the understanding of their ministry, in theory, in principle, and in doctrine, in all things pertaining to the kingdom of God on the earth, the keys of which kingdom have been conferred upon you.

15. And inasmuch as my people build a house unto me in the name of the Lord, and do not suffer any unclean thing to come into it, that it be not defiled, my glory shall rest upon it;

16. Yea, and my presence shall be there, for I will come into it, and all the pure in heart that shall come into it shall see God.

17. But if it be defiled I will not come into it, and my glory will not be there; for I will not come into unholy temples.

3. A Temple to be Built in Zion.

10-17. In these paragraphs the Lord informs the Saints that a Temple was to be built in Zion, according to the pattern given by revelation (v. 10). It was to be built speedily (v. 11). It was to be a "place of thanksgiving for all Saints," and a "place of instruction" for those who were called to the ministry (v. 13). No unclean thing was to enter it, and on that condition, "my glory," the Lord says, "shall rest upon it" (v. 15) as upon the Tabernacle in the wilderness (Ex. 40:34), and the Presence of God would be there (v. 16).

God was, if we may say so reverently, anxious that His people should rear a Temple in which they could be endowed with power from on high before the conflict with the adversary. The history of Temples teaches us that the people of God have been strong, or weak, in proportion to the faithfulness with which they have attended to their sanctuaries. The history of the Temple of Jerusalem is, as Dr. Joseph Angus, in his *Bible Handbook,* notes, "an index to the history of the Jews. When it fell, they were scattered; as it rose from its ruins, they gathered round it again; and history dates the captivity, with equal accuracy, from the destruction of the Temple, or from the first capture of Jerusalem." Speaking of the Temples in this dispensation, someone has declared that the completion of the Nauvoo Temple was the salvation of the Church from annihilation, although the Saints were forced to flee into the desert. Since the completion of the Salt Lake Temple, the adversary has had less power to injure the Church than he had before. If we remember that the Temples are the palaces of God, where His Presence is manifested, we can understand why, when the adversary was marshalling his forces against the Church, our Lord urged the Saints to build the Temple speedily. We can also understand why the evil one planned to have them scattered before they could rear that sacred edifice.

18. And, now, behold, if Zion do these things she shall prosper, and spread herself and become very glorious, very great, and very terrible.

19. And the nations of the earth shall honor her, and shall say: Surely Zion is the city of our God, and surely Zion cannot fall, neither be moved out of her place, for God is there, and the hand of the Lord is there;

20. And he hath sworn by the power of his might to be her salvation and her high tower.

21. Therefore, verily, thus saith the Lord, let Zion rejoice, for this is Zion—THE PURE IN HEART; therefore, let Zion rejoice, while all the wicked shall mourn.

4. PROSPERITY PROMISED.

18-21. The promise is definite: "If Zion do these things, she shall prosper" (v. 18).

Parley P. Pratt, in his *Autobiography*, writes:

"This Revelation was not complied with by the leaders of the Church in Missouri as a whole, notwithstanding many were humble and faithful; therefore, the threatened judgment was poured out to the uttermost, as the history of the five following years shows."

22. For behold, and lo, vengeance cometh speedily upon the ungodly as the whirlwind; and who shall escape it?

23. The Lord's scourge shall pass over by night and by day, and the report thereof shall vex all people; yea, it shall not be stayed until the Lord come;

24. For the indignation of the Lord is kindled against their abominations and all their wicked works.

5. VENGEANCE OF THE WICKED.

22-4. Students of the prophetic writings of the Bible are aware of the fact that the prophets, while predicting the calamities that were to overtake Israel, also foretold the fate that would befall their enemies. The people of God would be redeemed in due time, while the enemies would be utterly destroyed.

23. *Scourge shall pass over*] A mixed metaphor, also found in Isaiah (28:15, 18), referring to the invasion of Israel by the Assyrian army, in spite of the secret alliance between Israel and Egypt, which the leaders of the people had entered into and ratified as a compact with death and hell. The country would, nevertheless, be invaded. The enemies of the Saints had also made a compact, but that did not save the State from the "scourge," when the horrors of the Civil War rolled over the country.

25. Nevertheless, Zion shall escape if she observe to do all things whatsoever I have commanded her.

26. But if she observe not to do whatsoever I have commanded her, I will visit her according to all her works, with sore affliction, with pestilence, with plague, with sword, with vengeance, with devouring fire.

27. Nevertheless, let it be read this once to her ears, that I, the Lord, have accepted of her offering; and if she sin no more none of these things shall come upon her;

28. And I will bless her with blessings, and multiply a mul-

tiplicity of blessings upon her, and upon her generations forever and ever, saith the Lord your God. Amen.

6. ZION SHALL ESCAPE.

25-8. This is a promise that the Saints would escape the scourge, if they would do what God commanded them. He had prepared a refuge for His people, in the mountains, and, in the language of Isaiah, He urged the Church, "Enter thou into thy chambers, and shut thy doors about thee, hide thyself, as it were for a little moment, until the indignation be overpast" (Isaiah 26:20). Or, in the language of the Apocalypse, the Church, under the protection of the wings of a great eagle, fled into the wilderness, "into her place," where she "is nourished for a time, and times, and half a time, from the face of the serpent" (Rev. 12:14). The Latter-day Saints, from this experience in the Eastern States, learned the necessity of obedience to the Word of the Lord. They followed their divinely-appointed leaders into the Valleys of the Mountains, and, as a consequence, they have had blessings showered upon them, as a people and as individuals. They did escape the scourge of the Civil War.

GENERAL NOTES

"We are infinitely more blessed by the persecution and injustice we have suffered, than we could have been, if we had remained in our habitations from which we have been driven—than if we had been suffered to occupy our farms, gardens, stores, mills, machinery, and everything we had in our former possessions. Had we not been persecuted, we would now be in the midst of the wars and bloodshed that are desolating the Nation" (Brigham Young, *Jour. of Dis.,* Vol. X., p. 38).

It has been customary among a certain class of critics of the Latter-day Saints to say that the Church itself was largely responsible for the persecutions through which it passed in the early years of its existence. The saints, they claim, were undesirable citizens, who even deemed it their privilege to appropriate for their own use the property of their peaceful neighbors. For that reason, it is alleged, they were driven from Jackson County, Missouri, in 1833, and from Nauvoo, Illinois, in 1846. This is not true. Even non-"Mormons" admit that the Saints in Missouri and Illinois were innocent of wrong-doing.*

° An article illustrating this, is quoted in a publication called "The Journal of History." It is by one Alexander Majors, a son of Benjamin Majors, who was a member of the committee that represented the lawless crowd by which the Saints were driven from Independence. In his book called, "Seventy Years on the Frontier," he says, in part, as quoted:

"They [the Saints] established their headquarters at Independence, where some of their leading elders were located. There they set up a printing office, the first that was established within one hundred and fifty miles of Independence, and commenced printing their Church literature, which was very distasteful to the members and leaders of other religious denominations, the community being composed of

SECTION 98.

REVELATION *given through Joseph Smith the Prophet, at Kirtland, Ohio, August 6, 1833.——Patience in persecution enjoined—Good to come out of affliction—The constitutional law of the land to be supported by the Saints—Good men to be supported for secular office—The Saints to proclaim peace— Offenders in the Church at Kirtland reproved—The Saints to forgive their enemies—When resistance is justified—The Saints to be blessed if they will forgive their enemies.*

VERILY, I say unto you my friends, fear not, let your hearts be comforted; yea, rejoice evermore, and in everything give thanks;

2. Waiting patiently on the Lord, for your prayers have entered into the ears of the Lord of Sabaoth, and are recorded with this seal and testament—the Lord hath sworn and decreed that they shall be granted.

3. Therefore, he giveth this promise unto you, with an immutable covenant that they shall be fulfilled; and all things wherewith you have been afflicted shall work together for your good, and to my name's glory, saith the Lord.

Methodists, Baptists of two different orders, Presbyterians of two different orders, and Catholics, and a denomination calling themselves Christians.

"In that day and age it was regarded as blasphemous or sacrilegious for anyone to claim that he had met angels and received from them new revelations, and the religious portion of the community especially, was very much incensed and aroused at the audacity of any person claiming such interviews from the invisible world * * * Finally the citizens, and particularly the religious portion of them, made up their minds that it was wrong to allow them to be printing their literature and preaching, as it might have a bad effect upon the rising generation; and on July 4, 1833, there was quite a gathering of citizens, and a mob was formed to tear down their printing office."

*   *   *   *

"It has been claimed by people who were highly colored in their prejudice against the Mormons, that they were bad citizens; that they stole whatever they could get their hands on, and were not law-abiding. This is not true with reference to their citizenship in Jackson County, where they got their first kick, and as severe a one as they ever received, if not the most severe. There was not an officer among them, all the offices in the county being in the hands of their enemies, and if one had stolen a chicken, he could and would have been brought to grief for so doing, but it is my opinion that there is nothing in the county records to show that a Mormon was ever charged with any misdemeanor in the way of violation of the laws for the protection of property."

God is continuing to reveal His will concerning His people. As Section Ninety-seven was addressed more especially to the Saints in Missouri, so this Section is given to those in Kirtland and the East, but both contain instructions applicable to the Saints anywhere and at all times.

In this Revelation our Lord (1) gives the Saints a glorious promise (1-3); (2) instructs them to be law-abiding citizens (4-10); (3) commands them to forsake evil and cleave to that which is good (11-17); (4) offers consolation and warning (18-22); (5) gives instructions concerning how to treat enemies (23-48).

1. A GLORIOUS PROMISE.

1-3. This Revelation begins with a glorious promise. "Fear not!" "Let your hearts be comforted!" "Rejoice" and "give thanks," notwithstanding the trials that were coming; wait patiently on the Lord, for your prayers are heard (v. 2), and the promise is that all things "shall work together for your good, and to my name's glory" (v. 3).

3. *All things wherewith you are afflicted*] The meaning is that even the evil designs of men, in the hands of the Masterworkman, will turn out for the benefit of the people of God, and for His glory. The divine Will overrules all things for the *final* good of His children. We can see this exemplified in the history of the Latter-day Saints.

4. And now, verily I say unto you concerning the laws of the land, it is my will that my people should observe to do all things whatsoever I command them.

5. And that law of the land which is constitutional, supporting that principle of freedom in maintaining rights and privileges, belongs to all mankind, and is justifiable before me.

6. Therefore, I, the Lord, justify you, and your brethren of my church, in befriending that law which is the constitutional law of the land;

7. And as pertaining to law of man, whatsoever is more or less than this, cometh of evil.

8. I, the Lord God, make you free, therefore ye are free indeed; and the law also maketh you free.

9. Nevertheless, when the wicked rule the people mourn.

10. Wherefore, honest men and wise men should be sought for diligently, and good men and wise men ye should observe to uphold; otherwise whatsoever is less than these cometh of evil.

2. THE SAINTS MUST BE LAW-ABIDING.

4-10. In this section, our Lord reveals the important truth that it is the duty of the Saints to be loyal, law-abiding citizens. Two obligations are imposed upon them. They must (a) keep the Constitutional laws of the land, and (b) use their influence for the election of good officials. This Revelation should be studied closely.

4. *My people should observe to do all things whatsoever I command them*] That is the great, fundamental principle in the kingdom of God. God's law comes first, and if man, either through an autocratic ruler or through a representative assembly, should make laws contrary to the law of God, it would be the duty of men to keep the divine law, and let the consequence follow. Peter and John fearlessly appealed to the Sanhedrin, when that Jewish court made it juridically unlawful to preach in the name of the Nazarene. They said, "Whether it be right in the sight of God to hearken unto you more than unto God, judge ye" (Acts 4:19). Peter, when brought before the Sanhedrin for having ignored its injunction, being, in a modern term, in contempt of court, again asserted that it was his duty to obey God "rather than men" (Acts 5:29). All Christians are agreed on this.

Sometimes, however, a difference of opinion may arise as to whether a certain line of conduct is in accordance with the divine law, or not. There are as many views, almost, on that question, as there are religious denominations. How can a legislative assembly, then, be certain that it does not trespass by law-making contrary to the divine laws? By not enacting any laws on religious subjects, but leaving such matters to the conscience of each individual, and by protecting everyone in the exercise of what he conceives to be his religious duty. There can be only one exception to this rule. If anyone should claim the right, in the name of religion, to injure his fellowmen, or unlawfully deprive any of them of life, property, honor, or liberty to pursue lawful happiness, it would be the duty of the State to interfere.

5. *Law * * * which is constitutional*] The first duty of loyal citizens is to keep the commandments of God. Their next is to keep every law of the land which is constitutional. In the United States, every State makes its own laws, and Congress legislates for all. It is the duty of the Saints to keep the laws which are Constitutional; that is, which do not conflict with the Constitution. If either Congress or a State Legislature should enact an unconstitutional law, there are certain constitutional means provided by which it can be set aside. Loyal citizens will avail themselves of those means, if necessary, in preference to revolutionary measures. If there is any doubt as to the constitutionality of a law, the Supreme Court will pass upon it, if appealed to for a decision, and when the Supreme Court has spoken, the doubt is removed, and the controversy is ended.

7. *Whatsoever is more or less * * * evil*] Laws in conflict with the Constitution are not for the benefit of the people, and are, therefore, evil. The Prophet Joseph, in an address to the City Council of Nauvoo, delivered February 25th, 1843, said, in part:

"Powers not delegated to the States, or reserved from the States, are Constitutional. The Constitution acknowledges that the people have all power not reserved to itself * * * The Constitution is not a law to us, but it makes provision for us whereby we can make laws. Where it provides that no one shall be hindered from worshiping God according to his own conscience, is a law. No legislature can enact a law to prohibit it. The Constitution provides to regulate bodies of men and not individuals" (*Hist. of the Church*, Vol. V., pp. 289-90).

This embodies a general principle, by which laws can be tested as to their constitutionality.

8. *I, the Lord God, make you free*] The Constitution is the instrument through which God has secured and guaranteed the freedom of those of His children who are living under its provisions.

9. *Nevertheless, when the wicked rule, the people mourn*] Good officers of the law are essential to freedom. For, in the hands of wicked men, even good laws can be perverted and made to serve evil purposes.

10. *Honest men, and wise men should be sought for diligently*] The first duty of a loyal citizen is to obey the laws of God and the Constitutional enactments of man. The second is, to use his influence for the election of honest, wise, and good men to the offices created by law, and to uphold such men in their administration. In the United States the people elect legislatures to make their laws, executives to make them effective, and judges to interpret them. Honest, wise, and good men are needed in these branches of the government. Men of an opposite character will endanger the liberty guaranteed by the Constitution. The people of democratic countries may yet have to take up for serious consideration the question whether the aims and purposes of the Constitution are best served by party governments; or whether some better method of securing the offices for honest, wise and good men cannot be found.

11. And I give unto you a commandment, that ye shall forsake all evil and cleave unto all good, that ye shall live by every word which proceedeth forth out of the mouth of God.

12. For he will give unto the faithful line upon line, precept upon precept; and I will try you and prove you herewith.

13. And whoso layeth down his life in my cause, for my name's sake, shall find it again, even life eternal.

14. Therefore, be not afraid of your enemies, for I have decreed in my heart, saith the Lord, that I will prove you in all

things, whether you will abide in my covenant, even unto death, that you may be found worthy.

15. For if ye will not abide in my covenant ye are not worthy of me.

16. Therefore, renounce war and proclaim peace, and seek diligently to turn the hearts of the children to their fathers, and the hearts of the fathers to the children.

17. And again, the hearts of the Jews unto the prophets, and the prophets unto the Jews; lest I come and smite the whole earth with a curse, and all flesh be consumed before me.

3. FORSAKE EVIL; CLEAVE TO GOOD.

11-17. It is the will of God concerning the Saints that they shall forsake *all* evil and cleave unto *all* good (v. 11). *All* evil includes everything that is contrary to the will of God and detrimental to the advancement of His children in holiness before Him. The Saints must forsake not only the sins and crimes common in the world, but a great many evils which are not recognized by the world as evils. Evil companionship, evil amusements, evil aspirations for worldly power and honor, evil conversation, evil thoughts, and evil sentiments are all included. *All* good includes all that is in harmony with the will of God, no matter whence it comes. Saints cannot be clannish or partisan. They must be cosmopolitans, for there is some good everywhere for them to recognize and to cleave to.

Obedience to this commandment opens the door to the revelations of God—line upon line, precept upon precept (v. 12). It enables the Saints to endure trials and persecution (v. 13); to renounce war and proclaim peace, and to devote themselves to their special mission of uniting the hearts of fathers and children (v. 16), Jews and Gentiles (v. 17).

12. *He will give unto the faithful,* etc.] We are here taught that divine revelation is dependent on obedience to the commandment in Verse 11. If we forsake evil and cleave to that which is good, the channel of communication between God and us will be kept open, and we shall be enabled to "live by every word that proceedeth forth out of the mouth of God." But if we forsake good and cling to evil, the channel will be closed.

13. *Whoso layeth down his life in my cause * * * life eternal*] This is an intimation that the Saints would be tried even unto death. The storm of persecution had already broken loose over the Church, in Jackson County, though the brethren in Kirtland were not yet aware of it. When the time for the supreme test came, they had this comforting Revelation.

14. *Be not afraid of your enemies*] The Saints were not at the mercy of the enemy, any more than was Job. Their heavenly Father was trying

them, to see if they would abide in His covenant, "that you may be found worthy." The Prophet, in a letter dated December 5, 1833, and addressed to the Saints in Zion, encouraged them to have faith in God, and endurance. He wrote:

"Call to mind a Daniel, the three Hebrew children, Jeremiah, Paul, Stephen, and many others, too numerous to mention, who were stoned, sawn asunder, tempted, slain with the sword, and wandered about in sheep skins and goat skins, being destitute, afflicted, tormented, of whom the world was not worthy. They wandered in deserts and in mountains, and hid in dens and caves of the earth; yet they all obtained a good report through faith; and amidst all their afflictions they rejoiced that they were counted worthy to receive persecution for Christ's sake" (*Hist. of the Church*, Vol. I., p. 450).

16. *Renounce war and proclaim peace*] If the people of God obey the commandment to forsake evil and cleave unto all good (v. 11), they will labor for the abolition of militarism and the establishment of the king-dom of peace. There is no greater evil than war; there is no greater blessing than peace. Lucifer is the prince of war. The Son of God is the Prince of Peace.

Frank Crane, in an article in *The Christian Work* of September 2nd, 1916, strikingly depicted war as the work of the adversary of man, by stating what he (Crane) would do, "if he were the devil." The following paragraphs from that article are quoted:

"Here is murder, not the cheap and shameful knifing or shooting by the drunken thug in some dark alley, but murder beautiful, magnificent, where a thousand men are dismembered by one salvo, or lie quivering and shrieking on the ground after a charge; where trenches swarm with human creatures going mad with noise and terror, sitting with gangrened wounds in muddy water, suffocated with the stink of their dead companions, fly-blown and maggot-eaten by their side, or falling asleep from exhaustion while rats eat their living cheeks and lips."

*   *   *   *

"Add to murder the cruelty of vain and petty officers driving their men into sure destruction, and horrors of the civilians hunted from their homes, shot down at their own thresholds or burned alive in the fire of their own goods, and the old women brained for sheer deviltry, and the nameless crimes committed upon the young women, and their children stamped out by military heel like scampering mice; and over all the blur or unchecked hate, the sound of blasphemy, the ribald songs of the raging warmen, the futile prayers smashed by mailed fists upon the palsied mouths that utter them, the whole hoarse rattle and roar swinging up in a majestic orchestration and hallelujah chorus worthy of hell's gala day."

*   *   *   *

"I would glorify all this diabolism of destruction with the utmost enthusiasm, bands playing, men singing, priests and preachers telling

how they were serving Jesus, statesmen vaunting the bravery and manliness of murderers, women adoring them and praying for them, and
little children standing by admiring their gay uniforms."

Can there be any doubt that the Lord is in earnest, when He says,
"Renounce war and proclaim peace?"

Turn the hearts of the children, etc.] This is the great mission of the
Church of Jesus Christ of Latter-day Saints. War is one of the evils they
must forsake; peace is one of the blessings they must cleave to. For they
are to link together the hearts of the ancestors and their descendants.
They are to turn the hearts of the Jews to their Prophets, and this is
essentially a work of peace. It is temple work, and men of blood cannot
build, or administer in, temples.

17. *Lest I come and smite the whole earth with a curse*] Unless
the people of God are faithful to their trust as the *heralds of peace,*
the whole Earth will be smitten with a curse—even the curse of war—
"and all flesh be consumed before me." Such a condition would not
permit of work for the dead in the temples of God.

18. Let not your hearts be troubled; for in my Father's
house are many mansions, and I have prepared a place for you;
and where my Father and I am, there ye shall be also.

19. Behold, I, the Lord, am not well pleased with many who
are in the church at Kirtland;

20. For they do not forsake their sins, and their wicked
ways, the pride of their hearts, and their covetousness, and all
their detestable things, and observe the words of wisdom and
eternal life which I have given unto them.

21. Verily I say unto you, that I, the Lord, will chasten them
and will do whatsoever I list, if they do not repent and observe
all things whatsoever I have said unto them.

22. And again I say unto you, if ye observe to do whatsoever
I command you, I, the Lord, will turn away all wrath and indignation from you, and the gates of hell shall not prevail against
you.

4. CONSOLATION AND WARNING.

18-22. *Let not your hearts be troubled*] This is consolation. It is
quoted from the last discourse of our Lord, before His crucifixion. On
that occasion He said to His faithful disciples, "Let not your heart
be troubled" (John 14:1). Now in view of the approaching trials of the
Saints, He repeats that comforting exhortation.

18. *Many mansions*] Many "dwellings," many "homes." There is
room for all, and there are places suitable for all.

Where my Father and I am * * * *also*] This is a promise of celestial glory, for that is the glory in which the Father dwells. Comp. Sec. 76:62.

19. *I, the Lord, am not well pleased*] This was a warning to the Saints in Kirtland.

20-1. The reason for the divine displeasure is here stated. They do not forsake their sins, their wicked ways, the pride of their hearts, their covetousness, etc. They do not observe the Word of Wisdom; and, as a consequence, they will be chastised. This should be a warning to the Saints everywhere, at all times. It is, perhaps, easy to forsake grosser sins which are disapproved by law and social requirements; to forsake pride and covetousness, and similar sins may be more difficult. Many do not even know that they are sins.

22. *The Lord will turn away all wrath and indignation*] This is the reward of obedience.

23. Now, I speak unto you concerning your families—if men will smite you, or your families, once, and ye bear it patiently and revile not against them, neither seek revenge, ye shall be rewarded;

24. But if ye bear it not patiently, it shall be accounted unto you as being meted out as a just measure unto you.

25. And again, if your enemy shall smite you the second time, and you revile not against your enemy, and bear it patiently, your reward shall be an hundred-fold.

26. And again, if he shall smite you the third time, and ye bear it patiently, your reward shall be doubled unto you four-fold;

27. And these three testimonies shall stand against your enemy if he repent not, and shall not be blotted out.

28. And now, verily I say unto you, if that enemy shall escape my vengeance, that he be not brought into judgment before me, then ye shall see to it that ye warn him in my name, that he come no more upon you, neither upon your family, even your children's children unto the third and fourth generation.

29. And then, if he shall come upon you or your children, or your children's children unto the third and fourth generation, I have delivered thine enemy into thine hands;

30. And then if thou wilt spare him, thou shalt be rewarded for thy righteousness; and also thy children and thy children's children unto the third and fourth generation.

31. Nevertheless, thine enemy is in thine hands; and if thou rewardest him according to his works thou art justified; if he has sought thy life, and thy life is endangered by him, thine enemy is in thine hands and thou art justified.

32. Behold, this is the law I gave unto my servant Nephi, and thy fathers, Joseph, and Jacob, and Isaac, and Abraham, and all mine ancient prophets and apostles.

5. How to Treat Enemies.

(a) *The Law of Retaliation.*

23-32. The Lord here states what may, perhaps, be called *the lex talionis* of the gospel. "An eye for an eye and a tooth for a tooth," was the highest ideal of justice to which the majority of the Children of Israel could rise under the Mosaic law. Our Lord enunciated a higher ideal, "But I say unto you, that ye resist not evil; but whosoever shall smite thee on thy right cheek, turn to him the other also. And if any man will sue thee at the law, and take away thy coat, let him have thy cloak also" (Matt. 5:39-40). This principle is set forth in further detail in the paragraphs before us. If men will smite you, or your families, and ye will bear it patiently, and not seek revenge, ye shall be rewarded (v. 23). If the offense is repeated, and ye bear it patiently, your reward shall be a hundred fold (v. 25). If it is repeated again, and ye bear it patiently the reward shall be multiplied four times (v. 26), and the Lord will judge the offender (v. 27). If he still persists, he must be solemnly warned, and if he does not heed the warning, the victim is justified in "rewarding him according to his works" (v. 31); but if the wronged party will spare the offender, the reward for his righteousness will surely come (v. 30).

As the world is constituted at present, it is impossible to live in it without being wronged some time. What to do, when wronged, is one of the great problems of a Christian life. The world says, "Get even!" The Master says, "Forgive!" "Absurd!" the world exclaims; "what are laws and courts and jails for?" Christ bids us remember that our worst enemy is, after all, one of God's children whom Christ came to save, and that we ought to treat him as we would an erring brother. Very often Christian love in return for a wrong proves the salvation of the wrong-doer. It always has a wonderful effect upon those who practice it. It makes them strong, beautiful and God-like, whereas hatred and revenge stamp, upon the heart in which they dwell, the image of the devil.

33. And again, this is the law that I gave unto mine ancients, that they should not go out unto battle against any nation, kindred, tongue, or people, save I, the Lord, commanded them.

34. And if any nation, tongue, or people should proclaim war

against them, they should first lift a standard of peace unto that people, nation, or tongue;

35. And if that people did not accept the offering of peace, neither the second nor the third time, they should bring these testimonies before the Lord;

36. Then I, the Lord, would give unto them a commandment, and justify them in going out to battle against that nation, tongue, or people.

37. And I, the Lord, would fight their battles, and their children's battles, and their children's children's, until they had avenged themselves on all their enemies, to the third and fourth generation.

38. Behold, this is an ensample unto all people, saith the Lord your God, for justification before me.

(b) *The Law of War.*

33-8. Israel was a war-cradled nation, but the divine law placed many restrictions on their military life. All men from twenty years of age, capable of carrying arms, were liable to military service (Numbers 1:3), but all the priests and Levites, who were engaged in the Temple service, were exempt (Numbers 1:47); so was also a man who had built a house and had not yet dedicated it; one who had planted a vineyard and had not yet eaten of its fruit, and one who was engaged to be married and had not yet taken his betrothed home (Deuteronomy 20:5-7). A newly-married man was exempt for one year (Deut. 24:5), and, finally, every one who was afraid, or "faint-hearted," was barred from the service, lest "his brethren's heart faint as well as his heart" (Deut. 20:8). By these sweeping restrictions, the Temple service, industrial and agricultural pursuits, and domestic happiness were exalted above militarism, at a time when the military cast wielded the predominating influence in many countries.

Israel was enjoined from going to war with any city or nation, until a peace-offer had been refused (Deut. 20:10; compare Deut. 2:26-9). When war became inevitable, the Israelites were expressly commanded not to cut down the fruit trees in the territory of the enemy (Deut. 20:19). Unnecessary vandalism was prohibited.

Compare the instructions given to the Nephites, Alma 48:10-25.

38. *This is an ensample*] Note that war is justifiable when God commands it, but that such commandments cannot be expected, until the nation attacked has done all in its power to preserve peace (vv. 33, 36).

39. And again, verily I say unto you, if after thine enemy has come upon thee the first time, he repent and come unto thee

praying thy forgiveness, thou shalt forgive him, and shalt hold it no more as a testimony against thine enemy—

40. And so on unto the second and third time; and as oft as thine enemy repenteth of the trespass wherewith he has trespassed against thee, thou shalt forgive him, until seventy times seven.

41. And if he trespass against thee and repent not the first time, nevertheless thou shalt forgive him.

42. And if he trespass against thee the second time, and repent not, nevertheless thou shalt forgive him.

43. And if he trespass against thee the third time, and repent not, thou shalt also forgive him.

44. But if he trespass against thee the fourth time thou shalt not forgive him, but shalt bring these testimonies before the Lord; and they shall not be blotted out until he repent and reward thee four-fold in all things wherewith he has trespassed against thee.

45. And if he do this, thou shalt forgive him with all thine heart; and if he do not this, I the Lord, will avenge thee of thine enemy an hundred-fold;

46. And upon his children, and upon his children's children of all them that hate me, unto the third and fourth generation.

47. But if the children shall repent, or the children's children, and turn to the Lord their God, with all their hearts and with all their might, mind, and strength, and restore four-fold for all their trespasses wherewith they have trespassed, or wherewith their fathers have trespassed, or their father's fathers, then thine indignation shall be turned away;

48. And vengeance shall no more come upon them, saith the Lord thy God, and their trespasses shall never be brought any more as a testimony before the Lord against them. Amen.

(c) *The Law of Forgiveness.*

39-48. In paragraphs 23-32 the Saints are taught to bear persecution patiently, and not to seek revenge; here they are instructed to go still farther, and forgive an enemy as often as he repents of his evil-doing, and a stated number of times, even if he does not repent (v. 43). If, however, he continues to trespass and does not repent, the case is to be brought before the Lord, in the hope that the sinner may be brought to repentance; when that object is gained, he is to be forgiven (vv. 44, 45);

if there is no repentance, the matter is to be left entirely in the hands of the Lord.

40. *Until seventy times seven*] That means, practically, an unlimited number of times. In the days of our Lord, the Rabbis taught that no one was under obligation to forgive a neighbor more than three times. Peter, asking the Master for a ruling on that question, suggested that perhaps seven times would be a liberal improvement on the rule of the Jewish teachers, but our Lord answered, "seventy times seven." And then He taught the disciples that the indebtedness of one brother to another is insignificant, when compared with the debt which God has freely forgiven us. The kingdom of heaven, He said, is likened to a certain king who called his governors and other officials before him to render an account of their administration. One of them was then found to be owing ten thousand talents—something like ten million dollars. Evidently he had for many years failed to give an honest return to the sovereign of the taxes he had collected. The king, in his wrath, commanded that he and his family be sold as slaves, and that his property be confiscated. But, when this governor humbled himself, the king, filled with compassion, forgave him. The same servant, our Lord continues, found a fellow-servant who owed him a hundred denarii, or "pence"—say fifty dollars—and because he could not meet this obligation, he was cast into prison. When the king heard what his governor had done, he promptly delivered him to the "tormentors" or jailers, at whose hands he would find no mercy. "So likewise," our Lord adds, "shall my heavenly Father do also unto you, if ye from your hearts forgive not everyone his brother their trespasses" (Matt. 18:15-35).

It is one of the proofs of the divine origin of the Revelation in this volume that they inculcate forgiveness at a time when the flames of persecution were about to break out over the Saints. Those who reject the gospel as proclaimed by the Prophet Joseph, also reject the divine principle of forgiveness which is an essential part of it—the principle which Jesus exemplified on the cross, when He prayed, "Father, forgive them."

The gospel teaches us that if we have a grudge against any man, in our hearts, we should drive it out. It teaches us to do good to all, even to enemies, and thereby it makes us as happy as only a heart full of sunshine can be.

47. *If the children shall repent*] Note that the Lord expects the children, and even children's children, to right the wrongs committed and not righted by their fathers, if they can do so. A notable illustration of the repentance of children on behalf of their fathers is found in the history of Massachusetts. In 1633, the Assembly of that colony banished Roger Williams, a champion of religious freedom. Almost three centuries later, the State of Massachusetts, by its Legislature, annulled this proceeding.

GENERAL NOTES

"With regard to elections, some say all the Latter-day Saints vote together, and vote as I say. But I never tell any man how to vote, or whom to vote for. But I will show you how we have been situated, by bringing a comparison. Should there be a Methodist society here and two candidates running for office [and] one says, 'if you will vote for me and put me in governor, I will exterminate the Methodists, take away their charters, etc.'; the other candidate says, 'If I am governor, I will give all an equal privilege'; which would the Methodists vote for? Of course they would vote *en masse* for the candidate that would give them their rights. Thus it has been with us" (Joseph Smith, *Hist. of the Church,* Vol. V., p. 490).

The Prophet Joseph did not aspire to military honor or power. Concerning the position he held in the Nauvoo Legion, he says that when the Saints came to Illinois, the State demanded that they should bear arms and do military duty. But they had been robbed of all their worldly possessions and could not comply with the demand. The Prophet, therefore, advised them to organize themselves into independent companies and ask the State for arms, and he added that, though he was exempt from military service, because of lameness in one leg, he would join them. On that condition, the Saints formed the Legion. The Prophet was recognized as the Lieutenant-general, and the law was complied with. The Prophet says:

"All the power that I desire, or have sought to obtain, has been the enjoyment of the Constitutional privilege for which my fathers shed their blood, of living in peace in the society of my wife and children, and enjoying the society of my friends and their religious liberty which is the right of every American citizen, of worshiping according to the dictates of his conscience and the Revelations of God" (*Ib.*).

The Prophet Joseph was one of the staunchest supporters of the Constitution of the United States that ever lived, but he did not entertain a high regard for the party politics of his day. In a letter to the editor of the *Wasp,* he wrote:

"I have of late had repeated solicitations to have something to do in relation to the political farce about dividing the county; but as my feelings revolt at the idea of having anything to do with politics, I have declined, in all instances, having anything to do on the subject. I think it would be well for politicians to regulate their own affairs. I wish to be let alone, that I may attend strictly to the spiritual welfare of the Church" (*Hist. of the Church,* Vol. V., p. 259).

This letter is dated January 23rd, 1843. On the 6th of August, the same year, he said:

"In relation to National matters, I want it to go abroad unto the whole world that every man should stand on his own merits. The Lord has not given me a Revelation concerning politics. I have not asked Him for one. I am a third party and stand independent and alone. I desire to see all parties protected in their rights" (*Ibid.,* p. 526).

"It is said that Brother Joseph, in his lifetime, declared that the Elders of this Church should step forth at a particular time when the Constitution should be in danger, and rescue it, or save it. This may be so; but I do not recollect that he said exactly so. I believe he said something like this—that the time would come when the Constitution and the Country would be in danger of an overthrow; and, said he, if the Constitution be saved at all, it will be by the Elders of this Church. I believe this is about the language, as nearly as I can recollect it" (Orson Hyde, *Jour. of Dis.,* Vol. VI., p. 152).

SECTION 99.

REVELATION *given through Joseph Smith the Prophet, at Kirtland, Ohio, August, 1833.——Directions to John Murdock concerning his work in the ministry.*

BEHOLD, thus saith the Lord unto my servant John Murdock —thou art called to go into the eastern countries from house to house, from village to village, and from city to city, to proclaim mine everlasting gospel unto the inhabitants thereof, in the midst of persecution and wickedness.

2. And whoso receiveth you receiveth me; and you shall have power to declare my word in the demonstration of my Holy Spirit.

3. And whoso receiveth you as a little child, receiveth my kingdom; and blessed are they, for they shall obtain mercy.

4. And whoso rejecteth you shall be rejected of my Father and his house; and you shall cleanse your feet in the secret places by the way for a testimony against them.

5. And behold, and lo, I come quickly to judgment, to convince all of their ungodly deeds which they have committed against me, as it is written of me in the volume of the book.

6. And now, verily I say unto you, that it is not expedient that you should go until your children are provided for, and sent up kindly unto the bishop in Zion.

7. And after a few years, if thou desirest of me, thou mayest go up also unto the goodly land, to possess thine inheritance;

8. Otherwise thou shalt continue proclaiming my gospel until thou be taken. Amen.

This is a Revelation calling Elder John Murdock to go on a mission to the Eastern States. He was one of the men who received the gospel in Kirtland when Oliver Cowdery and companions passed through that city on the first western journey to the Lamanites, and together with Sidney Rigdon, Edward Partridge, Isaac Morley, Lyman Wight, and others, he was called to the ministry at that time. He held many important positions in the Church and discharged his duties faithfully. One of his children, Joseph S., died at the age of eleven months, as a result of exposure during the night of mob assault upon the Prophet at Hiram. Emma Smith, the Prophet's wife, had given birth to twins on the 30th of April, 1831. On the same date the home of the Murdocks had been blessed with twin children, Joseph S. and Julia. Sister Emma Smith's babies lived but three hours, and, when Sister Murdock passed away, Sister Emma took the motherless infants to rear. During the mob outrage, the infant boy contracted a cold that ended fatally, a few days later.

1. *In the midst of persecution*] The Lord, in calling His servant to go on a mission, did not conceal the fact that persecution would be his reward at the hands of men. Of Saul of Tarsus He said, "I will show him how great things he must suffer for my name's sake" (Acts 9:16). Similar information was given to Elder John Murdock.

3. *As a little child*] Those who receive the servants of the Lord must do so as little children; not as masters, or as critics. Children are willing to learn; they are confiding, eager to be assisted, full of trust and hope for the future. That is the spirit in which to receive the servants of God.

6. *Not * * * go, until your children are provided for*] He was permitted to postpone his departure for the mission, until his motherless children had been sent to Zion.

7. *After a few years * * * thou mayest go up also*] John Murdock was a member of Zion's camp, and made the journey to Zion in that choice company of men. In 1834, he was appointed a member of the High Council in Clay County, and in 1837, of the High Council in Far West. In 1838, he and George M. Hinckle, as trustees for the Church, purchased a townsite at De Witt, on the Missouri River, and in 1842, he was appointed Bishop of the Nauvoo Fifth Ward.

SECTION 100.

REVELATION *given to Joseph Smith the Prophet, and Sidney Rigdon, at Perrysburg, New York, October 12, 1833. The two had been long absent from their families and felt some concern over them.——Comforting assurances as to their families—Many of the Lord's people in that region—Sidney Rigdon to be a spokesman unto the Prophet and to be mighty in expounding the Scriptures—Assurances concerning affairs in Zion.*

VERILY, thus saith the Lord unto you, my friends Sidney and Joseph, your families are well; they are in mine hands, and I will do with them as seemeth me good; for in me there is all power.

2. Therefore, follow me, and listen to the counsel which I shall give unto you.

It is a very striking fact that the Church of Jesus Christ of Latter-day Saints, ever since its organization, has proceeded on its onward course, no matter what the outward circumstances have been. There has been no turning back, no hesitation, no vacillation. As a mighty ship with its precious cargo, it has steered straight for the goal. The wind may have been adverse at times; the waves may have been breaking over it from stem to stern; it may have been assailed by hostile craft from above and from below, and from all sides. There may have been disaffection and even mutiny among the crew, but the command has always sounded clear and high above the storm and the din of conflict, "Forward, full speed!"

These reflections are suggested by the fact that while the enemies in Missouri were gathering their lawless forces for an assault upon the Church there, the Lord inspired the Prophet Joseph to go on a mission and proclaim the gospel message. He was not to mind the enemies. His calling was to testify to the world. And he went on this mission as far as Canada, as full of faith and hope as if there had been no storm-clouds in the sky. What a testimony to his divine commission!

On the 5th of October, 1833, Joseph, in company with Sidney Rigdon and Freeman Nickerson, started on a journey east. Nickerson was a veteran of the war of 1812. He received the gospel at Dayton, New York, in April, 1833, and the same year went on a mission to Kirtland. Joseph and Sidney made this trip in his conveyance. On the 12th of October, the travelers arrived in Perrysburg, where Freeman Nickerson lived, and the same day this Revelation was received, in which the Lord (1) comforts His servants regarding their families (1-2); (2) encourages them to continue their missionary labors (3-8); (3) instructs them concerning their special gifts (9-12); and (4) comforts them concerning Zion (13-17).

1. REGARDING THEIR FAMILIES.

1-2. The Lord is mindful of His servants. Knowing that they would be unable to put their best efforts into missionary work if they were full of anxiety for their families, He gave them the assurance that their loved ones at home were well, and that He would take care of them during the temporary separation (v. 1). Having received this promise, they were prepared to continue their labors (v. 2).

"In going forth to do our duty in warning mankind, we should not have our minds troubled and perplexed on account of our families being destitute * * * if a man has no cause of trouble, he can engage, heart and soul, in the work of the ministry and think of nothing else but the work in which he is engaged. 'But,' says one, 'I cannot forget my wife and child that are at home.' You are not required to forget them. I could always remember my wife and child, but did I sorrow over them and fear that they were starving to death? No. * * * when absent on missions, we kneel down and pray, 'God bless the distant ones at home,' and then go on about our business" (Amasa M. Lyman, *Jour. of Dis.*, Vol. X., p. 181).

3. Behold, and lo, I have much people in this place, in the regions round about; and an effectual door shall be opened in the regions round about in this eastern land.

4. Therefore, I, the Lord, have suffered you to come unto this place; for thus it was expedient in me for the salvation of souls.

5. Therefore, verily I say unto you, lift up your voices unto this people; speak the thoughts that I shall put into your hearts, and you shall not be confounded before men;

6. For it shall be given you in the very hour, yea, in the very moment, what ye shall say.

7. But a commandment I give unto you, that ye shall declare whatsoever thing ye declare in my name, in solemnity of heart, in the spirit of meekness, in all things.

8. And I give unto you this promise, that inasmuch as ye do this the Holy Ghost shall be shed forth in bearing record unto all things whatsoever ye shall say.

2. CONDITIONS OF SUCCESS IN THE MISSION.

3-8. The Lord assures His servants that He has much people in Perrysburg and vicinity (v. 3), but they must comply with certain conditions, if they would achieve success in their labor among them. They must speak as guided by the Spirit (v. 5), for they would be given what to say (v. 6); and they must speak "in solemnity of heart" and humility (v. 7). If they would accept these conditions, the Holy Spirit would be poured out upon the people and testify of the truth (v. 8).

5. *Lift up your voice*] The servants of the Lord must make themselves heard. They have a message of salvation, of which they need not be ashamed.

Speak the thoughts that I shall put into your hearts]

Missionary work is God's work. Missionaries are but His messengers.
His ambassadors. They must deliver His message to the world. That does
not mean that they need no preparation. An ambassador from one nation
to another needs a great deal of training to fill that position efficiently and
worthily. The ambassadors of our Lord need more preparation than any
representative of a mere worldly kingdom. It is a missionary's duty to
"get an understanding of the gospel, and teach it, as the Spirit directs";
but to get an understanding of the gospel, he must both study it and
practice it. That is his preparation. When he is thus prepared, the Spirit
will direct his utterance.

6. *It shall be given you * * * what ye shall say*] Our Lord promised
the Twelve that, when they were brought before governors and kings
for His sake, they would be given in the same hour what to say in defense. They should not waste time on the legal phase of their position
but deliver their message (Matt. 10:16-20). This promise is here extended
to the testimony of the servants of God in general. If they are prepared,
by study and practice of the gospel, to testify of it to the world, they are
also prepared to speak in its defense in courts and legislative assemblies.
We have had a modern illustration of this truth in the remarkable
testimony of President Joseph F. Smith before a Committee of the
United States Senate, in the famous case against Senator Reed Smoot,
a testimony which extended over five days, and by which the witness
gained the respect of all who heard him, and turned public opinion to
a perceptible extent in favor of the cause he represented.

7. *Solemnity of heart*] This is a beautiful adornment of one who
speaks in the name of the Lord. Trivial comparisons, laughable stories,
ridiculous gestures and attitudes are contrary to the dignity of the calling
of a servant of the Lord. Humorous anecdotes or personal adventures,
may be introduced by a missionary as illustrations of a principle, or
doctrine, but if they are told to excite merriment, or to magnify the
speaker, they must be condemned. They should be left for the minstrel
show, or the music hall.

9. And it is expedient in me that you, my servant Sidney,
should be a spokesman unto this people; yea, verily, I will ordain
you unto this calling, even to be a spokesman unto my servant
Joseph.

10. And I will give unto him power to be mighty in testimony.

11. And I will give unto thee power to be mighty in expounding all scriptures, that thou mayest be a spokesman unto him,
and he shall be a revelator unto thee, that thou mayest know the

certainty of all things pertaining to the things of my kingdom on the earth.

12. Therefore, continue your journey and let your hearts rejoice; for behold, and lo, I am with you even unto the end.

3. EACH HAS HIS OWN GIFT.

9-12. The Lord recognizes the fact that each of His servants has his own gifts. Sidney Rigdon was qualified to be the "spokesman" of Joseph (v. 9), while Joseph was specially qualified to bear testimony, as a witness (v. 10). Sidney Rigdon had the gift of expounding the Scriptures, and by that means to bring to light the truth. Joseph had the gift of receiving revelations of the truth, by direct communication from God. These gifts were to be utilized in God's service.

9. *Spokesman*] Sidney Rigdon was raised up to be a spokesman to Joseph, in accordance with a prophecy by Father Lehi shortly before his departure (II. Nephi 3:18). Aaron was such a spokesman to Moses (Ex. 4:15, 16).

10. *Mighty in testimony*] The Prophet Joseph was indeed "mighty in testimony." As one who had seen the heavens opened and heard the voice of God, the Father, and His Son, and had conversed with angels, he could "testify," and his words had the force of those of an eye witness. Parley P. Pratt says that "even his most bitter enemies were overcome generally if he could once get their ears." He tells the familiar story of Joseph rebuking the blasphemous guards in Richmond jail. These had made the night hideous with their filthy language and stories of rapine and murder. All of a sudden Joseph rose and said, "Silence, ye fiends of the infernal pit! In the name of Jesus Christ I rebuke you, and command you to be still. I will not live another minute and hear such language." Elder Pratt continues:

"He ceased to speak. He stood erect in terrible majesty. Chained, or without a weapon; calm, unruffled and dignified as an angel, he looked upon the quailing guards, whose weapons were lowered or dropped to the ground; whose knees smote together, and who, shrinking into a corner, or crouching at his feet, begged his pardon, and remained quiet till a change of guards."

11. *Expounding all scriptures*] Sidney Rigdon was a powerful speaker as an expounder of the Scriptures. At the dedication of the Kirtland Temple he spoke for two hours and a half on Matt. 18:20. The Prophet says he was "forcible and sublime," and in the course of his remarks he "drew tears from many eyes."

13. And now I give unto you a word concerning Zion. Zion shall be redeemed, although she is chastened for a little season.

14. Thy brethren, my servants Orson Hyde and John Gould,

are in my hands; and inasmuch as they keep my commandments they shall be saved.

15. Therefore, let your hearts be comforted; for all things shall work together for good to them that walk uprightly, and to the sanctification of the church.

16. For I will raise up unto myself a pure people, that will serve me in righteousness;

17. And all that call upon the name of the Lord, and keep his commandments, shall be saved. Even so. Amen.

4. CONCERNING ZION.

13-17. Joseph's thoughts were continually on Zion, and at this time he must have felt very anxious about the Saints. The Lord, therefore, gives him the assurance that Zion will be redeemed (v. 13), and that all things shall work together for good to them that walk uprightly; and to the sanctification of the Church (v. 15). The Church will come out of the fire of persecution, purified, for God will raise up unto Himself a pure people (v. 16). How long a time it will take to raise up a people willing to serve God in righteousness, He does not say. But it will be done. Israel was in Egypt 400 years, and the Babylonian captivity lasted 70 years. But the purposes of God were accomplished.

14. *My servants Orson Hyde and John Gould*] Soon after the arrival of Oliver Cowdery in Kirtland as a messenger from the brethren in Zion, Orson Hyde and John Gould were sent to Jackson County with instructions from the First presidency. They arrived there towards the end of the month of September, 1833. The Prophet was assured that the two messengers were the special objects of divine care, and that they would be safe, if they would keep the commandments of God. During the entire history of the Latter-day Saints, the Lord has preserved His faithful servants, often miraculously, in dangers on land and sea, among enemies and false friends, until their mission was completed.

GENERAL NOTES

Shortly after the arrival in Jackson County, of the two messengers from Kirtland, W. W. Phelps and Orson Hyde were despatched with a petition from the Saints in Missouri to the Governor of that State, Daniel Dunklin, in which the outrages committed were set forth and redress was asked for. The Governor, in a letter dated October 19th, 1833, advised the Saints to bring suits against the violators of the law, and, in compliance with this suggestion, lawyers were engaged. But the mob was not looking for legal proceedings. They had already broken the law, and their only chance of escape from the consequences was to trample the fragments into the dust. And so, on the 31st of October, 1833, about fifty men, armed with guns, went to a Branch of the Church west of the Big Blue, and unroofed and partly demolished the dwellings of the Saints, and unmercifully beat several of the men, amid the shrieks and screams of women and children. The day following, a little settlement about 12 to 14 miles west of Independence was attacked. The same night a party stoned the houses of the Saints in Independence and broke windows and doors. The store belonging to Gilbert and Whitney was broken open and the goods scattered in the streets. Appeals for protection were ignored by justices of the peace. One judge at Lexicon is said to have advised the Saints to fight and kill the mob whenever the latter came upon them.

On the 5th of November, Independence was crowded with individuals from different parts of the county, all eager for violence. Word reached the Saints in the settlements that several of their brethren were imprisoned, and the lives of all were in danger. A company of about a hundred brethren led by Lyman Wight, was then formed and marched toward Independence. Colonel Pitcher had command of the "militia." He demanded that the Saints leave the county; that those who had arms deliver them to him, and that certain men be tried for murder. The brethren surrendered what few guns they had, and those "wanted" gave themselves up for "trial." The latter were not held. There was no case against them, but the arms were kept, and the mob could now break into houses and molest the people without fear of resistance. On the 5th and 6th of November, women and children fled in every direction before the merciless mob. On the 7th, the shores of the Missouri were lined with exiles. Hundreds of people were seen in every direction. Husbands were searching for their wives, and wives for their husbands; parents for children, and children for parents. Some of the Saints found a refuge in Clay County. Those who fled to Van Buren and Lafayette Counties were soon expelled by mobs. The condition of the scattered Saints was lamentable. "No regular order," writes W. W. Phelps, "can be enforced, nor any usual discipline kept up; among the world, yea, the most wicked part of it, some commit one sin and some another (I speak of the rebellious, for there are Saints that are as immovable as the everlasting hills), and what can be done? We are in Clay, Ray, Lafayette, Jackson, Van Buren, and other Counties, and cannot hear from one another oftener than from you. I know it was right that we should be driven out of the land of Zion, that the rebellious might be sent away. But, brethren, if the Lord will, I should like to know what the honest in heart shall do. Our clothes are worn out; we want the necessaries of life" (*Hist. of the Church*, Vol. I., p. 457).

As soon as the Prophet received definite information of the expulsion from Jackson County, Missouri, he sent a comforting affectionate letter to the scattered Saints. It was dated December 10th, 1833. In it he said, in part:

"Now there are two things of which I am ignorant; and the Lord will not show them unto me, perhaps for a wise purpose in Himself—I mean in some respects—and they are these: Why God has suffered so great a calamity to come upon Zion, and what the great moving cause of this great affliction is; and, again, by what means He will return her back to her inheritance, with songs of everlasting joy upon her head. These two things, brethren, are in part kept back that they are not plainly shown unto me; but there are some things that are plainly manifest which have incurred the displeasure of the Almighty" (*Hist. of the Church,* Vol. I., p. 454).

About the time of the expulsion of the Saints from Jackson County, Missouri, particularly on the 13th of November, 1833, there was a great meteoric display. The Prophet writes:

About 4 o'clock a. m., I was awakened by Brother Davis knocking at my door, and calling on me to arise and behold the signs in the heavens. I arose, and, to my great joy, beheld the stars fall from heaven like a shower of hailstones; a literal fulfilment of the word of God, as recorded in the Scriptures and a sure sign that the coming of Christ is close at hand" (*Hist. of the Church,* Vol. 1., p. 439).

SECTION 101.

REVELATION *given to Joseph Smith the Prophet, at Kirtland, Ohio, December 16, 1833. At this time the Saints who had gathered in Missouri were suffering great persecution. Mobs had driven them from their homes in Jackson County, and some of the Saints had tried to establish themselves in Van Buren County, but persecution followed them. The main body of the Church was at that time in Clay County, Missouri. Threats of death against individuals of the Church were many. The people had lost household furniture, clothing, livestock and other personal property, and many of their crops had been destroyed. See History of the Church, vol. 1, p. 456.———Affliction permitted to befall the Saints because of their transgression—The Lord's indignation to be poured out upon all nations—The pure in heart among those who had been expelled from Zion to return —Other stakes of Zion to be established—Blessed state incident to the millennial era of peace—Parable of the nobleman and the olive-trees—Gathering of the Saints to be continued—Those who have been oppressed by their enemies to importune for re-*

dress—Creation of the Constitution of the United States directed by the Lord—Parable of the woman and the unjust judge.

VERILY I say unto you, concerning your brethren who have been afflicted, and persecuted, and cast out from the land of their inheritance—

2. I, the Lord, have suffered the affliction to come upon them, wherewith they have been afflicted, in consequence of their transgressions;

3. Yet I will own them, and they shall be mine in that day when I shall come to make up my jewels.

In his letter to the scattered Saints in Missouri, dated December 10th, 1833, the Prophet stated that the spirit withheld from him definite knowledge of the reason why the calamity had fallen upon Zion. Here is another striking evidence of his sincerity. If he had been in the habit of writing revelations without divine inspiration, he could have done so at this time. But it is perfectly evident that he did not speak in the name of the Lord except when prompted to do so by the Spirit. On the 16th of December, however, this Revelation was received concerning the Saints in Zion, and the Lord (1) states why they had been afflicted (1-3); (2) explains the twofold object of the experience they had passed through (4-8); (3) gives promises concerning the Saints (9-21); (4) commands them to gather (22-5); (5) speaks of the final victory (26-36); (6) reminds them that they are "the Salt of the Earth" (37-42); (7) and that Zion will be redeemed (43-62); (8) sends special instructions to the Churches (63-75); (9) and to the scattered Saints (76-80); (10) applies the parable of the unjust judge (81-95); and (11) closes with instructions and promises (96-101).

1. WHY THE SAINTS WERE AFFLICTED.

1-3. The Spirit of revelation here says that the tribulations through which the Saints in Missouri had passed, had come upon them because of transgression (v. 2). Sin brings suffering, always, inevitably. As surely as fire burns, so surely sin ends in misery. It is a law as well established as the law of gravitation. However, the Lord had not rejected His people. "Yet," He says, "I will own them" (v. 3).

3. *When I shall come to make up my jewels*] Comp. Sec. 60:4. This does not refer to the day of final judgment but to the day of the restoration of the Earth to its lawful Ruler and King, our Lord Jesus Christ. (See Malachi 3:16-18). On that day, the Lord will own them and value them as jewels.

4. Therefore, they must needs be chastened and tried, even as Abraham, who was commanded to offer up his only son.

5. For all those who will not endure chastening, but deny me, cannot be sanctified.

6. Behold, I say unto you, there were jarrings, and contentions, and envyings, and strifes, and lustful and covetous desires among them; therefore by these things they polluted their inheritances.

7. They were slow to hearken unto the voice of the Lord their God; therefore, the Lord their God is slow to hearken unto their prayers, to answer them in the day of their trouble.

8. In the day of their peace they esteemed lightly my counsel; but, in the day of their trouble, of necessity they feel after me.

2. The Twofold Object of Affliction.

4-8. Our Heavenly Father had two objects in view, in permitting the enemy to afflict the Saints: To chastise them for their sins, and to try them, as He tried Abraham (v. 4). The sins referred to are enumerated. There were jarrings, and contentions, envyings, strife, lustful and covetous desires; the people were slow to hearken to the voice of God, when they had peace, though in the days of trouble they prayed fervently. These were their sins. It behooves us to search ourselves to see whether we are better in these respects than they were.

"Some may ask why we did not tarry at the Center Stake* of Zion when the Lord planted our feet there. We had eyes, but we did not see; we had ears, but we did not hear; we had hearts that were devoid of what the Lord required of His people; consequently, we could not abide what the Lord revealed to us. We had to go from there to gain an experience. Can you understand this? I think there are some here who can. If we could have received the words of life and lived according to them, when we first gathered to the Center Stake of Zion,* we never would have been removed from that place" (Brigham Young, *Jour. of Dis.,* Vol. XI., p. 102).

9. Verily I say unto you, notwithstanding their sins, my bowels are filled with compassion towards them. I will not utterly cast them off; and in the day of wrath I will remember mercy.

3. Promises Concerning the Saints.

(a) *God is Merciful.*

9. *In the day of wrath * * * mercy*] When the Saints were exiled and scattered, it appeared to human eye as if they had been utterly cast

---

* The brethren frequently speak of the "center stake in Zion." What they mean is Zion itself. The term "stake" is taken from the writings of Isaiah (Ch. 33:20 and 54:2). See *Essentials in Church History,* pp. 146-147, and *Saturday Night Thoughts—* Whitney, page 183.

off by their heavenly Father; but in the very day of wrath He would remember mercy. He would turn the curse of man into a blessing to His people. This was true of the exile from Zion, and also of the exodus, later, to the Rocky Mountains. A greater blessing could, possibly, not have come to the Church at that time. John Taylor remarks:

"We were driven out of Missouri—we were driven from one place to another in Missouri before we were driven out altogether. Then we were driven from Illinois to this Territory. But what of that? I know some men who thought the work was at an end. I remember a remark made by Sidney Rigdon—I suppose he did not live his religion; I do not think he did—his knees began to shake in Missouri; and on one occasion he said, 'Brethren, every one of you take your own way, for the work seems as though it had come to an end.' Brigham Young encouraged the people, and Joseph Smith told them to be firm and maintain their integrity, for God would be with His people and deliver them. I never saw a time that the Saints enjoyed themselves better than when they, apparently, were wading through their deepest troubles; I never saw them more full of the Holy Ghost" (*Jour. of Dis.,* Vol. XI., pp. 25-6).

10. I have sworn, and the decree hath gone forth by a former commandment which I have given unto you, that I would let fall the sword of mine indignation in behalf of my people; and even as I have said, it shall come to pass.

11. Mine indignation is soon to be poured out without measure upon all nations; and this will I do when the cup of their iniquity is full.

(b) Enemies will be punished.

10-11. It is no consolation, no pleasure, to the children of God to know that their persecutors are bringing upon themselves the wrath of the Almighty; they cannot glory in the sufferings of anyone; but it is strengthening to their faith to contemplate the unerring justice of God, and to know that "Whatsoever a man soweth, that shall he also reap" (Gal. 6:7); for this assures them of perfect justice in the distribution of eternal rewards. Here on Earth men's fortunes do not always show perfect justice, but all will be made right, finally. "I have seen the wicked in great power and spreading himself like a green bay tree; yet he passed away, and, lo, he was not: yea, I sought him, but he could not be found. Mark the perfect man, and behold the upright: for the end of that man is peace" (Psalm 37:35-7).

11. *Mine indignation * * * all nations*] This is another prediction of the wars that were to come on the Earth, beginning with the Civil War in the United States.

12. And in that day all who are found upon the watch-tower, or in other words, all mine Israel, shall be saved.

13. And they that have been scattered shall be gathered.

14. And all they who have mourned shall be comforted.

15. And all they who have given their lives for my name shall be crowned.

(c) Israel to be Gathered.

12-15. The people were now scattered, but they would be gathered again.

15. *All they who have given their lives*] At the time this Revelation was given, the Prophet knew of only one casualty, viz., that of Brother Andrew Barber,* who was killed on the 4th of November, 1833, by Robert Patten, in the encounter with the mob west of the Big Blue. There were others, however, especially women, who had died on account of exposure. One lady, named Keziah Higbee, without shelter against a terrible rainstorm, on the banks of the Missouri River, gave birth to a child. She did not survive. The Revelation includes in the promise of reward, all who had given their lives for the cause of the Master.

16. Therefore, let your hearts be comforted concerning Zion; for all flesh is in mine hands; be still and know that I am God.

17. Zion shall not be moved out of her place, notwithstanding her children are scattered.

18. They that remain, and are pure in heart, shall return, and come to their inheritances, they and their children, with songs of everlasting joy, to build up the waste places of Zion—

19. And all these things that the prophets might be fulfilled.

20. And, behold, there is none other place appointed than that which I have appointed; neither shall there be any other place appointed than that which I have appointed, for the work of the gathering of my saints—

21. Until the day cometh when there is found no more room for them; and then I have other places which I will appoint unto them, and they shall be called stakes, for the curtains or the strength of Zion.

(d) Zion not to be Removed.

16-21. The Revelations of God are exceedingly clear and definite in stating that the location of Zion had not been moved, although the people

---

* He has been called the first martyr of the Church in this dispensation.

were scattered (v. 17). Heber C. Kimball expresses his faith in this Revelation, as follows:

"I am pretty sure of one thing—we shall go to Jackson County, Missouri; that is, those who do right and honor their calling, doing what they have been told to do. You will be blessed, and you will see the day when Presidents Young, Kimball, and Wells, and the Twelve Apostles will be in Jackson County, Missouri, laying out your inheritances. * * * We shall be there in the flesh,* and all our enemies cannot prevent it. Brother Wells, you may write that. You will be there, and Willard will be there, and also Jedediah, and Joseph and Hyrum Smith, and David and Parley; and the day will be when I will see those men in the general assembly of the Church of the Firstborn, in the great council of God in Jerusalem, too" (*Jour. of Dis.,* Vol. IX., p. 27).

21. *I have other places*] The gathering, according to the plan, as first revealed, was to begin in Zion, but this plan was modified and the Saints were directed to build up other places before they established Zion.

"We are going to try to save ourselves, and when we come to under-standing we will then be counted worthy to possess Zion, even the Center Stake of Zion. It is true this is Zion,—North and South America are Zion, and the land where the Lord commenced His work, and where He commenced, He will finish. This is the land of Zion; but we are not yet prepared to go and establish the Center Stake of Zion. The Lord tried that in the first place * * * now it is for you and me to prepare to return back * * * and by and by to build up the Center Stake of Zion" (Brigham Young, *Jour. of Dis.,* Vol. XI., p. 324).

22. Behold, it is my will, that all they who call on my name, and worship me according to mine everlasting gospel, should gather together, and stand in holy places;

23. And prepare for the revelation which is to come, when the veil of the covering of my temple, in my tabernacle, which hideth the earth, shall be taken off, and all flesh shall see me together.

24. And every corruptible thing, both of man, or of the beasts of the field, or of the fowls of the heavens, or of the fish of the sea, that dwells upon all the face of the earth, shall be consumed;

25. And also that of element shall melt with fervent heat; and all things shall become new, that my knowledge and glory may dwell upon all the earth.

---

* As resurrected beings; some of the brethren mentioned had already passed away.

4. THE SAINTS TO GATHER.

22-5. The Lord commands His Saints to gather and to establish them-selves in "holy places" (v. 22); that is, in Stakes and Wards of Zion, and prepare themselves for the appearance of the Son of Man (v. 23).

"He comes! The earth shakes, and the tall mountains tremble; the mighty deep rolls back to the north as in fear, and the rent skies glow like molten brass. He comes! The dead Saints burst forth from their tombs, and 'those who are alive and remain are caught up' with them to meet Him. The ungodly rush to hide themselves from His presence, and call upon the quivering rocks to cover them. He comes! with all the hosts of the righteous glorified. The breath of His lips strikes death to the wicked. His glory is a consuming fire. The proud and rebellious are as stubble; they are burned and 'left neither root nor branch.' He sweeps the Earth as with 'the besom of destruction.' He deluges the Earth with the fiery floods of His wrath, and the filthiness and abominations of the world are consumed. Satan and his dark hosts are taken and bound —the prince of the power of the air has lost his dominion, for He whose right it is to reign has come, and 'the kingdoms of this world have be-come the kingdom of our Lord and His Christ' " (Charles W. Penrose, *Millennial Star,* Vol. XXI., pp. 581-4).

26. And in that day the enmity of man, and the enmity of beasts, yea, the enmity of all flesh, shall cease from before my face.

27. And in that day whatsoever any man shall ask, it shall be given unto him.

28. And in that day Satan shall not have power to tempt any man.

29. And there shall be no sorrow because there is no death.

30. In that day an infant shall not die until he is old; and his life shall be as the age of a tree;

31. And when he dies he shall not sleep, that is to say in the earth, but shall be changed in the twinkling of an eye, and shall be caught up, and his rest shall be glorious.

32. Yea, verily I say unto you, in that day when the Lord shall come, he shall reveal all things—

33. Things which have passed, and hidden things which no man knew, things of the earth, by which it was made, and the purpose and the end thereof—

34. Things most precious, things that are above, and things that are beneath, things that are in the earth, and upon the earth, and in heaven.

35. And all they who suffer persecution for my name, and endure in faith, though they are called to lay down their lives for my sake yet shall they partake of all this glory.

36. Wherefore, fear not even unto death; for in this world your joy is not full, but in me your joy is full.

5. THE MILLENNIUM.

26-36. In the paragraphs immediately preceding, the coming of the Lord is referred to as the great and important event for which the Saints are to be prepared. This coming marks the beginning of the Millennium. In this section we are told of certain wonderful features that will characterize that period. (a) The enmity between man and beasts shall cease (v. 26), as well as enmity between men; (b) prayers will be heard (v. 27); (c) Satan shall have no power to tempt man (v. 28); there shall be no sorrow because there is no death (vv. 29-31); the light of revelation will shine in its fulness (vv. 32-4); and the martyrs will partake of this glory (vv. 35-6).

27. *Whatsoever any man shall ask, it shall be given unto him*] Because in that day men will ask for only those things which the Spirit prompts them to pray for. We, ourselves, do not always know our deepest needs, and we often pray for things that would be harmful if given, but when the Spirit teaches us to pray, our prayers will be answered.

> "Not what we wish, but what we need,
>   Thy bounteous grace supply;
>   The good, unasked, in mercy grant;
>   The ill, though asked, deny."

28. *Satan shall not have power to tempt man*] At present he has that power. Says President George Q. Cannon:

"I have no doubt that many of my brethren and sisters have sensibly felt, in various places and at various times, evil influences around them. Brother Joseph Smith gave an explanation of this. There are places in the Mississippi Valley where the influence, or the presence, of invisible spirits is very perceptibly felt. He said that numbers had been slain there in war, and that there were evil influences or spirits which affect the spirits of those who have tabernacles on the Earth. I myself have felt those influences in other places besides the Continent of America; I have felt them on the old battle grounds of the Sandwich Islands * * * We call it the spirit of the evil one; but he has numerous agencies at work, even as the Lord has numerous agencies to assist Him" (*Jour. of Dis.*, Vol. XI., p. 30).

29. *There is no death*] Those who are resurrected with the just will not die again, and those who still live in mortality will reach a great age, and finally be changed in the twinkling of an eye (v. 31).

30. *The age of a tree*] Some trees grow quite old. An authority of the Forestry Service at Washington is quoted to the effect that the pine tree may attain 700 years as a maximum length of life; the silver fir 425 years; the red beech, 245; the aspen, 210; the birch, 200; the ash, 170 years. The heart of the oak begins to decay when the tree is about 300 years old. When man lives in accordance with the laws of God, and is clean and temperate in all things, there is no reason, as far as known, why he should not live to the same age as the Patriarchs before the flood.

32. *He shall reveal all things*] During the Millennium the knowledge of the Lord will be widely diffused among the children of men. One reason for this is that there will be numerous Temples, and the Lord and His messengers will visit these and teach the Saints. Resurrected beings will visit the Earth. Brigham Young says:

"By-and-by Zion will be built up; Temples are going to be reared, and the Holy Priesthood is going to take effect and rule, and every law of Christ will be obeyed, and He will govern and reign King of nations as He now does King of Saints. Pretty soon you will see Temples reared up, and the sons of Jacob will enter into the Temples of the Lord. What will they do there? They will do a great many things. When you see Zion redeemed and built up—when you see the people performing the ordinances of salvation for themselves and for others (and they will hereafter), you will see simply this (but I have not time this morning to tell you only a little part of it): About the time that the Temples of the Lord will be built and Zion is established—pretty nigh this time you will see (those who are faithful enough), the first you know, there will be strangers in your midst, walking with you, talking with you; they will enter into your houses and eat and drink with you, go to meeting with you, and begin to open your minds, as the Savior did the two disciples who walked out in the country in the days of old. About the time the Temples are ready, the strangers will be along and will converse with you, and will inquire of you, probably, if you understand the resurrection of the dead. * * * They will expound the Scriptures to you, and open your minds, and teach you of the resurrection of the just and the unjust, or the doctrine of salvation; they will use the keys of the holy Priesthood, and unlock the door of knowledge, to let you look into the palace of truth. You will exclaim, That is all plain: why did I not understand it before? And you will begin to feel your hearts burn within you as they walk and talk with you "(Brigham Young, *Jour. of Dis.,* Vol. VI., pp. 294-5).

37. Therefore, care not for the body, neither the life of the body; but care for the soul, and for the life of the soul.

38. And seek the face of the Lord always, that in patience ye may possess your souls, and ye shall have eternal life.

39. When men are called unto mine everlasting gospel, and

covenant with an everlasting covenant, they are accounted as the salt of the earth and the savor of men;

40. They are called to be the savor of men; therefore, if that salt of the earth lose its savor, behold, it is thenceforth good for nothing only to be cast out and trodden under the feet of men.

41. Behold, here is wisdom concerning the children of Zion, even many, but not all; they were found transgressors, therefore they must needs be chastened—

42. He that exalteth himself shall be abased, and he that abaseth himself shall be exalted.

6. THE SALT OF THE EARTH.

37-42. The Saints are "the salt of the Earth." Salt is essential to organized life, and a preservative against corruption. But if it loses its savor, it becomes useless. It cannot be made savory again. It can only be cast out and trodden under foot. As the salt of the Earth, the Saints have certain obligations. They must pay more attention to the soul, or the spirit, than to the body (v. 37); they must communicate with God in prayer (v. 38); and they must be humble (v. 42). The Children of Zion had failed, partly, in these respects.

During the Mosaic dispensation, a great deal of salt was used with the sacrifices, and large quantities were stored near the Temple. Rock salt, in time, lost its savor and was then scattered on the pavement.

43. And now, I will show unto you a parable, that you may know my will concerning the redemption of Zion.

44. A certain nobleman had a spot of land, very choice; and he said unto his servants: Go ye unto my vineyard, even upon this very choice piece of land, and plant twelve olive-trees;

45. And set watchmen round about them, and build a tower, that one may overlook the land round about, to be a watchman upon the tower, that mine olive-trees may not be broken down when the enemy shall come to spoil and take upon themselves the fruit of my vineyard.

46. Now, the servants of the nobleman went and did as their lord commanded them, and planted the olive-trees, and built a hedge round about, and set watchmen, and began to build a tower.

47. And while they were yet laying the foundation thereof, they began to say among themselves: And what need hath my lord of this tower?

48. And consulted for a long time, saying among themselves: What need hath my lord of this tower, seeing this is a time of peace?

49. Might not this money be given to the exchangers? For there is no need of these things.

50. And while they were at variance one with another they became very slothful, and they hearkened not unto the commandments of their lord.

51. And the enemy came by night, and broke down the hedge; and the servants of the nobleman arose and were affrighted, and fled; and the enemy destroyed their works, and broke down the olive-trees.

52. Now, behold, the nobleman, the lord of the vineyard, called upon his servants, and said unto them, Why! what is the cause of this great evil?

53. Ought ye not to have done even as I commanded you, and—after ye had planted the vineyard, and built the hedge round about, and set watchmen upon the walls thereof—built the tower also, and set a watchman upon the tower, and watched for my vineyard, and not have fallen asleep, lest the enemy should come upon you?

54. And behold, the watchman upon the tower would have seen the enemy while he was yet afar off; and then ye could have made ready and kept the enemy from breaking down the hedge thereof, and saved my vineyard from the hands of the destroyer.

55. And the lord of the vineyard said unto one of his servants: Go and gather together the residue of my servants, and take all the strength of mine house, which are my warriors, my young men, and they that are of middle age also among all my servants, who are the strength of mine house, save those only whom I have appointed to tarry;

56. And go ye straightway unto the land of my vineyard, and redeem my vineyard; for it is mine; I have bought it with money.

57. Therefore, get ye straightway unto my land; break down the walls of mine enemies, throw down their tower, and scatter their watchmen.

58. And inasmuch as they gather together against you,

avenge me of mine enemies, that by and by I may come with the residue of mine house and possess the land.

59. And the servant said unto his lord: When shall these things be?

60. And he said unto his servant: When I will; go ye straightway, and do all things whatsoever I have commanded you;

61. And this shall be my seal and blessing upon you—a faithful and wise steward in the midst of mine house, a ruler in my kingdom.

62. And his servant went straightway, and did all things whatsoever his lord commanded him; and after many days all things were fulfilled.

7. ZION TO BE REDEEMED.

43-62. This section contains a parable concerning the redemption of Zion. The Saints understood it, as soon as it was explained to them, but to the world it was as unintelligible as was the Parable of the Sower to the Jews. Our Lord, in the discourse found in Matthew 21:33-46, employs, practically, the same parable. The Prophet Isaiah has a somewhat similar parable (5:1-7).

Our Lord, in this part of the Revelation, compares Zion to a choice piece of land, owned by a nobleman who has commanded his servants to plant twelve olive trees upon it (v. 44); to set watchmen round about them, and to build a tower from which the grove could be watched (v. 45). The servants planted the trees, built a hedge, appointed watchmen, and began to build the tower. But while they were laying the foundations, they decided that there was no need of a tower (v. 48).

The settlements of the Saints were the olive trees; the officers of the Church were the watchmen, and the Temple, the site of which was dedicated August 3, 1831, would have been the tower from which the movements of the enemy could have been observed by inspiration. But, as nothing more was done to complete that tower, the enemy came by night and broke down the hedge, and the servants of the nobleman fled, leaving the enemy in possession (v. 51).

The nobleman rebuked his servants for their disobedience, but at the same time he commanded one of his men to gather them together again, and to take "the strength of mine house" and proceed to the land where the olive grove had been planted, and rescue it from those who held possession of it illegally (vv. 55-6). Here, then, is a Revelation containing the divine instructions that were carried out, afterwards, by those who formed the historic Zion's Camp.

44. *The vineyard*] In this Revelation, the vineyard is regarded as separate from the olive grove, for the nobleman planted olive trees in his vineyard, doubling its value.

45. *Build a tower*] The safety of the settlement of the Saints depends on the Temple, or rather on the power of God manifest in His holy House.

50. *While they were at variance * * * slothful*] This never fails. Strife always engenders slothfulness and neglect of duty.

53. *Watchmen upon the walls*] Watchmen upon the tower or walls, has reference to those who are appointed to positions of responsibility. The watchman on the tower is the presiding officer in the stake, ward or community.

55. *Unto one of his servants*] The Prophet Joseph (See Section 103:21).

56. *Redeem my vineyard*] The Prophet Joseph is commanded to gather up a company of men, faithful and true, and proceed to Zion and scatter the enemies; but he was not to make war upon them, but redeem the land by purchase (See Sec. 103:23).

62. *After many days*] The Prophet did as directed by Revelation, and in due time "all things were fulfilled."

63. Again, verily I say unto you, I will show unto you wisdom in me concerning all the churches, inasmuch as they are willing to be guided in a right and proper way for their salvation—

64. That the work of the gathering together of my saints may continue, that I may build them up unto my name upon holy places; for the time of harvest is come, and my word must needs be fulfilled.

65. Therefore, I must gather together my people, according to the parable of the wheat and the tares, that the wheat may be secured in the garners to possess eternal life, and be crowned with celestial glory, when I shall come in the kingdom of my Father to reward every man according as his work shall be;

66. While the tares shall be bound in bundles, and their bands made strong, that they may be burned with unquenchable fire.

67. Therefore, a commandment I give unto all the churches, that they shall continue to gather together unto the places which I have appointed.

68. Nevertheless, as I have said unto you in a former commandment, let not your gathering be in haste, nor by flight; but let all things be prepared before you.

69. And in order that all things be prepared before you, observe the commandment which I have given concerning these things—

70. Which saith, or teacheth, to purchase all the lands with money, which can be purchased for money, in the region round about the land which I have appointed to be the land of Zion, for the beginning of the gathering of my saints;

71. All the land which can be purchased in Jackson county, and the counties round about, and leave the residue in mine hand.

72. Now, verily I say unto you, let all the churches gather together all their moneys; let these things be done in their time, but not in haste; and observe to have all things prepared before you.

73. And let honorable men be appointed, even wise men, and send them to purchase these lands.

74. And the churches in the eastern countries, when they are built up, if they will hearken unto this counsel they may buy lands and gather together upon them; and in this way they may establish Zion.

75. There is even now already in store sufficient, yea, even an abundance, to redeem Zion, and establish her waste places, no more to be thrown down, were the churches, who call themselves after my name, willing to hearken to my voice.

8. Instructions to the Churches.

63-75. The Saints in the various Branches of the Church are here instructed to continue to gather (v. 64). But they must remember that gathering is not the final sorting out of the wheat from the tares. That will be done later (vv. 65, 66). At present all kinds will be found among the gathered Saints. Their gathering, however, should not be in haste, "but let all things be prepared before you" (v. 68); let land be purchased in Jackson County and adjacent counties, and then leave the matter in the hands of God (v. 71). Further, let agents be appointed to purchase the land (v. 73). There was no excuse for delay in acquiring all the land that was for sale, for the Saints had accumulated enough property to redeem Zion, and they could have done it by united efforts (v. 75).

76. And again I say unto you, those who have been scattered by their enemies, it is my will that they should continue to importune for redress, and redemption, by the hands of those who are placed as rulers and are in authority over you—

77. According to the laws and constitution of the people, which I have suffered to be established, and should be maintained for the rights and protection of all flesh, according to just and holy principles;

78. That every man may act in doctrine and principle pertaining to futurity, according to the moral agency which I have given unto him, that every man may be accountable for his own sins in the day of judgment.

79. Therefore, it is not right that any man should be in bondage one to another.

80. And for this purpose have I established the Constitution of this land, by the hands of wise men whom I raised up unto this very purpose, and redeemed the land by the shedding of blood.

9. Instructions to the Scattered Saints.

76-80. The scattered Saints are commanded to "importune for redress" (v. 76), as guaranteed by the Constitution and Constitutional laws (v. 77). The Lord suffered, that is, permitted, the establishment of Constitutional government in the United States for the protection of everybody in the enjoyment of religious liberty (v. 78). In the United States no man should be in bondage to another in matters over which conscience is the sole judge (v. 79), although most men like to force others to think and to act as they do. The Lord raised up wise men and inspired them to frame the Constitution for the very purpose of setting men at liberty, and the land was, furthermore, redeemed, to be a refuge for all oppressed, and the home of the free (v. 80).

It is strange that many men should have such a strong desire to force others to adopt their views and practices. It is strange to contemplate that prisons, torture, and death have been employed in the service of compulsory religion. No doubt, most of those who have resorted to such means have done so believing that they were trying to benefit their fellow-men by compelling them to believe and to do right. They did not call themselves persecutors. Nor do their modern successors regard themselves as persecutors, if they slander the members of unpopular churches, boycott them socially, and otherwise, and do everything in their power to prevent people from becoming interested in them. But, no matter how they regard themselves, they are persecutors, and as such they are in the service of Satan, who is the originator of the compulsory plan of salvation, and who has tried to enforce it among men from the beginning. God's kingdom is founded on perfect liberty.

81. Now, unto what shall I liken the children of Zion? I will liken them unto the parable of the woman and the unjust judge, for men ought always to pray and not to faint, which saith—

82. There was in a city a judge which feared not God, neither regarded man.

83. And there was a widow in that city, and she came unto him, saying: Avenge me of mine adversary.

84. And he would not for a while, but afterward he said within himself: Though I fear not God, nor regard man, yet because this widow troubleth me I will avenge her, lest by her continual coming she weary me.

85. Thus will I liken the children of Zion.

86. Let them importune at the feet of the judge;

87. And if he heed them not, let them importune at the feet of the governor;

88. And if the governor heed them not, let them importune at the feet of the president;

89. And if the president heed them not, then will the Lord arise and come forth out of his hiding place, and in his fury vex the nation;

90. And in his hot displeasure, and in his fierce anger, in his time, will cut off those wicked, unfaithful, and unjust stewards, and appoint them their portion among hypocrites, and unbelievers;

91. Even in outer darkness, where there is weeping, and wailing, and gnashing of teeth.

92. Pray ye, therefore, that their ears may be opened unto your cries, that I may be merciful unto them, that these things may not come upon them.

93. What I have said unto you must needs be, that all men may be left without excuse;

94. That wise men and rulers may hear and know that which they have never considered;

95. That I may proceed to bring to pass my act, my strange act, and perform my work, my strange work, that men may discern between the righteous and the wicked, saith your God.

10. THE UNJUST JUDGE.

81-95. In the minds of the Saints there would, naturally, be a doubt as to the effect of further petitions for redress. The Lord therefore reminds them of the parable of the woman and the unjust judge (Luke 18:1-8). This judge boasted of his atheism: He feared neither God nor man; yet, because the widow troubled him, by continually coming, he decided to "avenge her"; that is, to settle her case by according justice to her. For she was asking for justice, not for revenge. The Children of Zion are commanded to follow the example of this widow and "importune at the feet of the judge" (v. 86); and to carry the case from the judge to the Governor (v. 87), and from the Governor to the President, if need be (v. 88). And then, if they were not accorded justice, the Lord Himself would deal with the Nation (v. 89). When the leaders of the Nation refuse to do what is right, the Nation will suffer. This is perfectly just in a country where the people are responsible for their rulers.

The Saints did importune the rulers for redress. After having knocked at the doors of judges, they addressed several communications to Governor Dunklin of Missouri. In a letter dated February 4th, 1834, this official acknowledged the duty of the authorities to reinstate the Saints in their homes and to inquire into the proceedings of Col. Pitcher in depriving them of their arms. He also admitted that the entire State was interested in the faithful execution of the laws; "for that which is the case of the *Mormons* to-day, may be the case of the *Catholics* to-morrow, and after them, any other sect that may become obnoxious to a majority of the people of any section of the State." He proposed to provide protection for the people while suing in the courts and returning to their homes, but he did not guarantee protection in the continued possession of the homes, and the Saints, therefore, wisely declined to return and invite the mob to commit new outrages. Petitions were sent, and, finally, the Prophet Joseph appealed in person to the President of the United States, but this only elicited the famous answer, "Your cause is just, but I can do nothing for you."

96. And again, I say unto you, it is contrary to my commandment and my will that my servant Sidney Gilbert should sell my storehouse, which I have appointed unto my people, into the hands of mine enemies.

97. Let not that which I have appointed be polluted by mine enemies, by the consent of those who call themselves after my name;

98. For this is a very sore and grievous sin against me, and against my people, in consequence of those things which I have decreed and which are soon to befall the nations.

99. Therefore, it is my will that my people should claim, and hold claim upon that which I have appointed unto them, though they should not be permitted to dwell thereon.

100. Nevertheless, I do not say they shall not dwell thereon; for inasmuch as they bring forth fruit and works meet for my kingdom they shall dwell thereon.

101. They shall build, and another shall not inherit it; they shall plant vineyards, and they shall eat the fruit thereof. Even so. Amen.

11. Instructions and Promises.

96-101. Sidney Gilbert is instructed not to sell the Lord's storehouse, and the Saints are directed not to give up their claims. The Lord promises them that they shall come into possession of them in the Millennium, if not before. All things will finally be adjusted. Wrongs will be righted and all injustice removed. Then, and not till then, will there be lasting peace on Earth.

General Notes

When the gospel of Jesus Christ was first proclaimed in this dispensation by the Prophet Joseph and his associates, the world did not realize the immense importance of the movement. Joseph told the story of his prayer and the miraculous answer, the appearance of Moroni, the angel, and coming forth of the Book of Mormon, the restoration of the Priesthood and the organization of the Church. Then, the Witnesses related what they had seen and heard, and committed their testimony to writing. But very few of those who heard this wonderful story understood that a new era was about to dawn upon the world. They were, generally, inclined to regard it as a fairy tale or a deliberate scheme to deceive.

But before the Church was three years old, the world began to realize that a new moral force had been brought into operation. The gospel proved that the religious world was in error in its conception of the Godhead, in its views of the origin, nature, and final destiny of man, in its understanding of the plan of salvation, and its mode of worship. The gospel raised a higher ethical standard than that which was known in the world. It proposed to make men *equal* in temporal things, and to abolish destitution and poverty; it proposed to make men and women physically strong, by teaching them how to live; it proposed to establish peace in the home, in the fields of industry, and in international relations. It touched the ramparts of Satan at every point of prominence, and it proposed to undermine them, in spite of religious, business, and other interests arrayed against it.

Hence the onslaught on the Saints in Missouri, which God permitted for certain purposes. But that was only an incident. The "little stone" was rolling on. It is still moving in its onward course, and growing, and it is now evident that, in time, it will fill "the whole earth."

SECTION 102.

MINUTES *of the organization of the first High Council of the Church of Jesus Christ of Latter-day Saints, at Kirtland, Ohio, February 17, 1834.*

THIS day a general council of twenty-four high priests assembled at the house of Joseph Smith, Jun., by revelation, and proceeded to organize the high council of the church of Christ, which was to consist of twelve high priests, and one or three presidents as the case might require.

2. The high council was appointed by revelation for the purpose of settling important difficulties which might arise in the church, which could not be settled by the church or the bishop's council to the satisfaction of the parties.

3. Joseph Smith, Jun., Sidney Rigdon and Frederick G. Williams were acknowledged presidents by the voice of the council; and Joseph Smith, Sen., John Smith, Joseph Coe, John Johnson, Martin Harris, John S. Carter, Jared Carter, Oliver Cowdery, Samuel H. Smith, Orson Hyde, Sylvester Smith, and Luke Johnson, high priests, were chosen to be a standing council for the church, by the unanimous voice of the council.

4. The above-named councilors were then asked whether they accepted their appointments, and whether they would act in that office according to the law of heaven, to which they all answered that they accepted their appointments, and would fill their offices according to the grace of God bestowed upon them.

5. The number composing the council, who voted in the name and for the church in appointing the above-named coun-

cilors were forty-three, as follows: nine high priests, seventeen elders, four priests, and thirteen members.

6. Voted: that the high council cannot have power to act without seven of the above-named councilors, or their regularly appointed successors are present.

7. These seven shall have power to appoint other high priests, whom they may consider worthy and capable to act in the place of absent councilors.

8. Voted: that whenever any vacancy shall occur by the death, removal from office for transgression, or removal from the bounds of this church government, of any one of the above-named councilors, it shall be filled by the nomination of the president or presidents, and sanctioned by the voice of a general council of high priests, convened for that purpose, to act in the name of the church.

9. The president of the church, who is also the president of the council, is appointed by revelation, and acknowledged in his administration by the voice of the church.

10. And it is according to the dignity of his office that he should preside over the council of the church; and it is his privilege to be assisted by two other presidents, appointed after the same manner that he himself was appointed.

11. And in case of the absence of one or both of those who are appointed to assist him, he has power to preside over the council without an assistant; and in case he himself is absent, the other presidents have power to preside in his stead, both or either of them.

12. Whenever a high council of the church of Christ is regularly organized, according to the foregoing pattern, it shall be the duty of the twelve councilors to cast lots by numbers, and thereby ascertain who of the twelve shall speak first, commencing with number one and so in succession to number twelve.

13. Whenever this council convenes to act upon any case, the twelve councilors shall consider whether it is a difficult one or not; if it is not, two only of the councilors shall speak upon it, according to the form above written.

14. But if it is thought to be difficult, four shall be appointed; and if more difficult, six; but in no case shall more than six be appointed to speak.

15. The accused, in all cases, has a right to one-half of the council, to prevent insult or injustice.

16. And the councilors appointed to speak before the council are to present the case, after the evidence is examined, in its true light before the council; and every man is to speak according to equity and justice.

17. Those councilors who draw even numbers, that is, 2, 4, 6, 8, 10, and 12, are the individuals who are to stand up in behalf of the accused, and prevent insult and injustice.

18. In all cases the accuser and the accused shall have a privilege of speaking for themselves before the council, after the evidences are heard and the councilors who are appointed to speak on the case have finished their remarks.

19. After the evidences are heard, the councilors, accuser and accused have spoken, the president shall give a decision according to the understanding which he shall have of the case, and call upon the twelve councilors to sanction the same by their vote.

20. But should the remaining councilors, who have not spoken, or any one of them, after hearing the evidences and pleadings impartially, discover an error in the decision of the president, they can manifest it, and the case shall have a rehearing.

21. And if, after a careful re-hearing, any additional light is shown upon the case, the decision shall be altered accordingly.

22. But in case no additional light is given, the first decision shall stand, the majority of the council having power to determine the same.

23. In case of difficulty, respecting doctrine or principle, if there is not a sufficiency written to make the case clear to the minds of the council, the president may inquire and obtain the mind of the Lord by revelation.

24. The high priests, when abroad, have power to call and organize a council after the manner of the foregoing, to settle difficulties, when the parties or either of them shall request it.

25. And the said council of high priests shall have power to appoint one of their own number to preside over such council for the time being.

26. It shall be the duty of said council to transmit, immediately, a copy of their proceedings, with a full statement of the testimony accompanying their decision, to the high council of the seat of the First Presidency of the Church.

27. Should the parties or either of them be dissatisfied with the decision of said council, they may appeal to the high council of the seat of the First Presidency of the Church, and have a rehearing, which case shall there be conducted, according to the former pattern written, as though no such decision had been made.

28. This council of high priests abroad is only to be called on the most difficult cases of church matters; and no common or ordinary case is to be sufficient to call such council.

29. The traveling or located high priests abroad have power to say whether it is necessary to call such a council or not.

30. There is a distinction between the high council or traveling high priests abroad, and the traveling high council composed of the twelve apostles, in their decisions.

31. From the decision of the former there can be an appeal; but from the decision of the latter there cannot.

32. The latter can only be called in question by the general authorities of the church in case of transgression.

33. Resolved: that the president or presidents of the seat of the First Presidency of the Church shall have power to determine whether any such case, as may be appealed, is justly entitled to a re-hearing, after examining the appeal and the evidences and statements accompanying it.

34. The twelve councilors then proceeded to cast lots or ballot, to ascertain who should speak first, and the following was the result, namely: 1, Oliver Cowdery; 2, Joseph Coe; 3, Samuel H. Smith; 4, Luke Johnson; 5, John S. Carter; 6, Sylvester Smith; 7, John Johnson; 8, Orson Hyde; 9, Jared Carter; 10, Joseph Smith, Sen.; 11, John Smith; 12, Martin Harris.

After prayer the conference adjourned.

OLIVER COWDERY,
ORSON HYDE,
Clerks.

General Notes

The Prophet carefully guarded, against error, the report of the meeting in which this Council was organized. On February 18, he reviewed and corrected the minutes, and on the following day he assembled the Council to pass on the revised copy. The members then first engaged in prayer, asking God for the Spirit by which spiritual things are discerned. Then the minutes were read three times and, finally, adopted. It now forms what may be called the Constitution of the High Council of the Church of Christ.

A few days before the organization of this High Council, the Prophet addressed a council of High Priests and Elders on the subject of the proper order in such gatherings. "In ancient days," he said, "councils were conducted with such strict propriety, that no one was allowed to whisper, be weary, leave the room, or get uneasy in the least, until the voice of the Lord, by revelation, or the voice of the Council, by the Spirit, was obtained, which has not been observed in this Church to the present time" (*Hist. of the Church,* Vol. II., p. 25).

"I remember very well the organization of the High Council at Kirtland as a permanent institution. There had been several councils of twelve High Priests called for special cases, but they organized it permanently on the 17th of February, 1834. On the 19th, the first case that was brought up was that of Elder Curtis Hodge, Sen., who, while speaking in meeting, had gone into a spasm, shouting and screaming in such a manner as caused one of the Elders to rebuke him. Brother Hodge was brought before the Council for so doing. A great deal of instruction was imparted to the people, who were assembled in a room, sixteen feet by eighteen. The decision was that the charges in the declaration had been fairly sustained by good witnesses; that Elder Hodge ought to have confessed when rebuked by Elder Ezra Thayre; also that, if he had the Spirit of the Lord at the meeting where he shouted, he must have abused it and grieved it away, and all the Council agreed with the decision" (George A. Smith, *Jour. of Dis.,* Vol. XL., p. 7).

A very important Council meeting was held on the 20th of February, 1834. The attention of the Council had been called to the fact that, at a meeting at Springfield, Pa., held by Elders Orson Pratt and Lyman E. Johnson, some of the members of the Church had refused to partake of the Sacrament, because the Elder administering it did not keep the Word of Wisdom. Elder Lyman E. Johnson argued that they were justified in refusing, while Elder Orson Pratt held that Church members ought to receive the emblems from any Elder who retains his office, or license. Six councilors were appointed to speak on the question. When they had finished, the President gave the decision:

"No official member in this Church is worthy to hold an office, after having the Word of Wisdom properly taught him and he, the official member, neglecting to comply with or obey it."

This decision was confirmed by the vote of the Council (*History of the Church,* Vol. II., p. 34-5).

SECTION 103.

REVELATION *given through Joseph Smith the Prophet, at Kirtland, Ohio, February 24, 1834. For explanation of unusual names see heading to Section 78.——Cause of the persecutions permitted against the Saints in Jackson County, Missouri—The Saints to prevail if they follow the counsel of the Lord—Otherwise the powers of the world to prevail against them—The angel of the Lord and the Lord's presence to go before the people— Moneys to be collected and sent up to Zion for the purchase of lands—Individual instructions to certain Elders.*

VERILY I say unto you, my friends, behold, I will give unto you a revelation and commandment, that you may know how to act in the discharge of your duties concerning the salvation and redemption of your brethren, who have been scattered on the land of Zion;

2. Being driven and smitten by the hands of mine enemies. on whom I will pour out my wrath without measure in mine own time.

3. For I have suffered them thus far, that they might fill up the measure of their iniquities, that their cup might be full;

4. And that those who call themselves after my name might be chastened for a little season with a sore and grievous chastisement, because they did not hearken altogether unto the precepts and commandments which I gave unto them.

ON THE REDEMPTION OF ZION.

In a previous Revelation (Section 101:55-60), it was made known to the Prophet that he would be required, at some future time, to lead "the strength of mine house" to the land of Zion, in order to "redeem" it. The Revelation in this Section was received four months and twelve days afterwards, directing him to begin to gather up the strength of the Church for a relief expedition. Elders Lyman Wight and Parley P. Pratt had just arrived in Kirtland, from Missouri, with a message from the Saints. A meeting of the High Council was called. The messengers from Zion told the Council that the scattered Saints had obtained food and clothing in exchange for labor, and that they were quite comfortable for the time being; but they were grief-stricken because they had been driven from their homes in Zion, and they earnestly desired to know, if possible, how and by what means Zion was to be redeemed. This Revelation, given before the meeting of the Council was held, is an answer to that very question. When the messengers had stated the case, the Prophet had the answer ready. He had prepared to announce that he was going to Zion and that he would call for volunteers to accompany him. The Council endorsed this, and between thirty and forty men volunteered to go, whereupon the Prophet Joseph was elected Commander-in-Chief of the expedition.

In this Revelation, our Lord (1) makes known the reason why the Saints had been driven from Jackson County (1-4); (2) promises them power over the enemy, if they would obey (5-10), and (3) an opportunity to return (11-14); (4) speaks of the redemption of Zion "by power" (15-20), (5) of the mission of the Prophet Joseph (21-8), and (6) of others (29-30); (7) names the number of men needed for the expedition (31-4); and (8) gives sundry instructions (35-40).

1. WHY THE SAINTS HAD BEEN EXILED.

1-4. Our Lord reiterates the assurance given on several occasions that the exile was not an evidence that God had rejected His people. It was chastisement (v. 4) for the purpose of correction. It was necessary that the Saints should know this when they were about to furnish men and means for a relief expedition. Chastisement is not never-ending. In this case it was to be only for a "little season." If the Saints would submit and obey the Lord, their chastisement would be over.

It is to be noted that the Saints in Ohio and elsewhere were put to the test by this commandment to form a relief expedition. If they obeyed, Zion would be redeemed; if not, it would remain in bondage, and the churches in other places would also be set upon by enemies and scattered. The Prophet was well aware of this, for on the 21st of April, 1834, in a conference of Elders at Morton, Ohio, he prophesied:

"If Zion is not delivered, the time is near when all of this Church, wherever they may be found, will be persecuted and destroyed in like manner" (*Hist. of the Church,* Vol. II., p. 53).

Little did the Saints realize the purport of this prediction.

5. But verily I say unto you, that I have decreed a decree which my people shall realize, inasmuch as they hearken from this very hour unto the counsel which I, the Lord their God, shall give unto them.

6. Behold they shall, for I have decreed it, begin to prevail against mine enemies from this very hour.

7. And by hearkening to observe all the words which I, the Lord their God, shall speak unto them, they shall never cease to prevail until the kingdoms of the world are subdued under my feet, and the earth is given unto the saints, to possess it forever and ever

8. But inasmuch as they keep not my commandments, and hearken not to observe all my words, the kingdoms of the world shall prevail against them.

9. For they were set to be a light unto the world, and to be the saviors of men;

10. And inasmuch as they are not the saviors of men, they are as salt that has lost its savor, and is thenceforth good for nothing but to be cast out and trodden under foot of men.

2. THE SAINTS TO PREVAIL.

5-10. The promise is here given that the Saints shall begin to prevail against the enemies "from this very hour" (v. 6), provided they hearken to the counsel of the Lord. On that condition they are, furthermore, promised that they shall prevail until "the Earth is given unto the Saints, to possess it for ever and ever" (v. 7). On the other hand, if they did not keep the commandments of God, they would not prevail, but, as salt without savor, be cast out (v. 10. See also Sec. 101:39-41).

This is not difficult to comprehend. If Noah had not kept the commandment of God and built the Ark, he would not have escaped the flood. If Lot had not obeyed and left Sodom, he would have perished. If Israel had refused to obey Moses, they would not have been delivered from the bondage in Egypt. In any family, if the children refuse to follow the counsel dictated by the wisdom and love of the parents, they will not escape trouble.

5. *I have decreed a decree*] There was no uncertainty in the commandment for the rescue of the Saints. It was a decree issued by the Almighty.

7. *The earth is given unto the saints*] The Earth in its glorified condition will be the abode of celestial beings (See Sec. 88:15-20).

11. But verily I say unto you, I have decreed that your brethren which have been scattered shall return to the lands of their inheritances, and shall build up the waste places of Zion.

12. For after much tribulation, as I have said unto you in a former commandment, cometh the blessing.

13. Behold, this is the blessing which I have promised after your tribulations, and the tribulations of your brethren—your redemption, and the redemption of your brethren, even their restoration to the land of Zion, to be established, no more to be thrown down.

14. Nevertheless, if they pollute their inheritances they shall

be thrown down; for I will not spare them if they pollute their inheritances.

3. THE SCATTERED SAINTS TO RETURN.

11-14. Not only were the Saints to begin to prevail, but they were to be re-instated in their inheritances (v. 11). They were to be established, never more to be "thrown down" (v. 13), except they should pollute the place, by sin (v. 14).

This promise is yet to be fulfilled. The Saints have not yet been in a condition to receive this blessing, but the promise will be kept.

15. Behold, I say unto you, the redemption of Zion must needs come by power;

16. Therefore, I will raise up unto my people a man, who shall lead them like as Moses led the children of Israel.

17. For ye are the children of Israel, and of the seed of Abraham, and ye must needs be led out of bondage by power, and with a stretched-out arm.

18. And as your fathers were led at the first, even so shall the redemption of Zion be.

19. Therefore, let not your hearts faint, for I say not unto you as I said unto your fathers: Mine angel shall go up before you, but not my presence.

20. But I say unto you: Mine angels shall go up before you, and also my presence, and in time ye shall possess the goodly land.

4. REDEMPTION OF ZION BY POWER.

15-20. When the redemption of Zion comes, it will be by "power." The power of God will be manifested, as unmistakably as it was in the exodus of Israel. God will raise up a man who shall lead the Saints, as Moses led His people (vv. 17-18), and God's Presence will be with them, and angels shall go before them (v. 20).

15. *By power*]
"When God shows forth His power among the Latter-day Saints, it will be because there is unity in regard to doctrine, and in regard to everything that God has placed in their hands; and not only unity, but sanctification on their part, that there shall not be a spot or wrinkle, as it were, but everything shall be as fair as the sun that shines in the heavens" (Orson Pratt, *Jour. of Dis.,* Vol. XV., p. 361).

16. *A man * * * like as Moses*]
"Whether that man is now in existence, or whether it is someone yet to be born; or whether it is our present leader [Brigham Young] who

has led us forth into these valleys of the mountains; whether God will grant unto us the great blessing to have his life spared to lead forth His people like a Moses, we perhaps may not all know * * * Would to God that his life may be prolonged like Moses, in days of old, who, when he was eighty years old, was sent forth to redeem the people of Israel from bondage. God is not under the necessity of choosing a young man. He can make a man eighty years of age full of vigor, strength and health * * * But whether it be he or some other person, God will surely fulfil His promise * * * Many of us, no doubt, thought, when that Revelation was given, that Joseph would be the man * * * I do not know but that he will yet * * * We are living in the dispensation of the fulness of times, the dispensation of the resurrection, and there may be some who will wake from their tombs for certain purposes and to bring to pass certain transactions on the Earth, decreed by the great Jehovah; and if the Lord see proper to bring forth that man just before the winding-up scene to lead forth the army of Israel, He will do so" (*Ibid.*, p. 362-3).

17. *Ye are the children of Israel*] "They which are the children of the flesh, these are not the children of God: but the children of the promise are counted for the seed" (Rom. 9:8).

Led out of bondage] The conditions in the world, notwithstanding our boasted liberty, have produced "bondage." Those who have accumulated wealth command influence and power, and govern the affairs of kingdoms and republics to suit themselves, regardless of the needs of the poor. Class distinction is sharply drawn, and while there is oppression on one side, there is servitude on the other. Militarism is one fruit of existing conditions, and that is slavery in the most aggravated form. Another result is conflict between classes.

"Is this right or wrong? It is wrong, materially wrong, and we have continued in this wrong * * * When shall it come to an end? When will we learn to keep the commandments of God and become one, not only in doctrine but in the bands of earthly things? Such a time must come, and if we do not comply with it, we shall fall behind" (Orson Pratt, *Jour. of Dis.*, Vol. XV., p. 357).

19. *Angel * * * presence*] God appeared to Moses in different ways. When any of the Children of Israel in the wilderness sought divine counsel he went to the Tent of Meeting outside the camp. Moses entered the Tent, and the pillar of cloud descended and stood at the entrance, while the Lord spake to Moses, and the people were worshiping (Ex. 33:7-11). This was the Presence of the Lord. The Tent, or tabernacle, was constructed that the Lord might *dwell* therein, and His glory rested on the *mercy seat,* His throne between cherubim. The Angel or messenger of the Lord was His representative. When Israel disobeyed God, He said, "I will send an angel before thee * * * for I will not go up in the midst of thee; for thou art a stiffnecked people: lest I consume thee in the way" (Ex. 33:1-3). The Saints have the promise that when Zion

is to be redeemed by power, angels will go before them and also the divine Presence (v. 20).

21. Verily, verily I say unto you, that my servant Baurak Ale [Joseph Smith, Jun.] is the man to whom I likened the servant to whom the Lord of the vineyard spake in the parable which I have given unto you.

22. Therefore let my servant Baurak Ale [Joseph Smith, Jun.] say unto the strength of my house, my young men and the middle aged—Gather yourselves together unto the land of Zion, upon the land which I have bought with money that has been consecrated unto me.

23. And let all the churches send up wise men with their moneys, and purchase lands even as I have commanded them.

24. And inasmuch as mine enemies come against you to drive you from my goodly land, which I have consecrated to be the land of Zion, even from your own lands after these testimonies, which ye have brought before me against them, ye shall curse them;

25. And whomsoever ye curse, I will curse, and ye shall avenge me of mine enemies.

26. And my presence shall be with you even in avenging me of mine enemies, unto the third and fourth generation of them that hate me.

27. Let no man be afraid to lay down his life for my sake; for whoso layeth down his life for my sake shall find it again.

28. And whoso is not willing to lay down his life for my sake is not my disciple.

5. Missions of the Prophet Joseph.

21-8. The Lord here directs His servant Joseph Smith to call upon the young and middle-aged men of the Church to assemble in the land of Zion (v. 22); and upon "wise men" to go there with money enough to purchase all the land that might be for sale (v. 23). If the enemy then came upon them, the Lord would interfere in behalf of His people (v. 25).

24. *Ye shall curse them*] The expression may sound harsh to a refined ear, but it is strictly Scriptural. Abraham received the divine assurance, "I will bless them that bless thee, and him that curseth thee will I curse" (Gen. 12:3). Isaac said to Jacob, "Cursed be every one that curseth thee, and blessed be every one that blesseth thee" (Gen. 27:29).

To "curse" means to "imprecate," to "call down evil" upon somebody or something; but it also means to foretell evils that will befall those who persist in wickedness, as for instance, when Noah cursed Canaan, by predicting that his descendants would live in servitude, while those of Shem and Japheth would flourish and prosper. In that sense of the word it may be said that our Lord cursed Jerusalem, when He predicted its destruction, though He shed tears over the doomed City. The Saints are not authorized to return evil for evil, but they are commanded to cast off the dust of their feet, as a testimony against enemies, and then leave them in the hands of the Lord (See Sec. 24:15). In this connection it may be stated that *Baurak Ale* (vv. 21, 22) are Hebrew words, meaning, "The Lord blesses." The Prophet Joseph was sent to the world to be a blessing, not a curse.

29. It is my will that my servant Sidney Rigdon shall lift up his voice in the congregations in the eastern countries, in preparing the churches to keep the commandments which I have given unto them concerning the restoration and redemption of Zion.

30. It is my will that my servant Parley P. Pratt and my servant Lyman Wight should not return to the land of their brethren, until they have obtained companies to go up unto the land of Zion, by tens, or by twenties, or by fifties, or by an hundred, until they have obtained to the number of five hundred of the strength of my house.

6. SIDNEY RIGDON, PARLEY P. PRATT, AND LYMAN WIGHT.

29-30. Special instructions are here given to Sidney Rigdon, Parley P. Pratt, and Lyman Wight, regarding the gathering of the strength of the Church for the redemption of Zion. Sidney Rigdon is directed to visit the Branches in the Eastern States, and Parley P. Pratt and Lyman Wight, who had just arrived from Missouri, were not to return, until a company, preferably five hundred strong, had been formed for a relief expedition to Jackson County.

31. Behold this is my will; ask and ye shall receive; but men do not always do my will.

32. Therefore, if you cannot obtain five hundred, seek diligently that peradventure you may obtain three hundred.

33. And if ye cannot obtain three hundred, seek diligently that peradventure ye may obtain one hundred.

34. But verily I say unto you, a commandment I give unto you, that ye shall not go up unto the land of Zion until you have obtained a hundred of the strength of my house, to go up with you unto the land of Zion.

7. NUMBER OF MEN NEEDED.

31-4. Five hundred men were needed for the expedition. Five hundred were to be asked for; but, as men do not always comply with the requirements of the Almighty, three hundred, or even one hundred, were to be accepted (v. 33), but the expedition should not be attempted with a smaller number (v. 34).

35. Therefore, as I said unto you, ask and ye shall receive; pray earnestly that peradventure my servant Baurak Ale [Joseph Smith, Jun.] may go with you, and preside in the midst of my people, and organize my kingdom upon the consecrated land, and establish the children of Zion upon the laws and commandments which have been and which shall be given unto you.

36. All victory and glory is brought to pass unto you through your diligence, faithfulness, and prayers of faith.

37. Let my servant Parley P. Pratt journey with my servant Joseph Smith, Jun.

38. Let my servant Lyman Wight journey with my servant Sidney Rigdon.

39. Let my servant Hyrum Smith journey with my servant Frederick G. Williams.

40. Let my servant Orson Hyde journey with my servant Orson Pratt, whithersoever my servant Joseph Smith, Jun., shall counsel them, in obtaining the fulfilment of these commandments which I have given unto you, and leave the residue in my hands. Even so. Amen.

8. SUNDRY INSTRUCTIONS.

35-40. The Saints are instructed to pray that the Prophet Joseph may be permitted to go to Zion and organize the kingdom of God upon the consecrated land, and establish the Saints in accordance with laws given, or still to be given (v. 35). Parley P. Pratt is appointed the companion of Joseph on his journey in behalf of the redemption of Zion (v. 37); Lyman Wight is made the traveling companion of Sidney Rigdon (v. 38); Hyrum Smith and Frederick G. Williams and Orson Hyde and Orson Pratt, are to travel together (vv. 39, 40).

GENERAL NOTES

Five hundred men were called for. On the 5th of May, 1834, one hundred left Kirtland for Missouri. On the way, the company was reinforced and, finally, consisted of 205 members. The organization is known as Zion's Camp. The members were mostly Elders, Priests, Teachers, and Deacons. They crossed the Mississippi early in June, and in the latter part of that month pitched their tents between two forks of the Fishing River, Mo., between Richmond, in Ray Co., and Liberty, Clay Co., There, some of the exiles from Jackson County met them and told them of further outrages perpetrated against the Saints. The appearance at Fishing River of Zion's Camp caused considerable excitement in Missouri, and armed bands went out to meet them. On one occasion they were miraculously saved from a murderous attack, by a terrible storm which prevented the mob from crossing the River. Afterwards Colonel Sconce, of Ray Co., and Sheriff Gillium, of Clay Co., visited the Camp and satisfied themselves that the "Mormon" leaders had no other intention than to try to effect an amicable settlement of the existing difficulties.

On the 27th of May, 1834, Joseph made this note in his journal:

"Notwithstanding our enemies were continually breathing threats of violence, we did not fear neither did we hesitate to prosecute our journey, for God was with us, and His angels went before us, and the faith of our little band was unwavering. We know that angels were our companions, for we saw them."

Zion's Camp was organized on military lines, and the brethren were well armed for defense, but the mission was one of peace and good will. They carried clothing and provisions for the destitute Saints, and their object was to make peace, if possible, between the two classes of citizens. In some respects the mission appeared to be a failure, but in others it was a grand success. During the journey of a thousand miles, with trials and hardships innumerable, the sterling character of some of the men who afterwards became leaders of the Church was made manifest, and the Saints knew they could trust them. During this historic expedition, too, Brigham Young, the great Moses of the latter-day Israel, received his first lessons, under the eyes of the Prophet, in that leadership which became his special mission, after the martyrdom at Carthage, and the exodus from Illinois, and which made him famous in the annals of history. See Whitney's *Life of Heber C. Kimball,* pp. 77-9.

SECTION 104.

REVELATION *given to Enoch* [*Joseph Smith the Prophet*] *April 23, 1834, concerning the United Order, or the order of the Church for the benefit of the poor. The occasion was that of a council meeting of the First Presidency and other High Priests, in which the pressing temporal needs of the people had been given consideration. For explanation of unusual names see head-*

*ing to Section 78.——Some who had broken their covenants in
the United Order had come under condemnation—The Lord will
not be mocked—Care of the poor an imperative duty of the
Saints—The United Order in Kirtland was segregated from that
in Zion, Missouri—This separation partly because of transgression on the part of members, and partly because of the scattered
condition of the Saints in Missouri—A treasury for the order
provided for—On conditions of faith and humility, the Lord
promises to deliver his people this once out of financial bondage.*

VERILY I say unto you, my friends, I give unto you counsel,
and a commandment, concerning all the properties which belong
to the order which I commanded to be organized and established,
to be a united order, and an everlasting order for the benefit
of my church, and for the salvation of men until I come—

2. With promise immutable and unchangeable, that inasmuch
as those whom I commanded were faithful they should be
blessed with a multiplicity of blessings;

3. But inasmuch as they were not faithful they were nigh
unto cursing.

Before the brethren of Zion's Camp were ready to begin the journey
to Missouri, the Prophet received this Revelation concerning the property
belonging to the United Order. This Order had been established by
Revelation (See Sec. 82), and its temporal affairs were to be placed on
a solid foundation, before the journey to Zion. The brethren were going
to face the lion in his den. They did not know whether they would return. Heber C. Kimball says of the departure, on the 5th of May, "Truly,
this was a solemn morning to me. I took leave of my wife and children
and friends, not knowing whether I would see them again in the flesh,
as myself and brethren were threatened, both in that country and
Missouri, by enemies, that they would destroy us and exterminate us
from the land.

In this Revelation the Lord (1) characterizes the United Order as an
everlasting Order (1-3); (2) threatens transgressors of its rules with
severe punishment (4-10); (3) directs His servants to organize (11-18);
(4) specifies stewardships (19-46); (5) commands them to dissolve
partnership with the United Order in Zion (47-53); (6) explains what
stewardship means (54-59); (7) directs them to establish two treasuries
(60-77); and (8) to pay their debts (78-86).

1. THE UNITED ORDER.

1. *An everlasting order*] The Lord established the United Order, or
the Order of Enoch, when it had been demonstrated that the Saints

were not able to practice the celestial law of consecration. This Order was to be permanent, but when the Saints also proved themselves unequal to its requirements, the Lord again released them, temporarily, and gave them the law of tithing.

"Says one, 'What, God revoke a commandment!' Yes, that is what He did in ancient times, and He is the same God yet. He did it for our good; for if that law had been in full force, this people would not have been in these mountains this day. Our selfishness and covetousness are so great that, as a people, we never would have complied with it. A few amongst us might have done so, but as a people we should have been overcome and ruined; but owing to that law being revoked, many of us will now, perhaps, be saved" (Orson Pratt, *Jour. of Dis.,* Vol. XVI., p. 5).

4.   Therefore, inasmuch as some of my servants have not kept the commandment, but have broken the covenant through covetousness, and with feigned words, I have cursed them with a very sore and grievous curse.

5.   For I, the Lord, have decreed in my heart, that inasmuch as any man belonging to the order shall be found a transgressor, or, in other words, shall break the covenant with which ye are bound, he shall be cursed in his life, and shall be trodden down by whom I will;

6.   For I, the Lord, am not to be mocked in these things—

7.   And all this that the innocent among you may not be condemned with the unjust; and that the guilty among you may not escape; because I, the Lord, have promised unto you a crown of glory at my right hand.

8.   Therefore, inasmuch as you are found transgressors, you cannot escape my wrath in your lives.

9.   Inasmuch as ye are cut off for transgression, ye cannot escape the buffetings of Satan until the day of redemption.

10.   And I now give unto you power from this very hour, that if any man among you, of the order, is found a transgressor and repenteth not of the evil, that ye shall deliver him over unto the buffetings of Satan; and he shall not have power to bring evil upon you.

2. Consequences of Breaking Covenants.

4-10. Some of those who were called to become members of the United Order entered into covenants, as required, but soon broke their pledges because of covetousness (v. 4). Over these the wrath of God hovered as a thunder cloud; they might be destroyed by the enemy at any time (v. 5). Transgressors were to be cut off from the Order, for the protection of the innocent (v. 7), and when they were cut off, the adversary had power over them (v. 10).

4. *Covetousness*] Elder George A. Smith observes:

"The worship of money, the love of earthly goods, the desire to possess property, to control wealth, has been planted in the breast, soul, and heart of almost every man in the world, from generation to generation. It has been the great, ruling deity, the object worshiped by the whole Christian world. * * * No man seems to desire an office * * * for the public good, but the first thing to be considered is, 'What will it pay?' * * * The god of this world has dominion over the souls of men" (*Jour. of Dis.*, Vol. IX., p. 197).

Very few are saved from this sin. Those who broke their covenants because of covetousness had been saved, perhaps, from profanity, or from drunkenness, or from other sins of a similar nature, but covetousness still held them in chains. If we desire an illustration of the power of the adversary over some men—even some who are Church members— we need only consider their dealings with their fellowmen when a dollar is at stake. When the gospel becomes the "power of God unto salvation" to such an extent that man is saved from selfishness, of which covetousness is a manifestation, there will be no difficulty in living under the rules of the United Order; nor under the celestial law of consecration.

11. It is wisdom in me; therefore, a commandment I give unto you, that ye shall organize yourselves and appoint every man his stewardship;

12. That every man may give an account unto me of the stewardship which is appointed unto him.

13. For it is expedient that I, the Lord, should make every man accountable, as a steward over earthly blessings, which I have made and prepared for my creatures.

14. I, the Lord, stretched out the heavens, and built the earth, my very handiwork; and all things therein are mine.

15. And it is my purpose to provide for my saints, for all things are mine.

16. But it must needs be done in mine own way; and behold this is the way that I, the Lord, have decreed to provide for my saints, that the poor shall be exalted, in that the rich are made low.

17. For the earth is full, and there is enough and to spare; yea, I prepared all things, and have given unto the children of men to be agents unto themselves.

18. Therefore, if any man shall take of the abundance which I have made, and impart not his portion, according to the law of my gospel, unto the poor and the needy, he shall, with the wicked, lift up his eyes in hell, being in torment.

3. ORGANIZE AND APPOINT STEWARDSHIPS.

11-18. In this section the servants of the Lord are directed to effect an organization and appoint stewardships. The underlying principle is stated: The Lord, as the Creator of the heavens and the Earth, is the real owner of all that is therein (v. 14); He is perfectly willing that His children should use earthly things for their benefit (v. 15), and this is God's way of providing for them (v. 16). The United Order, then, is a divine institution.

19. And now, verily I say unto you, concerning the properties of the order—

20. Let my servant Pelagoram [Sidney Rigdon] have appointed unto him the place where he now resides, and the lot of Tahhanes [the tannery] for his stewardship, for his support while he is laboring in my vineyard, even as I will, when I shall command him.

21. And let all things be done according to the counsel of the order, and united consent or voice of the order, which dwell in the land of Shinehah [Kirtland].

22. And this stewardship and blessing, I, the Lord, confer upon my servant Pelagoram [Sidney Rigdon] for a blessing upon him, and his seed after him;

23. And I will multiply blessings upon him, inasmuch as he will be humble before me.

24. And again, let my servant Mahemson [Martin Harris] have appointed unto him, for his stewardship, the lot of land which my servant Zombre [John Johnson] obtained in exchange for his former inheritance, for him and his seed after him;

25. And inasmuch as he is faithful, I will multiply blessings upon him and his seed after him.

26. And let my servant Mahemson [Martin Harris] devote his moneys for the proclaiming of my words, according as my servant Gazelam [Joseph Smith, Jun.] shall direct.

27. And again, let my servant Shederlaomach [Frederick G. Williams] have the place upon which he now dwells.

28. And let my servant Olihah [Oliver Cowdery] have the lot which is set off joining the house, which is to be for the Laneshine house [printing office], which is lot number one, and also the lot upon which his father resides.

29. And let my servants Shederlaomach [Frederick G. Williams] and Olihah [Oliver Cowdery] have the Laneshine house [printing office] and all things that pertain unto it.

30. And this shall be their stewardship which shall be appointed unto them.

31. And inasmuch as they are faithful, behold I will bless, and multiply blessings upon them.

32. And this is the beginning of the stewardship which I have appointed them, for them and their seed after them.

33. And, inasmuch as they are faithful, I will multiply blessings upon them and their seed after them, even a multiplicity of blessings.

34. And again, let my servant Zombre [John Johnson] have the house in which he lives, and the inheritance, all save the ground which has been reserved for the building of my houses, which pertains to that inheritance, and those lots which have been named for my servant Olihah [Oliver Cowdery].

35. And inasmuch as he is faithful, I will multiply blessings upon him.

36. And it is my will that he should sell the lots that are laid off for the building up of the city of my saints, inasmuch as it shall be made known to him by the voice of the Spirit, and according to the counsel of the order, and by the voice of the order.

37. And this is the beginning of the stewardship which I have appointed unto him, for a blessing unto him and his seed after him.

38. And inasmuch as he is faithful, I will multiply a multiplicity of blessings upon him.

39. And again, let my servant Ahashdah [Newel K. Whitney] have appointed unto him the houses and lot where he now resides, and the lot and building on which the Ozondah [mercantile establishment] stands, and also the lot which is on the corner south of the Ozondah [mercantile establishment], and also the lot on which the Shule [ashery] is situated.

40. And all this I have appointed unto my servant Ahashdah [Newel K. Whitney] for his stewardship, for a blessing upon him and his seed after him, for the benefit of the Ozondah [mercantile establishment] of my order which I have established for my stake in the land of Shinehah [Kirtland].

41. Yea, verily, this is the stewardship which I have appointed unto my servant Ahashdah [N. K. Whitney], even this whole Ozondah [mercantile establishment], him and his agent, and his seed after him.

42. And inasmuch as he is faithful in keeping my commandments, which I have given unto him, I will multiply blessings upon him and his seed after him, even a multiplicity of blessings.

43. And again, let my servant Gazelam [Joseph Smith, Jun.] have appointed unto him the lot which is laid off for the building of my house, which is forty rods long and twelve wide, and also the inheritance upon which his father now resides;

44. And this is the beginning of the stewardship which I have appointed unto him, for a blessing upon him, and upon his father.

45. For behold, I have reserved an inheritance for his father, for his support; therefore he shall be reckoned in the house of my servant Gazelam [Joseph Smith, Jun.].

46. And I will multiply blessings upon the house of my servant Gazelam [Joseph Smith, Jun.], inasmuch as he is faithful, even a multiplicity of blessings.

4. DISPOSITION OF THE PROPERTY OF THE ORDER.

19-46. Specific directions are here given for stewardships. Sidney Rigdon is given charge of the tannery (v. 20). He had, at one time, been engaged in the very useful business of a tanner and was competent in this stewardship. Martin Harris, who was a successful farmer, is given charge of a piece of land (v. 24). He was also to manage a publication business, under the direction of the Prophet (v. 26). Oliver Cowdery and Frederick G. Williams are given charge of the printing office (v. 30). John Johnson is to be a real estate agent (v. 36). Newel K. Whitney is assigned to the mercantile establishment (v. 39). Joseph Smith is given charge of the Temple lot (v. 43). He is also to take care of his father (v. 45), for the Lord recognizes the duty of children to provide for their parents, as well as the duty of parents to care for their children.

47. And now, a commandment I give unto you concerning

Zion, that you shall no longer be bound as a united order to your brethren of Zion, only on this wise—

48. After you are organized, you shall be called the United Order of the Stake of Zion, the City of Shinehah [Kirtland]. And your brethren, after they are organized, shall be called the United Order of the City of Zion.

49. And they shall be organized in their own names, and in their own name; and they shall do their business in their own name, and in their own names;

50. And you shall do your business in your own name, and in your own names.

51. And this I have commanded to be done for your salvation, and also for their salvation, in consequence of their being driven out and that which is to come.

52. The covenants being broken through transgression, by covetousness and feigned words—

53. Therefore, you are dissolved as a united order with your brethren, that you are not bound only up to this hour unto them, only on this wise, as I said, by loan as shall be agreed by this order in council, as your circumstances will admit and the voice of the council direct.

5. DIRECTIONS TO DISSOLVE PARTNERSHIP.

47-53. According to a Revelation given April 26th, 1832 (Sec. 82:11, 12), the temporal affairs of the western and eastern divisions of the Church were to be under one management. In this Section instructions are given for the formation of two separate organizations, one to be called *The United Order of the Stake of Zion, the City of Shinehah* (Kirtland); the other, *The United Order of the City of Zion* (v. 48). Each was to be independent of the other (vv. 49, 50). The brethren in Kirtland were not to suffer on account of the losses inflicted by the mob on the Saints in Zion. As an independent organization, they would be in a position to render financial aid to the exiles. As a part of the organization in Zion, the financial disaster engendered by mob rule would have affected them also, and they might have been unable to come to the aid of their brethren.

54. And again, a commandment I give unto you concerning your stewardship which I have appointed unto you.

55. Behold, all these properties are mine, or else your faith is vain, and ye are found hypocrites, and the covenants which ye have made unto me are broken;

56. And if the properties are mine, then ye are stewards; otherwise ye are no stewards.

57. But, verily I say unto you, I have appointed unto you to be stewards over mine house, even stewards indeed.

58. And for this purpose I have commanded you to organize yourselves, even to shinelah [print] my words, the fulness of my scriptures, the revelations which I have given unto you, and which I shall, hereafter, from time to time give unto you—

59. For the purpose of building up my church and kingdom on the earth, and to prepare my people for the time when I shall dwell with them, which is nigh at hand.

6. WHAT STEWARDSHIP MEANS.

54-5. The Lord assigned certain properties to each of His servants (vv. 19-46), but He retained the ownership (v. 56). They were to manage the property for Him, and they were accountable to Him. Their office, power, and authority were those of stewards.

58. *Print my words*] The Lord gives special directions concerning the printing of the Scriptures, including the Doctrine and Covenants— "the revelations which I have given unto you, and which I shall, hereafter, from time to time give unto you." This volume is given for the building up of the Church (v. 59), and it should be studied diligently by all who are interested in the kingdom of God. Elder Joseph F. Smith, on one occasion, after having pointed out that the Bible and the Book of Mormon bear record of the truth that Jesus is the Christ, said:

"But is this all? No. We have here another book, the Doctrine and Covenants, which contains Revelations from God, through the Prophet Joseph Smith, who lived contemporary with ourselves. They are Christ's words, declaring that He was the same that came to the Jews, that was lifted up on the cross, was laid in the tomb, burst the bands of death, and came forth out of the grave. * * * Here, then, is another testimony of this divine truth; hence we have three witnesses" (*Jour. of Dis.*, Vol. XIX., p. 262).

60. And ye shall prepare for yourselves a place for a treasury, and consecrate it unto my name.

61. And ye shall appoint one among you to keep the treasury, and he shall be ordained unto this blessing.

62. And there shall be a seal upon the treasury, and all the sacred things shall be delivered into the treasury; and no man among you shall call it his own, or any part of it, for it shall belong to you all with one accord.

63. And I give it unto you from this very hour; and now see to it, that ye go to and make use of the stewardship which I have appointed unto you, exclusive of the sacred things, for the purpose of shinelane [printing] these sacred things as I have said.

64. And the avails of the sacred things shall be had in the treasury, and a seal shall be upon it; and it shall not be used or taken out of the treasury by any one, neither shall the seal be loosed which shall be placed upon it, only by the voice of the order. or by commandment.

65. And thus shall ye preserve the avails of the sacred things in the treasury, for sacred and holy purposes.

66. And this shall be called the sacred treasury of the Lord; and a seal shall be kept upon it that it may be holy and consecrated unto the Lord.

67. And again, there shall be another treasury prepared, and a treasurer appointed to keep the treasury, and a seal shall be placed upon it;

68. And all moneys that you receive in your stewardships, by improving upon the properties which I have appointed unto you, in houses, or in lands, or in cattle, or in all things save it be the holy and sacred writings, which I have reserved unto myself for holy and sacred purposes, shall be cast into the treasury as fast as you receive moneys, by hundreds, or by fifties, or by twenties, or by tens, or by fives.

69. Or in other words, if any man among you obtain five talents [dollars] let him cast them into the treasury; or if he obtain ten, or twenty, or fifty, or an hundred, let him do likewise;

70. And let not any among you say that it is his own; for it shall not be called his, nor any part of it.

71. And there shall not any part of it be used, or taken out of the treasury, only by the voice and common consent of the order.

72. And this shall be the voice and common consent of the order—that any man among you say to the treasurer: I have need of this to help me in my stewardship—

73. If it be five talents [dollars], or if it be ten talents [dollars], or twenty, or fifty, or a hundred, the treasurer shall give

unto him the sum which he requires to help him in his steward-ship—

74. Until he be found a transgressor, and it is manifest be-fore the council of the order plainly that he is an unfaithful and an unwise steward.

75. But so long as he is in full fellowship, and is faithful and wise in his stewardship, this shall be his token unto the treasurer that the treasurer shall not withhold.

76. But in case of transgression, the treasurer shall be sub-ject unto the council and voice of the order.

77. And in case the treasurer is found an unfaithful and an unwise steward, he shall be subject to the council and voice of the order, and shall be removed out of his place, and another shall be appointed in his stead.

7. Two Treasuries.

60-77. Directions are here given for the establishment of two sepa-rate treasuries. One was to be called *The Sacred Treasury of the Lord.* The proceeds from the publication of the Scriptures were to be kept in this treasury, and they were to be used for sacred purposes, as directed by the Order. The other was to hold all the funds accumulated by the business transactions of the various stewardships (v. 69). This, too, was to be common property, to be used as directed by the Order (v. 71). Each member was entitled to draw upon it, according to his needs, as long as he was in full fellowship (v. 75); but, in case of transgression of the rules of the Order, the transgressor would be subject to the decision of the organization (v. 76).

78. And again, verily I say unto you, concerning your debts —behold it is my will that you shall pay all your debts.

79. And it is my will that you shall humble yourselves before me, and obtain this blessing by your diligence and humility and the prayer of faith.

80. And inasmuch as you are diligent and humble, and exer-cise the prayer of faith, behold, I will soften the hearts of those to whom you are in debt, until I shall send means unto you for your deliverance.

81. Therefore write speedily to Cainhannoch [New York] and write according to that which shall be dictated by my Spirit; and I will soften the hearts of those to whom you are in debt, that it shall be taken away out of their minds to bring affliction upon you.

82. And inasmuch as ye are humble and faithful and call upon my name, behold, I will give you the victory.

83. I give unto you a promise, that you shall be delivered this once out of your bondage.

84. Inasmuch as you obtain a chance to loan money by hundreds, or thousands, even until you shall loan enough to deliver yourself from bondage, it is your privilege.

85. And pledge the properties which I have put into your hands, this once, by giving your names by common consent or otherwise, as it shall seem good unto you.

86. I give unto you this privilege, this once; and behold, if you proceed to do the things which I have laid before you, according to my commandments, all these things are mine, and ye are my stewards, and the master will not suffer his house to be broken up. Even so. Amen.

8. Directions to Pay Debts.

78-86. The servants of the Lord are here commanded to pay the debts incurred. If they had organized, as directed when the commandment was first given in 1832, and if they had been wise and faithful stewards, they would not have incurred indebtedness, but since they had contracted debts, their obligations must be met. Note, that the Lord expected them to pray for deliverance from debt, and then to work for it. God often answers prayers through natural agencies (vv. 80-2).

General Notes

The commandment to wipe out all indebtedness was obeyed. President Brigham Young says:

"Joseph was doing business in Kirtland, and it seemed as if all creation was upon him, to hamper him in every way, and they drove him from his business, and it left him so that some of his debts had to be settled afterwards; and I am thankful to say that they were settled up; still further, we have sent east to New York, to Ohio, and to every place where I had any idea that Joseph had ever done business, and inquired if there was any man left to whom Joseph Smith, Jr., the Prophet, owed a dollar, or a sixpence. If there was, we would pay it (*Jour. of Dis.*, Vol. XVIII., p. 242).

"We desire to get closer to the mark, to have closer communion with God, to be prepared for the day that is approaching, when we will have to go and build up the Center Stake of Zion, where the Order of Enoch, as is recorded in the book of Doctrine and Covenants, will be established (*Ibid.*, Vol. XII., p. 221).

"I say to the Latter-day Saints that the only reason why we do not take up the subject and enter into the organization of Enoch, or a City of Enoch, is simply this that we have not yet been able to find every item of law bearing upon this matter, so as to organize in a way that apostates cannot trouble us" (*Ibid.*, Vol. XVI., p. 122).

SECTION 105.

REVELATION *given through Joseph Smith the Prophet, on Fishing River, Missouri, June 22, 1834. Mob violence against the Saints in Missouri had increased; and organized bodies from several counties had declared their intent to destroy the people. The Prophet had come from Kirtland, at the head of a party known as Zion's Camp, bringing clothing and provisions. While this party was encamped on Fishing River the Prophet received this revelation. See History of the Church, vol. 2, chaps. 5 to 8 inclusive. For explanation of unusual names see heading to Section 78.——But for their transgressions the people might have been redeemed from their enemies—Unwillingness to impart to the poor condemned—The redemption of Zion deferred—The people to appeal to the officers of the law for redress—Lands in Jackson and adjoining counties to be purchased—Endowment to be given in the House of the Lord in process of erection at Kirtland—The day of calling followed by the day of choosing—The Saints to lift an ensign of peace.*

VERILY I say unto you who have assembled yourselves together that you may learn my will concerning the redemption of mine afflicted people—

Zion's Camp arrived at Fishing River on the 19th of June, 1834. On the 22nd, Sheriff Gillium, of Clay County, visited the Camp in order to find out the intention of the brethren. The Prophet addressed him and his companions and then issued a signed statement in which the following occurs, "We are willing for twelve disinterested men, six to be chosen by each party, and these men shall say what the possessions of those men are worth who cannot live with us in the County: and they shall have their money in one year; and none of the 'Mormons' shall enter that County to reside, until the money is paid. The damages that we have sustained in consequence of being driven away, shall also be left to the twelve men; or, they may all live in the County if they choose, and we will never molest them if they let us alone and permit us to enjoy our rights. We want to live in peace with all men; and equal rights is all we ask." The opponents refused to listen to this fair proposition.

The very day on which Sheriff Gillium visited the Camp, the Prophet received this Revelation, in which the Lord (1) reveals why Zion could not be redeemed at that time (1-10); (2) promises Endowments (11-15); (3) rebukes the disobedient and promises rewards to the faithful (16-19); (4) gives instructions for the discharge of the Camp (20-22), and (5) counsel on many subjects (23-32); (6) reiterates His gracious promises of Endowments (33-37); and (7) defines the mission of the Church in the world as one of peace (38-41).

2.   Behold, I say unto you, were it not for the transgressions of my people, speaking concerning the church and not individuals, they might have been redeemed even now.

3.   But behold, they have not learned to be obedient to the things which I required at their hands, but are full of all manner of evil, and do not impart of their substance, as becometh saints, to the poor and afflicted among them;

4.   And are not united according to the union required by the law of the celestial kingdom;

5.   And Zion cannot be built up unless it is by the principles of the law of the celestial kingdom; otherwise I cannot receive her unto myself.

6.   And my people must needs be chastened until they learn obedience, if it must needs be, by the things which they suffer.

7.   I speak not concerning those who are appointed to lead my people, who are the first elders of my church, for they are not all under this condemnation;

8.   But I speak concerning my churches abroad—there are many who will say: Where is their God? Behold, he will deliver them in time of trouble, otherwise we will not go up unto Zion, and will keep our moneys.

9.   Therefore, in consequence of the transgressions of my people, it is expedient in me that mine elders should wait for a little season for the redemption of Zion—

10.   That they themselves may be prepared, and that my people may be taught more perfectly, and have experience, and know more perfectly concerning their duty, and the things which I require at their hands.

1. Why Zion Was Not Redeemed.

1-10. The reasons why Zion had not been redeemed, and why it could not be redeemed at this time, are stated here.

2. In the first place, the transgressions of the Church, in failing to carry out the commandments of God concerning the celestial law, formed an obstacle. The Church as an organization suffered for the sins of individuals.

3. In the second place, many members of the Church were disobedient, full of evil, and guilty of selfishness.

*Do not impart * * * to the poor and afflicted*] Perhaps the selfishness manifested by Sylvester Smith during the journey of Zion's Camp was quite general. It appears that one evening Parley P. Pratt asked him for some bread, and that he refused to give it, although he was well supplied (*Hist. of the Church,* Vol. II., p. 153).

4. *Not united*] They were not living in the United Order, and the Lord expressly says that "Zion cannot be built up unless it be by the principles of the law of the celestial kingdom" (v. 5). The law of the celestial kingdom is the law of equality (See Sec. 76:95. Comp. 70:14; 78:6).

6. *Until they learn obedience*] Those who are prepared for celestial glory have learnt, somewhere, somehow, to live in accordance with celestial law.

8. *Where is their God?*] Some of the Saints were full of unbelief. They saw their brethren scattered and tormented, and they asked, "Where is their God?" If He will not deliver them, we will keep our money and not spend a cent on relief work. They were doubting. They had no faith. That was one reason why Zion could not be redeemed at that time.

9. *Wait for a little season*] The redemption of Zion was postponed "for a little season." There is no intimation of how long, by human measurement of time, that "season" would be. The Prophet evidently expected and hoped that the time of tribulation would be short. For, on the 16th of August, 1834, he wrote from Kirtland to Lyman Wight and others of the High Council in Zion:

"In case the excitement continues to be allayed, and peace prevails, use every effort to prevail on the Churches to gather to those regions and locate themselves, to be in readiness to move into Jackson County in two years from the 11th of September next, which is the appointed time for the redemption of Zion. If—verily I say unto you—if the Church with one united effort perform their duties; if they do this, the work shall be complete" (*Hist. of the Church,* Vol. II., p. 145).

Elder Orson Pratt has this to say:

"When the Saints were driven out from Jackson County, almost all in the Church expected that they would speedily be restored; and a person was considered almost an apostate that would say, they would not come back in five years, or ten at the furthest: but the prevailing opinion seemed to be that it would take place immediately. When Zion's Camp came up, and found the Saints all scattered abroad, what did we hear? Why all in Camp were on tiptoe to have Zion redeemed immediately; perhaps some would stretch their faith and put it off for five years; but those were considered weak in the faith" (*Journal of Discourses,* Vol. III., p. 17).

The history of the Church shows us that the "little season" extended over more than two years, or five, or even ten. Still, since the Spirit of revelation has characterized it as "little," we may hope that the redemption of Zion will not be postponed for a great while.

11. And this cannot be brought to pass until mine elders are endowed with power from on high.

12. For behold, I have prepared a great endowment and blessing to be poured out upon them, inasmuch as they are faithful and continue in humility before me.

13. Therefore it is expedient in me that mine elders should wait for a little season, for the redemption of Zion.

14. For behold, I do not require at their hands to fight the battles of Zion; for, as I said in a former commandment, even so will I fulfil—I will fight your battles.

15. Behold, the destroyer I have sent forth to destroy and lay waste mine enemies; and not many years hence they shall not be left to pollute mine heritage, and to blaspheme my name upon the lands which I have consecrated for the gathering together of my saints.

2. ENDOWMENTS PROMISED.

11-15. In the 10th paragraph we are taught that the redemption of Zion was postponed until the Saints should have attained more knowledge and more experience. Here we learn that it was necessary that the Elders should be "endowed with power from on high" (v. 11); the Lord had "prepared a great Endowment and blessing" for the faithful (v. 12). They were to have a Pentecostal outpouring of the Spirit, and then they would be in a position to teach the people "the things which I require at their hands" (v. 10). The Elders were not to fight "the battles of Zion" (v. 14); the Lord would do that in His own way (v. 15).

12. *Endowment*] See v. 33.

13. *A little season*] See v. 9.

15. *The Destroyer*] The cholera was at this time raging in Detroit, Cleveland, Buffalo, and many other places. The Prophet says he found

it almost in every place he passed through on his return journey to Kirtland, "It is," he wrote, "an awful and solemn day, but this is only the foreshadowing of what is to come" (*Hist. of the Church*, Vol. II., p. 146).

Not many years hence] The time of the enemies of the people of God is short. They flourish only as the flower which stands to-day but tomorrow falls before the scythe of the reaper.

16. Behold, I have commanded my servant Baurak Ale [Joseph Smith, Jun.] to say unto the strength of my house, even my warriors, my young men, and middle-aged, to gather together for the redemption of my people, and throw down the towers of mine enemies, and scatter their watchmen;

17. But the strength of mine house have not harkened unto my words.

18. But inasmuch as there are those who have hearkened unto my words, I have prepared a blessing and an endowment for them, if they continue faithful.

19. I have heard their prayers, and will accept their offerings and it is expedient in me that they should be brought thus far for a trial of their faith.

3. DISOBEDIENCE REBUKED: FAITHFULNESS REWARDED.

16-19. The Prophet Joseph had been commanded to gather the young and the middle-aged for the redemption of Zion (v. 16), but they did not respond in sufficient numbers (v. 17); some, however, had been faithful, and they were to receive the blessing and Endowment promised in vv. 11-12.

The Prophet, evidently, did not regard the command to gather "the strength of my house" as annulled when Zion's Camp was dismissed; for in the letter to the High Council in Zion, dated the 16th of August, he wrote, "If we do not exert ourselves to the utmost in gathering up the strength of the Lord's house that this thing may be accomplished, behold there remaineth a scourge for the Church, even that *they shall be driven from city to city,* and but few shall remain to receive an inheritance" (*Hist. of the Church*, Vol. II., p. 145).

19. *A trial of their faith*] The Lord knew what the outcome would be of the journey of Zion's Camp to Missouri; but the main object was gained. It was a trial of faith and integrity, by which the worth of those who stood the test became known to all the Saints.

20. And now, verily I say unto you, a commandment I give unto you, that as many as have come up hither, that can stay in the region round about, let them stay;

21. And those that cannot stay, who have families in the east, let them tarry for a little season, inasmuch as my servant Joseph shall appoint unto them;

22. For I will counsel him concerning this matter, and all things whatsoever he shall appoint unto them shall be fulfilled.

4. Permission to Disband.

20-2. The long journey being almost ended, permission was given to disband. Those of the Camp who could remain in Missouri might do so; the others would return home as soon as convenient.

On the 3rd of July, 1834, Lyman Wight was authorized to give to every man in the Camp, who had been faithful, a formal discharge.

23. And let all my people who dwell in the regions round about be very faithful, and prayerful, and humble before me, and reveal not the things which I have revealed unto them, until it is wisdom in me that they should be revealed.

24. Talk not of judgments, neither boast of faith nor of mighty works, but carefully gather together, as much in one region as can be, consistently with the feelings of the people;

25. And behold, I will give unto you favor and grace in their eyes, that you may rest in peace and safety, while you are saying unto the people: Execute judgment and justice for us according to law, and redress us of our wrongs.

26. Now, behold, I say unto you, my friends, in this way you may find favor in the eyes of the people, until the arm of Israel becomes very great.

27. And I will soften the hearts of the people, as I did the heart of Pharaoh, from time to time, until my servant Baurak Ale [Joseph Smith, Jun.] and Baneemy [mine elders], whom I have appointed, shall have time to gather up the strength of my house,

28. And to have sent wise men, to fulfil that which I have commanded concerning the purchasing of all the lands in Jackson county that can be purchased, and in the adjoining counties round about.

29. For it is my will that these lands should be purchased; and after they are purchased that my saints should possess them according to the laws of consecration which I have given.

30. And after these lands are purchased, I will hold the armies of Israel guiltless in taking possession of their own lands,

which they have previously purchased with their moneys, and of throwing down the towers of mine enemies that may be upon them, and scattering their watchmen, and avenging me of mine enemies unto the third and fourth generation of them that hate me.

31. But first let my army become very great, and let it be sanctified before me, that it may become fair as the sun, and clear as the moon, and that her banners may be terrible unto all nations;

32. That the kingdoms of this world may be constrained to acknowledge that the kingdom of Zion is in very deed the kingdom of our God and his Christ; therefore, let us become subject unto her laws.

5. DIVINE COUNSEL ON MANY SUBJECTS.

23-32. The Saints are here instructed on many subjects. They must be faithful, prayerful, and humble, and also discreet. They were not to publish broadcast the Revelations concerning the redemption of Zion, until the proper time came (v. 23). The Saints have no secret doctrines, no secret practices, but as there is a time for everything, so there is a proper time for the promulgation of revealed truth. Even the disciples of our Lord were charged not to testify, prematurely, to the fact that He was the Messiah (Luke 9:21. See also Matt. 9:30, Mark 5:43).

Another rule to observe is stated in verse 24. The Saints were not to threaten their neighbors with the judgments of the Almighty; nor were they to boast of faith, or mighty works. This follows from their duty of being humble. Humility neither threatens nor boasts.

Further, the Saints were to continue to supplicate the people for justice under the law (v. 25). If they would do this, they might find favor, and increase in numbers (v. 26) and in influence (v. 27), and thus be able to obey the commandment concerning the purchase of land (v. 28). No concerted effort to return to the land purchased should be made, until the army of the Lord had become "very great" (v. 31) and also "sanctified before me."

26. *The army of Israel becomes very great*] Although the Saints are referred to as an "army," the intention was not to take possession of the land purchased, by military operations. Zion was not to be redeemed by bloodshed. But if the Saints were numerous, they would have a correspondingly weighty influence by means of the ballot, and they would be safe under the law from molestation.

31. *Sanctified before me*] Numbers alone, however, do not count in the plans of God. His people must be *sanctified,* to gain the victory. This means that they must be clean; that they must have a clear conscience;

that they must strive to overcome the principle of evil and live so that the Holy Spirit may control not only their acts, but their words, thoughts, and sentiments. When the Saints are thus sanctified, they may be sure of victory, even if they die as martyrs for the kingdom of God.

33.   Verily I say unto you, it is expedient in me that the first elders of my church should receive their endowment from on high in my house, which I have commanded to be built unto my name in the land of Kirtland.

34.   And let those commandments which I have given concerning Zion and her law be executed and fulfilled, after her redemption.

35.   There has been a day of calling, but the time has come for a day of choosing; and let those be chosen that are worthy.

36.   And it shall be manifest unto my servant, by the voice of the Spirit, those that are chosen; and they shall be sanctified;

37.   And inasmuch as they follow the counsel which they receive, they shall have power after many days to accomplish all things pertaining to Zion.

6. ENDOWMENTS AGAIN PROMISED.

33-7. The promise of Endowment is reiterated. They were to be received in the Kirtland Temple, when that building should be completed. They were to be given only to those who were considered worthy (v. 35). And if the Elders, after their Endowments, would follow counsel, they would be given power to redeem Zion, after many days.

35. *A day of calling * * * choosing*] All were *called* through the preaching of the gospel. A few were now to be *chosen* to receive Endowments.

37. *After many days*] The word "days" here must be understood to mean an indefinite length of time.

38.   And again I say unto you, sue for peace, not only to the people that have smitten you, but also to all people;

39.   And lift up an ensign of peace, and make a proclamation of peace unto the ends of the earth;

40.   And make proposals for peace unto those who have smitten you, according to the voice of the Spirit which is in you, and all things shall work together for your good.

41.   Therefore, be faithful; and behold, and lo, I am with you even unto the end. Even so. Amen.

7. A MISSION OF PEACE.

38-41. Our Lord is the Prince of Peace (Is. 9:5). When He came in the flesh, angels heralded His advent, in the song,

"PEACE ON EARTH!"

The mission of His Church, therefore, is one of peace. "The Lord will bless His people with peace" (Ps. 29:11); and they are instructed to pray for the "peace of Jerusalem" (Ps. 122:6). Some churches of the world have proved their apostasy from the Prince of Peace by committing themselves to the policy of blood. The Church of Christ stands for peace among nations, as well as among individuals. It believes that nations should be bound by the standards of morality recognized by individuals.

38. *Sue for peace*] In obedience to this command, an Appeal was issued, in July, 1834, by a number of brethren, on behalf of the Church, in which the grievances of the Saints were set forth, and justice was asked for. The applicants said, in part:

"Now, therefore, as citizens of the United States and leading Elders in the Church of the Latter-day Saints, residing in the State of Missouri, in behalf of the Church, we the undersigned do make this solemn appeal to the people and constitutional authorities of this nation, and to the ends of the Earth, for peace; that we may have the privilege of enjoying our religious rights and immunities, and worship God according to the dictates of our own consciences, as guaranteed to every citizen by the Constitution of the National and States governments; that * * * we may be enabled to regain and enjoy our rights and property, agreeable to law, in this boasted land of liberty" (*Hist. of the Church*, Vol. II., p. 128).

39. *Lift up an ensign of peace*] An ensign is a flag, or a standard. When the Church has raised a Standard of Peace, it will be in a position to make a proclamation for peace "unto the ends of the Earth." And then the Millennium will not be far off. Just now* the ploughshares are being turned into swords (Joel 3:10); then the swords will be turned into ploughshares (Is. 2:4).

GENERAL NOTES

The object aimed at by the formation of Zion's Camp and its remarkable journey, was the peaceful reinstatement of the exiled Saints in their homes. This object would have been gained, if the Saints had complied with the requests made. The Revelation called for 500 men (See Sec. 103:23, 30) with sufficient means to purchase the land in Jackson County that was for sale. An addition of 500 young, energetic men, and their families, to the number of settlers that had been driven away, especially if they had means enough to make comfortable homes, would have strengthened the Church considerably. Governor Dunklin acknowledged the rights of the Saints to live unmolested in their homes, and he vacillated between the call of duty to protect the victims, and the clamor of

---

° This was penned in 1916.

the mob. An increase of the number of the Saints might have turned the Governor to the path of duty. He might, if necessary, have called out the militia to maintain order, if the Saints in Jackson County had been as strong as, or stronger than, their persecutors. At all events, there would have been no *political* incentive for siding with the mob. But the Saints did not respond as liberally as they might have done. In 1846, when the Federal Government asked the exiled "Mormons" to furnish 500 young men to march to California, the response was instantly given. In 1834, when 500 men were asked for, to go to Zion, only about 200 could be found for that purpose.

Zion might have been redeemed even with this number, if they had been united. But a spirit of rebellion developed, and when the Camp came to Missouri, the Lord deemed it necessary to punish the brethren, whereupon the cholera broke out among them. "Our ears," the Prophet says, "were saluted with cries, and moaning, and lamentations on every hand; even those on guard fell to the earth with their guns in their hands; so sudden and powerful was the attack of this terrible disease." About sixty-eight suffered more or less, and thirteen died. A cholera-stricken camp could, of course, exercise but little political influence upon the situation.

The promises of Endowments given in the Revelation were fulfilled in 1836, when the Kirtland Temple was dedicated. Heber C. Kimball tells the wonderful story thus:

"We had been commanded to prepare ourselves for a solemn assembly. At length the time arrived for this assembly to meet; previous to which the Prophet Joseph exhorted the Elders to solemnize their minds, by casting away every evil from them, in thought, word, or deed, and to let their hearts become sanctified, because they need not expect a blessing from God without being duly prepared for it, for the Holy Ghost would not dwell in unholy temples. This meeting took place soon after the House of the Lord had been dedicated * * * When the Prophet Joseph had finished the Endowments of the First Presidency, the Twelve, and the Presiding Bishops, the First Presidency proceeded to lay hands on each one of them, to seal and confirm the anointing; and at the close of each blessing the whole of the Quorums responded to it with a loud shout of Hosanna! Hosanna! etc. While these things were being attended to, the beloved disciple, John, was seen in our midst by the Prophet Joseph, Oliver Cowdery, and others. After this, all the Quorums rose in order, together with the three presidencies; and the Twelve then presented themselves separately and individually before the First Presidency, with hands uplifted towards heaven, and asked of God whatever they felt to desire; and after each individual petition, the whole of the Quorums answered aloud, 'Amen; Hosanna! Hosanna! Hosanna! to God and the Lamb, forever and ever, amen, and amen'" (Whitney's *Life of Heber C. Kimball,* p. 103-4).

The Prophet organized the High Council of Zion, July 3rd, 1834. On the 9th of the same month, he started for Kirtland, where he arrived early in August.

SECTION 106.

REVELATION *given through Joseph Smith the Prophet, at Kirtland, Ohio, November 25, 1834.——Warren A. Cowdery is named as a local presiding officer—Great blessings promised him on condition of his obedience—Nearness and suddenness of the Lord's future advent.*

IT is my will that my servant Warren A. Cowdery should be appointed and ordained a presiding high priest over my church, in the land of Freedom and the regions round about;

2. And should preach my everlasting gospel, and lift up his voice and warn the people, not only in his own place, but in the adjoining counties;

3. And devote his whole time to this high and holy calling, which I now give unto him, seeking diligently the kingdom of heaven and its righteousness, and all things necessary shall be added thereunto; for the laborer is worthy of his hire.

4. And again, verily I say unto you, the coming of the Lord draweth nigh, and it overtaketh the world as a thief in the night—

5. Therefore, gird up your loins, that you may be the children of light, and that day shall not overtake you as a thief.

6. And again, verily I say unto you, there was joy in heaven when my servant Warren bowed to my scepter, and separated himself from the crafts of men;

7. Therefore, blessed is my servant Warren, for I will have mercy on him; and, notwithstanding the vanity of his heart, I will lift him up inasmuch as he will humble himself before me.

8. And I will give him grace and assurance wherewith he may stand; and if he continue to be a faithful witness and a light unto the church I have prepared a crown for him in the mansions of my Father. Even so. Amen.

On his journey among the churches to gather up the strength of the Lord's House, the Prophet came to the City of Freedom, N. Y., where he was entertained by Warren A. Cowdery. He held several meetings there. One of the converts was Heman Hyde, and shortly after his bap-

tism, March 11, 1834, his parents and thirty or forty others were baptized and organized into a Branch, from which nucleus the light spread
and souls were gathered into the fold in all the regions round. In this
Revelation, Warren A. Cowdery is called to the office of presiding High
Priest over the Branch in Freedom and vicinity (v. 1). His duties are
stated (vv. 2, 3). He was to preach the everlasting gospel, and warn the
people. He was to devote his whole time to the ministry, and depend upon
the Lord for his reward, "for the laborer is worthy of his hire." He was
to remember that "the coming of the Lord draweth nigh" (v. 4) and warn
the world, lest the day should overtake them "as a thief." Gracious promises are given (vv. 7, 8).

2. *Everlasting gospel*] The everlasting gospel (Rev. 14:7) is this,
"Fear God, and give glory to him; for the hour of His judgment is come:
and worship him that made heaven, and earth, and the sea, and the
fountains of waters." That is the everlasting gospel. Worship the Creator,
as He is revealed in the story of creation. Worship Him, in whose image
man was made.

4. *The coming of the Lord*] This is an essential doctrine of the gospel.
The redemption of the world cannot be completed until after the second
advent of the Son of God.

7. *Vanity of his heart*] Here is another instance of the Seeric gift of
the Prophet while under divine inspiration. Warren A. Cowdery, owing
to this weakness, on one occasion, in a letter to the Presidency of the
Church, accused Thomas B. Marsh and others of the Twelve of having
neglected to teach the Saints their duty to contribute means for the building of the Temple. But he was honest enough to acknowledge his error
publicly, as soon as it was pointed out to him (*Hist. of the Church,* Vol.
II., p. 374).
Several events of great importance in the history of the Church trans-
pired in the year 1834, in addition to the journey of Zion's Camp from
Kirtland to Clay County, Mo. On the 17th of February the first High
Council of the Church was organized at Kirtland, with the Prophet Joseph
and his counselors as the presiding officers. On the 3rd of July, a High
Council was organized in Clay County, Mo., with David Whitmer, Wm.
W. Phelps, and John Whitmer as the presidency. On the same date, David
Whitmer was sustained as President of the Church in Zion, in the absence
of the Prophet, who was sustained as the First President of the Church.
In a conference held on May 3rd at Kirtland, on motion by Sidney Rig-
don, seconded by Newel K. Whitney, it was decided that the Church be
known as THE CHURCH OF THE LATTER-DAY SAINTS. On June 23rd, the
following were chosen to receive their Endowments: Edward Partridge,
William W. Phelps, Isaac Morley, John Corrill, John Whitmer, David
Whitmer, Algernon Sidney Gilbert, Peter Whitmer, Jr., Simeon Carter,
Newel Knight, Parley P. Pratt, Christian Whitmer, Solomon Hancock,
Thomas B. Marsh, and Lyman Wight. On November 29th, the Prophet

Joseph and Oliver Cowdery entered into a solemn covenant with the Lord, for themselves and their descendants, that, if He would prosper them and enable them to pay their debts, they would give to Him a tenth part of all that He would give them; also that they would be faithful in the use of that which might be entrusted to their care. On December 5th, Oliver Cowdery was ordained Assistant President, in accordance with the Revelation (Sec. 20:3) that designates him the Second Elder of the Church.

SECTION 107.

REVELATION *on Priesthood, given through Joseph Smith the Prophet, at Kirtland, Ohio, dated March 28, 1835. On the date named the Twelve met in council, confessing their individual weaknesses and shortcomings, expressing repentance, and seeking the further guidance of the Lord. They were about to separate on missions to districts assigned. See History of the Church, vol. 2, p. 209.——Distinction between the Aaronic and the Melchizedek Priesthoods—The right of presidency belongs to the Melchizedek Priesthood—High authority of the Presidency of the High Priesthood—The Bishopric as the presidency of the Aaronic Priesthood—Duties of the several quorums and of the presiding officers thereof—The Twelve constitute the Traveling Presiding High Council—The Twelve to ordain evangelical ministers, or Patriarchs—Descent of the patriarchal order from Adam to Noah—Bishops to be chosen from the High Priesthood unless literal descendants of Aaron are made known —The order of Church tribunals—No one in the Church exempt from accountability.*

THERE are, in the church, two priesthoods, namely, the Melchizedek and Aaronic, including the Levitical Priesthood.

2. Why the first is called the Melchizedek Priesthood is because Melchizedek was such a great high priest.

3. Before his day it was called *the Holy Priesthood, after the Order of the Son of God.*

4. But out of respect or reverence to the name of the Supreme Being, to avoid the too frequent repetition of his name, they, the church, in ancient days, called that priesthood after Melchizedek, or the Melchizedek Priesthood.

5. All other authorities or offices in the church are appendages to this priesthood.

6. But there are two divisions or grand heads—one is the Melchizedek Priesthood, and the other is the Aaronic or Levitical Priesthood.

7. The office of an elder comes under the priesthood of Melchizedek.

On the Two Priesthoods. Apostles Chosen.

On the 14th of February, 1835, a meeting was held at Kirtland, to which all the members of Zion's Camp had been invited. On this occasion the Prophet Joseph stated that "it was the will of God that those who went to Zion, with a determination to lay down their lives, if necessary, should be ordained to the ministry, and go forth to prune the vineyard for the last time, or the coming of the Lord, which was nigh—even fifty-six years should wind up the scene" (*Hist. of the Church,* Vol. II., p. 182). The assembly, by vote, expressed unanimous agreement, whereupon the Prophet submitted a proposition for the selection of Twelve Apostles, which was accepted by all present. After an interval of an hour, the meeting convened again, and the Three Witnesses, viz., Oliver Cowdery, David Whitmer, and Martin Harris, in accordance with a previous Revelation (See Sec. 18:37), selected Twelve, to be special witnesses, with them, to the truth of the gospel. Those chosen were, Lyman E. Johnson, Brigham Young, Heber C. Kimball, Orson Hyde, David W. Patten, Luke S. Johnson, William E. McLellin, John F. Boynton, Orson Pratt, William Smith, Thomas B. Marsh, and Parley P. Pratt.

Brigham Young relates the following:

"After we returned from Missouri, my brother Joseph Young, and myself had been singing after preaching in a meeting; and when the meeting was dismissed, Brother Joseph Smith said, 'Come, go down to my house with me.' We went and sang to him a long time, and talked with him. He then opened the subject of the Twelve and Seventies for the first time I ever thought of it. He said, 'Brethren, I am going to call out Twelve Apostles. I think we will get together, by and by, and select a Quorum of Seventy from those who have been up to Zion, out of the Camp boys.' In 1835, the last of January or in February, or about that time, we held our meetings from day to day, and Brother Joseph called out Twelve Apostles at that time. He had a Revelation when we were singing to him" (*Jour. of Dis.,* Vol. IX., p. 89).

On the 28th of February, the Church, in council assembled, commenced the selection of men to be Seventies. The Seven Presidents of the First Quorum were, Hazen Aldrich, Joseph Young, Levi W. Hancock, Leonard Rich, Zebedee Coltrin, Lyman Sherman, and Sylvester Smith.

On March 28th, 1835, the Twelve held a council meeting. They were about to separate and go to their various fields of labor. They were humble and contrite, confessing their shortcomings and forgiving each other, and they desired a Revelation for their comfort. "Our worthiness," they said, "has not inspired us to make this request, but our unworthiness." In answer to this humble petition the Revelation in the first fifty-eight paragraphs of this Section was given.

This is a Revelation on the Priesthood. It may be divided as follows: (1) Two Priesthoods (1-7); Authority of the Melchizedek Priesthood (8-12); (3) Authority of the Aaronic Priesthood (13-20); (4) Presiding Officers, (a) First Presidency (21-2); (b) Twelve Apostles (23-4); (c) Seventies (25-6); (d) Valid Decisions (27-32); Duties of the Twelve (33), and (f) of the Seventies (34-5); (5) Standing High Councils (36-7); (6) Seventies to Preach (38); (7) Patriarchs (39); (8) Lineage of the Priesthood (40-52); (9) Adam's Blessing (53-7); (10) Addenda on the duties of the various officers in the Priesthood (58-100).

1. Two Priesthoods.

Opinions differ concerning the character of the *Priesthood* in the Church of Christ. Romanists affirm that the ministers are *priests,* in the Old Testament meaning of the word; that they are mediators between God and the people; that they are offering a propitiatory sacrifice in the consecrated emblems, and that, in the absolution, they intercede for sinners, rendering the Sacrifice effectual in its application to individuals. The Roman clergy claim to be priests because the people must draw near to God through them, as Israel through Aaron; because they alone can present the real body and blood of the Son of God as a sacrifice, and because they have the power to bind and to loose, or to forgive sins, on Earth.

Protestants deny this claim. They hold that there are no *priests* in the Church of Christ. Jesus Christ, they argue, is our only Priest. He alone has access to God. All other men must approach the Father through Him. His death is the only sacrifice that takes away sin, and it is only through Him that the favor of God is conveyed to His people. Clergymen are only His ministers; not priests. In the Old Testament there were priests, but their office was abolished when Christ came. No priestly function, they say, is ever attributed to Christian ministers, in the Word of God. This is the Protestant view.

Romanists err in making the Priesthood a caste, a privileged class, a "hierarchy," with autocratic power over the faith and practice of their fellowmen. Our Lord warned His disciples against the temptation to assume the position of Rabbis and masters; "for one is your Master, even Christ; and ye are all brethren" (Matt. 23:8, 10). Romanists have ignored this principle and erected an ecclesiastical empire patterned after imperial Rome. The Protestants err in regarding the Priesthood as abolished in the Church. It is true enough that Christ is *the* Priest of the New Covenant. He is a Priest "for ever after the order of Melchizedek" (Heb. 7:17). He is "the Apostle and High Priest of our profession" (Heb. 3:1). But, as there was a Priesthood in each of the old dispensations, with power and authority to officiate in His stead, until He came and accomplished the work for the salvation of man, which was typified in the ordinances of those dispensations, so He commissioned His servants and gave them power and authority to officiate in His stead in the ordinances of the gospel, after His ascension. Those who hold this power and authority, hold the Priesthood; for Priesthood means divine authority to act for the Lord, be it as a preacher of the gospel or as one administering divine ordinances, etc. He commissioned the Twelve to continue His work after Him, for He said, "As thou hast sent me into the world, even so have I also sent them into the world" (John 17:18). He delegated to them His power and authority; that is, He clothed them with the authority of the Holy Priesthood. "Fear not," He said, "little flock; for it is your Father's good pleasure to give you the kingdom" (Luke 12:32). And again, "I appoint* unto you a kingdom, as my Father hath appointed unto me" (Luke 22:29). But in the Church there is no priest caste, no "hierarchy." Nearly all the male members in the Church hold the Priesthood. Peter had this fact in view, when he wrote to the Church, "Ye also, as lively stones, are built up a spiritual house, an Holy Priesthood to offer up spiritual sacrifices" (I. Peter 2:5). As many as are living stones in God's Temple—the Church—belong to the Priesthood. "Ye are a chosen generation, a royal Priesthood, an holy nation, a peculiar people" (I. Pet. 2:9). The Priesthood embraces the entire people, wherefore the Redeemed sing praise to Him who "hath made us kings and priests unto God and His Father" (Rev. 1:6).

1. *Two Priesthoods*] There are, then, two Priesthoods in the Church. But those who hold the authority of these Priesthoods are not the masters but the servants of the people; for they remember the word of the Lord, "Whosoever will be chief among you, let him be your servant; even as the Son of Man came not to be ministered unto, but to minister, and to give his life a ransom for many" (Matt. 20:27, 28).

"Although there are two Priesthoods, yet the Melchizedek Priesthood comprehends the Aaronic, or Levitical Priesthood, and is the grand head, and holds the highest authority which pertains to the Priesthood, and the keys of the kingdom of God in all ages of the world to the latest posterity on the Earth, and is the channel through which all knowledge, doctrine, the plan of salvation, and every important matter is revealed from heaven" (Joseph Smith, *Hist. of the Church*, Vol. IV., p. 207).

"What is this power that is conferred upon us in the holy Priesthood? What particular power do you give when you send a man to some other

---

* The word translated "appoint" is *diatithemai*, which means "to appoint by bequest." The kingdom went to the Apostles at the death of our Lord.

land to transact business in your name? You give him a power of attorney, authorizing him to transact in your name the business that you wish to be performed; and in that letter of appointment would be conveyed all your power, your authority, and ability to transact that business, even as effectually as if you yourself were present to perform it" (Orson Hyde, *Jour. of Dis.*, Vol. VIII., p. 20).

2. *Melchizedek Priesthood*] So called after Melchizedek, king of Salem and Priest of the Most High God. In Psalm 110:4 it is foretold that the Messiah would be a "Priest for ever after the order of Melchizedek." Paul applies this prophecy to our Lord (Heb. 6:20), and the Jews generally regarded Melchizedek as a type of the royal Priesthood which the Messiah would hold.

3. *The holy Priesthood after the Order of the Son of God*] This was the original name of the Melchizedek Priesthood. The reason why it was changed is stated in the next verse.

6. *Aaronic Priesthood*] So called after Aaron, the brother of Moses, who was made the High Priest, or presiding officer, of the Old Testament Priesthood and the Tabernacle service, an office which he filled for nearly forty years. It is also called the Levitical Priesthood, because Aaron was a descendant of Levi, the third son of Jacob and Leah, whose descendants were all set apart and consecrated for the sacred service. They had charge of the Sanctuary and the furniture belonging thereto. They acted as porters, guards, general servants, and singers.

8. The Melchizedek Priesthood holds the right of presidency, and has power and authority over all the offices in the church in all ages of the world, to administer in spiritual things.

9. The Presidency of the High Priesthood, after the order of Melchizedek, have a right to officiate in all the offices in the church.

10. High priests after the order of the Melchizedek Priesthood have a right to officiate in their own standing, under the direction of the presidency, in administering spiritual things, and also in the office of an elder, priest (of the Levitical order), teacher, deacon, and member.

11. An elder has a right to officiate in his stead when the high priest is not present.

12. The high priest and elder are to administer in spiritual things, agreeable to the covenants and commandments of the church; and they have a right to officiate in all these offices of the church when there are no higher authorities present.

2. Authority of the Melchizedek Priesthood.

8-12. There are two divisions in the Melchizedek Priesthood, viz., Elders and High Priests. The Presidency of the High Priesthood have authority to officiate in all the offices of the Church (v. 9). The High Priests, under the direction of the Presidency, have authority to officiate in their own calling, which is to administer in spiritual things; and also in the office of an Elder, Priest, Teacher, Deacon, or member (v. 10). An Elder has authority to officiate instead of a High Priest, when he is absent (v. 11). And the authority of both Elders and High Priests is to administer in spiritual things (v. 12). As the Melchizedek Priesthood holds the right of Presidency (v. 8), Elders and High Priests may officiate in all the offices of the Church, when there is no higher officer present.

"If anybody wants to know what the Priesthood of the Son of God is, it is the law by which the worlds are, were, and will continue forever and ever. It is that system which brings worlds into existence and peoples them—gives them their revolutions—their days, weeks, months, years, their seasons and times, and by which they are rolled up as a scroll, as it were, and go into a higher state of existence" (Brigham Young, *Jour. of Dis.*, Vol. XV., p. 127).

"There is a matter that has of late become a subject of a good deal of conversation * * * namely, that of the High Priesthood, or the place and calling of a High Priest. In the Revelation on this subject I find these words, 'And again, I give unto Don C. Smith, to be a President over the Quorum of High Priests, which ordination is instituted for the purpose of qualifying those who shall be appointed standing Presidents or servants over the different Stakes scattered abroad.' What are they organized for? It is instituted for the purpose of qualifying those who shall be appointed standing Presidents over the different Stakes * * * a sort of normal school, if you please, to prepare men to preside, to be fathers of the people" (John Taylor, *Jour. of Dis.*, Vol. XIX., p. 242).

13. The second priesthood is called the Priesthood of Aaron, because it was conferred upon Aaron and his seed, throughout all their generations.

14. Why it is called the lesser priesthood is because it is an appendage to the greater, or the Melchizedek Priesthood, and has power in administering outward ordinances.

15. The bishopric is the presidency of this priesthood, and holds the keys or authority of the same.

16. No man has a legal right to this office, to hold the keys of this priesthood, except he be a literal descendant of Aaron.

17. But as a high priest of the Melchizedek Priesthood has authority to officiate in all the lesser offices, he may officiate in

the office of bishop when no literal descendant of Aaron can be found, provided he is called and set apart and ordained unto this power by the hands of the Presidency of the Melchizedek Priesthood.

18. The power and authority of the higher, or Melchizedek Priesthood, is to hold the keys of all the spiritual blessings of the church—

19. To have the privilege of receiving the mysteries of the kingdom of heaven, to have the heavens opened unto them, to commune with the general assembly and church of the First-born, and to enjoy the communion and presence of God the Father, and Jesus the mediator of the new covenant.

20. The power and authority of the lesser, or Aaronic Priest-hood, is to hold the keys of the ministering of angels, and to ad-minister in outward ordinances, the letter of the gospel, the bap-tism of repentance for the remission of sins, agreeable to the covenants and commandments.

3. AUTHORITY OF THE AARONIC PRIESTHOOD.

13-20. The Aaronic Priesthood is also called the Lesser—not because it is inferior in sacredness, but because its scope, being concerned, prin-cipally, about "outward ordinances" (v. 14), is restricted to a smaller circle than the Melchizedek Priesthood. Its authority is to "hold the keys of the administering of angels, and to administer in outward ordi-nances, the letter of the gospel—the baptism of repentance for the remis-sion of sins" (v. 20).

20. *Ministering of angels*]

"In all their affliction He was afflicted, and the Angel of His Presence saved them; in His love and in His pity He redeemed them: and He bore them, and carried them all the days of old. The angels that have gone forth at sundry times to execute the decrees of God fully substanti-ate this fact. Abraham, Hagar, Jacob, Balaam, Joshua, Gideon, together with the enemies of the Lord are witnesses who knew the power and offices of angels on Earth. * * * The action of the angels or messengers of God, upon our minds, so that the heart can conceive things past, present, and to come, and revelations from the eternal world, is, among a majority of mankind, a great mystery" (*Millennial Star,* Vol. V., p. 180-1).

21. Of necessity there are presidents, or presiding officers growing out of, or appointed of or from among those who are ordained to the several offices in these two priesthoods.

22. Of the Melchizedek Priesthood, three Presiding High Priests, chosen by the body, appointed and ordained to that office, and upheld by the confidence, faith, and prayer of the church, form a quorum of the Presidency of the Church.

4. PRESIDING OFFICERS.

(a) *The First Presidency.*

21-2. Three High Priests, chosen and upheld by the Church, "form a quorum of the Presidency of the Church." This Council is at the head of all the affairs of the Church. Its President only is authorized to receive revelations for the Church. He is *the* Prophet, Seer and Revelator, and, together with his two Counselors, he leads and directs the Church, as Moses did the Children of Israel.

23. The twelve traveling councilors are called to be the Twelve Apostles, or special witnesses of the name of Christ in all the world—thus differing from other officers in the church in the duties of their calling.

24. And they form a quorum, equal in authority and power to the three presidents previously mentioned.

(b) *The Twelve Apostles.*

23-24. The Twelve bear the title of Apostles, or Messengers, because they are special witnesses of the name of Christ in all the world. They are also called Traveling Councilors. They constitute a traveling Presiding High Council, and from their decisions, when exercising judiciary functions abroad, there is no appeal. Their calling is to direct the affairs of the Church abroad under the instructions from the First Presidency, and to take the leadership of the Church when the First Presidency becomes disorganized, through death or otherwise. They form a Quorum, or Council, equal in authority to the First Presidency. (v. 24).

25. The Seventy are also called to preach the gospel, and to be especial witnesses unto the Gentiles and in all the world—thus differing from other officers in the church in the duties of their calling.

26. And they form a quorum, equal in authority to that of the Twelve special witnesses or Apostles just named.

(c) *Seventies.*

The Seventies are Elders called to preach the gospel to all the world under the direction of the Apostles. They are the missionaries of the Church and have no local authority of presiding. "The difference between this quorum and the quorum of the elders is that one is to travel continually, and the other is to preside over the churches from time to time; the one has the responsibility of presiding from time to time, and the other has no responsibility of presiding, saith the Lord our God." (Sec. 124:140.) There can never be two or three quorums of equal authority at the same time; therefore in the revelation where it reads that the Twelve Apostles form a quorum equal in authority with the First Presidency, and that the Seventies form a quorum equal in authority with the Twelve, it should be understood that this condition of equality could prevail only when the ranking quorum is no longer in existence, through death or otherwise. When the First Presidency becomes disorganized on the death of the President, then the Apostles become the presiding quorum, or council, of the Church with all the power to organize again the First Presidency, when they fall back again as the second ranking quorum of the Church. So with the Seventies, they would become equal only on the condition that the first two quorums ceased to exist. In regard to the Seventies, this provision, of course, concerns the first quorum of the Seventies.

On the 6th of April, 1837, a solemn assembly was held in Kirtland. It had been ascertained that most of the Presidents of the Seventies were High Priests and that the common practice was to confer the High Priesthood upon Elders when they were ordained and set apart for the Quorum of Seventy. "This was declared to be wrong, and not according to the order of heaven. New Presidents of Seventies were accordingly ordained to fill the places of such of them as were High Priests, and the *ex-officio* Presidents, and such of the Seventies as had been legally ordained to be High Priests, were directed to unite with the High Priests' Quorum" (*Hist. of the Church,* Vol. II., p. 476).

"If the first Seventy are all employed, and there is a call for more laborers, it will be the duty of the seven Presidents of the first Seventy to call and ordain other Seventy and send them forth to labor in the vineyard, until, if needs be, they set apart seven times seventy, and even until there are one hundred and forty-four thousand thus set apart for the ministry * * * The Twelve and the Seventy have particularly to depend upon their ministry for their support, and that of their families; and they have a right, by virtue of their offices, to call upon the churches to assist them" (*Joseph Smith, Ibid.,* p. 221).

27. And every decision made by either of these quorums must be by the unanimous voice of the same; that is, every member in each quorum must be agreed to its decisions, in order to make their decisions of the same power or validity one with the other—

28. A majority may form a quorum when circumstances render it impossible to be otherwise—

29. Unless this is the case, their decisions are not entitled to the same blessings which the decisions of a quorum of three presidents were anciently, who were ordained after the order of Melchizedek, and were righteous and holy men.

30. The decisions of these quorums, or either of them, are to be made in all righteousness, in holiness, and lowliness of heart, meekness and long suffering, and in faith, and virtue, and knowledge, temperance, patience, godliness, brotherly kindness and charity;

31. Because the promise is, if these things abound in them they shall not be unfruitful in the knowledge of the Lord.

32. And in case that any decision of these quorums is made in unrighteousness, it may be brought before a general assembly of the several quorums, which constitute the spiritual authorities of the church; otherwise there can be no appeal from their decision.

(d) *Unity in Decisions.*

27-32. There is an essential difference between the rules governing the deliberations of these Church Councils and those that are followed in the deliberative assemblies of the world. In Church Councils every decision must be unanimous (v. 27). In the world, "the majority rules," and the minority is set aside. It is possible to obtain unanimity in the Church Councils, because there is no one there who has any selfish interests to "fight for." In those assemblies everything is done, when the Spirit of the Lord prevails, "in all righteousness, in holiness, and lowliness of heart, meekness and longsuffering, and in faith, and virtue, and knowledge, temperance, patience, godliness, brotherly kindness, and charity" (v. 30). When each member endeavors to conform his views on every question that comes up for consideration, to these requirements, and eliminates all personal preferences, unity can be maintained. In these Councils each member freely states his views, but when the opinion of the majority is ascertained, this is always found to be based on truth, and the minority gladly falls in line. For it is of such Councils that it can be said absolute truth, *vox populi, vox Dei.*

33. The Twelve are a Traveling Presiding High Council, to officiate in the name of the Lord, under the direction of the Presidency of the Church, agreeable to the institution of heaven; to build up the church, and regulate all the affairs of the same in all nations, first unto the Gentiles and secondly unto the Jews.

(e) *Duties of the Twelve.*

33. See notes under vv. 23-4.

34.   The Seventy are to act in the name of the Lord, under the direction of the Twelve or the traveling high council, in building up the church and regulating all the affairs of the same in all nations, first unto the Gentiles and then to the Jews;

35.   The Twelve being sent out, holding the keys, to open the door by the proclamation of the gospel of Jesus Christ, and first unto the Gentiles and then unto the Jews.

(f) *Duties of the Seventies.*

34-5.   See notes under vv. 25-6.

36.   The standing high councils, at the stakes of Zion, form a quorum equal in authority in the affairs of the church, in all their decisions, to the quorum of the presidency, or to the traveling high council.

37.   The high council in Zion form a quorum equal in authority in the affairs of the church, in all their decisions, to the councils of the Twelve at the stakes of Zion.

5. STANDING HIGH COUNCILS.

36-7.   At the time this Revelation was given, there were two standing High Councils in the Church: One in Kirtland, organized February 17th, 1834, and one in Clay County, Mo., organized July 3rd, the same year.

"In Kirtland, Ohio, a great many things were revealed through the Prophet. There were then a First Presidency that presided over the High Council in Kirtland; and that High Council and another, which was in Missouri, were the only High Councils in existence. As I have said, the High Council in Kirtland was presided over by Joseph Smith and his Counselors; and hence there were some things associated with this that were quite peculiar in themselves. It is stated that when they were at a loss to find out anything in their Council, the Presidency were to inquire of the Lord and get Revelations on those subjects that were difficult for them to comprehend. * * * All High Councilors, and all Presidents of Stakes, and Bishops, and, in fact, all men holding the Priesthood * * * if they seek unto God with that faith which He requires of us, He will give them wisdom under all circumstances and on all occasions, and the Holy Spirit will never fail to indicate the path they should pursue" (John Taylor, *Jour. of Dis.*, Vol. XIX., p. 241).

37.   *High Council in Zion*] When this Council was organized, the Prophet, in his instructions, said that if he should now be taken away, he had accomplished the great work the Lord had laid before him, and that which he had desired of the Lord. He had done his duty in organizing the High Council "through which Council the will of the Lord

might be known on all important occasions, in the building up of Zion, and establishing truth in the Earth" (*Hist. of the Church,* Vol. II., p. 124).

This indicates the importance attached to the organization of the High Council in Zion. The standing High Councils in the various Stakes are presided over by the Stake presidency, and their jurisdiction is confined to the Stakes in which they are located.

38. It is the duty of the traveling high council to call upon the Seventy, when they need assistance, to fill the several calls for preaching and administering the gospel, instead of any others.

6. THE TWELVE AND THE SEVENTY.

38. See notes under vv. 25-6.

39. It is the duty of the Twelve, in all large branches of the church, to ordain evangelical ministers, as they shall be designated unto them by revelation—

7. PATRIARCHS.

39. *Evangelical Ministers*] Also called Patriarchs. In an address delivered on the 27th of June, 1839, the Prophet said:

"An Evangelist is a Patriarch, even the oldest man of the blood of Joseph, or of the seed of Abraham. Wherever the Church of Christ is established in the Earth, there should be a Patriarch for the benefit of the posterity of the Saints, as it was with Jacob in giving his Patriarchal blessings unto his sons."

"December 18, 1833, a number of elders assembled in the printing office in Kirtland and dedicated the printing press, with all that pertained thereunto, unto the service of the Lord. * * * While they were assembled in the printing office on this occasion the Prophet gave the first patriarchal blessings in this dispensation. It was his privilege to do this, for he held the keys of all the authority in the Church, and was spoken of as the first patriarch in the Church because of this fact, in the minutes which were kept at that time. Those who received blessings under his hands on this occasion were: Oliver Cowdery, the father and mother of the Prophet, and three of his brothers, Hyrum, Samuel and William Smith. Oliver Cowdery, who held the keys of Priesthood with the Prophet, also gave a number of patriarchal blessings. Joseph Smith, Sen., was ordained to the Patriarchal Priesthood, to hold the keys of blessings on the heads of all the members of the Church, the Lord revealing that it was his right to hold this authority. He was also set apart as an assistant counselor to the Prophet Joseph Smith." (*Essentials in Church History,* pp. 168-169.)

"It is the function of their Priesthood to pronounce blessings upon the heads of the people, and more especially to bless those who are fatherless. To them is given the power by the inspiration of the Lord to designate the lineage of the Saints, and in their blessings point out the possibilities to which they can attain through their faithfulness" (B. H. Roberts).

40. The order of this priesthood was confirmed to be handed down from father to son, and rightly belongs to the literal descendants of the chosen seed, to whom the promises were made.

41. This order was instituted in the days of Adam, and came down by lineage in the following manner:

42. From Adam to Seth, who was ordained by Adam at the age of sixty-nine years, and was blessed by him three years previous to his (Adam's) death, and received the promise of God by his father, that his posterity should be the chosen of the Lord, and that they should be preserved unto the end of the earth;

43. Because he (Seth) was a perfect man, and his likeness was the express likeness of his father, insomuch that he seemed to be like unto his father in all things, and could be distinguished from him only by his age.

44. Enos was ordained at the age of one hundred and thirty-four years and four months, by the hand of Adam.

45. God called upon Cainan in the wilderness in the fortieth year of his age; and he met Adam in journeying to the place Shedolamak. He was eighty-seven years old when he received his ordination.

46. Mahalaleel was four hundred and ninety-six years and seven days old when he was ordained by the hand of Adam, who also blessed him.

47. Jared was two hundred years old when he was ordained under the hand of Adam, who also blessed him.

48. Enoch was twenty-five years old when he was ordained under the hand of Adam; and he was sixty-five and Adam blessed him.

49. And he saw the Lord, and he walked with him, and was before his face continually; and he walked with God three hundred and sixty-five years, making him four hundred and thirty years old when he was translated.

50. Methuselah was one hundred years old when he was ordained under the hand of Adam.

51. Lamech was thirty-two years old when he was ordained under the hand of Seth.

52. Noah was ten years old when he was ordained under the hand of Methuselah.

8. From Adam to Noah.

40. *The order of this Priesthood*] The Priesthood of a Patriarch. It was confirmed to be handed down from father to son. Comp. Sec. 124:91.

41-52. How this Priesthood descended from Adam to Noah is here recorded. Adam ordained Seth, Enos, Cainan, Mahalaleel, Jared, Enoch and Methuselah. Seth ordained Lamech, and Methuselah ordained Noah. All these Patriarchs, except Noah, were born before Adam died; so that from him they might have received a full and authentic account of the creation, the fall, and the promise of redemption, as well as the ordination to the Priesthood.

53. Three years previous to the death of Adam, he called Seth, Enos, Cainan, Mahalaleel, Jared, Enoch, and Methuselah, who were all high priests, with the residue of his posterity who were righteous, into the valley of Adam-ondi-Ahman, and there bestowed upon them his last blessing.

54. And the Lord appeared unto them, and they rose up and blessed Adam, and called him Michael, the prince, the arch-angel.

55. And the Lord administered comfort unto Adam, and said unto him: I have set thee to be at the head; a multitude of nations shall come of thee, and thou art a prince over them forever.

56. And Adam stood up in the midst of the congregation; and, notwithstanding he was bowed down with age, being full of the Holy Ghost, predicted whatsoever should befall his posterity unto the latest generation.

57. These things were all written in the book of Enoch, and are to be testified of in due time.

9. Adam in Adam-ondi-Ahman.

53-7. This is a remarkable account of the last public appearance in a family re-union of our first Ancestor. Seven generations were represented by heads of families, holding the holy High Priesthood, and there were, besides, a numerous attendance. The meeting was held in the Valley of Adam-ondi-Ahman (v. 53). There the Lord appeared (v. 54) and administered comfort to Adam, who prophesied of the future of the race (v. 56).

53. *Adam-ondi-Ahman*] See Section 78:15.

54. *Michael, the Prince*] Adam, at this meeting, was sustained as Michael, the Prince, the Archangel, *Michael* means, "Who is as God." Adam was created in the image, after the likeness of God, and the name expresses this wonderful fact. *Prince* is a title. Jesus, the Son of God, is the *Prince of Peace*. Adam, Son of God, is also a prince. That title was, later, given to each of the twelve heads of the tribes of Israel (Numb. 1:16), who were to the people of the Old Covenant what the Twelve Apostles were, and are, to the Church of Christ. The Apostles are princes in the kingdom of God, and Adam was sustained as Michael, the Prince.

Archangel] This denotes an office. As one of the arch-angels, or chief messengers, of God, Adam has a special work to perform in connection with the divine plan of salvation. In Daniel 10:13-21 he is represented as having special charge of the Hebrew nation, and in Dan. 12:1 it is said that he will "stand up" for that nation, for its deliverance, at the time of the end. In Jude 9 he is said to have disputed with Satan about the body of Moses, and in Rev. 12 he is represented as being at war with the adversary.

55. *At the head*] Adam holds his position as the head of the human race, under the direction of our Lord.

56. *Adam stood up*] He was 927 years old on this occasion, but, evidently, he was not decrepit.

57. *The Book of Enoch*] The account is from the Book so named, but not from any book of Enoch now known to scholars. There is an alleged Book of Enoch extant, but it is no older than the second century B.C. Some time the genuine Book of Enoch will be revealed, from which some chapters in the Pearl of Great Price are copied, through the Spirit of Revelation.

Here ends the Revelation given on the 28th of March, 1835. What follows was received at sundry times.

58. It is the duty of the Twelve, also, to ordain and set in order all the other officers of the church, agreeable to the revelation which says:

59. To the church of Christ in the land of Zion, in addition to the church laws respecting church business—

60. Verily, I say unto you, saith the Lord of Hosts, there must needs be presiding elders to preside over those who are of the office of an elder;

61. And also priests to preside over those who are of the office of a priest;

62. And also teachers to preside over those who are of the office of a teacher, in like manner, and also the deacons—

63. Wherefore, from deacon to teacher, and from teacher to priest, and from priest to elder, severally as they are appointed, according to the covenants and commandments of the church.

64. Then comes the High Priesthood, which is the greatest of all.

65. Wherefore, it must needs be that one be appointed of the High Priesthood to preside over the priesthood, and he shall be called President of the High Priesthood of the Church;

66. Or, in other words, the Presiding High Priest over the High Priesthood of the Church.

67. From the same comes the administering of ordinances and blessings upon the church, by the laying on of the hands.

68. Wherefore, the office of a bishop is not equal unto it; for the office of a bishop is in administering all temporal things;

69. Nevertheless a bishop must be chosen from the High Priesthood, unless he is a literal descendant of Aaron;

70. For unless he is a literal descendant of Aaron he cannot hold the keys of that priesthood.

71. Nevertheless, a high priest, that is, after the order of Melchizedek, may be set apart unto the ministering of temporal things, having a knowledge of them by the Spirit of truth;

72. And also to be a judge in Israel, to do the business of the church, to sit in judgment upon transgressors upon testimony as it shall be laid before him according to the laws, by the assistance of his counselors, whom he has chosen or will choose among the elders of the church.

73. This is the duty of a bishop who is not a literal descendant of Aaron, but has been ordained to the High Priesthood after the order of Melchizedek.

74. Thus shall he be a judge, even a common judge among the inhabitants of Zion, or in a stake of Zion, or in any branch of the church where he shall be set apart unto this ministry, until the borders of Zion are enlarged and it becomes necessary to have other bishops or judges in Zion or elsewhere.

75. And inasmuch as there are other bishops appointed they shall act in the same office.

76. But a literal descendant of Aaron has a legal right to the presidency of this priesthood, to the keys of this ministry, to act in the office of bishop independently, without counselors, except in a case where a President of the High Priesthood, after the order of Melchizedek, is tried to sit as a judge in Israel.

77. And the decision of either of these councils, agreeable to the commandment which says:

78. Again, verily, I say unto you, the most important business of the church, and the most difficult cases of the church, inasmuch as there is not satisfaction upon the decision of the bishop or judges, it shall be handed over and carried up unto the council of the church, before the Presidency of the High Priesthood.

79. And the Presidency of the council of the High Priesthood shall have power to call other high priests, even twelve, to assist as counselors; and thus the Presidency of the High Priesthood and its counselors shall have power to decide upon testimony according to the laws of the church.

80. And after this decision it shall be had in remembrance no more before the Lord; for this is the highest council of the church of God, and a final decision upon controversies in spiritual matters.

81. There is not any person belonging to the church who is exempt from this council of the church.

82. And inasmuch as a President of the High Priesthood shall transgress, he shall be had in remembrance before the common council of the church, who shall be assisted by twelve counselors of the High Priesthood;

83. And their decision upon his head shall be an end of controversy concerning him.

84. Thus, none shall be exempted from the justice and the laws of God, that all things may be done in order and in solemnity before him, according to truth and righteousness.

85. And again, verily I say unto you, the duty of a president over the office of a deacon is to preside over twelve deacons, to sit in council with them, and to teach them their duty, edifying one another, as it is given according to the covenants.

86. And also the duty of the president over the office of the teachers is to preside over twenty-four of the teachers, and to

sit in council with them, teaching them the duties of their office, as given in the covenants.

87. Also the duty of the president over the Priesthood of Aaron is to preside over forty-eight priests, and sit in council with them, to teach them the duties of their office, as is given in the covenants—

88. This president is to be a bishop; for this is one of the duties of this priesthood.

89. Again, the duty of the president over the office of elders is to preside over ninety-six elders, and to sit in council with them, and to teach them according to the covenants.

90. This presidency is a distinct one from that of the seventy, and is designed for those who do not travel into all the world.

91. And again, the duty of the President of the office of the High Priesthood is to preside over the whole church, and to be like unto Moses—

92. Behold, here is wisdom; yea, to be a seer, a revelator, a translator, and a prophet, having all the gifts of God which he bestows upon the head of the church.

93. And it is according to the vision showing the order of the Seventy, that they should have seven presidents to preside over them, chosen out of the number of the seventy;

94. And the seventh president of these presidents is to preside over the six;

95. And these seven presidents are to choose other seventy besides the first seventy to whom they belong, and are to preside over them;

96. And also other seventy, until seven times seventy, if the labor in the vineyard of necessity requires it.

97. And these seventy are to be traveling ministers, unto the Gentiles first and also unto the Jews.

98. Whereas other officers of the church, who belong not unto the Twelve, neither to the Seventy, are not under the responsibility to travel among all nations, but are to travel as their circumstances shall allow, notwithstanding they may hold as high and responsible offices in the church.

99. Wherefore, now let every man learn his duty, and to act in the office in which he is appointed, in all diligence.

100. He that is slothful shall not be counted worthy to stand,

and he that learns not his duty and shows himself not approved shall not be counted worthy to stand. Even so. Amen.

10. DUTIES OF THE OFFICERS OF THE CHURCH.

64. *High Priesthood * * * the greatest of all*] John Taylor compares the Quorum of High Priests to a Normal School in which the members are being educated for their duties of presiding officers in the Church. The other divisions of the Priesthood may be said to be the preparatory grades of the same school. The young members are first made Deacons, and then Teachers, and then Priests, in order that they may learn thoroughly the duties and privileges of the Aaronic Priesthood. After that they are advanced to Elders, in the Melchizedek Priesthood, and finally to High Priests, "which is the greatest of all."

65-6. The President of the Church is the Presiding High Priest over the High Priesthood, and only through him do the ordinances and blessings come to the Church.

68. *The office of a Bishop*] The Bishop, as such, is a Priest who presides over the Aaronic Priesthood, under the direction of the First Presidency, and his duty is to administer in temporal affairs. However, if no literal descendant of Aaron is found to fill the office of a Bishop, a High Priest, with two counselors, holding the same Priesthood, may be set apart to officiate in the Bishopric (v. 76), as administrators of temporal affairs and judges.

77-84. The Latter-day Saints have been taught not to indulge in lawsuits, if not compelled to. The Church has a perfect judiciary, and the members need not suffer the expenses and inconvenience of so-called legal proceedings. The Teachers are peacemakers. They visit the Saints in their homes, as their friends, and they can generally remove, in their incipiency, all causes of trouble between members. But if they do not succeed, the matter may be taken to the Bishop's Court, where the evidence is heard and a decision may be taken to the High Council of the Stake, and the decision there given is final, unless the First Presidency, after a review of the evidence, orders a re-hearing. The Bishop's Court may, if deemed necessary, excommunicate a member who holds only the Aaronic Priesthood, and disfellowship one who holds the Melchizedek Priesthood. The High Council can excommunicate any member.

"When we take a High Priest and set him apart to officiate in the office of a Priest, or as a Bishop, while he is acting in this calling, do we expect him to officiate as a High Priest? When Bishop Miller finds that the Seventies in his Ward are teaching doctrine that he does not believe in, he has nothing to do with the matter while acting in the capacity of a Bishop. He would say, 'I stand here as your Bishop, and I have nothing to do with the doctrines you teach. I cannot control the higher Priesthood, while in my present calling. I cannot officiate here as an Apostle, as a revelator, as one who has authority to say, Thus saith the Lord, to the people concerning spiritual things' * * * In the capacity of a Bishop, has any person a right to direct the spiritual affairs of the kingdom of God? No. In that capacity his right is restricted to affairs of a temporal and moral nature. He has a right to deal with the transgressor. I do not care what office a transgressor bears in the Church and kingdom of God. * * * What! One of the Seventies? Yes. One of the High Priests? Yes. One of the Twelve Apostles? Yes, anybody that happens to come into this neighborhood and transgress the moral law. On the other hand, can the Seventies try a Bishop? No. Can the High Priests try him? No, unless they call twelve High Priests in the capacity of a High Council; and then you must have the Presidency of the Melchizedek Priesthood to preside over the Council" (Brigham Young, *Jour. of Dis.,* Vol. IX, p. 91).

85-9. Twelve Deacons constitute a Quorum (v. 85); twenty-four form a Quorum of Teachers (v. 86), and forty-eight, of Priests (v. 87). There are ninety-six Elders in an Elders' Quorum (v. 89). There is no given number for a High Priests' Quorum. All the High Priests in a Stake generally belong to the same Quorum, but Brigham Young tells us that, "Three High Priests form a Quorum; five form a Quorum, seven form a Quorum; twelve form a Quorum" (*Jour. of Dis.,* Vol. IX., p. 91).

90. The Seventies are Elders, but their Presidency and organization are distinct from those of the Elders.

91-2. The President of the Church is the Moses of the Church of Christ—leader, lawgiver, revelator, judge, and Prophet.

93. *According to the vision*] It has been said that the organization of the Church is the most nearly perfect on Earth. This is true. For it was given to the Prophet in a vision of the organization existing in the realm beyond the veil, just as the Tabernacle in the Wilderness was constructed according to a heavenly pattern shown to Moses on the Mount.

GENERAL NOTES

It should be noted that the organization of the Church was gradual. The Aaronic Priesthood was first conferred upon Joseph Smith and Oliver Cowdery, on the 15th of May, 1829. A short time afterwards they received the Melchizedek Priesthood. In June, 1831, other High Priests were ordained. The same year Edward Partridge was called to be the first *Bishop* in the Church (see Sec. 41). On the 18th of March, 1833, the *First Presidency* was organized in Kirtland. The Councils of Apostles and of Seventies were organized in 1835. And thus the organization grew and developed, until it reached the indescribable beauty and world-conquering strength which it has attained.

"When the Church is organized, in all its various departments with the President at the head, the Twelve in their place, the High Priests, Seventies, and Elders in theirs, together with the Bishops and lesser Priesthood * * * then the whole becomes as the body of a man, sound and complete in all its members, and everything moves harmoniously and pleasantly along" (John Taylor, *Jour. of Dis.,* Vol. XIX., p. 54).

"A High Priest is a member of the same Melchizedek Priesthood with the Presidency, but not the same power and authority in the Church. The Seventies are also members of the same priesthood (i.e. Melchizedek Priesthood), are a sort of traveling council or Priesthood, and may preside over a church, or churches, until a High Priest can be had. The Seventies are to be taken from the Quorum of Elders, and are not to be High Priests" (Joseph Smith, *Hist. of the Church,* Vol. II., p. 477).

SECTION 108.

REVELATION *given through Joseph Smith the Prophet, at Kirtland, Ohio, December 26, 1835.——Lyman Sherman is commended and admonished—His ordination to the office of Elder promised.*

VERILY thus saith the Lord unto you, my servant Lyman: Your sins are forgiven you, because you have obeyed my voice in coming up hither this morning to receive counsel of him whom I have appointed.

2. Therefore, let your soul be at rest concerning your spiritual standing, and resist no more my voice.

3. And arise up and be more careful henceforth in observing your vows, which you have made and do make, and you shall be blessed with exceeding great blessings.

4. Wait patiently until the solemn assembly shall be called of my servants, then you shall be remembered with the first of mine elders, and receive right by ordination with the rest of mine elders whom I have chosen.

5. Behold, this is the promise of the Father unto you if you continue faithful.

6. And it shall be fulfilled upon you in that day that you shall have right to preach my gospel wheresoever I shall send you, from henceforth from that time.

7. Therefore, strengthen your brethren in all your conversation, in all your prayers, in all your exhortations, and in all your doings.

8. And behold, and lo, I am with you to bless you and deliver you forever. Amen.

Lyman Sherman was one of the little band that made the journey to Missouri in company with the Prophet, in 1834, and when the Seventy were organized, he was chosen one of the first Seven Presidents. The day after Christmas, 1835, he went to the home of the Prophet and expressed a desire to have the Word of the Lord through him. "For," said he, "I have been wrought upon to make known to you my feelings and desires, and was promised that I should have a Revelation which should make known my duty" (*Hist. of the Church,* Vol. II., p. 345). This Revelation was given the same day, in answer to prayer.

1. *Your sins are forgiven you*] From this verse and the two following paragraphs it is evident that Lyman Sherman had passed through one of those mental struggles in which faith is tried to the utmost. It had been a question with him whether to go forward, or to turn back. It is evident, also, that he had conquered doubt and had determined to continue in the faith. At this stage of the trial, it occurred to him that he had sinned by resisting the voice of the Lord, and that perhaps he had lost his standing among the brethren. Tortured by this thought, he heard the voice of the Spirit whispering in his soul and prompting him to visit the Prophet and ask for the Word of God through His servant. The very first assurance was, "Your sins are forgiven you." What comfort! The Prophet knew nothing of the mental struggle through which his visitor had passed, or the condition in which it had left him. And yet he uttered the very word needed to restore peace to the troubled heart. And this word was spoken by one who had the authority of the Priesthood. It was no empty phrase.

4. *Solemn assembly*] A series of meetings, beginning on the 13th of January, 1836, and culminating in a solemn assembly shortly after the dedication of the Temple, was held in Kirtland. At the first meeting, vacancies in the Bishoprics and High Councils of Kirtland and Zion were filled. On the 22nd of January the Twelve and the Presidency of the Seventy received their anointments and blessings (*Hist. of the Church,* Vol. II., p. 383).

SECTION 109.

PRAYER *offered at the dedication of the Temple at Kirtland, Ohio, March 27, 1836. According to the Prophet's written statement, this prayer was given to him by revelation. See History of the Church, vol. 2, p. 410.*

THANKS be to thy name, O Lord God of Israel, who keepest covenant and showest mercy unto thy servants who walk uprightly before thee, with all their hearts—

2. Thou who hast commanded thy servants to build a house to thy name in this place [Kirtland].

3. And now thou beholdest, O Lord, that thy servants have done according to thy commandment.

4. And now we ask thee, Holy Father, in the name of Jesus Christ, the Son of thy bosom, in whose name alone salvation can be administered to the children of men, we ask thee, O Lord, to accept of this house, the workmanship of the hands of us, thy servants, which thou didst command us to build.

5. For thou knowest that we have done this work through great tribulation; and out of our poverty we have given of our substance to build a house to thy name, that the Son of Man might have a place to manifest himself to his people.

6. And as thou hast said in a revelation, given to us, calling us thy friends, saying—Call your solemn assembly, as I have commanded you;

7. And as all have not faith, seek ye diligently and teach one another words of wisdom; yea, seek ye out of the best books words of wisdom, seek learning even by study and also by faith;

8. Organize yourselves; prepare every needful thing, and establish a house, even a house of prayer, a house of fasting, a house of faith, a house of learning, a house of glory, a house of order, a house of God;

9. That your incomings may be in the name of the Lord, that your outgoings may be in the name of the Lord, that all your salutations may be in the name of the Lord, with uplifted hands unto the Most High—

10. And now, Holy Father, we ask thee to assist us, thy people, with thy grace, in calling our solemn assembly, that it may be done to thine honor and to thy divine acceptance;

11. And in a manner that we may be found worthy, in thy sight, to secure a fulfilment of the promises which thou hast made unto us, thy people, in the revelations given unto us;

12. That thy glory may rest down upon thy people, and upon this thy house, which we now dedicate to thee, that it may be sanctified and consecrated to be holy, and that thy holy presence may be continually in this house;

13. And that all people who shall enter upon the threshold of the Lord's house may feel thy power, and feel constrained to

acknowledge that thou hast sanctified it, and that it is thy house, a place of thy holiness.

14. And do thou grant, Holy Father, that all those who shall worship in this house may be taught words of wisdom out of the best books, and that they may seek learning even by study, and also by faith, as thou hast said;

15. And that they may grow up in thee, and receive a fulness of the Holy Ghost, and be organized according to thy laws, and be prepared to obtain every needful thing;

16. And that this house may be a house of prayer, a house of fasting, a house of faith, a house of glory and of God, even thy house;

17. That all the incomings of thy people, into this house, may be in the name of the Lord;

18. That all their outgoings from this house may be in the name of the Lord;

19. And that all their salutations may be in the name of the Lord, with holy hands, uplifted to the Most High;

20. And that no unclean thing shall be permitted to come into thy house to pollute it;

21. And when thy people transgress, any of them, they may speedily repent and return unto thee, and find favor in thy sight, and be restored to the blessings which thou hast ordained to be poured out upon those who shall reverence thee in thy house.

22. And we ask thee, Holy Father, that thy servants may go forth from this house armed with thy power, and that thy name may be upon them, and thy glory be round about them, and thine angels have charge over them;

23. And from this place they may bear exceedingly great and glorious tidings, in truth, unto the ends of the earth, that they may know that this is thy work, and that thou hast put forth thy hand, to fulfil that which thou hast spoken by the mouths of the prophets, concerning the last days.

24. We ask thee, Holy Father, to establish the people that shall worship, and honorably hold a name and standing in this thy house, to all generations and for eternity;

25. That no weapon formed against them shall prosper; that he who diggeth a pit for them shall fall into the same himself;

26. That no combination of wickedness shall have power to

rise up and prevail over thy people upon whom thy name shall be put in this house;

27. And if any people shall rise against this people, that thine anger be kindled against them;

28. And if they shall smite this people thou wilt smite them; thou wilt fight for thy people as thou didst in the day of battle, that they may be delivered from the hands of all their enemies.

29. We ask thee, Holy Father, to confound, and astonish, and to bring to shame and confusion, all those who have spread lying reports abroad, over the world, against thy servant or servants, if they will not repent, when the everlasting gospel shall be proclaimed in their ears;

30. And that all their works may be brought to naught, and be swept away by the hail, and by the judgments which thou wilt send upon them in thine anger, that there may be an end to lyings and slanders against thy people.

31. For thou knowest, O Lord, that thy servants have been innocent before thee in bearing record of thy name, for which they have suffered these things.

32. Therefore we plead before thee for a full and complete deliverance from under this yoke;

33. Break it off, O Lord; break it off from the necks of thy servants, by thy power, that we may rise up in the midst of this generation and do thy work.

34. O Jehovah, have mercy upon this people, and as all men sin forgive the transgressions of thy people, and let them be blotted out forever.

35. Let the anointing of thy ministers be sealed upon them with power from on high.

36. Let it be fulfilled upon them, as upon those on the day of Pentecost; let the gift of tongues be poured out upon thy people, even cloven tongues as of fire, and the interpretation thereof.

37. And let thy house be filled, as with a rushing mighty wind, with thy glory.

38. Put upon thy servants the testimony of the covenant, that when they go out and proclaim thy word they may seal up the law, and prepare the hearts of thy saints for all those judgments thou art about to send, in thy wrath, upon the inhabitants

of the earth, because of their transgressions, that thy people may not faint in the day of trouble.

39. And whatsoever city thy servants shall enter, and the people of that city receive their testimony, let thy peace and thy salvation be upon that city; that they may gather out of that city the righteous, that they may come forth to Zion, or to her stakes, the places of thine appointment, with songs of everlasting joy;

40. And until this be accomplished, let not thy judgments fall upon that city.

41. And whatsoever city thy servants shall enter, and the people of that city receive not the testimony of thy servants warn them to save themselves from this untoward generation, let it be upon that city according to that which thou hast spoken by the mouths of thy prophets.

42. But deliver thou, O Jehovah, we beseech thee, thy servants from their hands, and cleanse them from their blood.

43. O Lord, we delight not in the destruction of our fellow men; their souls are precious before thee;

44. But thy word must be fulfilled. Help thy servants to say, with thy grace assisting them: Thy will be done, O Lord, and not ours.

45. We know that thou hast spoken by the mouth of thy prophets terrible things concerning the wicked, in the last days— that thou wilt pour out thy judgments, without measure;

46. Therefore, O Lord, deliver thy people from the calamity of the wicked; enable thy servants to seal up the law, and bind up the testimony, that they may be prepared against the day of burning.

47. We ask thee, Holy Father, to remember those who have been driven by the inhabitants of Jackson county, Missouri, from the lands of their inheritance, and break off, O Lord, this yoke of affliction that has been put upon them.

48. Thou knowest, O Lord, that they have been greatly oppressed and afflicted by wicked men; and our hearts flow out with sorrow because of their grievous burdens.

49. O Lord, how long wilt thou suffer this people to bear this affliction, and the cries of their innocent ones to ascend up in thine ears, and their blood come up in testimony before thee,

and not make a display of thy testimony in their behalf?

50. Have mercy, O Lord, upon the wicked mob, who have driven thy people, that they may cease to spoil, that they may repent of their sins if repentance is to be found;

51. But if they will not, make bare thine arm, O Lord, and redeem that which thou didst appoint a Zion unto thy people.

52. And if it cannot be otherwise, that the cause of thy people may not fail before thee, may thine anger be kindled, and thine indignation fall upon them, that they may be wasted away, both root and branch, from under heaven;

53. But inasmuch as they will repent, thou art gracious and merciful, and wilt turn away thy wrath when thou lookest upon the face of thine Anointed.

54. Have mercy, O Lord, upon all the nations of the earth; have mercy upon the rulers of our land; may those principles, which were so honorably and nobly defended, namely, the Constitution of our land, by our fathers, be established forever.

55. Remember the kings, the princes, the nobles, and the great ones of the earth, and all people, and the churches, all the poor, the needy, and afflicted ones of the earth;

56. That their hearts may be softened when thy servants shall go out from thy house, O Jehovah, to bear testimony of thy name; that their prejudices may give way before the truth, and thy people may obtain favor in the sight of all;

57. That all the ends of the earth may know that we, thy servants, have heard thy voice, and that thou hast sent us;

58. That from among all these, thy servants, the sons of Jacob, may gather out the righteous to build a holy city to thy name, as thou hast commanded them.

59. We ask thee to appoint unto Zion other stakes besides this one which thou hast appointed, that the gathering of thy people may roll on in great power and majesty, that thy work may be cut short in righteousness.

60. Now these words, O Lord, we have spoken before thee, concerning the revelations and commandments which thou hast given unto us, who are identified with the Gentiles.

61. But thou knowest that thou hast a great love for the children of Jacob, who have been scattered upon the mountains for a long time, in a cloudy and dark day.

62. We therefore ask thee to have mercy upon the children of Jacob, that Jerusalem, from this hour, may begin to be redeemed;

63. And the yoke of bondage may begin to be broken off from the house of David;

64. And the children of Judah may begin to return to the lands which thou didst give to Abraham, their father.

65. And cause that the remnants of Jacob, who have been cursed and smitten because of their transgression, be converted from their wild and savage condition to the fulness of the everlasting gospel;

66. That they may lay down their weapons of bloodshed, and cease their rebellions.

67. And may all the scattered remnants of Israel, who have been driven to the ends of the earth, come to a knowledge of the truth, believe in the Messiah, and be redeemed from oppression, and rejoice before thee.

68. O Lord, remember thy servant, Joseph Smith, Jun., and all his afflictions and persecutions—how he has covenanted with Jehovah, and vowed to thee, O Mighty God of Jacob—and the commandments which thou hast given unto him, and that he hath sincerely striven to do thy will.

69. Have mercy, O Lord, upon his wife and children, that they may be exalted in thy presence, and preserved by thy fostering hand.

70. Have mercy upon all their immediate connections, that their prejudices may be broken up and swept away as with a flood; that they may be converted and redeemed with Israel, and know that thou art God.

71. Remember, O Lord, the presidents, even all the presidents of thy church, that thy right hand may exalt them, with all their families, and their immediate connections, that their names may be perpetuated and had in everlasting remembrance from generation to generation.

72. Remember all thy church, O Lord, with all their families, and all their immediate connections, with all their sick and afflicted ones, with all the poor and meek of the earth; that the kingdom, which thou hast set up without hands, may become a great mountain and fill the whole earth;

73. That thy church may come forth out of the wilderness of darkness, and shine forth fair as the moon, clear as the sun, and terrible as an army with banners;

74. And be adorned as a bride for that day when thou shalt unveil the heavens, and cause the mountains to flow down at thy presence, and the valleys to be exalted, the rough places made smooth; that thy glory may fill the earth;

75. That when the trump shall sound for the dead, we shall be caught up in the cloud to meet thee, that we may ever be with the Lord;

76. That our garments may be pure, that we may be clothed upon with robes of righteousness, with palms in our hands, and crowns of glory upon our heads, and reap eternal joy for all our sufferings.

77. O Lord God Almighty, hear us in these our petitions, and answer us from heaven, thy holy habitation, where thou sittest enthroned, with glory, honor, power, majesty, might, dominion, truth, justice, judgment, mercy, and an infinity of fulness, from everlasting to everlasting.

78. O hear, O hear, O hear us, O Lord! And answer these petitions, and accept the dedication of this house unto thee, the work of our hands, which we have built unto thy name;

79. And also this church, to put upon it thy name. And help us by the power of thy Spirit, that we may mingle our voices with those bright, shining seraphs around thy throne, with acclamations of praise, singing Hosanna to God and the Lamb!

80. And let these, thine anointed ones, be clothed with salvation, and thy saints shout aloud for joy. Amen, and Amen.

GENERAL NOTES

The dedication of the Temple in Kirtland, on the 27th of March, 1836, was an ever memorable event in the history of the Church. That structure was reared in compliance with Revelations received (See Sec. 88:119; 95:8-9), at a time when the Saints were few and poor, and when to raise the money required (between sixty and seventy thousand dollars) meant a great deal of self-sacrifice on their part. "While the brethren labored in their departments," says Tullidge, "the sisters were actively engaged in boarding and clothing workmen not otherwise provided for— all living as abstemiously as possible, so that every cent might be appropriated to the grand object." And thus they toiled on from the 23rd of

July, 1833, when the corner stones were laid, until it was completed for dedication.

In the Revelation given on the 1st of June, 1833, the Lord indicated the special object for which this house was to be built: "I gave unto you a commandment, that you should build an house, in the which house I design to endow those whom I have chosen, with power from on high" (Sec. 95:8). It was to be a place in which the Church would receive a Pentecostal baptism in the fire of the Holy Spirit. A special house, consecrated and dedicated, was needed for that purpose. Hence the commandment of God to the Saints concerning this house.

Now the day of dedication had come. The people assembled early, full of joy and gratitude, and they were not disappointed in their expectations. The manifestations of the divine presence were such as to leave no room in the minds of the true Saints for doubt concerning the nature of the work in which they were engaged. Heber C. Kimball relates that during the ceremonies of the dedication, an angel appeared and sat near Joseph Smith, Sr., and Frederick G. Williams, so that they had a fair view of his person. He was tall, had black eyes and white hair; wore a garment extending to near his ankles, and had sandals on his feet. "He was sent," President Kimball says, "as a messenger to accept of the dedication" (Whitney's *Life of Heber C. Kimball,* p. 103). A few days afterwards, a solemn assembly was held in accordance with a commandment received (See Sec. 108:4), and blessings were given. "While these things were being attended to," Heber C. Kimball says, "the beloved disciple John was seen in our midst by the Prophet Joseph, Oliver Cowdery, and others" (*Ibid.,* p. 104). On the 6th of April, a meeting was held which was prolonged into the night. On this occasion the spirit of prophecy was poured out upon the Saints, and many in the congregation saw tongues of fire upon some of those present, while to others angels appeared. "This," President Kimball says, "continued several days and was attended by a marvelous spirit of prophecy. Every man's mouth was full of prophesying, and for a number of days and weeks our time was spent in visiting from house to house, administering bread and wine, and pronouncing blessings upon each other to that degree, that from the external appearances one would have supposed that the last days had truly come, in which the Spirit of the Lord was poured out upon all flesh," (*Ibid.,* p. 105; see also *Hist. of the Church,* Vol. II., p. 427). Nor were the Saints the only ones who were aware of supernatural manifestations at this time. Elder George A. Smith rose to prophesy, when a noise was heard like the sound of a rushing wind. All the congregation arose, and many began to speak in tongues and prophesy. And then people of the neighborhood came running together (hearing an unusual sound within and seeing a bright light like a pillar of fire resting upon the Temple), and were astonished at what was taking place. This continued until the meeting closed, at 11 p.m. (*History of the Church,* Vol. II., p. 428).

The dedicatory prayer opens with an expression of gratitude to God

for His faithfulness and mercy (v. 1). Then the Prophet humbly asks
Him to accept the house which had been built in obedience to His command (v. 4). It was not a magnificent building, compared with the Temple
of Solomon, for instance, but, the Prophet says, "Thou knowest that we
have done this work through great tribulation" (v. 5). Then he asks
the Lord to bless His people in the solemn assembly that is to be called
(vv. 10-13), and to grant that those who shall worship in the Temple
may be instructed and learn wisdom (vv. 14-20). He asks for blessings
upon the servants of the Lord (v. 22), and on the Saints generally (vv.
24-8), and that the enemies may be confounded (vv. 29-31). He prays
for all nations (v. 54), for kings, princes, etc., (vv. 55-8); for the Church
(v. 59); for the children of Jacob; the children of Judah (v. 64); for
Israel (v. 67); and then he prays for himself and his house (vv. 68-70);
for the officers of the Church (v. 71), and for the Church (vv. 72-6).
This remarkable prayer can be studied, profitably, in connection with the
dedicatory prayer of King Solomon. See I. Kings 8:23-53, and II. Chron.
6:14-42.

Elder George A. Smith says of the Kirtland Temple:

"We considered it a very large building. Some 960 could be seated,
and there would be room for a few to stand; the congregation was swelled
to a little over a thousand persons at the time of the dedication. It was a
trial of faith. The Elders from every part of the country had come together. * * * The congregation was so large that we could not all get
in; and when the house was full, then, of course the doors were closed
and no more admitted. This caused Elder Frazier Eaton, who had paid
$700 towards building the house, to apostatize, because he did not get
there early enough to the meeting. When the dedication prayer was read
by Joseph, it was read from a printed copy. This was a great trial of faith
to many, 'How can it be that the Prophet should read a prayer?' " (*Jour.
of Dis.*, Vol. XI., p. 9).

"The erection of the Temple at Kirtland seemed to increase the hostile
opposition to which the Church had been subjected since its organization;
and persecution soon became so violent that all of the Saints who could
dispose of their property and leave did so and joined their fellow religion-
ists in Missouri. Within two years following the dedication, a general
exodus of the Saints had taken place, and the Temple soon fell into the
hands of the persecutors" (Dr. James E. Talmage, *The House of the
Lord,* p. 123).

Nor is this to be wondered at. The rearing of a Temple of God in the
world is the construction of a citadel by the followers of Prince Immanuel
in the territory claimed by Diabolus. Hence his rage when the people of
God build Temples. But the Temple in Kirtland served its divine purpose, as did that in Nauvoo, though both were abandoned. In it the
Saints received that power from on high which enabled the Church to
withstand, successfully, the attacks of all enemies. Owing to that baptism
by the Holy Spirit received in the Temples, the Church, notwithstanding

persecution, exile, and apostasy, has grown in spiritual power and become able to make itself felt in the world as a regenerating force. But for the Temples and the communion with God established through the Temple service, the Church might have been overwhelmed in the persecutions of Missouri and Illinois, just as the Primitive Church might have perished in the early persecutions but for the power it received on the day of Pentecost. Comp. Acts. 1:8.

SECTION 110.

VISIONS *manifested to Joseph Smith the Prophet, and Oliver Cowdery, in the Temple at Kirtland, Ohio, April 3, 1836. The occasion was that of a Sabbath day meeting. The Prophet prefaces his record of the manifestations with these words: In the afternoon, I assisted the other presidents in distributing the Lord's Supper to the Church, receiving it from the Twelve, whose privilege it was to officiate at the sacred desk this day. After having performed this service to my brethren, I retired to the pulpit, the veils being dropped, and bowed myself, with Oliver Cowdery, in solemn and silent prayer. After rising from prayer, the following vision was opened to both of us.——Personal manifestations of the Lord Jesus Christ—His acceptance of the Temple—Visitation by Moses and his commitment of the keys of the gathering—Visitation by Elias and his conferment of authority—Visitation by Elijah in direct fulfilment of Malachi's prediction.*

THE veil was taken from our minds, and the eyes of our understanding were opened.

2. We saw the Lord standing upon the breastwork of the pulpit, before us; and under his feet was a paved work of pure gold, in color like amber.

3. His eyes were as a flame of fire; the hair of his head was white like the pure snow; his countenance shone above the brightness of the sun; and his voice was as the sound of the rushing of great waters, even the voice of Jehovah, saying:

There were two stands, one on the west end and one on the east end, each consisting of four pulpits, one rising above the other, like terraces. The pulpits on the west end were reserved for presiding officers of the

Melchizedek Priesthood, and those on the east end for the Aaronic Priesthood. Each of these pulpits could be separated from the others by means of veils of painted canvas, which could be let down or rolled up at pleasure.

On Sunday, April 3rd, 1836, in the afternoon, after the Sacrament, the Prophet Joseph and Oliver Cowdery retired to the pulpit in order to engage in silent prayer. The veils were dropped. When they rose from their devotion, the visions recorded in this Section were given to both. (1) Our Lord appears (1-3); (2) His message is delivered to them (4-10); (3) Moses appears (11); (4) Elias appears (12); (5) Elijah appears (13-16).

1. OUR LORD APPEARS.

1-3. Glorious manifestations had indeed been given during the dedication services of this sanctuary. This vision surpasses any of those previously granted, for our Lord Himself indeed came to His Temple, "suddenly," as predicted (Mal. 3:1).

1. *The veil was taken from our minds*] The pulpit veil had been lowered, so that Joseph and Oliver were by themselves, but to their mind's eye the veil was removed, and the eyes of their understanding were opened.

2. *We saw the Lord*] He was standing upon the breastwork of the pulpit; that is, close to them. In Ex. 24:9-11, we are told that Moses, Aaron, Nadab, and Abihu, and seventy Elders "saw the God of Israel," and there was under His feet "a paved work of sapphire stone, and as it were the body of heaven in clearness." They saw the divine Manifestation, not close by, but standing on a pavement which in color could be compared only to the clear, blue sky. In this Revelation, the God of Israel, our Lord, was seen standing upon a pavement of pure gold, like amber in color and resting on the breastwork.

3. *His eyes, etc.*] They saw His features. The description resembles that of Daniel's vision of the Ancient of Days (Adam), and also that of John's vision of the Son of Man (See Dan. 7:9, and Rev. 1:14).

Rushing of great waters] There is wonderful harmony in the apparently unending tune of a waterfall. Some one with an analytical ear claims to have found that the sound produced by a cataract is composed by the chord C, E, G, and a deep F. The Song of the Redeemed sounded to the Revelator "as the voice of many waters," accompanied by the voice of thunder and the music of harps. It was at once majestic, awe-inspiring, and sweet.

4. I am the first and the last; I am he who liveth, I am he who was slain; I am your advocate with the Father.

5. Behold, your sins are forgiven you; you are clean before me; therefore, lift up your heads and rejoice.

6. Let the hearts of your brethren rejoice, and let the hearts of all my people rejoice, who have, with their might, built this house to my name.

7. For behold, I have accepted this house, and my name shall be here; and I will manifest myself to my people in mercy in this house.

8. Yea, I will appear unto my servants, and speak unto them with mine own voice, if my people will keep my commandments, and do not pollute this holy house.

9. Yea the hearts of thousands and tens of thousands shall greatly rejoice in consequence of the blessings which shall be poured out, and the endowment with which my servants have been endowed in this house.

10. And the fame of this house shall spread to foreign lands; and this is the beginning of the blessing which shall be poured out upon the heads of my people. Even so. Amen.

2. OUR LORD'S MESSAGE TO HIS SERVANTS

4. *The First and the Last*] Our Lord addresses His servants under a name by which He was well known to them (See Sec. 19:1). There was to be no mistake, as to His identity. It was not an angel, but our Lord Himself, who stood before them in the vision.

5. *Your sins are forgiven you*] This joyful assurance, which alone can bring peace to a human heart, was again given to Joseph and Oliver (See Sec. 29:3). Our Savior lives, although He was slain on Calvary, and He is our advocate (See Sec. 45:3) with the Father. Therefore He can forgive sins.

You are clean] He whose sins are forgiven is clean.

*Therefore * * * rejoice*] The wonderful manifestations they had witnessed were not comparable to the fact that their sins were forgiven. Jesus said to the Seventy: "In this rejoice not, that the spirits are subject unto you; but rather rejoice, because your names are written in heaven" (Luke 10:20).

7-10. *I have accepted this house*] This verse and the following three paragraphs contain a direct answer to the dedicatory prayer. But the condition is,—"If my people will keep my commandments, and do not pollute this holy house" (v. 8). When His people suffer His Sanctuary to be polluted, He is not greatly concerned if the hordes of Nebuchadnezzar carry away the consecrated vessels for Belshazzar to use in drunken orgies; or if the Roman soldiers level its walls with the ground and run the plow over it, so as to make sure that not one stone is left undisturbed.

11. After this vision closed, the heavens were again opened

unto us; and Moses appeared before us, and committed unto us the keys of the gathering of Israel from the four parts of the earth, and the leading of the ten tribes from the land of the north.

3. MOSES APPEARS.

11. *Gathering of Israel*] This means all the descendants of Jacob. Comp. Sec. 133:13, 26. In a communication to a Rochester paper, written by divine commandment and dated Kirtland, January 4th, 1833, the Prophet says, in part:

"By it [the Book of Mormon] we learn that our Western Indians are descendants of that Joseph who was sold into Egypt, and that the land of America is a promised land unto them, and unto it all the tribes of Israel will come, with as many of the Gentiles as shall comply with the requisitions of the new covenant. But the tribes of Judah will return to old Jerusalem. The City of Zion, spoken of by David in the 102nd Psalm, will be built upon the land of America, 'and the ransomed of the Lord shall return, and come to Zion, with songs of everlasting joy upon their heads' (Is. 35:10), and then they will be delivered from the overflowing scourge that shall pass through the land. But Judah shall obtain deliverance at Jerusalem. See Joel 2:32, Isa. 26:20-1; Jer. 31:12; Ez. 34:11-13" (*Hist. of the Church*, Vol. I., p. 315).

12. After this, Elias appeared, and committed the dispensation of the gospel of Abraham, saying that in us and our seed all generations after us should be blessed.

4. ELIAS APPEARS.

12. *Elias*] From a discourse delivered by the Prophet Joseph, at Nauvoo, on the 10th of March, 1844, the following is quoted:

"The spirit of Elias is first, Elijah second, and Messiah last. Elias is a forerunner to prepare the way, and the spirit and power of Elijah is to come after, holding the keys of power, building the Temple to the capstone, placing the seals of the Melchizedek Priesthood upon the house of Israel, and making all things ready; then Messiah comes to His Temple, which is last of all. Messiah is above the spirit and power of Elijah, for He made the world, and was that spiritual Rock unto Moses in the wilderness. Elijah was to come and prepare the way and build up the kingdom before the coming of the great day of the Lord, although the spirit of Elias might begin it" (*Hist. of the Church*, Vol. VI., p. 254).

13. After this vision had closed, another great and glorious vision burst upon us; for Elijah the prophet, who was taken to heaven without tasting death, stood before us, and said:

14. Behold, the time has fully come, which was spoken of

by the mouth of Malachi—testifying that he [Elijah] should be sent, before the great and dreadful day of the Lord come—

15. To turn the hearts of the fathers to the children, and the children to the fathers, lest the whole earth be smitten with a curse—

16. Therefore, the keys of this dispensation are committed into your hands; and by this ye may know that the great and dreadful day of the Lord is near, even at the doors.

5. Elijah Appears.

13. *Elijah*] See notes under Section 2. Elijah appeared to our Lord on the Mount of Transfiguration (Matt. 17:3), and according to II. Chron. 21:12, he wrote a letter eight years after his translation, to the wicked king, Jehoram, rebuking him for his apostasy. Here he appears, not as an avenger, but as a messenger of peace.

Elias was the representative of the Patriarchal dispensation; Moses, of the Mosaic, and Elijah of the dispensation preparatory to the coming of the Lord. Each delegated part of his authority and mission to the Prophet Joseph.

SECTION 111.

Revelation *given through Joseph Smith the Prophet, at Salem, Massachusetts, August 6, 1836. The Prophet with one of his Counselors and two other Elders had journeyed from Kirtland, Ohio, to Salem, Massachusetts; and, at their destination had entered upon the work of teaching the people from house to house, and preaching publicly as opportunity presented. See History of the Church, vol. 2, p. 463.——Directions for further labor—The Lord's assurances as to Zion.*

I, THE Lord your God, am not displeased with your coming this journey, notwithstanding your follies.

2. I have much treasure in this city for you, for the benefit of Zion, and many people in this city, whom I will gather out in due time for the benefit of Zion, through your instrumentality.

3. Therefore, it is expedient that you should form acquaintance with men in this city, as you shall be led, and as it shall be given you.

4. And it shall come to pass in due time that I will give this

city into your hands, that you shall have power over it, insomuch that they shall not discover your secret parts; and its wealth pertaining to gold and silver shall be yours.

5. Concern not yourselves about your debts, for I will give you power to pay them.

6. Concern not yourselves about Zion, for I will deal mercifully with her.

7. Tarry in this place, and in the regions round about;

8. And the place where it is my will that you should tarry, for the main, shall be signalized unto you by the peace and power of my Spirit, that shall flow unto you.

9. This place you may obtain by hire. And inquire diligently concerning the more ancient inhabitants and founders of this city;

10. For there are more treasures than one for you in this city.

11. Therefore, be ye as wise as serpents and yet without sin; and I will order all things for your good, as fast as ye are able to receive them. Amen.

On the 25th of July, 1836, the Prophet Joseph, in company with Sidney Rigdon, Hyrum Smith, and Oliver Cowdery, left Kirtland for a mission to the East. They passed through Albany, New York, Providence, Boston, and arrived, early in August, in Salem, Mass., where they hired a hall in which they held meetings for about a month, and visited sections of the surrounding country. While there, this Revelation was received.

1. *Notwithstanding your follies*] A merciful God overlooks the follies of His children, when the motives are pure. "Like as a father pitieth his children, so the Lord pitieth them that fear Him" (Ps. 103:13). They had come East for a good purpose, and the Lord assured them that He was not displeased with them, notwithstanding the folly of the undertaking.

2. *Much treasure * * * many people*] The Lord, further, assured them that He had much treasure and many people in the City of Salem, that would ultimately be gathered for the benefit of Zion. This is, undoubtedly, true of many other cities. When the time comes for the gathering of the Saints to the Land of Zion, the thinking people of the world, weary of international wars and industrial conflicts, will hail with joy any practical effort that promises to bring peace to man. Then "the sons of strangers shall build up the walls, and their kings shall minister unto thee" (Is. 60:10).

3. *That you should form acquaintance*] A successful missionary has the faculty of making friends. He takes an interest in all that interests his fellowmen, and brings to the society in which he moves the sweet in-

fluence of the gospel, even when he does not say a word on the subject of religion. Hermits are useless as missionaries.

4. *I will give this city into your hands*] When the Millennial reign comes, all the kingdoms of the world will be the kingdom of the Son of God, and He will administer the government through His faithful servants. Then some will be given authority over ten cities; others, over five (Luke 19:17).

5. *Concern not yourselves about your debts*] When the Kirtland Temple was dedicated, the Church was indebted to the amount of between thirteen and fourteen thousand dollars, and this debt, no doubt, was a heavy burden upon the shoulders of the leaders. But the Lord knew that the Saints had exerted themselves to the utmost, and He, therefore, gave this comforting promise.

6. *Concern not yourselves about Zion*] Another source of anxiety at this time was the condition of Zion. The Saints had been driven from Jackson County, and there was no prospect of a speedy change in the public sentiment. The Lord, therefore, told His servants not to harbor undue anxiety for the scattered Saints. He would be merciful to them. The plans and purposes of God concerning His people were not frustrated.

9. *This place*] The hall in which to hold meetings.

Inquire diligently concerning the more ancient inhabitants and founders of this city] History is, perhaps, the most useful knowledge a missionary can have, next to a thorough understanding of the principles of the gospel, but "ancient inhabitants" refers more particularly to the ancestors of the Prophet. The Revelation was given at Salem, the county seat of Essex County, Massachusetts. It was in that county that Robert Smith, the first of the Smith family in America, settled. It was the residence of many more of the pioneer immigrants to America, whose descendants joined the Church. At Salem, the county seat, the records for all the towns in the county were kept, and the Smiths' record, among others, were there. The matter of genealogy evidently entered into the inquiry concerning the "ancient inhabitants," for a purpose which was manifest later, of the salvation of the dead.

General Notes

The Prophet Joseph notes the persecution in the early days of Baptists and Quakers in Boston; the insane prosecutions of witches at Salem, and the destruction, in more recent days, by a mob, of a Catholic convent near Charleston, and adds:

"Well did the Savior say concerning such, 'By their fruits you shall know them.' And if the wicked mob who destroyed Charleston Convent, and the cool, calculating religious lookers on, who inspired their hearts with deeds of infamy, do not arise, and redress the wrong, and restore the injury four-fold, they, in turn, will receive of the measure they have meted out, till the just indignation of a righteous God is satisfied. When will man cease to war with man, and wrest from him his sacred rights of worshiping his God according as his conscience dictates? Holy Father, hasten the day!" (*Hist. of the Church,* Vol. II., p. 465).

Most of the famous Reformers of the world have clamored for religious liberty for themselves and their own followers; the Prophet Joseph demanded liberty of conscience for *all* men and *all* religions.

SECTION 112.

REVELATION *given through Joseph Smith the Prophet, to Thomas B. Marsh, at Kirtland, Ohio, July 23, 1837. The word of the Lord unto Thomas B. Marsh, concerning the Twelve Apostles of the Lamb. The Prophet records that this revelation was received on the day on which the Gospel was first preached in England. Thomas B. Marsh was at this time president of the quorum of the Twelve Apostles.——The Twelve to send the gospel abroad among all nations—They are to act under the direction of the First Presidency—Others may be authorized by the Twelve for ministry among the nations—The keys of power in the Priesthood committed to the First Presidency and the Twelve—The present designated as the dispensation of the fulness of times.*

VERILY thus saith the Lord unto you my servant Thomas: I have heard thy prayers; and thine alms have come up as a memorial before me, in behalf of those, thy brethren, who were chosen to bear testimony of my name and to send it abroad among all nations, kindreds, tongues, and people, and ordained through the instrumentality of my servants.

2. Verily I say unto you, there have been some few things in thine heart and with thee with which I, the Lord, was not well pleased.

3. Nevertheless, inasmuch as thou hast abased thyself thou shalt be exalted; therefore, all thy sins are forgiven thee.

4. Let thy heart be of good cheer before my face; and thou shalt bear record of my name, not only unto the Gentiles, but also unto the Jews; and thou shalt send forth my word unto the ends of the earth.

5. Contend thou, therefore, morning by morning; and day after day let thy warning voice go forth; and when the night cometh let not the inhabitants of the earth slumber, because of thy speech.

6. Let thy habitation be known in Zion, and remove not thy house; for I, the Lord, have a great work for thee to do, in publishing my name among the children of men.

7. Therefore, gird up thy loins for the work. Let thy feet be shod also, for thou art chosen, and thy path lieth among the mountains, and among many nations.

8. And by thy word many high ones shall be brought low, and by thy word many low ones shall be exalted.

9. Thy voice shall be a rebuke unto the transgressor; and at thy rebuke let the tongue of the slanderer cease its perverseness.

10. Be thou humble; and the Lord thy God shall lead thee by the hand, and give thee answer to thy prayers.

11. I know thy heart, and have heard thy prayers concerning thy brethren. Be not partial towards them in love above many others, but let thy love be for them as for thyself; and let thy love abound unto all men, and unto all who love my name.

At the end of the year 1836 and the beginning of 1837, a spirit of disaffection made itself manifest among the Saints in Kirtland. The United States was passing through a financial crisis, brought about by over-speculation, and other causes, and the Saints who had been drawn into the maelstrom suffered with the rest of the victims. "As the Saints," says Eliza R. Snow, "drank in the love and spirit of the world, the Spirit of the Lord withdrew from their hearts, and they were filled with pride and hatred towards those who maintained their integrity." George A. Smith, speaking of these times, says, "A man that would stand up in the streets and say he was Joseph's friend, could not get a greater compliment than being called a 'lick-skillet.' Joseph had few friends; but among the leading Elders of the Church in Kirtland, the High Council, one of the members of the First Presidency, some of the seven Presidents of the Seventies, and a great many others were so darkened that they went astray in every direction * * * They boasted of the talent at their command, and what they would do. Their plan was to take the doctrines of the Church, such as repentance, baptism for the remission of sins, throw aside the Book of Mormon, the Prophet and Priesthood, and go and unite the whole Christian world under these doctrines" (*Jour. of Dis.*, Vol. XI., p. 11). They even went so far as to claim that the Temple was theirs. The Prophet says:

"In this state of things, and but a few weeks before the Twelve were expecting to meet in full Quorum * * * God revealed to me that something new must be done for the salvation of His Church. And on, or about, the 1st of June, 1837, Heber C. Kimball, one of the Twelve, was set apart by the spirit of prophecy and revelation, prayer and laying on of hands of the First Presidency, to preside over a Mission to England, to be the first foreign mission of the Church of Christ in the last days" (*Hist. of the Church*, Vol. II., p. 489).

Heber C. Kimball, Orson Hyde, Willard Richards, and Joseph Fielding left for this mission on the 13th of June, 1837, accompanied, as far as Fairport, on Lake Erie, by Brigham Young and others. In New York City, they were joined by John Goodson, Isaac Russel, and John Snyder. The party arrived in Liverpool, England, on the 20th of July, 1837, and proceeded to Preston, where Heber C. Kimball, on the 23rd, preached the first sermon in a chapel belonging to the congregation of the Rev. James Fielding, a brother of Joseph Fielding.

The Revelation in this Section was given through Joseph, the Prophet. to Thomas B. Marsh concerning the Twelve Apostles, on the very same day on which the first gospel sermons were preached at Preston, England.

In this Revelation the Lord (1) addresses Thomas B. Marsh on his own status (1-11); (2) gives him instructions concerning the Twelve (12-22); (3) concerning their duties to the world (23-32); and (4) closes with an admonition and promises (33-4).

1. THE LORD SPEAKS TO THOMAS B. MARSH.

1. *I have heard thy prayers*] With all his faults, Thomas B. Marsh, at this time, was sincere in his prayers and sacrifices, which is proved by the fact that the Lord had accepted them. As the President of the Council of Twelve Apostles, he had their welfare at heart.

3. *All thy sins are forgiven thee*] Not because he was an Apostle, a leader in the Church, but "inasmuch as thou hast abased thyself." Forgiveness comes only to those who are humble and truly repentant.

4. *Thou shalt bear record of my name*] No one can be a messenger of the Lord, who has not received the forgiveness of his sins, so that he is pure and unspotted, and has a conscience void of offense toward God and man.

Thou shalt send forth my word] It is the office and calling of an Apostle to preach the gospel, administer the ordinances of the Church, heal the sick, and perform mighty works, plant and set churches in order, and ordain to the Priesthood and offices in the Church (Comp. Matt. 10:1, 28:19; Acts 14:23; I. Cor. 3:6.

5. *Contend thou * * * morning by morning, and day after day*] As eternal vigilance is the price of liberty, so it is also the price of the salvation of souls. The Gospel records the fact that our Savior very often taught the people and healed the sick during the day, and then retired to some secluded spot for prayer, sometimes spending the entire night in

communion with God, His Father, and then He was prepared, the next morning, for another day's work (See, for instance, Mark 1:21-35). See also pp. 277-78.

6. *Let thy habitation be known in Zion*] In 1832, Thomas B. Marsh received an inheritance—about thirty acres—on the Big Blue river, Missouri, and there he built a comfortable log house. When the Saints were driven from Jackson County, he went to Lafayette County, while most of the exiles sought refuge in Clay County. In 1834, he, too, went to Clay County. After an extended visit to Kirtland, he returned to his home on Fishing River, Clay County. In 1836, he built a house in Far West. In June 1837, he again visited Kirtland. It was necessary, for the success of his mission, that his residence in Zion should be known, and that his house should not be moved.

7. *Gird up thy loins * * * let thy feet be shod*] Be ready to travel. In 1837, Thomas B. Marsh accompanied the Prophet Joseph and Sidney Rigdon to Canada.

9. *Thy voice shall be a rebuke, etc.,*] Thomas B. Marsh was a powerful speaker. In 1836 he was a member of a committee selected to pass resolutions on behalf of the exiled Saints, at a meeting at the city of Liberty. On that occasion, he spoke of the persecution the Saints had suffered, so eloquently that General Atchinson and others wept.

10. *Be thou humble*] Pride was the weakness of Thomas B. Marsh. If he had been humble, he would not have fallen. He began by defying the righteous decisions of the High Council and the First Presidency, in a trivial case in which his wife was interested, and he ended by becoming a traitor to the Church.

12. And pray for thy brethren of the Twelve. Admonish them sharply for my name's sake, and let them be admonished for all their sins, and be ye faithful before me unto my name.

13. And after their temptations, and much tribulation, behold, I, the Lord, will feel after them, and if they harden not their hearts, and stiffen not their necks against me, they shall be converted, and I will heal them.

14. Now, I say unto you, and what I say unto you, I say unto all the Twelve: Arise and gird up your loins, take up your cross, follow me, and feed my sheep.

15. Exalt not yourselves; rebel not against my servant Joseph; for verily I say unto you, I am with him, and my hand shall be over him; and the keys which I have given unto him, and also to youward, shall not be taken from him till I come.

16. Verily I say unto you, my servant Thomas, thou art the

man whom I have chosen to hold the keys of my kingdom, as pertaining to the Twelve, abroad among all nations—

17. That thou mayest be my servant to unlock the door of the kingdom in all places where my servant Joseph, and my servant Sidney, and my servant Hyrum, cannot come;

18. For on them have I laid the burden of all the churches for a little season.

19. Wherefore, whithersoever they shall send you, go ye, and I will be with you; and in whatsoever place ye shall proclaim my name an effectual door shall be opened unto you, that they may receive my word.

20. Whosoever receiveth my word receiveth me, and whosoever receiveth me, receiveth those, the First Presidency, whom I have sent, whom I have made counselors for my name's sake unto you.

21. And again, I say unto you, that whosoever ye shall send in my name, by the voice of your brethren, the Twelve, duly recommended and authorized by you, shall have power to open the door of my kingdom unto any nation whithersoever ye shall send them—

22. Inasmuch as they shall humble themselves before me, and abide in my word, and hearken to the voice of my Spirit.

2. Concerning the Twelve.

12-13. Our Lord instructs the President of the Council to continue to pray for the members, and also to admonish them "sharply." Admonition without prayer is barren of results. He promised to feel after them, when they had passed through the tribulations awaiting them because they had yielded to temptations. And then, if they would not harden their hearts, they would be converted and healed.

Orson Hyde, who had imbibed of the spirit of speculation, freely acknowledged his faults and asked forgiveness. Parley P. Pratt, too, at one time was overcome by the evil spirit, of strife, but, he says, "I went to Brother Joseph Smith in tears, and with a broken heart and contrite spirit, confessed wherein I had erred. * * * He frankly forgave me, prayed for me, blessed me." Others did not repent. Luke S. Johnson, Lyman E. Johnson, and John F. Boynton were rejected and disfellowshiped by the Church on the 3rd of September, 1837, less than a month and a half after this Revelation was given.

14. *Take up your cross*] This seems to have been a common expression in religious circles at this time. Newel Knight said that he "would try and take up his cross and pray vocally during meeting" (*Hist. of the*

Church, Vol. I., p. 82). It is a Scriptural expression. Our Lord says, "If any man will come after me, let him deny himself, and take up his cross daily, and follow me" (Luke 9:23). The performance of duty is a task that requires continual effort. If anybody should join the Church because the services are "grand," or the sermons "beautiful," he would be disappointed, but he who comes determined to do his duty, will find life eternal. Paul says, "For thy sake we are killed all the day long" (Rom. 8:36); again, "I die daily" (I. Cor. 15:31). The followers of Christ "carry the cross."

16-20. The Prophet Joseph, Sidney Rigdon, and Hyrum Smith were the First Presidency, and on them rested the burden of all the Churches (v. 18). But the Twelve had the authority (keys) to regulate the affairs of the Church among all nations (v. 16). "Whosoever receiveth my word receiveth me, and whosoever receiveth me, receiveth those (the First Presidency) whom I have sent" (v. 20). Our Lord does not visit all men in person, but He sends His servants, His ambassadors. Those who reject these, would also reject Him, if He came in person to them.

23. Verily, verily, I say unto you, darkness covereth the earth, and gross darkness the minds of the people, and all flesh has become corrupt before my face.

24. Behold, vengeance cometh speedily upon the inhabitants of the earth, a day of wrath, a day of burning, a day of desolation, of weeping, of mourning, and of lamentation; and as a whirlwind it shall come upon all the face of the earth, saith the Lord.

25. And upon my house shall it begin, and from my house shall it go forth, saith the Lord;

26. First among those among you, saith the Lord, who have professed to know my name and have not known me, and have blasphemed against me in the midst of my house, saith the Lord.

27. Therefore, see to it that ye trouble not yourselves concerning the affairs of my church in this place, saith the Lord.

28. But purify your hearts before me; and then go ye into all the world, and preach my gospel unto every creature who has not received it;

29. And he that believeth and is baptized shall be saved, and he that believeth not, and is not baptized, shall be damned.

30. For unto you, the Twelve, and those, the First Presidency, who are appointed with you to be your counselors and your leaders, is the power of this priesthood given, for the last

days and for the last time, in the which is the dispensation of the fulness of times.

31. Which power you hold, in connection with all those who have received a dispensation at any time from the beginning of the creation;

32. For verily I say unto you, the keys of the dispensation, which ye have received, have come down from the fathers, and last of all, being sent down from heaven unto you.

3. The Duties of the Twelve to the World.

23-7. In these paragraphs the Spirit indicates that a storm was about to burst over the Church. "Darkness"—the very opposite of the light of revelation— "covereth the earth" * * * "and all flesh has become corrupt," as in the days of Noah. For that reason, "a day of wrath, a day of burning, a day of desolation, of weeping, of mourning," is coming, "as a whirlwind," and "upon my house shall it begin." The day of wrath came, and the Church was first sifted. Those who professed to be Saints and were not, were separated from the Church, through persecution, and the Church itself was then brought to a place of safety, in the mountain chambers.

28. *Purify your hearts*] "Hearts," is a figure used frequently in the Scriptures and stands for "affections," "understanding," "courage," "joy," etc. "Broken heart" means one that is humble and willing to be obedient to the will of the Lord. "Stony heart," means that the individual is unrepentant, unbelieving. These messengers who were to go forth were to purify their hearts so that the Spirit of the Lord might be their guide as they went forth into all the world.

33. Verily I say unto you, behold how great is your calling. Cleanse your hearts and your garments, lest the blood of this generation be required at your hands.

34. Be faithful until I come, for I come quickly; and my reward is with me to recompense every man according as his work shall be. I am Alpha and Omega. Amen.

4. Admonition and Promises.

33. The Lord repeats His admonition to His servants, that they must cleanse their hearts (See v. 28), and adds this solemn warning, that, unless they do so, the blood of this generation will be required at their hands. The responsibility of the position of a messenger of the Lord is overwhelming. But—and this is the promise—"I come quickly." The time is short, in which to carry this responsibility, and the reward is sure.

GENERAL NOTES

In the fall of 1833, the Saints were expelled from Jackson County, Mo. Many of the exiles settled in Clay County. For three years they enjoyed peace there, but on the 29th of June, 1836, they were requested, by a mass meeting, held at Liberty, to move on to a place "where the manners, the habits, and customs of the people would be more consonant with their own." No charge was preferred against them; only their religion was not "consonant" with the habits and customs of their neighbors. The Saints, after a protest as citizens of the United States, agreed to leave, and within three months they were on their way to a wilderness almost unoccupied, in the Shoal Creek region, where they settled and organized a county government of their own. They named their new location Caldwell County, and founded the city of Far West there, during the winter of 1836-7.

In Kirtland the spirit of apostasy continued rampant. Warren Parrish, John F. Boynton, Joseph Coe, and others, combined with some Missouri Elders and planned the destruction of the Church. Outsiders joined them. Brigham Young, who had exposed the villainy of some of them—in connection with the failure of the Kirtland Bank—became an object of their rage, and he left for Missouri on the 22nd of December, 1837. Three weeks later, the Prophet and Sidney Rigdon fled. They arrived in Far West, about the middle of March, 1838.

In Kirtland, on the 3rd of September, 1837, Frederick G. Williams had been rejected as one of the First Presidency, and Hyrum Smith sustained in his place. Lyman E. Johnson, Luke S. Johnson, and John F. Boynton, three Apostles; John Gould, one of the Presidents of Seventies, and several High Councilors were also rejected.

In Far West, at the April conference, Thomas B. Marsh, Brigham Young, and David W. Patten were sustained Presidents over the Church in Missouri, and under their administration Oliver Cowdery, David Whitmer, Luke S. and Lyman E. Johnson, John F. Boynton, and William E. McLellin were excommunicated.*

SECTION 113.

ANSWERS *to certain questions on Scripture, given by Joseph Smith the Prophet, March, 1838.*

WHO is the Stem of Jesse spoken of in the 1st, 2d, 3d, 4th, and 5th verses of the 11th chapter of Isaiah?

2. Verily thus saith the Lord: It is Christ.

---

*Oliver Cowdery and Luke S. Johnson rejoined the Church, but the others remained outside.

This Revelation was given shortly after the arrival of the Prophet at Far West. The 11th chapter of Isaiah is a prophecy of the establishment of the kingdom of Christ on Earth. It sets forth His character (1-2), His government (3-5), and the peaceful conditions that will prevail when He reigns (6-9). With the 10th verse begins a prophecy concerning the gathering of the people of God, previous to the Millennium.

1. *Stem*] This word means here "the *stock* which remains in the earth after the tree is cut down."

3. What is the rod spoken of in the first verse of the 11th chapter of Isaiah, that should come of the Stem of Jesse?
4. Behold, thus saith the Lord: It is a servant in the hands of Christ, who is partly a descendant of Jesse as well as of Ephraim, or of the house of Joseph, on whom there is laid much power.

3. *Rod*] This means a "shoot" or branch coming out of the "stem" of Jesse—a descendant.

5. What is the root of Jesse spoken of in the 10th verse of the 11th chapter?
6. Behold, thus saith the Lord, it is a descendant of Jesse, as well as of Joseph, unto whom rightly belongs the priesthood, and the keys of the kingdom, for an ensign, and for the gathering of my people in the last days.

5. *Root of Jesse*] A branch from the root. Jesse was the father of David.

7. Questions by Elias Higbee: What is meant by the command in Isaiah, 52d chapter, 1st verse, which saith: Put on thy strength, O Zion—and what people had Isaiah reference to?
8. He had reference to those whom God should call in the last days, who should hold the power of priesthood to bring again Zion, and the redemption of Israel; and to put on her strength is to put on the authority of the priesthood, which she, Zion, has a right to by lineage; also to return to that power which she had lost.
9. What are we to understand by Zion loosing herself from the bands of her neck; 2d verse?

10. We are to understand that the scattered remnants are exhorted to return to the Lord from whence they have fallen; which if they do, the promise of the Lord is that he will speak to them, or give them revelation. See the 6th, 7th, and 8th verses. The bands of her neck are the curses of God upon her, or the remnants of Israel in their scattered condition among the Gentiles.

In Isaiah 52:1, 2, the Prophet summons Zion and Jerusalem to put on garments befitting the dignity of a bride of the Son of God. These garments are the authority and power of the Priesthood.

SECTION 114.

REVELATION *given through Joseph Smith the Prophet, at Far West, Missouri, April 17, 1838.——Directions to David W. Patten—Positions occupied by the unfaithful to be given to others.*

VERILY thus saith the Lord: It is wisdom in my servant David W. Patten, that he settle up all his business as soon as he possibly can, and make a disposition of his merchandise, that he may perform a mission unto me next spring, in company with others, even twelve including himself, to testify of my name and bear glad tidings unto all the world.

2. For verily thus saith the Lord, that inasmuch as there are those among you who deny my name, others shall be planted in their stead and receive their bishopric. Amen.

David W. Patten is instructed to settle up his affairs and be prepared to take a mission. He was born in the State of New York, about the year 1800, and was baptized June 15th, 1832, by his brother, John Patten. He performed several missions and gradually rose to prominence. On February 15th, 1835, he was ordained an Apostle. He was absolutely fearless. His testimony was powerful and through him God performed many mighty works. In 1838, the mobbings in Missouri commenced anew, and Patten was foremost in the defense of the Saints. He died as the result of a wound received on the 25th of October, 1838, in a conflict with a lawless rabble at a place called Crooked River. His mission was on the other side of the veil.

SECTION 115.

REVELATION *given through Joseph Smith the Prophet, at Far West, Missouri, April 26, 1838, making known the will of God concerning the building up of that place, and of the Lord's House. This revelation is addressed to the presiding officers of the Church.——The official name, The Church of Jesus Christ of Latter-day Saints, confirmed by the Lord—Far West to be a holy and consecrated place—Commandment to build a house of the Lord there—The First Presidency not to incur debts for the building of a house unto the Lord.*

VERILY thus saith the Lord unto you, my servant Joseph Smith, Jun., and also my servant Sidney Rigdon, and also my servant Hyrum Smith, and your counselors who are and shall be appointed hereafter;

2. And also unto you, my servant Edward Partridge, and his counselors;

3. And also unto my faithful servants who are of the high council of my church in Zion, for thus it shall be called, and unto all the elders and people of my Church of Jesus Christ of Latter-day Saints, scattered abroad in all the world;

4. For thus shall my church be called in the last days, even The Church of Jesus Christ of Latter-day Saints.

1-4. This Revelation is addressed to the First Presidency and their counselors; the Presiding Bishop in Zion and his counselors; the High Council in Zion, and all the Elders and members of the Church.

3. *The Church of Jesus Christ of Latter-day Saints*] Here the name of the Church is given. The world, from the beginning, gave to the Saints the name "Mormons," or "Mormonites." The Saints called their organization, "The Church of Christ," or "The Church of Jesus Christ." At a conference held at Kirtland, in May, 1834, it was called, "The Church of the Latter-day Saints." Here the full and true name is revealed. The grammatical construction is unusual, but the name is full of meaning. It means, "The Church which belongs to Jesus Christ and which consists of Latter-day Saints." That is the force of the two *genitives*. It is the Church which Daniel saw (7:18) in his vision of the latter days, so that the very name fulfils a prophecy (Comp. Sec. 102:1; Ps. 50:5).

Bible scholars have said that since the name "Christ" is a title which means, "the Anointed One," sometimes interpreted "the Messiah," it ought to have the definite article, and we ought to say, "Jesus, *the* Christ, and not Jesus Christ, as given in the name of the Church. These learned men have overlooked the fact that the name of our Redeemer is "Jesus Christ," and this name refers to him individually as a being as well as to His title. We, therefore, disagree with them, and maintain that we should not use the definite article except in the case where we are referring to the Messiahship of our Redeemer. At other times when referring to His name, we should say "Jesus Christ." The greatest reason why we should do this is because our Lord calls Himself by that name repeatedly in the revelations to the Church.

"Wherefore, as I said unto you, it must needs be expedient that Christ —for in the last night the angel spake unto me that this should be his name—should come among the Jews." (2 Nephi 10:3.)

5. Verily I say unto you all: Arise and shine forth, that thy light may be a standard for the nations;

6. And that the gathering together upon the land of Zion, and upon her stakes, may be for a defense, and for a refuge from the storm, and from wrath when it shall be poured out without mixture upon the whole earth.

5-6. *Standard for the nations*] The truth revealed to the Saints is their "light," and it must be sent forth and become a "standard" for the nations. In the latter days, many people shall say, "Come ye, and let us go up to the mountain of the Lord * * * and he will teach us of his ways, and we will walk in his paths" (Is. 2:3.) The Saints should raise a standard for the nations, as regards moral, religious, and political conduct. They must lead the world, not ape its fashions. The gathering is to enable them to raise God's standard high.

7. Let the city, Far West, be a holy and consecrated land unto me; and it shall be called most holy, for the ground upon which thou standest is holy.

8. Therefore, I command you to build a house unto me, for the gathering together of my saints, that they may worship me.

9. And let there be a beginning of this work, and a foundation, and a preparatory work, this following summer;

10. And let the beginning be made on the fourth day of July next; and from that time forth let my people labor diligently to build a house unto my name;

11. And in one year from this day let them re-commence laying the foundation of my house.

12. Thus let them from that time forth labor diligently until it shall be finished, from the corner stone thereof unto the top thereof, until there shall not anything remain that is not finished.

13. Verily I say unto you, let not my servant Joseph, neither my servant Sidney, neither my servant Hyrum, get in debt any more for the building of a house unto my name;

14. But let a house be built unto my name according to the pattern which I will show unto them.

15. And if my people build it not according to the pattern which I shall show unto their presidency, I will not accept it at their hands.

16. But if my people do build it according to the pattern which I shall show unto their presidency, even my servant Joseph and his counselors, then I will accept it at the hands of my people.

7-16. The command is here given to build a Temple at Far West (v. 8). The date of beginning the work is appointed (v. 10); the important instruction is given that indebtedness should not be contracted by Temple construction (v. 13), and that sanctuaries must be built according to the plan revealed (vv. 14-16).

At this time there were about 150 houses at Far West, and among them were stores, hotels, and a fine school house. The City had sprung up, as by magic, in the midst of a rolling prairie. It might have been a large center of population today, into which would have been poured the wealth of continents, instead of a spot in a desert, but for the bigotry and strange madness of the neighbors.

The corner stones of the Temple were laid on the 4th of July, 1838. The excavation, one historian says, 120 by 80 feet in area, and 5 feet in depth was completed in half a day, more than 500 men being employed in the work. Little else was done, however, for the storm of persecution broke loose in all its fury, and the Saints at that place went into exile again.

17. And again, verily I say unto you, it is my will that the city of Far West should be built up speedily by the gathering of my saints;

18. And also that other places should be appointed for stakes in the regions round about, as they shall be manifested unto my servant Joseph, from time to time.

19. For behold, I will be with him, and I will sanctify him before the people; for unto him have I given the keys of this kingdom and ministry. Even so. Amen.

17-19. It is quite probable that if the Saints had gathered in greater numbers and built up their Stakes and cities more rapidly, the enemies would have had less power to execute their designs. That they did not do their duty in this respect, may be inferred from Section 117:1-6.

SECTION 116.

REVELATION *given to Joseph Smith the Prophet, near Wight's Ferry, at a place called Spring Hill, Daviess County, Missouri, May 19, 1838, wherein Spring Hill is named by the Lord:*

ADAM-ONDI-AHMAN, because, said he, it is the place where Adam shall come to visit his people, or the Ancient of Days shall sit, as spoken of by Daniel the prophet.

ADAM-ONDI-AHMAN was the place in which Adam blessed his descendants, three years before his death (Sec. 107:53). It is the place where he will sit in judgment, previous to the taking possession of the kingdom by the Saints (Daniel 7:9-14, 22). The Prophet Joseph, in a discourse delivered June 2, 1839, said:

"Daniel speaks of the Ancient of Days. He means the oldest man, our Father Adam (Michael). He will call his children together and hold a council with them, to prepare them for the coming of the Son of Man. He (Adam) is the father of the human family, and presides over the spirits of all men; and all that have the keys must stand before him in this grand council. This may take place *before some of us leave this stage of action*" (*Jour. of Dis.,* Vol. VI., pp. 237-8).

The Prophet here teaches us that the gathering spoken of by Daniel was, in the year 1839, an event of the near future, and that *all* men holding authority were to stand before Adam on that occasion.

SECTION 117.

REVELATION *given through Joseph Smith the Prophet, at Far West, Missouri, July 8, 1838, concerning the immediate duties of certain Elders, William Marks, Newel K. Whitney, Oliver Granger.——Imperative commands—What is property unto the Lord?*

VERILY thus saith the Lord unto my servant William Marks, and also unto my servant Newel K. Whitney, let them settle up their business speedily and journey from the land of Kirtland, before I, the Lord, send again the snows upon the earth.

2. Let them awake, and arise, and come forth, and not tarry, for I, the Lord, command it.

3. Therefore, if they tarry it shall not be well with them.

The Lord had commanded the Saints to gather and build up Far West speedily (See Sec. 115:17). A company of 515 souls, known as the *Kirtland Camp,* left Kirtland on the 6th of July, 1838, for Zion. On the 14th of September, it appears only 260 members were left, the others having been scattered "to the four winds." The camp arrived in Adam-ondi-Ahman on the 4th of October. Neither Marks, Whitney, nor Granger were members of this company. Joseph Smith at Far West had no means of knowing, at that time, who had, or who had not, left for Zion; but the Lord knew. Hence this Revelation in which He (1) calls William Marks and Newel K. Whitney to come to Zion and instructs the Saint concerning the property in Kirtland (1-6); (2) promises them blessings, if they will obey (7-11); and (3) gives instructions to Oliver Granger (12-16).

4. Let them repent of all their sins, and of all their covetous desires, before me, saith the Lord; for what is property unto me? saith the Lord.

5. Let the properties of Kirtland be turned out for debts, saith the Lord. Let them go, saith the Lord, and whatsoever remaineth, let it remain in your hands, saith the Lord.

6. For have I not the fowls of heaven, and also the fish of the sea, and the beasts of the mountains? Have I not made the earth? Do I not hold the destinies of all the armies of the nations of the earth?

I. CONCERNING THE PROPERTY OF KIRTLAND.

1-6. The Saints had private property in Kirtland, and there was property belonging to the Church. Many of them lingered there, reluctant to sacrifice their temporal interests. Our Lord regards this disposition as a sin (v. 4), and calls upon the people to repent and to let the property go for the liquidation of debt (v. 5). He would recompense them for any sacrifice they might make in His service.

7. Therefore, will I not make solitary places to bud and to blossom and to bring forth in abundance? saith the Lord.

8. Is there not room enough on the mountains of Adam-ondi-Ahman, and on the plains of Olaha Shinehah, or the land where Adam dwelt, that you should covet that which is but the drop, and neglect the more weighty matters?

9. Therefore, come up hither unto the land of my people, even Zion.

10. Let my servant William Marks be faithful over a few things, and he shall be a ruler over many. Let him preside in the midst of my people in the city of Far West, and let him be blessed with the blessings of my people.

11. Let my servant Newel K. Whitney be ashamed of the Nicolaitane band and of all their secret abominations, and of all his littleness of soul before me, saith the Lord, and come up to the land of Adam-ondi-Ahman, and be a bishop unto my people, saith the Lord, not in name but in deed, saith the Lord.

2. BLESSINGS PROMISED.

7. *Solitary places to bud and to blossom*] This promise has been miraculously fulfilled in the history of the Latter-day Saints. Wherever they have settled, the land has been blessed, the moisture of the air has increased, and the rigor of the climate has been tempered. The so-called "Great American Desert" exists no longer. In its place, there is an inland empire with a teeming population, centers of industry, and busy marts, and this modern wonder was performed by the location of the Church in the mountains. Compare the present conditions of Kirtland, Independence, Far West, and Nauvoo, with those of the cities of Utah!

8. *Olaha Shinehah*] *Shinehah* means "sun" (Book of Abraham 3:13), and *Olaha* is, possibly a variant of the word *Olea,* which is "the moon" (*Ibid.*). If so, the Plains of Olaha Shinehah would be the Plains of the Moon and the Sun, so called, perhaps because of astronomical observations there made. That the inhabitants of ancient America paid attention to astronomy is proved by the calendar stone and sun dials found among the ruins of old cities, and also by the pyramids they constructed. That the study of astronomy dates back to our first ancestor, there is no reason to doubt.

10. *Ruler over many*] William Marks was made President of the stake at Nauvoo. Unfortunately for him, he did not remain faithful, but after the martyrdom at Carthage he sided with Sidney Rigdon against the authority constituted by Revelation, viz., the Twelve Apostles (See Sec. 107:24), and the result was that he lost the blessings he might have obtained.

11. *Newel K. Whitney*] Bishop Whitney hearkened to the voice of the Lord. He did not follow the Kirtland apostates, but remained with the Church in all its trials. He went to Salt Lake City. In 1848 he was sustained as Presiding Bishop.

12. And again, I say unto you, I remember my servant

Oliver Granger; behold, verily I say unto him that his name shall be had in sacred remembrance from generation to generation, forever and ever, saith the Lord.

13.   Therefore, let him contend earnestly for the redemption of the First Presidency of my Church, saith the Lord; and when he falls he shall rise again, for his sacrifice shall be more sacred unto me than his increase, saith the Lord.

14.   Therefore, let him come up hither speedily, unto the land of Zion; and in the due time he shall be made a merchant unto my name, saith the Lord, for the benefit of my people.

15.   Therefore let no man despise my servant Oliver Granger, but let the blessings of my people be on him forever and ever.

16.   And again, verily I say unto you, let all my servants in the land of Kirtland remember the Lord their God, and mine house also, to keep and preserve it holy, and to overthrow the money-changers in mine own due time, saith the Lord. Even so. Amen.

3. INSTRUCTIONS TO OLIVER GRANGER.

12-16.   Oliver Granger was a man of faith and business ability—two qualities which form a rare combination. He characterized the Kirtland Camp as the greatest undertaking since the organization of the Church, and he firmly believed that God would bless that endeavor (*Hist. of the Church,* Vol. III., p. 96). When the Prophet fled from Kirtland, he appointed Granger his business agent, and so well did he perform this duty that he was commended by business men. At a conference held at Quincy, May 4th to 6th, 1839, he was appointed to return to Kirtland and take charge of the Temple and Church there. This makes the concluding verses of the Revelation perfectly clear. His name is to be held in remembrance for his faithful services as a man of business, having sanctified his talent to the service of the Lord.

SECTION 118.

REVELATION *given through Joseph Smith the Prophet, at Far West, Missouri, July 8, 1838, in response to the supplication: Show us thy will, O Lord, concerning the Twelve.——Commandment given to fill the places of those who had fallen—Future mission of the Twelve beyond the seas—Date of their departure fixed.*

VERILY, thus saith the Lord: Let a conference be held immediately; let the Twelve be organized; and let men be appointed to supply the place of those who are fallen.

2. Let my servant Thomas remain for a season in the land of Zion, to publish my word.

3. Let the residue continue to preach from that hour, and if they will do this in all lowliness of heart, in meekness and humility, and long-suffering, I, the Lord, give unto them a promise that I will provide for their families; and an effectual door shall be opened for them, from henceforth.

4. And next spring let them depart to go over the great waters, and there promulgate my gospel, the fulness thereof, and bear record of my name.

5. Let them take leave of my saints in the city of Far West, on the twenty-sixth day of April next, on the building-spot of my house, saith the Lord.

6. Let my servant John Taylor, and also my servant John E. Page, and also my servant Wilford Woodruff, and also my servant Willard Richards, be appointed to fill the places of those who have fallen, and be officially notified of their appointment.

1. *Let a conference be held*] This conference convened on the 9th of July. Five Apostles were present, viz., Thomas B. Marsh, David W. Patten, Brigham Young, Parley P. Pratt, and William Smith. The Council of the Twelve was completed, on this occasion, by the appointment of John Taylor, John E. Page, Wilford Woodruff, and Willard Richards, in the place of those who had fallen by the wayside. (See general notes under Section one hundred and twelve.) Thomas B. Marsh was instructed to notify Wilford Woodruff; Parley P. Pratt was to notify Orson Pratt, and Sidney Rigdon, Willard Richards. The older absent members were to be called home, as well as those recently chosen. Heber C. Kimball and Orson Hyde were in England. Willard Richards was with them, and received his ordination at Preston, April 14th, 1840.

5. *Let them take leave * * * on the 26th of April next*] Enemies of the Church threatened to make compliance with this command impossible, but when the day came, the Twelve and others met on the Temple ground at Far West, and Alpheus Cutler laid the foundation stone again, by rolling up a stone and placing it near the southeast corner, according to the Revelation (Section 115:11), whereupon the Twelve engaged in prayer. Then they sang, "Adam-ondi-Ahman," and, finally, took leave of the Saints. Then they were ready for their respective missions. When

the enemies heard of the proceedings, they were very much chagrined because they had forgotten the *date*.

GENERAL NOTES

This date, the 8th of July, 1838, is remarkable for the many revelations given. In addition to those recorded in Sections 117-120, one Revelation nowhere published, was received, making known the duty of William W. Phelps and Frederick G. Williams. Their former standing was taken from them on account of transgression, and they were called to travel "from land to land" (See *Hist. of the Church,* Vol. III., p. 46).

SECTION 119.

REVELATION *given through Joseph Smith the Prophet, at Far West, Missouri, July 8, 1838, in answer to the supplication: O Lord, show unto thy servants how much thou requirest of the properties of thy people for a tithing.*

VERILY, thus saith the Lord, I require all their surplus property to be put into the hands of the bishop of my church in Zion,

2. For the building of mine house, and for the laying of the foundation of Zion and for the priesthood, and for the debts of the Presidency of my Church.

3. And this shall be the beginning of the tithing of my people.

4. And after that, those who have thus been tithed shall pay one-tenth of all their interest annually; and this shall be a standing law unto them forever, for my holy priesthood, saith the Lord.

5. Verily I say unto you, it shall come to pass that all those who gather unto the land of Zion shall be tithed of their surplus properties, and shall observe this law, or they shall not be found worthy to abide among you.

6. And I say unto you, if my people observe not this law, to keep it holy, and by this law sanctify the land of Zion unto me, that my statutes and my judgments may be kept thereon, that it may be most holy, behold, verily I say unto you, it shall not be a land of Zion unto you.

7. And this shall be an ensample unto all the stakes of Zion. Even so. Amen.

The law of tithing, as now understood, had not been given to the Church previous to this Revelation. The term "tithing" in the prayer quoted in the headlines, and in previous Revelations (64:23; 85:3; 97:11), is, therefore, synonymous with "free-will offering," or "contribution" to the Church funds. The question presented in the petition to the Almighty was not how much a *tenth* part of the property of the people amounted to, but how much of that property He required for sacred purposes. The answer was this Revelation on the Law of Tithing. The Lord required, first, "all the surplus property" (v. 1), for the building of temples, etc. (v. 2); this is the "beginning of tithing" (v. 3); then He required one-tenth of all the interest annually (v. 4). This law was to become obligatory upon all who gathered to Zion (vv. 5-7). See also page 492.

The Prophet Joseph and Oliver Cowdery, on the 29th of November, 1834, entered into covenant with the Lord, as follows:

"That if the Lord will prosper us in our business and open the way before us that we may obtain means to pay our debts, that we be not troubled nor brought into disrepute before the world, nor His people; after that, of all that He shall give unto us, we will give a tenth to be bestowed upon the poor in His Church, or as He shall command; and that we will be faithful over that which He has entrusted to our care, that we may obtain much; and that our children after us shall remember to observe this sacred and holy covenant, and that our children, and our children's children may know of the same, we have subscribed our names with our own hands" (*Hist. of the Church,* Vol. II., p. 175).

"We do not ask anybody to pay tithing unless they are disposed to do so; but if you pretend to pay tithing, pay it like honest men" (Brigham Young, *Jour. of Dis.,* Vol. VIII., p. 202).

"The law of tithing is of very ancient origin. How early it was observed by the people of God is not clearly set forth in the Scriptures, but we have an account of its observance as early as the days of Abraham and Melchizedek. We have also, anterior to that, an account given us in the Scriptures of the bringing forward of offerings by Cain and Abel, one bringing the first fruits of the earth, and the other the first fruits of his flocks, as offering unto the Lord their God. From the days of Abraham down to the days of Jesus the law of tithing was observed by the people of God" (George Q. Cannon, *Jour. of Dis.,* Vol. XV., p. 145).

From the original text of Heb. 11:4, it may be gathered that Cain did not bring an honest tithing before the Lord, while Abel did; for the author of that Epistle says, literally translated, "By faith Abel offered unto God a more *abundant* [*pleiona*] sacrifice than Cain." The *Septuagint* version renders Gen. 4:6, 7 as follows, "And the Lord God said to Cain, wherefore didst thou become vexed, and wherefore did thy countenance fall? If thou didst rightly offer, *but didst not rightly divide,* didst thou not sin?" (Henry Lansdell, D. D. *The Sacred Tenth,* Vol. I., p. 41).

Ancient Israel paid three-tenths. One was for the support of the Levites and the Temple service (Lev. 27:30-3; Numb. 18:21-4). The second was to be spent by the head of the family and those dependent on him on yearly journeys to the conferences, on which occasions he was supposed to offer sacrifices and to feast with his friends (Deut. 14:22-7). He was expected to spend one-tenth of his income, yearly, on religious rites and social entertainments, at the annual festivals—the Passover, the Feast of Tabernacles, and the Feast of Weeks—in addition to the sacred tenth, which was the Lord's. A third tenth was paid every third year, for the benefit of Levites, strangers, orphans (Deut. 14:28, 29).

SECTION 120.

REVELATION *given through Joseph Smith the Prophet, at Far West, Missouri, July 18, 1838, making known the disposition of the properties tithed as named in the preceding revelation, Section 119.*

VERILY, thus saith the Lord, the time is now come, that it shall be disposed of by a council, composed of the First Presidency of my Church, and of the bishop and his council, and by my high council; and by mine own voice unto them, saith the Lord. Even so. Amen.

This Revelation is dated July 18th, but from the *History of the Church* (Vol. III., p. 44) it appears that it was given on the 8th, the same day on which the Revelations contained in Sections 117, 118, and 119 were received. It is a promise that the Lord will guide His servants by His Spirit in the expenditure of the offerings of the Saints—a promise that, as the results prove, has been fulfilled.

GENERAL NOTES

The Saints, expelled from Jackson County in the fall of 1833, and requested to leave Clay County in the summer of 1836, had found refuge in Caldwell County, and become quite prosperous. But the enemies were not inactive. On Aug. 6th, 1838, a State election was held. William P. Penniston, one of the candidates for the State legislature and generally known as an anti-"Mormon," naturally supposed that no Church member would vote for him. Acting on this assumption, he organized a mob for the purpose of preventing all the Saints from voting. This was, of course, illegal. Twelve "Mormons" went to Gallatin, to exercise their rights as citizens. They were set upon by Penniston's men. A conflict ensued. No lives were lost, but the election riot, for which Penniston's supporters were responsible, was followed by a general rising against the Saints.

Lilburn W. Boggs, one of the active leaders of the mob in 1833, was the governor of Missouri then. This emboldened the mob to plan an attack upon the little settlement of Diahman, which, however, was not carried out, owing to the firm stand taken by General Doniphan, who declared that the people had been deceived by designing, half-crazy men.

The mob, temporarily thwarted in their designs upon Diahman, turned against Dewitt, Carroll County. For nine days, that settlement was besieged and bombarded. An appeal to the governor only elicited the unsympathetic reply that the combatants might "fight it out." The Saints rather than to engage in civil war, left Dewitt and fled to Far West. The mob then marched upon Diahman.

On the advice of General Doniphan, the Saints in Far West sent a force to the assistance of their brethren in Daviess County, where houses were being plundered and burned, and other outrages committed. Colonel Lyman Wight, having obtained authority, organized a command for the protection of the Saints. At first the marauders fled before this organized resistance, but their bitterness increased. On the 25th of October, 1838, a marauding band was met and, after a short engagement, dispersed, and this, the so-called "Crooked River Battle," was heralded abroad as a "Mormon atrocity," on the strength of which Governor Boggs, on October 27th, 1838, issued an order for the extermination of the "Mormons."

Among the first results of this truly Herodian edict for the slaughter of innocents, was the Haun's Mill massacre, in which nearly a score of inoffensive "Mormon" settlers were mercilessly killed. Then the Governor's force marched against Far West. Colonel George M. Hinckle, commanding the defenders of that City, treacherously entered into a secret agreement with the commander of the assailants, General Lucas, to deliver up the leaders of the Church, and to disarm the "Mormons." Under pretense of having arranged a conference between the Church leaders and the militia generals, Hinckle induced Joseph Smith, Sidney Rigdon, Parley P. Pratt, Lyman Wight, and George W. Robinson to meet General Lucas, whereupon they were surrounded and, as "prisoners of war," condemned to be shot. This order, however, was not executed, because Generals Doniphan and Graham denounced it as a crime, and threatened to withdraw, if it were carried out.

The militia now advanced upon the defenseless city and compelled the Saints to sign away their property, "to defray the expenses of the war." The town was given up to pillage. Women were abused publicly, and nameless horrors were committed. The Prophet and his companions were taken, first to Independence, then to Richmond, and later, to Liberty, Clay County. While in jail at this place, he received the Revelations in Sections 121, 122, and 123.

The prisoners were treated outrageously. Several times their food was poisoned, but God preserved their lives. They passed the winter in prison, where they were held illegally. During this winter, from ten to twelve thousand Latter-day Saints, under the direction of Brigham Young, who, as President of the Twelve, had charge of the Church in the absence of the First Presidency, left Missouri for Illinois and thus placed themselves outside the reach of the Missourians. Most of the exiles found a kind welcome at Quincy, Ill., and there the Prophet Joseph and Hyrum joined the Saints during the latter part of April, or early in May, 1839, having been delivered, by the providence of God, from their enemies in Missouri.

President Joseph Fielding Smith was born at Far West, a few days after his saintly mother had been separated from her husband by the brutal captors and traitors. "The child, thus born amid these warlike scenes," was, as Elder Orson F. Whitney observes, "drinking in with his mother's milk a wholesome hatred of tyrants and mobs, and the courage to denounce them fearlessly" (*Hist. of Utah,* Vol. I., p. 160).

The repeated mobbings and drivings of the Latter-day Saints were a severe discipline, but they served a great purpose in God's plan. While the Saints were prosperous, many hypocrites joined the Church. They were the chaff. The blasts of adversity blew these to the four winds, and only the good wheat remained. The Church was purified by persecution.

SECTION 121.

PRAYER AND PROPHECIES, *written by Joseph Smith the Prophet, while a prisoner in the jail at Liberty, Missouri, dated March 20, 1839. The Prophet with several companions had been months in prison. Their petitions and appeals directed to the executive officers and the judiciary had failed to bring them relief. See History of the Church, vol. 3, p. 289.——Fervent appeals to the Lord in behalf of the suffering Saints—The curse of the Lord to fall upon those who contend against his will—Men though called may not be chosen—The rights of the Priesthood inseparably connected with the powers of heaven—Unrighteous exercise of the powers of the Priesthood leads to apostasy—Powers of the Priesthood to be exercised in justice and mercy.*

O GOD, where art thou? And where is the pavilion that covereth thy hiding place?

2. How long shall thy hand be stayed, and thine eye, yea thy pure eye, behold from the eternal heavens the wrongs of thy

people and of thy servants, and thine ear be penetrated with their cries?

3. Yea, O Lord, how long shall they suffer these wrongs and unlawful oppressions, before thine heart shall be softened toward them, and thy bowels be moved with compassion toward them?

4. O Lord God Almighty, maker of heaven, earth, and seas, and of all things that in them are, and who controllest and subjectest the devil, and the dark and benighted dominion of Sheol—stretch forth thy hand; let thine eye pierce; let thy pavilion be taken up; let thy hiding place no longer be covered; let thine ear be inclined; let thine heart be softened, and thy bowels moved with compassion toward us.

5. Let thine anger be kindled against our enemies; and, in the fury of thine heart, with thy sword avenge us of our wrongs.

6. Remember thy suffering saints, O our God; and thy servants will rejoice in thy name forever.

In the *History of the Church,* (Vol. III., pp. 289-305) an epistle is found, addressed "to the Church of Latter-day Saints at Quincy, Ill., and Scattered Abroad, and to Bishop Partridge in Particular." It is signed by Joseph Smith, Jr., Hyrum Smith, Lyman Wight, Caleb Baldwin, and Alexander McRae, and dated, "Liberty Jail, Clay County, Missouri, March 25, 1839." The letter, it appears, was commenced on the 20th and finished on the 25th. Sections 121, 122, and 123 are extracts from this communication.

In the opening paragraph of the letter, the Prophet refers to the fearful crimes committed against the Saints. He hears the cries of orphans and widows; he sees the innocent blood that stains the soil of the State; he contemplates the inhumanity of the people, that "shocks all nature," and "beggars and defies all description," and then he pours out his soul in lamentation before his God, as Jeremiah of old wept upon the ruins of Jerusalem: "O God! Where art thou?" And he prays, "Remember thy suffering Saints."

4. *Thy pavilion * * * thy hiding place*] These are expressions used by the authors of the Bible. When David says, "He made darkness his hiding-place, his pavilion round about him; darkness of waters, thick clouds of the skies" (Ps. 18:11), he considers the darkness of the thundercloud as a tent, or pavilion, in which Jehovah dwells in His majesty. The thunder-bolts, the hail, the wind, are His messengers. The Prophet Joseph, by using this grand, poetic conception, entreats the Lord to manifest Himself in His power for the salvation of the Saints from their enemies.

5. Let thine anger be kindled against our enemies] Can a prophet of God pray for vengeance? David could. Wrongs must be righted before the reign of perfect justice can prevail. It is perfectly consistent with the gospel to ask God to execute justice in behalf of His people. It is contrary to the gospel for man to take vengeance into his own hands, but not to pour out his soul's bitterness under injustice and wrong, before God in prayer.

7. My son, peace be unto thy soul; thine adversity and thine afflictions shall be but a small moment;

8. And then, if thou endure it well, God shall exalt thee on high; thou shalt triumph over all thy foes.

9. Thy friends do stand by thee, and they shall hail thee again with warm hearts and friendly hands.

10. Thou art not yet as Job; thy friends do not contend against thee, neither charge thee with transgression, as they did Job.

11. And they who do charge thee with transgression, their hope shall be blasted, and their prospects shall melt away as the hoar frost melteth before the burning rays of the rising sun;

12. And also that God hath set his hand and seal to change the times and seasons, and to blind their minds, that they may not understand his marvelous workings; that he may prove them also and take them in their own craftiness;

13. Also because their hearts are corrupted, and the things which they are willing to bring upon others, and love to have others suffer, may come upon themselves to the very uttermost;

14. That they may be disappointed also, and their hopes may be cut off;

15. And not many years hence, that they and their posterity shall be swept from under heaven, saith God, that not one of them is left to stand by the wall.

16. Cursed are all those that shall lift up the heel against mine anointed, saith the Lord, and cry they have sinned when they have not sinned before me, saith the Lord, but have done that which was meet in mine eyes, and which I commanded them.

17. But those who cry transgression do it because they are the servants of sin, and are the children of disobedience themselves.

18. And those who swear falsely against my servants, that they might bring them into bondage and death—

19. Wo unto them; because they have offended my little ones they shall be severed from the ordinances of mine house.

20. Their basket shall not be full, their houses and their barns shall perish, and they themselves shall be despised by those that flattered them.

21. They shall not have right to the priesthood, nor their posterity after them from generation to generation.

22. It had been better for them that a millstone had been hanged about their necks, and they drowned in the depth of the sea.

23. Wo unto all those that discomfort my people, and drive, and murder, and testify against them, saith the Lord of Hosts; a generation of vipers shall not escape the damnation of hell.

24. Behold, mine eyes see and know all their works, and I have in reserve a swift judgment in the season thereof, for them all;

25. For there is a time appointed for every man, according as his works shall be.

7-25. God's answer to the Prophet's prayer begins with these verses. The Prophet is assured that his sufferings will last only a moment (v. 7), and then God will exalt him (v. 8). He is reminded that he has not been tried to the extent that Job suffered (v. 10); and that his friends are faithful, and the assurance is given that those who accuse him falsely shall be disappointed (v. 14). "For there is a time appointed for every man, according as his works shall be" (v. 25).

9. *Thy friends do stand by thee*] This statement is made again in Section 122:3: "Thy people shall never be turned against thee by the testimony of traitors." It is a notable fact that no accusation, no false testimony turned the hearts of the Latter-day Saints from Joseph: they knew him, and they knew the accusers.

11. *Their hope shall be blasted*] The name of the Prophet Joseph lives in history and in the hearts of the Saints. The names of his friends, who were faithful, such as John Taylor, Willard Richards, Brigham Young, Wilford Woodruff, Orson Pratt, etc., are revered in the Church all over the world. But where are men like Hurlburt, McClellin, Boggs, and other persecutors? It has come to pass that they and their posterity have been "swept from under heaven" (v. 15). Especially is that true of Governor Ford. The ungodly are indeed "chaff which the wind driveth away" (Ps. 1:4).

16. *Cursed are all those that shall lift up the heel against mine anointed*] Those who say that the servants of the Lord have sinned, when they are innocent, take a grave responsibility.

18. *Those who swear falsely*] Thomas B. Marsh, who apostatized at a critical period, went to Richmond and swore falsely to an affidavit in which he called the Prophet a second Mohammed, who would "make it one gore of blood from the Rocky Mountains to the Atlantic Ocean."

20. *Their basket shall not be full*] Note the punishment on such apostates (vv. 19-22).

26. God shall give unto you knowledge by his Holy Spirit, yea, by the unspeakable gift of the Holy Ghost, that has not been revealed since the world was until now;

27. Which our forefathers have awaited with anxious expectation to be revealed in the last times, which their minds were pointed to by the angels, as held in reserve for the fulness of their glory;

28. A time to come in the which nothing shall be withheld, whether there be one God or many gods, they shall be manifest.

29. All thrones and dominions, principalities and powers, shall be revealed and set forth upon all who have endured valiantly for the gospel of Jesus Christ.

30. And also, if there be bounds set to the heavens or to the seas, or to the dry land, or to the sun, moon, or stars—

31. All the times of their revolutions, all the appointed days, months, and years, and all the days of their days, months, and years, and all their glories, laws, and set times, shall be revealed in the days of the dispensation of the fulness of times—

32. According to that which was ordained in the midst of the Council of the Eternal God of all other gods before this world was, that should be reserved unto the finishing and the end thereof, when every man shall enter into his eternal presence and into his immortal rest.

26-32. The Prophet, in the Epistle, reminds the Saints that, in the past, they have been vain and trifling both in public gatherings and private intercourse; he exhorts them to reform "both old and young, teachers and taught, both high and low, rich and poor, bound and free, male and female." "Let," he adds "honesty, and sobriety, and candor, and solemnity, and virtue, and pureness, and meekness, and simplicity crown our heads in every place; and, in fine, become as little children, without malice, guile, or hypocrisy. * * * If you do these things, and exercise fervent prayer and faith, * * * God shall give unto you knowledge," etc. God gives knowledge only to those whose minds are prepared to receive it.

28. *Whether there be one God or many gods*] The doctrine of the godhead is one about which the world seems unable to reach unity of faith. Is there a personal God, extia-mundane, the Creator, Preserver, and Governor of the world? Or, is the universe, itself, God? Is God knowable or unknowable? Are there three persons in the Godhead, or is there only one? Such are the questions on which opinions are ever divided. God reveals the truth to the Saints who are capable of receiving the testimony of the Holy Spirit. Then they *know* God.

29. *Thrones, and dominions, principalities and powers*] Not only will the Holy Spirit reveal God, but also the truth concerning the celestial beings who hold power and authority under His sovereignty, and who are here enumerated. Comp. Col. 1:16, where the literal translation is, "thrones, or lordships, or governments, or authorities."

30-1. Concerning the universe, too, the Holy Spirit will reveal the truth to the Saints. The world is God's and He desires His children to know something about its marvelous construction and operations.

33. How long can rolling waters remain impure? What power shall stay the heavens? As well might man stretch forth his puny arm to stop the Missouri river in its decreed course, or to turn it up stream, as to hinder the Almighty from pouring down knowledge from heaven upon the heads of the Latter-day Saints.

33. The Prophet observes that "ignorance, superstition, and bigotry, placing itself where it ought not, oftentimes are in the way of the prosperity of this Church; like the torrents of rain from the mountains, that floods the most pure stream with mire;" but the Lord here reminds him that rolling, or running waters do not long remain impure. The mountain streams that rush to their destination over a rocky bed, where they are broken up into small drops and silvery sprays are purified by every particle coming in contact with the oxygen in the air. God who purifies the mountain streams can pour knowledge from heaven upon the Latter-day Saints.

34. Behold, there are many called, but few are chosen. And why are they not chosen?

35. Because their hearts are set so much upon the things of this world, and aspire to the honors of men, that they do not learn this one lesson—

36. That the rights of the priesthood are inseparably con-

nected with the powers of heaven, and that the powers of heaven cannot be controlled nor handled only upon the principles of righteousness.

37. That they may be conferred upon us, it is true; but when we undertake to cover our sins, or to gratify our pride, our vain ambition, or to exercise control or dominion or compulsion upon the souls of the children of men, in any degree of unrighteousness, behold, the heavens withdraw themselves; the Spirit of the Lord is grieved; and when it is withdrawn, Amen to the priesthood or the authority of that man.

38. Behold, ere he is aware, he is left unto himself, to kick against the pricks, to persecute the saints, and to fight against God.

39. We have learned by sad experience that it is the nature and disposition of almost all men, as soon as they get a little authority, as they suppose, they will immediately begin to exercise unrighteous dominion.

40. Hence many are called, but few are chosen.

41. No power or influence can or ought to be maintained by virtue of the priesthood, only by persuasion, by long-suffering, by gentleness and meekness, and by love unfeigned;

42. By kindness, and pure knowledge, which shall greatly enlarge the soul without hypocrisy, and without guile—

43. Reproving betimes with sharpness, when moved upon by the Holy Ghost; and then showing forth afterwards an increase of love toward him whom thou hast reproved, lest he esteem thee to be his enemy;

44. That he may know that thy faithfulness is stronger than the cords of death.

45. Let thy bowels also be full of charity towards all men, and to the household of faith, and let virtue garnish thy thoughts unceasingly; then shall thy confidence wax strong in the presence of God; and the doctrine of the priesthood shall distil upon thy soul as the dews from heaven.

46. The Holy Ghost shall be thy constant companion, and thy scepter an unchanging scepter of righteousness and truth; and thy dominion shall be an everlasting dominion, and without compulsory means it shall flow unto thee forever and ever.

The Prophet, in his letter, warns the Saints not to labor for their own aggrandizement, or the accumulation of wealth, while so many of their brethren are groaning under the burden of poverty. Unless they heeded this warning, they could not have the intercession of the Holy Spirit. In this connection he is led to say, "There are many called, but few are chosen," and then he considers the reasons why this is so.

35. *Because their hearts * * * world*] He who only burrows in the ground, like a mole, soon loses all appreciation of the spiritual world.

36. *The rights of the Priesthood*] These are founded in principles of righteousness. There are no other *rights*.

37. *Compulsion*] An important truth is here announced. If anyone should undertake to exercise control, or dominion, or compulsion in unrighteousness, he could do so, only outside the authority of the Priesthood. He would then act in accordance with the plan of Lucifer. Compulsion is the basis of his form of government.

38. *Left unto himself*] That is the consequence of any attempt to exercise the authority of the Priesthood in unrighteousness, and he who is "left to himself" generally becomes a persecutor.

39. *Unrighteous dominion*] How true it is that men are prone to use their authority unrighteously! Many of the brethren, prominent in the early history of the Church, fell because they used the authority they held, for selfish ends.

41-6. Here the proper exercise of the power of the Priesthood is illustrated. The Priesthood should make those who hold it kind, full of knowledge, honest and virtuous. Where these qualities exist, the Holy Spirit will be. And only those that retain the Spirit are chosen, though many are called.

SECTION 122.

THE WORD OF THE LORD *to Joseph Smith the Prophet, while a prisoner in the jail at Liberty, Missouri, March, 1839. See History of the Church, vol. 3, p. 300.——Comforting assurances —Further persecutions of the Prophet and his possible martyrdom foreshadowed—The Son of Man had likewise suffered.*

THE ends of the earth shall inquire after thy name, and fools shall have thee in derision, and hell shall rage against thee;

2. While the pure in heart, and the wise, and the noble, and the virtuous, shall seek counsel, and authority, and blessings constantly from under thy hand.

3. And thy people shall never be turned against thee by the testimony of traitors.

4. And although their influence shall cast thee into trouble, and into bars and walls, thou shalt be had in honor; and but for a small moment and thy voice shall be more terrible in the midst of thine enemies than the fierce lion, because of thy righteousness; and thy God shall stand by thee forever and ever.

5. If thou art called to pass through tribulation; if thou art in perils among false brethren; if thou art in perils among robbers; if thou art in perils by land or by sea;

6. If thou art accused with all manner of false accusations; if thine enemies fall upon thee; if they tear thee from the society of thy father and mother and brethren and sisters; and if with a drawn sword thine enemies tear thee from the bosom of thy wife, and of thine offspring, and thine elder son, although but six years of age, shall cling to thy garments, and shall say, My father, my father, why can't you stay with us? O, my father, what are the men going to do with you? and if then he shall be thrust from thee by the sword, and thou be dragged to prison, and thine enemies prowl around thee like wolves for the blood of the lamb;

7. And if thou shouldst be cast into the pit, or into the hands of murderers, and the sentence of death passed upon thee; if thou be cast into the deep; if the billowing surge conspire against thee; if fierce winds become thine enemy; if the heavens gather blackness, and all the elements combine to hedge up the way; and above all, if the very jaws of hell shall gape open the mouth wide after thee, know thou, my son, that all these things shall give thee experience, and shall be for thy good.

8. The Son of Man hath descended below them all. Art thou greater than he?

9. Therefore, hold on thy way, and the priesthood shall remain with thee; for their bounds are set, they cannot pass. Thy days are known, and thy years shall not be numbered less; therefore, fear not what man can do, for God shall be with you forever and ever.

1-9. The Lord continues speaking words of comfort to His servant through the Spirit of Revelation. He assures him that his name shall be known all over the world; that fools shall scoff and hell rage, but that the pure, wise, and noble will embrace the truth (vv. 1-2). He assures him that traitors shall not be able to injure him except for a moment, but that his voice shall be like the roar of a lion among enemies (v. 4). He assures him that whatever happens to him shall be for his good (v. 8), and promises him divine assistance for ever and ever (vv. 5-7). And He reminds him that the Son of God suffered (v. 9). God never forsakes His servants in times of trouble.

1. *Fools shall have thee in derision*] Never was a truer word spoken. It is the fool who says in his heart that there is no God, and who holds "Mormonism" in derision. A man may have university education but, as a scoffer he is a fool, no matter how many doctor degrees he may have.

It is also true that the wise, noble and virtuous embrace "Mormonism," when they understand it. It appeals to them and to none else.

5. *False brethren*] There were many, but perhaps none exhibited more diabolical cunning than Samson Avard. This individual proposed to form a secret organization for the purposes of plunder and robbery, and succeeded in gathering a band of outlaws around him under the name of Danites. As soon as his plans and designs became known to the Church leaders, he was expelled from the Church, and then, to save himself, he swore that his band was a Church organization. His advice to Oliver Olney was "to swear hard against the heads of the Church." "I intend to do it," said he, "in order to escape, for if I do not, they will take my life" (*Hist. of the Church,* Vol. III., p. 209).

6. *If thine enemies fall upon thee*] The Prophet is contemplating the heartrending parting scene, when he and the brethren were torn from their loved ones, after having been betrayed into the hands of General Lucas. Before being hurried off to prison, they were allowed to see their families a moment. Joseph writes:

"I found my wife and children in tears, who feared we had been shot by those who had sworn to take our lives, and that they would see me no more. When I entered my house, they clung to my garments, their eyes streaming with tears, while mingled emotions of joy and sorrow were manifested in their countenances. I requested to have a private interview with them for a few minutes, but this privilege was denied me by the guard. I was then obliged to take my departure * * * My partner wept, my children clung to me, until they were thrust from me by the swords of the guards" (*Hist. of the Church,* Vol. III., p. 193).

Parley P. Pratt, in his *Autobiography,* writes:

"I went to my house, being guarded by two or three soldiers. The cold rain was pouring down without, and on entering my little cottage, there lay my wife sick of fever, with which she had been for some time confined. At her breast was our son Nathan, an infant of three months, and by her side a little girl of five years. On the foot of the same bed lay a woman in travail, who had been driven from her house in the night, and had taken

momentary shelter in my hut of ten feet square—my larger house having
been torn down. I stepped to the bed; my wife burst into tears; I spoke
a few words of comfort * * * I then embraced and kissed the little
babes and departed."

7. *Into the hands of murderers*] The prisoners were technically in
the hands of the civil authorities of the State, and were guarded by soldiers
of the militia, but, according to unimpeachable testimony, the guards at
Richmond boasted to each other of their deeds of rapine, murder, and
robbery, until the Prophet rebuked them in the name of Jesus Christ, and
they quailed before him as the evil spirits before the Son of God.

SECTION 123.

DUTY OF THE SAINTS *in relation to their persecutors, as set
forth by Joseph Smith the Prophet, while a prisoner in the jail
at Liberty, Missouri, March, 1839. See History of the Church,
vol. 3, p. 302.——All facts relating to the sufferings and abuses
of the people by their persecutors to be recorded—The record
of persecution to be published.*

AND again, we would suggest for your consideration the propriety of all the saints gathering up a knowledge of all the facts,
and sufferings and abuses put upon them by the people of this
State;

2. And also of all the property and amount of damages which
they have sustained, both of character and personal injuries, as
well as real property;

3. And also the names of all persons that have had a hand
in their oppressions, as far as they can get hold of them and find
them out.

4. And perhaps a committee can be appointed to find out
these things, and to take statements and affidavits; and also to
gather up the libelous publications that are afloat;

5. And all that are in the magazines, and in the encyclo-
pedias, and all the libelous histories that are published, and are
writing, and by whom, and present the whole concatenation of
diabolical rascality and nefarious and murderous impositions that
have been practised upon this people—

6. That we may not only publish to all the world, but present

them to the heads of government in all their dark and hellish hue, as the last effort which is enjoined on us by our Heavenly Father, before we can fully and completely claim that promise which shall call him forth from his hiding place; and also that the whole nation may be left without excuse before he can send forth the power of his mighty arm.

This Revelation is a continuation of the two previous Sections. The Lord (1) instructs the Saints to gather up all available material for a history of the Missouri persecutions, including the value of the property destroyed, and all defamatory literature (1-6); (2) gives the reasons for such a work (7-17).

1. A CHAPTER OF THE HISTORY OF HELL ON EARTH.

1. *All the facts*] Since the diabolical crusades against the Albigenses in Languedoc and the Waldenses in their mountain valleys, during the Dominican Inquisition, no greater outrage has been committed against humanity than the persecution of the Saints in Missouri. The Spirit of Revelation prompted the Prophet to suggest that all the facts be ascertained and placed on record.

5. *And all that are in Magazines, etc.*] The best refutation of anti-"Mormon" literature is a complete exhibition of it, by which a comparison is facilitated; for the statements by anti-"Mormons" are so contradictory, so improbable, so irrational, that no reasonable person can accept them after an examination of them. They have, moreover, originated with individuals whose truthfulness is of the lowest possible value.

6. *Before we can * * * claim that promise*] The Lord had promised to come out of His hiding place (See Sec. 101:89; 121:1), but before this promise could be fulfilled, the facts must be put before the world "in all their dark and hellish hue." There would then be no excuse for the refusal to render justice to the Saints, and there would be no reason why divine justice should be kept back.

At a conference held near Quincy, Ill., May 4th-6th, 1839, Almon W. Babbitt, Erastus Snow, and Robert B. Thompson were appointed a committee to gather up the historical material required by this Revelation.

7. It is an imperative duty that we owe to God, to angels, with whom we shall be brought to stand, and also to ourselves, to our wives and children, who have been made to bow down with grief, sorrow, and care, under the most damning hand of murder, tyranny, and oppression, supported and urged on and upheld by the influence of that spirit which hath so strongly riveted the creeds of the fathers, who have inherited lies, upon the hearts

of the children, and filled the world with confusion, and has been growing stronger and stronger, and is now the very mainspring of all corruption, and the whole earth groans under the weight of its iniquity.

8.   It is an iron yoke, it is a strong band; they are the very handcuffs, and chains, and shackles, and fetters of hell.

9.   Therefore it is an imperative duty that we owe, not only to our own wives and children, but to the widows and fatherless, whose husbands and fathers have been murdered under its iron hand;

10.   Which dark and blackening deeds are enough to make hell itself shudder, and to stand aghast and pale, and the hands of the very devil to tremble and palsy.

11.   And also it is an imperative duty that we owe to all the rising generation, and to all the pure in heart—

12.   For there are many yet on the earth among all sects, parties, and denominations, who are blinded by the subtle craftiness of men, whereby they lie in wait to deceive, and who are only kept from the truth because they know not where to find it—

13.   Therefore, that we should waste and wear out our lives in bringing to light all the hidden things of darkness, wherein we know them; and they are truly manifest from heaven—

14.   These should then be attended to with great earnestness.

15.   Let no man count them as small things; for there is much which lieth in futurity, pertaining to the saints, which depends upon these things.

16.   You know, brethren, that a very large ship is benefited very much by a very small helm in the time of a storm, by being kept workways with the wind and the waves.

17.   Therefore, dearly beloved brethren, let us cheerfully do all things that lie in our power; and then may we stand still, with the utmost assurance, to see the salvation of God, and for his arm to be revealed.

2. Reasons for this Revelation.

7.   *It is an imperious duty that we owe to God*] God knew that the Saints were not guilty of the crimes charged to them by enemies, and that they did not hold the doctrines credited to them, but inasmuch as

they claimed to be the people of God, their vindication was, in a sense, the vindication of the Deity. If a master has a servant who is falsely accused of crime, in vindicating himself he vindicates the master, since his character reflects, to some extent, the character of his master. "As a master, so the servant."

To angels] The angels who are sent to administer to the Saints have a right to know whether such accusations are true or false.

To ourselves, to our wives and children] Silence is sometimes more eloquent than words; but at this time it was necessary to place the accusers and persecutors in the limelight of public opinion, because wives and children had a right to know the full truth.

11. *To all the rising generation*] The falsehoods promulgated against the Saints had blinded many honest men and women and turned them away from the gospel. For their sake the truth should be made known.

15. *There is much * * * which depends upon these things*] The people of Missouri will some day be glad to make whatever amends they can for the wrongs the Saints suffered in that State—not because anybody will endeavor to compel them to do so, but because they will esteem it a privilege to obliterate the mistakes of the past. Then the facts will be considered important, and should be on record.

General Notes

"We read in that book [Book of Mormon], that not only a Church should arise, etc., but that the blood of the Saints who should embrace its faith, should cry from the ground to the God in heaven * * * How unlikely a thing to be fulfilled! Here, upon this land, is one of the most free governments given to man, bestowing upon all civil and religious liberty; * * * The people said such a thing could never come to pass; Joseph Smith was an impostor. But how long was it before this met with its fulfillment? History shows that three years after the rise of this Church, the Latter-day Saints, numbering some 1200 persons * * * were driven *en masse* from their possessions, their homes were torn down and destroyed, their animals were shot down * * * and many of the Saints were also shot dead by the persecutors. Was it because they had committed crimes that merited this treatment? No, their court records do not show a single instance of our people having broken the laws. Was it polygamy? No, for the principle of plural marriage was not known among us then" (Orson Pratt, *Jour. of Dis.*, Vol. XVIII., pp. 223-4).

SECTION 124.

REVELATION *given to Joseph Smith the Prophet, at Nauvoo, Illinois, January 19, 1841. Because of increasing persecutions and illegal procedures against them by public officers, the Saints had been compelled to leave Missouri. The exterminating order issued by Lilburn W. Boggs, Governor of Missouri, dated October 27, 1838, had left them no alternative. See History of the Church, vol. 3, p. 175. In 1841, when this revelation was given, the city of Nauvoo, occupying the site of the former village of Commerce, Illinois, had been built up by the Saints, and here the headquarters of the Church had been established.——Proclamation to the president of the United States, the governors of the States, and to the rulers of all nations—Blessed state of former members of the Church who had died—George Miller called to the bishopric—A house of entertainment for strangers to be erected—A Temple to be built at Nauvoo—No baptismal font upon the earth for the administration of baptisms for the dead—Reason for the command to Moses to build a tabernacle in the wilderness—Promise of revelations concerning sacred things thus far hidden—Men who prevent the Saints from carrying out the commandments of God to be held accountable—Delay in building a Temple in Jackson county, Missouri, tolerated—The house of entertainment to be known as Nauvoo House—Directions for its building and administration—William Law called to be a counselor in the First Presidency—Hyrum Smith called to be the Patriarch to the Church—His great powers and privileges—He receives the same office in the Priesthood once conferred upon Oliver Cowdery—General, stake and local officers of the Church named.*

VERILY, thus saith the Lord unto you, my servant Joseph Smith, I am well pleased with your offering and acknowledgments, which you have made; for unto this end have I raised you up, that I might show forth my wisdom through the weak things of the earth.

2. Your prayers are acceptable before me; and in answer to them I say unto you, that you are now called immediately to make a solemn proclamation of my gospel, and of this stake which I have planted to be a corner-stone of Zion, which shall be polished with the refinement which is after the similitude of a palace.

3. This proclamation shall be made to all the kings of the world, to the four corners thereof, to the honorable president-elect, and the high-minded governors of the nation in which you live, and to all the nations of the earth scattered abroad.

4. Let it be written in the spirit of meekness and by the power of the Holy Ghost, which shall be in you at the time of the writing of the same;

5. For it shall be given you by the Holy Ghost to know my will concerning those kings and authorities, even what shall befall them in a time to come.

6. For, behold, I am about to call upon them to give heed to the light and glory of Zion, for the set time has come to favor her.

7. Call ye, therefore, upon them with loud proclamation, and with your testimony, fearing them not, for they are as grass, and all their glory as the flower thereof which soon falleth, that they may be left also without excuse—

8. And that I may visit them in the day of visitation, when I shall unveil the face of my covering, to appoint the portion of the oppressor among hypocrites, where there is gnashing of teeth, if they reject my servants and my testimony which I have revealed unto them.

9. And again, I will visit and soften their hearts, many of them for your good, that ye may find grace in their eyes, that

they may come to the light of truth, and the Gentiles to the exaltation or lifting up of Zion.

10. For the day of my visitation cometh speedily, in an hour when ye think not of; and where shall be the safety of my people, and refuge for those who shall be left of them?

11. Awake, O kings of the earth! Come ye, O, come ye, with your gold and your silver, to the help of my people, to the house of the daughters of Zion.

12. And again, verily I say unto you, let my servant Robert B. Thompson help you to write this proclamation, for I am well pleased with him, and that he should be with you;

13. Let him, therefore, hearken to your counsel, and I will bless him with a multiplicity of blessings; let him be faithful and true in all things from henceforth, and he shall be great in mine eyes;

14. But let him remember that his stewardship will I require at his hands.

Most of the Saints expelled from the State of Missouri during the winter 1838-9, found their way into Illinois and Iowa. A majority of them went to Quincy, Ill., about 200 miles from Far West, and there they were kindly and hospitably received. Governor Carlin of Illinois, legislators, and private citizens vied with each other in proffering assistance and sympathy.

Among the prominent citizens who, at this time, extended a helping hand to the Saints were Daniel H. Wells, a native of Trenton, New York, and Dr. Isaac Galland. Daniel H. Wells was the owner of a tract of land, which he divided into lots and which the exiles were offered, practically on their own terms. Dr. Galland, also, sold his land at a reasonable price and on the most favorable terms.

The Prophet arrived at Quincy on the 22nd of April, 1839, and two days after, a Council was convened and resolutions were passed directing some of the Saints to go to Zion, and some to settle on Dr. Galland's land, near Commerce, Ill. This location soon became the central gathering place, and its name was changed to Nauvoo. In the year 1841, when this Revelation was given, this beautiful city had about 3,000 inhabitants. A charter had been granted by the Illinois Legislature, by which Nauvoo was given a liberal municipal government, with authority to form a militia and erect a university. A Temple was about to be built. The scattered Saints were gathering, and the settlements in Illinois were growing rapidly. The mission in Great Britain was highly successful. Such were the general conditions when this Revelation was given. The Church had a moment's rest. There was calm before the next storm.

In this Revelation the Lord (1) shows the Prophet that his prayers are answered (1-14), and (2) that He knows His servants (15-21); then (3) He commands the building of the Nauvoo House (22-4), and (4) the Temple (25-48); He then (5) gives the Saints a key by which they may know that their work is accepted (49-55), and (6) imparts further instructions concerning the Nauvoo House (56-83); then (7) comes the Word of the Lord to some of His servants (84-118), and (8) further instructions are given concerning the Nauvoo House (119-22); finally (9), the Officers of the Priesthood are named (123-45).

1. GOD ANSWERS PRAYER.

2. *Your Prayers are acceptable*] The Prophet Joseph always had the interests of the Church at heart. It was the burden he carried day and night. Like the Master, he was a man "despised and rejected" by many; "a man of sorrows, and acquainted with grief," but he never lost sight of his great mission. God, therefore, assured him that the sacrifices he had made, and the acknowledgment of his weakness, were pleasing to Him (v. 1), and that his prayers had been heard. What had been the subject of his prayers? Undoubtedly, the triumph of the kingdom of God on Earth. The Lord had heard those prayers, and directed him what to do.

Make a solemn proclamation] This was the immediate duty of the Prophet. The Revelation was read to the Saints at the General Conference, Nauvoo, April 7th, 1841. What further action was taken, the minutes do not show. But several letters concerning Nauvoo and the gathering were addressed to the Saints, and the literature of the Church was, in due time, made available to high and low. *The Voice of Warning* and a *Letter to Queen Victoria* were published by Parley P. Pratt. Orson Hyde wrote *An Address to the Hebrews* and a pamphlet addressed more particularly to the German nation. The Book of Mormon has been presented to at least two Sovereigns; to Queen Victoria, in 1842, by Elder Lorenzo Snow, and to King Oscar II., of Sweden, on the 22nd of September, 1897, by Elder Janne M. Sjodahl. This may all be said to be in accordance with this command.

7. *They are as grass*] It is natural to common mortals to "look up" to kings and potentates with a feeling of timidity and awe. Henry Ward Beecher, in an address in Brooklyn, in 1886, told a rather humorous anecdote of his nervousness when in the presence of Napoleon II. He forgot to address the Emperor as "Sire," although, before the audience took place, he was told to do so. The servants of the Lord are encouraged to proclaim the Gospel to kings and rulers without fear, for "they are as grass." Their power and glory are transient. The gospel is the only permanent factor in human history. The Priesthood is eternal.

12. *Robert B. Thompson*] Was born in Great Driffield, England, October 1st, 1811. For a number of years he was a Methodist preacher, but he embraced the gospel in Canada and was baptized in 1836. He lived in Far West when the fires of persecution were kindled, and was

compelled to flee for his life. He was a colonel in the Nauvoo militia, but he made the request, before he died (August 27th, 1841), that no military "flummery" should be permitted at his funeral services.

2. The Lord Knows His Servants.

15-21. In this section the comforting lesson is taught, that the Lord takes cognizance of, and knows, His servants individually. Moses could not be personally acquainted with all the people under his care, but God is not subject to human limitations.

15. And again, verily I say unto you, blessed is my servant Hyrum Smith; for I, the Lord, love him because of the integrity of his heart, and because he loveth that which is right before me, saith the Lord.

(a) Hyrum Smith.

15. *Bcause of the integrity of his heart*] That was a prominent feature of his character. Integrity is the best inheritance that parents can bequeath to children. The word of Solomon is well illustrated in the descendants of Hyrum Smith: "The just man walketh in his integrity: his children are blessed after him" (Prov. 20:7). For biographical notes, see Secs. 11, and 23:3.

16. Again, let my servant John C. Bennett help you in your labor in sending my word to the kings and people of the earth, and stand by you, even you my servant Joseph Smith, in the hour of affliction; and his reward shall not fail if he receive counsel.

17. And for his love he shall be great, for he shall be mine if he do this, saith the Lord. I have seen the work which he hath done, which I accept if he continue, and will crown him with blessings and great glory.

(b) John C. Bennett.

16. *John C. Bennett*] Was born in Massachusetts in 1804. He was well educated and possessed many gifts and accomplishments. He was a physician, a university professor, and a brigadier-general. On the 27th of July, 1840, he offered his services to the Church. The Prophet Joseph replied, inviting him to come to Commerce, if he felt so disposed, but warned him at the same time not to expect exaltation "in this generation," from devotion to the cause of truth and a suffering people; nor worldly riches; only the approval of God. The outcome of the correspondence was that he joined the Church and rose to prominent positions among the Saints. His fellowship with the people of God did not last long, however. On the 25th of May, 1842, he was notified that the leaders of the Church did no longer recognize him as a member, because of his

impure life, and shortly afterwards the Church took action against him. Then he became one of the most bitter enemies of the Church. His slanders, his falsehoods and unscrupulous attacks, which included perjury and attempted assassination were the means of inflaming public opinion to such an extent that the tragedy at Carthage became possible.

Why, then, did his name appear, in this Revelation, as that of a trusted assistant of Joseph? John Taylor furnishes the answer to that question. He says, "Respecting John C. Bennett: I was well acquainted with him. At one time he was a good man, but fell into adultery, and was cut off from the Church for his iniquity" (*Hist. of the Church*, Vol. V., p. 81). At this time he was a good man. But he was overcome by the adversary and made the slave of his carnal desires. The Lord knew him and warned him. "His reward shall not fail *if* he receive counsel." "He shall be great * * * *if* he do this," etc. Bennett did not heed these warning "ifs" from Him who knew what was in his heart.

"Bennett lived to be despised by all who knew him. "For some years before his death he suffered from violent fits; he also partly lost the use of his limbs and of his tongue, and it was difficult for him to make himself understood. He dragged out a miserable existence, without a person scarcely to take the least interest in his fate, and died without a soul to mourn his departure" (Andrew Jenson, *Hist. Rec.*, p. 496).

18.   And again, I say unto you that it is my will that my servant Lyman Wight should continue in preaching for Zion, in the spirit of meekness, confessing me before the world; and I will bear him up as on eagles' wings; and he shall beget glory and honor to himself and unto my name.

19.   That when he shall finish his work I may receive him unto myself, even as I did my servant David Patten, who is with me at this time, and also my servant Edward Partridge, and also my aged servant Joseph Smith, Sen., who sitteth with Abraham at his right hand, and blessed and holy is he, for he is mine.

(c) *Lyman Wight.*

18-19.   See Secs. 52:7; 103:30. David Patten, martyred on Oct. 25th, 1838. Edward Partridge, died in Nauvoo, May 27th, 1840. The Lord says these were "with Him;" not in a purgatory.

20.   And again, verily I say unto you, my servant George Miller is without guile; he may be trusted because of the integrity of his heart; and for the love which he has to my testimony I, the Lord, love him.

21.   I therefore say unto you, I seal upon his head the office of a bishopric, like unto my servant Edward Partridge, that he

may receive the consecrations of mine house, that he may administer blessings upon the heads of the poor of my people, saith the Lord. Let no man despise my servant George, for he shall honor me.

(d) George Miller.

20-1. George Miller, as long as the Prophet Joseph lived, seemed to be a faithful Latter-day Saint. He was chosen to fill the important place of Bishop, left vacant by the death of Edward Partridge. He accompanied the Prophet on his journeys, on several occasions. He and Newel K. Whitney were appointed Trustees-in-trust of the Church, after the death of the Prophet. And when the Saints left Nauvoo, he was among the first to cross the river. But from now on he changed. In the Camp of Israel, slowly wending its way westward, he became disaffected. He always wanted to be ahead of the main body, and be a law unto himself. At Winter Quarters he expressed the view that Texas was the place to go to, and not the Rocky Mountains, and when Brigham Young refused to listen to him, knowing that the Prophet had pointed to the Great Basin as the gathering place of the Saints, he left the Camp with a few followers, and joined Lyman Wight in Texas. Shortly afterwards he disagreed with this schismatic and joined Strang, unable to find peace and rest anywhere. Here is another career, beginning in integrity and love of the gospel and ending in failure, because of lack of humility.

22. Let my servant George, and my servant Lyman, and my servant John Snider, and others, build a house unto my name, such a one as my servant Joseph shall show unto them, upon the place which he shall show unto them also.

23. And it shall be for a house for boarding, a house that strangers may come from afar to lodge therein; therefore let it be a good house, worthy of all acceptation, that the weary traveler may find health and safety while he shall contemplate the word of the Lord; and the corner-stone I have appointed for Zion.

24. This house shall be a healthful habitation if it be built unto my name, and if the governor which shall be appointed unto it shall not suffer any pollution to come upon it. It shall be holy, or the Lord your God will not dwell therein.

3. THE NAUVOO HOUSE.

22-4. The Spirit of Revelation directs the Saints to build a fine hotel for the entertainment of strangers. There is no greater inducement for travelers to visit a place than good hotel accommodations. This Revelation proves that the Lord wanted the tourists of the world to visit and become acquainted with the Saints. These were not to be surrounded by a wall of isolation. They had nothing to hide from the world.

The erection of the hotel here referred to, generally known as the Nauvoo House, was commenced in the spring of 1841, and in 1846, when the Saints left Nauvoo, the walls were up above the windows of the second story. It fronted two streets, 120 feet on each. The estimated cost was $100,000. It was planned to be the most magnificent hotel in the West, at the time. When the Saints left the City, the unfinished building became the property of the Prophet's widow, and was subsequently claimed by her second husband, Mr. L. C. Bidamon. In 1872 he put part of it under roof and fitted it up as an hotel, known as the Bidamon House.

25. And again, verily I say unto you, let all my saints come from afar.

26. And send ye swift messengers, yea, chosen messengers, and say unto them: Come ye, with all your gold, and your silver, and your precious stones, and with all your antiquities; and with all who have knowledge of antiquities, that will come, may come, and bring the box-tree, and the fir-tree, and the pine-tree, together with all the precious trees of the earth;

27. And with iron, with copper, and with brass, and with zinc, and with all your precious things of the earth; and build a house to my name, for the Most High to dwell therein.

28. For there is not a place found on earth that he may come to and restore again that which was lost unto you, or which he hath taken away, even the fulness of the priesthood.

29. For a baptismal font there is not upon the earth, that they, my saints, may be baptized for those who are dead—

30. For this ordinance belongeth to my house, and cannot be acceptable to me, only in the days of your poverty, wherein ye are not able to build a house unto me.

31. But I command you, all ye my saints, to build a house unto me; and I grant unto you a sufficient time to build a house unto me; and during this time your baptisms shall be acceptable unto me.

32. But behold, at the end of this appointment your baptisms for your dead shall not be acceptable unto me; and if you do not these things at the end of the appointment ye shall be rejected as a church, with your dead, saith the Lord your God.

33. For verily I say unto you, that after you have had suffi-

cient time to build a house to me, wherein the ordinance of baptizing for the dead belongeth, and for which the same was instituted from before the foundation of the world, your baptisms for your dead cannot be acceptable unto me;

34. For therein are the keys of the holy priesthood ordained, that you may receive honor and glory.

35. And after this time, your baptisms for the dead, by those who are scattered abroad, are not acceptable unto me, saith the Lord.

36. For it is ordained that in Zion, and in her stakes, and in Jerusalem, those places which I have appointed for refuge, shall be the places for your baptisms for your dead.

37. And again, verily I say unto you, how shall your washings be acceptable unto me, except ye perform them in a house which you have built to my name?

38. For, for this cause I commanded Moses that he should build a tabernacle, that they should bear it with them in the wilderness, and to build a house in the land of promise, that those ordinances might be revealed which had been hid from before the world was.

39. Therefore, verily I say unto you, that your anointings, and your washings, and your baptisms for the dead, and your solemn assemblies, and your memorials for your sacrifices by the sons of Levi, and for your oracles in your most holy places wherein you receive conversations, and your statutes and judgments, for the beginning of the revelations and foundation of Zion, and for the glory, honor, and endowment of all her municipals, are ordained by the ordinance of my holy house, which my people are always commanded to build unto my holy name.

40. And verily I say unto you, let this house be built unto my name, that I may reveal mine ordinances therein unto my people;

41. For I deign to reveal unto my church things which have been kept hid from before the foundation of the world, things that pertain to the dispensation of the fulness of times.

42. And I will show unto my servant Joseph all things pertaining to this house, and the priesthood thereof, and the place whereon it shall be built.

43. And ye shall build it on the place where you have contemplated building it, for that is the spot which I have chosen for you to build it.

44. If ye labor with all your might, I will consecrate that spot that it shall be made holy.

45. And if my people will hearken unto my voice, and unto the voice of my servants whom I have appointed to lead my people, behold, verily I say unto you, they shall not be moved out of their place.

46. But if they will not hearken to my voice, nor unto the voice of these men whom I have appointed, they shall not be blest, because they pollute mine holy grounds, and mine holy ordinances, and charters, and my holy words which I give unto them.

47. And it shall come to pass that if you build a house unto my name, and do not do the things that I say, I will not perform the oath which I make unto you, neither fulfil the promises which ye expect at my hands, saith the Lord.

48. For instead of blessings, ye, by your own works, bring cursings, wrath, indignation, and judgments upon your own heads, by your follies, and by all your abominations, which you practice before me, saith the Lord.

4. THE NAUVOO TEMPLE.

25-48. In this section the Lord commands the Saints to build a Temple in Nauvoo. It was not unknown to Him that their stay in Illinois would be brief. They needed the blessings they were to receive in that sacred building, in order to pass the fiery furnace of the exodus and come out unscathed.

26. *Send ye swift messengers*] Missionaries. The Nauvoo Temple was to be built by contributions from the Saints in all parts of the world. It required united effort to complete it in the time allowed. It was necessary to send out missionaries who were experienced and could travel fast, to awaken an interest among the Saints in the great undertaking. On April 8th, a committee was appointed to this mission.

27-28. *For the Most High to dwell therein*] The Church is the kingdom of God on Earth. The Temple is the palace of the King.

29-30. *A baptismal font there is not upon the earth*] Baptism for the dead was performed by the Saints for some time following the resurrection of our Savior, but this practice soon became discarded as the apostasy set in and from that time until the time of the building the Nauvoo Temple, there was no baptismal font any place on the earth where baptisms for the dead could be performed. It now became necessary to prepare a font for this purpose, and the Lord gave the commandment that one be placed in the Nauvoo Temple. There was no font in the Kirtland Temple, because the work of salvation for the dead had not been revealed when that Temple was built. For a short time, while a place in the Nauvoo Temple was being prepared, the Lord granted the saints the privilege of being baptized for their dead in the Mississippi River, but explained that this could only be done when there was no House of the Lord where this ordinance could be performed, "for the ordinance belongeth to my house, and cannot be acceptable to me, only in the days of your poverty, wherein ye are not able to build a house unto me."

31-35. *I grant unto you a sufficient time to build a house*] This passage has been misinterpreted by some, especially by enemies of the Church who profess a belief in the mission of the Prophet Joseph Smith, but do not accept the doctrine of salvation for the dead. A careful reading of these verses will show that it was not the failure to build a house, but the failure to perform the ordinances for the dead in the house after it was prepared for those ordinances that would cause the rejection. In the months when the saints were without a Temple the Lord granted them the privilege of baptizing for their dead in the Mississippi River, but with the understanding that this was a special privilege which would end when they had been given sufficient time to prepare a place in the Temple where this ordinance could be performed. For baptism for the dead, as well as other ordinances for the dead, are to be performed in a house built to the name of the Lord and for that holy purpose. Therefore we find the members of the Church engaging in baptisms for the dead in the river from the time the privilege was granted until the time arrived when the font in the house of the Lord was prepared for that ordinance, and when that time arrived all baptisms for the dead in the river ceased by divine command. The Lord said (v. 32) "But behold, at the *end of the appointment* (i.e. the sufficient time) your baptisms for your dead shall not be acceptable unto me [in the river] and if ye do not these things *at the end of the appointment* ye shall be rejected as a church with your dead, saith the Lord your God.

"For verily I say unto you, that after you have had sufficient time to build a house to me, wherein the ordinance of baptizing for the dead belongeth, and for which the same was instituted from before the foundation of the world, your baptisms for your dead cannot be acceptable unto me." (i.e. acceptable in the river, or any other place outside the house of the Lord; v. 35.)

"And if ye do not these things at the end of the appointment, obviously does not mean 'if ye do not build a temple at the *end* of the appointment,' as our critics infer it does, but it refers to the *ordinances* that were

to be performed in the temple, and the failure on the part of the Saints to perform these ordinances for their dead was the thing that would cause their rejection with their dead, and not the failure to build the temple, which was merely the edifice in which the saving principles were to be performed. This is in harmony with the teachings of the Prophet Joseph Smith, who said that if we neglect the salvation of our dead, we do it at the peril of our own salvation! Why? Because we without them cannot be made perfect. (Doc. and Cov. 128:15.)" (Joseph Fielding Smith—*Salvation Universal,* page 22.)

At the conference of the Church held Sunday, October 3, 1841, the Prophet announced: "There shall be no more baptisms for the dead, until the ordinance can be attended to in the Lord's House; and the Church shall not hold another general conference, until they can meet in said house. For *Thus saith the Lord!*" (D.H.C. 4:426.) Thus the "end of the appointment" had arrived, and no more baptisms outside of that house were acceptable to the Lord. The reason for this startling proclamation was the fact that the font in the house of the Lord was prepared for that sacred ordinance. On the eighth day of November 1841, this font in the basement of the Temple was dedicated for the ordinance of baptism for the dead. The Prophet wrote in his journal of this event: "Monday, (Nov.) 8.—At five o'clock p.m., I attended the dedication of the baptismal font in the Lord's House. President Brigham Young was spokesman." (D.H.C. 4:446.) On the 21st day of that month Elders Brigham Young, Heber C. Kimball and John Taylor baptized about forty persons for the dead, and Elders Wilford Woodruff and George A. Smith confirmed them. Thus the great work of baptism for the dead commenced in the House of the Lord and continued until the Saints were driven from Nauvoo. After arriving in the valleys of the Rocky Mountains, a place was prepared in another House of the Lord, and this work for the salvation of the dead has continued on ever since.

It may be added that God did not reject the Church but saved it as by a miracle, from destruction. Says President George Q. Cannon:

"If any proof of this is needed, let us reflect upon the wonderful deliverance that God hath wrought out for us since we left Illinois. Up to that period, or up to the time that the Temple was partly finished, and the blessings of God bestowed within its walls, our enemies to a very great extent had triumphed over us. We had been driven from place to place; compelled to flee from one town, county, and State to another; but how great the change since then! We started out a poor, friendless people, with nothing but God's blessing upon us. His power overshadowing us and His guidance to lead us in the wilderness; and from the day that we crossed the Mississippi River until this day—the 8th of April, 1871—we have had continued success and triumphs * * * God has done for us as He did for His ancient covenant people, when he caused the waters of the Red Sea to separate, that they might pass through and escape the destruction their enemies threatened" (*Jour. of Dis.,* Vol. XIV., p. 125).

36. *In Zion * * * her stakes, and in Jerusalem * * * shall be places for your baptisms*] Temples must be built where they can be supervised by the President of the Church, who holds the keys of the sealing power. During the millennium, President Brigham Young has said, the work of salvation will be accomplished for the dead: "We trust in God. I reckon he will fight our battles and we will be baptized for and in behalf of the human family during the thousand years; and we will have hundreds of temples and thousands of men and women officiating therein for those who have fallen asleep, without having had the privilege of hearing and obeying the Gospel, that they may be brought forth and have a glorious resurrection, and enjoy the kingdom which God has prepared for them." (*Discourses of Brigham Young*, p. 615.)

38. *A Tabernacle*] Here we are taught that ordinances similar to those performed in our Temple were part of the ancient Tabernacle service. But little is known, from the Old Testament, concerning those ordinances, but it is stated that Aaron and his sons were to be washed and anointed "at the door of the Tabernacle" (Ex. 29:4-7; comp. 30:21; 40:12). A special laver, or font, was provided for that purpose (Ex. 40:11). In the Temple of Solomon, the laver was of immense size, and was, therefore, called a "molten sea" (I. Kings 7:23-6; comp. Rev. 4:6; 15:2). Baptisms were certainly performed as part of the services of the Mosaic covenant.

There were no ordinances performed for the dead in Solomon's Temple, or at any time before the resurrection of our Lord. Before that day there was a great gulf fixed which separated the righteous from those who had not received the Gospel, which none could pass. (Luke 16:26.) Until our Savior opened the gates through the resurrection all ordinances were confined to the living. President Smith's vision of the redemption of the dead is in harmony with this doctrine. (*Gospel Doctrine*, pp. 596-601.) "Jesus was the first man that ever went to preach to the spirits in prison, holding the keys of the Gospel of salvation to them. Those keys were delivered to him in the day and hour that he went into the spirit world, and with them he opened the door of salvation to the spirits in prison." (President Brigham Young, *Discourses of Brigham Young*, p. 379.)

39. *Oracles*] In this verse, the purposes for which the Temples are reared are indicated. They are for "washings," "anointings," "baptisms," "solemn assemblies," "memorials for sacrifices by the sons of Levi," and for "oracles."

"Memorials" refers, possibly, to records of sacrifices that will be kept when the Levitical service shall have been restored, and "oracles" means the place in which the divine revelations are received. The name is applied to the sacred Scriptures, which contain the Word of God, and also to the part of the Temple called the Holy of Holies, where the presence of God was manifested (I. Kings 8:6; II. Chron. 4:20; Ps. 28:2).

Municipals] Stakes and Wards.

41. *I deign to reveal unto my Church, etc.*] In verse 38 we are taught that ordinances were performed in the Mosaic Sanctuary, but we are not to understand that the people then had the truth revealed in the same fulness as it has been given to the Church now. Truths pertaining to "the dispensation of the fulness of times" were kept hid "from before the foundation of the world."

45. *If my people will hearken* * * * *shall not be moved out of their place*] The Saints generally labored diligently and with sublime self-abnegation upon the Temple, but the spirit of apostasy possessed many of the leading men in Nauvoo, as had been the case in Jackson County and in Kirtland. They polluted the sanctuary and all pertaining thereto. They brought upon themselves and the Church wrath, indignation, and judgment (v. 48). Because of their disobedience the Church was subjected to another sifting process by which the chaff was separated from the wheat.

49. Verily, verily, I say unto you, that when I give a commandment to any of the sons of men to do a work unto my name, and those sons of men go with all their might and with all they have to perform that work, and cease not their diligence, and their enemies come upon them and hinder them from performing that work, behold, it behooveth me to require that work no more at the hands of those sons of men, but to accept of their offerings.

50. And the iniquity and transgression of my holy laws and commandments I will visit upon the heads of those who hindered my work, unto the third and fourth generation, so long as they repent not, and hate me, saith the Lord God.

51. Therefore, for this cause have I accepted the offerings of those whom I commanded to build up a city and a house unto my name, in Jackson county, Missouri, and were hindered by their enemies, saith the Lord your God.

52. And I will answer judgment, wrath, and indignation, wailing, and anguish, and gnashing of teeth upon their heads, unto the third and fourth generation, so long as they repent not, and hate me, saith the Lord your God.

53. And this I make an example unto you, for your consolation concerning all those who have been commanded to do a work and have been hindered by the hands of their enemies, and by oppression, saith the Lord your God.

54. For I am the Lord your God, and will save all those of

your brethren who have been pure in heart, and have been slain in the land of Missouri, saith the Lord.

55. And again, verily I say unto you, I command you again to build a house to my name, even in this place, that you may prove yourselves unto me that ye are faithful in all things whatsoever I command you, that I may bless you, and crown you with honor, immortality, and eternal life.

5. The Efforts of the Saints Accepted.

49-55. The comforting truth is here stated that the Lord accepts the will for the deed, when His children endeavor with all diligence to obey God but are prevented from doing so by the enemy. On that ground the offerings of the Saints in Jackson County were accepted, and the wrath of God would be poured out upon the enemies. That the Saints were diligent in the building of the Nauvoo Temple is amply attested by history.

"That structure cost more than one million dollars; the Saints were poor, and a great deal of the time the Temple was in course of erection they were harassed by their enemies. The Prophet Joseph was forced into exile to avoid his enemies who tried to drag him into Missouri, and therefore he could not devote his personal attention to the building of the Temple, as he otherwise could have done; and in this way the work was retarded in some degree by the enemies of the people. Moreover, the building of that structure was not like building one to-day. The Saints could not order their timber from the lumberyard in a state of preparation for the Temple. There were no iron foundries from which they could obtain the required metal properly prepared; but, on the contrary, every detail had to be performed by the Saints. The timber had to be hewed in the far off forests of Wisconsin, carried to Nauvoo, and cut into boards and for the various uses of the Temple. The stone had to be cut and polished from the quarries, and the whole work had to be supplied out of the tithing of the people" (Joseph Fielding Smith, *Origin of the "Reorganized" Church*, p. 21).

56. And now I say unto you, as pertaining to my boarding house which I have commanded you to build for the boarding of strangers, let it be built unto my name, and let my name be named upon it, and let my servant Joseph and his house have place therein, from generation to generation.

57. For this anointing have I put upon his head, that his blessing shall also be put upon the head of his posterity after him.

58. And as I said unto Abraham concerning the kindreds of

the earth, even so I say unto my servant Joseph: In thee and in thy seed shall the kindred of the earth be blessed.

59. Therefore, let my servant Joseph and his seed after him have place in that house, from generation to generation, forever and ever, saith the Lord.

60. And let the name of that house be called Nauvoo House; and let it be a delightful habitation for man, and a resting-place for the weary traveler, that he may contemplate the glory of Zion, and the glory of this, the corner-stone thereof;

61. That he may receive also the counsel from those whom I have set to be as plants of renown, and as watchmen upon her walls.

62. Behold, verily I say unto you, let my servant George Miller, and my servant Lyman Wight, and my servant John Snider, and my servant Peter Haws, organize themselves, and appoint one of them to be a president over their quorum for the purpose of building that house.

63. And they shall form a constitution, whereby they may receive stock for the building of that house.

64. And they shall not receive less than fifty dollars for a share of stock in that house, and they shall be permitted to receive fifteen thousand dollars from any one man for stock in that house.

65. But they shall not be permitted to receive over fifteen thousand dollars stock from any one man.

66. And they shall not be permitted to receive under fifty dollars for a share of stock from any one man in that house.

67. And they shall not be permitted to receive any man, as a stockholder in this house, except the same shall pay his stock into their hands at the time he receives stock;

68. And in proportion to the amount of stock he pays into their hands he shall receive stock in that house; but if he pays nothing into their hands he shall not receive any stock in that house.

69. And if any pay stock into their hands it shall be for stock in that house, for himself, and for his generation after him, from generation to generation, so long as he and his heirs shall hold that stock, and do not sell or convey the stock away out of their

hands by their own free will and act, if you will do my will, saith the Lord your God.

70. And again, verily I say unto you, if my servant George Miller, and my servant Lyman Wight, and my servant John Snider, and my servant Peter Haws, receive any stock into their hands, in moneys, or in properties wherein they receive the real value of moneys, they shall not appropriate any portion of that stock to any other purpose, only in that house.

71. And if they do appropriate any portion of that stock anywhere else, only in that house, without the consent of the stockholder, and do not repay four-fold for the stock which they appropriate anywhere else, only in that house, they shall be accursed, and shall be moved out of their place, saith the Lord God; for I, the Lord, am God, and cannot be mocked in any of these things.

72. Verily I say unto you, let my servant Joseph pay stock into their hands for the building of that house, as seemeth him good; but my servant Joseph cannot pay over fifteen thousand dollars stock in that house, nor under fifty dollars; neither can any other man, saith the Lord.

73. And there are others also who wish to know my will concerning them, for they have asked it at my hands.

74. Therefore, I say unto you concerning my servant Vinson Knight, if he will do my will let him put stock into that house for himself, and for his generation after him, from generation to generation.

75. And let him lift up his voice long and loud, in the midst of the people, to plead the cause of the poor and the needy; and let him not fail, neither let his heart faint; and I will accept of his offerings, for they shall not be unto me as the offerings of Cain, for he shall be mine, saith the Lord.

76. Let his family rejoice and turn away their hearts from affliction; for I have chosen him and anointed him, and he shall be honored in the midst of his house, for I will forgive all his sins, saith the Lord. Amen.

77. Verily I say unto you, let my servant Hyrum put stock into that house as seemeth him good, for himself and his generation after him, from generation to generation.

78. Let my servant Isaac Galland put stock into that house, for I, the Lord, love him for the work he hath done, and will forgive all his sins; therefore, let him be remembered for an interest in that house from generation to generation.

79. Let my servant Isaac Galland be appointed among you, and be ordained by my servant William Marks, and be blessed of him, to go with my servant Hyrum to accomplish the work that my servant Joseph shall point out to them, and they shall be greatly blessed.

80. Let my servant William Marks pay stock into that house as seemeth him good, for himself and his generation, from generation to generation.

81. Let my servant Henry G. Sherwood pay stock into that house, as seemeth him good, for himself and his seed after him, from generation to generation.

82. Let my servant William Law pay stock into that house, for himself and his seed after him, from generation to generation.

83. If he will do my will let him not take his family unto the eastern lands, even unto Kirtland; nevertheless, I, the Lord, will build up Kirtland, but I, the Lord, have a scourge prepared for the inhabitants thereof.

6. INSTRUCTIONS CONCERNING THE NAUVOO HOUSE.

56-83. In this section special instructions are given concerning the Nauvoo House. It was to be dedicated to the Lord. The Prophet Joseph, or one of his descendants after him from generation to generation (v. 56), was to live there. This does not imply that the Presidency of the Church should be transmitted as an inheritance from father to son. It refers only to the shares of stock in the Nauvoo House Association. The Prophet Joseph owned a portion of that stock that was transferable property, and it was perfectly proper that he and any of his descendants who owned the stock should have their residence in the House as part of the dividend on the money invested, when that condition was understood and agreed on from the beginning. A building committee is appointed (v. 62), and instructions are given for the adoption of a constitution for the corporation (v. 63-72). Other individuals, besides Joseph, are mentioned as worthy to become stockholders. They are Vinson Knight (v. 74), Hyrum Smith (v. 77), Isaac Galland (v. 78), William Marks (v. 80), Henry G. Sherwood (v. 81), and William Law (v. 82).

7. THE WORD OF THE LORD TO INDIVIDUALS.

84-118. In these verses the Spirit of Revelation speaks to the individuals mentioned by name, giving counsel, instruction, encouragement, or warning and reproof, as each case may require.

84. And with my servant Almon Babbitt, there are many things with which I am not pleased; behold, he aspireth to establish his counsel instead of the counsel which I have ordained, even that of the Presidency of my Church; and he setteth up a golden calf for the worship of my people.

85. Let no man go from this place who has come here essaying to keep my commandments.

86. If they live here let them live unto me; and if they die let them die unto me; for they shall rest from all their labors here, and shall continue their works.

(a) *Almon Babbitt.*

84-6. The Lord severely rebukes Almon Babbitt. From these verses it may be gathered that his chief ambition was to make money, and that he advised the Saints to leave Nauvoo, contrary to the counsel of the Church leaders. Perhaps he was interested in the sale of land elsewhere. At all events, when the Saints left Nauvoo, he was appointed one of the real estate agents in whose hands the abandoned property was left, to be disposed of on the best terms obtainable. How he discharged this duty, we may infer from the following statement of Heber C. Kimball: "My house was sold at $1,700, intended to be used to help to gather the Saints; but Almon W. Babbitt put it in his pocket, I suppose" (*Jour. of Dis.,* Vol. VIII., p. 350).

87. Therefore, let my servant William put his trust in me, and cease to fear concerning his family, because of the sickness of the land. If ye love me, keep my commandments; and the sickness of the land shall redound to your glory.

88. Let my servant William go and proclaim my everlasting gospel with a loud voice, and with great joy, as he shall be moved upon by my Spirit, unto the inhabitants of Warsaw, and also unto the inhabitants of Carthage, and also unto the inhabitants of Burlington, and also unto the inhabitants of Madison, and await patiently and diligently for further instructions at my general conference, saith the Lord.

89. If he will do my will let him from henceforth hearken to the counsel of my servant Joseph, and with his interest support the cause of the poor, and publish the new translation of my holy word unto the inhabitants of the earth.

90. And if he will do this I will bless him with a multiplicity of blessings, that he shall not be forsaken, nor his seed be found begging bread.

(b) William Law.

87-90. William Law is here instructed to trust in the Lord and not fear for the safety of his family, although there was sickness among the people (v. 87). Fear is the great friend of disease-carrying microbes. It opens the door to them. If there is an epidemic abroad, it is certain to find the cowards. On the other hand, faith in God is an excellent foundation for both physical and moral health. William Law was, next, called to take a mission to Warsaw, Carthage, Burlington, and Madison (v. 88); to remember the poor and to publish the new Bible translation (v. 89). The Lord promises him certain blessings, if he will do these things— blessings extending to his posterity after him (v. 90); and commands the Prophet Joseph to appoint him counselor in the First Presidency, to take the place of Hyrum Smith (v. 91).

Wonderful opportunities were offered to Wm. Law, which he neglected to embrace. If he had done faithfully what God here gave him to do, he would have received the blessings promised, but when he failed to obey the Lord, even his appointment in the First Presidency could not save him from falling. When he lost the Spirit of God he became one of the most bitter enemies of the Church. Apostates and persecutors rallied around him, and he tried to form a church of his own of such material.

91. And again, verily I say unto you, let my servant William be appointed, ordained, and anointed, as counselor unto my servant Joseph, in the room of my servant Hyrum, that my servant Hyrum may take the office of Priesthood and Patriarch, which was appointed unto him by his father, by blessing and also by right;

92. That from henceforth he shall hold the keys of the patriarchal blessings upon the heads of all my people,

93. That whoever he blesses shall be blessed, and whoever he curses shall be cursed; that whatsoever he shall bind on earth shall be bound in heaven; and whatsoever he shall loose on earth shall be loosed in heaven.

94. And from this time forth I appoint unto him that he may be a prophet, and a seer, and a revelator unto my church, as well as my servant Joseph;

95. That he may act in concert also with my servant Joseph; and that he shall receive counsel from my servant Joseph, who

shall show unto him the keys whereby he may ask and receive and be crowned with the same blessing, and glory, and honor, and priesthood, and gifts of the priesthood, that once were put upon him that was my servant Oliver Cowdery;

96. That my servant Hyrum may bear record of the things which I shall show unto him, that his name may be had in honorable remembrance from generation to generation, forever and ever.

(c) Hyrum Smith.

91-6. In the preceding paragraph Hyrum Smith is pointed out as the legal successor of his father in the Patriarchal office; it is his "by right" of lineage, no less than by Patriarchal blessing. The following is the blessing pronounced upon Hyrum Smith by his father:

"My son Hyrum, I seal upon your head your patriarchal blessing, which I placed upon your head before, for that shall be verified. In addition to this, I now give you my dying blessing. You shall have a season of peace, so that you shall have a sufficient rest to accomplish the work which God has given you to do. You shall be as firm as the pillars of heaven unto the end of your days. I now seal upon your head the patriarchal power, and you shall bless the people. This is my dying blessing upon your head in the name of Jesus. Amen." (*Origin of the Reorganized Church and Question of Succession,* by Joseph Fielding Smith, p. 71.)

"We learn from the Doctrine and Covenants that there are two offices in the Church that descend from father to son. One is that of the Bishopric, for upon Aaron and his sons the Lord conferred this Priesthood (Section 68:16-18). The other is that of the Evangelist. This we learn in Section 107" (*Ibid.* p. 51).

In this section (v. 92-6) the Lord explains the power and authority of the Patriarch. "Whoever he blesses shall be blessed, and whoever he curses shall be cursed" (v. 93); "whatsoever he shall bind on earth shall be bound in heaven; and whatsoever he shall loose on earth shall be loosed in heaven."

In addition to the Patriarchal Priesthood which was conferred upon Hyrum Smith, he received another great and special blessing, for the Lord called him to be a "prophet, and a seer, and a revelator unto my church as well as my servant Joseph" (v. 94), and to him was transferred "the blessing and glory and honor and Priesthood and gifts of the Priesthood," that once were given to Oliver Cowdery, who stood as the "second Elder of the Church," holding the keys with the Prophet, before he (Oliver) transgressed. All these blessings were given to Hyrum Smith who, by this special calling, in addition to becoming the Patriarch of the Church, also became a President of the Church, holding the keys of the kingdom in conjunction with his brother Joseph. Moreover, he was given the promise that his name should be had in "honorable remembrance from generation to generation for ever and ever" (v. 96). How literally this has been fulfilled! (See remarks by Elder Joseph Fielding Smith, April Conference Report 1930.)

97. Let my servant William Law also receive the keys by which he may ask and receive blessings; let him be humble before me, and be without guile, and he shall receive of my Spirit, even the Comforter, which shall manifest unto him the truth of all things, and shall give him, in the very hour, what he shall say.

98. And these signs shall follow him—he shall heal the sick, he shall cast out devils, and shall be delivered from those who would administer unto him deadly poison;

99. And he shall be led in paths where the poisonous serpent cannot lay hold upon his heel, and he shall mount up in the imagination of his thoughts as upon eagles' wings.

100. And what if I will that he should raise the dead, let him not withhold his voice.

101. Therefore, let my servant William cry aloud and spare not, with joy and rejoicing, and with hosannas to him that sitteth upon the throne forever and ever, saith the Lord your God.

102. Behold, I say unto you, I have a mission in store for my servant William, and my servant Hyrum, and for them alone; and let my servant Joseph tarry at home, for he is needed. The remainder I will show unto you hereafter. Even so. Amen.

(d) A Last Warning to William Law.

97-102. The Spirit of Revelation again calls William Law to consider what he might gain by humility and lose by following his own inclination. Our Lord, who was full of compassion for Jerusalem, undoubtedly pitied this man, who was greatly exalted but fell so low. He was offered the choicest blessings of heaven; they would be his, if he would pray, be humble, and without guile. God knew his weaknesses. One of them was "guile," which means "deceitful cunning," "duplicity." By prayer, these might have been overcome.

103. And again, verily I say unto you, if my servant Sidney will serve me and be counselor unto my servant Joseph, let him arise and come up and stand in the office of his calling, and humble himself before me.

104. And if he will offer unto me an acceptable offering, and acknowledgments, and remain with my people, behold, I, the

Lord your God, will heal him that he shall be healed; and he shall lift up his voice again on the mountains, and be a spokesman before my face.

105. Let him come and locate his family in the neighborhood in which my servant Joseph resides.

106. And in all his journeyings let him lift up his voice as with the sound of a trump, and warn the inhabitants of the earth to flee the wrath to come.

107. Let him assist my servant Joseph, and also let my servant William Law assist my servant Joseph, in making a solemn proclamation unto the kings of the earth, even as I have before said unto you.

108. If my servant Sidney will do my will, let him not remove his family unto the eastern lands, but let him change their habitation, even as I have said.

109. Behold, it is not my will that he shall seek to find safety and refuge out of the city which I have appointed unto you, even the city of Nauvoo.

110. Verily I say unto you, even now, if he will hearken unto my voice, it shall be well with him. Even so. Amen.

(e) Sidney Rigdon.

103-10. Sidney Rigdon, according to a generally prevailing impression, was more or less, under the influence of a spirit of apostasy. It is related that, in Liberty jail, he declared to his fellow-prisoners that the sufferings of the Lord were nothing compared with his, and while the faithful Saints were straining every nerve to complete the Nauvoo Temple, he had no word of encouragement to them. As a consequence of his disposition, he did not have good health. Like the Corinthians who partook unworthily of the Sacrament (I. Cor. 11:30), he was "weak and sickly." The Lord, therefore, points out to him the cause of his ailments and promises to heal him, if he will do his duty and stand by the Prophet as a true counselor.

Sidney Rigdon had a remarkable experience some months after this Revelation was received. His daughter Eliza took sick and was pronounced dead by the physician. Some time after her departure, she rose up in the bed and said she had returned to deliver a message from the Lord. She then called the family around her. To her sister Nancy she said, "It is in your heart to deny this work; and if you do, the Lord says it will be the damnation of your soul!" To her sister Sarah she said, "We have but once to die, and I would rather die now, than wait for another time." After having spoken for some time she fainted, but recovered again. The following evening she called her father and said to him that the Lord would make her well, if he would cease weeping for her. Sidney Rigdon related this manifestation of the power of God, in a public meeting on the 20th of August, 1842, and added a strong declaration of his allegiance to the Prophet Joseph and the Church. On the same occasion, Hyrum Smith cited Sidney Rigdon's mind back to this Revelation, in which the Lord promised that if he would move into the City and defend the truth he would be healed, and showed that Rigdon's improvement in health was a fulfilment of this Revelation (*Hist. of the Church,* Vol. V., pp. 121-3). But, notwithstanding all, Rigdon finally lost his way. It can be said, however, that, according to his son, John Rigdon, who joined the Church, he never was an enemy of the Church.

111.   And again, verily I say unto you, let my servant Amos Davies pay stock into the hands of those whom I have appointed to build a house for boarding, even the Nauvoo House.

112.   This let him do if he will have an interest; and let him hearken unto the counsel of my servant Joseph, and labor with his own hands that he may obtain the confidence of men.

113.   And when he shall prove himself faithful in all things that shall be entrusted unto his care, yea, even a few things, he shall be made ruler over many;

114.   Let him therefore abase himself that he may be exalted. Even so. Amen.

(f) Amos Davies.

111-14.   From this Revelation it is evident that Amos Davies, notwithstanding his prominence, had some weaknesses. He was slow to obey counsel, and he shunned work. He is, therefore, commanded to "labor with his own hands" and prove himself faithful in all things. It is to be feared that he heeded this commandment only in part, for on the 9th of March, 1842, he indulged in abusive language concerning the Prophet, whereupon the court bound him over, to keep the peace (*Hist. of the Church,* Vol. IV., p. 549).

115.   And again, verily I say unto you, if my servant Robert D. Foster will obey my voice, let him build a house for my servant Joseph, according to the contract which he has made with him, as the door shall be open to him from time to time.

116.   And let him repent of all his folly, and clothe himself with charity; and cease to do evil, and lay aside all his hard speeches;

117.   And pay stock also into the hands of the quorum of the

Nauvoo House, for himself and for his generation after him, from generation to generation;

118. And hearken unto the counsel of my servants Joseph, and Hyrum, and William Law, and unto the authorities which I have called to lay the foundation of Zion; and it shall be well with him forever and ever. Even so. Amen.

(g) *Robert D. Foster.*

115-18. Robert D. Foster was one of the men who fell from a high position of honor to the lowest depths of wickedness. The Prophet befriended him again and again, hoping that he would mend his ways. According to a statement made to Cyrus H. Wheelock, shortly before the tragedy at Carthage, he was one of a number of conspirators who were determined to take the life of the Prophet, even if the court declared him innocent.

116. *Hard speeches*] They should never be indulged in. Hard words are the offspring of uncharitable feelings, and they engender such feelings, keeping the race of unkind thoughts and sentiments alive. Brigham Young says:

"When my feelings are aroused to anger by the ill-doings of others, I hold them as I would hold a wild horse, and I gain the victory. Some think and say that it makes them feel better, when they are mad, as they call it, to give vent to their madness in abusive and unbecoming language. This, however, is a mistake. Instead of its making you feel better, it is making bad worse" (*Jour. of Dis.,* Vol. XI., p. 255).

8. Concerning the Nauvoo House.

119-22. Further instructions concerning the Nauvoo House are given here.

119. And again, verily I say unto you, let no man pay stock to the quorum of the Nauvoo House unless he shall be a believer in the Book of Mormon, and the revelations I have given unto you, saith the Lord your God;

120. For that which is more or less than this cometh of evil, and shall be attended with cursings and not blessings, saith the Lord your God. Even so. Amen.

(a) *Stockholders.*

119, 120. The Nauvoo House was to be an hotel, but only those who believed in the Book of Mormon and the Doctrine and Covenants were permitted to hold stock in the association. Unity of faith may not seem essential to a business enterprise, but this house was to be erected for religious purposes; the weary traveler would there "contemplate the glories of Zion" (v. 60). It was essential that the owners of the house should all be of one faith; otherwise those who did not believe in the gospel might object to its principles being taught on their premises.

121. And again, verily I say unto you, let the quorum of the Nauvoo house have a just recompense of wages for all their labors which they do in building the Nauvoo House; and let their wages be as shall be agreed among themselves, as pertaining to the price thereof.

122. And let every man who pays stock bear his proportion of their wages, if it must needs be, for their support, saith the Lord; otherwise, their labors shall be accounted unto them for stock in that house. Even so. Amen.

(b) Compensation.

121, 122. In these paragraphs compensation is provided for work done by all engaged in furthering the interests of the association. "A laborer is worthy of his hire."

123. Verily I say unto you, I now give unto you the officers belonging to my Priesthood, that ye may hold the keys thereof, even the Priesthood which is after the order of Melchizedek, which is after the order of mine Only Begotten Son.

124. First, I give unto you Hyrum Smith to be a patriarch unto you, to hold the sealing blessings of my church, even the Holy Spirit of promise, whereby ye are sealed up unto the day of redemption, that ye may not fall notwithstanding the hour of temptation that may come upon you.

125. I give unto you my servant Joseph to be a presiding elder over all my church, to be a translator, a revelator, a seer, and prophet.

126. I give unto him for counselors my servant Sidney Rigdon and my servant William Law, that these may constitute a quorum and First Presidency, to receive the oracles for the whole church.

127. I give unto you my servant Brigham Young to be a president over the Twelve traveling council;

128. Which Twelve hold the keys to open up the authority of my kingdom upon the four corners of the earth, and after that to send my word to every creature.

129. They are Heber C. Kimball, Parley P. Pratt, Orson Pratt, Orson Hyde, William Smith, John Taylor, John E. Page, Wilford Woodruff, Willard Richards, George A. Smith;

130. David Patten, I have taken unto myself; behold, his priesthood no man taketh from him; but, verily I say unto you, another may be appointed unto the same calling.

131. And again, I say unto you, I give unto you a high council, for the corner-stone of Zion—

132. Namely, Samuel Bent, Henry G. Sherwood, George W. Harris, Charles C. Rich, Thomas Grover, Newel Knight, David Dort, Dunbar Wilson—Seymour Brunson I have taken unto myself; no man taketh his priesthood, but another may be appointed unto the same priesthood in his stead; and verily I say unto you, let my servant Aaron Johnson be ordained unto this calling in his stead—David Fullmer, Alpheus Cutler, William Huntington.

133. And again, I give unto you Don C. Smith to be a president over a quorum of high priests:

134. Which ordinance is instituted for the purpose of qualifying those who shall be appointed standing presidents or servants over different stakes scattered abroad;

135. And they may travel also if they choose, but rather be ordained for standing presidents; this is the office of their calling, saith the Lord your God.

136. I give unto him Amasa Lyman and Noah Packard for counselors, that they may preside over the quorum of high priests of my church, saith the Lord.

137. And again, I say unto you, I give unto you John A. Hicks, Samuel Williams, and Jesse Baker, which priesthood is to preside over the quorum of elders, which quorum is instituted for standing ministers; nevertheless they may travel, yet they are ordained to be standing ministers to my church, saith the Lord.

138. And again, I give unto you Joseph Young, Josiah Butterfield, Daniel Miles, Henry Herriman, Zera Pulsipher, Levi Hancock, James Foster, to preside over the quorum of seventies;

139. Which quorum is instituted for traveling elders to bear record of my name in all the world, wherever the traveling high council, mine apostles, shall send them to prepare a way before my face.

140. The difference between this quorum and the quorum of elders is that one is to travel continually, and the other is to preside over the churches from time to time; the one has the responsibility of presiding from time to time, and the other has no responsibility of presiding, saith the Lord your God.

141. And again, I say unto you, I give unto you Vinson Knight, Samuel H. Smith, and Shadrach Roundy, if he will receive it, to preside over the bishopric; a knowledge of said bishopric is given unto you in the book of Doctrine and Covenants.

142. And again, I say unto you, Samuel Rolfe and his counselors for priests, and the president of the teachers and his counselors, and also the president of the deacons and his counselors, and also the president of the stake and his counselors.

143. The above offices I have given unto you, and the keys thereof, for helps and for governments, for the work of the ministry and the perfecting of my saints.

144. And a commandment I give unto you, that you should fill all these offices and approve of those names which I have mentioned, or else disapprove of them at my general conference;

145. And that ye should prepare rooms for all these offices in my house when you build it unto my name, saith the Lord your God. Even so. Amen.

9. OFFICERS OF THE CHURCH.

123-145. The officers of the Church are here enumerated in the following order:

1. Patriarch, Hyrum Smith (v. 124).

2. First Presidency, Joseph Smith, Sidney Rigdon, William Law (v. 125-6).

3. President over the Twelve, Brigham Young (v. 127). The Council of the Twelve:
   Heber C. Kimball, Parley P. Pratt, Orson Pratt, Orson Hyde, William Smith, John Taylor, John E. Page, Wilford Woodruff, Willard Richards, George A. Smith.

4. The High Council:
   Samuel Bent, H. G. Sherwood, George W. Harris, Charles C. Rich, Thomas Grover, Newel Knight, David Dort, Dunbar Wilson, Aaron Johnson, David Fullmer, Alpheus Cutler, William Huntington.

5. President of the Quorum of High Priests, Don C. Smith (v. 133), and Counselors, Amasa Lyman and Noah Packard.

6. Presidency of the Quorum of Elders: John A. Hicks, Samuel Williams, Jesse Baker (v. 137).

7. First Council of Seventies:
Joseph Young, Josiah Butterfield, Daniel Miles, Henry Harriman, Zera Pulsipher, Levi Hancock, James Foster (v. 138).

8. The Bishopric: Vinson Knight, Samuel H. Smith, Shadrach Roundy (v. 141).

9. For Priests: Samuel Rolfe and Counselors.

10. Teachers.

11. Deacons.

12. Presidency of Stakes (v. 142).

127. *Brigham Young*] Was born in Whitingham, Windham County, Vermont, June 1st, 1801: In his 22nd year he joined the Methodist church. For a number of years he followed the trades of carpenter, joiner, glazier, and painter. In 1830 he saw, for the first time, a Book of Mormon, which had been left at the house of his brother Phineas, by Samuel H. Smith. In the fall of 1831, he heard some Elders preach and believed. Shortly afterwards he went to Canada, in company with John P. Green, where he visited his brother Joseph and related what he knew of "Mormonism." His brother accepted the truth and accompanied Brigham to Mendon, where the latter resided. Brigham Young was baptized on the 14th of April, 1832, by Eleazar Miller. After the death of his wife, Brigham Young made his home with Heber C. Kimball, and in September, the same year, the two friends went to Kirtland, where they visited the Prophet Joseph.

GENERAL NOTES

President Brigham Young says:
"Brother Heber and I never went to school until we got into 'Mormonism'; that was the first of our schooling. We never had the opportunity of letters in our youth, but we had the privilege of picking up brush, chopping down trees, rolling logs, and working amongst the roots and getting our shins, feet, and toes bruised. * * * I learned to make bread, wash the dishes, milk the cows, and make butter. * * * Those are about all the advantages I gained in my youth" (*Jour. of Dis.,* Vol. V., p. 97).

"Up to the time that 'Mormonism' came to me, I did earnestly pray, if there was a God (and I believed there was), 'Lord God, Thou who gavest the Scriptures; who didst speak to Abraham and reveal Thyself to Moses and the ancients, keep my feet that they may not be entangled in the snares of folly.' * * * I could not more honestly and earnestly have prepared myself to go into eternity than I did to come into this Church; and when I had ripened everything in my mind, I drank it in, and not till then" (Brigham Young, *Jour. of Dis.*, Vol. VIII., p. 38).

SECTION 125.

REVELATION *given through Joseph Smith the Prophet, at Nauvoo, Illinois, March, 1841, concerning the Saints in the Territory of Iowa.*

WHAT is the will of the Lord concerning the saints in the Territory of Iowa?

2. Verily, thus saith the Lord, I say unto you, if those who call themselves by my name and are essaying to be my saints, if they will do my will and keep my commandments concerning them, let them gather themselves together unto the places which I shall appoint unto them by my servant Joseph, and build up cities unto my name, that they may be prepared for that which is in store for a time to come.

3. Let them build up a city unto my name upon the land opposite the city of Nauvoo, and let the name of Zarahemla be named upon it.

4. And let all those who come from the east, and the west, and the north, and the south, that have desires to dwell therein, take up their inheritance in the same, as well as in the city of Nashville, or in the city of Nauvoo, and in all the stakes which I have appointed, saith the Lord.

When the Saints left Missouri, a large number of fugitives found their way into the Territory of Iowa. Large tracts of land were purchased, and several settlements were built up in the southeastern portion of that Territory. Before the arrival of the Saints, there were only 2,839 inhabitants in Lee County. In 1846 the population was estimated at 12,860. So rapidly did the County develop, when touched by the magic wand of "Mormon" industry. Nauvoo was the central point of gathering at this time, and the question, stated in the first verse of this Revelation, arose. The answer follows. The Saints were to gather and build cities in Iowa.

2. *Essaying to be Saints*] This expression is both instructive and comforting. To "essay" means to "endeavor," to "make an effort." All the

exiles, notwithstanding their faith and patience in sufferings, may not have been "Saints," but if they were trying to be worthy of that name, they were acceptable to God. Children who are earnestly striving to do their best, please their parents, even if they do not always succeed.

*Let them gather * * * and build up cities*] They did build up Montrose, Zarahemla, Ambrosia, Augusta, Keokuk. A Stake was organized in 1839, with John Smith as president.

3. *Zarahemla*] This settlement was founded by the Saints in 1839, on the uplands about a mile west of the Mississippi River, near Montrose and opposite Nauvoo, Ill. The Church had bought an extensive tract of land here. At a conference held at Zarahemla, August 7th, 1841, seven hundred and fifty Church members were represented, of whom three hundred and twenty-six lived in Zarahemla. But when the Saints left for the Rocky Mountains, that city was lost sight of.

4. *Nashville*] "A little town, pleasantly situated on the Mississippi River, at the head of Des Moines Rapids, in Lee County, Iowa, three miles by rail southeast of Montrose, and eight miles north of Keokuk, was purchased by the Church, together with 20,000 acres of land adjoining it, June 24th, 1839, * * * It continued to exist as a 'Mormon' town until the general exodus in 1846" (*Hist. Rec.* p. 983).

SECTION 126.

REVELATION *given through Joseph Smith the Prophet, in the house of Brigham Young, at Nauvoo, Illinois, July 9, 1841. At this time Brigham Young was president of the quorum of the Twelve Apostles.*

DEAR and well-beloved brother, Brigham Young, verily thus saith the Lord unto you: My servant Brigham, it is no more required at your hand to leave your family as in times past, for your offering is acceptable to me.

2. I have seen your labor and toil in journeyings for my name.

3. I therefore command you to send my word abroad, and take especial care of your family from this time, henceforth and forever. Amen.

The career of Brigham Young was that of a missionary. Shortly after his baptism, he went to Canada, in company with his brother, Joseph, and as a result of their labors, several families joined the Church and went to Kirtland. Brigham Young labored at his trade and preached the gospel whenever an opportunity was found. He joined Zion's Camp when that organization was formed. He and his brother were the "sweet singers" of the Camp, always cheerful and true. Brigham Young was chosen to be one of the Twelve Apostles, and early in May, 1835, he went to the Eastern States, as did the other Apostles, for the purpose of preaching the gospel, gathering the Saints, and collecting means to purchase land in Missouri. In 1836, after having attended the solemn assembly at Kirtland and received a promised endowment, he went on another mission to the Eastern States, traveling through New York, Vermont, Massachusetts, and Rhode Island, returning to Kirtland in the fall, where he became one of the chief supports of the Prophet, during the time of financial crash and apostasy. In 1840, Brigham Young, accompanied by Heber C. Kimball, Parley P. Pratt, Orson Pratt, George A. Smith, and Reuben Hedlock, left New York for a mission to Great Britain, where he labored with indomitable zeal and great success. On the 20th of April, 1841, he set sail for New York on his return journey. While in the British mission field, he had been instrumental in performing a great work. He says "Through the mercy of God we have gained many friends, established churches in almost every noted town and city of Great Britain, baptized between seven and eight thousand souls, printed 5,000 Books of Mormon, 3,000 hymn books, 2,500 volumes of the *Millennial Star,* and fifty thousand tracts." It was shortly after the arrival of Brigham Young in Nauvoo, after his British mission, that this Revelation was received, in which the Lord expresses approval of his labors and commands him to leave his family no more, but to send His word abroad and provide for his family.

In order to grasp fully the significance of this Revelation, an incident from the first meeting, in 1832, between the Prophet Joseph and his successor should be recalled. They had spent the evening in conversation on the gospel, and when the time for parting had come, Brigham Young was invited to lead in prayer. While he was praying, the Spirit of the Lord came upon him, and he spoke in tongues—the first instance of the bestowal of that gift upon anyone in this dispensation. Afterwards, it is asserted, the Prophet said, "A time will come when Brother Brigham will preside over this Church" (Whitney's *Hist. of Utah,* Vol. I., p. 112).

It should, further, be remembered that, at a Conference held at Nauvoo, August 16th, 1841, the Prophet Joseph, with this Revelation in mind, stated that, "The time has come when the Twelve should be called upon to stand in their place *next to the First Presidency,* and attend to the settling of emigrants and the business of the Church at the Stakes, and to assist to bear off the kingdom victoriously to the nations" (*Hist. of the Church,* Vol. IV., p. 403). By this Revelation, therefore, Brigham Young, the President of the Twelve (Sec. 124:127), was called to stand next to the First Presidency. Why? To take his place, whenever the Prophet should be called to another sphere of action. By this Revelation, the Spirit indicated that Brigham Young was to be the successor of Joseph Smith, as the Prophet had predicted in 1832.

SECTION 127.

AN EPISTLE *from Joseph Smith the Prophet to the Latter-day Saints at Nauvoo, Illinois, containing directions on baptism for the dead; dated at Nauvoo, September 1, 1842.——Because of intense persecution and consequent interference with his labors, the Prophet purposes to go into retirement for a short period— He rejoices in the eventual triumph of the cause of God—He gives the word of the Lord respecting the records to be made of baptisms for the dead.*

FORASMUCH as the Lord has revealed unto me that my enemies, both in Missouri and this State, were again in the pursuit of me; and inasmuch as they pursue me without a cause, and have not the least shadow or coloring of justice or right on their side in the getting up of their prosecutions against me; and inasmuch as their pretensions are all founded in falsehood of the blackest dye, I have thought it expedient and wisdom in me to leave the place for a short season, for my own safety and the safety of this people. I would say to all those with whom I have business, that I have left my affairs with agents and clerks who will transact all business in a prompt and proper manner, and will see that all my debts are canceled in due time, by turning out property, or otherwise, as the case may require, or as the circumstances may admit of. When I learn that the storm is fully blown over, then I will return to you again.

2. And as for the perils which I am called to pass through, they seem but a small thing to me, as the envy and wrath of man have been my common lot all the days of my life; and for what cause it seems mysterious, unless I was ordained from before the foundation of the world for some good end, or bad, as you may choose to call it. Judge ye for yourselves. God knoweth all these things, whether it be good or bad. But nevertheless, deep water is what I am wont to swim in. It all has become a second nature to me; and I feel, like Paul, to glory in tribulation; for to this day has the God of my fathers delivered me out of them all, and will deliver me from henceforth; for behold, and lo, I shall triumph over all my enemies, for the Lord God hath spoken it.

3. Let all the saints rejoice, therefore, and be exceedingly

glad; for Israel's God is their God, and he will mete out a just recompense of reward upon the heads of all their oppressors.

4. And again, verily thus saith the Lord: Let the work of my temple, and all the works which I have appointed unto you, be continued on and not cease; and let your diligence, and your perseverance, and patience, and your works be redoubled, and you shall in nowise lose your reward, saith the Lord of Hosts. And if they persecute you, so persecuted they the prophets and righteous men that were before you. For all this there is a reward in heaven.

5. And again, I give unto you a word in relation to the baptism for your dead.

6. Verily, thus saith the Lord unto you concerning your dead: When any of you are baptized for your dead, let there be a recorder, and let him be eye-witness of your baptisms; let him hear with his ears, that he may testify of a truth, saith the Lord;

7. That in all your recordings it may be recorded in heaven; whatsoever you bind on earth, may be bound in heaven; whatsoever you loose on earth, may be loosed in heaven;

8. For I am about to restore many things to the earth, pertaining to the priesthood, saith the Lord of Hosts.

9. And again, let all the records be had in order, that they may be put in the archives of my holy temple, to be held in remembrance from generation to generation, saith the Lord of Hosts.

10. I will say to all the saints, that I desired, with exceedingly great desire, to have addressed them from the stand on the subject of baptism for the dead, on the following Sabbath. But inasmuch as it is out of my power to do so, I will write the word of the Lord from time to time, on that subject, and send it to you by mail, as well as many other things.

11. I now close my letter for the present, for the want of more time; for the enemy is on the alert, and as the Savior said, the prince of this world cometh, but he hath nothing in me.

12. Behold, my prayer to God is that you all may be saved. And I subscribe myself your servant in the Lord, prophet and seer of the Church of Jesus Christ of Latter-day Saints.

JOSEPH SMITH.

This Section contains a letter by the Prophet Joseph to the Saints on the subject of baptism for the dead. In a meeting of the Relief Society, August the 31st, 1842, he made the remark, "a few very important things have been manifested to me in my absence respecting the doctrine of baptism for the dead, which I shall communicate to the Saints next Sabbath, if nothing should occur to prevent me." He did not wait, however, till the following Sabbath, but wrote this epistle on the Thursday preceding, and it was well he did, for on the Saturday he received word that the Missourians were again on the move, and the same day men well armed entered his house, and, without legal authority, searched for him. He was then at Newel K. Whitney's house, having escaped unobserved through a cornfield. In the evening the Prophet proceeded to the home of Edward Hunter, where he was safe for the time being.

The special thought which the Prophet desired to convey to the Saints at this time is expressed in paragraphs 6-9. Baptisms must be witnessed by a recorder, who can testify to the performance, as a witness, and the records must be preserved. On this subject the Prophet said in the Relief Society meeting referred to in the preceding paragraph:

"I have one remark to make respecting the baptism for the dead to suffice for the time being, until I have opportunity to discuss the subject at greater length—all persons baptized for the dead must have a recorder present, that he may be an eye-witness, to record and testify of the truth and validity of his record. It will be necessary in the Grand Council, that these things be testified to by competent witnesses. Therefore, let the recording and witnessing of baptisms for the dead be carefully attended to from this time forth. If there is any lack, it may be at the expense of our friends; they may not come forth" (*Hist. of the Church,* Vol. V., p. 141).

In an epistle written by the Prophet Joseph Smith to the "Traveling High Council and Elders of the Church of Jesus Christ of Latter-day Saints in Great Britain," dated October 19, 1840, the following in relation to baptism for the dead was revealed:

"I presume the doctrine of 'baptism for the dead' has ere this reached your ears, and may have raised some inquiries in your minds respecting the same. I cannot in this letter give you all the information you may desire on the subject; but aside from knowledge independent of the Bible, I would say that it was certainly practiced by the ancient churches; and St. Paul endeavors to prove the doctrine of the resurrection from the same, and says, 'Else what shall they do which are baptized for the dead, if the dead rise not at all? Why are they then baptized for the dead?'

"I first mentioned the doctrine in public when preaching the funeral sermon of Brother Seymour Brunson; and have since then given general instructions in the Church on the subject. The Saints have the privilege of being baptized for those of their relatives who are dead, whom they believe would have embraced the Gospel, if they had been privileged with hearing it, and who have received the Gospel in the spirit, through the instrumentality of those who have been commissioned to preach to them while in prison." (*Documentary History*, 4:231.)

SECTION 128.

AN EPISTLE *from Joseph Smith the Prophet to the Church of Jesus Christ of Latter-day Saints, containing further directions on baptism for the dead; dated at Nauvoo, Illinois, September 6, 1842.——More detailed instructions concerning the general recorder, local recorders, and their duties—Witnesses required —The keeping of records shown to be in conformity with the ordinances of the Lord—Records kept on earth as well as those kept in heaven to be used in judgment—What is bound on earth by the power of the Holy Priesthood is bound in heaven, and what is loosed here is loosed there—The baptismal font a similitude of the grave—The mission of Elijah the Prophet— Baptism for the dead a welding link between the departed fathers and the living children—The Prophet's gladsome summary of heavenly visitations to him—The voice of gladness— Glad tidings for the dead—Glad tidings from Cumorah—The voice of the Three Witnesses to the Book of Mormon—The voice of Michael, of Peter, James and John—Records of the work done for the dead to be made acceptable to the Lord.*

AS I stated to you in my letter before I left my place, that I would write to you from time to time and give you information in relation to many subjects, I now resume the subject of the baptism for the dead, as that subject seems to occupy my mind, and press itself upon my feelings the strongest, since I have been pursued by my enemies.

2. I wrote a few words of revelation to you concerning a recorder. I have had a few additional views in relation to this matter, which I now certify. That is, it was declared in my former letter that there should be a recorder, who should be eye-witness, and also to hear with his ears, that he might make a record of a truth before the Lord.

3. Now, in relation to this matter, it would be very difficult

for one recorder to be present at all times, and to do all the business. To obviate this difficulty, there can be a recorder appointed in each ward of the city, who is well qualified for taking accurate minutes; and let him be very particular and precise in taking the whole proceedings, certifying in his record that he saw with his eyes, and heard with his ears, giving the date, and names, and so forth, and the history of the whole transaction; naming also some three individuals that are present, if there be any present, who can at any time when called upon certify to the same, that in the mouth of two or three witnesses every word may be established.

4.   Then, let there be a general recorder, to whom these other records can be handed, being attended with certificates over their own signatures, certifying that the record they have made is true. Then the general church recorder can enter the record on the general church book, with the certificates and all the attending witnesses, with his own statement that he verily believes the above statement and records to be true, from his knowledge of the general character and appointment of those men by the church. And when this is done on the general church book, the record shall be just as holy, and shall answer the ordinance just the same as if he had seen with his eyes and heard with his ears, and made a record of the same on the general church book.

5.   You may think this order of things to be very particular; but let me tell you that it is only to answer the will of God, by conforming to the ordinance and preparation that the Lord ordained and prepared before the foundation of the world, for the salvation of the dead who should die without a knowledge of the gospel.

6.   And further, I want you to remember that John the Revelator was contemplating this very subject in relation to the dead, when he declared, as you will find recorded in Revelation 20:12—*And I saw the dead, small and great, stand before God; and the books were opened; and another book was opened, which is the book of life; and the dead were judged out of those things which were written in the books, according to their works.*

7.   You will discover in this quotation that the books were

opened; and another book was opened, which was the book of life; but the dead were judged out of those things which were written in the books, according to their works; consequently, the books spoken of must be the books which contained the record of their works, and refer to the records which are kept on the earth. And the book which was the book of life is the record which is kept in heaven; the principle agreeing precisely with the doctrine which is commanded you in the revelation contained in the letter which I wrote to you previous to my leaving my place—that in all your recordings it may be recorded in heaven.

8. Now, the nature of this ordinance consists in the power of the priesthood, by the revelation of Jesus Christ, wherein it is granted that whatsoever you bind on earth shall be bound in heaven, and whatsoever you loose on earth shall be loosed in heaven. Or, in other words, taking a different view of the translation, whatsoever you record on earth shall be recorded in heaven, and whatsoever you do not record on earth shall not be recorded in heaven; for out of the books shall your dead be judged, according to their own works, whether they themselves have attended to the ordinances in their own *propria persona,* or by the means of their own agents, according to the ordinance which God has prepared for their salvation from before the foundation of the world, according to the records which they have kept concerning their dead.

9. It may seem to some to be a very bold doctrine that we talk of—a power which records or binds on earth and binds in heaven. Nevertheless, in all ages of the world, whenever the Lord has given a dispensation of the priesthood to any man by actual revelation, or any set of men, this power has always been given. Hence, whatsoever those men did in authority, in the name of the Lord, and did it truly and faithfully, and kept a proper and faithful record of the same, it became a law on earth and in heaven, and could not be annulled, according to the decrees of the great Jehovah. This is a faithful saying. Who can hear it?

10. And again, for the precedent, Matthew 16:18, 19: *And I say also unto thee, That thou art Peter, and upon this rock I will build my church; and the gates of hell shall not prevail*

against it. And I will give unto thee the keys of the kingdom of heaven: and whatsoever thou shalt bind on earth shall be bound in heaven; and whatsoever thou shalt loose on earth shall be loosed in heaven.

11. Now the great and grand secret of the whole matter, and the *summum bonum* of the whole subject that is lying before us, consists in obtaining the powers of the Holy Priesthood. For him to whom these keys are given there is no difficulty in obtaining a knowledge of facts in relation to the salvation of the children of men, both as well for the dead as for the living.

12. Herein is glory and honor, and immortality and eternal life—The ordinance of baptism by water, to be immersed therein in order to answer to the likeness of the dead, that one principle might accord with the other; to be immersed in the water and come forth out of the water is in the likeness of the resurrection of the dead in coming forth out of their graves; hence, this ordinance was instituted to form a relationship with the ordinance of baptism for the dead, being in likeness of the dead.

13. Consequently, the baptismal font was instituted as a similitude of the grave, and was commanded to be in a place underneath where the living are wont to assemble, to show forth the living and the dead, and that all things may have their likeness, and that they may accord one with another—that which is earthly conforming to that which is heavenly, as Paul hath declared, 1 Corinthians 15:46, 47, and 48:

14. *Howbeit that was not first which is spiritual but that which is natural; and afterward that which is spiritual. The first man is of the earth, earthy; the second man is the Lord from heaven. As is the earthy, such are they also that are earthy; and as is the heavenly, such are they also that are heavenly.* And as are the records on the earth in relation to your dead, which are truly made out, so also are the records in heaven. This, therefore, is the sealing and binding power, and, in one sense of the word, the keys of the kingdom, which consist in the key of knowledge.

15. And now, my dearly beloved brethren and sisters, let me assure you that these are principles in relation to the dead and the living that cannot be lightly passed over, as pertaining to our salvation. For their salvation is necessary and essential to

our salvation, as Paul says concerning the fathers—that they without us cannot be made perfect—neither can we without our dead be made perfect.

16. And now, in relation to the baptism for the dead, I will give you another quotation of Paul, 1 Corinthians 15:29: *Else what shall they do which are baptized for the dead, if the dead rise not at all? Why are they then baptized for the dead?*

17. And again, in connection with this quotation I will give you a quotation from one of the prophets, who had his eye fixed on the restoration of the priesthood, the glories to be revealed in the last days, and in an especial manner this most glorious of all subjects belonging to the everlasting gospel, namely, the baptism for the dead; for Malachi says, last chapter, verses 5th and 6th: *Behold, I will send you Elijah the prophet before the coming of the great and dreadful day of the Lord: And he shall turn the heart of the fathers to the children, and the heart of the children to their fathers, lest I come and smite the earth with a curse.*

18. I might have rendered a plainer translation to this, but it is sufficiently plain to suit my purpose as it stands. It is sufficient to know, in this case, that the earth will be smitten with a curse unless there is a welding link of some kind or other between the fathers and the children, upon some subject or other —and behold what is that subject? It is the baptism for the dead. For we without them cannot be made perfect; neither can they without us be made perfect. Neither can they nor we be made perfect without those who have died in the gospel also; for it is necessary in the ushering in of the dispensation of the fulness of times, which dispensation is now beginning to usher in, that a whole and complete and perfect union, and welding together of dispensations, and keys, and powers, and glories should take place, and be revealed from the days of Adam even to the present time. And not only this, but those things which never have been revealed from the foundation of the world, but have been kept hid from the wise and prudent, shall be revealed unto babes and sucklings in this, the dispensation of the fulness of times.

19. Now, what do we hear in the gospel which we have re-

ceived? A voice of gladness! A voice of mercy from heaven; and a voice of truth out of the earth; glad tidings for the dead; a voice of gladness for the living and the dead; glad tidings of great joy. How beautiful upon the mountains are the feet of those that bring glad tidings of good things, and that say unto Zion: Behold, thy God reigneth! As the dews of Carmel, so shall the knowledge of God descend upon them!

20. And again, what do we hear? Glad tidings from Cumorah! Moroni, an angel from heaven, declaring the fulfilment of the prophets—the book to be revealed. A voice of the Lord in the wilderness of Fayette, Seneca county, declaring the three witnesses to bear record of the book! The voice of Michael on the banks of the Susquehanna, detecting the devil when he appeared as an angel of light! The voice of Peter, James, and John in the wilderness between Harmony, Susquehanna county, and Colesville, Broome county, on the Susquehanna river, declaring themselves as possessing the keys of the kingdom, and of the dispensation of the fulness of times!

21. And again, the voice of God in the chamber of old Father Whitmer, in Fayette, Seneca county, and at sundry times, and in divers places through all the travels and tribulations of this Church of Jesus Christ of Latter-day Saints! And the voice of Michael, the archangel; the voice of Gabriel, and of Raphael, and of divers angels, from Michael or Adam down to the present time, all declaring their dispensation, their rights, their keys, their honors, their majesty and glory, and the power of their priesthood; giving line upon line, precept upon precept; here a little, and there a little; giving us consolation by holding forth that which is to come, confirming our hope!

22. Brethren, shall we not go on in so great a cause? Go forward and not backward. Courage, brethren; and on, on to the victory! Let your hearts rejoice, and be exceedingly glad. Let the earth break forth into singing. Let the dead speak forth anthems of eternal praise to the King Immanuel, who hath ordained, before the world was, that which would enable us to redeem them out of their prison; for the prisoners shall go free.

23. Let the mountains shout for joy, and all ye valleys cry aloud; and all ye seas and dry lands tell the wonders of your

Eternal King! And ye rivers, and brooks, and rills, flow down with gladness. Let the woods and all the trees of the field praise the Lord; and ye solid rocks weep for joy! And let the sun, moon, and the morning stars sing together, and let all the sons of God shout for joy! And let the eternal creations declare his name forever and ever! And again I say, how glorious is the voice we hear from heaven, proclaiming in our ears, glory, and salvation, and honor, and immortality, and eternal life; kingdoms, principalities, and powers!

24.　Behold, the great day of the Lord is at hand; and who can abide the day of his coming, and who can stand when he appeareth? For he is like a refiner's fire, and like fuller's soap; and he shall sit as a refiner and purifier of silver, and he shall purify the sons of Levi, and purge them as gold and silver, that they may offer unto the Lord an offering in righteousness. Let us, therefore, as a church and a people, and as Latter-day Saints, offer unto the Lord an offering in righteousness; and let us present in his holy temple, when it is finished, a book containing the records of our dead, which shall be worthy of all acceptation.

25.　Brethren, I have many things to say to you on the subject; but shall now close for the present, and continue the subject another time. I am, as ever, your humble servant and never deviating friend,

JOSEPH SMITH.

This Section contains another letter from the Prophet on the subject of baptism for the dead, written while he was in seclusion at the home of Edward Hunter—his temporary Wartburg. The Prophet makes the following note. "The important instructions contained in the foregoing letter made a deep and solemn impression on the minds of the Saints; and they manifested their intentions to obey the instructions to the letter."

2-5.　In the preceding Section, the Prophet instructed the Saints to keep a record of Temple ordinances performed. In this letter, further instructions are given on this subject, and the information is added that it is all in accordance with preparations made, before the foundation of the world, for the salvation of the dead.

6-11.　The Prophet gives Scripture proofs for this. (1) John the Revelator saw the books opened and the dead judged out of the things which were written. (2) The power and authority of the Priesthood are such that, "whatsoever you loose on Earth shall be loosed in heaven," etc.; which means, "Whatsoever you record on Earth shall be recorded in heaven," etc.

12-15. From the subject of recording, the Prophet turns to the subject of baptism, and explains its significance. Baptism is a representation of burial and resurrection, as the Sacrament is a representation of His death.

15. *"They without us cannot be made perfect"; neither can we without our dead*] The words quoted seem to imply that the fulness of the gospel could not have been revealed to the fathers and Patriarchs of former dispensations, for the revelation of the gospel in its fulness ushers in the close of the ages, the winding-up scene, and the end cannot come until all the spirits, destined to tabernacle on this Earth, have been here; thus, they cannot be made perfect without us; neither can we without them.

As Paul says] Note that the Prophet credits this quotation from *Hebrews* to Paul. Among scholars, opinions concerning the authorship of that Epistle are divided. Some believe Apollos wrote it; others Luke, or Titus, or some other companion of Paul. Here the Spirit of Revelation ascribes the authorship to Paul. In favor of the Pauline origin it can be said that fathers of the Eastern and Alexandrian churches, in the third and second centuries, state that the "Ancients" had handed down the tradition that Paul wrote it. Clement of Alexandria, Origen, and Eusebius considered this testimony sufficient, and it must be admitted that it has a great deal more weight than a surmise in favor of Barnabas, or even Apollos, especially as there is no writing from the pen of either of them, with which the Epistle can be compared for critical purposes.

16. *Baptism for the dead*] "Else what shall they do which *are baptized for the dead?*" The Prophet quotes this from St. Paul's first letter to the Corinthians as a proof that vicarious baptism was practiced in the first Christian churches. To many Bible students this appears to be incredible, because they do not understand the revealed doctrine of baptism for the dead, and they are unable to find any sense in this Scripture passage. The Latter-day Saints are not at a similar disadvantage. To them, it is clear and instructive, because they know what the Apostle refers to. They know that in his day as in ours, faithful members of the Church were baptized for their departed kindred. They are aware that this practice continued in the churches for some time, for Tertullian, in the third century, referred to it as existing then. It furnished a striking argument in favor of the reality of the resurrection, the very point Paul has in view, because, if there were no resurrection, baptism for the dead would be an empty ceremony, void of virtue and merit. "If the dead rise not,"—this is the argument—"why are you baptizing for the dead?"

But may not baptism "for the dead" mean baptism "on the graves of the dead"? No, "*for* the dead" means "instead of," "for the benefit of" the dead.*

But may not "baptism" for the dead mean "persecution to death," "martyrdom?" No, for persecution does not prove the resurrection, and that is the subject Paul is treating on. But if God had revealed the doctrine of vicarious baptism for the benefit of the dead, that would indeed be an unanswerable argument in favor of the resurrection.

17. *Behold I will send you Elijah*] This promise was given in a Revelation received September 21st, 1823 (see Sec. 2). It was not understood then. Here the meaning of it is made clear.

20-21. In these paragraphs the Prophet reviews, enraptured, the wonderful story of the origin of the work in which the Saints were engaged. Scene after scene is unrolled before him, from the uncovering of the treasures of the Hill Cumorah to the last glorious Revelations on the salvation† of the dead;—from the unveiling of the ancient records of the Nephites to the opening of the books from which mankind shall be judged.

° The Greek preposition hyper with a genitive means "instead of," or "in behalf of," as in I. Thess. 5:10, where it is said that Christ died for us (hyper hemon); or "because of," as in I. Cor. 15:3. Those to whom Paul refers were baptized instead of the dead, not over their graves.

† "The latest word upon this interesting theme comes in the form of a 'Vision of the Redemption of the Dead,' a manifestation vouchsafed to President Joseph F. Smith, only a short while before his death. It is a description of the Savior's visit to the World of Spirits, as recorded in the First Epistle of Peter (3:18-20). The beholder of the vision says:

" 'I saw the hosts of the dead, both small and great, and there were gathered together in one place an innumerable company of the spirits of the just ° ° ° They were filled with joy and gladness, and were rejoicing together because the day of their deliverance was at hand ° ° ° the Son of God appeared ° ° ° and ° ° ° preached to them the everlasting gospel, the doctrine of the resurrection, and the redemption of mankind from the fall and from individual sin, on condition of repentance.

" 'I perceived that the Lord went not in person among the wicked and disobedient who had rejected the truth, to teach them; but behold from among the righteous He organized His forces and appointed messengers, clothed with power and authority, and commissioned them to go forth and carry the light of the gospel to them that were in darkness, even to all the spirits of men.

" 'I beheld that the faithful elders of this dispensation, when they depart from mortal life, continue their labors in the preaching of the gospel ° ° ° among those who are in darkness and under the bondage of sin in the great world of the spirits of the dead.'

"The new light here thrown upon the subject proceeds from the declaration that when the Savior visited the inhabitants of the Spirit world, it was by proxy and not in person so far as the wicked were concerned. He ministered to the righteous directly, and to the unrighteous indirectly, sending His servants bearing the authority of the Priesthood and duly commissioned to speak and act in His name and stead. President Smith's Pronouncement is a modification of the view commonly taken, that the Savior's personal ministry was to both classes of spirits (Compare III. Nephi 15:21-24)." (Orson F. Whitney, *Saturday Night Thoughts*, pp. 292-293. See *Gospel Doctrine*, pp. 596-601.)

20. *The voice of Peter, James, and John*] Referring to the restoration of the Melchizedek Priesthood, some time shortly before the organization of the Church.

21. *In the chamber of old Father Whitmer*] The Church was organized there.

Raphael] From the Revelations we know that Adam is Michael, and Noah, Gabriel; John the Baptist is called an angel (See Sec. 13). So is Moroni. Who Raphael was in the flesh is not revealed. In the Apocryphal book called Tobit (12-15) he is represented as saying, "I am Raphael, one of the seven holy angels, which present the prayers of the Saints, and which go in and out before the glory of the Holy One."

23. This verse, whether the sentiments expressed or the language in which they are clothed is considered, is worthy to stand side by side with the most exalted poetic compositions of Hebrew prophets. It is a fitting conclusion to the main theme of the letter, and an appropriate prelude to the announcement that follows, "Behold the great day of the Lord is at hand."

SECTION 129.

REVELATION *given to Joseph Smith the Prophet, at Nauvoo, Illinois, February 9, 1843, making known the three grand keys by which good or bad angels or spirits may be distinguished.—— Two kinds of beings besides mortals—Resurrected personages having bodies of flesh and bones—Disembodied spirits and spirits that have never been embodied—Means of detection.*

THERE are two kinds of beings in heaven, namely: Angels, who are resurrected personages, having bodies of flesh and bones—

2. For instance, Jesus said: *Handle me and see, for a spirit hath not flesh and bones, as ye see me have.*

3. Secondly: The spirits of just men made perfect, they who are not resurrected, but inherit the same glory.

4. When a messenger comes saying he has a message from God, offer him your hand and request him to shake hands with you.

5. If he be an angel he will do so, and you will feel his hand.

6. If he be the spirit of a just man made perfect he will come in his glory; for that is the only way he can appear—

7. Ask him to shake hands with you, but he will not move, because it is contrary to the order of heaven for a just man to deceive; but he will still deliver his message.

8. If it be the devil as an angel of light, when you ask him to shake hands he will offer you his hand, and you will not feel anything; you may therefore detect him.

9. These are three grand keys whereby you may know whether any administration is from God.

About the time this Revelation was received, a man came to the Prophet Joseph and told him he had seen an angel. He described his dress. The Prophet told him that he was mistaken, for in heaven there was no such dress as he had described. The man then became furious and commanded fire to come down from heaven and consume the Prophet and his house (*Hist. of the Church,* Vol. V., p. 267).

It should be noted that this Revelation came about a year before so-called spirit-rapping had been discovered, or invented, by the Fox family at Hydeville, N. Y., in March, 1844, giving birth to Spiritism with all its delusions. By this Revelation the Saints were forewarned and therefore saved from being deceived by false pretensions or by evil spirits.

Most Bible students have a very imperfect understanding of the nature of angels. They regard them as superior to man in intelligence, without material bodies, sexless, enjoying perpetual youth and immortality. Farther than that, the idea formed of angelic beings does not, as a rule, go. How clear and rational the information conveyed in this Revelation!

There has been considerable confusion arise because of the statement by the Prophet in this revelation that there are in heaven two kinds of beings, namely "angels who are resurrected personages, having bodies of flesh and bones * * * 2nd, spirits of just men made perfect—they who are not resurrected, but inherit the same glory." * * * When a messenger comes, saying he has a message from God, offer him your hand, and request him to shake hands with you. If he be an angel, he will do so, and you will feel his hand. If he be the spirit of a just man made perfect, he will come in his glory; for that is the only way he can appear." From this the thought has been conveyed to the minds of some that a personage cannot be an angel unless he is resurrected and has a body of flesh and bones. Any messenger sent from the presence of the Lord with a message is an angel. This term has even been applied to translated beings.

"In the broadest sense, any being who acts as a messenger for our Heavenly Father, is an angel, be he a God, a resurrected man, or the spirit of a just man; and the term is so used in all these senses in the ancient scriptures. In the stricter and more limited sense, an angel is, as the Prophet Joseph Smith states, a resurrected personage, having a body of flesh and bones; but it must be remembered that *none* of the angels who appeared to men before the death of the Savior could be of that class, for none of them was resurrected. He was the first-fruits of them that slept. He Himself appeared often to His servants before he took His mortal body; for instance, to the brother of Jared, to Abraham, to Moses, to the seventy Elders and to many others." (President George Q. Cannon in the *Juvenile Instructor,* Vol. 26; January 15, 1891.)

2. From what is here stated concerning the nature of the different classes of beings in heaven, the rules given in paragraphs four to eight are easily comprehended.

SECTION 130.

IMPORTANT ITEMS OF INSTRUCTION *given by Joseph Smith the Prophet, at Ramus, Illinois, April 2, 1843.——When the Savior appears he will be in his true form, that of a man—The abode of the angels—The earth in its sanctified and immortalized condition—Prophecy of great difficulties involving much bloodshed to begin in South Carolina—Time of the Lord's coming not definitely made known—Intelligence acquired in this life will abide with its possessor—The law decreed in heaven, that blessings are obtained only by obedience to the laws upon which they are predicated—The Father and the Son possess bodies of flesh and bones—The Holy Ghost a personage of spirit.*

WHEN the Savior shall appear we shall see him as he is. We shall see that he is a man like ourselves.

2. And that same sociality which exists among us here will exist among us there, only it will be coupled with eternal glory, which glory we do not now enjoy.

3. John 14:23—The appearing of the Father and the Son, in that verse, is a personal appearance; and the idea that the Father and the Son dwell in a man's heart is an old sectarian notion, and is false.

On the 2nd of April, 1843, the Prophet Joseph attended a meeting at which Orson Hyde spoke and, alluding to the coming of the Savior, said, "When He shall appear, we shall be like Him, etc. He will appear on a white horse as a warrior, and may be we shall have some of the same spirit. Our God is a warrior. It is our privilege to have the Father and Son dwelling in our hearts."

At dinner time the Prophet called the attention of Orson Hyde to these statements and told him that he would offer some corrections. Orson Hyde replied that they would be thankfully received, whereupon the Prophet gave the explanations contained in these paragraphs, first privately and afterwards in the meeting.

2. *That same sociality*] The Scriptures teach us that the social instinct of man remains after death. Our Lord assured the Jews, who boasted of their relationship with Abraham, that "many shall come from the east and west, and shall sit down with Abraham, Isaac, and Jacob, in the kingdom of heaven (Matt. 8:11). He also says to His disciples, "I appoint unto you a kingdom, as my Father hath appointed unto me; that ye may eat and drink at my table in my kingdom, and sit on thrones judging the twelve tribes of Israel" (Luke 22:29, 30). Lazarus, after death, had the place of honor at a social function* where Abraham presided (Luke 16:19-31). Sociability here is necessary to happiness. Even the hermit is happy in the thought that there is somebody who knows of his seclusion and admires his asceticism. It may safely be concluded that it is as necessary to happiness hereafter. Nobody cares to sing the Hallelujah Chorus all alone, or to shout Hosannah! by himself, on either side of the veil.

3. *Personal appearance*] The verse referred to reads, "If a man loves me, he will keep my word: and my Father will love him, and we will come unto him and make our abode with him." This, the Prophet says, does not mean that the Father and the Son will dwell in the "heart" of men, as some imagine. And he is right. It is the Spirit of God that dwells in man, not the Father, or the Son.

God dwelt among the people of Israel; His abode was the Tabernacle, and afterwards, the Temple, and His presence was manifested in the glory which rested between the cherubim on the Mercy Seat. In a similar manner He dwells in the hearts of the sanctified, by His Holy Spirit. But when the Father, or the Son, appears, he does so as a personage with the very body in the image of which man was made.

4. In answer to the question—Is not the reckoning of God's time, angel's time, prophet's time, and man's time, according to the planet on which they reside?

5. I answer, Yes. But there are no angels who minister to this earth but those who do belong or have belonged to it.

When the Prophet, at the little dinner party, had given his views on these subjects, questions were asked and a conversation ensued. The first question was answered in these verses.

---

* "Abraham's bosom" is by commentators considered to be an expression depicting the banquet of Paradise (Numb. 11:12; John 13:23).

4. *God's time, angel's time, etc.*] The truth is here revealed that time on each inhabited globe is measured according to the conditions existing. Astronomers say the same thing. They tell us that a year on Mercury, for instance, is equal to only eighty-eight of our days, that being the time in which that planet completes its revolution around the sun. On the other hand, Jupiter's year is equal to 4,332 of our days, while that of Saturn equals 10,767 days, or twenty-nine and a half of our years. The year of Mars equals 687, and that of Venus 224 Earth-days.

God's time, we read in the Pearl of Great Price (Book of Abraham 3:1-9), is measured by the revolutions of Kolob, the central orb of the system of worlds to which our solar system belongs, and a day to Him is one thousand of our years. This is in harmony with Psalm 90:4 and II. Pet. 3:8.

Prophet's time] The prophets count days and years as the people among whom they live and to whom they speak, or write. The people of Bible times and lands, it is thought, measured the years according to the phases of the moon and counted 354 days in a year, instead of 365, as now, and the prophets, of course, used the same time measure.

5. The striking information is added that no angels are sent to administer to this Earth except those who "belong, or have belonged to it."

"We have no doubt of the correctness of the statement of the Prophet Joseph Smith that 'there are no angels that minister to this earth but those who do belong or have belonged to it;' but that does not necessarily imply that they did not belong to the earth before they took a mortal body. In our opinion they belonged to this earth from the time of its creation, when they covenanted to come and take bodies thereon, at the time that the morning stars sang together and all the sons of God shouted for joy. In just this same way was Jesus 'the Lamb slain from before the foundation of the world.'

"We are taught to believe that Adam was the first man who took a body on this earth. There was no death before the fall. Who, then, was the angel who taught him the law of sacrifice, or of faith and baptism, or who was the cherubim with the flaming sword who guarded the tree of life? We cannot admit that the scriptures are false, and that these beings were not angels; neither can we admit that the Savior was not the first-fruits of the resurrection. Therefore, we are forced to the conclusion that the word 'angel' is used in the scriptures for any heavenly being bearing God's message or fulfilling His commands; and, further, that all beings who were created with the design that they should inhabit this earth, belong to it, and to no other planet. Taking this view, all difficulty vanishes. On the other hand, if this is not the case, how can the sayings of Joseph and the scriptures—the Bible, the Book of Mormon and modern revelation—be harmonized, as these all declare that angels were frequent visitors to this earth from the time of the creation to the days of the coming of the Redeemer." (President George Q. Cannon, *Juvenile Instructor*, January 15, 1891.)

6. The angels do not reside on a planet like this earth;

7. But they reside in the presence of God, on a globe like a sea of glass and fire, where all things for their glory are manifest, past, present, and future, and are continually before the Lord.

7. *Reside in the presence of God*] The Prophet is speaking of angels who have once belonged to this Earth; they reside on a glorified globe somewhere near where God dwells.

8. The place where God resides is a great Urim and Thummim.

9. This earth, in its sanctified and immortal state, will be made like unto crystal and will be a Urim and Thummim to the inhabitants who dwell thereon, whereby all things pertaining to an inferior kingdom, or all kingdoms of a lower order, will be manifest to those who dwell on it; and this earth will be Christ's.

8. The statement made in the 7th verse leads to two remarkable revelations: (1) God dwells on a glorified globe, which is a Urim and Thummim;

9. (2) this Earth will become a Urim and Thummim. It will then be a fit dwelling place for celestial beings.

10. Then the white stone mentioned in Revelation 2:17, will become a Urim and Thummim to each individual who receives one, whereby things pertaining to a higher order of kingdoms will be made known;

11. And a white stone is given to each of those who come into the celestial kingdom, whereon is a new name written, which no man knoweth save he that receiveth it. The new name is the key word.

10-11. Furthermore, each inhabitant on the glorified Earth will be given a "white stone"—a Urim and Thummim, whereby all things pertaining to a higher order of kingdoms will be made known.

12. I prophesy, in the name of the Lord God, that the commencement of the difficulties which will cause much bloodshed previous to the coming of the Son of Man will be in South Carolina.

13. It may probably arise through the slave question. This a voice declared to me, while I was praying earnestly on the subject, December 25th, 1832.

12-13. The subject of conversation now turns to the remarkable prophecy on war given on the 25th of December, 1832 (See Sec. 87). The statement is reiterated that the trouble would begin in South Carolina and that the paramount issue would be the slave question. Note that the series of wars, beginning with the Civil War of the United States, is said to be "previous to the coming of the Son of Man"; that is to say, shortly before His advent.

14. I was once praying very earnestly to know the time of the coming of the Son of Man, when I heard a voice repeat the following:

15. Joseph, my son, if thou livest until thou art eighty-five years old, thou shalt see the face of the Son of Man; therefore let this suffice, and trouble me no more on this matter.

16. I was left thus, without being able to decide whether this coming referred to the beginning of the millennium or to some previous appearing, or whether I should die and thus see his face.

17. I believe the coming of the Son of Man will not be any sooner than that time.

14-17. The mention of the coming of the Son of Man reminds the Prophet of an incident which he relates. He was once praying to know when the Lord would come, just as Christ's disciples on one occasion desired to know, "When shall these things be?" Our Savior did not enlighten the Twelve on the time for His coming (See Matthew 24:36) but He spoke of the signs by which they would know that the day was drawing near (Luke 21:31). Nor did God satisfy Joseph's curiosity concerning the time, but He gave him the remarkable answer recorded in the 15th verse: "If thou livest until thou art 85 years old, thou shalt see the face of the Son of Man." At the April Conference, 1843, the Prophet spoke of the preparations foretold in the Scriptures:

"Judah must return, Jerusalem must be rebuilt, and the Temple, and water come out from under the Temple and the waters of the Dead Sea be healed. It will take some time to rebuild the walls of the city and the temple, etc., and all this must be done before the Son of Man will make His appearance" (*Hist. of the Church,* Vol. V., p. 337).

16. *I was left thus*] At the April Conference referred to, the Prophet says, "I took the liberty to conclude that if I did live to that time, He would make His appearance. But I do not say whether He will make His appearance [on Earth] or I shall go where He is" (*Hist. of the Church,* Vol. V., p. 336).

18. Whatever principle of intelligence we attain unto in this life, it will rise with us in the resurrection.

19.   And if a person gains more knowledge and intelligence in this life through his diligence and obedience than another, he will have so much the advantage in the world to come.

18, 19.   Intelligence * * * will rise with us. The Prophet teaches us that, "A man is saved no faster than he gets knowledge, for if he does not get knowledge, he will be brought into captivity by some evil power in the other world, as evil spirits will have more knowledge, and consequently more power, than many men who are on the Earth" (*Hist. of the Church*, Vol. IV., p. 588). It would be useless, as far as life after death is concerned, to study and gain knowledge, if death ended it all.

20.   There is a law, irrevocably decreed in heaven before the foundations of this world, upon which all blessings are predicated—

21.   And when we obtain any blessing from God, it is by obedience to that law upon which it is predicated.

20-1.   This is indisputable. If we want to live we must conform to the physical laws by obedience to which life is sustained. We must take nourishment, exercise, keep clean, etc. If we desire to become musicians, painters, orators, we must obey certain laws by which the respective talents are developed. In the same way, if we desire to obtain any spiritual blessings, we must obey the laws upon which they are predicated.

22.   The Father has a body of flesh and bones as tangible as man's; the Son also; but the Holy Ghost has not a body of flesh and bones, but is a personage of Spirit. Were it not so, the Holy Ghost could not dwell in us.

23.   A man may receive the Holy Ghost, and it may descend upon him and not tarry with him.

22-3.   See Lectures on Faith, 5:1-3. If we believe the Scriptures that Jesus Christ ascended with a body of flesh and bones, and that He dwells with the Father, it is not difficult to accept the fact that the Father also has a material body, for the Son is His "express image" (Heb. 1:3).

SECTION 131.

INSTRUCTIONS *by Joseph Smith the Prophet, given at Ramus, Illinois, May 16 and 17, 1843. See History of the Church, vol. 5, p. 392, 393.——Degrees in the celestial glory—Significance of the new and everlasting covenant of marriage—The more sure word of prophecy—Impossibility of a man being saved in ignorance—Spirit is matter.*

IN the celestial glory there are three heavens or degrees;

2. And in order to obtain the highest, a man must enter into this order of the priesthood [meaning the new and everlasting covenant of marriage];

3. And if he does not, he cannot obtain it.

4. He may enter into the other, but that is the end of his kingdom; he cannot have an increase.

5. (May 17th, 1843.) The more sure word of prophecy means a man's knowing that he is sealed up unto eternal life by revelation and the spirit of prophecy, through the power of the Holy Priesthood.

6. It is impossible for a man to be saved in ignorance.

7. There is no such thing as immaterial matter. All spirit is matter, but it is more fine or pure, and can only be discerned by purer eyes;

8. We cannot see it; but when our bodies are purified we shall see that it is all matter.

Ramus, where this Revelation was received, was a settlement situated about 22 miles southeast of Nauvoo. The Prophet often visited this place and preached some powerful discourses there.

On the 16th of May, 1843, a little company, consisting of Joseph Smith, George Miller, William Clayton, Eliza and Lydia Partridge, and J. M. Smith, went to Ramus. The Prophet and William Clayton stayed at Benjamin F. Johnson's over night. Before retiring, the little party of friends engaged in conversation on spiritual topics. The Prophet told them that "except a man and his wife enter into an everlasting covenant and be married for eternity, while in this probation, by the power and authority of the holy Priesthood, they will cease to increase when they die; that is, they will not have any children after the resurrection." Then he spoke of the unpardonable sin, explaining that it consists in shedding innocent blood, or being accessory thereto. "All other sins," he said, "will be visited with judgment in the flesh, the spirit being delivered to the buffetings of Satan until the day of the Lord Jesus." Then he spoke of the three heavens in the celestial glory, as recorded in the first four verses of this Revelation. See also footnote, page 285.

2. *The new and everlasting covenant*] The new and everlasting covenant is the fulness of the Gospel, in other words, the sum total of all the

covenants, contracts, bonds, obligations, etc. that belong to the Gospel. Marriage for time and eternity is not *the* new and everlasting covenant, but one of the covenants which belong to the new and everlasting covenant.

On the 17th of May the Prophet preached a discourse on II. Pet. 1, and showed that knowledge is power. Among the truths announced at this time was that recorded in the 5th and 6th verses of this Revelation.

In the evening the Prophet went to hear a Methodist preach. After the sermon he offered some corrections. On Gen. 2:7 he observed that it ought to read, "God breathed into Adam his [that is, Adam's] spirit or breath of life;" but when the word *ruach* applies to Eve, it should be translated "lives."

He added the truths recorded in the 7th and 8th verses of this Revelation.

GENERAL NOTES

On his return home from Ramus, on the 18th of May, 1843, the Prophet took dinner with Judge Stephen A. Douglas, at Carthage, and gave him, at his request, a detailed account of the persecutions the Saints had suffered. He concluded his narrative with a prophecy which B. H. Roberts considers "one of the most remarkable prophecies either in ancient or modern times" (*Hist. of the Church,* Vol. V., p. 395). The Prophet concluded as follows:

"Judge, you will aspire to the presidency of the United States; and if ever you turn your hand against me or the Latter-day Saints, you will feel the weight of the hand of the Almighty upon you; and you will live to see and know that I have testified the truth to you; for the conversation of his day will stick to you through life."

Judge Douglas did aspire to the presidency so effectively that, on the 23rd of June, 1860, he was nominated by the Democratic party. Judging from appearances, his election was sure, for his party, in the preceding election, polled over half a million votes more than the opposing parties. But the Judge failed miserably. On the 12th of June, 1857, he turned his hand against the Latter-day Saints, in spite of the warning of the Prophet, when, in a speech delivered at Springfield, Ill., he accused the Latter-day Saints, then living in Utah, of all the crimes known to the penal code, well knowing that he did so falsely, to gain favor among the enemies of the Church. The result was as the Prophet had told him would be the case, he was defeated. Abraham Lincoln carried 18 States; Breckinridge, 11; Bell, 3; and Judge Douglas, only *one!* Less than a year after his nomination he died, disappointed, heartbroken, only 48 years of age (*Hist. of the Church,* Vol. V., pp. 393-8). The prophecy was fulfilled to the letter, and, incidentally, the Lord demonstrated to the world that He recognized the Church in the Valleys of the Mountains as His people; for it was because of his attitude towards the Saints there that he sealed his own doom.

SECTION 132.

REVELATION *given through Joseph Smith the Prophet, at Nauvoo, Illinois, recorded July 12, 1843, relating to the new and everlasting covenant, including the eternity of the marriage covenant, as also plurality of wives.——The Prophet's inquiry of the Lord—He is told to prepare himself to receive the new and everlasting covenant—Conditions of this law—The power of the Holy Priesthood instituted by the Lord must be operative in ordinances to be in effect beyond the grave—Marriage by secular authority is of effect during mortality only—Though the form of marriage should make it appear to be for time and eternity, the ordinance is not valid beyond the grave unless solemnized by the authority of the Holy Priesthood as the Lord directs—Marriage duly authorized for time and eternity to be attended by surpassing blessings—Essentials for the attainment of the status of godhood—The meaning of eternal lives—Plurality of wives acceptable only when commanded by the Lord—The sin of adultery—Commandment to Emma Smith, wife of the Prophet.*

VERILY, thus saith the Lord unto you my servant Joseph, that inasmuch as you have inquired of my hand to know and understand wherein I, the Lord, justified my servants Abraham, Isaac, and Jacob, as also Moses, David and Solomon, my servants, as touching the principle and doctrine of their having many wives and concubines—

2. Behold, and lo, I am the Lord thy God, and will answer thee as touching this matter.

This Revelation is dated the 12th of July, 1843. William Clayton, who was Temple Recorder and private clerk of the Prophet Joseph at that time, relates the following:

"On the morning of the 12th of July, 1843, Joseph and Hyrum Smith came into the office of the upper story of the 'Brick-store,' on the bank of the Mississippi River. They were talking of the subject of plural marriage, [and] Hyrum said to Joseph, 'If you will write the Revelation on celestial marriage, I will take and read it to Emma, and I believe I can convince her of its truth, and you will hereafter have peace.' Joseph smiled and remarked, 'You do not know Emma as well as I do.' Hyrum repeated his opinion, and further remarked, 'The doctrine is so plain, I can convince any reasonable man or woman of its truth, purity, and heavenly origin,' or words to that effect. * * * Joseph and Hyrum then sat down, and Joseph commenced to dictate the Revelation on Celestial Marriage, and I wrote it, sentence by sentence, as he dictated. After the whole was written, Joseph asked me to read it through slowly and carefully, which I did, and he pronounced it correct" (*Hist. Rec.* pp. 225-6).

This was not the first mention of the subject among the Saints. Sarah Ann Kimball and many others knew of it in 1842, and Joseph B. Noble heard of it in the fall of 1840. Orson Pratt says that the Prophet Joseph, in the forepart of 1832, while he was living at the house of Father Johnson at Hiram, Ohio, told Church members that he had enquired of the Lord concerning this doctrine, and received the answer that it was true, but that the time to practice it had not come (*Discourse by Orson Pratt,* Salt Lake City, October 7th, 1869). Consequently, the Law of the Church remained as stated in Doctrine and Covenants 42:22, and as it is to-day, "Thou shalt love thy wife with all thy heart, and shall cleave unto her and none else."

The Revelation is divided into two parts. The first, comprising vv. 3-33, deals mainly with the principle of celestial marriage, or marriage for time and all eternity; the second, comprising the remaining verses, deals with plural marriage. The doctrine of celestial marriage remains in force; the practice of plural marriage was abandoned by the acceptancy by the Church, in Conference assembled October 6th, 1890, of the *Manifesto* of President Woodruff.

Section 132 contains (1) an introductory statement (1-2); (2) a reminder to the Prophet that knowledge demands obedience (3-6); (3) a definition of the celestial law (7-14); and (4) how the law applies to marriage covenants (15-20); (5) a demand for obedience (21-7); (6) the Law of the Priesthood (28-33); (7) the doctrine of plural marriage (34-40); (8) a declaration that plurality of wives is not adultery (41-9); (9) that it is a sacrifice (50-7); (10) that it is a law of the Priesthood (58-66).

1. INTRODUCTORY STATEMENT.

1-2. From this introductory statement it is evident that the Prophet had made the question of marriage a subject of earnest prayer, as he did with matters concerning which he was perplexed and desired to know the truth. He did not understand how the Patriarchs, and David and Solomon could find favor with the Lord, while living in a manner contrary to certain modern moral standards, and he asked the Lord for light. Elder B. H. Roberts (*Hist. of the Church,* Vol. V., Intr., p. 29) suggests that it was in the year 1831, when the Prophet was studying the lives of the Patriarchs in the Old Testament, in the course of his Bible revision, that he was led to offer the prayer referred to in the first verse, and received the answer contained in this Section, though it was not then committed to writing.

3. Therefore, prepare thy heart to receive and obey the instructions which I am about to give unto you; for all those who have this law revealed unto them must obey the same.

4. For behold, I reveal unto you a new and an everlasting covenant; and if ye abide not that covenant, then ye are damned; for no one can reject this covenant and be permitted to enter into my glory.

5. For all who will have a blessing at my hands shall abide the law which was appointed for that blessing, and the conditions thereof, as were instituted from before the foundation of the world.

6. And as pertaining to the new and everlasting covenant, it was instituted for the fulness of my glory; and he that receiveth a fulness thereof must and shall abide the law, or he shall be damned, saith the Lord God.

2. KNOWLEDGE DEMANDS OBEDIENCE.

3-6. The truth is here emphasized that when the Lord reveals a law, man must obey it. Knowledge entails this responsibility. God may, as Paul expresses it, "wink at" the time of ignorance (Acts 17:30), but when the ignorance is removed, obedience is expected.

3. *Prepare thy heart*] That is the first step. God demands the obedience that comes from the "heart." He demands obedience as a result of affection.

4. *A new and everlasting covenant*] The marriage covenant had, for many centuries, been considered valid only "till death doth us part"; now a new covenant was about to be revealed, which would cover both eternity and time. It would be everlasting as well as new. It is new; and yet, it is as old as the gospel; it is as old as the plan of salvation adopted in the Council of Heaven, before the foundations of the world were laid (v. 5). It is part of that plan, that covenant, of which Jesus Christ is the Representative and Mediator.

*If ye abide not that covenant * * * damned*] That is to say, when the eternity of the marriage covenant has been revealed, those who reject that revelation and neglect to enter married life through the holy Priesthood, in which alone the authority to seal for eternity is vested, will be "damned." Their damnation will consist in not being permitted to enter into "my," that is, celestial glory.

This verse has sometimes been supposed to refer to plural marriage. But that is not the case. It refers to celestial marriage—marriage for eternity.

6. *For the fulness of my glory*] The eternal marriage covenant is

precedent to increase, to eternal posterity, and as our Lord is the Head of the race, man's posterity, ever increasing, means to Him eternal glory, power, and dominion. Isaiah had this in view, when he said, "When thou shalt make his soul an offering for sin, *he shall see his seed,* he shall prolong his days, and the pleasure of the Lord shall prosper in his hand" (Is. 53:10). The redeemed are his seed, for they belong to Him. By not entering into an eternal marriage covenant, according to celestial law, we neglect to contribute our share to the fulness of the glory of our blessed Lord and Redeemer, because there can be no eternal increase outside that law. What difference is there between deliberately taking a course that ends in no further increase in eternity, and the course taken by many who already in this life are guilty of what has been called "race suicide"?

7. And verily I say unto you, that the conditions of this law are these: All covenants, contracts, bonds, obligations, oaths, vows, performances, connections, associations, or expectations, that are not made and entered into and sealed by the Holy Spirit of promise, of him who is anointed, both as well for time and for all eternity, and that too most holy, by revelation and commandment through the medium of mine anointed, whom I have appointed on the earth to hold this power (and I have appointed unto my servant Joseph to hold this power in the last days, and there is never but one on the earth at a time on whom this power and the keys of this priesthood are conferred), are of no efficacy, virtue, or force in and after the resurrection from the dead; for all contracts that are not made unto this end have an end when men are dead.

8. Behold, mine house is a house of order, saith the Lord God, and not a house of confusion.

9. Will I accept of an offering, saith the Lord, that is not made in my name?

10. Or will I receive at your hands that which I have not appointed?

11. And will I appoint unto you, saith the Lord, except it be by law, even as I and my Father ordained unto you, before the world was?

12. I am the Lord thy God; and I give unto you this commandment—that no man shall come unto the Father but by me or by my word, which is my law, saith the Lord.

13. And everything that is in the world, whether it be or-

dained of men, by thrones, or principalities, or powers, or things of name, whatsoever they may be, that are not by me or by my word, saith the Lord, shall be thrown down, and shall not remain after men are dead, neither in nor after the resurrection, saith the Lord your God.

14. For whatsoever things remain are by me; and whatsoever things are not by me shall be shaken and destroyed.

3. THE CELESTIAL LAW.

7-14. The celestial law is here explained. All covenants, agreements, promises, etc., not entered into for eternity are of no force after death. Only the covenants that are sealed by the Holy Spirit of Promise, through one who holds divine authority, remain in force after death.

7. *Him who is anointed*] Refers to the President of the Church, who holds the keys of the kingdom of God on Earth.

*But one * * * at a time*] Only one man at a time holds this authority. He may delegate others to act for him, but he remains responsible for the administration of the kingdom. For "mine house is a house of order" (v. 8).

13. *Everything that is in the world * * * shall not remain*] The important truth is here taught that all institutions in this world, not founded on divine law but erected by human ingenuity, cease to exist on this side of the veil. Man-made governments are obliterated, as are the sand castles children build on the tide-swept beach. Man-made religions and churches are swallowed up in death. Not a trace of them will be seen on the shores of eternity. Social customs and habits not sanctioned by God, will not continue. On the other hand, all institutions founded on the Word of God will remain throughout all eternity. The Church will remain. The family will remain. All the organizations of which God is the author are eternal (v. 14).

15. Therefore, if a man marry him a wife in the world, and he marry her not by me nor by my word, and he covenant with her so long as he is in the world and she with him, their covenant and marriage are not of force when they are dead, and when they are out of the world; therefore, they are not bound by any law when they are out of the world.

16. Therefore, when they are out of the world they neither marry nor are given in marriage; but are appointed angels in heaven; which angels are ministering servants, to minister for those who are worthy of a far more, and an exceeding, and an eternal weight of glory.

17. For these angels did not abide my law; therefore, they cannot be enlarged, but remain separately and singly, without exaltation, in their saved condition, to all eternity; and from henceforth are not gods, but are angels of God forever and ever.

18. And again, verily I say unto you, if a man marry a wife, and make a covenant with her for time and for all eternity, if that covenant is not by me or by my word, which is my law, and is not sealed by the Holy Spirit of promise, through him whom I have anointed and appointed unto this power, then it is not valid neither of force when they are out of the world, because they are not joined by me, saith the Lord, neither by my word; when they are out of the world it cannot be received there, because the angels and the gods are appointed there, by whom they cannot pass; they cannot, therefore, inherit my glory; for my house is a house of order, saith the Lord God.

19. And again, verily I say unto you, if a man marry a wife by my word, which is my law, and by the new and everlasting covenant, and it is sealed unto them by the Holy Spirit of promise, by him who is anointed, unto whom I have appointed this power and the keys of this priesthood; and it shall be said unto them— Ye shall come forth in the first resurrection; and if it be after the first resurrection, in the next resurrection; and shall inherit thrones, kingdoms, principalities, and powers, dominions, all heights and depths—then shall it be written in the Lamb's Book of Life, that he shall commit no murder whereby to shed innocent blood, and if ye abide in my covenant, and commit no murder whereby to shed innocent blood, it shall be done unto them in all things whatsoever my servant hath put upon them, in time, and through all eternity; and shall be of full force when they are out of the world; and they shall pass by the angels, and the gods, which are set there, to their exaltation and glory in all things, as hath been sealed upon their heads, which glory shall be a fulness and a continuation of the seeds forever and ever.

20. Then shall they be gods, because they have no end; therefore shall they be from everlasting to everlasting, because they continue; then shall they be above all, because all things are subject unto them. Then shall they be gods, because they have all power, and the angels are subject unto them.

4. The Celestial Law Applied to Marriage.

15-20. From the preceding paragraphs (7-14) it follows that a marriage contract, entered into by worldly authority alone, ends at death. It is binding and perfectly legal and honorable as far as this life is concerned, but it is dissolved by the grim reaper's work. Nor is it sufficient for a man and a woman to make a private contract on the supposition that such an agreement will be binding for eternity (v. 18). The covenant must be sealed by the Holy Spirit of Promise, through him who is divinely authorized to do so. Then it is valid for eternity. Then it is a celestial marriage (v. 19).

Note the incomprehensible and immeasurable glory and exaltation that are the attendants in eternity on celestial marriage, provided the contracting parties live worthy and pure lives.

16. *Appointed angels*] Those who do not enter their family relations under the celestial law remain single in eternity; for there "they neither marry, nor are given in marriage." They are appointed *angels;* that is, "messengers," with the special duty to minister to those who, under the celestial law, are worthy of a greater exaltation.

"He [God] has revealed to us * * * that marriage is destined for eternity as well as time—that the marriage covenant between male and female must be entered into in this life, and the ordinance performed here by those whom God has appointed and ordained to hold the keys and authority to seal on earth that it may be sealed in heaven; for in heaven there is neither marrying nor giving in marriage; no such thing can be attended to there. Now, persons among the Latter-day Saints who do not enter this covenant of marriage, but prefer to lead a single life, can not enjoy all that fulness of exaltation which will be possessed by those who have this covenant sealed upon them. They might not have forfeited the right to have wives by which only they could have a posterity in the eternal worlds. Who will be the subjects in the kingdom which they will rule who are exalted in the celestial kingdom of our God? Will they reign over their neighbor's children? Oh, no! Over whom will they reign? Their own children, their own posterity will be the citizens of their kingdoms; in other words, the Patriarchal order will prevail there to the endless ages of eternity, and the children of each Patriarch will be his, while eternal ages roll on" (Orson Pratt, *Jour. of Dis.*, Vol. XV., p. 319).

19. *And it shall be said * * * next resurrection*] The first resurrection was at the resurrection of Jesus Christ; but we speak of the first resurrection as that which will take place at his coming, which is the first to us. There will be some who will not come forth until the second resurrection.

20. *Then shall they be gods*] What a wonderful Revelation this is, when compared with the narrow ideas held in the world! Children of kings are princes and princesses, associating on terms of equality with

their royal parents, and having a good chance of becoming kings and queens themselves. But when we say that the privilege of God's children is to associate with Him in the eternal mansions, and that they may become gods, then the world does not understand us, and many deem us guilty of blasphemy. They seem to think that they honor God by supposing that His children are infinitely inferior to Him. What kind of father is He, then, that He should feel it an honor to be the progenitor of an inferior offspring? Is there a king on earth that would feel honored by having degenerates and beggars for children? Do not fathers and mothers rejoice in the progress of their children? Is it not their ambition to educate and train their loved ones, until these shall reach the highest possible degree of intelligence and efficiency? Surely, we can do no greater honor to God, our Father, than to admit the divine possibilities which He has implanted in His offspring, and which will be developed under His tuition in this life and hereafter, until His children are perfect as He is perfect. Says President Brigham Young:

"Man is made an agent to himself before his God; he is organized for the express purpose that he may become like his Master. You recollect one of the Apostle's sayings, that when we see Him, we shall be like him; and again, 'We shall become gods, even the sons of God.' Do you read anywhere that we shall possess all things? Jesus is the elder brother, and all the brethren shall come in for a share with Him * * * We are created, we are born, for the express purpose of growing up from the low estate of manhood, to become gods, like unto our Father in heaven" (*Jour. of Dis.*, Vol. III., p. 93).

21. Verily, verily, I say unto you, except ye abide my law ye cannot attain to this glory.

22. For strait is the gate, and narrow the way that leadeth unto the exaltation and continuation of the lives, and few there be that find it, because ye receive me not in the world neither do ye know me.

23. But if ye receive me in the world, then shall ye know me, and shall receive your exaltation; that where I am ye shall be also.

24. This is eternal lives—to know the only wise and true God, and Jesus Christ, whom he hath sent. I am he. Receive ye, therefore, my law.

25. Broad is the gate, and wide the way that leadeth to the deaths; and many there are that go in thereat, because they receive me not, neither do they abide in my law.

26. Verily, verily, I say unto you, if a man marry a wife according to my word, and they are sealed by the Holy Spirit of

promise, according to mine appointment, and he or she shall commit any sin or transgression of the new and everlasting covenant whatever, and all manner of blasphemies, and if they commit no murder wherein they shed innocent blood, yet they shall come forth in the first resurrection; and enter into their exaltation; but they shall be destroyed in the flesh, and shall be delivered unto the buffetings of Satan unto the day of redemption, saith the Lord God.

27. The blasphemy against the Holy Ghost, which shall not be forgiven in the world nor out of the world, is in that ye commit murder wherein ye shed innocent blood, and assent unto my death, after ye have received my new and everlasting covenant, saith the Lord God; and he that abideth not this law can in nowise enter into my glory, but shall be damned, saith the Lord.

5. Obedience Required.

21. *Except ye abide my law * * * glory*] To "abide my law" means to "conform to," and then to remain obedient to, that law, in all its requirements. Celestial glory cannot be obtained except through obedience to celestial law. That is reasonable. If, in any country, an alien desire to obtain the highest possible honor and advantage that can be conferred on a naturalized citizen, he must submit to the laws and rules of the country. The same is true of the celestial kingdom of our God.

24. *This is eternal lives*] "Lives" here and in v. 22 means posterity in the Hereafter. To *know* God and our Lord Jesus Christ is to be on the road to exaltation, and this includes eternal increase. But to *know* God is not merely to have heard of Him. It is "to walk" with Him, as Enoch did; it is to "believe," or "live by" Him, as Abraham did; it is to be familiar with Him, as a child with its father.

This verse is not a quotation of John 17:3, where our Lord teaches His disciples that His mission was to give eternal *life* to those whom the Father had given Him, "in order that they may know" the true God and His Son. Earthly life is too short for that study. This is a new Revelation, in which we are taught that eternal increase, or "lives," is part of the glory of eternal life; but the language closely resembles that of John, as is frequently the case in these Revelations.

25. *The way that leadeth to the deaths*] The parallel passage, Matt. 7:13, has "destruction" for "deaths." In this paragraph "deaths" stands for the opposite of "lives" in vv. 22 and 24. It is the end of eternal increase. Note that there are only two gates and two roads. One gate is broad and one is strait; one road is wide and one is narrow; there is no middle road; few find the strait gate and the narrow way; many enter the broad gate and walk on the wide way.

The illustration seems to be drawn from a mansion having a large portal at which many enter, and a narrow entrance known only to a few.

26. *Any sin or transgression*] This verse has been greatly misunderstood and by some grossly abused. Unfortunately there are some who seem to think that after they are married for time and all eternity, the Lord, in this passage, grants them immunity against sin, as long as they do not shed innocent blood or deny the Holy Ghost. It should be remembered that the Lord taught during his ministry this same doctrine as given in the Doctrine and Covenants. (Matt. 12:31-32.) He has never granted to any person the privilege of sinning wilfully and then obtaining the reward of faithfulness without repentance. John said:

"If any man see his brother sin a sin which is not unto death, he shall ask, and he shall give him life for them that sin not unto death. There is a sin unto death; I do not say that he should pray for it." (I. John 5:16.)

In this passage we are taught that all manner of sin which is forgivable on repentance, or "not unto death," may be forgiven on repentance, but some sins may call for a most dreadful punishment even then—the destruction in the flesh and being turned over to the buffetings of Satan until the day of redemption. This punishment is most severe. The Lord has not at any time contradicted Himself and he has said: "And no unclean thing can enter into his kingdom; therefore nothing entereth into his rest save it be those who have washed their garments in my blood, because of their faith, and the repentance of all their sins, and their faithfulness unto the end. (III. Nephi 27:19.) The wilful sinners who remain in their sins, "shall return unto God, and behold his face, and remain in their sins." (II. Nephi 9:38. Compare Mormon 9:3-4.)

Blasphemies] A blasphemy is an indignity offered to God in words or acts, and in the Scriptures it means also "heresies." Hymenæus and Alexander, whom Paul "delivered to Satan" (I. Tim. 1:20), were blasphemers," but their "blasphemy" seems to have consisted in teaching the false doctrine that the resurrection had already taken place (II. Tim. 2:17).

27. *Blasphemy against the Holy Ghost*] This unpardonable sin is explained to mean "murder, wherein ye shed innocent blood, and assent unto my death, after ye have received my new and everlasting covenant." Some of those who have been instrumental in shedding the blood of the martyrs, from Stephen, who was stoned in Jerusalem, to Joseph and Hyrum, who were slain at Carthage, may ultimately be found among those who come under this condemnation. God alone is their judge.

28. I am the Lord thy God, and will give unto thee the law of my Holy Priesthood, as was ordained by me and my Father before the world was.

29. Abraham received all things, whatsoever he received, by

revelation and commandment, by my word, saith the Lord, and hath entered into his exaltation and sitteth upon his throne.

30. Abraham received promises concerning his seed, and of the fruit of his loins—from whose loins ye are, namely, my servant Joseph—which were to continue so long as they were in the world; and as touching Abraham and his seed, out of the world they should continue; both in the world and out of the world should they continue as innumerable as the stars; or, if ye were to count the sand upon the seashore ye could not number them.

31. This promise is yours also, because ye are of Abraham, and the promise was made unto Abraham; and by this law is the continuation of the works of my Father, wherein he glorifieth himself.

32. Go ye, therefore, and do the works of Abraham; enter ye into my law and ye shall be saved.

33. But if ye enter not into my law ye cannot receive the promise of my Father, which he made unto Abraham.

6. The Law of the Priesthood.

28-33. The celestial law, an explanation of which has been given in vv. 7-20, is here called, "The law of my Holy Priesthood." It was ordained by God before the world was (v. 28). In accordance with that law, Abraham received "all things" by revelation and commandment. Among the things received were promises concerning his seed—that his children should continue in this world and in the next, as innumerable as the stars (v. 30). This law is celestial, because by obedience to it, the works of God, the Father, continue, to His glory (v. 31).

29. *Hath entered into his exaltation*] This is said of Abraham. He has already ascended his throne. When this took place is not stated, but it evidently occurred after our Lord ascended in glory. If Abraham is exalted and occupies a throne, others must enjoy a similar privilege.

30. *Innumerable*] Abraham's children were to be innumerable. If we believe in an eternal increase, under the Celestial Law this promise is intelligible, for then there is no end to the increase.

34. God commanded Abraham, and Sarah gave Hagar to Abraham to wife. And why did she do it? Because this was the law; and from Hagar sprang many people. This, therefore, was fulfilling, among other things, the promises.

35. Was Abraham, therefore, under condemnation? Verily I say unto you, Nay; for I, the Lord, commanded it.

36. Abraham was commanded to offer his son Isaac; nevertheless, it was written: Thou shalt not kill. Abraham, however, did not refuse, and it was accounted unto him for righteousness.

37. Abraham received concubines, and they bore him children; and it was accounted unto him for righteousness, because they were given unto him, and he abode in my law; as Isaac also and Jacob did none other things than that which they were commanded; and because they did none other things than that which they were commanded, they have entered into their exaltation, according to the promises, and sit upon thrones, and are not angels but are gods.

38. David also received many wives and concubines, and also Solomon and Moses my servants, as also many others of my servants, from the beginning of creation until this time; and in nothing did they sin save in those things which they received not of me.

39. David's wives and concubines were given unto him of me, by the hand of Nathan, my servant, and others of the prophets who had the keys of this power; and in none of these things did he sin against me save in the case of Uriah and his wife; and, therefore he hath fallen from his exaltation, and received his portion; and he shall not inherit them out of the world, for I give them unto another, saith the Lord.

40. I am the Lord thy God, and I gave unto thee, my servant Joseph, an appointment, and restore all things. Ask what ye will, and it shall be given unto you according to my word.

7. PLURAL MARRIAGE.

34-40. In the preceding sections, this Revelation deals with celestial marriage—marriage for eternity. In this section and those following, plural marriage is the subject; and it is first shown that some of the greatest characters in the Old Testament had wives and concubines.

34. *Because this was the law*] Sarah gave Hagar to Abraham in accordance with law. It is known now that, according to the Code of Hammurabi, which, in many respects, resembles the later Mosaic law. if a man's wife was childless, he was allowed to take a concubine and bring her into his house, though he was not to place her upon an equal footing with his first wife, or the first wife might give her husband a maid-servant. This was the law in the country from which Abraham came. A concubine was a wife of inferior social rank.

37. *Isaac also*] There is no other record of any plural marriage of this Patriarch, but, aside from this Revelation, the probability is that he followed the custom of his age. How is it, on any other supposition, to be explained that Jacob accepted Laban's arrangement without protest? Where, if not in his home, had he learned that plural marriage was not at that time unlawful?

"It is not to be supposed that, in a time when polygamy was usual, the young sheyk remained celibate till forty. The marriage to one of the kin, Rebekah, was the political marriage for the clan, to set up a fresh chieftainess after Sarah was dead." (W. M. Flinders Petrie, *Egypt and Israel,* p. 24.)

Have entered into their exaltation. See verse 29.

40. *Restore all things*] The mission of the Prophet Joseph was that of a restorer of all things in accordance with the divine plan of redemption.

41. And as ye have asked concerning adultery, verily, verily, I say unto you, if a man receiveth a wife in the new and everlasting covenant, and if she be with another man, and I have not appointed unto her by the holy anointing, she hath committed adultery and shall be destroyed.

42. If she be not in the new and everlasting covenant, and she be with another man, she has committed adultery.

43. And if her husband be with another woman, and he was under a vow, he hath broken his vow and hath committed adultery.

44. And if she hath not committed adultery, but is innocent and hath not broken her vow, and she knoweth it, and I reveal it unto you, my servant Joseph, then shall you have power, by the power of my Holy Priesthood, to take her and give her unto him that hath not committed adultery but hath been faithful; for he shall be made ruler over many.

45. For I have conferred upon you the keys and power of the priesthood, wherein I restore all things, and make known unto you all things in due time.

46. And verily, verily, I say unto you, that whatsoever you seal on earth shall be sealed in heaven; and whatsoever you bind on earth, in my name and by my word, saith the Lord, it shall be eternally bound in the heavens; and whosoever sins you remit on earth shall be remitted eternally in the heavens; and whosoever sins you retain on earth shall be retained in heaven.

47. And again, verily I say, whomsoever you bless I will bless, and whomsoever you curse I will curse, saith the Lord; for I, the Lord, am thy God.

48. And again, verily I say unto you, my servant Joseph, that whatsoever you give on earth, and to whomsoever you give any one on earth, by my word and according to my law, it shall be visited with blessings and not cursings, and with my power, saith the Lord, and shall be without condemnation on earth and in heaven.

49. For I am the Lord thy God, and will be with thee even unto the end of the world, and through all eternity; for verily I seal upon you your exaltation, and prepare a throne for you in the kingdom of my Father, with Abraham your father.

8. Plural Marriage is not Adultery.

41-9. The Prophet, in his prayer on this subject, had asked the Lord for information concerning the ground on which the Patriarchs were justified in their domestic relations, and the answer was the definition of adultery here given. Plural marriage, the Revelation says, in substance, is not adultery, but to violate the marriage covenant is to commit that sin, the penalty being destruction (vv. 41, 52); but God Himself will execute that judgment (v. 54).

50. Behold, I have seen your sacrifices, and will forgive all your sins; I have seen your sacrifices in obedience to that which I have told you. Go, therefore, and I make a way for your escape, as I accepted the offering of Abraham of his son Isaac.

51. Verily, I say unto you: A commandment I give unto mine handmaid Emma Smith, your wife, whom I have given unto you, that she stay herself and partake not of that which I commanded you to offer unto her; for I did it, saith the Lord, to prove you all, as I did Abraham, and that I might require an offering at your hand, by covenant and sacrifice.

52. And let mine handmaid, Emma Smith, receive all those that have been given unto my servant Joseph, and who are virtuous and pure before me; and those who are not pure, and have said they were pure, shall be destroyed, saith the Lord God.

53. For I am the Lord thy God, and ye shall obey my voice; and I give unto my servant Joseph that he shall be made ruler

over many things; for he hath been faithful over a few things, and from henceforth I will strengthen him.

54. And I command mine handmaid, Emma Smith, to abide and cleave unto my servant Joseph, and to none else. But if she will not abide this commandment she shall be destroyed, saith the Lord; for I am the Lord thy God, and will destroy her if she abide not in my law.

55. But if she will not abide this commandment, then shall my servant Joseph do all things for her, even as he hath said; and I will bless him and multiply him and give unto him an hundred-fold in this world, of fathers and mothers, brothers and sisters, houses and lands, wives and children, and crowns of eternal lives in the eternal worlds.

56. And again, verily I say, let mine handmaid forgive my servant Joseph his trespasses; and then shall she be forgiven her trespasses, wherein she has trespassed against me; and I, the Lord thy God, will bless her, and multiply her, and make her heart to rejoice.

57. And again, I say, let not my servant Joseph put his property out of his hands, lest an enemy come and destroy him; for Satan seeketh to destroy; for I am the Lord thy God, and he is my servant; and behold, and lo, I am with him, as I was with Abraham, thy father, even unto his exaltation and glory.

58. Now, as touching the law of the priesthood, there are many things pertaining thereunto.

59. Verily, if a man be called of my Father, as was Aaron, by mine own voice, and by the voice of him that sent me, and I have endowed him with the keys of the power of this priesthood, if he do anything in my name, and according to my law and by my word, he will not commit sin, and I will justify him.

60. Let no one, therefore, set on my servant Joseph; for I will justify him; for he shall do the sacrifice which I require at his hands for his transgressions, saith the Lord your God.

61. And again, as pertaining to the law of the priesthood—if any man espouse a virgin, and desire to espouse another, and the first give her consent, and if he espouse the second, and they are virgins, and have vowed to no other man, then is he justified; he cannot commit adultery for they are given unto him; for he

cannot commit adultery with that that belongeth unto him and to no one else.

62. And if he have ten virgins given unto him by this law, he cannot commit adultery, for they belong to him, and they are given unto him; therefore is he justified.

63. But if one or either of the ten virgins, after she is espoused, shall be with another man, she has committed adultery, and shall be destroyed; for they are given unto him to multiply and replenish the earth, according to my commandment, and to fulfil the promise which was given by my Father before the foundation of the world, and for their exaltation in the eternal worlds, that they may bear the souls of men; for herein is the work of my Father continued, that he may be glorified.

64. And again, verily, verily, I say unto you, if any man have a wife, who holds the keys of this power, and he teaches unto her the law of my priesthood, as pertaining to these things, then shall she believe and administer unto him, or she shall be destroyed, saith the Lord your God; for I will destroy her; for I will magnify my name upon all those who receive and abide in my law.

65. Therefore, it shall be lawful in me, if she receive not this law, for him to receive all things whatsoever I, the Lord his God, will give unto him, because she did not believe and administer unto him according to my word; and she then becomes the transgressor; and he is exempt from the law of Sarah, who administered unto Abraham according to the law when I commanded Abraham to take Hagar to wife.

66. And now, as pertaining to this law, verily, verily, I say unto you, I will reveal more unto you, hereafter; therefore, let this suffice for the present. Behold, I am Alpha and Omega. Amen.

58-66. The truth is here reiterated, that whatever is done in the name of God, according to His law and by His direction, cannot be sin. What human law regards as a crime may, or may not, from the Divine point of view, be a sin. Sometimes the Innocent dies on Calvary, because criminals have acted as judge and jury.

General Notes

As has been stated in the introductory notes, the doctrine of plural marriage was made known to the Prophet in 1831, or 1832, although the Revelation on the subject was not committed to writing until the year 1843. It should be noted that even then it was not given to the *Church.* This step was taken on the 29th of August, 1852, when the Revelation was read to a General Conference in the "Old Tabernacle," Salt Lake City, and accepted by the assembly as a revelation from God and part of the law of the Church. In voting for the Revelation, the Saints firmly believed that they were only exercising their legal right as American citizens. They believed that, as a majority, they had the indisputable constitutional right to regulate their domestic affairs, within the boundaries of their own territory, and that the Supreme Court of the United States would uphold this view, even if Congress should be of a different opinion. And they were strengthened in their position by the fact that not until ten years after the action taken by the Church in 1852 was any effort made by Congress to stamp plural marriage as illegal.

The first Congressional enactment against plural marriage, passed in 1862, remained a dead letter for twenty years. By that time, the anti-Mormons had evidence that the Supreme Court would uphold legislation of that kind, and laws more drastic than the first were passed by Congress. The Church leaders appealed to the Supreme Court, as was their prerogative. For years there was a legal conflict. At last, when the Supreme Court had declared the anti-polygamy laws constitutional and there was no prospect that there would be a reversal of this decision, the Church loyally and gracefully accepted it. President Wilford Woodruff issued his Manifesto against the practice of plural marriage, and this was accepted by a unanimous vote of the General Conference assembled in Salt Lake City, Oct. 6th, 1890. This was done by divine revelation to President Wilford Woodruff.

This is the full text of the Manifesto:

"Press dispatches having been sent for political purposes, from Salt Lake City, which have been widely published, to the effect that the Utah Commission, in their recent report to the Secretary of the Interior, allege, that plural marriages are still being solemnized and that forty or more such marriages have been contracted in Utah since last June or during the past year, also that in public discourses the leaders of the Church have taught, encouraged and urged the continuance of the practice of polygamy,

"I, therefore, as President of the Church of Jesus Christ of Latter-day Saints, do hereby, in the most solemn manner, declare that these charges are false. We are not teaching polygamy or plural marriage nor permitting any person to enter into its practice, and I deny that either forty or any other number of plural marriages have during that period been solemnized in our temples or in any other place in the Territory.

"One case has been reported, in which the parties allege that the marriage was performed in the Endowment House, in Salt Lake City, in the spring of 1889, but I have not been able to learn who performed the ceremony; whatever was done in this matter was without my knowledge. In consequence of this alleged occurrence the Endowment House was, by my instructions, taken down without delay.

"Inasmuch as laws have been enacted by Congress forbidding plural marriages, which laws have been pronounced constitutional by the court of last resort, I hereby declare my intention to submit to those laws, and to use my influence with the members of the Church over which I preside to have them do likewise.

"There is nothing in my teachings to the Church or in those of my associates, during the time specified, which can be reasonably construed to inculcate or encourage polygamy, and when any Elder of the Church has used language which appeared to convey any such teaching, he has been promptly reproved. And I now publicly declare that my advice to the Latter-day Saints is to refrain from contracting any marriage forbidden by the law of the land.

WILFORD WOODRUFF,
President of the Church of Jesus Christ of Latter-day Saints."

After the Manifesto had been read to the Conference, President Lorenzo Snow offered the following:

"I move, that, recognizing Wilford Woodruff as the President of the Church of Jesus Christ of Latter-day Saints, and the only man on the earth at the present time who holds the keys of the sealing ordinances, we consider him fully authorized by virtue of his position to issue the manifesto which has been read in our hearing and which is dated Sept. 24th, 1890, and that as a Church in General Conference assembled, we accept his declaration concerning plural marriages as authoritative and binding."

The vote to sustain the foregoing motion was unanimous.

By this action the Church voted to conform to the laws of the land as interpreted by the highest tribunal, and to leave the issue with God. Since that conference, and, in fact, for some time previous to the acceptance of the Manifesto, no plural marriage has been performed anywhere with the sanction of the Church, or the approbation of the First Presidency, or anyone representing them, as was fully proved during the so-called Smoot investigation in the United States Senate, which commenced January 16, 1904.

"I want to say to this congregation, and to the world, that never at any time since my presidency in the Church of Jesus Christ of Latter-day Saints have I authorized any man to perform plural marriage, and never since my presidency of the Church has any plural marriage been performed with my sanction or knowledge, or with the consent of the Church of Jesus Christ of Latter-day Saints; and therefore such unions as have been formed unlawfully, contrary to the order of the Church, are null and void in the sight of God, and are not marriages" (President Joseph F. Smith, at the General Conference of the Church, Oct. 4th, 1918).

SECTION 133.

REVELATION *given through Joseph Smith the Prophet, at Hiram, Ohio, November 3, 1831. Prefacing this revelation the Prophet wrote: At this time there were many things which the*

Elders desired to know, relative to preaching the Gospel to the inhabitants of the earth, and concerning the gathering; and in order to walk by the true light, and be instructed from on high, on the 3rd of November, 1831, I inquired of the Lord and received the following important revelation, which has since been added to the book of Doctrine and Covenants and called the Appendix.——A proclamation to the people of the Church to gather to Zion—This proclamation to be carried by the Elders to the peoples of the world—Zion and Jerusalem both to be established—The voice of the Lord to issue from each of these centers—The Lost Tribes to be remembered by the Lord and to be brought forth from the north countries—These to receive their blessings at the hand of Ephraim—Graves of the Saints to be opened at the coming of the Lord—The doom of those who reject the Lord's message.

HEARKEN, O ye people of my church, saith the Lord your God, and hear the word of the Lord concerning you—

2. The Lord who shall suddenly come to his temple; the Lord who shall come down upon the world with a curse to judgment; yea, upon all the nations that forget God, and upon all the ungodly among you.

3. For he shall make bare his holy arm in the eyes of all the nations, and all the ends of the earth shall see the salvation of their God.

4. Wherefore, prepare ye, prepare ye, O my people; sanctify yourselves; gather ye together, O ye people of my church, upon the land of Zion, all you that have not been commanded to tarry.

5. Go ye out from Babylon. Be ye clean that bear the vessels of the Lord.

6. Call your solemn assemblies, and speak often one to another. And let every man call upon the name of the Lord.

7. Yea, verily I say unto you again, the time has come when the voice of the Lord is unto you: Go ye out of Babylon; gather ye out from among the nations, from the four winds, from one end of heaven to the other.

8. Send forth the elders of my church unto the nations which are afar off; unto the islands of the sea; send forth unto foreign

lands; call upon all nations, first upon the Gentiles, and then upon the Jews.

9. And behold, and lo, this shall be their cry, and the voice of the Lord unto all people: Go ye forth unto the land of Zion, that the borders of my people may be enlarged, and that her stakes may be strengthened, and that Zion may go forth unto the regions round about.

10. Yea, let the cry go forth among all people: Awake and arise and go forth to meet the Bridegroom; behold and lo, the Bridegroom cometh; go ye out to meet him. Prepare yourselves for the great day of the Lord.

11. Watch, therefore, for ye know neither the day nor the hour.

12. Let them, therefore, who are among the Gentiles flee unto Zion.

13. And let them who be of Judah flee unto Jerusalem, unto the mountains of the Lord's house.

14. Go ye out from among the nations, even from Babylon, from the midst of wickedness, which is spiritual Babylon.

15. But verily, thus saith the Lord, let not your flight be in haste, but let all things be prepared before you; and he that goeth, let him not look back lest sudden destruction shall come upon him.

16. Hearken and hear, O ye inhabitants of the earth. Listen, ye elders of my church together, and hear the voice of the Lord; for he calleth upon all men, and he commandeth all men everywhere to repent.

This Revelation was given on the 3rd day of November 1831, just two days after the Revelation was received known as the *Preface* to the Book of Commandments. It came in response to questions by the Elders of the Church relative to the preaching of the gospel, the gathering of the Jews to Palestine, and the return of the lost tribes of Israel, and other questions of great importance pertaining to the Dispensation of the Fulness of Times.

As it was given while the Prophet Joseph Smith was compiling the Revelations for publication, after the special Conference of the Church which ordered that work done, it was agreed that it should appear in the forthcoming volume. It is one of the most important Revelations the Prophet received and has continued to appear in all editions of the

Doctrine and Covenants from the beginning, notwithstanding many other Revelations were received since this was given.

1. *Hearken, O ye people of my church*] This expression, or "ye Elders of my church," occurs in a number of the Revelations. The significant feature of the expression is the recognition given by the Lord to those who have made covenant with Him in the waters of baptism and have received the Priesthood, and are members of the only Church upon the earth which the Lord recognizes as His (See Sec. 1:30). It brings to our attention clearly the great fact that a divided "Christianity" cannot be acceptable unto the Lord, that His house is a house of order (Sec. 132:8) in which all things are of necessity governed by law (Secs. 88: 34-39; 132:11-12).

2. *The Lord shall suddenly come to his temple*] At no time has the Lord declared the day nor the hour when He shall appear to take vengeance upon the wicked and make bare His holy arm in the eyes of the nations (v. 3). He did reveal to Malachi the fact that, in the latter days, He should suddenly come to His Temple, but before that day, He should send His messenger to prepare the way before Him, that the people might not be taken in their sins without a chance of repentance. Where could the Lord come to a temple, except among the Latter-day Saints? This prediction has in part been fulfilled, for the Lord appeared to Joseph Smith and Oliver Cowdery in the Kirtland Temple and there ministered to them in 1836; but this prophecy has a broader meaning, and the Lord shall come, without a doubt, to His Temple, where He will sit as "a refiner and purifier of silver," purging the house of Israel and ministering to His people. This appearing will be separate and distinct from the great coming in the clouds of heaven, when He will appear with power and great glory (Matt. 24:30) with a curse to judgment (v. 2) upon all the nations that forget God. This coming will be for the blessing and benefit of the most faithful of His saints, and when He comes to take final vengeance on the world, He will be preceded by a sign (Matt. 24:30; Sec. 88:93), that all peoples shall see and judgment shall be poured out upon the wicked.

5. *Go ye out from Babylon*] The Lord commanded all the Saints, excepting those who were specially commanded to tarry for the preaching of the gospel and the warning of the nations, to gather on the land of Zion (v. 4; see pp. 7, 186; also Index on "gathering"). They were to go out of Babylon. This term the Lord, in a number of revelations, and also in John's Revelation, applied to the wicked world and the great and abominable church which rules a large portion of the earth (see Sections 1:16; 35:11; 64:24; Rev. 16:19; 17:5; 18:2), and has made the nations drunken with her sins.

8. *Send forth the elders * * * to the nations*] This gospel of the kingdom is to be preached in all the world for a witness unto all nations

(Matt. 24:14) before the great day of the Lord shall come. The Lord calls attention to the necessity of carrying on this great labor, for the appointed time has come. Therefore, the Elders of the Church were to be sent forth "unto the nations which are afar off and to the inhabitants of the islands of the sea" (Sec. 1:1-4). Their attention is called to the important fact, however, that the words of life should first be declared among the Gentiles and afterwards unto the Jews. In the dispensation of the Meridian of Time, the gospel was first taken to the Jews. Jesus declared that He was not sent but to the lost sheep of the house of Israel (Matt. 15:24), and His disciples, when He sent them forth, were commanded to go only among those of the house of Israel and avoid the "way of the Gentiles and the Samaritans" (Matt. 10:5). After His resurrection, however, he sent them forth into all the world, first to the Jews then to the Gentiles. Their mission to the Gentiles was deferred until the Jews had received full opportunity of hearing the truth. In this dispensation the condition is reversed. The Elders are commanded to go first to the Gentiles and, after these have had the opportunity of receiving the gospel, it is to be carried to the Jews. The first shall be last and the last shall be first.

The curse pronounced upon the Jews for their rejection and crucifixion of the Lord was that they should be scattered among all nations and should thus remain downtrodden until the "times of the Gentiles be fulfilled" (Luke 21:24; Sec. 45:30). The capture of the Holy Land from the Turks by the British forces under General Allenby in 1917-18, is bringing to pass greater freedom for the Jews in their own land. They are now preparing to return in considerable numbers, and the indication is that the remnant spoken of by the prophets will soon stand on their native land. This means that the times of the Gentiles are rapidly drawing to their close.

> "The Gentile fulness now comes in,
> And Israel's blessings are at hand;
> Lo! Judah's remnant, cleansed from sin,
> Shall in their promised Canaan stand."

The Gentiles who obeyed the Gospel were commanded (v. 12) to gather in Zion, and those of the house of Judah were to flee to Jerusalem (v. 13). This is in harmony with the prediction of Isaiah and Micah, that out of Zion shall go forth the law, and the word of the Lord from Jerusalem. For from both these centers the Lord shall judge. Jerusalem shall be re-built and become a holy city, the capital for Judah, and Zion shall be the capital and city of our God, for Ephraim and his fellows. Both shall be seats of government in unison with each other, and the Lord shall dwell in both.

17.   For behold, the Lord God hath sent forth the angel crying through the midst of heaven, saying: Prepare ye the way of

the Lord, and make his paths straight, for the hour of his coming is nigh—

18. When the Lamb shall stand upon Mount Zion, and with him a hundred and forty-four thousand, having his Father's name written on their foreheads.

19. Wherefore, prepare ye for the coming of the Bridegroom; go ye, go ye out to meet him.

20. For behold, he shall stand upon the mount of Olivet, and upon the mighty ocean, even the great deep, and upon the islands of the sea, and upon the land of Zion.

21. And he shall utter his voice out of Zion, and he shall speak from Jerusalem, and his voice shall be heard among all people;

22. And it shall be a voice as the voice of many waters, and as the voice of a great thunder, which shall break down the mountains, and the valleys shall not be found.

23. He shall command the great deep, and it shall be driven back into the north countries, and the islands shall become one land;

24. And the land of Jerusalem and the land of Zion shall be turned back into their own place, and the earth shall be like as it was in the days before it was divided.

25. And the Lord, even the Savior, shall stand in the midst of his people, and shall reign over all flesh.

19. *Prepare ye for the coming of the Bridegroom*] All nations are called upon to repent and receive the gospel, for it is "unto all men, and there is none to escape" (Sec. 1:2). The vision which John saw (Rev. 14:6) has been fulfilled (v. 17 and 36). The angel has gone forth through the midst of heaven and has declared the everlasting gospel and committed it into the hands of man (v. 36), that it might go forth to the ends of the earth, to every creature as a warning before the coming of the Lord. He shall stand upon Mount Zion (v. 18), the Mount of Olivet (v. 19), the ocean, the islands of the sea (v. 20), and on the land of Zion (21), and shall be heard among all people (v. 21). The mountains shall be leveled, the valleys exalted, and the earth shall appear as it was before it was divided (v. 24). The righteous shall be received with joy and gladness, and the wicked shall be punished for their rejection of the gospel (See Zech. 12:10 and 14th chapter).

26. And they who are in the north countries shall come in remembrance before the Lord; and their prophets shall hear his

voice, and shall no longer stay themselves; and they shall smite the rocks, and the ice shall flow down at their presence.

27. And an highway shall be cast up in the midst of the great deep.

28. Their enemies shall become a prey unto them.

29. And in the barren deserts there shall come forth pools of living water; and the parched ground shall no longer be a thirsty land.

30. And they shall bring forth their rich treasures unto the children of Ephraim, my servants.

31. And the boundaries of the everlasting hills shall tremble at their presence.

32. And there shall they fall down and be crowned with glory, even in Zion, by the hands of the servants of the Lord, even the children of Ephraim.

33. And they shall be filled with songs of everlasting joy.

34. Behold, this is the blessing of the everlasting God upon the tribes of Israel, and the richer blessing upon the head of Ephraim and his fellows.

35. And they also of the tribe of Judah, after their pain shall be sanctified in holiness before the Lord, to dwell in his presence day and night, forever and ever.

36. And now, verily saith the Lord, that these things might be known among you, O inhabitants of the earth, I have sent forth mine angel flying through the midst of heaven, having the ever-lasting gospel, who hath appeared unto some and hath com-mitted it unto man, who shall appear unto many that dwell on the earth.

26. *And they who are in the north countries shall come in remem-brance*] It is understood that the ten tribes of Israel, after their liberation from the captivity of the Assyrians, departed into the land northward and eventually were lost to the knowledge of other nations. Just where they went and where they are we do not know more than what the Lord has revealed. We learn from the Book of Mormon (III. Nephi, 15th and 16th chapters) that the Savior visited them and taught them the gospel. They have their records, and prophets have been among them to teach them in part, at least, the gospel. That they are in the north we learn from this Revelation, also from Jeremiah 31:8, and other Scripture.

At a conference of the Church held in June 1831, the Prophet said that John the Revelator was then among the ten tribes of Israel who had been led away by Shalmaneser, king of Assyria, to prepare them for their return from their long dispersion. (*Essentials in Church History,* p. 126).

27. *And an highway shall be cast up in the midst of the deep*] A great many skeptical people rejoiced when the announcement was made that Commodore Peary had discovered the North Pole, and they declared that this proved beyond a doubt that the lost tribes were not in the north. The Lord never said that they were at the North Pole. No matter whether Commodore Peary discovered the Pole or not, there is a great deal of country in the north that no man, to our knowledge, has visited. The fact remains that the Lord can take care of these people and keep them hidden from the knowledge of others, until the time comes for that Revelation to be made known, wherever they are. A highway shall be cast up in the midst of the sea and the ice shall flow down at their presence, when the time comes for their journey to Zion. It shall no longer be said, "the Lord liveth that brought up the children of Israel out of the land of Egypt; but the Lord liveth, that brought up the children of Israel from the land of the north" (Jer. 16:14-15), so great shall be the miracle of their deliverance.

29. *And in the barren deserts there shall come forth pools*] This prediction has in part been fulfilled. It is a well-known fact that in many parts of the western country, inhabited by the Latter-day Saints, barren places have become fruitful, streams of water have increased in volume, and the deserts have been made to blossom. These miracles have taken place since the coming of the pioneers to Utah. The fulfilment of this promise, however, is not complete, for when the Lord restores the lost tribes and establishes His kingdom in power, a far greater manifestation of this nature will be seen. Then the waste places shall become fruitful and the Saints shall inhabit them; yet it shall come about naturally, for it is on natural principles that the Lord works.

31. *The boundaries of the everlasting hills*] This, without question, refers to the great Rocky Mountain range. When Jacob blessed his son Joseph, he said, "The blessings of thy father have prevailed above the blessings of my progenitors unto the utmost bound of the everlasting hills; they shall be on the head of Joseph, and on the crown of the head of him that was separate from his brethren." Moses also recorded the following, pertaining to Joseph's blessing: "And for the chief things of the ancient mountains, and for the precious things of the lasting hills * * * Let the blessing come upon the head of Joseph and upon the top of the head of him that was separated from his brethren." Again, Jacob referred to Joseph as "a fruitful bough by a well whose branches run over the wall." We have quite generally understood these references to indicate and point to Joseph's inheritance in America, for he received a double portion. As Joseph was separated from his brethren by their choice, so by the will of the Lord he received a greater blessing and,

besides his inheritance in Palestine, he also received as an inheritance the land of Zion—America—separated from the inheritance of the other tribes. His blessing which his father gave him "prevailed above the blessings of his [Jacob's] progenitors," in that the Lord gave to him the choicest of all land possessions. When the tribes of Israel come to Zion with songs of joy, the everlasting hills will tremble (v. 31) at their presence, as in gladness at their deliverance from their long separation from the rest of the world.

32. *And they shall * * * be crowned * * * by * * * the children of Ephraim*] Joseph, son of Jacob, was blessed by the Lord with the birthright in Israel, and stood first among the sons of Jacob. This blessing was also the inheritance of Ephraim, the second son of Joseph. We read in the fifth chapter of Chronicles the following: "The sons of Reuben, the firstborn of Israel, (for he was the firstborn; but forasmuch as he defiled his father's bed, his birthright was given unto the sons of Joseph, the son of Israel: and the genealogy is not to be reckoned after the birthright. For Judah prevailed above his brethren, and of him came the chief ruler, but the birthright was Joseph's.") The Lord confirmed this through Jeremiah when he said: "I am the father of Israel, and Ephraim is my firstborn" (Jer. 31:9). Thus, holding the first place in Israel, it is the right of Ephraim among the tribes to take the place of honor and stand at the head to minister unto the others. The Lord has called him to this mission in this dispensation. As the Tribes departed on their northern journey, many of the people fell by the way and mingled with the inhabitants of the land through which they passed. It is quite evident that those of Ephraim mingled with the nations in this way more than the people of any other tribe, for we have learned through revelation to Joseph Smith, that most of those now being gathered from the nations where the gospel has been preached, are of the lineage of Ephraim. This information has been imparted to thousands by our Patriarchs as they have been inspired to make the prediction on the heads of those who have received blessings at their hands. The Lord scattered the children of Ephraim that He might gather them in the latter days, to prepare the way for the coming of the other tribes to Zion. As the firstborn among the tribes, the Ephraimites receive the richer blessings and will be prepared through the fulness of the Priesthood to crown the people from the north with greater power pertaining to the gospel and their salvation when they come.

35. *Judah shall be sanctified*] When the Lord feels that Judah has been punished enough for his transgression, he will bring him back to his land and cleanse him from all sin (See Isa. 11:11; Jer. 12:14; 32:37; 33:7-10; Joel 2:32).

37. And this gospel shall be preached unto every nation, and kindred, and tongue, and people.

38. And the servants of God shall go forth, saying with a loud voice: Fear God and give glory to him, for the hour of his judgment is come;

39. And worship him that made heaven, and earth, and the sea, and the fountains of waters—

40. Calling upon the name of the Lord day and night, saying: O that thou wouldst rend the heavens, that thou wouldst come down, that the mountains might flow down at thy presence.

41. And it shall be answered upon their heads; for the presence of the Lord shall be as the melting fire that burneth, and as the fire which causeth the waters to boil.

42. O Lord, thou shalt come down to make thy name known to thine adversaries, and all nations shall tremble at thy presence—

43. When thou doest terrible things, things they look not for;

44. Yea, when thou comest down, and the mountains flow down at thy presence, thou shalt meet him who rejoiceth and worketh righteousness, who remembereth thee in thy ways.

45. For since the beginning of the world have not men heard nor perceived by the ear, neither hath any eye seen, O God, besides thee, how great things thou hast prepared for him that waiteth for thee.

46. And it shall be said: Who is this that cometh down from God in heaven with dyed garments; yea, from the regions which are not known, clothed in his glorious apparel, traveling in the greatness of his strength?

47. And he shall say: I am he who spake in righteousness, mighty to save.

48. And the Lord shall be red in his apparel, and his garments like him that treadeth in the wine-vat.

49. And so great shall be the glory of his presence that the sun shall hide his face in shame, and the moon shall withhold its light, and the stars shall be hurled from their places.

50. And his voice shall be heard: I have trodden the wine-press alone, and have brought judgment upon all people; and none were with me;

50. *I have trodden the wine-press alone*] When the Savior comes in glory, "red in his apparel," it shall be made manifest to all that salvation

and redemption are by and through His holy name; that He, by the shedding of His blood, redeemed the world, and besides Him there is no Savior. Every knee must eventually bow in honor to Him, and every tongue confess this great truth, that without the redemption which He wrought, we should all be in our sins and subject to the will of the devil.

51. And I have trampled them in my fury, and I did tread upon them in mine anger, and their blood have I sprinkled upon my garments, and stained all my raiment; for this was the day of vengeance which was in my heart.

52. And now the year of my redeemed is come; and they shall mention the loving kindness of their Lord, and all that he has bestowed upon them according to his goodness, and according to his loving kindness, forever and ever.

53. In all their afflictions he was afflicted. And the angel of his presence saved them; and in his love, and in his pity, he redeemed them, and bore them, and carried them all the days of old;

54. Yea, and Enoch also, and they who were with him; the prophets who were before him; and Noah also, and they who were before him; and Moses also, and they who were before him;

55. And from Moses to Elijah, and from Elijah to John, who were with Christ in his resurrection, and the holy apostles, with Abraham, Isaac, and Jacob, shall be in the presence of the Lamb.

55. *And from Moses to Elijah * * * John*] From this information we learn that Moses, Elijah, who was translated in a chariot of fire, and John the Baptist, received their resurrection at the time of the resurrection of Jesus Christ.

56. And the graves of the saints shall be opened; and they shall come forth and stand on the right hand of the Lamb, when he shall stand upon Mount Zion, and upon the holy city, the New Jerusalem; and they shall sing the song of the Lamb, day and night forever and ever.

57. And for this cause, that men might be made partakers of the glories which were to be revealed, the Lord sent forth the fulness of his gospel, his everlasting covenant, reasoning in plainness and simplicity—

58. To prepare the weak for those things which are coming on the earth, and for the Lord's errand in the day when the weak

shall confound the wise, and the little one become a strong nation, and two shall put their tens of thousands to flight.

59. And by the weak things of the earth the Lord shall thrash the nations by the power of his Spirit.

60. And for this cause these commandments were given; they were commanded to be kept from the world in the day that they were given, but now are to go forth unto all flesh—

61. And this according to the mind and will of the Lord, who ruleth over all flesh.

56. *The graves * * * shall be opened*] When Christ comes, the righteous shall come forth from the dead to meet Him (Sec. 88). That all might have the privilege of redemption and partake of the first resurrection, if they would, He sent into the world the fulness of the gospel and the everlasting covenant, with the promise that all who obey shall be given eternal life.

62. And unto him that repenteth and sanctifieth himself before the Lord shall be given eternal life.

63. And upon them that hearken not to the voice of the Lord shall be fulfilled that which was written by the prophet Moses, that they should be cut off from among the people.

64. And also that which was written by the prophet Malachi: For, behold, the day cometh that shall burn as an oven, and all the proud, yea, and all that do wickedly, shall be stubble; and the day that cometh shall burn them up, saith the Lord of hosts, that it shall leave them neither root nor branch.

65. Wherefore, this shall be the answer of the Lord unto them:

66. In that day when I came unto mine own, no man among you received me, and you were driven out.

67. When I called again there was none of you to answer; yet my arm was not shortened at all that I could not redeem, neither my power to deliver.

68. Behold, at my rebuke, I dry up the sea. I make the rivers a wilderness; their fish stink, and die for thirst.

69. I clothe the heavens with blackness, and make sackcloth their covering.

70. And this shall ye have of my hand—ye shall lie down in sorrow.

71. Behold, and lo, there are none to deliver you; for ye obeyed not my voice when I called to you out of the heavens; ye believed not my servants, and when they were sent unto you ye received them not.

72. Wherefore, they sealed up the testimony and bound up the law, and ye were delivered over unto darkness.

73. These shall go away into outer darkness, where there is weeping, and wailing, and gnashing of teeth.

74. Behold the Lord your God hath spoken it. Amen.

63. *Cut off from among the people*] Those who reject the testimony of His servants shall be cut off from among the people, as Moses predicted (Deut. 18:15, 18; I. Nephi 22:20), because they obeyed not His voice and believed not His servants (v. 71), when they came preaching the gospel of the kingdom. These shall be judged and found guilty and shall go "into the outer darkness where there is weeping and wailing, and gnashing of teeth because they would not receive that which they might have received (See 88:32), and the judgment is just.

SECTION 134.

A DECLARATION OF BELIEF *regarding Governments and Laws in general, adopted by unanimous vote at a general assembly of the Church of Jesus Christ of Latter-day Saints, held at Kirtland, Ohio, August 17, 1835, with the following preamble: That our belief with regard to earthly governments and laws in general may not be misinterpreted nor misunderstood, we have thought proper to present at the close of this volume our opinion concerning the same.——This was inserted near the end of the Book of Commandments, as compiled at that time. See History of the Church, vol. 2, p. 247.*

WE believe that governments were instituted of God for the benefit of man; and that he holds men accountable for their acts in relation to them, both in making laws and administering them, for the good and safety of society.

2. We believe that no government can exist in peace, except such laws are framed and held inviolate as will secure to each individual the free exercise of conscience, the right and control of property, and the protection of life.

3. We believe that all governments necessarily require civil officers and magistrates to enforce the laws of the same; and that such as will administer the law in equity and justice should be sought for and upheld by the voice of the people if a republic, or the will of the sovereign.

4. We believe that religion is instituted of God; and that men are amenable to him, and to him only, for the exercise of it, unless their religious opinions prompt them to infringe upon the rights and liberties of others; but we do not believe that human law has a right to interfere in prescribing rules of worship to bind the consciences of men, nor dictate forms for public or private devotion; that the civil magistrate should restrain crime, but never control conscience; should punish guilt, but never suppress the freedom of the soul.

5. We believe that all men are bound to sustain and uphold the respective governments in which they reside, while protected in their inherent and inalienable rights by the laws of such governments; and that sedition and rebellion are unbecoming every citizen thus protected, and should be punished accordingly; and that all governments have a right to enact such laws as in their own judgments are best calculated to secure the public interest; at the same time, however, holding sacred the freedom of conscience.

6. We believe that every man should be honored in his station, rulers and magistrates as such, being placed for the protection of the innocent and the punishment of the guilty; and that to the laws all men owe respect and deference, as without them peace and harmony would be supplanted by anarchy and terror; human laws being instituted for the express purpose of regulating our interests as individuals and nations, between man and man; and divine laws given of heaven, prescribing rules on spiritual concerns, for faith and worship, both to be answered by man to his Maker.

7. We believe that rulers, states, and governments have a right, and are bound to enact laws for the protection of all citizens in the free exercise of their religious belief; but we do not believe that they have a right in justice to deprive citizens of this privilege, or proscribe them in their opinions, as long as a regard

and reverence are shown to the laws and such religious opinions do not justify sedition nor conspiracy.

8. We believe that the commission of crime should be punished according to the nature of the offense; that murder, treason, robbery, theft, and the breach of the general peace, in all respects, should be punished according to their criminality and their tendency to evil among men, by the laws of that government in which the offense is committed; and for the public peace and tranquility all men should step forward and use their ability in bringing offenders against good laws to punishment.

9. We do not believe it just to mingle religious influence with civil government, whereby one religious society is fostered and another proscribed in its spiritual privileges, and the individual rights of its members, as citizens, denied.

10. We believe that all religious societies have a right to deal with their members for disorderly conduct, according to the rules and regulations of such societies; provided that such dealings be for fellowship and good standing; but we do not believe that any religious society has authority to try men on the right of property or life, to take from them this world's goods, or to put them in jeopardy of either life or limb, or to inflict any physical punishment upon them. They can only excommunicate them from their society, and withdraw from them their fellowship.

11. We believe that men should appeal to the civil law for redress of all wrongs and grievances, where personal abuse is inflicted or the right of property or character infringed, where such laws exist as will protect the same; but we believe that all men are justified in defending themselves, their friends, and property, and the government, from the unlawful assaults and encroachments of all persons in times of exigency, where immediate appeal cannot be made to the laws, and relief afforded.

12. We believe it just to preach the gospel to the nations of the earth, and warn the righteous to save themselves from the corruption of the world; but we do not believe it right to interfere with bond-servants, neither preach the gospel to, nor baptize them contrary to the will and wish of their masters, nor to meddle with or influence them in the least to cause them to be dissatisfied

with their situations in this life, thereby jeopardizing the lives of men; such interference we believe to be unlawful and unjust, and dangerous to the peace of every government allowing human beings to be held in servitude.

GENERAL NOTES

This "Declaration of Belief Regarding Governments and Laws in General," is not a revelation. It was not written by the Prophet Joseph Smith, but was prepared by Oliver Cowdery and was read at the General Assembly of the Church, August 17, 1835, at the time the revelations, which had been prepared for publication, were submitted for the vote of approval by the elders of the Church. At the time this conference, or General Assembly, was held, the Prophet Joseph Smith and his second counselor, Frederick G. Williams, were in Canada on a missionary journey, and the Prophet did not return to Kirtland until Sunday, August 23rd, one week after the Assembly had been held. Since the Assembly had voted to have this article on government and one on marriage, also prepared by Oliver Cowdery, published in the Doctrine and Covenants, the Prophet accepted the decision and permitted this to be done.

It should be noted that in the minutes, and also in the introduction to this article on government, the brethren were careful to state that this declaration was accepted as the belief, or "opinion" of the officers of the Church, and not as a revelation, and therefore does not hold the same place in the doctrines of the Church as do the revelations. In fact the first sentence could be improved by a slight change. The Lord in the very beginning revealed to Adam a perfect form of government, and this was "instituted of God for the benefit of man;" but we do not hold that all governments, or any man-made government, was instituted of God although the Lord holds a controlling hand over them. It was not long after the Lord established His government with Adam, and had commanded him to teach correct principles to his children, that men began to rebel and turn away. It is written in the Pearl of Great Price.

"And Adam and Eve blessed the name of God, and they made all things known unto their sons and their daughters.

"And Satan came among them, saying: I am also a son of God; and he commanded them, saying: Believe it not; and they believed it not, and they loved Satan more than God. And men began from that time forth to be carnal, sensual, and devilish." (Moses 5:12-13.)

From that time forth the authority to rule was usurped by men and, with few exceptions ever since, the governments in the earth have been and are the governments of men, and the guiding hand of the Lord by revelation and authority vested in his servants has been ignored. The day is to come, and is near at hand, when the Lord will come in his power and make an end of all man-made governments and take His rightful place as King of kings, and Lord of lords. He has decreed to make a "full end of all nations." It is true that the Lord holds men accountable for their acts and they will be brought to judgment. This is an excellent article and we can subscribe to its provisions until that day comes when the Savior will come to rule. Until that day he has commanded us to "be subject to the powers that be, until he reigns whose right it is to reign, and subdues all enemies under His feet." (Doc. & Cov. 58:22. Compare I. Peter 2:15-17.)

SECTION 135.

MARTYRDOM *of Joseph Smith the Prophet, and his brother, Hyrum Smith the Patriarch, at Carthage, Illinois, June 27, 1844. See History of the Church, vol. 6, p. 612.*

TO seal the testimony of this book and the Book of Mormon, we announce the martyrdom of Joseph Smith the Prophet, and Hyrum Smith the Patriarch. They were shot in Carthage jail, on the 27th of June, 1844, about five o'clock p.m. by an armed mob —painted black—of from 150 to 200 persons. Hyrum was shot first and fell calmly, exclaiming: *I am a dead man!* Joseph leaped from the window, and was shot dead in the attempt, exclaiming: *O Lord my God!* They were both shot after they were dead, in a brutal manner, and both received four balls.

2. John Taylor and Willard Richards, two of the Twelve, were the only persons in the room at the time; the former was wounded in a savage manner with four balls, but has since recovered; the latter, through the providence of God, escaped, without even a hole in his robe.

3. Joseph Smith, the Prophet and Seer of the Lord, has done more, save Jesus only, for the salvation of men in this world, than any other man that ever lived in it. In the short space of twenty years, he has brought forth the Book of Mormon, which he translated by the gift and power of God, and has been the means of publishing it on two continents; has sent the fulness of the everlasting gospel, which it contained, to the four quarters of the earth; has brought forth the revelations and commandments which compose this book of Doctrine and Covenants, and

many other wise documents and instructions for the benefit of the children of men; gathered many thousands of the Latter-day Saints, founded a great city, and left a fame and name that cannot be slain. He lived great, and he died great in the eyes of God and his people; and like most of the Lord's anointed in ancient times, has sealed his mission and his works with his own blood; and so has his brother Hyrum. In life they were not divided, and in death they were not separated!

4. When Joseph went to Carthage to deliver himself up to the pretended requirements of the law, two or three days previous to his assassination, he said: "I am going like a lamb to the slaughter; but I am calm as a summer's morning; I have a conscience void of offense towards God, and towards all men. I SHALL DIE INNOCENT, AND IT SHALL YET BE SAID OF ME—HE WAS MURDERED IN COLD BLOOD."—The same morning, after Hyrum had made ready to go—shall it be said to the slaughter? yes, for so it was—he read the following paragraph, near the close of the twelfth chapter of Ether, in the Book of Mormon, and turned down the leaf upon it:

5. *And it came to pass that I prayed unto the Lord that he would give unto the Gentiles grace, that they might have charity. And it came to pass that the Lord said unto me: If they have not charity it mattereth not unto thee, thou hast been faithful; wherefore thy garments are clean. And because thou hast seen thy weakness, thou shalt be made strong, even unto the sitting down in the place which I have prepared in the mansions of my Father. And now I . . . . bid farewell unto the Gentiles; yea, and also unto my brethren whom I love, until we shall meet before the judgment-seat of Christ, where all men shall know that my garments are not spotted with your blood.* The testators are now dead, and their testament is in force.

6. Hyrum Smith was forty-four years old in February, 1844, and Joseph Smith was thirty-eight in December, 1843; and henceforward their names will be classed among the martyrs of religion; and the reader in every nation will be reminded that the Book of Mormon, and this book of Doctrine and Covenants of the church, cost the best blood of the nineteenth century to bring them forth for the salvation of a ruined world; and that if

the fire can scathe a green tree for the glory of God, how easy it will burn up the dry trees to purify the vineyard of corruption. They lived for glory; they died for glory; and glory is their eternal reward. From age to age shall their names go down to posterity as gems for the sanctified.

7. They were innocent of any crime, as they had often been proved before, and were only confined in jail by the conspiracy of traitors and wicked men; and their *innocent blood* on the floor of Carthage jail is a broad seal affixed to "Mormonism" that cannot be rejected by any court on earth, and their *innocent blood* on the escutcheon of the State of Illinois, with the broken faith of the State as pledged by the governor, is a witness to the truth of the everlasting gospel that all the world cannot impeach; and their *innocent blood* on the banner of liberty, and on the *magna charta* of the United States, is an ambassador for the religion of Jesus Christ, that will touch the hearts of honest men among all nations; and their *innocent blood,* with the innocent blood of all the martyrs under the altar that John saw, will cry unto the Lord of Hosts till he avenges that blood on the earth. Amen.

This article on the Martyrdom of the Prophet Joseph Smith and his brother Hyrum, the Patriarch, touches the heart of every sincere believer in the Gospel of Jesus Christ and the restoration of the Church. This article was written by Elder John Taylor who offered his life with his beloved brethren in this tragedy in Carthage, Illinois. President Taylor was severely wounded and carried the balls with which he was wounded to his grave. His devotion and willingness and that of his companion, Willard Richards, bear a strong testimony of their conviction and integrity to the truth of the mission of the Prophet Joseph Smith. There were others who were willing also to remain with the Prophet and Patriarch to the end; but they were denied entrance to the jail after they had departed on important errands. The Patriarch Hyrum Smith never wavered in his devotion and loyalty to his younger brother whom the Lord called to stand at the head of the great dispensation of the Fulness of Times. It was necessary that Hyrum Smith, as well as Joseph Smith, seal his testimony with his blood, as he had taken the place of Oliver Cowdery as the second Elder of the Church and the Second Witness of the restoration. At the time of his death he was holding with the Prophet, jointly, the keys of this dispensation. The following paragraphs are taken from the remarks of Elder Joseph Fielding Smith at the conference of the Church, April 8, 1930.

"My grandfather, the Patriarch Hyrum Smith, was called to hold the keys of this dispensation jointly with the Prophet Joseph, his younger brother. * * *. Joseph Smith could not have stood alone, else his work would have failed, just as the work of the Savior required the confirmation of another witness, and who could testify for Christ other than his Father? And so the Lord called another man to stand with Joseph Smith and to hold the keys of salvation in this dispensation as a witness with him. The Prophet Joseph was alone in his first vision. He was alone when the Angel Moroni first came to him and revealed the Book of Mormon, but whenever keys were to be bestowed; when the Lord had light and information to reveal in which the power of the Priesthood was to play a part, Joseph Smith and one other witness received the blessings.

"It was Oliver Cowdery who was appointed to stand with Joseph Smith, to hold the keys of this dispensation. It was Oliver Cowdery who, with Joseph Smith, received the Priesthood of Aaron under the hands of John the Baptist. It was Oliver Cowdery who received the authority of the Melchizedek Priesthood with Joseph Smith from Peter, James and John. It was Oliver Cowdery who knelt with the Prophet Joseph in the Kirtland Temple in 1836, when Moses and Elias and Elijah came with the keys of their dispensations. I am convinced that if we had the full record, we would discover that Oliver Cowdery was associated with Joseph Smith the Prophet when the keys of all the other dispensations were revealed and restored in this dispensation. In this manner Oliver Cowdery was appointed and ordained to stand with the Prophet Joseph Smith as an associate and witness, holding all the authority and keys of this most glorious of all dispensations—the Dispensation of the Fulness of Times.

"Unfortunately—at least unfortunately for Oliver Cowdery, who was called to this wonderful and responsible position, jointly associated with Joseph Smith holding all the authority and presidency in this dispensation—Oliver Cowdery, in a spirit of rebellion and darkness, turned away. * * *

"That this testimony of witnesses might be continued and made complete, the Lord chose another to take the place of Oliver Cowdery, and that other witness was the Patriarch Hyrum Smith. By revelation through Joseph Smith, Hyrum was called and ordained to the Priesthood and standing once held by Oliver Cowdery. Hyrum Smith received a double portion, not only was he called to become the Patriarch to the Church, which was his birthright, but at the same time the Lord said to him: 'And from this time forth I appoint unto him that he may be a prophet, and a seer, and a revelator unto my Church, as well as my servant Joseph.' * * *

"Thus, we see, Hyrum Smith became a president of the Church with Joseph Smith which place Oliver Cowdery might have held had he not wavered and fallen from his exalted station. I am firmly of the opinion that had Oliver Cowdery remained true to his covenants and obligations as a witness with Joseph Smith, and retained his authority and place, he, and not Hyrum Smith, would have gone with Joseph Smith as a prisoner and to Martyrdom at Carthage.

"The sealing of the testimony through the shedding of blood would not have been complete in the death of the Prophet Joseph Smith alone; it required the death of Hyrum Smith who jointly held the keys of this dispensation. It was needful that these martyrs seal their testimony with their blood, that they 'might be honored and the wicked might be condemned.' "

SECTION 136.

THE WORD AND WILL OF THE LORD, *given through President Brigham Young, at the Winter Quarters of the Camp of Israel, Omaha Nation, West Bank of Missouri River, near Council Bluffs, Iowa, January 14, 1847.——Plan of organization for migration to the West—Admonitions to righteousness—The Lord to be praised both in times of joy and of sorrow—Needful that Joseph Smith the Prophet should have sealed his testimony with his blood.*

THE Word and Will of the Lord concerning the Camp of Israel in their journeyings to the West:

1-2. *The word and will of the Lord*] The Saints were driven from their homes in Nauvoo under the most trying circumstances and in poverty and destitution in large measure, for they had been robbed by their enemies. Therefore it was extremely needful for a revelation from the Lord for their guidance in their journeyings to the Rocky Mountains. The Lord did not fail them in this hour of distress and gave this revelation to President Brigham Young to guide them in their journeyings and admonishing them to keep His commandments. All the members of the Church were to be organized in companies and were required to keep the commandments faithfully that they might have the guidance of His Spirit with them in all their trying circumstances. These companies were to be on the order followed by Zion's Camp in their remarkable march from Kirtland to Missouri, with captains, over hundreds, fifties and tens and all under the direction of the council of Apostles.

2. Let all the people of the Church of Jesus Christ of Latter-day Saints, and those who journey with them, be organized into companies, with a covenant and promise to keep all the commandments and statutes of the Lord our God.

3. Let the companies be organized with captains of hundreds, captains of fifties, and captains of tens, with a president and his two counselors at their head, under the direction of the Twelve Apostles.

4. And this shall be our covenant—that we will walk in all the ordinances of the Lord.

5. Let each company provide themselves with all the teams, wagons, provisions, clothing, and other necessaries for the journey, that they can.

6. When the companies are organized let them go to with their might, to prepare for those who are to tarry.

7. Let each company, with their captains and presidents, decide how many can go next spring; then choose out a sufficient number of able-bodied and expert men, to take teams, seeds, and farming utensils, to go as pioneers to prepare for putting in spring crops.

8. Let each company bear an equal proportion, according to the dividend of their property, in taking the poor, the widows, the fatherless, and the families of those who have gone into the army, that the cries of the widow and the fatherless come not up into the ears of the Lord against this people.

9. Let each company prepare houses, and fields for raising grain, for those who are to remain behind this season; and this is the will of the Lord concerning his people.

10. Let every man use all his influence and property to remove this people to the place where the Lord shall locate a stake of Zion.

11. And if ye do this with a pure heart, in all faithfulness, ye shall be blessed; you shall be blessed in your flocks, and in your herds, and in your fields, and in your houses, and in your families.

4-11. *And this shall be our covenant*] How essential it was then in the days of tribulation for the saints to walk by covenant as they journeyed towards a new home. Moreover it was necessary that they provide themselves the best they could with teams, clothing and provisions, for the journey was a difficult one. Some members of necessity would be left behind until such time as they could be prepared. The officers of the companies were to decide who might go and who would better remain behind until a more suitable day. These who were to remain were to put in crops and wait until the coming harvest. Each company was to bear an equal proportion of the means for the benefit of all. Those who had substance were to share with those who were destitute, in the true spirit of charity and faith. There were among them the widows and fatherless and the wives and families of those who had gone into the "Mormon Battalion." If they would do this the Lord would pour out upon them his blessings. They should have flocks and herds and their fields would not fail them.

12. Let my servants Ezra T. Benson and Erastus Snow organize a company.

13. And let my servants Orson Pratt and Wilford Woodruff organize a company.

14. Also, let my servants Amasa Lyman and George A. Smith organize a company.

15. And appoint presidents, and captains of hundreds, and of fifties, and of tens.

16. And let my servants that have been appointed go and teach this, my will, to the saints, that they may be ready to go to a land of peace.

17. Go thy way and do as I have told you, and fear not thine enemies; for they shall not have power to stop my work.

18. Zion shall be redeemed in mine own due time.

19. And if any man shall seek to build up himself, and seeketh not my counsel, he shall have no power, and his folly shall be made manifest.

20. Seek ye; and keep all your pledges one with another; and covet not that which is thy brother's.

21. Keep yourselves from evil to take the name of the Lord in vain, for I am the Lord your God, even the God of your fathers, the God of Abraham and of Isaac and of Jacob.

22. I am he who led the children of Israel out of the land of Egypt; and my arm is stretched out in the last days, to save my people Israel.

23. Cease to contend one with another; cease to speak evil one of another.

24. Cease drunkenness; and let your words tend to edifying one another.

25. If thou borrowest of thy neighbor, thou shalt restore that which thou hast borrowed; and if thou canst not repay then go straightway and tell thy neighbor, lest he condemn thee.

26. If thou shalt find that which thy neighbor has lost, thou shalt make diligent search till thou shalt deliver it to him again.

27. Thou shalt be diligent in preserving what thou hast, that thou mayest be a wise steward; for it is the free gift of the Lord thy God, and thou art his steward.

18-27. *Zion shall be redeemed*] The members of the Church had been disappointed, if not discouraged, because Zion had not been redeemed. No doubt it was trying to the faith of some to be on the way to the unknown region of the Rocky Mountains. All that they had heard of this territory was discouraging and the redemption of Zion seemed farther away than ever from fulfillment. Now they were to take courage, for the Lord had not forgotten Zion, and it should be redeemed in the due time of the Lord. It was well, therefore, for the members to obey counsel and not seek to build themselves at the expense of others; should this be done they would lose the reward. The Lord would lead them as he led the children of Israel, and he was just as mindful of the Saints today as he was then. Every man should respect the rights and property of the rest, and all should be wise stewards.

28. If thou art merry, praise the Lord with singing, with music, with dancing, and with a prayer of praise and thanksgiving.

28. *If thou art merry praise the Lord*] The Lord knew that the members of the Church would be weary and discouraged as they journeyed, and therefore he gave to them a remedy by which their despondency and discouragement could be overcome. They were to "praise the Lord with singing, and music, with dancing," with prayer and thanksgiving. This advice was followed, and after the camp was made for the night, frequently someone with a violin furnished music for dancing and for singing the favorite hymns and melodies familiar to the group, and thus their spirits were revived. They were not to worry or complain about their enemies, for they were in the hands of the Lord.

29. If thou art sorrowful, call on the Lord thy God with supplication, that your souls may be joyful.

30. Fear not thine enemies, for they are in mine hands and I will do my pleasure with them.

31. My people must be tried in all things, that they may be prepared to receive the glory that I have for them, even the glory of Zion; and he that will not bear chastisement is not worthy of my kingdom.

31. *My people must be tried*] Suffering and trials are essential to the eternal welfare of man. Those who seek a place in the celestial kingdom in exaltation may be called upon to pass through tribulation. At an earlier day the Lord had declared that it would be after much tribulation that the blessings would come.

"For verily I say unto you, blessed is he that keepeth my commandments, whether in life or in death; and he that is faithful in tribulation, the reward of the same is greater in the kingdom of heaven. Ye cannot behold with your natural eyes, for the present time, the design of your God concerning those things which shall come hereafter, and the glory which shall follow after much tribulation." (Doc. & Cov. Sec. 58:2-3.)

32. Let him that is ignorant learn wisdom by humbling himself and calling upon the Lord his God, that his eyes may be opened that he may see, and his ears opened that he may hear;

33. For my Spirit is sent forth into the world to enlighten the humble and contrite, and to the condemnation of the ungodly.

34. Thy brethren have rejected you and your testimony, even the nation that has driven you out;

35. And now cometh the day of their calamity, even the days of sorrow, like a woman that is taken in travail; and their sorrow shall be great unless they speedily repent, yea, very speedily.

36. For they killed the prophets, and them that were sent unto them; and they have shed innocent blood, which crieth from the ground against them.

37. Therefore, marvel not at these things, for ye are not yet pure; ye can not yet bear my glory; but ye shall behold it if ye are faithful in keeping all my words that I have given you, from the days of Adam to Abraham, from Abraham to Moses, from Moses to Jesus and his apostles, and from Jesus and his apostles to Joseph Smith, whom I did call upon by mine angels, my ministering servants, and by mine own voice out of the heavens, to bring forth my work;

38. Which foundation he did lay, and was faithful; and I took him to myself.

39. Many have marveled because of his death; but it was needful that he should seal his testimony with his blood, that he might be honored and the wicked might be condemned.

40. Have I not delivered you from your enemies, only in that I have left a witness of my name?

41. Now, therefore, hearken, O ye people of my church; and ye elders listen together; you have received my kingdom.

42. Be diligent in keeping all my commandments, lest judgments come upon you, and your faith fail you, and your enemies triumph over you. So no more at present. Amen and Amen.

34-42. *For they killed the prophets*] The Lord declares that the nation rejected the prophets and permitted the saints to be driven out, and by doing so there would come upon them calamity and sorrow. The blood of Joseph and Hyrum Smith and the others who had been slain for the Gospel's sake cried to the Lord from the ground against them. The Prophet laid a foundation upon which all men could build, but they refused and the Lord took the Prophet to himself. While many marveled that the Lord would permit his enemies to slay his servant, yet it was needful that he seal his testimony with his blood "that he might be honored, and the wicked be condemned."

A CLOSING WORD

We know of no inspired word more appropriate as a finishing touch of this volume, than that with which John prefaces his Revelation, "Blessed is he that readeth, and they that hear the words of this prophecy, and keep those things which are written therein; for the time is at hand" (Rev. 1:3).

These Revelations should be read and studied diligently. They show us the road to life eternal; they tell us of the pitfalls on the way, and how to avoid them; they furnish us with light in the darkness; strength in temptations and trials; comfort when we mourn; and hope in times of despair. They tell us what is needed for the world's salvation from error and ignorance, from poverty and disease, from strife and war, from sin, death, and damnation. They proclaim the advent of the Son of God and point to the signs by which we may know that the establishment of His kingdom is near at hand. They tell us how to live so that we may enjoy citizenship in that kingdom, and exaltation in the presence of God. "Blessed is he that readeth * * * and they that KEEP THOSE THINGS which are written therein."

Reading is not sufficient. We must KEEP THE REVELATIONS in our memories and meditate upon them; we must keep them in our affection, so that we love them, as we would a message from our dearest friends; we must put their teachings into practice. If we are weary and exhausted, hungry and thirsty, it is no satisfaction to sit down to a table laden with food and pure water, and to admire the things provided; we must partake thereof, until our wants are supplied, and we must do so every day. It is the same with the spiritual nourishment. We must make it part of ourselves by putting into practice the truths revealed.

As an illustration: The Doctrine and Covenants proclaims the Millennial reign, when "the law shall go forth from Zion and the word of the Lord from Jerusalem." But it also makes it clear that this blessed era will not come, until we are prepared for it, and it gives directions for the preparations that are necessary,

These directions we must follow. We must do the work required of us. It would be in vain to preach the Millennium and sing of its glories without DOING something for it. As well might the farmer rejoice in the anticipation of a bountiful harvest and prosperity, without plowing his fields and putting the seed into the ground.

"Blessed is he that readeth." No inspired, or uninspired, writings more fully, or clearly, state the gospel of Jesus Christ than does this volume; none more solemnly warns against the evils of sin. It becomes us to read, hear, keep, and obey what God has revealed, for every word of God is pure. Well says the inspired Psalmist:

> "Thy word is true from the beginning,
> and every one of thy righteous judgments
> Endureth forever" (Psalm 119:160).

In October, 1880, at the General Conference of the Church held in Salt Lake City, Elder Joseph F. Smith of the Council of Twelve proposed the following, which was unanimously adopted:

"I move that we receive and accept the revelations contained in these books, as revelations from God to the Church of Jesus Christ of Latter-day Saints, and to all the world."—Millennial Star, Vol. 42, p. 724.

INDEX

INDEX

AARON, gift of, 35, 43; Priesthood of, conferred, 68; its duties etc., 69; the spokesman of Moses, 144; his descendants to be bishops, 411; upon A. and his seed, 501.

Aaronic Priesthood, 501; organized in the wilderness, 503; mission of the A. Priesthood, 503; why so called, 696; authority of, 698.

Abel, paid an honest tithing, 749.

Abideth forever, 502.

Abominations in the Church, 290.

Abraham, seen by the Prophet in celestial glory, 460; promise to A., 664.

Acquaintance, that you should form, 728.

Act, my strange, 603.

Adam, is Michael, 136, 139, 706, 743; being tempted, 158; transgressed, 158; seen by the Prophet in celestial glory, 460; the first man, 500; the seventh angel, 562; the son of God, 591, 599; A. in Adam-ondi-Ahman, 706; at the head of the race, 706.

Adam-ondi-Ahman, 482, 706; why so named, 743; Kirtland Camp at, 744; the song, 747.

Admonition without prayer futile, 734.

Address to the Saints in Nauvoo, 798, 801.

Adultery, 236.

Adversary, his plan of salvation, 7, 51, 759.

Advocate, I am their, 170, 253, 369.

Afflicted, all things wherewith you are, 616; why the Saints in Zion were, 637.

Affliction, twofold object of, 637.

Age of a tree, 644.

Agency of man, 595.

Agent, let there be an a. appointed, 298; his duties, 298; Sidney Gilbert, an a., 312, 313; a. of the Church, 344; Newel K. Whitney, an a., 381.

Ahashdah, 480, 490.

Ahman, meaning of, 484.

Alam, 490.

Albigenses, 763.

Alike, be, 298.

All-knowing, our Lord is, 198, 199.

Alms of your prayers, 540.

Alpha and Omega, 90, 91, 180, 198, 314, 361.

Alphus, * * * Omegus, 604.

Alvin Smith, seen by the Prophet in celestial glory, 460.

America, free to all nations, 56.

America, North and South, are Zion, 641.

American Indians, descendants of Lamanites and a few Nephites, 22.

—Civil War, xv, 10, 266.

Amherst, conference appointed, 431, 433.

Ancient of Days, 743.

Angel, a ministering, 41; of the bottomless pit, 158; flying in mid-heaven, 348; a. of God rebelled, 450; ascending from the east, 475; a. * * * presence, 663; angel's time, 814.

Angels, the servants of God are,

41; names of, 139, 810; a. waiting, 201; an innumerable company of, 459; of the devil, 465; four a., 475; shall fly, 558; executing the decrees of God, 560; accompanied Zion's Camp, 667; ministering of, 698; have a right to know the truth, 765; good and bad, how to know, 811; where a. reside, 815; appointed a., 826.

Anger, God's against rebellious, 321; let thine a. be kindled, 754; a. of the Lord kindled, 7, 373.

Angus, Joseph, on faith, 284.

Animal life, not to be wasted, 286.

Answer, God's, to Joseph's prayer in Liberty jail, 755.

Answers by revelation to questions on Scripture, 737.

Anthropology, 555.

Apocrypha, meaning of, 585; John Bunyan on, 586.

Apostasy in Nauvoo, 779.

Apostate condition of mankind, 7, 9.

Apostates, two classes, 295.

Apostle, Joseph to be called, 115, 116.

Apostles, Revelation on their calling, 81, 86, 87; in former dispensations, 87; their duty and power, 88, 105; special instructions to, 88; Joseph F. Smith on their mission and duty, 88-9; were to be selected by Oliver Cowdery and David Whitmer, 89; first Council of Twelve selected, 89; are Elders, 107; to judge the house of Israel, 149; succeed the First Presidency, 242; first Council to prune the vineyard, 693; A. chosen, 693; Brigham Young, on the first selection of, 693; the Twelve,

699; revelation to Thomas B. Marsh concerning, 732; John Taylor, John E. Page, Wilford Woodruff, and Willard Richards appointed, 747.

Appeal, an, for peace, 687.

Appearance of our Lord, 724.

Appoint, except to a. another, 241.

Archangel, 706.

Arm of Mercy, 146.

Armor, the whole of God, 137.

Army of Israel, 685.

"Art to Grow Old and Keep Young," on the, 574.

Ashley, Major N., 436.

Asylum denied the Saints, 332.

Assemble, to agree on God's word, 215.

Athanasius on militarism, 387.

Atonement, 94, 101-3.

Attention, God demands, 373, 433.

Augustine on election, 182; on militarism, 387.

Authority, this is mine, 5; a. of my servants, 5; C. W. Penrose on, 177, 178; Dean Farrar on, 178; the Prophet Joseph on, 178; civil a. of divine origin, 339; a. of the Melchizedek Priesthood, 697; of the Aaronic Priesthood, 698.

Avard, Sampson, 294.

BABYLON, the great, shall fall, 7; meaning of, 186.

Babbitt, Almon, 784.

Baneemy, 492.

Banquet hall, Zion a, 336.

Baptism for the dead, 775-8; instructions on, 776; an address on, 801; Scripture proofs, 807-9.

Baptism, requirement of an applicant for, 105; a covenant, 110; how to be administered, 110;

the manuscript to Zion, 417, 419; the MS. dedicated, 417; the Saints accept the work, 419; a committee for its publication, 419; how the proceeds were to be disposed of, 420; the laws of the United order applied, 420; the public to be prepared for its appearance, 423.
Book of Enoch, 139, 706.
Book of God, 459.
Book of Life, 459.
Book of Mormon, a collection of books, xii; why preserved, 21, 56, 57; a marvelous work, 23; two written copies of, 50; an attempted spurious version, 50; does not take the place of the Bible, 56; is a new witness, 57; prophesied of, 100; important truths in, 102; what we learn by it, 726; prophecy concerning the Church, 765; presented to sovereigns, 769.
Book of the Law of the Lord, 61.
Book, sealed, 474; the little b., 477; B. of Revelation, 478.
Books for schools, 319; b. good, to be studied, 580.
Booth, Ezra, 306, 307, 390, 392, 423, 487.
Bought, He has b. us, 91.
Boynton, John F., 320; rejected, 737.
Breastplate, 69, 78, 137.
Brethren in Zion warned, 517.
Brightness of my coming, 28.
Brinkworth, Reuben, miraculously healed, 525.
Broken mine everlasting covenant, 7.
Brunson, Seymour, 439.
Building committee, School of Prophets, 587, 601; issues a circular, 603.
Burned, shall not be, 394.
Burnett, Stephen, 439, 486.

CAHOON, Reynolds, 308, 438.
Cain, not an honest tithe payer, 749.
Cainhannock, 492.
Calamity, God's foreknowledge of, 8, 9.
— the Prophet Joseph called to warn the world, 9.
Caldwell County, 737, 750.
Calendar, error in, 98.
Call upon me while I am near, 551.
Called and chosen, 318.
Calvin on faith, 85.
Camp, Zion's, journey of, 666; the object of it, 687; rebellion in, 688; members of, for the ministry, 693.
Cannon, George Q., on revelation, 104-5; on the object of the restoration of the gospel, 204, 205; on the spiritual gifts, 515; on the Word of Wisdom, 575; on the triumph of the Church, 777; on prophetic evidence, 238, 239; on evil influences, 643.
Capernaum, 519.
Carlin, governor of Illinois, 768.
Carter, Jared, 485.
— Simeon, 308, 439.
— William, 308.
— Gideon, 440.
Cease from light speeches, 565; to be covetous, 565.
Celestial Kingdom of God, seen by the Prophet, 460; who are the heirs of it, 460; c. glory, 468; c. body, Earth to become, 472; c. glory, 541; c. truth, the Church founded upon, 542; c. marriage, Revelation on, 820; c. law explained, 824; applied to marriage, 826.
Celibacy, 226.
Center place of Zion, Revelation on, 189, 327; Saints to return

Eve, on the fall, 158.

"Evening and Morning Star", 394; on warning the world, 526.

Events of the last days, 557.

Events that will occur at the coming of the Lord, 264.

Everlasting gospel, 690.

Everlasting Order, the United Order, 668.

Everlasting punishment, 454; e. burnings, 460.

Evil, all, must be forsaken, 619.

Evil spirits, seen by Heber C. Kimball, and others, 471.

Exaltation, Abraham has entered into, 830.

Excel, a desire to, may be pride, 343.

Exile, not an evidence of rejection by God, 660.

Expenses of a missionary trip, how paid, 359.

Expound the mysteries, 422; expounding the Scriptures, Sidney Rigdon, 633.

Extortion, meaning of, 354.

Eye to eye, 520.

Face, shall see my, 588.

Facts, all the f. of the Missouri persecution to be placed on record, 763.

Faith, 24; without f. can do nothing, 44; how to study f., 78; to precede testimony, 78, 79; Lothian on, 85; Calvin on, 85; they shall have f., 175; who overcome by, 457.

Faithful in temporal affairs, 301; f. and wise, 425; if f., many sheaves, 434; revelations promised to the faithful, 619.

Fall, man fell, 101, 102; history of not a myth, 160.

False brethren, 761.

Falsehoods, different kinds, 225; how to be met, 765.

Family, human, must be united, 16; Saints to become one, 332.

Farrar, Dean, on authority to preach, 178.

Far West, Presidency over the Church in Missouri, 737; Revelations at, 737, 739, 740, 743, 746, 748, 750; concerning the building up of, 740; to build a Temple at, 742; Temple lot dedicated, 747; city given up to pillage, 751.

Fasting and prayer, 352; a sign of mourning, 555.

Father, Son and Holy Ghost one God, 103; Father, the, and I are one, 589.

Father, and the Son, 182; a doctrinal Exposition by the First Presidency and the Twelve, 448; F., has a body of flesh, 817.

Fathers, estranged from their children, 16.

Fear of man, displeasing, 358.

Fears, there were f. in your hearts, 405.

Feet, cleanse your, 360, 519; washing of, 566, 576.

Field, white to harvest, 22, 24, 32, 60, 66, 173.

Fifty-six years, should wind up the scene, 246.

Fig tree, parable of, 184, **186**.

First and the Last, the, 725.

Firstborn, Jesus Christ, the, 593.

First President, 710; is the Moses of the Church, 711.

First Presidency, when organized, 578; a symbol of the unity of the Church, and the means of preserving it, 582; on the Father and the Son, 589; on Jesus Christ, the Firstborn, 593; house for, 600; the F. P., 699; their burden, 735.

First resurrection, 377.

INDEX 881

Henry IV., 270.

Hiding-place, the Lord to come out of His, 763.

Higbee, Keziah, her death, 640.

High Council, organization of, 654; in Zion, 688, 702; standing High Councils, 702.

Highmindedness and pride, 581.

High Priest, of the Aaronic Priesthood, 69.

High Priesthood, first ordination to, 302, 303; the Prophet Joseph sustained as president of, 433; authority of the Presidency, 697; a normal school, 697; H. P., the greatest of all, 710.

High Priests, seven, appointed to preside in Zion, 294, 331; ordained at a conference in Kirtland, 425; three form a quorum, 711; hold the same Priesthood as the Presidency, 712.

Hills, Zion to flourish upon the, 189, 213.

Hinckle, Geo. M., 294, 751.

Hiram, Portage Co., Ohio, 11; the Prophet Joseph removes to, 388, 397; special conferences at, 403, 417, 419; mobbing at, 487.

History and general Church Record, 527; the Prophet Joseph instructed to study, 556, 599.

Hodge, on marriage, 285; on the Trinity, 103.

Holy Ghost and Spirit of God, Joseph F. Smith quoted, 184.

"Holy, holy, holy," 468.

Holy land, shall the children of the kingdom pollute my? 510.

Holy places, 263, 642.

Holy Spirit, necessary for the ministry, 192, 193; power to give, 319.

Honest men to be sought for, 618.

Honor those who serve me, 445.

Honorable men of the earth, 462.

Hope, what it is, 24.

Horah, 491.

Hosanna, meaning of, 192.

Hospitality, a mark of discipleship, 519.

House to house, 437.

House of God, a house of order, 109.

House of the Lord for the First Presidency, 600; h. for literary purposes, 600; tardiness in preparing for building, 602.

Houses, set in order your, 581.

Hubble, claims to have revelations, 240.

Human nature, successive portraits of, 173.

Humble, be thou, 733.

Humility, shown by prayer and faith, 29; a Christian virtue, 67, 231.

Humorous anecdotes, 632.

Humphrey, Solomon, 294, 309.

Hurlburt, D. P., 188.

Hyde, Orson, on Priesthood, 16; on the coming of the Lord, 264; Revelation to, 408; biographical notes, 409, 435; dedicates Palestine, 409; on evil spirits, 514; on the authority of the Priesthood, 695; goes to England, 732; asks for forgiveness, 734.

— Heman, 689.

Hyrum, meaning of name, 64.

"I AM," meaning of, 86, 588; "I am He," meaning of, 91, 146; you shall see me and know that, 406.

Idle, thou shalt not be, 231, 359.

Idlers in Zion, 415.

Illinois, Saints settle there, 768.

Image of God of the world, 7; man created in God's, 102.

Immutable, God is, 445.

was in the beginning, 590; was the word, 591; was the messenger of salvation, 591; was the light, 591; the Redeemer, 591; the truth and the life, of men, 591; He was also the Creator, 591; received all power, 592; the first born, 593; appears in the Kirtland Temple, 724.

Jewels, 358, 637.

Jews, this generation of, 261; to be gathered, 261; will be converted to go first to the Gentiles, then to the J., 579.

John, the beloved, our Lord's promise to, 39, 40; traditions concerning, 41; his Gospel, when written, 42; restores the Melchizedek Priesthood, 42; his influence on the religious thought of the world, 42; his spirit in these revelations, 67; among the ten tribes, 250; visions on Patmos, 449; I, John, bear record, 591-2.

John the Baptist confers Priesthood of Aaron, 68.

Johnson, Father of, 11, 411; to be a member of the United Order, 607; biographical note, 607.

— Luke S., 320; Revelation to, 408; biographical note, 410, 435; rejected, 737.

— Eli, 390.

— Lyman E., biographical note, 410, 436; on the misery of apostates, 470; rejected, 737.

Joseph, meaning of, 84.

Josephites, 21.

Jubal, 574.

Judge in Israel, Edward Partridge to be, 339; J., the unjust, 652.

Judged according to their works, 469, 470.

Judges, you shall be, 437.

Judging every man, 92.

Judgment which is to come, 518; prepare the Saints for the hour of, 556.

Judgments, to come upon the earth, 13; God revokes not, 93; upon nations, 154, 155, 264, 519; the Elders to warn the world, when directed by the Spirit, 526; Saints not to threaten with, 685.

Just, resurrection of the, 457; their glory, 458, 459; just men made perfect, 460.

Justice, Saints to supplicate for, 685.

Justification, defined, 104.

KANT, Emanuel, 269.

Kaw, Township, 328.

Key to John's Revelations, 471, 478.

Keys, not to be taken from the Prophet Joseph, 390; of the Kingdom of God, 398; keys of the kingdom, Revelation concerning, 576, 577; the Prophet a keeper of the keys forever, 576; of the School of the Prophets, 579; k. whereby to know angels and spirits, 810.

Kill, thou shalt not, 224; if any, 231.

Kimball, Heber C. on the new and everlasting Covenant, 4; on the Sacrament, 111; on the signs in the heavens, 269; on equality, 299; on endurance, 313; on the Clay and the Potter, 374; on receiving Revelations, 407; combats evil spirits, 471, 514; on the resurrection of the body, 545; on Zion's Camp, 668; goes to England, 732.

Kindled, let thine anger be, 754.

Kingdom of God, Brigham Young

on, 147, 148; given to the Saints, 252; keys of the, 398; K. of God and K. of Heaven, 399.

Kingdom of Heaven, 57; is at hand, 174; is yours, 371; on endowments in Kirtland, 688.

Kingdom of the Devil, 58.

Kingdoms, with you I will rend, 524; many, each governed by law, 548.

Kirtland, the Prophet's arrival there, 215; conditions existing, 215; first Revelation in, 214; first conference in, 249; falsehoods circulated about the Saints, 252; return journey to K., 359; the Prophet arrives in, 373; a strong hold, 393; visions in, 407; Bishop appointed for K., 425, 426; duties of Bishop in, 427; consecrated for a stake of Zion, 491; dedication of Temple accepted of our Lord, 588; City of Kirtland Stake, 600; dimensions of the Temple revealed, 604; the subject discussed, 605; Oliver Cowdery arrives in K., from Jackson County, 634; Temple, dedicatory Prayer, 713; K. Temple accepted, 725; disaffection among the Saints at, 731; apostasy in, 737; Kirtland Camp, 744; concerning the property at K., 744.

Kjerkegaard, 114, 326.

Knight, Newel, visits Harmony, 134; confirmed, 134; biographical note, 309; Revelation to, 314; at Thompson, 322; Bishop's counselor, 413; rescued from the power of an evil spirit, 513.

Knight, Joseph, Sr., Revelation to, 65, 66, 119; biographical note, 122.

Knight, Sister Polly, 348.

Knowledge is power, 819.

Know my power, 452; all shall k. me, 520.

Kolob, 814.

LABAN, sword of, 78.

Labor with their own hands, 310; with your might, 434.

Lake of fire, 377, 453.

Lamanites, 21, 56; mission to, 142, 144; "on the borders by," 142; L. blossom as the rose, 287; God's children, 471.

Lamech, 574.

Land should be purchased, 328; Partridge to divide, 339; blessed, 365.

Language, of divine Revelations accords with the language of those through whom they are given, 9.

Laughable stories, 632.

Laughter, not with much, 353; excess of, 552; cease from, 565.

Law-abiding, Saints must be, 617.

Law, to be received by prayer, 216; L. of the Gospel, a Revelation on, 218; L. concerning preaching, 219; L. of ordination, 221; L. of moral conduct, 222; L. of charity, 228; L. concerning transgressors, 229; L. of renumeration, 234; L. of leadership, succession, and consecration represents truth, 324; my, shall be kept, 339; L. of Enoch, not kept, 492; women and children under L. of Enoch, 494, 495; that which is governed by, 546; he hath given a L. unto all things, 550; God's and man's, relative importance of, 617; law which is constitutional, 617; L. of Retaliation, 623; L. of War, 624; L. of Forgiveness, 625; L. of the

Mighty and Strong, one; who is he? 528.

Mighty in testimony, the Prophet, 633.

Mighty One of Israel, 191.

Mighty works, do not keep men from falling, 17.

"Millennial Star," 169, 441.

Millennium, 147-9; the m., 643; after the, 153, 154; history of the doctrine, 160; holy men of old to see it, 255; the gospel to be preached during the, 346; Satan loosed after the Millennium, 563; languages during the, 579; prayer during the, 643; Satan bound, 643; there is no death, 643; man's age as the age of a tree, 644; resurrected beings to visit the Earth, 644.

Miller, George, 772.

Miller, Wm., his error, 149.

Militarism, 269; church fathers on, 387.

Ministers, must be ordained, 384; shall speak as moved upon, 410; their word is scripture, 410; must bear record of Christ, 410.

Ministry, instructions, 63; qualifications for, 22, 24; elementary truths for ministers, 66; directions concerning the, 409; preparation for, 554.

Miracles, when required, 125; meaning of, in New Test., 185, 513; m. and the laws of nature, 516; Saints do not boast of m., 525.

Miraculous directors, 78; m. manifestations, 407.

Mission of the Prophet for the redemption of Zion, 664; a mission of peace, 687; mission, the first, to England, 732.

Missionaries, promises to, 288; called, 439; not to accumulate means, 521; what preparation they need, 632; successful, makes friends, 728.

Missionary work, preparation for, 554; God's w., 632.

Missouri, mission to, 304, 307; land of inheritance, 302, 311; land of promise, 328; m. persecution, facts, to be recorded, 763.

Mississippi River, 366.

Misunderstanding between Sidney Rigdon and Edward Partridge, 489.

Mob in Kirtland, 487; in Jackson County, 609, 635.

Mobocrats come to a tragic end, 488.

Mocked, God not to be, 384.

"Molten sea," 778.

Moon, turned into blood, 150, 151.

Moral laws immutable, 223, 550.

Morley, Isaac, 294, 307, 413; M. farm, 382, 392, 393.

"Mormon," or "Mormonites," 740.

"Mormonism" and Irvingianism compared, 33; embraces all truth, 57; cosmopolitan character of, 57; a practical religion, and therefore hated, 423.

Moses, instead of God, 144; sons of M., 498, 504; this M. plainly taught the children of Israel, 502; a man like, 662; how the Lord communicated with Him, 663; appears in the Kirtland Temple, 726; a resurrected being, 847.

Murderer, has no forgiveness, 237.

Murderers, the Prophet and companions in the hands of, 762.

Murdock, John, martyrdom of his child, 11, 629; "bound," 303; Revelation calling him to go on a mission, 628; biographical note, 629.

Shakers, 282.

Shalemanasseh, 491.

Sherman, Lyman, Revelation concerning, 712.

Shield of faith, 138.

Shinehah, 491, 745.

Sinneth, unto the soul who, 490.

Sick, they shall heal the, 514.

Sickle, meaning of, 24; thrust in his s., 60.

Sign, a great, in heaven, 560; s. of the dove, 592.

Signs of the times, men slow to comprehend, 28; signs of the end of the times of the gentiles, 261-3; of the "day of the Lord," 264; in the heavens, 268; he that seeketh, 376; follow faith, 376; the Saints can read them, 410.

Sign-seekers, adulterers, 376.

Sin, God does not look upon, with the least degree of allowance, 9; lying, always a sin, 53; "sin not," 88; sin no more, 123; theories concerning origin of, 160; original or individual, 182; s. of the world, 182; warning against, 489; tardiness a grievous s., 603; contention a grievous s., 603; covetousness a s., 670; the unpardonable, 829; the man of, 250.

Sins, your s. have come up unto me, 324; thy s. are forgiven, 576; your s. are forgiven, 713, 725, 732.

Sinned, there are those who have, 389; nevertheless he has, 390; all of you have, 489.

Sinner, meaning of, 88.

Sjodahl, J. M., 769.

Slanderers to be refuted, 423.

Smith, Emma, at Hiram, Portage Co., Ohio, 11; Revelation to, 127; an elect lady, 128; murmur not, 128; her office and calling, 128, 129; after the martyrdom, 130; confirmed, 134.

Smith, George A., on the language of divine Revelations, 9; tells an anecdote of Thomas B. Marsh. 167; on impurity, 225; on false spirits, 240, 290; his baptism, 294; on the prosperity of the Saints, 334, 369; on the Sabbath, 354; on elders who said the Prophet was going wrong, 391; on miraculous manifestations, 407; on the organization of the High Council, 658; on disaffection at Kirtland, 731.

Smith, Hyrum, Revelation to, 59; biographical notes, 60; "the friend of God," 61; his special gift, 62; called to preach, 63; his sufferings, 65; his duty in the Church, 120; on Word of Wisdom, 286, 573-4; succeeds Fred G. Williams in the First Presidency, 737; his character, 770; legal successor of his father, 785; his patriarchal blessing, 786; called to be a prophet, seer, and revelator, 786; a President of the Church, 786, 855-57.

Smith, Joseph F., Jr., on the succession, 241; on the Nauvoo Temple, 780; on two hereditary offices, 786.

Smith, Joseph F., on "thine own" property, 95; on duty of the apostles, 88-9; visits Emma S., 130; on apostasy, 206; on death, 232; on the Sabbath, 351; on the care of children, 414; on the Spirit of God and the Holy Ghost, 509; on the Doc. and Cov., 675; biographical note, 752; vision of, 809.

Smith, Joseph, Sr., Revelation to, 22, 119; accepts the gospel, 23; patriarchal blessing upon his